DICTIONARY OF
ANCIENT
DEITIES

DICTIONARY OF
ANCIENT
DEITIES

PATRICIA TURNER

and

CHARLES RUSSELL COULTER

OXFORD
UNIVERSITY PRESS

OXFORD
UNIVERSITY PRESS

Oxford   New York
Athens   Auckland   Bangkok   Bogotá   Buenos Aires   Cape Town
Chennai   Dar es Salaam   Delhi   Florence   Hong Kong   Istanbul   Karachi   Kolkata
Kuala Lumpur   Madrid   Melbourne   Mexico City   Mumbai   Nairobi   Paris   São Paulo
Shanghai   Singapore   Taipei   Tokyo   Toronto   Warsaw

and associated companies in
Berlin   Ibadan

First published by McFarland & Company, Inc., Publishers, 2000
as Encyclopedia of Ancient Deities
Box 611, Jefferson, North Carolina 28640

First issued as an Oxford University Press paperback, 2001
198 Madison Avenue, New York, New York 10016

Library of Congress Cataloging-in-Publication Data
Coulter, Charles Russell, d. 1997.
[Encyclopedia of ancient deities]
Dictionary of ancient deities / Patricia Turner and Charles Russell Coulter
p.   cm.
Originally published: Encyclopedia of Ancient Deities. Jefferson, N.C. : McFarland, 2000.
Includes bibliographical references and index.
ISBN 978-0-19-514504-5

1. Gods—Dictionaries. I. Turner, Patricia. II. Title.
BL473.C67 2002
291.2'11'03—dc21   00-068457

Printed in the United States of America
on acid-free paper

In memory of
Charles Russell Coulter
—*Patricia Turner*

TABLE OF CONTENTS

ON ALPHABETIZATION AND SPELLING

The Encyclopedia Proper

For a number of reasons having to do with the intermingling of Western name styles, indigenous and non–Western styles, phrases in English, and alternate name forms (including, for instance, two or more elements closed up as one word, such elements linked with hyphens, and such elements separated as two words), it was determined that the most useful alphabetization scheme would be what is commonly known as word-by-word (as opposed to letter-by-letter spread over any number of words or word parts). In this scheme, in the encyclopedia proper, two or more elements linked by hyphens are treated as separate words (the hyphen being purely a recent Western orthographical construct).

Thus in the encyclopedia (i.e., main) portion of the book, "Aka, Aka-Kanet, Aka Maneh, Akadja" is one sequence and "Ti-yu, Tiamat" is another.

Many, probably most of the entry names have two or more spellings (as distinct from the matter of two or more elements closed up, hyphenated or separated). This is especially true of names that have for a long time been a part of or adapted by Western culture (e.g., Greek, Norse, Egyptian, Indian, Chinese). Some names have four to six or even more alternate spellings or similar versions.

Many but not all alternate versions of a name are entered into the main entry sequence as "see" references. The one entry to which they all refer may well list yet additional spellings or alternate forms of a name.

In effect there has been, out of necessity, an effort in many but not all cases to discover or decide upon the most common form of a name for purposes of determining where in the alphabetical sequence a main entry shall appear. No similar effort was, however, extended to regulating the spelling or form of any name appearing secondarily within the text of an entry. In some cases a "most common form" was not identifiable or was considered a matter of cultural or linguistic bias or in some way was almost entirely subjective; in these cases, one main entry form was simply chosen and the others subordinated as "see" references.

The Index

The index must serve numerous purposes, not least of which is as an alternate to or clarification of the main entry alphabetization sequence. Accordingly, it is arranged similarly, in a word-by-word fashion, but with hyphenated forms now considered one word (so that the reader has additional opportunities to locate a name form for which they search).

Thus, there appears the sequence

Aka	Akadja	Akalo
Aka Manah	A-Kahiwahiwa	Aka-Manah
Aka Mano	Aka-Kanet	Akamas

and the sequence

All	Al-lat	Alligator
All Merciful, The	Allath	Alloprosallos
All Pitying One	Allatu	All-pervader
All Sinned One	All-Caring	All-seeing
Allah	All-Devouring	almond trees
Allat	Allecto	

Virtually all alternate spellings and forms of a name appear in the index (whereas in the encyclopedia proper only several of what were determined to be the most

ix

important alternate forms were entered as "see" references). Index references are to pages upon which any appearance of a name exists, notably in the text of entries under other deities or subjects.

The reader must therefore consult the index under two or more alternate spellings to be sure of locating all references to the appearance of a name: that is, under both "Algonquian" and "Algonquin," both "Texcatlipoca" and "Tezcatlipoca," and both "Viracocha" and "Virococha." The great majority of alternate spellings in the index nevertheless simply refer to the main entry, not to subsidiary appearances under other entries.

The index also contains, as subjects, many ordinary English-language words and phrases, a major reason for the adoption of the word-by-word approach.

PREFACE

Throughout history, humans have pondered the question of their existence. In nearly every society, part of the answer has included some form of god or goddess involved in the creation of the universe.

This encyclopedia was compiled to give the general reader and scholars easy access to a broad range of mythologies related to deities. In addition to ancient deities, other mythology is included that will facilitate a comprehensive understanding of the deities — so there are entries for spirits, places, festivals, sacred objects, heroes, monsters, demigods and mythical beasts.

The research was extensive, covering a century of book publishing activity. We made use of a large personal library, collected over many years, on this topic. Research was carried out in a number of libraries outside the United States, and the Bibliography includes citations to many books published in those countries. As a result the reader will find deities often missing from standard collections, notably from the Inuit, Native American and African cultures.

At over 10,000 entries, this is the most comprehensive collection of information on this topic. The primary name of the deity is followed by alternate spellings or translations of the primary name. Then in parentheses the group of people (tribes, cultures, civilizations or people who lived in a geographic region) who recognized the deity or mythology is named. All alternate names are then given. All alternate names and alternate spellings are cross-referenced. An explanation of the origin, history and function of the subject of the entry is followed by any needed cross-references to guide the reader to related topics.

A comprehensive index permits direct access to any name by any of its spelling variants, as well as to the religions, cultures and places identified in the text. Also indexed are subjects, especially including those with which a deity is associated; a reader may, for example, locate goddesses of *lightning* or gods represented by *toads* by consulting the respective entries in the index.

My coauthor, Charles Coulter, passed away in 1997 shortly after we delivered this manuscript, which had occupied much of his time and mental energy during his last ten years. I am deeply grateful for his effort.

PATRICIA TURNER • *August 1999*

1

THE ENCYCLOPEDIA

A

A (Maya People, Yucatan)

A is a death god who is similar to the Aztec god of the dead, Miclantecutli. A major difference is that A presides over the west and his Aztec People, Mexico, counterpart presides over the north or south. His hieroglyph is a skull, a corpse's head and a flint knife used for sacrifices. *See also* Miclantecutli.

A-Kahiwahiwa (Polynesia)

"Fiery Black Clouds." One of the thirteen children of the god of winds, storms and hurricanes, Tawhiri-ma-tea.

A-shih (India) *see* Abheda; Ajita.

Aa (Mesopotamia)

Also known as: *Aah, Aos, Iah, Khensu, Sirdu, Sirrida.*

Aa as a Chaldean deity was known as Aos. Her emblem is a disk with eight rays. As the Akkadian and Sumerian moon goddess she is the consort of the sun god, Shamash. In this aspect, she is the mother of Tammuz. Ra, in Egypt was called Aa (the sun), as a high or sky god. Aa or Aah is another name for the Egyptian moon god, Khensu (q.v.). Aa is also an Egyptian root word meaning "great." Compare Aa to Gula. *See also* Aah; Aos; Shamash; Tammuz.

Aa Sekhemu (Egypt) *see* Aaru.

Aaai (Egypt) *see* Aai.

Aaan (Egypt) *see* Aani; Ab (B).

Aaapef (Egypt) *see* Aai; Apepi; Apophis.

Aaetes (Greek) *see* Medea.

Aah *Ah, Aa* (Egyptian, Middle East)

Also known as: *Aah-Djuhty, Aah Tehuti, Aah Te-huti, Ai, Aos* (Sumerian), *Iah, Khons, Khonsu, Knosu, Thoth.*

One of the names for the god of the moon. Aah is often represented as a regal young man wearing the lunar crescent and solar disc. Aah is also a general reference to the moon, and prefix or suffix to the primary name of a deity. The combination of the gods Aah and Thoth is the god Aah-Djuhty. *See also* Aa; Aah-Djuhty; Agu; Alignak; Aningan; Anunit; Arianrod; Artemis; Khonsu; Thoth.

Aah-Djuhty (Egypt) *see* Aah.

Aah Te-Huti *Aah-Tehuti*

Also known as: *Aah, Thoth* (Egypt).

A manifestation of Thoth, this moon god is represented by an ibis head surmounted by a crescent and a disk. *See also* Aah; Tehuti; Thoth.

Aah-Tehuti (Egypt) *see* Aah Te-Huti.

Aahes (Egypt) *see* Min.

Aai (Egypt)

Also known as: *Aai Gods.*

The Aai are three guardian gods who watch over the sunboat of Ra, in the Ninth Hour or Ninth Division of the underworld known as Tuat. (Tuat is divided into twelve parts, each of which corresponds to one of the hours of the night, and the divisions are called "Field," or "City" or "Hall," or "Circle.") The specific duty of the Aai gods is to destroy the monstrous serpent Apophis. The pylon of the Ninth Division or Ninth Hour is called Aat-shefsheft. It is guarded by the serpent

Ab-ta. The guardians of the corridor are Anhefta and Ermen-ta. Nine gods in mummified forms guard the wall. On the right side of the sun god Ra's boat are four gods of the south. They each wear the white crown, and are grasping a rope that is also held by a man who is called "the master of the front." Between the four gods and the man is a pillar surmounted by a bearded head, with a white crown on it, which is being raised by the rope. There is a hawk-headed sphinx with the white crown on his head, and a bearded head with a white crown on it, resting on his hind quarters. Standing on his back is a human figure that is surmounted by the heads of Horus and Set. In attendance as well are the four gods of the north. They are each wearing the red crown and grasping a rope. The rope is also held by a man known as "the master of the back." Between the man and the four gods is a pillar surmounted by a bearded head wearing a red crown. It is being raised by the rope. A man known as Apu is holding Shemti, the serpent with four heads at each end of his body. Another person is holding Bath, the serpent with a head at each end of his body. On Bath's back stands Tepi the serpent. Tepi has four human heads, breasts and arms and four pairs of human legs at each end of his body. There are also two men holding what might be a rope. On the left side of Ra's boat are sixteen human forms. These forms represent the souls of Amentet, the followers of Thoth, the followers of Horus, and the followers of Osiris. The first four have the heads of men, the second four, the heads of ibises, the third four the heads of hawks, and the fourth the heads of rams. These sixteen beings draw a rope. The rope is attached to Khepri, the double serpent with four heads, two at each end of his body. On one of his folds, the hawk Heru-tuati is perched. Eight human forms called Akhmiu are at the other end of the rope. In the center of this Division, Ra's sun boat is being towed. Marching before Ra are six human forms, four apes and four women who appear to be holding ropes. The three Aai gods are men holding a rope that is thrown over the head and held in the hands of the prostrate ass-eared man who is also called Aai. In front of the man are the serpent Apepi and the serpent-headed crocodile, Shesshes. These beings work magic for Ra on the monstrous Apepi. They beckon the serpent to come to them to be slain. The three drive their spears into Apepi and also destroy the serpent Sesi. They tightly hold the rope of Ai, and do not let the serpent rise toward Ra's sun boat. Text found on the alabaster sarcophagus of Seti I. indicates the Aai gods drive their pikes (spears) into Apophis and also destroy the serpent Sisi. Aai is listed as one of the gods in the Second Corridor of the Tomb of Seti along with the following gods: Aaai, Aakebi, Aana-tuati, Aatiu, Amam-ta, Amen-ha, Amen-khat, Ameni, Ament, Antheti, Aper-ta, Ast, Auai, Ba-Ra, Besi-shemti, Entuti, Hai, Her-ba, Heru, Hetchuti, Huaaiti, Ketuiti, Khenti-Amenti, Khenti-qerer, Khepera, Kheperi, Khepi, Kheprer, Maa-uat, Mau-aa, Mauti, Metu-khut-f, Nakiu-menat, Neb-baiu, Neb-senku, Nebt-het, Nef-em-baiu, Nehi, Netch-Baiu, Netchesti, Nethert, Nu, Nut, Qererti, Qu-ba, Ra-ateni, Rekhi, Remi, Seb, Sehetch-khatu, Sekhem-hra, Sekhen-ba, Sekheper-khati, Semaahut, Senk-hra, Senki, Seraa, Serqi, Seshetai, Shai, Shepi, Shu, Tchemtch-hat, Tebati, Tefnut, Tem, Temtemtch, Then-aru, Thenti, Theta-enen, Tuati, Uben, Urshiu. *See also* Abta; Abuk and Inet; Apepi; Apophis; Horus; Khenti Amenti; Khepri; Osiris; Ra; Set; Thoth; Tuat; Tefnut.

Aai Gods (Egypt) *see* Aai.

Aaiu-f-em-kha-Nef (Egypt) *see* Ap-Taui.

Aakebi (Egypt) *see* Aai.

Aakhui (Egypt) *see* Ab (A); Achet.

Aalu (Egypt) *see* Aaru.

Aamu (Egypt)

The Aamu are one of four classes of mortals as described by Horus in the Fifth Division or Fifth Hour of Tuat. The others are Nehesu, Egyptians, and Themehu. *See also* Aai; Horus; Tuat.

Aana (Egypt) *see* Aani.

Aana-tuati (Egypt) *see* Aai.

Aani *Aana* (Egypt)

Also known as: *Dog-faced Ape.*

Aani, a protector deity, is a dog-headed ape sacred to the god Thoth and a companion or associate of Thoth or Khnemu. In the First Hour of the night, unnamed, singing apes opened the way for the great god Ra and guided his boat through the hall to the Tuat. Two ape-gods, Benth and Aana, ministered to Osiris during the Second Hour of the night of the journey to Tuat. Khnemu is also associated with a group of eight apes; four of the apes are collectively called the Bentet apes, who are individually named Aaan, Bentet, Hetet-sept, and Qeften. Their duty was to praise the morning sun. The other four apes are known as the Utennu apes, named Ap, Asten, Kehkeh, and Utennu, and it was their responsibility to praise the evening sun. Aani is generally depicted as an ape, or an ape with the head of a dog. *See also* Aai; Ab; Khnemu; Osiris; Thoth; Tuat.

Aaru (Egypt)

Also known as: *Aa Sekhemu, Aalu, Aat, Sekhet-Aaru, Sekhet-hetep.*

Aaru is a place of bliss for good souls. This is the heaven where the soul (ka) rests after traveling through Amenti (Hades), through Aukar, and being absorbed with Osiris in a place called Ker-neter. References are made in the Book of the Dead where prayers are made for the soul to travel to Sekhet-hetep (possibly another name for Aalu). One must pass through the Underworld to get to this place and it contains either eighteen or twenty-one pylons (towers on either side of temple entrances). The domain of Osiris is sometimes called Sekhet-Aaru and is divided into fifteen or twenty-one Aats (pylons). Each pylon is guarded by demons armed with long knives. Although the Aats are named, not all the guardian gods are mentioned. The Aats are Sekhet Aaru, whose god is Ra-Heru-Khuti; Apt-ent-khet with Fa-akh, whose god is Tu-qa-Aat; The Aat of the spirits, Ammehet, whose god is Sekher-remu; Asset, Hasert whose god is Fa-pet; Apt-ent-qahu, Atu, with Sept; Unt, with Hetemet-bau; Apt-net, with Aa-Sekhemu; Kher-aha, with Hap; Atru-she-en-nesert-f-em-shet, Akesi with Maa-thet-f; Amentet-nefert or Amentet. Aaru is sometimes described as a tower or field of peace. The fields in Aaru are cultivated for food for the dead. *See also* Amentet; Elysian Fields; Ka; Nirvana; Tuat.

Aarvak *Arvak, Arvakr* (Norse; Teutonic)

Also known as: *Early Waker, Frost Mane, Hrim-faxi.*

Aarvak, also called "Early Waker," is one of the horses that pulls Sol the sun in its chariot along its course. His companion horse is Alsvid, "the fleet one," who represents the dawn. The animals were created in Muspells-heim, the land of warmth and brightness. The shield, Svalin, was formed to protect the horses and the earth from the harmful rays of the sun. A third horse, Alsvider, pulls Mani the moon in its cart along its course. Alsvider does not require the protection of the shield because of the weak rays of the moon. Aarvak may be associated with the horse mentioned in tales as Hrim-faxi, who pulled the dark chariot of Nott (Natt) through the heavens. *See also* Alsvid; Austri; Helius (Greek); Hrim-faxi; Muspells-heim; Natt; Nordri; Pegasus (Greek); Sol; Sudri; Westri.

Aat-shefsheft (Egypt) *see* Aai; Ab-ta.

Aati (Egypt)

He is one of the forty-two assessors or judges of the dead. In the hymns to Osiris from the "Book of the Dead," there are twenty-one deities on each side of the hall of the Maat (also called Maati) goddesses. These goddesses may be the goddess Maat in dual form or they may represent the goddesses from the South and North of Egypt. Two goddesses often referred to are likened to the two solar boats called Maaty. Although Aati is named he is not one of the primary deities of Egypt. *See also* Amit; Assessors; Maat; Osiris; Tuat.

Aatiu (Egypt) *see* Aai.

Aats (*Pylons*) (Egypt) *see* Aaru.

Aau (Egypt)

Aau, a jackal-headed mummy, stands at one end of the corridor of the Fifth Division or Fifth Hour (the pylon named Arit) of Tuat where the serpent Teka-hra guards the entrance. The other end of the corridor is guarded by the mummy Tekemi-aau. *See also* Aai; Tuat.

Ab (A) *Ib* (Egypt)

Also known as: *Shahar* (Arab).

The Ab, an amulet representing the heart, is said to contain the soul of Khepri, the immortal self-created god. Khepri, in the form of a beetle is made into an amulet believed to give new life. Ab is also the heart, thought to be the origin of energy, intellect, feelings and emotions. Achet, also known as Aakhui, is an amulet made of red stones or glass. It is representative of the rising sun and is said to give the owner the qualities of the sun god Ra. Another well known amulet is Tyt, a symbol of protection, said to be made from the knot of the magic girdle of Isis. The amulet Weres (Urs) was put under the pillow of the mummy to protect it from being decapitated in Tuat (the underworld). Ab is also the name of one of the numerous gods who minister to Osiris during the Second Hour of the night. Many other amulets were made to represent divine figures, animal figures, body parts (wedjat-eye), and symbols of royalty. Small amulets of the Ba made of gold and semiprecious stones were placed on the breast of the mummy to insure everlasting life. Instructions from the "Book of the Dead" were recited to endow the amulets with magic powers. The upper part of the Ab amulet was sometimes in the form of a human head. Made of red stones, it is inscribed in the chest of a mummy to represent the heart, which was buried in its own container. *See also* Abu; Anni; Ba; Ka; Khepri; Isis; Shahar; Tuat.

Ab (B) (Chaldean, Sumerian)

He is the Lord of Wisdom and Father of the Waters.

Ab-esh-imy-duat *Ab-sha-am-tuat* (Egypt)

Also known as: *Ab-she, Akhen.*

Ab-esh-imy-duat is a monster crocodile who guards the tomb of Osiris in the seventh section (hour) of Tuat (the underworld). In this section, the hidden abode of Osiris is found. It is said that when the great sun god Ra passes the monster, the god mesmerizes the beast with magic words. This allows the deceased Osiris, in the ground under the monster, to raise his head and gaze at Ra, which in turn allows the followers of Osiris to look upon Ra and be restored to life. Another demon crocodile is Ab-she who is said to eat lost souls, also in the Seventh Section or Seventh Hour of Tuat. Another serpent encountered during this portion of the journey, is Neha-hra. He attempts to stop the sun boat when it has reached a shallow junction where it appears to be impossible to go forward. Isis steps in and murmurs magical words; Neha-hra is held back at knife-point by the scorpion-goddess, Serqet and Her-tesu-f. Ra, protected by the serpent Mehen, continues his journey. *See also* Ab-ta; Akeneh; Apepi; Apophis; Ba, Shepes; Tuat.

Ab-ramu (Arabic, Babylonian, Hebrew) *see* Abram.

Ab-sha-am-Tuat (Egypt) *see* Ab-esh-imy-duat.

Ab-she (Egypt) *see* Ab-esh-imy-duat; Akhen.

Ab-ta (Egypt)

Ab-ta is a monster serpent guarding the Ninth Hour or Ninth Division of Tuat. This division is called Aat-shefsheft and here the Aai gods reside with a multitude of interesting beings. The corridor guardians are Anhefta and Ermen-ta and nine deified mummies guarding the wall. On the sun boat's right side are four gods of the South, a pillar with a bearded head wearing a white crown on top of it and a hawk-headed sphinx wearing a white crown. There is yet another bearded head, wearing a white crown with a human figure standing on his back and on top of this figure are the heads of Horus and Set. There are also the four gods of the North wearing red crowns, another pillar with a bearded head atop it, also wearing a red crown. There are two people holding serpents; one serpent, named Shemti, has four heads at each end of his body. He is held by Apu. Someone else holds a serpent with a head at each end of his body. This serpent is Bath, and Tepi, yet another serpent stands on his back. Tepi is equipped with four human heads, breasts, arms and four pairs of human legs. There are two other people who appear to have normal attributes. On the left side of the boat, there is another intriguing group. We find sixteen deities, four with the heads of men, four with the heads of ibises, four with the heads of hawks and four with the heads of rams. A double serpent with four heads is there, along with the well-known Khepri, who has Heru-tuati, the hawk poised on his back. The famous evil serpent, Apepi is there along with Shesshes, the crocodile, who has a tail which terminates in a serpent's head. The serpent Sesi meets his fate in this hour. *See also* Aai; Ab-esh-imy-duat; Abuk and Inet; Akhenet; Apophis; Ra.

Ab-u (Middle East) *see* Abu; Tammuz.

Aba (Choctaw People, North America)
Also known as: "*Great Spirit.*"
Aba is the name of the Great Spirit of the Choctaws. Originally known as mound builders, the Choctaw's important structures were made of wood and erected on huge earthen mounds, sometimes sculpted in the form of exalted animals. In legend, they believed they came from the internal regions of the earth along with grasshoppers. But, because their mother was killed by man, the revengeful grasshoppers persuaded Aba to close the opening and the men remaining inside became ants. The principal tribes known as mound builders are the Cherokee, Choctaw, Creek, Hitchiti, and Natchez who were located in what is now the Mississippi and Ohio regions of the United States. The mound builders originated from three separate cultures: Mississippians, Hopewell and the Adena. Carved stone figures thought to represent heroes, (placed in their wooden temples) and examples of fine engravings have been found on bone and copper (dating from C.E. 1000–1600).

Abaangui (South America) *see* Abaangui and Zaguaguaya.

Abaangui and Zaguaguaya (Guarayo People, South America)
Heroes, possibly divine beings. The brothers Abaangui and Zaguaguaya are culture heroes. A culture hero is a mythological creator figure, often presented in human or animal form, who shaped mortals and endowed them with their material and spiritual heritage.

Abaasy *Abasy* (Yakut People, Siberia)
Also known as: *Chebeldei.*
The Abaasy are wicked spirits from the lower regions, ruled by the great god, Ulu Tojon, or Arson Duolai (ruler of the dead). The son of the Abaasy chief is a cyclops with one eye and seven gigantic iron teeth. All these underworld spirits have one thing in common: they are each partly or fully composed of iron. They are depicted as one-eyed cyclops with seven large iron teeth. *See also* Arson Duolai; Chebeldei; Ulu Tojon.

Ababinili (Chickasaw People, North America)
He is the great or supreme spirit who is possibly a fire or sun god. Ababinili is generally thought of as the life, light, and warmth of spirit.

Abac (Irish) *see* Addane.

Abaeus (Greek) *see* Apollo.

Abaia (Melanesia)
Abaia, an evil eel was said to have caused a flood when a woman caught a fish in his lake. The only survivor was an elderly woman who had eaten a magical fish. In Saddle Island, Melanesia, there is said to be a pool "into which if any one looks he dies; the malignant spirit takes hold upon his life by means of his reflection on the water." *See also* Aokeu.

Abaios (Greek) *see* Apollo.

Abakan-Khan (Siberia) Rain or storm god.

Abanathabla (Middle East) *see* Abraxas.

Abans (Persia) Spirit of iron. Protector of iron miners.

Abantiades (Greek)
The Abantiades are the descendants of Abas, his son Acrisius, and Perseus, his great-grandson by Acrisius' daughter Danae. *See also* Abas (A); Acrisius; Danae; Perseus.

Abaris (Greek)
Priest, messenger, and possibly a Druid. Abaris, the servant of Apollo, in the land of the Hyperboreans, was transported to Greece on a golden arrow to visit Pythagoras. Abaris was the legendary instructor of Pythagoras and was described by Hecateus as a Druid apparently because Abaris had visited the area and had an impressive knowledge of the people and their philosophy. *See also* Aethalides; Apollo.

Abas (A) (Greek)
Renowned warrior. Abas, a former king of Argos, is the son of Lynceus, husband of Aglaia or Ocaleia, father of Chalcodon, twin sons Acrisius and Proetus, and a daughter, Idomene. Another son, Lycrus, was born outside of his marriage. Abas had inherited the magic shield of his grandfather Danaus, which was sacred to Hera. It was seized by Aeneas during his strife with Turnus, the Roman lord of darkness. *See also* Abantiades; Acrisius; Danaus; Hera.

Abas (B) (Greek)
Abas is the son of the great prophet Melampus and his spouse Lysippe. His brothers are Mantius and Antiphates. He married Talaus and had two children, Coeranus and Lysimache. *See also* Lysippe; Melampus.

Abas (C) (Greek)
A centaur, Abas was either the son of Ixion and Nephele or King Celeus of Eleusis and Metaneira. His brothers were thought to be Demophon and Triptolemus. He may have been the friend who traveled with Aeneas from Troy to Italy. His background, though vague, indicates that he was a skilled warrior. In one myth he roused Demeter's ire and was transformed into a lizard. *See also* Aeneas; Demeter; Ixion.

Abasoms (Africa) *see* Abonsam and Abosom.

Abasy (Siberia) *see* Abaasy.

Abathur (Gnostic)
Also known as: *B'haq Ziva.*
Abathur, a divine being known as an Uthra, is an angel. He brought forth another divine being in his own image by contemplating his reflection on black water. This being was named Ptah-il-Uthra. *See also* Ptah-il-Uthra; Uthra.

Abatwa (Africa)
The Abatwa are tiny spirits who hide under leaves of grass and sleep in anthills. They shoot their enemies with poison arrows.

Abderus (Greek, probably Thrace)
In some legends, Abderus is the hero son of Hermes from Opus. He is also said to be the son of Opian Menoetius, which would make him the brother of Patroclus. He was reputed to be the lover and armor bearer of Heracles. Heracles left him to guard the man-eating mares of Diomedes and when he returned he found that Abderus had been brutally ripped apart and eaten.

Heracles built the city of Abde'ra in honor of his friend. The city had the reputation for having a population of intellectually inferior inhabitants. *See also* Diomedes; Heracles; Hermes; Menoetius; Patroclus.

Abdu and Inet (Egypt) *see* Abuk and Inet.

Abel *Abelus, Abil* (Arabic)
Also known as: *Habel, Habil, Habl, Hebel, Hobal* (Persian, Arabic), (Hebrew, Muslim).

In the Hebrew and Christian tradition, Abel is the second son of Adam and Eve. He was the first man to sacrifice a lamb to God. The tale is told that Cain, a farmer, jealous of his brother, Abel, a herdsman and nomad, killed him. In the Islamic tradition, Abel (known as Abil or Habil) is Kabil's (Cain) younger brother. They are the eldest sons of forty children; twenty sets of twins. Abil was about to present his twin sister to Kabil so they could be man and wife. Kabil would not return the gesture by giving his brother his twin sister. The earth was without other females. Abil and Kabil's father, Adam, had been instructed by God to let the brothers marry each other's twin. God demanded to be appeased by sacrifices from the brothers. Abil offered his best ram. Kabil offered wild fruits. He then provoked a quarrel. Satan, standing nearby, was privy to the incident. He offered a large stone to Kabil, who accepted. He took the weapon and smashed his brother's skull. Abil, the first man to die, was buried by Kabil, his brother, and murderer. *See also* Adam; Cain; Eve; Hab'al.

Abellio (Celtic, Gaul)
Abellio, the apple tree god, was worshipped by the ancient Druids as were Robur, the oak tree god; Fagus, the beech tree god; and Buxenus, the box tree god. In the Gaulish "Biliomagus," a number of sacred trees are mentioned; the Oak of Mughna, the Ash of Uisnech, the Yew of Ross and others. *See also* Buxenus; Fagus; Robur.

Abeona (Roman)
She is the goddess who protects the child during his or her first efforts at walking and first departure from home. The city of Rome is protected by Abeona and she is also thought of as the protective goddess of travelers.

Abere (Melanesia)
Demoness. Abere was known as a wild, provocative woman who murdered men. It was said that the mimia reed grew around her to hide her from her victims. She was known for having a number of young female companions. Mesede, the marksman rescued Abere's son from a crocodile and then captured her young women. His jealous wife had the most beautiful of the captives beheaded and thrown into the sea and the other captives were slaughtered. In myth, the original victim's body became hard from the water and resembled a log which was washed ashore. Flies hollowed it out. The hero Morave found it, covered it with skin and made a drum. *See also* Mesede.

Aberewa (Ashanti) *see* Asase Yaa.

Abheda (Buddhist; India)
Also known as: *Mi-che-pa* (Tibet), *Mi-p'yed* (Tibet).
Abheda, meaning steadfast, is a deified mortal, the sixteenth

of sixteen arhats (saints). His symbol is the caitya (the stupa which holds sacred relics). This is also the symbol for Kuvera and Maitreya (qq.v.). *See also* Ajita; Medicine Buddhas; Stupa.

Abhijnaraja (Buddhist; Tibet)
One of the Medicine Buddhas (q.v.).

Abhimanyu *Saubhadra* (Hindu; India)
Son of Arjuna, spouse of Uttara and father of Parikshit, the king of Hastinapura. *See also* Arjuna; Parikshit.

Abiku (A) (Yoruba People, Africa)
The Abiku are hungry, thirsty, evil spirits who victimize children. To satisfy their desires, they enter the body of the child and the child can die. To drive the Abiku away, the parents leave food for it and ring bells, which the Abiku dislike. If they rub pepper into open cuts on the child the Abiku will depart to escape the pain. *See also* Abiku (B); Ifa; Olodumare; Olori; Olorun.

Abiku (B) (Dahomey People, Africa)
A forest spirit who can enter the womb of a woman, be born and dwell on earth, die, and be reborn into the same family. If the parents believe their child is an Abiku, they can dedicate the child to a Vodu (god). The Vodu protects the child from being taken back to the forest. In the past, sometimes the child's face would be scarred to deliberately make him or her ugly and unappealing to the spirits. Such a child would often be fitted with iron anklets to hold him or her to the earth or bells to keep them from running away. *See also* Vodu.

Abjaja "Born from a Lotus" (India) *see* Brahma.

Abjayoni (India) *see* Brahma.

Ablathanabla (Gnostic) *see* Abraxas.

Ablu (Etruscan) *see* Apollo.

Aboatia (Africa) *see* Mmoatia.

Abok (Africa) *see* Deng.

Abokas (Malaysia) Home of the dead.

Abonsam (Guinea, Africa)
Also known as: *Abasoms.*
Evil spirits. Water or tree deities. To drive the Abonsam from the village or home and to cleanse the area it was necessary to have four weeks of silence. During this period, it was hoped that the evil spirits would be frightened away. This was followed by a night of creating noise; thunderous sounds by rattling pots, beating sticks together and screaming loudly. They are possibly the same as the Abosom, the spirits of the Ashanti people (q.v.). *See also* Asase Ya; Nyame; Tano.

Abore (Warrau People, Guyana)
A culture hero who learned his skills from Wowta, a frogwoman. She kept him as a slave when he was a young man. He escaped the evil woman by enticing her to a hollow tree full of honey where she became stuck.

Aborigine People — Creation Legend *see* Bunjil; Dijanggawls (Australia)

Abosom *Obosom* (Ashanti People, Africa)
Also known as: Probably the same as *Abonsam.*

Tree or water spirits. There are thought to be several hundred Abosoms who are descendants of Nyame (Nana Nyankopon), a rain god and Asase Ya, his wife. They had four children. The most famous child is the former thunder god Tano who is now known as a river god. Two of the other children are Bia and Ananse. The fourth is not named. *See also* Abonsam; Asase Ya; Nyame; Tano.

Abou (Egypt) *see* Abu.

Abracadabra (Gnostic) *see* Abraxas.

Abraham (Hebrew) *see* Abram.

Abram *Ab-ramu, Abraham* (Hebrew, Christian, Arab), *Ibrahim* (Islamic).

"Father of a multitude." In the Islamic and Hebrew traditions the story is basically the same. The iniquitous King Nimrod, son of Caanan, a shrewd astrologer, foretold the birth of Abram (later to become known as Abraham) by reading the stars. When he was told that a man would be born who would rise up against him, he gathered his advisors together. A plan was devised to alter the promised course of events. A large building would be erected to house all the pregnant women. They were to be held under lock and key. If a woman gave birth to a male child, it was to be murdered. Seventy thousand newborns were slaughtered. Terah, heavy with child and extremely frightened, decided to leave the city. She headed toward the desert and passing along the edge of a valley, she came upon a cave where she sought refuge. Abram was born the next day surrounded by the brilliant light of his countenance. His mother wrapped him in her garment and abandoned him. The baby cried and wailed for sustenance. God sent the angel Gabriel down to the baby with milk. Gabriel devised a method for Abram to have access to the milk by sucking the little finger of his right hand. The infant remained in the cave feeding himself for ten days. At that time not only was he fully grown, but through Gabriel he came to the realization that for him there was only one true god. In the *Old Testament* the story continues that the shepherd Abram, following his god's orders, left Haran (he came from Ur in Babylonia) and went to Canaan. It was here he made a covenant with his god. He was promised that if he followed his command, he would be given the land of Canaan. He was also given the name Abraham. God also promised him a son in his old age. When his wife Sarah gave birth to Issac, Abraham's god tested his faith by asking him to sacrifice the child. (In the Muslim tradition, it is Ishmael, Abraham's son by the slave Hagar, who was offered as sacrifice). As Abraham was about to fulfill his god's bidding, the deity showed him a ram in the bush to be sacrificed instead. He was then promised by the god that his seed would multiply like the stars in the heavens. The Hebrew tradition adds to the *Old Testament* version of Abraham's story many "hero" stories. Abraham so detested Chaldean astrology that he smashed his father's idols. His mission in the world was as the spokesperson for one, living god. He was a giant, and a typical culture hero who discovered superior methods of agriculture, the alphabet, and knowledge of magic. He was a healer who used the precious stone around his neck to heal the sick. He also introduced circumcision to his people which became known as "Abraham's seal." Described as a monster with the strength of seventy-four

men, Abram died at one hundred and seventy-five years of age. Compare Abram to Brahma; Buddha; Krishna; Zeus; Zoroaster. *See also* Gabriel; Noah; Zam Zam.

Abrasax (Middle East) *see* Abraxas.

Abraxas (Egypt, Semitic, Syria)
Also known as: *Abanathabla, Ablathanabla, Abracadabra, Abrasax.*

Sun god. Abraxas is found in the doctrine of Simon Magus (the "father of Gnostics"). Abraxas and Ildebaoth were serpent symbols with the head of a lion surrounded by rays and were used at Gnostic ceremonies. It is said that the name was created to replace the unmentionable name of the Supreme Being. Basilides, the Gnostic, was thought to have declared that between the unknown Father of All and this world there were interposed a series of 365 heavens corresponding to the days of the year, chief of these being Abraxas. The Persian sun god had this name and in Syria, Abraxas was a form of Iao (Yahveh, or Yahweh). The word Abraxas was used on a seal or amulet to exorcise evil spirits. Sometimes Abraxas is shown with the body of a man, the legs formed of serpents, and holding the shield of Sophia. *See also* Iao; Sophia.

Abrayanti (India) A Krittika sister. *See also* Rishi.

Abru-el (Arab) *see* Adam; Gabriel.

Abruel (Arab) *see* Gabriel.

Absusu (Sumerian) *see* Abtagigi; Ishtar.

Absyrtus (Greek)
Also known as: *Phaethon.*

King of Colchis. An Argonaut. His grandfather is the sun god Helios, his father is Aeetes and his mother is rumored to be one of any number of women including Hecate. He is the nephew of Phaethon, son of Helios and Clymene. *See also* Adon; Aeetes; Helios; Phaethon.

Abt (Egypt) *see* Anhur.

Abta (Egypt) *see* Aai.

Abtagigi (Assyrian, Babylonia, Sumer)
Also known as: *Absusu, Aphrodite, Ishtar, Kilili.*

Goddess of harlots. She is an evil spirit who preys on men. Abtagigi is the name used for Ishtar in her aspect as the patron of sacramental promiscuity. In Babylonia and Assyria she was known as Kilili. The Greek goddess of love, Aphrodite, is said by some to be an aspect of Abtagigi. *See also* Aphrodite; Ishtar; Kilili.

Abtu and Ant (Egypt) *see* Abuk and Inet.

Abu *Abou* (Arabic, Egypt)
Also known as: *Elephantine* (Greek), *Elephantis.*

Light deity. Vegetation deity. Abu was an early Egyptian god of light who was likely worshipped in the city of the same name that was the site of the temples of Khnum (Kneph). The Greek name for this deity was Elephantis from Elaphas who was an Osirian god of light or sun. Abu or Abou can mean father when used as a prefix in the ancient Arabian language. One source says the ancient Sumerians thought of this deity as a vegetation god. In ancient Sumerian texts Abu was a god of vegetation. He is possibly similar to Ab whose hieroglyph is the phallus. *See also* Ab; Khnum.

Abu-Turab (Persia) *see* Ali.

Abuda (Japan) *see* Jigoku.

Abugupham-Bumo (Dhammai People, India)

Abugupham-Bumo and Anoi-Diggan-Juje were the first mortals. Their parents are the sister and brother frogs, Lujju-phu and Jassuju. The first mortals gave birth to Lubukanlung, Sangso-Dungso and Kimbu-Sangtung. *See also* Shuznaghu.

Abuk (Dinka People, Africa)

Abuk is a creator goddess and a goddess of women and gardens. She is an ancestor of Nyalitch, creator of the world and lord of the spirits. Aywil, thought to be the founder of the Dinka religion, learned and taught the people to pray to the supreme god Nyalitch through Deng, who is said to have adopted the role of a divine ancestor, or Abuk. Diing, the first man, opposed this law and after a fight, agreed that Aywil (also a divine ancestor) and his sons would have dominion over the sky and rain and Diing and his sons would rule the food-producing earth. In one myth, Abuk and Garang were the first man and woman. It is said that they were tiny but fully formed creatures made of clay. They were placed in a bean-pot overnight and swelled to full size. Abuk's emblem is a little snake. *See also* Aywil; Deng; Nyalitch.

Abuk and Inet (Egypt)

Also known as: *Abdu and Inet, Abtu and Ant.*

Guardians. Abuk and Inet were two fish that swam on either side of the boat of the sun god Ra to drive away all the evil entities in the water. *See also* Aai; Ab-ta; Apepi; Ra. *Note:* Abuk (Dinka people) is a completely different deity.

Abundantia (Teutonic) *see* Fulla.

Abundia (Teutonic) *see* Fulla.

Abundita (Roman) Farm Goddess.

Abyrga (Central Asia)

This deified serpent or sea-monster lives at the foot of the Tree of Life and dwells in a lake of milk. In some myths he is wound around Sumur, the world mountain. The Garide bird lives at the top of the tree. Compare Abyrga to Yggdrasil.

Abyzu (Gnostic, Semitic)

Abyzu is a demoness nightmare figure who frightens children while they sleep and causes the mother's milk to turn cold. It is said that St. Michael was able to break her spell by coercing her to reveal her forty names. She corresponds to Lamassu (q.v.).

Abzu (Sumerian) *see* Apsu.

Acacallis *Acalle* (Greek)

Also known as: *Chione, Deione.*

Acacallis, a deified mortal, is the daughter of Minos and Pasiphae. Her famous siblings are Androgeus, the famous athlete, winner of all events in the Panathenaea, who was killed by a bull; Ariadne, who aided Theseus in his escape from the Labyrinth; Catreus, who was killed accidentally by his son

Althaemenes; Deucalion, an Argonaut; Euryale, the mother of the famous giant and hunter, Orion; Lycastus; Glaucus, who almost died in a honeypot as an infant but was saved by Poly-eidus; Phaedra, who committed suicide; and Xenodice. Apollo seduced Acacallis and she bore a son, Miletus. Enraged, her hypocritical father exiled her from Crete and sent her to Libya. She had another son by Apollo named Amphithemis, also known as Garamas, who married Tritonis and became the father of Caphaurus (also called Cephalion) and Nasamon. In some legends she is also the mother of Phylacides and Philandros. Acacallis is also the mother of Cydon by Hermes or Tegeates. It may be that Acacallis was Chione, the daughter of Daedalion. She is possibly the same as Chione, who was probably the real wife of Hermes. *See also* Apollo; Ariadne; Hermes; Minos; Orion; Pasiphae; Theseus.

Academus (Greek)

Also known as: *Echedemus.*

Hero and possibly a god of light. Academus, an Arcadian living in Attica as a guest of Theseus, informed Castor and Pollux (the Dioscuri) where Theseus had incarcerated their sister, Helen. The Spartans treated him with respect and honor while he was alive and spared his property which was a short distance from Athens and is now called Academia. In another version of Helen's rescue, the Dioscuri rampaged through Attica until the people of Deceleia, who disliked Theseus, led the brothers to their sister. *See also* Castor and Pollux; Helen; Theseus.

Acala *Acara* (Buddhist; India, Nepal, Tibet)

Also known as: *Chandamaharoshana, K'ro-bo-mi-gyo-ba* (Tibet), *Mahachandrarosana, Vajrapani.*

Acala is an epithet of the Bodhisativa Vajrapani. He is depicted with four heads. *See also* Vajrapani.

Acalle (Greek) *see* Acacallis; Pasiphae.

Acamas (A) *Acamus, Akamas* (Greek)

Hero. Joint king of Melos. Acamas is the son of the hero Theseus and Phaedra. His siblings are Demophoon and two half-brothers: his father's illegitimate son, Hippolytus, and in some versions, Melanippus, (his mother being Perigune). His father, exiled from Athens, sent Acamas and Demophoon to King Elephenor in Euboea. As adults, they joined Elephenor and fought in the Trojan War, where they were able to rescue their grandmother Aethra, said to be Helen of Troy's slave. Acamas was one of the group who climbed into the belly of the Trojan horse. In one legend, he married Phyllis, declined her father's kingdom (offered as a dowry), and sailed away promising to return. Before his departure, Phyllis gave him a box that she said contained an object sacred to the goddess Rhea. She warned him to open it only if he decided not to return. Leaving her behind, he sailed to Cyprus and decided to settle there. When he didn't return, Phyllis cursed him and hung herself. Eventually, he opened the box. Terrified by its contents, he bolted away on his horse, was thrown to the ground and died by his own sword. A variation of this story is that Acamas and Phyllis were in love and possibly married. He went to fight in Troy and when his ship didn't return with the rest of the fleet, Phyllis, certain that he had been killed, died of grief. Athene, the goddess, transformed her into an almond tree and when

Acamas returned the next day he had only the trunk of the tree to embrace. The same story is told of Demophoon, although some think there were two Phyllises, both princesses, who died of grief and turned into almond trees. In another legend Acamas falls in love with Laodice, daughter of Priam, before meeting Phyllis and either he, or possibly his brother Demophoon, fathered a son, Munitus. In this version, he returned home from the war via Thrace where he fell in love with Phyllis and later deserted her. He comes to the same end in Cyprus where he fell off his horse and was killed by his own sword. Acamas was also known as the companion of Diomedes, king of Argos, whom he accompanied to Troy to demand the return of Helen after her elopement with Paris. *See also* Demophoon; Helen; Helius; Phaedra; Theseus.

Acamas (B) (Greek)

Acamus (B) is the son of the Trojan seer, Antenor, and his wife Theano, a priestess of Athena at Troy. His siblings are Agenor; Archelous; Coon, who was killed in the Trojan War; Crino, a sister; Demoleon, who was also killed in the war; Glaucus, who fought in the war; Helicaon, who also fought and was wounded; Iphidamas, who was killed; Laocoon; Laodamas; Lycaon, who was wounded in the war; Pedaeus, a half-brother; Polydamas, who was accused of being a traitor in the Trojan War, and Polybus. Acamas was a leader of the Dardanian forces in the Trojan War along with Aeneas and Archelous. He was killed by the archer, Meriones, who was also a commander of the Cretan forces. *See also* Aeneas; Antenor; Archelous; Meriones.

Acamas (C) & (D) (Greek)

Acamas (C) was a Thracian captain killed in the Trojan War by Ajax the Greater. Acamas (D), a cyclops, is mentioned as being one of the companions of Hephaestus when he lived on Mount Etna. Three other cyclopes are named, Brontes, Pyracmon, and Steropes. *See also* Ajax the Greater; Hephaestus.

Acan (A) (Chaldean)

Serpent god. Chaldean name meaning "great one."

Acan (B) (Maya People, Yucatan)

God of intoxication. Probably a deity of wine.

Acantum (Maya People, Yucatan) *see* Becabs.

Acara (Tibet) *see* Acala.

Acaragui (Native North American) *see* Niparaya.

Acaryavajrapani (India) *see* Vajrapani.

Acastus (Greek)

Acastus is the Argonaut son of Pelios and Anaxibia or Phylomache. He married Hippolyte or according to some texts, Astydameia, who is elsewhere known as his daughter. His daughters are Laodamia, Sterope, Sthenele and unnamed sons. Against his father's wishes he joined Jason, his father's enemy, as an Argonaut and later participated in the Calydonian Boar Hunt. His wife became infatuated with Peleus, king of the Myrmidons, who rebuffed her advances. Scorned, she lied to her husband and accused Peleus of attempting to seduce her. A short time later while on a hunting trip, Acastus stole Peleus' sword while he was asleep, leaving him defenseless. Peleus was almost killed by centaurs but was saved by the centaur Cheiron. With the assistance of Jason and the Dioscuri, he returned to Iolcus, destroyed the area and murdered the treacherous woman and according to some, Acastus. *See also* Acastus; Argonauts; Calydonian Boar Hunt; Jason; Pelios; Peleus.

Acat (Maya People, Yucatan)

God of Life. God of Tattooers. Acat is one of the Bacabs who are the four wind gods and the four pillars of heaven. They are the sons of Itzama, a hero who later became sacred. Their name list differs but four common names are Yuncemil, Echua, Backlum Chaam, and Chin. Acat is also responsible for the development of children in the womb. *See also* Acatl; Bacabs.

Acatl (Aztec People, Mexico)

Year god. Acatl is one of the four year bearers or year gods. He is in charge of the east region. Acatl is the god of those persons who dwell in this space and time. The other three gods are Tecpatl (north), Calli (west) and Tochthli (south). Possibly the same as Acat of the Maya People, who along with his brothers, the Becabs, were called pillars of heaven. Also similar to the Incan Tahuantin Suyu Kapac who were lords of the four quarters. Acatl corresponds to the skybearer, Tlauixcalpantecuhtli. *See also* Acat; Becabs; Calli; Tahuantin-Suyu-Kapac; Tecpatl; Tochtli.

Acca (Roman)

Acca was the wife of Heracles and is thought to be the counterpart of the Peloponnesian White Goddess, Acco. *See also* Acco; Heracles.

Acca Larentia *Acca Laurentia* (Etruscan, Roman)

Also known as: *Lupa.*

Mother goddess. Some feel that there is only one Acca Larentia, while others believe there are two. In both instances Acca Larentia is the nurse of Romulus and Remus. Acca Larentia (A) was won by Heracles in a game of dice with the king of Rome, Ancus Martius. Heracles was not able to collect his "prize" as the servant had locked her away. Eventually, she married Carutius and became the mother of the Fratres Arvales, twelve sons. When her husband died he left her a substantial estate. Upon her death she willed money to the people of Rome. Her festival, known as Larentalia is a rowdy celebration observed on December 23. Acca Larentia (B) is the wife of Faustulus, who was the shepherd of either the flocks of Numitor or Amulisu. Faustulus found Romulus and Remus, and Acca Larentia was their nurse. *See* Lares; Lupa; Mercury (A); Romulus.

Acca Laurentia (Roman) *see* Acca Larentia.

Acesidas (Greek) Another name for Idas, one of the Dactyli.

Acestes *Acestis* (Greek)

Hero and ancient king. Acestes is the son of the river-god Crimisus and the nymph Segesta or the Trojan woman Egesta. He was the king of Eryx or Drepanum, a Trojan settlement in Sicily. A Trojan War hero, the city of Acesta was named in his honor. During the funeral games after the burial of Anchises, he became the winner of the archery contest. Acestes may have been considered a god of lightning. *See also* Anchises; Crimisus; Egesta; Rivers.

Acestis (Greek) *see* Acestes.

Acetes (Greek) *see* Evander (B).

Ach-Chazu (Babylon) *see* Ahhazu.

Achachilas (Aymara People, Bolivia; Andeans)
Also known as: *Machulas.*
Mountain deities. Frost spirits. The Achachilas are objects of reverence and worship found in nature. Many Achachilas are mountain peaks that are often claimed as ancestors and have numerous myths attached to them. When two peaks face one another, they are identified as male and female entities. The People of the Andean highlands identify the Achachilas and Machulas as good and evil spirits and identify them with objects of nature and often with the spirits of famous deceased persons. Compare to Fuji (Japan). *See also* Anchancho; Ekkekko.

Achaeans (Greek) *see* Achaeus.

Achaei (Greek) *see* Achaeus.

Achaemenides (Greek) *see* Odysseus.

Achaeus (Greek)
Also known as: *Achates.*
Achaeus is the hero son of the Thessalian Xuthus (known as "the thievish one") and Creusa. His siblings are Diomede, Ion, and in some legends, Dorus. A descendant of Prometheus and the grandson of the hero Hellen, he had two sons, Archander and Architekes (Architeles). Achaeus and Ion went to Aegialus, in the Peloponnesus, with their father. Ion eventually became the king. Achaeus and allies from Athens and Aegialus banded together and reclaimed the Thessalian throne which had once belonged to Xuthus. The general area then became known as Achaea. Achaeus' sons moved to Argos, married daughters of Danaus and became so renowned that the Argives name was replaced by Achaeans, after Achaeus. *See also* Diomede; Hellen; Prometheus.

Achamoth (Gnostic)
Achamoth was an ousted god hurled into the abyss and deemed a fallen aspect of the lower Sophia. He represents the lower Wisdom; the form where spirit succumbs to matter and becomes the basis of the real world. *See also* Aeons; Pistis Sophia.

Achates (Greek, Roman) *see* Achaeus; Aeneas.

Acheloos (Greek) *see* Achelous.

Achelous *Acheloos* (Greek)
A river god. Shape changer. Achelous is the eldest of the three thousand sons (known as the Rivers) of Oceanus and Tethys. He is also been said to be the son of Sol by Terra or Helios by Gaea. Mating with Calliope or Terpsichore, he became the father of the three Sirens: Leucosia, Ligeia, and Parthenope. He is also thought to be the father of Callirrhoe, who was the mother of Ganymede. Achelous and Hercules were the suitors of Deianira (Dejanira). After a major competition for her hand Achelous was overthrown by Hercules. He turned himself into a serpent, was nearly strangled by his foe and then turned himself into a bull. Heracles wrenched off his horn, which the Naiads presented to the Goddess of Plenty, Amaltheia, who stuffed her treasures in its hollow. It has since become the legendary "Cornucopia." Achelous changed five nymphs into islands and seduced Perimele who was also turned into an island by Poseidon. Achelous is shown with the body of a bull and the head of a bearded and horned man, and sometimes as a snake. To compare to other river gods, *see* Acheron; Amaltheia; Alpheus; Asopus; Calydonian Boar Hunt; Cephissus; Cocytus; Helius; Heracles; Melpomene; Muses; Naiads; Oceanids; Oceanus; Rivers; Sirens.

Acheren (Greek) *see* Acheron.

Acheron *Acheren* (Greek)
Also known as: *Acherusia.*
A river god. Acheron is one of the three thousand sons of Oceanus and Tethys, Gaea, or Demeter. He was also said to be the father of Asclepius by Orphne or Gorgyra. In legend, he was punished and sent to Hades by the gods for providing drinks to the Titans during their battle with the Olympians. A variation of this story is that Acheron was banished to Hades when he had outlived his usefulness on earth. Acheron, the river, is the name of one of five rivers that are said to be connected with Hades. The very name, Acheron, was a synonym used in place of Hades to signify hell and was known as the "River of Woe and Sadness." The other rivers are Cocytus (wailing or groans), Lethe (forgetfulness), Phlegethon or Pyriphlegethon (fire) and Styx (the gods sealed their oaths by this name). The ancient and difficult Charon ferried souls of the dead across the Acheron, Cocytus and Styx rivers. *See also* Achelous; Alpheus; Asopus; Cephissus; Charon; Cocytus; Furies; Inachus, Lether; Oceanids; Oceanus; Rivers; Styx; Tartarus. The Acheron is similar to the Celtic Achren (q.v.).

Acherusia (Greek) *see* Acheron.

Achet (Egypt) *see* Aakhui; Ab.

Achilles *Achilleus*
Also known as: *Pyrrha* (Greek).
Achilles, the principal character of the Homeric epic of the *Iliad*, is the son of Peleus, king of the Myrmidons in Thessaly, and of Thetis, a sea goddess. He is thought to be the father of Neoptolemus (Pyrrhus) by Deidamia. There are various accounts of his youthful years. One version states that his mother, in an attempt to bestow immortality upon him, held him in fire all night, and during the day anointed him with magical potions so that his mortal parts might be consumed. Another account relates that to make him invincible she held him in the river Styx, holding him by his heel, which became the vulnerable part of his body. It had been foretold by Calchas, a famous seer, that Troy could not be taken in battle without Achilles. Thetis, fearing for her son's safety, disguised him as a female and placed him among the daughters of Lycomedes of Scyros, where he was known as Pyrrha. Odysseus, disguised as a merchant came, to the court of Lycomedes under divine inspiration searching for the hero who would conquer Troy. The fair Achilles, looking through Odysseus' merchandise, ignored the feminine merchandise and seized upon the weapons and was said to have discovered that he was a male. His mentors were Cheiron the centaur, and the warrior Phoenix, king of the Dolopes. At the urging of Odysseus, he and his closest friend and lover, Patroclus, joined the Greeks in the Trojan War. It is said that Peleus gave Achilles his golden armor, an ashen spear

and two horses to protect him in battle. He became famous for his bravery during the war and for his influence with the gods. During a campaign in Lyrnessus, Achilles slaughtered the family of Briseis and captured her as his concubine. In the tenth year of the war, Agamemnon was instrumental in taking Briseis from Achilles. Achilles then shut himself up in his tent and refused to participate in battle. Patroclus begged Achilles to lend him his golden armor so that he could lead the Myrmidons back into battle. Achilles agreed. Subsequently, Patroclus was slain by Hector, the Trojan prince, who confiscated the armor. Grief-stricken, Achilles arranged a splendid funeral for his friend and had his mother obtain new armor from Hephaistos. After slaying many Trojans, Achilles finally killed Hector by pursuing him around the walls of Troy three times, tying his body to his chariot, and dragging him in the dust to the front of the city. Xanthus, the faithful and immortal horse who had the power of speech, warned his master Achilles of his impending death. The Homeric version of Achilles' death relates that he was slain by an arrow from the bow of Paris, directed by Apollo, which struck him in his heel. Another tells how he loved the daughter of Priam, Polyxena. Hoping to wed her he went among the Trojans unarmed, and was slain by Paris at the temple of Apollo. After his cremation his ashes were placed in Patroclus' urn. For the origins of Achilles' armor, *see* Hephaistos. For the disposition of his armor after his death, *see* Sigurd (regarding vulnerability). He is associated with Helen of Troy and with Aeacus; Aphrodite; Chiron; Peleus; Phoenix; and Thetis. To compare the friendship of Achilles and Patroclus, *see* Enkidu, and Gilgamesh. Compare Achilles to Krishna (India). *See also* Agamemnon; Ajax the Greater; Amazons; Briseis; Calchas; Cassandra; Hector; Iphigeneia; Odysseus; Patroclus, Polyxena; Styx; Zephyrus.

Achilleus (Greek) *see* Achilles.

Achillides (Greek) *see* Neoptolemus.

Achiyalatopa (Zuni People, North America)
   Achiyalatopa is a celestial monster, thought to be a knife or feather deity.

Achren *Acheron, Ochren* (Celtic)
   Aspects or known as: *Annfwn* (Welsh), *Annwn, Annwvyn, Donn.*
   Achren (in Brythonic legend) is the underworld of the ancient Celts. Often called "The Plain of Two Mists," it is very similar to the Greek Acheron (q.v.). In Welsh legend, the underworld is known as Annfwn and is ruled by Arawn. As the Celts accept death as another stage in life, Achren is not a place of hell and damnation, but a place where ancestors gather, and mortals may visit. A place out of human time, a visitor could find it a garden of delights, or a monster-filled nightmare, and could return to earth much older, and could even disintegrate. Achren is not found in a specific location but can be found in many places. Likewise, the routes to reach Achren are innumerable; even sudden understanding can take one there. Although punishment does not exist in this underworld, all is not love and light; conflict exists and is settled by the intervention of a human mediator. *See also* Annfwn; Arawn; Pwyll.

Achtaroth (Assyrian) *see* Asherah.

Achtoret (Assyrian) *see* Asherah.

Achyuta (India) *see* Vishnu.

Acidalia (Greek) *see* Venus.

Acis (Greek) River god.

Acis (Greek)
   River god. Acis is the son of Faunas and Marcia, the nymph of the River Stercutus. (Some say his mother is Symoethis.) His siblings are the man-hating Dryas and Latinus, the mortal king. A handsome, young herdsman of Sicily, Acis fell in love with the sea-nymph, Galatea, a Nereid. Polyphemus, a crude, one-eyed giant who also adored the beautiful nymph surprised the lovers in a compromising position (chatting by the shore, in a grotto, or in bed, depending on the myth). Enraged, he yanked a boulder from Mount Aetna and lunged at his rival, crushing his skull. Galatea plunged into the sea to avoid certain death. She gave her loved one immortality by transforming him into the god of a stream that flows to Mount Aetna. His blood formed the stream which bears his name. *See also* Cylcops; Faunas; Galatea; Nereids; Pan.

Acmon (Greek) *see* Oceanus.

Acmonides (Greek) *see* Cyclops.

Acolnauacatl (Mexico) *see* Mictlantecutli.

Acolnauactl (Mexico) *see* Miclantecutli.

Acotzentli (Aztec People, Mexico)
   Tree of Life. It gave food for the people during the second age of man. *See also* Legend of the Four Suns.

Acrea (Greek) *see* Rhea.

Acrisius (Greek)
   Acrisius, king of Argos, is the son of Abas and Aglaia or Ocaleia and the twin brother of Proetus. Sibling rivalry between the twins began in the womb. His other brother was Chalcodon, king of the Abantes of Euboea. He led the Euboeans in the battle between Thebes and Euboea and was killed by Amphitryon. Chalcodon's people were known as the Abantes. Acrisius married Eurydice, the daughter of the king of Sparta, Lacedaemon. Sparte, or in some versions Aganippe was the father of Danae and Evarete. It was prophetically foretold that Danae would give birth to a son who would slay him. He hid her in a brass tower to protect himself but that did not stop the great god Zeus. He gained access to her in a golden shower, and as a result, she became the mother of Perseus. The fearful Acrisius then encapsuled them in a chest and had it thrown into the sea. The chest landed on the island of Seriphus (Seriphos), and the mother and child were rescued by Dictys, the seaman of Acetes. Danae and Perseus were shipped off to live with Dictys' brother, Polydectes, the king of the country. Eventually, the prophecy became reality when Perseus threw a disc which accidentally hit his grandfather Acrisius in the foot and killed him. The golden shower is said to represent the sun's rays, necessary for fertilization. Another interpretation is the golden shower as a cloudburst that makes the earth fertile. The cloudburst could also represent a sacred marriage between heaven and earth. Compare Acrisius to Balor. *See also* Abas (A); Aganippe; Aglaia; Danae; Dictys; Oenamaus; Perseus.

Actaea (Greek) *see* Nereids; Nereus.

Actaeon (Greek)

Actaeon is the hero son of Aristaeus and Autonoe, brother of Macris, and possibly the grandson of Cadmus. He became a celebrated hunter and hero trained by the renowned hunter, Cheiron, said to be the wisest of the centaurs. Artemis caught him spying on her as she was bathing with some nymphs. Annoyed or embarrassed, she splashed him with water; he changed into a stag and was devoured by his own dogs. Less popular variations of this legend are that Actaeon bragged to Artemis, herself a skilled hunter, that he was the better hunter; irate, she killed him. Another is that Artemis, angry that he wanted to marry her aunt Semele, whom Zeus was wooing, killed him. Yet another version is that Actaeon tried to rape Artemis and she killed him in self defense. *See also* Argus (F); Aristaeus; Artemis; Cheiron; Semele.

Actaeus (Greek) *see* Agraulos.

Actis (Greek) *see* Heliades.

Actor (A) (Greek)

Hero. An Argonaut. There are various genealogies attributed to the hero Actor. As the king of Phocis, he is the son of Deion and Diomede and the brother of Aenetus, Asteropeia, Cephalus and Phylacus. His union with Aegina produced Irus, Menoetius (an Argonaut) and Polymela. He was the grandfather of Patroclus (Menoetius' son). Peleus, king of Myrmidons, who was an Argonaut, killed Actor's half-brother Phocus. Actor purified Pelus and was said to have given him one-third of his kingdom and either Polymela or Antigone for a bride. In another legend, he is the son of Mymidon and Peisidice and brother of Antiphus and Eupolemeia. He became the king of Phtia and was said to have died childless and to have left his estate to Peleus. Yet again, he is said to have had a son, Eurytion, who was adopted. For Actor's father's background, *see* Aeolus (A). *See also* Actor (B); Actor (C); Aegina; Argonauts; Patroclus; Peleus.

Actor (B) (Greek)

Actor is the son of Phorbas and Hyrmina and brother of Augeias and Tiphys. He is said to be the father of the twins, Ceatus and Eurytus, known as the Moliones (Molionides) after their mother; though it is also said that Poseidon is their father and Moliones their mother. *See also* Actor (A); Actor (C); Moliones; Poseidon.

Actor (C) (Greek)

Actor, the Argonaut and hero, is identified as the son of either Deion, the Phoenician, or one of the many men named Hippasus. Actor has also been called the son of Poseidon and Agamede. Agamede, celebrated for her knowledge of the healing arts, had two other sons, Belus and Dictys, also by Poseidon. She is the daughter of Augeas and wife of Mulius, an early healer who knew the healing properties of all plants. Actor has also been referred to as the father of Echecles and in other legends, Astyoche. A hero, Actor was said to have been conquered by Turnus, the Roman poet and soldier. *See also* Actor (A); Actor (B); Argonauts; Poseidon.

Acuecueyotl (Aztec People, Mexico)

She is the personification of waves and an aspect of Chalchiuhtlicue (q.v.).

Acyuta (India) "Immovable" *see also* Krishna.

Ad-Ama (Hebrew) *see* Adam.

Adad (A) *Addad, Addu* (Aramean, Assyrian; Babylonian; Canaanite; Sumerian).

Also known as: *Baal of Mt. Lebanon* (possibly), *Baalsamame, Balsamem, Balshameme, Balshamin, Bardad* (Syria), *Belshim, Ber, Bir, Birqu, Birque, Dadu* (Amorite), *Hadad* (Syrian), *Haddad* (Phoenician), *Ilhallubu* (Babylonian), *Ilumarru* (Akkadian), *Iluwir, Ishkur* (possibly), *Iskur, Jashar* (possibly; Hebrew), *KurGal, Kurgal* (Canaanite; "Great Mountain"), *Marri* (Sumerian), *Marru, Martu* (Amorite), *Ramman, Rammanu, Rammon* ("The Thunderer"; Amorite), *Rimmon, Riummon* (possibly; Syrian).

God of Storms and Floods. Prophet. Adad, son of Asherat of the Sea, replaced Enlil when Enlil was promoted to ruler of the earth. As his power could be used for beneficial and for destructive purposes he is both feared and worshipped. He is also a god of justice and punishment. His consort was the storm-goddess, Shala. Adad was the god who carried out the order for the Deluge given by Bel, or as others say, Ishtar. He was also known as the "Lord of Foresight." Adad is usually shown wearing a pointed helmet with his horns mounted on a bull and grasping three-pronged thunderbolts in each hand. See Enlil, or Shamash, who also could reveal the future. Adad is also similar to Hadad of Phoenician mythology. He was possibly merged with Marduk at a later date and he could be the forerunner of Zeus. He is thought to be the Amorite god Martu. Adad might be another name for Balshamin. He is also identified with Imi, Iskur, Mer, Mermer, Nigir, Nimgigri, Nimgirgirri, and Riummon. He is possibly the same as Bel, Ea, Hadad, Ishkur, Jashar, Marduk, Riummon, Yahveh, and Zeus.

Adad (B) (Syrian)

Also known as: *Hadad, Martu* (Amorite).

The spouse of Adargyns, the earth, Adad is a sun god. When husband and wife merged, creativity evolved. In Babylonia-Assyria, Adad was known as a god of thunder, storms and rainfall. *See also* Hadad.

Adad (C) (Assyrian)

The son of Anu, Adad is a god of storms who is associated with Baal and Hadad (qq.v.).

Adad-Ea (Babylonian)

In the Gilgamesh epic Adad-Ea ferried Gilgamesh. He is also credited with ferrying souls across the waters of death to Ut-Napishtim's abode. *See also* Charon; Gilgamesh.

Adam (A) *Ad-ama, Adamah*

Also known as: *Ade, Edie, Edom, Mahre* (Ancient Persian), *Odem* (Arabic, Babylonian, Hebrew, Persian, Syrian).

Adam is said to have been the first human formed by god from dust gathered by the angel Michael. His name may signify Ad-ama "father of the race." Eve (Khavah), the first female, was created from Adam's rib. According to the standard biblical version, Adam and Eve had two sons, Cain and Abel. Disobeying God's instructions, and succumbing to temptation, they were banished from the Garden of Eden and subsequently held responsible for humans becoming mortal. In some schools of thought, the story of Adam was of Babylonian origin, later repeated in Persian legends. The Arabs differ in thought from the Christians in that Cain was the son of Lilith and not Eve. While the Christians say God created Adam from dust, the Koran speaks of Allah sending four Archangels, (Gabriel, Michael, Asraphel [Israfel] and Asrael [Azrael]) for four handfuls of earth in different colors and texture. Only Asrael brought earth which God molded into the form of man. Adam awoke one morning to find Haiwa (also known as Eve), the first woman. God taught Adam, in Arabic, the names of all the "things" surrounding him. He warned Adam not to eat the fruit from one particular tree. To do so would mean banishment from the paradisical Janna to a life of hardship on earth. Iblis, the evil serpent demon who was hovering nearby in the garden, persuaded Haiwa to eat the fruit. Adam decided to join her. Both fell to earth. In another version Adam begot demons (Shedim and Lilith) originally and it was Lilith who bore Samael, Leviathan, and Asmodeus and the rest. In tales from the Apocryphal or pseudepigrapha legends they were also the parents of the sisters, Luluwa and Aklemia. In an ancient tale, Adam was created by God from the elements of the universe. His spirit was formed from the wind, his thoughts from the clouds, his eyes from the sun, his flesh and bones from the earth and roots, and his blood from water. Adam is symbolized as a pillar or pole. This story is similar to the Akkadian legend of Adapa where the great god is Ea. *See also* Abel; Adapa; Adhibuddha (India); Azazel; Cain; Ea.

Adam (B) *Sabaoth Adamas* (Gnostic)

Underworld god. From text of the post–Christian sect of the Ophites, and referenced in the text of the "Pistis Sophia," Adam is known as Sabaoth Adamas. He is a chief of Archons, the underworld. The god Melchizidek ("Receiver of Light"), opposed Adam. *See also* Hades; Pistis Sophia.

Adam and Balujen (Tinguian People, Philippine Islands)

The sons of the creator Kadaklan (q.v.).

Adamah (Hebrew) *see* Adam.

Adamanthea (Greek) *see* Zeus.

Adapa (Mesopotamian)

Also known as: *Addu* (Aramaean).

Created by the god of wisdom, Ea, to rule over the human race, Adapa is the chief-priest of Eridu, and some say, Ea's son. Fishing one day, Adapa's boat was overturned by the southwest wind demoness, Shutu. Angered, he cursed her and crippled her wings. The celestial deity, Anu, alarmed by the mortal man's power, sent his messenger Ilabrat to summon Adapa to his court. Ea informed Adapa to expect to be greeted at the heavenly gates by the gods Tammuz and Gizida (also known as Ningizzida), who would escort him to Anu and offer him bread and water. Possibly jealous, Ea instructed Adapa to refuse the nourishment, and lying, told him that it would cause his death. Anu instructed him to appear before the great god Ea. The court had to decide if they should kill the powerful mortal Adapa or raise him to the rank of a god. Tammuz and Gizida intervened and explained that since all wisdom had been revealed to Adapa by Ea, he needed only eternal life to become a god. It was

decided that Adapa would be made immortal. When he appeared before the gods he was offered bread and water, which unknown to him was the food of everlasting life. Adapa, following Ea's instructions, refused the nourishment. Not only did he lose the opportunity of immortality for all humans but it is said that he also brought illness, disease and death to other humans. The goddess of healing, Ninkarrak (said to be Anu's daughter), was able to cure all the ill effects of his act, except death. Adapa is often called the forerunner of Adam. This myth is similar to that of Yahweh and Adam (qq.v.). Compare Adapa's story to the tale of the Greek Persephone. *See also* Addu; Anu (B); Ea; Ilabrat; Ninkarrak; Tammuz.

Adar (A) (Persia) *see* Atar.

Adar (B) (Akkadian, Semitic)

Also known as: *Atar, Bar, En-ge, Nin-ib, Ninib, Nin-lil, Uras.*

Weather god. Adar is the son of the lord of ghosts and hell, Mul-lil. Known as the "Sun of the South," he controlled lightning and thunder. Adar in Hebrew means "splendid" or "shining." Uras, in Akkadian, means "the shining"; Nin-ib, "the Lord"; and Bar, "the bright" or "living." In Babylonian myth, Adar was another name for Ninib as god of the summer sun. *See also* Ninib.

Adargyns (Syrian)

"The Earth." She is the wife of Adad. *See also* Adad (B).

Adda-nari (Hindu) *see* Addanari.

Addad (Babylon) *see* Adad.

Addanari *Adda-Nari* (Hindu)

Goddess of nature, religion and truth. Addanari uses the same symbols as the Roman Mercury: a circle, cup, sword and magician's rod. She is identified with the Egyptian Isis. *See also* Mercury.

Addane (Celtic)

Also known as: *Abac* (Irish), *Avanc* (Celtic).

A water monster, sometimes described as a dwarf, Addane's abode is Lake Llyon Llion. After causing a great flood, he was dragged from his home by oxen belonging to Hu Gadarn. In a variation, he was killed by Peredur.

Addephagia (Roman)

Goddess of good cheer. She is generally shown as a smiling matronly woman surrounded by emblems of eating and drinking.

Adder (British Isles, Christians, Druids)

Evil serpent deity. The sly and crafty adder is thought by some to be an aspect of Eris, the goddess of strife. The Christians believed that the adder was a form of the devil. And, the Druids carried amulets (adder stones) as charms. An adder is said to have caused the Battle of Camlan (between Arthur and Mordred) and is also said to be the source of power of the ancient goddess Cailleach Bheur. Even though snakes were said not to exist in Ireland, the story is historically documented that the Milesius (natives of Ireland) carried banners with the symbol of a snake twisted around a rod, rather than the usual coat of arms. In Ireland, the adder was depicted as a green snake god. *See also* Arthur; Cailleach Bheur; Eris.

Addittee (India) *see* Aditi.

Addu (Aramaean)
Also known as: *Adad, Adapa, Marduk.*
Storm god. Addu is one of the fifty names that Anu proclaimed should be bestowed upon Marduk. Addu could have been a forerunner of Marduk or he could have merged with Marduk. It is possible that Addu is only an aspect of Adad. *See also* Adad; Adapa; Marduk.

Ade (Hebrew) *see* Adam.

Adee (Haida, Kwakiutl, Tlingit, Tsimshian People, North America)
Also known as: *Idi.*
Semi-divine creature. Adee, also known as the "Thunderbird" is described as an eagle with an extra head on its abdomen. Adee lives in a mountain lake and is strong enough to carry a whale with its talons.

Adekagagwaa (Iroquois People, North America)
A name for the sun as a Great Spirit. He controls the wind god Ga-oh, the thunder or storm god Hino and the god of winter, Gohone. *See also* Hino.

Adharma (India)
Brahma as the destroyer of all things. *See also* Anrita; Brahma; Maya People, Yucatan (C).

Adhibudda (India) *see* Adhibuddha.

Adhibuddha *Adi-buddha, Adhibudda* (Buddhist; India)
Also known as: *Buddha, Swayambhu* (Nepal).
Adibuddha is the primordial Buddha without beginning or end. He was manifested from the syllable AUM, and is self-existent. All things are manifested by him and emanate from him. The Dyhani Buddhas evolved from Adhibuddha. Adibuddha is said to be revealed in the form of a blue flame coming out of a lotus. *See also* Adam (Arabic, Christian, Semitic); Amida; Buddha; Dhyani Buddhas, P'an Ku (China); Purusha; Samantabhadra, Vajrasatwa.

Adhidevatas (India) *see* Devis.

Adhiratha (India) *see* Radha.

Adi (India) A shape changing demon. *See also* Vasistha.

Adi-Buddha (India) *see* Adhibuddha.

Adi-Pati (India) *see* Ganesha.

Adi-Siki-Taka-Pikone-no-Kami (Japan) *see* Three Goddesses of Munakata.

Adit (India) *see* Aditi.

Aditi *Addittee, Adit.* (Brahmanic, Hindu, Vedic; India, Iran)
Also known as: *Deva-Matri* (Mother of the Gods), *Devaki* (Inca People), *Shakti.*
Aditi, the "Mother of Worlds" is said to be self-formed. Originally, she was the mother of the early Persian Asuras and Asuris (demons), and the gods and goddesses known as the Suras and the Suris. Later, she was considered the mother of all gods. In some texts, she is called the daughter of Daksha, the wife of Kasyapa and mother of Vishnu in his avatar as Vamana. In her avatar as Devaki, she gave birth to Vishnu in his avatar as Krishna. For this reason, Vishnu is sometimes referred to as Aditi. In other texts she is the daughter of Vasus the god of wealth, the sister of the Aditya, the wife of Vishnu and mother of the Rudras. She is also portrayed as the mother of Daksha, and the mother of Indra, or the attendant of Indra. Danu (Diti) is said to be her sister and rival. There are indications that she could be the mother of Agni, the fire god. More frequently, she is known as the mother of the Adityas, a group of six, seven, eight, or twelve gods. Varuna is known as chief of the Adityas. In one well known myth, she has twelve children and she throws one of them, Martanda (the sun) also known as Vivasvat, into the sky. Her son, Indra, is said to have given his mother earrings which appeared on the water's surface when the gods churned the ocean. These earrings were stolen by the demon Naraka and returned to her by Krishna. Aditi is often invoked with Mitra and Varuna for protection, freedom from disease, and forgiveness from sin. Aditi has many titles; among them are; "The Boundless Whole," "Eternal Space," "Mystic Space," "Cosmic Space," "The Celestial Virgin," and "The Supporter of the Sky." She is invoked for the cure of headaches, epilepsy and insanity. The goddess Devaki is an incarnated form of Aditi. There is a close correspondence between Aditi and the Tibetan goddess Tho-ag, also spelled Tho-og, who is known as "The Eternal Mother," "Space," "The Eternal Ever-Present Cause of All," and "The Form of All Existence." In one description, Aditi is described as an earth cow milked by the earth goddess Prithu. Her milk appeared in the form of grain and vegetables. Aditi as the "Boundless Whole," or "Cosmic Space" and similar titles, represents infinite space. Her children, the Adityas symbolize the stars. Aditi corresponds with the goddesses Vach and Diti (also known as Danu). For information about Diti, *see* Maruts. *See also* Adityas; Asuras; Daksha; Devaki; Devis; Indra; Kasyapa; Krishna; Maruts; Mitra; Rudra; Shakti; Surya; Vach; Vamana; Varuna; The Vasus; The Vedas; Vishnu; Vivasvat.

Aditya (India) *see* Adityas.

Adityas, The *Aditya* (singular), *Agni* (Hindu, Vedic; India, Persia)
Originally the Adityas, known as great warriors, thought to be of Persian origin, were a triad of three divinities: Varuna (guardian of the night), Mitra (guardian of the day), and Angra Mainyu. In time, the deities of the triad changed to Agni, Vayu and Surya and then to Agni, Indra and Surya. At a later date they were the six, seven, eight or twelve sons of the goddess Aditi. Immortal sun gods, their element was eternal light. In one record, Aditi has seven sons: Ansa, Aryaman, Bhaga, Daksha, Mitra, Surya and Varuna. Dhatri, Indra, Martanda, Savitri, and Vishnu were added later, increasing their number to twelve. The leader of the Adityas was Varuna. Martanda the sun, also known as Vivasvat, was born from a dead egg and thrown into the sky by his mother. Groups of Vedic gods, like the Adityas, Maruts, Vasus and Ribhus, often appear as rays of the sun, as stars or as constellations. They are sometimes spoken of in human form or as having been ancient sacrificers. In astrological traditions, the number of Adityas is given as twelve. This identifies them with the positions of the sun in each of the months of the year and with the astrological signs. Compare the

Adityas to the Amesha Spentas (Persia). *See also* Adita; Angra Mainyu; Bhaga; Daityas; Daksha; Devaki; Dhatri; Indra; Kasyapa; Mitra; Parjanya; Pushan; Ribhus; Sakra (named by some as an Aditya); Savitri; Surya; Varuna; Vasus; Visasvat; Vishnu; Vrita.

Adlet (Eskimo People, Canada and Greenland)
Also known as: *Erqigdlit.*
An Eskimo woman who was the spouse of a red dog bore him ten offspring. Five of the children were dogs who were put in a boat and set to sea. They are the ancestors of the Caucasians. The other five offspring are blood-drinking monsters known as Adlet. Their offspring are the Erqigdlit.

Adlinden (Eskimo) *see* Adlivun.

Adliparmiut (Eskimo) *see* Adlivun.

Adlivun (Eskimo People)
Also known as: *Adlinden.*
Adlivun, the home of the sea goddess Sedna is located at the bottom of the ocean. It is the place of judgment for mortals who died a non-violent death. They stay in Adlivun for one year. Guarded by a huge dog, Adlivun can only be reached through a shaman known as an angakok. The Greenland Eskimo people say that all the dead, except murderers, eventually reach Adliparmiut. Located further away than Adlivun, it is a dark and stormy place, but it is not as bad as Adlivun. In some myths it is said that spirits from Adlivun, dressed in old clothes, bring disease and death to their villages. *See also* Agoolik; Aipaloovik; Nerivik; Sedna.

Ad'meta (Greek) *see* Admete.

Admeta (Greek) *see* Admete.

Admete *Ad'meta, Admeta* (Greek)
Admete, a deified mortal, is the daughter of Eurystheus and Antimache, and a priestess of Hera's temple. Hippolyte, the queen of the Amazons, owned a girdle (belt) that Admete coveted. Her father, who designated the twelve labors of Heracles, made Heracles fetch the girdle as his ninth labor. Initially, this labor did not seem taxing. Heracles and his friends docked their ship at Themiscyra. Hippolyte boarded, they entertained one another and she promised him the belt. The goddess Hera, aggravated at the ease of the transaction, disguised herself as an Amazon and spread the rumor that Heracles had abducted their leader. The warrior women attacked the ship and Heracles, thinking he had been duped by Hippolyte, killed her and took the belt. *See also* Eurytheus; Hera; Heracles; Hippolyte.

Ad'metos (Greek) *see* Admetus.

Admetus *Ad'metos* (Greek)
Admetus, a deified mortal, and the king of Pherae, is the son of Pheres and Periclymene (Clymene). His maternal grandfather, Minyas, was said to have built the first treasury. His siblings are Idomene, Lycurgus, and Periopis. He joined his cousin Jason's Argonauts and both were members of the Calydonian Hunt Club. In some legends, Jason gave Pelias' daughter Alcestis to Admetus to marry after he helped him reclaim his father Aeson's throne from Pelias. The more popular version is that Zeus sent Apollo to work in Admetus' court for a year as part of his punishment for slaying the cyclops. Admetus was extremely kind to the god, and Apollo, in gratitude, insured that his cattle (or ewes) all bore twins. Pelias, the father of Alcestis, a beautiful and popular woman, consented to her marriage to Admetus provided that he pick her up in a chariot pulled by lions and boars. Apollo insured that Admetus could keep the promise. It is said that Admetus neglected to offer the traditional sacrifice to the goddess Artemis prior to his marriage. On his wedding night, instead of finding his wife in bed, he found the bed full of snakes. Again, Apollo came to the rescue and placated Artemis. Later, after having two children, Eumelus and Perimele, Admetus fell ill. The Fates, dying to destroy Admetus, promised to spare his life, after Apollo, or in some myths, Zeus, intervened and it was agreed that he would be saved if a family member would voluntarily die in his place. Admetus asked his elderly parents, but they refused. So, Alcestis, out of love for her husband, swallowed poison. In some tales Heracles arrived and rescued her from death and in others Persephone, queen of the underworld, sent her back to the world. Admetus became a god when Apollo gave both him and his wife immortality. *See also* Alcestis; Apollo; Argonauts; Artemis; The Fates; Jason; Pelias.

Adn *Adan, Aden, Dar al Thawab* (House of Recompense); (Islamic)
Good souls will live in mansions in this paradise. *See also* Eden.

Adonaios (Greek) *see* Adonai.

Adon (A) *Adonai* (Semitic)
A title of honor meaning "lord." In the Old Testament Adonai is substituted for the Hebrew tetragram YHWH. *See also* Adonis.

Adon (B) (Middle East) The brother of Astarte (q.v.).

Adonaios (Greek) *see* Adonis.

Adonay (Greek) *see* Adonis.

Adonia (Greek)
A festival following harvest to mourn the death and celebrate the rebirth of Adonis (q.v.).

Adonis *Adon* (Egypt), *Adonai* (Hebrew), *Adonay, Adonaios, Aidoneus*
Also known as: *Alevin, Emut* (Egypt), *Hey-Tau* (Egypt) (Phoenicia, Syrian, later, Greek).
Of Semitic origin, the worship of Adonis was widely spread throughout the ancient world. Adonis is the son of Cinyras who was the king of Paphos in Cyprys and Cenchreis or Metharme, or the son of Phoenix and Alphesiboea, or the son of Cinyras and Cinyras' daughter Myrrha (Smyra). The prevalent myth is that Cinyras, himself a handsome man, bragged that his daughter Myrrha (Smyra) was more beautiful than Aphrodite. Incensed, Aphrodite made Myrrha, under the influence of wine, seduce her father. Cinyras, angry when Myrrha became pregnant, chased her with a sword. The gods changed her into a myrrh tree which eventually split open revealing the infant Adonis. To save the child from being slain by his father, Aphrodite stole him, hid him in a box and entrusted him to Persephone. When Persephone opened the box and saw the beauty of the

child she decided to keep him for herself. Aphrodite appealed to Zeus to judge who should keep Adonis. In one rendition, Zeus appointed the muse Calliope to be the mediator. It was decided that Adonis would spend equal portions of the year between the goddesses, Aphrodite in the celestial realm and Persephone in the underworld. Furious, Aphrodite caused the death of Calliope's son, Orpheus. Aphrodite and Adonis had two children, a son Golgos, founder of Cyprian Golgi and a daughter Beroe, founder of Beroea in Thrace. Some say that Adonis not Dionysus was the father of Aphrodite's son Priapus. It is said that Adonis was killed by a boar while hunting. A variation is that the boar was a weapon of the god Ares who, jealous of Aphrodite's love for Adonis, killed him. Identified with Eshmun (Phoenicia), Tammuz (Babylon) and Osiris (Egypt). Adonis was considered a prototype of Hay-Tau. The story of Adonis and Aphrodite is similar to Diana (of the Wood) and Virbius. The rivalry between Aphrodite and Persephone for the love of Adonis is similar to the rivalry of Artemis and Phaedra for the love of Hippolytus. The gods Diarmuid (Celtic), Osiris and Tammuz were all associated with fertility and killed by boars. A large stone carving found at Ghineh portrays Adonis at rest with a spear awaiting the attack of a boar while Aphrodite is seated as though in mourning. The boar represents the slayer and the slain. Following the annual harvest a festival known as Adonia is held to mourn the death and celebrate the rebirth of Adonis. See also Angus (Celtic); Aphrodite; Ares; Calliope; Cinyras; Naiads; Persephone; Priapus (A).

Adranos (Italy) see Adranus.

Adranus *Adranos* (Sicilian) An ancient deity of Italy.

Adrastea (Greek) see Adrastia.

Adrasteia (Greek) see Adrastia.

Adrastia *Adrastea, Adrasteia, Adrestea* (Greek)
Nymph of fate. Adrastia, a nymph of Crete, is a daughter of the beekeeper Melisseus and sister of the nymph Ida (also called Io) of the Cretan Mount Ida. It has been said that their father, Melisseus, is also their mother, Melissa the goddess, the Queen-bee who annually kills her male consorts. Adrastia and Ida were given the responsibility to care for the infant Zeus after he had been left in Crete by his mother Rhea because she was frightened that Cronus, her brother who was also her husband, would kill him. They fed the infant milk from the goat Amaltheia and probably honey, considering their origins. To keep Cronus from hearing the baby cry, the artistic Curetes, who assisted them, beat their shields with swords. In another version Adrastia is the goddess of fate who was later called Nemesis. Amaltheia (meaning "tender") the maiden-goddess; Io, the nymph-goddess; and Adrastis ("the inescapable one") are one of the moon-triads. Adrastia gave her charge a beautiful ball which Aphrodite, the goddess of love, later used to try to bribe her son, Eros. Adrastia may be the same as Nemesis and may have been another name for Rhea. See also Adrastis; Amaltheia; Cronus; Curetes; Rhea; Zeus.

Adrastos (Greek) see Adrestus.

Adrastus (Greek) see Adrestus.

Adrestea (Greek) see Adrastia.

Adrestus *Adrastos, Adrastus* (Greek)
King of Argos. Adrestus, the king of Argos, is the son of Talaus and Lysimache, though some think that his mother was Eurynome or Lysianassa. His siblings are Astynome; Eriphyle, who with her husband was killed by their son; Mecisteus; Aristomachus; Metidice; Pronax; and Parthenopaeus, one of the Seven Against Thebes. Adrestus married his niece Amphithea, the daughter of his brother Pronax, and became the father of Aegialeus; Aegialeia; Argeia, who was killed by Creon; Cyanippus, a king of Argo; Hippodameia; and Deipyle. Adrestus was the leader and thanks to his magic winged horse Arion, he was the only survivor of the Seven Against Thebes. This campaign was facilitated to aid Polynices, the son of Oedipus, gain the throne of Thebes from his brother, Eteocles. Since the city had seven gates, it was decided that each side would post a hero at each gate. The seven attackers were Adrestus; Polynices; Tydeus (Tydus) of Calydon; Capaneus, the nephew of Adrestus; Hippomedon, the cousin or nephew of Adrestus; Parthenopaeus, the Arcadian chieftain and brother of Adrestus; and Amphiaraus, the brother-in-law of Adrestus and the greatest prophet of his time, who knew the event would fail. The Thebans defending the city were Actor, Hyperbius, Lasthenes, Melanippus, Megareus, and Polyphontes. The brothers, Eteocles and Polynices, ended up in one-on-one combat and destroyed one another fulfilling the curse of their father, Oedipus. It was a barbaric battle and although the deities Athene and Zeus were on hand, for the most part they merely observed the mortals at war. Ten years later, the sons of the Seven Against Thebes decided to avenge their fathers. This group was known as the Epigoni ("those who come later"). In this battle, Aegialeus, the son of Adrestus, was killed and Adrestus, an old man, died of grief. Seven Against Thebes is known as one of the main episodes in the Theban cycle of myths. The list of attackers varies slightly. Some say that Meciteus, the brother of Adrestus was one of the group and that Tydeus was excluded. See also Adrastia; Amphithea; Apsyrtus; Eurydice (C); Hippodamia (A); Oedipus.

Adrija (India) "Mountain Borne." See also Parvati.

Adrika (India) see Apsarases and Satyavati.

Adrisyanti (India) see Parashara.

Adsullata (Celtic)
She is a river goddess and patroness of the river Savus in Noricum.

Adu Ogyinae (Ashanti People, Africa)
The first people to inhabit earth came from holes in the ground made by a worm. Seven men, some women, a dog and a leopard were created. Their leader was Adu Ogyinae.

Adununkisum *Uyungsum* (Saora People of India)
Sun god. See also Angajan; Babusum; Bomersum; Ilinbongasum; Labosum; Ringesum; Tobardasum.

Aeacides (Greek) The descendants of Aeaucus (q.v.).

Aeacus *Aiakos* (Greek)
Aeacus, the king of Aegina became a demi-god and a judge in the underworld. He is the son of Zeus and Aegina, or possibly Europa. He married Endeis, the daughter of Cheiron, and

fathered Peleus and Telamon, and another son, Phocus, by the nereid Psamathe. He became the grandfather of Achilles and Ajax. His sons, Peleus and Telamon, killed their half-brother Phocus, and the population of Oenone (Oenopia) was decimated by the plague; ants covered everything. In other myths it is written that this tragedy was the consequence of Pelops' murder of Stymphalus or Aegeus' treacherous acts toward Androgeus. Nonetheless, Zeus transformed the insects into humans, whom Aeacus called the Myrmidons (ants). Some legends say that Aeacus, the son of Aegina, as a young man, lived alone on the island. Lonely, he prayed for companionship; his prayers were heard; the ants were converted to mortals. He renamed the island Aegina after his mother and became king. Aeacus, Apollo, Poseidon and others built the walls of Troy. While they were working, they were attacked by three snakes. Two of the reptiles died and the third attacked the section of the wall built by Aeacus. Apollo correctly interpreted this incident as an omen that Aeacus' descendants would wreak havoc over Troy for the following thirty years. After his death, Aeacus, renowned for his integrity, was made a judge in Hades along with Minos and Rhadamanthys. Other myths say that he was a lonely gatekeeper. The descendants of Aeacus are known as Aeacides. *See also* Aegina; Ajax the Greater; Cheiron, Europa; Hades; Minos; Myrmidons; Peleus; Rhadamanthys; Styx; Telamon.

Aeaea (Greek) An epithet of Circe (q.v.).

Aebh *Aobh* (Celtic; Irish)
Goddess of mist (or personification of mist). Foster daughter of Bodb Dearg, and wife of Ler. Her three children were changed into swans by her sister, Aeife (or Aoife). *See also* Bodb Dearg; Ler.

Aeculapius (Greek, Roman) *see* Aesculapius.

Aed *Aedh, Aodh* (Celtic)
Also known as: *Hugh.*
Possible weather god. Son of Dagda. Slain for seducing Conchean's wife. As Hugh he was changed into a swan by Aeife. In one version Aedh was the mortal son of Eochail Lethderg, Prince of Leinster. He was carried off by two Sidh-women. After escaping their clutches he was restored to human life by St. Patrick.

Aedh (Celtic) *see* Aed.

Aedon *Aedon* (Greek)
Also known as: *The Nightingale.*
Aedon was either the daughter or wife of Zethus (king of Thebes), and mother of Itylus, whom she murdered accidentally, mistaking him for her nephew Amaleus, the son of Niobe. In a variation; Aedon is the daughter of Pandareus and Harmothoe (Hormothoe). Intensely jealous of her sister, Niobe, who is adored by her six sons and six daughters, she attempts to murder her sister's son, Sipylus, and kills her own son, Itylus by mistake. Grief-stricken, she attempts suicide, fails, and is transformed into a nightingale. It is said that the mournful song of the bird is Aedon lamenting her dead son. In another myth, she is the wife of the artist, Polytechnus of Colophon. Here, Aedon is an artist as well and it is said that the competition between the couple caused bitter quarreling. Polytechnus

further enraged his wife when he allegedly raped her sister, Chelidon. In revenge, the two women killed his son, Itys, and gave his flesh to Polytechnus as food. Appalled, Zeus turned them all into birds. Aedon became a nightingale, Chelidon, a swallow, Polytechnus, a woodpecker, her father, Pandareus, an osprey, her mother, Hormothoe, a halcyon, and her brother, a hoopoe (an Old World bird, with patterned plumage, a fan-like crest, and a slender, down-ward curving bill). *See also* Niobe; Tereus; Zethus.

Aeegeus (Greek) *see* Medus.

Aeeiouo (Coptic)
This is one of the gods Jesus is supposed to have prayed to. *See also* Pistis Sophia.

Aeeta (Greek) *see* Aeetes.

Aeetes *Aeeta* (Greek)
Aeetes, king of Colchis was the son of Helios and Perseis (Perse), and the brother of Perses, Pasiphae who gave birth to the monster Minotaur, and Circe the sorceress. His first marriage to the nymph Asterodeia resulted in the birth of Chalciope (also known as Iophossa) and perhaps Absyrtus (also spelled Apsyrtus.) Others feel that Absyrtus was the son of Aeetes and his second wife, Eidyia (daughter of Oceanus), by whom he became the father of the sorceress and moon goddess, Medea. Aeetes was known as a cruel leader and his people were said to be barbarians. He lived in a marvelous palace built by the famous smith and artisan, Hephaistos. Phrixus arrived on the back of the golden flying ram trying to escape from his wicked stepmother and eventually married Chalciope. The ram was sacrificed and its fleece entrusted to Aeetes, who had it guarded by the monster Argus. When the hero Jason arrived to claim the fleece, Aeetes initially resisted but later gave Jason an extremely difficult task to perform before handing over the magic fleece. Aeetes was paranoid because an oracle had said that he would die at the hands of a foreigner. He also feared that one of his sons would kill him as they had befriended the Argonauts, who as outsiders were a worry to him. It was his daughter Medea who magically arranged for Jason to capture the fleece and who eloped with the Argonaut. Aeetes was deposed by his brother, Perses, but Medea returned to Colchis, killed her uncle and restored her father to the throne. Aeetes death is questionable. In some versions, he is cruelly murdered by Medea and Jason, or by Medea's son, Medus (Medeius), and in other versions he is killed during a fight with the Argonaut Meleager. This is part of the story of Jason and the Argonauts. *See also* Apsyrtus; Argus (D); Chalciope; Golden Fleece; Hephaistos; Helius; Jason; Oceanids; Pasiphae; Phrixus.

Aega (Greek) *see* Aex.

Aegaeon *Aegeon* (Greek)
Also known as: *Briareus, Obriareus.*
According to the Olympian Creation Myth, the weather god Aegaeon was one of the first children born of the sky god Uranus and his mother, Gaea, although Poseidon has been called the father. His siblings were Cottus and Gyges. They were said to be semi-humans giants, each with one hundred hands and some say each had fifty heads. Following their births came the three cyclopes: Brontes, Steropes and Arges. Aegaeon was called Bri-

areus, meaning strong, or Obriareus by the gods and Aegaeon by mortals. The three brothers were known as the Hecatoncheires and the Centimani. Briareus is said to represent hurricanes; Cottus, volcanoes; and Gyges, earthquakes. The brothers assisted Zeus in his battles with the Titans, but not willingly. Aegaeon (Briareus) was chosen to arbitrate in a contest between Poseidon and Helios over the ownership of Corinth. He divided the isthmus between the two. Aegaeon represents violent seas or storms. Compare to the storm deities and destructive natural forces: harpies and chimaera. *See also* Aegaeon; Briareus; Chaos; Cyclopes; Gaea; Hecatonchires; Tartarus; Titans.

Aege (Norse; Teutonic)
This little known god of the sea was once an enemy of the Aesir, but later gave feasts for them in his golden hall.

Aegeon (Greek) *see* Aegaeon.

Aeger (Teutonic) *see* Aegir.

Aegeria (Roman) *see* Egeria.

Aegeus (Greek) *see* Aegis.

Aegiale (Greek)
One of the Heliades. Daughter of Apollo or Helios and Clymene. *See also* Aegle (A).

Aegialeia (A) (Greek)
She is the daughter of Adrastus and Amphithea. Her siblings are Aegialeus, Argeia, Cyanippus, Deipyle and Hippodameia. She married Diomedes and later had an affair with her husband's friend's son Cometes. *See also* Adrestus; Amphithea; Heliades; Hippodameia; Sthenelus.

Aegialeia (B) (Greek)
This is an older name of the city of Sicyon.

Aegialeius (Greek) *see* Aegialeus.

Aegialeus (A) (Greek)
He is the son of Inachus the river god who was also and first king of Argos and his father's sister, Melia. His siblings are Io, Hera's attendant, and Phoroneus, who was the first to erect an altar in honor of Hera. *See also* Inachus; Melia.

Aegialeus (B) (Greek)
He is the son of Adrestus and his father's niece Amphithea. His siblings are Aegialeia, Argeia; Cyanippus (he may be his son and not his brother); Deipyle; and Hippodameia. Aegialeus was the only one of the Epigoni, who are the "Sons of the Seven against Thebes," to be killed. His father was the only survivor of the "Seven Against Thebes." *See also* Amphithea; Apsyrtus; Phoroneus.

Aegimius (Greek)
He was the progenitor and king of the Dorians.
Aegimius' paternal grandparents were Hellen and the nymph Ortheis (Orseis). His father was Dorus and his mother was one of Cretheus' daughters. His brother, Tectamus, became the king of Crete. In conflict with the Lapiths (*Lapithæ*) of Mount Olympus, Aegimius called upon Heracles for assistance. The demigod led the Dorians in battle and defeated the Lapiths, killing

Coronus. In payment, Aegimius offered Heracles a third of his kingdom. Heracles refused but requested Aegimius to hold it in trust for his sons. After the death of their father, the Heraclids lived in Doris and assisted the Dorians in their invasion of the Peloponnesus. Aegimius' sons, Pamphylus and Dymas, were killed. Subsequently, the Dorians honored the men by naming three main divisions of their people for them and for Hyllus. *See also* Coronus; Heracles.

Aegina *Aigina* (Greek)
A river nymph, Aegina is the daughter of the river god Asopus, and Metope. She has nineteen sisters and three brothers. Impregnated by Zeus, possibly in the form of a flame, he whisked her to the island of Oenone (Oenopia), where she gave birth to a son, Aeacus. Her father, anxious to know who abducted his daughter, manipulated the king of Corinth, Sisyphus, into telling him that the perpetrator was Zeus. This disclosure is thought by many to be the reason that Sisyphus ended up in Hades, doomed for eternity to push a huge boulder to the top of a hill, only to have it roll down again. Zeus had to throw thunderbolts at the bereft father to end his persistent haranguing of the god. The jealous goddess Hera dropped a snake into Aegina's water supply and killed the woman. In time, her son Aeacus renamed the island Aegina, in honor of his mother. The island of Aegina became the home of the Myrmidons, the ants who were changed into mortals by Zeus. According to some, Aegina was also the mother of Menoetius by Actor. There are myths that say that Europa and not Aegina was the mother of Aeacus. Compare Aegina to Europa. To compare to women who were seduced by Zeus in other forms; *see* Antiope, Danae, Europa and Leda. *See also* Actor (A); Aeacus; Asopus; Hera; Menoetius; Pelasgus (B); Sisyphus.

Aegipan *Aigi'pan* (Greek)
Also known as: *Pan.*
Some authorities say Aegipan was another name for Pan, but early writers said that he was a son of Zeus and the nymph Aex or the goat Boetis. Aex, the daughter of Pan or the sun god Helius may have been a goat and not a nymph. It was the hide of Aex or Amaltheia which was used to make the sacred Aegis of Zeus. Aegipan assisted Hermes in recovering the sinews belonging to Zeus and stolen by Typhoeus. Aegipan is either the constellation Capricorn or Capra. He is sometimes shown as a goat with the lower body of a fish. *See also* Aegis; Aegisthus; Almaltheia; Hermes; Pan; Typhon for other goat-related myths.

Aegir *Aeger* (Norse; Teutonic)
Also known as: *Alebrewer, Gymir, Hler.*
Aegir, "master of the sea," was the son of the giant Fornjotr (also known as Farbuti). His siblings were Kari (the air) and the god of evil, Loki (fire). A giant, he married the pale, sea goddess of death, Ran (robber), who in some legends is also his sister. They had nine daughters, also giants, who represented the waves and were all the mothers of Heimdal, the defender of heaven. Although Aegir was not included in the ranks of the gods, he was very friendly with them. And, as a brewer for the gods, he often entertained, especially during flax harvesting, in his sea palace in the western ocean of Vanaheim by the island of Hlesey (also known as Cattegat). His abode was said to be

well-lit by the gold he had collected from shipwrecks, for if he appeared above the waves, it was to sink ships and ransack them of their cargo. A portion of his wealth came from the tithes offered to him from Saxon pirates who hoped to stay on good terms with him. His servants were Fimafeng and Eldir. Aegir is depicted as an elderly man with a long white beard, claw-like fingers, wearing a black helmet. Sometimes he is depicted as a dragon that surrounds the worlds. For an account one of Aegir's banquets, *see* Loki. *See also* Fornjotr; Heimdal; Kari; Loki; Mimir; Niord; Ran; Thor.

Aegis *Aegeus, Aigis, Egis* (Greek)

In early Greek mythology, the Aegis was the storm cloud that surrounded Zeus' thunderbolt. Later in myth it became his sacred shield. It was created by the fire god Hephaistos from the hide of the goat Amaltheia, who nursed Zeus at birth. In other versions, the Aegis was made from the hide of Aex (also spelled Aega), thought by some to be a goat and by others to be a nymph who was the daughter of either the sun god Helius or of Pan, the shepherd god. Occasionally Zeus loaned his shield to other deities and eventually he gave it to Athena (Athene). When Perseus, the son of Zeus, chopped off Medusa's head and presented it to Athena, she had it attached to her Aegis. This magical breastplate had the capacity to make the wearer invulnerable and to turn enemies to stone. In some writings Aegis was an early king connected in legend with Minos. In Roman mythology, the Aegis was the breastplate of Jupiter and Minerva. Some say Aegeus was a form of Poseidon. For goat-related legends *see* Amaltheia, Aegisthus and Aegipan. *See also* Aegeus; Athena; Fafnir; Hephaistos; Jupiter; Medusa; Minerva; Minos; Minotaur; Perseus; Poseidon.

Aegisthus *Aighistos, Aigisthus* (Greek)

Aegisthus, the prince of darkness and deity of murderers, was born as the result of an incestuous relationship by his father, the king of Mycenae, Thyestes, and Pelopia, who was also Aegisthus' sister. Married to Clytemnestra, they were the parents of Erigone, who later committed suicide, and Aletes, who was murdered. As an abandoned infant, Aegisthus was suckled by a goat. His sister/mother Pelopia married her father's brother, Atreus; they recovered Aegisthus and raised him. In time, his true identity came to light and he murdered his stepfather/uncle and some say he also killed his natural father. The silence broken, his mother Pelopia, who did not know that it was her father who had raped and impregnated her, committed suicide. Aegisthus also conducted an affair with his stepbrother Agamemnon's wife, Clytemnestra, despite a warning from Hermes. The lovers plotted and murdered Agamemnon and the doubted prophetess, Cassandra, whom Agamemnon had won as a prize when the Greeks overcame Troy. They settled down, had their family and Aegisthus ruled Mycenae for seven years. Then another step-brother, Orestes, the son of Agamemnon, returned from exile and with the aid of his childhood friend, Pylades, he murdered Clytemnestra and Aegisthus. This act drove Orestes temporarily insane. For goat-related legends, *see* Amaltheia, Aegis, Aegipan. *See also* Agamemnon; Cassandra; Clytemnestra.

Aegle (A) *Aglaea, Aigle* (Greek)

One of the Heliades. Goddess of radiance. Aegle is the daughter of Apollo and Clymene, or Helios and Clymene. Her siblings are Aegiale (also known as Phoebe), Aetheria and Phaethon. She is the half-sister of Phaethusa, Lampetie and Lampethus. When her brother Phaethon died, her grief was so overwhelming that she turned into a poplar tree and wept tears of amber. In other renditions, the sisters, Aegiale, Aetheria, Aegle, Lampetie and Phaethusa were transformed by the gods into poplar trees when they died. Compare Aegle to Hesperides. *See also* Aglaia; Graces; Heliades; Helius; Phaethon.

Aegle (B) (Greek)

Also known as: *Charis.*

One of the Graces. She is the daughter of Zeus and Eurynome. *See also* Graces.

Aegle (C) (Greek)

One of the Hesperides, who are the guardians of the golden apples. *See also* Hesperides.

Aegle (D) (Greek) She is the daughter of Asclepius (q.v.).

Aegle (E) (Greek)

She is the daughter of Panopeus and Neaera, sister of Epeius and lover of Theseus (q.v.).

Aegle (F) (Greek) Aegle is the name used for more than one nymph.

Aegus (Greek) *see* Aether.

Aegyptus (Greek)

King of Egypt. He is the son of Belus and Anchinoe, the twin brother of Danaus, brother of Phineus, Thronia and Cepheus (possibly). Following the instructions of the Oracle at Delphi, he sacrificed his daughter Aganippe to save Egypt from a drought. His fifty sons married the fifty daughters of Danaus. *See also* Agenor (A); Danaides; Danaus; Eurydice (C).

Aeithlius (Greek) *see* Aeolus (A).

Aello *Aellopuus* (Greek)

A whirlwind deity, Aello, one of the harpies, is a daughter of Thaumas and Electra, or Neptunus and Terra, or Poseidon and Gaea, or Typhon and Echida. Her sister harpies were Podarge (Celaeno) and Ocypete. Initially depicted as beautiful, swift bird-like maidens, who could carry mortals, they evolved into loathsome creatures who harangued and sometimes snatched mortals. The harpies personify the sudden destructive forces of nature such as tornadoes or whirlwinds. Aello is possibly the same as Aeolus who was a son of Hellen and the nymph Orseis. This male version was also a keeper of the winds. The three harpies may be Athena in her triple-goddess form as a sudden destroyer. Aello is shown with a body of a bird, the pale face of emaciated woman and having claws of a lion on her hands. *See also* Aeolus (B); Briareus; Chimaera; Graeae; harpies; Phineus; Sirens.

Aellopuus (Greek) *see* Aello.

Aeneas *Aeneus, Aineias* (Greek)

A deified mortal, and sun deity, Aeneas is often called the founder of the Roman race. He is the son of Anchises the king of Dardania and the love goddess Aphrodite. He had one brother, Lyrus, who died childless. Raised by nymphs and trained by Cheiron the centaur, he grew up to become a war-rior. With Acamas and Archelous, he was a leader of the Dar-danian troops. During the Trojan War, armed with weapons forged by the fire god Hephaistos, he was seriously injured by Achilles. His mother rescued him from the battlefield and he was nursed to health by the goddess of hunting, Artemis, and the powerful goddess, Leto. He was kept from returning to battle by Poseidon, who explained to the gods that Aeneas and his descendants would one day rule Troy. At the fall of Troy, he escaped, holding high the sacred flame and carrying his elderly father on his back. Married to Creusa, they were separated dur-ing the flight and she died. Their son, Iulus (also known as Ascanius), stayed with him. He enlisted twenty ships of Tro-jans and went in his search of his promised empire. He encoun-tered many obstacles: a miserable run-in with the harpies; wretched weather whipped up by Aeolus, the god of winds; and an obsessive affair with Dido deliberately instigated by Venus, which threw him off track. He obtained permission from the gods to visit his father in the underworld for advice and purification. Eventually, he arrived in Italy where he fought bit-terly with the fearless warrior and king of Rutali, Turnus, whom he killed. He married his opponent's daughter Lavinia and they became the parents of Aeneas Silvia (Silvius). Aeneas died in western Sicily with great honors bestowed upon him. To com-pare to others who visited the underworld; *see* Heracles and Orpheus. *See also* Aeolus (B); Anchises; Evander (B); Golden Bough; Hephaistos; Poseidon; Venus.

Aenetus (Greek) *see* Actor.

Aeneus (Greek) *see* Aeneas.

Aengus (Celtic) *see* Angus.

Aeoina Kamui (Japan) *see* Okikurumi.

Aeolia (Greek)
She is the daughter of Amythaon, who with his half-brother Neleus re-instituted the Olympic Games and Idomene or pos-sibly Bias, the king of Argos and Pero. She married Calydon, the son of Aetolus and Pronoe and became the mother of Epi-casta, who married Agenor and Protogeneia. *See also* Agenor; Amythaon; Bias; Calydon; Pero.

Aeolus (A) (Greek)
Also known as: *Aeolus (B) (possibly)*.
The ruler Aelous is the great grandson of Prometheus, known as the father of mortals, the grandson of Deucalion the builder of the ark and a survivor of the Deluge. He is the son of Hellen, the king of Phthia (some say founder of the Greek race) and the nymph Orseis (also known as Ortheis). Hellen divided up the Greek lands between his three sons, Dorus of the Dorians, the thievish Xuthus who was possibly the king of Athens, and Aeo-lus. Aeolus received Thessaly and called the inhabitants of this area, Aeolians. He married Enarete, the daughter of Deimachus. Their sons are Cretheus the first king of Iolcus, Athamas who was possibly the king of Achaea, and the cunning Sisyphus. Salmoneus the king of Elis, and Perieres the king of Messenia are also their sons, as are Magnes the human magnet, Macar (also known as Marareus), and Deion the king of Phocis. It is possible that Aeolus is the father of Aeithlius by Protogeneia, although he is generally thought to be the son of Zeus. Their daughters are Canace, Peisidice, Alcyone who drowned herself,

Calyce, Perimele who was thrown into the sea by her father and turned into an island by Poseidon, Tangara and Arne (her mother may have been Hippe). Canace was instructed to kill herself with a sword for committing incest with her brother Macar who also killed himself. Aeolus then committed suicide. *See* Aeolus (B) the god of the winds who is often regarded as the same as Aeolus (A) by many late authors. For details of Deion's marriage *see* Actor (A). For detail's of Perieres' mar-riage, *see* Gorgophone. *See also* Argus (D); Arne; Boreas; Deu-calion; Hellen; Promethus; Sisyphus.

Aeolus (B) (Greek)
Also known as: *Hippotades, Aeolus (B) (possibly)*.
God of the winds, and father of the winds, Aeolus is the son of Poseidon and Arne (also known as Melanippe), who is the daughter of Aeolus (A) and the brother of Boeotus, or the son of Hellen the king of Phthia, and Hippe who was the daughter of Cheiron the centaur. Aeolus married Gyane (Cyane), the daughter of King Liparus. They took up residence on the cloud island Lipara (Liparus) that floated around the celestial realm. The couple had six daughters and six sons. Each son married one of his sisters. Initially, either Zeus or Hera appointed Aeo-lus to be a guardian of the winds. In time his status was raised to father of the winds. In myth, he is said to have invented the sail. His position allowed him to order the invisible energy to do his bidding; he could whip up a storm or delicately rustle a blade of grass. It is said that Odysseus docked his ship at the Lipara Islands and was entertained by the wind god. When he was ready to depart, Aeolus gave him a wind bag and cautioned him not to open it. His suspicious or curious crew decided to throw caution to the winds, opened it, and let loose a tempest which caused a torturous journey until they reached Laestry-gones. For other wind deities *see* Astraeus; Boreas; Notus; Zephyrus. To compare to storm deities *see* Chimaera; Harpies. Compare Aeolus to Fu-jin (Japan). *See also* Aello; Aeneas; Aeo-lus (A); Aquilo; Astraeus; Cheiron; Eos; Harpies; Hellen; Hera; Poseidon; Zeus.

Aeons *Aion* (Post-Christian Gnostics)
Also known as: *Eon*.
Age of the universe. Aeons are also deities who were the offspring of Bathos and possibly Sige. Nous and Aletheia begot Logos and Zoe. From this pair came Agape, Ageratos, Anthro-pos, Autophyes, Bythios, Ecclesia, Ecclesiasticus, Elpis, Heno-sis, Macaria, Metricos, Mixis, Monogenes, Paracletos, Patricos, Pistis, Sophia, Synerasis and Theletas. Each of these were paired as male and female. The feasts of Agape were held in worship at many of the rites of these deities. *See also* Achamoth; Archons; Pistis Sophia.

Aepytus (A) (Greek)
King of Messenia. He is the youngest son of Cresphontes and Merope. His two brothers and his father were killed by Polyphontes, who overthrew the throne. Aepytus was raised by Cypselus, his mother's father. He regained the throne when he killed Polyphontes (q.v.).

Aepytus (B) (Greek)
King of Arcadia. He is the son of Eilatus, who is the son of Merope. Aepytus raised Evadne, the daughter of Poseidon and

Pitane. She became the mother of the prophet Iamus by Apollo. *See also* Merope.

Aer and Arura (Phoenicia)

In the beginning there was Time. From time came Desire and Darkness. From these two deities came Aer (air) and Arura (breath). Aer was intelligence, and Aura represented movement. From these two came the cosmic egg. In some versions Aer was the offspring of Uranus. Compare to Aether (Greek).

Aeracura (Celtic, Irish, Greek)

It is possible that Aeracura was a forerunner of Dis Pater. In ancient mythology she was thought to be an earth deity and is identified with the god of fields, trees and forests, Silvanus. She is also known as the Celtic earth mother of the Rhine Valley. Aeracura is shown with a basket of fruit or a horn of plenty. *See also* Dis; Dis Pater; Silvanus.

Aerolith (Syria)

Followers of Baal worshipped this stone which is said to have fallen from heaven. *See also* Baal.

Aeron (Celtic) Goddess of war and slaughter.

Aerope (Greek) *see* Agamemnon; Ares.

Aeropus (Greek) He is the son of Ares and Aerope. He is also the father of Echemus who was the king of Arcadia. *See also* Ares.

Aerth (Teutonic) *see* Hertha.

Aertha (Teutonic) *see* Hertha.

Aes Sidhe (Celtic) *see* Dana.

Aesar (A) (Teutonic) *see* Aesir.

Aesar (B) (Celtic, Irish)

Also known as: *Aesus, Asus* (Roman), *Dia, Logh.*

Aesar is thought to be an ancient creator god or god of fire and intelligence. He may have been a Druid deity and possibly a god of destruction. He was a consort of Eire. *See also* Aesir; Aesus.

Aesculapius (Greek) *see* Asclepius.

Aeshma (Zoroastrian; Persia)

Also known as: *Aesm* (Pahlavi dialect).

One of Angra Mainyu's assistants, Aeshma is the demon of wrath, fury, lust, and outrage. He constantly stirs up strife and war. If he is not successful in creating chaos among the good, he will do so among his colleagues, the demons. Aeshma assails the souls of the dead as they approach Chinvat Bridge. This fiend is in opposition to the Amesha Spenta Vohu Manah and is held in check by Sraosha, the personification of obedience and devotion, who will eventually defeat him. Aeshma may be the same as Asmodeus (q.v.). *See also* Ahura Mazda; Amesha Spentas; Angra Mainyu; Chinvat Bridge; Daevas; Sraosha; Vohu Manah; Yazatas.

Aesir *Aesar, Aisar, A'sas* (Norse; Teutonic)

Originally a race of war gods, the Aesir are sky deities led by Odin and Frigg. Their home is in Asgard. The Aesir are the opponents of the sea gods known as the Vanir who are led by the god Njord's children Freyr and Freyja. After a long battle which no one won, they agreed to a peaceful settlement and exchanged hostages. The Vanir gave Njord and his son Fryr to the Aesir. The Aesir gave Henir to the Vanir. There are several lists with the names of the Aesir. One list names Balder, Heimdall, Loki, Odin, Thor and Tyr. Usually the number of Aesir is said to be twelve. They are Balder, Bragi, Hermoder, Henir, Hodur, Loki, Odin, Svipdag, Thor, Tyr, Vali, and Vidar. In another list the following names are given of deities who at one time or another were considered Aesir: Balder, Baugi, Bragi, Forseti, Frey, Heimdal, Henir, Hodur, Loki, Njord, Odin, Thor, Ullur, Vali, and Vidar. Their female counterparts are the Asynjor. Their names are Beda, Bil, Eir, Fimila, Fjorgyn (also known as Jord), Freyja, Frigga, Frimla, Fulla, Gefion, Gerd, Gna, Hnossa, Horn, Mardoll, Nanna, Saga, Sif, Sigyn, Skadi, and Vanadis. The name Aesir may be derived from the Sanskrit Asura, or possibly the Egyptian cognate name of Asar who was form of Osiris. The name Aesir is similar to Asar (Egyptian), Asari (Babylonian), Assur (Assyrian), Azur (Hebrew) and Esar (Turkish). The name may have originated in Asia. *See also* Aesar; Asgard; Balder; Bil; Bor; Bragi; Forseti; Frejya; Freyr; Frigga; Fullar; Gefton; Gerd; Gladsheim; Gna; Heimdall; Henir; Hodur; Hofud; Jord; Jotun-heim; Mimir; Nanna (A); Odin; Sif (A); Sigyn; Skadi; Thor; Tyr; Vali; Vanadis; Vanir; Vidar; Yggdrasil; Ymir.

Aesm (Persia) *see* Aeshma.

Aeson (Greek) *see* Jason and Admetus.

Aesus *Æsus* (Roman)

Also known as: *Aesar.*

Aesus is possibly a fire god or a supreme deity, or possibly a Druid supreme being. Aesus is also the Roman name for deity. Not much else is known. *See also* Aesar (B); Dia.

Aether *Aethre, Aithre* (Greek)

Also known as: *Ether.*

He is the god of storms and winds, god of light, and god of the upper air or sky. Aether is the son of Erebus and Nyx. His siblings are Cer the goddess of violent death, Charon the ferryman of the dead, Hemera who personifies day, Hynos the god of sleep, Moros the god of destiny, Nemesis the goddess of retribution, and Thanatos the god of death. Aether has also been called the father of Uranus or Nxy and Uranus. In the Orphic tradition, Aether and Chaos sprang from Chronos or Time. In certain renditions Aether appears in the feminine form as the daughter of Pittheus (a mortal king) and Aegeus (sea) who deserted her. She is also said to be the mother of Theseus (Sun). Aether represents the upper sky, or upper air, the realm closest to the earth, as opposed to air. As a geographical location it was said by some to be the abode of Zeus. For additional information on the Orphic tradition, *see* Phanes. Compare Aether to the Phoenician Aer and Arura. *See also* Chaos; Erebus; Uranus.

Aetheria (Greek)

She is one of the Heliades. Her parents are Helios and Clymene. *See also* Aegle (A); Heliades.

Aethiolas (Greek) *see* Helen.

Aetholides (Greek)

Also known as Pythagora (possibly).

Renowned for his perfect memory, he is the son of Hermes and Eupolemia. During the Argonautic expedition, he was the herald. *See also* Abaris; Eupolemia.

Aethon (Greek) *see* Helius.

Aethra (A) (Greek)

Aethra is the mother of Theseus. She was abducted by the Dioscuri and taken to Troy where she became the servant of Helen of Troy. Her grandsons, Acamas and Demophoon, liberated her. *See also* Acamas (A); Demophoon; Dioscuri; Theseus.

Aethra (B) (Greek)

Another name for the Oceanid Pleione (q.v.).

Aethre (Greek) *see* Aether.

Aethus (Greek) *see* Arethusa (A); Arethusa (B).

Aetna (Roman) Mountain goddess. *See also* Fuji; Pele.

Aetolus (Greek) *see* Apis (B).

Aex (Greek)

Also known as: *Aega* (Greek). *See also* Aegipan; Aegis; Helius.

Af (A) (Egypt)

Af is the spirit of Ra during the first hour of the night as he journeys through the underworld. At that time he is called the "Sun of Night" which is a dead god (body) or flesh.

Af (B) (Africa) *see* Afa.

Af (C) (Hebrew)

In Gehenna (Hebrew), Af is one of the three angels: Af, Khema and Mashkhith.

Af-Osiris (Egypt) *see* Osiris.

Afa (A) (Samoan) Storm god.

Afa (B) (Dahomey People, Africa)

Also known as: *Af.* The androgynous god of wisdom, Afa was consulted on matters of marriage and sexual problems.

Afau (Egypt)

One of the gods who accompany Osiris during the Second Hour of the Night. *See also* Osiris; Shesat Maket Neb-S; Tuat.

Afi (Norse; Teutonic)

Also known as: *Grandfather.*

Deified mortal. Afi and Amma are the ancestors of the race of peasants. Heimdall slept between Afi and Amma who were Grandfather and Grandmother. From the union with Amma Karl was born. He later married Snor. They had ten sons and ten daughters. Of the ten sons there is Breid, Boddi, Bondi, Brattskegg, Bui, Bundinskeggi, and a daughter named Brud. *See also* Heimdall; Karl; Rig.

Afreet *Affreet* (Arabic)

Also known as: *Afrit, Ifrit.*

Unclean spirits, or evil genii.

Afrit (Arabic) *see* Afreet.

Afu, The (Egypt)

Protectors. They are gods who are mentioned in the Pyramid Texts. Their duty is to minister to Osiris in Second Hour of the Night. *See also* Tuat.

Ag (India) *see* Agni.

Aga-mi-ketsu-no-Kami (Japan)

Probably a deity of food. She was sent by the Emperor Yuryaku to be the companion of Amaterasu. She might be the same or similar to Ukemochi-no-Kami (q.v.). *See also* Amaterasu.

Agaku (Babylonia) *see* Marduk.

Agamede (Greek) *see* Actor (C).

Agamemnon (Greek)

Sun hero. Argonaut. Agamemnon is the son of Atreus and Aerope or according to some, the son of Atreus' son Pleisthenes and Cleolla. As the son of Atreus, he and his brother Menelaus were known as the Atreidae, meaning sons of Atreus. He may have been the brother of Pleisthenes and Anaxibia. Agamemnon married Clytemnestra and became the father of Iphigenia (Iphigeneia), Iphianassa, Electra (also known as Laodice), Chrysothemis, and Orestes. Homer names Iphigenia, Iphianassa, and Electra, Laodice. Others say that Iphigenia was raised by Clytemnestra but was actually the daughter of Helen and Theseus. He was also the father of Chryses by his slave Chryseis, and the father of the twins Pelops and Teledamas by his "war prize," Cassandra. Agamemnon murdered Clytemnestra's first husband, Tantalus, and brutally killed their baby before he married her. Agamemnon was a rich and powerful king of Mycenae who became the commander of Greek forces at Troy. He was able to convince Clytemnestra and Helen's father, Tyndareus, to choose his brother Menelaus as Helen's fiancé. In the meantime, Helen was abducted by Paris, the Trojan prince and Menelaus appealed to Agamemnon to take his forces to rescue her. As he was preparing to do so, he boasted to the huntress Artemis that he was more skilled then she. Infuriated, she sent either calm seas or violent storms to immobilize his ships. The prophet Calchas advised Agamemnon that only the sacrifice of his daughter Iphigenia would quell the rage of Artemis. Pulled between his duties as a father and as a commander-in-chief he prepared his daughter for sacrifice. It is said that at the last moment, Artemis or Hera substituted a stag for the young woman and took her away to be a priestess. In some legends, she became the goddess Hecate. Agamemnon's act incurred the wrath of Clytemnestra, who was never certain if her daughter had been sacrificed, for she never saw her again. For details about his relationship with Cassandra, *see* Cassandra. For details pertaining to the murderous deaths of Agamemnon and Cassandra *see* Aegisthus; Cassandra; Cinyras; Clytemnestra. *See also* Achilles; Calchas; Helen; Iphigenia; Menelaus; Orestes.

Aganippe (Greek)

Fountain of the Muses. Nymph of the fountain. Aganippe lived in the spring of the same name at the foot of Mt. Helicon and provided inspiration to all who drank from her waters. Aganippe, known as the nymph of inspiration, is the daughter of Permessus, a river god. See Naiads for other classes of water nymphs. *See also* Danae; Muses.

Aganju (Yoruba People, Africa)

In some myths Aganju is the son of Odudua and the brother/spouse of Yemoja. They became the parents of several river goddesses and of Ogun, Olokun, Orunjan, Shango, Shankpanna and others. *See also* Obatala; Ogun; Yemoja.

Aganus (Greek) *see* Helen.

Agapae (Greek) *see* Agape.

Agape *Agapae* (Greek)

Early Christian love feasts which were forbidden by the Church in C.E. 391. Epiphanius, before he became a saint, was lured into a Syrian Gnostic group, the Phibionites. He reported their rituals in detail and went on to renounce the group and approximately eighty of his associates. *See also* Aeons.

Agas Xenas Xena *Aqas-Xena-Xenas* (Chinook People, United States)

This deity of the evening star became the father of Siamese twins who were separated by Blue Jay (q.v.).

Agasaya "The Shrieker" (Semitic) *see* Ishtar.

Agassou (Dahomey People, Africa)

He is a panther fetish god of the royal household.

Agastya (Hindu; India)

Also known as: *Dattoli, Kalasi-Suta* (Son of a Jar).

A Rishi and a divine teacher of science, religion and literature, Agastya was also a priest and poet. After death he was assigned a place in the heavens where he became the ruler of Canopus, the South Star. In one legend, Agastya was born as a result of the seed spilled by Varuna and Mitra (in some versions it is Surya, not Varuna), when they were filled with desire for the beautiful nymph Urvasi. Their sperm was collected in a jar of water, and in time, Agastya was born in the shape of a beautiful fish. He was later reborn as a child. The Vindya mountains wanted to be higher than Meru Mountain and were growing at a rate that threatened to block the sun's rays. The gods asked Agastya for assistance. He packed up his family and journeyed to the south. When he met Vindya, he requested the boon of the mountains to not grow until he returned at another time. His boon was granted, but Agastya continued south and never returned. Since that time, the mountains have never grown. When he was offended by the ocean he drank it up and found his enemies the Daityas, who were at war with the gods, hidden under the water. From various animal parts he molded a beautiful young woman who became his spouse Lopamudra. In later years, while living as a hermit on the mountain slopes, he provided lodging for Lakshmana, Rama, Sita, who were in exile. He gave Rama the bow of Vishnu, the quiver of Indra and the dart of Brahma. In southern India he lives invisibly on Agastya's hill in Travancore and is venerated as the divine teacher of science, Sanskrit literature, and the Hindu religion. *See also* Brahma; Daityas; Indra; Mitra; Rakshasas; Ravana; Rishi; Surya; Urvasi; Vishnu; Vrita.

Agathadeamon (Greek) *see* Agathos Diamon.

Agathodiamon (Greek) *see* Agathos Diamon.

Agathos Diamon (Greek)

Also known as: *Agathadeamon, Agathodiamon.*

Deity of health, good fortune and life. This ancient Greek spirit is the oracle of the future and teacher of wisdom. He is the spouse of Tyche Agathe (also known as Agatha).

Agave (Greek)

Agave is the daughter of Cadmus and Harmonia. Her siblings are Autonoe, Illyrius, Ino, Polydorus, and Semele. She married twice, her first husband was Echion. They had a child, Pentheus, who became the King of Thebes. Pentheus and his mother Agave ridiculed Dionysus, who in turn forced her and her sisters, to rip Pentheus to pieces. Her second husband was the king of Illyria, Lycotherses whom she murdered so her father Cadmus could take over the throne. Dionysus drove Agave insane after being ridiculed by her and her son, Pentheus. Agave and her sisters ripped Pentheus to pieces. *See also* Cadmus; Dionysus; Harmonia (A); Ino; Nereids; Semele.

Agbe (Dahomey People, Africa)

Also known as: *Arge Woyo* (Haitian).

Agbe, the son of Mahu and Lisa is the chief god of the Xevioso or Thunder pantheon. His mother (also known as Sogbo) placed him in charge of world affairs. Agbe's abode is the sea. When he has a conference with his mother he must join her where the sky and the sea meet. Although powerful, he was never instructed in the art of rain-making. He sends the water from the sea up to his mother, who causes it to fall from the sky as rain. Lightning at sea is caused by Agbe and lightning on ground by Sogbo. The Haitian deity Arge Woyo belongs to the Rada Pantheon and is also a sea deity. He has a son Agweto and a daughter Agweta. *See also* Aylekete; Leza; Mahu; Rada.

Agdistis *Agdos* (Greek)

Also known as: *Cybele.*

Deified object. In some renditions, Agdo was a natural rock from which the world sprang forth. The "Great Mother" is said to have slept on this rock. (Cybele of Asia Minor was known as "Great Mother.") Zeus couldn't impregnate her so he impregnated Agdo, the rock and produced Agdistis. Agdistis, born with both male and female organs, frightened the other gods. Liber, the ancient Roman god of fertility drugged a well from which Agdistis drank. After he fell asleep, Liber tied his foot and phallus together with a strong hair rope. In trying to get free Agdistis castrated himself and his blood fertilized the earth. It is thought by some sources that the castrated Agdistis grew up to become Cybele. Nana (also known as Naa), a river nymph, placed a pomegranate from a tree that grew in the area in her bosom and from this came her son Attis (Atys, Atos) who became the consort of Cybele. In a variation of this portion of the myth, Attis was born from an almond that grew from the severed genitals of Agdistis. Attis also castrated himself and became a pine tree. *Note:* Liber is often confused with the Greek Iacchus who is the son and possibly husband of Demeter and is identified with Bacchus. *See also* Attis; Cybele.

Agditis (Greek) *see* Agdistis.

Agdos (Greek) *see* Agdistis; Cybele.

Agemo (Africa)

Also known as: *Sky God's Messenger.*

He is a chameleon.

Agenor (A) (Sidon, Syria, then to Greece)

Also known as: *Auga-nur* (Semitic).

Deified mortal or sun god. Fire deity. Agenor, the king of Phoenicia, is the son of Poseidon and Libya who is the daughter of Epaphus and Memphis. Agenor is the twin brother of Belus and brother of Lelex. His mother Libya may have been the mother of Lamis by Agenor's uncle Belus. Agenor married Telephassa also known as Argiope. Their sons are Argus (possibly); Cadmus who became king of Thebes; Cilix who accompanied Cadmus and Phoenix in their search for the kidnapped Europa; Phineus the king of Thrace; Phoenix who became king of Phoenicia; and Thasus. They had one daughter Europa, who was raped by Zeus in the form of an eagle. Belus, king of the Egyptians married Anchinoe who was the daughter of the god Nile. They were the parents of twins, Aegyptus and Danaus, a daughter, Thronia, and possibly Cepheus. Aegyptus had fifty sons and Danaus had fifty daughters who were known as the Danaids. Agenor and Belus were thought to be ancestors of Dido, queen of Carthage and the Persian kings. *See also* Aegyptus; Agenor (B); Danaids; Danaus; Dido; Europa.

Agenor (B) to (G) (Greek)

There are numerous men named Agenor in Greek mythology. Agenor (B) was the king of Argus, son of either Ecbasus, Triopas, or Iasus. Agenor (C) is the son of Pleuron and Xanthippe (*see* Hippodamus). Agenor (D) is the brave Trojan, the son of Antenor and Theano. Agenor (E) was or Belus the father of Dido, Anna and Pygmalion, but not thought to be Agenor (A). Agenor (F) was the name of a man engaged to Andromeda and killed by Perseus. Agenor (G) is the son of Phegeus. *See also* Agenor (A).

Ageratos *see* Aeons; Nous.

Aghyu Gugu (Cherokee People, North America) *see* Unelanuhi.

Agilma (Babylonia) *see* Marduk.

Aglaea (Greek) *see* Aglaia.

Aglaia *Aegle, Aglaea* (Greek)

Also known as: *Charis, Ocaleia, The Shining One.*

Nymph. Worshipped throughout Greece. Aglaia, the daughter of Zeus and Eurynome is one of the Graces. Three of her sisters are Euphrosyne, Thalia and Pasithea. Homer called Aglaia by the name of Charis (Grace). Like the Muses with whom they lived on Olympus, they loved to sing and dance, and like the Muses, they were companions and attendants of Athena or Aphrodite. Early writers indicate that Aglaia was the wife of the fire god Hephaestus while later poets name Aphrodite as his wife. For other possibilities of Aglaia's parentage, *see* Graces. Not to be confused with Aglaea the mother of the twins Acrisius and Proetus by Abas. *See also* Charities; Muses; Proetus.

Aglaope (Greek) *see* Sirens.

Aglauros (Greek) *see* Agraulos.

Aglaurus (Greek) *see* Agraulos.

Agloolik (Eskimo)

Good spirit. Agloolik, a good spirit who lives under the ice, aids the hunters and fishers in overcoming obstacles in their daily lives. *See also* Adlivun; Aipaloovik; Sedna.

Agnar (Norse; Teutonic)

Hero or god of light. Brother of Geirrod. In a complicated tale they were saved by Odin and Frigga.

Agnayi (Hindu; India) *see* Agni.

Agne (India) *see* Agni.

Agnen (Tupinamba People, Brazil)

A fisher deity. *See also* Ariconte.

Agneya (India) Son of Agni. *See also* Karttikeya.

Agneyastra (India) A magic weapon. *See also* Sagara.

Agneyi *Suada* (India)

Daughter of Agni. *See also* Agni; Rishi.

Agni *Agne, Agnis* (Brahmanic, Hindu, Tantric, Vedic; India; possibly of Persian origins).

Also known as: *Ag, Agni Yavishta, Agoni* (Slavic), *Anala, Asani* (Lightning), *Bhava* (Existence), *Brhaspati* (Lord of Devotion), *Dhumakety, Grahapati, Grhapati* (Lord of the House), *Hotar* (The Invoker), *Isana* (Ruler), *Jatavedas* (All-knowing), *Mahadeva* (Great god), *Moloch, Narasamsa* (Praise of Men), *Ogoni* (Slavic), *Pasupati* (Lord of Cattle), *Pav, Pavaka* (The Purifier), *Pramati, Rudra* (Roarer), *Sarva* (All), *Skambha* (Support), *Slayer of Rakshasas* (Slayer of Evil Spirits), *Surya, Tanunapat* (Son of Self), *Trita, Tryambaka,* (Three-Mothered or Three-Eyed), *Ugra* (Dread), *Vaishwanara* (Universal Man), *Yavishta.*

Agni's name means "The Knower." The master of the universe, he is also the god of fire, sun and lightning. In the Vedic tradition, his parents are the earth goddess Prithivi and Dyaus the sky god. Born fully grown and eternally youthful as an all-consuming flame, he immediately devoured his parents. To sustain himself, he lapped up the clarified butter known as *ghee,* which was poured on the sacrificial fire. Sometimes, like his rival, and some say twin brother Indra, he sustained himself on the magic soma. His other siblings are the goddess of dawn Ushas and the goddess of the starlit night, Ratri. Other legends pertaining to his birth: he was born in wood from plants and springs to life whenever fire is ignited; he was born of the sky god Dyaus and brought to earth by the demigod Matarisvan; he was created from the friction of two stones generated by Indra; he was born of the waters and generated the first germ of life; he was created by Indra and Vishnu; he was created by the friction of fire sticks, his mother the lower and his father the upper; the fire sticks are his two mothers; he was generated by the ten fingers called ten maidens; he was the son of Prajapati (the Creator) and Ushas and was given eight names, which constitute his eight forms; he was born from the breath of Prajapati along with Indra, Soma and Parameshthin Prajapatya; Agni was the supreme ruler of the earth, Vayu or Indra ruled the air, and Surya ruled the sky; Angi encompassed all three worlds and their gods; therefore he was thrice-born. He is constantly born and reborn in the celestial realm as the sun. He is born again in the atmosphere, where he ignites the rain clouds and appears on earth as lightning. He is born a third time by priests and followers in the form of the sacrificial fire. He also presides at the altar and hearth where he is kindled at dawn or immediately before day breaks. In this form, known as

Grhapati, he constantly dies and is reborn. He offers warmth, protection and nourishment to mortals. To worshipers, he bestows domestic health and welfare, and consumes their enemies. The smoke from his fires rises to the heavens and becomes the clouds, which form the rain. In the form of lightning, he is known as Trita, and blazes at the heart of the sun. As the sun, he is known as Surya. When Agni is worshipped as the fire, lightning and sun, he is known as Tryambaka the Three-mothered. So it is, that wherever there is fire, there is Agni. The followers of Brahma consider his mother as Sandili. The goddess Lakshmi is also indicated as his possible mother. It is also said that he is the son of Brahma, Kasyapa and of Aditi or Angiras the king of the Manes. He is said to be the husband of Suada (also spelled Suadha, Svaha and Swaha and known as Agnayi) and father of Pavaka, Pavamana and Suci. He is the father of Karttikeya (also known as Skanda). Agni carries the Asu or Manas which is the spiritual principle to the sun after cremation of the body. He is invoked as a celestial deity and a domestic deity for he knows the realm of the gods as well as he knows the realm of the household. Agni is invoked to dispel the powers of the evil spirits known as rakshasa. A slayer of demons, he battles the flesh-eating Kravyad, who is a rakshasa (evil spirit). When ill, Agni is invoked alone or with Soma and Varuna, to drive away the fire of fever. He is invoked for abundance and prosperity and the forgiveness of sins. The river goddess Saraswati appears as his attendant or consort. Agni has two faces (Sun fire and Earth fire), three heads growing red flames and three legs (one perhaps a euphemism for the phallus, or the three fires of an individual's life), wearing a garland of fruit. He is said to have tawny flowing hair, golden teeth and he is flame red in color. He is equipped with seven tongues, each with a name, with which he laps up the ghee (sacrificial butter) and a distended stomach. The name of Agni's first tongue is Kali the goddess of destruction. She represents the dark side of Agni, his ashes and ambers. Agni has seven arms (to span the continents) and has also been depicted with three bodies. He rides on a ram. He symbolizes the creative life-giving spark of the universe. In his hideous form, he has iron tusks and roars like a bull. Agni's three heads symbolize his triple birth. His seven arms are rays of light. His two faces represent the creative and destructive nature of fire. Depicted on his ram with four arms and two heads, he holds his attributes: a fan to fan fire, an ax, a torch and the sacrificial ladle. Flames shoot from his mouth and seven rays are emitted from his body. The eight aspects of Agni are Asani (lightning), Bhava (existence), Isana (ruler), Mahadeva (great god), Pasupati (lord of cattle), Rudra (roarer), Sarva (all), Ugra (dread). Agni's mount is the ram. In the practice of yoga, Agni relates to mindfulness and wakefulness, or the fire of the mind and the Kundalini, or fire at the base of the spine. The goddess Sarasvati represents the element of water. The etymology of the goddess Suada's name means "a good offering through fire." Mystically, it means "so be it" which is the ending of many mantras. Kravyad (Flesh Eater) is depicted with red hair and shiny fangs. Sometimes Brhaspati (also called Brahmanaspati) is considered to be the same as Agni. In Agni's creation myth, Matarisvan is not to be confused with a later wind god of the same name. Agni is identified as the Rudra Shiva aspect of Shiva (destructive). Compare Agni to Cronus (Greek), Fuji (Japan), Hephaistos (Greek), Hestia (the Greek hearth goddess), Pele (Hawaiian), Vahagn (Armenian), and Vesta (Roman). For a myth about Agni and Bhrigus see Bhrigus. The mythology of Agni and Indra is similar (q.v.). See also Angirasa; Apam Napat (Inod-Iranian); Arjuna; Asuras; Brahma; Brhaspati; Daksha; Dikpalas; Durga; Dyaus; Garuda; Jogina; Kali; Kama (A); Karttikeya; Kasyapa; Kravyad; Krishna; Kuhu; Lokapalas; Matarisvan; Mitra; Moloch; Parvati; Prajapati; Prithiva; Ratri; Ravana; Rishi; Rudra; Saraswati; Skamba; Soma; Surya; Tvashtri; Urvasi; Ushas; Vahagn; Varuna; Vasistha; Vasus; Vedas (The); Vishnu; Vourukasha; Yama.

Agni Yavishata (India) *see* Agni.

Agnimukha (India) "Fire Face." *See also* Yaksha and Yakshini.

Agnis (India) *see* Agni.

Agoneus (Greek) *see* Hermes.

Agoni God of Fire (Slavic) *see* Agni.

Agothyathik (Africa) *see* Aywel.

Agras (Finnish)
God of twins. God of grain (possibly). In some myths, Agras is the patron of turnips.

Agrasandhani (India) List of mortal's deeds. *See also* Yama.

Agrat Bat Mahalat *Igirit* (Hebrew)
On Wednesday and Friday evenings, Agrat Bat Mahalat, the ruler of 180,000 demons, climbs into her chariot and hunts everything that moves. *See also* Lilith (queen of the demons).

Agraulos *Aglauros, Aglaurus* (Greek)
The goddess of agriculture and fertility Agraulos is the daughter of Cecrops, the king of Attica, and Agraulos, the daughter of Actaeus. Her sisters are Herse, Pandrosus, and possibly Erysichthon. Hermes approached Agraulos and paid her for the opportunity to have sex with her youngest sister, Herse. The young woman took his gold but denied Hermes his wish as she was jealous of her sister's good luck. What she didn't know was that the goddess Athene had instilled feelings of envy within the young woman. Infuriated, Hermes turned Agraulos to stone and raped Herse who had two sons by him, Cephalus and Ceryx. Her sisters and her mother were asked to care for a casket and instructed not to open it. Ignoring the command, they lifted the lid and found hidden inside, the child Erichthonius, who had serpent's tails for legs. The sight of him drove two of the sisters insane. They leapt to their deaths from the top of the Acropolis. Agraulos and her sisters are known as the Augralids. Agraulos is not to be confused with Agraulus (Aglaurus), the daughter of Actaeus and the mate of Cecrops. Cecrops, the father of Agraulos has a man's body and a snake's tail. *See also* Ares; Cecrops.

Agreaskoui (Iroquois) *see* Areskoui.

Agreus (Greek) *see* Agrius (A).

Agri-manios (Greek) *see* Angra Mainyu.

Agriskoue (Iroquois) *see* Areskoui.

Agrius (A) *Agreus* (Greek, Sumerian)
Also known as: *Agrotes.*

Giant. High god. Agrius is the son of Gaea and brother of Thoas, and one of the Giants. In the war between Giants and gods, Agrius and Thoas were battered to death by the Fates who used brazen clubs or they were killed by Heracles. As Agreus, he was said to be part of the pantheon of Melqart (Melkart) of the Sumerians. The name is said to mean "hunter." One of the names of the Babylonian god Gebal was Agroueros. *See also* Fates; Gaea; Giants; Hippolytus; Melkart.

Agrius (B) to (E) (Greek)
There are other men by the name of Agrius in Greek mythology. Agrius (B) was a Centaur who attempted to kill Heracles but was killed by him. Agrius (C) was possibly the father of Thersites, who was known as the ugliest man in the Trojan War; not to be confused with Agrius the king of Calydon. Agrius (D) was the son of Odysseus and Circe. Agrius (E) was the king of Calydon, son of Porthaon and Euryte who committed suicide when his sons were killed by Diomedes the son of Tydeus. *See also* Agrius (B); Agrius (D); Agrius (E); Circe; Diomedes; Heracles; Odysseus.

Agro-manyus (Persia) *see* Angra Mainyu.

Agroata (Greek) *see* Agrius (A).

Agros *Agrotes, Agroueros* (Phoenician)
Also known as: *El.*
Hunter, or high god. Son of Technites and Geinos. Grandson of Agreus and Halieus. Associated with Melqart. *See also* El.

Agrotes (Greek) *see* Agrius.

Agroueros (Phoenician) *see* Agros.

Agrouneros (Greek) *see* Agrius (A).

Agu (Akkadian)
Also known as: *Aku.*
Male Moon God. *See also* Aah (Egypt); Sinu (Semitic).

Aguilo (Greek) *see* Aquilo.

Agunua *Argunua* (Solomon Islands, Melanesia)
Serpent deity. Agunua created men and one woman, as well as the sea, land and storms. It is said that he created rain because he was thirsty. He instructed his brother to plant a yam from which sprang the original banana, coconuts, and almond trees. One day, his brother planted a batch of yams incorrectly and from that time forth certain plants became inedible forever. *See also* Gainji; Tagaros.

Agusaya (Babylon)
Also known as: *Ishtar.*
Goddess of loud-crying. She is an aspect of Ishtar, who is also a the goddess of loud-crying or wailing. Agusaya is associated with Ea and Saltu (discord). *See also* Ishtar.

Agwe (Haitian)
Voodoo god of waters, wind, thunder, boats and seashells. He lives on an underwater island. A blue-colored ram is sacrificed in his honor. Similar to St. Ulrique of the Catholics.

Agweta (Dahomey People, Africa) *see* Agbe.

Agweto (Dahomey People, Africa) *see* Agbe.

Agyieus (Greek) *see* Apollo.

Agyieyus (Greek) *see* Apollo.

Ah (Egypt) *see* Aah; Astarte.

Ah (Egypt) *see* Astarte.

Ah-hetep (Egypt)
Sovereign Chief. One of the four chiefs guarding the Fifth Division (hour) of Tuat. *See also* Tuat.

Ah-Kiuic (Maya People, Yucatan)
Also known as: *Echauc.*
God of plenty and of merchants. He is one of the triad of Chac and Hobnel. *See also* Chac Mol; Hobnil.

Ah Puch (Maya People, Yucatan) *see* Ahpuch.

Ah Puchah (Maya People, Yucatan People, Yucatan People, Yucatan) *see* Ah Puch.

Ah-uuc-chek-nale (Maya People, Yucatan) *see* Ahmucen-Cab.

Aha (Egypt) *see* Bes.

Ahalya (Brahmanic, Hindu; India)
An early goddess, some say that Ahalya, "Night," was the first woman created by Brahma. The spouse of the sage Gautama, her great beauty caught the attention of the promiscuous god Indra. His overtures to her were on the verge of being satisfied when Gautama walked in on them. He cursed Indra with a thousand marks of the yoni (female sex organ). Later, he reconsidered his curse and transformed the yoni to one thousand eyes. The lighter sentence was given because the actual sex act had not taken place. Indra, overcome with passion, convinced the moon to assume the shape of a cock and to crow while it was still night. When Gautama heard the familiar sound, he rose and left to perform his morning prayers. Indra seized the opportunity and assumed Gautama's form and entered Ahalya's bed. This time Gautama caught them and turned his wife to stone. She remained in that state until many years later, when Vishnu, in his incarnation as Rama, kicked her. Once again alive, she was reunited with Gautama. Indra was cursed to become a eunuch and was only saved from his fate by the intervention of the gods. *See also* Brahma; Indra; Indrani; Rama; Vishnu.

Ahana (India) *see* Athena.

Ahans (India) *see* Asvins.

Aharman (Persia) *see* Angra Mainyu.

Ahat (Egypt)
Also known as: *Ahet, Ahit, Ehat, Ehet.*
Protector deity. Ahat is the cosmic cow who nurses and protects the sun god, Ra. *See also* Amen; Ra.

Ahau-Chamahez (Maya People, Yucatan)
Lord of the Magic Tooth. A god of medicine.

Ahayuta Achi (Zuni People, North America)
They are twin culture heroes, or according to some, twin

gods of war. They protect gamblers and mischief-makers. They are also responsible for destroying monsters and rapists. Protectors of Zuni villages, they live inside mountains. The Ahayuta Achi provided men with implements, and taught them to hunt. The twins are the sons of Dripping Water but were raised by Spiderwoman, their grandmother.

Aherat (Middle East) *see* Asherah.

Ahet (Egypt) *see* Ahat.

Ahhazu *Ach-Chazu* (Babylonia, Sumer)
Also known as: *Labasu.*
Demon of death, disease and pestilence. Ahhazu is probably the same as Labasu and one of the group of twelve demons of the Sumerians. These include Alu, Lamashtu, Lilith, Lilu, and Utukku. *See also* Als; Lilith.

Ahi (Egypt, Persia, India.)
Also known as: *Azi, Azhi Dahaka, Vrita.*
Ahi is the Persian Azhi Dahaka (meaning "biting snake"). The Vedic Ahi, (his alternate name is Vrita) is the celestial snake who withheld rain, and was defeated by Indra. In other interpretations, Ahi is the son of the serpent god Danu and Vrita. To the Egyptians Ahi represented daytime. Ahi is depicted as a dragon or a snake. Ahi is comparable to Visvarupa and Azhi Dahaka (qq.v.). *See also* Angra Mainyu; Azi; Ihi; Vrita; Zohak.

Ahi-Mu (Egypt)
One of the forty-two Assessors (judges of the dead). *See also* Assessors.

Ahiah (Hebrew) *see* Jehovah.

Ahimsa (India) *see* Narayana (C).

Ahit (Egypt) *see* Ahat.

Ahkinshok (Aztec People, Mexico)
No particular function, but may be one of the day gods. He lives below the earth and has several titles: Guardian of Bees, Owner of the Days, and Spirit of New Fire. *See also* Kasin; Yumchakob.

Ahkushtal (Aztec People, Mexico)
Birth deity. Little shown, but appears to be associated with other gods below the earth. *See also* Kasin; Yumchakob.

Ahmakiq (Aztec People, Mexico)
Wind deity. His function is to lock up the winds that destroy crops. Patrons of medicine and other workers who tend ill humans can be locked up or otherwise controlled by this god. He lives below the earth. *See also* Yunchakob.

Ahmes-Neferatari (Egypt) *see* Amenhotep I.

Ahmucen-Cab (Maya People, Yucatan)
Creator. The legend is rather confusing, but essentially the deity came down and covered the faces of the Oxlahun-ti-Ku, who were thirteen gods. Ahmucen-cab had other names, a sister and children but neither his other names nor the names and faces of any of them were seen. It is possible Oxlahun-ti-Ku was one of his names and he was captured by Bolon-ti-Ku (nine gods) after he brought down stones and trees. In the legend the Bolon-tsac-cab (nine orders) covered the world with a blanket of seeds and went back to the thirteenth heaven. The world was then formed. After this the legend follows that of the Legend of the Four Suns, except the four Becab (also known as Cantul-ti-Ku) destroyed this world then placed the mortal Kanxib-yui on the new world they created. The story proceeds with the goddess Itzam-kab-ain, who is a female whale with alligator feet, impregnated by Ah-uuc-chek-nale. Thus, the world began. *See also* Bacabs; Legend of the Four Suns.

Ahoeitu (South Pacific)
He is the king of Tonga, the son of the sky god Eitumatupua, and the earth goddess Ilaheva. *See also* Eitumatupua.

Ahpuch *Ah Puch, Ah Puchah* (Maya People, Yucatan)
Also known as: *Ahpuch Yum Cimil, Eopuco, Hanhau.*
God of death. A demon, Ahpuch slayed the Becabs. In one of his several aspects, he is the ruler of the ninth sector (or layer) of the underworld. In another version he was called a "Demon Destroyer" and "Lord of Death." *See also* Becabs; Ek Ahau; Hanhau.

Ahpuch Yum Cimil (Maya People, Yucatan) *see* Ahpuch.

Ahrenkonigin (Austrian) Goddess of the Harvest.

Ahriman (Persia) *see* Angra Mainyu; Drujs.

Ahrimanes (Persia) *see* Aryaman.
Ahsonnutli and Yolaikaiason (North America) *see* Atseatsan and Atseatsine.

Ahti *Ahto* (Finland)
Also known as: *Kaukomieli, Lemminkainen.*
God of the waters and fishermen. Consort of Wellamo (also spelled Vellamo). They live deep under the sea in a place known as Ahtoia (Atola). He is holder of the treasure Sampo. Some say Lemminkainen bore the epithet Ahti so he could be both god and hero. His servants are Vetehinen, and Tursa a sea monster. He is shown with a beard of moss. *See also* Lemminkainen; Naaki.

Ahto (Finland) *see* Ahti.

Ahu (Egypt)
One of the principal gods shown in the Pyramid Texts.

Ahuehuete (Aztec People, Mexico)
Tree of life. The only two survivors of the great deluge were a man and woman who climbed this tree. Some say their names are Nala and Nina.

Ahura (Persia) *see* Ahura Mazda.

Ahura Mazda *Ahura, Asura, Auramazda* (Manichean, Zoroastrian, Zurvan; Persian, Iranian)
Also known as: *Bag-Mazda, Horomazes* (Greek), *Hormazu, Ohrmazd* (Iranian), *Ormazd* (the later name of Ahura Mazda under the Sassanians), *Oromazez, Ormuz, Ormuzd, Thraetaona.*
Ahura Mazda ("Wise Lord") is the creator of all good, and the Supreme God of the Zoroastrians. His adversary and opposite is Angra Mainyu. Ahura Mazda is the president of the council of six ministers (sometimes seven), known as the Amesha

Spentas, also called the "Augmentative Immortals." The Amesha Spentas, three male and three female, are said to be aspects, personifications, or attributes of Ahura Mazda. Some scholars believe that they are based on ancient gods. In later times they were thought of as gods or archangels. Ahura Mazda revealed himself to humans through the Amesha Spentas. After the creation of the Amesha Spentas, the Yazatas were created, followed by the creation of the universe and mortals. In one myth, Angra Mainyu was born from Ahura Mazda during a moment of doubt. In another, Ahura Mazda and Angra Mainyu existed but were separated by the Void. It happened that Angra Mainyu came upon Ahura Mazda and his light and following his nature attempted to destroy him. He refused Ahura Mazda's offer of peace, which was conditional upon him praising the Good Creation. In the orthodox tradition, an agreement was reached. History spans twelve thousand years. The first three thousand years were allocated to creation. The second three thousand years passed according to the will of Ahura Mazda. The third three thousand years are mixed with the will of Ahura Mazda and Angra Mainyu. In the fourth three thousand year period, Angra Mainyu and all evil will be destroyed. There are variations of this creation myth, and some are based on a nine thousand year cycle. The Zurvan tradition considers the first nine thousand years as the period of the rule of evil. Evil will be defeated during the final three thousand years. In the Zoroastrian tradition, Angra Mainyu created the sky. It served as a cover to enclose the world and to trap Angra Mainyu. Originally, the world was in an ideal state. The first man, Gaya Maretan, shone like the sun, until Angra Mainyu, persuaded by the female demon, Jahi, woke from a deep sleep and attacked creation. In the Manichean tradition, there are two realms: light, ruled by the Father of Greatness, and dark, ruled by the Prince of Darkness. Originally, the two realms existed in a balanced state. The Prince of Darkness, attracted by the light, upset this balance by permeating light, including the light of the Primeval Man. The god Mithra attempted to punish the demons of darkness. From the skins of the defeated demons, he created the skies; the mountains were made from their bones. The earths (four or eight in number), the ten firmaments, the zodiac, the constellations and planets were created from their flesh and excrements. Uncontaminated light particles were used to create the sun and moon, while the stars contained partially contaminated substance. The animal and vegetable world, came into existence, and because of their origin, they contained undelivered light particles. Ahura Mazda is depicted as a bearded man with a winged, plumed body and a sacred tree. In an ancient bas relief Ahura Mazda is depicted in the same costume that King Darius I (521–486 B.C.E.) wore: a wide-sleeved tunic with a circle representing the sun's disk at the waist of his long robe, a cap on his head and a long beard on his face. He has wings and is poised in the air. He is also shown enclosed in a winged circle. He appears bearded, stately in demeanor, in a stance of benediction. In another depiction, he is shown putting on the solid heavens as a garment and covering himself with his symbol, flames of fire. The Zoroastrians use one hundred and eight names to denote the attributes of Ahura Mazda. He is vaguely connected with Khaldi (Armenian, Iranian). See also Aeshma; Akhtar (The); Ameretat; Amesha Spentas; Anahita; Angra Mainyu; Aramzad (Armenia); Asha Vahishta; Asuras (India); Atar; Avesta; Bag-Mashtu; Bundahish; Chinvat Bridge (for life after death); Fravashi; Gaokerena Tree; Gaya Maretan; Haoma; Hariati (Mount); Hvare-khshaeta; Jahi; Khshasthra Vairya; Mitra; Nairyosangha; Rapithwin; Rashu; Spenishta (sacred fire); Spenta Armaiti; Thrita; Tishtrya; Varuna (India); Vayu; Vohu Manah; Yazatas; Yima.

Ahy (Egypt) see Herusmatauy.

Ai (A) (Akkadian, Egypt) see Aah.

Ai (B) (Norse; Teutonic)
Also known as: *Great Grandfather.*
God of Serfs. Ancestor of the race of serfs. Husband of Edda. Heimdall (also known as Rig) slept between Ai and Edda. From his union with Edda came Thrall who married Thir and from their union sprang the race of Thralls or serfs. See also Aah; Heimdall; Thrall.

Ai (C) (Estonian)
Also known as: *Hai* (Hebrew).
Thunder god.

Ai (D) (Teutonic) see Dwarfs.

Ai-Willi-Ay-O (Eskimo) see Sedna.

Aiai (Hawaii)
Aiai, the son of Ku-ula-kai, the god of abundance in the sea, followed his father's instructions and set up numerous fishing grounds around the island. When his son Punia came of age he too was instructed in this trade. Father and son worked together and expanded to other islands. See also Ku-ula-kai; Ku and Hina.

Aiaiakuula (Hawaii, Polynesia)
Goddess of fishers. See also Kuula.

Aiapakal (Tierra del Fuego)
The shamans, known as Yakamouch, converse with the god Aiapakal and gain their power from the spirit, Hoakils. See also Yakamouch.

Aiakos (Greek) see Aeacus.

Aiapaec (Peru) Supreme Deity.

Aias (Greek) see Ajax the Greater.

Aibheaog (Celtic) Ancient fire goddess.

Aida-Wedo (Haiti)
The rainbow snake goddess. See also Damballah.

Aides (Greek) see Cocytus; Hades.

Aidne (Celtic)
Fire god. He created fire for the Melesians by rubbing his hands together.

Aido Hwedo (Dahomey People, Africa; Haiti)
Aido Hwedo is the great rainbow serpent who served as the vehicle for the goddess Mahu as she created the universe. His excrement formed the mountains. When Mahu had completed her creation, she realized that the earth was too heavy. She had Aido Hwedo coil himself beneath the planet to keep it from toppling. Heat disturbs Aido Hwedo, so the seas were created to keep him comfortable. Whenever he shifts, an earthquake

occurs. When he has finished eating the iron bars beneath the sea, he will devour his tail and the world will come to an end. Believers are careful not to incur the wrath of the great serpent, for he is very jealous. Before marriages take place, special offerings are presented to Aido Hwedo and relatives invoke him not to harm the newlyweds. *See also* Damballah; Mahu.

Aidoneus (Greek) *see* Adonis.

Aife (Celtic) *see* Aeife.

Aigamuchab (Hottentot, Africa)
Ogre. Little known about this fellow, except he is a cannibal with eyes on top of his feet.

Aighistos (Greek) *see* Aegisthus.

Aigi'pan (Greek) *see* Aegipan.

Aigina (Greek) *see* Aegina.

Aigis (Greek) *see* Aegis.

Aigisthus (Greek) *see* Aegisthus.

Aigle (Greek) *see* Aegle.

Ailanthus (China)
This tree of paradise has a beautiful flower that has an offensive aroma. Tenacious, it can grow under the most adverse of conditions.

Aileili (Celtic) *see* Mider.

Aillen (Irish) *see* Aine.

Ailo (Hebrew) *see* Lilith.

Ailuros (Egypt) *see* Bast.

Aimon Kondi (Arawak People, New Guinea)
In the Creation Legend, Aimon Kondi set the world on fire. Marerewana and his people sought refuge in caves. A great deluge followed, and the survivors escaped in canoes. *See also* Makonaima.

Aindra (India) *see* Aindri.

Aindri *Aindra* (India) *see* Arjuna; Indra; Indrani.

Aine (Irish)
Aine was known as the Irish goddess of love and thought by some to be a moon goddess, fertility goddess and goddess of cattle. She is variously called the sister of Aillen and daughter of the fertility Eogabal, or the sister of Fenne (Fennen) and daughter of Eogabal. Eogabal in this version was a king of the Tuatha de Danann, and Aine was the wife of Gerold, the Earl of Desmond. Their child was Earl Fitzgerald. A variation on this theme is that Gerold Iarla (Earl Gerald of Desmond) came upon Aine bathing in a river and raped her. Gerald, a magician of repute, turned into a goose and disappeared, although others say that Aine killed him with her magical powers. He is said to live in the waters of Loch Gur. Every seven years he makes an appearance mounted on a white horse which trots around the perimeter. In another rendition, Aine is known as the wife and daughter of Manannan Mac Llyr. A feast, Midsummer Night, was held in her honor. Farmers waved straw torches over the fields and cattle to insure replenishment. In later times, as Aine she was worshipped as a fairy queen in South Munster. Aine is sometimes identified with Dana, and she has been said to be identical to Anu. *See also* Anu; Dana; Manannan Mac Llyr.

Aineias (Greek) *see* Aeneas.

Aino (Finland) *see* Vainomoinen.

Ainu-rak-kur (Japan) *see* Okikurumi.

Aion (A) (Gnostic) *see* Aeons.

Aion (B) (Phoenician) *see* Kolpia.

Aior-Pata (Greek) *see* Amazons.

Aipaloovik (Eskimo)
Evil god of the sea. Aipaloovik lives deep in the ocean and is a danger to all fishermen or those who venture out to sea. *See also* Adlivun; Agloolik.

Air (A) (Phoenician)
In the Creation Legend of Damascisu, Air is the son of Omicle and Potos (meaning desire), who with his sister Aura became the parent of Otos (meaning reason). *See also* Air (B); Aura; Kolpia (for the Creation Legend of Philos Byblos).

Air (B) (Phoenician)
In the beginning, Air and Chaos existed. Their union produced Kolpia (Wind) and Potos (Desire). (From the Creation Legend of Philo Byblos). *See also* Air (A); Chaos; Kolpia.

Air (C) (Phoenician)
Air and Ether engendered Oulomos in the Creation Legend of Mochus. *See also* Air (A); Air (B); Oulomos.

Air, God of (Egypt) *see* Shu.

Airavarta (India) *see* Airavata.

Airavata *Airavarta, Airawata* (India)
Indra's divine white elephant. *See also* Dikpalas; Indra; Kurma; Lokapalas; Swarga.

Airawata (India) *see* Airavata.

Aireskoi (Iroquois) *see* Areskoui.

Aireskouy (Iroquois) *see* Areskoui.

Airmid (Celtic)
The goddess of witchcraft and herb lore, she is the daughter of Dia'necht and the sister of Miach. It was Airmid and Miach who healed King Nuada. *See also* Dia'necht; Nuada.

Airya *Iraj* (Persian) *see* Thrita.

Airyano Vaejo (Iranian)
Heaven or Eden. This is a place of bliss where no one grew old until Ahriman (earlier known as Angra Mainyu) came and brought ten months of winter each year.

Ais (A) (Armenia) *see* Devs.

Ais (B) (Greek) *see* Hades.

Aisar (Norse) *see* Aesir.

Aither *Aither* (Greek)

Deities of light. Heavenly light. In Hesiod's version of creation, the god Aither and goddess Hemera (Day) were born of Gaea (Earth), Tartarus (Underworld) or Eros (Love). In other traditions, Hermera is the daughter of Erebus (Darkness) and Nyx (Night). She is also said to be the mother of Phaethon by Cephalus. Phaethon was kidnapped by Aphrodite to be the protector of her shrine. For siblings of Hemera, *see* Aether.

Aithre (Greek) *see* Aether; Aither.

Aithuia (Greek) *see* Athena.

Aitvaras (Prussian, Lithuanian)

This little demon of good fortune is found behind the big stove in the house. He feeds on leftover food. In Lithuanian legend, he is known to steal items, usually corn, milk, meal and coins to bring to his master. When he is flying he appears like a fiery tail. In the house he looks like a cock. A family can purchase him or acquire him from the egg of a seven-year-old cock. He must be fed omelets. For the price of one's soul he can be purchased from the devil. Once in a while, he is found and his identity is not known when he is brought into the house. Once ensconced, it is difficult to drive him away, although he can be killed. *See also* Domovoi.

Aiwel (Africa) *see* Aywil.

Aiwel Longar (Africa) *see* Aywel.

Aiyai (Tamil People, India)

Aiyai is an ancient goddess of hunters. Followers' severed heads were offered to her in sacrifices. Dressed in leopard skin and wearing a tiger's teeth necklace, she wields a black sword and carries a bow. Her mount is a stag decorated with snakes. *See also* Kali; Karitay.

Aiyanar (India) *see* Gramadeveta.

Aizen Myo-O (Japan) *see* Aizen-Myoo.

Aizen-Myoo *Aizen Myo-O, Aizenmyo-o, Aizenmyo-wo* (Buddhist, Shinto, Japan)

Also known as: *Raga-vidyaraja* (Buddhist).

God of Love and Sexual Desire. His look is supposed to portray the suppression of passionate lusts. In some versions he is regarded as secret. According to legend he manifests the state when agitation becomes enlightenment and the passion of love becomes the compassion for everything that lives. According to some the moment of agitation takes the form of a Vajrasattva and becomes Aizen-Myoo. Pictured as a red, glaring, three-eyed, frowning god, with six arms, and an unusual hair arrangement. He also has a lion head nestled in his hair. He carries a bell, a stick, a bow and arrow, a thunderbolt and a lotus in his hands. In some forms he can have two heads and two, four or six arms.

Aizenmyo-o (Japan) *see* Aizen-Myoo.

Aizennyo-wo (Japan) *see* Aizen-Myoo.

Aja (Babylon) *see* Aya.

Aja Ekapada (Hindu; India)

Aja is a lightning god and the name signifies a one-footed goat. Aja Ekapada may symbolize the swiftness of the strike of the lighting bolt. In the Vedic tradition, the goat is called Aja. A-ja means "unborn." *See also* Rama.

Ajagava (India) Shiva's Sacred Bow. *See also* Shiva.

Ajan (Islamic) *see* Jinn.

Ajatar *Ajattara* (Finnish)

Devil of the Woods.

An evil female dragon who suckles snakes and causes disease.

Ajattara (Finnish) *see* Ajatar.

Ajax the Greater (Greek)

Also known as: *Aias*.

Warrior and hero. Ajax, the son of Telamon and Periboea or possibly Eriboea, is known as "the greater" because of his height. It has been said that he was the tallest of the Greeks. His consort was Tecmassa and their child was Eurysaces. A prince or king of Salamis, and one of Helen's suitors, Ajax was considered almost as powerful and brave as Achilles and proved himself a hero when the Greeks attacked Troy. It was Ajax who lifted Achilles' body from the battle while Odysseus held the enemy at bay. Later it was decided that either Ajax or Odysseus should be given the armor of Achilles. A secret vote was taken and Odysseus received the honors. Ajax, ashamed and humiliated, suffered a breakdown and began to slaughter sheep, believing the animals to be his enemies. A vestige of sanity remained and it is said that he committed suicide rather than taking the chance of killing his colleagues. In other versions of his death he was said to have been murdered by Paris, Odysseus or Teucer and from his blood the purple hyacinth sprang forth. *See also* Acamas (C); Achilles; Aeacus; Ajax the Lesser; Helen.

Ajax the Lesser (Greek)

Ajax the Lesser is the hero son of Oileus, the king of Locris, who was an Argonaut and one of Apollo's lovers. Ajax's mother was either Eriopis or Rhene. Swift of foot, he had a reputation for being able to outrace all but Achilles, although in another legend he was placed at the funeral games of Patroclus and he lost a race to Odysseus. He was often in the company of Ajax the Greater and although he was a courageous warrior, he was also a brute and a braggart. It is said that when the Greeks conquered Troy, Ajax the Lesser raped Cassandra, one of Athena's priestesses. Athena struck back by causing a shipwreck when he was en route home. He survived by clinging to a rock and declaring that he did not need the assistance of the gods to remain alive. This incensed the sea god Poseidon who with his trident ruptured the rock and Ajax sank to his death in the sea. *See also* Ajax the Greater; Athena; Cassandra; Poseidon.

Ajbit (Maya People, Yucatan)

Creator deity. One of thirteen gods who tried to create man from wood after two other attempts had failed. *See also* Ajtzak; Tzakol.

Aji-suki-Taka-hi-kone (Japan) *see* Aji-suki-takahikone.

Aji-suki-takahikone *Aji-suki-Taka-hi-kone* (Japan) *see* Take-mi-kazuchi; Taki-tsu-hiko.

Ajita (Buddhist; India)
Also known as: *A-shih, Ma-p'am-pa* (Tibet), *Me-phem-pa* (Tibet), *Maitreya, Mi-Lo Fu* (China).
A deified mortal who is the second arhat (one of sixteen, later eighteen apostles). He is usually depicted in a meditative pose with his head covered. *See also* A-shih; Abheda; Maitreya; Mi-Lo Fu (China).

Ajnesvara (India) *see* Vishnu.

Ajorsum (Saora People, India)
This snake god lives in streams. For other deities *see* Adunnkisum; Arsi Basum.

Ajtzak (Maya People, Yucatan)
Creator deity. Ajtzak belongs to a group of creator gods who attempted to create humans from wood. The other deities are Hunahpu, Hunahpu-Guch, Ixmucane, and Ixpiyacoc.

Ajuna (India) *see* Garuda.

Ajy-khoton (Yakut) *see* Ajysyt.

Ajysit (Yakut) *see* Ajysyt.

Ajysyt *Ajysit, Ijaksit* (Yakut People, Siberia)
Also known as: *Ajy-khoton.*
Ajysyt is goddess of childbirth and domestic animals, particularly cattle. She brings the new soul from heaven to the child being born and writes the child's fate. She is always depicted laughing. *See also* Khotun.

Ak (Akkadian) *see* Nebo.

Aka (Turkish) *see* Akha.

Aka-Kanet (Araucanian People, Chile) *see* Akanet.

Aka Manah *Aka-Manah, Akah Manah, Ako-Mano, Akoman* (Persia)
He is known as the demon of vile thoughts and discord. Aka Manah was created by Ahriman to be one of his assistants. *See also* Angra Mainyu; Daevas; Darvands; Vohu Manah.

Akadja (Dahomey People, Africa; Haitian) *see* Bossu.

Akalo (Solomon Islands)
The Akalo is the friendly ghost of the dead or the soul of the living. The Akalo is caught with a diminutive rod and placed in a container with the skull, jawbone, tooth and a lock of hair from the deceased. When illness strikes offerings are made to the Akalo. Offerings are also presented at the beginning of the yam harvest. The ghosts of mortals with spiritual power become Li'oa. *See also* Agunua.

Akamas (Greek) *see* Acamas (A).

Akanet (Araucanian People, Chile)
Also known as: *Aka-Kanet, Algue.*
Although a protector of man, this deity of fruit and grain can be cruel at times. He may have originated as a culture hero. Akanet presides over harvest festivals. His counterpart and possible twin is the evil Guecubu (his name means "The Wanderer Without"). *See also* Epunamun; Pillan.

Akar (Egypt) *see* Aker.

Akara (Egypt) *see* Aah.

Akasagarbha (Japan) *see* Dhyanibodhisattvas; Gundari-Myoo; Kokuzo-Bosatsu; Kshitigarbha; Samantabhadra.

Akatauire (Polynesia) *see* Rangi.

Akbal (Aztec People, Mexico) *see* Huecomitl.

Ake (Polynesia) *see* Aokeu.

Akebiu (Egypt)
Deities of crying. "The Wailers." These are four bearded gods found in the eleventh sector of Tuat. *See also* Tuat.

Akeneh (Egypt)
Akeneh is a serpent demon mentioned in "The Text of Unas," a king in the fifth dynasty. This text describes magical methods to destroy serpents and barbarous beasts. Other serpents mentioned are, Amen, Antaf, Hau, Heka, Hekret, Hemth, Nai, Senenahemthet, Setcheh, Tcheser-tep, Thethu, and Ufa. *See also* Ab-esh-imy-duat; Ab-ta; Apepi; Apophis.

Aker (Egypt)
Also known as: *Akar, Akeru.*
Guardian animal. Earth god. A double-headed lion god who guards the gate of the dawn through which Ra the sun god passes each morning. He is connected with Set as a deity of gloom and of early dawn and twilight when demons are about. The keeper of the gates that open to the underworld address the deceased soul by saying, "the gates of the earth-god [Aker] are opened unto you." (From "The Pyramid Texts.") Aker is represented in one version as a narrow piece of land with a human or lion head at either end. In another version these symbols guard the entrance and exit of the underworld and are depicted as a double-headed lion or sphinx seated back to back. One faces the west, where the sun begins its travels into the night and one the east, where the sun appears each morning. *See also* Teta, and Unas (the god-eating god), who were early kings in the fifth and sixth dynasties. Because the kings were as powerful in the afterworld as when mortal, it is said that the bones of Aker tremble when these deified kings pass through. Aker is sometimes identified with Qeb. *See also* Unas.

Akeru (Egypt) *see* Aker.

Akesi (Egypt) *see* Aaru.

Akethor (Teutonic) *see* Thor.

Akewa (Toba People, Argentina) Sun goddess.

Akh (Egypt)
The Akh is thought of as a spirit of a god who dwells in heaven and matches the human counterpart. At death, the Ka (double) splits and turns into a bird, the Akh, which flies into the afterlife and turns again into the Ka. The Ba (soul) stays behind on earth. *See also* Ba; Ka.

Akha *Aka* (Assyro-Babylonia, Burait, Turkey)
Also known as: *Acca Larentia* (Roman), *Alka, Akha,* (Lapp), *Ekhi* (Accadian), *Sar-Akha* (Lapp), *Ummu* (Assyrian).
A Mother Goddess. The Lapps call her Sar-Akha ("Lady Mother"). The Akkadian word Ekhi is rendered Ummu (mother) in Assyrian. *See also* Acca Larentia.

Akhekh (Egypt)

Akhekh is an aspect of the evil god Set. Shown as a griffin, he has the body of an antelope and the head of a bird. The head is surmounted by three uraei and wings. *See also* Set.

Akheloos (Greek) *see* Achelous.

Akhem-Sek (Egypt)

Celestial beings who are called "Those who never go down."

Akhen (Egypt)

Also known as: *Ab-esh-imy-duat, Ab-She.*

Serpent monster. The meaning of Akhen's name is likely indicative of his personality; it means "to split" or "wear out the eyes." A monster serpent, his responsibility is to guard the seventh section of the underworld (Tuat) as Ra, the sun god passes in his boat. *See also* Ab-Esh-Imy-Duat; Ab-she; Ab-ta; Akeneh; Apepi; Apophis.

Akhet-nen-tha *Akhenaten, Ikhnaten* (Egypt)

Also known as: *Amenhotep IV.*

Akhet-nen-tha is the son of Amenhotep III and Queen Tiy. When he succeeded his father, he moved his court from Akhenaten in Thebes to Tell el-Amarna. He forbade the worship of Amen and devoted himself to the worship of Aten. This period in Egyptian history is known as the Amarna Heresy. He was married to the beautiful Nefertiti. For further information on this period, *see also* Amen; Aten.

Akhmiu (Egypt) *see* Tuat.

Akhrokhar (Gnostic) *see* Pistas Sophia.

Akhtar, The (Persia)

They are the twelve constellations created by Ahura Mazda, who are regarded as generals of his army. Other stars or constellations mentioned are Hapto-iringa, Satavaesa, Tishtrya and Vanant. *See also* Ahura Mazda; Hapto-iringa; Tishtrya; Yazatas.

Akhtya (Zoroastrian; Persia)

Chief of the demon magicians and sorcerers known as the Yata. *See also* Pairikas; Yata.

Aki-bime-no-Kami (Japan) *see* Ukemochi.

Aki-Yama no Shitabi-onoko (Japan)

God of Winter. He is called the frost man of the autumn mountain. His brother is Haru-Yama-no-Kasumio-noko.

Akinetos (Gnostic) *see* Aeons; Nous.

Akka (A) *Aka* (Estonian, Finnish)

Also known as: *Emader-Akka, Rauni.*

Harvest deity. Wife of Jumala and later, Ukko. She is sometimes said to be a goddess of female sexuality. She created the bodies of mankind after Jumala created their souls. Akka is shown as a triangle or six-sided polygon. The mountain ash is her symbol. *See also* Jumala.

Akka (B) *Aka, Ekki* (Turkey) Mother goddess.

Akkruva *Avfruvva* (Finno-Ugric)

Also known as: *Havfru.*

Goddess of rivers. This presumably lovely half-woman, half-fish, fills the rivers with fish. *See also* Havfru.

Akna (A) (Maya People, Yucatan)

Mother goddess. Birth goddess (possibly). Wife of Akanchob. She is associated with the Becabs (q.v.).

Akna (B) (Eskimo)

"Mother." Goddess of childbirth.

Ako-Mano (Persia) *see* Aka Manah.

Akoman (Persia) *see* Aka Manah.

Akongo (Nagombe People, Africa)

Supreme god. This god once lived with people on earth or as some say, heaven. The turmoil created by humans was unbearable to him. He went off into the forest and has not been seen again. Akongo placed the giant Libanja in the east and the giant Songo in the west to hold up the sky with poles. When they let go of the poles it will be the end of the world. *See also* Amma; Nommo.

Akra (Persia) *see* Simurgh.

Akrura (India)

Chief Demon of Kansa's Court. *See also* Kansa; Syamantaka.

Aksak (Chaco People, South America)

Creator. Beetle who created men and women from clay.

Akselloak (Eskimo) The good spirit of rocking stones.

Akshobhya *Akshyobhya* (Nepal), *Aksobhya* (Tibet); (Buddhist; India)

Also known as: *Dhyani Buddha Gozanze-Myoo* (Japan), *Gozanze-Myoo* (Japan), *Heruka* (wrathful aspect), Trailokyavijaya (terrible aspect).

Akshobhya, the god of consciousness, is the second of the Dhyani Buddhas (Buddhas of meditation). He is the guardian of the East. His consort (sakti) is Locana, known as the Buddha Eye and in some renditions, Mamaki. The Japanese deity, Gozanze-Myoo, one of the Godai-Myoo (Five Great Kings), is an aspect of Akshobhya and one of the protectors of Buddhism. In some traditions of Buddhism, particularly in Nepal, Akshobhya is said to originate from the blue syllable "Hum." He is believed to represent the primordial cosmic element of Vijnana (consciousness). In Bardo, the Tibetan Buddhism after-death state, Akshobhya and Locana appear embracing. They are accompanied by two male bodhisattvas, Kshitigarbha the Essence of Earth and Maitreya the Loving One. There are also two females: Lasya, a bodhisattva of dance, and the bodhisattva Puspa, the goddess of flowers. The name Akshobhya means "Immovable." Akshobhya has one face and two arms and is blue in color. He exhibits the bhusparsa mudra (pose), which is the earth-touching gesture. This gesture commemorates Gautama Buddha's victory over temptation by the demon Mara. The right arm rests over the right knee. The palm is turned inward and the fingers extended downward with the middle fingers touching the ground. The left hand rests on the lap with the palm upward. This gesture is also characteristic of Sakyamuni. When represented in the shrine he always faces the east as this is the area he protects. His symbol is the thunderbolt, denoting spiritual and mystical power. His vehicle is a pair of elephants. His consort Locana's color is blue. Her emblems are the kapala (skull cap) and vajra (thunderbolt). Her mudras are varada; the arm pendant, fingers extended outward, palm turned outward, and vitarka; the arm bent, fingers extended upward, except index finger, which touches the tip of the thumb, palm turned outward. The varada signifies charity and the vitarka signifies argument. The Buddha Eye, in this case, means spiritual awakening. *See also* Amida; Avalokitesvara; Bhaishajyaguru; Chandamaharoshana; Dhyani Buddhas; Gozanze-Myoo; Heruka; Maitreya; Mamaki; Mara; Prajna-paramita; Ratnasambhava; Trailokyavijaya; Vairocana; Vajrapani; Vajrasatwa.

Akshyobhya (Nepal) *see* Akshobhya.

Aksobhya (India) *see* Akshobhya.

Aktiophi (Greek) *see* Hecate.

Aku (Akkadian) *see* Agu.

Aku-Thor (Teutonic) *see* Thor.

Akua (Polynesia) *see* Atea.

Akuj (Kenya, Africa)
This benevolent deity may be consulted by anyone by throwing a sandal in the air. The way the sandal lands will indicate the answer to a question.

Akupara (Hindu, India)
The tortoise upon which the earth rests.

Akusaa (Egypt) Sunset goddess.

Akycha (Eskimo People, United States) God of the Sun.

Al (A) (Afghanistan)
A female of about twenty years old who feeds upon corpses. She has long nails and teeth and her feet are reversed.

Al (B) (Ugarit, Syria) *see* El.

Al Ait (Phoenician) God of fire.

Al-Amin (Arabic) *see* Mohammed.

Al-lat (Arabic) *see* Allat.

Al Ussa (Arabic) *see* Al-uza.

Al-Uza *Al Ussa, Al-Uzza, Al'uzzah* (Arabic)
Also known as: *Uzzah.*
An early Arabic goddess, she formed a triad of desert goddesses with Allat and Menat. Some texts say she is a little known goddess who may represent the planet Venus. In other versions she is an angel whose idol was destroyed by Mohammed. She may have been a sky deity. *See also* Allat; Unsas.

Ala (A) (Arab) *see* Alilah; Allah.

Ala (B) *Ale* (Ibo People, Nigeria)
Also known as: *Ane, Lawgiver of Society, Queen of the Dead.*
Ala the earth mother is the creator of the living and queen of the underworld. A lawgiver and guardian of morality, her name is used in courts of law to uphold oaths. During planting first fruits and harvest, sacrifices are given at her sacred tree. She is sometimes depicted with a child.

Ala (C) (Sumer)
Bisexual demons who can be impregnated by humans.

Alaghom Naom *Alaghom Naum* (Gnostic)
Also known as: *Iztat Ix, Mother of the Mind.*
Alaghom Naom is the supreme goddess and mother of wisdom. She is the creator of mind and thought. Her spouse is the chief deity, Patol. *See also* Sophia-Prunikos.

Alah (Arabic) *see* Allat.

Alaisiagae (Teutonic)
Alaisiagae is a name for the goddesses of fate, the Valkyries (q.v.).

Alaka (India) Sacred City. *See also* Kuvera.

Alakaluf (Tierra del Fuego, South America)
Also known as: *Ona, Vaghan.*
Supreme deity. He is the spirit who created the world but it was refashioned by others. His abode is beyond the stars. Alakaluf never eats or drinks. If he is angered he can cause sickness of death.

Alakh (Khumbu-patas People, India)
Supreme god who revealed himself to the mendicant Govind, and 63 other disciples in the Himalayas in 1864. They worshipped a leader known as Bhima and his wife.

Alalus (Hittite, Hurrian)
Known as the father of the gods and the king of heaven, Alalus reigned for nine years until he was deposed by his son Anus. Upon leaving the heavenly throne, Alalus descended to Earth where he was fed by Kumarbis, the son of Anus, who later deposed his father. *See also* Anus; Kumbaris; Ullikummis.

Alambusha (India) *see* Apsarases.

Alan (Philippines) Deformed forest spirits.

Alastor (Greek)
He is the father of Alastor, who was killed in the Trojan war by Achilles.

Alat (Arabic) *see* Allat.

Alatuir (Slavic)
The waters under this sacred stone on the paradisaical island of Bouyan cured all illnesses. In later myths, Alatuir became the stone at the crossroads which warned of danger. That myth dissolved into the myth that Alatuir was the stone which served as the base for the Christian cross. *See also* Bouyan.

Alberich (Teutonic) *see* Andavari.

Albion (Greek) *see* Amphitrite.

Albiorix (Celtic)
Also known as: *Rigisamos.*
War god. Equivalent to Mars (Roman). His titles are "King of the World," and "Most Royal." *See also* Cocidius; Tuetates.

Albors, Mount (Persia) *see* Alburz, Mount.

Albunea (Greek) A local goddess who wasn't too well known.

Alburz, Mount *Albors, Mount* (Persia)
This largest of the cosmic mountains developed over an eight hundred year span when evil plunged through the sky, into the waters, and up through the center of world. The intense quake

that resulted caused the growth of Mount Alburz which spreads throughout the cosmos. The base is attached to the sky and the roots hold the earth together. From these roots, all other mountains are created. The peak of this mountain is Mount Tera, located in the middle of earth. Arezur ridge, the gateway to hell, is on the rim of the mountain. Shaken from their places in the universe by the arrival of evil, the sun, moon, and constellations began to revolve around the earth. They now enter the sky each day through one of the one hundred and eighty apertures on the east, and set through the one hundred and eighty apertures on the west side of the mountain. Beyond its peak lies Vourukasha the cosmic ocean. Mithra observes the world from his dwelling on Mount Alburz. *See also* Chinvat Bridge; Hariati (Mount); Mithra; Tree of Many Seeds; Vourkasha.

Alcaeus (A) (Greek)
He is the son of Perseus and Andromeda (qq.v). *See also* Gorgophone.

Alcaeus (B) (Greek)
Heracles' name at birth. His son by Omphale, the queen of Lydia, was also named Alcaeus. Heracles was her slave for three years. They had two other children, Algelaos and Lamus. *See also* Heracles; Omphale.

Alcaeus (C) (Greek)
He ruled Thasos on the island of Paros with his brother, Sthenelus. They are the sons of the famous athlete, Androgeus.

Alcathous (A) (Greek)
King of Megara. He is the son of Pelops and Hippodamia. For family lineage, *see* Pelops. *See also* Calydonian Boar Hunt; Hippodamia (C); Pelops.

Alcathous (B) (Greek)
He is the son of Porthaon and Euryte. He died at the hands of his nephew, one of the Seven Against Thebes, Tydeus or by Oenomaus, the king of Pisa.

Alcemene (Greek)
Alcemene is the daughter of the king of Mycenae, Electryon, and Anaxo, the daughter of Alcaeus and Hipponome, or Electryon and Eurydice. Her first marriage was to Amphitryon. Her twin sons, Heracles and Iphicles have different fathers. Zeus is the father of Heracles. *See also* Eurydice (C).

Alcestis (Greek)
She is the daughter of Pelias, the king of Iolcus, and possibly Anaxibia, who is the daughter of Bias and Iphianassa. She married the kindly Argonaut Admetus, and became the mother of Eumelas, who won the chariot race at the funeral games of Achilles and Perimele. Alcestis volunteered to die in her husband's place when he was ill. For details, *see* Admetus. *See also* Pelias; Savriti (B).

Alcides (Greek) Epithet of Heracles.

Alcimede (Greek)
She is the daughter of Phylacus and Clymene, who is the daughter of Minyas. The Argonaut Iphiclus is her brother. She married Aeson, the king of Thessaly and became the mother of the Argonaut Jason and possibly Promachus (some say Polymede is his mother). *See also* Clymene; Jason; Minyas.

Alcimenes (Greek)
He is the possible son of Jason the Argonaut and Medea, the sorceress. See Medea for the siblings of Alcimenes. *See also* Jason; Pheres (A).

Alcippe (A) (Greek)
Her parents are Ares, the god of war, and Agraulos. Her fraternal grandparents are the great god Zeus and the queen of heaven, Hera. *See also* Ares.

Alcippe (B) (Greek)
She is the possible mother of Oeneus by Ares. Some say Demonice is his mother.

Alcithoe (Greek) She is the daughter of Minyas (q.v.).

Alcis (Teutonic)
Sky gods; little known twin gods who may be connected with Castor and Pollux (Greek).

Alcmaon (Greek)
He is the son of Thestor and Megara. His siblings are the prophet Calchas, Leucippe and Theonoe. *See also* Calchas.

Alcmene (Greek) *see* Eurydice (C); Rhadamantus.

Alcyone (Greek)
She is one of six sisters and seven brothers who are the children of Aeolus and Enaret. *See also* Aeolus (A); Canace; Enaret.

Alcyoneus (Greek)
Alcyoneus, an evil giant, is the son of Gaea (the earth) born of the blood of the castrated Uranus. His brother, Porphyrion, was the leader of the giants. He and Alcyoneus were known as the strongest of the group. Alcyoneus lived in Pallene, a peninsula in the Aegean Sea. Using magic, he twice stole the sacred cattle belonging to Helius the sun god. Alcyoneus was invincible only if he stayed in his own area. During the battle of the giants and the gods on Mount Olympus, Heracles clubbed or shot him and then dragged him outside of his home territory and he died. In some renditions of this legend, Telamon accompanies Heracles on this adventure. Compare Alcyoneus to Antaeus. For the names of siblings see Giants. *See also* Aloeides; Gaea; Hippolytus (B); Lamia.

Aldoneus (Greek) *see* Hades.

Ale (Nigeria) *see* Ala (B).

Ale-im (Arabic; Hebrew) *see* Abram.

Alecto *Alektro, Allecto* (Greek)
Alecto is one of the Erinyes, the goddesses of retributive justice, and personifies of enduring hate. *See also* Erinyes.

Alegeus (Greek) *see* Andromeda.

Aleion (Phoenicia) Water Spirit. *See also* Aleyin.

Alektro (Greek) *see* Alecto.

Alemona (Roman)
The goddess Alemona is the "Guardian of the Fetus."

Aletes (Greek) *see* Aegisthus.

Aletheia (Greek) *see* Aeons; Nous.

Alexander (Greek) Another name for Paris (q.v.).

Alevin (Greek) *see* Adonis.

Alexandra (Greek) *see* Cassandra.

Aleyin *Aleion* (Phoenicia)
Also known as: *Aleyn Baal, Amurru, Ba'al of the Earth, Resheph* (Egypt). (Akkadia, Babylonia, Canaan, Phoenicia, Sumer, Ugarit)
Aleyin is the god of clouds, winds, rain, spring, and possibly air or winter. He is the son of Ba'al and the brother of the goddess Anat. Aleyin acted as the intermediary between his father and Mot during their ongoing battle of death and resur-·rection. Described as a rider of the clouds, he is usually accompanied by seven companions and eight wild bears. As Amurru he is the brother of Qadesh. He is probably the same as Aleyn Baal. *See also* Anat; Baal; Marduk; Mot; Qadesh; Resheph.

Aleyn (Mesopotamian) *see* Aleyn-Baal.

Aleyn-Baal *Aleyn* (Akkadian, Babylonian, Canaanite, Phoenician, Sumerian, Ugarit)
Also known as: *Baal, Baal Hammon* (Carthage), *Baalshamin, Ba'al-zebub* (Canaan, Phoenicia, Ugarit), *Bel* (Akkadian, Babylonian, Sumerian), *Hadad, Marduk, Melkart.*
"God of the Waters." Storm and Weather God. He has four hundred and fifty prophets and four hundred priestesses. He perishes at the coming of every summer. *See also* Aleyin; Ba'al-zebub; Baal; Hadad.

Alf (Teutonic) *see* Dwarfs.

Alf-heim (Teutonic) *see* Alfheim.

Alfadir (Teutonic) *see* Odin.

Alfadur (Teutonic) *see* Odin; Ragnarok.

Alfar (Norse; Teutonic)
There are two groups of Alfar, both dwarfs. One group, the artistic Liosalfar are light elves who live in Alfheim and are ruled by Freyr. The other group, known as evil elves, are the Dockalfar. They live in the underground in Svart-alfa-heim, and are ruled by Wayland the Smith. *See also* Alfheim; Alvis; Dwarfs; Elves; Freyr; Sindri; Svart-Alfa-Heim.

Alfheim *Alf-heim, Alvheim* (Norse; Teutonic)
Also known as: *Ljosalfaheim.*
Alfheim, located in Asgard between heaven and earth is the home of the Liosalfar, or light elves. It is also the abode of Freyr as king of the Alfar. Alfheim is near the sacred well of the Norns at the root of the sacred tree, Yggdrasil. The evil dwarfs live in Svart-alfa-heim. In later myths from England and France, the king of dwarfs was known as Oberon and he ruled along with his wife, Titania. *See also* Alfar; Andvari; Asgard; Svart-Alfa-Heim; Yggdrasil.

Alfhild (Scandinavia)
Alfhild is a young goddess who dressed as a male warrior to avoid marriage to King Alf. They engaged in battle and found that they were equals in strength. She then agreed to wed him.

Alfrigg (Norse; Teutonic)
He is one of four dwarfs who are gods of smiths. The oth-ers are Berling, Dvalin and Grerr. Freyja slept with all four in order to procure the "Necklace of the Brisings." *See also* Freyja, Loki.

Algue (Araucanian People, Chile) *see* Akanet.

Ali (A) (Teutonic) *see* Vali.

Ali (B)
Also known as: *Abu-Turab, Ali ibn, Haidar, Murtaza.* (Islamic, Shi'a sect)
The son of Abu Talib, Ali is the cousin of Mohammed, and the husband of Mohammed's daughter Fatimah. Their mar-riage ceremony was celebrated in heaven with the archangel Jibril acting as the bride's guardian. The couple became the par-ents of two sons, Hassan (also called Hasan and Al-Hasan) and Husayn (also spelled Hussein). Ali became the second Muslim. Mohammed's wife, Khadija, was the first Muslim. In the Shi'a tradition, Ali is known as the person who received the testament of Mohammed when the prophet knew that death was immi-nent. See Alah; Mohammed.

Alidat (Babylonyian, Canaanite, Semitic) *see* Ashtoreth.

Alignak (Eskimo)
Also known as: *Aningan, Anningan.*
He is the god of the moon, god of the falling snow, storms, eclipses, earthquakes and tides. He is also the protector of ani-mals, the disinherited, and orphans. He can cure sterility in women. Alignak is a ward against the mighty anger of Sedna, goddess of the sea. *See also* Pinga; Sedna.

Aliki (Hawaii) *see* Kariki.

Alilah (Arabic)
Also known as: *Ala, Allah.*
Supreme deity. Ancient deity of the Northern Arabians. In some versions he is the mate of Allat. He is similar to El and Jehovah. Alilah later became Allah.

Alilat (Arabic, Babylonia).
Also known as: *Alilta, Halitta, Ilat.*
Alilat is a mother goddess, and an earth goddess. She is also thought to be a war goddess similar to Athena. The name Alilat is another name for the early Arabic mother goddess, Ilat. The Greek sage, Herodotus, claimed that Aphrodite was called Alilat. *See also* Al-Uza; Alilah (A); Aphrodite; Athena; Ilat.

Alilta (Arabic, Babylonia) *see* Allath.

Alinda (Aborigine People, Australia)
Also known as: *The Moon Man.*
A god of death. He and Dirima the parrot fish man killed each other and the spirit of Alinda threw himself into the moon. He decreed that all living things must die, but he would die for only three days, then return to move across the sky. Each dead moon drops into the sea and becomes the empty shell of the nautilus. In a sense he also controls the tides. At high tide the water rushes to fill the moon, then drains back into the ocean until the moon is empty and the ocean is at low tide. *See also* Purukupali.

Alittu (Mesopotamia) *see* Ashtoreth.

Aliyan (Canaan)
Son of Baal. Husband of Anat. He was killed by Mot.

Alka (Lapp) *see* Akha.

Alkuntam (Bella Coola People, Canada)
Also known as: *Alkuntam, All-Father.*
Great sky-god. Alkuntam is the highest in the hierarchy of deities. With the assistance of Senx, (the sun), mortals were created. The mother of Alkuntam is a cannibal (mosquito) who inserts her long nose into the ears of men and sucks out their brains.

All-Father (Teutonic) *see* Yggdrasil.

All Swift (Teutonic) *see* Alsvid.

Allah (Mohammedanism, Islamic; South Arabia)
Also known as: *Ala, Alilah.*
Sole divinity. The name may derive from Ailiah, a god of Arabia's pre–Islamic, polytheistic tradition. Similar to El, Il, Ilah, Jehova. Certain descriptions of Allah seem to draw upon pre–Islamic tradition as well, especially the characteristics of certain moon deities such as Ilmugah, Kahil, Shaker, Wadd, and Warah. *See also* Aliliah; El.

Allat *Alat, Ilat*
Also known as: *Alah* (Babylonia), *Al-Lat, Allath, Allatu, Asa* (Syria), *Beltis-Allat, El-Lat, Ellat* (Sumer), *Hallat, Lat* (local name), *Sad* (masculine form); (Arabic, Assyria, Assyro-Babylonia, Chaldea, Sumer).
As Allat, the Nabataean mother goddess, she is called the Queen of Heaven; she is a fate deity, and a defender of cities. She is the morning and evening star. As the morning star, she is a goddess of war. As the evening star, she is the patron of love and prostitutes. Her attributes are a turreted crown and a cornucopia. In pre–Islamic Arabia, she was worshiped by the Arabic people in the form of a large stone. Under the stone, (housed in a wooden structure), precious stones were kept. She was the patron of travelers. Trees in the area were sacred to her (the Valley of Wajj). Allat is one of three desert goddess worshiped by the Arab people before Islam. She was later condemned by the *Koran.* The other two are Al-Uza and Menat. As a triad, they are known as Unsas. Some think that there is a connection between the Unsas and Arabic angels. She may be the same as the earlier Arabic goddess, Ilat (q.v.). She is comparable to the Semite sun goddess Samas. Compare Allat and Aphrodite (Greek), and Allat and Tyche (Greek). *See also* Al-Uza; Allah; Allatu; Astarte (Phoenician); Athena (Greek); Ereshkigal; Ishtar; Quadesh (Egypt); Unsas.

Allath (Arabic) *see* Allat.

Allatu
Also known as: *Beltis-Allat* (Chaldea), *Ereshkigal* (Mesopotamia).
Allatu with her mate the god of pestilence and fever, Nergal, rules the underworld, Arallu. Her messenger is Namtaru. Allatu, also the goddess of copulation, is depicted with the body of a woman, the head of a lioness, and the talons of a bird of prey. In each hand she holds a serpent. She is shown suckling two lions. Her name Ereshkigal was borrowed from the Sumerian people of Babylonia. She is thought to be the same as the Phoenician Astarte and the Babylonian Ishtar. She parallels the Greek Persephone. (The name and mythology of Allatu is sometimes attributed to Allat, and vice versa.) *See also* Allat; Anat; Arallu; Ereshkigal, Ilat; Ishtar; Kore; Namtaru; Nergal; Persephone; Tyche.

Allecto (Greek) *see* Erinyes.

Allfather (Teutonic) *see* Ginnunga-gap; Odin.

Alloprosallos (Greek) *see* Ares.

Almus (Greek) *see* Sisyphus.

Aloadae (Greek) *see* Aloeides.

Aloeidae (Greek) *see* Aloeides.

Aloeides *Aloadae, Aloeidae* (Greek)
The twin giants, Otus and Ephialtes are known as the Aloeides. They are the children of Iphimedeia and the sea god Poseidon or Aloeus. Some say that Canace was their mother. The noble-looking giants grew a fathom a year. At a very young age, they abducted Ares, the god of war, and imprisoned him in brass chains. They were devoted to one another. Their mischief and constant bragging pressed the nerves of Zeus. He decided to shut them up by hurling a thunderbolt at them but was dissuaded by Poseidon. They stayed on good behavior for a short time and then decided to abduct the warrior goddess Artemis. She appeared to them in the shape of a white doe. They chased her over land and sea and finally caught her in an open space. One brother was in front of her and the other at her back. Artemis darted around and when they threw their javelins, neither saw the other. They each died by the other's hand. In another tradition, the twins were nine years old when they fought the gods and were killed by Apollo and Artemis. Otus and Ephialtes were the first mortals to worship the Muses of Helicon. *See also* Alcyoneus; Aloeus; Antaeus; Ares; Canace; Giants; Iphimedeia (A); Muses.

Aloeus (Greek)
He is the son of Poseidon and Canace, or some say Uranus and Gaea (the earth). As the son of Poseidon and Canace, he is the brother of Epopeus, Hopleus, Nireus and Triopas. He married his brother's daughter, Iphimedeia, and became the father of Pancratis. With his second wife, Eeriboea, either he or Poseidon became the father of the Aloeides. *See also* Aloeides; Athamas; Canace; Cretheus; Epopeus; Giants; Iphimedeia (A); Poseidon.

Aloka *Aloke Nang-sal-ma* (Tibet) *see* Avalokitesvara.

Aloke (Tibet) *see* Aloka.

Alom (Maya)
Also known as: *Hunahpuguch.*
Creator. One of the regents who attempted to create men. The others were Tzakol, Bitol and Qaholom (also known as Cajolom). *See also* Hunahpu; Tzakol.

Aloros (Greek) *see* Alulim (Sumerian).

Alphaeus (Greek) *see* Alpheus.

Alphee (Greek) *see* Alpheus.

Alpheios (Greek) *see* Alpheus.

Alpheius (Greek) *see* Alpheus.

Alpheous (Greek) *see* Alpheus.

Alphesiboea (Greek) *see* Adonis.

Alpheus *Alphaeus, Alphee, Alpheios, Alpheous, Alpheius* (Greek)
A river god. Alpheus was one of the three thousand sons of Oceanus and Tethys and a brother of the three thousand Oceanids. He was said to be the father of Orsilochus. As the principal river of Elis, Alpheus saw the nymph Arethusa bathing in his water and changed into human form to pursue her. She fled from him and possibly with the assistance of the goddess of hunting, Artemis, she was transformed into a spring a great distance away from Alpheus. Undaunted, he became a river again and flowed along until he found her and was able to merge with her waters. In some legends, Heracles used the waters of Alpheius in his labors when he had to flush out the Augeian stables. To compare to other river gods, *see* Achelous, Acheron, Asopus, Cephissus, Cocytus, Inanchus, Rivers, Oceanus. *See also* Artemis; Heracles.

Alphito (Greek)
Barley or grain goddess. Ancient deity who could be the same as Dione. *See also* Aphrodite; Dione.

Alrinach (Eastern Europe)
This demon is associated with shipwrecks. It is shown in the form of an old woman.

Als (Armenia, Babylonia, Persia)
Aspects of known as: *Al* (singular), *Alu* (Babylonia).
Originally the Als were disease demons. In later times they became childbirth demons who abduct babies from the womb at seven months. They cause blindness to the unborn and miscarriages. Their homes are made in damp, dark corners of stables or houses. They are half-beast, half-human and can be male or female. Als have fingernails of brass, iron teeth, and snake-like hair. They carry iron scissors. Sometimes they are depicted with the tusks of a boar. The king of the Als is chained away in a deep, dark place where he wails continuously. To keep his cohorts away, the woman must surround herself with iron implements. The Babylonian Alu is said to crush men while they are sleeping. Similar to the Jewish Lilith, the Greek Lamia and the Armenian Thepla. *See also* Ahhazu; Aluqa; Jinn.

Alsvid *Alsvider, Alsvinn, Alswid* (Norse; Teutonic)
Also known as: *All Swift, Hrim-faxi* (possibly).
Alsvid, meaning "All Swift" and his companion, Aarvak, meaning "Early Waker," are the horses that pull the sun chariot of Sol along its course. *See also* Aarvak; Nat (B); Pegasus (Greek); Sol (B); Svalin.

Alsvider (Teutonic) *see* Alsvid.

Alsvinn (Teutonic) *see* Alsvid.

Alswid (Teutonic) *see* Alsvid.

Altan-Telgey (Mongolian) Earth Goddess.

Althaea (Greek) *see* Althea.

Althaemenes (Greek) *see* Acacallis; Pasiphae.

Althaia (Greek) *see* Althea.

Althea *Althaea, Althaia* (Greek)
Probably a mother or earth goddess. In legend Althea was the mother of Atabyrius (the pagan Hebrew deity who was represented as the golden calf). She is also known in Greek mythology as the daughter of Thestius and Eurythemis. Her siblings are Hypermnestra, Leda and Plexippus. She became the wife of her uncle Oeneus, and mother of Meleager by Oeneus or possibly Ares. Some say she is the mother of Deianeira (Deianira), Gorge and Toxeus by Dionysus. She may also be the mother of Tyedeus and may possibly have had a son by Poseidon. When her son Meleager was born the Fates predicted a hero's future for him but Atropos foresaw his death if a brand burning in the fire was not extinguished. Althea removed the brand and hid it. Meleager joined the Argonauts when he was so young that his father sent his cup-bearer, Meleager's uncle, Laocoon, along to care for him. He went on to marry Cleopatra and became the father of Polydora. When Artemis in anger sent the Caly-donian Boar to ravage his father's lands, he led the hunt, killed the monster and was awarded the skin for a trophy. During the hunt he met and fell in love with the Arcadian huntress Ata-lanta and it is possible that he may have fathered Parthenopaeus. According to Homer, a fight developed between the Curetes, who felt they should have the boar skin, and the Calydonians. Meleager killed his mother's brothers and quit fighting when Althea became angry with him. Without his leadership, the Curetes attempted to scale the walls of Calydon. Cleopatra urged him to put aside his anger and act on behalf of the city, which he did and died during the ensuing battle. In another version, Meleager gave the prized boarskin to his love, Ata-lanta, rousing the ire of his uncles who tried to wrest it from her. Angered, Meleager killed them thus infuriating Althea, who remembered the prophecy of Atropos. She pulled out the brand, rekindled it and watched her son die an agonizing death. Remorseful, she then hung herself. Grief-stricken, Cleopatra also committed suicide. The remaining women in the house of Oeneus were turned into guinea fowl by the revengeful Artemis. Some say she is represented by a flower. *See* Calydonian Boar Hunt for details about her husband Oeneus. *See also* Ares; Artemis; Atropos; Fates.

Altjira (Arunta People, Australia)
The All-Father or Sky Dweller, is indifferent to mortals. His voice is like thunder and he has the feet of an emu.

Alu (Babylonian, Sumerian)
Alu is a wicked devil who covers a man like a garment and smothers him. Alu is also one of twelve devils mentioned along with Lilith. The Alu are in the same category as the Als (q.v.). *See also* Ahhazu; Aluqa; Lilith; Utukku.

Alukah (Canaanite) *see* Ereshkigal.

Alulei (Marshall Islands, Micronesia)
Also known as: *Aluluei.*
God of Navigators. He is the son of Palulop. His two brothers are Big Rong and Little Rong. His children are Longorik and Longolap. Alulei has two faces, one looking forward and one looking back. Rata (Polynesia) is similar to Alulei. He is associated with the carpenter god, Solang. *See also* Palulop.

Alulim (Sumerian)
Also known as: *Aloros* (Greek).

First man. He descended from the celestial realm and became one of the antediluvian kings. He ruled earth before the flood for either 28,000 or 67,000 years depending on the myth. He corresponds to Adam (Hebrew).

Aluluei (Micronesia) *see* Alulei.

Aluqa (Arabic)
A seductive female demon who is known to suck her victim's blood after intercourse. Exhausted, he commits suicide. *See also* Als.

Al'uzzah (Arabic) *see* Al-Uza.

Alvheim (Teutonic) *see* Alfheim.

Alvis *Alviss* (Teutonic)
Also known as: *All Knowing Wise Dwarf.*
He is a dwarf who was turned into a stone by Odin or Thor because he had the temerity to woo Thor's daughter, Thrud. Alvis lives in the underground caves. He promised that he could marry Thor's daughter. When he went to get his bride he was detained by Thor who asked him questions until daybreak. He was forced to leave alone. *See also* Alfar; Thor; Thrud.

Alxion (Greek) *see* Oenamaus.

Am (Egypt) *see* Amen (B).

Am-Beseku (Egypt) *see* Assessors.

Am-Kehuu (Egypt) *see* Tcheser-tep-f; Unas.

Am-Khaibetu (Egypt) *see* Assessors.

Am-Mit *Am-mut* (Egypt) *see* Amit.
Door guard in the Fourth Hour of Tuat. The goddess Ammit consumes souls with fire from her mouth. *See also* Sekhemus.

Am-Senf (Egypt) *see* Assessors.

Am-Sit (Egypt) *see* Amset.

Am-Ta (Egypt) A name for Sekhem.

Ama (A) (Sumerian)
Also known as: *Mama, Mami.*
Mother goddess. Probably derived from Ana. Similar to Ariadne, Arianrhod, Athena, Marian, and Marianna.

Ama (B) (Teutonic) *see* Amma (B); Eire.

Ama (C) (Japan) *see* Ama NoUzume; Ama-tsu-Kami; Kami.

Ama (D) (India) *see* Parvati.

Ama-Amta (Egypt) A name for Sekhem.

Ama-No-Hashadate (Japan) *see* Izanami; Kami.

Ama No Hashidate (Japan) *see* Kami.

Ama-No-Hohi (Japan) *see* Ame no-Oshido-Mimi.

Ama-No-Kagaseo (Japan) *see* Amatsu-mikaboshi.

Ama-no-minaka-nushi *Ama-no-minakanushi-no-Kami, Ame-no-minaka-nushi,* (Shinto; Japan)
Also known as: *Kuni-toko-tachi no mikoto* (Eternal Land Ruler).
Supreme deity. Ama-no-minaka-nushi (Heavenly Central Lord) is the head of the triad known as the three creator Kami who sprang from chaos (darkness). The secondary deities are Taka-mimusubi (High Producing), and Kamu-mimusubi, (Divine or Mysterious Producing). These deities are also called Kuni no sa-tsuchi no Mikoto (Land of Right Soil of Augustness) and Toyo-kumu-no Mikoto (Rich Form Plain of Augustness). It is thought that Taka-mimusubi represents Kami-rogi (the Divine-Male) and Kamu-mimusbi represents Kami-romi (the Divine-Female). In some traditions, Ama-no-minaka-nushi and Taka-mimusubi are one and the same. The next deities were Uhiji-ni no Mikoto (Mud Earth) and Suhiji-ni no Mikoto also called Suhiji-ne no Mikoto (Sand Earth). They were followed by Oho-to nochi no Mikoto (Great After Door) and Oho-to mahe no Mikoto (Great Before Door). The next deities were Omo-taru no Mikoto (Face Pleasing) and Kashiko-ne no Mikoto (Awful) also called Aya-Kashiko-ne no Mikoto, Imi kashiki no Mikoto, or Awo-kashiki-ne no mikoto, or Aya-kashiki no Mikoto. The next deities were Izanagi (Male-who-Invites), and Izanami (Female-who-Invites). In other traditions, Taka-mimusubi and Kamu-mimusubi appeared after Izanagi and Izanami and Taka-mimusubi was their child. These deities are known as celestial deities, Ama-tsu-Kami (Gods of Heaven). The mission of Izanagi and Izanami was to unite and give birth to earthly manifestations, known as Kuni-tsu-Kami. The first created was the Japanese archipelago, followed by Kami; nature, food and fire. Kami is all things that were produced; Kami is the forces of nature. Izanagi and Izanami brought into being the divine rulers of the world. Known as their children, they were Ama-terasu Ohmi-Kami, also known as Amaterasu (Heaven-Illumining Goddess), Tsukiyomi-no-mikato (Moon-Ruler) and Takehaya Susanowo (Valiant-Swift-Impetuous-Hero). The *Kojiki* ("Records of Ancient Matters"), is the oldest chronicle in Japan. It was written in C.E. 712 by Futo no Yasumuro, the court noble. The *Kojiki* records the earliest doctrines of Shinto mythology concentrating primarily on the age of the gods. In C.E. 720 the *Nihongi* ("Chronicles of Japan") further recorded the myths of the land and included the reigns of the emperors. Mythology and history entwined called the mythical Jimmu Tenno (Sun of Heaven) a great-grandson of the sun goddess Amaterasu. He was also credited with being the founder of the empire. All following emperors dated from him and were called divine. In 1946 the emperor Hirohito renounced his divinity. The deities created after the triad emerged from chaos up to and including Izanagi and Izanami are known as the Seven Generation Deities. *See also* Amaterasu; Amatsu-Mikaboshi, Hiruko; Izanagi and Izanami, Jimmu Tenno; Kami; Kamu-Mimusubi; Susanowo; Takama-no-hara; Three Goddesses of Munakata; Tsuki-Yomi.

Ama-no-Minakanushi-no-Kami (Japan) *see* Ama-no-minaka-nushi.

Ama-no-oshiho-Mimi (Japan) *see* Ame-no-Oshido-Mimi.

Ama-no-Saug-Me (Japan) *see* Ame no-Oshido-Mimi.

Ama-no-Uki-Hashi (Japan) *see* Izanami.

Ama No Uzume (Japan) *see* Ame-no-uzume.

Ama-no-Uzume *Ame-no-Uzume-no-Mikoto* (Heavenly Alarming Female), (Shinto; Japan)
Also known as: *Ama, Otafuku, Udzume, Uzume.*
Fertility goddess. Shaman. When the sun goddess Amaterasu descended into the cave named Ame-no-Iwato (Rock Cave of Heaven), she left the universe in darkness. The eight hundred myriad of deities convened to create a plan which would entice her back into the world. The plan included a boisterous dance by the goddess Ama-no-Uzume to be performed at the mouth of the cave. Caught up in the passion of her dance, Ama-no-Uzume stamped loudly on the ground, lowered her skirt and exposed her breasts. Uproarious laughter from the audience of deities piqued Amaterasu's curiosity. She could not understand the frivolity on the outside when she was secreted in the depths of the cave. They had after all, been saddened by her absence and the resulting darkness, and until now, had been wooing her in attempts to persuade her to leave the cave. She glanced out to investigate, caught sight of herself in a mirror and attracted by her beautiful image stepped out of the cave, bringing light back into the world. This dance became known as the karuga, a pantomimic dance performed at Shinto festivals. The Sarume, an ancient family ruled by female Kimi (a hereditary title), are said to have descended from Ama-no-Uzume. The members of the family performed in ritual dances at court. Later, as recorded in the "Kojiki," Ama-no-Uzume was requested by Amaterasu to accompany her grandson Ninigi to earth. Her function was to deal with possible enemies. On earth she encountered the hostile giant Saruta-biko and was able to woo and enchant him with her beauty and gestures. In the translation of the *Nihongi* by Aston, Ama-no-Uzume bares herself before Saruta-biko whom some say she married. The karuga represents the planting of the seed and awaiting the return of the summer sun to nourish its growth. The mirror known as Kagami and also Yata-Kayami was created by the goddess Ishikoridome-no-Mikoto. *See also* Amaterasu; Kami; Ninigi.

Ama-terasu-o-Kami (Japan) *see* Amaterasu.

Ama-terasu-o-mi-Kami-me no Mikoto (Japan) *see* Amaterasu.

Ama-terasu Ohmi-Kami (Japan) *see* Ama-no-minaka-nushi; Amaterasu.

Ama-terasu-Oho-hiru-me no Mikoto (Japan) *see* Amaterasu.

Ama-tsu-Kami (Japan)
Also known as: *Kami, Kuni-tsu-Kami.*
Celestial deities. The Ama-tsu-Kami are the celestial deities who reside in Takama-no-hara (abode of the gods). Their earthly counterparts are known as Kuni-tsu-Kami. For the Shinto creation myth, *see* Ama-no-minaka-nushi. *See also* Ama-no-minka-nushi; Kami; Takama-no-hara.

Ama-tsu-mika-hoshi (Japan) *see* Okuni-Nushino-Mikoto.

Ama-Tu-piko-nasgisa-take-u-Gaya-puki-apezu-no-mikoto (Japan) *see* Jimmu Tenno; Toyo-Tama-Bime.

Ama-Tu-Pikone-no-mikoto (Japan) *see* Amaterasu.

Ama-waka-hiko (Japan) *see* Ame-no-Oshido-Mimi.

Amaethon *Amathaon* (British, Celtic, Welsh)
God of Agriculture. He is the son of Don and Beli. His siblings are Govannon, Llud and possibly Gwydion. He is credited with bringing domestic animals to earth from the "land of the gods." *See also* Amathaon; Llud.

Amagandar (Tungus People, Africa)
Also known as: *Orokannar.*
Family of protective female spirits of happiness.

Amahraspands (Persian) *see* Amesha Spentas.

Amairgin (Celtic) *see* Amergin.

Amaite-Rangi (Mangaia Island, Polynesia)
A male sky demon. *See also* Ngaru.

Amalivaca (Orinoco River People, South America)
He is the culture hero who taught the people the arts of life and agriculture.

Amalthaea (Greek) *see* Amaltheia.

Amalthea (Greek) *see* Amaltheia.

Amaltheia (A) *Amalthaea, Amalthea* (Greek)
Also known as: *Sibyl* (Roman).
A goat. Raised by Pan, Amaltheia is the goat who suckled the infant Zeus in a cave at Lyktos on the island of Crete. One of her horns flowed with ambrosia (a cornucopia) and her other horn flowed with nectar. After her death Zeus kept the horn filled with golden fruit from the Garden of Hesperides to honor Amaltheia. It became known as the "Horn of Plenty." He used her hide to cover his shield and it became known as the Aegis. It is said that in later times he hung the goat and horn in the sky and it is now known as the constellation of Capricorn. Legend associates Amalthea with Adrastia and Ida as a moon-triad. For goat-related legends, *see* Aegipan, Aegis, Aegisthus. *See also* Achelous; Adrastia; Aegis; Amaltheia (B); Cornucopia; Ida; Pan; Zeus.

Amaltheia (B) (Greek)
She is the daughter of the king of Crete, Melissus, and sister of Melissa. This Amaltheia may have fed Zeus the milk from the goat Amaltheia. *See also* Amaltheia (A).

Amaltheia (C) (Roman)
She is referred to as the Cumaean Sibyl, the prophetess of the Sibylline oracles of Rome. She owned and possibly wrote the nine books of oracular advice. Three of the nine books remained in the Temple of Jupiter until it was destroyed by fire in 83 B.C.E.

Amaltheia (D) (Roman)
She is also known as Deiphobe, Demo, Demophile or Herophile. *See also* Sibyl.

Amam (Egypt) *see* Amit.

Amam-Mitu (Egypt)
One of the seven goddess who minister to Osiris in the Second Hour of the Night. *See also* Shesat Maket Neb-S; Tuat.

Amam-ta (Egypt) *see* Aai.

Amamet (Egypt) *see* Amit.

Amamet the Devourer (Egypt) *see* Amit.

Aman (A) (Egypt) *see* Amen (B).

Aman (B) (Japan) *see* Shichi Fukujin.

Amanki

Also known as: *Enki* (Babylonian).

A water god, Amanki is an aspect of the Sumerian god Enki (q.v.).

Amano-Iwato (Japan) *see* Amaterasu.

Amanoro (Armenian) Spring goddess.

Amaravati *Devapura* (City of Gods) (Hindu; India)

Amaravati is the capital city in the celestial kingdom of Swarga. Located on the eastern spur of Meru Mountain, it is said to have a thousand gates and contains fruits of all seasons, jewels and other objects of pleasure. Temperatures do not exist, nor does depression or sadness. The lovely Apsarases add to the beauty of the city. This land of bliss is Indra's heaven; it is the land of fallen warrior heroes or those who perform penance and sacrifice. The name means "Full of Ambrosia." Compare to Valhalla (Teutonic). *See also* Ambrosia; Apsarases; Swarga; Visvakarma.

Amardad (Persia) *see* Ameretat; Haurvatat.

Amarud (Babylonian) *see* Marduk.

Amarudu (Babylonian) *see* Marduk.

Amaruduk (Babylonian) *see* Marduk; Nimrod.

Amashilamma (Sumerian) Cow Goddess.

Amaterasu (Buddhist, Shinto; Japan) *Ama-terasu-o-mi-Kami, Ama-terasu-o-mi-Kami* (the Heaven-great-shining-Kami), *Amaterasu Ohmi-Kami, Ama-terasu-Oho-hiru-me No Mikoto, Amaterasu-Oho-hiru-me, Amaterasu-Oho-mi-Kami, Amaterasu-omi-gami, Shimmei.*

Also known as: *Oho-hiru-me No Muchi* (Great Noon Female of Possessor or Great Mistress of the Day), *Ten-sho-dai-jin, Tenshodaijin, Tenshoko-daijin, Tenshokodaijin.*

Amaterasu is a sun goddess, the founder of sericulture, the guardian of agriculture, the deity of peace and order and the ancestor of the ruling family. She is the daughter of Izanagi and Izanami. She rules the realm of light on ama (heaven) and earth and the Plain to Heaven. She is the sister of the storm god Susanowo (also known as Takehaya Susanowo, Valiant-Swift-Impetuous-Hero) and the moon ruler and ruler of the night, Tsuki-Yomi. Her younger sister, Wakahiru-Me (Wakahirume), is possibly a solar deity. She is the weaver who assisted Amaterasu in weaving garments for the gods in the Plain of Heaven. (*See* Amatsu-Mikaboshi.) In some traditions, she has an older brother, Hiruko. When Amaterasu was a young goddess, her father, Izanagi, gave her a necklace of jewels named Mi-kura-tana-no-Kami, which was an emblem of fertility. She offered her son Ama-No-Oshido-Mimi the opportunity to rule the earth. When he saw the confusion on the planet, he refused to leave the celestial realm. She is the mother of the goddesses

Takiri-bime-no-mikoto, Ikiti-simapime-no-mikoto also named Sa-yori-bime-no-mikoto, and Takitu-pime-no-mikoto. Her other sons are Masa-katu-a-katu-kati-paya-pi-Ame-no-oso-po-Mimi-no-mikoto, Ame-no-po-pi-no-mikoto, Ama-Tu-Pikone-no-mikoto, Iku-Tu-Pikone-nomikoto and Kumano-kusubi-no-mikoto. She also has a favored grandson, Ninigi, who was destined to become the ruler of Izuwo province. After her brother, Susanowo, committed atrocities against her, Amaterasu withdrew into a cave and took the light of the world with her. During this period, many evil demons conducted underhanded activities without observation. A multitude of deities approached the cave named Ame-no-Iwato (Sky-Rock-Cave) to show their support and to persuade the goddess to bring her light back to the heavens and earth. Finally they resorted to a plan suggested by the god Hoard Thoughts. A mirror named Kagami (also called Yata-Kayami) and a necklace were hung in a tree. The goddess Ame-no-uzume-no-mikoto, also known as Ama-no-Uzume (Heavenly Alarming Female) performed a frenzied dance called the Kagura. She became boisterous and stripped off her clothing, causing glee in the audience. The gods howled with laughter. Curious, the sun goddess peeked out to investigate the commotion. She was told that they had found a more beautiful woman to take her position. She caught sight of the reflection of a beautiful woman in the mirror and cautiously moved closer to examine it. Several deities apprehended the goddess. Tajikaroo (Prince Mighty Power) placed a barrier made of straw rope named Shiri-kume-na-nawa (Don't Retreat-Rope) across the entrance to the cave. The light of the world returned and overcame darkness. Other deities involved in convincing her to shine were Ame-no-tajikara-wo and Tuto-Tamu. Dignified, honest, meek in temper, Amaterasu was a brilliant and wise ruler. Besides protecting rice fields, she invented and constructed irrigation canals, organized religious rites, and wove clothing for the gods. In some traditions of her following, she is associated with the god Taka-mi-musubi, (High Producing). He accompanies her as her hidden or higher entity. She also has a female companion, a food goddess, Toyo-uke-no-Kami (Abundance-Bounty Goddess) also known as Toyo-uke-hime (Plentiful-Food-August). Though shrines have been dedicated to her, little is known about her and her origin is disputed. The monk Gyogi (670–749) initiated an offshoot of Shinto, known as Ryobu-Shinto and proclaimed that Amaterasu and Buddha were the same. The name Ten-sho-dai-jin is a current name used for Amaterasu. Amaterasu is depicted as a beautiful woman. The cock is her sacred bird as it greets the morning sun. As well as a sun symbol, the cock is the emblem of vigilance and activity. In early times, a sacred crow named Yata-Garasu, who had several feet, was her messenger. (*See* Jimmu Tenno for crow symbolism.) She owned three divine rice fields, the Easy-Rice-Field-of-Heaven, the Level-Rice-Field-of-Heaven, and the Village-Join-Rice-Field-of-Heaven. She also developed the art of raising silkworms. The sacred mirror is the symbol of purity. The necklace is a symbol of fertility and spiritual power. One of the rites of worship of the sun goddess is the dance known as the Kagura. It is one of the oldest of the Japanese dances and was later the basis for the No dramas. During an eclipse, another ceremony of the sun goddess is performed. Participants gather and clash metal objects together to signify the occasion when Amaterasu peeked out of the cave to discover why it was so noisy. A great shrine was dedicted to this goddess in the province of Ise. The founder of sericulture, Amaterasu put silkworms in her mouth and reeled silk from them. The goddess Ukemochi had at this time already produced the silkworm from her eyebrows. The act of weaving symbolizes creation and life which represents accumulation, multiplication, and growth. Straw rope is tied around trees at Shinto shrines. At Amaterasu's principal shrine in Ise, the rope stretches across a ravine through which the sun is seen at dawn. For the Shinto creation myth, see Ama-no-minaka-nushi. For details of her birth, see Izanagi and Izanami. For details of her brother's outrageous behavior toward her, see Susanowo. See also Ninigi (her grandson), Hikohohodemi (her great-grandson), Hosuseri (her great-grandson), Jimmu-Tenno (her great-great grandson). She is sometimes identified as an aspect of Amita (Amida). She is sometimes identified with Dainachi Nyorai (an aspect of Buddha). Compare Amaterasu's necklace (Mi-kura-tana-no-Kami) to the Teutonic goddess Freyja's necklace (Brisinga-men) and the Greek Amazon goddess Hippolyte's girdle. For details of the sacred treasures of Shintoism, see Susanowo. Compare to Kami-mimusubi, who collected the seeds for food produced by Ogetsu-hime-no-Kami. For the origins of Amaterasu's food supply, see Ukemochi. See also Amano-Uzume; Ame-no-Oshido-Mimi; Haya-ji; Ishikoridome-no-Mikoto; Kusanagi; Ninigi; Okuni-Nushino-Mikoto; Sengen, Take-mi-kazuchi; Three Goddesses of Munakata; Toyo-Tama-Bime.

Amaterasu-Oho-hiru-me (Japan) *see* Amaterasu.

Amaterasu-Oho-mi-kami (Japan) *see* Amaterasu.

Amaterasu-omi-gami (Japan) *see* Amaterasu or Ama-Terasu-Oho-Hiru-Me No Mikoto.

Amaterasu Takehaya Susanowo (Japan) *see* Ama-no-minaka-nushi.

Amathaon *Amatheon* (Celtic)
   The son of Anu, he is a wizard who taught his art to his brother Gwydion. When Amathaon stole a dog and a roebuck from Arawn, a fight broke out between Arawn and Gwydion which became known as "The Battle of the Trees." *See also* Anu (A); Arawn; Gwydion.

Amathaounta *Amathaunta* (Egypt, Sumer)
   Also known as: *Ashima.*
   She is a goddess of the sea.

Amathaunta (Egypt) *see* Amathaounta.

Amatheon (Celtic) *see* Amathaon.

Amatsu-Mikaboshi (Early Shinto; Japan)
   Also known as: *Ama-no-kagaseo* (The Brilliant Male).
   God of Evil. God of Stars.
   Amatsu-Mikaboshi (The August Star of Heaven) in early times was later identified with the Pole Star, Myo-ken, and later assimilated with Ama-no-Minaka-nushi (The Heavenly Central Lord), the head of the triad who sprang from Chaos. The *Nigongi* speaks of Amatsu-Mikaboshi. *See also* Ama-no-Minaka-nushi.

Amatsu-Otome (Japan)
   Japanese angels. They are all young, virgin females. Carv-ings of Buddhist angels from the Asuka period (C.E. 552 to C.E. 645) hang from a canopy in the Kondo (Golden Hall) at Horyu-ji, in Nara, Japan. *See also* Apsarases (India).

Amatupiko-Pikonagisa (Japan) *see* Toyo-Tama-Bime.

Amayicoyondi (Pericu People, North American) Sky Mother.

Amazons (Greek, Scythian)
   Also known as: *Aior-pata, Kakasians, Sauromatai.*
   Hunters and warrior women. The Scythians thought of them as Airo-pata or "man-slayers," while the Greeks said the name meant "without breast." It was their custom to integrate with males from neighboring tribes from time to time. If the children born of these unions were male, they were sent back to their fathers, mutilated, or used as slaves. Female children had a breast removed so they could handle their weapons more effectively. In early times, Io in her cow shape encountered the female warriors. Later, Heracles, in an attempt to secure the girdle of Hippolyte was involved in a battle with them. During the latter part of the Trojan War, they joined Priam, the last king of Troy, in fierce battle against their hated enemies, the Greeks. Their queen, Penthesileia (some say Thalestris), was killed by Achilles. The Amazon female warriors of South America were similar to their valiant sisters. The Amazons worshiped the moon. They are associated with Artemis (q.v.). *See also* Antiope (A); Hippolyte.

Amba (A) (India) "Mother."
   An epithet for Uma-Parvati. *See also* Parvati.

Amba (B) (India) A Krittika sister. *See also* Rishi.

Ambalika (India) *see* Pandavas; Vyasa.

Ambi (India) *see* Ambika.

Ambika *Ambi, Amvika Devi.*
   (Hindu, Vedic; India) Ambika, "the Mother" is the moon goddess aspect of the great goddess Devi. She is the spouse and perhaps the sister of Rudra. *See also* Devi; Parvati; Purusha; Rudra; Sati (A); Vyasa.

Ambrosia (Greek)
   Also known as: *Amrita* (Sanskrit).
   Nectar of the gods. Ambrosia is the honey-flavored food of the gods. When served with nectar it preserved their immortality and gave them eternal youth. It was also the ointment used for anointing sacred stones. Ambrosia is similar to the Indian Amrita and Soma. *See also* Amaravati; Amrita; Chandra; Haoma; Soma.

Amburaja (India) *see* Varuna.

Amchimalghen (Araucanian People, South America)
   Every person has an invisible, beneficent nymph known as Amchimalghen in attendance.

Ame-no-hohi (Japan) *see* Ama-no-oshido-mimi; Amaterasu.

Ame-no-ina-fune (Japan) *see* Izanami.

Ame-no-iwato (Japan) *see* Amaterasu.

Ame-no-minaka-nushi (Japan) *see* Ama-no-minaka-nushi.

Ame-no-murokumo-no-tsurugi (Japan) *see* Kusanagi.

Ame-no-Oshido-Mimi *Ama-no-oshiho-mimi* (Shinto; Japan)
Also known as: *His Augustness Truly Conqueror, I Conquer Conquering, Swift Heavenly Great Ears.*
Celestial deity. Son of the sun goddess, Amaterasu. Ame-no-Oshido-Mimi was instructed by his mother, the sun goddess Amaterasu to descend to earth as the sovereign to calm the warlike mortals. Before departing, he stopped on the Floating Bridge of Heaven, observed the tumult below and told his mother that he could not fulfill her request. The eight hundred deities held a conference and appointed the God-Who-Hoards-Thoughts to determine a plan. They decided that Ame-no-Hohi would descend to earth and organize worldly affairs in Izumo. They waited three years for a report from the god. Nothing. They sent his son and never heard from him again. Earthly attractions may have seduced them. The divine group reconvened and delegated the courageous warrior, Ame-no-Wakahiko (Ama-Waka-Hiko), equipped him with a sacred bow and arrows, and sent him on the mission. When he arrived to take up his duties, he fell in love with Shita-teru-Hime, the daughter of Okuni-nushino-mikoto, and neglected to contact the deities in the celestial realm. Eight years later, the gods sent a pheasant named Nakime (also known as Nanaki or Na-naki-me) to investigate. She perched on a branch outside Ame-no-Wakahiko's home. The women of the household saw her and became alarmed fearing that it was an evil omen. Ame-no-Wakahiko took charge and shot the bird with one of his divine arrows. Some say he followed the advice of his servant, Ama-no-sagu-me. The arrow punctured the pheasant and landed at the feet of Amaterasu in the heavens. She recognized the sacred arrow, hurled it back to earth and it pierced Ame-no-Wakhiko in the heart. He died. The tears of his grief-stricken widow were so penetrating that the gods heard them, took pity and sent her parents from the celestial realm to attend the funeral. The divine delegation sent two more deities to earth. They informed Okuni-nushi-mikoto that Amaterasu was taking control of the land. A skirmish developed but the sun goddess prevailed and sent her grandson Ninigi to bring order to the land. In other renditions of this legend, the arrow fell at the feet of Amaterasu's adjunct Taki-mi-Mushubi, who hurled it back to earth and killed Ame-no-Wakahiko. The pheasant and the cock have similar symbolic definitions. For a variation of the myth of Ame-no-Wakhiko, see Haya-ji. *See also* Amaterasu; Ninigi; Okuni-nushino-mikoto.

Ame-no-puya-kinu-no-kami (Japan) *see* Kushi-nada-hime.

Ame-no-tajikara-no (Japan) *see* Amaterasu.

Ame-no-tajikara-wo (Japan) *see* Amaterasu.

Ame-no-uki-hashi (Japan) *see* Izanami.

Ame-no-uzume-no-mikoto (Japan) *see* Ama-no-Uzume.

Ame-no-wakahiko (Japan) *see* Ame-no-wo-ha-bari; Haya-ji; Okuni-Nushino-Mikoto.

Ame-no-wo-ha-bari (Shinto; Japan)
Also known as: *Itsu-no-wo-ha-bari.*
Sacred object. Ame-no-wo-ha-bari (Heavenly-Point-Blade-Extended) is the sword Izanagi used to remove head of his son, the fire god, (Fire-Burning-Swift Male Spirit) whose birth caused the death of his mother Izanami. From his blood sixteen deities were born. The fire god meeting with the cold metal blade could indicate the severing of earth from heaven. When the sword is associated with fire it often symbolizes purification. After slaying his son, Izanagi went to the sea to purify himself. Compare to the sacred sword, Kusanagi. *See also* Izanagi and Izanami.

Amehetp (Egypt) *see* Amenhotep I.

Amen (A) (British)
The magic cauldron which belonged to Keridwen (q.v.).

Amen (B) *Aman, Ammon, Amon, Amum, Atum* (Egypt; possibly Nubian and Syrian)
Also known as: *Am, Amen-ra, Amen-ur, Amon-ra* ("King of Gods"), *Amun-re, Hammon, Jupiter-Ammon, Niu.*
"The Hidden One." Patron deity of the city of Thebes. Son of Thoth and Maat. A primeval deity, Amen was originally a god of the dead. His association with death may indicate that he was an agricultural god. His name signifies "the hidden one," the soul (ba) of all things. His influence waxed and waned throughout many dynasties. He is known as a supreme creative god, a god of war, and the force behind the wind. His name appeared as early as the fifth dynasty and he is said to have introduced civilization to Egypt. Prior to being elevated to a supreme god (Amen-Ra) around the Twelfth Dynasty, he was a local god, probably of Apt (a section of Thebes) where he was said to have ousted the war god Mont (Month). During the eighteenth dynasty he was the Supreme God of Egypt and the Great God of Thebes. Amen and his consort Ament (also called Amenet), are described in the Pyramid Texts as members of the Ogdoad, a company of eight gods who were worshipped as mothers and fathers of the world. He is shown with the potter's wheel forming the egg said to create mortals. During the New Kingdom, he was the husband of the mother goddess Mut and one of the Triad of Thebes with Mut and his son, the moon, Khensu. In other forms he was the god Par (lord of the phallus), or Ahat (a form of the goddess Meh-urt, or Net). As a creator god he was worshipped chiefly as a goose (symbol of sexual power). The ram with curved horns (his fertility aspect) is generally regarded as his sacred animal. Amen (as Amun) is depicted as Amun-Min and has as an aspect the snake Kematef ("He Who Has Completed His Time"). When he is with Ament, she is uraeus-headed (serpent-headed) and he is shown with a frog's head; and if he is shown with the uraeus, she appears with the head of a cat. As Amen-Ra he is shown as a bearded, blue man, with a tail (lion or bull), wearing a double plumed headdress, either red and green, or red and blue. He wears a tight skirt, a large neck-piece and numerous bracelets. He holds an ankh in his right hand and a scepter in his left hand. He is also depicted with a hawk's head and as Amen-Ra-Temu he has the head of a hawk. In some cases he is shown as having the head of a crocodile or with the head of a man and the body of a beetle with the wings of a hawk, the legs of a man and the claws of a lion. He is also shown with the head of a goose or a ram. As Amen he has been depicted as a black lingam (stylized phallus) in the Ammonium of the Libyan desert. In Greece he was

identified with Zeus, in Rome with Jupiter; thus the name, Jupiter Ammon. Under this name he was worshipped at Siwa. Amen is also identified with Amsu and Khnemu, and the Greek Harsaphes (q.v.). *See also* Ahat; Akeneh; Akhet-Nen-Tha; Amen-Ra; Ament; Amentet; Amsu; Amunet; Aten (for period when worship of Amen was forbidden); Hehui; Heru-Khu; Horus; Khensu; Kheperi; Maat; Min; Mont; Mut; Nau and Nen; Nu; Ogdoad; Par; Ra; Sekhemus; Temu; Thoth.

Amen-ha (Egypt) *see* Aai.

Amen-khat (Egypt) *see* Aai.

Amen-khum (Egypt) *see* Khnum.

Amen-Ra (Egypt)

The priest of Amen created the deity Amen-Ra in an attempt to establish a connection between Amen and the cult of the sun god, Ra. *See also* Amen (B); Ament; Amun; Maat; Min; Nekhbet.

Amen-Ra-Temu (Egypt) *see* Amen (B).

Amen-Ur (Egypt) *see* Amen (B).

Amenaber (Armenian) *see* Aramazd.

Amenet (Egypt) *see* Ament.

Amenhetep (Egypt)

Also known as: *Son-of-hapu.*

God of healing. Amenhetep, an architect as a human, was one of the few humans deified after death. He was close to Amenhetep III of the Eighteenth Dynasty. As a god, he had a small following. *See also* Imohotep; Pedesi; Pehor.

Amenhotep, Son of Hapu (Egypt)

Also known as: *Amenophis* (Greek).

Sage. Master builder. Amenhotep, (1379–1417 B.C.) was renowned as a sage and an architect and his reputation continued to grow throughout the centuries. He was a devoted follower of Thoth and was said to have written books of magic. Many myths were built around this creative man who was the master builder for Amenhotep III. Although statues were erected in his honor, and a temple was dedicated to him along with Hathor and Imhotep, he never became a bona-fide deity. Amenhotep, son of Hapu is usually depicted as a scribe, in a crouching position, with a roll of papyrus on his knees. *See also* Imhotep.

Amenhotep I *Amehetp* (Egypt)

Also known as: *Amenophis I* (Greek).

Deified Pharaoh. God of protection. Am-henth-f (1557–1530 B.C.), worshipped west of Thebes with his mother, Ahmes-Nefertari. He became a god of protection by saving the life of a worker, who had been bitten by a snake. He is one of the gods mentioned in the Pyramid Texts. Am-henth-f is depicted as a bearded, black man.

Amenhotep III (Egypt) *see* Amenhotep, Son of Hapu.

Ameni (Egypt) *see* Aai.

Ameno-uzume-no-kami (Japan) *see* Ama-no-Uzume.

Amenophis (Egypt) *see* Amenhotep, son of Hapu.

Amenophis I (Egypt) *see* Amenhotep I.

Amenotsudoe-chine-no-kami (Japan) *see* Kushi-nada-hime.

Ament (Egypt) *see* Aai and Amentet.

Also known as: *Amenet, Ament-ra, Amentet; Amenti, Amonet, Amunet, Iment.*

Goddess of the Underworld. Earth Mother. Originally from Libya, Ament was said to live in a tree near the World Gates. Her name means "hidden" from the word Amenti. Amentet, also called Amenti, Ker-neter, Tan, The West, or The Land of the Setting Sun, is where the dead assembled waiting for the sun god Ra's boat to pass. Her function was to offer nourishment to approaching souls. If they accepted, they were bound to follow the gods, live in the realm of Osiris and never return to earth. She was an early Egyptian deity, possibly the mother of Ra, and said to be an aspect of Isis in Thebes. As Ament or Amunet, she was a consort of Amen at Karnak, a primeval deity, member of the Ogdoad, and mentioned in the Pyramid Texts. From the hymn inscribed on the walls of the temple of Hebt, in the Great Oasis, it is indicated that Ament had all the attributes of the goddess, Net. She is shown as Ament-Ra, the wife of Amen, who in this context is a local god in Apt. She appears as a ram-headed goddess breast-feeding Horus. In time, Ament was usurped by the goddess, Mut. Ament's emblems are the hawk and the feather. She is depicted with the head of a cat, ram, sheep or serpent and is often portrayed with the crown of Lower Egypt. For goddesses of the west who welcomed the dead, *see* Aai, Amentet, Hathor, Isis, Maat, Neith, and Nut. *See also* Amen; Mut; Ogdoad.

Ament-Nefert (Egypt)

One of the seven goddesses who minister to Osiris in the Second Hour of the Night. *See also* Aaru; Shesat Maket Neb-S; Tuat.

Ament-Ra (Egypt) *see* Ament.

Amentet (Egypt)

Also known as: *Amenthes, Amenti, Ker-neter, Tan, The West.*

The Underworld. The Egyptian meaning for Amentet is "hidden place." In Plutarch's account of the introduction of the deity Sinope into Egypt, he used the word Amenthes as a "subterraneous region." In Egyptian mythology, Amentet is where the sun sets and the dead come into contact with the deities; a hidden place. When the deceased souls encountered the deity they had worshipped while alive, and if they knew the magic words necessary for entry, they were granted admission to Ra's sun boat for the journey through Tuat (the underworld). When the sun rose at daybreak, they were allowed to roam around until sunset when they again continued their journey. Osiris (Khenti Amentet) was another name for him when he usurped the god An-her. *See also* Aaru; Amen; Ament; An-her; Apis (A); Hathor; Hell; Maat; Neith; Nut; Seker; Serapis; Sinope (Greek).

Amentet-Nefert (Egypt) *see* Aaru.

Amenthes (Egypt) *see* Amentet.

Amenti (Egypt) *see* Aaru; Ament; Amentet.

Ameretat *Amardad, Amererat, Murdad* (Persia)
He is the god of all green plants, health, and long life. Ameretat is also one of Ahura Mazda's attendants. *See also* Ahura Mazda; Amesha Spentas; Haurvatat.

Amergin *Amairgen, Amairgin, Amhairghin* (Celtic)
A divine judge, a bard, and a shape-changer, Amergin was one of the leaders of the Milesian conquerors of Ireland. A poem by Amergin dating to the seventh century C.E. is said to be the oldest Celtic literary record (in the "Yellow Book of Lecan"). A Druid, he was known as the chief counsellor of the Sons of Mil (Melesians, Milesians), who are descendants of the Gaels. In some myths, the Celtic goddesses, Banbha, Fotia and Eriu separately approached him to request that the island, named after her. Eriu, an eponym for Ireland, was chosen. When the Sons of Mil encountered the Tuatha De Danann and demanded surrender, the Tuatha De Danann decided to let Amergin judge who should stay on the island. His decision was that the Sons of Mil should leave for the magical boundary known as the ninth wave. They did as requested but in time returned and landed again. The Tuatha De Danann mystically whipped up a wind storm that sailed them back into the sea. Amergin, with a change of heart, in turn invoked the wind and the sea to be still, permitting the Sons of Mil to return. Amergin's poetry is often compared to the ancient British poet, Taliesin. For the results of this episode see Tuatha De Danann. *See also* Banbha; Cu Chulain; Tuatha De Danann.

Amesha Spentas *Amahraspands, Amesho Spends, Ameshospends Amshashpands* (Pahlavi dialect), *Amshaspends* (Zoroastrian; Persia)
Ahurha Mazda is the president of the council of six ministers known as the Amesha Spentas. They are Vohu Manah, who represents "Good Mind" or "Benevolence," protects animals and is responsible for taking the souls of the just to Paradise; Asha Vahishta ("Perfect Order"), who is the protector of fire and of the physical and moral order of the world against demons; Khshasthra Vairya ("Good Power," in Pahlavi Shahriver), the protector of metals and the defender of the poor; Spenta Armaiti ("Devotion and Wisdom") the ancient and wise patroness of the earth, who appears devoted, adoring and submissive; Haurvatat ("Wholeness," "Health," "Prosperity") who represents water, and brings prosperity and health to mortals; and Ameretat ("Immortality"), who oversees plants. Haurvatat and Ameretat are usually joined to represent their position of presiding over all the necessaries of life, including fruit and vegetation. Sometimes Sraosha ("Obedience") is included to complete the holy number of seven when Ahura Mazda is not included in the group. The Amesha Spenta, three males and three females, are said to be aspects, personifications, or attributes of Ahura Mazda. Some scholars believe that they are based on ancient gods. In later times they were thought of as gods or archangels created by Ormazd (the later name for Ahura Mazda) out of sun matter. Their function is to assist him in creating and governing the universe. Ormazd reveals himself to humans through the Amesha Spenta. These gods are depicted seated on golden thrones in the House of Song on the heaven or bridge known as Chinvat where all mortals pass at death.

Compare the Amesha Spentas to Adityas (India) and Kudai (Siberian). *See also* Aeshma; Ahura Mazda; Ameretat; Apo; Asha Vahishta; Atar; Chinvat; Haurvat; Khshasthra Vairya; Pairika; Rashnu; Spenta Armaiti; Vayu; Vohu Manah; Yata; Yazatas.

Amesho Spend (Persia) *see* Amesha Spentas.

Ameshospend (Persia) *see* Amshaspands; Amesha Spentas.

Amet-tcheru (Egypt)
One of the seven goddesses who minister to Osiris in the Second Hour of the Night. *See also* Shesat Maket Neb-S; Tuat.

Amhairghin (Celtic) *see* Amergin.

Ami-Hemf (Egypt)
Also known as: *Dweller in His Flame.*
He is a mighty serpent fifty feet long who lives on top of Bakhau, the Mountain of the Sunrise. He is possibly connected with the underworld. *See also* Apepi.

Amida (Buddhist; Japan; originally India)
Also known as: *A-mi-t'o-fo* (China), *Amidas* (Japan), *Amita* (Japan), *Amitabha* (The Buddha of Immeasurable Light, India), *Amitayus,* (The Buddha of Immeasurable Life Duration; India), *Avalokitesvara* (India), *Bato Kannon* (India), *Bato-kwannon* (India), *Dai Itoku-Myoo* (Japan), *Dhyani Buddha Amitabha* (India), *Hod-dpag-med* (The Buddha of Immeasurable Light; Tibet), *Kanro-o* (Japan), *Muryoju* (Japan), *Muryoka* (Japan), *Od-dpag-med* (Tibet), *Omito, Omit'o-fo, Omito-fu, O-mi-t'o Fo* (China), *O-pa-me* (Tibet).
Amida is the same as Amitabha (India). While still a Bodhisattva, Amida Buddha refused enlightenment for himself unless he was granted the ability to bring Nirvana to anyone who appealed to his name. He vowed not to enter Nirvana until he saved all humans. His western abode, Sukhavati, meaning "Land of Bliss," is known as Gokuraku-Jodo (Japan), Nirvana (India), and Hsi T'ien (China). Nirvana is open to all who call on his name. Here one has the opportunity for rebirth. The Sanskrit original of the name Amita is Amitabha. Amitabha is the incarnation of Gautama, who became Buddha. Amida, known as Omito-fu (see above for variant spellings), in China, was brought to that country by the middle of the second century C.E. although the transcription of Sanskrit to Chinese began in approximately C.E. 65. The worship of the Amida Buddha was taught in Japan by the monk Kuya in 951 and Genshin (942–1017). Initially, Amita was one of the innumerable deities in the Shingon pantheon; later he became the primary deity of the Jodo and Shinshu sects in Japan. Amida in his aspect as one of the Five Dhyani Buddhas is known as Amitabha in Japanese Buddhism, and is favored by the Shinshu and Jodo-Shu traditions of Buddhism. The worship of Amida was never as popular in India proper as it was in Central Asia and the Far East. In India, Amida, known as Amitabha, was thought to be the incarnation of Buddha as compassionate spirituality. The esoteric traditions recognize three Amidas: Muryoju, Muryoko, and Kanro-o. In some traditions, Avalokitesvara is the spiritual son of Amitabha and the ruler of Sukhavati. His sakti (consort) is Pandara. Amitabha or Amitayus rules the Western Paradise known as Sukhavati; Aksobhya rules the Abhirati universe in

the east; the Master Physician, Bhaisajyaguru is also in the east. Dharmadhvaja was the first Tashi Lama of Tibet (also called Panchen Rimpoches) and is considered to be an incarnation of Amitabha. His Tibetan name is bLo-bzan-chos-kyi-rgyal-mtsan or Lob-sang-chho-chi-gyal-tshen. Amida is often depicted sitting with crossed legs on a lotus. He is often shown with his two palms folded face up, one on top of the other resting on his lap. He is also shown standing with an uncovered head, dressed in Indian costume, with one arm bent, fingers pointing skyward. The other arm is extended, with the fingers directed to the earth. He is usually red, which is the color of paradise, and is frequently shown enthroned in the center of paradise. His arm and hand positions indicate that heaven and earth are witness to his vow not to enter Nirvana until all human beings have been saved. His escort is the peacock. In the Japanese iconography, he is usually red and is frequently shown enthroned in the center of paradise. This depiction is known as "Kuwarishiki no Amida." Another popular Japanese depiction shows Amida appearing behind the mountains. This is known as "Yamagoshi no Amida." His emblems are the bell (ghanta) and the begging bowl (patra). His symbol is the pink lotus which he often holds. The lotus represents purity and the acceptance of situations outside of itself. When shown on the alter (stupa), he always faces west (the location of paradise). In the World of Forms mandala, Muryoju (Amitayus) is in the central group underneath the Dainichi-nyorai; in the World of Ideas mandala, he is above the head of Dainichi-nyorai. Amida in his Dhyani Buddha form as Amitabha or Amitayus is red and is seated in a meditative posture. His station is west and his vehicle is the swan. Amitabha sits on the Peacock Throne, symbolizing openness and acceptance. The peacock symbolizes the power and beauty of transmutation. The peacock is said to have the ability to eat poisons and transform them into the beauty of its feathers. Amitabha is the symbol of passion and desire. The wisdom corresponding to the poison is discrimination, which gives the detachment for passion to become compassion. In Japanese Buddhism, Amida is considered by some to be a manifestation of the Shinto sun goddess Amaterasu. For a description of Amida's dwelling place, see Sukhavati. As Amitabha, he is on the mandala of the five Tathagatas; see Dai Itoku-Myoo (Japan), Vairocana, and Yamantaka for Amida's wrathful manifestation. Compare to Adam. See also Aksobhya; Amaterasu; Avalokitesvara; Bhaishajyaguru; Dai Itoku-Myoo; Dainichi-nyorai; Dhyani Buddhas; Fuji; Heruka; Miroku-Bosatsu, Monju-Bosatsu; Pandara; Stupa; Sukhavati.

Amida Buddha (Japan) see Amida.

Amidas (Japan) see Amida.

Amighavajra (India) see Amoghasiddhi.

Amirini (Yoruba People, Africa) An early goddess.

Amisodaurus (Greek) see Chimaera.

Amit *Amam, Am-mit*

Also known as: *Amamet, Amamet the Devourer, Ammut, Amunet, Eater of the Dead, Devourer of Amenti;* (Egypt).

Demonic goddess. Heart-eater of sinful dead souls. Amit, a monster deity, with the head of a crocodile, the body of a lion and the rear end of a hippopotamus, stands by in the Hall of Judgment, ready to chew up the hearts of departed souls who are judged as guilty. It appears that Amit was likely hungry as records do not indicate that he ever performed this task. The Egyptians presented a list known as the "Negative Confession" list to the judges. It was prepared before death and placed in the tomb upon death. This list prefaced every unacceptable act with the phrase, "I have not," thus insuring safe passage through the Hall of Judgement, if a series of other questions were answered properly. See also Aati; Anubis; Maat; Negative Confession; Thoth.

Amita (Japan) see Amida.

Amitabha (India) see Amida.

Amitayus (India) "The Buddha of Immeasurable Light." See also Amida.

Amitolane (Zuni People, United States) "The rainbow."

Amm (South Arabia)

The meaning is either ancestor or uncle in the ancient tongue. It can also be construed to be a name for the moon. See also Ab; Shahar.

Amma (A) (Dogon People, West Africa)

Supreme creator and god of fertility and rain. His wife is Earth. They are the parents of the twins. The twins have snake-like appearances including forked tongues. After leaving his wife he created four males and four females which were the first humans. He was said to have created the first jackal named Ogo. In a variation of the myth, the goddess Akongo created the first mortal. Amma mated with her and they created the twins. See also Akongo; Nommo.

Amma (B) (Teutonic)

Also known as: *Ama, Grandmother.*

In Teutonic belief, Amma was a mortal woman. Heimdall (also known as Rig), slept between Amma and her husband Afi. From Heimdall's union with Amma, Karl, the founder of the race of peasants was born. See also Afi.

Amma (C) (India) Goddess of the Kaveri River.

Amma (D) (India) see Gramadeveta.

Amma-Ana-Ki (Assyro-Babylonian) see Ea.

Ammanavaru (India) see Gramadeveta.

Ammehet (Egypt) see Aaru.

Ammi-Seshet (Egypt) A form of Maat as a fire goddess.

Ammon (Egypt) see Amen.

Ammon, Oracle of (Greek) see Andromeda.

Ammut (Egypt) see Amit.

Amogha-Siddhi (India) see Amoghasiddhi.

Amoghapasa Lokeswar (Buddhist; Nepal)

Also known as: *Avalokitesvara.*

Amoghapasa Lokeswar is shown four-faced, with eight arms. He stands on a lotus. In his four right hands, he holds the Vajra, the sword, the goad and the bow. In his four left hands he holds the Ghanta (bell), the Tridandi, the noose and an arrow. He is honored to prevent poverty. *See also* Avalokitesvara; Vasundhara.

Amoghasiddhi (Buddhist; India)
Also known as: *Amogha-Siddhi* (Almighty Conqueror; Sanskrit), *Amoghasiddi, Amoghavajra* (Sanskrit), *Dhyani Buddha Amoghasiddhi, Don-yo-dup-pa* (Tibet), *Don-yod-grub-pa* (Tibet), *Fuku* (Japan), *Heruka.*
Amoghasiddhi is the fifth Dhyani Buddha, the Buddha of meditation. On the mandala of the five Tathagatas, he represents the cosmic element of confrontation (sanskara), and the pure quality of air and wind. He is the embodiment of the rain season. Known as the "Omnipotent Conqueror," he is from the powerful Karma family. He appears on the fifth day in Bardo from the Realm of Accumulated Actions. His name means "Accomplishing All Actions, All Powers." His spiritual consort (sakti) is Samaya-Tara, also known as Dolma, or the Green Tara, an aspect of Tara. With him on the fifth day are the male bodhisattvas Vajrapani (also known as Sgrib-pa-rnam-sel in Tibet) who is the "Clearer of Obstructions," and Sarvanivaranaviskambhin (Sgrib-pa-rnam-sel in Tibet), known as the "Clearer of Obturations." There are also two female bodhisattvas, Ganda, also known as Gandhema (and as Dri-chha-ma in Tibet), meaning "She Spraying Perfume" and Naivedya (also known as Nidhema in the Sanskrit language and as Zhalzas-ma in Tibet), meaning "She Holding Sweetmeats." She is associated with the light of wisdom and is depicted as green in color. In front of Amoghasiddhi's shrines in Nepal, a small square pit is found which is meant for the snake, a symbol of protection from the rain. The wrathful manifestation of Amoghasiddhi is the green Heruka Buddha. Amoghasiddhi is green in color and his symbol is the sword (khadga) or the double thunderbolt (visvavajra). Green is the color of envy and is also called the light-path of the all-performing wisdom. The visvavajra, indestructible, is the symbol of fulfilling all actions. He always faces his region, the north. Seated in a meditative pose (asana dhyana), his left hand lies open on his lap and his right hand is held in the gesture of protection (abhaya mudra). In this gesture the arm is elevated and slightly bent. The hand is lifted to shoulder level with the palm turned outward and all the fingers extended upward. Sometimes he is depicted with a seven-headed serpent in the background which serves as an umbrella. His mount (vahana) is a dwarf or Garuda (half-bird and half-man). He is sometimes mounted on an eagle. When Amoghasiddhi and Samaya-Tara are depicted embracing on the back of the Garuda, who is a musician, it plays the cymbals as it flies through the air. This particular type of Garuda is known as shang-shang and is sometimes called the Harpy-throne. In Greek mythology, the Harpy is female. In the Buddhist tradition, the harpy can be either sex. It symbolizes mightiness, conquest over all the elements and fulfillment. The goddess Ganda ("She Spraying Perfume") is depicted holding a shell-vase of perfume. She represents sense-perception required to accomplish skillful activity. The sweetmeats held by Naivedya represent meditation as the food required to nourish skillful action. For the five Tathagatas; *see* Avalokitesvara; Ganda; Heruka; Vairocana; Vajrapani. *See also* Dhyani Buddhas; Tara (B); Vajrasatwa.

Amoghasiddi (India) *see* Amoghasiddhi.

Amon (Egypt) *see* Amen (B); Atum.

Amon-Ra (Egypt) *see* Amen.

Amon-Re (Egypt) *see* Amen.

Amonet (Egypt) *see* Ament.

Amor (Roman, Greek)
Also known as: *Cupid, Cupido, Eros* (Greek).
Boy-god of love. He is the son of Venus and Mars or Mercury. *See also* Cupid; Eros.

Amphianax (Greek) Another name for Iobates (q.v.).

Amphiaraus (Greek) *see* Adrestus; Argonauts.

Amphibia (Greek)
Another name for Nicippe, the daughter of Pelops and Hippodameia. *See also* Nicippe.

Amphinome (Greek) *see* Jason.

Amphion (Greek)
Amphion is the hero son of Zeus and Antiope and the twin brother of Zethus. Abandoned at birth, the brothers later became joint rulers of Thebes. Amphion married Niobe, the daughter of Tantalus, and they became the parents of twelve children. The brothers later became co-rulers of Thebes and settled into a friendly partnership. Amphion played a lyre given to him by Hermes and provided the cultural atmosphere. Zethus, more pragmatic, was interested in breeding cattle. His family life fell into chaos when Niobe began bragging about her numerous children and berated the goddess Leto for only giving birth to two offspring. The offended goddess instructed her children, the deities Apollo and Artemis, to slaughter the offensive women's pride and joy, her children. Some say only two survived, Amyclas and Chloris. Amphion was either killed in melee, or grief-stricken committed suicide. Zethus also encountered tragedy that he could not bear. For details about Amphion's birth, *see* Antiope. For details about the deaths of their children, *see* Niobe. *See also* Apollo; Leto; Tantalus (A); Zethus.

Amphithea (Greek)
She is the daughter of Pronax and the sister of Lycurgus. Amphithea married her uncle, Adrestus. She became the mother of Aegialeus, Aegialeia, Argeia, Cyanippus, Hippodameia, and possibly Deipyle. *See also* Adrestus; Anticleia (A); Apsyrtus; Autolycus (A).

Amphithemis (Greek) *see* Acacallis.

Amphitrite (Greek)
Also known as: *Salacia* (Roman).
Sea goddess. Amphitrite, the personification of the sea, is the daughter of Nereus and Doris or of Oceanus and Tethys. As the daughter of Oceanus and Tethys, she is one of their fifty daughters, known as the Nereids. Poseidon fell in love with her and attempted to court her. She rebuffed him and ran to Atlas for protection. Undaunted, Poseidon sent scouts the world over in search of her. One of his envoys, Delphin, found her and convinced her to marry the sea god. To show his gratitude,

Poseidon placed the Dolphin constellation in the sky in Amphitrite's honor. Poseidon and Amphitrite were the parents of many children, including Albion, Benthesicyme, Charybdis, Rhode, and Triton. As Salacia, she is the Roman goddess of springs. Amphitrite is shown riding in a chariot with Poseidon drawn by Tritons blowing conch-shells. She carries a trident in her hand. *See also* Nereids; Poseidon; Scylla.

Amphitryon (Greek) *see* Acrisius; Alcestis; Rhadamantus.

Amra (Afghanistan) *see* Imra.

Amraphel (Babylonian) *see* Hammurabi.

Amrata (India) *see* Amrita.

Amrita *Amrata, Amrta* (Hindu, Vedic; India)
Also known as: *Nia-Jara, Pi-Yusha.*
Amrita, the "Elixir of Life" or "Water of Immortality," is what the gods searched for during the Churning of the Ocean of Milk. The vial containing the beverage is known as Amrita-Kumbha. Amrita is sometimes said to be the fruit of a tree. The celestial goddess associated with Amrita is Amritika. In the Vedas, the name Amrita is used to signify various items that are sacrificed, but it is particularly applied to soma juice. Often Amrita and soma are confused but are considered to be closely associated and the mythology is often the same. *See also* Admida; Ambrosia (Greek); Amida; Amrtakundali; Haoma (Indo-Iranian); Indrani (regarding the Parijata Tree); Kurma (regarding the Churning of the Ocean of Milk); Sesha; Soma; Vishnu.

Amrita-Dhari (Tibet) *see* Amritahari.

Amrita-Kumbha (India) *see* Amrita.

Amrita Kundika (Japan) *see* Gundari-Myoo.

Amrita Surabki (India)
Buddha's begging-bowl. *See also* Buddha.

Amritahari *Amrita-Dhari* (Tibet) *see* Ankusha; Kinkini-Dhari.

Amrite Kundalin (Japan) *see* Gundari-Myoo.

Amritika (India) *see* Amrita; Soma.

Amrta (India) *see* Amrita.

Amrtakundali *Amitra-Dhara* ("Urn of Nectar"), *Gundari-Myoo* (Japan); (Buddhist; Tibet)
Amrtakundali (Coil of Nectar) is one of the four wrathful guardians of the gates in Bardo, the after-death state between death and rebirth. He is responsible for the northern gate and for the distribution of Amrita, the beverage of immortality. The other guardians are Vijaya the Victorious, who guards the eastern gate; Yamantaka, Destroyer of Death, the guardian of the southern gate; Hayagriva the Horse-Necked, who guards the western gate. There are also four female guardians: Ankusa, the Hook; Pasa (Pashadhari), the Noose; Srnkhala, the Chain; and Ghanta, the Bell. On the sixth day in Bardo, along with the guardians, the five Dhyani Buddhas appear. Vairocana and his consort appear from the central realm. The central realm is the All-pervading Circle. Amoghasiddhi and his consort appear

from the northern realm, the Realm of Perfected Actions. Vajrasattva and his consort appear from the eastern realm, the Realm of Complete Joy. Ratnasambhava and his consort appear from the southern realm, The Glorious Realm. Amitabha (Amida) and his consort from the western realm, the Blissful Realm of Lotuses. Each Buddha and his consort have their attendants with them. The six sages, known as the Blessed Ones also appear. They represent the six realms of the world. They are Indra, of the hundred sacrifices, sage of the gods; Vemacitra, Splendid Robe, sage of the jealous gods; the Lion of the Sakyas, sage of the mortals; Dhruvasinha, Steadfast Lion, sage of the animals; Jvalamukha, Flaming Mouth, sage of the Pretas (hungry ghosts); and Dharmaraja, the Dharma King, who presides over the hell-beings. The All-Good Mother and Father of all the Buddhas, Samantabhadra and Samantabhadri also appear. A total of forty-two deities appear. The four goddesses who guard the doors of Bardo are known as the Wang-Chug-mas. They have human-like bodies and animal heads and appear on the twelfth day in Bardo. To compare to the Four Great Kings, *see* Dhritarashtra. Compare to the Lokapalas. *See also* Gundari-Myoo; Hayagriva; Yamantaka.

Amset *Am-Sit* (Egypt)
Also known as: *Imseti, Meslam, Mestha, Mesti.*
A guardian spirit, Amset is one the the four divine sons of Horus. His brothers are Tuamutef, who guards the east, Hapy, who guards the north, and Qebhsneuf, who guards the west. Amset is the guardian of the south. (Some say he guards the northern section.) He is the Canopic guardian of the stomach, liver, and lower or large intestines. (Canopic vases hold the viscera of the dead.) Amset and his brothers are all connected with the life in the underworld. Amset assisted Horus when Osiris was mummified. He is represented by a human head on an egg shaped vase. *See also* Hapy (A); Horus; Osiris; Qebhsneuf; Tuamutef.

Amseth (Egypt) A god who is associated with Thoth.

Amshashpands (Persia) *see* Amshaspands.

Amshaspands *Amahraspands, Ameshospend, Amshashpands* (Pre-Christian Gnostics; Simon Magus sect; Zoroastrian; Persia)
Also known as: *Amesha Spentas.*
Immortal spirits. Archangels. A half–Gentile, half–Jewish sect of Gnostics who believed, as did Zoroaster that there were six "roots" or aspects of the Supreme Being. (Some ancient texts say seven.) These later deities are Ameretat (Immortality), Asha Vahishta (Truth), Haurvetat (Good Health), Khshathra Vairya (Right Law), Spenta Armaiti (Wisdom), Vohu Mano (Good Mind). Simon called them Mind, Thought, Voice, Name, Desire, and Reason. Ahriman created six evil archangels to oppose the Amshashpands. Among them were Tauru, Zairicah, also spelled Zairicha (sickness and death), Khurdad and Murdad (hunger and thirst) and others. Some say they were created out of sun matter by Ormazd. They are a form of Amesha Spentas (q.v.).

Amshaspends (Persia) *see* Amesha Spentas.

Amsu (Egypt)
Also known as: *Amsu-Amen, Min-Amen.*

Local creator deity. A god worshiped in the nomes (cities or districts) of Herui and Amsu. In one of the hymns Amsu-Amen or Min-amen is called "Maker of Everlastingness" and "Lord of Eternity." Amsu is depicted as a human figure wearing the double plume headdress and holding a flail in his left hand. Identified with Amen-Ra. *See also* Amen; Amsu; Min.

Amsvartner (Teutonic)

This is the ocean that surrounds the island where Fenrir the wolf is chained. *See also* Fenrir.

Amu-Aa (Egypt)

One of the gods who accompany Osiris during the Second Hour of the Night. *See also* Shesat Maket Neb-S; Tuat.

Amulet

This is a charm worn to ward off evil or to bring good fortune. *See also* Ab; Guabonito; Kagu-tsuchi; Khepri; Lilith; Marduk; Scarab; Shina-tsu-hiko; Stupa; Talisman; Tet; Vessavana.

Amulets (Egypt) *see* Ab.

Amun (Egypt) *see* Amen (B); Atum; Keket; Khensu; Min; Nut.

Amun-Kneph (Egypt) *see* Khnum.

Amun-Min (Egypt) *see* Amen (B).

Amun-Re (Egypt) *see* Amen (B).

Amunet (Egypt)

Also known as: *Nuit.*

Goddess of Mystery. She and Amen created light. *See also* Amen; Flame; Island of Flame; Neith; Niut.

Amurru (Babylonian, Phoenician) *see* Aleyin; Anat; Qadesh; Reshep.

Amvika (India) *see* Ambika; Sati (A).

Amyclas (A) (Greek)

He is one of the six sons of Amphion and Niobe. He also has six sisters. Apollo murdered his brothers and Artemis murdered all of his sisters except Chloris. Amyclas is thought to have survived as well. *See also* Amphion; Apollo; Artemis; Leto.

Amycus (A) *Amykos* (Greek)

Amycus is the son of Poseidon and the ash nymph Melie and the brother of Mygdon. He was the king of the Bebryces who challenged all strangers to boxing matches. A giant, known for his strength, he was reputed to have killed many opponents. His brother Mygdon had died in an earlier battle with Dascylus the king of Mariandyni or his son Lycus over a land dispute. Amycus was killed in a match with Polydeuces when the Argonauts landed on his shores. *See also* Argonauts; Polydeuces; Poseidon.

Amycus (B) (Greek) *see* Ixion, Nephele.

Amycus (C) (Greek)

He was the companion of Aeneas. They were both killed by Turnus (q.v.). *See also* Aeneas.

Amykos (Greek) *see* Amycus (A).

Amymone (Greek)

River goddess.

A Danaid, she is one of the fifty daughters of Danaus and Europa. She is the mother of Nauplius by Poseidon. She married Enceladus, the son of Aegyptus and murdered him on their wedding night. After having sex with Poseidon, in arid Argos, a perpetual spring issued forth. In another story, she was attacked by a Satyr but rescued by Poseidon who told her to draw his trident from a rock. This she did and a spring came forth. In that spot, the monster Hydra was born. *See also* Aegyptus; Danaides; Danaus; Europa; Hydra; Hypermnestra; Poseidon.

An (A) (Akkadian, Assyrian, Babylonian, Sumerian; possibly Egyptian)

Also known as: *Ana, Anat, Anath, Anatu, Anu, Anum.*

High God of Heaven. The goddess Nammu who personified the eternal primeval sea is the mother of the Sumerian sky god An. With Ki, the earth goddess, An became the father of the god of air, Enlil. In later times, Enlil superseded An as chief of the Sumerian pantheon. Semitic Assyrians referred to Anu and Anatu (Anath) as god and goddess of heaven. He was part of the Sumerian triad of high gods: An, Enlil, and Ninhursag. Some say the trinity was An, Enlil and Enki. There is a possibility that Babbar was included. In another tale, it is related how the cosmos was divided among a slightly different tripartite: the sky to An, the Earth to Enlil, and the underworld to the goddess Eriskigal. Some writers say the goddess Innini represented the female principle of An. Most legends refer to Anu, but An might have been a separate deity. In a separate tale An was the brother of Ki and they were the sons of Nammu. Both were depicted in the shape of a mountain. They were also said to be the creators of Enlil. In the Babylonian Genesis, "Enuma Elish," the tale is told of the conflict between Anu and Kumarbi. It is in this narrative that the theme of castration first appears. The tale of An is similar to that of Ra of the Egyptians where Isis refers to the supreme god. The Egyptians called An a form of Osiris. Some say the name Anu is the Akkadian form of An. *See also* Ana; Anat; Anath; Anatna; Anatu; Anu (Celtic); Anum; Innini; Nammu.

An (B) (Teutonic) *see* Dwarfs.

An (C) A title for Osiris meaning sun or moon god.

An Ut (Egypt) *see* Anubis.

An-a-f (Egypt)

A little known Egyptian god, possibly of the underworld. One of the forty-two assessors or judges of the dead. *See also* Assessors.

An-Aareretef (Egypt)

Also known as: *An-Aretf.*

Assessors of a section of the Tuat (q.v.).

An-Aretf (Egypt) *see* An-Aareretef.

An-her *see* Amentet; Anhur.

An-hetep-f (Egypt).

One of the forty-two assessors or judges of the dead. *See also* Assessors.

An-Hur *Anher, Anhur* (Egypt)

Sun god. An-hur was a form of the Egyptian sun god Ra. He

is the son of Hathor (goddess of beauty, love and joy) in her form of Her-t. An-hur stood in the prow of the sun's boat as "Slayer of the Enemies."

An-Kung (China)
Goddess of Sailors. Wife or consort of H'ien-hou.

An-mut-f (Egypt) One of the gods in the Pyramid Texts.

An-pu (Egypt) *see* Anubis.

An-tcher-f (Egypt) One of the gods in the Pyramid Texts.

Ana (A) (Celtic) *see* Anu (A).

Ana (B) (Middle Eastern) *see* Anat; Anu (B).

Ana-Hid (Armenian) *see* Anahita.

Ana Nse Kukuroko (Ashanti People, Africa) *see* Ananse.

Ana-purna *Anapurna, Anna Perenna* (Roman), *Anna-Purna, Annapurna* (Hindu; India)
Also known as: *Parvati.*
Ana-Purna is the ancient Indian goddess of daily bread. Her name means "full of food." Her abode is on the top of Anna-purna mountain. She is often shown seated, feeding a child. The Romans called her Anna Perenna the goddess of spring, who personified life, health, and plenty. Mars used her to secure Minerva for himself. She is often identified with Devi (q.v.). *See also* Durga; Parvati.

Anadyomene *see* Aphrodite.

Anahit (Persia) see Anahita.

Anahita *Anahit, Anahite, Anait, Anaitis* (Chaldean, Iranian, Persian, Semitic [possibly])
Also known as: *Anaitis* (name in later times), *Anta* (Asia Minor), *Ardevi Sura Anahita* (The High, Powerful, Undefiled One), *Nane, Venus* (Roman).
Female Yazata water genius. Goddess of procreation. During the times of the Achaemenians (558–330 B.C.), Anahita was widely worshipped. She is the ancient Persian Great Mother; goddess of fertility and fertilizing waters; particularly the spring among the stars from which all the rivers of the earth flow. She appears in the Mazdaism pantheon as a chief deity associated with Ahura Mazda and Mithra. Known as Ardevi Sura Anahita in the "Avesta," she purified the seed of all males, sanctified the womb of all females and purified their breast milk. Women in childbirth appealed to her for aid and comfort. She was also called upon in times of severe illness. In Armenia, she was the Mother Goddess, known as the mother of all wisdom, the giver of life, and the daughter of Ahura Mazda. She is approached by female followers of marriageable age for guidance. Men desiring strong females as spouses call upon her. In the past, green branches accompanied sacrifices to her. Her followers, nobility of both sexes, entered her services as slaves; the women engaged in sacred prostitution at her shrine before marriage. In Chaldean astrology she was associated with the planet Venus. The bull was her sacred animal and sacred herds of white heifers were branded with her mark, a torch. The heifers were also sacrificed to her. She drives a chariot pulled by four horses who represent the wind, rain, clouds and sleet. She is depicted as strong, tall, beautiful, and pure. She wears a golden crown with eight rays and a hundred stars, a golden mantle and a golden necklace around her neck and is adorned with thirty otter skins. Compare Anahita to the Vedic sun goddess, Surya (B). *See also* Ahura Mazda; Apam Napat; Hvare-khshaeta; Mitra; Qadesh; Tishtrya; Vourukasha (A); Vourukasha (B); Yazatas.

Anahite (Persian) *see* Anahita.

Anait (Persian) *see* Anahita.

Anaitis *Anahita* (Persia)
The goddess Anahita was called Anaitis in later times. As Anaitis, she was popular in Asia Minor and the Mediterranean. *See also* Anahita.

Anakhai (Mongol)
Spirit of the dead. Anakhai is the soul that haunts its former home. It is dangerous to infants.

Anakim (Hebrew) *see* Rephaim.

Anala (India) *see* Agni; Vasus.

Anamaqkiu (Menominee People, United States)
This malignant spirit who caused the great flood by dragging Moqwais (the wolf) under the sea.

Anan (Celtic) *see* Eire.

Ananda (India) "Joy, Happiness." An epithet for Shiva.

Ananga (Hindu; India)
God of Love consumed by the fire of Shiva's third eye. *See also* Kama; Kami (A); Shiva.

Ananke (Greek)
Another name for the goddess of law and justice Themis.

Ananse *Anansi, Annancy* (Ashanti People, Africa)
Also known as: *Ana Nse Kukuroko, Annancy* (Native American People).
Creator and trickster deity. He is the son of Asase Ya and Nyame. Known as "The Enormous Spider," he is the creator of the sun, moon, stars, day and night. He often intercedes between gods and mortals and aids mortals by giving them the first grain. He is the first king of human beings. Some say Ananse won his stories (power) from the sky-god, Nyankopon. He is generally known in Native American lore as Annancy, who is also a spider. *See also* Abosom.

Anansi (Africa) *see* Ananse.

Ananta (India) An epithet of the world serpent Sesha (q.v.).

Ananta-Shayana (India) Epithet of Vishnu (q.v.).

Anaplades (Greek) *see* Hermaphroditus.

Anapurna (India) *see* Ana-Purna.

Anar *Annar* (Norse; Teutonic)
Also known as: *Onar.*
Creator. He is a creating father, who was the second husband to Nat (night). His child is Jord (the earth). Anar is possibly associated with water. *See also* Nat; Onar.

Anat (Assyria, Canaan, Chaldea, Sumer then Egypt)

Also known as: *Ana, Anata, Anath, Anath-yahu, Anatha, Anatu, Anna-nin, Annuthat, Anta, Antit, Antum, Hanata, Quadesh* (Phoenician).

"Lady of Heaven." "Mistress of the Gods." Mother goddess. Earth goddess. She is the virgin daughter of Baal and sister of Aleyin, although in some legends she is the sister of Baal. As his sister, she is grief-stricken when he is murdered by the harvest-god Mot, who had attempted to woo her sexually. Overwhelmed, she wandered through the fields mutilating herself by gashing her cheeks. The goddess Shaphash came to her aid and together they went in search of the murderer. When they located him, they made him vomit his rival Baal. Then Anat murdered Mot in a particularly horrific manner. When he did not remain dead, he was killed again by her brother, Aleyin. Introduced in Egypt by the Hyskos (shepherd kings) Anat was said to be the consort of Baal-Sutekh. Her epithet is Qadesh and she is depicted as a warrior, defender of cities and dragon-slayer. She is the female counterpart of the god of war and thunder, Reshef, and was said to be his consort. The Sumerians regarded her, under the name Anatu, as the wife of Anu while the Egyptians considered her the wife of Set. She is the mother of Lamashtu, the Anunnaki and the seven Utukki. She, or as some say, the goddess Athirat, interceded to have El build a palace for Baal. As Anat, she is depicted with a helmet, shield and battle ax. When she is seated she is shown holding a shield and spear in her right and a club in her left. When standing, she is shown dressed in a panther skin and holding a papyrus scepter in her right hand and the ankh (emblem of life) in her left. She wears a white-feathered crown, sometimes with a pair of horns at the base. As Anat she compares to Aphrodite and Athena, and is the same as Anaitis. Anat is the northern Semitic name of Allat. She may have been a composite of Ashera, Astarte and Ishtar. Her name is connected with the Semitic word "ayn" ("source"). *See also* Aleyin; Allat; Asherah; Astarte; Baal; Qadesh; Reshef; Shaphash.

Anata (Middle East) *see* Anat.

Anath (Middle East) *see* Anat.

Anath-Yahu (Middle East) *see* Anat.

Anatha (Middle East) *see* Anat.

Anatis (Arthurian) *see* Vivien.

Anatu (Middle East) *see* Anat.

Anax (Greek) *see* Giants.

Anaxibia (A) (Greek)

There is a possibility that she is the daughter of Crisus. Her siblings are Astyoche and Strophius I. *See also* Acastus; Agamemnon; Antilochus; Helios.

Anaxibia (B) (Greek)

She is the daughter of Bias and Iphianassa. Her husband is possibly Pelias. Her children are Acastus, Alcestis, Hippothoe, Pelopia and Pisidice. *See also* Acastus; Alcestis; Hippothoe; Pelias.

Anaxibia (C) (Greek)

She is the sister of Agamemnon and Menelaus. Pylades is her son by Strophius I. She had a number of other children by Nestor, including, Antilochus, Perseus, Polycaste and Peisidice. *See also* Agamemnon; Antilochus; Menelaus; Perseus; Pylades.

Anaye (Navajo People, North America)

Also known as: *Alien Gods, Child of the Waters.*

Evil spirits. Destroyers of mortals. It was thought that the Anaye were destroyed long ago by the brothers Nayanezgani and Thobadzistshini some of them remain. They are Cold, Hunger, Old Age, and Poverty. The Anaye are monsters, giants and beasts. They are similar to the Tshindi devils. The Anaye are opposites of the Yei. *See also* Nayanezgani; Thobadzistshini.

Ancaeus Great (Greek) *see* Argonauts.

Ancaeus Little (Greek) *see* Argonauts.

Anchancho (Collao People, South America)

Also known as: *The Supay.*

Evil spirits. The Anchancho dispense all diseases and are sometimes thought to be the disease. They take possession of humans while they are asleep or frightened. They also entice mortals with an evil eye, enter their body, suck their blood and cause death. The Anchancho frequent mountain peaks, especially during storms. Their voices, sounding like the braying of an ass, can be heard during storms. *See* Ekkekko (good spirits) for a myth pertaining to the Anchancho and the Ekkekko. *See also* Achachilas; Supay.

Anchile, The *Ancile* (Roman)

The Anchile is the sacred shield belonging to Mars. It is guarded by the priests of Mars, the Salii. *See also* Mars.

Anchinoe (Greek) *see* Agenor (A); Danaus.

Anchises (Greek)

Light deity. Anchises and his brother Laocoon are the sons of Capys, who was the son of Assaracus, and Hieromneme. His cousin Themiste is the daughter of Ilus and Eurydice. Anchises, a king of Dardania, noted for his beauty was the lover of Aphrodite and the father of Aeneas, Hippodameis and Lyrus (about whom little is known). It is also thought by some that Hippodameis and Lyrus may be the children of Anchises and a mortal woman. Zeus, tired of listening to Aphrodite brag about the numerous affairs that she had magically arranged between unsuspecting deities and mortals, arranged a liaison between the great goddess and the youth. Overwhelmed by passion, she had the Graces anoint her with oil and bedeck her in a blazing red dress and jewels. She appeared to Anchises disguised as a mortal as he was tending his herd on Mount Ida. Delighted to accommodate her desires, he spent a heavenly night with her. The following morning, Aphrodite stood before him in all her glory and revealed her true identity. Anchises was astonished and fearful, for he had heard that mortal men who slept with goddesses would age prematurely. Cautioning him to keep their relationship a secret, she assuaged his fears and promised him a son who would be like a god. Drunk one night, Anchises forgot his promise and began to brag about his affair with the beautiful goddess. A very angry Zeus thrust a lightning bolt at him and from that day Anchise walked with a limp. Their son, Aeneas, known as "the pious one," went on to become a national hero of Rome. Compare this myth to the myths of Attis; Cybele. In each case the male is wary of being depleted by sleeping with a goddess. *See also* Acestes; Aeneas; Aphrodite; Eurydice (C).

Ancient Spider (Micronesia) *see* Areop-Enap.

Andarta (Celtic) Bear Goddess.

Ander (Persia)
Ander is one of the evil spirits created by Ahriman to be his assistants. *See also* Ahriman.

Andhaka (Hindu; India)
Andhaka is the son of Kasyapa and Diti. This demon, who had a thousand heads and two thousand hands and feet, was a general nuisance to the gods. He walked around pretending to be blind although he had perfect vision. The great Hindu triad of gods, Brahma, Shiva and Vishnu, held a meeting to decide how to handle this menace. As they discussed the issue, the energy from their eye contact manufactured a brilliant feminine form. When they gazed upon her multi-colored beauty, each deity wanted to possess her. She divided herself into the three goddesses, the white Sarasvati, the red Lakshmi and the black Parvati. When Andhaka attempted to steal the magic Parijata tree from Swarga, he was slain by Shiva. Andhaka represents famine and the goddesses represent the past, present and future. *See also* Brahma; Diti; Kasyapa; Lakshmi; Parijata Tree; Parvati; Sarasvati; Shiva; Swarga; Vishnu.

Andhrimner (Teutonic) *see* Andrimne.

Andra (Persian)
Also known as: *Indra* (India).
Andra waits on Chinvat Bridge for the souls of sinners which he hurls into hell. *See also* Asha Vahishtra; Chinvat Bridge; Indra.

Andreus (Greek) *see* Cephissus.

Andriamanitra & Andrianahary (Madagascar)
Good and evil gods who created the earth and mortals. Andriamanitra made domestic animals and the hive with honey. Andrianahary made wild animals, and hornets. This in turn caused Andrianahary to create magical cures for the evil caused by Andrianahary and Zanahary (qq.v.).

Andrianahary (Madagascar) *see* Andriamanitra and Andrianahary.

Andrimne *Andhrimner, Andhrimnir* (Norse; Teutonic)
Cook for the gods. Andrimne is the cook who roasts the meat from the boar Saerimne (also spelled Saehrimnir) in the cauldron Eldrimne, which never runs out of food. After the feasting on the meat the boar is restored to its former self, alive, well and ready to be eaten during the next meal. *See also* Odin.

Androgeus (Greek)
Also known as *Eurgyes*.
He is the son of Minos and Pasiphae. His siblings are Acacallis, Ariadne, Catreus, Deucalion, Euryale, Glaucus, Lycastus, Phaedra, Xenodice and others. His children are Alcaeus and Sthenelus. A famous athlete, Androgeus, under the name of Eurgyes, won every race at the Panathenaean games. While on his way to race in Athens, he was killed by the Bull of the Marathon. That incident was the cause of Athenians being sacrificed to the Minotaur. *See also* Acacallis; Aeacus; Ariadne; Minos; Minotaur; Pasiphae; Sthenelus.

Andromeda (Greek) Lunar deity.
Hero. Andromeda is the daughter of Cepheus (Ethiopian king of Joppa) and Cassiopeia. She is the wife of Perseus and mother of Alcaeus, Electryon, Heleus, Mestor, Perses, Sthenelus and Gorgophone. Andromeda's mother bragged that she and Andromeda were more beautiful than the Nereids. The incensed sea-nymphs complained to their protector Poseidon. To placate them, he sent a flood and a sea-monster to Philistia. Andromeda's father Cepheus consulted the Oracle of Ammon and was told that the only hope was to sacrifice his daughter. Naked, save for a few jewels, she was chained to a rock and left to be devoured by the sea-monster. Perseus, flying overhead saw her and swooped down. He consulted with her parents and agreed to rescue her if they would allow her to marry him. Reluctantly, they agreed. Andromeda was saved and the marriage followed immediately. Her fiancé, who was Agenor, the father of Phineus, or by some accounts, her uncle Phineus, barged into the wedding festivities with friends and a fight ensued. Perseus ended the fray by turning the upstarts to stone with the head of Medusa. This myth may come from the Babylonian tale of Marduk and Tiamat. It also parallels Heracles' rescue of Hersione. *See also* Ariadne; Gorgophone; Marduk; Nereids; Persus; Tiamat.

Anduruna (Mesopotamia)
In Babylonian mythology, Anduruna is one of the ancient names for the underworld. In Mesopotamian mythology it is defined as a heaven where the gods play. *See also* Arallu.

Andvare (Teutonic) *see* Andvari.

Andvari *Andvare* (Norse; Teutonic)
Also known as: *Alberich, Elbegast, Gondemar, Laurin, Oberon.*
Andvari, the fish-shaped dwarf king, guarded treasures of the gods, including the ring of magic, Draupnir (also called Andvarinaut). From this golden ring other golden rings constantly dropped. Hreidmar was holding the gods prisoners because Loki had killed his son Ottor (also spelled Otr). (Earlier, Ottor had been changed into an otter.) The price of the gods release was a quantity of gold. Loki stole the treasures and the ring Draupnir from Andvari to gain the prisoners release. Andvari, however, had put a curse on the ring. So it was that when Hreidmar received the ransom, he was killed by Fafnir, who in turn was killed by Sigurd. The House of Hredimar was torn apart with jealousy over the golden treasure and as noted, it was the cause of the downfall of Sigurd. As a pike, Andvari frequented waterfalls that came to be known as the Cascade of Andvari. *See also* Alberich; Andvarinaut; Fafnir; Hreidmar; Loki; Sampo; Sigurd.

Ane (A) (Nigeria) *see* Ala (B).

Ane (B) (Arabic) *see* Ala.

Anean People — Creation Legend (Peru, South America) *see* Sibu.

Anga-Raja (India) *see* Karna.

Angada (India) *see* Bali (A).

Angajan (Saora People, India) Moon goddess. *See also* Adununkisum.

Angana (India) *see* Apsarases.

Angara (India)
She is an Apsaras and monkey queen, the wife of Kesari and mother of monkey god Hanuman. *See also* Apsarases; Hanuman.

Angels (Arabic, Christian, Hebrew, Syrian)
Also known as: *Angel* (Singular), *Archangels, Cherubim, Lords, Powers, Seraphim, Thrones, Rulers.*
Messengers. When confronted with the problem of worshiping both the supreme god and the lesser divinities under one name, the early priests invented the orders of angels who were assistants to the primary deity. The Koran classifies them in various ways. Nineteen are in charge of hell-fire, eight support the god's throne on Judgment Day, several remove the souls of the righteous at death, two accompany every mortal during life; one writes the good deeds, and the other the evil deeds. Four of these are Archangels: Gabriel, Azrael, Israfel, Michael. The Syrians had three classes of angels: the upper are Cherubim, Thrones, Seraphim; the middle, Lords, Powers, and Rulers; the lower Angels, Archangels, Principalities. Some believe Gabriel was the highest of all angels. The early Hebrews grouped the angels into ten classes: the Bene Elohim, Cherubim, Erelim, Hashmalim, Ishim, Malachim, Ophannim, Seraphim, Sishanim, and Tarshishim. According to some authors all of the angels originated from the Egyptians who classed the inferior or lesser deities under one god. Some say they have two or more pair of wings. When Mohammed saw the archangel Jibril (Gabriel) he reported that he had six hundred pairs of wings. *See also* Angirasa; Anunaki; Apsarases; Cherub; Rishi.

Angerboda *Angerbodha, Angrboda, Angrbodha* (Norse; Teutonic)
Also known as: *Iormungandr, Jormungandr, Ljod, Midgard Serpent, Midgardsormen.*
Giant. Angerboda is a giant who lives in Utgard. She is in charge of the East wind. She is either mother or foster-mother of Loki, Fenrir the wolf, the death queen Hel and Jormungandr, who is also known as the Midgard Serpent. Under the name Ljod she became the maidservant of Freyja. Some say that she is the mate of Loki, the trickster god *See also* Fenrir; Gullveig; Hel; Loki; Midgard.

Angerbodha (Teutonic) *see* Angerboda.

Angerona (Etruscan, Roman)
Angerona is the ancient Goddess of the Winter Solstice and sometimes called a goddess of death. She is associated with the practice of keeping the name of a god from the enemy. She may represent the silence of winter and the fragility of the ecosystem. She is shown with her mouth sealed and one finger placed on it. Her feast known as Angeronalia or the Divalia is held on December 21. *See also* Ceres.

Angervadil (Icelandic; Teutonic)
Also known as: *Angurvadel.*
Magic sword. This sword belongs to the Icelandic hero, Frithiof (also spelled Fridthjof). It blazes in time of war and shines with a dim light in times of peace. The saga of Frithiof was created in later times (approximately C.E. 1300).

Angeyja (Norse; Teutonic)
Water goddess. Angeyja is the personification of the waves. She is one of Heimdall's nine mothers (for the names of the other eight mothers, *see* Heimdall). *See also* Ran.

Angiras *Angiris* (India) *see* Agni; Brihaspati; Daksha; Kuhu; Rishi.

Angirasa (Hindu; India)
The Angirasa are descendants of the fire god Agni who are charged with protecting the sacrificial fires. These celestial bodies are deities of fire and light and may be seen as meteors. *See also* Agni; Brihaspati.

Angiris (India) *see* Angiras.

Angitia (Italian)
Also known as: *Circe* (Greek).
Goddess of healing, herbs, oration and witchcraft. *See also* Circe.

Angoi (Borneo) Creator.
Angoi gave breath to mortals, but was cut to pieces by another deity. From the god's pieces, noxious animals were created.

Angpetu Wi (Dakota People, North America)
Name of the sun.

Angra Mainyu *Angro Mainyus* ("Angry Spirit") *Anro-mainyus* (Mazdaism, Zoroastrian; Persia)
Also known as: *Agri-manios* (Greek), *Agro-manyus, Aharman* (name used in later times), *Ahriman* (Pahlavi dialect), *Ahrimanes, Drauga* (Old Persian), *Druj, Manyu.*
This wicked, evil prince of demons is the chief opponent of Ahura Mazda, the god of light. It is said that he may have been created by Ahura Mazda in a moment of doubt, or that he arose from the abyss of endless darkness. At the resurrection he will be slain by Keresaspa on Mount Damavand, or imprisoned for eternity. With his disposal, all evil will be removed from the world. Angra Mainyu created a host of demons to assist him in his quest to overcome good. Azhi Dahaka, the dragon, was created by Angra Mainyu to destroy the faithful. A great lizard was formed by him to destroy the Gaokerena Tree which grows in the cosmic ocean, Vourukasha. Other demons who fall under his command are the Drujs, who were his servants and the Daevas. His epithet, Druj, signifies Ahura Mazda as the embodiment of deception. In some renderings, Druj is said to be at his side representing the female embodiment of evil. All sorrow, pain, disease, and death are caused by Angra Mainyu. The greatest satisfaction for this "demon of all demons" is when a mortal turns away from Ahura Mazda. Angra Mainyu presides over a host of Drugas who are monstrous female fiends, Daevas, Pairikas, and the Yata. The Kavis and Karapans, who are priests of false religions, also fall under his jurisdiction. Jahi, a female fiend, roused Angra Mainyu from a long sleep and convinced him to pour poison over the body of Gaya Maretan, the first man. By doing so, Angra Mainyu created sin, misery and disease in the world. He can change his outward appearance to a lizard, snake, or a youth. When Zoroaster was born this arch

demon attempted to seduce him into evil. *See also* Aeshma;
Ahi; Ahura Mazda; Asha Vahishtra; Azazel (Islamic); Azi
Dahaka; Daevands; Drujs; Gaokerena Tree; Gaya Maretan; Jahi; Keresaspa; Nasu; Pairikas; Sraosha; Vayu; Vourukasha; Yata; Zahhak; Zoroaster.

Angrboda (Teutonic) *see* Fenrir.

Angrbodha (Teutonic) *see* Angerboda.

Angro Mainyus (Persia) *see* Angra Mainyu.

Anguissance (Celtic) *see* Arawn.

Angurvadel (Teutonic) *see* Angervadil.

Angus *Aengus, Cengus, Engus, Oengus, Oenghus* (Celtic, Irish)
Also known as: *Angus Mac Og, Angus Od, Angus of the
Brugh, Mac Ind Og, Mac Oc, Mac Og, Oengus of the Bruigh.*

Angus is a god of love, a patron deity of young people, the
deity of youth and beauty and a shape-changer. A Tuatha De
Danann, he is the son of Dagda and the river-goddess, Boann.
In some myths, Dana, (Danu) is mentioned as his mother. As
was the custom for royal children, he was raised by a foster parent, in his case, the god, Midir. A minor deity, his tale is one
of magic, music and romance with several variations. A musician, he played a golden harp and all who heard it were
enchanted and fell under his spell. In this version of his story
we are told that he slept all winter and arose at spring's dawn.
In a dream, the beautiful Caer Ibormeith (Caer Yewberry)
appeared from the Otherworld and he instantly fell in love.
Determined to make his dream a reality, he set out in search of
her with the help of Bodb, king of the Sidi of Munster. Although
he had the gift of eternal youth, he was sick with love and
became gravely ill during his travels. Eventually he found his
loved one, bound by silver chains to one hundred and forty-
nine other young women, all in the images of swans. He
changed himself into a swan and rescued her. Together, as they
flew off to the safety of his palace in the fairy mounds, their
beautiful swan song put everyone to sleep for three days and
three nights. Angus' dark, obsessive side was illustrated when
he abducted his brother Mider's wife Etain, kept her encased
in glass and carried her with him all the time. In this vein, it is
said that Angus, after being away, returned to find that his
father, Dagda, had not given him a castle *(sidhe)*, as he did the
other members of the Tuatha De Danann. Furious, he evicted
his father from his dwelling and took it for himself. In other
versions of this myth, Angus ousted Elcmhaire (Elcmar) and
not his father from the castle, Brugh na Boinne and it became
his residence. Elcmhaire was his mother Boann's husband.
Angus was the result of an illicit affair she had with Dagda.
Angus' sacred animal is the pig. He is similar to other dying
gods, Adonis, Attis, Dumuzi, and Tammuz. Compare him to
Mabon. *See also* Boann; Cailleach Bheur; Dagda; Dana; Etain;
Mider.

Angus Mac Og (Celtic) *see* Angus; Cailleach Bheur.

Angus Od (Celtic) *see* Angus.

Angus of the Brugh (Celtic, Irish) *see* Angus.

Angusta (Eskimo) *see* Anguta.

Anguta (Eskimo)
Also known as: *Angusta.*

Anguta is called the shadowy father of the sea-goddess Sedna.
In myth he cut off her fingers when she ran from the sea-birds.
See also Sedna.

Anhefta (Egypt)
Anhefta is the protective spirit who guards one end of the
corridor in the Ninth Sector of Tuat. Ermen-ta guards the other
end. *See also* Ab-ta; Tuat.

Anher (Egypt) *see* Anhur.

Anhert (Egypt) *see* Anhur.

Anhir (Egypt) *see* Anhur.

Anhoret (Egypt) *see* Anhur.

Anhorte (Egypt) *see* Anhur.

Anhur *Anher, An-her, Anhert, Anhir, An-hur* (Egypt)
Also known as: *Anhur-Shu, Anhoret, Anouris, Onouris*
(Greek), *Onuris, Theb-ka* (as God of the Underworld).

Sky god. God of the dead. God of war. Anhur is the son of
Hathor in her form of Her-t. His wife was the lion-headed goddess Mehit. As a solar deity he was worshiped at Abydos. In the
metropolitan area of Heliopolis he was often associated with
Shu (a local god) and called Anhur-Shu; his consort was Tefnut.
Anhur was also known as the divine huntsman of This in Upper
Egypt. He stands in the prow of the sun god Ra's boat as "Slayer
of the Enemies." Anhur is shown as a warrior wearing a headdress with four plumes. He wears a long embroidered robe and
carries a spear. Sometimes he holds a cord leading the sun. The
Greeks identified Anhur with Ares. In the Christian era, he was
identified with St. George. *See also* Ares; Hathor.

Anhur-Shu (Egypt) *see* Anhur.

Ani (Egypt)
His residence is in Tuat (the underworld). He is possibly a
lord of festivals and the new moon. Ani is mentioned in one of
the ancient hymns in relationship to Amen-Ra. *See also* Amen-Ra;
Tuat.

Anila (India) *see* Vasus.

Animiki (Ojibway People, North America)
He is the god of thunder and the creator of the west wind.

Aningan (Eskimo) *see* Alignak; Idlirvirissong.

Anioch (Greek)
Also known as: Eniocha.

It was either Anioch or Eurydice who was married to king
Creon of Thebes. Anioch is the mother of Enioche, Haemon,
Megara, Menoeceus and Pyrrha. *See also* Eurydice (C); Megara;
Pyrrha.

Aniran (Persia) *see* Khshasthra Vairya.

Aniruddha (India) *see* Bana; Kama (A); Krishna; Pradyuma.

Anit (Egypt) A goddess of one of the cities of ancient Egypt.

Anith (Celtic) *see* Eire.

Anitsutsa (Cherokee People, North America) The Pleiades.

Anjama (India) *see* Dikpalas.

Anjana (India) *see* Lokapalas.

Anjea (Australia)
Creator. She forms babies from mud and places them in the womb of women.

Ank (Egypt) *see* Ankh.

Ankamma (India)
She is one of the Mutyalamma goddesses who are deities of the household. She is the goddess of cholera or sometimes as disease in general. *See also* Mutyalamma.

Ankh (A) (Egypt)
Also known as: *Ank.*
Emblem. The ankh is the symbol of "life." It is a T-shaped figure with a loop on top. The name is similar to the Ankus which is the scepter of Indra and is also an elephant goad.

Ankh (B) (Egypt)
Also known as: *Anukis* (Greek), *Khnum.*
Ankh is another name for Khnum as a creator. *See also* Anuket, Khnum.

Ankhat (Egypt) *see* Isis.

Ankhi (Egypt)
A monster serpent with a bearded mummiform god growing out from each side of its body.

Ankt (Egypt) *see* Anouke.

Ankusha (India)
Also known as: *Chak-yu-ma* (Tibet)
This tiger-headed goddess is a Shakti. With her consort Vijaya, she is the Door-keeper of the East. On the Sixth Day in the Bardo World, she is found with three other female goddesses: Kinkini-Dhari, Pashadhari, and Vajra-shringkhala. There are also four male Door-keepers: Amritahari, Hayagriva, Vijaya, and Yamantaka. *See also* Amrtakundali; Hayagriva; Kinkini-Dhari; Shakti; Vijaya; Yamantaka.

Anna-Nin (Middle East) *see* Anat; Nana.

Anna Perenna (Roman) *see* Ana-Purna.

Anna-Perenna (India) *see* Ana-Purna.

Annancy (Africa) *see* Ananse.

Annapurna (India) *see* Ana-purna.

Annar (Teutonic) A dwarf. *See also* Anar; Dwarfs.

Annfwn (Celtic) *see* Achren.

Anningan (Eskimo) *see* Alignak.

Annis (A) (Celtic) *see* Ked.

Annis (B) (Sumer) *see* Inanna.

Annun (Celtic) *see* Annfwn.

Annunaki (Sumer) *see* Anunnaki.

Annuthat (Middle East) *see* Anat.

Annwn (Celtic)
Also known as: *Annfwn.*
This is the home of the dead, ruled by Arawn. Annwn is a beautiful paradise island that permeates serenity. In later legends Arthur sailed with a large crew to raid Annwn and carry off a magic cauldron. *See also* Achren; Arawn; Pwyll.

Annwvyn (Celtic) *see* Achren, Pwyll.

Anobret (Greek) *see* Cronus.

Anoi-Diggan-Juje (Dhammai People, India)
Anoi-Diggan-Juje and Abugupham-Bumo were the first mortals. Their parents are the brother and sister frogs, Lujju-phu and Jassuju. *See also* Shuznaghu.

Anonach (Celtic) *see* Eire.

Anos (Mesopotamia) *see* Anu (A); Anu (B).

Anouke (Egypt)
Also known as: *Ankt.*
Goddess of War. Anouke is a member of a Nubian triad. She wears a curved feathered crown, and carries a spear. Anouke may be the same as Anta or Anath who is an Egyptian deity originating from the Asiatic people.

Anouris *see* Anhur.

Anpao (Dakota People, North America)
A Janus-like two-faced being.

Anpu (Egypt) *see* Anubis.

Anquat (Egypt) *see* Isis.

Anquet *Anuket* (Egypt)
"Giver of Life." With Khnum and Satis this goddess is one of the Elephantine Triad. *See also* Anukis; Isis; Khnum.

Anrita (India)
She is the wife of Adharma and mother of Maya. *See also* Maya (C).

Anro-mainyus (Persia) *see* Angra Mainyu.

Ansa (India) *see* Adityas; Mitra; Varuna.

Anshar *Anshur, Ashur, Asshur* (Assyro-Babylonia, Sumer)
Also known as: *Assorors, Shar.*
God of Sky and Heavens. Warrior god. Anshar and his sister-wife Kishar are the offspring of Lakhame and Lakhumu. They in turn produced the gods Anu, Anatu, and Ea. Some say they are also parents of Enlil. Anshar and Kishar were the grandparents of Marduk. Anshar is the progenitor of the Babylonian pantheon. He was victorious over the Dragon of Chaos during the great work of Creation. Sometimes his principal consort was the goddess Ninlil. As Ashur, he is the head of the Assyrian pantheon. He is shown as a winged disk, or mounted on a bull. Sometimes he is depicted floating in the air. Anshar is similar to Apsu. He might be the same as the Greek Assoros and Kissare. Anshar is associated with Ea in the legend of Tiamat. *See also* Apsu; Anu (B); Ea; Enlil; Igigi; Lahamu and Lahmu; Marduk; Ninlil; Tiamat.

Anshashpands (Persia) *see* Amesha Spentas.

Anshumat (India) *see* Sagara.

Anshur (Sumer) *see* Anshar; Ashur.

Ansuman (India)
This god keeps vital organs functioning properly. *See also* Surya.

Anta (Asia Minor) *see* Anahita.

Antaeus (Greek)
God of Darkness. Antaeus, a Libyan giant, is the son of Gaea (the Earth) and the sea god Poseidon, or perhaps Gaea and the blood of the castrated Uranus. His sister, Charybdis, guarded the straits of Messina with Scylla. His brother Ogyges, was a king of Athens who married Thebe, the daughter of Zeus. A wrestler, Antaeus would challenge all strangers visiting his kingdom. Occasionally he was thrown, but when his feet touched earth he was immediately revitalized and became even stronger. The roof of the temple he had built in Poseidon's honor was adorned with the skulls of his former opponents. When Heracles discovered that the earth was the source of his strength, he lifted him above the ground and gave him a bear hug that killed him. Tinga, the widow of Antaeus, became the mother of Sophax, by Heracles. Compare Antaeus to Alcyoneus. For siblings names, see Giants. *See also* Charybdis; Gaea; Poseidon; Scylla.

Antaf (Egypt) *see* Akeneh; Apepi.

Antaka (India) "He Who Ends Life." *See also* Yama.

Antanzah (Mesopotamia) *see* Anu.

Antares (Persia) *see* Hapto-iringa.

Antariksha (Vedic; India)
The atmosphere where gods and demons struggle for supremacy. *See also* Prithiva.

Antauges (Greek) *see* Dionysus.

Antea (Greek) Another name for Stheneboea (q.v.).

Antenor (Greek)
Antenor was a Trojan prophet and advisor. His spouse is Theano who was one of Athena's priestesses. His sons are Acamas, one of the leaders of the Trojan War, who was killed in the war; Agenor, a Trojan hero; Archelous, a leader in the Trojan War; Coon, who was killed by Agamemnon in the Trojan War; Demoleon, who was also killed in the Trojan War; Glaucus, who was also killed by Agamemnon in the Trojan War; Helicaon, wounded in the Trojan War; Iphidamas, also killed by Agamemnon in the Trojan War; Laocoon; Laodamas; Lycaon, also wounded in the Trojan War; Pedaeus, who was Antenor's son by another woman; Polybus; Polydamas, accused of being a traitor. Antenor has one daughter, Crino. The idea for Odysseus to steal the Palladium came from Antenor. It was also Antenor's idea to built the Wooden Horse. *See also* Acamas (B); Agenor; Archelous; Palladium; Polydamas.

Antero Vipunen *Antero Wipunen* (Finnish)
Deity of Wisdom. Wainamoinen received the three lost words of magic from this giant by entering his body and working magic.

Antero Wipunen (Finnish) *see* Antero Vipunen.

Anteros (Greek)
God of Passion. God of mutual love. God of tenderness. Avenger of unrequited love. Anteros is the son of Ares and Aphrodite. (In some versions of his legend, he is said to be the son of Aphrodite and her husband, the fire god, Hephaistos.) His twin brother and adversary is Eros, the god of love. His other siblings are Phobos, the god of panic; Pallor, the god of terror; Deimos, sometimes known as the god of dread; Enyo, goddess of war; Harmonia (Hermoine), goddess of harmony. His brother, the beautiful god of love, Eros received most of the attention. Anteros is mentioned as his attendant. *See also* Aphrodite; Ares; Eros; Harmonia (A); Hephaistos.

Antetu (Egypt) Another name for Sekhem or possibly Ra.

Antevorta (Roman)
Goddess of Prophecy. The Future. She is the sister of Postverta (at one time they were one goddess), the goddess of the past. *See also* Postverta.

Anthat (Asia Minor)
Also known as: *Anta*.
Mother goddess. She is possibly a horse deity or a goddess of battle. Little else is known. She is sometimes shown in battle garments. *See also* Anat.

Antheia (Greek)
Antheia was Hera's name when she was an adolescent. *See also* Hera.

Antheti (Egypt) *see* Aai.

Antheus (Greek) *see* Dionysus.

Anthios (Greek) *see* Dionysus.

Anti (Egypt)
God of the Ferrymen. Anti is the ferryman who brought Isis across to the island where Seth had isolated himself. *See also* Isis; Seth.

Anticleia (A) *Antikleia* (Greek)
Dawn goddess. Anticleia is the daughter of the thief Autolycus and Amphithea. She was seduced by the cunning Sisyphus and became pregnant. In some renditions she was married to Laertes, the king of Ithaca, at the time and in others Sisyphus arranged the marriage upon learning about her pregnancy. The father of the child, Odysseus, could have been either man. Anticleia adored her son and when she thought that he had been killed at Troy she died of grief or killed herself. Anticleia is often identified with dawn's light or evening light. She is also associated with Odysseus in his visit to hell. *See also* Autolycus; Odysseus; Sisyphus.

Anticleia (B) (Greek)
Also known as: *Philinoe*
She is the daughter of Iobates (also known as Amphianax) the king of Lycia. Her sister is Stheneboea (q.v.). *See also* Bellerophon; Iobates.

Anticleia (C) (Greek)

She is the wife of the surgeon Machaon, the co-ruler of parts of Thessaly, who was one of Helen's suitors. *See* Machaon.

Anticleia (D) (Greek)

She is the mother of Periphetes, by Poseidon or Hephaestus.

Antigone (A) (Greek)

Dawn goddess. Antigone is the daughter of Oedipus and Jocasta or possibly Euryganeia. She is the sister of Eteocles, Ismene and Polynices. When her blind father Oedipus was exiled by the Thebans, Creon and his own sons, Polynices and Eteocles, Antigone guided and cared for him. His sons stayed behind, squabbled over the throne and finally killed one another in the war of Seven Against Thebes. The disgraced father and his loving daughter finally found solace in Colonus, near Athens. On his deathbed, the king of Athens, Theseus restored honor to the old man. Before her father's death, Antigone was abducted by Creon, who wanted to capture the old man. Theseus rescued her. When she heard of her brothers' deaths she defied an order by Creon and administered rites to Polynices. Enraged, Creon punished her by incarcerating her in a cave or burying her alive in her brother's grave. She committed suicide or was killed by Haemon, Creon's youngest son. It has also been said that when Haemon found her dead, he killed himself. In a different rendition, Hyginus wrote that Haemon aided her escape from his father Creon. They had a son together, who in later years, traveled to Thebes. The young man was recognized by his grandfather Creon, who identified him by a family birthmark. The bitter man would not forgive his son Haemon for defying his orders. Haemon then murdered Antigone and killed himself. *See also* Actor; Anticleia; Oedipus.

Antigone (B) (Greek)

She is the daughter of Laomedon and the sister of Priam. Hera turned her into a stork for comparing her own beauty to Hera's. *See also* Hera; Priam.

Antigone (C) (Greek)

She is the daughter of Pheres and mother of the Argonaut Asterion. Her husband Cometes committed adultery with Aegialeia, Diomedes' wife. *See also* Aegialeia; Pheres.

Antigone (D) (Greek)

She is the daughter of Euryton the Argonaut and king of Ohthia who was accidentally killed by Peleus. She married Peleus and became the mother of Polydora. When Peleus deserted her, she committed suicide. *See also* Peleus; Polydora.

Antikleia (Greek) *see* Anticleia.

Antilochus (Greek)

He is the eldest son of the wise, brave Nestor, the king of Pylos, and Anaxibia or possibly Eurydice. His siblings are Aretus, Echephron, Paeon (he is possibly the son and not the brother of Antilochus), Peisidice, Peisistratus, Perseus, Polycaste, Stratius and Thrasymedes. He was one of Helen's suitors and fought in the Trojan War. He died while defending his father Memnon and was buried in the same grave as his dear friend Achilles and Patroclus. *See also* Achilles; Memnon; Patroclus; Perseus.

Antimache (Greek) *see* Admete.

Antimachus (A) (Greek)

A Trojan, he is the father of Hippolochus, Hippomachus and Peisander.

Antimachus (B) (Greek)

His parents are Heracles and one of the fifty daughters of Thespius.

Antion (Greek)

Antion is associated with Perimele and is possibly the father of Ixion (q.v.).

Antiope (A) (Greek)

Also known as: *Hippolyta, Melanippe.*

Queen of the Amazons. Antiope is the daughter of the god of war, Ares, and the Queen of the Amazons, Otrera. She is the sister of Hippolyte. A warrior, Antiope had a child named Hippolytus by the hero, Theseus. It is debatable if Antiope fell in love with Theseus and left her territory willingly or was kidnapped by this adventurer. He did campaign against the Amazons, with the assistance of Peirithous, the king of Lapith, and possibly Heracles and left with the Amazon queen, variously called Antiope, Melanippe or Hippolyta. The Amazons, led by Antiope's sister Hippolyte, descended on Athens in retaliation and a fierce battle ensued. Many of the Amazons were slaughtered and it is said that Hippolyte died of a broken heart. After the birth of her son, Hippolytus, Antiope also died. There is the possibility that Theseus, generally known as a just person and defender of the oppressed killed her when she opposed his marriage to Phaedra, the daughter of Minos. *See also* Amazons; Ares; Arne; Minos; Phaedra; Theseus.

Antiope (B) (Greek)

Lover of Zeus. She is the daughter of the river god Asopus and Metope, or Nyceteus and Polyxo. Antiope is the mother of the twins Amphion and Zethus. Zeus, who lusted after the beautiful young woman, came to her disguised as a satyr and impregnated her. Fearful of her father's wrath, she escaped from Thebes to Sicyon were she married King Epopeus, the son of Poseidon and Canace. Her father pursued her, intending to vent his wrath on her husband and either killed him or found him dead. In some renditions, Epopeus committed suicide when he found out that Antiope was pregnant by Zeus. Asopus died as well, either from a wound suffered in the encounter with Epopeus or from the humiliation of his daughter's pregnancy. With his last breath he begged his brother Lycus to punish Antiope. On the way back to Thebes with Lycus, she gave birth to twins, Amphion and Zethus. Her uncle made her abandon the babies and he dragged her home. Once there she was imprisoned and treated cruelly by Lycus' wife, Dirce. Years passed, Antiope managed to escape and was reunited with her sons. Outraged when they heard how their birth mother had been treated they went after Dirce and Lycus. Lycus was either murdered or driven from the throne and Dirce was tied to a bull and dragged to her death. In a variation of the theme; Dirce was punished with insanity by the god Dionysus. She wandered around Greece until she met Phocus, who cured and married her. Not to be confused with Antiope, also known as Hippolyta, the wife of Theseus. To compare to other women who were seduced by Zeus in different forms, *see* Aegina; Danae; Europa; Leda. *See also* Amphion; Zethus.

Antiope (C) (Greek) *see* Muses.

Antiope (D) (Greek)

She is the wife of Eurytus and the mother of Clytius, Iole and Iphitus. When Eurytus refused to give her to Heracles, he was killed.

Antiphates (Greek) *see* Abas (B).

Antit (Middle East) *see* Anat.

Antiu and Hentiu (Egypt)

Assistants and protectors. The Antiu are four beings, each having four serpent heads, and armed with knives and ropes, on the right hand of Ra's sun boat. They are found in the Tenth Division of Tuat. *See also* Tuat.

Antu (Assyro-Babylonian)

Also known as: *Antum.*

Antu was the first consort of the sky god, Anu. Their offspring are the underworld gods, the Anunnaki and the seven evil demons, the Utukki. She was replaced by Anu's second consort, Ishtar (Inanna), who is sometimes called her daughter. *See also* Anat; Anu; Anunnaki; Enlil; Utukki.

Antum (Assyro-Babylonian) Another spelling for Antu.

Anu (A) (Celtic)

Also known as: *Ana, Black Annis, Buan-Ann, Dana, Danu, Don, Nanu.*

Mother of gods. Goddess of fertility. Wind goddess (possibly). Culture hero. Anu is an ancestor of the Tuatha De Danann. She is said by some to be the daughter of Dagda. In another myth she is known as the sister of King Math, the spouse of the powerful Irish lord of life and death, Bile, and the mother of Amathaon, Arianrhod, and Gwydion. She is sometimes confused with Danu as part of a triple concept of one deity. "The Paps of Anu" in Co. Kerry were named after Anu. She is also known as Don, the spouse of Beli (the British name for Bile). In the Dane Hills of Leicestershire, where she was known as Black Annis, she was offered human sacrifices. Compare Anu to Aine. *See also* Amathaon; Arianrhod; Bile; Brigit; Dana; Tuatha De Danann.

Anu (B) (Akkadian, Babylonian, Hittite, Hurrian, Sumerian, Syrian)

Also known as: *An* (Sumer), *Ana* (Sumer), *Anos, Anum* (God of Storms, Wind and Waves).

"Heaven." In Mesopotamian mythology, Anu, lord of the firmament, is considered the source of order and the divine king of the natural and supernatural worlds. In Babylonian mythology, Anu the sky god is the son of Anshar and Kishar. He is the father of Ea or others say Ea's father is Anshar. Anu's first consort was Antu by whom he became the father of the underworld gods known as the Anunnaki and the seven evil demons known as the Utukki. His second consort was Innini (Ishtar). The star spirits and the demons of darkness, rain and cold were created by Anu. His shooting stars, known as kishrus, have great strength. Anu is the chief of a triad with Ea and Enlil. In Hurrian-Hittite mythology, tales are told of Anu, Ea and Enlil and the conflict between the older and younger gods. This triad has been credited with teaching divination by pouring oil on water. It is said that Anu created the

heavens, and Ea created the dry land. When he was castrated by Kumbaris, Anu announced to his gleeful foe that in turn he had impregnated Kumbaris with three fearful gods; Atanzah, Teshub and Tigris. Anu has little to do with mortals, although in some instances he is called on to cure illnesses. One of his primary functions is to act as arbiter of the disputes of the gods. His power and authority are wielded with the aid of his creation, the stars, which are his troops, and whose place it is to punish the wicked. Other gods were later identified with him and took on the name Anu. The goddesses Ninkarrak and Gula are both thought to be daughters of Anu, as is Ishtar, who is also known as his second consort. Some of the demons of disease are said to be the offspring of Anu and Enlil. Anu's throne is in Atrahasis, the third or highest heaven. This is where he keeps the Bread and Water of Life (food of immortality). The gate to his heaven is guarded by Tammuz and Nigishzida. From a piece of clay, Anu created the brick god Kulla. Numbers played an important role in Babylonian society. Every proper name could be written in numbers. Anu, the father of the gods, had the perfect number sixty (60). He is shown as a tiara or turban placed on a throne. Anu is the counterpart of the god An of the Sumerians (q.v.). He is associated with Adapa and Marduk. Anu's son, Enlil, was originally the leader of the pantheon. Anu later took over that position. *See also* Adapa; An; Anath; Anshar; Anunnaki; Anus; Apsu; Damkina; Ea; Enki; Enkidu; Enlil; Gula; Igigi; Ishtar; Kishar; Kulla; Kumbaris; Mirsu; Ninkarrak; Nusku; Tammuz; Tigris; Utukki.

Anubis (Egypt)

Also known as: *An-pu, Anpu, Am Ut, Hermanubis* (Greek), *Khent Sehet, Mercury* (Roman), *Sekhem Em Pet, Tep-tu-f.*

Underworld deity. Early god of the dead. God of the cemetery. Guardian God. God of the soul through the Land of the Shades. Director of embalming. Anubis, known as the jackal-headed god, may be the son of Osiris, Set or Ra and Nephthys or Isis. One myth states that he was abandoned by his mother and raised by Isis. In the Pyramid Texts, he is known as the fourth son of Ra, and his daughter is Kebehut. As the son of Osiris and Nephthys he is said to have swallowed his father (this myth alludes to the night swallowing day). He is the judge and protector of the dead, and possibly the messenger of Osiris. Some say he was replaced by Osiris. He was also the protector of tombs and one of the eight early Egyptian gods. He is the dog or jackal-headed god of funerals and mummification. He is in charge of the scales that weigh the hearts of the dead against the Feather of Truth in the Hall of Judgment before Osiris and the forty-two gods. His duty is to cast the dead to the Eaters of Souls if the heart is not in balance. Anubis accompanies Osiris during the Second Hour of the Night. He is also the guardian of Khersek-Shu, the door which the deceased enter (see Tuat or Shesat Maket Neb-S). Anubis is the Greek rendering of the Egyptian name Anpu. As Anpu he is the god of the nomes of Anpu and Sep. It is suggested that Anubis was originally a jackal who became a god because he devoured corpses. An image of a reclining black jackal is depicted on the doors of numerous rock tombs. He is represented as a bushy tailed black jackal, or a black skinned man with the head of a dog, or with a human body and the head of a jackal. The antelope is sacred to Anubis. The sharp eyesight of this animal deemed it prophetic. As conductor of the souls, he was also given the name Hermanubis by the Greeks. The Romans identified him with Mercury. *See also* Amit; Ap-uat; Hermes; Horus; Osiris.

Anuket (Egypt) *see* Anukis.

Anukis *Anqet, Anquet, Anuket, Anukisuas, Anukit* (Egypt, Greek, Sudan; possibly introduced from Ethiopia)
Anukis is the Greek rendering of the name Anuket. She is the second wife of the god Khnum and the mother of Satis. She was charged with controlling the the narrow course of the upper Nile and the Cataracts. She is one of the Triad of Elephantine with Khnum and Satis. Her principal place of worship was in Nubia. She is depicted as a woman wearing a crown of feathers, usually found with a red parrot, or as a woman holding a tall papyrus scepter and wearing a high crown of feathers. Her sacred animal is the gazelle. *See also* Khnum; Satis

Anukit *see* Anukis.

Anulap (Island of Truk, Micronesia)
Possibly a creator. Husband of the creator Ligoububfanu. Teacher of magic and knowledge. *See also* Ligobund.

Anum (Mesopotamia) *see* Anu (B).

Anumati (India)
The moon worshiped as a goddess during the latter half of the lunar cycle immediately before becoming full.

Anunaki (Sumer) *see* Anunnaki.

Anungite (Pawnee People, North America)
The abode of spiritual power.

Anunit (Assyria, Babylon, Sumer)
Also known as: *Anunitum.*
Moon goddess. She is known variously as the daughter of Baal, Samas or Sin. Sometimes she is known as the sister of Samas and the wife of Sin. Anunit is the mistress of battle, the bearer of the bow and quiver. Her symbol of the sun with eight rays is similar to that of the goddess Ishtar (q.v.).

Anunitum (Babylon)
An early goddess worshiped at Sippar. She later merged with Ishtar (q.v.).

Anunnaki *Annunaki, Anunaki, Ennuki* (Assyro-Babylonia, Sumer)
Assembly of high gods representing the Sumerian pantheon. Presided over by An and Enlil, the Anunnaki is composed of Anu, Ea and the Igigi who are the children of Anshar and Kishar. (Some say the Anunnaki were created by Marduk and others say the Anunnaki were created by Anu.) The Assyrians and Babylonians believed that the Anunnaki were the three hundred gods of the lower of the three heavens. It is also said by some that the Anunnaki created Babylon, Eridu and Esagilla from the sea. When the Anunnaki decided to destroy humankind with a great flood, one of the gods informed Ziusudra, King of Shurappak, of the decision. He built an ark in which the seeds of the mortals were preserved during the seven days and seven nights the waters raged. After surviving the deluge, he was accepted as a deity and put in charge of the country of Dilmun. The Anunnaki lived in or below Arallu, the place of the dead. Their palace is known as Diligina or Ekalgina. Anunnaki corresponds to the Igigi who were gods of the middle or upper heaven. As the offspring of Anu and Antu, the Anunnaki are the siblings of the seven evil demons known as the Utukki. *See also* Anat; Anu; Apsu; Arallu; Dilmun; Igigi; Utukki.

Anunu (Egypt) *see* Neith; Net.

Anup (Egypt) *see* Anubis.

Anus (Hittite, Hurrite)
Alulus, the sky god, was king of heaven for nine years before his son Anus ousted him. Anus ruled for nine years, then he in turn was overcome by his son Kumarbis. Kumarbis swallowed his father's testicles. Anus cursed him and fled to Heaven, where he hid. Anus is comparable to the Akkadian Anu (q.v.). *See also* Alulus; Kumarbis; Ullikummis.

Anush (Armenian)
The first queen of Azdahak. Mother of dragons.

Anzety (Egypt)
He was a local god of the town of Busiris, who preceded Osiris. Later his attributes were incorporated into those of Osiris. Anzety was depicted by a human head on a pole. His arms hold the crook and the flail. *See also* Osiris.

Anzu (Persian, Sumerian) *see* Zu.

Ao (A) (Polynesia, New Zealand)
First element. Ao represents light and the opposite of Po, the primeval darkness. Ao is also considered the first ancestor of the Maori People. *See also* Aos; Po; Tangaloa.

Ao (B) (China)
In Chinese cosmology, Ao is a fish or a monster. *See also* Dragon Kings.

Ao Ch'in *Ao K'in* (China) *see* Dragon Kings.

Ao-Jun (China) *see* Dragon Kings.

Ao-Kahiwahiwa (Polynesia) *see* Tawhiri-ma-tane.

Ao-Kanapanapa (Polynesia)
"Glowing Red Clouds." One of the children of the god of winds, storms and hurricanes, Tawhiri-ma-tea.

Ao Kuang (China) *see* Dragon Kings.

Ao-Marama (Polynesia)
This light deity is one of Po's children. *See also* Ao.

Ao-Nui (Polynesia)
"Dense Clouds." One of the thirteen children of the god of turbulent weather, Tawhiri-ma-tea.

Ao-Pakakina (Polynesia) *see* Tawhiri-ma-tea.

Ao-Pakarea (Polynesia)
"Wildly Drifting Clouds." *See also* Tawhiri-ma-tea.

Ao-Potango (Polynesia)
"Dark Heavy Clouds." *See also* Tawhiri-ma-tea.

Ao-Pouri (New Zealand, Polynesia)
Also known as: *Po.*
World of darkness. When Rangi the sky lay in union on Papa the earth, in the beginning, all the gods were held under their

bodies. This was the darkness called Ao-pouri. The gods involved in the separation of Rangi and Papa are Tu-matauenga, Tane-mahuta, Tawhiri-ma-tea, Rongo-ma-tane, Tangaroa, and Haumia-tikitiki. See also Papa; Po; Rangi; Tangaroa.

Ao-Roa (Polynesia) see Tawhiri-ma-tea.

Ao Shun (China) see Dragon Kings.

Ao-Toto (Polynesia)
An ancestor of Tawhiri, Ao-Toto is either a god or an early culture hero. See also Tawhiri-ma-tea.

Ao-Whekere (Polynesia) see Tawhiri-ma-tea.

Ao-Whetuma (Polynesia) "Fiery Clouds." See also Tawhiri-ma-tea.

Aobh (Celtic) see Aebh; Aed.

Aoi (Coptic)
This was a god that Jesus prayed to. See also Pistis Sophia.

Aoide (Greek)
She is the Boeotian muse of song. Her sisters are Melete, the muse of practice, and Mneme, the muse of memory.

Aoife (Irish)
Also known as: Aeife, Aife.
Aoife was a warrior woman who resided in Scotland. She was a rival of Scathach the Amazon queen who is the eponymous goddess of Skye. Aoife was defeated in battle by CuChulainn, the mortal son of the deity Lugh. A peace treaty was drawn up with a provision that Aoife would bear CuChulainn's son. She abided by the agreement. When she heard that CuChulainn had mated with Emer, she decided to get even. She raised her son Conlaoch to excel in every skill. She also instructed him never to refuse a challenge, never to back down from anyone and never to reveal his name. The last dictate cost him his life, for he was killed by his father, CuChulainn, who did not know his identity. In another version, Aoife began life as the adopted daughter of Bodb Dearg. She replaced her sister Aebh as the mate of Ler and became the step-mother to Aed, Conn, Fiachra and Fionnuala. Extreme jealousy of the children caused her to turn them into swans. She designated that they would roam the world for nine hundred years. Boadh Dearg in turn changed Aeife into a witch of the air and assigned her the duty of sweeping the wind forever. See also Bodb Dearg; Manannan Mac Llyr.

Aokeu (Polynesia)
Also known as: Aokeu and Ake.
Probably a sky or flood deity. He and the sea god, Ake, quarrelled about who was the greatest and most powerful. To prove himself Ake caused the sea to rise dramatically while Aokeu poured rain down on the land. The resulting flood destroyed all but Rangi (a mortal in this case) who prayed to Rongo. Rongo brought things back to normal. See also Rangi; Rongo.

Aokeu and Ake (Polynesia) see Aokeu.

Aos (Chalean, Greek, Sumerian)
Also known as: Aa, Hoa, Oannes.
God of light. Some say that Aos is the Greek rendering of

the god Ea. The Assoros and Kissare descended from Aos. See also Aa; Aah.

Ap (Egypt) see Aani; Apepi; Apophis; Utennu.

Ap-Taui (Egypt)
Attendant deity. Ap-taui is one of the gods responsible for administering to Ra in the Eleventh Hour (Section) of Tuat. Five of the gods are armless, and from the neck of one, juts two serpents' heads. Ra's breath gives them life. Their souls live on the sun god's hidden light and their soul food comes from provisions stored in his sun boat. The other attendants' names are Aaiu-f-em-kha-nef, Aunaauif, Hepa, Khnem-renit, Maa, Merenaaui-f, Meskhti, Nerta, Rest-f, Tua-Heru.

Ap-Uat (Egypt)
Also known as: Ophois, Ophois Wepwawet, Sekhem Taui, Upuaut, Upwuat, Wepwawet.
Ap-uat, one of the principal gods mentioned in the Pyramid Texts, is often referred to as Wepwawet in mythology and is often been confused with Anubis, who is his brother. A wolf or jackal-headed god, Ap-uat is mentioned as "The Opener of the Ways," in the First Section (Hour), of the night (which is an ante-chamber of Tuat). Ap-uat rides on the bow of Ra's boat acting as a guide, and a protector. He is also mentioned in connection with the god of the Nile, Hapi, in the text of the Unas, where they are commanded to raise the waters of the great river so that grain could be grown for the king to eat on his journey to the Underworld, and for his future home in the Elysian Field. He was specifically "The Opener of the Ways" to the south, while Anubis was responsible for the northern ways. He is a friend and companion of Osiris. Ap-uat, the oldest-known god worshipped in Abydos (Aabdju) was deposed by Khenty-amentiu. At Asyut or Siut, he was a cemetery god. The standards of Ap-uat and Anubis were the same: a human head wearing a white crown which projects from the back of a lizard. Ap-uat, wolf or jackal-headed, is depicted with a grey or white head, often standing, dressed in a soldier's uniform. See also Anubis; Elysian Field; Khenty-amentiu; Tuat.

Apa (India) see Vasus.

Apam Napat (Indo-Iranian; Hindu)
Known as "Grandson of Waters," he is the son of Vourukasha, the cosmic sea, who was born on a cloud, and became the lover of Anahita. Apam Napat represents lightning and is identified with the Hindu fire god Agni (q.v.). He is the purifier of the seed of the earth and in the animal kingdom. See also Anahita; Vourukasha (A).

Apaosha (Zoroastrian; Persia)
Draught demon. See also Ahriman; Tishtrya.

Apap see Apophis.

Aparna (India) see Shiva.

Apason (Assyro-Babylonia) see Apsu; Belus (B).

Ape (Egypt)
Also known as: Hedj-wer.
This baboon god, called the "Great White One" during the Archaic Period was regarded as a form of Thoth during the Pyramid Age. His duty is to keep watch over Thoth. Thoth is

depicted with the ape god sitting on the back of his head or shoulders. *See also* Thoth.

Apep (Egypt) *see* Aai.

Apepi (Egypt)
Also known as: *Aaapef, Ap, Apap, Apep, Apophis, Pepi.*
Deity of darkness. Ruler of the underworld. Enemy of the sun. Apepi is the fiery, serpent-devil of mist, darkness, night and storms. In order to destroy him, it was necessary to curse him by every name he was known: Am, Aman, Amen, Beteshu, Hau-hra, Hemhemti, Hem-taiu, Iubani, Iubau, Karau-ane-memti, Kenememti, Khak-ab, Khan-ru, Khermuti, Khesef-hra, Nai, Nesht, Qerneru, Qettu, Saatet-ta, Sau, Sebv-ent-seba, Sekhem-hra, Serem-taui, Sheta, Tetu, Turrupa, Uai, and Unti. The priests of Amen-Ra burned wax figures of Apep who daily endeavored to prevent the sun from rising. There are other feared serpents mentioned by the ancient Egyptians. They are Akeneh, Amen, Antaf, Hau, Heka, Hekret, Hemth, Senena-hemthet, Setcheh, Tcheser-tep, and Thethu. Although some have the same names as gods, they are different entities entirely. One serpent named Ami-Hemf who lived on the top of Bakhau, the Mountain of Sunrise, is described as being fifty feet long. Apepi could be associated with Rahabh (Hebrew). Compare Apepi to Tiamat. *See also* Aai, Ab-esh-imy- duat; Ab-ta; Abuk; Aken; Akeneha; Apophis, Gehenna (Hebrew underworld); Hades (Greek); Tuat.

Aper-ta (Egypt)
Another name for Sekhem and possibly Ra. *See also* Aai.

Apet *Epet* (Egypt) *see* Taueret.

Aphangak (Brazil, Peru; South America)
A class of demon. *See also* Kilyikhama.

Aphareus (Greek) *see* Gorgophone.

Apheliotes (Greek) *see* Boreas; Eurus.

Aphrodite (Greek, possibly of Phoenician origins)
Also known as: *Acidalia* (surname); *Acraea* (surname), *Alilat, Alitta, Amathusia* (surname), *Ambologera* (surname), *Anadyomene* (surname; Rising from the Sea), *Androphonos* (Man-slayer), *Antheia* (surname), *Apaturia* (surname), *Aphaci- tis* (surname), *Aphrodite Genetrix, Aphrodite Nymphia, Aphrodite Pandemos, Aphrodite Porne, Aphrodite Urania, Apotrophia, Aracynthias* (surname), *Areia* (surname), *Argennis* (surname), *Callipygos* (surname), *Cnidia* (surname), *Colias* (surname), *Ctesylla* (surname), *Cypria* (surname), *Cythera* (sur- name), *Delia* (surname), *Despoena* (surname), *Dionaea* (sur- name), *Epidaetia* (surname), *Epitragia* (surname), *Epitymbria* (Of the Tombs), *Erycina* (Roman; surname), *Euplios* (fair voy- age), *Genetyllis* (surname), *Hecaerge* (surname), *Hippodameia* (surname), *Idalia* (surname), *Ishtar* (Babylonian), *Kypris, Lime- nia* (surname), *Mechanitis* (surname), *Melaenis* (Black One; surname), *Melinaea, Migonitis* (surname), *Morpho* (surname), *Nicerphoros* (surname), *Pandemos* (surname), *Paphia* (sexual love; surname), *Peitho Suadela* (Roman), *Pelagia, Philia* (sur- name), *Pontia* (she who arose from the sea), *Scotia* (Dark One), *Urania* (surname), *Venus* (Roman), *Zephyritis* (surname), *Zerynthia* (surname).
One of the twelve Olympians. Goddess of love, beauty and sensual desire. Patron of courtesans. She is the beautiful, sen- sual daughter of Zeus and his aunt Dione, or Cronus and Euonyme, or Uranus and Hemera. Some say her mother is Eilei- thyia, the goddess of birth, who is said to be the daughter of Zeus and Hera. Alternately, she was born of sea foam where the severed genitals of Uranus were thrown into the sea by Cronus. Using the prior scenario, she landed either at Paphos in Cyprus or at Cythera, hence her epithets "Kypris" and "Cythera" which also indicate her connection with the goddesses Ishtar and Astarte. Zeus arranged her marriage with his half-brother, the god of fire, Hephaistos. He is an ugly god who has a lame leg. From appearances, their marriage was an unlikely match. Hep- haistos, however, made her beauty shine through his works of art as a smith to the gods. Aphrodite was renowned for her extra-marital affairs with gods and mortals. Her lovers' stations in life were not of importance to her. She delights in her sexu- ality. Some of her lovers were Adonis, Anchises, Ares, Butes, Dionysus, Hermes, Poseidon and Zeus. Her favorite lover was the god of war, Ares, who is the son of Zeus. They had children together: Phoebus, Deimos, Harmonia, Eros, and Anteros. Her other children by gods are Hermaphroditus by Hermes; Eryx by Poseidon; Priapus by Dionysus. Children from her relation- ships with mortals are Aeneas and Lyrus by Anchises; and a boy and a girl by Adonis. She is also the mother of Aeneas, Beroe, Golgos, Hymen, Herophilus, and Rhodos. She was worshipped as Aphrodite Urania (goddess of the sky or, goddess of higher intellectual love), and Aphrodite Pandemos (goddess of the folk, marriage and family life). The red poppy, the rose, the myrtle, the apple, the dove, swan and swallow, the tortoise, ram, the planet Venus and the month of April are sacred to her. She is usually shown nude or slightly clothed in diaphanous drapery material. She is also identified with Astarte, the Egyptian Hathor, the Roman Syria Dea and Venus. Comparable to Ben- ten (Japan) and Sarasvati (India). She is connected to the Oceanids (q.v.). For more information regarding her relation- ships, *see* Adonis; Anchises; Ares; Dionysus; Hermes; Posei- don. *See also* Achilles; Adonis; Adrastia; Aeneas; Aglaia; Aither; Alitta; Anat; Anchises; Anteros; Ariadne; Asopus; Atalanta; Chaos; Eos; Fates; Gaea; Graces; Harmonia (A); Helius; Hep- haistos; Hermaphroditus; Hymen; Ishtar; Sirens; Tiamat; Venus.

Aphson (Babylonia) *see* Apsu.

Api (Egypt) One of the gods in the Pyramid Texts.

Apis (A) (Egyptian)
Also known as: *Asar-Hap* (Greek), *Asar-Hapi* (Greek), "Bull of Amentet," "Bull of the Underworld," *Epaphus* (Egypt), *Hap, Hapi, Hapi-Ankh, Osiris-Apis* (Greek), *Osiris-Hapi* (Greek), *Osorapis* (Greek), *Ptah, Serapis* (Greek).
Originally Apis was considered to be the god of Memphis, Ptah. The bull symbolized the sacred life of Ptah (q.v.). Apis is the Greek modification of the name Hap. Later in the same ani- mal shape the bull was regarded as Osiris. At that time Osiris was called the "Bull of Amentet" or the "Bull of the Under- world." Apis became the most important of the sacred bulls in Egypt. He was Osiris incarnated in bull form. He went to earth as his own representative in the shape of a bull. He was recog- nized by his black hide, triangle of white on his forehead, white

crescent spot on the right side and a knot under his tongue.
When the original Apis died, mourning for him continued until
a new bull fitting the description of the original Apis was found.
The new bull symbolized resurrection. Each apis was venerated
by the priests who gave him food and shelter. During his
twenty-fifth year he was drowned in a holy spring. Later, before
the Roman invasion when the Greeks ruled Egypt, Apis was
worshiped as Serapis. In another myth the sacred bulls Apis of
Memphis, and Mnevis of Heliopolis were dedicated to Osiris.
It was commanded that all Egyptians worship these animals as
they had assisted in the discovery of corn and in sowing the
seed, thus spreading the benefits of agriculture to the people.
After the Late Period Apis was depicted on many coffins as a
sacred bull running with the mummy of the deceased to the
tomb. After the New Kingdom he turned up with a sun-disk
on his head. Apis is pictured as a bull with a star or crescent
between his horns and with an amulet hanging from his neck.
Sometimes Isis sits on his back. He has also been seen wearing
the disk and figure of a sacred serpent (Uraeus) on his head.
Apis is linked to Epaphos, the son of Io. In Greek mythology
Epaphus, the son of Zeus and Io, became the King of Egypt, was
married to Memphis, and founded the city of Memphis. He
was rumored to be the bull Apis. *See also* Amentet; Cherub;
Hap; Mnevis; Osiris; Ptah; Serapis.

Apis (B) (Greek)

Ruler of Apia. Seer. Apis is the son of Phoroneus and Teledyne and the brother of Car and Niobe. A cruel and unjust
ruler, he was deposed by Thelxion and Telchis and killed by the
son of Endymion, Aetolus. He died childless and his nephew
Argus, son of Niobe, succeeded him. Aeschylus wrote that Apis
was a son of Apollo, a seer and a physician originally from Nau-
pactus, who practiced in Argos. *See also* Niobe (B).

Apisirahts (Blackfeet People, North America)

Also known as: *The Morning Star, The Morning Venus God.*
A deified mortal, Apisirahts is the son of the sun god. He
took a mortal girl to heaven. She was allowed to dig for every
root but that of the "forbidden turnip." Out of curiosity, she
disobeyed and uncovered the hole to earth. Forced to return to
earth, she was let down by Spider Man's web. She died longing
for Apisirahts. *See also* Napi.

Apit (Egypt)

One of the goddesses of the city of Unnu or Hermopolis or
possibly another of the many cities of ancient Egypt.

Aplu (Greek) see Apollo.

Apo (Persian)

He is a water deity and a Yazata (q.v.). *See also* Amesha Spentas; Anahita.

Apocatequil (Inca, Peru)

A popular god of lightning, he is the son of the first mortal
Guamansuri (posthumously), and the twin brother of Piguero.
The mother of the twins was brutally murdered by her brothers, the Guachimines. Apocatequil brought his mother back to
life and killed the Guachimines. Ataguchu showed them how
to make a hole from Pacari, the Cave of Refuge, that would lead
them to the land of the Incas. The twins released the first Peruvians from the underworld. They are possibly deities of night

and day. *See also* Creation Legends of the Inca; Pacari (for other
versions of the Inca Creation Legend).

Apochquiahuayan (Aztec, Mexico)

This is another name for the Aztec underworld, Mictlan
(q.v.).

Apoconallotl (Aztec) see Chalchiuhtlicue.

Apollo *Apollon* (Greek)

Also known as: *Abaeus, Abaios, Acersecomes* (surname meaning Unshorn), *Aguieus, Agyieus, Agyieyus, Aplu, Cynthius* (born
on Mount Cynthius), *Delius, Far Darter* (Dealer of Death),
Helios, Hobal, Loxias, Lycean, Lykeious (wolf god), *Moiragete*
(guide of the Moirae), *Musagetes* (patron of the Muses), *Namios*
(He of the Pastures), *Paean* (the Healing God), *Phaenops, Phoebus* (the Shining One), *Phoebus Apollo, Reshep* (Babylon),
Smintheus (mouse-god), *Tushna* (Etruscan).

God of light. God of prophecy. Patron of medicine, music,
the lyre and archery. One of the twelve Olympians. Apollo may
have originated in Asia and was possibly a Hittite god (Hobal).
There is a remote possibility he originated from a Nordic divinity. He is the son of the great god Zeus and Leto (also known as
Latona), the twin of the goddess Artemis and the father of the
physician god Asclepius. Apollo and Artemis, were born on
Delos. He spent three months of the year with the Hyperboreans. The remaining months were spent at Delphi. His various
lovers and numerous children are by Acacallis, Amphithemis
and Miletus; Acantha (no children); by Arsinoe, Eriopis; Asteria, no children; Bolina, no children; by Calliope, Orpheus; by
Calaeno or Thyia, Delphus; Cassandra, no children; Castalia, no
children; by Chione, Philammon; by Chrysorthe, Corona; Clymene, no children; by Coronis or Arsinoe, Asclepius; by Creusa,
Cyrene, Autychus, Idom (possibly), Aristaeus; by Daphne, no children; by Dryope, Amphissus; by Evadne, Iamus; by Issa, Hecuba
(possibly) Troilus; Melia, no children; by Ocyrrhoe, Phasis; by
Parthenope, Lycomedes; by Phtia, Dorus, Laodocus, Polypoetes;
by Procleia, Tenes; by Psamathe, Linus; by Rhoeo, Anius; by
Stilbe, Centaurus, Lapithus; by Syllis, Zeuxippus; by Thyia, Delphus; by Thyria, Cygnus and Phylisu. His homosexual lovers
were Cyparissus and Hyacinthus. Apollo killed the Python and
the Cyclops. The Cyclops, manufacturers of Zeus' thunderbolts,
made the thunderbolt that killed Apollo's son, Asclepius. Apollo
in retaliation killed the Cyclops. As a result of the Cyclops' death,
Apollo was forced to serve, in the capacity of a herdsman, the
Argonaut Admetus for one year. After Tityus, the Euboeoan
giant attempted to rape their mother, Leto, Apollo and Artemis
killed him (some say he died by Zeus' hand). They were also
responsible for slaying Niobe's children. As a sun symbol,
Apollo's spreading golden hairs on his head are likened to rays
of the sun. The bow and arrow represents the same symbology,
as well as depicting the male-female principles. In Greece and
Pre-Columbian America, the arrow represented the sun's rays.
As well as being a phallic symbol, the arrow symbolizes the light
of supreme power. Apollo's sacred birds are the raven and the
swan. His sacred tree is the laurel. His sacred instrument the
lyre, and his sacred island, Delphos. Compare Apollo to the
Hindu god, Vishnu, the Babylonian, Shamash, and the Egyptian god, Horus. *See also* Abaris; Acacallis; Achilles; Actaeon;
Admetus; Aeacus; Aegle; Ajax the Lesser; Aloeides; Amphion;

Apis (B); Ares; Argus (A); Artemis; Aristaeus; Asclepius; Behedety (Egypt); Bel (Celtic); Borvo; Cassandra; Clytia; Curetes; Cyclops; Eurydice (C); Graces; Helius; Hestia; Hymen; Leto; Muses; Niobe; Oceanus; Sinope; Tityus; Zephyrus.

Apollodorus (Greek) Mythologist of the 2nd century B.C.E.

Apollon (Greek) *see* Apollo.

Aponbolinayen *Aponitolau* (Philippine) *see* Ina-Init.

Apophis *Apopophis*
Also known as: *Aaapef, Ap, Apap, Apep, Apepi* (Egypt).
Underworld deity. Apophis is the serpent-devil of mist, darkness, storm, and night. His fiends are called the "the children of rebellion." This immense serpent lives in the other Nile that flows through the vault of heaven. He constantly attempts to thwart the god Ra as he rides daily across the sky in his sun-boat. Whenever Apophis is successful, an eclipse occurs. Apophis represents darkness and its struggle against the light of the sun. Because he is the sun's enemy, he was confused and identified with Seth, the enemy of the gods, in later times. Existing ritual texts refer to the "overthrowing of Apophis" and offer magical protection. It is said that each morning when the sun rises and each evening as it descends, the sun boat is attacked by Apophis causing the sky to turn red from the defeated serpent. In the "Book of the Dead," the "great cat" cuts off the head of Apophis when his body threatens the sacred Persea Tree. Apophis is generally pictured as a massive animal, sometimes pierced with spears or knives by Horus. He is similar to the Babylonian Tiamat. *See also* Aai; Ab-esh-imy-duat; Ab-she; Ab-ta; Akeneh; Akhen; Apepi.

Apsaras (India) *see* Apsarases.

Apsarases *Apsaras, Apsarases* (Brahman, Buddhist, Hindu, Vedic; India)
Also known as: *Devaki, Kshiti-Apsarases* (terrestrial Apsarases), *Vrikshakas* (tree nymphs).
The Apsarases are music-making angels in the Buddhist faith. In Hinduism they reside in Indra's heaven Amaravati as water nymphs or celestial dancers. According to the Ramayana, they rose from the Churning of the Ocean. In later Hindu mythology they are depicted as beautiful courtesans of the sky who were the consorts of the Gandharvas. The Apsarases were given as rewards to heroes slain in battle. They often lived in the sacred Banyan tree (*Ficus benghalensis*). It is a species of the fig tree and is sacred because it is believed that a woman who desires children will be blessed if she prays under its leaves. When wedding processions passed the trees they were asked to bless the wedding party. The Apsarases, who are shape changers, have a dark side that is employed when the gods want holy people driven mad so they will not become too powerful. They bring good or bad luck to the gambler. One of the legends of Ganga, the Hindu river goddess of the sacred river Ganges, is connected with the Apsarases. They are sometimes thought of as clouds but are generally shown flying through the clouds. They are shown as beautiful, voluptuous, large-hipped, lightly clad, young women. In Cambodia they are often depicted dressed in long skirts, holding flowers, or dancing with their knees apart. In Cham representation, the Apsarases are shown to the waist, holding a lotus bud and appearing as though they are coming out of a wall. In one reference, it is stated that there are five hundred Apsarases. Some of their names are Adrola, Alambusha, Angana, Bhima (Terrible), Caksusi (the Clairvoyant), Harini, Lavangi (She of the Clove Tree), Manasi (the Intelligent One), Marisha, Menaka, Misrakesi, Pramlocha, Purvachitti, Rambha, Sahaganya, Sanumati, Sasilekha, Saudamani, Shakuntala, Sukanthi, Surabhidatta, Surapamsula, Urvasi. The Apsarases are associated with Ganga, the Hindu river goddess of the Ganges. *See also* Amaravati; Amatsu-otome (Japan); Angara; Devaki; Devas (A); Gandharvas; Ganga; Hanuman; Kama (A); Kurma (regarding Churning of the Ocean); Marisha; Menaka; Pramlocha; Pishachas; Rambha; Sarasvati; Satyavati (regarding Adrika); Shakuntala; Swarga; Urvasi.

Apsarasras (India) *see* Apsarases.

Apsu *Abzu* (Sumerian), *Apzu* (Assyro-Babylonian)
Also known as: *Apason* (possibly), *Aphson* (Babylonian), *Rishtu, Zigarun* (Akkadia, "The Mother Who Has Begotten Heaven and Earth").
In the very beginning, in Assyro-Babylonian mythology, only the primordial oceans existed. The Apsu was sweet water which encircled the earth. Earth was a round plateau bounded by mountains. The vault of heaven rested on the mountains which floated on the Apsu. Apsu fused with the female principle, Tiamat, in the form of salt water, and all things were created, beginning with Lahamu and Lahmu (also known as Lakhmu and Lakhamu), who possibly represented a type of silt and have been described as monstrous serpent gods. They were followed by Anshar, possibly the earth aspect, and Kishar, possibly the sky aspect. They created the sky god Anu, and Anu created the earth god and god of wisdom, Nudimmud (also called Ea or Enki), and Inlil. As the gods grew they attempted to create order out of chaos. Their rebelliousness angered Apsu and Tiamat. They called upon Mummu, to assist them in slaying their offspring. Before this feat was accomplished Tiamat had a change of heart and declined to be involved. Ea, with the aid of a magic incantation, killed Apsu and locked Mummu away. Later, after establishing his abode on the corpse of Apsu, he and his spouse, Damkina, became the parents of Marduk. Tiamat, with an army of monsters and renegade gods attempted to avenge her spouse's death. Marduk overcame her, split her corpse in two, and created heaven and earth. With the assistance of his father, Ea, mortals were created from the blood of the renegade god Kingu's blood. At first Apsu was a feminine deity, but later, as a god, he was the dragon husband of Tiamat and father of the other gods. The Babylonian version gives Apsu the mate named Mummu. In other versions Mummu is known as the commander-in-chief or messenger of Apsu. In a Sumerian version where Apsu is thought to be a river or sea, Ea gathered clay from the Apsu and created the gods. In one tale, Apsu was kept awake by the noise of the gods and wanted to destroy them, but was captured by the overlord Ea. Ea cast a spell on him that caused him to fall into a deep sleep. While sleeping Ea killed him and took over his dwelling. Ea cast the same spell on Mummu and became powerless. The Sumerians believed this was the sea where the Anunnaki and Igigi dwelled and where they were ruled by Marduk. As Aphson, in the Babylonian Creation Myth of Damascius, he was the spouse of Tauthe. Compare Apsu to the Greek Oceanus. *See also* Anshar; Anu (B);

Anunnaki; Damkina; Ea; Enuma Elish; Igigi; Kingu; Kishar; Lahamu and Lahmu; Marduk; Mummu; Nudimmud; Tiamat.

Apsyrtus *Apsyrtos* (Greek)
Also known as: *Aegialeius, Aegialeus, Phaethon* (Shining One).

Apsyrtus was born with the name Aegialeus and became known as Apsyrtus, meaning "swept down" after his death. His father was Aeetes, the ruthless king of Colchis and his mother was either Asterodeia or his father's second wife Eidyia (the daughter of Oceanus and Tethys). In one myth it is related that Aeetes sent Apsyrtus in pursuit of the ship Argos, which carried his daughter Medea, Jason the Argonaut and the Golden Fleece. He trapped the ship at the mouth of the Danube. The Argonauts agreed to set Medea ashore on an island while they debated whether she should return home or follow Jason to Greece and who should have possession of the Golden Fleece. Meanwhile, Medea sent an untruthful message to Apsyrtus telling him that she had been abducted and begging him to rescue her. When he arrived on the island he was murdered and dismembered by Jason. In the version by the Greek poet Apollonius Rhondius, Jason killed Apsyrtus but Medea dismembered him and threw his body parts into the sea. Aeetes then abandoned his pursuit of the Argos to collect his son's remains. There are accounts of this myth wherein Jason also kills Aeetes. For various accounts of the route taken by the Argos, see Aeetes, Jason, and Medea. There are two other figures named Aegialeus. One is the son of Inachus and Melia, and the brother of Io and Phoroneus; the other is the son of Adrastus and Amphithea. This man was the only Epigoni killed in the taking of Glias by Laodamas. *See also* Aeetes; Aegialeus; Golden Fleece; Jason; Medea.

Apt *Apet, Aptu* (Egypt) *see* Apet; Aptu; Hathor.

Apt-ent-khet (Egypt) *see* Aaru.

Apt-ent-qahu (Egypt) *see* Aaru.

Apt-net (Egypt) *see* Aaru.

Aptu (Egypt)
Also known as: *Apet, Apt.*
A water monster. Also, the ark on which Osiris floats. *See also* Apet; Osiris.

Apu (Egypt)
A god in the ninth sector of Tuat. He holds the serpent Shemti, which has four heads at each end of his body. *See also* Ab-ta; Tuat.

Apu-Hau (Polynesia)
"Fierce Squalls." The son of the god of winds, Tawhiri-ma-tea.

Apu-Matangi (Polynesia)
"Whirlwind." The child of Tawhiri-ma-tea.

Apu Punchau (Peru) *see* Inti.

Apu-Punchau *Apu Punchau* (Inca, Peru) *see* Inti.

Apzu (Assyro-Babylonian) *see* Apsu.

Apzu-Rishtu (Assyrian) Counterpart to Tiamat (q.v.).

Aqas-Xena-Xenas (Chinook People, North America) *see* Agas Xenas Xena.

Aquila (Greek)
This is the eagle that flew Aphrodite's slipper to Hermes, or the eagle that took Ganymede to the celestial realm. It could also be Metope, after she was transformed by the goddess Hera.

Aquilo *Aguilo* (Roman)
North wind personified. Equivalent of the Greek Boreas (q.v.).

Ar-Ast-Neter (Egypt)
One of the gods who accompany Osiris during the second hour of the night. *See also* Tuat or Shesat Maket Neb-S.

Ara (Armenian, Phrygian)
Culture hero. Possible sun-god. Ara is the husband of Nvard. He was captured and possibly killed by Queen Semiramis. He is possibly related to, or the same as Er, the son of Armenius. There are similarities in Ara's life to the story of Gilgamesh.

Ara-Mi-Tama (Japan) *see* Amaterasu.

Ara-mi-tama (Japan)
Susanow's wicked soul. His beneficent soul is known as Nigi-mi-tama. *See also* Susanow.

Ara Tiotio (Morai People, New Zealand)
Also known as: *Awhiowhio* (Australia).
God of tornadoes. *See also* Awhiowhio.

Arabus (Greek)
He is the son of Hermes, brother of Daphnis and father of Cassiopeia (q.v.)

Arachne (Greek)
Deity of weaving.
She is the daughter of Idmon and Colophon. She challenged Athena to a weaving contest. They came out even. The jealous goddess Athena took her competitor's cloth and destroyed it. Arachne hung herself. Athena then changed her into a spider. *See also* Amaterasu (Japan); Athena.

Araga (India) This is another name for Vishnu as Rudra (q.v.).

Arak (Cambodia)
A family guardian spirit, the Arak lives in the house or a tree. When someone is seriously ill, a shaman (kru) is called to have the Arak incarnated in himself. The Arak tells the shaman what evil spirit is torturing the patient. The patient is then gashed and rice wine is poured over him or her. Special festival days are set aside for the Araks between January and March.

Aralez (Armenian) *see* Arlez.

Arallu *Aralu* (Assyro-Babylonian, Sumer)
Also known as: *Anduruna, Ganzir, Shualu.*
The underworld. Arallu is a kingdom ruled by Ereshkigal and her consort, Nergal. This is the place where the dead are judged. Sometimes it is depicted as a lower world and sometimes a mountain. There are seven entrances by seven gates in the west, the place of the setting sun. Arallu is infested with monster and demon souls of the wicked dead, the etimmu and gigim. In the legend of Gilgamesh the goddess, Irkalla or Allat

was possibly the ruler Arallu. The goddess Ishtar followed Tammuz in his annual descent into Arallu. The watchman of Arallu is Nedu (also known as Neti). *See also* Anduruna; Ishtar; Tammuz.

Aralu (Babylonian) *see* Arallu.

Aram (Armenian) *see* Armenak; Ba'al Shamin.

Aramaiti (Persia) *see* Amesha Spentas; Amshaspends; Daevas.

Aramati (India) Goddess of devotion.

Aramazd (Armenian, Persian)
  Also known as: *Ahura Mazda, Ormizd.*
  Supreme god. Creator. He is the chief deity, possibly of the Zoroastrianism cult, in early Armenia. Some say he is the father of Anahita, Mihr and Nane. He is probably a sky god and a fertility god similar in nature to the Persian Ahura Mazda. In some versions, he is thought to be the son of Zervana Akarana and twin brother of Ahriman. Although called the father of gods, there is no indication of a wife or consort. There is a vague reference in some texts that Anahit was his wife but, although possible, there is no direct evidence. Aramazd's messengers or angels are the Hreshtak which might be the same as the Persian, Firistak. Some of Aramazd's attributes are similar to those of Dionysus. *See also* Ahura-Mazda; Anahita; Aramazd (for Firistak); Dionysus; Tiur.

Aranunna (Babylonia) *see* Marduk.

Arawak People — Creation Legend (New Guinea) *see* Makonaima; Sigu.

Arawn (Celtic, Irish)
  Also known as: *Anguissance, Augusel.*
  God of the underworld. Arawn, the ruler of the underworld, Annwn and owner of the magic cauldron, frequently contended with would-be usurpers for his title. In one myth, Arawn, said to be the originator of pigs, gave Pwyll the underworld animals as a gift in return for ridding him of his rival Hafgan (also spelled Havgan). Hafgan was Arawn's enemy from the otherworld whom he had to fight yearly. Once, Arawn and Pwyll magically exchanged bodies for a year and a day so that Pwyll could get Hafgan out of Arawn's life. In the Arthurian cycle, he was known as one of the kings of Scotland. Arawn is depicted as a huntsman, with a pack of red-eared dogs, chasing a white stag. *See also* Achren; Amathaon; Annfwn; Pwyll.

Arazu (Akkadian, Sumer)
  God of crafts. Arazu is one of the gods created by Ea at the beginning. From an ancient prayer, it could be construed to mean Arazu was a priest. "[He] Created the god of carpenters, molders, and Arazu, as completers of the work of his creation."

Arbhu (India) *see* Ribhus (The).

Arbidihist (Persia) *see* Asha Vahishta.

Archelous (Greek) *see* Acamas (B) and Aeneas.

Archander and Architekes (Greek) *see* Achaeus.

Archons (Post-Christian Gnostics, the Ophites)
  Also known as: *The Great Archon, Ruler According to Valentinus.*

They are the seven ruling spirits created by the god Ophiomorphus, the serpent son of Ialdabaoth. The first was either Adonaeus or Adonai; the second, Ialdabaoth; third, Iao; fourth, Sabaoth; fifth, Astaphaios; sixth, Ailaiosastaphaios; seventh, Horaios. They are associated with Abraxas (q.v.). *See also* Pistis Sophia.

Ardabahisht (Persia) *see* Asha Vahishta.

Ardevi Sura Anahita (Persian) *see* Anahita.

Ardhanari (India) *see* Ardhanariswara; Shiva.

Ardhanari-Ishvara *Ardhanari, Ardhanari-Ishavara, Arhhanariswara* (Hindu; India)
  Also known as: *Hara Gauri.*
  Brahma, unhappy with his creation of male deities, called forth Shiva, who appeared in the form of Ardhanari-Ishavara, "The Lord Who Is Both Male and Female." Ardhanari-Ishavara is the combination of Shiva and his wife Devi, who were so in love, they became one. Ardhanari-Ishavara is depicted with a bare torso, and one of two breasts, obviously female, is full and sensuous. The forehead is extremely high and represents the lingam. When the image is of half–Shiva and half–Gauri it is called Hara Gauri. *See also* Brahma; Devi; Lakshmi; Shiva.

Ardhanariswara (India) *see* Ardhanari-Ishvara.

Ardi-bahisht (Persia) *see* Asha Vahishta.

Ardusht (Persia) *see* Zoroaster.

Ardvi Sura Anahita *see* Anahita.

Ardvi Vaxsha (Persia)
  Goddess of Water and Moisture.

Areimanios (Roman) *see* Mithras.

Areius (Greek)
  He is the Argonaut son of Bias, the king of Argos and the beautiful daughter of Neleus and Chloris, Pero. For a list of siblings, *see* Pero. *See also* Bias.

Arekoi (Iroquois People, North America) *see* Areskoui.

Aremata-Rorua and Aremata-Popoa (Polynesia)
  "Long Wave and Short Wave." These are two powerful ocean demons.

Arene (Greek)
  Arene is the daughter of Oebaulus, the king of Sparta and Gorgophone. *See also* Gorgophone; Hippocoon.

Areop-Enap (Gilbert and Nauru Islands, Micronesia)
  Also known as: *Ancient Spider.*
  This creator god floats in space. He created the moon from a snail he found in a large mussel, then created sun from another snail. He then made earth from the lower half of the mussel shell with the help of a worm or grub (Rigi). The sweat from the grub in his efforts to raise the top of the shell became the sea. *See also* Nareau; Rigi; Yelafaz.

Ares (Greek; possibly worshiped in Thrace and Scythia. May have originated as a Minoan deity).
  Also known as: *Alloprosallos, Enualios* (possibly), *Enyalius*

(possibly), *Gradivus* ("Leader of Armies"), *Maris, Mars, Tues, Tuesco, Tui.*

Storm god. God of war. Ares is the only son of Zeus and Hera. His sisters are Aphrodite the goddess of love; his twin Eris (also known as Discordia), the goddess of strife and discord, the nymph Arge, Eileithyia, the goddess of childbirth, and Hebe (also known as Ganymeda), the goddess of eternal youth. Ares never married but he had numerous affairs with goddesses and mortal women and he fathered many children. One of his great loves was his sister Aphrodite and they had a number of children even though she was married to the fire god Hephaistos. They were the parents of Deimos (Fear), Phobos (Panic), the god of fear and terror, Harmonia, who was turned into a snake by Ares, Pallor (Terror), Anteros, the god of passion, and possibly Eros, the god of love. Their affair ended when Helius, the sun god, betrayed them. They were discovered when Aphrodite's husband was away. Ares took his usual advantage of the time to slip into bed with the love goddess. Helius, the sun god, arranged to have a net fall over the naked lovers and then invited other Olympian gods into the bedroom to look and laugh. Poseidon stepped in and convinced the wronged husband to accept reparation from Ares and he let the guilty couple go their opposite ways. The virile Ares also had children by Demonice, the daughter of the Calydonian Agenor; Evenus, who eventually committed suicide, and possibly Thestius, Pylus, Molus and Oeneus (their mother may be Alcippe). Dryas, the Argonaut, was his son by an unknown woman in Aetolia. He may have been the father of the Argonaut Meleager, by Althea, who eventually hung herself. He was the father of Ialmenus and Ascalaphus, both Argonauts, by Astyoche. By either Dotis or Chryse (also known as Comana) he was the father of Phlegyas who became the king of Orchomenus and had a daughter who was raped by Apollo. By the nymph Cyrene, who loved to wrestle lions, or possibly Asteric, he was the father of Diomedes who was made to eat his flesh-eating horses by Heracles. Cygnus, who was turned into a swan, is Ares' son by Pelopia or Pyrene. Some say he was the father of Parthenopaeus by the huntress Atalanta. By Otrere (Otrera), he was the father of the Amazon queen, Penthesileia, and Antiope (Melanippe) and Hippolyte, who was either killed by Heracles or died of a broken heart. He was also the father of Tereus, who after raping his sister-in-law, cut out her tongue. By Asterope or Harpina, he is thought by some to be the father of King Oenomaus, who killed all but the last of his daughter's suitors. King Oxlus was also his son by Protogeneia. It is possible that he is the father of Ixion. Another son, Aeropus, was born from his union with Aerope, who died in childbirth; the child was miraculously saved by Ares. He also had an affair with the dawn goddess Eos. When his lover-sister, Aphrodite found out, she punished Eos by making her be perpetually in love. Ares seduced Agraulus and they had a daughter, Alcippe. Halirrhothius, the son of Poseidon, raped Alcippe, and an inflamed Ares killed him. This action resulted in him being the first person, mortal or divine to be tried for murder. He was acquitted by his daughter's testimony. Though Ares is called a warrior, he fared better in the bedroom then on the battlefield. He was captured by the twin giants Otus and Ephialtes and stuffed into a bronze encasement for thirteen months. Hermes apparently rescued him. Heracles overcame him four times in battles. He was so gravely injured during the Trojan War that he fled the battle arena screaming and ran off to complain to Zeus, who was not impressed. Zeus told him that he was hated by the other gods. Whenever he was at war he was accompanied by his sons, Deimus (Fear) and Phobus (Panic). He was able to redeem his warrior character to an extent when he killed the Giant Mimas during the battle between the gods and the Giants. Menoeceus, the son of Creon, sacrificed himself to Ares to save the city of Thebes from destruction. His symbols are a spear or an arrow or the burning torch, and a spear. Ares is sometimes shown as a helmeted warrior dressed in armor. The cock is his emblem and he is associated with the dog and vulture. Some say he is identified with the Egyptian god, Anhur, and is similar to Eres (Teutonic) and Maruts (Vedic). He is sometimes associated with Athene. Ares is frequently identified with the Roman Mars. He is deified for his warlike spirit rather than as war god. Similar to the Norse god of war Thor. *See also* Adonis; Aloeides; Althea; Anhur; Anteros; Enyalius; Graiae; Harmonia (A); Hephaistos; Ixion; Mars; Oenamaus.

Areskoui *Agreaskoui, Agriskoue, Aireskoi, Aireskouy, Arekoi* (Iroquois People, North America)

Also known as: *Great Spirit.*

A creator god. He was offered first fruits of the chase, and woman captives were sacrificed to him. Possibly a god of hunting and war. *See also* Kitshi Manito.

Arete (Greek)

Goddess of virtue. Representative of courage. Wife of Alcinous (King of the Phaeacians). She accompanied and guided Hercules along a thorny path where he did many virtuous things. She was also worshiped by Jason of the Argonauts. *See also* Argonauts; Heracles; Jason; Odysseus.

Arethusa (A) *Aethusa* (Greek)

Wood nymph. Nymph of springs and fountains. Artemis' attendant. Arethusa, the daughter of Oceanus. She was pursued by the river god Alpheus until Artemis changed her into a spring on the island of Ortygia. She is forever joined to the river Alpheus. Heracles had to divert the river's waters in order to clean the Augeian stables, one of his labors. Arethusa may be an aspect of Artemis. *See also* Alpheus; Artemis; Heracles; Oceanus.

Arethusa (B) *Aethusa* (Greek)

She is the daughter of Atlas and Pleione (also known as Aethra). She is one of the Hesperides (Aegle, Erythia, Hesperia). Her other siblings are the Hyades, Pleiades, Hyas and Calypso. *See also* Atlas; Calypso; Hesperia; Hesperides.

Aretia (Chaldea)

Also known as: *Horchia, Titae-Aretia, Titaea Magna.*

Little known Earth Goddess. Some say Aretia is connected with Janus. She is possibly the same as the Greek Arete.

Aretus (A) (Greek)

Son of Nestor and Anaxibia. *See also* Anaxibia; Antilochus.

Aretus (B) (Greek)

He is one of fifty sons of Priam, the last king of Troy.

Arganthone (Thracian) Goddess of Hunting.

Argayu (Yoruba People, Africa)

He is the sun god and god of the desert. *See also* Ogun; Olodumare.

Arge (Greek) *see* Ares; Argos; Cyclops; Hephaistos.

Arge Woyo (Haitian) *see* Agbe (Dahomey People, Africa).

Argeia (Greek) *see* Adrestus; Amphithea; Argus (C).

Arges (Greek) *see* Aegaeon; Gaea.

Argetlam "The Silver Handed" (Celtic) *see* Llud.

Argia (Greek) *see* Inachus; Meliae.

Argiope (A) (Greek) Nymph.

She is the spouse of the poet and musician, Philammon, and the mother of Thamyris, the minstrel of Thrace. *See also* Agenor (A); Europa.

Argiope (B) (Greek)

Argiope may be the same as Telephassa (q.v.), or they could be two different people.

Argonauts (Greek)

Heroes. The Argonauts are the crew of heroes recruited by Jason in his quest for the Golden Fleece. They sailed to Colchis on the Argos about eighty years before the Trojan War. Because a number of the Argonauts, including Jason, were said to have sprung from the blood of Minyas' daughters, they are also known as the Minyans. *See also* Actor (A); Actor (C); Amycus; Argonauts (Names of); Argus (C); Argus (D); Argus (E); Harpies; Heperides; Hylas; Jason; Nereids.

Argonauts (Names of) (Greek)

Acasus, son of King Pelias; *Actor*, son of Deion the Phocian; *Admetus*, prince of Pherae, son of Pheres and Periclymene; *Amphiaraus*, the Argive seer; *Great Ancaeus* of Tegea, son of Poseidon; *Little Ancaeus*, the Lelegian of Samos; *Argus* the Thespian, builder of the Argo; *Ascalaphus* the Orchomenan, son of Ares; *Asterion*, son of the Pelopian Cometes and Antigone; *Atalanta* of Calydon, the virgin huntress; *Augeias*, son of King Phorbas of Elis; *Butes* of Athens, the bee-master; *Caeneus* the Lapith (he had once been a woman); *Calais*, the winged son of Boreas; *Canthus* the Euboean; *Castor*, the Spartan wrestler, one of the Dioscuri; *Cepheus*, son of Aleus the Arcadian; *Coronus* the Lapith, of Gryton in Thessaly, son of Caenus; *Echion*, the herald, son of Hermes and Eupolemeia; *Erginus* of Miletus; *Euphemus* of Taenarum, the swimmer; *Euryalus*, son of Mecisteus, one of the Epigoni; *Eurydamas* the Dolopian, from Lake Xynias, son of Ampycus and Chloris; *Heracles* of Tiryns, the strongest man who ever lived, now a god; *Hylas* the Dryopian, squire to Heracles; *Idas*, son of Aphareus of Messene; *Idom* the Argive, son of Abas or Apollo and Asteria or Cyrene; *Iphiclus*, son of Phylacus or Cephalus and Clymene or of Thestius the Aetolian; *Iphitus*, son of Naubolus the king of Phocis; *Jason*, the captain of the expedition, son of Aeson and Alcimede; *Laertes*, son of Acrisius the Argive; *Lynceus*, the look-out man, brother to Idas; *Melampus* of Pylus, son of Poseidon; *Meleager* of Calydon; *Mopsus* the Lapith, son of Ampycus and Chloris; *Nauplius* the Argive, a noted navigator, son of Poseidon; *Oileus* the Locrian, father of Ajax; *Orpheus*, the Thracian poet, son of Oeager and Calliope; *Palaemon*, son of Hephaestus, an Aetolian; *Peleus* the Myrmidon; *Peneleos*, son of Hippalcimus, the Boeotian; *Periclymenus* of Pylus, the shape-shifting son of Poseidon; *Phalerus*, the Athenian archer; *Phanus*, the Cretan son of Dionysus; *Poeas*, son of Thaumacus the Magnesian; *Polydeuces*, the Spartan boxer, one of the Dioscuri; *Staphylus*, brother of Phanus; *Tiphys*, the helmsman, of Boeotian Sipae, son of Hagnias or Phorbas and Hyrmina; *Zetes*, the brother of Calais.

Argos (Greek) *see* Argus.

Argrius (Greek) *see* Calydonian Boar Hunt.

Argunis (Greek) *see* Arjuna (India).

Argus (A) *Argos* (Greek)

King of Argos. Argus is the son of Zeus and Niobe, a mortal who is the daughter of Phoroneus. He was the first child born of a god and a mortal woman. His siblings are Osiris, who was murdered by his other brother Typhon; Pelasgus, who became the first king of Arcadia. Argus married Evadne, the daughter of Strymon and Neaera. They became the parents of Peiras, Ecbasus, Criasus and possibly Epidaurus. (In other accounts he is the son of Pelops or Apollo.) Argus was said to have introduced the cultivation of grain to the city of Argos (named after him) where he remained king for seventy years. The city of Argos was founded by Phoroneus and was originally named Phoronea. The main deity of the city of Argos from Pre-Hellenic times was Hera. *See also* Apis (B); Niobe (B); Osiris; Phoroneus; Typhon; Zeus.

Argus (B) *Argos* (Greek)

Also known as: *Argus of the Hundred Eyes, Argus Panoptes* (All-Caring).

Monster. Argus was either born of Gaea (the earth) or he was the son of Agenor or Inachus, river gods and brothers. His grandfather, a monster also named Argus, killed the dragon Echidna. His grandson Argus inherited his looks; he was a monster giant with one hundred eyes all over his body; fifty watched while fifty slept. Argus was sent by Hera to guard Io from the amorous Zeus. He was killed by Hermes when Hera felt that he had over-stepped his boundaries. She used his eyes to decorate the tail feathers of the peacock. *See also* Echidna; Gaea; Hera; Hermes; Io.

Argus (C) *Argos* (Greek)

Builder of the magic ship, Argo. An Argonaut. Argus is the son of Argeia who was the wife of Polybus. He was a Thespian who was asked by Jason to build a ship capable of carrying his men on the journey to retrieve the Golden Fleece. Argus built the famous Argo, a fifty-oared ship empowered with magic from Athene's beam in the prow built from Zeus's oak tree. Argus joined the crew and became an Argonaut for the famous expedition. *See also* Argonauts; Golden Fleece; Jason.

Argus (D) (Greek)

Argus (D), the oldest son of Phrixus and Chalcipe, persuaded his grandfather, Aeetes, to give the Golden Fleece to Jason. In an escape, he was rescued by the Argonauts. It is thought by some that Argus was the father of Magnes, the human magnet, and not Aeolus. *See also* Aeetes; Golden Fleece; Jason; Magnes, Medea; Phrixus.

Argus (E) (Greek)

The son of Jason and Medea. It was thought that he was murdered by his mother. *See also* Jason; Medea; Phrixus.

Argus (F) *Argos* (Greek)

Faithful pet. Argus was the only one to recognize his master, the warrior Odysseus, when he returned after his twenty year sojourn. He was so delighted to see his master that he died of joy. Actaeon also had a dog by the same name. *See also* Odysseus.

Argus (G) (Greek) *see* Agenor (A).

Argyron (Greek) *see* Telchines.

Arhats (Buddhist, Taoist; China)

Also known as: *Shi-pa Lo-han.*

Protectors and instructors. Either sixteen, eighteen or five hundred spirits who protect the Buddhist religion and instruct followers in the Buddhist and Taoist law. The Arhats are usually associated with the Eight Immortals. Various names are given to these deities. Among them are Han Chung-Li, Lu Tung-pin, Chang-Kuo-Lao, Lan-Ts'ai-ho, Han Siang-Tzu, Tsao-kuo-chia, Ho-hsien-ku and T'ieh-Kuai Li (also called Li). *See also* Buddha; Chang-Kuo-Lao; Chung-Li-Ch'uan; Eight Immortals; Han Chung-Li, Han Siang-Tzu Ho-hsien-ku; Lan-Ts'ai-ho; Lu Tung-pin; T'ieh-Kuai Li; Tsao-kuo-chia.

Ari-em-ab-f (Egypt) *see* Assessors.

Ari-hes (Egypt) *see* Bast.

Ari-hes-nefer (Egypt)

Protector deity. Ari-hes-nefer's statue, in the form of a lion-headed god, was found by the entries of palaces and tombs to protect the living and the dead from evil spirits.

Ariadne (Greek)

Also known as: *Aridella.*

Goddess of dawn. Moon goddess. Fertility goddess. Vegetation goddess. She is the daughter of Minos, the king of Crete and the moon goddess, Pasiphae. Her siblings are Acacallis; Androgeus; Catreus; Deucalion; Eurydale; Glaucus; Lycastus; Phaedra; Xenodice. It was Ariadne's ball of thread that enabled Theseus to find his way out of the Labyrinth and survive certain death from the Minotaur. He married her as promised and then deserted her, leaving her on the island of Dia (Naxos). The rationale for his actions varies. Some think that she was abducted by Dionysus and died of grief, or that she was rescued by Dionysus and married him. Perhaps Thesesus abandoned her of his own free will. There is also a possibility that she married Oenarus, who was Dionysus' priest. Others say Theseus died in a storm at sea; he did not abandon her. An early story is that Artemis killed her because of something Dionysus had told her about Ariadne, or Artemis killed her while she was giving birth to twins. It is agreed that she had children by Dionysus: Ceramus, Peparethus, Phanus, and Thoas. Her other two children, Oenopion and Staphylus, are thought to be by Theseus. In another rendering of her story, Ariadne hung herself. After her death, Dionysus placed the constellation Corona Borealis, which he had given to her when they were married, in the sky in her honor. In another tradition, it is Theseus who placed this symbol of her in the heavens. After her ascension, she became known as Aridella. Her cults practiced orgiastic rites and males were sacrificed to her. The fire god Hephaistos forged her wedding tiara. The inventor Daedalus built a dance floor

for her at Cnossus. Compare Ariadne to Andromeda and Medea. She is identified with Aphrodite in some areas. The ball of thread given to Theseus is compared to Clotho's thread of life. Compare to the Cymric moon goddess, Arianrhod. *See also* Daedalus; Dionysus; Minos; Minotaur; Pasiphae; Theseus.

Arianrhod *Arianrod* (Celtic)

Also known as: *Ethne* (possibly).

Moon goddess. Goddess of birth. Mistress of the Otherworld Tower of Initiation. She is one of "The Children of Don," who are children from the lineage of the ancient goddess Don who has been associated with Danu. Don is represented as the mother of the Cymric pantheon as recorded in the "Mabinogion" also known as the "Four Branches." The "Mabinogion" is a collection of stories usually called British, although most of the stories are set in Wales. She is the daughter of Don and Beli and sister of Gwydion. Her brother had offered her services to Math as his footholder, a position of honor. The stipulation was that she had to pass a virginity test. She took the test, failed, and then gave birth to two twin sons, Dylan and Llew. Either Arianrhod or Math threw Dylan into the sea where he became a sea deity. Llew was rescued by Gwydion. Humiliated, Arianrhod cast a spell on her son Llew, stating that he would never have a name, weapons, or a wife. Gwydion, with the use of magic, was able to revoke her "guise." It has been suggested that perhaps Gwydion tricked his sister into having an incestuous relationship and when she realized the circumstances, she rejected her children. Her name means "Silver Wheel." The constellation Corona Borealis is said to be named after Arianrhod and Ariadne. It is sometimes called Arianrhod's castle. Corona Borealis is also known as a purgatory. Arianrhod is described as pale and very beautiful. She is compared to the Greek Ariadne as both names link them to the spider and both are associated with Corona Borealis. *See also* Ama (A); Anu (A); Ariadne; Bile; Don; Gwydion; Llew Llaw Gyffes; Lugh; Math.

Arianrod (Celtic) *see* Arianrhod.

Ariconte *Aricoute, Arikute* (Tupi-Guarani People, Brazil)

This god of night is generally known as the twin of Timondonar (also spelled Tamendonar and Tamanduare), the god of light. They are the sons of either the culture hero Maira Ata or the mortal Sarigoys. The brothers struggle with one another daily. Once, during a quarrel, Tawenduare stamped his foot with great emphasis and caused the great deluge. All were killed except the brothers and their wives, who climbed trees in search of safety. From the survivors, the Tupinamba and the Tominu people were born. They constantly fought with one another. In some myths the brothers are opposed by a fisher deity known as Agnen. *See also* Irin Mage; Maira Ata; Monan.

Aricoute (Tupi-Guarani People of Brazil) *see* Ariconte.

Aridane (Greek) *see* Bacchus.

Aridella (Greek) *see* Ariadne.

Arikute (Tupi-Guarani People, Brazil) *see* Ariconte.

Arimans (Persia) *see* Angra Mainyu.

Arinitti (Hittite) *see* Arinna.

Arinna (Hittite)

Also known as: *Arinitti, Ishtar* (possibly), *Wurusemu.*

Goddess of the sun or fertility goddess. War goddess (possibly). Arinna shares the same attributes as Cybele, the mother goddess of Phrygia and Asia Minor and the Roman Ma-Bellona. As the sun goddess, Wurusemu, she was originally the goddess Hepat. She is sometimes called an aspect of Ishtar. *See also* Cybele; Hepat; Ishtar.

Arion (Greek) *see* Adrestus; Demeter; Gaea.

Arishta (India) "The Bull-fiend." *See also* Krishna.

Aristaeus *Aristaios* (Greek, Libyan)

Also known as: *Agreus, Nomus.*

Benevolent deity. Agricultural deity. Instructor of beekeeping. Protector of beekeepers. Possibly a deified man. He is the son of Apollo and Cyrene, brother of Autychus. His wife is Autonoe, the daughter of Cadmus. Their children are Actaeon and Macris. (In some versions, Aristaeus is called the son of Uranus and Ge.) He is the half-brother of Orpheus and the spouse of Autonoe. The Centaur Cheiron taught Aristaeus the art of healing. In one legend, Aristaeus was born in Libya, raised by the Horae and as a god lived on nectar. He worked as a beekeeper and cheese maker and was the inventor of bookkeeping. He fell in love with Eurydice, the new bride of Orpheus. As she was fleeing from a swarm of his bees, she was killed by a snake. His mother advised him to seek the advice of the sea god Proteus, who instructed him to sacrifice cattle in Eurydice's memory. He found new swarms of bees in the carcasses of the cattle. He disappeared near Mt. Haemus. Aristaeus is associated with Proteus. *See also* Actaeon; Cheiron; Eurydice (A); Macris.

Aristaios (Greek) *see* Aristaeus.

Aristomachus (Greek) *see* Adrestus.

Arisudana (India) "Slayer of Enemies." *See also* Krishna.

Arjuna *Arjuni, Arjunis* (Hindu; India)

Also known as: *Aindri* (possibly).

Arjuna is the third son of Pandu and one of the five Pandava princes. As a result of his virgin birth by Kunti with Indra, he is also known as Indra's son. He shared his wife Draupadi with his four brothers to honor his mother's request. His eldest brother Yudhisthira lost everything in a gambling match with his cousins, the Kauravas. Arjuna and his family were forced to spend twelve years in exile. The following year they spent in bondage as King Virata's servants. During his years in exile, he performed twelve labors. Vishnu in his sixth avatar as Parashur Rama taught Arjuna the use of weapons. He became a brilliant archer and warrior. Arjuna journeyed to the Himalayas to request celestial weapons to use in an upcoming battle against the Kauravas. From there he went on to Indra's heaven, Swarga, to improve his battle skills. In Swarga, he fought the Daityas and emerged the victor. With a celestial bow named Gandevi (also spelled Gandiva), given to him by Agni and originally owned by Soma, he fought his own father, Indra. When Indra was threatened by the indestructible demon Niwatakawaca, he sought help from Arjuna. Before doing so, he felt it necessary to test Arjuna's inner strength. He sent the beautiful nymphs Tilottama and Suprabha to tempt him during his meditation. Although they perfumed and beautified themselves, they were not successful. (Tilottama in another escapade was able to captivate the Asura brothers, Sunda and Upasunda.) In another episode, Arjuna unknowingly fought Shiva who was disguised as a Kirata. When he returned to battle the Kauravas, Krishna acted as his charioteer. Before marching into war, Krishna recited the *Bhagavad-Gita* to the hesitant soldier who was about to engage in warfare against his cousins. One of his wives was Subhadra, the sister of Krishna, with whom he had a son Abhimanyu also known as Saubhadra. He also mated with Ulupi, the Naga princess, and had a son, Iravat. They were married in her abode in Patala (the underworld). He was killed by his own son, but was revived by a Naga charm given to him by Ulupi. Some say that Arjuna is a form of Indra called Aindri. Arjuna is similar to Heracles (Greek). *See also* Abhimanya; Agni; Asuras; Bhishma; Daityas; Draupadi; Duryodhana; Indra; Jara-Sandha; Kamadhenu; Karna; Kauravas; Krishna; Kunti; Kuvera; Naga and Nagini; Pandavas; Pandu; Parashur Rama; Parikshit; Prajapati; Patala; Shiva; Soma; Subhadra; Swarga; Varuna; Vishnu; Yama; Yudhisthira.

Arjuni (India) *see* Arjuna.

Arjunis (India) *see* Arjuna.

Arkate (Etruscan)

An obscure god who cautioned Favnu against another obscure deity, the goddess Alpanu. Arkate appears as an old man in a cloak.

Arkharokh (Gnostic) *see* Pistis Sophia.

Arkheokh (Gnostic) *see* Pistis Sophia.

Arlez *Aralez* (Armenia)

Also known as: *Jaralez.*

Benevolent spirits. By licking the wounds of brave men who fell in battle, they are able to restore their lives. The Arlez are the invisible spirits of dogs. *See also* Devs.

Armaita (Persia) *see* Spentas Armaiti.

Armat (Armenia) *see* Perkunis.

Armati (Persia) *see* Armaita; Spentas Armaiti.

Armen (Semite) *see* Baal.

Armenak (Armenian)

Sky god and folk-hero. He is the son of Hayk and possibly the same as the Teutonic god, Irmin. He is similar to the hero, Aram of Armenia. *See also* Hayk; Irmin.

Arnaeus (Greek) Another name for Irus (q.v.).

Arnaknagsak (Eskimo) *see* Sedna.

Arnamentia (British) Ancient goddess of spring waters.

Arnarquagssaq (Eskimo) *see* Sedna.

Arne (Greek)

Also known as: *Melanippe.*

She is the daughter of Aeolus and Hippe or Enarte. She has seven brothers and six sisters (for a list of their names, *see* Canace). She became pregnant by Poseidon when he was in the shape of a bull. They became the parents of Aeolus II and Boeotus. *See also* Aeolus (A); Boeotus; Enarte; Poseidon.

Arohi-rohi (Maori People, New Zealand)
Also known as: *Mirage.*
Creator. He created the first woman, Ma-riko-riko (Glimmer) from the warmth of the sun. According to some he created Echo.

Aroueris (Egypt) *see* Horus.

Arpacana (Tibet) *see* Arpacanamanjusri.

Arpacanamanjusri *Arpacana* (Buddhist; Tibet)
Also known as: *Jam-pa-i-dbyans, Jam-pe-yang, Manjusri* (Tibet).
God of wisdom. He is a manifestation of Manjusri.

Arrets (Egypt) Seven halls of the underworld. *See also* Tuat.

Arsa (Syria) *see* Allat.

Arsai (Canaan, Syria, Ugarit)
Arsai is the symbol of the earth. Her sister, Pidray (meaning "mist"), is a nature goddess who symbolizes light. Another sister, Tallai, symbolizes dew and rain. They are the daughters of Baal.

Arsan Duolai (Yakut) *see* Arson Duolai.

Arsaphes (Egypt)
Also known as: *Herishef, Hershef.*
Fertility god. Known as "Lord of Awe." Arsaphes refers to the Egyptian Herishef (He Who Is Upon His Lake). Hershef appeared in Herakleopolis as an image of the sun god. He was a primitive fertility god in the form of a ram. Arsaphes was praised as a giver of sustenance. In the Ninth and Tenth Dynasty he was identified with Ra and with Osiris. The ram's head served as a symbol for worship by his followers. He is shown with a solar disc headdress or the Atef crown. He assimilated with Heracles according to Greek interpretation. *See also* Hershef.

Arsi Basum (Saora People, India)
Monkey god. *See also* Ajorsum.

Arson Duolai *Arsan Duolai, Arsan-duolai* (Yakut People, Siberia)
Also known as: *Syga Tojon, Ulu Tojon.*
Ruler of the dead or underworld deity. Arson Duolai is the king or chief of the Abasy. He is a devourer of souls and bestower of diseases, who was assuaged only by blood sacrifices. His mouth is in his forehead and his eyes are at his temples. *See also* Abaasy; Ulu Tojon.

Arta (Persia) *see* Asha Vahista.

Artemis (Greek; possibly originated in Asia)
Also known as: *Artemis Calliste* ("Artemis the Fairest"), *Artemis Caria, Artemis Caryatis, Artemis Laphria, Auge, Cynthia, Delia, Diana* (Roman), *Dictyanna, Dictynna, Diktynna, Hecate, Kalliste* (Fairest), *Lukea, Luna, Parthenos* (Virgin), *Phoebe, Pythia, Selene.*
Nature goddess. Goddess of fertility. Moon goddess. Birth goddess. Goddess of hunting. Guardian of the Forest, Lady of Wild Things. This virgin goddess is the daughter of Zeus and Leto (also known as Latona). As "Lady of the Wild Things," she was patroness of all the totem clans and was annually offered a sacrifice of animals, birds and plants, a ritual which survived the Classical time at Patrae, in Calydonia. When Oeneus, the king of Calydon, neglected to give her the proper sacrifices, she sent the Calydonian Boar to destroy his crops and plunder his land. Later she was associated with Selene (Moon) and Hecate (Night). A similar burnt offering was presented by the Curetes at Messens and yet another is recorded from Hierapolis. As Lukea, the Greeks called her "Goddess of Light." She turned Actaeon into a stag and he was killed by his own hounds. She had only one love, the hunter god Orion whom she accidentally killed with an arrow. However, in another writing, we are told that she had a scorpion sting him to death for having the temerity to touch her. Artemis withheld the wind in an attempt to prevent the Greeks from reaching Troy. Like her brother, Apollo, Artemis was adept at using the bow and arrows and had the ability to send plagues and pestilences. Attended by a train of nymphs, she ranged at night through the land hunting deer. Artemis represented the feminine principle. She presides over births. Sudden deaths of women were attributed to her arrows. Rites performed in her honor included erotic dances, the clashing of cymbals, and the sacrificing of live animals over fire. The Laconians built a temple to Artemis from which Caryatids, female statues used as columns, are named. She is often represented with a bow, arrows, and quiver attended by hounds, or in a chariot drawn by two white stags and sometimes as a young virgin wearing a short tunic. Her sacred animal is the tragelphus, which is part goat and part stag. As the Priapian Diana, she appears with male organs. She is sometimes identified with Athene, Bast, Hecat, Isis, and Nephthys. As Artemis of Ephesus she is identified with Roman Diana. Compare Artemis to Lakshmi (India). *See also* Aah; Actaeon; Admetus; Aeneas; Agamemnon; Aloeides; Alpheus; Amazons; Amphion; Ariadne; Atalanta; Britomartis; Callisto; Calydonian Boar Hunt; Car; Ceto; Curetes; Diana; Ephesus; Leto; Mama Allpa; Napaeae; Orion; Pelops; Sekhmet.

Artemis Calliste (Greek) *see* Artemis.

Artemis Caria (Greek) *see* Artemis.

Artemis Caryatis (Greek) *see* Artemis.

Artemis Laphria (Greek) *see* Artemis.

Artemis of Ephesus (Greek) *see* Artemis.

Arthur (British, Celt)
Also known as: *Artus.*
Hero. Arthur is the son of Uther Pendragon and Igerna or he is an illegitimate son or a creation of Merlin the Magician. The original tales of Arthur date to Roman times. Some identify Arthur with the word Aruthr, meaning "great." Most of the current information comes from the work of Geoffrey of Monmouth (C.E. 1147) He is related to Mordred. In some myths, he is the nephew of Merlin and creator of the "Round Table." Arthur proved his right to the throne by withdrawing the sword "Excalibur" from a rock. His sister is Morgan Le Fay. Most of Arthur's legends center around his Round Table, knights, and the Holy Grail. Arthur's wife is Guinevere. Arthur is similar to

Mercury Artaeus (Gaul). His final resting place is in Avalon. *See also* Adder; Vivien.

Artimpaasa (Sythian) Ruler of the moon. Goddess of love.

Artinis (Armenian, but probably originally from a prior civilization called Urartians [from the Assyrians]).

Sun god. Artinis is one of a triad of early gods with Khaldi (high god or moon god) and Theispas (weather god). They are possibly the forerunners of Babylonian Shamasa; Sin, and Ramman (qq.v.). *See also* Khaldi; Theispas.

Artio (Celtic)

Goddess of wildlife, who appeared as a bear. She may have been the spouse of Essus. Artio was also worshiped at Berne (meaning "bears") in Switzerland.

Artus (British) *see* Arthur.

Aruna *Arushi* (Plural), *Rumar* (Hindu; India)

Aruna is the dawn god and charioteer of the sun. With Garuda, they are the horses that draw Surya's or Vishnu's chariot. Aruna is also called Rumar the son of Kasyapa. He is sometimes shown as a bird. The name means red, rosy-colored, ruddy or tawny. *See also* Garuda; Kaspaya; Surya; Vishnu.

Arundhati (India)

"The Morning Star." One of the Krittika sisters, and the faithful spouse of Vasistha. *See also* Karttikeya; Rishi; Vasistha.

Aruru (Assyro-Babylonia, Chaldea, Sumer)

Also known as: *Belet-ili, Mami, Ningal, Ninhursag, Ninmah, Nintue.*

Mother Goddess. Goddess of Creation. Earth goddess. This goddess helped Marduk mould the first human and create mankind. In one version, at the request of the gods, Aruru molded Enkidu (or Esbani) from mud or clay to be the rival of Gilgamesh. She was also the creator of Gilgamesh by some accounts. Aruru is the personification of earth. In the Sumerian version, at Nippur, it was the earth goddess Aruru or Mami who was said to have created men from clay. Some say Aruru was the sister or wife of Enlil. She might have been given the additional title of "Goddess of Childbirth." Her son or husband might have been Nesu. She is sometimes identified with the Sumerian earth mother, Ki, and sometimes Nammu. Sometimes she is said to be the sister of Enlil. Aruru is possibly identified with Mah or Belit-ili. *See also* Belit; Mah (B); Mami; Marduk; Nammu; Ningal, Ninhursag; Ninlil; Ninmah; Ninsun; Nintu.

Arushi (India) *see* Aruna.

Arusyak (Persia) *see* Anahit; Vahagn.

Arvak (Teutonic) *see* Aarvak.

Arvakr (Teutonic) *see* Arvak.

Arya Achalanatha (Japan) *see* Fudo-Myoo.

Arya Sarasvati (Tibet) *see* Sarasvati.

Arya Tara (Nepal)

Protector goddess. Arya Tara is from the group of twenty-one Green Taras. She protects mortals from the eight evils: fire, theft, lightning, flood, earthquake, enemies, famine and untimely death. Arya Tara is depicted sitting gracefully in the Ardhapayanka position. *See also* Tara.

Aryaman (Persia)

Also known as: *Ahriman, Ahrimanes.*

Might be a god of marriage. He is the third member of the Aryan trinity (the Adityas), with Mitra and Varuna. In one rendition he is known as the evil prince of the kingdom of darkness. In another, Aryaman is an Aditya, the son of Aditi, the Mother of All Gods. His name means "Bosom Friend." Aryaman brings sacrifices to fruition. He is associated with Ohrmazd and is said to be his elder twin. Each controls the world for 6,000 years. Aryaman is identical to Angra Mainyu. *See also* Aditi; Adityas; Armenak (Armenian); Ariman; Mitra; Surya; Vahagn; Varuna.

Aryong-Jong (Korea) Goddess of rainfall.

Asa (A) (Persia) *see* Asha Vahishta.

Asa (B) (Teutonic) *see* Bifrost.

Asa Poorna (India) *see* Shakti.

Asabru (Teutonic) *see* Bifrost.

Asag (Sumer) Underworld demon. *See also* Ninurta.

Asaheim (Teutonic) *see* Asgard.

Asakku (Assyro-Babylonia) *see* Lahamu and Lahmu.

Asama (Japan) *see* Sengen.

Asamanjas (India) *see* Sagara.

Asapishachikis (India) Female Demons. *See also* Pishacha.

Asar (A) *Asir* (Egypt)

Also known as: *Osiris.*

Aspect of a god. One of the gods in the Pyramid Texts. An aspect of Osiris. Similar to Assur (Assyrian), Asari (Babylonian), Azur (Hebrew) Aesir (Teutonic). *See also* Marduk.

Asar (B) (Babylonian) *see* Marduk.

Asar-Apis (Egypt) *see* Serapis.

Asar-hap (Egypt) *see* Serapis.

Asar-Hap (Greek, Egypt) *see* Apis (A); Serapis.

Asar-Hapi (Greek, Egypt) *see* Apis (A); Serapis.

Asarhap (Egypt) *see* Serapis.

Asari *Asarri* (Assyro-Babylonia)

Originally a Syrian god of agriculture, Asari later became confused with Osiris (q.v.). *See also* Ea; Marduk.

Asarri *Asaru* (Babylonian, Sumerian) *see* Marduk.

Asartaiti (Egypt) *see* Osiris.

Asaru (Babylonia) *see* Marduk.

Asarualim (Babylonia) *see* Marduk.

Asarualim Nunna (Babylonia) *see* Marduk.

Asaruludu (Babylonia) *see* Marduk.

A'sas (Teutonic) *see* Aesir.

Asase Efua (Africa) *see* Asase Yaa.

Asase Ya *Asae Yaa* (Ashanti People, Africa)
Also known as: *Aberewa, Asase Efua.*

Asase Ya, "Old Woman Earth," is the great goddess who created humanity and at death returns them to her fold. The earth, and specifically the plowed field, is her temple. A goddess of fertility, the farmers pray to her and their ancestors at planting. She is mate of Nyame and Mother of the Gods. Her name-day is Thursday and is considered a sacred day of rest. She is petitioned when land is cultivated or when a grave must be dug. Some say she is androgynous. *See also* Abosam; Nyame; Tano.

Asbet (Egypt)
In the Pyramid Texts she is associated with Isis and Nephthys.

Asbru (Teutonic) *see* Bifrost.

Ascalaphus (A) (Greek)
An Argonaut. He was the co-ruler of Orchomenus with his brother, Ialmenus. Both men were suitors of Helen of Troy. They took thirty ships to Troy. Their parents are Ares and Astyoche. *See also* Ares; Argonauts; Ialmenus.

Ascalaphus (B) (Greek)
His parents are the river god Acheron and Gorgyra or Orphe. When it was learned that he had spied on Persephone, he was turned into an owl by Demeter. *See also* Acheron; Demeter; Persephone.

Ascanius (Greek)
Another name for Iulus (q.v.). *See also* Aeneas.

Ascension, The (Islamic) *see* Mohammed.

Asclepius *Aeculapius, Aesculapius, Ascalaphus, Asklepios, Esculapius* (Greek, known in Carthage; possibly originated in Egypt)
Also known as: *Eshmun* (Carthage).

God of healing and medicine. Physician for the Argonauts. Deified mortal. Asclepius is the son of Apollo and the nymph Coronis or possibly Arsinoe. He might be the son of Acheron and Orphne. He married Epione, the daughter of Merops. His daughters are Acesis (meaning "remedy"), Aegle, Iaso (cure), Janiscus, Hygieia (health) and Panacea (all-healing). His sons are Machaon and Podalirius. As an infant, his mother was burned to death for adultery. Asclepius was saved from the flames by a dog. Later, he learned the art of healing from the Cheiron the Centaur. Zeus, fearing that mortals would be revived from death, threw a thunderbolt at Asclepius and killed him. In one tale, Asclepius was able to copy Apollo and bring the dead back to life. The ruler of the underworld, Cronus, worried that Asclepius would depopulate Hades, was frantic. So, the great god Zeus was about to hurl his thunderbolt at Asclepius when Apollo interceded and pleaded for Asclepius. Instead of murdering him, Zeus relented and placed Asclepius among the stars as Serpentarius the snake-bearer. His staff with coiled snakes is our modern day symbol of medicine. He later became a god of medicine with the symbol of a snake. There are tales that indicate that he was loved by the Phoenician goddess and Mother of Gods, Astronoe. Sometimes he is shown as a serpent, but more often as a benign middle-aged man. Sometimes he is with the dog Cerberus, who is at his feet. The staff is his attribute (as it is for Bacchus Dionysus, Hermes, and Mercury). The dog is the sacred animal of Asclepius, who was said to have been raised by a bitch. The animal symbolizes fidelity and love. In past days, followers offered sacrifices to dogs in his temples. The tongue of the dog was thought to have healing properties. To dream of a dog signified a cure for the follower. He is sometimes confused with the Egyptian god Serapis. The Greeks say this god is identified with a son of Ptah, Imhotep. He is associated with Persephone and Demeter. He is sometimes identified with Eshmun. Compare Asclepius to the twin Vedic healers, the Asvins. *See also* Acheron; Astronoe; Athene; Cerberus; Dia'necht (Celtic); Eshmun; Fates; Lycurgus (A); Serapis.

Asdar (Sumer) *see* Ashdar; Astarte.

Aser (Hebrew) *see* Asherah.

Aset (Greek) Greek rendering of Isis.

Asfandarmad (Persia) *see* Spentas Armaiti.

Asgard (Norse; Teutonic)
Also known as: *Asaheim.*

The dwelling place of the Aesir (gods) known as Asgard is located in Midgard, the middle earth. Gladsheim Castle, built by the gods, is located in Asgard. Inside is the great banquet hall of Valhalla with thrones for Odin and the twelve highest gods. It has 640 doors and 960 warriors can walk abreast through each door. The ceiling is made of spears and the roof of shields. The hall and everything in it is solid gold. The twelve Aesir (gods) and twenty-four Asynjur (goddesses) assemble in the hall at the bidding of Odin. In one myth, Lidskjalv, Odin's throne, is located in the meadow Idavollen. Frigga and other goddesses have their own hall known as Vingolv (Hall of Friendship). Another hall for the gods, known as Valaskjalv, is covered with silver. Jotunnheim, the home of the giants; Svartheim, the home of the dark elves; and Mannheim, the home of mortals, are all a part of the Norse world. The Bifrost, also known as the Rainbow Bridge, connects the Norse world to the outside world. *See also* Aesir; Alfheim; Bifrost; Valaskjalv.

Asgaya Gigagei (Cherokee People, North America)
Also known as: *The Red Man, The Red Woman.*

Asgaya Gigagei is a bisexual thunder deity.

Ash (Egypt of foreign import)
Also known as: *Lord of the Land of the Olive Tree, Lord of the Land of Tehennu.*

A minor three-headed deity: lion, vulture, and snake. He is mentioned five times in inscriptions from the eleventh to the eighteenth dynasty. In the fifth dynasty, he was known under the names noted above.

Ash-hrau (Egypt)
Five headed-monster serpent in the sixth sector of Tuat. Its body is twisted so that its tail almost touches one of its heads. *See also* Tuat.

Ash of Uisnech (Celtic) *see* Abellio.

Ash-Vahishta (Persia) *see* Asha Vahishta.

Asha (Persia) *see* Asha Vahishta.

Asha Vahishta (Persia) *Ash-Vahishta, Asha Vahista*

Also known as: *Arbidihist* (Pahlavi), *Ardabahisht, Ardibahisht, Asa, Asha, Arta, Rta* (Old Persian).

The most beautiful of the Amesha Spentas, Asha Vahishta is representative of divine law, good thought, and moral order in the world. The protector of fire, and the protector of the physical and moral world against demons. In hell Asha Vahista assures that mortals do not suffer more punishment than they deserve. Believers say that all who do not know Asha Vahishta are outside the whole order of god and therefore must forfeit heaven. Asha's chief opponent is Indra (known in the Avesta as Andra), who represents the Spirit of Apostasy. Asha Vahishta is associated with the Yazatas (q.v.). *See also* Ahura Mazda; Amesha Spentas; Angra Mainyu; Avesta; Daevas; Vohu Manah.

Asha Vahista (Persia) *see* Asha Vahishta.

Ashanti People — Creation Legend (Africa) *see* Adu Ogyinae.

Asharu (Babylonia) *see* Marduk.

Ashdar *Asdar, Ashtar, Astar, Athtar;* (Akkadian, Arabic, Semitic, Sumerian)

Mother goddess. She was originally a Sumerian deity who was adopted by the Akkadians. She is likely from the South Arabian god Athtar which was the name of the planet Venus. The only Semitic name in early history of a deity was Asdar. The South Arabians speak of Astar or Athtar which meant Venus. Ashdar may have been the original creator deity of the Semitic people of that region. Possibly a moon goddess. She could be a mother goddess of the Abyssinians and mother/sister/wife of Tammuz. Ashdar is associated with Shamash. Possibly identified with Innini and Ishtar. *See also* Athtar; Babbar; Utu.

Ashem (Egypt)

One of the messenger gods mentioned in the Pyramid Texts.

Ashemu *Ashen* (singular) (Egypt)

They are a class of beings associated with Heru, the hawk god and Sekhem. The Ashemu are sometimes referred to as the form in which a god is visible. *See also* Afa; Henmemet; Unas; Utennu.

Ashen (Egypt) *see* Ashemu.

Asher (Hebrew) *see* Asherah (B).

Ashera (Hebrew) *see* Anat; Asherah (B).

Asherah (A) (Phoenician) *see* Hathor.

Asherah (B) *Asher, Ashera, Aser* (Assyria, Canaanite, Phoenician, Ugarit; Mesopotamia)

Also known as: *Achtaroth; Achtoret; Anath-Yahu, Asherat; Ashertu; Asirat* (Hittite); *Asirtu; Asratu; Assir; Astar; Astarte* (Phoenician); *Astert; Astirati; Astereth; Ashtoreth* (Phoenician); *Athrar; Ess-eorradh* (Celtic); *Istar* (Akkadian); *Kaukabhta* (Syrian).

Mother goddess. Fertility goddess. National goddess of Sidon. Originally, she was the wife of the father god, El. She is often shown nude and holding her breasts. Her hair is done in two long ringlets (attributes of the goddess Hathor). A number of oval pottery plaques show her nude figure holding lily stalks or serpents similar to the poses of the Egyptian deity Hathor. She is identified with Venus (Greek), Ishtar (Babylon), and Isis (Egypt). She is sometimes identified with the goddess Astarte as Kaukabhta (Syrian), and Anahit (Armenian). *See also* Anat; Astarte; Baal; El; Qadesh.

Asheratian (Ugarit) *see* Astarte.

Ashertu (Middle East) *see* Asherah (B).

Ashi Vanguhi (Persia) *see* Yazatas.

Ashima (Egypt, Sumeria) *see* Amathaounta.

Ashir (Assyria, Sumer) *see* Ashur.

Ashmadai (Middle Eastern) *see* Asmodeus.

Ashnan (Chaldea, Sumer)

Ashnan, the goddess of grain, is a kind and bountiful deity sent to earth by Enki. She, along with Lahar, Ningizzida, Ninsar and Siris, were created at the same time by either Anu or the gods he created. In some myths, the god of wisdom, Enki, suggested to Enil that he create Ashnan and Lahar. Ashnan and Lahar, the cattle god, were created to control the crops and cattle and to supply food and drinks to the gods. One day they imbibed heavily and were unable to carry out their duties. Mortals were formed to take over their chores. Ashnan is similar to the Chaldean goddess of grain, Nisaba (not to be confused with Nisaba the architect goddess). *See also* Ea; Enki; Enlil; Lahar; Nisaba.

Ashrapa (India) "Drinkers of Blood." *See also* Dakinis.

Ashshur (Assyria, Sumer) *see* Ashur.

Ashtareth (Babylonia, Canaan, Semite) *see* Ashtoreth.

Ashtaroth (Palestinian, Syrian) *see* Astarte; Chaos; Ishtar.

Ashtart (Phoenician) *see* Astarte.

Ashtoreth *Ashtareth* (Babylonian, Canaanite, Semitic)

Also known as: *Alidat, Alittu, Belit, Mylitta.*

Earth goddess. Alittu and Alidat were originally titles of Ishtar as a Babylonian mother goddess. Later it became Mylitta, then Ashtoreth. The name Mylitta was used by the Assyrians for Aphrodite. *See also* Astarte; Belit; Ishtar.

Ashur *Anshar, Anshur, Ashir, Ashshur, Asur, Asshur, Assur, Azur* (Assyria, Sumer)

Chief deity. A creator god with many powers. He was the National God of Assyria known originally as Ashir. According to some, his attributes were borrowed from the Sumerian gods Enlil and Marduk. He has the attributes of Anu and is similar to Yahweh. Ashur is a dragon slayer and a warrior. Sometimes Belit is his consort. Ashur is the Lord of the Four Cardinal Points. He is a god of four faces: the bull, eagle, lion, and man. Sometimes he is depicted standing above a bull, sometimes as a huge winged god wearing bracelets and carrying a basket and arrows. His emblems are the winged disk, the fir cone, and the bow and arrow. *See also* Anshar; Ashur; Ashura; Marduk; Tiamat.

Ashura (Canaanite, Semitic)

A goddess who is thought to be the wife or mate of Yahweh (q.v.).

Ashvamukhi (India)

"Horse-face." *See also* Yaksha and Yakshini.

Ashvatthaman (India) *see* Duryodhana; Parikshit.

Ashvins (India) *see* Asvins.

Ashwins (India) *see* Asvins.

Ashyggr-drasil (Teutonic) *see* Yggdrasil.

Asi (India) Sacred Sword. *See also* Brahma.

Asi-na-duti (Japan) *see* Kushi-nada-hime.

Asia (A) (Greek) Another name for Hesione (q.v.).

Asia (B) (Greek)

An Oceanid. She is the daughter of Oceanus and Tethys. *See also* Oceanids.

Asiaq (Eskimo)

This goddess, who was originally human, is the spirit of the weather. She is one of the triad of spirits with Pinga and Sila. She produces thunder by rubbing two pelts together and brings rain by shaking out a pelt dipped in urine (thunder). *See also* Pinga; Sila.

Asir (Egypt) *see* Asar (A).

Asirat (Middle East) *see* Asherah (B).

Asiri (Egypt) *see* Osiris.

Asitanga (India) "With Black Limbs." *See also* Shiva.

Ask *Askr* (Norse; Teutonic)

In the Norse creation myth, Ask is one of two trees or blocks of wood, possibly from an Ash tree, that were used by Odin, Ve, and Vili to carve the first mortals. (The word Ash is frequently used as a prefix to the tree of life, Yggdrasil [q.v.].) The first male was named Ask and the female, Embla. Odin gave them breath and life, Vili gave them understanding, and Ve gave them human senses and attributes. In a variation of this myth, Ask and Embla were saved by Odin and his brothers during the great deluge. *See also* Embla; Midgard; Odin; Ve; Vili; Ymir.

Askefruer (Danish) Forest spirits who cure diseases.

Asken (Egypt) One of the gods in the Pyramid Texts.

Asklepios (Greek) *see* Asclepius.

Askr (Teutonic) *see* Ask.

Asman (Persia) *see* Khshasthra Vairya.

Asmegir Citadel (Teutonic)

Home of deities. This citadel had eight architects, all dwarfs, to design it. Presently, it is guarded by the dwarf Delling. Asmegir is also the name of the spirits who dwell with Balder.

Asmodeus (A) (Arabic, Hebrew)

Also known as: *Ashmadia.*

Demon. He probably originated from the demon of Arabia named Aeshma-deva. He is the lame, demon husband of Sarah who was the daughter of Raguel. As Ashmadia, he was said to have made Noah drunk. In legend he killed Sarah's seven bridegrooms, then he fled to Egypt where he was bound by the angel Raphael. In another legend he was captured by Solomon. *See also* Aeshma.

Asmodeus (B) (Semitic)

Spirit of lust. Asmodeus is the beautiful goddess daughter of the fallen angel Shamdon and sister of Tubal-Cain.

Asogguano (Yoruba People, Africa)

Representative of health matters and epidemics. *See also* Olodumare.

Asoka (India) Shiva's sacred plant. *See also* Shiva.

Asopus (A) (Greek)

River god. Asopus is the son of Oceanus and Tethys and the brother of the three thousand river gods, known as Rivers, and the three thousand goddesses known as Oceanids. A river god of Boeotia, he married Metope, and they became the parents of twelve or twenty daughters and two sons. Some of the daughters are Aegina, Cleone, Corcyra, Salamis, Sinope, Thebe. Their sons are Ismenus and Pelasgus. Under false guise, Zeus seduced, abducted and impregnated Aegina. Asopus went to Corinth in search of his daughter. Sisyphus, who knew what had happened, would not reveal it to the distraught father until he promised to produce a spring of water behind Aphrodite's temple. Asopus produced the spring, known as Peirene, found that the culprit was the great god Zeus, and went in pursuit of him. He attempted to make Zeus accountable for his actions but the powerful deity, Asopus with his famous thunderbolts, drove to his river bed and subsequently punished Sisyphus for betraying him. To compare to other Greek river gods, *see* Achelous, Acheron, Alpheus, Cephissus, Cocytus, Inachus, Oceanids, Oceanus, Rivers, Tethys. *See also* Aeacus; Aegina; Antiope; Oenamaus; Sinope; Sisyphus.

Asopus (B) (Greek) He is the son of the sea god Poseidon and Eurynome.

Aspelenie (Lithuanian)

Aspelenie is a household goddess who rules the area behind the cooking range. She appears as a small, harmless snake who can keep the area free from rodents and can be treated as a pet.

Asrafel (Mohammed) *see* Gabriel.

Asrapa (India) *see* Dakinis.

Asratu (Middle East) *see* Asherah.

Asri (India) Goddess of fortune.

Ass (Egypt)

Another name for the sun god Ra, who in this form, was devoured by a gigantic serpent.

Assara Mazaas (Persia)

Creator god of Ashurbanipal. *See also* Ahura Mazda.

Assarac (Assyrian)

Little known except this deity was worshiped on a mound called Birs.

Assaracus (Greek) *see* Anchises.

Assessors (Egypt)

Also known as: *Forty-two Assessors or Judges.*

Assessors or judges of dead souls. The Forty-Two Assessors were located in the Judgment Hall (also known as the Hall of the Maati Goddesses). Twenty-one assessors lined either side of the wall and heard the Negative Confessions of the deceased soul. The confessions were forty-two denials declaring that the deceased had not committed certain "sins" during his or her lifetime. The names of the Assessors according to the "Papyrus of Nebsent" in the British Museum are Usekht-nemmat, Hept-shet, Fenti, Am-khaibetu, Neha-hau, Rerti, Maati-f-em-tes, Neba-per-em-khetkhet, Set-kesu, Uatch-nes, Qerti, Hetch-abehu, Am-senf, Am-beseku, Neb-Maat, Thenemi, Aati, Tutu-f, Uamemti, Maa-an-f, Heri-seru, Khemi, Shet-kheru, Nekhen, Ser-kheru, Basti, Hra-f-ha-f, Ta-ret, Kenemti, An-hetep-f, Neb-hrau, Serekhi, Neb-abui, Nefer-Tem, Tem-sep, Ari-em-ab-f, Ahi-mu, Utu-rekhit, Neheb-nefert, Neheb-kau, Tcheser-tep, An-a-f. *See also* Maat; Negative Confessions; Tuat.

Asset (Egypt) *see* Aaru.

Asshur (Assyria, Sumer) *see* Anshur; Assur.

Assorors (Sumer) *see* Anshar.

Assorus (Babylonia) *see* Anu (C); Belus (B).

Assur (Assyria, Sumer) *see* Ashur.

Assuras (India) *see* Asuras.

Assyro-Babylonian — Creation Legend (from the Tablets of Ashurbanipal) *see* Apsu; Bel (B); Tiamat.

Ast (Egypt)

One of the gods in the Pyramid Texts. *See also* Aai; Astarte.

Astaik *Astik* (Armenian, Semitic, Syrian)

Also known as: *Aphrodite.*

"Little Star." She is the spouse of Ba'al Shamin. Vahagn, the god of fire, abducted her. In later Armenian tales, Astaik is identified with Arusyak ("Little Bride"). Astaik is also a title of Anahit (q.v.). She is thought to be a rival of Anahit and Nana. She might represent the planet Venus. *See also* Astarte; Baal Shamin; Ishtar; Nana; Vahagn.

Astamatrikas (Hindu; India)

Also known as: *Saktis.*

In Hindu mythology, the Astamatrikas are divine mother goddesses. They are known as Saktis when they are seven or ten in number. When they are eight in number they are called Astamatrikas.

Astanpheus (Gnostic) *see* Astaphaeus.

Astaphaeus (Ophite of the post–Christian gnostics)

Also known as: *Astanpheus, Astaphaios.*

Possibly another name for Yahweh. He is associated with the seven spheres of the planets: Adonai, Ailoaios, Astaphaios, Horaios, Ialdabaoth, Iao and Sabaoth. *See also* Yahweh.

Astaphaios (Gnostic) *see* Astaphaeus.

Astar (Sumer) *see* Ashdar; Asherah (B).

Astarete (Phoenicia) *see* Astarte.

Astarte *Astar, Ashtart, Astart* (Greek), *Astarete, Astartu.* (Assyro-Babylonia, Canaan, Carthage, Egypt, Phoenicia, Sumer, Syria)

Also known as: Ah (Egypt), Ast (Egypt), Ashdar, Asherah, Ashtareth (Babylonia), Asherah, Asheratian (Ugarit), Ashtaroth, Ashtoreth (Hebrew), Astoreth, Innini (possibly), Ishtar (Babylon), Kaukabhta (Syrian), Qadesh, Qedeshet (Semite).

Astarte is a goddess of love, battle, war, sex, fertility and maternity. She is the Near Eastern mother goddess worshiped in Egypt in the Eighteenth Dynasty, possibly in relation with Seth and thought to be the daughter of the sun god Ra or Ptah. She is both a mother goddess and a warrior goddess. Astarte is said to be the sister of Anat and Baal. She is the sister and bride of Tammuz. Some say she was worshiped in Egypt as the goddess Ah or Ast (Isis). Her origin might go back as far as the goddess of Sumer, Innini. She could be a goddess of harlots since one of her titles is Qadesh which is similar to the Babylonian Qadishtu, a word for harlot. The singular of the name Ashtaroth is Asthoreth and is a title (meaning "Lady") of the ancient Semitic deities, and similar to that of Baal or Baalim, which means "lord." She is identified with the planet Venus. Babylonian astronomers charted her changes from a morning to an evening star. She was shown with the head of a lioness topped by the disk of the sun. She drove a chariot pulled by four horses. Sometimes Astarte was shown armed with a shield and club, riding a horse into battle. Sometimes she is depicted with the head of a cow or bull. In Egypt she appears naked riding bareback on a horse wearing the Atef-crown and carrying weapons. She also appears sketched on limestone flakes possibly by workers in the Necropolis. She is possibly derived from the Phoenician goddess Tanit. Sometimes she is confused with Hathor and Isis. There are some writers who say the Canaanite gods Adon, Eshmun, Kemosh and Melquart were regarded as brothers, sons, or husbands of Astarte who was then considered as an earth goddess. She corresponds to the early Arabian male deity, Athtar. Astarte is also identified with Aphrodite and Mylitta and sometimes Tyche. She is also identified with the deities Istaru of the Assyrians and Ashtoreth of the Hebrews. Compare her to Hathor, Isis and Tanit. *See also* Adon; Allatu; Anat; Asherah (B); Ashtoreth; Athar (B); Baal; Chemosh; Ishtar; Isis; Qadesh; Tyche.

Astartu (Phoenicia) *see* Astarte.

Asten (Egypt) *see* Aani; Thoth; Utennu.

Aster paeus (Greek)

He is the son of Pelagon who was killed in the Trojan War by Achilles.

Asteria (A) (Greek)

Her parents are the Titans Phoebe and Coeus. She is the sister of Leto (also known as Latona). She married Perses, the Titan son of Crius and Eurybia. Asteria committed suicide by drowning and was turned into a quail. *See also* Ceos; Leto.

Asteria (B) (Greek)

She is one of the fifty daughters of Danaus, known as the Danaids. *See also* Danaus.

Asterie (Greek) *see* Ares.

Asterion (A) (Greek)

River god. He is the son of Oceanus and Tethys. In a contest between Hera and Poseidon, the judges were Asterion, Cephissus and Inachus. The Asterion river was in Peloponnesus. *See also* Hera; Inachus; Poseidon; Rivers.

Asterion (B) (Greek)

An Argonaut, he is the son of Cometes and Antigone, the daughter of Pheres. *See* Argonauts.

Asterios (Greek) *see* Minotaur; Zeus

Asterius (A) (Greek)

King of Crete. He adopted Minos, Rhadamanthys and Sarpedon, the sons of Zeus and Europa. *See also* Argonauts; Europa; Minos; Minotaur; Sarpedon (A).

Asterius (B) (Greek)

"Star." Another name for the Minotaur (q.v.).

Asterius (C) (Greek) Another name for Asterion.

Asterius (D) (Greek) The Argonaut brother of Amphion.

Asterodeia (Greek)

A nymph, she is the first wife of Aeetes, the king of Colchis, and the mother of Chalciope (also known as Iophossa). *See also* Aeetes; Apsyrtus.

Asterope (A) (Greek)

An epithet of Sterope (q.v.). *See also* Ares; Oenamaus; Sirens.

Asterope (B) (Greek)

She is the wife of Hippalcimus and mother of Penelaus, the Argonaut.

Asterope (C) (Greek)

She is the daughter of the river god, Cebren, and the wife of Aesacus.

Asteropeia (Greek) *see* Actor.

Astert (Assyro-Babylonian) *see* Asherah (B).

Asthertet (Egypt)

Associated with the goddess Hathor, she is known as "The Mistress of Horses." *See also* Hathor.

Asti (Egypt) A name given to Thoth by the sun god Ra.

Astik (Middle East) *see* Astaik.

Astika (India)

Astika, a sage, is the son of the serpent goddess Manasa. Injury or death by a snake bite can be avoided by uttering Astika's name when bitten. *See also* Manasa; Takshaka.

Astioche (Greek)

It was either Astioche or Axioche who was the mother of Chrysippus who was murdered either by his half-brothers or by Hippodameia, the wife of Pelops. *See also* Danaus; Hesione; Pelops.

Astirati (Middle East) *see* Asherah (B).

Astoreth (Phoenician) *see* Asherah (B); Astarte.

Astovidad (Persian) Demon of Death *see* Varuna (India).

Astraea (Greek)

Also known as: *Dike, Virgo.*

Goddess of justice. Astraea is the daughter of Zeus and Themis, who was also the personification of justice. Astraea's sisters are the Horae and the Moirai. Astraea, fed up with mortals, left the earth during the bronze and iron ages. She is now seen as Virgo in the heavens. *See also* Ceos; Dike; Horae; Justitia; Moirai; Themis.

Astraeus (Greek)

He is the Titan son of Crius and Eurybia. His brothers are Pallas and Perse. With Eos, the goddess of dawn, he became the father of all the stars and the winds: Boreas, Hesperus, Notus, Phosphorus, Zephyrus, and perhaps Aura. *See also* Boreas; Eos; Notus; Zephyrus.

Astrerodeia (Greek)

She is the nymph wife of Aeetes and mother of Chalciope. *See also* Apsyrtus.

Astronoe (Phoenician)

She turned Eshmun into a god using generative heat. *See also* Asclepius; Cybele; Eshmun.

Astrope (Greek)

One of the sun god Helius' horses who pulled the chariot Quadriga through the sky. *See also* Helius.

Astydameia (A) (Greek)

Pelops and Hippodameia are her parents. She married Acastus and became the mother of Laodamia, Sterope, Sthenele and sons who are not named. It appears that she fell in love with Peleus, the king of the Myrmidons, and Argonaut, who ignored her. Slighted, she took revenge and in the end was cut into pieces by her would-be lover. For a list of her siblings *see* Pelops. For details regarding her attack on Peleus, *see* Acastus. *See also* Peleus.

Astydameia (B) (Greek)

Also known as.

Her parents are Amyntor and Cleobule. Her siblings are Crantor and Phoenix. By Heracles, she could be the mother of Ctesippus and Tlepolemus.

Astynome (Greek)

Her parents are Talaus the Argonaut and Lysimache or Lysianassa. She married Hipponous, the king of Olenus, and became the mother of Capaneus, one of the Seven against Thebes and Periboea. *See also* Adrestus; Capaneus; Hipponous.

Astyoche (A) (Greek)

Daughter of Laomedon and Strymo, or daughter of Actor. *See also* Actor (C).

Astyoche (B) (Greek)

The daughter of the river god, Simoeis, she married Erichthonius, who at the time was the richest man in the world. Their son was Tros, the eponym of Troy. *See also* Ares; Erichthonius.

Astyoche (C) (Greek) Daughter of Crisus (q.v.).

Astyoche (D) (Greek)

Daughter of Phylas. Mother of Tlepolemus by Heracles.

Asu-Niti (India) *see* Yama.

Asu-su-namir (Assyro-Babylonian) *see* Asushunamir.

Asur (Sumer, Assyria) *see* Ashur.

Asura (Persia) *see* Ahura Mazda.

Asuras *Assuras*

Also known as: *Ahura Mazda, Asuris* (female Asuras), *Danavas, Hormusda* (Mongolian); (Vedic; India).

In the Vedic tradition, Asuras are beings who existed before the creation of our universe. Roughly translated, the name means "living power," and in ancient Vedic texts meant "god." Agni, Indra and Varuna were known as Asuras. In later times, the meaning of the word changed and the Asuras, said to be born from Brahma's hip, became enemies of the gods. The word that once meant "god" became "Sura." The Asuras, according to the Satapatha Brahmana, are descendants of Prajapati and are described as giant shape changers who can become invisible. In their constant battles with the gods, many Asuras have been killed. Shukra, the seer and son of Bhrigus, is the guru of the Asuras. He personifies the planet Venus. Jalandhara, the son of the goddess Ganga, is an Asura who married Vrinda, the daughter of a heavenly nymph. Other well known Asuras are the demons Vrita and Kansa. The Asuras live in Patala, the underworld, in surroundings said to surpass the splendor of the celestial realm. The names of their towns are Shining, Startassel, Deep and Golden. Historically, they were thought to have been connected to mining. The Asuras are associated with Karttikeya, the god of war, and Parvati. *See also* Adidti; Agni; Ahura Mazda (Persia); Amitra; Arjuna; Bhima (A); Brahma; Brighus; Daityas; Danavas; Devas (A); Devas (B); Ganga; Hiranyakasipu, Indra; Jalandhara; Kansa; Kurma; Patala; Prajapati; Rakshasa; Upasunda; Varuna; Vishnu; Vrita.

Asuris (Persia) Female Demons. *See also* Asuras.

Asus (Roman) *see* Aesus.

Asushunamir *Asu-su-namir, Asushu-namir, Uddushunamir* (Assyro-Babylonian)

The beautiful eunuch Asushunamir was created by the great god Ea for one purpose. He was to travel to the underworld to wield his charms on Ereshkigal and persuade her to release Ishtar. *See also* Ea; Ishtar; Tammuz (for a variation of this myth).

Asva (India) "The Dawn"; "The Mare." *See also* Ushas.

Asvaghosa (Buddhist; India)

Originally a Brahmin, Asvaghosa converted to Buddhism (circa C.E. 100). He is The Twelfth Ancestor in the Ch'an line that begins with Gautama Buddha and ends with Bodhidharma. *See also* Buddha.

Asvamedha (India) Early Vedic horse sacrifice. *See also* Rama.

Asvamuttakha (India) *see* Ma-mien (China).

Asvinau (India) *see* Asvins.

Asvins *Ahans, Ashvins, Ashwins, Asvinau, Atvins* (Brahmanic, Hindu, Vedic; India)

Also known as: *Dasra* (Wonder Workers), *Dasra and Nasatya, Dioskouroi* (Greek), *Divo Napata, Nakula and Sahadeva, Naonghaithya* (called this name in later times).

In Vedic mythology, the Asvins are cosmic deities, the sons of Dyaus, or of the sun god Surya, or Savitri and the nymph Sanja, or Surya and the nimble cloud goddess Saranyu. She is also said to be the mother of twins Yami and Yama, which would make them the siblings of the Asvins. They are variously said to be the cosmic gods of the dawn, of heaven and earth, of day and night, sun and moon, or morning and evening (one half dark, the other light). In the *Rig-Veda*, they are called the joint husbands of Surya, the sun maiden. Tales are told of their rescue of Bhujyu (the Sun), who was thrown into the ocean by his evil father. The twins renewed him by taking him in their chariot on the path of the gods. In Brahman mythology they are twin healing deities who cure all infirmities. The elder is Dasra and the younger twin is Sahadeva. As the physicians of Swarga, the heavenly abode of Indra, they were known independently or collectively as Nasatya, or Nasatya and Dasra. In the *Mahabharata*, it is written that they rejuvenated the aged and wealthy sage Chyavana. Other patients of the Asvins were Vispala, for whom they fitted an iron leg, and Upamanyu who had his eyesight restored. The Asvins were the fathers of Sahadeva and Nakula, the youngest Pandu princes, by the goddess Madri. According to the *Ramayana*, they were the fathers of the monkeys Dvivida and Mainda. The goddess Vadaba (also spelled Vadava), the wife of Vivasvat, is said by some to have given birth to the twins while in the form of a mare. The Asvins are invoked by warriors in battle, by the heavy burdened and down trodden, the ill, the humble, and by brides who wish to be fertile. In later times, the Asvins declined in mythological status and became the Zoroastrian archdemon Naonghaithya. The Asvins are described as being handsome young twins, one light and one dark in color, on horseback or in a golden three-seated, three-wheeled car drawn by horses, a bird, an ass, or a buffalo. Their vehicle was made by the three generous elves known as the Ribhus. The Asvins' color is red. When Ratri, the goddess of night, dissolves, the Asvins bring up the morning light and make a path for the goddess of dawn, Ushas. They are depicted as the drivers and the horses for the sun's chariot. They are symbolized by two circles, two mountain peaks, two eyes, or two wheels. The name Nasatya indicates that they were either born from the nose of their mother or may have been elephant (long nosed) deities. In astrology, they represent Gemini. They are associated with the lotus and used honey for many of their healing activities. Bhujyu represents the sun at its ebb during the winter solstice and its restoration in spring or summer. Bhujyu also represents consciousness lost in a materialistic world. The monster Mada represents thought. Other Vedic physicians are Agni, Indra, Rudra, Soma. Regarding Naonghaithya, *see* Spentas Armaiti. The Asvins are comparable to the Greek Dioscuri, and the Greek healer Asclepius. They are associated with Mitra and Ratri. For another myth involving the Asvins, *see* Mada. *See also* Bhrigu; Chandra; Pandavas; Pushan; Ribhus; Sanja; Saranyu; Surya-Bai; Swarga; Ushas; Vivasvat.

Aswini (India) *see* Surya.

Asyngur (Teutonic) *see* Asynjor.

Asynja (Teutonic) *see* Asynjor.

Asynje (Teutonic) *see* Asynjor.

Asynjor *Asynja* (singular form), *Asyngur, Asynje* (Teutonic)

The Asynjor are the female counterparts to the Aesir (q.v.). *See also* Aesir; Asgard; Fjorgyn; Jord.

At-Em (Egypt) Mother goddess of all-devouring time.

At-en-ra (Egypt) *see* Adon.

Ata (Middle Eastern) *see* Atargatis.

Atabei *Attabeira* (Haiti; Taino People, Antilles)

Also known as: *Guacarapita, Guimazoa, Iella, Illa, Mamona, Momona.*

Atabei is the First Woman or Mother Earth. She is the mother of the Haitian sky god Joca-huva and, in some versions, Iocauna. Her messengers are Coatrischie the hurricane goddess and Guatauva. Atabei is associated with Guabanex (q.v.). *See also* Guamaonocon; Iella; Iocauna.

Atabyrius (Greek) *see* Althea.

Ataensic (Iroquois Indian People). *See also* Ataentsic.

Ataentsic *Ataensic, Ataeusic* (Huron, Iroquois People, North America)

A water goddess. High goddess. Spouse of the Chief of Heaven. She is a mortal woman who was sent to the upper regions. After enormous pain and suffering she was sent back to earth with the gift of maize and meat. Ataentsic became the Great Earth Mother. Her twins Yoskeha (also spelled Ioskeha) and Tawiscara caused her death during childbirth. Her next tribulation was to fall or be kicked from heaven. The animals who created the emerging earth came to her rescue. In some legends, it is Ataentsic's daughter "Breath of Wind" who gave birth to Yoskeha and Tawiscara. *See also* Yolkai Estan; Yoskeha and Tawiscara.

Ataeusic (Huron, Iroquois People, North America) *see* Ataentsic.

Atago-Gongen (Buddhist, Shinto; Japan)

Also known as: *Atago-Sama, Kagu-tsuchi no Kami, Susanowo.*

God of fire and destruction. The son of Izanagi and Izanami, this deity is worshiped on the mountain Atago. He is shown as a warrior mounted on a horse who carries a pearl and a crozier. Atago-Gongen is possibly the same as Jizo. *See also* Izanagi; Kagu-Tsuchi.

Atago-sama (Japan) *see* Atago-Gongen.

Ataguchu (Inca) *see* Apocatequil; Pacari.

Atahocan (Algonquin, Montagnais People, North America)

Also known as: *The Great Spirit.*

Supreme Being. Atahocan is the creator of all things. *See also* Gitchi.

Ataksak (Eskimo)

God of joy. This good spirit lives in heaven. When he dies his body will shine. Ataksak is shown as a sphere with many brilliant cords on his body.

Atalanta (A) *Atalante* (Greek)

Atalanta, goddess of the hunt, may have originally been a death goddess. She is the daughter of Iasus and Clymene. Her father abandoned her on Parthenia because he wanted a son. Artemis, the goddess hunter, sent a bear to raise her in the woods. Later, hunters found her and took her under their wings. Her upbringing gave her superior skills as a hunter, runner and warrior and she became famous for her foot racing. Her father reappeared on the scene and claimed the paternal right to choose her mate. She agreed, with the stipulation that she would not mate with any man who could not outrun her and if she could outrun him, she could kill him. Renowned for her beauty, there were many contenders for her hand who ended up dead. She was finally defeated in a foot race by Melanion (also spelled Meilanion and Milanion) who threw three golden apples in her path. The apples from the garden of Hesperides were given to him by Aphrodite. (His adventures are often attributed to Hippomenes.) In time, the couple were turned into lions by Zeus for desecrating his temple or for desecrating the temple of Cybele. In another version, they were punished because Melanion forgot to thank Aphrodite for the Golden Apples. Atalanta might be a form of Artemis or Diana (qq.v.). *See also* Althea; Aphrodite; Ares; Argonauts; Calydonia Boar Hunt; Cybele; Hesperides; Jason; Paris (A); Zeus.

Atalanta (B) (Greek) She is the daughter of Schoeneus, king of a section of Boeotia. She had wanted to remain a virgin, but eventually changed her mind and married Hippomenes.

Atalanta (C) (Greek) The daughter of Maenalus.

Atalante (Greek) *see* Atalanta.

Atamas (Greek) *see* Ino.

Atanea (Polynesia) *see* Atunua.

Atanua *Atanea* (Polynesia). Dawn goddess. *See also* Atea.

Atanzah (Mesopotamia) *see* Anu (B).

Ataokoloinona (Madagascar, Africa) Messenger.

He is the son of Ndriananahary who sent him to earth to see if it was a good place to inhabit. Because earth was hot and dry Ataokoloinona buried himself in the ground and was never seen again. *See also* Ndriananahary.

Atar *Adar, Atarsh* (Zoroastrianism; Persia)

Chief of the Yazatas. Atar, the son of Ahura Mazda, is a god of fire. Sometimes he is classified as an Amesha Spentas and said to be one of the assistants of Asha Vahishta who presides over righteousness in the moral sphere and is the spirit of fire in the material sphere. Atar conquered the evil dragon Azi Dahaka in a battle for the control of Divine Glory. Personified, he is a source of comfort to mortals. He offers wisdom, virility, and a paradise for the virtuous. In the eyes of Atar, only one sin is unforgivable: to burn or cook dead flesh. He is comparable to the Hindu god of fire, Agni (q.v.). *See also* Ahura Mazda; Amesha Spentas; Asha Vahishta; Azhi Dahaka; Fravashis; Yazatas.

Atarate (Middle Eastern) *see* Atargatis.

Atargate (Middle Eastern) *see* Atargatis.

Atargatis *Atarate, Atargate, Atergatis, Ataryatis, Atharate.* (Aramaic, Hittite, Roman [later], Syrian)

Also known as: *Ata* (possible original name), *Ataryatis Derketo, Dea Syria* (Syria), *Derceto, Derketo, Tar-Ata.*

Atargatis was originally a goddess of fertility. She descended as an egg from heaven and emerged as a mermaid goddess. Her origins lead some to call her the mother of mermaids. A jealous rival cursed her with an unabiding love for a handsome young man. To ensure his fidelity, she caused him to disappear. A daughter, Semiramis, resulted from the union. Atargatis left her daughter in the care of doves in the wilderness and then threw herself into a lake and became a fish. She may have been the mate of Hadad. At a later date, she was worshiped by the Romans. Devoted eunuchs self-abused themselves and performed ecstatic dances in her honor. Atargatis is depicted with the tail of a fish, as a sky-goddess in a diaphanous veil with eagles around her head, and as sea goddess with a dolphin crown. She may be a combination of Athar and Ate. *See also* Ate; Cybele; Ishtar; Oannes; Semiramis.

Atarsh (Persian) *see* Atar.

Ataryatis Derketo (Syrian)
Another name for the fish goddess Atargatis (q.v.).

Atchet (Egypt) *see* Ra.

Ate (Greek)
She is the goddess of infatuation, rash actions, and mischief. The daughter of either Zeus or Eris, Ate is the sister and friend of Ares (war and storm). After Zeus threw her out of heaven for causing Eurystheus to be born before Heracles, she took refuge among men and led them to impulsive actions. Zeus sends the Litai (prayers) to follow her around, trying to straighten up the trouble she creates. Her toy, the Apple of Discord, has caused numerous conflicts and was the cause of the Trojan War. Ate is identified with Atargatis. She is similar to the Erinyes, Furies, and the Roman goddess Discordia. *See also* Ares; Atargatis; Zeus.

Atea *Akua, Atua, Autu, Etua, Otua* (Polynesia)
Also known as: *Atea Rangi, Rangi, Te Tumu* ("The Source"), *Vatea, Wakea.*
"Great Expanse of the Sky." The Sky. Atea and Papa are the primeval couple, the procreators of all who followed. In some myths however, we are told that Atea, the god of light, is the son of the god of darkness, Tanaoa. He is the brother of Ono, spouse of the dawn goddess Atunua, and father of Hakaiki. He is one of the triad with Ono and Hakaiki. The Mangaians say that Atea and Papa's first son was Tangaroa. The people of Tuamotu have Atea married to Fa'ahotu. Their first son is Tahu who became a renowned magician. Their second son is Tane (some say). Their third son is Ro'o. At one time, Atea and Tane were fastened in a deadly embrace. Finally, Tane used his thunderbolt Fatu-Titi to kill Atea. In other myths, Atea is released from Rua, the god of darkness, by Ru, Hina, Maui, Tane or Atea depending on the legend. Sometimes all five deities were involved in the release of the god of light. *See also* Atuna; Hina; Maui; Mutuhei; Ono; Papa (A); Rangi; Rongo; Rua; Ta'aroa; Tanaoa; Tane; Tangaroa; Vari (A); Vatea.

Atea Rangi (Polynesia) *see* Atea; Rangi.

Atem (Egypt) *see* Atum.

Aten *Adon, Aton, Atum* (Egypt)
Also known as: *Horus, Khepri, Ra, Ra-Harakhte, Shu, Tem.*
God of the sun, light, providence and life. Depending on the position of the sun, he was called Aten, Khepri, Ra or Atum. Under the name of Horus, he was joined with Ra and was then called Ra-Harakhte. Called Aten, Pharaoh Amenhotep IV took the name Ikhnaton or Akhenaton (Akhenaten), meaning "pleasing to Aten." Married to the beautiful Nefertiti, he declared Egyptian religion to be monotheistic, although the god was probably worshiped at an earlier date. The monotheistic worship of Amenhoteps lasted from fifteen to seventeen years until the death of this Pharaoh. (It has been suggested that he and Nefertiti were murdered.) His reign initiated a revolutionary change in Egyptian art. During this period, artistic forms took on a naturalistic, as opposed to a stylized, form. The priests of Amen-Ra destroyed the records of his reign, and Akhenaten's son-in-law, Tutankhaten, who changed his name to Tutankhamen, restored the worship of Amen-Ra. Aten is usually pictured in the form of a large red disk with rays tipped with hands. At times he is shown as a falcon with speckled wings. *See also* Yahweh, the only god for the Egyptians at the time. Sometime during the reign of Amenhotep, Aten was changed to Shu, then changed again to Re or Ra. *See also* Akhet-nen-tha, Amen (B), Atum; Khepri.

Atene (Greek) *see* Ares.

Ater-Asfet (Egypt) One of the gods in the Pyramid Texts.

Atergata (Middle Eastern) *see* Atargatis.

Atergatis (Middle Eastern) *see* Atargatis.

Ateseatine (Pueblo People, United States) *see* Atseatsan.

Atesh (Persia) *see* Atar.

Athamas (Greek)
Athamas is one of seven sons of Aeolus and Enarete. He has six brothers and seven sisters (for a list of their names *see* Canace). His first of three marriages was to the nymph Nephele. He became the father of Helle and Phrixus. His second marriage to Ino produced two more children, Learchus and Melicertes. When he married his third wife, Themisto, he became the father of Erythrius, Leucon, Ptous and Schoeneus. Except for Leucon and Learchus, all of his children were accidentally killed by Themisto (she subsequently committed suicide). Athamas killed his son Learchus accidentally when he mistook him for a stag. When this happened, he was exiled to Thessaly. He renamed Thessaly, Athamantia. *See also* Aeolus (A); Canace; Helle; Nephele; Phrixus.

Athar (A) (Southern Arabic)
Male counterpart of the Assyro-Babylonian goddess Ishtar, who came into being after matriarchy was rejected.

Athar (B) (Ugarit)
One of the children of Asheratian of the sea. *See also* Astarte.

Atharate (Middle East) *see* Atargatis.

Atharvan (India) *see* Matarisvan.

Athena *Athenaa, Athenaia, Athene* (Greek)
Also known as: *Aithuia* (Diver Bird), *Baze, Bulaia* ("She of the Council"), *Glauk-Opis* ("Owl-faced"), *Gogopa* (Death Goddess), *Grogopa, Merchanitis, Minerva* (Roman), *Nice, Nike* (Goddess of Victory), *Pallas* (Storm Goddess), *Pallas Athene, Parthenia, Parthenos* ("Virgin"), *Polias* (Goddess of the City), *Soteira, Tritogeneia, Victoria* (Roman).

Assimilated from Minerva (Roman) and originally part of the triad of Jupiter, Juno and Minerva, the name Athena may have come from the Albanian goddess Ethona or Vedic Ahana. Hesiod connected her with Eris (strife) and at first she was a goddess of battle and storms. The Greeks identified her with the Egyptian sky goddess Neith. The grey-eyed Greek virgin goddess of war, wisdom, and handicrafts, and patroness of Athens, Athena is the daughter of Zeus and Metis. Zeus, fearing that Metis would bear a son stronger than himself, turned her into a fly and swallowed her. The child, Athena, sprang from his head fully armed with helmet, shield, and spear. Some say Prometheus or Hephaestus split open Zeus's head with an axe for this miraculous birth. Athena won the contest with Poseidon for Athens by producing the olive tree which the Athenians judged more useful than Poseidon's salt spring. The Parthenon was her temple. The owl is her bird. She is often depicted as a maiden in warlike array attended by the owl and the serpent, both emblems of wisdom. She is credited with the taming of horses and the use of chariots. In the form of Gogopa she is a death goddess. As Pallas, she was a storm goddess presiding over war. During times of peace she instructed people in useful crafts. Aithuia is her name when she is in the shape of a seabird. In the Wars of the Gods with the Giants and Titans, she defeated the monstrous giant Enceladus. She also assisted Heracles in various tasks. Athena taught Danus to build a two-prowed ship and helped Epeius build the wooden horse. Athena invented the loom, the spindle and the flute. It is said that she remained a virgin, rejecting all suitors. On the third year of each Olympiad, a festival, celebrated by games, banquets and sacrifices, was held in her honor. The prize was a jar of olive oil pressed from one of her sacred trees. Some old texts refer to Minerva using the name of Athena, and some consider them one and the same deity. As Athena, she was associated with the legend of Prometheus when he was considered a creator god. The Greeks also associated Athena with the goddess Net by representing her as a vulture and a scarab. She is shown with a conical cap surmounted with a cock's comb. She wields a spear and wears a scaly tunic trimmed with snakes. Between her breasts, she wears an ornament symbolizing the head of Medusa. She is associated with Hermes (q.v.). Athena is comparable to the goddess of dawn, Eos, and the Roman Aurora. *See also* Aegis; Aello; Aglaia; Agraulos; Ajax the Lesser; Anat; Argus (C); Artemis; Belleraphon; Cassandra; Corybantes; Enceladus; Epeius; Eris; Hephaistos; Hesperides; Inachus; Kore; Medea; Medusa; Minerva (Roman); Naiads; Neith; Nike; Pallas; Pegasus; Perseus; Stymphalian Birds; Zeus.

Athenaa (Greek) *see* Athena.

Athenaia (Greek) *see* Athena.

Athene (Greek) *see* Athena.

Athensic (Iroquois People, North America)
An ancestor, she fell from heaven during the great deluge. When the waters receded, she was on dry land which became a continent. *See also* Enigohatgea; Enigorio; Itapalas.

Ather (Greek) *see* Nemesis; Nox.

Atheret (Ugarit, Syria) *see* Athirat.

Athirat *Atheret* (Ugarit, Syria)
Mother of the gods, and known as "Athirat the Merciful," she is the official wife of El, the Supreme God. She suckled two of the gods, Shahar and Shalim, who were fathered by El. She rides a donkey with a silver harness. Athirat is often depicted seated at the seashore, spinning. *See also* Anat.

Athor (Egypt) *see* Hathor.

Athrar (Middle Eastern) *see* Asherah (B).

Athtar (Arabic, Babylonian, Canaanite)
Also known as: *Ashdar, Ishtar.*
Sky deity. In South Arabia Athtar was the planet Venus, but later Sumerian and Babylonians converted him to a female version who became Ashdar and Ishtar. *See also* Astarte; Innini.

Aththar (Ugarit, Syria) God of irrigation.

Athuma (Egypt) *see* Atum.

Athwya (Persian) *see* Haoma; Thraetaona.

Athyr (Greek) *see* Hathor.

Ati-Auru (Polynesia) *see* Tiki.

Atira (Pawnee People, North America) *see* H'uraru; Tirawa.

Atius (Pawnee People, North America) *see* Shakuru; Tirawa.

Atius Tirawa (Pawnee People, North America) *see* Tirawa.

Atlacamini (Aztec)
Storm god aspect of Chalchiuhtlicue (q.v.). *See also* Apoconallotl.

Atlantiades (Greek) *see* Hermaphroditus.

Atlantius (Greek) *see* Hermaphroditus.

Atlas (Greek)
Also known as: *Hyas.*
King of Mauretania. He is the Titan son of Iapetus and Asia (the consort of Prometheus) or Clymene, the river nymph daughter of Oceanus and Tethys. Others say he is the son of Uranus and Gaea. His siblings are Epimetheus, who opened Pandora's box; Menoetius, who was hurled into the underworld by Zeus' thunderbolt; and Prometheus, who was chained to a rock for thirty years while eagles nibbled daily on his regenerating liver. Atlas owned one thousand flocks of every type and fruit-bearing trees. He married Pleione (also known as Aethra) and was the father of Asterie, the Hesperides, the Pleiades, Hyades, Hyas, and Calypso. (Some write that Hesperis is the mother of the Hesperides.) He was also the father of Dione. Atlas fought with the Titans against Zeus. The unhappy Zeus doled out heavy punishment and sentenced Atlas to carry the weight of the world on his shoulders. At a later time, Heracles tricked Atlas into giving him the three Golden Apples. Atlas eventually was turned to stone by Perseus. Atlas is similar to the Egyptian god Shu. In the Pelasgian creation myth, Atlas was coupled with the Titan Phoebe as the rulers for the Moon. He is usually shown holding the sky with outstretched arms. *See also* Amphitrite; Calypso; Clymene; Epimetheus; Eurynome (A); Harmonia (A); Maia; Mercury (A); Oceanids; Orion; Pelops; Perseus; Prometheus; Themis.

Atlatonan (Aztec, Mexico)

Goddess of the coast. She is generally associated with Tez-catlipoca in festivals. In some legends Atlantonan, Uixtochi-huatl, Xilonen and Xochiquetzal were assigned to Tezcatlipoca as wives. *See also* Tezcatlipoca; Uixtochihuatl; Xilonen.

Atmu (Egypt) *see* Atum.

Atnatu (Aborigine People, Australia)

This High Being constructed himself out of nothing and gave himself a name. He has a wife and sons. All his sons have his name, Atnatu. He is described as a "great black man."

Aton (Egypt) *see* Aten.

Atonatiuh (Aztec, Mexico)

In the Creation Legend, this god caused the deluge of the "first earth." He was later equated with Tlaloc (q.v.). *See also* Legend of the Four Suns; Nata and Nena; Tlazolteutl.

Atreidae (Greek) *see* Agamemnon.

Atreus (Greek)

King of Mycenae. He is the son of Pelops and Hippodameia. His siblings are Alcathous, Astydameis, Chrysippus, Copreus, Lysidice, Nicippe, Pittheus, Thyestes and Troezen. He married Aerope who earlier had been the wife of Pleisthenes. Aerope had an affair with her brother-in-law, Thyestes, resulting in the birth of twins. The twins Tantalus and (possibly) Aglaus or Pleisthenes were slaughtered by Atreus who served them as a meal to Thyestes. Atreus is the father of Agamemnon and Menelaus. There is a possiblity that he is the father of Anaxibia and Pleisthenes. In another scenario, Thyestes married Pelops (who is actually Thyestes' exiled daughter), whom he believed was the daughter of Thesprotus. She was already pregnant by Thyestes at the time of their marriage. Atreus' death, in this case, was caused by the son of Thyestes and Pelops, Aegisthus. *See also* Aegisthus; Agamemnon; Hippodameia (B); Pelops.

Atri (India) Son of Brahma. *See also* Brahma; Rishi; Soma.

Atropos (Greek)

Also known as: *Fates, Moirai.*

Goddess of life. "The Unbending." One of the Fates. Her parents are Zeus and Themis, and Clotho and Lachesis are her sisters. Atropos, who carries the scissors to cut the thread of life, is said to be the smallest of the Fates, and the most terrible. Similar to Roman goddess Morta. *See also* Fates.

Atroposy (Greek) *see* Fates.

Atru-she-en-nesert-f-em-shet (Egypt) *see* Aaru.

Atse Estsan and Atse Hastin (Native American) *see* Atseat-san and Atseatsine.

Atseatsan and Atseatsine *Atse Estsan and Atse Hastin.* (Navaho, Pueblo, and Iroquois People, North America)

Also known as: *Ahsonnutli and Yolaikaiason.*

Creators. First man and first woman. God and goddess who raised the sun in the heavens. Ahsonnutli, with the help of twelve men, created a blaze from a crystal, but it was too hot so Atseatsan and Atseatsine appeared to give assistance. With a great deal of effort and much stretching of the earth, they raised the blaze to its present position in the sky. The twelve men who are the Yiyantsinni still hold the sun or heaven up with poles. In another version these were the first woman and man. They were created out of ears of corn by the four strange beings who suddenly appeared. These beings were Bitsis Lakai (also known as Hasteyalti), Bitsis Dotli'z (also known as To'nenili), Bitsis Litsoi, and Bitsis Lizi'n (also known as Hastezini). In another rendition, Atseatsan and Atseatsine intermarried with some underworld people named Kisani and from this inter-marriage came the human race. They are probably the same as Hasteyalti and Hastehogan. *See also* Anaye; Estsanatlehi; Kle-hanoai; Nayanezgani; Thobadzistshini.

Attabeira (Antilles Islands; Haiti) *see* Atabei; Iocauna.

Attes (Greek) *see* Attis.

Atthis (Greek) *see* Athena.

Attis *Attes, Attus, Atus, Atys* (Greek; Phrygian)

God of vegetation. Attis is the son of the Akkadian mother goddess, Nana, and an almond that had fallen to the ground. The almond had grown from the the genitals of Agdistis, who had castrated himself and turned into a pine tree. When Attis broke his vow of chastity and married the daughter of the river god Sangarius, he was driven insane by Cybele, who was supposedly his consort. He castrated himself and died. Violets grew from his blood and Cybele resurrected him in the form of a fir tree. Compare Attis to Anchises and to the Sumerian Dumuzi. *See also* Agdistis; Angus; Hephaistos; Uranus.

Atu (Egypt) *see* Aaru.

Atua (Polynesia) Flying ancestor spirits who live in trees. *See also* Atea.

Atugan (Mongol; Siberia)

Early goddess of the Mongols. Worshiped as one of the "Goddesses of Earth."

Atum (Egypt) *Atem*

Also known as: *Amen-Ra, Atmu, Atum-Ra, Atum-Re, Atumu, Khepri, Ra, Ra-Tem, Tem, Tem-Asar, Temu, Tum.*

Originally, Atum was a local god of the city of Annu or Heliopolis. His sacred animal was Merwer the bull. At a later time, he merged with Ra and was known as Ra-Tem. Later still, Atum was personified as the rising and the setting sun. He is generally thought to be the first born of the gods, father of the setting sun, and the ancestor of mortals. He is the son of the primeval Nun. In some accounts, he was created by four frogs and four snakes. In a variation, he is said to have originally been a serpent who changed into a man. At the end of the world he is to change back to a serpent and return to the primeval Nun. He became the father of the first divine couple, the twins Shu and Tefnut, by self-fertilization, either from his own spit or by self-copulation. His daughter Tefnut is also considered to be his consort. Later, when his cult spread, he had two female counterparts: Iusaas, (also called Iusaaset), and Nebhet Hotep (also called Nebt-Hetep). The births of Shu and Tefnut are also attributed to his union with Mebet Hotep. Atum is a member of the Ennead (the council of nine gods) which also includes Shu, Tefnut, Geb, Nut, Osiris, Isis, Set and Nephthys. The earliest records of him came from about 2350 B.C.E. during the fifth dynasty. He is shown with a human head, wearing the *pschent*, (the double crown of the Egyptian pharaohs), or shown as an old man leaning on a stick. A symbol of "Atum and his hand" appear as a divine couple on coffins of the Herakleopolitan period. Some think the Benu Bird is an aspect of Atum. Also see Benu. He is sometimes confused with Amon. *See also* Amen (B); Aten; Bennu; Ennead; Geb; Horus; Isis; Iusaas; Khepri; Nephthys; Nu; Nut; Ra; Set; Shu; Tefnut; Temu; Tum.

Atum-Ra (Egypt) *see* Atum.

Atum-Re (Egypt) *see* Atum.

Atuma (Egypt) *see* Atum.

Atumu (Egypt) *see* Atum.

Atus (Greek) *see* Attis.

Atvins (India) *see* Asvins.

Atymnius (Greek)
    The son of Zeus and Cassiopeia, Atymnius was the possible lover of Minos. If it was not him, it is thought to be Miletus. *See also* Cassiopeia; Minos; Sarpedon (A).

Atys *Attis* (Greek) *see* Attis, Cybele.

Au Sept (Egypt) Ancient creation goddess.

Auai (Egypt)
    Another name for Sekhem or possibly Ra. *See also* Aai.

Auchimalgen (Araucanian People, Chile, South America)
    Moon goddess, seer, protector of mortals and mate of the sun. Her face revealed everything. When red in color, it was an indication that an important person would die. *See also* Cherruve; Pillan.

Aud (Norse; Teutonic)
    Also known as: *Audr.*
    Deity of the night. Aud is the son of Nott (also known as Nat) by her first husband, Naglfari. He is the brother of Jord and Dag. *See also* Dag; Jord; Naglfari.

Audhumla *Audumla* (Norse; Teutonic)
    Audhumla, the divine cow, was created in Ginnunga-gap before the beginning of the world as we know it. The evil giant Ymir fed from the four rivers of milk that she produced. From his smelly armpits he produced his own offspring. Audhumla sustained herself by feeding from the salty ice. After eons had passed, she was still licking when a man's hair appeared. By the evening of the second day his head appeared, and by the evening of the third day the whole man appeared. He was the first man and his name was Buri. He became the father of Bor, who in turn was father of Odin, Ve, and Vili. Some say Audhumla was created by Surtr. Compare to Kamadhenu (India). *See also* Bor; Buri; Ginnunga-gap; Surtr; Ve; Ymir.

Audjal (Caroline Islands)
    A minor goddess of the earth. The care of the earth was given to her by the god Ifaluk.

Audumla (Teutonic) *see* Audhumla.

Auf (Egypt) *see* Ra.

Auga-nur (Semitic) *see* Agenor (A).

Auge (Greek) *see* Artemis.

Augeias (Greek) *see* Actor (B); Argonauts; Helius.

Augelmir (Teutonic) *see* Ymir.

Augralids, The (Greek) *see* Agraulos.

Augusel (Celtic) *see* Arawn.

Aukele-nui-aiku (Hawaii) *see* Kaneapeua.

Aukert *Aukar* (Egypt)
    Aukert is possibly another name for the underworld. It is mentioned in relation to Amen-Ra. *See also* Aaru; Tuat.

Aukhesia (Akkadian, Greek) *see* Lamia.

Aulanerk (Eskimo)
    Ocean deity. This naked deity lives in the ocean. His struggles cause the waves.

Auler (Teutonic) *see* Ull.

Aumakua (Hawaii)
    Guardian spirits. The Aumakua (spirits) come to meet the soul and protect it from the perils of the journey to the otherworld. *See also* Po.

Aumanil (Eskimo)
    Sea deity. He is a god of the whales, who lives on land.

Aun (Semitic, Syrian)
    Also known as: *An, On.*
    Ancient Semite fish god. The name may be associated with the fish god Dagon. The Syrians believed that Aun is the husband of Derketo. *See also* Atargatis; Dagon (A); Dagon (B).

Aunaauif (Egypt) *see* Ap-taui.

Aura (A) (Greek) *see* Aurora.

Aura (B) (Phoenician)
    In the Creation Legend of Damascius, Aura (meaning intelligence) and Air were the parents of Otos (meaning reason). Aura and Potos (meaning desire) were the parents of a daughter Omicle, who was known as "The Mother of All Things." *See also* Air (A).

Aura (C) (Greek)
    Her parents are Lelantos and Periboea. She became the mother of twins by Dionysus. During a mental breakdown, she tore one of her twins apart and ate it. She then committed suicide by drowning.

Auraka (Polynesian) "All-Devouring." Death deity.

Auramazda (Persia) *see* Ahura Mazda.

Aurboda (Teutonic) *see* Gulveig; Jotuns.

Aurentil (Teutonic) *see* Aurvandil.

Aurgelmir (Teutonic)
    This is another name for Ymir, the primeval frost giant (q.v.).

Aurgenimir (Teutonic) *see* Ymir.

Aurora (Roman)
Also known as: *Eos* (Greek).
Aurora, goddess of dawn, is the Roman name for the Greek dawn goddess, Eos. She is shown flying before the chariot of the sun, sometimes carrying a torch and flowers. Aurora is comparable to the Greek Athene, Ausera of the Lithuanians, the Vedic goddess of dawn, Ushas, and the Slavic Zorya Utrennyaya. *See also* Athena; Ausera; Eos; Gaea; Ushas.

Auroras, The Two *Auroras* (Serbian), *Zarya* (Slav), *Zoryas*
Also known as: *The Two Zarys or Zoryas*.
These two beautiful virgins sit at the side of the Sun King (possibly Dazhbog). One is Aurora of the Morning, the other, Aurora of the Evening. The Slavic people call Aurora of the Morning "Zorya Utrennyaya" and Aurora of the Evening "Zorya Vechernyaya." *See also* Aurora; Eos; Ushas; Zorya.

Aurva (India)
A Bhrigus sage, Aurva hated the Kshatriya race. *See also* Sagara.

Aurvandil *Aurentil, Orendil, Orvandel* (Norse; Teutonic)
Also known as: *Egil, Egilorvandel*.
A hero and a solar or wind deity, he is the spouse of the seer Groa, and the father of Hadding and Svipdag. His second wife was Sith the mother of Ull. He is also said to be the father of Roskva and Thjalfi. Aurvandil lives on the border of Jotunheim. Thor threw his frozen toe into the heavens where it became a star that some say is the morning star, or the constellation Orion. *See also* Groa; Thor.

Aus (Babylonian)
In the Creation Legend of Damascius, Aus is the brother of Anu and Illinus, and with his mate, Dauce, he is the father of Belus. *See also* Belus (B).

Ausaas (Egypt) She is the spouse of the sun god Harakhtes.

Ausar (Egypt) *see* Osiris.

Ausares (Egypt) *see* Osiris.

Ausera (Lithuanian)
She is the goddess of dawn comparable to Aurora, Eos, Saranyu and Ushas. *See also* Ausrine.

Aushedar (Persia) The First Savior. *See also* Zoroaster.

Aushedar-mah (Persia) The Second Savior. *See also* Zoroaster.

Ausiri (Egypt) *see* Osiris.

Ausrine (Lithuanian) Dawn goddess. *See also* Ausera; Breksta.

Aust (Egypt) *see* Isis.

Auster (Greek) *see* Notus.

Austi (Teutonic) A Dwarf. *See also* Dwarfs.

Austri *Austre* (Norse; Teutonic)
One of the four dwarfs who support the heavens (made from the skull of Ymir) on his shoulders. The other dwarves are Nordri, Sudri, and Westri. *See also* Aarvak; Muspells-heim; Ymir.

Autak (Persia)
The demon mother/spouse of Angra Mainyu and mother of Azhi Dahaka (qq.v.).

Authades (Gnostic)
Also known as: *The Proud God*.
The *Pistis Sophia* text is from an early gnostic sect similar in belief to that of the Ophites and of Valentinus. It is a composite of the writings of several scribes. The date of the original document is around the seventh century C.E. It is not known the age of the composite parts. There is a part of the universe called the Thirteenth Aeon which is controlled by a triad of vague unnamed deities called the Great Forefather or the Great Unseen One, a goddess named Barbelo, and a god named Authades. This triad from the book *Pistis Sophia* are variously named the Twenty-four Unseen Ones, the Three Tridynami or Triple Powers. Of these twenty-four powers, Pistis Sophia is the one whose name is the title of the book. *See also* Pistis Sophia.

Autolycus (A) (Greek)
Thief. Argonaut. He is the son of Hermes and Chione and the grandfather of Odysseus. He married Amphithea and they had several sons and Anticleia. He taught Heracles how to wrestle. Autolycus has the power of changing anything that he steals, and of never getting caught. He has only been outsmarted on one occasion, by Sisyphus (q.v.). *See also* Anticleia (A); Hermes; Odysseus.

Autolycus (B) (Greek) An Argonaut. Father of Polymede.

Autonoe (Greek)
She is the daughter of Cadmus and Harmonia. Her siblings are Agave, Illyrius, Ino, Polydorus and Semele. Her children, by her marriage to Aristaeus are Actaeon and Macris. After tormenting Semele, Dionysus drove her and her sisters insane. *See also* Actaeon; Aristaeus; Harmonia (A); Ino; Semele.

Autophyes (Gnostic) *see* Aeons.

Autu (Polynesia) *see* Atea.

Auxo (Greek) *see* Graces, Charities.

Avagdu *Avaggdu* (Celtic)
The ugly son of the fertility goddess Keridwen (q.v.).

Avaggdu (Celtic) *see* Avagdu.

Avaiki *Havai, Havaiki, Hawaiki* (Polynesia)
Avaiki is the coconut shell that is the universe. From the bottom of this shell came Vari and Take, the origin of all life. Some demons in Avaiki are Te-aka-ia-oe, Te-tangaengae or Te-vaerua, and Te-manava-roa. In the Tuamotuan version, a creator deity named Kiho dwelled beneath the foundations of Avaiki. *See also* Kiho; Vari (A); Vatea.

Avallon *Avilion* (Britain)
Also known as: *Avallach*.
God of the Underworld.

Avalokit-Isvara *see* Avalokitesvara.

Avalokitesvara (Buddhist; India)
Also known as: *Amitabha, Amoghapasa Lokeswa* (Nepal), *Avalokit-Isvara, Avalokiteswara* (Nepal), *Chen Resic* (Tibet),

Cheresi (Tibet), *Kuan Yin* (China), *Lokeswara, Mahakaruna, Padma-pam, Padmapani, Sahasrabhuja* (Nepal), *Samanta-mukha* (Nepal), *Sitatapatraparajita* (Tibet), *Tara.*

Avalokitesvara is known as the downlooking deity. One of five Dhyanibodhisattvas, he is the Bodhisattva of compassion and instruction, the protector of health from poisonous snakes, ferocious animals, robbers and demons. Avalokitesvara is one of the one hundred and eight forms of Lokeswara. Sharing in the misery of mortals, he symbolizes infinite compassion and a willingness to aid those in distress. He refuses to accept Nirvana since he considers such acceptance selfish because most mortals have not attained that stage. He appears in Bardo on the fourth day. In attendance with him are Amitabha and his consort Pandaravasini and Manjusri and two female Bodhisattvas, Gita and Aloka. Aloka (also spelled Aloke), who is also known as Nang-sal-ma, personifies light. She is associated with fire and her color is red. Avalokitesvara's invocation "Om Mani Padme Hum," which means "The Jewel of Creation in the Lotus," is found inscribed on rocks, loose stones, prayer wheels and other objects. In his manifestation with eleven heads he is known as Samantamukha. Avalokitesvara is often in the company of the goddess Tara. She is also the consort, according to some, of Amoghasiddhi and Akshobhya. Avalokitesvara, who has a million eyes and a hundred thousand hands, can appear in any guise. Sometimes he is shown as half-male and half-female. He is usually depicted standing and holding in his hand the indestructible jewel. He is shown in fifteen different shapes in sculptures. As Padmapani, he wears an effigy of Amitabha in his hair to indicate his divination and he holds a pink lotus. He corresponds to the Hindu Padmapami. *See also* Akshobhya; Amida; Amoghapasa; Amoghasiddhi; Dhyani Buddhas; Dhyanibodhisattvas; Kannon; Kharchheri; Kuan Yin (China); Lokeswara; Lu-ma; Manjusri, Matsyendranatha; Sahasrabhuja; Samantabhadra; Samantamukha; Shimhanada; Sristikanta; Tara; Vajrapani; Varuna.

Avalon (Celtic, Gaelic)
Also known as: *Avilion.*
Heaven. Avalon is an idyllic island in the west, the home of heroes after death. Some say that Avalon is near Glastonbury. It is also the place where King Arthur was buried by his sister, Morrigu (q.v.).

Avanc (Celtic) *see* Addane.

Avany (Ceylon)
Mother of Buddha Sakyamuni. *See also* Sakyamuni.

Avatar (Hindu, India)
Also known as: *Avatara.*
Reincarnated deity. An avatar is the reincarnation on earth of a deity in the form of an animal or human. For an example, see the section "Also known as" under the entry for Vishnu.

Avatea (Polynesia) *see* Vatea.

Aventina (Roman) *see* Diana.

Avesta (Zoroastrian)
The sacred book containing the teachings of Zoroaster (q.v.). *See also* Anahita; Bundahish; Yashts.

Avfruvva (Finno-Ugric) *see* Akkruva; Havfru.

Avilayoq (Eskimo People) *see* Sedna.

Avilix (Maya) *see* Xumucane.

Avlekete (Dahomey, Fon People, Africa) *see* Aylekete.

Awahili (Cherokee People, North America)
"The Sacred Eagle."

Awanawilona (Native American) *see* Awonawilona.

Awar (Islamic)
He is the crafty demon of evasion and lasciviousness who is the son of Iblis and the brother of Dasim Sut, Tir and Zalambur. His name means "one-eyed." *See also* Azazel.

Awejsirdenee (India) *see* Kalki.

Awhiowhio (Aborigine People, Australia)
Also known as: Ara Tiotio (New Zealand)
God of whirlwinds. As Ara Tiotio, he is the god of tornadoes.

Awitelin Tsita *Awitelin Ts'ta* (Zuni People, North America)
Also known as: *Awonawilona, Hatai Wugti* (Spider Woman).
Awitelin Tsita is the mother goddess who was created from the spit of Shiwanokia. As the mate of the sky god Apoyan Tachu, the two created life. In another legend she was created by Awonawilona (q.v.). *See also* Shiwanni and Shiwanokia.

Awo-kashiki-ne No Mikoto (Japan) *see* Ama-no-minaka-nushi.

Awo-mikoto (Japan) *see* Ama-no-minaka-nushi.

Awonawilona *Awonawilone* (Pueblo, Zuni People, North America), *Awonawilone*
Also known as: *Awitelin Tsita, Awitelin Ts'ta, He-She, Sun Father.*
"Maker and Container of All." "All-Father." Awonawilona created himself in the form of the sun. The sun brought light to the dark void and mist clouds from which the waters evolved. He impregnated the sea waters from the surface of his person and produced the scum. From the green scum, the "Four-fold Containing Mother Earth," known as Awitelin Tsita, and the "All Covering Father Sky," known as Apoyan Ta'chu, were created. From Awitelin Tsita and Apoyan Ta'chu, all terrestrial things were created. In other versions of the myth Awonawilona ruled above while Shiwanni and his wife Shiwanaokia ruled the earth. Awonawilona, the Supreme Spirit and life-giving power, is often thought of as the Sun Father. In another version of this myth, Awonawilona filled the sea with bits of his own flesh, then hatched the resulting mass into Father-sky and Mother-earth. He is associated with Achiyalatopa, the knife-feathered monster. *See also* Awitelin Tsita; Shiwanni and Shiwanokia; Tloque Nauaque.

Awun (Formosa) God of destruction.

Awwaw (Bantu Iyala People, Northern Nigeria, Africa)
Supreme God.

Axibia (Greek) *see* Helius.

Axioche (Greek) *see* Astioche.

Axiothea (Greek) *see* Hesione.

Axius (Greek) *see* Rivers.

Aya *Aja* (Assyrian, Babylonian, Chaldean)
"The Bride." Deity of the sea. Dawn goddess. She is the consort of Shamash and the mother of Misharu and Kittu. In later times, she merged with Ishtar (q.v.). Different versions say this deity may be male or female. Aya is a Babylonian goddess of dawn who later merged with Ishtar (q.v.). Compare Aya to Aurora, Eos, Saranyu and Usha.

Aya-kashiki No Mikoto (Japan) *see* Ama-no-minaka-nushi.

Aya-kashiko-ne No Mikoto (Japan) *see* Ama-no-minaka-nushi.

Ayar Aucca (Inca) *see* Tahuantin Suyu Kapac, and Manco Capac.

Ayar Cachi (Inca) *see* Tahuantin Suyu Kapac, and Manco Capac.

Ayar Manco (Inca) *see* Tahuantin Suyu Kapac, and Manco Capac.

Ayar Uchu (Inca) *see* Tahuantin Suyu Kapac, and Manco Capac.

Ayida (Haiti) Rainbow goddess. *See also* Damballaha.

Ayido (Haiti) *see* Damballah.

Aylekete *Avlekete* (Dahomey, Fon People, Africa)
Also known as: *Agbe.*
Thunder deity. A member of the Vodu family of gods. In the Dahomey belief, Aylekete is the chief god of thunder. *See also* Agbe; Rada; Vodu.

Ayllu (Inca)
The spirit of dead ancestors. *See also* Ka (Egypt).

Aymur (Ugaritic)
A magic weapon. *See also* Kothar and Khasis.

Ayodhya (India) Capital city of Rama. *See also* Sagara.

Aywil *Aiwel* (Dinka People, Africa)
Also known as: *Aiwil Longar.*
Spear god. Ancestor. Founder of Dinka religion. Born with great power and a full set of teeth, Aywil is the son of the creator goddess of women and gardens, Abuk. Aywil preached that people had to pray through his son, Deng, and his mother, Abuk. The first man, Diing, disagreed and finally it was decided that Aywil would control the sky and rain, while Diing would have the earth. As "spear master," he gave the first spears to men after an altercation with a man named Agothyathik. *See also* Abuk; Deng.

Az (Manicheism, Zoroastrian; Persia)
In the *Avesta*, Az appears as a minor male demon. In the Zoroastrian faith, Az is represented as the female prototype of "wrong-mindedness." In Manicheism, Az is also a female demon who is responsible for blinding man to his divine origin. *See also* Vohu Manah.

Azacca (Haitian)
God of agriculture. He is said to be brother of Ghede. His origin could be Indian rather than African.

Azai-Dahaka (Persian) *see* Azhi Dahaka.

Azapane (Sudan, Africa) *see* Bele.

Azariel (Hebrew)
This angel, invoked by people who fish, is responsible for the earth's waters.

Azazel *Azazil* (Arabic, Hebrew, Persian)
Also known as: *Eblis, Iblis* ("The Calumniator," Islamic), *Satan* ("The Hater"), *Shaitan, Taus, Zeraili* (Islamic; Africa).
A fallen angel, he is called a desert fiend and a seducer of women. He is the governor of the earth and the lowest heaven. In the African Islamic tradition he is the angel of death. Other accounts vary; one holds that after God created Adam, he commanded the angels to worship man. Azazel, at that time an angel, refused. God turned him into a devil and he became Iblis, the father of all evil genii. In another account, all the angels including Azazel gathered to look at the clay that their god intended to shape into the first man, Adam, who was to be superior to the angels. Azazel vowed never to accept man's superiority and kicked the clay until it rang. As Iblis, he had five sons Awar, Dasim, Sut, Tir, and Zalambur. In other accounts, he is the father of Sut and Ghaddar by a wife created by Allah. The thorny acacia bush was sacred to him according to Arab tribes. His name is pre–Jewish and pre–Islamic. Some speculate that he may have been an early Semitic goat god whose worship later became repulsive to the Jewish and Islamic faiths. Azazel is also known as Taus, the peacock angel. Sometimes Azazel is called Shaitan. *See also* Adam; Angra Mainyu (his Zoroastrian counterpart); Azrael; Daevas; Dasim; Devil; Jinn; Satan; Tiur.

Azazil (Middle Eastern) *see* Azazel.

Azdahak (Persia) *see* Azhi Dahaka.

Aze (Japan) Female pine tree spirit.

Azhdak (Persia) *see* Azhi Dahaka.

Azhi (Persia) *see* Azhi Dahaka.

Azhi Dahaka *Azai-Dahaka* (Iranian), *Azdahak, Azhdak, Azhi, Azi, Azi-dahak, Azi Dahaka* (Iranian, Zoroastrian; Persia)
Also known as: *Ahi* ("The Throttler; India) *Bivar-asp, Dahhak, Vishapa* ("Whose Saliva Is Poisonous"), *Zahhak, Zohak.*
His name means "Fiendish Snake." His greatest desire is to exterminate mortals from the face of the earth. He is one of the numerous demons created by Angra Mainyu to destroy the faithful. If he were cut open the whole world would be crawling with serpents, lizards and scorpions. In the *Avesta*, he ruled the second millennium of human history (the eighth of creation). In the "Bundahish," he is the son of fiendish demon Angra Mainyu by Angra Mainyu's mother, Autak. Azhi Dahaka, in an attempt to conquer Yima, was captured by Thraetaona and chained to Mount Demavand. He will remain there until the end of history. At that time, he will devour one-third of the mortals and one-third of the vegetation of the world. When Keresaspa is resurrected, he will slay Azhi Dahaka. This evil fiend evolved into the mythical king of Babylon, Zohak, who was an enemy of Persia. In Zoroastrian myth, Azhi Dahaka was

overcome by Faridun and chained to Mount Demavand. The last of his dynasty and that of the serpent-worshipping kings of Media is known as Bevarash. He is variously described as a three-headed serpent; a serpent with three mouths, triple heads, and six eyes; sometimes seven heads; or as a man with two serpents growing from his shoulders. *See also* Ahi; Ahura Mazda; Angra Mainyu; Atar; Avesta; Bundahish; Bushyansta; Demavand (Mount); Drujs; Faridun; Keresaspa; Thrita (for Thraetaona); Verethraghna; Yima; Zohak.

Azidahaka (Persia) *see* Azhi Dahaka; Azi; Drujs.

Aziza (Dahomey People, Africa)

Forest spirits who give magic and knowledge of the worship of gods to mortals.

Azrael (Hebrew, Muslim)

He is the angel of death who watches over the dying. At the moment of death he separates the soul from the body. At Judgement Day, Azrael will be the last to die. His death will come when the Archangel's horn sounds the second time. *See also* Angels; Azazel.

Azrua (Gnostic)

High god. A name for the supreme being who some believe is the equivalent of Zervan. (It is likely a corruption of Ahura Mazda or possibly the Sanskrit Asura.) In the context of the Manichaean belief it means the "King of the Paradise of Light," but not the highest god. That name is reserved for Fihrist. *See also* Ahura Mazda; Zervan.

Aztec People — Creation Legend (Mexico) *see* Chicomontoc, Legend of the Five Suns.

Aztlan (Aztec, Mexico)

Aztlan is the legendary home of the Aztecs. There are seven cities in Aztlan that correspond to the seven tribes, or seven sons, of Mixcoatl. *See also* Mixcoatl; Ixtaccihuatl.

Azur (Assyria, Sumer) *see* Ashur.

B

B (Maya)

Carrying the axe and fasces, this thunder god is depicted frequently on statues and in ancient manuscripts. He may be the thunder god Chac (q.v.). *See also* "K."

B-Iame (Australia) *see* Baiame.

Ba (Egypt)

Also known as: *Bia, Ka* (Spirit), *Kah, Khu* (Mummy), *Ta* (Shade).

Soul of the Dead. The Egyptians believed that each mortal was made up of three parts: the Ka (the double), Ba (the soul), and the Akh (glorified spirit). The Ba departs the body temporarily after death, returning to the mummy to preserve it. Once the body is buried, the Ba continues to visit the cemetery at night and is given refreshments by Neith, Hathor, or other tree of life goddesses. Ba is usually shown as a hawk with a human head. Ka is shown as a heron. *See also* Ab; Akh; Amenti; Assessors; Hathor; Ka; Neith.

Ba Neb Tetet (Egypt) *see* Banededet.

Ba-neb-tettu (Egypt)

Creator god. *See also* Hathor; Heru-pa-kaut.

Ba-Ra (Egypt) *see* Aai.

Ba-tau (Phoenician)

He is either the brother of Hay-Tau or an incarnation of Hay-Tau (q.v).

Ba Xian (China) *see* Eight Immortals.

Ba'al (Phoenicia) *see* Baal.

Baal *Ba'al Bal, Bel, Belu* (Babylonia, Phoenicia, Sumer, Syria)

Also known as: *Aleyn Baal, Armen, Ba'al Lebanon, Ba'al of Tyre, Ba'al Shamin, Ba'al Tsaphon* ("Lord of the North"), *Ba'alzebub, Ba'alim, Baalim, Baalsamame, Balsamem, Balshameme, Barshamina, Bel* (Sumer, Babylonian), *Belshim, Belu, Belus,* (Phoenician), *El, Elagabalus* (Roman), *Great Baal, Hadad, Melkart* ("God of the City"), *Rider of the Clouds.*

Baal is a title meaning lord, or master. The Phoenicians used the title to disguise the real name of the god. They feared that strangers would win the god's favor if they knew his true name. There were many local Baals. The greatest, known as the "Great Baal," is the son of the Father of the gods, El, and brother of the god of seas and rivers, Yam-Nahar. Baal, known as "Rider of the Clouds," is a fertility god representing the beneficent aspects of water as rain. His lightning and thunder depict his power, and the fertile earth his beneficence. In conflict with Yam-Nahar, who was El's favored son, Baal eventually subdued him. After his victory, his home of cedar and brick seemed inappropriate. Baal wanted a grander dwelling, like the other gods. With his sister Anath, he approached Asherah, goddess of the sea and mate of El, and asked her to intercede on his behalf and make his request known to his father El. Permission was granted and it was decided that the abode would be constructed from the tree of Lebanon, the cedar of Antilebanon, and with lapis-lazuli, gold, and silver. Kothar-u-Khasis, the god of crafts, was called in to work on the project. Baal argued with the contractor, insisting that his home be built without windows. It is thought that he did not want Yam-Nahar to see him frolicking with his lovers. Kothar-u-Khasis prevailed and it was finally agreed that there would be a window in the edifice. This window was ostensibly for Baal to use to send out his thunder and lightning. Upon completion of the home, Baal arranged a magnificent celebration. A host of family, including Asherah's seventy children, were invited. His father, El, had a new favorite: the god of the underworld and sterility, Mot, who represents aridity. Baal sent his messengers Gapn and Ugar to inform Mot that he was not invited to his celebration. Displeased, Mot returned a threatening message. Victorious over Yam-Nahar, Baal now had to deal with Mot. The message frightened him, and he responded that he was Mot's slave forever. In one interpretation, Baal was devoured by Mot. Mot was then forced to regurgitate him by Baal's sister, Anath, with the aid of Shapash. In another rendition, El, grief-stricken when he heard of his son's death, wandered around lamenting and gashing himself. Anath searched for her brother and when she found his body Shapash helped her carry it to Mount Zaphon. A great funeral feast was held in his honor. Anath went in search of her brother's murderer, Mot. When she found him, she brutally massacred him. After a time, El had a dream that Baal was still alive. Joyously, he announced the news to Anath and Shapash. His absence had left the soil dry and parched. Lady Asherah of the Sea had put her son Ashtar on the throne during Baal's absence. He found that his feet would not touch the footstool, nor his head the top of the throne, so he declined to rule in the heights of Mount Zaphon. Baal was eventually found and restored to the throne. His battle with Mot was renewed. After an intense struggle, they both fell to the ground and were separated by Shapash. It appears that they came to a meeting of the minds for Baal was restored to his throne. Baal's name as the god of thunder and lightning is Hadad. As Hadad, he sent monstrous creatures to attack Asherah and the moon god, Yarikh. They appealed to El for assistance. He advised them to hide in the wilderness and give birth to wild beasts so that Hadad would be distracted and chase the beasts. As forecast, Hadad hunted the monsters. He was captured by them and disappeared for seven years. During this period, the earth fell into what is described by some as chaos but may have been a severe draught. In a Canaanite myth, Anath is looking for Baal, and is told by his servants that he is hunting. She searches for him and when they meet he falls in love with her. Although she is in the shape of a cow, they have sex. From this union, a wild ox was born. Baal is portrayed as a bull, the emblem of animal and vegetable fertility. See also Anath; Asherah (B); Bod-Baal; El (the father god was the equivalent to Enlil and at times they were identified with each other); Hadad; Kothar and Khasis; Mot; Shapash; Yam-Nahar; Yarikh.

Baal Enet Mahartet (Ugarit)
Rain god.

Ba'al Hammon *Baal Hammon* (Carthage)
Also known as: *Aleyn-baal.*
Sky god. Fertility god. Husband of Tanit. He appears to have been worshiped along with Tanit Pene Ba'al (a little known goddess). Romans thought him to be the god Jupiter Ammon from Africa. He is shown as a bearded old man wearing ram's horns on his head. The bull is a manifestation of Baal among the Canaanites. See also Aleyn-Baal; Baal; Tanit.

Ba'al Lebanon (Semite)
God of lightning, rain, and thunder. See also Baal.

Baal-Peor (Moabite) see Chemosh.

Baal Sapon (Canaanite, Hurrite, Syrian)
Ancient god similar to Jupiter.

Baal Shamin see Baalshamin.

Ba'al Shamin *Balsamem, Balsamin, Balshamin, Balshameme, Belshim* (Arabic, Armenian, Hittite, Phoenician, Semitic, Syrian)
Also known as: *Baal, Adad.*
"Lord of the World." "Good and Rewarding God." "Master of the Skies." Ba'al is the head of the pantheon consisting of Dur-Europas, Hatra, Palmyra, Shahr and Shamash. His chief opponent is Vahagn. In some renditions, Vahagn was responsible for stealing Ba'al Shamin's wife Astaik. As a Syrian deity, he was destroyed by the Armenian god, Aram. As an Armenian god, originally from Phoenicia, Ba'al Shamin is known for his heroic deeds. See also Adad; Aleyn-Baal; Armenak; Astaik; Baal; Vahagn.

Baal-Sutekh (Egypt) see Anat.

Ba'al Tsaphon (Semite) see Baal.

Ba'al-zebub *Baalzebub, Ba'al-zebul, Beelzebub, Beelzebul* (Semite)
Also known as: *Fly.*
Demon. Lord of Flies. Lord of Zebulon. God of the city of Ekron. Although frequently called Beezlebub, it is an incorrect name for him. Some writers say the early Hebrews changed the name of Yahveh to Ba'al-zebub because they couldn't associate an idol with their god. He is similar to Satan. See also Baal.

Ba'al-zebul (Semitic) see Ba'al-zebub.

Ba'alat *Baalat, Baalath* (Semitic), (Phoenicia, later connected to the Egyptians and Semites)
Also known as: *Baaltis, Belili, Beltis, Belit.*
"The Lady." "Queen of Gods." Goddess of books, libraries, writers. She is the female equivalent of Baal. Her principal city is Byblos, which gave humans papyrus. (Papyrus was called Byblos by the Greeks, who then applied the same word to books.) She is depicted with an elaborate Egyptian hairstyle, wearing a tight robe, with shoulder straps. Her dress on a cylinder seal resembles that worn by the goddess Hathor. The Phoenicians depicted her generous body naked, with her hands covering her full breasts. She is sometimes identified with the Egyptians Isis and Hathor. Ba'alat corresponds to Baalti and Beltu. See also Cybele; Ishtar.

Baalath (Semite)
The female aspect of Baal. She is identical to Ba'alat, Baalti and Beltu.

Ba'alim (Semite) see Baal.

Baalim (Phoenician) see Baal.

Baalith (Middle East) *see* Belili.

Baalsamame (Phoenician) *see* Adad; Baal.

Baalshamin (Mesopotamian) *see* Ba'al Shamin.

Baalti *Belti* (Phoenician) *see* Belti.

Baalzebub (Phoenician) *see* Ba'al-zebub.

Baau (A) (Assyro-Babylonian) *see* Bau; Tiamat.

Baau (B) (Phoenician)
In the Creation Myth of "Philo Byblos," she is the spouse of Kolpia, and the mother of Aion and Protogonos. *See also* Kolpia.

Bab (Egypt)
Also known as: *Baba, Set, Seth.*
Trickster. In legend, this roguish god upset the tribunal during the trial between Osiris and Seth. *See also* Neith.

Baba (Egypt)
Another name of the evil god Seth. The name generally means parent or father. *See also* Ab.

Baba Yaga *Baba Jaga* (Russian, Slavic)
Deity of the dead. Baba Yaga is a thunder witch and the grandmother of the Devil. This supernatural hag lives in a house with a picket fence tipped with skulls. She rides through the sky in an iron cauldron and sweeps away the traces of her passage with her broom. (Some say her chariot is a mortar and pestle.) She eats or petrifies her victims. *See also* Bertha (German).

Babas (Armenia)
An ancient Armenian deity. The name may just mean "father." *See also* Ab; Baba.

Babbar (Sumer)
He is the sun god of Larsa, and a member of the earliest Sumerian pantheon. *See also* Shamash; Utu.

Babhru-Vahana *Babru-Vahana* (India)
He is the son of Arjuna and Chitrangada. *See also* Arjuna.

Babru-Vahana (India) *see* Babhru-Vahana.

Babusum (Saora People, India)
This guardian god rides on a horse through each village nightly. *See also* Ajorasum.

Babylonian — Creation Legend (from Berosus) *see* Belus (C).

Babylonian — Creation Legends (from Damascius) *see* Aus; Belus (C).

Babylonian — Creation Legend (Chinese, Greek) *see* Chaos.

Bacab (Maya) *see* Becabs.

Bacchantes *Bassarids* (Greek) *see* Dionysus; Maenads.

Bacchus *Bakchos, Bakkhos* (Roman, Arabic, Egypt, Ethiopia, Greek, Phoenicia, Roman, Semite)
Also known as: *Dionysus* (Greek), *Iacchus, Lakchos, Liber, Orotal, Salmoxis, Zalmoxis.*
Originally a nature god. Later a god of wine and revelry. Fertility god. The worship of Bacchus was carried into Greece where he became the Greek Dionysus. However, he was also known as Bacchus (indicating noisy and rowdy) by the Greeks and Romans. The eternally youthful Bacchus represents the social and beneficent aspects of wine, as well as its intoxicating prop-

erties. He is the son of Semele and Jupiter. Semele had encouraged Jupiter to come to her in his divine splendor. He reluctantly agreed. When he appeared before her as thunder, she was killed by lightning. Jupiter was able to save their unborn child, Bacchus. After the death of Semele, Jupiter placed Bacchus with the Nysaean nymphs. While growing up he became familiar with the properties of grape growing. Juno, the enemy of his mother, struck Bacchus with madness. Bacchus set off in his altered consciousness to wander the earth. The goddess Rhea cured him in Phrygia. He left the area and traveled through Asia and India teaching the people how to cultivate the grape vine. When he returned to Greece, the rulers, particularly Pentheus, who feared the negative effects of the grape juice, refused to receive him. Pentheus' mother, Agave, and her friends, members of the Bacchus cult, were extremely unhappy with his stance. Likely in a highly inebriated state and full of anger, she tore her son Pentheus apart. At another time in Bacchus' travels he was on a ship en route to Asia. The sailors, who were really pirates, came up with the idea that they could make extra money by selling Bacchus into slavery. They threatened Bacchus, who was not happy with their plan. Using his skills as a deity, he changed himself into a ferocious lion. The ship, at his command, became a vessel of serpents with jungle-thick plant life covering it. When he added music to the air, he terrified the pirates. They plummeted to their deaths in the sea where they became sweet, docile dolphins. Bacchus is shown in purple robes in peacetime and wearing panther skins in time of war. In early representation he was a pillar of stone and is sometimes shown as a goat. The goat is a symbol of fertility as well as lasciviousness, agility, and sociability. It also symbolizes stupidity and stench. He is also depicted seated in a chariot drawn by panthers, leopards or tigers. He is crowned with vine leaves, and is surrounded by a group of intoxicated satyrs and nymphs. The staff is his attribute as it is for Asclepius, Dionysus, Hermes and Mercury. The symbolism of the staff represents support or an instrument of punishment. Red wine symbolizes blood and sacrifice, as well as youth and eternal life. The grape represents fertility and sacrifice, for from the grape comes the wine. Bacchus is the personification of the sun as ripener. The ass was sacred to Bacchus as well as Silenus. This animal symbolized wisdom and prophetic powers. The bull with a human face represents Bacchus. (Pan wore the ears of an ass to indicate acute perception.) Compare Bacchus to Set (Egypt), for whom the ass was an insignia. Sometimes Bacchus is identified with Liber. *See also* Bes; Dionysus; Juno; Maenads; Rhea; Satyrs; Semele; Silenus.

Bach-ma (Indo-China) *see* Ma-Mien.

Bachis (Egypt) *see* Buchis.

Bachue (Chibcha People, Colombia, South America)
Also known as: *Turachogue.*
Goddess of water. Goddess of farming. Protector of vegetation and harvest. Bachue emerged from her home under the waters of Lake Iguaque bearing a small boy with whom she later mated. They had four or six children, although some myths say they created the human race. When she was content that mortals could live without her, she transformed herself and her mate into dragons. They returned to their home in the lake, where they still reside. *See also* Bochica; Chiminagua.

Backlum Chaam (Maya)

God of male sexuality. One of the Becabs, he is similar to Priapus of the Greeks (who is originally from Asia). *See also* Acat; Becabs.

Badari *Bhadri-Nath* (Hindu; India)

An ancient title for Shiva, later given to Vishnu as Lord of Badari, a shrine on the Ganges. Durga was called Bhandrakali. The name is connected with Bhadra or Bhandra which means "piety." In the Maratha country he was worshiped as Bhadra Vira. Under this name, he is depicted with the sun and moon, and is mounted on Nandi, the sacred cow. The goat-headed Daksha accompanies him. Badari is armed with a bow and arrow, sword, spear, and shield. *See also* Daksha; Durga; Nandi; Shiva; Vishnu.

Badava (India) *see* Vadava.

Badb Catha (Celtic, Irish)

Also known as: *Badb, Badhbh, Battle Raven, Cauth Bodva* ("War Fury," Gaul), *Morrigu* (possibly).

"Battle Raven." Goddess of war. Goddess of death. Storm goddess (possibly). Death is eminent when the Celtic fury Badb Catha appears. After the Battle of Moytura when the Tuatha De Danann's fought and drove away the Formonians, Badb recounted the event and prophesied doom. There is a possibility that Badb Catha is an incarnation of the goddess Morrigu. Badb later deteriorated into the Banshee. She is usually depicted as a crow, sometimes as a bear, wolf, cow, a foul hag, a gigantic woman, or a beautiful young woman. *See also* Banshee; Bean-Nighe; Morrigu.

Badessy (Dahomey People, Africa; Haiti)

Sky god. Badessy is a minor deity who was worshiped along with the male deities called hougouns and the females called mambos.

Baduh (Semite)

Invoked by writing the numerals 8, 6, 4, 2, (these numerals represent the letters in the Arabic alphabet that form his name), Baduh insures that messages are quickly delivered.

Baduhenna (Teutonic)

Goddess of war and storm goddess.

Baeldaeg (Teutonic) *see* Balder.

Bafur *Bavor* (Teutonic) *see* Dwarfs.

Bag-Mashtu (Iranian; possibly a local god of the earlier Urartian people)

Also known as: *Bag-Mazda*

Sky deity. He is often confused or identified with Ahura Mazda. There is a possibility that he is an ancient form of that god. Bagos Papaios, the Phrygian sky god, might be associated with Bag-Mashtu. *See also* Bagos Papaios; Khaldi.

Bag-Mazda (Persia) *see* Ahura Mazda.

Bagadjimbiri (Aborigine People, Australia)

Creators. They are two heavenly brothers who created everything. They started out as Dingos (wild dogs), but changed to giants, whose heads touched the sky. They had a great deal of hair that they pulled out and gave to every tribe. They were killed by a man, but Dilga, their mother, detected the odor of the corpses and sent the milk from her breasts underground to where they lay. It revived them and killed the man. The brothers eventually became water snakes.

Bagavatcbi (India) *see* Parvati.

Bagos Papaios (Pyrygian)

Sky deity. This little known deity of the early Pyrygian people might have been worshiped with the earth goddess, Semele. She is possibly identified with Kybele and Ma. *See also* Bag-Mashtu; Semele.

Bahman (Persia) *see* Vohu Manah.

Bahram (Islamic) Protector of travelers. *See also* Verethraghna.

Bahu (India) *see* Bau; Bohu; Sagara.

Bai Ulgan *Bai-Ylgon* (Altaic, Tartars)

Also known as: *Kudai Bai-ulgon*.

A high god, his name means "Most Grand." He lives in the sixteenth heaven on the Golden Mountain. His three sons are Pyrshak-khan, Tos-khan, and Suilap. Two of his grandsons, Kyrgys-khan and Sary-khan, are gods of happiness. Later, he was replaced by Tengere Kaira Kan, to whom horse sacrifices were offered. *See also* Tangri.

Bai-Ylgon (Altaic, Tartars) *see* Bai Ulgan.

Baiame (Aborigine People, Australia)

Also known as: *B-Iame, Biamban, Birral, Bunjil, Byamee, Daramulun, Kohin, Koin, Maamba, Munganngaua, Nurelli, Nurrundere.*

Father of all things and master of life and death, Baiame resides in a sky palace constructed of fresh water and quartz crystal. It is generally thought that at one time he lived on earth. Invisible, sometimes he appears as a human in the form of an old man. He is the father of Daramulun. Sometimes he is depicted as an old man sitting with his legs under him or sometimes asleep. Baiame, the force of good, is opposed by the Darawigal, the force of evil. *See also* Bunjil; Daramulun; Nurrundere.

Baidya-isvar (India) *see* Shiva.

Baidya-nith *Byju-Nath* (Hindu; India)

Little is known about this ancient deity, but some say Shiva changed his name to Byju to please an aboriginal worshiper at the shrine of Baidya-Nath. As Baidya is also the name for some of the peaks of the hills, it could signify Baidya-nith as a deity of the hills or mountains.

Bairam (Persia)

A later name for the god of victory Verethraghna (q.v.).

Bairavi (India) "The Terrible." *See also* Kali.

Baiyuhibi (Indonesia)

God of clouds, fog and rain. Creator of mountains and valleys.

Baj Bajaniai *Bajanai* (Yakut People, Siberia)

Forest god. God of hunters. His tears are rain and his voice the wind. In some instances, his game herd is called Baj Bajaniai.

Bajanai (Siberia) *see* Baj Bajaniai.

Bajang *Badjang* (Malaysia)
A malignant spirit who foretells disaster.

Bak (India) *see* Vach.

Bakasura (India) A demon. *See also* Krishna.

Bakchos (Greek) *see* Bacchus.

Bakh (Egypt) *see* Buchis.

Bakha (Egypt) *see* Buchis.

Bakkhos (Greek) *see* Bacchus.

Bala-Bhadra (India) *see* Bala-Rama.

Bala-Deva (India) *see* Bala-Rama.

Bala-Hadra (India) *see* Bala-Rama.

Bala-Rama (Vedic, Hindu; India) *Balarama*
Also known as: *Bala-Bhadra, Bala-Deva, Bala-Hadra, Gupta-Chara, Hala-Bhrit, Hala-Yudha, Halayudha* (Whose Weapon Is a Ploughshare), *Kam-Pala, Langali, Madhupriya* (Friend of the Wine), *Musali, Nila-Vastra, Sankashana, Sesha, Silappadikaram* (Tamil People, India).
Bala-Rama, the god of shepherds and ploughers, is the elder brother of Krishna. It had been ordained by the gods that order had to be restored to the earth. Vishnu, therefore, created an avatar of himself in the form of Krishna to combat the forces of evil. Vishnu plucked a white hair from Seshu the serpent that would become Bala-Rama and a black hair from his body that would become Krishna. These hairs were placed in the womb of Devaki, the wife of Vasudeva. When the demon Kansa heard about the impending birth of forces that would kill him, he ordered that Devaki's first six children be slaughtered. Bala-Rama was transferred to the womb of Rohini, the other wife of Vasudeva. The demon Kansa was told that Devaki had miscarried. When Bala-Rama was older, he ploughed the course of the river Yamuna with his ploughshare Hala, and created all things with his club, named Khetaka (also named Saunanda), and Musala, his pestle. Bala-Rama shared many of Krishna's adventures and assisted him in slaying many demons. He instructed Bhima and Duryodhana in the skills of warfare. Later, in the great war of the Mahabharata, he rescued Krishna's son Samba from Duryodhana. He did not participate in the battle between his cousins, the Kauravas and the Pandavas. King Raivata thought that his daughter Revati was too beautiful to be the wife of a mortal. He searched for and found the god Bala-Rama. Bala-Rama and Revati had two sons, Nishatha and Ulmuka. In the Vaishnava tradition, Bala-Rama is considered Vishnu's eighth avatar instead of Krishna, who is considered a god in his own right. Others say that Bala-Rama is an avatar of Vishnu's endless, thousand-headed serpent, Sesha. When he died, under the Banyan tree in Krishna's celestial abode Dvarka, Sesha slithered out of his mouth and flew to Vishnu's ocean. A marvelous funeral was held for Krishna and Bala-Rama. When Vasudeva, Devaki and Rohini heard of Krishna's death, they died of grief. Krishna's eight primary wives, Bala-Rama's wives, and King Ugrasena threw themselves on the funeral pyre and burned to death. Bala-Rama is described as being of fair com-plexion and wearing a blue vest. Compare Bala-Rama to Heracles. *See also* Bana; Bhima; Devaki; Duryodhana; Jagannath; Kaliya; Kansa; Kauravas; Krishna; Pandavas; Sesha; Sisupala; Syamantaka; Yami.

Balam (Quiche People, Central America)
A jaguar god. *See also* Gucumatz.

Balam-Agab (Maya) *see* Xumucane.

Balam-Quitze (Maya) *see* Xumucane.

Balamma (India)
She is one of the Mutyalammo goddesses who are deities of the household. Her function is to preside over the family carts. *See also* Mutyalammo.

Balams (Quiche People, Central America)
The Balams are the ancestor gods of the Quiche. *See also* Gucumatz.

Balan (Celtic) *see* Bel (B).

Balandhara (India) *see* Bhima (A).

Balarama (India) *see* Bala-Rama.

Balbog (Slavic)
Also known as: *Belbogh, Bjelbog.*
Sun god. He is often called the "Pale One," or the "Shining One." Balbog is similar to Balder.

Baldag (Teutonic) *see* Balder.

Balder *Baldr, Baldur* (Norse; Teutonic)
Also known as: *Baeldaeg, Baldag, Beldeg, Beldegg, Paltar, Wodan* (later Germanic form).
Sun god. God of innocence and piety. Balder is the son of Odin and Frigga, and the brother of Hermod. Nanna is his wife and their child is Forseti, the dispenser of justice. Balder lives in his zodiacal house, Breidablik, which corresponds to the sign of Gemini, the twins. When Balder had a series of troubling nightmares about death, he reported them to the Aesir council. The goddess Frigga listed all things and commanded that nothing would harm Balder, but she neglected to include mistletoe. In one myth, Loki the jealous fire god and trickster was aware of Frigga's omission. He persuaded the blind god of darkness, Hodur, to throw either the mistletoe branch, or sprig, or a spear, or in some myths, a magic sword named Mistelteinn. It hit Balder and he fell dead. His ship, Hringhorn, became his funeral pyre. Nanna committed suicide. Odin's son Hermod, who was a messenger for the gods, took his father's horse Sleipnir, and rode it to Hel in an attempt to rescue Balder. In one myth he offers to pay a ransom for Balder's return. Hel agreed, with the stipulation that everything in the world, dead and alive, must weep for Balder. The magic ring, Draupnir, which had been placed on his funeral pyre, was given to Hermod by Balder, to be given to Odin. Nanna, who also had a magic ring, gave it to Hel to give to Fulla. Hermod returned to earth where everything dead and alive wept for Balder, except for Loki, the trickster fire god, who had disguised himself as a female giant named Thok. Balder could not return to earth. He is expected to return with several other gods and two humans after Ragnarok (also known as "The Twilight of the Gods"). Balder's death was

avenged by Vali who is a son of Odin and Rind. Balder is depicted as a very handsome man. Balder is associated with Heimdall (q.v.). He corresponds to the Slavic Byelobog, and is similar to the Slavic god Balbog (qq.v.). *See also* Aesir; Asmegir Citadel; Balbog; Boe; Breidablik; Draupnir; Forseti; Frigga; Hel; Hermod; Hodur; Loki; Miming; Nanna (A); Njord; Ragnarok; Rind; Skadi; Sleipner; Thok; Thor; Vali; Vanir; Wodan.

Baldr (Teutonic) *see* Balder.

Baldur (Teutonic) *see* Balder.

Baleyg (Teutonic)
"One with Flaming Eyes." Another name for Odin.

Bali (A) *Balin, Wali, Valin* (Hindu; India)
The giant ape and monkey prince Bali is the son of Indra and the half-brother of Sugriva. They shared the same mother, who was a monkey queen. Bali had a long and powerful tail. Once, the king of the demons, Ravana, came up behind him and grasped it as Bali was performing ablutions. Without missing a beat, Bali used his tail to tie Ravana's hands and feet. He set out on a jaunt to visit the western, eastern and northern oceans with the demon held captive on his tail. He kept him that way for twelve years. As the son of Indra, he was endowed with more power than Sugriva. He had the ability to look at anyone and assume half of that person's strength. He usurped his brother from the throne and held reign as King of the Monkeys until he was killed by Rama. His spouse was Tara, also known as Dara, and he had a son, Angada. *See also* Indra; Rama; Ravana; Sugriva.

Bali (B) *Baly* (Brahman, Hindu; India)
He is the demon grandson of Prahlada; son of Virochana; spouse of Vindhyavali; and the father of Bana (also called Vairochi), the demon with a thousand arms, and a daughter Putana, who had poisonous breasts. His austere devotions earned him the authority to reign over the three worlds known as Triloka. Triloka consists of akasa (heaven) where the sun shines but there are no clouds, apas (atmosphere) where clouds are found, and vasumdhara (earth) where mortals are generally found. His power was a threat to the gods, so Vishnu, in his dwarf avatar as Vamana, asked Bali if he could have as much land as he could cover with three steps. When Bali consented, Vamana immediately assumed his cosmic size as Vishnu and with one step covered the earth from one end to the other. His second step covered the heavens. His third step could have covered the entire underworld but he left the lowest portion, known as Patala, for Bali. In another legend, a battle took place between Indra and the demons led by Jalandhara. Bali was struck, and when he fell, a flood of jewels came from his mouth. Indra threw his vajra (thunderbolt) at him and ripped him to pieces. Because of his severe austerities and pure conduct, precious jewels came from various parts of his body and his blood was changed to rubies. *See also* Bana; Daityas; Krishna; Nara-Simha; Patala; Prahlada; Surya; Vamana; Vishnu.

Balin (Celtic) *see* Bel (B).

Balius (Greek)
This immortal horse and his brother, Xanthus, belonged to Achilles. They are the sons of Boreas and Podarge, the Harpy. *See also* Achilles; Boreas; Harpies; Podarge; Xanthus; Zephyrus.

Balmarcodes (Phoenician)
God of revelry and the dance. He is probably another form of Hadad. *See also* Hadad.

Balmung (Teutonic)
Also known as: *Gram*.
The dwarfs fashioned this magic sword for Siegfried. *See also* Sigurd.

Baloi (Basuto People, Australia)
The Baloi haunt graves. They are also known for working harmful magic on an extracted tooth and on the person who previously owned the tooth.

Bal'or (Celtic) *see* Balor.

Balor *Bal'or* (Celtic, Irish)
"Evil Eye." King of the Fomorians. The god Balor is the monster son of Buarainech and the grandson of Net. One of his eyes had been poisoned. Everything he glanced at could be destroyed. This one-eyed monster was the champion of the Fomorians. He was killed by a stone from the sling of his grandson, Lugh, that hit him in his only eye and scattered his brains in all directions. This took place at the second Battle of Moytura. His corpse was hung on the sacred hazel tree. Since that time, the tree has dripped poison. Balor now lives under the sea. Compare him to the Greek Acrisius. *See also* Cian; Dagda; Lugh; Yspaddaden (Welsh).

Balsamem (Mesopotamia) *see* Adad; Baal; Ba'al Shamin.

Balshameme (Mesopotamia) *see* Adad; Baal, Ba'al Shamin.

Balshamin (Mesopotamia) *see* Adad; Ba'al Shamin.

Baltein (Celtic, Irish) *see* Beltine.

Baltis (Phoenician)
Cronus gave the city of Byblos to this goddess. *See also* Dione.

Balubaale (Africa)
Spirit beings of the Bantu people of Africa. Some say this is a collective name for all the gods of earth, death, lightning, plague and the rainbow. *See also* Kibuuka; Mukasa.

Balujen (Tinguian People, Philippine Islands) *see* Adam.

Baly (India) *see* Bali (B).

Bamun Owtar (India)
An avatar of Vamana (q.v.)

Bana *Vairochi* (Hindu; India)
Bana, a demon with one thousand arms, is son of Bali and brother of a sister, Putana. She is the demon who nursed Krishna with her poisoned breasts and was subsequently killed by the god. Bana's daughter Usha was in love with Krishna's grandson Aniruddha. Bana brought the couple together by using his magic powers. Krishna and Bala-Rama attacked Bana. Skanda (also known as Karttikeya) and Shiva attempted to protect him, but Skanda was injured and Bana's arms were cut off. Krishna and Shiva engaged in a fight which Krishna won. Shiva pleaded with Krishna to spare Bana and his wish was granted. Bana is usually shown with multiple arms, riding in a chariot

drawn by lions. *See also* Bala-Rama; Bali (B); Karttikeya; Krishna; Shiva; Usha.

Banaded (Egypt) *see* Banebdedet.

Banalingas (Hindu; India)

Sacred stones, small and elliptical with a natural polish produced by the action of the river water. They are frequently found in the Narmada river, one of the sacred rivers of the Hindus, and are used as a symbol for Shiva.

Banana (Sumer)

The coachman for the sun-god Shamash.

Banba (Celtic) *see* Banbha.

Banbha (Celtic, Irish)

Also known as: *Banba.*

Death goddess. Banbha, according to an ancient document, is said to be the first person to settle in Ireland. At that time it was known as "the Island of Banbha of the Women," or "Banbha of Fair Women." In some myths, her father is Cain and in others, Dagda. Her sisters are Erui and Fotia, said to be the daughters of Cain. The three, known as the "Goddesses of Sovereignty," were worshiped as triple goddesses. Following Banbha's arrival on the island came Cessair and her group. They died, leaving one survivor. The race of Giants, known as Fomorians, followed and they were defeated by the Partholanians from Spain. They, too, died, save one, and the Nemeds, also from Spain, came ashore. The Fomorians regrouped and subdued the Nemeds until the advent of the Firbolgs, who came from Greece via Spain. They battled the Fomorians but were in turn conquered by the Tuatha De Danann. Banbha was the goddess-queen of the Tuatha De Danann; she and her sisters were married to the kings: Mac Cuill, Mac Cecht, and Mac Greine, who are also known as the "Kings of Tara." Amergin, the poet and judge of the Milesians (also spelled Melesians), was allowed to bring his people to the island after promising the goddesses to name an island after each of them. They opposed the Milesians with magic but were overcome by them. Compare Banbha to Morrigu. The Milesians are thought by some to have been the original Celts. They are shown with bird-like characteristics. The name Banbha means "pig," which is connected to cults of the dead. *See also* Amergin; Bress; Cessair; Dagda; Firbolgs; Fomorians; Partholanians; Tuatha De Danann.

Baneb Djedet (Egypt) *see* Banebdedet.

Banebdedet (Egypt) *Banaded*

Also known as: *Ba Neb Tetet, Baneb Djedet, Binded.*

A local deity, who later acquired greater status, Banebdedet is a god of arbitration. During creation Banebdedet settled an argument between Horus and Set by having them write a letter to the goddess Neith for her opinion. Banebdedet is a member of the Mendean Triad with Hetmehit and Harpakhrad. He is depicted as ram, or goat-headed. *See also* Horus; Neith; Set.

Banitu (Assyro-Babylonian) *see* Ishtar.

Banka-Mundi (Khond People, India)

Goddess of hunting.

Bannik (Slavic, Russian)

Spirit of the Bath. Bannik is one of a group of household spirits known as Domovoi. He is the spirit of the bath and he lives in the out-house. He allows only three bathers to enter. He is the fourth, and if someone tries to take his place in line, he pours hot water on the person. Bannik can foretell the future. To do so, the subject must place his or her naked buttocks through the half-open door of the bath house and wait. If caressed softly, the future will be bright, but if clawed, it is a bad omen. He is depicted as a wizened little character with straggly white hair and a beard. Sometimes Bannik lives under the toilet seat. The bather is advised to leave a little bath water and soap for Bannik in case he decides to bathe. There are instances when Bannik takes up residence under the stove. *See also* Chlevnik; Domovoi; Kikimora; Ovinnik.

Ban'shee (Celtic) *see* Banshee.

Banshee *Ban'shee, Banshie.* (Celtic, Irish, Scots)

Also known as: *Ban'sith* (Gaelic), *Bansith, Baobhan Sith, Bean-Nighe* (Scotland), *Bean Si, Bean-Sidhe* (Irish), *Caoineag, Caointeach.*

Banshee is presented by some as a female fairy and by others as a wind or death spirit. Originally, she may have been a princess of the Celtic hill people. When her wail is heard under one's window, it foretells death in the house. She is depicted wearing a grey cloak over a green dress. Her hair is long and streaming, and she has red eyes from weeping. Sometimes she appears as a beautiful woman. The Bean-Nighe of Scottish Highlands is more like a female ghost who died in childbirth, although she is called a water spirit and seer. She appears as a small-boned woman with long breasts who dresses in green. You can't mistake her. She has one nostril, one tooth, and red, webbed feet. If you can grab and suck one of her breasts, you will be granted any wish. Baobhan Sith is similar to Banshee but is a dangerous kind of succubus who is similar to a fairy rather than a god.

Banshie (Celtic) *see* Banshee.

Ban'sith (Gaelic) *see* Banshee.

Bansith (Gaelic) *see* Banshee.

Banyan Tree (India)

Sacred tree. *See also* Apsarases; Bala-Rama.

Baobhan Sith (Celtic) *see* Banshee.

Bar (Akkadian) *see* Adar.

Bara (A) (Aborigine People, Australian)

God of the northwest winds. He brings the monsoons from November to March. During the rest of the year he resides in a large hollow tree. It is believed that spirit children riding in on Bara's winds hide in the grass until they see the woman who will become their mother. *See also* Maijunga, the god of the dry season.

Bara (B) (Babylonian) *see* Baragulla.

Baragulla (Babylonian)

Also known as: *Bara.*

The son of Ea, Baragulla is an oracle god who reveals the future. *See also* Ea.

Barashakushu (Babylonia) *see* Marduk.

Barbelo (Gnostic)
   Mother Goddess. Feminine power derived from the primordial father. She is the mother of Ialdabaoth or Sabaoth. Barbelo is associated with the Archons. Her origin is dated circa C.E. 150–180. Her name probably originated from the Gnostics who came from either Syria or Egypt. *See also* Archons; Sabizios.

Bardad (Semite) *see* Adad.

Barhishmati (India)
   Daughter of the divine architect Visvakarma and sister of Sanja. *See also* Sanja; Viskvakarma.

Barku (Syria) *see* Rimmon.

Baron Cimetiere, Baron La Croix, Baron Piquant (Haitian)
   Names used for Ghede, god of the dead. *See also* Ghede.

Barshamina (Mesopotamia) *see* Baal; Ba'al Shamin.

Bas (Egypt) *see* Bast.

Basileus (Greek) "The King." An epithet of Zeus.

Basilisk (Gnostic)
   Deified creature. This frightening-looking lizard is able to run on water. Those who annoy it can be frozen in their tracks by its angry glare. It is generally found by those who are not looking for it in the inaccessible regions of the Swiss Alps and the African deserts. It has the body and wings of a dragon and the head of a serpent. It is usually shown with its tail in its mouth. Sometimes it is depicted as half cock and half snake. Basilisk is connected with Gnostic Abraxas in that Agathodemon or "good spirit" was said to have hatched by a cock from a serpent's egg. *See also* Abraxas.

Bassareus *Bassarides* (Greek)
   They are the followers of Dionysus. *See also* Dionysus.

Bast *Bas* (Egypt)
   Thought by some to be of Semitic or Phoenician origin (perhaps connected with the Hebrew Bosheth).
   Also known as: *Bastet; Bubastis; Oubastet; Pakht; Pasht; Sekhmet.*
   Cat goddess of life, fruitfulness, pleasure, music, dance and cats. Bast is the mother of Mahes and wife of Bes (Bas). Bes was a form of Set (evil god of night), and she was a form of Sekhmet (a ferocious lion-headed goddess of sunset and fiery heat who is the daughter of the sun-god Ra). In another rendition, she is the wife of Ra and mother of Hes (a form of Horus). She is also regarded as the mother of the lion-god Miysis (lord of slaughter). Bast was worshipped at Bubastis in early times. During Bast's festival, it was forbidden to hunt lions according to an inscription of Rameses IV. Bast was known as the "Eye of the Moon." She is known by the Greeks as Artemis or possibly Pasht. As a male god, he might have been connected with Bosheth (a name of Baal). He was also thought to be a form of Set. As the male deity, Bes, or Bas, is the god of laughter. Because of this confusion, Bast was also thought to be a goddess of pleasure. She corresponds to the goddess Hathor. She is also identified with Artemis, Baal and Typhon. Sometimes she is confused with Mut and Sekhmet. Bast is represented as a cat-headed woman holding in her right hand either a sistrum or an aegis, and in her left hand, a basket. Sometimes, she is depicted as a cat. A bronze figure in the British Museum shows her holding her aegis in her left hand and a Hathor-headed sistrum in her right hand. *See also* Bes; Bosheth; Hathor; Mut; Sekhmet; Uadjit.

Bastet (Egypt) Festival of. *See also* Bast.

Basti (Egypt) *see* Assessors.

Bata (Egypt)
   Also known as: *Bet.*
   Agricultural deity. He is a farmer god who looks like a mummified bull or ram. Possibly connected with Anubis.

Batara Guru (Sumatra)
   Unhappy because they did not have children, Batara Guru and his wife moved to a hut by the sea and planted a garden. They hoped that by living a simple life they would have a family. Batara Guru's garden was destroyed by a serpent. When he tried to chase the serpent away, the serpent refused to leave until Batara Guru gave him food. He propped the serpent's mouth open and gave him nourishment. When Batara Guru withdrew his hand there was a ring on his finger. The ring enabled he and his wife to have children. The earth was created by one of his sons. It hung on cords from the sky. However, the earth kept light from reaching the god of the underworld. He was so furious that he destroyed the earth. Seven times his son attempted to recreate the earth. On the eighth attempt, with the help of Batara Guru, they were successful. They placed the earth on pillars. The underworld god shows his anger from time to time by causing earthquakes.

Bateia (A) (Greek)
   Mother of the Trojan People. She is the daughter of Teucer, king of Phrygia and wife of Dardanus. Her children are Erichtonius and Ilus. *See also* Dardanus; Erichtonius.

Bateia (B) (Greek)
   A Naiad. She could be the mother of Hippocoon, Icarius and Tyndareus by Oebaulus, the king of Sparta. The other possibility is Gorgophone (q.v.). *See also* Hippocoon; Icarius.

Bath (Egypt) *see* Ab-ta.

Bati Khan (Toda People, India) Hunting god.

Bato Kannon (Japan) *see* Amida.

Bato-Kwannon (Japan) *see* Amida.

Battle of the Trees (Celtic) *see* Amathon.

Battle Raven (Celtic)
   A name for the goddess of war, Badb Catha.

Battle Shaker (Teutonic)
   Another name for Vigrid, the plain where the Norse gods will fight on the day of Ragnarok. *See also* Vigrid.

Bau *Ba'u* (Akkadian, Babylonian, Phoenician, Sumerian)
   Also known as: *Baau* (possibly), *Bahu, Bohu, Gula, Gur, Ninhursag, Ninki.*
   "Goddess of the Dark Waters." A primeval goddess, early

references refer to her as the mother of Ea. She was Anu's spouse, the first wife of Ninib, the wife of Ningirsu. Sometimes she is referred to as the sister of Enlil. In some accounts, she is the wife of Ninurta. She is also said to be the consort of Tammuz. Most references to Bau are in relation to Ninurta. In Babylonia, at the end of harvest, a festival was held to celebrate the sacred marriage of Bau and Ningirsu. The festivities also ensured bountiful crops for the following year. She is possibly a water or creator goddess who preceded Tiamat, and is identified with Gula. She may be the same as the Phoenician goddess Baau. In later times, she was replaced by Ishtar. *See also* Bohu; Gula; Ninhursag; Tiamat.

Baubo *Babo* (Greek)
Also known as: *Ceres* (Roman).
Baubo was Demeter's nurse while she was mourning for her lost daughter Persephone, whom Hades had abducted. Baubo had the reputation for telling indecent jokes. She is depicted without a head or limbs. Her breasts appear as eyes and her genitals are shaped like a bearded mouth. Some scholars believe Baubo to be the same as Hecate (q.v.). She is similar to the Japanese Uzume (q.v.). *See also* Ceres; Demeter; Persephone.

Baucis (Greek)
Baucis is the wife of Philemon of Bithynia. While in their golden years of marriage, they received an unexpected visit from the great god Zeus and the messenger of the gods Hermes. The elderly couple were not aware that their visitors were gods or that they had been turned away from other shelters. They invited the gods into their home and made them comfortable. For their unselfish act they were saved from the Deluge. Their unpretentious cottage was turned into a magnificent palace. After death, Baucis became a linden tree and Philemon an oak tree. They were planted in front of the doors of the temple.

Baugi (Teutonic; Norse)
He is the giant brother of Sattung. When Odin, disguised as Bolverk, was on his journey to Jotun-heim to find the mead of poetry, he worked for Baugi. Sattung guarded the mead made from Kvasir's blood. The mead was distilled in the magic cauldron, Odraerir. The drinker of Kvasir was given the gifts of wisdom and poetry. Odin tricked Sattung into giving him the secret recipe for the production of Kvasir. *See also* Aesir; Bolverk; Jotun-heim; Kvasir; Odin; Odraerir; Sattung.

Baugreginn (Teutonic) *see* Mimir.

Baumbur (Teutonic) *see* Bombor.

Bavor (Teutonic) *see* Bafur.

Bayl (Sumer) *see* Bel.

Baze (Greek) *see* Athene.

bDe-mch-og-dpal-kor-lo-dom-pa   (Tibet) *see* Dorje Phagmo.

bDug-spos-ma (Tibet) *see* Dhupa.

bDul-Rgal (Tibet) King of Demons.

Bealtuinn (Celtic) *see* Beltine.

Bean Si (Celtic) *see* Banshee.

Bean-Nighe (Scots) *see* Banshee.

Beann (Egypt) *see* Benu.

Beanu (Egypt) *see* Benu.

Beav (Teutonic) *see* Vali.

Becabs *Bacabab, Becab* (Maya, possibly Toltec)
Also known as: *Acantun, Cantul-ti-ku, Four Wind Gods, Pillars of Heaven, Water Sprinklers.*
Wind gods. Deities of agriculture, rain, and fertility. Patrons of beekeepers. Representatives of the four winds, the four cardinal points, and one-quarter each of the 260-day calendar. The Mayan earth, created by the omnipotent god Hunab Ku, was flat and four-cornered. Above the earth are the thirteen levels of the upperworld, and below, nine levels of the underworld. Fashioned by Hunab Ku to hold up the heavens are the four Becabs. One list of their names, positions, and colors states that Cauac is in the south, his color is red. Ix is in the west, his color is black. Kan is in the east, his color is yellow. And Mulac is in the north, his color is white. Sometimes the lists of point names differ. These four gigantic gods are variously known as Acantun, "Water Sprinklers," "Four Wind Gods" and "Pillars of Heaven." Acantun is also the name used for the pillars or stones erected for the Becabs. As seasonal deities, the first Bacab is blue (some say yellow) for the south. The second is red for the east, the third white for the north, and the fourth black for the west. Each Becab also presided over one-quarter of the 260-day calendar. The Becabs are the divine intercessors for beekeepers. During Zotz, the fourth month, owners of beehives prepared for their feast, which was held in Tzec, the fifth month. The Becabs were consulted to determine the most auspicious day to hold the annual ceremony during their festival period. The brothers are often shown as old men with upraised arms. They are personified by animals and human-headed water jars. The Becabs are closely associated with the four Chacs. In another interpretation, Hunab Ku created the rain god Itzamna and his consort Ixchel, the goddess of childbirth, medicine, and weaving. They became the parents of all other deities, including the Becabs. In each case, when the deluge destroyed the world, the four Becabs escaped. Another Mayan belief to consider is that the sky is held up by four different species of trees, each tree a different color. In the center stands the green ceiba tree (also called the silk-cotton tree). *See also* Acat; Acatl; Backlum Chaam; Tahuantin Suyu Kapac.

Beda (Teutonic) An Asynor. *See also* Aesir.

Beelsamin (Phoenician).
A lord of the sky similar to the Greek Zeus (q.v.).

Beelzebub (Semite) *see* Ba'al-Zebub.

Beelzebul (Semite) *see* Ba'al-Zebub.

Befana (Roman)
Also known as: *Befana, La Strega, La Vecchia, Saint Befana.*
Spirit. An old woman who is as kind as she is ugly. Each January 5 she distributes sweets to good children and lumps of coal to naughty children. Befana is possibly a corruption of Epiphania or Epiphany. *See also* Bertha.

Begelmir (Norse; Teutonic)

Survivors of the flood. When Ymir flooded the earth with his own blood, the Begelmir, a husband and wife team, were the only survivors.

Begochiddy (Navajo People, North America)

A great god.

Behdety (Egypt)

Also known as: *Apollo* (Greek), *Hor Beditite, Hor Behdetite, Horus.*

Another name for Horus. As Behdety, he was worshiped at Behdet in ancient Edfu. He led the forces of Ra-Horakte against Set. Behdety is falcon-headed and is depicted with the winged disk of the sun. He is often shown in the form of a winged solar disk or a falcon with outstretched wings. His claws hold a fly-whisk and a ring. *See also* Horus; Set.

Bekotshidi (Navaho People, North America) *see* Klehanoai.

Bel (A) (Babylonian, Sumer)

Also known as: *Aleyn-baal, Bayl, Belit, Enlil, Marduk.*

A title meaning "lord." The Babylonians gave the title Bel to Marduk, calling him Bel-Marduk or simply Bel. When the deities of the Sumerians were integrated with their own, the god Enlil became identified with Bel. Belit, the feminine form, was the title given to Ninlil and was also an honorary title given to numerous other goddesses. *See also* Aleyn-Bel; Baal; Bel (B).

Bel (B) (Gaelic)

Also known as: *Balan, Balin, Belenos, Belenus, Belinus, Bellin.* God of the dead.

Bel (C) (British)

Also known as: *Bel (B).*

Sun god and mythical king of Britain. *See also* Bel (B).

Bel (D) (Celtic)

Also known as: *Bel (B).*

He is an ancient god who was appeased by human sacrifice. *See also* Belinus; Borvo.

Bel (E) (India) *see* Vilva.

Bel Marduk (Babylonia) *see* Marduk.

Bel Matati (Babylonia) *see* Marduk.

Belatucadros (Celtic)

He is a horned god of war, who is equated with Mars.

Belbogh (Slavic) *see* Balbog.

Beldeg (Teutonic) *see* Beldegg.

Beldegg (Teutonic) *see* Balder; Odin; Thor.

Bele (Eastern Sudan, Africa)

Also known as: *Azapane, Mba, Tul.*

A trickster god. Counterpart of the god Tere (q.v.).

Belenos (Celtic) *see* Bel (B); Borvo.

Belenus (Celtic) *see* Bel (B).

Beletersetim (Assyria, Sumer)

This is another name of Belit-Sheri, the scribe of Arallu, the underworld. *See also* Belit-Sheri.

Be'li (British) *see* Bel (B).

Beli (Celtic) *see* Arianrhod; Bel (B).

Belili *Belial* (Akkadia, Assyro-Babylonia, Hebrew).

Also known as: *Baalith, Belit-ili* (title for Ishtar).

Goddess of the Underworld. Sister of Tammuz. Some writers say she was also a goddess of the moon, trees, springs, love and wells. They also say she was the predecessor of Ishtar and mistress of Tammuz. As Belial, this deity is a male and chief of the demons and enemy of God. In New Testament times the name "Belial" is associated with Satan and is a demon of evil. *See also* Belit; Devil; Satan.

Belinus (Celtic) *see* Bel (B).

Belisama (Celtic)

She is the goddess of the Mersey River. Some scholars think that she is a version of the Roman goddess Minerva. *See also* Sequana.

Belit (Assyro-Babylonia, Sumer)

Also known as: *Ba'alat, Beltis, Belit-Ilani* (Mistress of the Gods), *Belit-Ile, Belit-Ili, Belit-Illi, Mylitta, Ninhursag, Nintud.*

Belit is considered to be a title of Astarte, Ninlil, or some say, Nintud. As Belit-Ili she was the "Lady of the Gods." As Nintud (Nintu), she was "Lady of Childbirth." Some say she was consort of Assur or Bel. Others say she was the wife or sister of Enlil. She is shown seated and dressed in a tight robe, her hair made up in the style of the Egyptians. She wears a disk with two horns on her head. She is also depicted with her right hand in an attitude of blessing the baby that she holds as it suckles her left breast. Similar to Hathor and possibly the same as Astarte and Ishtar. She is associated with Tammuz. *See also* Arura; Bel; Ninhursag; Nintud.

Belit-Ilani (Mesopotamia) *see* Nintud.

Belit-Ile (Mesopotamia) *see* Belit.

Belit-Ili (Mesopotamia)

"Lady of the Gods." *See also* Belit; Mah (B); Ninhursag; Ninki.

Belit-Illi (Mesopotamia) *see* Belit.

Belit-Sheri *Belit-Seri, Belit-tseri* (Assyro-Babylonian)

Also known as: *Beletersetim, Nana* (possibly).

Belit-Sheri, the scribe and goddess of writers, is the sister and lover of Tammuz and some say the sister of Ishtar. A scribe of the underworld, she sits in front of the Queen of Death, Ereshkigal, with recordings of the activities of mortals. Upon their deaths she calls out the judgments. *See also* Nana; Tammuz.

Belitis *Beltis* (Mesopotamia)

Also known as: *"Lady."*

Another name for Ninlil, goddess of fertility. *See also* Beltis; Ninhursag; Ninki; Ninlil.

Bellerophon *Bellerphontes* (Greek)

Also known as: *Deophontes, Hipponoos* (Slayer of horses or monsters), *Hipponous, Leophontes.*

Greek hero. One of the Seven Great Slayers of Monsters. Bellerophon is the grandson of Sisyphus and son of Glaucus and Eurymede (also known as Eurynome), although according to Homer, Poseidon was his father. His brother was generally known as Deliades. He married Philinoe and became the father of Deidamia, Hippolochus, Isander and Laodamia. Exiled from Ephyra for unintentionally killing Deliades or Bellerus the tyrant of Corinth, he went to Proetus for purification. Prodded by his spurned wife Anteia (also known as Stheneboea), Proetus had Bellerophon deliver a sealed letter to Iobates requesting that he kill Bellerophon. Indirectly, Iobates attempted to fulfill the request. He urged Bellerophon to search for and kill the Chimaera, a fire-breathing monster. Before departing, Bellerophon sought advice from the sage Polyeidus, who suggested that he enlist the aid of Pegasus, the winged horse. He directed him to the temple of Athene where the goddess presented him with a golden saddle and instructed him to go to the well of Peirene. There he found Pegasus, who upon seeing the golden saddle, allowed Bellerophon to mount him. On the back of the moon-horse, in mid-air, Bellerophon slaughtered the Chimaera by shooting arrows through him and in another version by also shoving lead down his throat, which, melted by his fiery breath, seared his intestines. Returning as the victor, the surprised Iobates tried another tactic. He sent him to fight the Solymians, a neighboring tribe, then the Carian pirates and the Amazons. Undaunted, Bellerophon emerged victorious after each battle. Finally, Iobates decided to send the strongest of his soldiers to kill him. Bellerophon petitioned Poseidon to flood the Xanthian Plain to drive the soldiers away. His request was answered and once again Bellerophon was undefeated. Iobates, convinced that Bellerophan was favored by the gods, offered him his daughter Philonoe in marriage and made him successor to his throne. Inflated by his successes and envious of the gods, Bellerophon mounted Pegasus and attempted to fly to the heavens. Annoyed, Zeus sent a gadfly which stung Pegasus and threw Bellerophon, seriously injuring him. Blinded, lame and spurned by the gods, he became an outcast who wandered the fields alone and died miserably with neither his death nor burial place marked. Another myth relates that Bellerophon finally evened the score with Antea by inviting her to ride Pegasus and then from a great height he shoved her to her death. Hyginus wrote that she committed suicide when she learned that Bellerophon married her sister. Other myths say that Bellerophon received Pegasus from either Athene or Poseidon. *See also* Athene; Chimaera; Iobates; Pegasus; Philinoe; Poseidon; Proetus; Sarpedon (A); Sarpedon (B); Sisyphus.

Bellerphontes (Greek) *see* Bellerophon.

Bellerus (Greek) *see* Bellerophon.

Bellin (Celtic) *see* Bel (B).

Bellona (Roman)
Also known as: *Enyo* (Greek), *Mah-Bellona* (in later times).
Bellona, the goddess of war, is the daughter of Phorcys and Geto, and either sister or companion of Mars. Her priests, called Bellonarii, inflicted wounds on themselves when offering sacrifices. Bellona is shown with dishevelled hair, dressed in full armor and holding a bloody lash. She is identified with the Greek Enyo. *See also* Aruru; Mah.

Bellonarii (Roman) Priests of the war goddess Bellona (q.v.).

Belos (Babylonia) *see* Marduk.

Belshim (Semitic) *see* Adad; Baal.

Beltaine (Celtic, Irish) *see* Beltine.

Beltan (Celtic, Irish) *see* Beltine.

Beltane (Celtic, Irish) *see* Beltine.

Belti *Baalti* (Babylonian, Phoenician, Semite, Sumer)
Also known as: *Baalath, Beltis, Belitis, Beltu.*
Mother goddess. Generally used as a name which signifies "lady." Usually indicates a term for Astarte and Ishtar. *See also* Baalath; Ishtar.

Beltine *Baltein, Bealtuinn, Beltaine, Beltan, Beltane* (Celtic, Irish)
Also known as: *Galan-Mai* (Welsh), *Shennda Boaldyn* (Isle of Man).
Festival day. Several historical days in mythology are said to have taken place on the first of May (of the old calendar). It is said that on this day the race of Partholon, led by Partholon and his queen Dealgnaid, one of the earliest settlers of Ireland, came ashore. On the same day three hundred years later they left Ireland. On this day the Tuatha De Danann were said to have first stepped foot on the island. The first Gaelic people are said to have arrived in Ireland on this day. May 1 marked the beginning of summer on the old calendar. Beltaine (Beltine) means "the fire of Bel" and relates to the deity Bel also known as Belinus. It is said that on the evening before May 1, all household fires were extinguished and relit from a main fire thought to be ignited by the Druids. Various rituals accompanied this tradition which were thought to protect the people from evil and illness. Later this became the feast for Saint Brigit. *See also* Bel (B); Brigit; Tuatha De Danan.

Beltis (Sumer, Babylon) *see* Belti.

Beltis-Allat (Arabic, Chaldean) *see* Allat; Allatu.

Beltiya (Assyro-Babylonian) *see* Zerpanitum.

Beltu (Sumer, Babylonian) *see* Belti.

Belu (Semitic) *see* Baal.

Belus (A) (Phoenician) *see* Baal.

Belus (B) (Greek)
King of the Egyptians. Belus is the son of the sea god Poseidon and Libya (eponym of Libya, which, to the ancients, was her homeland Egypt). He is the twin brother of Agenor and brother of Lelex. His spouse is Anchinoe (q.v.). *See also* Agenor (A); Danaus; Lamia; Lelex.

Belus (C) (Babylonian Creation Legend of Berosus, 280 B.C.E.) (Babylonian Creation Legend of Damascius, sixth century C.E.)
In the story of Berosus, Belus (who is the same as Bel) ripped Thalath in half. She ruled the abyss and its horrendous monsters. Belus destroyed the monsters and created heaven with one half of Thalath and earth with her other half. He ordered Kingu to cut off his head. From his blood and earth, mortals, animals, the five planets, the sun, and the moon were formed. In the story of Damascius, Tauthe and Apason (the same as

Apsu) existed in the beginning. They created the gods Moymis, Lakhe, Lakhus, Assorus, and Kissare. Assorus and Kissare were the parents of Anu, Illinus, and Aus. Aus and Dauce were the parents of the creator of the world, Belus. For the Creation Legend from the Tablets of Ashurbanipal (circa 650 B.C.E.) *see* Tiamat. *See also* Apsu; Aus; Bel (B); Bile.

Belus (D) (Greek)
Phoenix, the king of Phoenicia, is possibly his father.

Belus (E) (Greek)
He is possibly the father of Anna, Dido and Pygmalion. The other possibility is that Agenor is their father.

Bendegeit Vran (Celtic) *see* Bran.

Bendigeid Fran (Celtic) *see* Bran.

Bendigeid Vran (Celtic) *see* Bran.

Bendis (A) (Cappadocian) Earth goddess.

Bendis (B) (Thracian)
Moon goddess. Worship of Bendis spread from Thrace to Lemnos and later to Attica. Her worship involved the celebrated mysteries in Samothrace. She is identified with Artemis, Hecate, Persephone and Rhea. *See also* Artemis (possibly her counterpart); Cybele; Hecate; Persephone; Rhea; Sabazius.

Benen (Egypt)
Guardian of the eighth sector of Tuat. *See also* Tuat.

Benet (Egypt) *see* Aani.

Benjaiten (Japan) *see* Benten.

Bennu Bird (Egypt) *see* Benu.

Bensai-Ten (Japan) *see* Benten.

Bentakumari (Assamese People, India) Water Goddess.

Benten (Buddhist; Japan; Hindu origins)
Also known as: *Benjaiten, Bensai-Ten, Benten* ("Coin-washing Benten"), *Benzai-Ten, Benzai-Tennyo, Benzaiten, Ichiki-Shima-Hime* (an ancient name), *Sarasvati* (India), *Zeniari*.
Goddess of the sea, and of good luck. Originally, she was known as the Hindu love goddess, Benzaiten. As Benten she is a jealous goddess, however, she absorbed the qualities of her former rival, Kichijo-ten and became the only goddess of the Shichi Fukujin (the "Seven Deities of Good Fortune"). She rose from the sea as the daughter of the Dragon King Ryu-wo. As a sea goddess, she was worshiped primarily on the smaller islands. She is also the goddess of good fortune, the goddess of music and public speaking. Later, she became the Goddess of Waters, and in some way is associated with an obscure deity named Uga-jin. Benten's avid followers are business people, gamblers, actors, dancers, musicians and geishas. Some say she has two sisters. She is depicted as a beautiful woman dressed in ornate clothing. She variously holds a lute, sword or jewel in two hands. In other depictions, she is shown with eight arms holding various objects. Sometimes she is shown with her messenger, a white snake. She is also depicted riding on a dragon. As a Shichi Fukujin, she holds a lute. As with other images of the Shichi Fukujin, her image has been carved on rice grains. Women often carried her talisman as they believed that she made them more fruitful and accentuated their beauty and tal-

ents. As Zeniarai Benten, she increased the prosperity of all who threw coins into her well. She is similar to the Greek goddess of love, Aphrodite, and almost identical to the Indian goddess of the arts, Sarasvati. As Benzaiten, she is associated with Bishamon, the god of happiness and war. *See also* Bishamon; Kichijo-Ten; Sarasvati; Shichi Fukujin.

Bentet (Egypt) *see* Aani.

Bentet Apes (Egypt) *see* Aani.

Benth (Egypt) *see* Aani.

Benthesicyme (Greek)
Daughter of Poseidon and Amphitrite, she raised her half-brother, Eumolpus, who had been thrown into the sea by his mother Chione. *See also* Amphitrite; Chione; Eumolpus.

Benu (Egypt)
Also known as: *Atum* (possibly), *Beann, Beanu, Bennu, Byanu;* (possibly as the Phoenix; he flew from Arabia to Egypt).
Mythical bird. He is shown as a huge golden hawk with a heron's head. He makes his appearance once every 500 years. He came from Arabia with the body of his father enclosed in an egg of myrrh. Other sources indicate that the Benu Bird, in this case a heron, is an aspect of Atum. It was said to have flown through the first dawn, coming to rest on a rock in the primordial waters (the Nun), where it opened its beak and let out a cry breaking the silence of the Nun. His plumage was colored part gold and part red, and he was about the size of an eagle. Benu is sometimes called the soul of Osiris. The name Beanu or Beann is also that of the Celtic mother goddess. The Benu, like the phoenix, re-creates itself from fire. *See also* Atum.

Benu Bird (Egypt) *see* Atum.

Benzai-Ten (Japan) *see* Benten.

Benzai-Tennyo (Japan) *see* Benten.

Benzaiten (Japan) *see* Benten.

Berchta (Teutonic) *see* Bertha.

Berecyntia (A) (Greek)
A surname of Cybele derived from Mount Berecynthus in Phrygia, where Cybele was worshiped. *See also* Cybele.

Berecyntia (B) (Celtic, Gaul)
This earth goddess may be the same as Brigit.

Bergelmir *Bergelmer* (Norse; Teutonic)
This frost giant came from the feet of Thrudgelmir, who in turn was produced by Ymir. Bergelmir is the father of all the evil frost giants, who are known as Hrim-Thurs. He and his wife were the only ones to survive the war with Odin and his brothers. Bergelmir escaped and made his home in a place in Jotunheim. Here he began a new race of frost-giants who continued the war with Odin and his group. In another rendition, Bergelmir and his spouse were the only survivors of a deluge caused by the blood of Ymir. *See also* Bor; Buri; Jotun-heim; Ymir.

Berkta (Teutonic) *see* Bertha.

Berling (Norse; Teutonic)
Dwarf smith. One of four dwarfs who slept with Freyja in

return for the gift of the Brising Necklace. The others were Alfrigg, Dvalin, and Grerr. See also Alfrigg; Freyja.

Beroe (Greek) see Adonis; Semele.

Berserker (Teutonic) see Berserkir.

Berserkir Berserker, Berserks (Norse; Teutonic)
Also known as: Bear Shirts, Berserksgangr.
Deified mortals. They are the human warriors who went into a frenzy, possibly induced by drugs or by large quantities of alcohol, before battle. As warriors, they were immune to weapons. After battle, when their fury subsided, they became unusually weak. In their weakened state, they were captured. The Berserkir (Old Norse for "bear" and "shirt") fought wearing animal skins and are under the special protection of Odin. Originally, there were twelve Berserkir born on the island of Bolmso, the sons of Arngrim and Eyfura. Thor killed the serpent-wives of the Berserkir. They are the relatives of Ottar. The Berserkir are often described as "fantastically ugly," and are often mistaken for trolls. See also Odin.

Berserks (Teutonic) see Berserkir.

Berserksgangr (Teutonic) see Berserkir.

Bertha Berchta, Berkta, Brechta (Teutonic)
Also known as: Frigga, Frau Berchta, Gode, Holda, Huldra, Nerthus, Percht, Perchta, Precht, Vrou-elde, Wode.
"White Lady." Bertha could be a spirit of spring. Bertha is not attractive, but she is kind and sweet. Her duties are to watch over the souls of unborn children (who are known as "the Heimchen"). She also watches over children who die before baptism. Bertha is reputed to be the female form of Odin. In this form she is known as "Frau Gode," or "Frau Wode." In Holland she is known as Vrou-elde and in Germany she is known as Nerthus. In Scandinavia, they call her Huldra. She is identified with Freyja and the Slavic Baba Yaga. She is associated with Holda, Wera and other goddesses of the New Year. Bertha is similar to the Roman Befana (q.v.). See also Baba Yaga; Befana; Holda; Nerthus.

Bes (Egypt, Phoenicia, Sudan, and Nubia; possibly of Semitic origin)
Also known as: Aha (fighter), Bas, Besam Bisu.
Bes is the god of marriage, god of music, fighting, dancing, protector of women in childbirth and protector against terrors, evil spirits, dangerous beasts and insects. He may have been a god of birth. He was also a god of fashion, particularly of the adornment of women. Later he was known as a god of the dead or fate. He carried the sa (symbol of protection), a knife for defense, and musical instruments to ward off evil spirits. His image was found on mirrors and cosmetic pots to aid in averting the "Evil Eye." He is akin to Bacchus the Roman god of gaiety in nature. He does not resemble the other members of the Egyptian Pantheon in appearance. Bes might have a mate named Ta-weret. In some legends, he is the husband of Bast. He is depicted as an ugly, hairy dwarf god. He has a huge beard, protruding tongue, flat nose, shaggy eyebrows and hair, large projecting ears, long thick arms, and bowed legs. He wears an animal skin whose tail hangs down to the ground, and a tiara of ostrich feathers. There are those who say he had feathers

instead of hair. In the Eighteenth Dynasty, pictures of Bes with wings were popular. Bes is associated with Hathor and her son Ihy. Bes is the counterpart of the goddess Theoris. Compare Bes to Bacchus, Gilgamesh, Silenus. Some say he is Horus' nurse. See also Bast; Bastet; Hathor; Theoris.

Beset (Egypt)
She is a patron of art, music and childbirth, and the female counterpart of Bes (q.v.)

Besi (Egypt)
Otherworld deity. God in the tenth sector of Tuat (q.v.)

Besi-Shemti (Egypt) see Aai.

Besla (Teutonic) see Bestla.

Bestla Besla, Bettla (Teutonic)
Bestla is the giant daughter of Bolthorn, who became the mate of Bor and the mother of Odin, Ve and Vili. She is the daughter-in-law of Buri. In another myth, she is known as the daughter of Ymir and twin of Mimir. See also Bolthorn; Bor; Buri; Mimir; Odin; Ve; Vili; Ymir.

Besu (Slavic)
Devil or disagreeable god.

Bet (Egypt) see Bata.

Betsune Yeneca (Chippewa People, North America)
Star deity. Name of the Old Woman's Grandchild, a magic boy from the stars.

Bettla (Teutonic) see Bestla.

Bevarash (Zoroastrian; Persia)
The end of the dynasty of the fiendish snake, Azhi Dahaka (q.v.).

Beyla (Teutonic)
Earth goddess. Wife of Byggvir. Handmaiden of Freyr.

Bhadra Vira (India) see Badari.

Bhadracharu (India) see Rukmini.

Bhadrakali (India) see Badari; Durga; Karttikeya.

Bhadri-Nath (India) see Badari.

Bhaga (Hindu; India)
God of strength, beauty, good fortune and marriage. An Aditya, Bhaga, the "divine," is the brother of the god Varuna and Ushas the goddess of dawn. There was a time, when Daksha held an important event, to celebrate a sacrifice. He invited everyone from near and far—except Shiva. Enraged, Shiva created the monster, Virabhadra, who blinded Bhaga. See also Aditya; Daksha; Durga; Mitra; Parvati; Shiva; Ushas; Varuna.

Bhagavad-Gita Bhagavadgita (Hindu; India)
"Song of the Divine One."
This is the sixth book of the *Mahabharata*, in the form of a dialogue between Krishna, an avatar of Vishnu, and Arjuna, expounding philosophical theories on duty and death. The conversation took place when Arjuna was unwilling to do battle and questioned the remarks of Krishna, his charioteer, on the subject. The Bhagavad-Gita consists of 606 verses and is thought to have been written in the first century C.E.

Bhagavata Purana, The (Hindu; India)

Dedicated to Bhagavata (god, said to be Vishnu), this Sanskrit work by Vopdeva (c. 1300), is composed of 12 books, divided into 322 chapters. The name means "The Old Book of Divinity."

Bhagiratha (India)

Great grandson of King Sagara (q.v.).

Bhairab (Nepal)

One of Shiva's numerous destroyer forms, Bhairab is either dark blue or black and is depicted nude. In pictures he is occasionally shown as white. He has many arms and usually one head shown with rolling eyes and unruly hair. In his hands are a skull-cup, a wand with three skulls, or a noose. He may wear sandals and is often shown standing on a recumbent figure. *See also* Shiva.

Bhairava (Hindu; India, Indonesia, Tibet)

Also known as: *Jigs-Byed* (Tibet), *Shiva.*

Bhairava, the "destroyer," is one of eight (or twelve) terrifying aspects of Shiva. As Bhairava he destroys for the pleasure of destruction. He is depicted frowning. His eyes are angry, his hair flaming and his tiger teeth appear razor sharp. Naked, a snake is coiled around his neck and he wears a necklace of skulls. He carries his noose, trident and drum. He is often accompanied by demons, imps and a dog, sometimes said to be a jackal. In some locales, Bhairava and the village god Bhairon have merged. Bhairava is worshiped in northern and central agricultural districts of India as a black dog, a snake-girded drummer, or a red stone. Depictions of Bhairava are often very similar to depictions of the Buddhist god of death, Mahakala. *See also* Bhairon; Shiva.

Bhairavi (India)

"Terrifying Female." *See also* Durga; Kali; Parvati.

Bhairoba (India) *see* Bhairon.

Bhairon *Bhairava, Bhairoba* (Bombay), *Kala Bhairava* (Bombay); (Hindu; India)

A local village god, Bhairon is the personification of the field spirit. In some places, he has merged with Shiva's terrifying aspect as Bhairava. In Benares he serves as a guardian at Shiva's temples. As Kala Bhairava, or Bhairoba, he is depicted with a sword or club, carrying a bowl of blood. *See also* Bhairava; Gramadeveta.

Bhaisajyaguru (India) *see* Bhaishajyaguru.

Bhaishajyaguru *Bhaisajyaguru*

Also known as: *Man-la, Sang-gyeman-gyila-beduryr-o-chi-gyal-po* (Tibet); (Buddhist; India)

God of healing. God of sex change. A Bodhisattva and the fifth Buddha, he is the master physician and god of healing and of spells. He rules the east (as does Akshobhya) and is depicted as blue in color. He holds fruit in his right hand. *See also* Akshobhya; Amida; Yao-Shih Fu.

Bhama (India) Krishna's wrathful wife. *See also* Krishna.

Bhangi (Cambodian) *see* Rahu (B).

B'haq Ziva (Gnostic) *see* Abathur.

Bharadvaja *Bharadwaja, Bharawaya* (Hindu; India)

The son of the Rishi Brihaspati, Bharadvaja, a great poet and sage, was the spiritual leader of the Pandavas. He is the father of Drona (q.v.). *See also* Brihaspati; Pandavas; Rishi.

Bharadwaja (India) *see* Bharadvaja.

Bharata (A) *Bharatha, Bharati* (Hindu; India)

Bharata is one of four sons of King Dasaratha and Queen Kaikeyi. He was the spouse of Madavi (also called Mandavi) and the cousin of Sita. He reigned in place of his half-brother Rama during the latter's exile which was caused by Kaikeyi. His other siblings are Lakshmana and Satrughna. (He is not to be confused with Bharata, the Vedic king of the Bharatas, nor Bharata the hermit who was associated with Vishnu.) *See also* Dasaratha; Lakshmana; Rama; Sita.

Bharata (B) (Hindu; India)

An ancestor of the Kauravas and Pandavas and the son of King Dushyanta and the nymph Shakuntala (q.v.).

Bharatha (India) *see* Bharata (A).

Bharati (India)

Goddess of Speech. A name for Sarasvati (q.v.). *See also* Vach.

Bharawaya (India) *see* Bharadvaja.

Bhargavi (India) Wife of Shiva. *See also* Devi.

Bharundas (Hindu; India)

Birds who carry away the dead.

Bhava (India) "Existences." A title of Agni (q.v.).

Bhava-Siva (India) *see* Daksha.

Bhavani *Bhawani, Bhowanee, Bhowani, Devi, Devi-Uma, Kali, Mari, Parasu-Pani, Parvati* (Hindu; India; possibly Dravidian)

"Bestower of Existence." Bhavani is a name alternately used for Devi, Kali, or Parvati. In one depiction, she is shown as young, wearing a crown, and containing within her body a landscape incorporating the sun, moon and the sea. Perfume was burned in her honor by women in childbirth. The Korwa (also called Korama) people of India worship Bhavani as Mari, the goddess of death. *See also* Dakinis; Devi; Kali; Mari.

Bhawani (India) *see* Bhavani.

Bhiarav (Nepal) *see* Varahi.

Bhima (A)

Also known as: *Bhima-sena* ("The Terrible"), *Bhimul Pen, Bhimsen, Bish-nat* (as an earlier incarnation), *Vrikodara* ("Wolf's Belly"); (Hindu; India)

As the son of Vayu "the wind" and Kunti "the earth," Bhima has the ability to fly. The second of the five Pandavas, his older brother is Yudhisthira. Hanuman, the flying monkey, is his half-brother. A giant in size, he is the spouse of the Rakshasis Hidimbaa and the father of Ghatotkacha. She is the sister of the demon Hidimba whom Bhima killed. With princess Balandhara of Kasi, he has another son, Sarvaga. Trained by Drona and Bala-Rama to use the magic club, he became a ferocious warrior. His cousin Duryodhana once poisoned him and threw him into the Ganges River. His body sunk to the bottom but he was revived by resident serpents. The fiery-tempered god insulted the solar Karna and became his enemy for life. He killed the demon Vaka and so many other Asuras that they promised not to accost humans if he would leave them alone. When Jayadratha, and at another time, Kitchaka attempted to rape his spouse Draupadi, he trounced them thoroughly. Disguised as a demon and, aided by his magic club, he rescued Draupadi from death by fire. During the great Battle of the Mahabharata, he fought Bhishma, killed the two sons of the king of Magadha, fought his old master Drona, killed Duhsasana and smashed Duryodhana's thigh. When the devious king Dhritarashtra summoned him to his court, Krishna intervened and substituted an iron statue, which the enraged king crushed in an embrace. In another adventure, he set out for Lake Kubera and the life-giving lotus in the northeastern area of the celestial realm. He found the lake and killed the Yakshas who guarded the lotuses. The water from the lake gave him youth and strength. *See also* Bala-Rama; Bhishma; Draupadi; Duryodhana; Jara-Sandha; Karna; Krishna; Kunti; Pandavas; Rakshasa; Takshaka; Yaksha and Yakshini; Yudhisthira.

Bhima (B) (India) *see* Apsarases.

Bhima (C) (India) A name for Shiva or Rudra (q.v.).

Bhima-Devi (India) "Terrifying Goddess." *See also* Kali.

Bhima-sena (India) *see* Bhima (A).

Bhimsen (India) *see* Bhima (A).

Bhimul Pen (India) *see* Bhima (A).

Bhishma
Also known as: *Gangeya* ("Son of Ganga"), *Jalu-Ketu* (banner name), *Nadija* (River-born); (Hindu; India)
Bhishma, a deified mortal, is the son of the river goddess Ganga and the sage Santanu. He was known for his devotion and honor. When his aged father wanted a young wife, he accommodated him and gave him the woman he himself loved, Satyavati. To ensure that his father's new sons would become kings, he gave up his throne. Later, he found mates for his youngest half-brother. They were the daughters of the Raja of Kasi. When their husband died, Bhishma gave the women to his other half-brother Vyasa. Their children were Dhritarashtra, who was blind, and the pale Pandu. Bhishma tried to prevent the war between the Kauravas and Pandavas but ended up leading the Kauravas. He was killed, but not instantly, by a thousand darts shot by Arjuna at the Battle of Kurukshetra. His divine power permitted him to decide the day of his death, so he lay for fifty-eight days with the darts sticking out from his body. During this period he gave many discourses on morality. Bhishma was welcomed into Mount Meru where he became one of Indra's advisors. *See also* Arjuna; Bhima; Ganga; Indra; Meru Mountain; Pandavas; Satyavati; Vyasa.

Bhishmaka, King (India)
Father of Rukmini. *See also* Sisupala.

Bhisma (India) *see* Bhima (A).

Bhogavati (India) *see* Nagas and Nagis.

Bhogini (India) *see* Nagas and Nagis.

Bhowanee (India) *see* Bhavani; Devi.

Bhowani (India) *see* Bhavani; Devi.

Bhradrakali (Hindu; India)
Goddess of death.

Bhramara (India) "Relating to the Bee." *See also* Devi.

Bhrigu (India) *see* Bhrigus.

Bhrigus *Bhrgu* (singular) or *Bhrigu* (Hindu; India)
A Bhrigu, who was the first wise man, was married to Puloma, who in turn was betrothed to a demon. It was Bhrigus the sage who cursed Agni then repented and revoked his curse. Along with Matarisvan they represent the wind. In another version, the first wise man was Bhrigu and his descendants were the Bhrigus, meaning "the Shining Ones." A son of Bhrigus was the wealthy sage Chyavana who was rejuvenated by the healing twin deities, the Asvins. (Chyavana is also spelled Cyavana and Syavana.) Agni betrayed Bhrigus' wife into the hands of a Raksha. Bhrigus condemned Agni to forever consume everything. Agni retaliated by hiding himself from the gods and mortals. Realizing that Agni was indispensable, Bhrigus revoked his curse and Brahma urged him to return. They had to decide which of the three gods, Brahma, Shiva or Vishnu, was most deserving of the Brahmans' worship. Bhrigus was sent by the Bhrigu to find out who was the most deserving deity of the Hindu triad. He went to visit Shiva who was preoccupied with his wife and would not grant him an interview. Bhrigus, infuriated, cursed Shiva and decreed that henceforth the god would be worshipped as a lingam. Bhrigus went on to see Brahma, who was not remotely interested in granting the sage an audience. He then went on to Vishnu, and when he found him sound asleep, he kicked him in the ribs. Although rudely awakened, Vishnu's first concern was for Bhrigus. He asked him if his foot was injured from the kick. This concern won Bhrigus over, and he declared Vishnu to be the most deserving of adoration. Bhrigus is the father of the deity Shukra (meaning "Bright"), who became a guru to the Asuras. Blind in one eye, with the ability to bring the dead to life with his incantations, he personifies the planet Venus. As well as being a sage of the *Mahabharata*, he is thought of as a minor deity. Bhrigus foretold the life of all people born. His prophecies, written down, are known as the "Bhrigu Collection" ("Bhrigu Samhita"). *See also* Agni; Asuras; Asvins; Brihaspati; Lakshmi; Loka; Mada; Prajapati; Rishi; Shiva; Vishnu.

Bhu (Brahmanic, Hindu; India)
She is Mother Earth, who reclined at the bottom of the ocean before Creation. Brahma raised her to the surface where she appeared as a lotus flower which opened when the light enveloped her. *See also* Bhumi.

Bhu-Devi *Bhudevi* (India)
An earth goddess similar to Pritha. *See also* Bhumi; Darti Mai; Pritha; Prithivi; Sita.

Bhudevi (India) *see* Bhu-Devi.

Bhugangi (Hindu; India) *see* Kundalini.

Bhujagas (India) *see* Naga and Naginis.

Bhujangi (India) see Kundalini.

Bhujyu (India) The Sun. See also Asvins.

Bhumi *Bhumidevi* (Hindu, Vedic; India)

Bhumi is referred to as the fourth earth and the mother of the planet Mars. She is one of seven sisters who are not named, but may be associated with seven stars or planets. She is thought by some to be the spouse of Vishnu. Bhumi is the mother of Sita, known as Bhumija, who sprang from a furrow in the earth and in the end returned to Bhumi, the earth. The Indian goddesses Medini and Mahi are also known as the mother of Mars. Bhumi corresponds closely to Prithivi. Sometimes they are said to be two forms of the same goddess. See also Bhu; Bhu-devi; Bhumiya; Brihaspati; Sita; Varaha (Vishnu's avatar as a boar); Vishnu.

Bhumija (India) see Bhumi; Sita.

Bhumiya (Northern India)
Also known as: *Khetrpal, Rani* (feminine).
Bhumiya is an ancient earth god or goddess who is worshipped at the time of marriage, birth and harvest. He sometimes changes sex and is identified with the earth mother. People who are disrespectful to Bhumiya become ill. The Dangis People worship Bhumiya as a snake. See also Bhumi.

Bhumiya Rani (India) see Bhumiya.

Bhur-Loka (India) see Loka.

Bhura (India) see Bura-Penu.

Bhuri (India) see Bura-Penu.

Bhut (India) see Bhutas.

Bhuta (India) see Bhutas; Daksha.

Bhutanayaki (India) Spirit Leader. See also Devi.

Bhutapati (India) Prince of demons. See also Rudra; Shiva.

Bhutas *Bhut, Bhutias, Buta* (Hindu; India)
The Bhutas, children of Krodha, the daughter of Daksha, and her mate Bhuta, are malignant spirits, vampires, ghosts, or goblins who despise humans and frequent cemeteries. Mortals who have died a violent death become Bhutas. The Bhutas never rest on earth, so they can be avoided by lying down. Burning turmeric will also keep them away. Bhutas speak with a nasal twang, hate fire and do not have shadows. See also Daksha; Demons; Incubus; Jinn (Persian); Krodha; Nagas; Pishachas; Rakshasas; Satyrs (Greek).

Bhutesvara (India) Lord of Spirits and Demons. See also Shiva.

Bhutias (India) see Bhutas.

Bhuvana-Matri (India) "Mother of the World." See also Devi.

Bhuvanisvari (India) "Mistress of the World." See also Devi.

Bhuvar-Loka (India) see Loka.

Bia (A) (Greek, Egypt)
Also known as: *Ba, Ka.*
God of force and violence. He and his brother, Cratus (also spelled Kratos) helped Hephaestus nail Prometheus to a cliff.

They were also great helpers of Zeus. Another version tells that Bia (violence) was a daughter of the nymph Styx, who was the personification of the river Styx and the Titan Pallas. Bia was the sister of Zelos, Nike, and Caratus. She also helped the Olympians in the revolt of the Titans. See also Nike; Prometheus; Styx.

Bia (B) (Ashanti People, Africa)
He is the son of Nyame and Asase Ya and the older brother of Tano. Bia was deprived of his inheritance by his younger brother and was left poor land on the Ivory Coast. See also Asese Ya; Nyame.

Biadice (Greek) see Cretheus.

Biamban (Australia) see Baiame.

Biambun *Biamban* (Aborigine People, Australia)
Supreme deity. A god whose name is not to be spoken. He may be same as Biamban. See also Daramulun.

Bibhishan (India) see Vibishana.

Biblindi (Teutonic) see Odin.

Bielbog (Slavic) see Byelobog.

Bifrost *Bivrost, Bilrost* (Norse; Teutonic)
Also known as: *Asa, Asa Bridge, Asabru, Asbru.*
The Rainbow Bridge, Bifrost, links Asgard to the world of the mortals. The bridge stretches high above Midgard between the edges of Niflheim, or, some say, between Asgard and Midgard. It is built of fire, water, and air. It crosses the rivers of the dead (Kerlaug). The bridge is watched by the god Heimdall who is armed with a sword and carries a trumpet called Giallarhorn. The trumpet is used to announce the coming or going of the various gods. Only Thor is denied the privilege of using the bridge. During Ragnarok, Bifrost will be broken down by Sutur as he leads the sons of Muspell. See also Asgard; Niflheim; Thor.

Bifur (Norse; Teutonic)
Dwarf. One of the dwarfs who made Glepnir, the chain that binds the wolf Fenrir. The other named dwarfs are Bafur, Bombor, Dain, Nain, Nar, Niping and Nori. Skirnir, Freyr's messenger, was sent to the dwarfs to have them make the chain. See also Dain; Dwarfs; Fenrir; Yggdrasil.

Bihishan (India) see Shurpanaka.

Bijadari (India) Benevolent demigods. See also Vidyadhara.

Bil (A) (Teutonic)
This minor goddess, an Asynjor, is the waning moon, who with Hiuki (also known as Hjuki), follows Mani the moon god on his course. She is described as a little girl. See also Aesir; Asynjor; Mani.

Bil (B) (Celtic) see Bel (B).

Bila (Aborigine People, Australia)
Sun goddess or sun-woman. She is a bloodthirsty cannibal who was wounded by the lizard-man Kudnu with a boomerang because she ate his people. She disappeared and the world was in darkness. Kudnu threw his boomerangs to the north, west,

and south. It was only when he threw his last one to the east that she changed into a ball of fire and returned to the world.

Bildjiwararoju *Bildjiwruaroiju* (Australia) *see* Djanggawuls.

Bile (Celtic)
A culture hero, he is the spouse of Don and the father of Arianrhod, and Caswallwan. *See also* Arianrhod; Bel (B).

Bileyg (Teutonic)
"One with Evasive Eyes," an alternate name for Odin.

Bilflindi (Teutonic) *see* Odin.

Bilrost (Teutonic) *see* Bifrost.

Bilskirnir (Norse; Teutonic)
It is the dwelling place of the god Thor in Asgard. *See also* Asgard; Thor.

Bilva (India) Sacred Fruit. *See also* Shiva.

Bima (Aborigine People, Australia) *see* Purukupali.

Bimbo-Gami (Japan) *see* Bimbogami.

Bimbogami *Bimbo-Gami* (Japan)
A god of poverty who is exorcised by throwing away the bamboo tube that lights the household fire.

Binded (Egypt) *see* Banebdedet.

Bingo (Bantu People, Africa)
God of knowledge. Son of Nzame and a mortal woman known as Mboya. After a quarrel with his wife over the affections of Bingo, Nzame threw his son from heaven. Otoyum, a great sorcerer, saved and hid Bingo. When Bingo grew up, he became the teacher of mortals. *See also* Nzame.

Binzuru *Binzuku* (Buddhist; Japan)
Originally he was a mortal disciple of Buddha. He became a god because of his miraculous abilities to heal the sick. In some myths, Binzuru broke his vow of chastity and so is denied entrance to Nirvana.

Bir (Assyrian) *see* Adad.

Biral (Australia) *see* Baiame, and Bunjil.

Birque (Semite) *see* Adad.

Birral (Australia) *see* Baiame.

Birren (Celtic) *see* Bith and Birren.

Birushana (Japan) *see* Dainichi-nyorai.

Bis-Bis (Assyro-Babylonian) *see* Tiamat.

Bish-nat (India) *see* Bhima (A).

Bishamon (Buddhist, China; Buddhist, Japan; originally of Hindu origins)
Also known as: *Bishamon-Ten, Bishamon-tenno, Bishamon-ten, Tamon, Tamon-tenno, Tamontennu.*
God of war, happiness, wealth and good luck. Guardian. Bishamon ("Wide Hearing"), a Shi-Tenno, is the guardian of the north. He is also one of the Shichi Fukujin (seven deities of good luck), and in this capacity is the god of war and wealth.

As a warrior he is the protector of human life and chaser of demons. He is the brother of Kishijoten, a goddess of luck and beauty who corresponds to Lakshmi the Indian goddess of fortune and Sri the Indian goddess of prosperity. As a guardian, Bishamon is depicted as a soldier with a ferocious expression, usually shown with a small container in the shape of a pagoda in one hand and a spear in the other hand. As a Shichi Fukujin, he is also depicted as a soldier, holding similar items, sometimes with a halo in the shape of a wheel. *See* Lakshmi and Sri for similarities to Kishijoten. *See also* Benton; Daikoku; Jikoku-Ten; Kichijo-Ten; Komoku-Ten; Shi Tenno; Shichi Jukujin; Tamontennu; Zocho-Ten.

Bishamon-Ten (Japan) *see* Bishamon.

Bishamon-Tenno (Japan) *see* Bishamon.

Bishamonten (Japan) *see* Bishamon.

Bishen (India) *see* Devi; Gauri; Parvati.

Bishenjun (India) *see* Kalki.

Bisi-Bisi (Assyro-Babylonian) *see* Ishtar.

Bisimbi (Congo, Africa) *see* Nymphs.

Biswarupa (Nepal)
Biswarupa, a representation of many gods in one, has many heads and arms. The rear circle of arms has the hands in various hand poses. Other circles of arms hold implements and weapons. The heads, terrible and gentle, are those of the deities.

Bith and Birren (Irish)
This couple, similar to Adam and Eve, survived a deluge. They were the parents of Cessair (q.v.).

Bitje (Egypt)
A monster serpent with a head at each end, it is found in the ninth sector of Tuat.

Bitol (Maya)
Also known as: *Ixmucane.*
Creator deity. One of the council of Seven Gods of Creation. After the second attempt at creating mortals, four of the gods (regents) changed their names and sculpted men out of wood. Bitol became Ixmucane (q.v.). *See also* Alom.

Bivar-Asp (Persia) *see* Azi; Zahhak.

Bivrost (Teutonic) *see* Bifrost.

Bjelbog (Slavic) *see* Balbog.

Bjorno-hoder (Teutonic) *see* Hodur.

Black Annis (British)
Also known as: *Black Agnes.*
Black Annis lived in a cave alone. She hid in the branches of the last oak tree from her forest. This blue-faced hag feasted on people that she had snatched from their firesides. Others believed that she would grab children who played in her territory and scratch them to death. Early each spring, a dead cat would be dragged before a pack of hounds in front of her cave in Dante Hills to celebrate the death of winter. *See also* Cailleach Bheur.

Black Hactcin (Jicarilla Apache People, South America) *see* Hactcin.

Black Mother, The (India) *see* Kali.

Black Surt (Teutonic) *see* Surtr.

Blathine (Celtic) *see* Blathnat.

Blathnat *Blathine* (Celtic)
The daughter of King Mider, she married Curoi, who was the guardian of the king's magic cauldron. Blathnat conspired with Cuchulain to steal the cauldron from Curoi. *See also* Cuchulain; Curoi; Mider.

Bleifstr (Teutonic) *see* Loki.

Blodeuwedd (Celtic, Welsh)
Also known as: *Flower Face.*
She was created by Math and Gwydion from a tree and flower-blossoms. The spouse of Llew, she loved Gronw Pebyr. To him she divulged the secret of how Llew could be killed. Gwydion punished her by death, or by turning her into an owl. This myth is similar to the myth of Blathnat (q.v.). *See also* Gwydion; Llew Llaw Gyffes.

Blue Jay (Chinook People, Pacific Coast People, North America)
A creator god, Blue Jay decides how each animal and bird will live, make its home, and eat. He is also a protector of humans. In the Chinook belief Blue Jay was orginally a mischief-maker, the gods turned him into a zoomorphic being. His sister is Ioi. *See also* Agas Xenas Xena.

Bn-Ym (Ugarit) *see* Khoser-et-Hasis.

Bo (Ewe People, Dahomey; Africa)
Bo protects people in war. During ceremonial occassions, his priests carry bundles of painted red and white sticks that are four to six feet in length. They also carry brass axes. Bo is associated with the god of lightning, Khebieso (also known as So).

Boand (Celtic, Irish) *see* Boann.

Boann (Celtic, Irish)
Also known as: *Boand, Boannan, Buan.*
Mother deity. River nymph. Boann is the goddess or priestess of the Boyne River in eastern Ireland who, by her union with Dagda, became the mother of Angus, Bodb, Brigit, Mider, and Ogma. Some say she is the river nymph wife of Ecmar (also spelled Elcmar, Elcmhaire. Accused of adultery with Dagda, she drowned in Connla's well trying to prove her innocence. It is said the result of her infidelity was the birth of Angus. To conceal this from Ecmar she and Dagda held the sun still for the nine months of her pregnancy but made it seem like only one day had passed. Angus was raised by the underworld deity, Mider. For other river deities, *see* Brigantia, Sequana. Compare Boann to Tammuz. *See also* Angus; Dagda.

Boannan (Celtic, Irish) *see* Boann.

Boar with the Nine Tusks (Maya) *see* Cit-Bolon-Tum.

Bochica *Bochicha, Bokika* (Chibecha; Muyscaya People, Colombia, South America)

Also known as: *Chiminizagagua, Nempterequeteva, Nemquetheba, Xue, Zuhe.*
Sun God. Supreme creator and lawgiver. Bochica brought agriculture, social laws, crafts and other skills to the people. Before he left the mortal plane, he imprinted the shape of his foot on a rock. His wife was Chia (or possibly Huythaka or Cuchaviva) who brought a great flood which angered Bochica. He exiled his wife to the sky where she became the moon. He defeated the demon Chibchacum and forced him to carry the earth on his shoulders. Earthquakes are the result of Chibchacum getting restless. Bochica was possibly brought to Mexico by the Buddhist missionaries. In legend, an old bearded man clothed in robes came from the east to teach the people skills and crafts. Thinking he was one of the Apostles, they gave him the epithet "Chiminizagagua," meaning "messenger of Chiminingua" (q.v.). *See also* Bachue (goddess of water); Chaquen (god of boundaries); Chia; Chibchacum; Cuchavira (god of air and the rainbow); Fomagata (storm god); Nencatacoa (god of weavers).

Bochicha (Bogata, South Africa) *see* Bochica.

Bod-Baal (Ugarit)
He assisted Baal in his battle with the Son of the Sea, Khoser-et-Hasis, and the Lord of the Sea, Zabel, and the beast Suffete, the Lord of the River. *See also* Baal.

Bodb (Celtic)
Also known as: *Bodb Dearg, Bodb Derg, Bod the Red, Bov.*
Father of deities. Bodb is either the son of Dagda and Boann, or the father of Dagda. He succeeded his father as ruler of the gods. After the defeat of the Tuatha De Danann, he became their king. His daughter, Aoife (also spelled Aeife), turned his stepchildren into swans, so he punished her by transforming her into a wind demon. Bodb eventually retired to the retreat of the gods. The name Bodb is sometimes confused with Badb, who is a goddess of battle. *See also* Aebh; Angus; Balor; Boann; Dagda.

Bodb the Red (Celtic) *see* Bodb.

Boddhisattvas (India) *see* Bodhisattvas.

Boddi (Teutonic) *see* Heimdall.

Boden (Teutonic) *see* Bodn.

Bodhisats (India) *see* Bodhisattvas.

Bodhisattva Cakdor (Tibet) *see* Vajrapani.

Bodhisattva Cheresi (Tibet) *see* Avalokitesvara.

Bodhisattvas *Boddhisattvas, Bodisats, Bodisatvas, Buddhas*
Also known as: *Pu-sa* (China); (Buddhist, India)
Bodhisattvas originated in the Mahayana branch of Buddhism. They are spiritually advanced persons who have achieved complete enlightenment. This qualifies them for Nirvana, the state of detachment from suffering. However, Bodhisattvas have chosen to remain in the world to assist and guide humans who have not achieved enlightenment. Although there are numerous Bodhisattvas, the common Bodhisattva trinity is composed of Avalokitesvara, Manjusri and Vajrapani. Maitreya, the future Buddha, is the last of the Bodhisattvas. Bodhisattvas are usually

shown in a group of five, seated in an attitude of profound meditation (dhyana). Manjusri and Maitreya are shown seated on a throne. *See also* Dhyani Buddhas; Dhyanibodisattvas.

Bodisats (India) *see* Bodhisattvas.

Bodisatvas (India) *see* Bodhisattvas.

Bodn *Boden* (Norse; Teutonic)
Bodn is the crock used to create the mead of poetry which was brewed from Kvasir's blood. Two other vessels were used to mix the brew: the crock Son, and the kettle Odraerir. Kvasir was killed by the dwarfs Fjalar and Galar. *See also* Kvasir; Odraerir.

Boe (Teutonic)
Also known as: *Vale.*
One of the sons of Odin and Rind (the personification of the hard, frozen earth). He avenged the death of Balder by killing Hodur. *See also* Hodur; Odin; Rind.

Boeotus (Greek)
He is the son of Poseidon and Arne (also known as Melanippe), the brother of Aeolus, the father of Itonus, and grandfather of Hippalcimus. *See also* Aeolus (B); Arne.

Boetis (Greek)
This goat or the goat Aex became the mother of Aegipan with Zeus. *See also* Aegipan.

Bogatyri (Slavic)
Also known as: *Bogatyr* (singular).
Spirits or gods of the Christian era. Some say they are river spirits. Their names are Ilya-Muromyets, Mikula, Potok-Mikhailo-Ivanovich, Sadko, Svyatogor, Volkh (Volga). Epic poems, known as "byliny," were written about these deities. Eventually, the Bogatyri were beaten. They fled to caves where they turned to stone.

Bogu (Sumer) God of Wealth.

Bohu (Mesopotamia)
Also known as: *Baau, Bahu, Bau, Gur.*
Earth Mother. *See also* Bau; Ea.

Boi (Celtic, Gaelic) *see* Cailleach Bheare.

Bokika (Bogota, South America) *see* Bochica.

Bolon-Ti-Ku (Maya People, Yucatan) *see* Ahmucen-Cab.

Bolon-Tsac-Cab (Maya People, Yucatan) *see* Ahmucen-Cab.

Bolthorn (Norse; Teutonic)
He is the frost giant brother of the wise giant Mimir, and grandfather of Odin, Vili, and Ve. *See also* Bestla; Bor; Buri; Mimir; Odin; Odraerir.

Bolverk *Bolverkr, Boverkin* (Norse; Teutonic)
Also known as: *Evil Doer, Odin.*
Aspect of Odin. Bolverk is one of the names chosen by Odin when he journeyed to Jotun-heim to find the mead of poetry made from Kvasir's blood. He also uses this name when in the role of a war god. *See also* Baugi; Jotun-heim; Kvasir; Odin.

Bolverkin (Teutonic) *see* Odin.

Bombor *Baumbur* (Teutonic) *see* Dwarfs.

Bomersum (Saora People, India)
God of the marketplace. *See also* Adununkisum; Babusum.

Bomong (India) *see* Bong.

Bona Dea (Roman)
Also known as: *Fatua, Fauna.*
An ancient goddess of women. Possibly a goddess of fertility. She is reputed to be a relation of the god Faunus (possibly wife or daughter), or possibly just a female form of Faunus. She is supposed to be a goddess of fertility. Her true name is not known because she has refused to give one hint of it. She is a great prophet, a dispenser of healing herbs, and is quite chaste. She also permits no wine to be imbibed in her presence. Her name means "the Good Goddess." She was worshiped in early December in secret by women only. Bona Dea ("Good Goddess") was the most popular name used in the worship of Fauna Fatua. Bona Dea is identified with Maia and Rhea. *See also* Cybele; Faunus; Ops (a Sabine goddess).

Bondi (Teutonic) *see* Heimdall.

Bong and Bomong (Minyong People, India)
Sky and earth goddesses.

Bonus Eventus (Roman)
Agricultural deity. He is a rural god in charge of the harvest. Some say he is a god of success or luck.

Boodh (India) *see* Buddha.

Boodha (India) *see* Buddha.

Bor *Borr* (Norse; Teutonic)
He is the son of Buri and spouse of the giant Bestla, who is the daughter of Bolthorn. Bor and Bestla are the parents of Odin, Vili, and Ve, the ancestors of the Aesir. Odin, Vili, and Ve finally succeeded in slaying the great giant Ymir, and all of the other Giants except Bergelmir. *See also* Audhumla; Bergelmir; Bestla; Bolthorn; Buri; Midgard; Odin; Ve; Vili; Ymir.

Boreadae (Greek) *see* Boreas; Zetes.

Boreades (Greek) *see* Boreas; Zetes.

Boreas (Greek)
Also known as: *Aguilo* (Latin), *North Wind.*
God of the North Wind. Boreas is the son of the Titan Astraeus ("Starry Night") and Eos ("Dawn"). Boreas, who resided in Thrace, fell in love with the nymph Oreithyia (also spelled Orithyia) who lived in Athens. The match did not sit well with the Athenians, who hated the Thracians because of the despicable deeds of Tereus. Boreas, as the North Wind, took matters into his own hands and whisked his loved one off her feet and took her to Thrace. His mother is the goddess of dawn, Eos, who had earlier abducted her lover, the beautiful Cleitus. Boreas and Oreithyia became the parents of Chione, Cleopatra, the winged twins Zetes and Calais, and Haemus. In the Pelasgian creation myth, Boreas is the fertilizing force which impregnates Eurynome, the Goddess of All Things. Boreades (also spelled Boreadae) is generally used as a name for the twins, Calais and Zetes, but it is sometimes used when referring to

the children of Boreas. It is also used when referring to the twelve horses sired by Boreas in stallion form when he mated with the mares of Erichthonius (also spelled Erechtheus), king of Dardania, said to be the world's richest man. Astraeus is the daughter of Erechtheus who was referred to by Homer as the grandson of Erichthonius. Other sources write that they are one and the same person. Boreas is usually depicted with snake tails in place of feet, or as a young man flying about in a playful way and sometimes as being the father of rain, snow, hail and tempests and also as an old winged man, veiled in clouds. Compare to Fujin (Japan). Boreas is the equivalent of the Roman Aquilo. *See also* Aello; Chaos; Chimaera; Cleite; Eos; Eurus; Eurynome (A); Harpies; Notus; Tereus; Zephyrus.

Bori (Teutonic) *see* Buri.

Bormanus (Celtic, Gaul) *see* Borvo.

Bormo (Celtic, Gaul) *see* Borvo.

Borr (Teutonic) *see* Bor.

Borus (Greek)

He is the son of Perieres and Gorgophone. His siblings are Aphareus, Icarius, Leucippus and Tyndareus. Borus married Polydora (q.v.). *See also* Gorgophone; Icarius.

Borve (Celtic) *see* Borvo.

Borvo *Bormo* (Celtic, Gaul)

Also known as: *Belenos, Bormanus, Borve* (possibly), *Gramnnos.*

"God of Hot Springs." He is a divine healer who wards off illness, and a god of health giving springs. Borvo means "to boil." His consort was the Gaulish goddess of cattle, "The Divine Cow," Damona. In some renditions, he is thought to be the son of the early mother goddess, Sirona, (also known as Dirona), whom he displaced. Borvo may be the same as Borve, a Cymric king. The deity Bel, also known in the British tradition as Belinus, was called Belenos, as is Borvo. They are likely aspects of the same deity originating with Apollo (q.v.). *See also* Bel (B); Damona.

Bosheth (Hebrew) *see* Bast (Egypt).

Boshintoi (Siberia)

God of blacksmiths. Boshintoi and his nine sons made the horse post of the North Star.

Bossu (Dahomey People, Africa; Haiti)

Also known as: *Akadja.*

Malevolent spirit. A voodoo deity worshiped by the criminals of the underworld. Some say he might have been a mortal king named Kadja Bossu whom the Dahomey called Akadja. He is said to be a rival of the god of iron, Ogun. Bossu is related to the work god, Mounanchou. *See also* Ogun.

Bouddha (India) *see* Buddha.

Boulaia (Greek)

Another title of Athene as a goddess of council. *See also* Athene.

Bous (Teutonic) *see* Vali.

Bouto (Egypt, Greek) *see* Buto.

Bouyan (Slavic) An island paradise. *See also* Alatuir.

Bozaloshtsh (Slavic)

Messenger of death. She is described as a small woman with long hair who appears under the window of someone approaching death. Similar to Banshees (q.v.).

Brage (Teutonic) *see* Odin.

Bragi (Teutonic)

Also known as: *Brage, Odin* (possibly).

An Aesir, Bragi is the son of Odin and Frigga, and spouse of Idun (also known as Iduna). He is the lord of the sky and day, the god of poetry and eloquence, and the patron of bards. He may be an aspect of Odin. Bragi and Hermod welcomed all heros to Valhalla. Bragi is depicted as an old man with a long white beard. He carries a harp. *See also* Aesir; Hermod; Hoenir; Ull; Vali.

Brahma *Brahmans* (Brahmanic, Buddhist, Hindu; India)

Also known as: *Abjaja,* ("Born from a Lotus"), *Abjayoni, Adharma* ("Destroyer of All Things"), *Maha-pita* ("The Great Father"), *Narayana, Pitamaha* ("Grandfather"), *Prah Prohm* (Cambodian), *Prajapati* ("Lord of Creation"), *Purusha, Ts'ana-Pa* ("White Brahma"; Tibet).

Brahma, a creator god, received the basics of his mythological history from Purusha. During the Brahmanic period, the Hindu Trimurti was represented by Brahma with his attribute of creation, Shiva with his attribute of destruction and Vishnu with his attribute of preservation. The later Brahmans gave him the role of the Vedic Hiranyagarbha and Prajapati. He was born from Narayana, the golden primeval egg. The *Ramayana* states that he is self-existent, created himself as a boar, raised the world from the primeval waters with his tusks and formed the universe. In the *Mahabharata* epic he sprang from the right side of the great god Mahadeva. Others believe that Mahadeva sprang from Vishnu's forehead and Brahma sprang from Vishnu's navel, or from the lotus growing from Vishnu's navel, which makes him an avatar of Vishnu. In the "Laws of Manu," The "Self-Existent" Brahmam created the primeval waters and the golden egg with his seed within it. He emerged from the egg as Brahman and is simultaneously the son of the primal spirit, Narayana, the primal man, Purusha, and the creator god, Brahma. The "Vishnu Purana" presents Brahman as the essence of the world and the creator. In another creation myth, Brahama initially created ignorance, which he threw away. She survived and became Night. From Night came the Rakshasas and Yakshas, who are sometimes enemies but usually helpful. He then created the immortals. From his hip came the Asuras, who became enemies of the gods. The earth came from his feet, and all other elements of the world from other parts of his body. In other renditions, Brahma began the creation process and became discouraged, so he created four Munis (sages) to complete his work. Their interest in worshiping the universal spirit, Vasudeva, took precedence over their assignment from Brahma. This angered the great god and from his anger the deity Rudra was formed to complete the creation process. Brahma's paradise was Brahmaloka, located on Mount Meru. Some say that Surya, the sun god, may be the son of Brahma. The goddess of learning, Sarasvati, is Brahma's principal wife.

He is the father of the capable Daksha, who was born from his thumb, and the wise Atri. He is the grandfather of King Yudhishthira. Narayana is said by some to be an aspect of Brahma and by others an aspect of Vishnu. In some renditions of the Buddhist tradition, Brahma and Indra interacted with Buddha. In one myth the two gods bathed the newborn Buddha. The god Brahma initially was not the same as the neuter gender godforce of the "Upanishads," Brahman. In later times, however, Brahma did become identical with Brahman. Brahma, often in fish form, is usually depicted as having four bearded faces and four arms (representing the four Vedas) and seated on a lotus throne. With his four faces, he controls the four quarters of the universe. The lotus represents Mani, the earth. He holds the disk, alms dish, or spoon in his hands. Originally Brahma had five heads, but one was burnt off by Shiva's third eye when he discovered that Brahma lusted incestuously after his daughter Sandhya. Sometimes he is imaged with three faces. His color is red, and he is sometimes shown as a peacock or a swan. He is also shown riding on Hansa his goose, who has a spotted red and blue peacock's tail. Sometimes he is seated in his chariot, pulled by seven swans who symbolize the seven worlds, or some say clouds. He wears the skin of a black antelope and is dressed in white. His sword, named Asi, is the sun's ray born of a sacrifice made on his altar called Samantapancaka. In his aspect as Abjaja (also known as Abjayoni) he is depicted sitting on a lotus, rising out of the navel of Varuna, who is connected by a flower stem (umbilical cord) to Narayana-Vishnu. When Brahma surveyed the four corners of the universe before beginning the creation process, it symbolized the four functions of the consciousness that the mortal must achieve: thought, feeling, intuition, and sensation. At all rites for Brahma he is presented with a single flower and Ghee (sacrificial butter). During the full moon night in January, he is adorned with Vishnu and Shiva on either side. The next day, the images are cast into holy waters. The symbol of the Trimurti is the syllable om, made up of the three sounds, a, u, m. Brahma's arrow is named Naga-pasa. The Tibetan Ts'ana-pais is usually shown brandishing a sword and carrying a white bull. Compare Brahma to the creation myths of Manu and Varuna. Compare him to Abram. See also Agastya; Agni; Ahalya; Andhaka; Ardhanari-Ishvara; Asuras; Brahman; Buddha; Daksha; Dwaparayuga; Gandharvas; Ganesha; Garuda; Gramadeveta; Hansa; Hiranya-kasipu; Hiranyagarbha; Kama (A); Karttikeya; Kuvera; Loka; Manjusri; Manu; Marichi (B); Meru Mountain; Narada; Narayana (A); Narayana (B); Narayana (D); Prajapati; Purusha; Rakshasas; Ratri; Ravana; Rishi; Rudra; Sandhya; Sarasvati; Savitri (B); Shiva; Skambha; Surya; Tara (A); Vach; Vasistha; Vishnu; Visvakarmna; Yaksha and Yakshini.

Brahma-Kapla (India) see Kalpa.

Brahmaloka (India) Brahma's Paradise. See also Brahma.

Brahman (Hindu)
Also known as: *That, Absolute.*
"Truth." Infinity or the Absolute. According to some authorities, the world is illusion. It can exist inwardly or outwardly. It is the indescribable world of illusion. Brahman was the neuter gender world spirit, the All-god. In later times, Brahman and Brahma were considered the same. See also Brahma; Sarasvati.

Brahman — Creation Legaue (Hindu; Vedic) see Brahma; Prajapati (A); Purusha

Brahmanaspati (Hindu; India) see Brhaspati.

Brahmani (India)
Wife of Brahma. See also Brahma; Devi; Sarasvati.

Brahmans (India) see Brahma.

Brahmapura (India)
Brahma's heaven, located on Meru Mountain (q.v.).

Brahmarishis (India) see Rishi.

Brahmi (India) see Sarasvati.

Bramanaspati (India) see Brihaspati.

Bran (British, Celtic, Welsh)
Also known as: *Bendegeit Bran, Bendigeid Fran, Bendigeid Vran, Bran the Blessed, Leodegrance, Vron.*
A brave giant, Bran is the brother of Branwen and Manawyddan and the son of Llyr by Iweridd or, some say, Febal. He has two half-brothers, Nissyen and Evnissyen (also spelled Efnissien), who were enemies. Bran was the possessor of a cauldron with the power to bring the dead back to life, but without the restoration of the power of speech. When his sister, Branwen, married the king of Ireland, Matholwch, he gave the cauldron to the Irish. This gift was compensation for the humiliation Evnissyen had caused the Irish. The ungrateful Matholwch subsequently imprisoned his new wife in the castle kitchen and treated her like a servant. Bran, with the British fleet behind him, walked through the sea to rescue his sister. A battle ensued and the defeated Irish offered to get rid of Matholwch and allow Gwern, the son of Branwen and Matholwch, to assume the throne. Evnissyen reappeared on the scene and killed Gwern. The fighting resumed but neither side emerged the victor. The Irish brought their dead to life until Bran smashed the magic cauldron. Seven Britons survived: Pryderi; Manawydan; Glunen, the son of the culture hero Taran; Taliesin; Ynawc; Grudyen, the son of Muryel; and Heilyn, the son of Gwynn the Ancient. Bran, severely wounded by a poisoned arrow, asked the survivors to behead him. It was said that his head was buried in London with eyes toward France to ward off all invaders. His head, which supposedly lived for eighty-seven years, is variously called: Uther Ben ("Wonderful Head,") Uther Pendragon, or Urien. (A starling brought Bran the message of his sister's distress. The birds of Rhiannon kept his head distracted from discomfort by their sweet singing.) See also Branwen; Manawydan Ap Llyr; Pryderi; Rhiannon.

Bran the Blessed (Celtic) see Bran.

Branwen *Brangwaine, Brynwyn, Dwynwen* (Celtic, Irish, Welsh)
A deified mortal, Branwen was the daughter of Llyr by Iweridd, and sister of Bran and Manawyddan. Famous for her beauty, she attracted the king of Ireland, Matholwch (also spelled Matholwych). Their marriage temporarily united Britain and Ireland. When Bran heard from a starling that the king was keeping his sister prisoner in the castle kitchen, he went to rescue her. A battle developed and peace resulted for a brief period. Branwen's step-brother Evnissyen, murdered

their son Gwern, bringing about war. Grief-stricken, Branwen died. *See also* Bran; Evnissyen; Manawydan Ap Llyr; Pryderi.

Brathy (Phoenician)
One of the giants of the mountains. They were the inventors of incense. Three others were named Cassios, Lebanon, and Antilebanon.

Brattskegg (Teutonic) *see* Heimdall.

Breathmaker (Seminole People, North America)
The Milky Way was created by Breathmaker by blowing at the sky. This is the path the people and their animals follow when they die en route to a "city in the western sky." Breathmaker also taught the people how to dig wells and find fish.

Brechta (Teutonic) *see* Bertha.

Breg (Celtic) *see* Dagda.

Breid (Teutonic) *see* Heimdall.

Breidablik (Norse; Teutonic)
Also known as: *Broad Splendor.*
This is Balder's residence in Asgard. It has golden pillars and a silver roof. It became his zodiacal house, which corresponds to the sign of the twins, Gemini. *See also* Asgard; Balder; Gladsheim; Sovabek.

Breit-Hut (Teutonic) *see* Odin.

Breksta (Lithuania)
Goddess of the passing hours of darkness. Her companions are Ausrine, the dawn, and Zleja, the high day.

Bres (Irish) *see* Bress.

Bres mac Elatha (Celtic) *see* Bress.

Bress *Bres* (Celtic, Irish)
Also known as: *Bres mac Elatha.*
Sun deity. Bress "the beautiful" is the son of the Fomorian sea king, Elathan, and the Tuatha De Danann earth mother goddess, Eriu. He married the goddess Brigit, who is the daughter of Dagda. Bress was appointed king of the Tuatha De Danann when king Nuada had his hand severed during the First Battle of Magh Tuiredh against the giant Firbolgs. Their motive in appointing him was an attempt to appease their enemies the Firbolgs. He turned out to be a dreadful tyrant who raised taxes and monopolized food sources which humiliated the people and made them subservient. In legend, there are many horror stories about his evil practices. Fortunately, the Tuatha De Danann had a rule that kings who were physically maimed could not reign. King Nuada lost the throne to Bress under that edict. A poet could cause the disfigurement of a king by satirizing him. In one eventful happening, the chief poet Cairbre's words were so scathing they caused Bress' face to erupt in boils. The Tuatha ousted him and he joined the Fomorians. In the Second Battle of Magh Tuiredh, he fought against the people he had once ruled and was defeated. *See also* Banbha; Brigit; Dagda; Dia'necht; Lugh; Nuada; Tuatha De Danann.

Brhaspati *Brahmanaspati* (Hindu; India)
The "Lord of Devotion," he brought light to the world. His worshipers are given long life and victory. Brhaspati is sometimes thought to be the same as Agni (q.v.).

Brian (Celtic) *see* Cian; Dana.

Briareus (Greek)
Also known as: *Aegaeon, Obriareus.*
He is one of the Hecatonchires, sons of Uranus and Gaea. *See also* Aegaeon; Gaea; Hecatonchires.

Brid (Celtic) *see* Brigantia.

Bride (Celtic, Irish) *see* Brigantia; Brigit.

Bridge of Pain (China) *see* K'u-ch'u K'iao.

Bridge of the Gatherer (Persian) *see* Chinvat Bridge.

Bridge of the Requiter (Persian) *see* Chinvat Bridge.

Bridget (Celtic, Irish) *see* Brigantia; Brigit.

Brig (Irish) *see* Brigit.

Brigantes (Celtic) *see* Brigantia.

Brigantia *Brigindo* (British, Celtic, Irish)
Also known as: *Brid, Bride, Bridget, Brighid, Brighit, Brigid, Brigin-do, Brigit, St. Bridget.*
Protector deity. Multi-function goddess. Brigantia is a goddess of northern England, the protective goddess of the Brigantes, the largest tribe of Britain, which was named after her. It is said that she was raised on the milk of a magic cow from the Otherworld who was white with red ears. A goddess of the seasons, she watched over springs, streams, cattle and lambs. She is also a goddess of the hearth and fertility. She oversees the pain of women in childbirth. In Scottish mythology, she is Brigid, the goddess and saint, who oversees the coming of spring and ends the winter reign of Cailleach Bheur. Brigantia corresponds to the goddess Brigit of Ireland and also has aspects of the Irish Danu. She is often equated to the Romano-British goddess, Minerva. She is shown wearing a globe shaped crown, armed and wearing a breastplate, or bare-breasted. *See also* Bheur; Boann; Brigit; Cailleach Bheur; Dana; Minerva.

Brighid (Celtic) *see* Brigantia; Brigit.

Brighit (Celtic) *see* Brigantia; Brigit.

Brigid (Celtic, Irish) *see* Brigantia; Brigit.

Brigindo (Celtic) *see* Brigantia.

Brigit *Brighid, Bridget, Brigid* (British, Irish, Scottish)
Also known as: *Bride, Brig.*
Patroness of culture and learning. Goddess of healing. Brigit is the daughter of Dagda, who was a leader of the Tuatha De Danann. In some myths, she has two sisters of the same name; however, this could be her aspects as a triple-goddess, patroness of poets, healers and smiths. She is said to have a brother, Angus, who is the Irish Cupid. Brigit married a Fomorian, Bress, and had a son, Ruadan. Ruadan was slain by the Tuatha De Danann weapon-maker, Goibnui. In her grief, Brigit initiated the first "keening" in Ireland, a wailing lamentation. She is often equated with the Celtic Brigantia, as they share the attributes of fertility and abundance. However, Brigit had the additional aspects of culture and skills. She has been equated with Dana and Anu, but the worship of Brigit was more widespread as illustrated in the eventual adoration of St. Brigit. Like

Brigantia, she is referred to as the Celtic version of Minerva. *See also* Angus; Anu; Boann; Bress; Brigantia; Dagda; Dana; Minerva; Ruadan; Tuatha De Danann.

Brigitte (Haitian)

Also known as: *Maman Brigitte.*

Deity of cemeteries. Goddess of the dead. Female counterpart of Ghede who was an aspect of Baron Samedi. *See also* Ghede.

Brihadratha, King (India) Big Carriage. *See also* Jara-Sandha.

Brihaspati (Brahmanic, Hindu, Vedic; India)

Also known as: *Angirasa, Bramanaspati, Purohita* (the family priest of the gods), *Vyasa* (an incarnation in the fourth Divapara age).

He is a creator deity, a god of incantation and ritual, who is called the "Chaplain," "Master of Formula," "Creator of All Things," and "He Whom the Gods Themselves Would Consult." In the Vedic tradition, he is an abstract deity, known as the first of the Vedic priests. To the Brahmans, he is the divine sage Angirasa, son of Angiras. The Puranas tell of a battle between the gods, with Brihaspati leading the Angirasa line of seers, and the Asuras, led by Shukra (the personification of Venus) of the Brigus. His spouse, Tara (the personification of the stars), was abducted by the moon, Soma. A divine war, known as the Tarakamaya, erupted. Indra supported Brihaspati, and Rudra, the Daityas and the Danavas. The sage Usanas, who had an ancient feud with Brihaspati, supported Soma. The earth, Bhumi, was so unsettled that she appealed to Brahma to bring an end to the battle. He acknowledged her request and ordered Soma to allow Tara to return to Brihaspati. She gave birth to a dazzling son named Budha, who represents the planet Mercury, and had to admit to Brahma that he was the child of Soma. When Brihaspati found out, he was so enraged that he turned her to ashes. Brahma intercepted and returned her in a purified form and Brihaspati reunited with her. Soma was disinherited by Varuna as punishment for his role in the event. Brihaspati is one of the Rishis, who were poets, sages and prophets born from Brahma's mind. His son Bharadvaja also became a poet and sage to the Pandavas. Another son, Kacha, was sent to study with the chief priest of the Asuras to learn the secret of the charm that restores life to the dead. The Asuras killed him several times, but he was restored to life by his teacher. The Balis of Ceylon identified Brihaspati as the planet Jupiter, but worshiped him as phallic. He is depicted with a large halo of moon and stars over a conical headdress. His body is gold, his legs striped blue. In each hand he holds a phallus. Sometimes he is shown holding a container of soma in his left hand. He is also shown sitting or leaning on a tiger. At his feet rests a half-fish, half-human monster. His vehicle, the Niti-ghosha, is drawn by eight pale steeds. He is also shown with seven mouths, sharp horns, a hundred wings, holding an ax and a bow. His day of the week is Thursday and his zodiac sign is either Sagittarius or Pisces. *See also* Bharadvaja; Bhumi; Brighus; Daityas; Pandavas; Prajapati; Rishi; Rudra; Tara (A); Vach.

Brimir (Norse; Teutonic)

Giant. His hall will survive Ragnarok. It is a warm place where there will be plenty of food and drink. *See also* Ragnarok.

Brimo (Greek) *see* Demeter; Hecate; Persephone; Rhea.

Briseis (Greek) *see* Brises.

Brises (Greek) *see* Achilles; Calchas.

Brisingamen (Norse; Teutonic)

Also known as: *Brisings' Necklace, Sviagris.*

Freyja had sex with the four dwarfs, Alfrigg, Berling, Dvalin and Grerr, to gain ownership of the deified necklace, Brisingamen. Odin was so angry when he heard about Freyja and the dwarfs, he forced Loki to steal Brisingamen. In the meantime, Freyja broke the necklace when she heard that the giant Thrym demanded to marry her as compensation for returning to Thor his magic hammer, Mjollnir. *See also* Dvalin; Dwarfs; Freyja, Mjollnir; Thor; Thrym.

Brisings' Necklace (Teutonic) *see* Brisingamen.

Britomaris (Greek) *see* Britomartis.

Britomartis *Britomaris* (Crete, Greek)

Also known as: *Aphaea, Aphaia* (her name in Aegina, meaning "invisible"), *Dictynna* ("Lady of the Nets" or "Netted One").

Goddess of fishers, hunters, sailors. Britomartis, the daughter of Zeus and Carme, was a Cretan nymph. She received the name Britomartis from King Minos of Crete because she refused his advances and tried to kill herself. She flung herself from a cliff into the ocean. The fishing nets that she had invented as a gift to mortals saved her life. From that time, she was known as Dictynna ("netted one"). For protecting her chastity, Artemis placed her with the immortals in the heavens as a star. Other sources state she ruled the eastern end of the island as Britomartis and the western section as Dictynna. She became an aid to navigators. Her name became a title of Artemis as a fish goddess. As Aphaia, a local deity of Aegina, Britomartis is comparable to Athena, the goddess of wisdom. As she attempted to escape the advances of Minos, she was trapped in a fishing net and brought to Aegina by the fishermen. One of the men fell in love with her and ran into a densely wooded area and disappeared. In another rendition, her attempted escape from Minos caused her death. Her name was changed to Dictynna and she was made immortal. *See also* Artemis; Minos; Dictyanna; Pasiphae.

Broad Splendor (Teutonic)

Another name for Balder's residence, Breidablik (q.v.).

Brokk (Norse; Teutonic)

A dwarf who, along with Sindri or as some say Eitri, manufactured the golden hair for the goddess Sif after Loki cut off her real hair. Loki also received Skidbladnir, a magic ship for Freyr, and a magic spear named Gungnir for Odin. *See also* Dwarfs; Eitri.

Bromius and Evan (Greek) *see* Bacchus.

Bronte (Greek) *see* Helios.

Brontes (Greek)

"Thunder." Brontes, one of the Cyclopes, has a single eye in the middle of his forehead. *See also* Acamas (D); Aegaeon; Cyclopes; Gaea.

Broteas (Greek)

The son of Tantalus and Dione, the brother of Niobe and Pelops, Broteas was renowned for the figure of the Mother Goddess that he had carved in stone. When he was asked by the great hunter-warrior goddess Artemis to carve her likeness, he refused. Broteas went insane and burned himself to death. *See also* Artemis; Niobe; Pelops; Tantalus (A).

Broth of Oblivion (China) *see* Mi-Hung-T'ang.

Brownie (Scot)

This goblin is similiar to the elves. There is a possibility that Brownie was originally a pre–Celtic god. *See also* Dwarfs; Elves.

Brud (Teutonic) *see* Heimdall.

Brunhilde (Teutonic) *see* Brynhild.

Brut (Celtic)

Also known as: *Brute, Brutus.*

Deified mortal. In Geoffrey of Monmouth's account of early history, a descendant of Aeneas who, after his conquest of Albion, became king of the island, then called Britain after his name. At the direction of Diana, Brut the mortal and a group of Trojans founded Britain, which was at that time known as Albion and was inhabited by a race of giants.

Brute (Celtic) *see* Brut.

Brutus (Celtic) *see* Brut.

Brynhild *Brunhild, Brunhilde* (Teutonic)

As Brynhild, she was one of the Valkyries. In some versions she was queen of Iceland and wife of Gunther. Associated with Siegfried. *See also* Valkyries.

Buan-Ann (Celtic) *see* Anu (B).

Buana (Celtic, Irish) *see* Boann.

Bubastis (Greek) *see* Bast; Buto; Uadjit.

Buchis *Bacis* (Egypt)

Also known as: *Bakh, Bakha, Bkha, Bukhe* (Egypt), *Menthu-Ra, Mont.*

Buchis, the sacred bull, lived at Hermonthis in Upper Egypt. It is believed that Mont (also known as Menthu, Mentu, and Muntu) was often incarnated as Buchis. As Bacis or Bakh he was the Egyptian bull representing the sun-god Ra. Buchis is also the Greek rendering of the Egyptian Bukhe. Buchis is also thought to be an incarnation of Osiris. His counterpart was the sacred Apis bull at Memphis. He is shown with black hair that grows in the opposite direction from other animals. He changes his color every hour of the day. *See also* Aa Nefer; Apis (A); Mnevis; Mont.

Buddh (India) *see* Buddha.

Buddha *Boodh, Boodha, Bouddha, Buddh* (Buddhist, Hindu; India)

Also known as: *Buddha-Avatara* (Vishnu's ninth avatar), *Gautama, Gotama, Jina, Sakyamuni* ("Sage of Sakya"), *Siddartha* ("One Who Has Achieved His Purpose"), *Shih-Chia-mou-ni* (China), *Tathagata* ("One Who Has Thus Arrived").

The name Buddha means the "Awakened One." As the future Buddha or Bodhisattva (meaning the would-be-Buddha), he had passed through thousands of years before coming to earth. Most Western scholars agree that his birth date was 566–486 B.C.E. Others say the date is 563–486, or 558–478 B.C.E. While Buddha was in Tusita heaven, he determined the time, date, location, and the mother who would give birth to him. He came into the world as Gautama, the son of Maya and a Rajah, Suddhodhana, the chief officer of the Sakyas in Kapilavastu. Maya dreamed that a white elephant with six tusks entered her womb. Then she saw the full moon drop into her lap. Sixty-four Brahmans predicted the birth of a son who would be a Buddha or a universal emperor. The quasi-virgin birth of her son followed, as he issued forth from her right side. At the same moment, his future wife, his horse, elephant, charioteer and the bo-tree (*Ficus religiosa*) were born. Seven days after his birth, his mother died of joy. Raised by his mother's sister, Mahaprajapti, he grew up surrounded by luxury. When he was sixteen years old, he won his bride, Yasodhara, the daughter of Dandapani, in an armed contest. They became the parents of a son, Rahula. At twenty-nine years of age, Gautama tired of worldly ways. His faithful driver and confidant Channa prepared the horse Kanthaka for his master. Gautama left his wife and son and retired to contemplate in the wilderness for six years. During this period he survived torments and temptations and arrived at a state of complete enlightenment (bodhi) as he sat under a banyan tree. He could have entered Nirvana at that point, but his compassion led him back to the world to share his wisdom. Assisted by his son, he wandered throughout India and taught to anyone who would listen. In his eightieth year, he left the world and retired to Paranirvana, the highest state of absolute bliss. Buddha regarded himself as a Tathagata: one who has "arrived," one who has experienced and transcended the imperfections of life. Numerous stories of Buddha's life are found in a collection of stories known as the "Jatakas." According to some, Buddha was the ninth avatar of Vishnu (Buddha-Avatara). Buddhists do not accept this theory. The original Buddha was depicted as a wheel, empty throne, or a tree. The white elephant was a royal symbol. In later times, he was depicted with short, curly hair, seated on or in a lotus. In the Mayayana tradition, Buddha is sometimes depicted in princely attire complete with jewels and a diadem. Buddha, Vairocana and Maitreya share the same mudra: dharmacakra (both hands against the breast, left hand covering the right). This mudra is the mudra of preaching. Often he is shown with the jnana mudra (the hand held up with the thumb touching the tip of the index or middle finger; the sign of insight). The book containing the essential teachings of Buddha is known as "The Dhammapada" (q.v.). For a similar legend, *see* Mahavir. *See also* Arhats; Asvaghosa; Brahma; Dipamkara; Hariti; Jagannath; Manushi Buddhas; Mara; Marichi (A); Maya (A); Miroku-Bosatsu (Japan); Mucalinda; Sakra; Sakyamuni; Stupa; Tushita; Vairocana; Vajrapani; Vishnu.

Buddha-Avatara (India) *see* Buddha; Vishnu.

Buddha Dakini (Tibet) *see* Khados.

Buddha Dakinis (India) *see* Dakinis; Khados.

Buddhi (India)

Goddess of wisdom and knowledge. *See also* Ganesha; Karttikeya.

Buddhist Universe (India) *see* Chakravala.

Budha (India)
The son of Tara and Soma, and spouse of Ida. He personifies the planet Mercury. *See also* Brihaspati; Ida (B); Tara (A).

Bugan *Bigan* (Ifugao People, Philippines)
He is the son of the first woman and brother of Wigan, the mother of humanity after the Deluge. *See also* Wigan.

Bui (Teutonic) *see* Cailleach Bheare; Heimdall.

Bukhe (Egypt, Greek) *see* Buchis.

Bulaia (Greek) *see* Athena.

Bull of Amentet (Egypt) *see* Apis (A).

Bull of Confusion (Egypt) *see* Iti.

Bull of Meroe (Egypt) *see* Ra.

Bull of the Underworld (Egypt) *see* Apis (A).

Bull of the West (Egypt) *see* Osiris.

Bumba (Bantu, Bushongo People, Africa)
Also known as: *Chembe, Jambi* (possibly the same, or a similar creation god), *Nyambe, Nyambi, Nzambi.*
Bumba is the high god of creation, who established the tabus and appointed the rulers. After he returned to heaven, he only communicated with mortals in dreams. He is described as a giant white being who vomited up the sun, moon, stars and living creatures. He taught the mortal, Kerikeri, the secret of making fire. He is similar to Leza (q.v.) *See also* Nyambe.

Bumerali (Aborigine People, Australia)
Lightning goddess. *See also* Pakadringa.

Bunbulama (Aborigine People, Australia)
Goddess of Rain. *See also* Bumerali; Pakadringa.

Bundahish *Bundahisn, Bundahishn*
Also known as: *Zandagahih* (Zoroastrian; Persia).
Thought to have been translated from an original Zend manuscript, the "Bundahish" is an important Zoroastrian work encompassing the six days of creation, astronomy, the wars of Ahura Mazda and numerous other topics. Another important work is the "Denkart," an encyclopedia of religious lore. *See also* Ahura Mazda; Ahzi Dahaka; Avesta; Tishtrya; Yashts.

Bundahishn (Zoroastrian) *see* Bundahish.

Bundahisn (Zoroastrian) *see* Bundahish.

Bundinskeggi (Teutonic) *see* Heimdall.

Bunjil *Bun-Jil* (Kulin, Wurunjeri People, Australia)
Also known as: *Biral, Daramulun, Mami-Ngata, Ngurunderi, Pun-Gel.*
The supreme being. He is said to have two wives. His son is Binbeal, the rainbow. He could have other children. Bunjil created man out of clay while his brother, the Bat (Ngunung-ngunnut), brought women out of water. Bunjil is probably the same as Baiame, Daramulun, or Nurrundere. *See also* Daramulun; Gidja; Pun-Gel.

Bunomus (Greek) *see* Helen.

Bunosi (Melanesia)
Bunosi is the snake child of a normal woman and the brother of Kafisi. He coughed up the first plants and pigs. His large tail fills a room. *See also* Kafisi; Marruni.

Bunyip (Australia)
These water monsters were involved in the great deluge. Apparently, a group of men caught a small Bunyip. Its mother was so angry she flooded the land until it covered everything. The people who managed to escape were turned into black swans.

Bur (Teutonic) *see* Buri.

Bura-penu *Bhura* (India)
God of light and mate of Tari-penu, also known as Bhuri, goddess of darkness.

Buraq (Islamic) *see* Mohammed.

Bure (Teutonic) *see* Buri.

Buri *Bori, Bur, Bure* (Norse; Teutonic)
In the beginning, before earth and heaven existed, Buri was created from ice by the cow Audhumla. He had a son named Bor who married Bestla, the daughter of the frost giant Bolthorn. Their children, all males, were Odin, Vili, and Ve. In the war with the frost giants, Buri, along with his sons, succeeded in slaying Ymir and all the frost giants except for Bergelmir (q.v.). *See also* Audhumla; Bestla; Bor; Ve; Vili; Ymir.

Bursiris (Egypt) *see* Osiris.

Bushongo People — Creation Legend (Africa) *see* Bumba.

Bushyansta (Zoroastrian; Persia)
These yellow demons of lethargy and sloth cause men to oversleep and neglect their spiritual obligations. They are associated with Azhi Dahaka and the female demon of corpses, Nasu (q.v.). The Bushyasta are depicted with long hands.

Buso (Malay)
The Buso live in the branches of graveyard trees and feast upon the flesh of the dead. Forests and rocks are their favorite haunts. They have curly hair, two long pointed teeth, one eye which can be red or yellow, a flat nose and long bodies.

Buta (India) *see* Bhutas.

Butes (A) (Greek)
When Butes, the Argonaut son of Poseidon or Teleon and Zeuxippe, was sailing from Colchis, he jumped overboard to swim to the Sirens. Aphrodite, the goddess of love and beauty, rescued him. *See also* Argonauts; Poseidon; Sirens.

Butes (B) (Greek) He is the son of Boreas (q.v.).

Butes (C) (Greek)
Pandion and Zeuxippe are his parents. His twin brother is Erechtheus and other siblings are Philomela and Procne. His spouse is Cthonia, the daughter of Erechtheus and Praxithea (Butes is Cthonia's father's twin). They became the parents of Erechtheus II (also known as Erichthonius). *See also* Zetes (for Erechtheus).

Buto (A) *Bouto* (Egypt)
Also known as: *Edjo, Gozu Tenno* (Japan), *Inadjet, Uadjit, Uajet, Uatchet, Uatchura, Uazai.*

Protector goddess. Mother of the sun and moon. Buto is the Greek name of the goddess who protects Lower Egypt or as some say, a Greek transcription of the name of the town, Per Uadjit, where she was worshiped. Buto is also the name of the swamp where Isis hid the coffin containing the body of Osiris. Buto is a snake goddess often represented in the form of a cobra. She is often depicted with a red crown on her head. She was sometimes shown as a snake, often a cobra, or as a woman with her head topped by a vulture and crown. She is shown both with and without wings. Buto is sometimes shown beside the vulture-goddess Nekhebet. In this depiction, she is called Nebti (meaning two mistresses). Buto is identified with the goddesses Bast and Sekhmet when she is shown in cat or lion form. She is the equivalent to Leto and Latona. *See also* Gozu Tenno; Latona (mother of Apollo); Leto; Uatchet.

Buto (B) (Japan)

Also known as: *Gozu Tenno, Susanowo.*

As Buto crossed the earth in search of a spouse, he stopped in southern India and asked the wealthy King Kotan-Shorai for food and shelter. The king refused him entry. Buto carried on with his journey and went to a palace under the sea where he found his bride-to-be. On his return trip, he stopped in on the inhospitable Kotan, chopped his body into five pieces, and massacred his people. Kotan's poor brother Somin-Shorai, known as the god of hospitality, welcomed Buto. In exchange, for thanks and to discharge his indebtedness, Buto gave him a talisman to protect him from disease. Buto is an aspect of Gozu Tenno, the protector against plagues, and is thought to be of foreign import. Buto is also said to be an aspect of the storm god, Susanowo. The above myth pertaining to Buto is comparable to a myth about Susanowo. Buto is depicted as ox-headed.

Regarding the importance of hospitality, *see* Susanowo. *See also* Fuji; Gozu Tenno.

Butterfly Maiden (Hopi People, North America)

A kachina who rules springtime.

Buxenus (Celtic) Box-tree god. *See also* Abellio.

Byamee (Australia) *see* Baiame.

Byampsa (Tibet) *see* Maitreya; Mi-Lo Fu.

Byanu (Egypt) *see* Benu.

Byas River (India) *see* Vasistha.

Byelobog *Bielbog* (Slavic)

Also known as: *Bylun.*

God of light. Both names mean "White God." In Slavic mythology, Byelobog has an evil counterpart called Chernobog or "black god." Some say Byelobog only shows himself during daylight hours, and is a benevolent god of travelers who lose their way. He is shown as an old man with a white beard dressed in white robes. *See also* Chernobog.

Byelun (Slavic) *see* Byelobog.

Byleipt (Teutonic) *see* Loki.

Byleipter (Teutonic) *see* Loki.

Byleist (Teutonic) *see* Loki.

Bylun (Slavic) *see* Byelobog.

Byul-Soon (Korea)

Star goddess.

C

Cabaguil (Maya People, Yucatan)

One of seven creator gods. Called "Heart of the Sky."

Cabeiri (Greek) *see* Caberi.

Caberi *Cabeiri, Cabiri, Kabeiroi, Kabirs* (Greek)

Also known as: *Cyclopes, Qabirim* (Phoenicia).

Known in various parts of the ancient world, the Caberi of Samothrace are the children of Zeus and Calliope. Some say they are the children of Uranus. They could be the sons of Hephaestus as they were his helpers at the forge. Others call them descendants of Sydycos (Sydyk) and brothers of Esmun. The Caberi are variously known as spirits of the underground or of fire. They have also been called fertility spirits. They are associated with the tale of the Argonauts and with Demeter and Kore. They are similar to the Dactyls and similar to if not the same as the Cyclopes. The Caberi are identified with the Curetes, Dioscuri, the Corybantes, and sometimes with Persephone, Rhea and Hecate. There are similarities to Kubera of the Hindu and the Roman Penates. *See also* Ceres; Corybantes; Cyclopes; Dacytls; Demeter; Dioscuri; Ignis; Telchines.

Cabrakan (Maya People, Yucatan) *see* Hunahpu.

Caca (A) (Roman)

Also known as: *Vesta.*

Goddess of Excrements. Caca is associated with Cloacina, the Roman goddess who oversees sewers. It is possible that Caca's father is Vulcan, the god of metal-working. In later times, Caca was succeeded by Vesta, the goddess of the hearth. *See also* Cloacina; Medusa; Vesta; Vulcan.

Caca (B) *Cacia* (Greek)

She is the sister of the Italian cattle thief, Cascus. When she learned that he had rustled cattle belonging to Heracles, she told Heracles where to find his animals. Heracles killed Cascus and rewarded Caca with divine honors. A perpetual flame was kept in her sanctuary. *See also* Cacus.

Cacce-Olmai (Lapp)

This fish god is associated with water and fishermen. He can be destructive if not given the proper sacrifice.

Cacia (Greek) *see* Caca (B).

Caculha Huracan (Central, South America) *see* Huracan.

Cacus *Kakos* (Greek)

Also known as: *Coeculus.* (Originally, he was probably an ancient Roman god.)

A three-headed, fire-breathing giant. His residence was in a cave on Mount Palatine in Rome. He stole the cattle of Geryon and dragged them by their tails to his cave so their footprints could not be traced. It was one of Heracles' labors to retrieve the cattle. One of his twelve secondary labors was to kill the cattle thief. Heracles found the cattle, (thanks to Cacus' displeased sister, Caca) and killed Cacus. *See also* Caca (B); Heracles; Medusa.

Cadmus (Greek)

The son of King Agenor and either Telephassa or Argiope, Cadmus became the King of Thebes. His siblings are Cilix, Electra, Demodoce, Phineus, Thasus, Europa, Phoenix, and possibly Argos. The gods attended his wedding to Harmonia, the daughter of Aphrodite. He became the father of Agave, Autonoe, Illyrius, Ino, Polydorus and Semele. Sometimes his children are said to be Actaeon, Ino, Pentheus and Semele. When his sister, Europa, was raped by Zeus, King Agenor sent Cadmus to try to find her. He was advised by Apollo's oracle to follow a cow that he would come upon. When the cow stopped, Cadmus was to found a city and call it Thebes. While in the area he decided to share drinks with the gods. The fierce dragon of Ares turned up in the water well. Cadmus drew his sword and slaughtered it. He took the monster's teeth and buried half of them. From the teeth armed dragon-men issued forth from the ground and fought with Cadmus and his men. Eventually they reached a calm and the dragon-men helped him build Thebes. Four of his children died violently, and it was thought to be tied in with Cadmus' slaying of the dragon. Later, he and Harmonia moved to Illyria where they were changed into beautiful snakes. Cadmus introduced the alphabet and writing into Greece. *See* Actaeon; Agenor (A); Harmonia (A); Ino; Semele.

Caecinus (Greek)

He is the river god son of Oceanus and Tethys and possibly the father of Euthymus, the Olympic boxer. *See also* Oceanus; Rivers.

Caelestis (Greek) *see* Tanit.

Caelus (Greek) *see* Uranus.

Caeneus (A) (Greek)

Also known as: *Caenis.*

Caeneus was born a female and named Caenis. She is the daughter of the Arcadian Lapith chieftain, Elatus, and Hippea,

the daughter of Antiphus. Caeneus' siblings are of Ischys and Polyphemus. As Caenis, she changed her sex after being raped by the sea god Poseidon. Caeneus participated in a fracas between the Lapiths and the Centaurs at the wedding party for Perithous and Hippodameia and was changed into a bird by Zeus. *See also* Polyphemus; Poseidon.

Caeneus (B) (Greek)

He is the Argonaut father of two Argonaut sons, Phocus and Priasus.

Caenis (Greek)

The name taken by Caeneus when she changed her sex to male. *See also* Caeneus.

Caer Ibormeith (Celtic, Irish) *see* Angus.

Caer Yewberry (Celtic, Irish) *see* Angus.

Caesar (Roman) *see* Dis Pater; Mercury (B).

Cagn (Bushman, Hottentot People, Africa)

Also known as: *Coti, I Kaggen, Kaang, Kaggen.*

"Praying Mantis." Creator deity. A shape changer and creator god, his home is known only to the antelopes. Cagn rules with his two sons, Cogaz and Gewi. His wife's name is Hyrax, or some say Coti, although in some versions Coti is another name for Cagn. Cagn has daughters but their names are not known. Cagn's power is located in one of his teeth. *See also* Gaunab; Kaang.

Caillagh ny Groamagh (Isle of Man) *see* Cailleach Bheare.

Cailleach Bheare (Celtic, Gaelic)

Also known as: *Bherri* (Northern Ireland), *Black Annis* (Britain), *Boi, Bui, Cailleach Bherri, Cailleach Bheur, Cailleach ny Groamagh* (Isle of Man), *Cally Berry* (Northern Island), *Caolainn, Hag of Beare* (Ireland).

"Mountain Mother." Cailleach Bheare is known as the controller of the weather of winter months, a mover of islands and a builder of mountains. She is also known as queen of the Limerick fairies. She is the epitome of longevity and repeatedly passes from youth to old age. During these cycles, Cailleach Bheare has many husbands and numerous children. Her children, grandchildren, and great-grandchildren became people and races. She resides in the old southwest Munster, thought to be the home of the dead. Under the name of Boi she is the wife of the god, Lugh. As Caolainn, she is the ruler of a healing well in County Roscommon in Ireland. Cailleach has red teeth and one eye in the middle of her blue-black face. Her hair is matted and she wears a kerchief. Over her gray clothing she wears a faded plaid shawl. *See also* Cailleach Bheur; Cally Berry; Lugh.

Cailleach Bheur *Cailleach Bheare* (Irish, Scottish)

Also known as: *Cailleach Mor, Carlin.*

Winter season. Cailleach Bheur, a ferocious mother goddess known as a hag, is reborn every October 31. She is responsible for the falling of snow. During February, her power is dissipated by the appearance of Brigantia (also known as Brigit) in her aspect as springtime. With the approach of warmer weather, Cailleach Bheur places her staff under a holly bush and turns to stone. Her son is a god of youth (possibly an aspect of Mabon and Angus mac Og), whom she pursues battles with constantly. In other myths, she has more than one son; all giants, but none as powerful as she. *See also* Adder; Angus; Black Annis; Brigantia.

Cailleach Mor (Scottish) *see* Cailleach Bheur.

Cain *Kain* (Gnostic, Semite, Muslim)
Also known as: *Kabil* (Arabic).
Deity of soil or agriculture. Eldest son of Adam. Murderer of his brother, Abel. Father of Enoch, Irad, Mehiyya-El, Methusha-El, Lamech, Jabal, Jubil and Tubal-Cain (Tubal-Kain). The last three were said to be deities. The Koran names them Kabil (Cain) and Habil (Abel). Cain founded the city of Un-ug. *See also* Abel; Banbha; Itzamna.

Caipre (Celtic) *see* Etan.

Cairbe (Irish) *see* Bress.

Cairima *Salm* (Persian) *see* Thrita.

Caitya (Buddhist) *see* Stupa.

Cajolom (Maya People, Yucatan) *see* Hunahpu; Qaholom.

Cakra-Samvara (India) *see* Dorje Phagmo.

Caksusi (India) *see* Apsarases.

Calais (Greek)
An Argonaut. One of the Boreades. Calais is the son of the wind god Boreas and Oreithyia. He is the twin of Zetes. His other siblings are Chione, Cleopatra and Haemus. Calais and Zetes accompanied the Argonauts. When they rescued Phineus from the Harpies they were given wings. Heracles killed the twins and they were turned into birds or winds. *See also* Argonauts; Boreas; Harpies; Phineus; Zetes.

Calakomanas (Hopi, Zuni People, North America)
Corn or maize goddesses.

Calchas (Greek)
Soothsayer. Calchas, the son of Thestor and Megara and advisor to Apollo, was the most famous seer of the Greeks of his period. His siblings are Alcmaon, Leucippe and Theonoe (also known as Eidothea). He is the father of Cressida and Briseis (although some legends indicate that her father was Brises of Lyrnessus). Calchas' prophecies about the Trojan War were accurate as was his warning that the Greeks would lose the battle without the assistance of Achilles. He advised the Greeks to build the Trojan Horse. He also advised Agamemnon to sacrifice Iphigenia so the proper winds could guide his fleet to Troy. A vain man, he was certain that he was the most powerful seer and the he could not be outdone in his field. He accepted a guessing game challenge by Mopus and when he failed to ascertain the correct number of figs on a tree, he strangled on his own vanity or died of envy. *See also* Achilles; Agamemnon; Briseis; Iphigenia; Phineus.

Cale (Greek) *see* Charities.

Callalamma (India)
She is one of the Mutyalammo goddesses who are deities of the household. Her function is to preside over the buttermilk. *See also* Mutyalammo.

Calli (Aztec People, Mexico)
One of the four year-bearers or year gods. Calli is in charge of the west region. He is god of those mortals who live in that space and time. *See also* Acatl; Tecpatl; Tochtli.

Calliope *Kalliope* (Greek)
Muse of epic poetry. Talented musician on any instrument. One of the nine Muses. Calliope is the daughter of Zeus and Mnemosyne. She is said to be the mother of the Corybantes (lovers of music and wild dancing) by Zeus; of Hymen, the composer and god of marriage; Ialemus, also a composer; and Linus, composer of songs, by Apollo; of Rhesus, the Thracian prince, by the Strymon River; of the Sirens, all of whom had beautiful voices, by the river god Achelous; and of Orpheus, the most famous of poets by Oeagrus. Calliope taught her friend Achilles how to sing among friends at banquets. Zeus asked her to mediate the disagreement between Aphrodite and Persephone over Adonis. *See also* Adonis; Aphrodite; Corybantes; Muses; Persephone; Sirens; Zeus.

Callirius (Gallo-Roman) *see* Silvanus.

Callirrhoe (A) (Greek)
She is the Oceanid daughter of Oceanus and Tethyus. Her spouse was Chrysaor. She could be the mother of Cerberus; Echidna and Geryon. With Manes, she had a son, Cotys. *See also* Ceto; Chrysaor; Oceanids; Tethyus.

Callirrhoe (B) (Greek)
The river god, Scamander, is her father. Her spouse is Tros and her children are Assaracus, Cleopatra, Ilus and Ganymede. A fountain in Attica is named for her on the spot that she committed suicide.

Callirrhoe (C) (Greek)
She is the daughter of Amphione and Niobe. Callirrhoe and four of her sisters were killed by the warrior goddess, Artemis. Apollo killed five of her six brothers. *See also* Apollo; Artemis; Niobe.

Callirrhoe (D) (Greek)
Lycus of Libya is her father. When her lover, Diomedes, deserted her, she committed suicide. *See also* Diomedes.

Callirrhoe (E) (Greek)
Achelous, the river god, is her father. Her siblings are Castalia, Peirene and possibly the Sirens. She became the second wife of Alcmeon and the mother of Acarnan and Amphoterus. *See also* Achelous.

Callisto *Kalisto* (Arcadian, Pre-Hellenic, Greek)
Also known as: *Calliste, Kalliste.*
Originally Callisto was a Pre-Hellenic goddess. When Arcadia was invaded by the Greeks, she was reduced to the status of a nymph. Her attributes were given to the Greek goddess Artemis. As a nymph, she is the daughter of Lycaon, Nycteus, Ceteus, or Zeus. She is the sister of Pallas. Earlier, she was the nymph companion of Artemis. An affair with Zeus caused her death by the hands of Artemis, but she gave birth to a son named Arcas (ancestor of the Arcadians). She is depicted in animal form as a mother bear. In human form, she is shown as a young athlete racing through the woods. There is a tale wherein Artemis accidentally killed Callisto and was so upset that she

took her name and her symbols and called herself Artemis Calliste. She is sometimes confused with Artemis because her symbol is also a she-bear. *See also* Artemis; Zeus.

Cally Berry (Irish)

She is known as the "water hag" or the "old gloomy woman," who protects lakes from being drained and controls the weather. She is generally thought to be the same as Cailleach Bheare.

Calyce (Greek) *see* Aeolus (A); Canace.

Calydon (A) (Greek) He is the son of Thestius.

Calydon (B) (Greek)

His parents are Ares and Astynome. Artemis, the goddess of hunting, caught him peeking at her while she was bathing. She turned him to stone. *See also* Ares; Artemis; Astynome.

Calydon (C) (Greek)

He is the son of Aetolus, the king of Elis, and Pronoe, who is the daughter of Phorbus.

Calydonian Boar Hunt (Greek)

The boar represents the sun causing drought. Oeneus was the king of Calydon, husband of his niece Althaea and later Periboea. He was the father of Deianira who killed Heracles and then committed suicide, Gorge who was possibly changed into a guinea fowl by Artemis, Toxeus who was killed by Oeneus, Olenias, Perimede, Tydeus one of the Seven against Thebes, Laocoon (by a servant woman) and possibly Meleager an Argonaut. His parents are Porthaon, the first king of Calydon, and Euryte, the daughter of Hippodamas. His siblings are Alcathous who was slain either by his nephew Tydeus or Oenomaus the king of Pisa, Agrius who expelled Oeneus from the throne and eventually committed suicide, Melas the friend of Heracles, Sterope who was possibly the mother of the Sirens by Achelous and Leucopeus. When he neglected to make the expected annual sacrifices to the goddess Artemis, she sent a monstrous boar to his area to deplete the crops and ravish the land and its people. Oeneus sent word to other Greek cities for assistance with the offer of the boar's skin as a trophy to the victor. A marvelous assortment of warriors and heroes, including their hostile neighbors the Curetes, arrived to conquer the beast. Apparently the only female to join the hunt was the skilled Atalanta with whom Meleager fell in love. Meleager, the son of either Oeneus or Poseidon, felled the vicious boar and was awarded the skin which he gave to Atalanta. This caused dissension and resulted in a war between the Calydons and the Curetes. Artemis transformed Meleager into a guinea fowl after his death and Althaea's guilt for her role in his demise caused her suicide. Oeneus, the hospitable host of deities and celebrities, who introduced the art of wine making to his constituents, was said to have died in Argos at an advanced age. For details of the battle between the Calydonians and the Curetes *see* Althaea. *See also* Artemis; Jason.

Calypso *Kalypso, Kalupso* (Greek)

Immortal nymph. Death goddess. Calypso is either the daughter of Atlas and Tethys, Atlas and Pleione or of Oceanus and Tethys. She is said to be the sister of Hyas, the Hyades, the Hesperides, Maia and the Pleiades. The shipwrecked Odysseus was offered safe harbor and her love when he was washed ashore on her island Ortygia (also spelled Ogygia, Ogugia) in the Ionian Sea. They have two children, Nausinous and Nausithous. After seven years together Odysseus was homesick and longed for his wife and family. Calypso tempted him with the offer of eternal youth and immortality if he would remain with her, but Zeus sent Hermes with a message instructing her to let him go. In some versions of this myth, Calypso and Odysseus are said to be the parents of Telemachus and Telegonus. More often, Odysseus and Penelope are the parents of Telemachus and Odysseus and Circe are the parents of Telegonus. Calypso's name means "to hide." Calypso is shown in a cavern surrounded with alder (a shrub or tree that grows in cool moist places), which was sacred to the deity of death, Cronus. In the branches sit Cronus' sea-crows and Calypso's horned owls and falcons. To compare to other nymphs *see* Naiads. *See also* Hesperides; Oceanids; Oceanus; Odysseus; Scylla; Zeus.

Cama (India) *see* Kama.

Camalotz (Maya People, Yucatan People, Yucatan)

Demon. After the gods created mankind from various materials they decided to destroy them in a flood. Camalotz helped by cutting off the heads, while Xecotcovach ate their eyes, Cotzbalam devoured their flesh and Tucumbalam ground their bones and sinews. *See also* Alom; Cotzbalam; Tzakol; Xecotcovach.

Camaxte (Aztec People, Mexico; Mexico) *see* Texcatlipoca.

Camaxtle (Aztec People, Mexico; Mexico) *see* Xipe Totec.

Camaxtli (Aztec People, Mexico; Chichimees, Tlascalan People, Mexico)

Also known as: *Tezcatlipoca, Xipe Totec; Yoamaxtli.*

Creator deity. Son of Ometecuhtli (Tonacatecuhth) and Omecihuatl (Tonacacihuatl). Brother of Tezcatlipoca, red, blue, white and black; Quetzalcoatl, and Huitzilopochtli. One of the gods who were instructed by their parents to create the world. He was said to be a God of vegetation, God of thunderstorms and War God, sometimes associated with tornadoes and hunting. Some believe that Camaxtli is identical or similar to the deities of various early races: Curicaveri of the Tarascan, Mixcoatl of the Chichimec, Otontectli, and Xocotl of the Tepanec and Otomi people, and Huitzilopochtli of the Aztec People, Mexico. *See also* Coxcoxtli; Huitzilopochtli; Legend of the Four Suns; Mixcoatl; Tezcatlipoca; Yoamaxtli.

Camazotz (Maya People, Yucatan People; Yucatan)

Bat god of Xibalba. Hun Hunahpu and his twin brother Vukub Hunahpu were sacrificed by the people of the hellish underworld, Xibalba. The blood-thirsty bat god, Camazotz, used his claws to cut off Hun Hunahpu's head. The head was placed in a barren tree, likely to ward off ill-wishers. Hunahpu regained his life, but Camazotz was defeated. *See also* Hunahpu; Ixbalanque; Xibalba.

Camdhen (India) *see* Kamadhenu.

Camenae *Camena, Carmenai* (Roman)

Also known as: *Carmentes, Casmenae.*

They are fountain nymphs, spirits of springs and rivers and goddesses of prophecy in Roman mythology. Their leader is Carmenta. The most famous of the Camenae is Egeria. They are worshiped in the same month as the Fons. On October 13, their festival day, known as Fontinalia, wreaths are thrown into wells for good luck. They are identified with the Greek Muses. *See also* Egeria; Fons; Muses.

Cameiro (Greek) Another name for Cleothera (q.v.).

Campe (Greek)
   A monster female dragon who guarded the Hecatoncheires and Cyclopes in the underworld prison of Tartarus until Zeus released them. *See also* Cyclopes; Erebus; Hades; Hecatoncheires; Tartartus.

Camulos (Celtic) *see* Camulus.

Camulus *Camulos* (Celtic)
   Also known as: *Cumhal* (Gaelic), *Coel, Cole* (British), *Cocidius* (British).
   Ancient war god. As Cumhal, he is the father of Finn. Camulus equates with Mars. *See also* Albiorix; Cocidius; Tuetates.

Camunda (India) *see* Kali.

Canace (Greek)
   She is the daughter of Aeolus of Magnesia and Enaret. She has seven brothers and six sisters. Her brothers are Athamas, Cretheus, Deion, Macareus, Perieres, Salmoneus, Sisyphus, and six sisters: Alcyone, Arne, Calyce, Peisidice, Perimele and Tanagra. By Poseidon she became the mother of Aloeus, Epopeus, Hopleus, Nireus and Triopas. When her father found out that she was having sex with her brother Macareus, he demanded that she commit suicide. *See also* Aeolus (A); Aloeides; Aloeus; Arne; Epopeus.

Canache (Greek) *see* Aeolus (A).

Canapa (Peru) *see* Coniraya.

Canda (India) A Demon. *See also* Durga; Kali.

Candelifera (Roman)
   Goddess of childbirths.

Candi (India) *see* Kali.

Candra (India) *see* Chandra.

Candramas (India) *see* Chandra.

Candulus (Greek) *see* Heliades.

Canola (Irish)
   This goddess invented the Irish harp.

Canopic Vases (Egypt) *see* Amset; Horus.

Canopus (India) The South Star. *See also* Agastya.

Canthus (Greek) *see* Argonauts.

Cantul-Ti-Ku (Maya People, Yucatan People, Yucatan) *see* Ahmucen-Cab; Becabs.

Caoineag *Caointeach* (Scottish)
   Another name for the Banshee.

Capaneus (Greek)
   He is the son of Hipponous and Astynome. His marriage to Evadne produced Sthenelus, who is one of the Epigoni. Capa-

neus, the inventor of the scaling ladder and one of the "Seven against Thebes," was killed when Zeus hurled a thunderbolt at him for bragging that he could not be stopped from entering Thebes. There is a possiblity that Capaneus was brought back to life by the great physician, Asclepius (q.v.). *See also* Adrestus; Astynome; Hipponous.

Caphaurus (Greek)
   Also known as: *Cephalion.*
   He is the shepherd son of Ampithemis and Tritonis and brother of Nasamon. When the Argonauts Canthus and Eribotes attempted to steal his sheep, he killed them. Subsequently, he was killed by other Argonauts.
   See also Acacallis; Argonauts.

Capheira (Greek) *see* Telchines.

Capra (Greek) *see* Aegipan.

Caprakan (Maya People, Yucatan People, Yucatan)
   An evil spirit of mountains and earthquakes. Destroyer of mountains. He was put to death by the hero twins Hunahpu and Ixbalanque. Caprakan is the son of the giant Gukup Kakix and Chimalmat, and brother of Zipacna. *See also* Hunahpu and Ixbalanque.

Capricorn (Greek) *see* Aegipan; Amaltheia.

Capys (Greek) *see* Anchises.

Car (Greek)
   Also known as: *Carius, Carys, Great God Ker, Karu, Karus, Q're.*
   First king of Megara. Solar King. He is the son of Phoroneus and Cerdo, Peitho or Teledice. His siblings are Niobe and Teledice. Car founded Megara, the principal city of Megaris, on the Isthmus of Corinth and established the worship of Demeter. His hair was shaved off annually before his death. At the annual feast of Comyria (hair trimming), young men mourned him and had their hair shorn. These men were later known as Curetes. The name Car may have derived from Artemis the moon goddess, Caria or Caryatis. *See also* Apis (B); Curetes; Niobe (B); Phoroneus; Satyrs.

Caragabi (Choco People, Colombia, South America)
   Caragabi was born from the saliva of the high god Tatzitzebe. He is the creator of humans and animals (who were made from some humans), the sun, moon, and stars, and he filled the tree which holds the spirit of life. He taught the people to gather food plants. Tutruica, his rival, is always trying to reverse Caragabi's work. After the world has been destroyed by fire, Caragabi will return.

Cardea (Roman)
   Goddess of thresholds and door pivots. Hunter. Cardea had to devise numerous ways to protect her virginity. Her love was Janus, the god of beginnings and endings, who is also a god of doors. Cardea transferred her powers to Janus. *See also* Janus.

Caria (Greek) *see* Car.

Carian Pirates (Greek) *see* Bellerphon.

Cariclo (Greek) *see* Cheiron; Oceanus.

Caridad (Africa) *see* Ochun.

Caridwen (Celtic) Corn goddess. Patroness of poetry.

Carius (Greek) *see* Car.

Carlin (Scottish)

Spirit of Hallowmas, the eve of winter. On this night, ghosts of the dead appear on earth. To protect farmers from their visitations, ears of corn made in Carlin's likeness are put on display. *See also* Cailleach Bheur.

Carmenai (Roman) *see* Camenae.

Carmenta (Greek) *see* Carmentis.

Carmentes (Roman) *see* Camenae.

Carmentis *Carmenta* (Roman)

Also known as: *Nicostrata, Postverta.*

Birth Goddess. Goddess of Healing. Goddess of the Future. She is one of the Camenae (prophetic nymphs linked with the Muses). Carmentis, a fountain nymph, is possibly the mother and Hermes the father of Evander (he introduced the Greek alphabet, the flute, lyre and triangular harp into Italy). There are writers who say that Carmentis adapted the Greek alphabet to the Latin language. *See also* Evander (B); Postverta.

Carna (Roman) Goddess of the heart and other body organs. Goddess of over-hinges. *See also* Cardea.

Carpo (Greek)

"Autumn." Goddess of autumn season. Carpo, one of the Horae, is the daughter of Zeus and Themis, who is the Titan daughter of Uranus and Gaea. Carpo is worshipped with Thallo, who is the personification of spring. *See also* Horae; Thallo.

Carpus (Greek) *see* Chloris; Zephyrus.

Caryatids (Greek) *see* Artemis.

Caryatis (Greek) *see* Artemis; Car.

Carys (Greek) *see* Car.

Casmenae (Roman) *see* Camenae.

Cassandra *Kasandra* (Greek)

Also known as: *Alexandra.*

Goddess of prophecy. Cassandra is the daughter of the king of Troy, Priam, and the moon goddess Hecuba. She came from a large family of eleven sisters and fifty brothers. Some of her siblings were her twin Helenus, who was her only brother to survive the Trojan War; Paris, who was abandoned at birth; Polyxena, who was sacrificed; Hector, the brave leader of the Trojans who was killed by Achilles; Deiphobus, also a brave warrior, who was forced to marry Helen; and Creusa, who was captured by the Greeks, rescued, and then disappeared. Cassandra had twin sons, Teledamas and Pelops, by her master Agamemnon. Cassandra promised to marry Apollo if he conferred the gift of prophecy upon her. When he fulfilled her wish she reneged and refused to marry him. Incensed, he rendered her gift worthless by making everyone who heard her prophecies disbelieve her. She fled to Athena's sanctuary after the fall of Troy, was raped by Ajax the Lesser and awarded as a prize to Agamemnon. He ensconced her in his chariot and took her to his home in Mycenae. Like everyone else he ignored her accurate visions of doom. Cassandra, Agamemnon and their infant twins were murdered by his wife Clytemnestra and her lover Aegisthus. A shrine near Amyclae was erected in Cassandra's honor under the name of Alexandra. *See also* Aegisthus; Agamemnon, Ajax the Lesser; Apollo; Athena; Clytemnestra; Creusa; Hector; Hecuba; Paris; Pelops; Teledamas.

Cassiepeia (Greek) *see* Cassiopeia.

Cassiopea (Greek) *see* Cassiopeia.

Cassiopeia *Cassiepeia, Cassiopea, Kessiepeia* (Greek)

Night goddess. She is the daughter of Arabus who is the son of Hermes. She married Cepheus, the king of Ethiopia and became the mother of Andromeda. She is also the mother of Atymnius, by Zeus. (Atymnius was the possible lover of Minos.) Poseidon sent a flood to the country because of the displeasure of the Nereids caused by Cassiopeia's constant and irritating bragging about her daughter. Andromeda was offered as a sacrifice but was saved by Perseus. *See also* Andromeda; Hermes; Perseus.

Cassotis (Greek) *see* Naiads.

Castalia (Greek) *see* Naiads.

Castalius (Greek) *see* Cephissus.

Castor and Pollux *Castor and Pollus, Kastor and Polydeukes* (Greek)

Also known as: *Dioscures, Dioscuri, Polydeuces* (the name also used by the Greeks for Pollux).

Assistants to men and women in battle. Gods of weights and measures. Gods of commerce. Assistants to people traveling. Protectors of sailors. Zeus came to Leda in the form of a swan. They engaged in sex and she delivered two eggs. Each egg contained a brother and sister (Castor and Clytemnestra, Pollux and Helen). (In the Homeric version, Castor and Pollux are the sons of Leda and king Tydracus.) The brothers are commonly known as the Dioscuri. Castor became a famous horse trainer and Pollux became a well known boxer. When their sister Helen (the wife of Menelaus) was abducted by Theseus, the brothers were able to rescue her in Aphidnae. While they were there, they overtook the city. The brothers were also involved in the Argonauts expedition, and in the Calydonian Boar Hunt. They became involved in an episode with Lynceas and Idas (the sons of Alphaeus) where they stole a herd of oxen from Arcadia. Idas steered the oxen to his home in Messene. The displeased brothers ransacked the city and retrieved the oxen. From this incident a feud developed between Lynceas and Idas and Castor and Pollux. Castor was killed. The death of his dear brother sent the grieving Polydeuces begging to Zeus for his own death. Zeus told Polydeuces that he could make a choice of staying on Olympus with the gods for the rest of time, or he could share the fate of Castor and stay one day on earth and one day on Olympus for the rest of time. He chose the fate of his brother. After their deaths they became the constellation Gemini. Castor and Pollux were extremely popular in Greece and in Rome. *See also* Academus; Argonauts; Calydonian Boar Hunt; Curetes; Helen; Leda.

Castor and Polydeuces (Greek) *see* Jason.

Caswallwan (Celtic)
Son of Bile (q.v.).

Cataclothes (Greek) *see* Harpies.

Catamitus (Roman) The Roman name for the Greek Ganymede (q.v.).

Catequil (Inca People, Peru)
God of lightning and thunder. God of twins (possibly). In early times, he was propitiated by the sacrifice of children. He is one of the attendants of Mama Quilla (q.v.). Catequil is associated with Cuycha, the rainbow.

Catha (Etruscan)
Sun deity.

Cathena (Mojave People, North America)
Also known as: *Quakuinahaba.*
First woman. Virgin sister of Ku-yu.

Catreus (Greek) *see* Acacallis; Ariadne; Minos; Pasiphae.

Caucasian Eagle (Greek)
His parents are Typhon, the destructive one hundred-headed whirlwind, and the monster, half-woman half-snake, Echidna. For a list of his monster siblings, *see* Echidna. *See also* Chimaera; Typhon.

Cauldon of Dagda (Celtic) *see* Dagda.

Caurus (Greek) *see* Harpies; Zephyrus.

Cauth Bodva (Celtic)
"War Fury." This is a name for the goddess of war, Badb Catha.

Cave of Refuge (Inca People, Peru) *see* Pacari.

Cavern of the Seven Chambers (Aztec People, Mexico) *see* Chicomoztoc.

Cavillaca (Inca People, Peru) *see* Coniraya; Pacha-Camak.

Ce Acatl (Mexico) *see* Quetzalcoatl.

Ceacht (Celtic, Irish)
Goddess of medicine. *See also* Dagda; Dia'necht.

Cearas (Celtic, Irish)
God of fire. An aspect of Dagda (q.v.).

Ceasar (Irish) *see* Cessair.

Cebrew (Greek) *see* Rivers.

Cecrops (Greek) *see* Agraulos; Gaea.

Cedalion (Greek)
Cedalion is a dwarf, possibly the son or father of the fire god Hephaistos. The goddess Hera assigned Cedalion the job of teaching Hephaistos the art of metal working. When the giant hunter Orion was blinded, he hoisted Cedalion to his shoulders and the dwarf led Orion to the sun where he was healed by Apollo. *See also* Hephaistos; Orion.

Celaeno (A) (Greek) She is the daughter of Poseidon and Ergea.

Celaeno (B) (Greek) One of the Harpies (q.v.)

Celaeno (C) (Greek)
One of the fifty daughters of Danaus, known as the Danaids. *See also* Asteria; Danaids; Danaus; Hypermnestra.

Celaeno (D) One of the Pleiades (q.v)

Celestial Kings (China)
Guardians. These deities replaced the two door guards, Shen-t'u and Yu-lu, who in turn were replaced by the Sniffing and Puffing Generals. The Celestial Kings are similar to the Buddhist divinities, Dhartarastra, Vaisravana, Virudhaka and Virupaksha, who were entrance guards. *See also* Men-shen.

Celestial Mandarin (China) *see* Ch'eng Huang.

Celestial Toad (China)
A title for the moon goddess, Chang-O.

Celeus (King) (Greek)
King of Eleusis. With Eumolpus, the co-founder of Eleusinian Mysteries. Teacher of agriculture. Inventor of agricultural tools. King Celeus married Metaneira. Their children are Demophon, possibly Abas and Triptolemus, and four daughters. *See also* Abas (C); Demophon.

Celmis (Greek)
With Acmon and Damnameneus, Celmis is one of the three original Dactyls (q.v.).

Cenchreis (Greek)
The spouse of Cinyras, she is the mother of Adonis and Myrrha. *See also* Adonis; Cinyras; Myrrha.

Cengus (Celtic) *see* Aengus.

Cenn Cruaich (Celtic)
Known as the "Lord of the Mound," first born children were sacrificed to him. His likeness was produced in gold, surrounded by twelve stones.

Centauras (Greek) *see* Centaurs.

Centauroi (Greek) *see* Centaurs.

Centaurs *Centauras, Centauroi, Kentaurs, Kentauros* (Greek).
Cloud deities. The race of half-man, half-horse, Centaurs live in the mountains of Thessaly. They are the children of Ixion and Nephele, who is cloud-shaped like Hera, the queen of heaven. In some renditions of this myth, Centaurus is named as the Centaurs' father. It is possible that he is the father of some of the Centaurs. Only the centaur Cheiron is the son of Cronus and Philyra, and the centaur Pholus is the son of Selenus and an ash-nymph (possibly Philyra). It is always difficult for the Centaurs to bridle their passions. They are renowned for their abusive treatment of nymphs and human women. The name Centaurs is probably derived from the Turanian word for man-beast. They are described as half-man, half-horse, or the upper torso, arm and head of a man with the body of a horse or ass. Centaurs are similar to the Gandharva. They are associated with Atalanta. Generally, the Centaurs are said to be followers of Dionysus. *See also* Cheiron; Ixion; Nephele; Nessus.

Centeal (Mexico) *see* Cinteotl.

Centeatl (Aztec People, Mexico) *see* Cinteotl.

Centeol (Aztec People, Mexico) *see* Cinteotl.

Centeotl (Aztec People, Mexico) *see* Cinteotl.

Centimanes (Greek) *see* Hecatonchires.

Centimani (Greek)

This is the Roman name for the Hecatonchires (q.v.). *See also* Aegaeon.

Centipede (Egypt)

Also known as: *Sepa.*

Protector against harmful animals and enemies of the gods. Sepa (meaning "centipede") is a minor god mentioned in the Pyramid Texts. As a charm, he is summoned to ward off malevolent animals and enemies of the gods. He is connected with the necropolis and linked with Osiris as a mortuary god. *See also* Osiris.

Centzon Huitznahuas *Centzon Totochtin, Centzonhuitznauac, Centzonuitznaua* (Aztec)

Also known as: *The Four Hundred.*

Evil deities. Star gods of the South. They are the sons of Coatlicue born prior to the birth of her son Huitzilopochtli. When the Centzon Huitznahuas and their sister Coyolxauhqui found out about the impending birth of their brother they became enraged and attempted to murder their mother. Huitzilopochtli sprang from his mother dressed in full battle gear. He killed his siblings using his powerful weapon, a fire serpent named Xiuhcoatl. The Centzon Huitznahuas are also known as the "Four Hundred Southerners." The Four Hundred Northerners are called Centzon Mimixcoa. *See also* Centzon Mimixcoa; Coatlicue; Huitzilopochtli.

Centzon Mimixcoa

Also Known as: *The Four Hundred Northerners.*

(Aztec People, Mexico) Star gods. *See also* Centzon-Huitznahuas.

Centzon Totochtin (Aztec People, Mexico)

Also known as: *Four Hundred Rabbits, Pulque Gods.*

They are the four hundred deified rabbits who are gods of drunkenness and licentiousness, who were thrown into the face of the moon. Some of their names are Texcatzoncatl, Colhuatzincatl, and Ometochtli. They are associated with Xochipilli. *See also* Centzon Huitznahuas; Colhuatzincatl; Ometochtli; Patecatl (discoverer of peyote); Texcatzoncatl.

Centzonuitznaua (Aztec People, Mexico) *see* Centzon Huitznahuas.

Centzonhuitznauac (Aztec People, Mexico) *see* Centzon Huitznahuas.

Ceos *Coeus* (Greek)

God of night. Ceos, a Titan is the son of Gaea and Uranus. He is the father of Asteria by his sister, the original moon goddess Phoebe, and Mnemosyne by Leto, the goddess of the night. Hesiod called him the father of Leto and Asteria by Phoebe. He is also named the father of the witch goddess Hecate in some references. The name Ceos means "intelligence." *See also* Aurora; Cronus; Eos; Eurynome (A); Gaea; Hecate; Leto; Titans; (The) Two Auroras.

Cephalion *Caphaurus* (Greek)

Another name for Caphaurus (q.v.). *See also* Acacallis.

Cephalus (A) (Greek)

His parents are the god Hermes and the dew, personified by Herse, and his brother is Ceryx. He is the possible father of Phaethon by Hemera (Other possiblities for Phaethon's parents are Tithonus and Eos.) *See also* Eos; Hermes.

Cephalus (B) (Greek)

He is the son of the King of Phocis, Deion, and Diomede, the daughter of Xuthus, "the thievish one." His siblings are Actor, Aenetus, Asteropeia and Phylacus. His first wife was Procis, whom he accidentally killed. He was sentenced to the island of Taphos and while there he helped Amphitryon conquer Taphos. At a later time, Clymene became his second wife, and they became the parents of the Argonaut Iphicles. *See also* Actor (A); Diomede; Xuthus.

Cepheus (A) (Greek)

The King of Ethiopia. He married Cassiopeia and became the father of Andromeda (q.v.). *See also* Cassiopeia.

Cepheus (B) (Greek)

King of Tegea. Argonaut. His parents are Aleus and Neara. He is the father of Aerope, Echemus, Sterope, and unnamed others. The kingdom of Tegea could not be destroyed as he held a lock of hair from Medusa's head that had been given to him by the goddess of love, Athena. When he went to sail with the Argonauts, he gave the lock of hair to his daughter, Sterope. *See also* Aerope; Medusa; Sterope.

Cephissus (Greek)

River god. Cephissus is one of the three thousand sons of Oceanus and Tethys, known as the Rivers, and brother to his three thousand sisters, the Oceanids. As a river, the Cephissus flows into the Saronic Gulf near Athens. As a deity, Cephissus and the nymph Leiriope are the parents of the vain Narcissus. Cephissus is thought to be the father of Thyia, although Castalius has also been called her father. Either Cephissus or Andreus is the father of Eteocles, a king of Boeotian Orchomenus, who was the first man to name the three Graces and sacrifice to them. To compare to other river gods, *see* Achelous, Acheron, Alpheus, Asopus, Cocytus, Inachus. *See also* Graces; Narcissus; Oceanids; Oceanus; Rivers; Tethys.

Cer (Greek)

Goddess of violent death. She is the daughter of the underworld darkness, Erebus, and the goddess of the night, Nyx. Her siblings are Aether, the god of light; Charon, ferryman of dead souls; Oneiroi (also known as Dreams); Hypnos (also known as Somnus, the god of sleep); Momus, the god of fault-finding; Moros; Nemesis, the goddess of retribution; Thanatos, the god of death. *See also* Aether; Charon; Erebus; Hypnos; Keres; Nemesis; Nox; Thanatos.

Ceramus (Greek)

He is the son of Dionysus and Ariadne (qq.v.).

Cercaphus (Greek)

An intelligent man, known for his interest in astronomy, Cercaphus is one of the Heliades. It was either Cercaphus or

Macar who were the first to sacrifice to Athena. *See also* Athena; Heliades.

Cerberus *Kerberos* (Greek)

Watchdog of Hades. Cerberus, the offspring of Echidna and Typhon, is a three-headed (or fifty-headed) dog with a voice of bronze who is the watchdog of Hades. Stationed at the gates of death, Cerberus allows people to enter but devours them if they try to leave. Only twice has he been negligent in his duties. Once was when the sweet music of Orpheus put all his heads to sleep. The second time was when Heracles in his quest to accomplish his twelfth labor was to bring Cerberus from the underworld to King Eurystheus. He strangled each of the monster dog's heads and rendered it unconscious. Heracles then carted the animal to the king, who was so petrified at the sight of the beast that he hid and demanded that Heracles return it to the portals of Hades. Heracles merrily accommodated the king and returned Cerberus to his owner, Hades, demanding and receiving a payoff from him. In the Roman version it was Sibyl conducting Aeneas through hell who brought sleep upon Cerberus by feeding him honey-cake seasoned with poppy seeds. *See also* Chimaera; Echidna; Hades; Heracles; Orpheus; Tartarus; Typhon.

Cercopes (Greek)

The Cercopes are gnomes with two tails who are known for thievery. They are the sons of Oceanus and Theia. *See also* Oceanus; Passalus; Theia.

Cercyon (Greek)

King of Eleusis. This king, son of Hephaistos, required all visitors to wrestle with him. In the end, he was killed by Theseus. *See also* Hephaistos; Theseus.

Cerdo (Greek)

"The Wise." She is the wife of Phoroneus and the mother of Car. *See also* Car; Niobe (B); Phoroneus.

Ceres *Kerres* (Greek)

Also known as: *Angerona* (Etruscan), *Cabiria* (a derivative of Babylonian Kabiri or Cabiria), *Demeter* (Greek).

Earth Mother. Agricultural goddess. Goddess of grain and corn. Goddess of fruit and flowers. One of the twelve great Olympians. Chief of the Penates (household deities). Ceres is the daughter of Cronos and Rhea. She became the mother of Arion by Poseidon and Proserpine by Jupiter. It is thought that Ceres replaced the early agriculture goddess Tellus Mater or possibly Kerres. She is shown as a wheat ear. Ceres is associated with Liber and Libera, who were also earth deities. She is the Roman equivalent of the Greek Demeter. The word cereal is derived from her name. *See also* Angerona; Baubo; Cabiri; Demeter; Evander (B).

Ceridwen (British, Celtic) *see* Keridwen.

Cerklicing (Latvia)

God of fields and corn.

Cermait (Celtic) "The Honey-mouthed." *See also* Ogma.

Cernobog (Slavic) *see* Chernobog.

Cernunnos *Cernunnus* (Celtic)

Possibly a god of animals or an underworld deity. Various depictions indicate he might be a god of providence or plenty. Some writers think he might be a fertility deity. Later Christians tended to assimilate him to Satan. Cernunnos is depicted as horned, sitting cross-legged, holding a collar in one hand and a ram-headed serpent in the other hand. He is flanked by animals. Sometimes he is shown with a beard and sometimes with three heads. In some depictions he has the legs of a serpent. He is also depicted as the antlered stag of the Celts. Dances were performed around him near the small temples. He is similar to Shiva in his aspect as Pashupati. Cernunnus resembles the Slavic Chernobog. *See also* Sucellos.

Cerridwen (British, Celtic, Welsh) *see* Keridwen.

Ceryx (Greek)

He is the son of the messenger of the gods, Hermes, and Herse, the personification of dew, and brother of Cephalus. *See also* Agraulos; Hermes; Herse.

Cesair (Irish) *see* Cessair.

Cesar (Irish) *see* Cessair.

Cesara (Irish) *see* Cessair.

Cesarea (Irish) *see* Cessair.

Cessair *Ceasar, Cesar, Cesara, Cesarea, Cesair* (Irish)

Cessair, possibly a moon goddess, is said to be Noah's granddaughter, and the daughter of Bith and Birren. In legend, she was refused entry into the ark and fled with her husband, Fintan (also spelled Finntain), along with Ladru, another man and fifty women to Inisfail, which is now Ireland. Forty days after arriving on the island all except Fintan perished in the Great Flood. Ladru became known as the "first dead man of Erin." Fintan survived as a salmon. Through the centuries he assumed many shapes as he watched Ireland's history develop. He lived to be six hundred years old and he verbally transmitted this history to more recent generations. The next influx of people to the island were Partholon and his followers. *See* Banbha, said to be the first settler in Ireland. *See also* Partholon.

Cethe (Celtic)

He is the brother of Cian and Cu, and the son of Dia'necht (q.v.).

Ceto (Greek)

Sea monster. Ceto is the sea monster daughter of Pontus and Gaea, or Oceanus and Gaea. In one myth, she married her brother, Phorcys, and became the mother of Callirrhoe (also called Echidna), the sea monster Scylla, the Gorgons, the Graiae and the dragon Ladon. In other legends she is said to have been her brother Phorcys' daughter, a result of his union with their mother Gaea. They became the parents of the Gorgons. In yet another version of this myth she was one of the fifty Nereids, the water nymphs, who are children of Nereus and his sister/wife Doris. *See also* Callirrhoe; Doris; Echindan; Gaea; Gorgons; Graiae; Hesperides; Ladon; Medusa; Nereids; Nereus; Oceanus; Pontus; Scylla.

Ceus (Greek) *see* Ceos.

Cexochitl *see* Cinteotl.

Cezalcouati (Mexico) *see* Kukulcan.

Cghene (Isoko People, Southern Nigeria, Africa)
He is the Supreme Being and the creator of all. His abode is in the sky, which is a part of him. He rewards the just and punishes the unjust. The intermediary between Cghene and mortals is known as an *oyise*, also called uko Cghene ("messenger of Cghene"). It is made from the oyise tree, and is about eight feet long. It stands on the grounds of the eldest family member. Each morning he throws his used chewing stick before the pole and prays for the family and village members.

Ch-Ien Niu *Kien Niu (China)*
Heavenly cowherd. Husband of Chih-Nii (q.v.).

Cha-dog-ma (Tibet)
Also known as: *Vajra-Shringhala* (Sanskrit). *See also* Hayagriva; Kinkini-Dhari; Vajra-Shringhala.

Ch'an Tzu-fang (China)
God of the fire or furnace or hearth. *See also* Tsao Chun; Tsao-Shen; Tsao-wang.

Chaac (Maya People, Yucatan) *see* Chac.

Chac *Chaac* (Maya People, Yucatan)
Also known as: *"B"* (possibly), *Xib Chac.*
Rain god. Patron of agriculture. Chac is analogous to the Aztec god Tlaloc. The Mayas sacrificed to Chac for rain. Elsewhere he is referred to as one of a triad with Hobnel and Ah-Kluic, who are both gods of plenty. During festivals, human sacrifices, particularly children, were offered to the rain god. An important part of the ceremonies was to listen to the prophecies of a shaman named Chilam. He is often depicted in Mayan temples, wearing a mask, or sometimes as having a tapir's nose, tusks, and holding an axe. He is also shown with body scales, long whiskers, his abundant hair bound up above his head. One may also see him in wells, rivers, and streams, often net fishing. *See also* "B"; Chacs; Tlaloc.

Chacs (Maya People, Yucatan)
Minor rain deities. The ruler of the Chacs is Chac. Initially there were four Chacs, one for each point of the compass. During spring festivals, the hearts of wild animals were sacrificed to the Chacs. They are associated with the Becabs and Itzamna (q.v.). The Chacs, depicted as old men, are similar to the Tlalocs and their ruler, Tlaloc. *See also* Becabs; Chac; Tlalocs.

Chadanta (Buddhist; India)
Chadanta was the Bodhisattva in another life. He appeared as a white elephant with six tusks. As an elephant he had two wives, one who was jealous of the other. The jealous woman desired to be reincarnated as a human princess. Her wish was granted and in her next life she was a princess who grew up and married the King of Benares. When she remembered her prior life, she sent a hunter out to search for her husband, the white elephant with six tusks. His instructions were to kill him and return his tusks to her. The hunter tracked Chadanta, captured him in a pit, and wounded him with his arrows. Chadanta asked the hunter what motivated him to visit harm upon him. The hunter relayed his instructions to the elephant. When Chadanta realized that it was his fate to die in this manner, he helped the hunter fulfill his task. The hunter was unable to saw through

the elephant's tusks. Chadanta relieved him of his task by sawing off his own tusks. He died in his own blood. When the news reached the queen, she too died.

Chafura (Egypt) *see* Khepri.

Chahuru (Pawnee People, North America)
Water Spirit.

Chaitraratha (India) Celestial Garden. *See also* Kuvera.

Chak-na-rin-chhen (Tibet) *see* Ratnasambhava; Vairocana.

Chak-yu-ma (Tibet) *see* Ankusha.

Chakra (Hindu; India)
This magic weapon, shaped like a wheel, was given to Vishnu by Shiva to destroy demons. The Chakra symbolizes the sun.

Chakra Sambara *Heyvajra, Sambara* (Buddhist; Nepal)
Chakra Sambara, an aspect of Sambara, the deity of supreme bliss, is also a manifestation of Heyvajra, the central figure of Vajrayana Buddhism. Chakra Sambara is depicted embracing his consort Vajrabarahi in a mystic position which symbolizes the union between wisdom and method leading to ultimate bliss. *See also* Sambara (B).

Chakravala *Buddhist Universe* (Buddhist; India)
The Buddhist Universe of Chakravala has three planes above, around and below Mount Meru. The lower plane is the abode of a specific type of sinner. It contains one hundred and thirty-six hells reserved for the enemies of Buddha. The lowest realm of hells is known as Avici. The minimum stay in this realm is twenty-five thousand years until the soul is reborn. Around the peak of Mount Meru is the Heaven of the Four Great Kings. This plane is populated with pretas (ghosts), animals, demons and men. The Four Great Kings guard the entrance to Sukhavati, the Buddhist paradise. Above the Heaven of the Four Great Kings is the Heaven of the Thirty-three Divinities. This is also called the Heaven of Sakra (Indra). There are twenty-four heavens above the Heaven of the Thirty-three Divinities. Six of these heavens are for souls who relish the pleasures of the senses. The twenty remaining heavens are known as the Chyana Lokas and the Arupa Lokas. The Arupa Lokas are the regions of Abstract Meditation. The Chyana Lokas are the dwelling places of enlightened souls. *See also* Dhartarastra (for a description of the Heaven of the Four Great Kings); Lokapalas; Sukhavati (Paradise); Visvakarma; Yidak.

Chakrisvari (India)
A Yakshini with sixteen arms. *See also* Yaksha and Yakshini.

Chala (India)
Goddess of fortune.

Chalchihuitzli (Aztec People, Mexico) *see* Chimalmatl.

Chalchiuhcihuatl (Mexico) *see* Xilonen.

Chalchiuhtlicue *Chalchihuitli'cue, Chalchihuitlicue, Chalchiuhcueye* (Aztec People, Mexico)
Also known as: *Acuecueyotl, Apoconallotl, Atlacamini, "Emerald Lady," "I"* (possibly), *Petticoat of Blue Stones* (sometimes called this name).

Chalchiuhtlicue is known as a beneficent and a malevolent deity. She is the Goddess of the East, ruler of the water sun Nahuiatl, goddess of the sea, springs, and all running water. She is the protector of newborn babies and of marriages. She ruled the fourth universe, which the flood destroyed. Tlaloc is her brother and perhaps her spouse. In some renditions, she is the spouse of Tlaloctecutli who was created to rule the waters. Sometimes she appears as the wife of Quetzalcoatl. She is the Lord of the Third Hour of the Day, and the Sixth Hour of the Night. She wears a skirt covered with jade. Her headdress is similar to that of Tlazolteotl. Her colors are blue and white. She is associated with flowers and mushrooms and often carries amaranth stems. Sometimes she is depicted as a snake or frog. The Mayan water goddess "I" (q.v.) may be the same as Chalchiuhtlicue. She preceeded the Mayan rain and thunder god Chac (q.v.). *See also* Acuecueyotl; Legend of the Four Suns; Lords of the Day Hours; Lords of the Night Hours; Ometecutli and Omeciuatl; Quetzalcoatl; Tlaloc; Tlaloctecutli.

Chalchiuhtonatiuh (Aztec People, Mexico) *see* Legend of the Four Suns.

Chalchiuhtotolin (Aztec People, Mexico) *see* Tezcatlipoca.

Chalciope (Greek)
Also known as: *Iophossa*
She is the daughter of the king of Colchis and his first wife, the nymph Asterodeia, and half-sister of Absyrtus and Medea. Chalciope was the first wife of Phrixus. Their children are Argus, Cytissorus, Melas, Phrontis and Presbon. Thessalus is her son by Heracles. She persuaded her sister to help Jason in his search for the Golden Fleece, after the Argonauts rescued her four sons from a shipwreck. *See also* Aeetes; Argus; Golden Fleece; Medea; Phrixus.

Chalcipe (Greek) *see* Argus (D).

Chalcodon (Greek)
King of the Abantes of Euboea. The son of Abas and Ocaleia, his siblings are Acrisius and Proetus. Amphitryon killed him at Thebes. *See also* Abas (A); Acrisius; Amphitryon; Proetus.

Chalcon (Greek) A Myrmidon. *See also* Telchines.

Chalmecatciuatl (Aztec People, Mexico)
Paradise. This is the heaven where the Tree of Milk grows. It is reserved for children. When Tlaloc is in residence, it is called Tlalocan. May be similar to Iztaccihuatl (*see* Mixcoatl). *See also* Mictlan; Tlaloc.

Chalucas (Zoque People, Mexico; possibly originally Maya)
Also known as: *Homshuk* (Popoluca People), *Kondoy* (Mixe People).
Culture hero. There is little known about Chalucas. He might have been a corn spirit. The few legends available indicate he defeated enemies and started present day civilization.

Champ-pa (Tibet) *see* Maitreya; Mamaki.

Chamunda (India)
This is the name of the goddess Kali in her bloodthirsty manifestation as the slayer of the demons Chanda and Munda. In battle, her mount is the buffalo. *See also* Kali.

Chanda (India) *see* Durga.

Chanda Maharoshana (Nepal) *see* Chandamaharoshana.

Chandamaharoshana *Chanda Maharoshana* (Buddhist; Nepal)
Also known as: *Acala, Akshobhya, Mahachandrarosana.*
Chandamaharoshana is an aspect of Akshobhya. He bears on his crown the effigy of Akshobhya. Worshipped in secret, he is kept secluded from public gaze. He has one face, two arms and squinted, slightly red eyes. His bare fangs are framed by a beastly face. A jewelled headdress decorated with a garland of severed heads adorns his head. In his right hand he carries the sword and in his left hand the noose around his raised index finger against his chest. His left leg touches the ground and his right leg is slightly raised. Clothed in tiger skin, he is adorned with jewels. White snakes compose his sacred thread. *See also* Acala; Akshobhya; Tara.

Chandi (Buddhist, Hindu; India)
Also known as: *Devi, Durga-Kali, Tou Mu* (China).
Chandi, meaning "fierce," is an aspect of the Great Mother Devi. It is also the name applied to Durga-Kali, who is an aspect of Devi, in her terrifying aspect when she slays the demon Mahisha. Compare Chandi to Marichi (A) and Tou Mu (Chinese). *See also* Devi; Durga; Kali.

Chandika (India)
"The Burning," or "The Fierce." *See also* Durga; Kali.

Chandra *Candra* (Hindu, Vedic; India)
Also known as: *"Bright One," Candramas, Soma.*
Chandra the moon god was created from the churning of the milk ocean which produced soma and amrita, the beverages of the gods. Once considered an independent god, Chandra was later assimilated by Soma. In some renditions, Chandra is the lover of the beautiful goddess of dawn, Ushas, or Surya, the sun goddess. The goddess Rohini (also known as Red Cow) is the wife of Chandra and Soma. Chandra's steed is the antelope. He rises up from the ocean each night and influences the lives of mortals from birth until death. Chandrakanta is the moon-gem prized by healers. It is said to reduce fevers and eliminate headaches. The Chandrakanta is retrieved from ponds at midnight by divers who are willing to risk having spells cast upon them by water nymphs. The stone is created by the rays of the moon falling on water that is free of all pollutants. In Vedic mythology, Chandra is one of the eight attendants of Indra, who are known as the Vasus. *See also* Amrita; Asvins; Kurma; Parvati; Rohini; Soma; Surya (B); Ushas; Vasus.

Chandra-Prabha (India) *see* Gwakko-Bosatsu.

Chandrakanta (India) Sacred moon-gem. *See also* Chandra.

Chandraprabha (Jain; India)
Lord of the moon and ruler of the present age, Chandraprabha is the eighth of twenty-four forebears of Jainism.

Chang (Buddhism, Taoism; China)
Also known as: *Chang Hsien, Chang Kung, Chang-Sien, Chang Yuang-Hsiao, Immortal Chang.*
God of male children. This ancient deity of Szechwan is still worshiped in a ceremony using a bow of mulberry and arrows

of silkworm wood. Chang is the father of Kien t'an. He protects all children from the Celestial Dog, T'ien Kou (Sirius). Originally, Chang was responsible for the birth of male children, but later he was responsible for the birth of all children. He is the father of two mortal writers; Su Shi and Su Ch'e. Chang is shown as an old man bending a bow pointed at the sky. He is the counterpart to Avalokitesvara who is a deity of women. See also Avalokitesvara.

Chang Fei Khang Fei (China)
Deity of butchers. See also Fan K'uei.

Chang Hsien (China) see Chang.

Chang-Kuo-Lao Chang Kuo (China)
One of the Eight Immortals. He is known by his miraculous donkey. After traveling thousands of miles in a day, he is folded up like a piece of paper. Chang-Kuo-Lao is depicted as an old man, usually riding a donkey backwards and carrying a feather in his hand. See also Arhats; Chung-Li-Ch'uan; Eight Immortals; Han Chung-Li.

Chang-O Ch'ang-O (China)
Also known as: Heng-O, T'ai-Yin Huang-Chun, Yueh-Fu Ch'ang O.
Goddess of the moon. Chang-O's husband Yi, the Excellent Archer, possessed the drink, or pill, of immortality. He was furious to learn that his wife had taken the potion in his absence. Fearful, Chang-O sought refuge in the moon. This ancient legend is still part of traditional belief. Chang-O's other titles are "The Celestial Toad" and "The White Beauty." She is shown as a beautiful young lady. (In some versions Chang-O is a male deity.) See also "I" (A); Yi.

Ch'ang-Sheng T'u-Ti (China)
Also known as: God of the Place.
Guardian. They are a group of deities who guard the home and its contents. Ch'ang-Sheng T'u-Ti and his wife Jui-k'ing fu-jen are usually named as head of this group. See also Ch'uang-kung; K'eng-san-ku.

Chang-Sien (China) see Chang.

Chang Tao-ling (China)
Also known as: T'ien-shih (Celestial Master).
He is the founder of existing Taoism. Born in the second century (common era), he was deified in the eighth century. He was the recipient of numerous divine revelations during his life. Chang Tao-ling also prepared the drug of immortality. With the aid of his magic talismans and magic powers, he successfully overcame eight king-demons. After passing his wisdom and learnings on to his son, he ascended to the heavens with his wife and two disciples. See also Chang-O; Lao-tzu.

Chang Tung-Ch'ang (China) see Ch'eng Huang.

Chang Yuang-Hsiao (China) see Chang.

Chango (Africa, Caribbean, Central America, South America)
Warrior god. He defends mortals against enemies who want their land, wealth and women.

Channa (India) see Buddha.

Chantico (Aztec People, Mexico)
Fire goddess of the home and hearth. Fertility goddess. Chantico is generally associated with wealth and precious stones. She appears with a golden face. Her symbols are a red serpent and cactus spikes.

Chaos (Chinese, Babylonian, Greek)
There are variations of the creation myth in Greek mythology. Hesiod said that Chaos, also known as "The Gap" came into being first, followed by the earth, Gaea. Next followed Tartarus, the dark abyss below Hades, which was followed by Eros (Love). (Eros is not to be confused with Aphrodite's son, who appeared in later works.) All things followed these creations. Chaos gave birth to Nyx (Night) and Erebus (Darkness). Gaea bore Uranus (Sky), Ourea (Mountains), and Pontus (Sea). (See also Gaea.) In the Orphic creation myth, Chaos, Erebus, and Nyx existed at the beginning. In the Pelasgian creation myth, Eurynome, the Goddess of All Things, emerged from Chaos, and from the North Wind, also called Boreas, her consort Ophion was created. In the Olympian version, Mother Earth emerged from Chaos and bore her son, Uranus (Sky). In Greek mythology, Darkness existed first and Chaos sprang from Darkness, or that the God of All Things, sometimes called Nature, appeared in Chaos and separated the elements. It is also said that the goddess Aphrodite (foam born) who rose from the sea is the same as the wide-ruling goddess who emerged from Chaos, called Eurynome, in the Pelasgian creation myth, and in Syria and Palestine as Ishtar, or Ashtaroth. In Babylonian mythology, Chaos is a feminine principle meaning mother of all gods and is personified by the goddesses Neith and Tiamat. Air and Chaos, who existed in the beginning, created Kolpia (the wind) and Potos (desire) in the Phoenician Creation Legend of Philo Byblos. In a Chinese version Chaos was likened to an egg and from this egg was born Phan-ku. When the parts of the egg separated the heavy elements became earth and the light, pure elements became the sky. These became Yin and Yang. Also in Chinese mythology, Ch'i and Tien Li were created from Chaos. Phan-ku of China is represented as a squatting man holding the egg of Chaos which is symbolized as Yin and Yang. For the role played by Chaos in the Pelasgian creation myth see Eurynome (A). To compare to the Orphic creation myth see Phanes; for the Homeric version see Oceanus; for the Olympian version, see Gaea. See also Aether; Air; Boreas; Erebus; Nox; Pan-ku; Tartarus.

Chapala (India)
Goddess of fortune.

Chaquen (Chibcha People, Bogota, South America)
Guardian and god of boundaries. See also Bochica.

Char (Armenian) see Devs.

Charis Aegle (Greek) see Aegle; Aglaia; Graces.

Charites (Greek) see Graces.

Charities, The (Greek) see Aglaia; Graces.

Charon Kaharon (Greek)
Ferryman of the dead. Charon is the son of Erebus and Nyx. His siblings are Aether, Cer, Dreams, Hemera, Hypnos, Momus, Moros, Nemesis and Thanatos. He ferries the souls of the dead

over the waters of the rivers Styx and Acheron in a leaky rotting boat, to Hades. He receives payment for each passenger. (This is why the ancient Romans put a coin [the obolus or obol] into the mouth of a corpse before burial.) If a coin is not produced, the spirit must wait a hundred years, then Charon could ferry them across at no charge. Sometimes he is shown as an aged or grumpy boatman, sometimes with a scraggly white beard and wearing a dirty cloak hanging from his shoulders by a knot. *See also* Acheron; Aether; Cocytus; Erebus; Golden Bough; Heracles; Keres; Nemesis; Nox; Styx; Tartarus.

Charumati (India)
She is the daughter of Krishna and Rukmini. *See also* Rukmini; Sisupala.

Charun (Etruscan)
God of death. His hammer, which is normally used when he accompanies Mars in battle, is also used to kill his victims. *See also* Hades.

Charvi (India) *see* Kuvera.

Charybdis (Greek) *see* Amphitrite; Gaea; Nereids; Scylla.

Chasca (Inca People, Peru)
Dawn goddess. Created by Viracocha, Chasca brings forth flowers and protects young women. She is identified with the planet Venus and is worshiped as an attendant of the Sun. In depictions, she is shown surrounded by clouds who are her messengers. *See also* Viracocha.

Chavah (Babylonia) *see* Eve.

Chavva (Babylonia) *see* Eve.

Chebeldei (Siberia)
Also known as: *Abaasy, Abasy.*
Inhabitants or spirits of the underworld. Chebeldei is a black spirit of the underworld who has a very long nose. Many of these underworld spirits are partly or completely composed of iron, and black in color. Their noses are eighteen meters long. *See also* Abaasy.

Cheiron *Chiron, Kheiron, Kiron* (Greek)
Instructor. Cheiron is the immortal son of the underworld god Cronus and the nymph Philyra. Unlike his uncouth fellow Centaurs, Cheiron was intelligent, cultivated and gentle. Sometimes he is referred to as the chief of the Centaurs. He was renowned for his knowledge and skills in the healing arts, music and archery. Cheiron also had the gift of prophecy. He taught the art of war to many of the famous heroes; Actaeon, Achilles, Asclepius, Jason, Heracles and Podalirius. Cheiron was accidently shot by one of Heracles' poisoned arrows. Although he was immortal, he chose to die and pass his immortality to the Titan Prometheus (q.v.). Cheiron was said to have married Cariclo. He is the father of Endeis, Ocyrrhoe (Menalippe), and Thea. (The gods changed Ocyrrhoe into a horse because of her gift of prophecy.) Cheiron is depicted as a man with a horse's body. *See also* Acastus; Achilles; Actaeon; Aeacus; Aeolus (B); Aristaeus; Centaurs; Cronus; Nessus; Oceanus; Jason.

Chelidon (Greek) *see* Aedon.

Chelovek (Russia) *see* Domovoi.

Chem-pa (Tibet) *see* Mi-Lo Fu.

Chembe (Africa) *see* Bumba.

Chemosh *Kemosh* (Canaan, Moabite, Semite, Sumer; possibly of Egyptian origin)
Also known as: *Baal-Peor, Kammus, Kamus, Shamash* (Sumer).
Chemosh, thought by some to be a deified mortal king, was the national war god of the Moabites when they fought against Israel. He was worshiped along with Eshmun and Melqart, who were said to be the brothers, sons, or husbands of Astarte. Mentioned in the Bible, he was worshiped by Solomon. As Baal-Peor this deity was androgynous. As a male he was a sun god and as female, a moon goddess. Chemosh is shown as a phallus, cone, pillar or tree branch. He is associated with Ishtar (q.v.). *See also* Astarte; Baal; Eshmun; Shamash.

Ch'en (Maya People, Yucatan)
Also known as: *Grandmother.*
Moon goddess. She was the first woman to have sexual intercourse.

Ch'en Ch'i (China) *see* Men Shen.

Chen Wu *Cheng Wu* (China)
Also known as: *Hsuan T'ien Shang Ti, Pei-chi Chen Chun* ("God of the North Pole").
God of the north. God and ruler of the abode of darkness. He is the reincarnation of T'ien Pao. *See also* Hsuan T'ien Shang Ti (q.v.).

Chen Jen (Taoist; China)
"Perfect Ones."
Chen Jen is generally used to describe those who reached perfection and are suitable for worship. The Chen Jen do not have physical bodies. They can travel between the physical and spiritual worlds.

Chen Resik (Tibet) *see* Avalokiteswara.

Ch'eng Huang *Ch'eng-huang shen* (China)
Also known as: *Celestial Mandarin, Chang Tung-Ch'ang, Shui Jung, Yang Ki-Sheng, Yu-K'ien, Yung-Ku Wang.*
God of the city. God of walls and ditches. As Shui Jung, he is one of the "Eight Spirits" (Pa Cha). Double walls surrounded all cities. The ditch between the walls was called huang while the walls were called ch'eng. Worship of Ch'eng Huang is probably from the Yao dynasty around 2357 B.C.E. Each village had its own Ch'eng Huang. They are called T'u-ti (Gods of the Place). Some versions say the original god (or founder) has one name, and is usually worshiped instead of Ch'eng Huang. Some of the gods of walls and ditches are Yank Ki-sheng, Yu-K'ien, Chang Tung-ch'ang, and Yung-ku wang. Ch'eng Huang is associated with Mr. White (Po-lao-ye), Mr. Black (Hei-lao-ye), Mr. Horse-face, and Mr. Ox-face. *See also* Ma-Mien; Men Shen.

Cheng Lung (China) *see* Heng and Ha; Men Shen.

Cheng Wu (China) *see* Chen Wu.

Chenrezig *Chenrgzi* (Buddhist; Tibet)
An incarnation of Buddha and the national tutelary deity of

Tibet, Chenrezig is the four-armed herdsman. His mantra is "Om man-ni pad-me hum." *See also* Buddha.

Chenrgzi (Tibet) *see* Chenrezig.

Chent-Ament (Egypt) *see* Osiris.

Chepera (Egypt) *see* Khepri.

Cherakan-Ixmmucane (Maya People, Yucatan) *see* Chirakan-Ixmucane.

Cheresi *(Bodhisattva)* (Hindu; India) *see* Bodhisattva Cheresi.

Chernobog *Cernobog, Czarnobog, Zcernoboch* (Slavic)
Evil deity. Chernobog is the black god who is opposite of Byelobog, the spirit of light. *See also* Byelobog.

Cherruve (Araucanian People, Chile, South America)
Depicted as man-headed serpents, the Cherruve are spirits of shooting stars who are under the command of the weather and thunder god, Pillan. *See also* Auchimalgen; Pillan.

Cherub *Choreb, Kerub* (Roman; originally, possibly Assyrian)
Also known as: *Cherubim* (plural).
Messengers. In Biblical lore they were pictured as two figures of gold whose wings covered the mercy seat on the Ark. Although often shown as cupid-like figures, most scholars think they were fierce guardians of holy places. They were possibly derived from the Assyrian guardian creatures placed at the gates of temples. These were bulls with the head of a man and wings of an eagle. Some legends indicate they were of the higher order of angels and were the supreme god's messengers. The Bible describes them with four faces, four wings, and calf-like feet. *See also* Angels; Apis (A).

Cherubim (Semite) *see* Angels; Cherub.

Chespisichis (Greek) *see* Khensu.

Chhaya *Khaya, Shaya* (India)
Goddess of the shade. *See also* Sanja; Tapati.

Chhwaskamini (Buddhist; Nepal)
Also known as: *Tara*.
Evil spirit. Chhwaskamini is the evil form of the loving goddess Tara who fights off demons and wicked spirits. *See also* Tara.

Ch'i (A) (China)
The ether. In the beginning there was Ch'i, "ether," a single cell. This divided into Yin and Yang as a result of the vibrations set in motion by Tao, a force, and thus creation began with the appearance of two opposite ethers, able to produce the elements, which went on to combine and form everything in the universe. *See also* Chaos.

Ch'i (B) (China)
Ch'i is the son of Yu and the Girl of T'u. His grandfather is Kun. In some renditions, Yu was born from his dead father's stomach three years after his death. In another myth, Yu turned into a bear while digging through a mountain, possibly in an attempt to hold back flood waters. When T'u saw him in bear form she ran away and changed into a stone. Yu hollered after her "Give me my son." That stated, the stone split open and Ch'i was born. *See also* Kun (B).

Chi (China)
Chi is the soul or the total being; the unexplainable manifestation that controls the body.

Chi-Haya-Buru (Japan) *see* Kami.

Ch'i-Lin (China)
God of animals. This unicorn is one of the "Head of All Animals," known as Ch'i-Lin. It doesn't eat living vegetation and never walks on green grass. It appears at the birth of good leaders, or sages. Ch'i-Lin has the body of a deer, the tail of an ox, and the hooves of a horse. It is multi-colored on the back and yellow on the belly.

Chi Sheng Sien-Shi (China) *see* Confucius.

Ch'i-ti *Red Lord* (China) *see* Shang Ti.

Ch'i-You (China)
God of war, weapons, smiths and dancers. He is the son, grandson, or minister of Shen-nung ("Divine Farmer"). Ch'i-You eats stone, iron and sand. His head is iron, his brow bronze, he has sharp pointed horns, four eyes, six arms, eight fingers and eight toes. His hair bristles like spears. He either has a human body with feet of an ox, or a beast body and human voice.

Chia *Chie* (Muyscaya People, Colombia, South America)
Also known as: *Huytaca, Suetiva, Xubchasgagua*.
Chia is the moon goddess mate of Bochica, or in some myths, Cuchaviva. From jealousy and as a mischievous prank, Chia used her magic to flood the land. Bochica punished Chia by banishing her to a permanent home in the sky, where she was transformed into the moon, and became a primary goddess of women. In an alternate tale, Chia told mortals that merrymaking, joy and laughter should supplant the severe rule of laws made by Bochica. This angered Bochica, who turned her into an owl. To spite him, she helped Chibchachum flood the plain of Bogota. There were few survivors. If she became displeased with a man, he had to dress as a woman rather than being punished by her. Chia is often confused with Hunthaca, the spouse of Nemquetcha. She is the same as Suetiva (q.v.). *See also* Bochica.

Chibcha People — Creation Legend (Colombia, South America) *see* Bachue; Chimaqua.

Chibchacum *Chibchachum* (Muyscaya People, Colombia, South America)
He holds up the earth. When this god is tired, he shifts the weight on his shoulders and causes earthquakes. *See also* Bochica.

Chibiabos (Algonquin People, North America) *see* Chipiapoos; Manibozho.

Chibilias (Maya People, Yucatan) *see* Ix-chel.

Chichen Izta (Maya People, Yucatan) *see* Itzamna.

Chickcharney (Andros Island, Bahamas)
A small, feathered, furred spirit of the forest.

Chicomecoatl *Chicomexochit* (Aztec People, Mexico)
Also known as: *Seven Snakes, Xilonen.*
Goddess of crops, particulary maize. Goddess of plenty. She is associated with Coatlicue because of her powers of fertility. She is similar to Ceres, and is identified with Tonacacihuatl. Chicomecoatl is possibly represented as a red ear of corn. *See also* Ceres; Coatlicue; Xilonen.

Chicomexochitl (Mexico) *see* Tonacatecutli.

Chicomoztoc (Aztec People, Mexico)
Also known as: *The Seven Cities of Cibola* (possibly).
Place of origin. In the creation myth, the Aztec race emerged from the Cavern of the Seven Chambers, also known as Chicomoztoc, after a great natural disaster. *See also* Legend of the Four Suns.

Chiconamictlan (Aztec People, Mexico) *see* Chicunauhmictlan.

Chiconauapan (Aztec People, Mexico) *see* Chicunauhmictlan.

Chicuna (Andean People, Peru)
"Lord of All Things." Creator deity.

Chicunauhmictlan *Chiconamictlan* (Aztec People, Mexico)
Also known as: *Apochquiahuayan, Chiconauapan, Mictlan.*
Home of the Dead. Chicunauhmictlan, frequently shortened to Mictlan, is the ninth pit where the "lords of night" rule over the affairs of men. It is the abode of Mictlantecutli and Mictlanciuatl who live in a windowless home. Xiuhtecutli is also a resident of Chicunauhmictlan. The dead are given magical spells and a water vase for their trip to the Home of the Dead. They use spells to help them when they pass the monsters guarding the "clashing mountains." They also pass eight deserts, and eight hills. After meeting the "Lord of the Dead," Mictlantecuhtli, the dead souls mount a red dog sacrificed at their death and follow the nine-fold stream in the underworld. They are then allowed to take their rest in Chicunauhmictlan. Chicunauhmictlan is the opposite of Omeyocan (q.v.). *See also* Chicuna; Legend of the Four Suns; Mictlantecutli.

Chie (South America) *see* Chia.

Ch'ien Niu (China) *see* Kengiu (Japan).

Ch'ien-T'ang (Taoist; China)
Chief of the river gods. A Dragon King. He is the brother of Ling Hsu, who is a king of one of the local rivers. One of the legends associated with this deity is that he caused a nine-year flood. *See also* Dragon Kings.

Ch'ih Kuo (China) *see* Mo'li Shou.

Chih-Nii (China) *see* Chin Nu.

Chih Nu (China) *see* Chih Nii; Chin Nu.

Chih-Wen (China)
Water dragon. His depiction, sometimes shown as a fish with a raised tail, is carved on bridges and roofs to ward off fire.

Ch'ih Yeo (China)
Satan. He is the head of eighty-one brothers who are described as having the bodies of beasts. Huang-Ti captured him and cut him to pieces.

Chikisanti (Ainu People, Japan)
Goddess of elm trees. The ancient Ainu People believed that the elm tree was the first tree. Chikisanti is the mother of the first man, Pon Okikurumi, by Okikurumi. *See also* Okikurumi.

Children of Don, The (Britain, Wales)
Deities of Wales and Britain, similar to the Irish Tuatha De Danann. The two most important of the Children of the Don are the all-powerful god Gwydion, a beneficent teacher who controlled war and peace, and his sister-wife Arianrhod. *See also* Arianrhod; Gwydion.

Children of Llyr, The (Britain, Wales)
Popular deities of the ancient Welsh and British people. Llyr became the father of Manawyddan by Don's daughter Penardun and of Bran and Branwen by Iweridd. *See also* Llyr; Manawyddan.

Chilenga (Africa) *see* Lisa.

Chimaera *Chimera, Chimaira* (Greek)
A Lycian monster. Storm deity. The Chimaera is the offspring of the whirling hurricane Typhon and Echidna, an eternally youthful, half-nymph, half-snake monster. The Chimaera did not fare well in the appearance department, nor did her siblings who are the Sphinx, Hydra, Cerberus, the Caucasian Eagle, the Crommyonian Sow and the Vultures. Raised by the Lycian chieftain, Amisodaurus, the Chimaera, personification of evil, ravaged the land and killed the innocent. Bellerophon, the slayer of monsters, had been sent by Iobates, the king of Lycia, to perform numerous dangerous tasks. Outfitted with the golden bridle on the winged Pegasus, he flew through the air, confronted the monster and slew it. Chimaera is shown with three heads or the head of a lion, goat, or snake, or with the front parts of a lion, the center of a goat and a snake's tail, and she breathes fire. In medieval times, the Chimaera was associated with lust. In current interpretations, it has been seen as an allegory of an Achaean capture of the White Goddess's shrine on Mount Helicon. It is also thought to represent an initiation. To compare the Chimaera (the essence of a storm cloud) with wind deities *see* Aeolus, Borea, Eurus, Notus, Zetes, and Zephyrus. To compare the Chimaera to other destructive forces of nature *see* Aegeon, Aello, Bellerophon, Harpies, Pegasus, and Typhon (A). *See also* Cerberus; Echidna; Hambaris; Hydra; Sphinx.

Chimaira (Greek) *see* Chimaera.

Chimalman (Aztec People, Mexico) *see* Chimalmatl.

Chimalmatl *Chimalman* (Aztec, Toltec People, Mexico)
Also known as: *Chalchihuitzli* ("Precious Stone of Sacrifice").
Ancestor of the Toltec people. She is the earth-born virgin wife of Mixcoatl and the mother of Quetzalcoatl under his name Citlallatonac. She died during childbirth and was given the title Chalchihuitzli. In other renditions, she is known as the mother of Quetzalcoatl by Camaxtle (also known as Texcatlipoca). She might be related to Huitzilopochtli (q.v.). *See also* Camaxtle; Ilancue; Mixcoatl; Texcatlipoca.

Chimata-no-Kami (Japan)

Also known as: *Sanzu-no-Kawa.*

God of cross-roads. According to some, he was a phallic deity who was removed by Buddhism. He is one of the gods of roads known as Sae-no-kami. *See also* Sanzu-no-kawa.

Chimera (Greek) *see* Chimaera.

Chiminagua *Chiminigagua, Chiminiquagua* (Chibcha People, South America)

Also known as: *Bochica.*

Creator deity. Before anything existed, light was enclosed by Chiminagua. He rose and freed the light, then created mankind. In the tale of Chibcha myth, Chiminagua was the creator of all. When the world began, the light was in Chiminagua and all was darkness. He set the light free, creating blackbirds to carry it over the earth. In some renditions, Bochica was given the name Chiminizagagua, meaning "Messenger of Chiminagua." *See also* Bochica; Suetiva.

Chimini-Pagus (Chibcha, Muyscaya People, South America)

This is the name of the casket that contained light in the beginning. In the Creation Legend, it was sent to earth where blackbirds scattered the light. *See also* Chiminagua.

Chiminigagua (Colombia, South America) *see* Chiminagua.

Chiminiquagua (Colombia, South America) *see* Chiminagua.

Chiminizagagua (Chibcha People, Bogota, South America) *see* Bochica.

Chin (Maya People, Yucatan)

He is the god of death and one of the Becabs (q.v.). *See also* Acat.

Chin Chia (China)

Also known as: *Mr. Golden Cuirass.*

God of Scholars. Protector of weak students. Avenger of evil actions. Occasionally he sometimes accompanies Chu I or K'uei Hsing as an attendant of Wen Ch'ang. Chin Chia is shown with a flag and a sword. *See also* Chi I; Wen Ch'ang.

Ch'in Ch'iung (China) *see* Men Shen.

Chin Neu (China) *see* Chin Nu.

Chin Nu *Chih Neu, Chih-Nii, Chih Nu, Kien Niu* (China)

Also known as: *Heavenly Spinster, Spinning Damsel, Stellar Goddess, Weaver Damsel.*

The goddess of spinners and weavers, Chin Nu, is the daughter of the Jade Emperor Yu Huang. One day Chin Nu came to earth from heaven to bathe. An ox, who was the guardian spirit of a cowherd, advised him to take Chin Nu's clothing. She was unable to return to heaven without her clothes, so she stayed and wed the cowherd. They had two children. Seven years passed and Chin Nu found her clothes and returned to heaven. Her spouse was very upset. He consulted with the ox. It was agreed that he would carry the children in baskets on a pole across his shoulders, and he would grasp the ox's tail and go to heaven in search of his wife. When he encountered her father, he demanded that he be permitted to see Chin Nu. Yu Huang gave her husband, Ch'ien Niu, a star to the west. Chin Nu's star is to the east of the Heavenly River. Because of their positions they are only reunited on the seventh day of the seventh month each year. On that day all the magpies each take a twig and build a bridge for them across the Heavenly River. Her husband became known as the Celestial Herdsman. In a variation of this myth, Chin Nu wove fine garments without seams for her father Tung Wang Kung (also known as Yu-ti). This so pleased him that he gave her in marriage to Ch'ien Niu, the Heavenly Herdsman, a star in the constellation Aquila. Then, because the goddess had too little time for his robes, the Jade Emperor put the Milky Way between his daughter and her husband. It was believed that once a year, crossing by a bridge made by magpies, the couple was reunited. In some versions, it is the queen who placed the Milky Way between the lovers. *See also* Kengiu (Japan).

Ch'in Shu-Pao (China) *see* Hu King-te; Men-shen.

China — Creation Legend *see* Ch'i

Ching-Tu (Buddhist; China)

Also known as: *Kun-Lun Mountain.*

Heavenly paradise. The legend is the same as that of the Kun-Lun Mountain. *See also* Jodo; Kun-Lun.

Ching Yuh (Korea) *see* Kengiu (Japan).

Chinnamastica (India) *see* Kali.

Chinnigchinich (Native North American)

Creator. He is an orphan who created men and women out of clay. It is he who taught the people the art of medicine.

Chinnintamma (India)

She is one of the Mutyalammo goddesses who are deities of the household. She functions as head of the home. *See also* Mutyalammo.

Chinta-Mani (India) *see* Cintamani.

Chintamani Lokeswar (Nepal) *see* Lokeswar.

Chinvat Bridge *Chinvat Peretu, Cinvat* (Persian)

Also known as: *Bridge of the Gatherer, Bridge of the Requiter.*

This bridge spans from Mount Tera, the peak of the cosmic Mount Alburz, to heaven. Upon death, all souls cross Chinvat Bridge. The beams of the bridge are many-sided and of varying thickness. When a righteous soul arrives, the thick rim appears. When a sinner arrives, the thin and sharp beam is presented and the soul drops to a hell below. On the rim of Mount Alburz is the Arezur ridge, the gateway to hell, where demons congregate. Mithra, Sraosha and Rashnu are the judges of the dead souls. Indra made the bridge shrink as souls passed over it, thus dropping them into the abyss. *See also* Aeshma; Alburz (Mount); Amesha Spentas; Andra; Hariati (Mount); Mithra; Rashnu; Sraosha; Yazatas.

Chione (A) (Greek)

She is the daughter of Boreas and Oreithyia. Her siblings are Calais, Cleopatra, Haemus and Zetes. The seductive sea god, Poseidon, impregnated Chione and she bore Eumolpus whom she threw into the sea. He was rescued by his father and raised by his half-sister, Benthesicyme. *See also* Acacallis; Autolycus (A); Boreas.

Chione (B) (Greek)

In one day, Chione had two children by two different gods:

Autolycus by Hermes and Philamon by Apollo. *See also* Autolycus; Philamon.

Chipiapoos (Potawatomi People, North America)

God of the dead. Brother of the trickster, Nanabojo. Chipiapoos was pulled under the ice by demons. He is similar to Chibiabos. *See also* Manibozho; Nanabojo.

Chiquinau (Nicaragua, Central America)

"God of Nine Winds." God of the air. He is one of the creator gods who are ruled by Tamagostad and Zipaltonal. He is associated with Ciaga; Ecalchot; Misca; Quiateot; Vizetot.

Chirakan-Ixmucane *Cherakan-Ixmmucane* (Maya People, Yucatan)

Creator. This goddess was created when four of the gods who created the world split themselves and became four additional deities. She is associated with Ixpiyacoc, Ixmucane, Hunahpu-guch and Hunahpu-utiu. Chirakan-Ixmucane, Ajtzak and Ajbit were among the thirteen deities who tried to create mortals from various materials. *See also* Alom; Legend of the Four Suns.

Chiron (Greek) *see* Cheiron.

Chiruwi (Africa)

Spirits. The Chiruwi are both good and bad. They have half-bodies, one eye, one ear, one leg, and one arm.

Chitra-ratha (India) *see* Gandharvas.

Chitragupta (India) Registrar of the Dead. *See also* Yama.

Chitrangada (A) (India) Wife of Arjuna (q.v.).

Chitrangada (B) (India) Half-brother of Vyasa (q.v.).

Chiu Kung (China)

Also known as: *Chiu I.*

"Nine Palaces." "Mountains of the Immortals," (also known as Hsien Shan). "Territory of the Immortals," (also known as Hsien Ching). Chiu Kung is the residence of the Fairies. *See also* Hsi-hua; Tung Wang.

Chiun (Hebrew) *see* Rephaim.

Chiutcoatl (Aztec People, Mexico) *see* Cinteotl.

Chixu (Pawnee People, North America) The Ghosts.

Chlevnik (Russia, Slavic)

One of the Domovoi who are household spirits, the Chlevnik is the spirit of the cattle shed or barn. To prevent harm to new animals and to be successful in raising cattle, the Chlevnik must be appeased with an offering. In some areas, the farmers attempt to drive the Chlevnik away by beating on the walls to frighten it. *See also* Bannik; Domovoi; Kikimori; Ovinnik.

Chloris (Greek)

Also known as: *Meliboea, Flora* (Roman).

Goddess of flowers. Goddess of fertility. Chloris is the personification of spring. She is the daughter of Amphion and Niobe. Her eleven brothers and sisters were murdered by Apollo and Artemis. She alone survived. In some traditions she is the wife of Zephyrus (who is the West Wind) and a son, Carpus, the personification of fruit. She has also been called the wife of Neleus. As the wife of Neleus, she is the mother of thirteen children. Chloris was a participant and winner in the Heraean Games. The Heraean Games were held every four years at Olympia and were only for female participants. They were initiated by Hippodameia in honor of Hera. At one time, the women, classed by age, with the youngest first, ran with their hair flying loose and a bare shoulder. *See also* Amphion; Apollo; Artemis; Flora; Niobe; Zephyrus.

Chnemu (Egypt) *see* Khnum.

Chnoumes (Egypt) *see* Khnum.

Choco People — Creation Legend (Colombia, South America) *see* Caragabi

Choctaw People — Creation Legend (North America) *see* Aba

Chonchonyi (Araucanian People, Chile, South America)

This evil deity has a large head with long, flapping ears which he uses as wings to fly about as he preys on the sick and weak.

Chonsu (Egypt)

God of the Moon.

Choreb (Roman) *see* Cherub.

Chos-Rgyal Phyi-Scrub (Tibet) *see* Yama.

Choun (Inca People, Peru) *see* Inti; Manco Capac; Virococha.

Chousorus (Phoenician) *see* Oulomos.

Christ *Khristos* (Greek) "Anointed One." *See also* Jesus.

Chronos (A) (Greek) see Cronus.

Chronos (B) (Greek)

This is the name of one of the sun god Helius' horses. *See also* Helius.

Chrysaor (Greek)

Chrysaor and his brother, Pegasus, sprang from the blood of Medusa at the time she was decapitated by Perseus. His father is the sea god Poseidon. Chrysaor married the Oceanid Callirrhoe. He is the possible father of the female monster Echidna and Geryon, the owner of the flocks stolen by Heracles as his tenth labor. *See also* Callirrhoe; Echidna; Heracles; Medusa; Oceanids; Perseus.

Chryse (A) (Greek)

Also known as: *Comana*

She is the daughter of Halmus, the king of Boeotian Orchomenus. Her relationship with Ares produced a son, Phlegyas, who later became the king of Orchomenus. *See also* Ares; Phlegyas.

Chryse (B) (Greek)

She is the daughter of Pallas, who is the son of Lycaon and Cyllene. *See also* Pallas.

Chryseis (Greek)

Also known as: *Astynome.*

When she was captured by the Greeks during the battle at Troy, she became the concubine of Agamemnon (q.v.).

Chryses (A) (Greek)

He is the son of Chryseis and Agamemnon. *See also* Agamemnon; Chryseis.

Chryses (B) (Greek)

His parents are Poseidon and Chrysogeneia and his son is Minyas.

Chryses (C) (Greek)

He is one of the many children of Hermes (q.v.).

Chryses (D) (Greek) He is the father of Chryseis (q.v.).

Chrysippe (Greek) *see* Danaus.

Chrysippus (Greek) He is the son of Pelops (q.v.).

Chryson (Greek) *see* Telchines.

Chrysothemis (A) (Greek)

Also known as: *Iphianassa, Iphigeneia.*

She is the daughter of Agamemnon and Clytemnestra. Her siblings are Electra and Orestes. *See also* Agamemnon.

Chrysothemis (B)

In the Pythian games, the Cretan Chrysothemis won first prize for poetry and music.

Chthon (Greek)

An epithet of Gaea, the personification of earth. *See also* Gaea.

Chu (China)

Spirit of the Grain. Chu is the son of Shen-Nung, the god of agriculture. *See also* Hou Chi; Shen-Nung.

Ch'u Chiang (China) *see* Chu-kiang.

Chu I (China)

Also known as: *Lu Ch'i, Mr. Red Coat, Mr. Red Jacket.*

Chu I is an assistant to Wen Ch'ang (also known as Wench'ang ti-kun, or Wen-ti) the god of literature. Chu I's mortal name is Lu Ch'i and the dates given for his life are approximately C.E. 780–784. He is usually shown with K'uei Hsing (also spelled K'ue-sing), another assistant. Sometimes he is shown with Chin Chia. Chu I and Chin Chia are identified as helpers and protectors of weak candidates. Chu I has the green face of an Immortal, the lips of a dragon and the head of a panther. *See also* Chin Chia; Wen Ch'ang.

Chu Jung (China)

Also known as: *The Red Emperor.*

Chu Jung was originally the Red Emperor who reigned for two hundred years. Later he became the god of the Fourth Month and the god of fire. He punishes those who break the laws of heaven.

Chu-kiang *Ch'u Chiang* (Buddhist; China)

The ruler of the second of the Chinese hells (T'i-Yu), he judges thieves and murderers by placing them in front of a mirror which reflects their evil actions. *See also* Kshitigarbha; Ti-Yu.

Ch'uan Hou (China) *see* T'ien Hou.

Chuan-Lun *Chuan-Lun Wang* (China)

God of hell. Of the ten hells in Chinese mythology, Chuan-Lun is the ruler of the tenth and last hell. He pronounces the final sentence and assigns the soul to one of six states. *See also* Kshitigarbha; Ti-Yu.

Ch'uang-Kung (China)

Also known as: *Lord of the Bed.*

One of the deities of the bed or bedroom. Along with his mate, Ch'uang-mu, he protects the bed. He is possibly worshiped for his ability to allow a woman to have a child. Ch'uang-Kung is one of a group called "Gods of the Place." *See also* Ch'ang-sheng t'u-ti; Ch'uang-Mu.

Ch'uang-Mu (China)

Also known as: *Lady of the Bed.*

Goddess of the bed or bedroom. Paired with Ch'uang-Kung, lord of the bed. She is one of a group called "Gods of the Place." *See also* Ch'ang-sheng t'u-ti; Ch'uang-Kung.

Chuchulain (Celtic) *see* Cuchulain.

Chukum (Colombia)

God of boundaries and foot-races. He is one of deities worshiped with Bochica (q.v.).

Chukwu (Ibo People, Africa) Supreme god.

Chunda (A) (Buddhist; India)

Chunda, a benign goddess, is shown with a smiling face, four or sixteen arms, holding a lotus, rosary and a begging-bowl.

Chunda (B) (Hindu; India)

Chunda and Munda, two demon spies, were sent by Sumbha and Nisumbha to kill the goddess Durga. They approached her with their army, and she promptly devoured all of them. *See also* Durga.

Chung-Li-Ch'uan (China)

High god. He is sometimes known as the chief of the Eight Immortals (Pa Kung). His function is to revive the dead. Chung-Li-Ch'uan is shown as a fat bearded man, sometimes with a bare stomach, sometimes clothed. He carries a fan and the peach of immortality. *See also* Arhats; Eight Immortals; Han Chung-Li; Pa Hsien; Pa Kung.

Chung-Liu (China)

Also known as: *Tsao Shen.*

God of the Shaft. It refers to the air shaft in the center of the old houses. In some versions, Chung-Liu is one of the gods of the inner-doors. *See also* Tsao Shen.

Chupunika (India) A Krittika sister. *See also* Rishi.

Churning of the Ocean (India) *see* Kurma.

Chuvalete (Cora People, Central America)

This is the morning star who protects worshipers from the fierce sun.

Chuvash (Russian) *see* Kaba.

Chwezi (Uganda, Africa)

Tribal deities of the forces of nature. There are nineteen Chwezi, each with a function: earthquakes, rain, moon, et cetera. Some say the Chwezi are culture heros.

Chyavana (India) *see* Asvins; Mada.

Ciaga (Nicaragua, South America)

Water god. Under the rule of Tamagostad and Zipaltonal,

Ciaga shared in creation with Ecalchot, Quiateot, Misca, Chiquinau, and Vizetot. *See also* Chiquinau; Ecalchot; Quiateot; Vizetot; Zipaltonal.

Cian *Kian* (Celtic)

Minor sun deity. Later an evil deity. Cian, a shepherd, is the son of the divine physician, Dia'necht, and the father of Lugh by Ethlinn the moon goddess, who is the daughter of Balor. Cian permitted Gavidjeen, Go's cow, to return to Balor, its former owner. With the aid of the sea god, Manannan Mac Llyr (Manannan Mac Lir), he reached Balor's abode in the underworld of the sea (some say an island). Here he met Ethlinn, who had been locked in a tower by her father. They slept together and Lugh was born of their union. Cian deserted her with the cow and child in tow. Again, Manannan Mac Llyr rescued him, but now demanded compensation. Cian gave him his son, Lugh, whom the sea god raised to become the sun hero. Some time later, Cian noticed his enemies approaching: the three sons of Tuirenn (Brian, Iuchar and Iucharba). Magically, he turned himself into a pig. When they realized what he had done, they changed into hounds and gave chase, overcame, and killed him. They attempted to bury him six times but only on the seventh attempt did he stay under the ground. His son Lugh found the body and vowed vengeance. An addendum to this myth tells of Cian as a druid later in life. Evil, he delighted in changing his pupils, the children of Tuirenn, into hares and pursuing them as a hound. They banded together, struck him with his staff, thus causing Ireland to divide into the North and the South. For comparison *see* Danae and Zeus. *See also* Balor; Dia'necht; Lugh; Manannan Mac Llyr; Tuatha De Danann.

Cibola, The Seven Cities of (Aztec People, Mexico)

Also known as: *Chicomoztoc* (possibly).

In legend, the Seven Cities of Cibola are the cities from which the Aztec People originated.

Cigfa (Celtic) *see* Pryderi.

Cihauteto *Cihuateteo* (Aztec People, Mexico)

Also known as: *Cihuacoatl* (possibly).

The Cihauteto are five women who died in childbirth. They became demon goddesses who return to earth in terrible form to frighten humans. They are known to linger around crossroads.

Cihuatcoatl *Cihuacoatl, Ciuacoatl* (Aztec People, Mexico)

Also known as: *Ilamatecutli, Itzpapalotl, Quilaztli, Tamazcalteci, Teteoinnan, Tlaltecuhtli, Tlatecutli, Tonantzin.*

"Women Snake." Mother goddess. Earth goddess. Goddess of childbirth. She is the mother of Mixcoatl. She often comes to earth to weep at the crossroad market where she abandoned her infant son. Instead of finding her son, she finds a sacrificial knife. *See also* Ciuateteo; Ilamatecuhtli; Itzpapalotl; Tlaltecuhtli; Tonantzin.

Cihuateteo (Aztec People, Mexico) *see* Cihauteto.

Cilix (Greek)

His parents are King Agenor and Telephassa or Argiope. *See also* Agenor (A).

Cilla (Greek)

She is the daughter of the King of Troy, Laomedon, and Strymo, who is the daughter of the river god Scamander (also known as Xanthus). *See also* Hesione; Scamander.

Cin *Cinni* (Turkey)

One of a group of spirits known as Onlar, the Cin are spirits who can cause insanity, paralysis, or other illnesses. Shapechangers and tricksters, the Cin can appear visible or invisible. Certain prayers or curses can keep the individual safe from their evils.

Cinni (Turkey) *see* Cin.

Cintamani *Chinta-Mani* (Hindu; India)

Also known as: *Divya-ratna* (Divine Jewel), *Pearl of Price.*

The wish-granting gem, made by Brahma, that contains all of the world's knowledge. *See also* Kshitigarbha; Ratnasambhava.

Cinteotl *Centeal, Centeotl* (Aztec, Toltec People, Mexico)

Also known as: *Cexochitl, Chiutcoatl, Cihuatcoatl, Tonacajoha, Tzinteotl.*

God of maize. Grandson of "Our Grandmother," Toci. He is depicted as a young man with a yellow body. A jagged black line moves down his brow, across his cheek, and down to the base of his jaw. He often has maize in his headdress or maize growing from his head. *See also* Cihuatcoatl; Lords of the Night Hours; Tlazolteutl; Tzinteotl; Xilonen.

Cinvat (Persia) *see* Chinvat Bridge.

Cinyras (Greek)

His lineage is uncertain. He could be the son of Sandorcus of Syria, or of Paphus, Apollo, or Pygmalion. Cinyras was the king of Paphos in Cyrus, he was wed to either Cenchreis or Metharme. His children are Adonis and Myrrha. (There is a possibility that Myrrha is Adonis' mother.) His other children are Braesia, Laogore, Mygdalion and Orsedice. Cinyras, a suitor of Helen, did not go to the Trojan War. Instead, he promised Agamemnon that he would send fifty ships. Forty-nine of the ships were made of clay. The fiftieth ship was commanded by Cinyras' son Mygdalion. After an incestous relationship with his daughter Myrrha, Cinyras committed suicide. *See also* Adonis; Agamemnon; Cenchreis; Helen.

Cipactli (Aztec People, Mexico)

Also known as: *Coxcox, Coxcoxtli, Huehuetonacacipactli* (Fish God; "Old Fish God of our Flesh").

"Crocodile." Fish god. Sea monster. Cipactli is another name for Coxcoxtli (q.v.). *See also* Legend of the Four Suns; Tiamat.

Cipactonal *Cipactli, Cipattoval* (possibly) (Aztec People, Mexico) *see* Omeciutal.

Cirape (Crow People, North America)

Also known as: *Little Coyote.*

He is the younger brother of the Trickster.

Circe *Kirke* (Greek)

Also known as: *Aeaea, Angita* (Italian), *Marica* (Roman).

"The Enchantress." Sorceress. She is the daughter of the sun, Helios, and the Oceanid, Perse, and the sister of Aeetes, Pasiphae and Perses. Her first marriage was to Odysseus. Their children are Ardeas, Agrius and Telegonus (some say she was the mistress of Odysseus and had only one son by him). Her second marriage to Telemachus produced a son, Latinus (some say he is the son of Odysseus). She is also the mother of Comus by Bacchus. Her charms enticed men and her use of sorcery changed them into swine. Circe, madly in love with Glaucus, poisoned Scylla and turned her into a monster. Circe dwells alone in the western island of Aeaea, denoting the setting sun. Her visitors are changed into animals. Aeaea is one of two islands of the same name. Aeetes' abode was the eastern island, denoting the rising sun. *See also* Aeetes; Angita; Calypso; Glaucus; Helius; Oceanids; Odysseus; Pasiphae; Perses; Skylla.

Cisa *Ciza Zisa* (German)
Possibly a harvest goddess as her festival was September 28.

Cissos (Greek) *see* Dionysus.

Cit-Bolon-Tum (Maya People, Yucatan)
Also known as: *Boar with the Nine Tusks.*
God of medicine.

Citalicue (Aztec People, Mexico)
A name of the "God of All Existence." *See also* Tloquenahuaque.

Citlalatonac *Citlallatonac* (Aztec People, Mexico) *see* Nata and Nena.

Citlalinicue *Citlalicue* (Aztec People, Mexico) *see* Nata and Nena.

Ciuacoatl (Aztec People, Mexico) *see* Cihuatcoatl.

Ciuateteo *Cihuateteo, Ciuapipiltin* (Aztec People, Mexico) *see* Cihuateto; Tlaloc; Tlalocan; Xolotl.

Ciza (German) *see* Cisa.

Cleio (Greek)
Muse of history. She is one of the nine Muses. Her symbols are a wreath of laurel and a scroll. She is often shown with Cadmus, holding a writing implement. *See also* Cadmus; Muses.

Cleite (Greek)
She is the daughter of Meropes, the king of Percote. Her siblings are Adrastus, who was killed in the Trojan War by Diomedes; Arisbe, who was the first wife of Priam and the mother of Aesacus; and Amphius, who was also killed in the Trojan War by Diomedes. *See also* Adrastus; Danaus; Diomedes.

Cleitus (Greek)
He is the son of Mantius and brother of Polypheides. Eos, the goddess of dawn, fell in love with his beauty and abducted him. *See also* Boreas; Eos.

Clemenus (Greek) *see* Phaethon.

Cleodora (A) (Greek) A Danaid. She is one of the fifty daughters of Danaus. *See also* Danaid; Danaus.

Cleodora (B) (Greek)
She is the nymph mother of Parnassus by the sea god, Poseidon.

Cleolla (Greek)
Cleolla is the spouse of Pleisthenes, the king of Argos and Mycenae, and the mother of Anaxibia, and possibly Agamemnon and Menelaus. *See also* Agamemnon.

Cleone (Greek)
The river god Asopus is her father and Metope is her mother. *See also* Asopus; Metope.

Cleopatra (A) (Greek)
Her parents are the north wind, Boreas, and Oreithyia, the daughter of Erechtheus and Praxithea. *See also* Althea; Boreas; Danaus; Harpies; Phineus; Zetes.

Cleopatra (B) (Greek)
She is the daughter of Idas and Marpessa, the wife of Meleager and the mother of Polydora. *See also* Meleager; Polydora.

Cleopatra (C) (Greek)
One of the fifty daughters of Danaus known as the Danaids. *See also* Aegyptus; Danaids; Danaus.

Cleopatra (D) (Greek)
Her parents are Tros, the son of Erichthonius and Astyoche, and Callirrhoe, daughter of the river god, Scamander. *See also* Callirrhoe; Ganymedes; Scamander.

Cleopatra (E) The name of seven queens of Egypt.

Cleostratus (Greek)
His lover was a young man from Thespiae named Menestratus who saved him from being eaten alive by a dragon who attacked people in the area every year.

Cleta (Greek) *see* Graces.

Clio (Greek)
She is the mother of Hyacinth by Pierus. *See also* Muses.

Cloacina (Roman)
Also known as: *Venus.*
Underworld deity. This goddess looks after sewers. In ancient times, she was in charge of the sewers of the Cloaca Maxima which drained the Forum. *See also* Caca.

Clotho *Klotho* (Greek)
Goddess of fate. Clotho is the youngest of the three Moirai. Called the Spinner, she spins the thread of life. Her parents are Zeus and Themis. Her sisters are Lachesis and Atropos. *See also* Ariadne; Atropos; Fates; Moirai; Themis.

Clothru (Celtic, Irish)
Fertility goddess. Clothru and Ethne were the wives of Conchobar after Medb left him. She is known as the sister of Bres, Ethne, Lother, Medb, and Nar. In some renditions, Clothru is the wife of Cian.

Cluracan (Celtic, Irish) *see* Cluricaune.

Cluricanes (Celtic)
Depicted as wrinkled, old men, these elves are known for their knowledge of hidden treasure. *See also* Dulachan; Elves.

Cluricaune *Cluracan* (Celtic, Irish)
Wine deity. Cluricaune is similar to the Leprechaun, but is

associated with the caring of wine or beer barrels. He is also a shoemaker like the Leprechaun. *See also* Leprechaun.

Clutoida (Celtic) Goddess of the river Clyde. *See also* Sequana.

Clymene (A) (Greek)
She is the daughter of the extremely wealthy Minyas. *See also* Alcimede; Atalanta; Cephalus; Periclymene.

Clymene (B) (Greek)
Her parents are Oceanus and Tethys. She married Iapetos and became the mother of Atlas, Epimetheus, Monoetius and Prometheus. *See also* Epimetheus; Heliades; Minyas; Oceanids; Oceanus; Phaethon; Tethys; Themis.

Clymene (C) (Greek) She is one of the fifty daughters of Nereus and Doris known as the Nereids. *See also* Doris; Nereids; Nereus.

Clymene (D) (Greek) Catreus, the king of Crete, is her father. Her siblings are Aerope, Althaemenes and Apemosyne. *See also* Aerope; Catreus.

Clymenus (A) (Greek) He is the father of Eurydice. *See also* Eurydice (C).

Clymenus (B) (Greek) His father is Aeneas, king of Calydon.

Clymenus (C) (Greek)
King of Olympia. Fifty years after the flood, he went to Crete. Clymenus restored the Olympic Games.

Clymenus (D) (Greek) King of Arcadia.

Clymenus (E) (Greek)
King of Boeotian Orchomenus. His father is Presbon. Clymenus was killed in a fight with the Thebans. His death was avenged by his son, Erginus.

Clytemnestra (Greek) *see* Aegisthus; Cassandra; Helen; Leda.

Clytia *Clytie* (Greek)
Clytia, an Oceanid, is one of the three thousand daughters and three thousand sons of Oceanus and Tethys. She was the spiteful lover of the sun god Helius who informed King Orchamus of Persia, the father of Leucothoe, that the sun god was sleeping with his daughter. He punished her by burying her alive. The rejected Clytia withered away and became a flower, the heliotrope. In another myth, Clytia was the devoted lover of Apollo. Whenever the god would abandon her she would transform herself into a heliotrope. Heliotropes turn their heads to follow the journey of the sun through the sky each day. *See also* Apollo; Helius; Hyacintos; Oceanids.

Clytie (Greek)
Another name for Merope, the daughter of Pandareus and Harmothoe.

Clytius (Greek) *see* Giants; Hesione.

Cmok (Slavic) *see* Zmek.

Coatepec (Aztec People, Mexico)
"Serpent Mountain." The dwelling place of Coatlicue (q.v.).

Coatlicue *Couatlicue* (Aztec People, Mexico)
Also known as: *Tlazoltoeotl, Tonantzin, Serpent Lady* (sometimes called this name), *Serpent Petticoated, Serpent Skirt.*
"Serpent Skirt." Mother goddess. Earth goddess. She is the mother of a daughter, Coyolxauhqui, and four hundred sons known as the Centzon Huitznahuas. Coatlicue is one of the spouses of Mixcoatl. One day, when she was sweeping, a ball of feathers fell into her bosom. She became pregnant. Her four hundred sons and her daughter were so outraged they decided to murder her. As they were about to put Coatlicue to death, the new child Huitzilopochtli came out of his mother's womb, fully clad in armor. He killed both his sister and brothers with a serpent weapon called Xiuhcoatl. It is said that a few of his brothers escaped to Uitzlampa "Place of Thorns" in the south. Coatlicue's dwelling was on Coatepec mountain. She is presented as the crocodile Cipactli or as a giant frog. *See also* Centzon Huitznahuas; Chicomecoatl; Legend of the Four Suns.

Coatrischie (Haiti)
Hurricane goddess. *See also* Atabei; Guabancex.

Cocalus (Greek) *see* Minos.

Cocidius (British)
Also known as: *Alator, Albiorix* (Celtic), *Belatucador, Camulus, Condates, Coritiacus, Loucetius, Rigisamos* (Celtic), *Totates.*
War god. Cocidius was also worshiped under the above names. He is identified with Mars.

Cockatoo Man (Australia) *see* Mars.

Cocytus *Kokytus* (Greek)
Also known as: *The Wailing River.*
River god. As a river god, Cocytus is one of the three thousand sons (the Rivers) and three thousand daughters (the Oceanids) of Oceanus and Tethys. He is said to be the father of Menthe, who was discovered in a compromising situation with Aides, the son of Cronus and Rhea and she was changed into a mint plant by the jealous goddess Persephone. As a river, the Cocytus is a tributary of the river of sadness, the Acheron, in Epirus. The echoes of unburied souls are doomed to wander along the banks of the Cocytus wailing and groaning for one hundred years after death. If properly buried and with the correct fare, dead souls are allowed to board the boat of the ancient boatman Charon, who will ferry them across the river. The other rivers of the Underworld are the Phlegethon (river of fire), Lethe (river of forgetfulness) and Styx (river of the unbreakable oath). To compare to other river gods, *see* Achelous; Acheron; Alpheus; Asopus; Cephissus; Charon; Cronus; Erebus; Hades; Inachus; Lethe; Oceanids; Rivers; Styx; Tartarus. *See also* Cronus; Persephone; Rhea.

Coeculus (Greek, Roman) *see* Cacus.

Coelus (Greek) *see* Uranus.

Coem (Tupi-Guarani People, Brazil) *see* Hermitten.

Coeranus (Greek) *see* Abas (B).

Coeus (Greek) *see* Ceos.

Cogaz (Bushman, Hottentot People, Africa)
The son of Cagn and brother of Gewi, he is possibly a creator deity. *See also* Cagn.

Colhuacan (Aztec People, Mexico)
Emergence myths. *See also* Chicomoztoc.

Colhuatzincatl (Aztec People, Mexico)
One of the pulque gods, Colhuatzincatl is the son of Cinteotl. He is associated with the Centzon Totochtin. *See also* Patecatl.

Colla (Inca People, Peru) *see* Ayar Aucca; Manco Capac, Tahuantin Suyu Kapac.

Colossus of Rhodes (Greek) *see* Helius.

Comana (Greek) This is another name for Chryse (q.v.).

Combalus (Syrian)
God of vegetation. Knowing of his inevitable death and of his trip to the underworld, he rejected his earth goddess and castrated himself for the redemption of mortals.

Cometes (Greek)
He is the son of Sthenelus, brother of the king of Argos, Cylarabes, husband of Antigone, and father of Asterion. He committed adultery with Diomedes' wife, Aegialeia. *See also* Asterion; Diomedes; Sthenelus.

Comus *see* Bacchus; Circe.

Con (Inca People, Peru) *see* Coniraya.

Con Ticci Viracocha (Inca People, Peru) *see* Virococha.

Con Ticci Viracocha Pachayachachic (Inca People, Peru) *see* Virocorocha.

Conaire, King (Celtic) *see* Dagda.

Conchean (Celtic) *see* Aed.

Conchobar, King (Celtic) *see* Clothru; Cuchulain; Dech'tire.

Confucius (China, Japan)
Also known as: *Chi-Sheng Sien-Shi, Wen Chung.*
Deified mortal. Although much debate still reigns as to whether Confucius is considered a god and worshiped as such, the fact is that most think he was a mortal. His religion (Confucianism, Fu Chiao) is that of the learned and is generally associated with scholars and officials. He is the grandfather of Tsi-si. According to some history Confucius was born in 551 B.C.E. and died in 479 B.C.E. Confucius is usually shown seated and wearing imperial costume. He is said to be a reincarnation of Wen Chung (q.v.).

Coniraya (Inca People, Peru)
Also known as: *Coniraya Viracocha.*
Supreme being. Creator of all things. Responsible for irrigation, and terracing the fields. Coniraya came to earth dressed in ripped and torn rags, like a begger. He was scorned by everyone. He came upon Cavillaca, a beautiful young virgin goddess. She was sitting under a lucma tree. Coniraya turned himself into a bird, fashioned his sperm in the likeness of the lumca tree's fruit and watched her eat it. She became pregnant and

had a child. When the child was a year old she found out that the ragged Coniraya was the father. She was so full of shame and so angry that she took the child and ran off to the sea coast. When they arrived, mother and child walked into the water and became rocks. Coniraya went in search of Cavillaca and the child. Along the way, he encountered many adventures. When he finally reached the coast he found that they had turned to stone. While there he met Pachacamac's two daughters. He had sex with the eldest and then attempted to bed the younger woman. She apparently was not interested for she turned into a pigeon and flew away. Coniraya was so furious he took Urpihuachacs a few fish, which were the only fish in existence. He threw them into the sea. That is how fish came to populate the waters. *See also* Pachacamac; Viracocha.

Conopa (Inca People, Peru)
Also known as: *Huasi-Camayoc.*
Household deities. Little information is available about the Conopa. We do know that several thousand of these idols were destroyed by the Spaniards. *See also* Lars.

Consus (Roman)
Grain deity. Earth deity (possibly). Information is sparse regarding Consus. He is worshiped in the same month as Ops.

Coon (Greek) *see* Acamas (B).

Copacati (Inca People, Peru)
This lake goddess would not tolerate worship to other deities. She was known to have toppled temples or submerged them under the waters of Lake Titicaca. This lake is a few miles from the ruins at Tiahuanaco. With Mama Cocha, Copacati was a mother goddess of the lake. *See also* Mama Cocha.

Copreus (Greek) *see* Pelops.

Coqui-Xee (Mixtec People, Mexico)
Also known as: *Coqui-Cilla, Piye-Tao, Zapotec Quetzalcoatl.*
Creator deity. He is the creator of all things but himself uncreated. The Mixtec people were his first creation, followed by Cozaana, the deer god and Huichaana, the deer goddess. *See also* Mixcoatl.

Corb (Celtic) He is a god of the Fomonians (q.v.).

Corcyra (Greek) *see* Asopus.

Core (Greek) *see* Kore; Persephone.

Cori Ocllo (Inca) *see* Tahuantin Suyu Kapac.

Cornucopia *Cornu Copiae* (Greek)
Horn of Plenty. Under the secret care of the nymphs, the infant Zeus was suckled by the goat Amaltheia, whose horn he gave to the nymphs, endowing it with the power to be filled with whatever its possessor wished. According to another tradition, the cornucopia is Achelous' or Amalthea's broken horn which was filled with fruits and flowers by the Naiads. *See also* Achelous, Amaltheia.

Corona Borealis (Greek) *see* Ariadne.

Coronis (A) (Greek)
She is the Thessalian princess daughter of the king of

Orchomenus, Phlegyas, and the possible sister of Ixion, the King of the Lapiths of Thessaly. Apollo and Coronis had an affair that produced the great healer, Asclepius. Sometime later, she was unfaithful. As she prepared to marry Ischys, she was killed by Apollo or Artemis. See also Apollo; Artemis; Asclepius; Ischys.

Coronis (B) (Greek)
Coronis, the daughter of Coroneus of Phocis, was loved by Poseidon. Athena changed her into a white crow. After taking bad news to Athena, she was turned into a black crow by the fiery goddess.

Coronis (C) (Greek) She is the daughter of Ares.

Coronis (D) (Greek)
One of the Hyades, she is the daughter of Atlas and Pleione. See also Hyades.

Coronus (A) (Greek)
The son of Apollo and Chrysorthe, he was the king of Sicyon until Epopeus, the son of Poseidon and Canace, deposed him. See also Antiope; Epopeus.

Coronus (B) (Greek)
An Argonaut and leader of the Lapiths, Coronus, the son of Caeneus and father of Leonteus and Lyside, was killed by Heracles.

Corus (Greek)
Weather god. Known as the northwest wind, Corus is the son of Aeolus and Aurora. Wherever he goes, he drives clouds of snow before him. His five brothers are Aquilo, Boreas, Eurus, Notus and Zephyrus. See the individual entries for information about these brothers. See also Aeolus.

Corybantes Korybantes, Kurbantes (Phrygian)
Also known as: Curetes; Galli.
Known as the crested dancers and sometimes called divine, the priests, known as Corybantes, worship the Phrygian goddess Cybele in wild frenzied dances during which they clash spears and shields. They are thought to be the children of Apollo and Thalia or Athena, Zeus and Calliope, or Corybas or Cronus and Rhea. Ovid calls them people born of rainwater. The Corybantes rites are similar to the Satyrs who attend Dionysus. See also Adrastia; Curetes; Cybele; Helius; Rhea; Satyrs.

Corybas (Greek) see Corybantes; Cybele.

Corynetes (Greek) Another name for Periphetes (q.v.).

Cosmocrator (Gnostic) The devil.

Cosmology of Assur (Sumerian)
A myth that mentions the birth of the first two ancestors of mankind, Ulligarra and Zalgarra, from the blood of the gods known as Lamga.

Coti (Hottentot People, Africa) Another name for Cagn (q.v.).

Cottus Cotus, Cottys, Kottos (Greek)
Nature deity. One of three brothers known as the Hecatonchires. They fought on the side of Zeus in the war with the Titans. They each have fifty heads and a hundred hands. See also Aegaeon; Gaea; Hecatonchires; Titans.

Cottys (Greek) see Cottus; Hecatonchires.

Cotus (Greek) see Cottus; Hecatonchires.

Cotzbalam (Maya People of Yucatan)
Demon. The gods, dissatisfied with the men they had created with various materials, destroyed them by a flood. Cotzbalam assisted by devouring their flesh. See also Camalotz; Xecotcovach.

Couatlicue (Mexico) see Coatlicue.

Couretes (Greek) see Curetes.

Coventina (Celtic) Covetina (British)
Goddess of springs and waters. This water goddess is depicted holding a goblet in one hand as she lies comfortably on a leaf that floats on the water.

Covetina (British) see Coventina.

Coxcos (Aztec People, Mexico) see Coxcoxtli.

Coxcox Cox-cox (Aztec People, Mexico) see Coxcoxtli.

Coxcoxtli Coxcos, Cox-cox, Coxcox, Kox (Aztec People, Mexico)
Also known as: Teo-Kipaktli, Tezcatlipoca.
First man, survivor of flood. Husband of Xochiquetzal. The Aztec Noah. Some say their names were Nala (male) and Nina (female) or Nata and Nana. They escaped the flood (in a hollowed out tree) that destroyed all mankind and lived on the mountain, Colhuacan. Their children, who were dumb, were given speech by a dove but could not understand each other because all the languages were different. See also Cipactonal. This tale is similar to that of Nata and Nana (qq.v.). Associated with Tezcatlipoca, Citlallatonac and Citlalicue. See also Xochiquetzal.

Coyolxauhqui (Aztec People, Mexico)
Also known as: Golden Bells, Tecciztecatl (god of the moon).
Moon Goddess. She is the only daughter of Coatlicue. Her four hundred brothers are the Centzon Huitznahuas. With her brothers, she plotted to murder her mother who had been divinely impregnated with Huitzilopochtli. He emerged from his mother's womb fully dressed in battle gear, intent upon revenge. Coyolxauhqui was decapitated, and he threw her head to the sky where it became the moon. Some say her death was an accident, then in remorse he cut off her head. Huitzilopochtli killed most of his four hundred brothers. Coyolxauhqui replaced the moon god, Tecciztecatl. See also Centzon Huitznahuas; Coatlicue; Huitzilopochtli; Meztli; Tecciztecatl; Yohualticitl.

Coyote (Native North Americans)
Also known as: Ola'li (Maidu People, N.A.), Sedit (Wintun people), Ueuecoyotl (Aztec People, Mexico).
Coyote appears with many faces. He can be a creator or a teacher of the people. In some myths, Coyote is a cunning and creative trickster god, or folk-hero. He can appear with both attributes in the same story. Coyote is worshiped by numerous Indian People. He may be a god of dancers. In one myth, he

created the earth and all living creatures. He built a boat in which he drifted while the earth was covered with water. He then told two ducks to dive and bring back mud. One duck did not return, the other did what he was told. Coyote created earth from this mud. Sihu, the elder brother of Coyote, is identified with Montezuma. In a Maidu myth, Ola'li came out of the ground with his dog Kaudi (So'lla) or Rattlesnake. In legends of the Achomawi People of California, their creator emerged from a small cloud. The creator was assisted by Coyote who emerged from a mist over the land. The Zuni people say that Coyote taught them to live in peace. The Chemchuevi tell of Coyote and Puma creating man. The Crow people credit Coyote and his brother Cirape for creating the earth and everything on it. In the mythology of the Navaho, man and woman lived in the first world which was too small. They moved up to the second world, left it and went to the third world. This world was the home of the water monster Tieholtsodi. Coyote kidnapped the monster's children. Tieholtsodi retaliated by flooding the world. Coyote, the first man, and the first woman went up to the fourth world. The water monster followed them. They moved on to the fifth world which is our present world. Coyote finally returned Tieholtsodi's children. After death, people returned to the fourth world. The Poma People call Coyote the younger brother of the creator god, Madumda. Coyote is similar to Xolotl of the ancient Mexican people. *See also* Cirape; Italapas; Olle; Ueuecoyotl.

Cranaus (Greek) *see* Cronus.

Crantaeis (Greek) *see* Hecate.

Crataeis (Greek) *see* Phorcys; Scylla.

Cratus (Greek) *see* Styx.

Credne *Creidne, Creidhne* (Celtic)
God of Artificers and Braziers. Credne is a Tuatha De Danann, an ancient race of gods. One of the triad of divine craft-smith gods, his specialty was metal work. With his companions, Goibniu and Luchta (also known as Luchtaine), they forged the weapons used by the Tuatha De Dananns in the war known as the First Battle of Magh Tuiredh, against the evil Fomorians. Their weapons came with the guarantee that whomever was wounded by them would not survive. Credne also assisted the divine physician, Dia'necht, in forging an artificial hand for king Nuada. The Celts held the smiths in high esteem, as they were thought to possess magical abilities to heal through charms, spells and the implements they produced. These implements, weapons, ploughs and utensils were vitally important to their existence (not to be confused with Creidne, an Irish female warrior). Compare with the Greek metal workers, Dactyli. *See also* Dia'necht; Goibniu; Hephaistos; Tuatha De Danann.

Cree People, Canada — Creation Legend *see* Wisagatcak.

Creiddylad (Celtic)
Another name for Creudilad (q.v.). *See also* Llyr.

Creidhne (Irish) *see* Credne.

Creidiylad (British, Irish) *see* Creudilad.

Creidne (Irish) *see* Credne.

Creirwy (Celtic)
She is the beautiful daughter of Keridwen and sister of an extremely ugly brother Avagdu. *See also* Keridwen.

Crenae (Greek) *see* Naiads.

Creon (Greek) *see* Adrestus; Antigone; Ares; Eurydice (C).

Creseusa (Greek) *see* Creusa (A); Glauce.

Cresphontes (Greek) *see* Aepytus.

Cressida (Greek) *see* Calchas.

Crete (Greek) *see* Europa.

Cretheus (Greek)
He is the founder and first king of Iolcus. His parents are Aeolus and Enarete. He has six brothers and seven sisters (for a list of their names *see* Canace). His first marriage was to Sidero, his second to Tyro and the third to either Demodice or Biadice. *See also* Aeolus (A); Aegimius; Enaret; Tyro.

Creudilad *Creiddylad, Creidiylad, Creudylad* (British, Irish)
Goddess of spring. Part of a trio with Gwyn (sun god) and Gwyrthur (underworld god). She is the daughter of Llud, or some say Llyr. *See also* Gwinn.

Creudylad (British, Irish) *see* Creudilad.

Creusa (Greek)
There are numerous references to the name Creusa in Greek mythology. See the following entries.

Creusa (A)
Also known as: *Creseusa.*
Creusa and Glauce burned to death with her father Creon. *See also* Danaus; Glauce; Jason; Medea.

Creusa (B) A Nereid. *See also* Nereids.

Creusa (C) A Danaide. *See also* Aeneas; Danaides.

Creusa (D) A Naiad. *See also* Naiads.

Creusa (E)
Daughter of Priam and Hecuba, captured by the Greeks, rescued and disappeared. *See also* Hecuba; Priam.

Creusa (F)
Daughter of Erechtheus, married Xuthus, raped by Apollo and gave birth to Janus. *See also* Janus.

Creusa (G)
May be the mother of Telamon. *See also* Creusa (A); Danaus; Medea; Telamon.

Criasus (Greek)
His parents are Argus and Evadne. *See also* Argus (A); Evadne.

Crimisus (Greek)
River god. He is the son of Oceanus and Tethys. His spouse is Egesta, the daughter of Hippotes, and his son, Acestes. *See also* Acestes; Oceanus; Rivers; Tethys.

Crino (Greek)

She is the daughter of Antenor, the Trojan prophet, and Theano, who is the priestess of Athena at Troy. *See also* Acamas (B).

Crius *Crios* (Greek)

Crius was the Titan son of Uranus and Gaea and sibling of Thaumas, Phorcys, Ceto, Eurybia and Nereus. He married his sister Eurybia and was the father of Astraeus, Pallas and Perses. *See also* Cronus; Eurynome (A); Gaea; Nereus; Oceanus; Phorcys; Pontus; Styx.

Crnobog (Slavic)

Also known as: *Crnoglav.*

Underworld deity. The black god of the dead.

Crnoglav (Slavic) *see* Crnobog.

Crocodile (Egypt) (Greek) *see* Centipede; Helios; Horus; Suchos.

Crom-Eocha (Celtic) *see* Dagda.

Crommyonian Sow (Greek)

Also known as: *Phaea.*

The daughter of Typhon and Echidna, this feral sow raped the Corinth countryside. She is possibly the mother of the Calydonian Boar. She eventually died at the hand of the hero Theseus, the king of Athens. *See also* Calydonian Boar; Cerberus; Chimaera; Hydra; Typhon; Vultures.

Cronos (Greek) *see* Cronus.

Cronus *Chronos, Cranaus, Cronos, Khronos, Kronos* (Greek)

Also known as: *Saturn, Saturnus* (Roman).

God of the World. God of Time. High God. Harvest God. A Titan, Cronus is the son of Uranus, who personifies the Sky, and Gaea, the Earth. He is the father, by his sister, Rhea (who is known as the mother of the gods), of Zeus, Poseidon, Hades, Hestia, Demeter, and Hera. Some versions give him eleven brothers and sisters: Oceanus, Coeus, Crius, Hyperion, Iapetus, Theia, Rhea, Themis, Mnemosyne, Phoebe, and Tethys. He was also the possible father of the Centaur, Cheiron, by Philyra. Encouraged by his mother, he overthrew and castrated his father. From this point, the heavens and earth (creation) continued to develop separately. Cronus, now the supreme ruler, released his brothers, the Titans, with the exception of the Hecatoncheires and the Cyclopes. Next, he swallowed his offspring to prevent his sons from overthrowing him. His wife, Rhea, however, hid the young Zeus from him. When he was older, Zeus rebelled and Cronus was induced to vomit up his other children, who joined with Zeus in a war against their father and some of his Titan colleagues. Zeus also released the Hecatoncheires and the Cyclopes, flung his father and friends into Tartarus, the lowest realm of the Underworld, where the Hecatoncheires guarded them. With this act, the era of the Olympians began, followed by the war of the Olympians against the Titans. Another tradition calls the rule of Cronus the "Golden Age," where death did not exist and all mortals lived like gods. When his reign in Olympus ceased, he went on to become king on the Islands of the Blessed where mortals, favored by the gods went at death. Some believe he was a deified king who had a son named Anobret, whom he sacrificed and he

also may have had a son named Aides. The Orphics said that Aether and Chaos sprang from Cronus as Time. In the Pelasgian creation myth, Cronus is coupled with Rhea as the rulers for the planet Saturn. For the development of the heavens during this period, *see* Nox. Sometimes he is identified with the Egyptian god Geb. Compare to Agni (India). Compare to Indra (India). *See also* Adrastia; Ceos; Cocytus; Corybantes; Curetes; Eumenides; Eurynome (A); Gaea; Hecatoncheires; Hestia; Nut; Oceanus; Rhea; Styx; Telchines; Zeus.

Crow (Tlingit People, North American)

By beating his wings, Crow created dry land. He also gave light or fire. Compare to Coyote.

Cteatus (Greek)

He is the son of Actor or Poseidon and Molione. With his twin Eurytus (they are possibly Siamese twins), they are known as the Molionides. *See also* Actor (B).

Cu (Celtic)

He is the son of the god of medicine, Dia'necht (q.v.).

Cu Chulain (Celtic) *see* Cuchulain.

Cuchavira *Chuchaviva* (Chibcha People, Bogota, South America)

Also known as: *The Rainbow.*

God of air. Part of the Bochica mythology. He was master of the air and rainbow and healer deity. He protected women in childbirth. He was not greatly respected since he was also a god of drunkenness and a protector of drunkards. He is possibly the same as Nencatacoa (q.v.). *See also* Bochica.

Cuchaviva (South America) *see* Bochica; Chia.

Cuchu'lainn (Celtic) *see* Cuchulain.

Cuchu'linn (Celtic) *see* Cuchulain.

Cuchulain *Chuchulain, Cu Chulain, Cuchu'lainn, Cuchulainn, Cuchu'linn, Cuchullin, Culain, Culann, Koo-chul-inn* (Celtic)

Also known as: *Setanta, Hound of Chulain, Watchdog of Chulain.*

God of heat and light. He is the son of Lugh, the sun god, and the mortal woman Dech'tire, who was the wife of the prophet Sualtim (also said to be of virgin birth) and the sister of King Conchobar of Ulster. He is the spouse of Emer. Cuchulain is immune to most magic spells. The witch Scatbvach, "Queen of Darkness," taught him magic. He was known throughout Ireland as a fearless warrior and a great lover. He received his name when he killed the watchdog of Conchobor, and offered to take the dog's place. One version of his birth says he was born three times, and is sometimes shown with three heads. Fergus and Cathbad taught him wisdom, courage, and warfare. Amergin prepared him for his special role in society, then Scatbvach taught him sorcery. Cuchulain has seven pupils in each eye, seven fingers on each hand and seven toes on each foot. His hair is three colors and he wears a lot of jewelry. In battle he changes shape drastically; his feet and knees are to his rear and his calves and buttocks to the front. His hair stands on end and on the tip of each strand was a spot of blood or a spark of fire. His mouth spews fire and a long stream of black blood shoots up from his head. One eye is pushed to the rear of his skull and the other sits on his cheek. On his forehead there is a marking known as the "hero's moon." In this stage he cannot be contained and has to be doused in three tubs of cold water to keep him quiet. *See also* Amergin; Blathnat; Curoi Mac Daire; Dechter; Dech'tire; Devorgilla; Fand; Lugh; Manannan Mac Llyr; Morrigu.

Cuculcan (Mexico) *see* Kukulcan.

Culain (Celtic) *see* Cuchulain.

Culann (Celtic) *see* Cuchulain.

Cupara (Jivaro Indian People, Andes, South America)

Parents of the sun, Cupara and his spouse made the moon from mud. The moon became the wife of the sun. Their children were the animals and the tropical plant manioc. The ancestor of the tribe was the sloth.

Cupid *Cupido* (Roman) *see* Amor; Brigit; Eros.

Cupra (Etruscan)

An ancient goddess of fertility, she formed a triad with the fire god Tina and the goddess of wisdom, Minerva. Her weapon is the thunderbolt. *See also* Juno; Minerva; Tina.

Curche (Slavic) *see* Kurke.

Curetes *Couretes, Kouretes* (Greek, the aborigines of Aetolis)

Also known as: *Corybantes, Gegeneis* (children of the earth), *Imbrogeneis* (children of the rain), *Korubantes, Korybantes.*

The origins of the Curetes varies. They are said to be the children of Poseidon and Thalassa or Hecaterus and a daughter of Phoroneus. It is also thought that they might be descendants of Hephaestus, or descendants of the Semites or the most ancient people of Crete. One of their functions was to create a great deal of noise so Cronus would not hear the cries of the infant Zeus (the child Kouros) when Rhea gave birth in Crete. In one version, Hera ordered Zeus to put the Curetes to death for hiding his son by Eo, Epaphus. Some say they were priests attached to the worship of Cybele. An inscription was found in Crete, at Palaiokastro, containing the "Hymn of the Curetes," in honor of Zeus. The uproar made by Curetes, with their dancing, clashing of cymbals and swords in the Corybantic and Dactylic worship is similar to the "devil scaring" techniques practiced by the Chinese and other races in attempts to drive away the powers of evil by making noise. Other references state that the Curetes were the sacred king's armed companions. The Greek interpretation was "young men who have shaved their hair." At an annual feast called Comyria, the Curetes shaved their hair to honor Car, the solar king whose hair was shorn annually before his death. In this context they were known as Corybantes. This custom might be of Libyan origin. They are associated with Castor and Pollux, and the Corybantes. Dardunus founded a college of Salian priests who performed the same rites as the Cretan Curetes. Compare the Curetes to the Vedic Maruts. *See also* Adrastia; Althea; Apollo; Artemis; Calydonian Boar Hunt; Car; Cybele; Satyrs; Telechines.

Curicaveri (Tarascan People, Mexico) *see* Camaxtli; Huitzilopochtli.

Curoi Mac Daire (Celtic, Irish)

Curoi was a the King of Munster, and a priest of the sun god. He married King Mider's daughter, Blathnat. He was entrusted with guarding Mider's magic cauldron. His wife assisted Cuchulain in stealing it from him. When the Tuatha de Danann were defeated, Curoi was killed by Cuchulain, who became his successor. *See also* Blathnat; Cuchulain; Mider; Tuatha de Danann.

Curupira *Korupira* (Brazil)

This forest demon is known for his mischief making and his love for tobacco. A guardian spirit of the woods, he assists hunters in their search for game. Curupira has one eye, large ears and is bald. He rides a pig or a deer.

Cusco Huanca (Inca People, Peru) *see* Tahuantin Suyu Kapac.

Cuycha (Inca People, Peru)

A rainbow deity, Cuycha is one of Mama Quilla's attendants. Cuycha is associated with Catequil.

Cuzco (Inca People, Peru)

Sacred City. Originally Cuzco was thought to be the center of the earth. It was sought by the legendary family migrating to the east in prehistoric times. Cuzco is the home of Manco-Capak and his sister Mama Occlo.

Cyane (A) (Greek) She is the wife of Aeolus. Her six sons and six daughters married each other. *See also* Aeolus (B).

Cyane (B) (Greek)

Assaulted by her father, this nymph then offered him as an altar sacrifice.

Cyane (C) (Greek)

After attempting to halt the kidnapping of Persephone, this nymph was turned into a fountain by Hades. *See also* Hades; Persephone.

Cyanippus (Greek)

He was the king of Argos. His parents are Adrastus, who was the king of Argos, and his niece Amphithea. His siblings are Aegialeus, Aegialeia, Argeia, Deipyle, and possibly Cyanippus and Hippodameia. *See also* Adrastus; Amphithea; Apsyrtus.

Cyavana (India) *see* Bhrigus; Mada.

Cybebe (Greek) *see* Cybele.

Cybele *Cybebe, Cybelle, Kubele, Kybele* (Greek, Phrygian)

(Asia Minor, known as "Great Mother," then to Greece and Rome. Cybele may be derived from the Semitic Gebaliah [goddess of Gebal].)

Also known as: *Agdistis, Berecyntia* (Gaul), *Dindymene, Dindymus, Ma, Magna Mater* (Roman), *Mater Turrita* (Roman), *Ops, Rhea.*

Earth goddess. Healer. Builder of cities. Protector during war. Cybele was a fertility goddess and goddess of caverns, worshipped as mother of the gods in Phrygia and Asia Minor. Worship of Cybele traveled to Greece and Rome. If Cybele began life as Agdistis, her father was Zeus and she was born of the rock Agdos. Or, she could have been the daughter of Uranus and Gaea, or Meion and Dindyme. Cybele was the mother of King Midas by Gordius, king of Phrygia (Gordius of the knot fame) and may also have been the mother of Sabazius (Dionysus). Her great love was for Attis (Atys) and she was possibly the mother of Corybas (later identified with the Corybantes) and Sabazius. She made a pact with Attis to remain celibate. He broke the pact and to satisfy the terms of his agreement he had to castrate himself. When Attis died, Cybele transformed him into a pine tree. She conducted her mourning period under the tree and all growth stopped on the earth. Zeus promised her that the tree would always remain green (evergreen). In another version, Zeus, jealous of Attis' relationship with Cybele, sends wild boars to rip the handsome young man to pieces. Cybele's priests, all castrated in her honor or in honor of Attis, were known as the Galli. Cybele was a healer, a protector and she offered immortality to her devotees. Eventually Cybele and the goddess Rhea merged. She wore a turreted crown to signify that she was a war goddess and founder of cities. She was attended by the Corybantes and rode in a chariot pulled by lions; sometimes she held a whip. She was also associated with bees. As Cybele Phrygia, she bears branches in her hands and was associated with a sacred column. Cybele is identified with Rhea, Demeter, and Bona Dea. Cybele's legends are the same as the mythology attached to the Phoenician mother-goddess Astronoe. Compare Cybele and Attis to Inanna and Dumuzi, Ishtar and Tammuz. *See also* Agdistis; Arinna; Atalanta; Attis; Corybantes; Curetes; Midas; Rhea; Sabazius.

Cybelle (Greek) *see* Cybele.

Cyclopes *Cyclops, Ky-klopes, Kyklopes; Kyklops* (Greek)
Storm or volcano deities. The Cyclopes are the one-eyed giant children of Uranus and Gaea. Their names are Brontes, who personifies Thunder; Steropes, who personifies Lightning; Arges (who is also known as Acmonides and Pyracmon), who personifies sheet lightning. Hesiod and Homer include Acamas, Polyphemus and Pyracmon as Cyclopes. The first Cyclopes were subterranean divinities or fire genii and were assistants of Hephaistos. They were the ones who manufactured the thunderbolts for Zeus, since they were the only ones who knew the process. They helped Vulcan make the thunderbolts for him, the darts for Cupid, the trident for Poseidon, a bronze helmet for Hades, and a shield for Achilles. It was Homer who changed them in his "Odyssey." Then they became the familiar evil one-eyed giants. They were reported to live on the Island of Sicily. The most famous of these ugly creatures was Polyphemus, who loved Galatea, and who killed Acis. The Cyclopes were in turn killed by Apollo in vengeance for the death of his son Asclepius. The Cyclopes are giants with one eye centered in the forehead. Later the Cyclopes were replaced by the Caberi (q.v.). *See also* Acamas (D); Acis; Aegaeon; Cronus; Gaea; Galatea; Hecatonchires; Hephaistos; Titans.

Cydon (Greek)
He is the son of Hermes or Tegeates and Acacallis, the daughter of Minos and Pasiphae. *See also* Acacallis.

Cyena *Cyene* (India) *see* Garuda.

Cygnus (Greek)
He is the son of Ares and Pelopia or Pyrene. Cygnus wounded Heracles and Heracles killed him and turned him into a swan. *See also* Ares.

Cyhiraeth (Celtic)
Originally, she was a goddess of streams. Later, she became a spirit who haunts brooks. Her mysterious cry foretells death.

Cymodoce (Greek)
She is one of the fifty daughters known as Nereids, of Nereus and Doris. *See also* Nereids.

Cymothoe (Greek)
One of the fifty daughters, known as Nereids, of Nereus and Doris. *See also* Nereids.

Cynosura (Greek)
A nursemaid to the infant Zeus, this nymph of Mount Ida became the star, Ursa Minor. *See also* Zeus.

Cynthia (Roman)
Also known as: *Diana.*
As Cynthia, she is the goddess of the moon. *See also* Artemis; Diana.

Cynthius (Greek)
Also known as: *Apollo*
This epithet of Apollo was given because he was born on Mount Cynthius on the island of Delos. Diana was also born in the same place. *See also* Apollo.

Cyrene (Greek)
Cyrene, a nymph, became the queen of Libya after she killed a violent lion. She is the daughter of Hypseus and Chilidanope. By Apollo, she became the mother of Aristaeus and Autychus. By Apollo or Abas, she is the mother of Abas. Ares is her son by Diomedes. *See also* Ares; Aristaeus.

Cythera *Cythereia* (Greek) An epithet of Aphrodite (q.v.).

Cytissorus (Greek)
Cytissorus helped the Argonauts capture the Golden Fleece and assisted them in their escape from Colchis. *See also* Golden Fleece; Phrixus.

Czarnobog (Slavic) *see* Chernobog.

D

Da (Dahomey People, Africa; Tibet)
Also known as: *Dab-Iha.*
Little known Serpent.

Da-Bog (Slavic) *see* Dazbog.

Daauke (Assyro-Babylonia) *see* Damkina.

Dab-Iha (Africa; Tibet) *see* Da.

Dabaiba (Inca People, Peru)
The "Mother of Creation."

Dabog (Slavic) *see* Dazbog.

Dactls (Greek) *see* Dactyli.

Dactyli *Dactls, Dactyls, Daktuloi* (Greek)
Giant gods of metallurgy. Their name means "fingers." It is thought that there were three Dactyli originally. Their individual names are Acmon, Celmis, and Damnameneus. Over the years, the number of Dactyli has ranged from three to thirty-two. Fire and the forging of copper and iron were introduced to Crete by the Dactyli. In one of the Dactyli-related myths, they came from the earth when Rhea dug her fingers into the ground while giving birth to Zeus. Other reports state that they are the servants of Rhea, and that they live at the foot of Mount Ida. Some versions say they are metal workers of Hephaistos, who taught mortals how to work metals, the use of arithmetic, and letters of the alphabet. They are also known as the ten children of Rhea or Anchiale, a nymph. Yet in other tales, there are thirty-two Dactyli, all magicians. Others say that the Dactyli are five in number. As five Dactyli they are thought of as the five fingers: Heracles (thumb), Aeonius (forefinger), Epimedes (middle finger), Jasius, (ring or healing finger), Idas (little finger). There are similarities to the Telchines and to the Cyclopes (qq.v.). Compare to Irish metal workers, Cabiri, and Credne. *See also* Hephaistos; Rhea.

Dada (Yoruba People, Africa)
She is the goddess of the brain and senses. *See also* Olodumare.

Dadu (Middle Eastern) *see* Adad; Bir; Birqu; Rammanu.

Dadzbog (Slavic) *see* Dazbog.

Dae-Soon (Korea)
Moon goddess.

Daedalion (Greek)
When his father, Chione, committed suicide, Apollo changed Daedalion into a hawk. *See also* Acacallis; Chione.

Daedalus (Greek)
Deified mortal. Inventor. Builder of the Labyrinth. A brilliant inventor, Daedalus is the son of Metion or Eupalamus and Alcippe or Merope. His son is Icarus. Jealous of the talents of his nephew Talos, he murdered him. Exiled from Athens, he fled to Cnossus where he built the Labyrinth for the Minotaur. Father and son were confined within the maze. They made wings of wax and feathers to fly to safety, but Icarus flew so high, and came so close to the sun that his wings melted and he fell to his death. Daedalus fled to Sicily and sought refuge with Cocalus, the king of Camicus. In some versions, Daedalus murdered Perdix because of jealousy, since Perdix invented the saw. Daedalus also created a false bull which mated with the moon goddess, Pasiphae, the wife of Minos, the king of Phrygia. It was this union that created the Minotaur. Daedalus also invented the axe, the level, and sails for ships. *See also* Ariadne; Icarus; Labyrinth, Minos; Minotaur; Pasiphae; Perdix.

Daemon *Daemons and Daimones* (Plural); *Daimon* (Roman)
Also known as: *Demons.*
Personal spirits, both good and evil. In some traditions, daemons are thought to be the energy used to form gods. It is also said that daemons are two spirits, good and evil, who preside over mortals and areas. Zeus is said to have assigned a daemon to each individual at birth and after death as a guide to Hades. Genii, nymphs, satyrs, river gods and penates are described as daemons. Compare to Genius and Lares.

Daemons (Roman) *see* Daemon.

Daevas *Daeva, Daiva, Devas* (India); (Islamic, Mazdaism, Zoroastrian; Persia)
Also known as: *Devs* (Armenian), *Divs* (Persian).
These malevolent spirits are helpers of the prince of demons, Ahriman, earlier known as Angra Mainyu. Under the rule of Iblis, their function is to fight all that is good. Generally they are opposed to the Asuras. The Daevas are Aka Manah, the spirit of evil who opposes Vohu Manah; Indra, the deceiver of men (not the Vedic god) who opposes Asha Vahishta; Sauru, an anarchist and tyrant, opposes Khshasthra Vairya; Naonhaithya, the demon of stubborness, pride, rebellion and irreverance who opposes Spenta Armaiti; Taurvi and Zairisha, the demons who degrade men, lead them to failure, and cause old age, oppose Haurvatat and Ameretat; and Aeshma, the demon of lust and rage who opposes Sraosha. (The Vedic Daevas are gods.) *See also* Aeshma; Ameretat; Ameshas Spenta; Angra Mainyu; Azazel; Devs; Devas (A); Devas (B); Drujs; Haurvatat; Hoshang; Khshasthra Vairya; Peri; Spenta Armaiti; Sraosha; Vohu Manah; Yata.

Dag (A) (Norse; Teutonic) *see* Dagr.

Dag (B) (German)
Day goddess. She is possibly the female version of Dagr (q.v.).

Dagan (Semite) *see* Dagon.

Daganoweda (Huron, Iroquois People, North America)
Also known as: *Deganiwada, Hiawatha.*
Aspect. He is the son of the Great Spirit and a mortal woman, Djigonasee. It is also the name for Hiawatha or the deity who converted Hiawatha to the brotherhood.

Dagda *Dagde, Daghda, Daghdae, Daghdha, Dogdha* (Celtic)
Also known as: *Crom-Eocha, Daghdae-Cearas, Dagodevos, Eochaid Ollathair* (The Great Father), *Ruad Ro-Fhessa* (The Mighty One of Great Knowledge).
Omnipotent god of knowledge, life and death. Dispenser of plenty. Controller of weather and crops. Son of Eladu (knowledge), Dagda, usually referred to as "The Dagda," was one of the leaders of the Tuatha De Danann. He was known for his wisdom, magic and music. It is said that he could summon the seasons by playing his harp, named "the Oak of Two Greens." With Undry, his magic cauldron, and a magic pig that could be eaten daily and reappear cooked, he could provide an unending supply of food. It follows that he carried excessive weight. He also had difficulty controlling his sexual appetite. He was said to have mated with Morrigan and also with Boann by whom he had two children, the goddess Brigit and the god Angus. In another legend, Brigit appears as his wife, not his daughter. He was also said to have married a woman with three names, Breg (Lie), Meng (Guile) and Meabel (Disgrace). They had three daughters each named Brigit. The goddess Dana is said to be his child as is the goddess Bambha. Other children attributed to Dagda were Ogma, Midir, Bodb the Red, and Ceacht. As god of earth and fertility, he used a dual function magic club to heal, resurrect, wound and kill. As he dragged his gigantic club, the spikes would claw the ground leaving gaping paths behind him. When the Tuatha De Danann landed on the island they challenged the Firbolgs in the First Battle of Magh Tuiredh and emerged the victors. As a result of this engagement, the king of the Tuatha De Danann had his hand amputated. A rule of the people was that the monarch could not be physically maimed, so Nuada was replaced by the Fomorian, Bress, who was of mixed heritage. His mother, Eriu, was a Tuatha De Danann and his father, Elatha, a Fomorian. Bress turned out to be a tyrant, who subjected the Tuatha De Danann to severe penalties. Dagda and his son Ogma were reduced to menial activities and humiliating injustices by this king. Eventually, the Tuatha De Danann under the leadership of Lugh were able to topple the reign of the Fomorians in the Second Battle of Mag Tuiredh. Dagda, however was not able to retain ownership of his own property. It was not the enemy who evicted him from his castle, Bruigh na Boinne, it was his son, Angus. In some myths, we are told that this talented leader with a great zest for life ended up being a contented cook for king Conaire the Great. Dagda was shown as ugly, gross, and potbellied, usually wearing a short tunic and sandals. His two special attributes were his cauldron and his club. He is the equivalent of the Welsh Math and is similar in nature to his brother Lugh. For details involving his relationship with Morrigan *see* Morrigan. Compare Dagda's club to Thor's hammer, Indra's thunderbolt and Sucellos mallet. Compare to the mythology of Pushan (India) and Thor (Teutonic). For details of the Fomorians injustices to Dagda and his people, *see also* Angus; Anu (B); Balor; Banbha; Boann; Bress; Brigit; Dana; Nuada; Ogma; Tuatha De Danann.

Dagde (Celtic) *see* Dagda.

Daghda (Celtic) *see* Dagda.

Daghdae (Celtic) *see* Dagda.

Daghdae-Cearas (Celtic) *see* Dagda.

Daghdha (Celtic) *see* Dagda.

Dagini (India) *see* Dakinis.

Dagoba (Buddhist) *see* Stupa.

Dagodevas *see* Dagda.

Dagon (A) *Dagan, Daguaun, Dagun, Daguna* (Akkadian, Babylonian, Canaanite, Semitic, Sumerian, Ugarit)
Also known as: *Oannes, Zeus Arotrios* (Zeus the Farmer).
Dagon was analogous to Ea and the Phoenician god Dagon. He was worshiped in the city of Ashdod (Israel), where the Ark of the Covenant was kept. He has been referred to as an attendant of the great Enlil. In one legend he is one of the sons of Uranus and Ge. His brothers were Ilos (El-Cronus), Betylus, and Atlas. Sometimes he is known as one of an old Sumerian trinity with Shamash and Idurmer. Dagon was likely an androgynous deity. He is described as fish-tailed. He may be associated with Atargatis (Derketo). It is possible that he was replaced by Apollo. *See also* Atargatis; Dagon (B).

Dagon (B) *Dagan* (Phoenician)
Also known as: *Baal Dagon, Baal of Arvad, Siton, Zeus Arotrios* (Zeus the Farmer).
In the Phoenician Creation Legend of Philo Byblos, Dagon is the son of Ouranos and Ge; the brother of sisters Astarte, Rhea, Dione and probably Caribo (Cabira), the daughter of Astarte and Cronus. His brothers are Cronus, Betylus, and Atlas. He is thought of as a corn god, but later excavations (Graeco-Roman) indicate a relationship with Oannes the Chaldean fish god (q.v.).

Dagr *Dag* (Norse; Teutonic)
Also known as: *Day.*
God of the Day. Known as the "Bright and Fair." He is the son of Delling, the dwarf gatekeeper of Asmegir and brother of a sister, Nott, the personification of night. The All Father sends Dagr (Day) and Nott (Night) around the earth in a chariot every twenty-four hours. Day's horse is named Skin-faxi, and Nott's horse is Hrim-faxi. *See also* Delling; Nott.

Daguaun (Middle Eastern) *see* Dagon (A).

Dagun (A) (Middle Eastern) *see* Dagon (A).

Dagun (B) (Afghanistan) *see* Imra.

Dahak (Persia) *see* Zahhak.

Dahana (Greek) *see* Perseus.

Dahhak (Persia)
An evil spirit and enemy of Yima. *See also* Azhi Dahaka.

Dahomey People, Africa — Creation Legend *see* Aido Hweda.

Dai Itoku-Myoo *Amida, Goemmason, Yamantaka (Sanskrit).* (Buddhist; Japan)

Dai Itoku-Myoo is one of the Godai-Myoo. They are the protectors of Buddhism and incarnations of the five great Buddhas. Dai Itoku-Myoo is an incarnation of Amida and a manifestation of Amida's wrathful aspect. His function is to carry out the wishes of Amida. Dai Itoku-Myoo battles illnesses and poisons. He is reputed to be more powerful than the dragon. The name Goemmason (Destroyer of Death) is also used when applied to Dai Itoku-Myoo for he vanquished the King of the Underworld, Emma-O. Dai Itoku-Myoo is shown with six heads, six arms, and six legs. His faces show fierce expressions. He is usually seated on a white ox. He is also depicted sitting on a rock with three left legs folded and the three right legs set on the earth. In one of his right hands he holds a scepter, one is raised and holds a sword. In one of his left hands he holds a wheel, and in another hand a trident. He has been shown with one head, three eyes, bristling hair and two arms. He is seated on a rock with crossed legs. In his right hand, he holds a long stick with a trident at each end. In his left hand he holds the varja (thunderbolt). Dai Itoku-Myoo is always depicted with flames in the background. *See also* Amida; Emma-O; Fudo-Myoo; Godai-Myoo; Gozanze-Myoo; Gundari-Myoo; Yamantaka.

Daikoku (Japan) *see* Diakoku.

Daimon (Greek) *see* Daemon.

Daimones (Greek) *see* Daemon.

Dain (Norse; Teutonic)

He is one of the dwarfs who made the chain that bound the wolf Fenrir. He is also one of the dwarfs who ate the buds of the life tree, Yggdrasil. The other dwarfs are Dvalin, Duneyr, and Durathror. *See also* Bifur; Dvalin; Dwarfs; Yggdrasil.

Dainachi Nyori (Japan) *see* Dainichi-Nyorai.

Dainichi-nyorai *Dainachi Nyori* (Buddhist; Japan)

Also known as: *Birushana, Fudo-Myoo, Maha-Vairochana Tathagata (Sanskrit), Tathagata Mahavairokana.*

The secret doctrine that forms the tenets of the Tendai, the Shingon, the Kegon and other esoteric traditions, were said to have been transmitted through the Bodhisattva Vajrasatwa and Nagarjuna by Dainichi-nyorai (Great Sun Buddha). Known as the "Great Illuminator," Dainichi-nyorai is said to be a reincarnated form of Vairochana (meaning "belonging to or coming from the sun"). Dainichi-nyorai is sometimes considered an androgynous deity. The Shinto sun goddess Amaterasu was identified with Dainichi-nyorai when Buddhism was introduced to Japan. In some traditions, Dainichi-nyorai is thought to be a reincarnation of Amaterasu. Fudo-Myoo, said to be an incarnation of Dainichi-nyorai, is one of the Godai-Myoo (Five Great Kings). His function is to carry out the wishes of Dainichi-nyorai. When shown in the mandala of the World of Ideas (Vajradhatu), he is depicted seated in a meditative pose, wearing a crown, and holding his left index finger. The left hand pose indicates the intellectual element, the right hand, the five elements: earth, water, fire, air and the ether (or vital energy). This is known as the mudra of the Six Elements. Dainichi, as one of the Buddhist trinity, is shown wearing a replica of a dog's head on his head, the eleventh sign of the zodiac. He is also in the center of the mandala of the World of Forms immediately above

Muryoju (Amitayus). In the mandala of the World of Ideas (Kongokai), Dainichi-nyorai is below Muryoju. In the Garbhadhatu mandala, the divine physician, Yakushi-rurikwo-nyorai is identified with Dainichi-nyorai. *See also* Amaterasu; Amida; Fudo-Myoo; Godai-Myoo; Vairocana; Vajrasatwa; Yakush-nyorai.

Daityas *Daitya* (Singular), *Danavas*; (Hindu; India)

The giant evil spirits known as the Daityas are the offspring of the goddess Diti and Kasyapa. The Daityas were relegated to the ocean depths in a strata known as Patala by Indra for their opposition to sacrifice. Their city is called Hiranyapura. When it breaks the boundaries set by Indra, this city moves around under the earth or sails through the air. Hiranya-kasipu, his son Prahlada and great-grandson Bali and Hiranyaksha are Daityas. The Daityas are a category of Asuras, as are the Danavas, who are also giants, and the Adityas. The Daityas and Danavas were frequently in conflict with the gods. In contrast, the Adityas represent eternal light and the power of good. The female Daityas are described as giants who wear jewels the size of boulders. Compare the Daityas to the Rakshasas. *See also* Adityas; Agastya; Arjuna; Asuras; Bali (B); Brihaspati; Diti; Hiranya-kasipu; Hiranyaksha; Hiranyapura; Indra; Kasyapa; Krishna; Kurma (regarding the churning of the sea of milk); Maruts; Nara-Simba; Patala; Prahlada; Rahu; Savarbhanu; Vamana (Vishnu's avatar as a dwarf); Varaha (Vishnu's avatar as a boar); Varuna; Vrita.

Daiva (India, Persia) *see* Devas (A); Devas (B).

Dajdbog (Slavon) *see* Dazbog.

Dajoji (Iroquois People, North America)

Also known as: *The Panther.*

A panther deity and god of the west wind, Dajoji is called "west wind" in mythology. He is said to support the whirlwind. Ga-oh summons him to fight against storms. When Dajoji's cry pierces the night, the sun hides in fear.

Dakas (India) *see* Dakinis.

Dakini (India) *see* Dakinis; Kali.

Dakini Ye-she-tsho-gyal (India)

A recent incarnation of Sarasvati, said to have lived approximately twelve hundred years ago. Her powerful memory permitted her to remember everything she heard. *See also* Sarasvati.

Dakinis *Dagini* (Buddhist, Hindu, Lamaist; India)

Also known as: *Asrapa, Ashrapa (Drinkers of Blood), Dakis, Kadomas, (Tibet), Khadhomas, Khadomas, Khados, Khandros, Mka-gro-ma (Tibet).*

Dakinis are categorized as air spirits, fairies and a class of demon goddess. Their male counterparts are known as Dakas. They are attendants to the goddess Kali. The name translated literally means "sky walking woman." They are sometimes described as giants, and sometimes with the bodies of fish. They are shown eating flesh or drinking blood. Dakinis are used to designate the female partner in the tantric initiation, and thus are human and superhuman. In this tradition, they are called "mothers" and they are able to grant paranormal powers and spiritual insight to the sincere practitioner of Kundalini yoga. The Five Orders of Dakinis in Tibetan rites are: the Vajra

Dakinis, who are white and sometimes blue in color and have the attribute of peacefulness; the Ratna Dakinis, who are yellow and have the attribute of grandness; the Padma Dakinis, who are red with the characteristic of fascination; the Karma Dakinis, who are the Dakinis of action, are green in color and associated with sternness; and the Buddha Dakinis, who are the Dakinis of Understanding and are dark blue in color. The Tibetan Dakinis are described as being "majestically divine" in appearance. In the mythology of Lamaism, Dakini was a lion-headed goddess associated with Lha-mo. *See also* Bhavani; Dorje Phagmo; Kali; Khados, Mkah Hgroma; Varahi.

Dakis (India) *see* Dakinis.

Daksha (Hindu, Vedic; India)

Daksha is an early Vedic god who was both the son and father of Aditi. In the *Brahmanas* he is identified with the creator, Prajapati. In the *Mahabharata*, he is the son of Brahma, whose right thumb gave birth to him. He married Prasuti, the daughter of Manu, who in some legends is said to have been born from Brahma's left thumb. Daksha was the chief of the Prajapatis, who are the seven (and later ten) sages and poets born of Brahma and called rishis. He was the father of sixteen daughters who became the mothers of all living things, including gods, men and demons. The youngest, Sati, an incarnation of Uma, became Shiva's wife. This made Daksha Shiva's father-in-law. Thirteen of the daughters were given to Yama, one to Agni, one to the Pitris and one to Bhava-Siva. In other legends, the number of daughters is said to be 24, 50, or 60. He gave away two of his sixty daughters to Bhuta, ten to Dharma, twenty-seven to Soma, thirteen to Kasyapa, three to Trakshya, two to Agni, two to Angiras, and one (Sati) to Shiva. In one version Daksha neglected his twenty-six daughters who then put a curse on him. Since then, the moon becomes faint at times. One of his daughters, Suaha, was called the wife of Agni and possibly Rudra. Another daughter, Krodha, meaning "anger," was the wife of Kasyapa and was the mother of all four-footed predators and all birds of prey. Two other daughters, Puloma and Kalaka, were wives of Kasyapa and mothers of the 60,000 giant demon spirit Danavas. (Some say that Puloma and Kalaka are the daughters of Vaishvanara and that they were the mothers of thirty million Danavas.) Daksha is born and killed in every generation. Some scholars say that Daksha is Vishnu who is incarnated through him to create living beings. Others say that as the first man, he created from himself a woman and fell in love with her. Their many daughters married Soma. In the *Mahabharata*, it is written that Daksha initiated a giant sacrifice, known as a hecatomb, for all the gods. As he did not know Shiva, he neglected to give him a share of the sacrifice. Shiva was so enraged that he broke Pushan's teeth, Savitri's arms and tore out Bhaga's eyes. He was then given his portion and he returned the deities to health. In the Puranas, the gods were sacrificing to Vishnu and did not invite Shiva. His mate Uma persuaded him to show his power to the gods. From his anger the giant demon Virabhadra emanated. He caused a great melee that did not end until Daksha propitiated Shiva and acknowledged his superiority. In other interpretations, Daksha considered Shiva disreputable and never liked him. Later, he was forced to acknowledge Shiva's superiority over Brahma. After a long feud, Daksha was decapitated by the god in anger. *See*

also Aditi; Adityas; Agni; Badari; Bhaga; Bhutas; Brahma; Danavas; Devaki; Devi; Dharma; Diti; Durga; Garuda; Kadru; Karttikeya; Kasyapa; Lokapalas; Manu; Marisha; Medha; Mitra; Nagas and Nagis; Parvati; Pitris; Prajapati; Priti; Pushan; Rahu; Rishi; Rudra; Sati; Shiva; Simhika; Soma; Surabhi; Uma; Vasistha; Vinata; Virabhadra; Yajna; Yama.

Dakshaja "Born of Daksha" (India) *see* Devi.

Dakshina (India) *see* Devi.

Dakshina-Murti (Hindu; India)

Shiva's name, Dakshina-Murti, meaning "Facing South," is used when he sits on Mount Kailasa instructing the yogis.

Daktuloi (Greek) *see* Dactyli.

Dalhan (Arabic)

This is a species of cannibal demon who rides an ostrich in the desert. In other interpretations, the Dalhan is depicted as a man riding a camel. He lives on desert islands and feeds on shipwrecked sailors. *See also* Jinn.

Dam-c'an-r-do-rje-legs-pa *Dam-chen-dr-je-le-pa, Dor-le* (Buddhist; Tibet)

He is the chief of the demons who were subdued by Padmasambhava. He is shown in Tibetan clothing, carrying a kapala and Vajra. He is seated on a lion with a green mane. *See also* Samantabhabra.

Dam-chen-dr-je-le-pa (Tibet) *see* Dam-c'an-r-do-rje-legs-pa.

Dam-ki (Assyro-Babylonia) *see* Damkina.

Damanaka Tree (India) A sacred tree. *See also* Kama.

Damaru (Hindu; India)

Shiva's sacred drum. *See also* Nataraja.

Damballah (Haitian, of African origin)

Also known as: *Damballah-Wedo.*

Damballah, a powerful serpent deity of the Rada pantheon of Haitian voodoo gods is the patron of rains, streams and rivers. He is not concerned with mortal problems and is usually found around water. Special pools are built for his bathing. Although a sky god, he is also said to live in trees. His mate is Aida Wedo, the rainbow snake, also known as Ayida. Damballah is generally shown as an arch in the sky, colored like a rainbow. His symbol is an egg. Aida Wedo wears a jeweled headdress. During Voodoo rituals, she slithers along the floor. *See also* Aido Hwedo; Rada.

Dame du Lac (Arthurian) *see* Vivien.

Dames Vertes (Celtic, French)

Wind spirits and shape-changers, the "Green Ladies" entice travelers from their routes in the forest. Laughing, they hold their victims upside down over waterfalls. In human form, they dress in long green robes and are tall and attractive. As wind spirits, they stimulate all plant life in their paths.

Damgalnunna (Sumer) *see* Ninki.

Damia (Greek)

She is a goddess of health worshiped only by women.

Damke (Assyro-Babylonia) *see* Damkina.

Damkina *Davkina, Dawkina* (Assyro-Babylonia)

Also known as: *Daauke, Dam-ki, Damke, Damku, Dauke, Dauthe, Gashanki, Ninella, Ninhursag, Ninki.*

In Chaldean mythology, Damkina is possibly the daughter of Tiamat who personifies the primordial waters or Ki who personifies the earth. She is the sister/consort of Ea, and the mother of Marduk and possibly Tammuz. She may also be the mother of the sea goddess Gasmu. In Babylonian mythology, she is a sky deity, variously known as the consort of Ea, or Anu, who with one of them ruled the Apsu. With Ea, she is said to be the mother of Bel. In later Babylonian mythology a triad of goddesses is represented by Damkina, Belit, and Anath. In Sumerian mythology, she is the earth mother (her name in the Akkadian language means "Lady of Earth"). She is also known as the consort of Enki in some tales. Damkina is appealed to by women who are in labor. As Ninki she is the queen of the deep waters, and as Gashanki she is queen of the earth. *See also* Anath; Anu; Apsu; Bel (A); Ea; Enki; Gasmu; Ki; Marduk; Ninhursag; Ninkarrak.

Damku (Assyro-Babylonia) *see* Damkina.

Damnameneus *see* Dactyli.

Damona (Celtic, Gaul) Goddess of cattle. *See also* Borvo.

Damsel Ho (China) *see* Ho-hsien-ku.

Damu (Sumer) *see* Dumuzi; Tammuz.

Damu-zi-abzu (Babylonian) *see* Tammuz.

Dan (A) (Fon People, Africa)

Also known as: *Dan Ayido Hwedo, Danh.*

Snake god of unity and life. He is the son of the twins Lisa and Mahu. Dan is shown as a rainbow snake with his tail in his mouth. He is possibly the god Dan Petro of the Haitian people.

Dan (B) (Celtic) *see* Dana.

Dan Ayido Hwedo (Africa) *see* Dan.

Dan Petro (Haitian)

Also known as: *Danh.*

God of farmers. Originally, Dan Petro may have come from Africa as Danh. He is considered the father of tribal gods of the Haitians. His attributes are snake-like.

Dana (Celtic)

Also known as: *Ana, Anu, Danu* (Irish), *Don* (British, Welsh), *Donu* (Irish).

Goddess of plenty. Dana is the daughter of Dagda and the mother of Brian, Iuchar and Iucharbar (who may be a triple concept of one deity). As Dana, she is confused with the triad of goddesses: Danu, Anu (Ana) and Brigit (Bridgit). The Celtic race is descended from Dana. Her people, the Tuatha De Danann, came to Ireland many centuries ago from the Isles of the West and returned there at a later time. Some, who could not bear to leave the land they called Erinn, took the name Aes Sidhe and remained. It is believed they are the leprechauns who dwell beneath the surface of the land and vanish and reappear at will. In an ethical battle, they will fight beside mortals with lances of blue flame and pure white shields. Dana represents the earth, the fertility mother of all. The Welsh identified her with Don and she is comparable to their "Great Mother" Modron. She is associated with Aine the moon goddess. Compare to the moon goddess, Arianrhod. Dana is said to be the counterpart of Gaea. *See also* Aine; Angus; Anu (B); Bel (B); Brigantia; Brigit; Dagda; Don; Leprechaun; Tuatha De Danann.

Danae (Greek)

Also known as: *Abantias, Dahana.*

It is generally thought that Danae was the daughter of Acrisius and Eurydice, though some say that she may have been the daughter of Aganippe and Acrisius or his friend, Teutamias, the king of Larissa. Danae had been seduced by her uncle Proteus and later became the mother of Perseus by Zeus, despite her father's extraordinary attempts to shelter her from becoming pregnant. Danae, as a descendant of Abas, a king of Argos, was sometimes known as Abantias. *See also* Acrisius for the events surrounding Danae's pregnancy and the birth of Perseus. To compare with women who were seduced by Zeus in other forms, *see* Aegina; Antiope; Europa; Leda. *See also* Perseus; Zeus.

Danai (Greek) *see* Danaides.

Danaidae (Greek) *see* Danaides.

Danaides *Danaids, Danaidae* (Greek)

Also known as: *Danai.*

Deities of springs and waters. Possibly early agricultural deities. The Danaides are the fifty daughters of Danaus who married their cousins, the fifty sons of Aegyptus. On their wedding night, forty-nine Danaides murdered their husbands. *See also* Danaus for the complete legend of the Danaides. *See also* Agenor (A); Amymone; Eurydice (C); Hypermnestra.

Danaids (Greek) *see* Danaides.

Danaus (Greek)

King of Libya. Danaus is the son of Belus and Anchinoe. His siblings are his twin brother Aegyptus, Thronia and perhaps Cepheus (Phineus). He was given Africa as a gift from his father, and originally ruled as the king of Libya. Aegyptus ruled Arabia and later conquered the Melampodes and named it Egypt after himself. Danaus, fearful that Aegyptus might kill him for his land, fled. It is said that Athena assisted him and he sailed to Greece, reportedly in a vessel thought to be the first two-prowed ship. With him were his fifty daughters, known as the Danaides, who were escaping from their cousins, the fifty sons of Aegyptus, who wanted to marry them. When he arrived in the arid land, he supplanted the reigning king, Gelanor, and became king. It is said that he was the first person to water the land by the use of wells. The men found Danaus and demanded that he consent to the marriages of his daughters. Although the body of the story differs, the ending remains basically the same. He acquiesced, possibly under force, but on their wedding night he gave the women weapons and instructed them to murder their husbands. It is said that they beheaded the men, burying their torsos at the city gates of Argos and their heads in the marshes. Hypermnestra, who married Lynceus, was the only daughter who disobeyed her father. Later, Danaus tried to find husbands for his daughters, and of course encountered difficulties. He finally decided to offer the widows as prizes in a footrace and threw in attractive shields as added incentive. After death, the sisters (except Hypermnestra) were said to have been punished in Tartarus (the underworld). They were condemned to the useless task of pouring water continually into a sieve. In some accounts, Lynceus murdered Danaus to avenge his brothers' deaths and in others they reconciled and Lynceus succeeded Danaus, and the line of Argive kings stemmed from him. The Argives and eventually the Greeks were called Danai. The names of some of the Danaides are Celaeno, Cleite, Stenele, Chrysippe, Erato, Eurydice, Glauce (also known as Creusa), Polydore, Phylodameia, Asteria, Astioche, Cleodora, Amymone, and Cleopatra. Aegyptus, following the instructions of the Delphic Oracle, sacrificed his only daughter Aganippe to end a drought in Egypt. Eventually, Aegyptus arrived in Greece, heard of his sons' fate and fled to Aroe, where he died. Compare Danaus to Endymion and Nereus. *See also* Abas; Achaeus; Agenor (A); Amymone; Argos, Erato; Hypermnestra; Lynceus.

Danavas (India)
Sixty thousand, or thirty million, gigantic evil spirits. *See also* Brihaspati; Daityas; Daksha; Kuvera; Vritra.

Dancer of the Burning Ground (India) *see* Nataraja; Shiva.

Dandadhara (India) *see* Yama.

Dandapani (India) *see* Buddha.

Danh (Africa) *see* Dan.

Daniel (Assyro-Babylonia)
A diviner of dreams, able to cast spells on wild animals, Daniel was also a prophet. He destroyed a dragon by driving a storm wind into the dragon's mouth and splitting it in half. He is famous for being cast into a den of lions. His symbol is the four-horned goat. Daniel's story is similar to the Babylonian Marduk and Tiamat.

Danil *Daniyal* (Arabic)
Danil, like the Hebrew Daniel, was also a prophet and diviner of dreams. Imprisoned, he was released by the king to interpret a dream.

Daniyal (Arabic) *see* Danil.

Danu (A) (Celtic) *see* Anu (A).

Danu (B) (India)
One of Daksha's numerous daughters. Mate of Mitra-Varuna, the Asvins and Kasyapa. Mother of the Danavas and Danavis. *See also* Aditi; Diti; Kasyapa; Mitra; Varuna; Vritra.

Danu (C) (India)
The serpent god father of Vritra and Ahi (qq.v.).

Danus (Greek) *see* Eurydice (C).

Dao (Babylonian) *see* Tammuz.

Daonus (Babylonian) *see* Tammuz.

Daphne (Greek)
A nymph, Daphne, is a priestess of Gaea who personifies the earth. She led secret female rituals to celebrate the femininity of the earth. A mortal male, Leucippus, dressed in female attire in an attempt to gain access to her services. The sun, who sees all, suggested that the females perform their rituals nude so that males could not intrude. The true identity of Leucippus was revealed and he was killed. The sun god Apollo had his own agenda. When he saw Daphne he attempted to mate with her, but she rejected him. Infuriated, he chased her and attempted to rape her. She appealed to Gaea who responded immediately and turned the beautiful nymph into a laurel tree. From that time, Apollo wore laurel wreaths in his hair and the laurel tree was honored as a source of inspiration. Compare Dapne to the Indian Urvasi. *See also* Apollo; Gaea; Oenamaus; Rivers.

Dar el-Jannah (Islam) Islamic Paradise (q.v.)

Darago (Philippines)
She is a volcano goddess and warrior. In ancient times, she required human sacrifices to keep her from erupting.

Daramulum (Aborigine People, Australia) *see* Duramulun.

Daramulun *Darramulum* (Aborigine People, Australia)
Also known as: *Biamban, Baime, Bunjil, Ngurunderi, Nurrundere, Thuremlin.*
This supreme being made earth his home a long time ago. He is sometimes called Biamban (meaning master). He wasn't married and lived with his mother, Ngalalbal. Sometimes he is said to be the one-legged son of Baiame. Daramulun is connected with a flood myth. In some myths, he is known as a culture hero from whom later medicine men could draw their power. This power enabled them to kill their enemies, fly anywhere, including to the sky land, which is the land of ghosts. He is sometimes shown with an axe, or with his mouth filled with quartz and with an enlarged phallus. He is sometimes depicted with one leg. *See also* Bunjil; Thuremlin.

Darawigal (Australia)
This god represents the force of evil who opposes Baiame (q.v.).

Darbas (Hindu; India)
The Darbas are spirits who haunt cemeteries and eat dead bodies. *See also* Dasyus; Panis; Pishachas.

Darkness (Greek) *see* Chaos; Nyx.

Darramulum (Aborigine People, Australia) *see* Daramulun.

Daru-el-Bawar (Islam) Islamic Hell (q.v.).

Daru el-Qarar (Islam)
Meaning the "Dwelling which Abideth" and symbolized by green chrysolite, this is the third stage in Islamic Paradise (q.v.).

Daru el-Salam (Islam)
Meaning the "Dwelling of Peace" and symbolized by white pearls, this is the second stage in the Islamic Paradise (q.v.).

Darvands (Persia)
Evil spirits created by Ahriman to be his assistants. They are Aka Mano, Ander, Nasatyas, Sauru, Tarik, and Zarik. The Vedic Darwands were originally good spirits, but like the Devas,

became demons in Persia. *See also* Angra Mainyu; Devas; Nasatyas; Saura.

Darwands (Vedic) Good spirits. *See also* Darvands.

Darzamat (Latvia)
Goddess of Gardens.

Dasan (Pomo People, North America)
With his father, Makila, Dasan led the bird clan, who brought civilization from over the waters.

Dasarata, King (India) *see* Dasaratha.

Dasaratha, King *Dasarata, Dasharatha* (Hindu; India)
Father of Rama. *See also* Rama and Hanuman.

Dascylus (Greek) *see* Amycus (A).

Dasharatha (India) *see* Dasaratha, King.

Dasim (Islamic)
The son of Iblis, the devil, Dasim became the demon of discord. *See also* Azazel.

Dasra and Nasatya (India) Wonder Workers. *See also* Asvins.

Dasyus (Dravidian, Hindu; India)
These evil spirits are the enemies of the gods and mortals. They appear human in the guise of ugly robbers and thugs. *See also* Darbas; Panis; Pishachas.

Datan (Slavic, Polish)
Datan is one of a group of spirits who are in charge of the prosperity of the fields. Tawals is another spirit, as is Lawkapatim, who is only concerned with the tilling process. They are grouped with the goddess Marzann who looked into the growth of fruit. *See also* Lawkapatim.

Dattoli (India) *see* Agastya.

Dauce (Babylonian Creation Legend of Damascius) *see* Aus, and Belus (B).

Daughter of the Night (Greek) *see* Nemesis.

Daughter of Themis (Greek) *see* Furies; Themis; Zeus.

Daughters of the Evening (Greek) *see* Hesperides.

Dauke (Assyro-Babylonia) *see* Damkina.

Dauthe (Assyro-Babylonia) *see* Damkina.

Davalin (Teutonic) *see* Dain; Dvalin.

Davinka (Assyro-Babylonia) *see* Damkina.

Dawat Puja (India)
"Worship of the Inkstand." Festival day. *See also* Sarasvati.

Dawkina (Assyro-Babylonia) *see* Damkina.

Day (Teutonic) *see* Dagr.

Day Gods (Aztec People, Mexico) *see* Lords of the Day Hours.

Dazbog *Da-Bog, Dabog, Dadzbog, Dajdbog, Dazh-Bog, Dazhbog* (Poland); (Slavic)
Also known as: "*Son of Svarog*" (Son of the Sky).

Dazbog is the son of Svarog, who personifies the sky, and the brother of Stribog, the god of cold and frost. Initially a sun god, in later times Dazbog was reduced to demon status in Siberia. As a sun god, he was associated with Khors, the god of health and hunting; Perun, the god of thunder; and Stribog, the god of cold and frost. In some tales, he is the part-time spouse of Myersyats, who personifies the moon. He visits her during the summer. Dazbog is depicted in wood with a silver head and a golden moustache. He is similar to the Sumerian Dazibogu (q.v.). Dazbog is identified with the Greek Helius. Compare Dazbog to the Greek Hephaistos. *See also* Perun; Stribog.

Dazh-Bog (Slavic) *see* Dazbog.

Dazhbod (Sumer) *see* Dazibogu.

Dazhbog (Slavic) *see* Dazbog.

Dazibogu (Sumer)
Also known as: *Dazhbod*.
He is a sun god, similar to the Slavonic Dazbog (q.v.).

Dazima (Semite)
One of the goddesses created by Ninhursag.

Dbyar-Gyi-Rgyalmo (Tibet) *see* Grismadevi.

De Hi No (Huron People, North America) *see* Heng.

De-Hi-No (China) *see* Heng.

Dea Artio (Celtic) *see* Artio.

Dea Syria (Greek) *see* Atargatis.

Deae Matres (Celtic)
The trinity of mother goddesses who rule fertility and creativity.

Dealgnaid (Celtic) *see* Beltine.

Death Star (Pawnee People, North America) *see* Tirawa.

Debabou and De Ai *De Babou* (Oceanic)
Also known as: *Na Atibu, Te-Po-ma-Te-Maki*.
First people. The children of Nareau. Against the orders of Nareau, this couple bore three children: the sun, the moon and the sea. *See also* Nareau.

Debee (India) *see* Devi.

Deber (Babylonian, Semite)
Pest god. Deber is worshiped with Resheph (also called Ninib) in festivals. Deber could be the same as the goddess Diban, of the Babylonian flood legend. Possibly connected with Yahweh.

Dech'tire *Dechterecul, Dechtire* (Celtic, Irish)
Mother of Cuchulain, by either Conchobar, Lugh, or Sualtam, and sister of King Conchobar. In another version she is the daughter of Maga and half-sister of Cuchulain. In other versions, she swallowed a mayfly and conceived Cuchulain, or she was impregnated by Lug's soul, or that in the form of a bird, she flew away with Lug. Cuchulain was born by his mother's vomit. Dech'tire had an enormous appetite, as did her fifty female attendants. She had the ability to change herself and the women into birds. *See also* Cuchulain; Lugh.

Dechtire (Celtic, Irish) *see* Dech'tire.

Decima (Greek) *see* Fates.

Dechterecul (Celtic, Irish) *see* Dech'tire.

Deduska (Russia) *see* Domovoi.

Deduska Domovoy (Russia) *see* Domovoi.

Dedusky Domovoy (Russia) *see* Domovoi.

Dee (Celtic)
War or river goddess. Little known; there was a river of the same name.

Deganiwada (Huron, Iroquois People, North America) *see* Daganoweda.

Deianeira (Greek) *see* Deianira.

Deianira *Deianeira, Dejanira* (Greek)
She is the daughter of Dionysus or Oeneus and Althaea. Her children by her second marriage to Heracles are Ctesippus, Hyllus, and Macaria. The goddess of the hunt, Artemis, transformed Deianira into a guinea fowl after she accidentally killed Heracles and committed suicide. *See also* Althea; Calydonian Boar Hunt; Heracles; Nessus.

Deidamia (A) (Greek)
Another name for Astydameia. *See* Astydameia (B).

Deidamia (B) (Greek)
When Achilles, her lover, died, she married Helenus. Deidamia is the mother of Pyrrhus.

Deidamia (C) (Greek)
Her parents are Bellerophon and Philonoe, her siblings, Hippolochus, Isander, and Laodamia. She married Evander, and became the mother of Dyna, Pallantia, Pallas, Roman and Sarpedon II.

Deimachus (A) (Greek)
He is the father of Autolycus, Deileon and Phlogius. *See also* Autolcyus.

Deimachus (B) (Greek)
His wife is Aeolus and his son is Enarete. *See also* Aeolus (A).

Deimos *Deimus* (Greek)
God of fear and dread. Deimos is the son of the god of war, Ares, and the goddess of love, Aphrodite. His siblings are Pallor, the god of fear; Anteros, the god of passion; Enyo, the goddess of war; Eros, the god of love; and Harmonia and Phobos. He accompanied his father and his brother, the god of fear, Phobos, into battle. *See* Anteros; Aphrodite; Ares; Harmonia (A); Phobos.

Deion (Greek)
King of Phocis. Deion is the son of Aeolus and Enarete. He has six brothers and seven sisters. His spouse is Diomede, and his children are Actor, Aenetus, Asteropeia, Cephalus and Phylacus. *See also* Actor (C); Aeolus (A); Canace; Diomede; Enaret.

Deione (Greek)
This is another name for Acacallis, thought by some to be the mother of Miletus by Apollo. *See also* Acacallis.

Deiphobus (A) (Greek)
His parents are Priam and Hecuba. He is the brother of Aesacus, Cassandra, Creusa, Hector, Helenus, Paris, Polyxena and Troilus. Deiphobus was renowned for his bravery during the Trojan War. He was forced to marry Helen when Paris died, and met his death by her former spouse, Menelaus. *See also* Cassandra; Creusa; Helen; Paris.

Deiphobus (B) (Greek) He is the son of Hippocoon (q.v.).

Deipyle (Greek)
She is the daughter of Adrastus and Amphithea. She married Tydeus, one of the Seven against Thebes, and became the mother of Diomedes. *See also* Adrestus; Diomedes.

Deipylus (A) (Greek)
Deipylus could be the son of the Argonaut Jason and Hypsipyle. He is said by some to be the son of Polyxo who was married to the king of Rhodes, Tlepolemus. She tried to avenge Deipylus' death at Troy by killing Helen. Instead, she killed a servant. *See also* Jason.

Deipylus (B) (Greek) He is the son of Polymnestor and Ilione.

Deivi (Prussian)
A respectful term which means goddess.

Dejanira (Greek) *see* Deianira.

Dekla (Latvia)
The goddess of fate who oversees infants and weeps when a birth is tragic.

Delia (Greek) This is an epithet of Diana. *See also* Artemis.

Deliades (Greek)
Bellerophon accidentally killed his brother, Deliades, the son of Glaucus and Eurymede. *See also* Bellerophon; Eurymede; Glaucus.

Delka (Latvia)
This gentle goddess cradles the newborn child.

Delling (Norse; Teutonic)
Also known as: *Dellinger.*
The dwarf gatekeeper at the castle of the Asmegir, Delling is the third husband of Nat (Night) and father of Dagr (Day). *See also* Asmegir; Dagr.

Dellinger (Teutonic) *see* Delling.

Delphic Oracle (Greek) *see* Lamia; Themis.

Delphin (Greek) *see* Amphitrite.

Delphyne (Greek)
Dragon-woman. Before her death by Apollo, she was responsible for guarding the sinews of Zeus, which had been stolen by Zeus' son, Aegipan, and the messenger of the gods, Hermes. *See also* Aegipan; Hermes; Typhon (A).

Dem-chho-pal-khor-lo-dom-pa (Tibet) *see* Dorje Phagmo.

Dema (Marind-anim People, New Guinea)
Dema is the term given to the divine creators and primordial beings of mythical times. They are depicted in human form, and sometimes as animals or plants.

Demarus (Greek) *see* Melkart.

Demavand, Mount *Demavend, Mount* (Persia) *see* Verethraghna, Angra Mainyu, Azhi Dahaka and Thrita.

Demavend, Mount (Persia) *see* Verethraghna, Angra Mainyu, Azhi Dahaka and Thrita.

Demeter (Greek)

Also known as: *Brimo, Centeotl* (Mexican), *Ceres* (Roman), *Deo, Doso, Kore, Kore-Persephone, Isis* (Egyptian).

Demeter (the Roman Ceres), is one of the great Hellenic divinities. She is the Greek goddess of agriculture and vegetation, protector of marriage, and corn goddess. The daughter of Cronus and Rhea, she was swallowed by her father and rescued by Zeus. Her daughter Persephone's name was kept secret; she was known as Kore, which means "the girl." This gave Demeter a double name; Kore-Persephone as Demeter is identified both with herself and with her daughter. Persephone was kidnapped by the lord of the underworld, Hades. Demeter requested Zeus' aid in returning her. Initially, he refused. She left Olympus grief-stricken and wandered the earth while the human race starved. She used the name Doso when she discarded her duties as a goddess and went to live among mortals. As Doso the Cretan she was the nursemaid of Demophon. She attempted to make the boy immortal by holding him in a magic fire each night. When his mother, Metaneira, saw them she screamed and the spell was broken. Demeter revealed herself to Metaneira. She then instructed that a shrine be built for her at Eleusis. When it was completed she lived in it. Demeter may have initiated the Eleusinian mysteries. It is said that she taught the prince of Eleusis, Triptolemus, the art of corn cultivation. He in turn spread his knowledge to the Greeks and the rest of the world. Zeus finally relented and sent Hermes to bring Persephone back. As she had eaten pomegranate seeds, food of the underworld, she had to spend one-third of the year below ground. Demeter, in another legend was the daughter of Uranus and Gaea, and sister of Hades, Hera, Hestia, Poseidon and Zeus. Demeter is said to be the mother of Plutus and Philomelus by Iasion. Known as mare-headed, her union with Poseidon produced Arion, a black stallion. She had a son, Plouton (wealth), from her union with Iasion in a ploughed field. There is reference to the possibility of Demeter being the mother of Iacchus. In another myth, as Doso, she ate Pelops' shoulder by mistake and replaced it with an ivory shoulder. The name Brimo is also applied to Rhea, Hecate, and Persephone. Her legend is similar to that of Ashtar and Tammuz. Demeter is compared to the horse goddess Epona. *See also* Abas (C); Acheron; Angerona; Car; Cronus; Cybele; Erysichthon; Evander (B); Hades; Hecate; Hestia; Isis; Pelops; Persephone; Rhea; Styx; Tantalus (A).

Demiurge (Gnostic)

Also known as: *Metropator.*

Chief of the lowest order of eons. Demiurge is credited with introducing evil into the world. Some identify him with Jehovah.

Demne (Celtic, Irish) *see* Finn.

Demogorgon (Aborigine People, Australia)

An evil spirit, Demogorgon haunts graves at night. He strolls about in skeletons of the dead by day, and bites the unwary in the stomach.

Demoleon (Greek)

Killed in the Trojan War, he is the son of Antenor and Theano. *See also* Acamas (B); Agenor; Glaucus; Laocoon; Polydamas.

Demonice (Greek)

Her parents are Agenor and Epicasta, her siblings, Hippodamus, Porthaon, and possibly Thestius. By Ares, she is the mother of Evenus, Molus, Pylus and Thestius. *See also* Ares; Crethus.

Demons *Daimon*

In Babylonian mythology are included the vampire (Lamashtu), Alu (ghost of the breasts), Namtar (ghost of the throat), Uttuka (the shoulder), Gallu (the hand), Elimmu (the bowels), Rabisu (a spy), Ahhazu (the seizer), Labasu (the overwhelmer), Lilu (male lasciviousness) and Lilitu (female lasciviousness). The list of demons is long and is covered under separate names. Not all are listed, but a partial reference follows. Persian: Al, Akwan, Div, Nar, Nara, Damrukh Nara, Shelan Nara, Mardash Nara, Kahmaraj Nara, Tahmurath, Jinn, Jann. Buddhist: Lokapalas, Yakshas, Kumbhandas, Dhritarashtra, Gandharvas, Virupaksha, Nagas, Garudas, Pretas, Hariti, Yakshini, Panchika, Tara. India: Asvins, Vala, Panis, Sorama, Asuras, Panaka, Tripura, Mahishasura, Vasuki, Daitya, Danavas, Kshatriyas, Rakshasas. Asia, including Japan and China: Ts'en-kuang, Chu-kiang, Sung Ti, Wu Kuan, Yen-lo, Pien-Ch'eng, P'ing-teng Tu-shi, Ts'en-kuang, Chaun-lun, Jizo, Kishimojin, Kubira or Kuvera, Oni, Gaki. These demons can be male or female, good or bad. Some can be regarded as gods and goddesses in their own right. *See also* Bhut (India); Daemon (Greek); Jinn (Persian); Satyrs (Greek).

Demophon *Demophoon* (Greek)

Joint king of Melos. Demophon is the son of Theseus and Phaedra or Antiope (Theseus' mistress). He secured the Palladium from Diomedes for Athens. When Troy fell, Demophon was madly in love with Laodice. On a stopover in Thrace, on his way home from Troy, he met and fell in love with Phyllis. When he left her, she committed suicide. *See also* Acamas (A); Antiope; Laodice.

Demophoon (Greek) *see* Demophon.

Dendrites (Greek)

"He of the Trees." This is an epithet for Dionysus (q.v.).

Deng (Dinka People, Africa)

Also known as: *Deng-dit, Diing, Dinga-dit.*

God of Rain. Birth deity. Deng is the son of the goddess Abuk. He is in charge of the food-producing earth. Some say he is the ancestor of all the Dinka people and that lightning comes from his club. In one version as Deng-dit he appears as the creator god. His consort is L'wal, the essence of evil. Deng-dit instructed L'wal to form mankind from a bowl of fat. He left the bowl unguarded. L'wal appropriated it and created caricatures of Deng-dit and Abuk's creatures. Abuk was an evil spirit, said to be the grandchild of L'wal. Compare Deng to the Yoruba deity, Shango. *See also* Abuk.

Deng-Dit (Dinka People, Africa) *see* Deng.

Denga (Africa) *see* Aywil.

Denkart (Zoroastrian) *see* Bundahish.

Deo (Greek) An epithet of Demeter.

Deohako (Seneca People, North America)
They are the spirits of corn, beans and squash who lived together on a hill. Onatha, the spirit of corn, wandered away one day looking for dew. The evil spirit Hahgwehdaetgah (an alternate name for Taweskare) abducted her and took her underground. The sun searched for and found her. However, she must reside in the cornfields until it is ripe. Some say this is the collective name for the three daughters of the earth-mother. *See also* Yoskeha and Taweskare.

Derceto (Middle Eastern) *see* Atargatis.

Derketo *Derceto* (Middle Eastern) *see* Atargatis.

Dervaspa *Drvaspa, Gosh* (Zoroastrian; Persia)
A Yazata, and the guardian of cattle, he personifies the soul of the bull. *See also* Gaya Maretan; Yazata.

Destroyer, The (Persia) *see* Mahrkusha.

Deucalion (A) (Greek)
Survivor of the nine-day Deluge. He is the son of Prometheus. His mother was either Hesione, Pronoea or Clymene. His spouse is Pyrrha, the first mortal woman born. Their children are Amphictyon, Hellen, Pandora, Protogeneia and Thyia. Deucalion was issued a dictate from the gods to build an ark. He followed instructions and with Pyrrha they were the only survivors of the Deluge. Their ark landed on Mount Parnassus. The goddesses advised them to cover their heads and throw the "bones of their mother" behind them. They did not have bones, so instead they threw stones. These stones became the new human race. Usually Deucalion and Pyrrha are shown as a pair. *See also* Acacallis; Aeolus (A); Ariadne; Minos; Pasiphae; Prometheus; Telchines.

Deucalion (B) (Greek)
The Argonaut son of Minos and Pasiphae.

Deus (Greek) *see* Zeus.

Deus Clavigerus (Roman) *see* Janus.

Dev (India) *see* Daevas; Devas (A); Devas (B).

Deva-Kanya (India) *see* Savitri (B).

Deva-Kanyakas (India) *see* Devis.

Deva-Matri (India) Mother of the Gods. *See also* Aditi.

Deva-Parvata (India)
Sacred Mountain. *See also* Meru Mountain.

Devak (India)
A guardian deity, the Devak takes the shape of an animal, tree or the tool of a trade. It is considered an ancestor or head of the household and is usually worshiped at the time of marriage or when moving into a new home.

Devaka (India) *see* Devaki.

Devaki (Hindu; India)
Also known as: *Aditi, Apsarases, Deywuckee, Dhriti, Nit, Niti.*

Devaki is the daughter of Devaka and the youngest of seven sisters. She became the spouse of Vasudeva and the mother of a daughter, Subhadra, and eight sons. Her first six sons were killed by her cousin, King Kansa of Mathura. Her seventh child, Bala-Rama was conceived by her, but placed in the womb of and born by Rohini, the daughter of Rudra and the second wife of Vasudeva. When Kansa heard of her eighth pregnancy, he imprisoned Devaki and Vasudeva. At birth, her eighth child, Krishna, assumed the form of Vishnu and arranged, with the assistance of the gods, that he replace the baby daughter born to the poor cowherds Yasoda and her mate Nanda with himself. When Kansa heard of Devaki's delivery and found that she had given birth to a female child, he set the family free. The female baby took the form of the goddess Devi and announced to Kansa that he had been outwitted and that his future enemy had escaped. Kansa took the precaution of ordering all the male babies in the city to be killed not realizing that Krishna was safe in the forest with Yasoda and Nanda. Devaki is closely connected with Aditi and is sometimes said to be an incarnation or avatar of this goddess. Samnati, one of Daksha's numerous daughters, is also associated with Devaki. *See* Rudra for details about Rohini. *See also* Aditi; Adityas; Apsarases; Bala-Rama; Daksha; Kansa; Krishna; Subhadra; Vishnu.

Devananda (India) *see* Mahavira.

Devanganas (India) *see* Devis.

Devarishis (India) *see* Rishi.

Devas, The (A) *Daevas, Daiva or Dev* (singular); *Devis* (feminine); (Buddhist, Jain, Hindu, Vedic; India)
In the Vedas, the Devas were divine spirits of good and later became known as nature spirits. The name means "bright one." They are the masculine counterpart of the Devis and their leader is Indra. The Devas were prominent in the Churning of the Ocean of Milk. They enlisted the help of the Asuras (demons) by promising them a potion of soma, the sacred elixir of the gods. Even though the Asuras were suspicious of their intentions, they helped them dismantle Mount Mandara, which was used as the churning stick. The Asuras also enticed Vasuki the serpent from his underwater abode so he could be used as the churning instrument. Vishnu instructed the Devas to take his head and the Asuras, the tail. The Asuras did not like the arrangement and insisted on changing places with the Devas. This is what Vishnu had hoped they would request, for if the Asuras gained access to the magic soma, it would have given them powers equal to the gods. When the churning progressed, the Asuras were suffocated by the hot air from Vasuki's breath while the Devas at his tail were cooled by ocean air. In some versions the Devas are Dyaus (day) and Prithivi (earth). There are thirty-three Devas, eleven in each of the three Hindu worlds, although sometimes their numbers are given as eight or twelve. The Devas are said by some to be associated with the sun, as are the Gandharvas, Apsarases, Yatudhanis and Gramanis. *See also* Asuras; Daevas; Devas (B); Devis; Indra; Kurma (regarding Churning of the Ocean of Milk); Mandara Mountain; Vasuki; Vishnu.

Devas, The (B) (Zoroastrian; Persia)
In Persian mythology, the Devas were malevolent spirits,

genii of evil, created as counterparts of the Amesha Spentas by Angra Mainyu, who ruled over them. Other names are given: Divs, Drauga, Druj, and Durugh.

Devasena (India)

Also known as: *Kaumari; Sena. See also* Karttikeya.

Devatas (India) *see* Devis.

Devayoshas (India) *see* Devis.

Devee (India) *see* Devi.

Devera (Roman)

This goddess rules the brooms used to purify ritual sites.

Devi *Debee, Devee* (Brahmanic, Dravidian [possibly], Hindu, Vedic; India).

Also known as: *Ambika, Bhairavi* ("Terrible"), *Bhargavi* (Wife of Shiva), *Bhavani, Bhowanee, Bhowani, Bhuta-nayaki* (Spirit Leader), *Bhuvana-Matri* (Mother of the World), *Bhuvanisvari* (Mistress of the World), *Brahmani* (Wife of Brahma), *Bhramara* (Relating to the Bee), *Chandi* ("Fierce"), *Chinnamastica, Dakshaja* (Born of Daksha), *Dakshina* (Right-handed), *Devi-Uma, Devi-Uma-Kali, Digambari* (Clad with the Quarters), *Doorga, Durga* (Inaccessible), *Eka* (One), *Gauri* (The Golden Lady), *Gowree, Idika* (Mother), *Jaganmatri* (Mother of the World), *Kalee, Kali* (The Black Mother), *Kali-Durga, Kalika, Kamakshi, Kotari* (Naked), *Kumari* (The Maiden), *Lilavati* (Charming Woman), *Ma, Madira* (Of Spiritous Liquor), *Maha-Maya* (Illusion), *Maha-isvari* (Great Potentate), *Mahakalee* (The Great Black One), *Maharajni* (Great Queen), *Mangala* (The Auspicious One), *Mari, Matri* (Mother), *Menakshi, Minakshi* (Fish-Eyed), *Minakshidevi, Mridani, Nairriti* (South-Western), *Parbati, Parvati* (The Mountaineer), *Parwati, Purbutty, Rudrani* (Wife of Rudra) *Shakti, Sarasvati, Sarvamangala* (Universally Auspicious), *Sarvani, Sarvavasini, Sati* (Virtuous), *Shakti, Surisi, Surisvari* (Divine Lady), *Sutty, Tariki* (Delivering), *Triambika* (Wife of Rudra-Shiva), *Triganini* (Mother of Three Worlds), *Uma* (Light), *Vaishnavi* (Wife of Vishnu), *Vari* (Fair Faced), *Vigaya* (Victorious), *Vindhyavasini, Vindhyavarini* (Dwelling in the Vindhya Mountains), *Yogisvari* (Adept in Yoga).

Devi is known as a "Great Mother" or "Universal Mother." She is one of the most important of the Indian goddesses. She is a creator, maintainer and destroyer. In one of her earliest forms, Devi as Ambika is associated with Rudra and is said by some to be his wife and possibly his sister. She appears as the early fertility goddess Gauri, meaning the "Golden Lady" or the "Shining One." She is the granddaughter of Mahakali the "Great Black One" (also an epithet for Devi-Uma-Kali). She is the daughter of Sirsootee, the sister of Bishen and possibly the mother of a daughter, Manasa. Gauri is later used as a first name for Parvati (another aspect of Devi) when she rides on a tiger. We encounter her as Sati, the daughter of Daksha and the devoted wife of Shiva. After the death of Sati, she is reborn as Parvati the youngest daughter of Mena, the sister of the goddess Ganga, once again the wife of Shiva, and according to some legends, the mother of Karttikeya (also known as Skanda) and Ganesha. As Uma, the wife of Shiva, her skin is golden and she personifies light and beauty. As Durga, once again the wife of

Shiva, she is yellow, wears a menacing expression, rides a tiger and has ten arms. Kali, the "Black Mother," appears as the goddess of destruction and wife of Shiva. Devi also appeared as the female baby of Yasoda, the wife of Nanda who nurtured the baby Krishna when the demon Kansa wanted to kill him. Devi is worshiped as Mari the goddess of death, by the Korwas, also known as Korama people of India. Devi is also a name signifying any female deity. Devi as Kali-Durga killed the buffalo monster Mahisasura (Mahisha) who threatened to undo the world. Devi is depicted with four faces and four arms. She wears a diadem of shining colors. Her emblems include the bow, arrow, bowl, goad, hook, ladle, noose, prayer-book, rosary, sword and peacock's tail. For Minakshi, *see* Kuvera. *See also* Ana Purna; Ardhanari-Ishvara; Bhavani; Chandi; Daksha; Devaki; Devis; Durga; Ganesha; Ganga; Gauri; Kali; Kansa; Karttikeya; Krishna; Kumari; Laksahmi; Manasa; Mari; Maruts; Parvati; Rudra; Sarasvati; Sati (A); Shakti; Shiva; Sitala; Vishnu.

Devi-Kali (India) *see* Kali.

Devi Sri (India) Noble Goddess. *See also* Lakshmi.

Devi-Uma (India) *see* Bhavani; Devi.

Devi-Uma-Kali (India) *see* Devi.

Devil

Also known as: *Belial, Eblis, Iblis, Lucifer, Nergal, Satan, Sathan, Sathanas, Shaitan* (Islamic), *Shetan* (Islamic).

Evil spirit. Possibly from the Greek Diabolos or from the Indian meaning of "little Deva or demon." The Jews called these demons Shedim or Liliths and S'eirim in the Old Testament. In the Teutonic language they are called Deopul, Diabul, Duibhal, Duwel, and Teufel. The Egyptian devil was Set. The Islamic Shaitan more often inhabits the bodies of females. It tempts women to disobey their spouses. To rid her of the spirit, the name of the spirit must be known and the woman must be beaten. Same as the Saxon Deopul, Diabul, Diubhal and the German Teufel. In Judeo-Christian belief, the devil is the principal of evil and the archfiend. *See also* Azazel; Satan.

Deving Isching (Latvia) God of Horses.

Devis, The *Deva* (masculine); (Buddhist, Hindu, Jain; India)

If the word Devi is used as a name, it refers to Kali, Parvati, Uma and Durga. It is sometimes used to describe a female angelic, heavenly or divine being. The Devis are the daughters of Aditi. Other Devic beings are the Deva-Kanyakas, the Devayoshas and the Devanganas. Also included are the Devatas, who are divided into the following classes: the Adhidevatas, Digdevatas, Grihadevatas, Mangadevatas, Mantradevatas, Purvadevatas, Rajyadidevatas, Rakshodhidevatas, Sakunadevatas, Shastradevatas, Sthalidevatas, Ushodevatas, Vanadevatas, Vrikdevatas. The Vidyadevis are Devis who are described as Jain goddesses of knowledge. Gandhara is known as a Vidyadevis. In Cambodia, the Devatas are known as Thevadas. *See also* Aditi; Devas (A); Dorje-Naljorma; Durga; Kali; Parvati; Uma.

Devona (Celtic) River goddess. *See also* Sequana.

Devorgilla (Irish)

Her father, the king of Ireland, gave her to Cuchulain. He

rejected her and passed her on to another man. Wounded, she transposed herself and her female attendant into birds and they flew away. One day when Cuchulain was hunting, he threw a rock at the bird and it fell to earth and assumed the form of Devorgilla. The hero saved her life by sucking the stone from her flesh. In doing so, he swallowed some of her blood making them related by blood and therefore unable to have sex. See also Cuchulain.

Devourer of Amenti (Egypt) see Amit.

Devs (Armenian)
Also known as: Ais, Char.
Gigantic, shape-changing spirits, the Devs can appear as humans, serpents or in dreams as wild animals. They often have one or more eyes and seven heads. Usually harmful, sometimes they appear foolish and harmless. Their presence can be detected by insanity, itching around the throat, ear or tongue, sneezing or fainting. They can be deterred by cutting through the air with a sword or a stick. In the theological sphere the Devs are harmful spirits who are constantly riddling the path of truth with their snares. See also Arlez; Daevas; Hambaris; Kaches.

Dewtahs, The (India) Celestial Beings. See also Aditi.

Deywuckee (India) see Devaki.

Dhammai People, India — Creation Legend see Shuznagnu and Zumiang-nui.

Dhammapada, The (Buddhist)
This book contains the teachings of Gautama Buddha. The Pali version of The Dhammapada, which contains 423 verses divided into twenty-six chapters, is the most widely known. The Tibet and Chinese versions vary slightly from the Pali version. See also Buddha.

Dhana-Pati (India) see Kuvera.

Dhanada (India) "Giving Wealth." See also Kuvera.

Dhanus (India) The Sacred Bow. See also Kurma.

Dhanvantari (Hindu; India)
He is the physician of the gods and the keeper of soma. See also Kurma.

Dhara (India) see Vasus.

Dharani (India) see Lakshmi; Parashur Rama.

Dharini (Tantrayana Buddhism) Goddess of Memory.

Dharma (Buddhist, Hindu; India)
Dharma, a sage, and the personification of law and justice, was a judge of the dead. He married a number of Daksha's daughters who became the mothers of children who personified virtue. With his mate Sraddha, the goddess of faith, he became the father of Kama, the god of love. Dharma is the god who appears when mortals are being tested for strength of character. In the Mahabharata, Dharma is the father of the chief of the Pandavas, Yudhishthira. Dharma is an ancient title of Yama, who in his role of judge of the dead is known as Dharmaraja. In Buddhism, Dharma (The Dhamma) is the Ultimate Reality and the formulation of Buddha's teachings as presented in the sutras. See also Daksha; Dwaparayuga; Kama; Kunti; Medha;

Narayana (C); Pandavas; Sraddha; Tretayuga; Vyasa; Yama; Yudhisthira.

Dharma Palas (India) see Lhamo.

Dharmacakra (India)
Soft-voiced lord of speech. See also Manjusri.

Dharmapala (Buddhist; India)
Depicted as hideous giants with huge teeth, tongues sticking out, and hair standing on end, the Dharmapala are the "Protectors of Religion." See also Vajrapani.

Dharmaraha (India) see Mitra; Yama.

Dharmaraja (India)
King of Virtue. See also Amrtakundali; Yama.

Dharmavajra (India) see Samantabhadra.

Dhartarastra Jikokuten (Japan), Yul-khor-bsrun (Tibet); (Buddhist, Hindu; India)
Dhartarastra dwells in the Buddhist universe of Chakravala. He lives with the other guardians in the Heaven of the Four Great Kings near the peak of the sacred Mount Meru. This plane is populated with pretas (ghosts), animals, demons and men. The Four Great Kings guard the entrance to Sukhavati, the Buddhist paradise. Dhartarastra, lord of the Gandharvas (heavenly attendants), is the guardian of the east. Another Great King is Virudhaka, lord of the Kumbhandas (giant demons and gnomes), who is the guardian of the south. Virupaksha, lord of the Nagas (dragons or serpents) is the guardian of the west. Vaisravana, lord of the Yaksas (demon disease carriers) is the guardian of the north. As a group the guardians are known to the Hindu and Buddhist as Lokapalas. In the Hindu tradition, Agni guards the north, Indra the east, Varuna the west and Yama the south. In some traditions, Kubera guards the north and Ravana is the guardian of the fifth position, which is located in the center. Dhartarastra is white in color. He wears a plumed helmet, holds a stringed instrument and feeds on incense. See also Chakravala; Naga Naga Knaya; Sukhavati; Virudhaka; Virupaksha.

Dharti Mai Bhudevi, Dharti Mata; (Hindu; India)
Mother Earth who supports the earth. Her presence is everywhere in the ground. Pregnant women are placed upon her at the time of delivery. Pigs, goats, and fowl are sacrificed to her. She is worshiped as a pile of stones or a pot in many villages. See also Prithivi; Sinivali; Vishnu.

Dharti Mata (India) Earth Mother. See also Dharti Mai.

Dhata (India) see Prajapati; Surya.

Dhatr (India)
Creator of All Things. See also Prajapati; Surya.

Dhatri (Vedic; India)
Originally, Dhatri was sometimes included in the lists of Adityas. Later, he was known as a minor deity of health and domestic harmony. See also Adityas.

Dhenuka (India) King of the Hayas. See also Krishna.

Dhisana (Vedic; India) Goddess of plenty.

Dhritarashtra (India)

He is the blind son of Vyasa and Ambika, mate of Gandhari, and father of one hundred sons. The eldest son, Duryodhana, was the leader of the Kauravas, who fought the Pandavas in the war of the *Mahabharata*. *See also* Bhima (A); Bhishma; Duryodhana; Kauravas; Kunti; Pandavas; Radha; Vyasa.

Dhriti (India) *see* Devaki.

Dhruvasinha (India) *see* Amrtakundali.

Dhumaketu (India) *see* Agni.

Dhumbarahi (Nepal) *see* Varahi.

Dhupa (India) *see* Ratnasambhava.

Dhupema (India) *see* Dhupa.

Dhurva (India) *see* Vasus.

Dhyani Buddha Akshobhya (Nepal) *see* Akshobhya; Dhyani Buddhas.

Dhyani Buddha Amitabha (Nepal) *see* Dhyani Buddhas.

Dhyani Buddha Amoghshiddhi (Nepal) *see* Amoghshiddhi; Dhyani Buddhas.

Dhyani Buddha Vajrasatwa (Nepal) *see* Vajrasatwa.

Dhyani Buddhas *Dhyanibuddhas*

Also known as: *Panch Buddhas* (Kathmandu, Nepal), *Tathagata* (Nepal); (Buddhist; Nepal)

The five Dhyani Buddhas are abstract aspects of Buddhahood which emanate from the self-existent Adibuddha. From the meditations of the knowledge-holding Dhyani Buddhas evolved the five Dhyanibodhisattvas, who are the five Buddhist creators of the universe. The five Dhyani Buddhas are Vairocana, Akshobhya, Ratnasambhava, Amitabha and Amoghasiddhi. The consorts (saktis) of the Dhyani-Buddha are known as Dhyanibuddhasaktis. Vairocana's sakti is Vajradhatvisvari, Akshobhya's sakti is Locana (Buddhalocana), Ratnasambhava's sakti is Mamaki, Amitabha's sakti is Pandara, and Amoghasiddhi's sakti is Tara. The Dhyani Buddhas represent the five Skandhas. The Skandhas are the five cosmic elements: Rupa (form), Vedana (sensation), Samjna (name), Sanskara (conformation), and Vijnana (consciousness). The Dhyani Buddhas are exceptionally popular in Nepal where they are depicted in every shrine, often found in courtyards and in the main entrance of a Buddhist home. A Dhyani Buddha may incarnate as a mortal manifestation known as a Manushi-Buddha. The Dhyani Buddhas are shown together seated on an open lotus in the lotus position with their palms and soles are turned upwards in the dhyana mudra. Their bare heads are crowned by thick curls. Their eyes are usually half-closed. Sometimes they hold a cup in the open hand, symbolizing openness. Their undergarment, held by a scarf, reaches from the chest to the knee. The outer garment is a monk's costume, which leaves only the right arm bare. Sometimes a sixth Dhyani Buddha, Vajrasatwa, is added. Generally Vajrasatwa is regarded as the priest of the five Dhyani Buddhas. For more specific descriptions, see the individual names of the deities. *See also* Adibuddha; Akshob-

hya; Amida; Amoghasiddhi; Avalokitesvara; Boddhisattvas; Dhyanibodhisattvas; Maitreya; Mamaki; Manjusri; Manushi-Buddhas; Pandara; Ratnasambhava; Samantabhadra, Tara (B); Vairocana; Vajrapani; Vajrasatwa.

Dhyanibodhisattvas (Buddhist; Nepal)

The five Dhyanibodhisattvas evolved from the Dhyani Buddhas and are known as the creators of the cycles of the world. They are Avalokitesvara, Ratnapani, Samantabhadra, Vajrapani, and Visvapani. Over time, the number of Dhyanibodhisattvas increased. In Northern Buddhist temples a group of eight Dhyanibodhisattvas is often seen standing to the right of an important deity. They are Akasagarbha, Avalokitesvara, Kshitigarbha, Mahasthamaprapta, Maitreya, Manjusri, Sarvanivaranaviskambhin, Trailokyavijaya. Vajrapani or Samantabhadra are sometimes substituted for one of the eight. They wear a five-leafed crown and are garbed in a scarf on the upper body, and a shawl over the lower limbs. They wear earrings, bracelets, armlets, and anklets. *See also* Boddhisattvas; Dhyani Buddhas; Kshitigarbha; Maitreya; Manjusri; Samantabhadra; Trailokyavijaya; Vajrapani.

Dhyanibuddhas (Nepal) *see* Dhyani Buddhas.

Dhyanibuddhasaktis (Nepal) *see* Dhyani Buddhas.

Di (Roman) *see* Dii.

Di-do (Tibet) *see* Gro-bdog.

Dia (A) (Greek)

She is the wife of Ixion, and mother of Pirithous. She was seduced by Zeus, who was in the shape of a horse. *See also* Ixion.

Dia (B) (Celtic) *see* Aesar (B).

Dia Griene (Scotland)

She is the daughter of the sun who was a prisoner in the Land of the Big Women and escaped with Cailleach, who was disguised as a fox. *See also* Cailleach Bheur.

Diakoku *Daikoku* (pre–Buddhist, Buddhist, Shinto; Japan)

Also known as: *Daikoku Sama, Daikoku Ten, the Great Black Belt Deity.*

Diakoku combined with Okuni-Nushino-Mikoto to become the god of wealth and one of the seven gods of luck known as the Shichi Fukujin. His son, the god of labor Ebisu, is also a Shichi Fukujin. Diakoku, as well as being a god of wealth, is a god of happiness, war, artisans, and merchants. He is a god of heaven and the north. Diakoku is depicted as dark skinned with swollen ear-lobes (a symbol of omniscience), heavy-set, with a smile on his face. He is also shown as a soldier holding a pagoda and a lance or shown with a rice bale and a protruding stomach. The rice bale symbolizes the infinite source of wealth. He is also shown carrying a mallet which grants good fortune and happiness. Diakoku is often accompanied by a rat who acts as his messenger. (In the Hindu and Buddhist tradition a rat vomiting jewels is a rain symbol.) His likeness formed in gold is carried as a charm for prosperity. His colors are black and blue. He may be one of the Shinto kami (deity), as Okuni-Nushino-Mikoto is a Shinto kami. *See also* Ebisu; Hiruko; Shichi Fukujin; Stupa.

Diamond Kings (Buddhist; China)

Also known as: *Kings of Hell, Ssu Ta Chin-Kang.*

The Diamond Kings guard the register of judgments. *See also* Ssu Ta Chin-Kang.

Dian Cecht (Celtic) *see* Dia'necht.

Diana (Roman)

Also known as: *Artemis* (Greek), *Aventina, Cynthia, Lala* (Etruscan), *Lucina* (Light), *Phoebe, Selene, Tergemina, Trivia* (Three Ways).

Goddess of forests and groves. Goddess of slaves and plebeians. Diana is the daughter of Jupiter and Latona. She is the Roman equivalent for Greek goddess of hunting and the moon, Artemis. Diana's dwelling place is the forest. She loved Endymion, Pan, and Orion. She had three aspects, Hecate, Luna, and Phoebe. Some say she was a goddess of childbirth and the birthing of animals. Aventina is Diane as she was worshiped on Aventine Hill in Rome. Her epithet, Tergemina, refers to her triform divinity as a goddess of heaven, earth, and hell. She is generally shown as a woman, sometimes with three heads, a horse, a dog, and a boar. Her chariot is drawn by heifers, horses, two white stags, or a lion and panther. *See also* Actaeom; Adonis; Artemis; Atalanta; Ceto; Egeria; Gefion; Mama Quilla.

Diancecht (Celtic) *see* Dia'necht.

Dianchecht (Celtic) *see* Dia'necht.

Diane of Crete (Greek) *see* Isis.

Dia'necht (Celtic) *Dian Cecht, Diancecht, Dianchecht.*

Also known as: *The Leech.*

Dia'necht, the god of medicine and divine physician, is a member of the Tuatha De Danann, an ancient race of deities. He is the father of Airmid, Cethe, Cian, Cu, Etan, and Miach, and the grandfather of Lugh. Their king, Nuada, had his hand severed during a brutal battle with the demonic giants, the Fomorians. Dia'necht, with the assistance of Credne, the divine bronze worker, created a silver prosthesis for the ruler. However, a rule of sovereignty was that the monarch could not have any physical defects, so he was forced to resign. In an attempt to mend fences with their former enemies, the Tuatha's offered the throne to Bress, the son of the Fomorian king. This move almost crippled his subjects as he was a greedy, dictatorial monarch. In a twist of fate, Dia'necht's son, Miach, also a brilliant surgeon, was able to restore Nuada's severed hand. Dia'necht, insanely jealous, viciously attacked his son on three separate occasions and Miach survived. The fourth time, Dia'necht's assault generated a grave head injury and his son died. It is said that three hundred and sixty-five (365) different herbs grew on his grave which his sister Airmed tended. Meanwhile, the people removed Bress, who returned to his father's undersea kingdom to draw up battle plans, and King Nuada regained his throne. *See also* Asclepius; Bress; Cian; Credne; Lugh; Tuatha De Danann.

Dianus (Roman) *see* Janus.

Diarmait (Celtic)

He was the friend of Finn who was subsequently slain by him. *See also* Finn.

Diarmuid (Greek) *see* Adonis.

Diaus (India) *see* Dyaus.

Diban (Babylonia) *see* Deber.

Dice (Greek) Another spelling for Dike (q.v.).

Dictyanna *Dictynna* (Greek)

Also known as: *Britomartis.*

Dictyanna is an ancient Cretan goddess who is a follower of Artemis. She invented fishing nets. *See also* Artemis; Britomartis.

Dictynna (Greek) *see* Dictyanna.

Dictys (Greek)

The son of Magnes and a Naiad, he is the brother of Polydectes, and husband of Clymene. He was a fisherman in Crete until Perseus, the son of Zeus and king of Mycenae and Tiryns, made him the king of Seriphus in Crete. Dictys had rescued Perseus when he was an infant who had been thrown to sea by Acrisius. *See also* Acrisius; Clymene; Perseus; Polydectes.

Dido *Didon, Didone* (Greek)

Also known as: *Elissa* (possibly).

Founder and former queen of Carthage, Dido is the sister of Pygmalion and wife of Sychaeus. She is the daughter of Belus or Mutgo. Dido married her uncle, Acherbas (also called Sicharbas), whom Pygmalion killed for his money. When Aeneas was travelling to found the Roman race, he stopped in Carthage to visit her. She fell deeply in love with him. When he left to fufill his destiny, she threw herself on a flaming funeral pyre. Dido may have been worshiped as a goddess of love. *See also* Aeneas; Agenor (A); Pygmalion.

Didon (Greek) *see* Dido.

Didone (Greek) *see* Dido.

Digambara (India) An epithet of Shiva.

Digambari (India) *see* Devi.

Digdevatas (India) *see* Devis.

Dih (India) *see* Gramadeveta.

Dihwar (India) *see* Gramadeveta.

Dii Di (Roman)

Dii is the Roman name for the twelve great Greek gods: Ceres (Demeter), Mars (Ares), Phoebus (Apollo), Diana (Artemis), Mercury (Hermes), Venus (Aphrodite), Jupiter (Zeus), Minerva (Athena), Vesta (Hestia), Juno (Hera), Neptune (Poseidon), and Vulcan (Hephaistos).

Diing (Dinka People, Africa) *see* Abuk; Deng.

Diinga (Africa) *see* Aywil.

Dike (A) *Dice* (Greek)

Goddess of justice. The daughter of Zeus and Themis, Dike is one of the three Horae. Her sisters are Eirene and Eunomia. Dike is the personified goddess of justice. *See also* Dike (B); Horae; Themis.

Dike (B) (Greek)

Also known as: *Astraea*.

She is the daughter of Zeus and Themis, who was also called Dike. *See also* Dike (A).

Diko (Russia) *see* Domovoi.

Dikpalas *Dig-Gaja* (Buddhist; Nepal)

In Nepal, the Dikpalas are invoked in every religious ritual, particularly those associated with buildings. They are the guardians of the four corners and four directions. The guardians of the four corners are Agni, god of fire, ruler of the southeast; Vayu, god of wind, ruler of the northwest; Isana (a form of Shiva), the northeast; and Nairitya, (also spelled Nairrita) god of dread, the southwest. The gods of the four corners are: Indra, king of gods who presides over the east; Varuna, lord of the ocean, over the west; Kuvera, god of wealth, over the north; and Yama, god of death over the south. The eight elephant deities who support the eight corners of Dik (the universe), are also known as Dikpalas. They are Airavata, Pundarika, Supratika, Vamana, Kumunda, Anjanma, Pushpadanta and Suryabhauma. *See also* Agni; Indra; Kumunda; Kuvera; Lokapalas; Navagrahas; Varahi; Varuna; Vayu; Yaksha and Yakshini; Yama.

Diksha (India) *see* Soma.

Diktynna (Greek) *see* Dictyanna.

Dil (Ireland) Cattle goddess.

Dilbar (Babylonia)

This is Ishtar as the "Evening Star" who provokes war.

Dilmun (Sumerian)

Dilmun, the home of the gods, is the garden of paradise. Enshag (son of Enki and Ninhursag) is chief of this region. After the seven-day flood which destroyed humanity, King Ziusudra (the Sumerian Noah), who survived, was made a god and lived in Dilmun. Some say Nabu was connected with Dilmun as a scribe. It is also said that Eden is located in Dilmun. Tagtug, the gardener in Dilmun, ate a forbidden plant and lost his right to immortal life. Dilmun is associated with Enki (q.v.). The *Epic of Gilgamesh* may refer to Dilmun. It is possibly the same as Eridu. *See also* Irkalla; Nabu.

Dina-Kara (India) "Day-Maker." *See also* Surya.

Dinas (Arthurian) *see* Vivien.

Dindymene (Greek) *see* Cybele.

Dindymus (Greek) *see* Cybele.

Ding (Africa) *see* Abuk.

Dinija (Crete)

"Mistress of Wild Things," possibly the original Earth Mother. Dinija appears in connection with Zeus on records at Knossos.

Dinka People, Africa — Creation Legend *see* Abuk.

Diomede (A) (Greek)

Her parents are Xuthus, "the thievish one," and Creusa. Her siblings are Achaeus, Ion, and Dorus (possibly). Through marriage to Deion, she became the mother of Actor, Aenetus, Asteropeia, Cephalus and Phylacus. *See also* Achaeus; Actor; Asteropeia; Cephalus; Deion; Xanthippe.

Diomede (B) (Greek)

She is the wife of Amyclas and the mother of Argalus, Cynortas, Leaneira, and Hyacinthus. *See also* Amyclas.

Diomedes (A) (Greek)

King of the Bistones of Thrace. His parents are Ares and Cyrene or possibly Asterie. The eighth labor of Heracles was to kill and eat the human-eating horses belonging to Diomedes. *See also* Ares.

Diomedes (B) (Greek)

Also known as: *Tydides*.

King of Aetolia. Greatest hero at Troy (after Achilles). One of the Epigoni. Made immortal by Athena. His parents are Tydeus and Deipyle, his wife is Aegialeia. At one point, he fell in love with Callirrhoe. Diomedes was also one of Helen's suitors. He took a fleet of eighty ships to Troy from Argos. With Acamas, he threatened war if Helen was not returned. *See also* Abderus; Acamas (A); Ares; Epigoni.

Dionae (Greek) *see* Dione.

Dione *Dionae* (Greek)

Also known as: *Aphrodite*.

Goddess of water (moisture). She is the daughter of Atlas or Oceanus and Tethys, or possibly of Uranus and Gaea. It is thought by some that she was the first consort of Zeus. If that is so, she would be the mother of Aphrodite. Dione married Tantalus and is the mother of Broteas, Niobe and Pelops. In the Pelasgian creation myth, Dione is coupled with Crius as the rulers of the planet Mars. She could be a pre–Hellenic Greek goddess of sexuality and inspiration, who was later replaced by Hera. She is sometimes identified with Diana. *See also* Broteas; Eurynome (A); Pelops; Tantalus (A).

Dionusos (Greek) *see* Dionysus.

Dionysus *Dionusos, Dionysos, Dyanysos* (Greek, possibly of Thracian or Semitic origin)

Also known as: *Antauges, Antheus, Anthios, Bacchus* (Roman, God of Wine and Revelry), *Bassareus* (Lydian; pertaining to clothing worn by Dionysus' followers), *Bromius* (the Roarer), *Cissos, Dendrites* (He of the Trees), *Dithyrambos* (He of the Double-door), *Eleusis* (pertaining to Eleusinian Mysteries), *Eleutherios, Euios, Iacchus, Iakchos, Isodaites, Karpios, Kubebe, Laphystios, Lenaeus, Lenaios* (said to be his most ancient name), *Liber* (Roman), *Liknites* (as the resurrected child), *Nuktelios, Nyktelios, Osiris* (Egyptian), *Perikionios, Phytalmios, Plutodotes* (Wealth-giver), *Puripais, Sabazius* (as Thracian Corn God), *Sykites, Thyoneus, Zagreus* (Cretan).

Fertility or earth god. God of wine. God of ecstasy. God of drama. Prophetic deity. Dionysus is the son of Zeus and Semele or possibly Demeter, the goddess of agriculture. Other women said to be his mother are Io, Thyone and Dione. As Eleusis, his parents were said to be Ogygus and Daeira. As Dionysus Zagreus, he is the son of Zeus and Persephone and appears in snake form. The most popular version of his legend is with Zeus and Semele as his parents. He married Ariadne, the daughter of Minos, who first loved the hero Theseus. They had six sons: Oenopion (it is possible that his father was Theseus), Phanus, an Argonaut, Ceramus, Peparethus, Staphylus, and Thoas. He was also the father of Hymen (Hymenaeus) the god of marriage, possibly by Aphrodite, Deianira by Althaea who was the wife of Oeneus, he was possibly the father of Phlias by Araethyrea, of Narcaeus by Physcoa and of Arete. As a young man, the divine heritage of Dionysus was not recognized so he left Greece and traveled to Asia to develop his divine powers. His charisma inspired devotion wherever he went and he soon attracted a following and had numerous exciting adventures. Upon returning to Greece his empowerment was recognized by the deities and he was accepted as the son of Zeus and admitted to the company of the Olympians. He delighted in sharing his knowledge of the virtues of wine. He is depicted either as a bearded man or a youth with ivy leaves and grapes around his forehead, wearing a "nebris" (a fawn skin), and carrying a thyrsus (a pole with a pine cone or vine leaves decorating the top). Wine, particularly red wine, symbolizes blood and sacrifice and youth and eternal life. Grapes symbolize fertility and sacrifice, because from the grape comes the wine. Dionysus represented the fertile energy of all growing things and was eventually considered the god of the vine. The goat was central to the celebrations of Dionysus. It represented fecundity and lasciviousness. Worshipers tore the animal apart and ate it raw. The festivals provided the group with an opportunity to vent repressed inhibitions. View the depictions and symbols of Bacchus. For the circumstances surrounding Dionysus' birth by Semele, which is comparable to the circumstances surrounding Christ, Adonis, Moses, Perseus, and Llew Llaw, *also see* Semele. Dioynsus is sometimes associated with Osiris. He is compared to the Armenian Aramazd (q.v.). *See also* Althea; Antiope; Bacchus; Corybantes; Giants; Graces; Hymen; Naiads; Perseus; Satyrs; Serapis; Spantaramet; Theseus.

Dioscures (Greek) *see* Dioscuri.

Dioscuri *Dioscures* (Greek)
Also known as: *The Gemini Twins, Tyndaridae.*
The twins, Castor and Pollux, are known as the Dioscuri. *See also* Acastus; Castor and Pollux; Leda.

Dipamkara *Dipankar, Dipankara* (Buddhist; India)
The Buddha of the First World Cycle, Dipamkara, known as "The Enlightener" or "The Lightmaker" was born in the mythological city of Deepavati. He is said to have lived on earth for a million years. As a child, Gautama Buddha offered Dipamkara a handful of dust. It was at this time that Gautama made his decision to attain enlightenment. Dipankar Buddha is depicted Adhaya mudra (his right hand held up in the gesture of protection) and his left hand is Varada mudra (down with the palm facing out in the gesture of charity). He either sits or stands with a monastic garment draped over the left shoulder and wears a pleated flowing skirt. *See also* Buddha; Manushi-Buddhas.

Dipankar (India) *see* Dipamkara.

Dipankara (India) *see* Dipamkara.

Dirce (Greek)
Antiope was given to Dirce as a slave. Dirce is the wife of Lycus, a regent of Thebes. Their son is also known as Lycus. Dirce's husband killed Epopeus, Antiope's husband. In turn, Antiope's children killed Dirce by tying her to either the tails or the horns of an enraged bull. Dirce became a fountain. *See also* Antiope.

Dirona (Celtic) *see* Borvo; Sirona.

Dis (A) (Celtic, Norse, Greek)
Supreme deity. As a deity, Dis is thought to have originated with the Gauls or Celts. The Gauls claimed that they were direct descendants of this god. The Romans worshiped him as an underworld deity and a god of wealth. Dis is also a name used for the world of the dead and is often a name used for Pluto, which is another name for Hades. The Celtic Dis is depicted with the hammer (for creativity) and the cup (for abundance). *See also* Hades; Pluto, Tartarus. May be related to Dis Pater (Dispater). *See also* Aeracura; Hades.

Dis (B) The singular for Disir (q.v.).

Dis Pater *Dispater* (Roman)
Also known as: *Dis, Orcus, Pluto.*
Underworld deity and god of wealth. Dis Pater might have been called Dis and is possibly Celtic in origin. Not a fashionable god, he was named by Caesar and is thought by some scholars to have replaced an earlier Celtic goddess named Aeracura. Two of his aspects were Pluto (Plutos) the Greek god of the dead, and Orcus, the Roman deity of death. In some versions he was the chief of the underworld. His spouse is Persephone. Dis Pater is shown carrying keys and riding in a vehicle pulled by four black horses. Compare to Manes, Orcus and Pluto. *See also* Aeracura; Bel (B); Dis; Sucellos.

Disciplina (Roman) Goddess of discipline.

Discordia *Discord* (Roman)
Also known as: *Eris* (Greek).
Goddess of Strife. Discordia, the Roman goddess of strife, is identified with the Greek goddess of strife, Eris. Discordia was thought to be the consort of Mars. *See also* Adder; Ares; Eris; Hephaistos.

Disir (Teutonic)
Also known as: *Dis* (singular).
Disir is a term used to designate a certain group of goddesses who were concerned for the good of the home and family. The Valkyries and Norns were Disir. Certain goddesses were also called Disir, such as Freyja (q.v.). Special sacrifices were offered to the Disir. *See also* Norns; Valkyrie.

Dispater (Roman) *see* Dis Pater.

Dithrambos (Greek) *see* Dithyrambos.

Dithyrambos *Dithrambos* (Greek, Roman)
Also known as: *Bacchus* (Roman), *Dionysus* (Greek).
Dithyrambos is an epithet of Bacchus, the god of wine. It is also the name for a wild song sung by the Bacchanals. In Greek mythology, Dithyrambos, meaning "Him of the Double Door," is an epithet of Dionysus. *See also* Bacchus; Dionysus.

Diti (Hindu; India)
She is one of the sixty daughters of Daksha, and the mate of Kasyapa. They were the parents of the giant Daityas, the enemies of sacrifice. Indra had them confined to the depths of the ocean where they were ruled by Varuna. Diti harbored resentment toward Indra and begged Kasyapa for a son who would be indestructible. He agreed with the provisions that she remain pregnant for one hundred years and remain pious and pure

throughout her confinement. When Indra found out that she was pregnant, he watched her carefully to see if she was adhering to her bargain. Toward the end of her century-long term, she went to bed one night without washing her feet. Indra seized the opportunity and thrust his vajra (thunderbolt) up her womb to destroy the unborn child. It was so strong that it divided into seven weeping sections. Their crying unsettled Indra and he tried to comfort them. It did not stop them, their wailing only became louder. Angry, Indra divided each of the seven children into seven, creating forty-nine children, who survived as the forty-nine flying warriors known as the Maruts. In some references the Maruts are numbered at twenty-seven or one hundred and eighty. Diti and Kasyapa were also the parents of the thousand-headed demon, Andhaka, and two famous Daityas, Hiranya-kasipu and Hiranyaksa. There are correspondences between Diti, Aditi and Vach. *See also* Aditi; Andhaka; Asuras; Daityas; Daksha; Hiranya-kasipu; Hiranyaksa; Indra; Kasyapa; Maruts; Rudras; Vach; Varuna.

Diuturna (Roman) *see* Juterna.

Div (Zoroastrian) *see* Jin; Daevas.

Divali (India) A Jain festival to honor Mahavira (q.v.).

Diveriks (Lithuania) Deity of the Rainbow.

Divine Cow, The (Gaulish, Celtic) *see* Borvo.

Divji Moz (Slavic)
Storm demons. They are wild spirits of the forests who were accompanied by fierce winds. The Divji Moz cause travelers to lose their way.

Divo Napata (India) *see* Asvins.

Divs (Persia) *see* Daevas; Deva.

Divya-ratna (India) *see* Cintamani.

Diwali (India) A Festival. *See also* Lakshmi.

Diwata Magbabaya (Philippine Islands)
High god. A great spirit, who lives in a house of coins. No mortal can look at him, for if he does so, the mortal will melt into water.

Djadek (A) (Czech) *see* Domovoy.

Djadek (B) (Slavic) *see* Domovoi.

Djamar (Aborigine People, Australia)
Supreme Being, who made all things. He has a mother, but not a father. He is supposed to walk with a dog. He lives in the salt water, under a rock. In some versions Djamar is in charge of two other high gods, Marel and Minan, whom he placed with other tribes.

Djanggawuls (Aborigine People, Australia)
Creator and fertility deities. The sisters Miralaid (also spelled Miralaidj) and Bildjiwararoju (Bildjiwuraroiju), are daughters of the sun goddess. They are goddesses of fertility who created human beings and vegetation. Some say the Djanggawuls are two sisters and a brother. The sisters' names are Djanggau and Djunkgao and the brother's name is Bralbral. They originally lived on the island named Bralgu (Bu'ralgu), and later moved to Arnhem Land. The sisters, eternally pregnant, gave birth to plants and animals as they walked about the earth. With each birth, a portion of their long vulvae broke off and became the first sacred objects. One day, their brother and his friend stole the sacred objects and left the sister bereft of their superhuman powers. The women left to follow the path of the sun, all the while continuing to give birth to new creatures. *See also* Wawalag Sisters.

Djed (Egypt) Deified object.
A shape in which Osiris sometimes appeared, especially as a warrior leader. The Djed, a sacred object or fetish, was at first the trunk of an evergreen tree and was later stylized in the form of a column topped by four capitals.

Djehuti Orzehuti (Egypt)
Also known as: *Zehuti.*
This is a name by which the god Thoth was known in early times. The name derives from Djehut, a former province of Lower Egypt. *See also* Thoth.

Djeneta (Chippewa People, North America) Name of a giant.

Djigona (Huron People, North America) *see* Deganiwada.

Djigonsa (Huron People, North America)
Messenger. Mother of Deganiwada, and wife of the "Great Spirit." She was the messenger between her son of the Sky-world and the tribes of the Mohawks and Onondaga.

Djinn *Djinns* (Arabia) *see* Efrit; Jinn.

Djunggun (Australia) *see* Wondjina.

Dmyal-wa (Tibet) *see* Naraka (B).

Dockalfar (Teutonic) Dark Elves. *See also* Alfar.

Doda (Serb) *see* Dodola.

Dodol (Slavic)
Air god or goddess. This deity is pulled around the sky in a chariot by white horses.

Dodola *Doda* (Serb)
Goddess of rain.

Dog-Faced Ape (Egypt) *see* Aani.

Dogdha (Celtic) *see* Dagda.

Dogoda (Slavic) The west wind. *See also* Perun; Stribog.

Doh (Yenisei People, Siberia)
One of the greatest magicians. While traveling, Doh would fly over the waves until he became weary, then he would create islands to rest on.

Dohit *Dohitt* (Mosotene, Quechua People, South America)
Creator. The Mosotene say Dohit created the first mortals from clay. The Quechua say he created the world in the shape of a raft. Next, he created mortals and then retired. Later, he returned to change some of the mortals to animals and birds. He also taught the people how to farm. *See also* Keri and Kame.

Dola (Slavic)

Also known as: *Dolya, Sreca* (Serbia).

The spirit of mortal fate given to a newborn. *See also* Dolya (who is similar to Sreca of the Serbian people).

Dolgthrisir (Teutonic) *see* Dolgthvari.

Dolgthvari *Dolgthrisir* (Teutonic) *see* Dwarfs.

Dolma *Tara* (Tibet)

A common name in Tibet for the goddess Tara in all her forms.

Dolphin Constellation (Greek) *see* Amphitrite.

Dolya *Nedolya* (Russia, Slavic)

This goddess of fate lives behind stoves. When her spirits are high, she brings good luck. When her mood is bad, she is known as Nedolya, appears as an old hag, and brings with her bad luck. *See also* Bannik; Chlevnik; Domovoi; Kikimora; Ovinnik.

Domfe (Kurumba People, Africa)

This water god, god of rain and wind, gave the first food-bearing seeds to humans.

Domnu (Celtic)

The goddess of the sea, she is also the mother of one of the Fomorian kings, Indech. He was killed during a battle by Ogma, one of the chiefs of the Tuatha De Danann (q.v.). *See also* Ogma.

Domovik (Russia) *see* Domovoi.

Domovoi *Domovoj, Domovoy, Domovui* (Estonian, Finnish, Polish, Russian, Slavic)

Also known as: *Chelovek, Deduska, Deduska Domovoy, Dedusky Domovik, Domovoy, Djadek* (Slavic), *Dvorovoi* (Finno-Ugric), *Haldja* (Finnish), *Haltia* (Finnish), *Holdja* (Estonia), *Iskrychi* (Poland), *Karliki* (Slavic), *Khoromozitel, Susetka, Syenovik* (Russia), *Tsmok* (Russia).

These household spirits are thrown out of heaven by the great god. The benevolent Domovoi land on houses, barns and farmlands, the evil ones land in fields, woods and wild lands. They generally live near the stove because they like fire. If they are angry they can burn the house down. If the family moves, fire from the former home is moved to the new home to welcome the Domovoi. A Domovoi is depicted as an old, gray-bearded man. He protects the household against hostile spirits as he bustles through the house at night. If a hairy person brushes against the Domovoi at night, good luck is ensured. If the hands are smooth, bad luck follows. The female Domovoi called Kikimora, Domania, or Domovikha, live in the cellar, or in ovens. One species of the Domovoi is the Chlevnik, spirit of the cattle shed or barn. The kitchen spirit is called the Ovinnik and the bathroom spirit, the Bannik. They can appear in many shapes, such as small and hairy men, animals and even objects. Under the name of Haltia or Haldja this is the ruler who precedes men almost as a ghost or shadow. In some legends, this spirit comes in the shape of a dog or cat. Halti and Holdja are house goddesses. They live in the beam of the roof in each room. If acknowledged when entering the house, they bring the occupants good luck. They are similar to the Aitvaras of Prussia and the Roman Lares (qq.v.). *See also* Bannik; Chlevnik; Dolya; Dvorovoi; Khoromozitel; Kikimora; Krukis; Ovinnik.

Domovoj *Domovui* (Russia)

Also known as: *Karliki* (Slavic) *Iskrzychi* (Poland), *Syenovik and Tsmok* (Russia), *Haltia, Haldja* (Finnish), *Holdja* (Estonia).

House spirit. These domestic dwarf spirits are similar to Domovoy of the Slavs, and Aitvaras of Prussia. Under the name of Haltia or Haldja, this spirit was the ruler who precedes men almost as a ghost or shadow. Sometimes the Domovoj come in the shape of a dog or cat. Halti and Holdja are house goddesses. They live in the beam of the roof in each room. If acknowledged when entering the house, they bring the occupants good luck.

Domovoy (Russia) *see* Domovoi; Dvorovoi.

Domovui (Russia) *see* Domovoi; Dvorovoi.

Don (British, Celtic)

Also known as: *Dana.*

Goddess of fertility. Don is known as the mother of the Welsh pantheon as related in the fourth branch of the Mabinogion. She is associated in Wales and Britain with the Irish earth mother Dana. Some of the Children of Don (meaning ancestors) were Gwydion, Govannon, Ludd, and Arianrhod. Don is thought of as the mother of the sacred tribe. Some renditions place her as mother of Math and wife of Beli. *See also* Arianrhod; Dana; Gwydion; Math.

Don the Enchanter (Celtic) *see* Gwydion; Pryderi.

Donar (Teutonic)

Also known as: *Thor, Thunar* (Anglo Saxon).

Donar is an alternate name for Thor, the thunder god. As Donar, his symbol is the swastika. *See also* Thor.

Dongo (Songhoi People, Africa)

God of Thunder. Legend says Dongo threw his axe into heaven to try it out, then when one of the villagers made a spark, Dongo threw his axe at it killing all his companions. His grandfather told him to fill his mouth with water and spray it on his companions which brought them back to life.

Donn (Celtic) *see* Achren.

Donu (Celtic) *see* Dana.

Door Guards (China) *see* Men-shen.

Doorga (India) *see* Devi.

Dor-le (Tibet) *see* Dam-c'an-r-do-rje-legs-pa.

Dori (Teutonic) *see* Dwarfs.

Doris (Greek)

She is the sea goddess spouse of Nereus, and the mother of the Nereids. Her parents are Oceanus and Tethys. *See also* Amphitrite; Ceto; Nereids; Nereus; Oceanids; Oceanus; Tethys.

Dorje-Naljorma *Toma* (Tibet), *Vajra-Yogini* (Tibet)

This Tantric goddess personifies spiritual energy and intellect. She is described as sixteen years of age, with one face, three eyes and two hands. The Flames of Wisdom form a halo around her. She is in a dancing position, with her right leg bent and foot uplifted. Her left leg is on the breast of a prostrate human. *See also* Devis; Toma; Vajra-Yogini.

Dorje Phagmo *Dorje-phe-mo* (Tibet), *rDorje-P'ag-mo* (Buddhist; India, Tibet)

Also known as: *Vajra-Varahi, Vajrabarahi, Vajravarahi.*

Dorje Phagmo is known as the Thunderbolt Sow, the Great Diamond Sow, the Female Energy of All Good, and the Most Precious Power of Speech. She is a Khadoma (female demon) and a Bodhisattva (a person who has attained enlightenment). Once when her monastery in Tibet was threatened, she turned herself and her attendant monks and nuns into pigs for protection. When the invaders saw an empty monastery, they said they would not loot it. Dorje Phagmo and her populace returned to human form in front of the invaders and then metamorphized everyone back into swine. This terrified the would-be looters into a state of awe. Instead of taking items away, they presented the monastery with priceless gifts. When called upon, Dorje Phagmo can bestow supernatural powers on her followers. As Vajravarahi, she is the consort (sakti) of Cakra-samvara, the Buddha of sublime happiness. In Tibet, he is known as dDe-mch-og-dpal-kor-lo-dom-pa or Dem-chho-pal-khor-lo-dom-pa. A dorje is a type of thunderbolt. The name Dorje Phagmo is interpreted as "Thunderbolt Sow." As Vajravarahi, she is depicted excreting a sow's head from her right ear. Her color is red; her position (asana) is dancing. One of her emblems is the kapala (Sanskrit), also called the t'od-p'or (Tibetan), an altar object that is also the emblem of Buddhasaktis, Dakinis, Dharmapala, Ekajata and Yi-dam. The Khados correspond to the Indian Dakinis (female demons). *See also* Dakini; Sambara (B); Varahi.

Dorje-phe-mo (Tibet) *see* Dorje Phagmo.

Dorje-sem-pa (Tibet) *see* Vajrasatwa.

Dorobo (Masai People, Africa) *see* Ngai.

Doros (Greek) *see* Achaeus.

Dorr-Karing (Swedish)

Door spirit. Legend says she stands by the doorway and blows out the candles of those entering or leaving. *See also* Uksakka.

Dorus (A) (Greek)

He is the son of Hellen and Ortheis. His siblings are Aeolus and Xuthus. Aegimius and Tectamus are his children. *See also* Aeolus (A); Hellen.

Dorus (B) (Greek)

Apollo and Phthia are his parents, and Laodocus and Polypoetes are his siblings. He is the father of Xanthippe. *See also* Polypoetes.

Dorus (C) (Greek) He is the son of Xuthus and Creusa (qq.v.).

Doso (Greek)

Doso is the name Demeter used while she nursed Demophon in disguise. *See also* Demeter; Demophon.

Dotis (Greek) *see* Ares.

Doto (Greek) One of the fifty Nereids (q.v.).

Drac (A) *Draca* (Middle Eastern)

The Drac are female water spirits who entice women and children into the water and devour them.

Drac (B) (French) A spirit feared by peasants.

Dragon Kings (Taoist; China)

Also known as: *Lung-Wang.*

Weather deities. There were either four, eight, or ten of these deities. Creatures said to represent the yang force (*see* Yin and Yang). They were associated with the waters of lakes, rivers, and the sea, and all fell under the rule Yu-ti. Four brothers, Ao Kuang (Eastern sea), Ao Jun (Western sea), Ao Shun (Northern sea) and Ao Ch'in (also spelled Ao-K'in (Southern sea), were lords of the seas surrounding the earth. Each had his crystal palace, court, and attendants. In the Taoist belief there are four kings; Kuang-te, Kuang-li, Kuang-jun and Kuang-she. In a similar legend, a dragon called Enlightener of the Darkness had control over light and darkness by the opening and closing of his eyes. His breath brought wind and rain, cold and fire. The Dragon Kings are generally shown as a serpent or dragon. Similar to the Nagas (q.v.). *See also* Lung; Nine Songs; Ssu-ling; Yama Kings.

Drauga (Persia) *see* Angra Mainyu.

Draupadi, Princess *Panchali* (India)

See also Arjuna; Duryodhana; Karna; Kunti; Pandavas.

Draupner (Teutonic) *see* Draupnir.

Draupnir *Draupner* (Norse; Teutonic)

Also known as: *Dropper.*

Emblem of fertility. A magic ring. Eight similar rings dropped from the original ring every night. Some say the ring produced eight rings on every ninth night. The rings were manufactured by the dwarfs who presented them as a gift to Odin. The dwarf, Sindri, is sometimes referred to as the manufacturer of the rings. Other writers say it was the dwarfs Eitri and Brokk who forged the original ring. It is pictured as a large red gold ring shaped as a snake with its tail in its mouth. *See also* Dwarfs; Odin; Sindri.

Dreams (Greek)

Also known as: *Oneiroi.*

The Oneiroi are the children of Nyx or Hypnos, or Erebus. They guard the Underworld entrance. *See also* Aether; Hypnos; Keres; Nemesis; Nox.

Dri-chab-ma (Tibet) *see* Ganda.

Dri-chha-ma (Tibet) *see* Ganda.

Dripping Water (Zuni People, North America)

She is the mother of the twins, the Ahayuta Achi (q.v.).

Dromi (Norse; Teutonic)

Dromi is the second of three chains that bind Fenrir the wolf. The other chains are Laeding and Gleipnir. *See also* Fenrir; Gleipnir.

Drona (A) (India)

Drona, a martial arts expert, is the son of Bharadvaja (q.v.). *See also* Bhima (A); Duryodhana.

Drona (B) (India)

Wife of Kripa, Mother of Ashvatthaman. *See also* Duryodhana.

Dropper (Teutonic) *see* Draupnir.

Droudje (Persia) *see* Drujs.

Druantia (Celtic) Goddess of fir trees.

Drudge (Teutonic) *see* Thor.

Drugas (Persia) *see* Angra Mainyu.

Druge (Persia) *see* Drujs.

Druj (Persia) *see* Angra Mainyu; Drujs.

Drujs *Droudje, Druge, Duruge, Nasu* (India, Persia)
These monstrous demons of deceit, often female, were adversaries of the Amesha Spentas. Nasu and Ahzi Dahaka were Drujs. Nasu, the female demon, disguised as a fly, would land on corpses to assist in their corruption. Ahzi Dahaka was a three-headed serpent with six eyes and three pairs of fangs. He was later assimilated into the mortal king, Zohak, the enemy of Persia. He was also said to be an adversary of Yima. Another Druj was Jahi who was associated with Ahriman. Originally, Druj was a goddess. Druj is also an epithet for Angra Mainyu (q.v.). The Drujs are associated with the Pairikas and Yata (qq.v.). *See also* Ahzi Dahaka; Amesha Spentas; Angra Mainyu; Jahi; Mashya and Mashyoi; Nasu; Yima.

Drukh (Hindu; India)
Malignant spirits who were companions of Vritra (q.v.).

Drumalika (Hindu; India)
During the second age of the world, Drumalika, a demon, assumed the form of King Ugrasena, and raped his wife Queen Pavanarekha as she strolled through the forest. After his act of violence, he resumed his demon form and revealed to her that she would bear a son, who would rule nine divisions of the earth and would become the archenemy of Krishna. The son, Kansa, was born ten months later. Kansa, evil personified, murdered children, and forced King Jarasandha of Magadha to give him two of his daughters, whom he married. He deposed King Ugrasena who ruled the peaceful, agricultural kingdom of the Yadavas of Northern India and banned all worship of the god Vishnu. The gods decided that it was time to intervene and send Vishnu to earth in his avatar as Krishna to restore a balance between good and evil. *See also* Kansa; Krishna.

Drvaspa (Persian) *see* Dervaspa.

Dryades *Dryads* (Greek)
Also known as: *Hamadryads.*
In early times Dryades were the protectors of the forest; specifically the oak tree. In later periods, these nymphs were associated with the Hamadryads and would reside in any tree; with the exception of fruit trees which were reserved for Maliades. It is said that if a branch of her tree was thoughtlessly broken or injured, the mortal would be punished by a Dryade. They are depicted as females crowned with oak leaves and armed with axes. *See also* Hamadryads; Naiads; Nereids; Nymphs; Oceanids.

Dryads (Greek) *see* Dryades.

Dryas (A) (Greek) Son of Ares.

Dryas (B) (Greek)
She is the daughter of Faunas, and the sister of Acis. She hated men and never appeared in public. *See also* Acis.

Dryas (C) (Greek) He is a centaur associated with Peirithous.

Dryas (D) (Greek) Son of Lycurgus.

Dryas (E) (Greek)
Father of Lycurgus, who was the king of the Edonians of Thrace.

Dryh Basy (Persia)
A corpse demon who is the personification of the spirit of corruption, decomposition, contagion and impurity.

Dryope (A) (Greek)
She is a fountain nymph who was so in love with Hylas that she drew him into her fountain. *See also* Hylas.

Dryope (B) (Greek)
She is the daughter of Eurytus and the mother of Amphissus by Apollo.

Dryope (C) (Greek)
Aphrodite possessed Dryope's body. She used it to arouse the women of Lemnos to kill all their men.

Dryope (D) (Greek)
Pan is possibly her son by Hermes. Dryope is the daughter of Dryops and Polydore.

Dryops (A) (Greek)
He is the father of Dryope and spouse of Polydore.

Dryops (B) (Greek) Son of Apollo.

Dryops (C) (Greek) Son of Priam.

Dryops (D) (Greek)
He is associated with Aeneas, the son of Anchises and Aphrodite.

Dsam-Bha-La (Tibet) *see* Jambhala.

Dsovean (Armenia)
Storm god. Husband of the storm goddess Dsovinar. Some think Dsovean is the same as the old god Vahagn. *See also* Agni; Vahagn.

Dsovinar (Armenia)
Storm goddess. Wife of the storm god Dsovean. *See also* Dsovean.

Duamutef (Egypt) *see* Tuamutef.

Duat (Egypt) *see* Tuat.

Dubbisag (Sumer) *see* Nabu.

Dubh Lacha (Irish) Sea-goddess.

Dufr (Teutonic) *see* Dwarfs.

Dug-Po-Ma (Tibet) *see* Dhupa.

Dughda *Dughdhova* (Persia)
Virgin mother of Zoroaster (q.v.).

Dughdhova (Persia) *see* Dughda.

Duhsasana *Dushasana* (India) *see* Bhima (A).

Dula (India) A Krittika sister. *See also* Rishi.

Dulachan (Celtic)
Similar to the Cluricanes, the Dulachan are malicious goblins or elves. *See also* Cluricanes; Dwarfs; Elves.

Dumazu (Sumer) *see* Dumuzi.

Dumu-e-zi (Sumer) *see* Dumuzi.

Dumu-zi (Sumer) *see* Dumuzi.

Dumuduku (Babylonia) *see* Marduk.

Dumunzi (Sumer) *see* Dumuzi.

Dumuzi *Dumazu, Dumu-e-zi, Dumu-zi, Dumunzi, Dumuziabzu, Dumuziapsu, Dumuzida* (Sumerian; Accadian)
Also known as: *Damu, Tammuz* (Babylon), *Ziapsu.*
This Sumerian vegetation god and shepherd god was later identified with the Babylonian god, Tammuz. To the chagrin of Enkidu and Utu, he became the mate of Inanna. His sister Gestinanna interpreted his nightmares and deduced that he was being attacked by demons. He fled and she vowed that she would never divulge his whereabouts. When the demons arrived, they attacked her but she remained steadfast in her vow of silence. (Her name means "Lady of Desolation.") Eventually, the demons discovered Dumuzi in the form of a gazelle hiding among his sister's sheep. They carried him off to the underworld. She pursued them, and in time was able to convince the underworld deities to allow Dumuzi to live six months on earth each year if she remained six months of each year in the underworld. The three most important females in his life were his devoted sister Gestinanna, his wife Inanna, and his mother, Ninsun. The dying Dumuzi is shown with the three women surrounding him. Some say he was the son of Ea and husband/son of Innini. The goddess Gula-Bau has also been called his mother/wife. His animal is the bull. Compare Dumuzi to the Babylonian Tammuz and Ishtar and the Phrygian Cybele and Attis. Some compare him to the Greek Adonis (q.v.). Compare Dumuzi to the Celtic Angus. *See* Inanna for another interpretation of his descent into the underworld. *See also* Ea; Enki; Enkidu; Gestinanna; Gula; Ninsun; Nintud; Shala; Utu.

Dumuziabzu (Sumer) *see* Dumuzi.

Dumuziapsu (Sumer) *see* Dumuzi.

Dumuzida (Sumer) *see* Dumuzi.

Duneyr (Teutonic) *see* Dain; Dwarfs; Yggdrasil.

Dunga (Assyro-Babylonia)
A name for Ea as the deity of singers and psalmists.

Dup Shimate *Dup Shimati* (Sumer)
The name of the Tablets of Fate (q.v.).

Dup Shimati (Sumer) *see* Tablets of Fate.

Dur-Europas Ba'al Shamin *see* (Mesopotamia).

Duramulun *Daramulum* (Aborigine People, Australia)
Also known as: *Baiame, Thuremlin.*

Creator. He was the first to dwell on earth, but he created man on a planet that had only animals. He gives the medicine man his powers. Some versions call him the son of Baiame of Ngalaibal. Duramulun was one of the survivors of the flood. *See also* Baiame.

Durapror (Teutonic) *see* Yggdrasil.

Durathror (Teutonic) *see* Dain; Dwarfs.

Durga (Hindu; India)
Also known as: *Ambika* (Mother), *Bhadrakali, Bhima, Chamunda, Chanda, Chandi, Chandika* (The Burning or Fierce), *Devi, Durga Mahisasuramardini, Gauri, Gaya* (The Conquering), *Jaganmatri, Kali, Karala* (The Formidable), *Karali, Kausiki* (Like an Owl), *Mahalaxmi, Mahishamardini* (Killing Mahisa), *Parvati, Pathalavati* (Pale Red), *Sarika* (Bird), *Sati, Shakti, Simharatha* (having a car drawn by lions), *Skanda, Uma* (Light), *Vetanda* (Like an Elephant), *Vetala* (Ghoul), *Vikathikarala* (Fearful).
Durga, the invincible destroyer, warrior and goddess of death, is an aspect of the Great Mother Devi, who was born from the wrath of Vishnu and Shiva. She was formed by the flames in their mouths to evict the demon Mahisasura from heaven. Equipped by the gods with the most powerful of weapons, she engaged in battle with Mahisasura who was disguised as a buffalo. After slaying the animal, she defeated the demons Kaitabha and Madhu who were born from Vishnu during his cosmic sleep. Next, the demon brothers Sumbha and Nisumbha attempted to reign over the deities. Once again, they called upon Durga. She appeared as the beautiful goddess Parvati to soothe the worried gods. After reassuring them, she marched into battle as Durga and confronted the demons Canda and Munda. As they approached her ready for combat, she furrowed her brow and the terrifying warrior goddess Kali emerged. Kali was ready for war. She flung the demons around, crushed them with her jaws and decapitated them with her sword. The heads were given to Durga as a gift. As the slayer of demons, Durga is often called Kali-Durga. Durga, meaning "inaccessible," resides on the sacred Mount Mandara. She is usually depicted as a full-breasted female clothed in yellow and riding a tiger or lion. She is shown with two to ten arms. Sometimes she has vampire teeth and four arms. She is also shown as a beautiful woman with ten arms holding the moon-disk and a skull. In her most common depiction, she has eight arms, holding a sword, arrow, chakra, shield, noose, javelin, bow and conch shell. In Indian depictions, a violent struggle is shown between Durga and the buffalo. In Javanese depictions, the buffalo is in a recumbent position and the dwarf-like figure of Mahisasura is seen emerging from the animal. In a specific rendering thought to be typical, Durga stands on its back and head with her feet apart. In her three left hands she holds a conch, shield, and bow. In three rights hands she holds a sic, sword and arrow. Her fourth hand pulls at the tail of the animal. Her festival is called the Durga-puja and is held from the seventh to the tenth days of the bright fortnight of Asvina (September–October). During this time, Durga is invoked on a twig from the sacred vilva tree. In another interpretation of Durga as an aspect of Devi, it is said the goddess Devi acquired the name Durga for her fierce form from the demon of the same name

whom she slaughtered after a fierce battle. He had taken over the three worlds and forced the gods to live in the forest and worship him. His power was so great that fires could not burn, stars disappeared and waters stood still. In desperation, the gods asked Shiva to attempt to rid the universe of the personification of evil. He turned to his mate Devi for a solution to the problem. Initially, she created the entity Kalaratri to rid the world of this foe, but he was unsuccessful. Devi decided to overcome him herself. The pronunciation of the name Durga is with a long final vowel when referring to the goddess and with a short final vowel when referring to the demon. *See also* Agni; Ana-Purna; Badari; Devi; Devis; Gauri; Kali; Mahalaxmi; Meru Mountain; Parvati; Rudra, Sati; Shakti; Shiva; Vilva; Vishnu.

Durga Mahisasuramardini (India) *see* Durga.

Durga Purga (India)
Hindu festival also known as Nava-ratri. *See also* Durga; Kali.

Durin (Norse; Teutonic)
Also known as: *Durinn.*
First of the Dwarfs. Assistant or second in command to Modsognir who was chief of the dwarfs. He helped create the dwarfs. *See also* Modsognir.

Duruge (Persia) *see* Drujs.

Durvasas (India) *see* Karna and Kunti.

Duryodhana (Hindu; India)
Duryodhana, a Kaurava, was the eldest of the one hundred sons of the blind king, Dhritarashtra. His father also raised his brother Pandu's five sons, the Pandavas. The Kauravas were jealous of the Pandavas and tried numerous methods to destroy them. Duryodhana's hatred was obsessive. He attempted to poison Bhima, and then set fire to his cousins' home. In desperation, he arranged a gambling match. The stakes were high. The losers were to forego their freedom. To ensure his victory, Duryodhana had the charlatan, Sakuni, prompt him. Yudhisthira, the eldest of the Pandavas, gambled and lost his own freedom and that of his brothers and their common wife, the princess Draupadi. When Duryodhana took advantage of the situation by humiliating her, Bhima swore revenge. Thirteen years later, after the great war of the Mahabharata, the defeated Duryodhana sought refuge under water. He emerged to duel with Bhima who extracted his revenge by smashing his thigh. Ashvatthaman, the son of Drona and Kripa, who was a Kaurava warrior, came upon him alone in a field. He promised to bring him the five heads of the Pandava brothers. When he returned, Duryodhana realized that Ashvatthaman had murdered the young sons of Draupadi, whom he did not hate. Duryodhana died at the grisly sight of their heads. *See also* Arjuna; Bala-Rama; Bhima (A); Dhritarashtra; Karna; Kauravas; Krishna; Pandavas.

Dus (Scrat; Teutonic) (Celtic) Demons.

Dusares *Dousares, Dusura* (Arabia, Greek, Roman)
Sun god or possibly a god of mountains. God of the vine. A local god of South Arabia, who was worshiped by the Romans. In some versions, his mother is a virgin goddess named Chaabu. He is depicted as a black stone pillar on a base of gold and sometimes as a human figure holding a cornucopia. Dusares is identified with Bacchus and Dionysus. Some identify him with Tammuz.

Dushasana (India) *see* Duhsasana.

Dushyanta (India) *see* Bharata (B); Shakuntala.

Dusii (Celtic)
They are demons comparable to the medieval European Incubus, the Persian Jinn, Greek Satyrs, and Samoan Hotua Poro. *See also* Demons.

Dusuara (Greek) *see* Dusares.

Duzakh (Persia) *see* Dzokh; Hades; Hell.

Dvalin *Davalin, Dvalinn* (Norse; Teutonic)
Dwarf smith. Dvalin was one of the dwarfs created by Modsognir. He is the son of Ivald, and brother of Sindri or Brock. He assisted Sindri in forging the sword, known as Tyrfing, or the spear, known as Gungnir, and Freyja's necklace, known as Brisingamen. He also fashioned the ship Skidbladnir for Odin. *See also* Brisingamen; Freyja; Loki.

Dvaraka (India) *see* Dvarka.

Dvarapala (Indonesia) Temple Guardians.

Dvarka (India)
Celestial Abode. *See also* Bala-Rama; Krishna; Parijata; Pradyuma; Swarga; Yadavas.

Dvergar (Teutonic) *see* Dwarfs.

Dvivida (India) Monkey Child. *See also* Asvins.

Dvorovoi (Finno-Ugric; Slavic)
Also known as: *Domovik, Domovoi, Domovoj, Domovoy, Domovui, Korka-kuzo* (Finno-Ugric), *Korka-murt* (Finno-Ugric).
These courtyard spirits hate all animals with white fur. They are not always friendly to humans. Sometimes they dwell under the floor of the house. As Korka-kuzo or Korka-murt, when they are not friendly, they cause nightmares. They have the power to substitute small children for changelings. Sacrificing a black sheep can placate them. *See also* Domovoi.

Dwaparayuga (Hindu; India)
Also known as: *Dwarpara.*
Part of the Kalpa cycle, (or Day of Brahma), Dwaparayuga is the third of the four Yugas (ages) of the current Mahayugas (epoch). The other Yugas are Krita, the first of the Yugas; Tretayuga, the second of the Yugas; Kaliyuga (named for the goddess Kali), the fourth Yuga. Dwaparayuga will last for 2,400 divine years. Each divine year is 360 human years. Dwaparayuga's total length is 864,000 human years. During this period, with virtue at 50 percent, Dharma, the god of justice and duty, is yellow in color, and walks on two legs. *See also* Brahma; Dharman; Kaliyuga; Kalpa; Krita; Tretayuga.

Dwarfs *Dwarves* (Norse; Teutonic)

Also known as: *Dvergar*.

Almost all mythology has tales of these diminutive beings. They are often called artisans, and many are smiths or gold workers. Some of the dwarfs mentioned in Norse mythology are Ai, Alf, Alvis, An, Andvari, Annar, Austi, Bafur, Bifur, Bombor, Brokk, Dain, Dolgthvari, Dori, Draupnir, Dufr, Duneyr, Durathror, Durin, Dvalin, Eikinskjaudi, Fal, Fili, Fith, Fjalar, Frosti, Fundin, Galar, Gandalf, Ginnar, Gloin, Har, Haur, Hornbori, Ingi, Jari, Kili, Lit, Loni, Mjodvitnir, Moin, Nain, Nali, Nar, Nibelung, Nidi, Nipingr, Nordri, Nyi, Nyr, Oinn, Ori, Radsuithr, Radsvid, Regin, Rekk, Sjarr, Skandar, Skirfir, Sudri, Thekkr, Thorin, Thror, Thrurinn, Vali, Veigur, Vestri, Vig, Vindalf, Virvir, Vithur, and Yingi. India had Agastya, Egypt called Bes a dwarf, and others were Cedalion (Greek), Gahongas (Iroquois), and Kaukis (Prussia). Elves and Dwarfs are frequently confused. The original elves, said to be of Norse origin, were called Alfar. There are two groups of Alfar: light (Lios Alfar) or dark (Svart Alfar). The Lios Alfar are ruled by Freyr, and the Svart Alfar, who live in the underground known as Svart-Alfa-Heim, are ruled by Wayland the Smith. If they break a rule and make an appearance during the day, they are turned to stone. Dwarfs, trolls and gnomes spend their time collecting gold, silver and valuable stones which they secret away. The fairies and elves live in a bright, airy realm located between heaven and earth. They spend their time flitting around enjoying the finery of nature or dancing in the moonlight. *See also* Alfar; Alvis; Berling; Bifur; Brisingamen; Brokk; Brownie; Dain; Draupnir; Durin; Dvalin; Elves; Fenrir; Fjalar; Freyja; Freyr; Gleipnir; Kvasir; Midgard; Nibelung; Nordri; Pusait; Regin; Sindri; Sudri; Svart-Alfa-Heim; Ymir.

Dwarka (India) *see* Krishna; Visvakarma.

Dwumwem (Celtic) *see* Dwyn.

Dwyn (Celtic)

Also known as: *Dwumwem, Oengus*.

God of Love. *See also* Angus.

Dwynwen (Celtic) *see* Oengus.

Dxui (Bushmen, Central Africa)

Also known as: *Thixo* (Ponda, Xhosa People), *Tsui* (Bushmen).

Creator god. For details, *see also* Tsui.

Dyai (Tucana People, Amazon, South America)

Dyai and his wicked brother Epi were the sons of Nutapa. Dyai was born from his father's right knee, and Epi was born from his father's left knee. When Nutapa was killed by a jaguar, his sons brought him back to life. Dyai was Epi's caregiver. He constantly rescued him from difficulties. The brothers caught a fish from which they created man. The two brothers eventually parted. Dyai went to the east, and Epi to the west.

Dyaus *Diaus, Dyu, Dyhu* (Hindu,Vedic; India)

Also known as: *Dyaus-Pita* (Sky-Father), *Dyaus-Pitar, Dyava-Prithivi* (used when speaking of Dyaus and Prithivi).

Dyaus a sky deity, god of thunder, rain and fertility, is an early Vedic deity, the husband of Prithiva (Earth). He was the father of Ushas (Dawn), Agni (Fire) and Indra and according to some the father of Surya the sun god and possibly the Asvins. Originally, the couple was considered to be the parents of the gods and mortals. Dyaus was murdered by Indra, who then established himself as ruler of the universe. Dyavan (the sky) or Varuna (heaven), is the home of Dyaus. He is sometimes confused with the Greek Dyeus or Zeus. Dyaus is called Father, Dyaus-Pital, similar to Zeus Pater and the Roman Jupiter and the Greek Zeus. Dyaus is depicted as a bull and Prithiva as a cow. *See also* Agni; Asvins; Devas; Indra; Prithiva; Ratri; Surya; Tvashtri; Ushas.

Dyaus-Pita *Dyaus-Pitar* (India)

Sky Father. *See also* Dyaus; Prithiva; Vedas.

Dyaus-Pitar (India) *see* Dyaus-Pita.

Dyaus-Pitri (India) *see* Prithiva.

Dyava-Matar (India) Earth Mother. *See also* Prithiva.

Dyava-Prithivi (India) *see* Dyaus.

Dyavaprithivi (India) *see* Prithiva.

Dyavaprthivi (India) *see* Prithiva.

Dyavo (Slavic) Serbian demons. *See also* Demons.

Dyhu (India) *see* Dyaus.

Dylan (Celtic)

Also known as: *Eilton* (Son of the Wave), *Endil*.

The brother of Llew, Dylan dove into the sea when he was born. As a sea god, he was known as Eilton and Endil. *See also* Arianrhod; Llew Llaw Gyffes; Pryderi.

Dymas (A) (Greek)

Dymas, a Trojan, disguised himself as a Greek during the Trojan War. He was killed by the Trojans. *See also* Aegimius.

Dymas (B) (Greek) King of Phrygia.

Dyna (Greek) *see* Evander (B).

Dynamene (Greek)

She is one of the fifty daughters of Nereus and Doris, known as the Nereids (q.v.).

Dyne (Greek) *see* Evander (B).

Dyotana (India) The Light Bearer. *See also* Ushas.

Dyu (India) *see* Dyaus.

Dzalarhons (Haida People, North America) *see* Dzelarhons.

Dzelarhons *Dzalarhons* (Haida People, North America)

Also known as: *Volcano Woman*.

She is a mountain spirit. Known as the Volcano Woman, she rules the creatures of the earth and punishes abusers of the creatures.

Dzhe Manito *The Good Spirit* (Algonquin, Chippewa People, North America)

He is the second in command to the Chief of Spirits, Gitche.

Dzokh (Armenia) *see* Duzakh; Hades; Hell; Santaramet.

E

E (Maya) Maize god.

Ea (Akkadian, Assyro-Babylonian, Sumerian)

Also known as: *Amma-Ana-Ki, Aos, Dunga, Enki* (Sumerian), *Engur, Enki-Ea, Hea, Hoa* (Chaldean), *Lumha, Nadimmud, Nidim, Ninbubu, Nindubarra, Ninigiku* (King of the Sacred Eye), *Ninigikug, Nudimmud, Nurra, Oannes.*

His early names were Nudimmud and Nidim. A creator deity, Ea is the god of earth and waters, god of the deep sea and god of wisdom. He is the author of the arts of life, the teacher of civilization, and the law-giver. With Anu and Enlil he is the third member of a triad. Ea, Anu and Enlil rule the cosmos, with Ea reserving the right to rule all waters surrounding the earth. He is the water god of Eridu. He is the patron of magicians, healers, and all who practice art and crafts. His magical incantations allowed him to battle and overcome his mother Apsu, the personification of sweet waters, and Mummu (in the Babylonian Creation Myth). He divided Apsu into sections, one of which became his resting place. When Tiamat, the personification of bitter waters, intent upon avenging Apsu's death, called upon her evil forces, Ea in turn invoked Anshar for assistance and appointed his son Marduk as the leader of an order of newly established gods. From the blood of Kingu, the leader of the opposition, Ea created mortals. As a creator god, he made the gods Kulla (also known as Ki-gulla), Ninildu, Nimsimug, Arazu, Gushkinbanda, Ninagal, Ninzadim, Ninkurra, Ashnan, Lahar, Siris, Gizidu (also known as Ningizzida), Ninsar, Umunmutamku, Umunmutamnag, and Kusug. As well as Marduk, Ea is the father of the goddess Nina and some say Nanshe, the goddess of springs and canals. Some say he has a son, Asari, who is his mediator for mortals. His name means "He who does good to men." Under his titles of Dunga and Lumha, he is deity of singers and psalmists. Under the name Ninbubu, he is a god of sailors. As Nindubarra he is god of shipbuilders and as Nurra he is god of potters. As Engur he is a water-deity. Later in history he had a spouse named Damkina or Ninki. Despite his wisdom, Ea's jealousy was the cause of mortals not being able to attain immortal life. (The Sumerian god Enki in later times [second-millennium B.C.E.] became the Babylonian god Ea.) Ea is sometimes shown as a goat with a fish tail or a human with water gushing from his shoulders or from a vase. *See also* Adad (A); Adam; Adapa; Adar; Agusaya; Anshar; Anu (B); Anunnaki; Aos; Apsu; Arazu; Asari; Ashnan; Asushunamir; Baragulla; Bel (A); Belit; Bohu; Dagon; Damkina; Dumuzi; Eden; Elish; Enki (he is the same as Enki and the opposite of Enlil), Enlil; Ennugi; Enuma Ereshkigal; Eridu; Ezuab; Gasmu; Gilgamesh; Ishtar; Khi-dimme-azaga; Kingu; Kishar; Kulla; Lagamal; Lahar; Lumha; Mami; Marduk; Mummu; Nanshe; Nimsimug; Nina (B); Ninib; Ninigiku; Ninildu; Ninki; Ninkurra; Nudimmud; Oannes; Saltu; Silik-mulu-khi; Tammuz; Tiamat; Ullikummis; Umunmutamku; Usma; Utnapishtim; Ziusudra; Zu.

Eabani (Sumer) *see* Enkidu; Gilgamesh.

Eadna (Celtic) *see* Eire.

Eadon (Ireland) Goddess of poetry.

Ealur (Babylon) Another name for Zerpanitum (q.v.).

Eanna (Sumer) The dwelling place of Anu on earth.

Early Waker (Teutonic) *see* Aarvak.

Earth (A) (Norse; Teutonic)

Also known as: *Fjorgyn, Jord.*

Earth is another name for the goddess Jord who is also known as Fjorgyn. *See also* Jord.

Earth (B) (Greek) *see* Gaea.

Earthmaker (Winnebago People, North America)

Creator deity. Supreme creator of the Winnebago, He is depicted as taking pity on the human race, because having created it last, all the gifts he possessed had already been distributed to the various spirits. He created an herb which had a pleasant odor and which all the spirits immediately desired. But to them he said, "To all of you I have already given something valuable. You are all fond of this herb, is it not so? I am myself." Then he took some of the leaves, mashed them up, and, filling a pipe, smoked. The odor was pleasant to inhale. All the spirits craved tobacco, so he gave each one a puff and said: "Whatever, from now on, the human beings ask of me and for which they offer tobacco, that I will not be able to refuse. I myself will not be in control of this herb and since, of all these I have created, the human beings alone are poor, if they offer us a pipe full and make some request, we shall always grant it."

East Wind (Greek) *see* Boreas; Eurus; Notus.

East Wind Hag (Teutonic) *see* Gullveig.

Eastre (Norse; Teutonic; Saxon)

Also known as: *Eostre, Ostra.*

Goddess of spring. Probably identical with Frigga as possibly a goddess of earth or rejuvenation of spring after a long winter. *See also* Eostre; Frigga.

Eater of Hearts (Egypt) *see* Sakhmet.

Eater of the Dead (Egypt) *see* Amit.

Eaynnes (Greek) *see* Erinyes; Eumenides.

Ebhlenn (Ireland) *see* Ebhlinne.

Ebhlinne *Ebhlenn* (Ireland)

The goddess Ebhlinne, the daughter of Guaire, married a king of Cashel, and ran away with his son. She was worshiped in the southern county of Tipperary and lived in the Twelve Mountains of Ebhlenn.

Ebisu (Buddhist, Shinto; Japan)

Also known as: *Hirugo, Hiruko* (in his form as a jellyfish), *Kotoshironushi-No-Mikoto.*

God of fishermen. Patron of trade and manual workers. Ebisu is the son of Daikoku, the god of prosperity. With his father, they were members of the Shichi Fukujin (seven deities of good fortune). Ebisu and Daikoku are thought to be Shinto kami (gods). Ebisu was known as the first angler and a deity of fishermen. He represented honesty and frankness. Ebisu is depicted holding a fishing line and a large fish on a string. Usually his earlobes are swollen (a symbol of omniscience) and he wears Japanese clothes. *See also* Daikoku; Fukujin; Hiruko; Shichi.

Eblis (A) (Islam) *see* Iblis.

Eblis (B) (Muslim) *see* Azazel; Jinn; Satan.

Ec (Yenisei People, Siberia)

Also known as: *Num, Tgorem* (Ugrian people), *Torum.*

Creator deity. Supreme god of the order of the universe. A Greek name adopted by the Mongols for their high god. He abides in the seventh sky which contains the water of life. His eyes are the sun and moon. *See also* Num; Tgorem; Torum.

Ecalchot (Niquiran People, Nicaragua)

Wind god. One of the creators who are ruled by Tamagostad and Zipaltonal. He is associated with Ciaga, Quiateot, Misca, Chiquinau, and Vizetot. *See also* Chiquinau; Ciaga; Quiateot; Vizetot.

Ecbasus (Greek)

He is the son of Argus and Evadne. *See also* Argus (A).

Echauc (Maya) *see* Ah-Kiuic.

Echecatl (Aztec) *see* Quetzalcoatl.

Echecles (Greek)

He is the son of Actor and husband of the daughter of Phylas, Polymele. *See also* Actor (C).

Echedemas (Greek) *see* Academus.

Echephron (Greek)

He is the son of Nestor and Eurydice or Anaxibia. *See also* Antilochus.

Echida (Greek) *see* Echidna.

Echidna *Echida* (Greek)

Also known as: *Echis.*

Eternally youthful half-nymph, half-snake monster. There are numerous couples known as her parents. They are either Chrysaor and Callirrhoe, Phorcys and Ceto, Tartarus and Gaea, or Styx and Peiras. Her mate is the destructive whirlwind Typhon. She is the mother of the following monsters: the Caucasian Eagle, Cerberus, the Crommyonian sow, the Chimaera, Geryon, Hydra, Ladon, the Nemean lion, Orthus the dog (pos-

sibly by Orthus), the Sphinx (possibly by Orthus) and the Vultures. It is also possible that she is the mother of three children by Heracles. *See also* Aello; Argus (B); Cerberus; Chimaera; Gaea; Harpies; Phorcys; Skylla; Tartarus; Typhon (A).

Echiodna (Greek)

She is the daughter of Phorcys and Ceto. For a list of her siblings *see* Medusa.

Echion (A) (Greek)

An Argonaut. Echion is the son of Hermes and Antianeira. In the Calydonian Boar Hunt, he threw the first spear. *See also* Argonauts; Hermes.

Echion (B) (Greek)

Husband of Cadmus, father of Pentheus, he is one of the surviving Sparti (dragon-men) who sprang from the sown teeth of the dragon of Ares. *See also* Cadmus.

Echis (Greek) *see* Echidna.

Echo (Greek)

Nymph. Daughter of Gaea, and one of the Oreads. Echo, was one of Hera's attendants. Under the assumption that Echo was covering up one of her husband Zeus' affairs with nymphs, Hera took Echo's normal voice from her. She could not begin sentences, but only repeat the words of others. Echo loved Pan but left him for the beautiful Narcissus. When he spurned her, she faded away until only her voice remained. *See also* Gaea; Hera; Oreads; Pan.

Echua *Ekchuah* (Maya) *see* Ekchuah.

Echuac (Maya People, Yucatan) *see* Icona.

Ecmar (Celtic, Irish) *see* Angus; Boann.

Edda (Teutonic) *see* Ai; Heimdall; Thrall.

Eden (Hebrew, Semitic, Sumerian)

Also known as: *Garden of Eden.*

Paradise. This legend is told in the Holy Bible, third chapter of Genesis. God planted a garden in Eden toward the east. Here he placed Adam and Eve, and food trees including the "tree of life." Compare to Dilmun. The story is similar to that of Adapa, Anu and Ea. *See also* Adam.

Edie (Hebrew) *see* Adam.

Edimmu (Sumer)

The evil genie. These Utukku are the souls of unburied dead or those dead who have not received proper burial and funeral rites. They are a ceaseless thorn of revenge on the living and difficult to appease. *See also* Utukku.

Edjo (Egypt) *see* Buto (A); Nekhbet; Uadjit.

Edom (Hebrew) *see* Adam.

Edusa (Roman)

Goddess who rules the weaning of children.

Eeriboea (Greek)

She is the second wife of Aloeus (q.v.). It is possible that she is the mother of Telamon's son, Ajax.

Eeyeekalduk (Eskimo)

God of healing. He can help heal the sick. It is dangerous to look into his eyes. A small man with a black face, Eeyeekalduk lives in a stone.

Ef (Egypt) *see* Khnum.

Efe (Pygmy People, Africa)
First man. Efe was sent to earth by the supreme being, but returned to heaven. When he returned to earth after a long time, he brought spears. *See also* Orish Nla.

Efnissien (Celtic, Welsh) *see* Evnissyen.

Efrit (Arabic)
Spirits of ancient Arabians. The Efrit are evil, shape-shifters who cheat mortals. *See also* Djinns.

Efu Ra (Egypt) *see* Ra.

Egeria *Aegeria* (Roman)
Originally Egeria was a goddess of wisdom and foresight. She may have been a form of Diana as she shared the shrine at Nemi with Diana and the Camenae. In some legends she appears as the water nymph wife of king Numa Pompilius. She was a prophet and served as his advisor on occult or mystical matters, taught methods of earth worship, and pronounced the first laws of the city. In later times, she was worshiped by pregnant women who prayed for an easy delivery and who were desirous of knowing the future of the baby. *See also* Camenae; Diana.

Egesta (Greek)
She is the daughter of Hippotes, the spouse of the river god, Crimisus, and the mother of Acestes. *See also* Acestes; Crimisus.

Egil (Teutonic) *see* Orvandel.

Egilorvandel (Teutonic) *see* Orvandel.

Egis (Greek) *see* Aegeus; Aegis.

Eglimi (Teutonic) *see* Englimi.

Egyptians (Egypt) *see* Aamu.

Ehat (Egypt) *see* Ahat.

Ehecatl (Aztec People, Mexico)
Also known as: *Ehecatl-Quetzalcoatl, Quetzalcoatl* (possibly an aspect), *Texcatlipoca.*
The god of the wind, Ehecatl begins the movement of the sun and sweeps the high roadways of the rain god with his breath. *See also* Quetzalcoatl; Texcatlipoca.

Ehecatonatiuh (Aztec) *see* Legend of the Four Suns.

Ehet (Egypt) *see* Ahat.

Eidothea *Theonoe* (Greek) *see* Calchas; Theonoe.

Eidya (Greek) *see* Aeetes.

Eidyia (Greek) *see* Apsyrtus; Medea; Oceanids.

Eight Immortals, The (Buddhist, Taoist; China)
Also known as: *Ba Xian, Pa Hsien, Pa Kung.*
The Eight Immortals, seven males and one female, have various duties (although none are specific), but are usually worshiped together. Some of the immortals can only perform in conjunction with others. Versatile, they can change shape at will and fly. They are appealed to when the faithful desire to ward off evil spirits, cure minor illnesses, achieve financial success, have a long life or want to produce a male child. Their names are Han Chung-Li (Han Zhung Li), Lu Tung-pin (also spelled Lu Dongbin and also known as Lu Yan), Chang-Kuo-Lao (also spelled Zhang Kuo Lau), Lan-Ts'ai-ho (Lan Cai Ho), Han Siang-tsi (Han Xiang Zi), Tsao-kuo-chia (Cao Kuo Qin), T'ieh-Kuai Li (Di Kuai Li) and the one female, Ho-sien-ku (also spelled Ho Xian Ku). In some versions, Chung-Li-ch'uan is the chief deity, in others, it is Lu Tung-pin. In another version, one of the deities is Li Theh-kuai. Lu Tung-pin, considered to be the most popular of the Immortals, is an historical figure. Quanzhen Taoism is based on his writings. Han Chung-Li, a general during the Han dynasty, converted to Taoism. Chang Kuo-Lao and Ho-sien-ku were ordinary people, who while alive, endured suffering and injustices without complaint. The gods had tested them sorely, found them worthy and deemed them immortal. Han-chung Li, associated with immortality, wears an old green mantle and carries a feather fan to calm the sea. Lu Tung-pin, a Taoist scholar was the author of the "Hundred Character Tablet." He always carries a sword and rides a donkey backwards. Associated with medicine, he tames evil spirits with his charms. Lan Ts'ai-ho, the patron of gardeners, is said to be slightly insane. He appears as a male or a female carrying a basket of magic flowers. He began life as a street singer but later renounced all human pleasures. In the summer, he wears a tattered garment with a wide wooden belt and one shoe. During the winter months, he wears cotton and sleeps on the snow. He was carried to heaven by a stork, or in other renditions his ascent was made on a waft of wine. He threw away his belt, shoe and garments en route. Han Siang-tsi is a boy with two small hair knots on his head. He is the patron of musicians and is renowned for his poetry and music. His symbol is the jade flute. Ts'ao Kuo-kiu is a judge who carries a tablet. Ho-sien-ku is a female who wears a lotus on her shoulder. T'ieh-Kuai Li is shown as an ugly beggar who is bald and bearded and leaning on an iron crutch, which is his symbol. He is bad-tempered and has unusual ways, but his cause is directed to the poor and the weak. Compare to Arhats. *See also* Chang-Kuo-Lao; Han Chung-Li; Chung-Li-Ch'uan; Han; Han Hsiang-tzu; Lu Tung-pin.

Eikinskjaudi (Teutonic) *see* Dwarfs.

Eil (Teutonic) *see* Eir.

Eileithya (Egypt) *see* Nekhbet.

Eileithyia *Eileithyia, Eilythia, Eleuthia, Ilithyia* (Greek)
Also known as: *Lucina* (Roman).
Goddess of Childbirth. She is one of four children of Zeus and Hera. The others are: Hebe, Hephaestus and Ares. Her presence is very important during childbirth. She brings both pain and relief. Eileithyia might have been one of the ancient Cretan deities. There are versions which say she was an attendant of Hera. She is shown as a kneeling woman holding a torch. *See also* Ares; Artemis; Hera; Nekhbet.

Eilton (Celtic) *see* Dylan.

Eilythia (Roman) *see* Eileithyia.

Einheriar (Teutonic) *see* Einherjar.

Einherjar *Einheriar* (Norse; Teutonic)

Heros. The Einherjar are the warriors who have died in battle in Valhalla. They fight during the day and feast at night. They await Ragnarok, the end of the world. Einherjar is also the name of the place where they feast on the meat of the divine boar, Saehrimnir, cooked by Andhrimnir, in the magic cauldron named Eldhrimir. *See also* Ragnarok; Valhalla.

Einridi (Teutonic) *see* Thor.

Eioneus (Greek)

He is the son of Magnes. His siblings are Pierus and Hymenaeus. He courted Hippodameia and was killed by her father, Oenomaus. *See also* Hippodameia; Ixion.

Eir (Norse; Teutonic)

Also known as: *Eil, Eira, Eyr, Eyra.*

Goddess of Healing. A skilled physician, she also is an attendant to Frigga. Eir lives on Lyfjaberg, the hill of healing, with Menglad, Hlif, Hlifthrasa, Thjodvara, Bjort, Bleik, Blid, Frid, and Aurboda. They are all deities of help and healing. Eir taught medicine to women who were the only physicians in ancient Scandinavia. *See also* Frigga.

Eira (Teutonic) *see* Eir.

Eire (Celtic)

Also known as: *Ama, Anan, Anith, Anonach, Anu, Eadna, Eirean, Eirin, Eirinn, Eoghana, Iath, Ith, Momo, Mumham, Nannan, Nanu, Ops, Sibhol, Tlachgo, Tlacht.*

A mother goddess, Eire is probably an earth deity or a deity of water or darkness. Eire is possibly the same as Eriu (q.v.). *See also* Aesar (B).

Eirear (Celtic) *see* Eire.

Eirene *Irene* (Greek)

Also known as: *Pax* (Roman).

Eirene, the goddess of peace, is the daughter of Zeus and Themis. She is one of the Horae. *See also* Dike; Horae; Irene; Plutus; Themis.

Eirin (Celtic) *see* Eire.

Eithinoha (Huron, Iroquois People, North America)

One of the lower powers. Mother of spirit of wheat, Onatha.

Eitri (Norse; Teutonic)

Dwarf smith. Eitri is a master smith who fashioned the three gifts for the gods. His brother is Brokk. They manufactured the magic ring, Draupnir, the golden boar, Gullinbursti, and the hammer, Mjollnir. He is associated with Loki in that Brokk sewed Loki's lips together with Eitri's awl. *See also* Brokk; Draupnir; Dwarfs.

Eitumatupua (South Pacific)

He is the sky god spouse of the earth goddess Ilaheva, and father of Ahoeitu the King of Tonga. Jealous of their earth-born brother Ahoeitu, Eitumatupua's heavenly sons attacked and ate him. When the father found out he gathered the sons together and made them vomit. With the aid of magic herbs, Eitumatupua pieced his son together and gave him the kingdom of Tonga.

Ek Oankar (Sikh; India) The Supreme Being.

Eka *"One."* (India) *see* Devi.

Eka Obasi (West Africa) *see* Isong.

Ekadanta (India) *see* Ganesha.

Ekadzati (Tibet) One-eyed Goddess of Wisdom.

Ekajata (India) *see* Tara.

Ekako (Collao) *see* Ekkekko.

Ekchuah *Echua* (Maya)

He is the god of travelers and of planters, specifically cacao planters. He was known to have battled the god "F," the god of war or sacrifice, unsuccessfully on numerous occassions. He may be the god "M." Ekchuah has a black face and an unusually large nose. *See also* Acatl; Becabs; Icona.

Ekeko (*Collao*) *see* Ekkekko.

Ekhi (Akkadian) *see* Akha.

Ekkekko *Ekako, Ekeko, Eq'eq'o* (Andean, Collao People, South America)

Prosperity deity. Domestic good luck deity. The Ekkekko is a popular icon of good luck and is the counterpart of the Anchancho. Numerous myths have been related about the good fortune bestowed upon mortals by Ekkekko. In one legend, the Anchancho are the children of Mallcu of Chacamita, a renowned prince and his mistresses. The Ekkekko are his children by his wife, Curaj Mama. The Ekkekko are usually small figures of a happy, fat, bald man often wearing a poncho and a peaked cap. *See also* Achachilas; Anchancho; Supay.

Ekki (Turkey) *see* Akka.

El *Al, Elah, Il* (Ugarit, Canaanite, Semite, Phoenician, Ugarit)

Also known as: *Agros, Allah, Elat* (femine form of El), *Elioun, Eloah, Elohim* (plural of El), *Elyon, Ilah, Ilu.*

Supreme Semitic god. Chief god in the hierarchy of the Phoenician pantheon. Father of gods, mortals and time. Fertility god. Sun god. The word "El" means god in the sense of the supreme deity. Husband of Athirat, father of Shahar and Shalim. He dwells in the hollow of the Abyss at the Source of All Rivers. Another authority states that his wife is Asherah of the Sea, though others call her a close advisor. El's son is Baal, who is often shown with horns, brandishing a club, and holding a thunderbolt. Some writers say his sons' names are Mot and Latpon, and that Mot was his favorite. Sometimes shown as a bull or an old bearded man. He was possibly replaced by Baal. El is similar to Yahweh. Some think that the Semitic El was originally a god of the oak tree. *See also* Agros; Anat; Asherah (B); Baal; Elohim; Mot.

El Gran Dios (Spanish) *see* Nukuchyumchakob; Yumchakob.

el-Khudr (Arabic) *see* Elijah.

El Lat (Arabic) *see* Allat.

Eladu (Celtic) *see* Dagda.

Elagabalus (Roman)

He is a Roman emperor, worshipped as a variant of Baal at Emesa (C.E. 218–22). *See also* Baal.

Elah (Ugarit) *see* El.

Elara *Elare* (Greek)

She is the daughter of Ochomenus. An affair with Zeus resulted in the birth of the Euboeoan giant, Titysus (q.v.).

Elat (Sumer) Female form of El.

Elatha (Celtic) *see* Bress; Dagda.

Elathan (Ireland) *see* Bress.

Elbegast (Teutonic) *see* Andvari.

Elcmar (Celtic, Irish) *see* Angus; Boann.

Elcmhaire (Celtic, Irish) *see* Angus; Boann.

Eldhrimir (Teutonic) *see* Odraerir.

Eldir (Teutonic) *see* Aegir.

Electra (A) *Elektra* (Greek)

Also known as: *Laodice.*

She is most frequently called the daughter of Agamemnon and Clytemnestra. Electra is also known as the daughter of Oceanus and Tethys, the daughter of Iris and mother of Dardanos and Iasion by Ilios the sky god, or the wife of Thaumas and mother of Iris and the Harpies. As the daughter of Agamemnon and Clytemnestra, her siblings are Orestes, the musician and poet, Chrysothemis and Iphigenia. She encouraged Orestes to kill their mother. The motive was to assuage her fury with her mother for having an affair with Aegisthus. This act also avenged the death of her father. Electra married her brother's childhood friend, Pylades, and became the mother of Medon and Strophius II. *See also* Aello; Agamemnon; Electra (B); Electra (C); Eumenides; Harmonia; Harpies; Oceanids; Orestes.

Electra (B) (Greek)

She is the daughter of Agenor and Telephassa. Her siblings are Cadmus, Cilix, Europa, Demodoce, Phineus, Thasus, and Phoenix.

Electra (C) (Greek)

Electra is one of Helen of Troy's attendants.

Electra (D) (Greek)

One of the Pleiades (q.v.). The daughter of Atlas and Pleione, her siblings are Alcyone, Celaeno, Maia, Merope, Sterope and Taygete. An affair with Zeus produced two children, Dardanus and Iasion. *See also* Atlas; Merope; Sterope; Zeus.

Electryon (Greek)

He was the king of Mycenae. His parents are Perseus and Andromeda. Electryon's son-in-law, Amphitryon, accidentally killed him. Amphitryon was later purified by Creon. *See also* Amphitryon; Andromeda; Gorgophone; Perseus; Sthenelus.

Eleggua (Yoruba People, Africa)

The ruler of all paths and opportunities in life. *See also* Olodumare.

Eleio (Hawaii)

A kuhuna (diviner) who sees spirits, cures diseases and resurrects the dead.

Eleithyia (Greek)

Also known as: *Lucina* (Roman).

She is the daughter of the great god Zeus and Hera, the queen of heaven. Her siblings are the god of war, Ares; the nymph, Arge; the goddess of strife, Discordia; the goddess of eternal youth, Hebe (also known as Ganymede); and the fire god, Hephaistos.

Eleius (Greek)

He is the son of Poseidon and Eurycyda, who became the king of Elis, following his uncle Aetolus' reign.

Elektra (Greek) Another spelling for Electra.

Elephantine, Triad of (Egypt)

This triad consists of Anquet, Satis, and Khnum. In ancient Egypt, their shrine was at Yebu (Elephantine), a southern frontier city. *See also* Khnum.

Elephantis (Greek) *see* Abu (Egypt).

Elephenor (Greek)

King of the Abantes of Euboea. He is the son of Chalcodon and Imenarete or Alcinoe. With Acamas and Demophon, he went with forty ships to Troy. Elephenor was killed at Troy by Agenor. *See also* Acamas (A); Agenor; Demophon.

Eleusis (Greek) *see* Dionysus.

Eleutherios (Greek) *see* Dionysus.

Eleuthia (Greek) *see* Eileithyia.

Elijah *Elish'a, Elisha* (Arabic, Hebrew)

Also known as: *el-Khudr* (Arabic), *Ilias* (Arabic), *Ilyas* (Islamic), *Ilyasin* (Islamic).

Prophet. The Jews regarded him as a mysterious being who guards men from life to death. His father is said to be Sabak. He lives in the fifth heaven under the tree of life. Some call him the angel of the covenant and the messenger. He is supposed to return three days before the coming of the Messiah. In legend, Yahweh promised him immortality because he destroyed the priest of Ba-al. In some versions Elisha was second in command under Elijah. He is called el-Khudr (the green one) or Ilias by the Arab People. He is similar to St. George and St. Elias (Christian).

Elioun (Ugarit) *see* El.

Elish'a (Arabic, Hebrew) *see* Elijah.

Elisha (Arabic, Hebrew) *see* Elijah.

Elissa (Tyrian)

She is an early goddess who may have been known as Dido in later times. *See also* Dido.

Elivagar (Norse; Teutonic)

Eleven or twelve rivers springing from the cauldron, or as some say, spring, or well named Hvergelmir (also called Kvergjelme) in Niflheim. The rivers froze into ice blocks which are said to be the source of the clay giant Ymir. The individual names of the rivers are Svol, Gunnthra, Fjorm, Fimbulthul, Slid, Hrid, Sylg, Ylg, Vid, Leipt and Gjoll. In other versions, only some of the streams are called Elivagar. *See also* Ginnungagap; Surtr; Ymir.

Eljudnir (Teutonic)

Home of a god. Hall of the dead in Hel. It is ruled by the underworld goddess, Hel. Located in Niflheim.

Ellat (Sumer) *see* Allat.

Ellen Douglas (Arthurian) *see* Vivien.

Elli (Norse; Teutonic)

Old age. This woman wrestled with Thor in the court of Utgard-Loki. Thor lost. She was actually "Old Age." *See also* Thor.

Ellil (Sumer) *see* Enlil.

Eloah (Ugarit) *see* El.

Eloaios (Hebrew) *see* Elohim.

Elohim *Elom* (Aramaic, Gnostic, Southern Hebrew)

Also known as: *El, Eloaios, Eterah, Ilmaqah, Jerah, Sahar, Terah.*

This moon god possibly originated with the Phoenician and Aramean deity, El. Elom is the name given to the moon by Southern Hebrews. Elohim may be the same as the Arabian deity Ilah or Il. Elohim may have been connected with Marduk. Perhaps the early Hebrew legends refer to Elohim, Shaddai and Elyon as a form of El (q.v.). *See also* Abram; Yahweh.

Elom (Hebrew) *see* Elohim.

Elves (Teutonic)

Also known as: *Elbes.*

Mischievous and often feared spirits of the woods, hills and streams, Elves are said to preside over metals. Elves could be helpful or detrimental to the individual. Elves and Dwarfs are frequently confused. The original elves, said to be of Norse origin, are called Alfar. There are two groups of Alfar: light (Lios Alfar) or dark (Svart Alfar). The Lios Alfar are ruled over by Freyr; and the Svart Alfar, who live in the underground, are ruled by Wayland the Smith. If they break a rule and come out during the day, they are turned to stone. Dwarfs, trolls and gnomes spend their time collecting gold, silver and valuable stones which they secret away. The fairies and elves live in a bright, airy realm located between heaven and earth. They spend their time flitting around enjoying the finery of nature or dancing in the moonlight. Elves are thought to be a Scandinavian form of the fairy. *See also* Alfar; Alfheim; Brownie; Cluricanes; Dulachan; Dwarfs; Freyja; Freyr.

Elyon (Ugarit) *see* El.

Elysian Field (Greek)

Also known as: *Blessed Isles, Elysium, Isles of the Blest, White Island.*

Elysian Field, ruled by either Rhadamanthys or Cronus, is the destination after death of the blessed. Its location is variously described as being in the center of the earth, in the sun, or in the Isles of the Blest. The Romans believed it was located in the underworld. The concept of Elysian Field possibly originated from the Minoan civilization. A few of the well-known residents of this paradise are Cadmus, Diomedes, Menelaus and Peleus. It is also the resting place for the nine horses of the sun god, Helius. *See also* Cadmus; Cronus; Diomedes; Harmonia (A); Helius; Lethe; Peleus.

Emathion (Greek)

King of Arabia, Emathion is the son of Tithonus and Eos. *See also* Eos.

Embla *Emla, Emola* (Teutonic)

The first woman, Embla was found by Odin in the rough form of a tree. She was improved upon by Odin, Vi, and Vili, from an elm, or elder tree. Sometimes she is thought to be the spouse of Ask (q.v.). *See also* Midgard; Odin; Ve; Vili; Ymir.

Emen (Egypt) *see* Kek.

Emer (Celtic, Irish)

She is one of the wives or consorts of Cuchulain. *See also* Cuchulain.

Emla (Teutonic) *see* Embla.

Emma (Japan) *see* Emma-O.

Emma-Hoo (Japan) *see* Emma-O.

Emma-O *Emma, Emma-Hoo, Emma-Sama, Yama-Raja, Yemma* (Buddhist; Japan)

Emma-O, a Buddhist god, is the ruler of Jigoku and judge of the dead. With two decapitated heads, he judges the deeds of sinners. He has the power to prolong life and to resurrect the dead. The deeds of each sinner are weighed before judgement is handed down, condemning the soul to an appropriate section of hell. Emma-O only judges men while his sister (possibly Miru-me, one of the heads) judges women. Souls that are to be judged are brought to Emma-O in a flaming chariot by devils or demons called the Oni. Emma-O is the chief of a large number of underlings: eighteen generals and eighty thousand men. Emma-O is depicted with a menacing expression and dressed in the robes of a judge, wearing a cap inscribed with his name. The mirror is his attribute. Compare Emma-O to Susanowo (Japan) and Yama (India). *See* Ishikoridome-no-Mikoto (regarding mirrors). *See also* Dai Itoku-Myoo; Jigoku; Oni.

Emma-Sama (Japan) *see* Emma-O.

Emola (Teutonic) *see* Embla.

Empousae *Empusa* (Greek)

Demonesses. Hecate uses the Empousae to frighten foreign travelers. They will withdraw if they are insulted. They may be derived from the Lilim who were devotees of Lilith, the first wife of Adam. They are also linked with the Lamiae, who are witches that suck blood. The Empousae have one leg of an ass and one leg of brass. *See also* Hecate.

En-Ge (Semitic) *see* Adar.

En-lil (Sumer) *see* Enlil.

En-Mersi (Sumer) *see* Ningirsu.

Enarete (Greek)

The wife of Aeolus, they became the parents of seven sons: Athamas, Cretheus, Deion, Macareus, Perieres, Salmoneus, Sisyphus; and seven daughters: Alcyone, Arne (her mother may have been Hippe), Calyce, Canace, Peisidice, Perimele, Tangara. *See also* Aeolus (A); Arne; Canace; Cretheus; Sisyphus.

Enbarr (Celtic, Irish, Welsh) *see* Lugh.

Enbilulu (A) (Sumer)
This god of canals was appointed by Enki to ensure that the Tigris and Euphrates rivers functioned properly. *See also* Enki.

Enbilulu (B) (Babylon) *see* Marduk.

Enceladus (Greek)
Giant. Storm demon. Enceladus is the son of Tartarus and Gaea or Gaea and the blood of the castrated Uranus. He is said to be the most powerful of the giants. In some renditions, Gaea sent Enceladus to avenge the death of the monster Typhon, who was killed by Zeus. Other myths say that he was killed by Heracles or Athena. He is still held by adamantine chains in the burning cave under Mount Aetna where Zeus or Athena placed him. Every now and then he changes position, and because of his huge size, causes our earthquakes. Enceladus is depicted as a hundred-armed giant. *See also* Athena; Giants; Hecatonchires; Typhon (A); Zeus.

Endil (Celtic) *see* Dylan.

Endumion (Greek) *see* Semele.

Endymion (Greek) *see* Apis (B).

Engidu (Sumer) *see* Enkidu.

Englimi *Eglimi, Eylime* (Teutonic) *see* Hjorids.

Engur (Assyro-Babylonia) Ea as a water god.

Engus (Celtic) *see* Aengus.

Enigohatgea (Iroquois People, North America) *see* Enigorio.

Enigorio and Enigohatgea (Iroquois People, North America)
These twin brothers were opposites. Enigorio was kindly, and good. He created rivers, fertile land, and fruit trees. His twin brother Enigohatgea created natural disasters, deserts, and harmful plants. They are similar to Ioskeha and Tawiscara of the Huron People.

Eniocha *Anioche* (Greek) *see* Anioche.

Enioche (Greek)
He is the son of Creon, the king of Thebes and Anioche (also known as Eniocha) or Eurydice. *See also* Eurydice (C).

Enki (Assyro-Babylonian, Sumerian)
Also known as: *Amanki* (Babylonian), *Ea* (Akkadian, Sumerian), *Lumha, Nudimmud*.
Wisdom is the attribute of Enki, a name meaning "Lord of the Earth." He is the Sumerian counterpart of the Akkadian god Ea. Enki is also called "Lord of the Watery Deep," meaning the primeval waters known as the Apsu. Enki existed in Dilmun, a place peopled by gods, and he possibly ruled the city of Eridu. He fertilized the swampy land with his own seed. His wife, the mother goddess Nintu, gave birth to Ninmu and Nindurra. After incest with Nindurra, Enki begot Uttu, the goddess of plants. He is also thought to have been the father of Marduk. In another myth, Enki and Ninhursag are married. They became the parents of Ninmu, the goddess of plants. An interesting note is that Ninhursag's gestation period was only nine days. Enki then impregnated his daughter Ninsar, who gave birth to the goddess Ninkurra. Enki also impregnated her and she gave birth to Uttu, also a goddess of plants. Ninhursag warned Uttu against Enki's advances and advised her how to deal with him. Following her advice, she asks for gifts of cucumbers, apples, and grapes. Enki fufills her request. Enki and Uttu have intercourse and from their union eight plants were born. Before Ninhursag could name the plants, Enki ate them. Infuriated, Ninhursag cursed Enki and departed. Presumably, from the curse, Enki was stricken with illness in eight parts of his body. A cunning fox was used to persuade Ninhursag to return and cure Enki. She did so by creating eight deities, one for each area of his body that had been stricken. These deities were regarded as Ninhursag's children. It was Enki who suggested that Enlil create Lahar, the cattle god, and Ashnan, the grain goddess to earth, to feed and cloth the gods. Enlil placed him in charge of supervising the earth. After ensuring that Sumerian land would be productive, he appointed a deity for each realm. Kabta, the god of bricks, was placed in charge of the pickaxe (created by Enlil) and the moulding of bricks. Buildings and foundations were allocated to the god Mushdamma, known as the "Great Builder of Enlil." The "King of the Mountain," Sumuqan, was in charge of vegetable and animal life. Dumuzi, the shepherd god, was the supervisor of sheepfolds and stables. The goddess Ishtar felt that she had been ignored by Enki, so he allocated certain provinces to her and gave her a personal insignia. Later, when the gods became aggravated and decided to destroy all mortals with a great flood, Enki disagreed. He instructed the mortal Ziusudra to build a boat to save himself, his family, along with a few other people and animals. The goddess Ninki is thought to have been one of Enki's wives, as is Nintu (see Ninmu). The Sumerian Enki became the Babylonian Ea in later times (second-millennium B.C.E.). Enki is associated with Inanna (q.v.). *See also* Anu (B); Anunnaki; Apsu; Ashnan; Damkina; Dumuzi; Ea; Enlil; Ishtar; Lahar; Lumha; Marduk; Nammu; Nanshe; Ninhursag; Ninki; Ninmu; Ninti; Nintu; Tammuz; Uttu.

Enki-Ea (Assyro-Babylonia) *see* Ea; Enki; Enuma Elish.

Enkidu *Engidu, Enkimdu*
Also known as: *Eabani, Enkita* (Hittite); (Sumerian)
The god of farmers, land owners, and grain growers, Enkidu, a primitive being, was shaped from mud by Aruru. He moulded him in the likeness of the god Anu to overcome Gilgamesh. A protector of animals, he interfered with the capture of game and led the flocks away. Once, a prostitute was sent to strip him of his primitive powers and to civilize him. After fighting with Gilgamesh they became dear friends. Ishtar, rejected by Gilgamesh, persuaded the gods to kill Enkidu. His death set Gilgamesh searching for immortality. It was Enkidu, according to some myths, that the goddess Ishtar originally wanted to marry. Her brother, the sun god Utu, preferred Dumuzi, the shepherd god, and he desperately wanted the goddess for his wife. Ishtar, the farmer god, offered him many gifts in return for Ishtar's hand, but Dumuzi rejected them. This myth deals with the competition between the pastoral and the argicultural modes of life. Compare the friendship between Enkidu and Gilgamesh to the friendship between Achilles and Patroclus. *See also* Anu; Aruru; Dumuzi; Gilgamesh; Inanna; Ishtar; Nudimmud; Utu.

Enkimdu (Sumer) *see* Enkidu.

Enkita (Hittite) *see* Enkidu.

Enlil *En-lil, Ellil* (Assyro-Babylonian, Sumerian)
Also known as: *Adad, Bel, Illillos, Ishkur, Lil.*

An air god, earth god, and storm god (particularly hurricanes), Enlil was the most important deity of the Sumerian pantheon. He is the son of heaven, personified as the god An, and earth, the goddess Ki. When he separated from his parents, heaven and earth, the universe was created as heaven and earth separated by air. He was known as lord of the storm, lord of the spirits on earth and in the air, and ghosts. He was the patron god of the city of Nippur, where his temple was called E-Kur (the mountain house). The center of his cult was in Babylon. The name Enlil means "lord of the ghost-world." In very early times, he was associated with the goddess Ninhursag. In later mythology, Enlil was sexually attracted to the goddess Ninlil. As she was sailing on Nunbirdu stream one day, Enlil raped her. He was sentenced by a council of gods and banished to the underworld. Ninlil, who became pregnant by his heinous act, insisted that she follow him. To avert having their child born in the darkness, Ninlil gave birth to three underworld deities to serve as substitutes. She was then able to make her ascension to heaven where Nanna, the moon god was born. Following the suggestion of the god of wisdom, Enki, Enlil created other deities to follow his instructions to bring order into the universe. He created Lahar, the god of cattle, and the grain goddess, Ashnan. These two minor deities were to provide food and clothing for the gods. Often drunk, they were unable to fulfill their duties. As a result, it was decided that mortals would be created to take over their tasks. Enlil placed Enki in charge of supervising the earth. It was Enlil who created the pickaxe and presented it to the people of Sumeria. When mortals became too boisterous for Enlil to tolerate, he used his weapon, the "amaru," or the great deluge, to regain control. Enlil generally resided on the Great Mountains of the East, although he had a special abode in heaven known as "Enlil's Way." Anu had an area in heaven known as "Anu's Way," but unlike Enlil, he preferred to stay in heaven. In later times, Bel and Marduk (q.v.) acquired his mythology and Anu took over his place as leader of the pantheon. Enlil's symbol is the seven small circles representing the Pleiades. Also see Ninlil (for another version of Nanna's conception). *See also* Adad; An; Anu; Ashnan; Bel (A); Belit; Ea; Enki; Igigi; Inanna; Ishkur; Ki; Lillity; Marduk; Nammu; Nanna (B); Ninhursag; Nusku; Utnapishtim; Utu.

Enmesarra (Babylon, Sumer) *see* Enmesharra.

Enmesharra *Enmesarra, Ennmeshara* (Babylon, Sumer)
Also known as: *Nergal.*

In some versions, he is a sun god, and the protector of flocks and vegetation. In other myths, he is a god of the underworld. Enmesharra is one of the names of Nergal (q.v.).

Enmessara (Assyro-Babylonian) *see* Nergal.

Ennammasht (Sumer) *see* Ninurta.

Ennead, The (Egypt)
Also known as: *Psedjet.*

Supreme beings. The deities of Heliopolis, consisting of Ra

and the eight gods and goddesses descended from him, namely, Shu and Tefnut, Geb and Nut, Osiris, Isis, Set, and Nephthys. Other deities, including Horus and Khenti Amenti, were sometimes considered to be among the company of gods of the divine Ennead. Usually there were nine deities grouped in threes. There were also the Greater and Lesser Enneads. The Greater Ennead had Horus, Isis, Nephthys, Nut, Set, Shu, Tefnut, Tem, Thoth.

Ennoia (Gnostic)
Goddess of thought. She probably originated with Simon Magus. He said the prostitute who accompanied him, named Helena, was a reincarnation of this goddess.

Ennugi (Babylonia)
He is the governor of the gods and also the god of irrigation. He watchs over canals and dikes. Ennugi is associated with Anu, Enlil, Ninurta and Ea.

Ennuki (Sumer) *see* Anunnaki.

Ennyo (Japan)
The Ennyo are female deities wearing fluttering veils. They fly around (without wings) scattering flowers in the air and playing music.

Enodia (Greek) An epithet of Hecate.

Enshagme (Semite)
Lord of Dilmun. One of the gods created by Ninhursag. Possibly a god of intelligence. *See also* Dilmun.

Entuti (Egypt) *see* Aai.

Enua (Polynesia) *see* Papa (A).

Enualios *Enyalius* (Greek) *see* Ares; Enyalius.

Enuma Elish (Babylonia, Sumer)
Babylonian Poem of Creation. Seven tablets in cuneiform text. *See also* Apsu; Ea; Enki; Gilgamesh.

Enyalius *Enulios* (Greek)
God of war. Enyalius is either the companion of Ares or his epithet. *See also* Ares.

Enyo (A) (Greek)
A Graiae. She is the daughter of "the Old Man of the Sea," Phorcys, and Ceto. *See also* Ceto; Graiae; Phorcys.

Enyo (B) (Greek)
Also known as *Bellona* (Roman)
Goddess of war. Enyo is the daughter of the god of war, Ares, and the goddess of love, Aphrodite. She went to battle with Ares. Her siblings are Anteros, Deimos, Eros, Harmonia, Pallor and Phobos. *See also* Anteros; Bellona; Eros; Harmonia (A); Pallor; Phobos.

Eo (Greek) *see* Curetes.

Eochaid Ollathair (Celtic) *see* Dagda.

Eogabal (Irish) *see* Aine.

Eoghana (Celtic) *see* Eire.

Eopuco (Maya) *see* Ah Puch.

Eos (Greek)

Also known as: *Aurora* (Roman).

Dawn goddess. Eos, the goddess of dawn, is the daughter of the Titan sun god Hyperion, and his sister Theia (also known as Thia or Euryphaessa). *She is the sister of Selene, the moon,* and Helius, the sun. She abducted her mortal husband Tithonus when he was a handsome young man. As he aged, she lost interest in him and is said to have locked him up so she didn't have to listen to his endless chattering. She had numerous affairs, among them one with Cephalus, another beautiful mortal whom she plucked from the earth to live with the gods. She has been called the mother of her husband Tithonus as well as the mother of Emathion the king of Arabia, who was killed by Heracles, and Memnon, the king of Ethiopia, by Tithonus or Cephalus, and Phaethon, who was abducted by Aphrodite, also by Tithonus or Cephalus. Some say that she was the mother of the goddess of breezes, Aura, and the morning star, Eosphorus, by Astraeus. From her relationship with Astraeus (his name means "Starry") they also produced the winds: Boreas the North Wind, Notus the South Wind, Zephyrus the West Wind, and Eurus the South East Wind. Some say they are the parents of the Evening Star Hesperus (Vesper). Eos rises from her bed each morning to travel across the sky with her brother, the sun god Helius. Together they bring the first rays of daylight to mortals. She is portrayed as saffron-robed, with flaming red hair, driving a purple chariot drawn by two horses; as riding the horse Pegasus and carrying a torch; or as a winged goddess sprinkling dew from an urn. Two of her horses are Lampus and Pegasus. Compare Eos to the Vedic goddess of dawn Ushas. *See also* Ares; Aurora; Ausera; Boreas; Ceos; Helius; Orion; Pegasus; Two Auroras; Zephyrus.

Eosphorus (Greek)

Also known as: *Lucifer*.

Eosphorus, the morning star, is the son of Eos and Astraeus. *See also* Eos.

Eostre (Anglo-Saxon)

Also known as: *Eastre*.

Goddess of the Spring. Protectress of fertility, goddess of rebirth and friend to all children. To amuse the children, Eostre changed her beautiful pet bird into a rabbit. The rabbit brought forth brightly colored eggs, which Eostre gave the children as gifts. *See also* Eastre.

Eous (Greek) *see* Helius.

Epadun (Babylonia) *see* Marduk.

Epaphus (Greek)

King of Egypt. Founder of the city of Memphis. His parents are Zeus and Io. He married Memphis, the daughter of the river god, Nile. *See also* Agenor (A); Apis; Curetes; Memphis; Nile.

Epeius *Epius* (Greek)

Founder of Pisa. The son of Panopeus and Neaera, and the brother of Aegle, Epeius was the Phoenician leader at Troy. With Athena, he built the Wooden Horse. A boxer, he won the boxing event at the funeral games of Patroclus. *See also* Athena.

Epet (Egypt) *see* Apet.

Epheseus (Greek) *see* Artemis.

Ephialtes (Greek)

He is the giant son of the sea god Poseidon (or Aloeus) and Iphimedeia. His twin is Otus. *See also* Aloeides; Giants.

Epi (Tucana People) *see* Dyai.

Epicaste *Jocasta* (Greek) *see* Jocasta.

Epidaurus (Greek)

He is the son of Argus and Evadne, or the son of Pelops, or the son of Apollo. Epidaurus is also the name of a town in the Peloponnesus. *See also* Argus (A); Evadne; Pelops.

Epigoni, The (Greek)

"Those who come later." The Epigoni are the sons of the Seven against Thebes. They successfully marched on Thebes ten years after the Seven against Thebes. For the names of the Epigoni, *see also* Adrestus.

Epimetheus (Greek)

Epimetheus is the Titan son of Iapetus and the Oceanid, Clymene, or Asia, the brother of the giants Menoetius, Prometheus and Atlas and possibly the husband of Pandora and father of Pyrrha (said to be the first woman born of a mortal). Known as moronic, he ignored a warning by Prometheus not to accept gifts from the gods (his name means "afterthought"). He accepted the gift of Pandora (the first woman) from Zeus, and she unleashed the evils of the world on mortals. In another myth, he assisted Prometheus in the formation of mortals, but he bestowed his attributes, swiftness, strength and courage, on animals and had nothing to contribute to mortals. He convinced Prometheus that man needed to be endowed with a special attribute, so Prometheus vaulted into heaven and stole fire from the sun and brought it to man in a hollow tube. *See also* Atlas; Iapetus; Oceanids; Pandora; Prometheus; Pyrrha.

Epius *Epeius* (Greek) *see* Epeius.

Epo'na (Gaul, Celtic, Roman) *see* Epona.

Epona *Epo'na, Lady Godiva* (Gaul, Roman)

Epona, known as the "Horse Goddess," was originally a Celtic tutelary deity who presided over the fecundity of the soil. Later she became goddess of the equine race. She was worshiped by Roman soldiers and shrines decorated with roses were placed in every stable. The English Lady Godiva is thought by some to be a later form of Epona. Epona is shown partially clothed, riding a mare sidesaddle or standing next to a foal. She is also depicted sitting on a throne with two foals feeding from her lap. In an ancient relief, she is shown sitting on a throne with triads of horses on either side, while a pig is being sacrificed. The key which unlocks the Underworld is one of her symbols. Compare Epona to the Celtic and Welsh mare goddess, Rhiannon.

Epopeus (A) (Greek)

King of Sicyon. He is the son of Poseidon and Canace. His siblings are Aloeus, Hopleus, Nireus and Triopas. He married Antiope, who was pregnant by Zeus. Epopeus deposed Coronis, the king of Sicyon. Epopeus was killed by Antiope's uncle Lycus. *See also* Aloeus; Antiope; Canace; Coronis; Lycus; Zeus.

Epopeus (B) (Greek)

The king of Asopia, spouse of Ephyraea and father of Marathon.

Epopeus (C) (Greek)

He was the king of Lesbos who raped his daughter, Nyctimene. She was subsquently turned into an owl by Athena.

Epopeus (D) (Greek)

Aloeus, the king of Asopia, is the son of the sun god Helius, and the father of Epopeus.

Epunamun (Araucanian People, Chile)

He is a war god, possibly of Inca origin. He is comparable to the Inca sun god Punchau (q.v.). *See also* Akanet; Pillan.

Eq'eq'o (Collao) *see* Ekkekko.

Erathipa (Aborigine People, Australia)

The erathipa is a fertility stone with a vaginal-like opening on one side.

Erato (A) (Greek)

Also known as: *Errato.*

The Muse of erotic poetry. Erato is the daughter of Zeus and the goddess of memory, Mnemosyne. She is shown holding her symbol, a small lyre. *See also* Mnemosyne; Muses.

Erato (B) (Greek) A Dryad (q.v.).

Erato (C) (Greek) One of the Danaids. *See also* Danaus.

Erato (D) (Greek) A Nereid, daughter of Nereus (q.v.).

Erda (Teutonic) *see* Jord; Odin.

Erebus (Greek)

Also known as: *Hades, Tartarus.*

Underworld god. Erebus, born from Chaos and darkness, is the brother of Nox (Night). With his sister Nox he became the father of Hemera (Day) and Aether (Sky); Cer, the goddess of violent death; Oneiroi (Dreams); Somnus, also known as Hypnos the god of sleep; the twin of Somnus, Thanatos (Death); Momus the fault finder; Nemesis the goddess of retributive justice; and Charon the ferryman of dead souls. As a deity of the lower world he is the personification of the terrible darkness through which departing souls pass to Hades. Erebus is also the name of the lower region of the underworld. The dark and mysterious place further below is often called Tartarus though many writers feel that Erebus and Tartarus are the same place. Hades is a general term used for the underworld or the deity in charge. *See also* Aether; Aither; Cocytus; Fates; Hades; Hesperides; Nemesis; Tartarus.

Erech (Sumer)

The Biblical name of Uruk.

Erechtheus I (Greek)

Also known as: *Erichthonius.*

King of Athens. Inventor of the chariot and chariot harness. He is the son of Hephaistos. When his father attempted to rape the goddess of war, Athena, his sperm fell on Mother Earth, Gaea. Erechtheus was born with the tail of a snake. Athena raised him at the Acropolis. *See also* Athena; Erechtheus II; Gaea; Hephaistos.

Erechtheus II (Greek)

Also known as: *Erichtonius.*

King of Athens. Successor of his grandfather, Erechtheus I.

His parents are Pandion, who was also a king of Athens, and Pandion's aunt, the Naiad, Zeuxippe. Erechtheus is the twin of Butes. His other siblings are Philomela and Procne. Some say that Erechtheus I and Erechtheus II are the same.

Eredatfedhri (Persia)

She is the virgin invoked to defeat evil. *See also* Jahi.

Ereint (Celtic) *see* Ludd; Nuada.

Eres (Greek) *see* Ares.

Erescheigal (Babylon, Sumer) *see* Ereshkigal.

Ereshkigal *Erescheigal, Erishkegal, Eriskigal* (Babylon, Greek, Sumer)

Also known as: *Allat, Allatu* (Akkadian), *Alukah* (Canaanite), *Ganzir, Ningirda.*

Goddess and queen of Arallu, the land of no return. She ruled the underworld alone until Nergal and his evil spirits marched into her territory and forced her to marry him. He also demanded that she designate him as the King of Arralu for the price of peace. When Ereshkigal's sister, the goddess Ishtar, went to Arralu searching for Tammuz, she was held prisoner. The great god Ea created Asushu-Namir to negogiate her release. Some say her spouse was Ninazu, the grandfather of Tammuz, and her son was Ningishzida, the father of Tammuz. Ereshkigal's messenger is Namtar. She may be an alter-ego of Inanna, queen of the sky and goddess of love. Sometimes, Inanna is referred to as the sister of Ereshkigal. She may be associated with the Greek Hecate and the Sumerian Nebo. In a curse from the Greek texts *Aktiophi*, Erescheigal is mentioned in relation to Hecate. *See also* Allat; Demeter; Hecate; Inanna; Nergal.

Erginus (A) (Greek)

This Argonaut piloted the Argo after the death of Tiphys. He is the son of either the god of the sea, Poseidon, or Clymenus. *See also* Argonauts; Rhadamantus.

Erginus (B) (Greek)

King of Boeotian Orchomenus. When his father was killed by the Thebans, he avenged his death.

Erh-Lang *Er-Lang* (China)

Hero. He drives away evil spirits using his dog, T'ien K'ou. Er-lang is from the family of the Jade Emperor, possibly a nephew. He is usually shown with Nu-kua. They are dressed in mandarin clothing and accompanied by oxen, buffaloes and horses. Sometimes they are accompanied by pigs. *See also* Jade Emperor.

Eriboea (A) (Greek)

She is the mother of Ajax the Greater (q.v.).

Eriboea (B) (Greek)

Also known as: *Merope, Periboea.*

Polybus is her spouse. She raised Oedipus, the king of Thebes who solved the riddle of the Sphinx. *See also* Oedipus; Polybus.

Eriboea (C) (Greek) She is the wife of Aeneus.

Eriboea (D) (Roman)

An epithet of the goddess of marriage, Juno.

Eriboea (E) (Greek)
    An epithet of the goddess of love, Aphrodite.

Erichthonius *Erichtonius* (Greek)
    He is the son of Dardanus and Arisbe. Erichthonius became the king of Dardania and at the time, he was the richest man in the world. His marriage to Astyoche produced a son, Tros. *See also* Agraulos; Boreas; Gaea; Hephaistos; Tros.

Erichtonius (Greek) *see* Erichthonius.

Eridanus (Greek)
    River god. Eridanus is the son of Oceanus and Tethys. *See also* Oceanus; Phaethon; Rivers; Tethys.

Eridu (Sumer)
    Heaven or paradise. Legends say this is the place where man was created and where the souls go after death. It is a great pine whose roots are in the very center of the earth and its crown extends into the sky. *See also* Aah.

Erigone (Greek)
    Harvest goddess. She is the daughter of the farmer, Icarius of Athens. When her murdered father's grave was discovered by her dog, Maera, Erigone hung herself. She became either the constellation Virgo, or Bootes. *See also* Aegisthus; Icarius (B).

Erinn (Celtic) *see* Dana.

Erinyes *Eaynnes, Erinys, Erinyes, Erynnes, Irinyes* (Greek)
    Also known as: *Eumenides, Furiae* (Roman), *Furies* (Roman).
    The Erinyes, goddesses of retributive justice, are Alecto (also spelled Allecto, Alektro), personifying enduring hate; Megaera, jealousy; and Tisiphone, revenge. They were born with the Giants and Meliae and are the daughters of Gaea (Earth) and the blood of their father, the castrated Uranus. They harangued, hassled and tormented the disloyal whether alive or dead and also thwarted mortals from acquiring knowledge about the future. The Erinyes represent the Triple Goddessess and are said to have lived in Erebus. A combination of the harsh and the benevolent; their work of punishment in life and death defends those whom human law fails to protect. They inflicted the tortures prescribed by the gods on villains such as Sisyphus and Tantalus when they were in Hades. The Erinyes are shown as black maidens with serpents in their hair and blood dripping from their eyes. Sometimes they are shown in snake form. The Erinyes are the same as the Roman Furies and sometimes said to be the same as the Eumenides. *See also* Eumenides; Fates; Gaea; Giants; Meliae; Nemesis; Sisyphus; Tantalus; Uranus.

Erinys (Greek) *see* Erinyes.

Erinyes (Greek) *see* Erinyes.

Eriopis (A) (Greek)
    She is the daughter of Jason and Medea. Her siblings are Alcimenes, Argus, Medeias, Mermerus, Pheres, Thessalus and Tisandrus. *See also* Alcimenes; Jason; Medea; Pheres (A).

Eriopis (B) (Greek)
    Her parents are Apollo and Arsinoe. She is the sister or possibly the half-sister of the god of healing, Asclepius. The king of Locris became her husband and they had one child, Ajax the Lesser (q.v.). *See also* Apollo; Arsinoe; Asclepius.

Eriphyle (Greek) *see* Adrestus.

Eris (Greek)
    Also known as: *Discordia* (Roman).
    Goddess of discord and strife. Eris is the daughter of Zeus and the goddess Hera. Her brother is the god of war, Ares. Her son by her father Zeus is Ate. Eris' purpose in life and the celestial realm is to cause discord, strife, lies, murders and even wars. She rolled the Golden Apple to the guests at the wedding of Peleus and Thetis and thereby indirectly caused the Trojan War. Her acts have caused competition and inspiration. She is noted with Athena for inspiring Heracles. The Adder (poisonous snake) is thought to be an aspect of Eris. *See also* Adder; Ares; Athena; Discordia; Lethe; Peleus; Thetis.

Erishgal (Babylon, Sumer) *see* Ereshkigal.

Erishkegal (Babylon, Sumer) *see* Ereshkigal.

Eriskigal (Babylon, Sumer) *see* Ereshkigal.

Erisvorsh (Slavic)
    God of the holy tempest. *See also* Perun; Stribog.

Eriu (Celtic) *see* Banbha; Bress; Dagda; Eire.

Erkir (Armenian) *see* Perkunis.

Erlik-Khan *Irlek-Khan* (Central Asia)
    Also known as: *Erlin* (possibly the same).
    God of the dead. He has a great many spirit helpers. Only those who have sinned go to his realm.

Erlin (Ural-Altaic People)
    First man, or brother of the creator. Eastern king of the dead. A confused god who thought humans would graze like cattle, but realized the mistake. He handed the sun and moon to the devil and his aides had to get them back. Other legends say there were too many suns and moons and Erlik shot the excess down with arrows. *See also* Nubti.

Erma-Ta (Egypt) *see* Ab-ta; Anherta.

Ermen-ta (Egypt) *see* Ab-ta.

Ermine (Teutonic) *see* Irmin.

Erna (Teutonic) *see* Jarl.

Ernutet (Egypt) *see* Renenutet.

Ernutit (Egypt) *see* Renenit.

Eros (Greek, Roman)
    Also known as: *Amor* (Roman), *Cupid* (Roman).
    God of love. Initially, Eros was born of Chaos with Gaea and Tartarus. Later he was known as the son of the goddess of love Aphrodite and either the god of war Ares or the god of fire Hephaestus. From this lineage his siblings are Anteros, Deimos, Enyo, Harmonia, Pallor, and Phobos. There are renditions stating that his mother was Venus, Iris, or Ilythiae. His father is variously named as Ares, Hermes, Mars, or Zeus. Eros pierces the hearts of gods and mortals with his gold-tipped arrows of desire. He is the most splendid in appearance of all the gods. He is shown as a chubby infant, or a handsome adult male. Often he has wings and usually carries his bow and arrow. Compare

Eros to Kama (Hindu). *See also* Adrastia; Aither; Amor; Anteros; Aphrodite; Ares; Cupid; Deimos; Graces; Harmonia (A).

Erqigdlit (Eskimo People, Canada, Greenland) *see* Adlet.

Errato (Greek) *see* Erato.

Erui (Irish) *see* Amergin; Banbha.

Erulus (Greek)
King of Italy. He is the son of the goddess of orchards, Feonia. *See also* Evander (B).

Eruncha (Australia)
These cannibalistic devils have the power to transform a man into a medicine man.

Erynnes (Greek) *see* Erinyes.

Erysichthon (A) (Greek)
He is the son of Triopas and Hiscilla. For the names of his siblings, *see* Iphimedeia (A). After destroying Demeter's sacred grove, the goddess punished him by hunger; no matter the amount of food he ate, he was hungry. He even sold his daughter, Mestra, into prostitution for food. In an attempt to quell his hunger pains, he ate his own legs. Still, he died of hunger. *See also* Demeter; Triopas.

Erytheis (Greek)
A guardian of the Golden Apples. She is the Hesperide daughter of Atlas and Pleione (some say Atlas and Hesperis). *See also* Golden Apples; Hesperides.

Erythrius (Greek)
He is the son of Athamas and Themisto (qq.v.).

Erythrus (A) (Greek)
His parents are Rhadamanthus and Alcmene. *See also* Rhadamanthus.

Erythrus (B) (Greek)
His parents are Hermes and Antianeira. The Argonaut Echion is his brother. *See also* Echion; Hermes.

Erytus (Greek) *see* Eurytus.

Erzulie (Haitian)
Goddess of beauty. The best description of this goddess is that she has all the attributes of Aphrodite. She is usually shown in elaborate dress. Erzulie was sexually involved with the Voodoo gods Damballah, Agwe, and Ogoun. *See also* Ogoun.

Es-u (Middle Eastern) *see* Abu; Tammuz.

Esagil (Sumer)
The sanctuary of Marduk in Babylon.

Esagila (Babylonian) Marduk's temple (q.v.).

Esaugetuh Emissee *Esaugeteh Emissee* (Creek People, North America)
A chief god, his name means "Lord of Wind." When the waters of the deluge receded, he moved to the mountain Nunne Chaha, and created his people from mud and clay. In another version, his home is in a cave. He created men from clay and built walls where he laid them out to dry.

Escalibor (Arthurian) *see* Excalibur.

Eschetewuarha (Chamacoco People, South America)
High goddess. Wife of the Great Spirit. She ruled over the world. Mother of birds or clouds that spread rain.

Eschu (Africa, Haiti) *see* Legba.

Esculapius (Greek) *see* Asclepius; Eshmun.

Esege Malan (Buryat People, Siberia)
A little known god who presides over the western sky.

Eset (Egypt) *see* Isis.

Esharra (Babylonia)
The sacred dwelling of the gods. *See also* Marduk.

Eshmoun (Phoenicia) *see* Eshmun.

Eshmun *Ashmun, Eshmoun, Esmoun, Esmounos, Esmun* (Phoenicia)
Also known as: *Aesculapius, Asclepius.*
God of health and healing. God of the city. Formerly a god of fertility. He became more powerful in Carthage than Melqart. He is identified with the Greek Adonis, the Babylonian Tammuz and the Egyptian Osiris. Eshmun is sometimes identified with Asclepius by the Greeks. He is possibly the same as Adonis and also the Egyptian god, Thoth. *See also* Adon; Asclepius; Astarte.

Eshu (Yoruba People, Africa)
Also known as: *Olus, Sigidi.*
Messenger and guardian spirit. God of discord. Trickster. Eshu is an important orisha who loves to test the true character of mortals. He often appears in disguise and causes confusion. Eshu is a servant of the supreme god, Olodumare, the orisha Ifa and the orisha Orish-nla. Eshu is also called Sigidi, although this name is usually used to conjure up power while meditating by a practitioner who has been paid to fulfill a request to hurt somebody. Followers worship Eshu for fear that if he is not appeased, he will cause disruption. In later times Eshu was compared to the devil of Christianity and called Olusi by the followers of the Yoruba religion, though this does not seem to be an accurate description aside from the devil as a spirit of temptation. He is usually shown with a large clever head and a knowing grin. He is thoughtfully chewing the top of his knuckle. His favorite food is cocks and the dog is his sacred animal. Eshu likes palm oil, but hates oil made from the palm kernel. The Yoruba, known for their bronze casting and stone carving from early times, have depicted Eshu in statue form. Eshu is comparable to the evil genius Legba of the Dahomeans. Eshu is also similar to Esu, the trickster deity of the Edo people. *See also* Fa (A); Ifa; Olodumare; Orish-nla.

Esmounos *Esmoun* (Greek, Phoenician)
Possibly a god of fire or heat. One of the Cabiri who was loved by Astronoe. In legend she was pursuing him and for some reason he cut off his genitals with an axe before being captured. Astronoe, in remorse, turned him into a god using her own heat. *See also* Asclepius; Cabiri; Eshmun; Sydycos. Possibly the same as Eshmun.

Esmun (Phoenicia) *see* Eshmun.

Eso (Edo People, Africa) *see* Eshu.

Essicalibur (Arthurian) *see* Excalibur.

Estanatlehi *Estsanatlehi* (Navajo People, North America)
Mother goddess. Goddess of youth. Helper of mortals. Estanatlehi recreates herself. When she ages, she turns herself into a young girl. Estanatlehi is the highest deity of a group of nature and household gods known as the Yei. Sometimes she is known as a goddess of rain and the west. She is called the mother of Nayanezgani and sister of Yolkai Estsan. Separately, she is known as the mother of Thobadestchin. The turquoise is her symbol. *See also* Ahsonnutli and Yolaikaiason; Atseatsan and Atseatsine; Yei; Yolaikaiason.

Estiu (Ireland)
Estiu is a bird goddess and a warrior woman.

Esus *Hesus* (Gaul)
God of vegetation and war. Little is known of Esus, but it is thought he was a wood-cutter and that human sacrifices were offered to him. His victims were hung from trees and ritually wounded. An ancient relief of Esus shows him dressed in woodman's clothing, chopping down a tree. His sacred animal is the bull. Esus is equated with Mars and Mercury of the Romans. Compare Esus to Odin who also hung his enemies from trees.

Etain (A) (Celtic, Irish)
A sun and horse goddess, she was the lover of Mider, in his form as Aileili. The obsessive Angus stole her away from Mider, and encased her in glass so that he could carry her around with him. *See also* Angus; Mider.

Etain (B) (Ireland)
A female fairy who died of grief when her mortal husband was killed. Her abode was Ben Edar Hill.

Etan (Celtic)
She is the daughter of Dia'necht, the god of medicine, and the spouse of Ogma, the god of literature, and mother of the bard Caipre. *See also* Dia'necht; Ogma.

Etana (Babylonia)
Originally an early king (Kish Dynasty), he merged with an earlier hero and became a god.

Eteocles (A) (Greek)
King of Thebes. He is the son of Oedipus and Jocasta or Euryganeia. His siblings are Antigone, Ismene and Polynices. He is the father of Laodamas. *See also* Antigone; Polynices.

Eteocles (B) (Greek)
King of Boeotian Orchomenus. He is the son of Andreus or Cephissus and Evippe, Eteocles named the Graces, and was the first to make sacrifice to them. *See also* Cephissus; Graces.

Eteoclus (Greek)
One of the Seven against Thebes, Eteoclus is also the brother of Evadne. *See also* Evadne; Seven Against Thebes.

Eterah (Ugarit)
Also known as: *Jarah, Jerah, Terah.*
This is the name used for the supreme god El, in his form of the moon god, spouse of the sun goddess. *See also* El; Elohim.

Ether (A) (Greek) *see* Aether.

Ether (B) (Phoencian) *see* Air (B); Air (C).

Ethinoha (Iroquois People, North America) *see* Nokomis.

Ethlenn (Celtic) *see* Ethlinn.

Ethlinn *Ethlenn, Ethne, Ethniu* (Celtic) *see* Cian; Clothru.

Ethne (Celtic) *see* Ethlinn.

Ethniu (Celtic) *see* Ethlinn.

Ethona (Greek) *see* Athena.

Etu (India) *see* Agni.

Etua (Polynesia) *see* Atua.

Etuda (Sumer) *see* Tammuz.

Eudora (A) (Greek)
She is the daughter of Atlas and Pleione. Eudora is a Hyade. Her other siblings are Calypso, Hyas, the Hesperides and the Pleiades. *See also* Atlas, Calypso; Hesperides; Hyades; Pleiades.

Eudora (B) (Greek)
One of the Nereids (q.v.).
Eudorus (Greek). His parents are the messenger of the gods, Hermes and his lover Polymele, the wife of Echecles. *See also* Hermes; Polymele.

Euios (Greek) *see* Dionysus.

Eumelus (A) (Greek)
Winner of the chariot race at the funeral games of Achilles. Eumelus is the son of Admetus and Alcestis, the brother of Perimele, and husband of Iphthime. *See also* Alcestis; Admetus.

Eumelus (B) (Greek)
He warned Aeneas that Trojan women were setting their ships on fire. *See also* Aeneas.

Eumelus (C) (Greek) The father of Antheias.

Eumenides (Greek)
Also known as: *Eaynnes, Erinyes, Erinyes, Furiae* (Roman), *Furies* (Roman), *Irinyes.*
Fertility deities. A name meaning "good-tempered ones," the Eumenides were given to placate the avenging spirits of the Romans, known as the Furies. Some say the Eumenides are the Erinyes; however, it is thought by others that the Eumenides had a kinder aspect to their personalities and were Chthonian goddesses (deities or spirits of the Underworld) worshipped under different names in different areas. In this role their duty was to insure the general fertility of the earth. In one version, as the Erinyes, they were given the new name, Eumenides, after a trial involving Electra and Orestes. Some say they led souls into the realm of the dead. The Eumenides have black skin, dogs' heads, snakes for hair, blood-shot eyes and bats' wings. They carry brass-studded scourges and wear soiled grey robes. They are similar to Moirai. The functions of Nemesis often overlapped those of the Eumenides. In some places they were

closely associated with the Graces. They are also similar to the Three Norns (Scandinavia). *See also* Erinyes; Furies; Graces; Morai; Orestes.

Eumolpus (A) (Greek)

With King Eleusis, the co-founder of the Eleusinian Mysteries. King of Thrace. His parents are the god of the sea, Poseidon, and Chione, the daughter of the north wind, Boreas, and Oreithyia. Chione threw her son Eumolpus into the sea. He was rescued by Poseidon and raised by his half-sister, Benthesicyme. Eumolpus is the father of Ismarus or Immaradus and Ceryx and possibly Phorbas. When he tried to seize the throne from Erechtheus, the king of Athens, during a war, he was killed. *See also* Eleusis.

Eunaomia *Eunomia* (Greek)

Goddess of seasons. The daughter of Zeus and Themis, Eunaomia is the personified goddess of law and order and one of the three Horae (q.v.).

Euneus (Greek)

King of Lemnos. Euneus is the son of Jason and Hypsipyle, the daughter of Thoas and Myrina. *See also* Jason.

Eunomia (Greek) *see* Eunaomia.

Euphemus (Greek)

The Argonaut son of the god of the sea, Poseidon, and Europa or Mecionice. Euphemus had the ability to run across water without wetting his feet. *See also* Argonauts; Europa; Lamia; Poseidon.

Euphrosyne (Greek)

"Joy." One of the Graces, she is the daughter of Zeus and Eurynome. *See also* Aglaia; Graces.

Eupolemia (Greek)

By Hermes, the messenger of the gods, she is the mother of Aetholides, the Argonauts herald, who has a perfect memory. Her parents are Myrmidon and Peisidice, the daughter of Aeolus and Enarete. *See also* Aeolus (A); Aetholides; Hermes.

Europa (A) (Greek, possibly Asian)

Europa is the daughter of Agenor, the king of Phoenicia, and Telephassa or Argiope. It is also possible that she was the daughter of Agenor's son, Phoenix. At a very young age Zeus fell in love with her. He assumed the shape of a beautiful white bull and lured her to his back. He carried her off to Crete and kept her as his mistress. Her sons by Zeus were Minos, Rhadamanthus, and Sarpedon. She later married Asterius and became the mother of a daughter, Crete (the same as the island), and he adopted her sons. In another version, she is the mother of Euphemus by Poseidon and possibly the mother of Aeacus by Zeus. In some legends, Europa and not Aegina is said to be the mother of Aeacus. The rose is associated with Europa. Compare her to Aegina, also carried off to an island by Zeus. Compare to other women seduced by Zeus in another form. *See also* Aegina; Agenor (A); Antiope; Apis; Danae; Leda; Oceanids; Poseidon; Rhadamantus; Sarpedon (A).

Europa (B) (Greek)

Danaus and Europa are the parents of fifty daughters known as the Danaids (q.v.).

Europa (C) (Greek)

An Oceanid, she is the daughter of Oceanus and Tethys. *See also* Oceanids; Oceanus; Tethys.

Europa (D) (Greek) She is the daughter of Tityus.

Europa (E) (Greek) Her parents are Phoenix and Perimede.

Eurus (Greek)

Also known as: *Apheliotes.*

God of the East Wind. Little is known of Eurus, the East Wind. He is the brother of Boreas, Notus, and Zephyrus and a son of Aeolus and Aurora. Compare to storm clouds, Chimaera, Harpies. For family history *see* Boreas; Zephyrus. *See also* Aeolus; Notus; Zetes.

Euryale (A) *Euryae* (Greek)

A Gorgon, Euryale is the daughter of Ceto and Phorcys. *See also* Ceto; Gorgons; Medusa; Stheno.

Euryale (B) (Greek) Queen of the Amazons.

Euryale (C) (Greek) She is a daughter of Proteus (q.v.).

Euryalus *Erytus* (Greek)

An Argonaut. One of the Epigoni. He is the son of Mecisteus. *See also* Argonauts; Epigoni.

Eurybatus (Greek)

He killed Lamia, the monster of Crissa. *See also* Lamia.

Eurybia (A) (Greek)

A Titan. She is the daughter of Oceanus and mother earth, Gaea. Her siblings are Ceto, Crius, Nereus, Phorcys and Thaumas. She wed Crius and became the mother of Astraeus, Pallas and Perses. *See also* Crius; Gaea; Oceanus; Perses; Phorcys; Styx.

Eurybia (B) (Greek) She is the daughter of Thespius.

Eurydamas (A) (Greek)

He is the Argonaut son of Irus and Demonassa. *See also* Argonauts.

Eurydamas (B) (Greek) He is one of Penelope's suitors.

Eurydamas (C) (Greek)

An interpreter of dreams for the Trojans.

Eurydice (A) (Greek)

Eurydice, the Dryad wife of the famed musician Orpheus, died on her wedding day. As she attempted to escape the amorous attentions of Aristaeus, the beekeeper, she was bitten by a snake. She was granted permission to leave the darkness of Hades and accompany her new husband on the condition that he not turn around to look at her until they reached the light of the world. In a moment of forgetfulness, he turned and Eurydice fell back into Hades and was punished by eternal death. *See also* Aristaeus; Orpheus.

Eurydice (B) (Greek)

Her parents are Lacedaemon and Sparte. She married Acrisius (q.v.).

Eurydice (C) (Greek)

There are numerous women in Greek mythology with the name Eurydice. King Nestor of Pylos was married to Eurydice who was the daughter of Clymenus. In another legend there is Eurydice the wife of Creon, who was the king of Thebes. She was the mother of Enioche (possibly), and a beautiful son, Haemon, who was killed by the Sphinx when he couldn't answer the riddle; a daughter, Megara, who married Heracles; and Menoeceus, her virgin son, who committed suicide to save the kingdom. Grief-stricken, she killed herself after his death. There was also Eurydice, one of the fifty daughters of Danaus called the Danaids, who was said to have murdered her husband Dryas, who was also her cousin and one of the fifty sons of Aegyptus. One of the numerous children of Pelops and Hippodameia was Eurydice, thought by some to be the mother of Alcmene, the last mortal love of Zeus, who became the mother of Heracles and his twin Iphicles. Eurydice, the daughter of Adrastus, married the fourth king of Troy, Ilus, who was a famous wrestler. Their children were Laomedon, who refused to pay Apollo and Poseidon for building the walls of Troy and was killed by Heracles, and a daughter, Themiste (Themis), who became the mother of Anchises and Laocoon (not to be confused with the Argonaut of the same name).

Euryganeia (Greek)
Possible wife of Oedipus, mother of Antigone, Eteocles, Ismene and Polynices. *See also* Antigone; Eteocles; Oedipus; Polynices.

Eurymede (Greek)
She is the sister of Scylla and Iphinoe. *See also* Bellerophon; Graces; Scylla.

Eurymedon (Greek)
Hermes is his father (q.v.). *See also* Eurynome (A); Perseus; Themis.

Eurynome (A) (Greek)
She is the goddess of all things, and a creation goddess. According to the Pelasgian creation myth, in the beginning Eurynome emerged from Chaos. In order to stand she had to divide the sea from the sky. She grasped the North Wind between her hands and the serpent Ophion emerged, and coiled itself around her limbs. It was the fertilizing North Wind also known as Boreas who impregnated her. In the form of a dove she laid the Universal Egg and had Ophion coil around it seven times until it hatched and spilt in half. From this egg came all things. Eurynome and Ophion lived on Mount Olympus for a time but it is said that he insisted upon being called author of the Universe which vexed Eurynome to the point that she physically removed him from their home and banished him to the Underworld. She then created the planetary powers. A Titaness and a Titan represented each planet. Theia and Hyperion, the sun; Phoebe and Atlas, the moon; Dione and Crius for Mars; Metis and Coeus for Mercury; Tethys and Oceanus for Venus; Rhea and Cronus for Saturn. The first man, however, was said to be Pelasgus, who rose up from the soil of Arcadia. Other mortals followed. It is said that Eurynome ruled until she was displaced by Cronus and Rhea and either fell into the sea or simply retired to Oceanus. Eurynome is shown in mermaid's form. Compare to the Olympian creation myth (which did not permit the influence of the planetary powers). To compare to the Homeric creation myth, *see* Oceanus. For the Orphic cre-

ation myth, *see* Phanes. *See also* Atlas; Boreas; Ceos; Chaos; Cronus; Dione; Eurynome (B); Hyperion; Rhea.

Eurynome (B) (Greek)
Sea deity. Eurynome, a Titan, is the daughter of Oceanus and Tethys. By Zeus she is the mother of the three Graces. She is not to be confused with Eurymede, who has as an alternate name, Eurynome. *See also* Aglaia; Eurynome (B); Graces; Oceanus; Tethys.

Eurynome (C) (Greek)
She could be the mother of Adrestus by Talaus. *See also* Adrestus.

Euryphaessa (Greek) *see* Eos.
She is the Titan mother of Eos, Helius and Selene. Some say Euryphaessa and Theia, the wife of Hyperion, the sun god, may be the same. *See also* Eos; Helius; Hyperion.

Eurysaces (Greek) He is the son of Ajax the Greater (q.v.).

Eurystheus (Greek) *see* Admete; Ate; Kerberos.

Euryte (Greek) *see* Calydonian Boar Hunt.

Eurythemis (Greek)
She is the wife of Thestius and the mother of numerous children, including Althea and Plexippus.

Eurytion (A) (Greek) He is a son of Actor.

Eurytion (B) *Eurytus* (Greek)
This Centaur caused chaos at the wedding of Peirithous and Hippodameia. He was killed.

Eurytus (A) *Eurytas* (Greek)
King of Oechalia. His parents are Melaneus and Oechalia. By his first marriage, he became the father of Dryope. His second marriage, to Antiope, produced Clytius, Iole and Iphitus. Heracles, who was taught the art of the bow and arrow by Eurytus, demanded that he give him Antiope, his wife. When he refused, Heracles killed him. *See also* Dryope; Melaneus; Melas.

Eurytus (B) (Greek)
He is the twin son of Actor or Poseidon and Molione.

Eurytus (C) (Greek)
He is the Argonaut son of the messenger of the gods, Hermes, and Antianeira and the brother of Echion.

Eurytus (D) (Greek)
Another name for Eurytion, the Centaur. *See also* Eurytion (B).

Euterpe (Greek)
She is the muse of lyric poetry. Her symbol is the flute. *See also* Muses.

Euthymus (Greek)
An Olympic boxer, he sailed on the Odysseus. *See also* Caecinus; Rivers.

Evadne (A) (Greek)
She is the daughter of Poseidon and Pitane. Evadne became the mother of Iamus by Apollo. *See also* Poseidon.

Evadne (B) (Greek)
Her father is Iphis, the former king of Argos. Her brother,

Eteoculus is one of the Seven Against Thebes (q.v.). *See also* Eteoculus.

Evadne (C) (Greek)

Her parents are the Thracian river gods, Strymon and Neaera. Her marriage to Argus, king of Argos, resulted in the birth of Criasus, Ecbasus, Epidaurus and Peiras.

Evaki (Bakairi People, South America)

She is the goddess of night or sleep. Evaki stole sleep from the eyes of lizards and then shared sleep with all living things. Evaki closes the lid on the pot which contains the sun each night. She reopens it at dawn.

Evan and Bromius (Greek) *see* Bacchus.

Evander (A) *Evandrus* (Greek)

Minor deity. Evander was the son of Hermes and a nymph who was the daughter of Ladon, the river god. He was associated with Pan and was worshipped in Arcadia. It is thought that he may have been an aspect of Hermes. Evander (A) and Evander (B) are thought by some to be one and the same person. *See also* Evander (B); Hermes; Pan.

Evander (B) *Evandrus* (Greek origins)

Fertility lord. Evander was thought to be a son of Hermes and Carmenta, or Sarpedon and Laodamia. As the son of Sarpedon and Laodamia it is said that he married Deidamia the sister of Laodamia and became the father of Pallantia, Pallas, who had fifty sons all slaughtered by Theseus, Dyne (or Dyna, meaning power), Roma the goddess of strength and Sarpedon (named after his father). He was the leader of a group of Arcadian colonists who settled in Italy and built the city of Pallanteum outside of Rome. Evander joined Aeneas (who with his followers had fled from Troy) and overcame the Rutali, the Italian tribe ruled by Turnus. It is said that Evander killed Erulus, the king of Italy, three times in one day. Erulus was the son of the goddess of orchards, Feronia, who had given her son three lives and three arms. In some legends, Evander was too old to assist Aeneas in battle, so he sent his son Pallas in his place. Some say that Evander was responsible for introducing the Greek gods and the Greek alphabet to Italy. *See also* Acetes; Carmentis; Sarpedon (A); Sarpedon (B).

Evandrus (Greek) *see* Evander (A); Evander (B).

Evarete (Greek)

The daughter of Acrisius and Eurydice, the sister of Dane, she married Oenomaus and became the mother of Hippodameia and Leucippus. *See also* Acrisius; Hippodameia; Keycuppus; Oenamaus.

Eve (Hebrew, Semitic, Babylonian)

Also known as: *Chavah, Chavva, Eva, Evita, Haiwa* (Arabic), *Hawwa, Heve, Mashye* (Persian).

First woman. After causing Adam to fall into a deep sleep, Yahveh took a rib from him and made Eve. In the original legend there was no mention of the name of Adam's mate. In the Koran, her name is not mentioned, and she is referred to as Adam's spouse. Later, she was called Haiwa. Adam and Haiwa had twenty sets of twins; each set a boy and girl. Eve is usually portrayed nude, her loins girded by grape leaves. Sometimes she is shown holding an apple. Her legend is similar to the legend of Adapa. *See also* Adam; Adapa.

Evenus (Greek)

He is the son of Ares and either Demonice or Alcippe. He married a woman named Alcippe. They had three children: Epistrophus, Marpessa and Mynes. When his daughter, Marpessa, was kidnapped by Apollo, Evenus committed suicide. *See also* Ares.

Evnissyen *Efnissien* (Celtic, Welsh), *Evenissyen*

The stepbrother of Bran, Branwen, and Manawyddan. Evnissyen caused a battle between Ireland and Britain when he killed Gwern, the son of Matholwch and Branwen, by casting him into the fire of the hearth. *See also* Bran; Branwen.

Excalibur (Arthurian) *see* Kusanagi; Vivian (Japan).

Excellent Archer (China) *see* Chang-O; "I" (A).

Exizkur (Babylonia) *see* Marduk.

Eylime (Teutonic) *see* Englimi.

Eyr (Teutonic) *see* Eir.

Ezuab (Sumer)

The home of Ea, Ezuab is located in the sacred city of Eridu. *See also* Ea; Eridu.

F

F (Maya People, Yucatan)

A god of war or sacrifice, F was the victor in numerous battles with the god of travelers and planters, Ekchuah (q.v.).

Fa (A) (Egypt, Africa, Dahomey people)

Also known as: *Ifa* (Dahomey, Africa); possibly *Orunmila*.

The Dahomey people consider this deity to be the greatest of all the gods. Generally thought of as the personal fate of each person. Fa may be associated with the African (Dahomey) god of destiny with the same name. In that sense the name means the soul or personal fate of each man. Some versions associate Fa with Legba and with Eshu. In general, Fa and Ka (Egypt) are the soul. Fa is associated with the palm nut. *See also* Ifa; Tuat.

Fa (B) (Egypt)

God of destiny. In the Egyptian cosmology the name is associated with the soul. In Egyptian mythology this is one of twelve gods in the eleventh sector of Tuat. He is the bearer or carrier who carries on his head the serpent Mehen to the eastern part of the sky. The other gods are Ermenu, Athpi, Netru, Shepu, Reta, Amu, Ama, Shetu, Sekhenu, Semsem, and Mehni. May be associated with the African (Dahomey) god of destiny with the same name. In that sense the name means the soul or personal fate of each man. In general, Fa and Ka (Egypt) are the soul.

Fa-Akh (Egypt) *see* Aaru.

Fa-Pet (Egypt) *see* Aaru.

Fa'a-ti (Polynesia)

Fa'a-ti is located within the inner shell, Timi-iti. The outer shell is known as Rumia. It existed in the primeval darkness, Po. The self-created, supreme god, Ta'aroa came from Fa'a-ti. *See also* Ta'aroa.

Fabruus (Roman) *see* Dis; Pluto.

Fachea (Irish) Goddess of poetry.

Fafnir *Fafner* (Norse, Teutonic)

A dragon deity. Brother of Otr (Otter) and Regin. Son of Hreidman (Hreidmar). When Loki killed Otr he was forced to cover Otr in gold. Because of disagreement between Otr and Regin, Fafnir turned himself into a dragon. Both brothers were slain by Sigurd. In one version Otr was killed by Loki. Fafnir wore a helmet named Aegis (helmet of dread).

Fagus (Celtic) Beech tree god. *See also* Abellio.

Fakahotu (Polynesia)

Also known as: *Hakahotu.*

The female force. The male source was Papa or Te Tumu. *See also* Papa.

Fal (Teutonic) *see* Dwarfs.

Falias (Celtic)

This is the Tuatha de Danann city of the north. The "Stone of Destiny," also known as the "Stone of Fal," came from this city. *See also* Tuatha de Danann.

Fama (Roman) *see* Pheme.

Famien (Africa, Guinea)

Fertility deity. Sometimes said to be a god of good health. If carried in the form of a knife in a bag it represents the true power of the god. Sometimes two knives are carried in the bag. Represented as a cave or carried around in a bag. Similar to grigris which are bundles of sacred objects.

Fan K'uei *Fan K'uai* (China)

God of butchers. Mortal whose occupation was a dog skinner in the Han era and was later adopted as a deity of butchers. In some legends the deity of butchers is Khang Fei or Chang Fei who was a pork seller.

Fan T'ao (China) *see* P'an-T'ao.

Fand (Celtic)

She is the abandoned wife of Manannan Mac Llyr. She became the mistress of Cuchulain. After a tryst in Mag Mell (Plain of Joy) she left him and returned to her husband. *See also* Cuchulain; Manannan Mac Llyr.

Fanus (Roman)

Also known as: *Fauna, Fauni* (Plural), *Faunus, Pan* (Greek).

God of crops. God of fertility. Inventor of herding, hunting, and husbandry. Protector of agriculture and shepherds. Inventor of poetry. Fanus is the grandson of Saturn, the nephew of Juno, the son of Picus, the prophet and demigod. His companion is Fauna (also known as Bona Dea), the fertility goddess and goddess of animals. Fanus is the father of Latinus, a mortal king, by Marica, a water nymph. He is possibly the father of Acis by a nymph. Fanus is identified with the Greek Pan. He is associated with Romulus and Remus. *See also* Bona Dea; Fauna; Picus; Saturn; Stercutius.

Faraguvaol (Antilles)

Faraguvaol is a a tree-trunk that wanders at will. It is one of the Zemis (spirits). It is shown as a wooden beam or a tree trunk. *See also* Zemis.

Faravai (Micronesia) *see* Palulop.

Farbauti (Teutonic) *see* Farbuti.

Farbuti *Farbauti* (Teutonic)

He is the mate of Laufey or Nal, and the father of Loki and Helblindi (q.v.). *See also* Forjotnr.

Faridun *Thraetana, Thraetaona, Thrita* (in earlier times); (Persia)

God of war. Bringer of fire. Faridun, a deified mortal, was an epic king who concealed his daughter. She became the mother of the hero Manushcithra (also known as Minucihr) who became Faridun's successor. The evil conqueror Zahhak was killed by Faridun with the assistance of the smith Kava. *See also* Thrita; Zahhak.

Farma-Tyr *see* Odin.

Faro (Mende People, Africa)

First man and twin of Pemba. According to legend Faro was sacrificed to atone for Pemba's sin of incest, and Faro was cut into pieces which became trees. Faro was sent back, alive, to earth in an ark which came to rest in a cave named *kaba karo*. The ark contained Faro and the eight ancestors of men. It also contained all the animals and plants that were the ancestors of those that exist now. Said to be depicted as a fish or fish-like. *See also* Mangala (B); Nyama; Pemba.

Fates *Fata, Fatum* (Greek)

Also known as: *Moirai, Moerae* (Greek), *Parcae* (Roman).

Personifications of implacable destiny. Triple Moon-goddess (in her death aspect). First identified in Hesiod's "Theogony," they were either the three daughters of Nyx (Night): Clotho (the spinner), Lachesis (Apportioner), and Atroposy (Atropos) (the cutter), or the daughters of Zeus and Themis. Their names imply the mortals' lot in life; the spinning, measuring and cutting of life. In another version, they are the daughters of Night and Erebus. The later poet Pindar makes them attendants of Themis when she married Zeus. They frequently appear in opposition to Zeus, which gave them greater power than Zeus.

As the Parcae they were Decima, Parca and Nona. Known to the Greeks as the Moirae, they aided the gods in their war with the Giants, killing Agrius and Thoas with bronze clubs. Although they usually remained distant from the affairs of gods and mortals it is recorded that they assigned Aphrodite with the one divine duty of making love, that they assisted Hermes in formulating the alphabet (although some attribute this to Io), the art of boxing, the use of weights and measures and the cultivation of the olive tree. They killed Typhon with poison fruit, and persuaded Zeus to kill Asclepius with a thunderbolt. Their number varies from one to three. In the single version Fate is called Moira and is associated with luck or fortune similar to the role Tyche plays. The Fates were worshipped in many parts of Greece. Sometimes they are associated or identified with the Keres and the Erinyes. They correspond to Tyche and to the Hebrew goddess, Meni. *See also* Admetus; Agrius (A); Clotho; Eumenides; Furies; Keres; Meliae; Moirae; Muses; Parcae; Sirens; Themis; Typhon (A).

Fatimah *Fatima* (Persia) *see* Ali (B); Mohammed.

Fatua (Roman) *see* Bona Dea; Fanus.

Faumea (Oceanic)
Also known as: *Haumea, Nona.*
Faumea, the eel-woman, taught the great god of the sea, Tangaroa, how to lure the man-killing eels out of her vagina. After sleeping together, Faumea gave birth to Tu-nui-ka-rere (or Ratu-nui) and Turi-a-faumea. Turi and his wife, Hina-arau-riki, were surfing one day, when Rogo-tumu-here, the demon octopus, captured Hina and spirited her away to the bottom of the ocean. Bereft, Turi assisted Tangaroa and Tu-nui-ka-rere in building a canoe, so he could search for his beloved. Faumea, who had withdrawn the wind into the sweat of her armpit, released it to power their canoe. When Turi and Tangaroa reached the ocean home of Rogo-tumu-here, Tangaroa baited his hook with sacred red feathers. Attracted to the bait, Rogo was pulled tentacle by tentacle into the vessel and each was sliced off by Tangaroa. When Rogo's head appeared, he decapitated him and from his head Hina, covered with the slime of the ocean, appeared. *See also* Haumea; Rata; Tangaroa.

Fauna (Roman)
Goddess of fertility. Counterpart to Fanus. Sometimes said to be either his daughter, sister or wife. Identified with Bona Dea.

Faunus (Roman, Greek) *see* Fanus.

Faustulus (Roman)
He is the herdsman spouse of Acca Larentia.

Favonius *Favonus* (Roman)
The west wind. *See also* Harpies; Zephyrus.

Febal (Celtic) *see* Bran.

Febris (Roman)
Febris is the goddess of fever and malaria. She is attended by Tertiana and Quartiana. The month of February is named after Febris.

Februus (Etruscan, Italian)
God of purification. He is probably a forerunner of Dis Pater

and he might be the same as Febris, the Roman goddess of malarial fever.

Feng Huang (China)
The Phoenix, and one of the Ssu-ling. The Feng Huang has five colors, and a song of five notes. It can raise its tail to the height of six feet. It is an omen of prosperity. According to some, the Phoenix represents the empress and the dragon represents the emperor.

Feng I (China) *see* Nine Songs.

Feng Po (China)
Also known as: *Earl of Wind, Feng Shih.*
Wind god. As a male he is God of the Wind. Sometimes replaced by Feng-P'o-P'o (Mrs. Wind) who is goddess of the wind, and is shown riding on the back of a tiger. Generally associated with Tien-Mu, Yu-tzu and Yun-t'ung, all weather deities. *See also* Feng Po-Po; Fujin.

Feng Po-Po *Feng P'o P'o* (China)
Goddess of the Wind. She replaced the Count of the Wind. Feng Po-Po travels over the clouds seated on a tiger. She carries a bag of winds in her arms. *See also* Feng Po.

Feng Shih (China) *see* Feng Po.

Feng-Tu (China)
Town of the dead. The chief city of Hell. There are three bridges that must be crossed to arrive at the gate. One gold, one silver and without railings, and one narrow and dangerous to cross. These bridges are for the gods and for the souls of the good and of those deserving punishment. Inside the gate are the palaces of the Yama Kings and the dwellings of the numerous officials and assistants and of all those who carry out the functions of the world of the dead. *See also* Kun-Lun Mountains; Yama Kings.

Fenga (Iceland) *see* Mysinger.

Fenne (Irish) *see* Aine.

Fennen (Irish) *see* Aine.

Fenrir *Fenrer, Fenris* (Norse; Teutonic)
Also known as: *Hrodvitnir.*
This wolf god is the offspring of Loki and Angrboda. He is so huge and fierce that only Tyr was able to chain him. Tyr lost a hand in the process. Fenrir was first bound by a chain called Laeding (also called Leding) made of strong iron links. Fenrir broke it. Then he was bound by an even stronger chain called Dromi that he also broke. The last chain, forged by dwarfs, was called Gleipnir. Made from invisible powers of the world, and small as a silken cord, it was unbreakable. Fenrir is still bound on an island in the sea (Amsvartner), waiting for the apocalypse known as Ragnarok. At that time, he will break loose. In some sources Fenrir is bound by a chain called Gelgja tied to or drawn through a black rock named Gjoll. Some say Fenrir had two sons by Gulveig-Hoder, one named Hati and the other Skoll. The two were called the Varns. In another version Hrodvitnir was the father of Skoll and Hati. *See also* Bifur; Dain; Dromi; Dwarfs; Gleipnir; Gullveig; Hati; Laeding; Loki; Ragnarok; Skoll; Thviti.

Fenris (Teutonic) *see* Fenrir.

Fenti (Egypt) *see* Assessors.

Fergus Mac Roig *Fergus Mac Roy* (Celtic, Irish)
Foster father of Cuchulainn. He possesses the strength of 700 men, and a sword as long as a rainbow. He fought Conchobar because of Deidre. *See also* Cuchulainn.

Feronia (Etruscan)
Goddess of fire and fertility. *See also* Evander (B); Flora.

Fiachna (Irish) *see* Manannan Mac Llyr.

Fialar (Teutonic) *see* Fjalar.

Fides (Roman)
Goddess of good faith. Goddess of fidelity. Fides is responsible for honesty, oaths and verbal contracts. She wears a wreath of laurel and olive. Her festival date is October 1.

Figonas *Higona, Hi'ona, Vigona* (San Cristobal)
Creators. Spirits who were named Hatuibwari, Aunua, and Walutahanga. Hatuibwari was a winged serpent with a human head, four eyes, and four breasts. Walutahanga was a female serpent born to a mortal woman. The Figonas are shaped like serpents. They are similar to the Kafisi spirits. *See also* Kafisi; Ndengei.

Fihrist (Gnostic)
High God. Fihrist is possibly a forerunner of Azrua in the context of "King of the Paradise of Light." He may be related to Zurvan and Ahura Mazda. *See also* Azrua; Zurvan.

Fili (Teutonic) *see* Dwarfs.

Fimafena (Teutonic) *see* Aegir.

Fimbulthul (Teutonic) *see* Elivagar.

Fimila (Teutonic) *see* Aesir.

Find (Celtic) "Fair-haired One." *See also* Finn; Lugh.

Fingal (Celtic, Irish) *see* Finn.

Finias (Celtic)
The Tuatha De Danann city of the south. Nuada's spear came from Finias. *See also* Nuada; Tuatha De Danann.

Finn (Celtic, Irish)
Also known as: *Demne, Fi'onn Mac Cumhal, Find, Fingal, Finn Mac Cool, Finn Mac Coul, Finn Og mac Cumhail, Fionn.*

Finn was a giant who could stand on two mountain tops and stoop to drink. Superhuman in all ways, he was the leader of the Fenians (fiana), a roving band of warriors. Known as Demne in his youth and raised by foster parents, he lived for over two hundred years. In one rendition, he was the son of Cumhal and Muirne (Murine). He became the father of Oisin, by Sadb and the grandfather of Oscar. He acquired the thumb of knowledge which allowed him to foresee the future by sucking his thumb. His dogs, Bran and Sceolan, had the reputation of being the wisest of all dogs. These pets were his nephews in dog-form. In one myth, Finn approached the High King of Ireland to ask for his daughter Grainme's (Grainne) hand in marriage. While at a banquet, Grainme spied Finn's friend Diarmait and instantly fell in love. After drugging the guests she declared her undying love to her fiance's friend. Gallantly, he refused to be involved with her. Determined, she cast a spell on him and they eloped. Furious at the unexpected turn of events, Finn set off in pursuit and although he caught the couple, the gods were with them and they escaped. In time, the fences were mended and they were embraced by the Fenians, not knowing that Finn still harbored a grudge. He enticed Diarmait on a hunt and caused his death by having him walk over a boar skin, in bare feet. Like Achilles, this was Darmait's only vulnerable spot, as his friend well knew. Finn lived a lengthy life as a poet, lover, rogue and hero. In some myths, he does not die but becomes very decrepit and drifts into the Otherworld, where he is said to be sleeping. Compare Finn and King Arthur for similar traits. Regarding the thumb of knowledge *see* Finneces. *See also* Murine; Oisin.

Finntain (Irish) *see* Cessair.

Fintan (Irish) *see* Cessair.

Finuweigh and Mehu (Philippines)
When the other gods attempted to create man from wax, they failed. Finuweigh and Mehu used a different approach. They made a man from dirt. Finuweigh put the man's nose on upside down. Mehu pointed out that if the nose was left in that manner, man would drown from rain running into his nostrils. Finuweigh refused to change the nose. When he turned away, Mehu quickly turned the nose around. He left his fingerprints on each side of the man's nose.

Fiorgyn (Teutonic) *see* Fjorgyn.

Fir Bholg (Celtic) *see* Firbolgs.

Firbolgs *Fir Bholg* (Celtic)
A mythological race defeated by the Tuatha De Danann. Considered by some to be the first fairies of Ireland, the Firbolgs are giant, grotesque creatures. Some claim they originally came from Greece. *See also* Banbha; Tuatha De Danann.

Fire (Phoenician)
With Flame and Light, Fire was one of the three children of Genos and Genea in the Phoenician Creation Legend. From Fire, his sons Hyposouranios, the first to build towns, and Ousoos, the first to use skins for garments, were born. *See also* Kolpia.

Firishtak *Firistak* (Persian) Angels. *See also* Aramazd.

Fith (Teutonic) *see* Dwarfs.

Five Blossoms (Mexico) *see* Macuilxochitl.

Five Suns (Aztec, Mexico) *see* Legend of the Four Suns.

Fjalar (Norse; Teutonic)
Also known as: *Havamal, Loki, Suttung, Utgard-Loke.*

The Red Cock. Fjalar, the symbol of fire, is the son of Surtr, the chief of the fire giants. When Ragnarok, the end of the world, is near, Fjalar will warn the giants. He is the giant from whom Odin stole the magic mead. He is also associated with the gods of frost. *See* Loki; Odin; Surtr.

Fjolnir (Teutonic) *see* Odin.

Fjorgyn *Fiorgyn* (Teutonic)

An Asynjor, also known as Jord, she is the giant mate of Odin, the mother of Frigga, and the mother of wife of Thor. *See also* Aesir; Earth; Jord; Odin.

Fjorgynn (Teutonic)

He is sometimes called the father, or the spouse of Frigga.

Fjorm (Teutonic) *see* Elivagar.

Flame (Phoenician) *see* Kolpia.

Flames (Teutonic) *see* Logi.

Flames of Wisdom (Tibet) *see* Dorge-Naljorma.

Flint (Huron, Iroquois People, North America) *see* Tawiscara.

Flora (Greek, Roman)

Also known as: *Chloris* (Greek), *Feronia* (Etruscan).

Goddess of fertility, and of flowering plants. Flora is an ancient deity of spring. Her festivals were called Floralia. It was a time of theater, dance, games and wonderful food. In some traditions, she is the Etruscan goddess of fire, Feronia. She is generally associated with Pomona, the goddess of fruit trees. She is also associated with Robigus. For Flora as Feronia *see* Evander (B). *See also* Zephyrus.

Flower Face (Celtic) *see* Blodeuwedd.

Fodla (Irish) *see* Amergin; Banbha.

Foge and Toafa (Samoa) Spirits in charge of rain.

Foland (Teutonic) *see* Volund.

Fomagata (Chibcha People, South America)

Also known as: *Thomagata*.

Storm god. Terrifying fire spirit. He is able to change men into animals. Bochica removed him. *See also* Bochica; Thomagata.

Fomorians (Celtic)

Also known as: *Fomors.*

Gods of darkness and evil. The Fomorians are a race of giants symbolized by darkness or evil. They were defeated in battle by the Partholanians, who then succumbed to the plague, with the exception of one member. *See also* Goibniu; Tuatha De Danann.

Fomors (Celtic) *see* Fomorians

Fongasigde (Andes, South America) *see* Naymlap.

Fons (Roman)

They are spirits of fresh water who were worshiped with the Camena who were also water deities.

Formorians *see* Banbha (Irish).

Fornax (Roman) *see* Inari; Vesta.

Fornjotnr *Fornjot, Fornjotnr, Forjotnro, Fornjotr* (Norse; Teutonic)

Also known as: *Farbuti, Ymir.*

Supreme first god. Storm god. It is commonly accepted that Ymir is the founder of the gods, but some say it was Fornjotnr. He had three sons: Hler (sea), Kari (air), Loki (fire). From his sons came the other frost giants: Mimir, Grendel, Gymir (sea giants); Thiassi, Thrym, and Beli (storm giants); Fenris and Hel (giants of fire and death). Fornjotnr is the father of Loki and Aegir by Haufey or Nai. *See also* Aegir; Fenrir; Kaare; Loki; Ymir.

Fornjotnro (Teutonic) *see* Fornjotnr; Ymir.

Forseti *Forsete* (Norse; Teutonic)

God of justice. He is the son of Balder and Nanna. Forset is one of the twelve major deities mention in the "Eddas." His home in Asgard, called Glitnir, is made of gold and silver. For a list of the other major deities *see* Ull.

Fortuna (Roman, Etruscan)

Also known as: *Fors, Muliebris, Primigenia, Tyche* (Greek), *Univirae.*

Goddess of good luck, chance and fortune. Deity of fate. Fortuna's festival date is June 24. She is shown on a round globe with a cornucopia in one hand and a rudder in the other hand. Her symbol is the wheel of fortune. She is also shown with the god of wealth, Ploutos, in her arms. *See also* Tyche.

Fotia (Irish) *see* Amergin; Banbha.

Fotla (Irish) *see* Amergin; Banbha.

Four Branches, The (Celtic) *see* Arianrhod.

Four Great Kings (India) *see* Dhartarastra; Lokapalas; Naga Knaya.

Four Hundred, The (Aztec) *see* Centzon-Huitznahuas.

Four Hundred Northerners, The (Aztec People, Mexico)

Star gods. *See also* Centzon Mimixoca.

Fraig (Teutonic) *see* Freyr.

Fratres Arvales (Roman)

The twelve sons of Carutius and Acca Larentia.

Frau Holle *Frau Venus* (Teutonic) *see* Holda.

Fraus (Roman) Goddess of treachery and fraud. *See also* Nox.

Fravahar (Persian) *see* Fravashi.

Fravak and Fravakain (Persia) *see* Mashya and Mashyoi.

Fravar (Persian) *see* Fravashi.

Fravartin (Persia) *see* Fravashi.

Fravashi *Fravartin* (Pre-Zoroastrian, Zoroastrian, Persia).

Also known as: *Fravahar* (Pahlavi dialect), *Fravar* (Persian), *Hrotik* (Armenian).

The Fravashi (meaning "genius") appear in the *Avesta* as one of a group of angels. Their function is to assist in making plant life grow and reproduce. In Zoroastrianism, they are the guardians of divine and human beings. The Fravashi is a spirit created by Ormazd (the later form of Ahura Mazda), who exists before the birth of a mortal, protects the mortal during life, and rejoins the soul at death. Fravashis are constantly at war against evil. Prosperity is visited upon the faithful followers who fulfill their duties to the Fravashi and burn incense in their honor. The 19th day of each month is devoted to them as are the last ten days of the year. The Chief of the Fravashis is Verethraghna, who personifies the idea of victory. In Armenian belief, the Fravashis live near the houses or tombs of followers. Devotions are offered on Saturdays and also before important festivals. Compare Fravashi to Manes (Roman) and Pitris (India). *See also* Ahura Mazda; Atar; Verethraghna; Zoroaster.

Fravashis *Fravartin* (Persia, Zend), *Hrotik* (Armenian)
Goddess of Souls. Guardian. Singular of the plural, Fravashi (meaning "Genius"). She-Who-Is-Many is Fravashi. Fravashi is composed of the souls of all living creatures, including the Not-Yet-Born. She is the defender of all living creatures. Said to be created by Ormazd. In some legends the Fravashis exist in heaven before birth and join the soul after death. The chief of the Fravashis is Verethraghna, who personifies the idea of victory. *See also* Atar; Verethraghna.

Frea (Teutonic) *see* Frigga.

Freki *Freke* (Norse; Teutonic)
Deified animal. With the wolf Geri, Freki, also a wolf, attends Odin.

Frey'a (Teutonic) *see* Freyja.

Freya (Teutonic) *see* Freyja; Vanadis.

Freyja *Frey'a, Freya* (Teutonic)
Also known as: *Gefjon, Gefn, Gondul* (possibly), *Horn, Mardal, Mardoll* ("Shining One over the Sea"), *Menglad, Menglod, Moertholl, Sessrymner, Syr, Vanadis.*
Goddess of Fertility. Freyja is the daughter of Njord and the twin sister and wife of Freyr. (Some writers say her husband is the mortal Od.) Her daughters are Hnoss (meaning jewel), by Odr who is possibly an aspect of Odin and Gersimi (Gerseme, meaning "precious one), and some say Frigg. Freyja is one of the Vanir. Her hall or home is called Sessrumnir. Loki borrowed Freyja's magic robe of feathers, which enabled him to fly to the land of the giants in search of Thor's hammer. Freyja's most famous possession is her amber necklace, known as "The Necklace of the Brisings." Freyja noticed four dwarves, Alfrigg, Dvalin, Berling, and Grerr, who were employed by the palace, working on a beautiful necklace. Overwhelmed with desire for the precious piece, she agreed to pay any price to call it her own. The only acceptable price to the dwarfs, who had many precious items stashed away, was to have the beautiful woman to spend a night in bed with each of them. Without second thoughts, she did so. In another attempt to procure his hammer from the giants, Thor disguised himself as Freyja and borrowed her necklace. Loki accompanied him dressed as a servant. At a later date, Loki, following Odin's orders, stole the necklace. He attempted to hide it but was apprehended by Heimdall, who was in the form of a seal. After a vicious encounter, Heimdall returned the necklace to Freyja. Gondul, the Valkyrie, who went to earth to retrieve the souls of kings who died in battle, is thought by some to be one of Freyja's disguises. Freyja is depicted in a robe of feathers, wearing her necklace and riding in a cart drawn by cats. Sometimes she is shown on the golden boar thought by some to be her brother Freyr. She loved decorative items, particularly jewelry, but she is also shown in

a helmet and breastplate. Compare Freyja's necklace to Hippolyte's girdle (Greek) and to the necklace of Amaterasu (Japan). Some associate Freyja with Cyble and Isis. Compare Freyja's mode of dress to Minerva. *See also* Aesir; Brisingamen; Disir; Dvalin; Dwarfs; Elves; Frey; Gefion; Heimdall; Loki; Menglad; Odin; Vanadis; Vanir.

Freyr *Fraig, Frey, Fro* (Norse; Teutonic)
Also known as: *Fricco, Ingun, Ingunnar-Frey, Ingvi-Frey, Sviagod* (Swedish), *Yngri* (Swedish), *Yngvi.*
Freyr is god of the world, earth, patron of married couples, a fertility god, and the ruler of the dwarfs. A Vanir, he is the son of Jjord (also known as Niord and Njord). He is also the twin brother and husband of Freyja. His magic ship, Skidbladnir, could carry all the deities, or it could be folded like a napkin and put into a pocket. Freyr is the owner of a horse named Blodughofi which can travel through flames and darkness. The dwarfs, who were ruled by Freyr, gave him a golden boar named Gullin-Bursti. Some say Freyr's name is the female form of Freyja and Frigga. *See also* Aesir; Alfar; Alfheim; Dwarves; Elves; Freyja; Frigga; Gerd.

Fria (Teutonic) *see* Frigga.

Fricco (Teutonic) *see* Freyr.

Fridthjof *Frithiof* (Icelandic) *see* Angervadil.

Frigga *Friga, Frigg, Frija, Frygga* (Norse; Teutonic)
Also known as: *Frea, Fria, Holda.*
Personalization of the civilized world. Goddess of the atmosphere or clouds. Perhaps also a goddess of love and fertility. Frigga is the principal wife of Odin and most revered of the Norse goddesses. She is the mother, by Odin, of Balder, Tyr, and Hermod. She is the sister of Jord or as some say, the daughter of Jord and Odin or Fiorgyn and Fiorvin (Ertha). She is the only goddess who has the privilege of sitting on the throne, known as Hlidskialf, next to Odin. Her own palace is known as Fensalir. She is represented wearing either snow-white or dark garments. She is tall, beautiful and stately and is shown wearing heron plumes in her headdress. Hanging from her girdle are a bunch of keys. Frigga may be the same as Holda (q.v.). *See also* Aesir; Balder; Bertha; Gladsheim; Hermod; Hlin; Jord; Loki; Odin.

Frimla (Teutonic) *see* Aesir.

Frithiof *Fridthjof* (Icelandic) *see* Angervadil.

Fro (Teutonic) *see* Freyr.

Frog Princess (Haida People, North American) *see* Dzelarhons.

Frost Mane (Teutonic) *see* Aarvak.

Frosti (Teutonic) *see* Dwarfs; Fjalar.

Frygga (Teutonic) *see* Frigga.

Fu Hsi (China) *see* Fu-Hsi.

Fu-Hsi *Fu Hsi* (China)
He is a legendary sage who instructed men in the skills of hunting and fishing and in the art of cooking. He invented writing,

made marriage rules, and discovered iron. Fu-Hsi drove wild animals out of China. He also discovered the "eight diagrams" which became the symbols of the teaching of Tao. A large water horse gave him the tablets bearing the inscriptions. Fu-Hsi is one of the Three Emperors who are half-man and half-serpent. He is usually shown with long nails worn by scholars. His sister/spouse is Nu-Kua (q.v.). *See also* Kun (B).

Fu-Hsing *Fu-Sing* (China) *see* Fu-Shen.

Fu-Jin *Fujin* (Japan)
    God of the winds. Fu-jin carries a large bag of winds across his shoulder. From this bag he selects the type of wind he wants to release ranging from a gentle breeze to a violent hurricane. The intensity of the wind depends on how wide the mouth of the bag is opened. In the Shinto tradition, the first wind god born from the breath of the god Izanagi was Shinaland. Fu-jin is blue in color. In the Ryobu-Shinto tradition, the wind deity Haya-ji is depicted in a contorted shape, carrying his wind bag on his shoulder. Compare to the wind deities, Tatsuta-Hiko and Tatsuta-Hime. Compare to the whirlwind god, Haya-ji (Haya-Tsu-muji-no-Kami). Compare to the Greek winds Argestes, Boreas, Notus and Zephyr. Compare to wind deities Saramaya, Trophonius, Vayu, Pan, Mercury, Linos, Aeolus, Amphion, Aeolus and Maruts. *See also* Raiden.

Fu-Shen *Fu-Hsing, Fu Shen, Fu Sing* (China)
    God of happiness. Fu-Shen is thought to have come into existence during the dynasty of Wu Ti (C.E. 502–550). Presumed to be small in stature, he began life as a mortal judge. During his career he issued an edict proclaiming that small men should have the same rights as other people. The emperor, who liked small men and who had many small men in his service, was touched by the ruling. He lifted the levy against small men. From that time, Fu-Shen was known as a god of happiness. He is often shown in the company of the god of long life and the god of salaries. His symbol is the bat.

Fu Shen (China) *see* Fu-Shen.

Fu Sing (China) *see* Fu-Shen.

Fuchi (Japan)
    Also known as: *Huchi Fuchi.*
    Fire deity. Fuchi is a fire-goddess who gave her name to Mount Fujiama. In some versions she was originally a goddess of the early, semi-nomadic Ainus People. It is possible that Fuji is a corruption of the Ainu goddess, Fuchi. *See also* Fuji.

Fudo (Japan) *see* Fudo-Myoo.

Fudo-Myoo *Fudo* (Buddhist; Japan)
    Also known as: *Arya Achalanatha* (Sanskrit), *Dainichi-nyorai* (Japan), *Konkara* (Japan), *Seitaka* (Japan), *Shiva* (India), *Vairochana* (Sanskrit).
    God of wisdom and righteousness. Fudo-Myoo is the most important of the Godai-Myoo (Five Great Kings) who protect the Buddhist world. An incarnation of Dainichi-nyorai, his function is to carry out the wishes of the great Buddha. Fudo-Myoo is the manifestation of Dainichi's wrath against evil and is presented in a terrifying form. He fights the opponents of Buddha and protects the believer against calamities, great dangers, fire and theft. He is fond of mortals and gives them his

complete support in their endeavors. He has two attendants, Seitaka Doji, also known as Seit Ka-Doji, and Kongara-Doji. A youthful incarnation of Fudo-Myoo was Konkara. It is said that in an elderly incarnation, he was named Seitaka. The Shingon sect consider Fudo-Myoo a form of the Hindu deity Shiva. Fudo-Myoo is depicted as seated or standing on a rock with the legs of his thick, muscular, ornamented body, crossed. He is also shown standing on a precipice. He has long hair with one lock falling from the left side of his head. His eyes bulge under thick scowling eyebrows. Fangs protrude from the corners of his mouth. He holds a sword in his right hand and a cord in his left. Usually there is a flaming halo behind him that resembles a raging fire. The sword is the sword of justice which conquers greed, anger and folly. The rock he stands on indicates his firmness and suggests that as his name indicates, he is "The Immovable." The cord held by Fudo-Myoo is to bind the enemies of Buddha. Seitaka Doji holds a stick in his right hand and a vajra (thunderbolt) in his left hand. The vajra is a symbol of divine or mystic power. Kongara-Doji appears in Indian costume. A sword which is still preserved was presented to Fudo-Myoo by the Emperor Shujaku (C.E. 931–946). This sword is said to cure insanity. *See also* Dai Itoku-Myoo; Dainichi-nyorai; Godai-Myoo; Gozanze-Myoo; Gundari-Myoo; Kongo-Yasha-Myoo.

Fufluns (Etruscan)
    Also known as *Puphluns.* God of growing things, including mortals, he is thought to be a version of Bacchus (q.v.).

Fugen Bosatsu (Japan) *see* Bodhisattva; Monju-Bosatsu; Samantabhadra.

Fugen En-myo (Japan) *see* Samantabhadra.

Fugi-San (Japan) *see* Fuji.

Fuji (Japan)
    Also known as: *Fuchi, Fugi-San, Fukiyi, Juji-Yama.*
    Sun goddess. Mountain goddess. Fire goddess. Goddess of the hearth. In one legend Fuji is a female and Mt. Haku (a male) who stands higher. When the Buddha Amida ran a pipe from the top of Haku to the top of Fuji and poured water into it, the water ran down Fuji's peak. Angry that she was not the highest mountain, Fuji beat Haku's head until it cracked. Her action created the eight peaks, making Fuji the highest mountain in Japan. Fuji was probably a volcano goddess of Mount Fujiyama. As Fuchi, she was also the guardian of home and hearth of the ancient, semi-nomadic Ainu people from the northern islands of Japan. The name Fuji is derived from Fuchi. It is said that the mountain derived its name from this sun goddess. Another deity known as the goddess of Mount Fujiyama is Sengen-Sama, the daughter of Oh-yama-tsumi (Great-Mountain-Possessor). Mount Fujiyama is considered sacred, as are other mountains in Japan. A fountain of youth is said to be hidden in the mountain. The wandering ancestor god Mi-oya-no-kami, approached the miserly god of the mountain for food and was turned away. Mi-oya-no-kami became angry and sentenced the mountain to an eternity of cold, snow and scant food supplies so that few mortals would visit her. When he visited the sacred Mount Tsukuba, he was treated hospitably and in return he insured that the mountain would have an abundance of food. Compare Fuji

to Achachilas. Regarding the importance of hospitality *see* Susanowo. *See also* Agni (India); Buto (B); Fuchi; Hestia (Greek); Pele (Hawaiian); Sengen; Vesta (Roman).

Fujin (Japan) *see* Fu-jin.

Fukaotsu (Japan) *see* Buddha; Vajrapani.

Fuku (Japan) *see* Fukurokujin; Shichi Fukujin.

Fuku-Roku-Ju (Japan) *see* Fukurokujin.

Fukurokujin *Fuku, Fuku-Roku-Ju, Fukurokuju, Jukurokujin* (Buddhist, Shinto; Japan, China)
God of wisdom, long life, good luck and happiness. Fukurokujin is one of the Shichi Fukujin (seven deities of luck). He is easily recognizable because the length of his head is nearly equal to the length of his body. Fukurokujin originated in China. In the Shinto tradition, he is known as the god (kami) of all trades. He is also known as the southern pole star god. It is thought that Fukurokujin was a Chinese philosopher and prophet in his earthly incarnation. He is depicted with a narrow, elongated head, a high forehead and white whiskers and is often accompanied by a tortoise, white crane or a stork; symbols of longevity. For details about the crane and tortoise, *see* Jorojin. Another symbol of longevity in Japan and China is fungus. The image of Fukurokujin is worn for good luck. *See also* Jorojin; Shichi Fukujin.

Fukurokuju (Japan) *see* Fukurokujin.

Fulgora (Roman)
Goddess of lightning.

Fulla (Norse; Teutonic)
Also known as: *Abundantia, Abundia, Habone* (Danish), *Vol, Vola, Volla.*
Goddess of the toilet of Frigga. She is the sister or friend of Frejya and Frigga's first and favorite attendant. Fulla protected Frigga from Odin's anger by having a dwarf pull down a statue erected by Odin. This indirectly caused a freeze by the ice-giants, known as Jotuns. She was responsible for carrying Frigga's valuables in a coffer. Fulla's hair is long and flowing, bound by a circlet shaped like a sheaf. *See also* Frigga; Hlin; Nanna.

Fundin (Teutonic) *see* Dwarfs.

Furies *Furiae* (Roman)
Also known as: *Dirae, Erinyes, Eumenides, Poenae.*
Goddesses of vengeance. Personified curses. Underground deities. The Furies were the names given to the Erinyes by the Romans. Three hideous winged females, Alecto, Tisiphone, and Magaera, they sprang from the blood of mutilated Ouranos. They are the daughters of Terra (earth). Avenging deities, the Furies pursued and punished the guilty, especially murderers. One has to pound on the ground to get their attention. Known in hell as the Furies and in heaven as the Dirae, they appealed to Dike, the goddess of justice, to punish the wicked. They are shown as black maidens with serpents in their hair and blood dripping from their eyes. *See also* Acheron; Eumenides; Nyx.

Futemimi-no-Kami (Japan) *see* Kushi-nada-hime.

Futsu-Nushi (Japan)
Lightning or fire deity. The Sharp-cutting Lord. A general of the Sun Goddess (Amaterasu), who appears to be a weapon deity. *See also* Ninigi; Take-mi-kazuchi.

Fylgia *Fylgja, Fylgjur* (plural) (Iceland, Norway)
This is a guardian spirit, an attendant spirit or a person's soul or double. The Fylgia can appear in dreams as a guardian and offer advice or give warnings. As the soul or double it is conceived in animal form, often a wolf bridled with snakes. If a person sees his or her Fylgia (except in dreams), it means death. When a person dies, the Fylgia passes on to another family member. The Fylgia are related to the Norns (q.v.) and the Hamingjur, who are usually invisible, feminine beings who accompany men and direct their course. *See also* Ba; Fylgukona; Norns.

Fylgjur (Iceland, Norway) *see* Fylgia.

Fylgukona *Hamingja* (Norway)
A female guardian spirit who represents a family or an individual. Similar to the Fylgia (q.v.).

Fylgya (Iceland, Norway) *see* Fylgia.

G

G (Maya)
This sun god is recognized by his filed front teeth, and the sun sign Kin. He may be the same as Kinich Ahau (q.v.).

Ga-Gaah (Iroquois People, North America)
A sacred crow, Ga-Gaah came from the sun and brought a grain of corn in his ear. This was planted by Hahgwediyu (an alternate name for Yoskeha) and became the food of mankind. *See also* Ga-Oh; Yoskeha.

Ga-Gorib (Africa) *see* Gaunab.

Ga-Oh *Gaoh* (Huron, Iroquois, Seneca People, North America)
The Great Spirit of the Winds, Ga-Oh is the giant who con-

trols the Bear, who is the north wind, the Panther of the west wind, the Moose of the east wind, and the Fawn of the south wind. Some legends say he was a cannibal who used stones as missiles and uprooted great trees. He is possibly related to the sacred crow Ga-Gaah (q.v.). He may be the same as Gahe of the Apache People (q.v.). *See also* Adekagagwaa; Hino; Manibozho.

Ga-Tum-Dug (Sumer)

Also known as: *Ninhursag, Ninki.*

Earth goddess. Little known goddess who was worshiped at Lagash where a temple was erected to her. She corresponds to the goddess Bau. *See also* Ninhursag; Ninki.

Gabil *Gerra, Gibil* (Assyria, Sumer)

Also known as: *Girau, Nusku.*

God of fire. Giver of light and the symbol of the sacrificial flame. He is the patron of those who work with metal and he also acts as an arbiter of law and order. Gabil is the son of Anu and sister of Nin-karrak, the healing goddess. The wizard Ashipu wanted to break the evil spell of a sorcerer so he burned a peeled onion and a crushed date and invoked the name of Gabil. *See also* Nin-karrak; Nusku; Shamash; Sin.

Gabriel *Abruel, Jibril, Jiburili* (Hebrew, Arabic)

Also known as: *Asrafel, Ruh el Amin* (faithful spirit), *Serafili* (Muslim; Africa).

Archangel. He is personified as an angel who appeared to Daniel as a man. At the end of the world, Gabriel will blow his horn. *See also* Abram.

Gabzur (Babylon) *see* Arallu.

Gad (Canaan, Hebrew)

God of Fortune. Biblical reference to "prepare a table for Gad and furnish a drink for Meni (deity of numbers or lots)." A similar deity from the Syrians is called Ba'al Gad who is a master of luck. Gad is represented as a lion. *See also* Menat; Menu.

Gaea (Greek, Roman)

Also known as: *Chthon, Gaia, Ge, Gea, Geb* (Egypt), *Gi, Rhea, Tellus* (Roman), *Terra* (Roman), *Titaea.*

According to the Olympian creation myth, Gaea sprang forth from Chaos. She is the personification of the earth. A virgin mother, she gave birth to her son, Uranus, who personifies the sky. From Gaea and Uranus the birds, beasts, seas, lakes, rivers, trees, flowers and grass were created. Her first children were the semi-human giants, Briareus, also called Aegaeon, Gyges, and Cottus, each with one hundred hands. They were followed by the three one-eyed Cyclopes: Brontes, Steropes and Arges, who were builders and smiths. Hesiod wrote that from Chaos, Gaea (Earth) was born, followed by Tartarus and Eros, "the love which softens hearts." Gaea then gave birth to Uranus (Sky) to cover her and formed Ourea (Mountains) and Pontus (Sea). Uniting with her son Uranus, she then created the first race, six females and six males, called the Titans. They were named Oceanus, Ceos, Hyperion, Crius, Iapetus, Cronus, Theia, Rhea, Mnemosyne, Phoebe, Tethys, and Themis. Next were born the one-eyed giants, the Cyclopes, Brontes, Steropes and Arges, followed by the monstrous Hecatonchires, named Cottus, Briareus and Gyges. Uranus, horrified with his offspring, shut them away deep in the earth. Angry with his actions, Gaea induced her son Cronus to sever the genitals of his father, Uranus. From his blood and semen, Gaea gave birth to the Erinyes, the Meliae and Aurora. From his severed genitals, Aphrodite was born. In the Olympian tradition, Gaea created the universe, and gave birth to the first race of gods and the first race of mortals. Other children attributed to Gaea are: Cecrops, Echo, Palaechthon, Rumor, and Alcyoneus. It is said that she was also the mother of Ceto, Crius, Eurybia, Nereus, Phorcys and Thaumas, all by Oceanus. By Hephaistos, she was the mother of Erichthonius. She is the mother of Echidna and Typhoeus, possibly by Tartarus; and Ogyges, and Charybdis, and Antaeus, by Poseidon. Some think that she was also the mother of the monster Arion, the guardian of the Golden Fleece. She is identified by the Romans as Terra or Tellus (q.v.). Gaea is said to be the counterpart of the Celtic goddess Dana. Compare to the earth goddess Prithiva (India), and Geb (Egypt). *See also* Acheron; Adrastia; Aegaeon; Aello; Agraulos; Agrius (A); Aither; Alcyoneus; Antaeus; Aphrodite; Aurora; Ceos; Ceto; Chaos; Cottus; Crius; Cronus; Cybele; Cyclopes; Echo; Enceladus; Erinyes; Eros; Eumenides; Giants; Golden Fleece; Harpies; Hecate; Hecatonchires; Helius; Hephaistos; Hesperides; Hyperion; Iapetus; Meliae; Mnemosyne; Nereids; Nereus; Nox; Oceanus; Orion; Phoebe (B); Phorcys; Pontus; Poseidon; Rhea; Styx; Tartarus; Tellus; Tethys; Themis; Titans; Typhon (A); Uranus; Zeus.

Gaelestis (Roman) *see* Janus.

Gaels, The (Celtic) *see* Tuatha De Danann.

Gaga (Sumer) The messenger of Anshar.

Gagnrad (Norse; Teutonic)

Another name used by Odin.

Gahe (Apache People, North America)

Wind deities. Mountain spirits who drive away disease. They have different colors representing different directions: black (east), blue (south), white (north), yellow (west). Gahe is probably the same as Ga-oh of the Iroquois People (q.v.).

Gahongas *Gahonga* (Iroquois People, North America)

Dwarf spirits who live in water and rocks. They might be deities of rocks or stones since legends tell of them having great strength and throwing stones. The Gahongas are part of a group of dwarfs along with Gandayahs and Ohdowas. *See also* Jogaoh.

Gaia (Greek) *see* Gaea.

Gajendra (India) *see* Ganesha.

Gajomartan (Iranian, Persian) *see* Gaya Maretan.

Gaki (Japan)

Also known as: *Preta* (India).

Demons. Ghosts. The Gaki, known as hungry ghosts, congregate wherever there is any waste of food or drink. These spirits are tormented by constant hunger and thirst. They can assume any shape yet in their real form are invisible to humans. They can be detected because they sing, whistle or talk. They consume the food in flames. Although the Gaki have the power to harm, they need human sympathy and pity. The Gaki are shown as wretched, footless beings, with wide mouths. They appear emaciated except for their bellies, which are swollen. The belief in footless ghosts is from the depictions of the late–eighteenth century artist, Maruyama Okyo. *See also* Kappa; Oni; Preta; Shiko-Me; Tengu.

Galan-Mai (Welsh) *see* Beltine.

Galar (Teutonic) *see* Dwarfs; Fjalar; Kvasir; Odraerir.

Galatea (A) (Greek)
A Nereid. She is the sea nymph daughter of Nereus and Doris, who fell in love with Acis. Polyphemus, a jealous admirer of Galatea, killed Acis in a fight. *See also* Acis; Amphitrite; Galatea; Nereids; Thetis.

Galatea (B) (Greek)
Pygmalion carved an ivory statue of a woman. It was so beautiful that the women-hating Pygmalion fell in love with it. The goddess of love, Aphrodite, brought the statue to life. She was named Galatea. By Pygmalion, she became the mother of Paphos.

Galeru (Australia) *see* Rainbow snake.

Galgavaldyr (Teutonic) *see* Odin.

Galli, The (Greek) *see* Corybantes; Cybele.

Gallu *Gello* (Babylonian, Sumerian, Semitic)
Also known as: *Gello* (Greek), *Gelou, Gilou.*
Demons. These seven demons love to eat flesh. They are similar to Sedu.

Gama (Africa)
Male spirits who eat the flesh of corpses. *See also* Gaunab.

Gamab (Hottentot People, Africa) *see* Gaunab.

Gamati (Africa)
Female spirits who eat the flesh of corpses. *See also* Gama; Gaunab.

Gamelios (Greek) Zeus as the god of marriage.

Gamlat (Babylonia) *see* Ishtar.

Gamr (Teutonic) *see* Garm; Hati.

Gamsu (Chaldean) Sea goddess. *See also* Zerpanitum.

Ganadevatas (Hindu; India)
Minor deities who are led by Ganesha. They are attendants of Shiva and live on Mount Kailasa. Included in this group are the Adityas, when they represent the twelve annual phases of the sun, and the Visvadevas, who attend to funeral offerings. Also included are the Vasus, who personify natural phenomena and live in Swarga, Indra's heaven. Dharma's twelve sons, the Sadhyas, belong to this group in their personification of Vedic rites and prayers, as do the Rudras or Maruts.

Ganapati (India) *see* Ganas.

Ganas (Hindu; India)
They are one of nine groups of minor deities. Demon dwarfs, they are the attendants of Shiva and Parvati. Their ruler is Ganesha, who is called Ganapati in this capacity. *See also* Ganadevatas; Ganesha.

Ganaskidi (Navaho People, North America)
They are also known as "The Humpbacks." The Ganaskidi are corn spirits or harvest deities and one of the group of deities called Yei (q.v.).

Ganda *Gandha, Gandhema* (Tibet) (Buddhist; country or origin, India)
Also known as: *Dri-chab-ma* (Tibet), *Dri-chha-ma* (She Spraying Perfume; Tibet), *Hlamos* (Tibet), *Matrikas.*
Ganda is one of the mother goddesses of Buddhism known as Matris. She appears in Bardo on the fifth day with a host of deities, including Amoghasiddhi. The Matris are also called the Matrikas, and in Tibet the Hlamos. They are usually numbered as eight, though some say there are seven, nine or sixteen Matris. They often appear in disguise, for in their true form they are so beautiful that they could arouse uncontrollable sexual desire. Ganda is depicted with two or four arms and is usually standing on one foot with the other foot lifted. This asana (position) is the dancing position, known as ardhaparyankasana. She holds a shell-vase of perfume. Her color is green, symbolizing the light of wisdom. The perfume, made from numerous herbs, represents sense-perception. Matris are not to be confused with Matrs, female Hindu spirits who dwell in cemeteries, crossroads and on mountains. The Matrs are said to practice witchcraft and are disease demons. *See also* Amoghasiddhi.

Gandalf *Gandalfr* (Teutonic) *see* Dwarfs.

Gandalfr (Teutonic) *see* Gandalf.

Gandarewa *Kundrav* (Persian)
This fiendish dragon is the "lord of the abyss" and master of the deep waters of Vourukasha, the cosmic sea, and the home of White Haoma. His epithet "golden heeled" is a reminder of the charitable side of his personality. At times he distributes the Haoma plant but generally he jealously guards it. A spy for Azhi Dahaka, his goal is to destroy the world. In a brutal battle, his skin was stripped off up to his head by the heroic Keresaspa, who then tied him up and dragged him to the seashore. Somehow, Gandarewa still managed to eat fifteen of Keresaspa's horses and attempted to abduct his family. After a battle that lasted nine days and nine nights in the cosmic ocean, Keresaspa finally overcame him. Compare Gandarewa to Gandharva (Hindu). *See also* Azhi Dahaka; Haoma; Keresaspa; Srvara.

Gandayah (Iroquois People, North America) *see* Gahongas; Jogaoh.

Gandayaks (Iroquois People, North America)
Benevolent spirits. They are dwarfs who are in charge of making vegetation fruitful. They also control fish. *See also* Dwarfs; Gahongas; Ohdowas.

Gandevi (India) *see* Gandiva.

Gandha (India) *see* Ganda.

Gandhara (India) Goddess of knowledge. *See also* Devis.

Gandhari *Gundhary* (India)
She is the daughter of Subala, spouse of Dhritarashtra and mother of Duroydhana and probably Dussasana. She and her spouse retired into the forest with Kunti (q.v.).

Gandharva-Loka (India) *see* Loka.

Gandharvas *Gandharvis* (feminine) (Vedic, Brahmanic, Hindu; India)

The first Gandharva, a Vedic deity, was the measurer of space, the sun steed and preparer and guard of soma, the elixir of the gods. In the "Brahmanas," the Gandharvas and their lovely spouses, the Apsarases, preside over fertility. They are said to be descendants of Brahma or Kasyapa and Muni. Their leader is Chitra-ratha, or according to some, Visvavasu (an enemy of Indra), and Tumburu. These spirits, half-man and half-bird, are skilled musicians and medical experts who are charged with caring for the precious soma juice. They are usually found in Swarga (Indra's heaven) frolicking with the Apsarases, although they have their own beautiful cities in the foothills of Meru Mountain. Their function is to entertain the gods with their music and minister to their needs. They haunt the air, forests and mountains. The Gandharvas usually get along well with mortals although occasionally they will fight with men. Vishnu was called upon to assist the Nagas when the Gandarvas descended to Patala and plundered their treasures. They sent the river Narmada (now known as the Nerbudda) to guide Vishnu to the underworld where he defeated the Gandarvas. Gandharvas are described as shaggy, half-bird, half-human demons, who are orgiastic, phallic, taboo-breakers. They can alter themselves into beautiful human men who have mystical power over women. Others say they were men with bird wings and legs. The *Mahabharata* refers to Gandarvas as a race of hill dwellers. Gandarva parallels the Persian Gandarewa (q.v.). *See also* Asparases; Brahma; Devas (A); Hanuman; Kasyapa; Krishna; Kuvera; Loka; Lokapalas; Meru Mountain; Nagas; Narada; Patala; Ravana; Soma; Swarga; Vishnu; Visvavasu.

Gandharvis (India) *see* Gandharvas.

Gandhema (India) *see* Ganda.

Gandiva *Gandevi* (India)

This is the celestial bow that originally belonged to Soma and later to the god of war, Arjuna. *See also* Arjuna; Soma.

Ganesha *Ganesa, Ganesh* (Hindu; India)

Also known as: *Adi-Pati* (the Ancient Lord), *Bhutesa*, *Chakra-Raja* (Lord of the Wheel), *Ekadanta* (One-toothed), *Gajana, Gajanana, Gajendra, Gana-Pati, Ganapati* (Chief of the Ganas or dwarf demons), *Heramba, Lambakarna* (Long-eared), *Lombodara* (hang-bellied), *Panpati, Pasu-Pati, Shasti* (his female form), *Shoden* (Japan), *Sidhi Data* (Bestower of Success), *Vinayaka* (God of Difficulties).

Ganesha is the god of wisdom and eloquence, arts and letters, the remover of obstacles, the first scribe and god of scribes and patron deity of literature. He is the god of science and skills, god of seductive eloquence, god of prosperity, and ruler of the demon dwarfs, known as the Ganas. Numerous myths surround this popular deity. In some accounts, he is the son of Parvati and Shiva and his siblings are Karttikeya and Kumara. In other renditions, he was born from a mixture of dust and Parvati's body moisture or the sacred water of the Ganges river. Many of his myths involve his head. Parvati was anxious to show her newborn to Shiva. His searing glance reduced the child's head to ashes. Brahma advised her to take the first head she could

find for her baby. Another myth relates that when Ganesha blocked Shiva's path to Parvati's bath, the angry god struck off his head. To keep Parvati happy he replaced it with an elephant's head. Ganesha's head is attributed to Parvati's wrath in another legend. She was jealous of his beauty and cursed him to be fat, with an elephant head. He has only one full tusk, the other tusk was lost in a fight with Parasuraman or broken to use as an implement to write the *Mahabharata* which was dictated by the sage Vyasa. Another tale tells us that Rama went to visit Shiva and was barred entrance by Ganesha. Indignant, Rama threw an axe at him. When Ganesha realized that the weapon belonged to his father he permitted it to strike him and his tusk was broken off. The goddesses Buddhi, who personifies intelligence and wisdom, and Siddhi, who personifies success, became his spouses when he won them in a contest with his brother Karttikeya. Ganesha's blessings must be obtained for any endeavor, venture or difficult matter to be successful. He is invoked before writing, weddings, trips, or opening a new business. At births, prayers are offered that every organ may receive strength from him. He is invoked at purification rites and by mothers, twelve days after the birth of the child. All household matters are under his care, particularly kitchen items. Only Ganesha can forgive one who kills a serpent. In the Smarta tradition, five principal deities are worshiped: Shiva, Vishnu, Shakti, Surya and Ganesha. Ganesha is invoked at the beginning of ceremonies, for as the remover of obstacles, he will ensure a beneficial service. He is usually depicted as red or yellow in color, with an elephant head, one full tusk and one partial tusk, four arms, and a big stomach. He holds the lotus or sacred thread, the Ankus (elephant goad), the sacred conch shell, and the Chakra (wheel). His mount is a mouse or rat. Sometimes he holds a small tooth. Ganesha must be appeased before worshiping other gods. His appetite is gargantuan and he particularly enjoys offerings of fruits and vegetables. The deep-rooted Durva-grass is his emblem. His festival is known as Ganesha-Chaturthi. It is celebrated towards the end of August on the fourth day of the first fortnight. His image is made from various substances, such as clay, wood or paper. It is placed on a platform in the house and surrounded by lamps and mirrors decorated with dyed red rice. He is offered rice pudding. After being worshiped for ten days, the images are thrown into the water. On his feast day followers are not to look at the moon. This directive stems from a story that Ganesha was once frightened by a snake and fell from his mount, the mouse. His stomach burst open and the full moon laughed at him. As Shasti, his female form, he is shown with four arms and four breasts. *See also* Brahma; Devi; Ganas; Karttikeya; Kumara; Parvati; Rama; Shakti; Shiva; Surya; Vishnu; Vyasa.

Ganesha-Chaturthi (India)

Feast day in honor of Ganesha.

Ganga *Gung, Gunga, Mai* (Hindu; India)

Ganga, the river goddess of the Ganges and fertility goddess, is the daughter of the Himalayas or Himavat (meaning "Owner of Snow") the mountain god, and consort of the gods, including Vishnu and Shiva. Her sister is the mountain goddess Parvati. The sage Bhagiratha, son of Dilipa, through prolonged asceticism prayed for her waters to bring relief to the parched land. The gods answered his prayers. Brahma warned the deities that she could not be allowed to flow freely from the celestial realm (where she circled Meru mountain three times), for her weight would cause massive floods. Shiva supported her waters before their fall onto Mount Kailasa by allowing the water to flow through his thick hair. She separated herself into seven streams and flowed onto the mountains and valleys amid great rejoicing. One of her streams became the sacred river Ganges. From earth, she followed Bhagiratha's chariot to Patala (the underworld) and hence is said to water the three worlds. Ganga married the mortal king Santanu (also spelled Shantanu) so that she could keep her promise to the Vasus to be their mother in their incarnations. They in return promised that her youngest son, Bhishma, would receive one-eighth of each of their power. In some legends, her son by Shiva is Karttikeya, though his mother is often said to be Parvati. A variation is that Karttikeya did not have a mother. His father, Rutra-Shiva, ejaculated into a fire; the fire went out and his seed spilled into the Ganges River and Karttikeya was born. In another myth, Ganga is said to be one of the Apsaras who married the mortal King Santanu. Ganga is depicted as a crowned mermaid or as a white queen. She is shown on the back of a sea monster called the makara. A name of praise for Shiva is Gangadhara (Carrying the Ganges). In this aspect, he is shown restraining the powerful river in his hair to protect the earth. Ganga is also shown as a beautiful woman with her waters flowing about her. She personifies prowess, health and abundance. Her annual festival, Dasara, is held on the tenth lunar day of the bright fortnight of Jyeshtha (May-June). All rivers are considered sacred in India, but the seven most sacred are the Ganges, Jumna, Godavari, Sarasvati Narmada, Indus and Kaveri. *See also* Apsarases; Asuras; Bhishma; Devi; Karna; Karttikeya; Kunti; Lakshmi; Makara; Meru Mountain; Parvati; Sagara; Sarasvati; Shiva; Vishnu; Yami.

Ganga-ja (India) "Born from the Ganges." *See also* Karttikeya.

Gangamma (India)
She is one of the Mutyalammo goddesses who are deities of the household. She functions as the goddess of water. *See also* Mutyalammo.

Ganges (India) *see* Ganga; Varuna.

Gangeya (India) *see* Bhishma; Ganga; Karttikeya.

Gangler (Teutonic) *see* Odin.

Gansam Deo (India) *see* Gramadeveta.

Ganumedes (Greek) *see* Ganymede.

Ganv-devata (India) *see* Gramadeveta.

Ganva-devi (India) *see* Gramadeveta.

Ganymeda (Greek)
This is another name for the goddess of eternal youth, and cup-bearer to the gods, Hebe.

Ganymede (Greek)
Also known as: *Catamitus* (Roman) *Ganumedes.*
Cup-bearer of the gods. He is the son of Tros and Callirrhoe. Ganymede, an exceptionally graceful, handsome youth was kidnapped by Zeus. He sent Ganymede on the back of an eagle to

Olympus. There he became Hebe's successor as cup-bearer. Ganymede later became the constellation Aquarius. *See also* Hebe.

Ganzir (Semitic) *see* Ereshigal.

Gaoh (Iroquois People, North America) *see* Ga-oh.

Gaokerelna Tree (Persia) *see* Gaokerena.

Gaokerena Tree *Gaokerelna Tree* (Persia)
See also Angra Mainyu; Haoma; Thrita; Tree of Many Seeds; Vourukasha.

Gapn (Ugaric) *see* Baal.

Garamas (Greek)
Another name for Amphithemis. *See also* Acacallis.

Garang (Dinka People, Africa) *see* Abuk.

Garden of Eden *see* Hesperides.

Garden of Hesperides (Greek) *see* Amaltheia; Nereus.

Gari (Teutonic) *see* Geri.

Garide (Central Asia)
He is the bird who resides at the top of the tree of life. *See also* Abyrga.

Garita (India) Bird goddess; mother of Garitari.

Garitari (India) *see* Garita.

Garkain (Aborigine People, Australia)
Evil spirit. Garkain lives in the jungle. He can walk and fly. His victims are captured by enfolding them in the loose skin that attaches his arms and legs. He eats his victims raw. *See also* Namarakains.

Garm *Garme, Gamr, Garnr* (Teutonic)
This ferocious, monster wolf-dog is the watchdog of the dead and the guardian of Hel. At the apocalypse, known as Ragnarok, he will break loose and attack Tyr. During their battle, they will kill one another. *See also* Hati; Ragnarok.

Garme (Teutonic) *see* Hati; Garm.

Garmr (Teutonic) *see* Hati; Garm.

Garnr (Teutonic) *see* Hati; Garm.

Garuda (Brahman, Hindu; India; Country of origin, Babylon)
Also known as: *The Kruth* (Cambodian), *Naga-Teka* (Snake Killer), *Simurgh* (Persian), *Taraswin* (The Swift One).
In the beginning, Garuda emerged from Brahma's eggshell. Following his birth, elephants were created from the same substance. In later mythology, as king of the birds, and a demi-god, he was hatched from an egg laid by his mother Vinata, one of Daksha's numerous daughters. His father is Kasyapa, his brothers are Aruna and the Suparnas, and his sister is Sumati. At birth his glow was so beautiful that he was worshiped as an incarnation of Agni. In the *Ramayana* he appears as the grandchild of Cyena and Cyene, the hawks who carried off Soma, the elixir of the gods. Another grandmother is Tamra, one of Kasyapa's mates. In the *Mahabharata*, Vinata and Kadru, the

mother of the serpents and Vinata's co-wife, fought. She was enslaved along with Garuda. The serpents promised freedom only if Garuda would bring them a cup of soma. This was not an easy task. He had to extinguish the protective ring of fire surrounding the valuable drink, break through a sharp-spoked revolving wheel, and kill the serpent guards. He succeeded, but as he flew toward the netherworld, he was pursued by the gods. Indra caught up with him and a terrific battle ensued. Garuda overcame the great god and Indra's famous vajra (thunderbolt) was damaged in the fray. Garuda flew into the serpent's territory with the ransom. Indra, again, was close behind and another battle occurred. The liquid spilled to the ground and the greedy serpents licked up enough to make themselves immortal. It is said that the strength they received from the soma caused their tongues to become forked. Indra was able to retrieve the balance of the soma and return it to its rightful place on celestial Mount Meru. In a variation of this myth, Garuda attempts to fly to the moon. He encounters numerous obstacles and is involved in a battle with the gods. The gods, realizing the strength of their opponent and wishing to maintain ownership of the moon, reach a compromise by bestowing immortality upon him and appointing him as Vishnu's personal mount. This giant bird watches the earth from his perch on a heavenly tree. Whenever dragons and serpents appear, he swoops down and devours them. Garuda may be appealed to for nullifying poison from snakebites. Generally his color is green, but can be gold. Emeralds spew forth from his spittle. He has an eagle's head, which is usually white or gold. Sometimes his face is white and he has red wings and talons. His torso and limbs are like a human male. He is also depicted as a peacock with a long tail. Vishnu and Lakshmi are shown together on Garuda's back as he wings towards the heavens. Garuda is the symbol of the soaring human spirit. It can also be interpreted that the serpents represent polluted waters which are dried up by Garuda, a solar deity representing the sun. Garuda's son Jatayu was the king of the eagles. In the plural form, Garudas are giant birds who feed upon their enemies the Nagas. They can assume human form and in India they are usually shown with small wings and a beak. *See also* Agni; Aruna; Indra; Janguli; Kaliya; Kasyapa; Krishna; Lakshmi; Mara; Nagas; Sampati; Soma; Sumati; Suparnas; Vasuki; Vishnu.

Garudi (India)
    One of Shiva's secret forms as a female bird of prey.

Gashan-Ki *Gashanki* (Assyro-Babylonian) *see* Damkina; Nin-ki.

Gashanki (Assyro-Babylonia) *see* Gashan-Ki.

Gasmu (Chaldaea)
    She is an ancient sea goddess who may be the daughter of Damkina and perhaps the wife of Ea. Gasmu is associated with Zerpanitum (q.v.). *See also* Damkina; Ea.

Gat Tooth (Teutonic) *see* Tanngrisni; Thor.

Gatamdug *Gula* (Assyro-Babylonia)
    A mother goddess who assimilated into Gula (q.v.).

Gaumaonocon (Antilles) *see* Iocauna.

Gaumukh (India) A Yaksha. *See also* Yaksha and Yakshini.

Gauna (Africa) *see* Gaunab.

Gaunab *Gamab, Gunab* (Hottentot People, Africa)
    Also known as: *Ga-Gorib, Gauna* (Hottentot), *Gawa* (Damaras), *Goub.*
    God of evil. Gaunab, who lives beyond the stars, is the constant adversary of the supreme, Heitsi-Eibib. Gaunab chooses mortals who will follow him through the abyss to the stars. Males who do so are called Gamagu and females, Gamati. The Gamagu and Gamati eat the flesh of dead humans. This is why only bones are left in graves. In some renditions, Gaunab lives under a pile of stones. He entices people to throw stones at him. If they do, the stone bounces back and kills the thrower. Gaunab is also challenged by Tsui-goab. And, a surprising addition — it is said that Gaunab created the rainbow. *See also* Heitsi-Eibib; Tsui.

Gauri *Gowrie* (Hindu; India)
    Also known as: *Devi, Gouri* (possibly), *Isani, Jaganmata, Kali, Lokamatri, Mahagauri, Parvati.*
    Gauri, a fertility goddess known as "The Golden Lady," is an early aspect of the great mother goddess Devi. She is said by some to be the daughter of the goddess Sirsootee and granddaughter of Mahakali. In other references, she is the daughter of Sirsootee, sister of Bishen and the niece of the goddesses Mahakali and Sri and the god Brahma. Gauri may be the mother of Manasa although it is generally stated that Manasa is the daughter of the sage Kasyapa and Kadru. Gauri may be the same as the goddess of abundance, Gouri, also known as Isani, a local goddess of Oodeypoor in Rajputana, India, who is the wife of Iswara. Gauri is also the first name used for Kali or Parvati when she rides on a tiger. It is also Parvati's name before her skin became lighter. Prior to Durga's entrance as a warrior she was known as Gauri. And, the name is sometimes used as another name for Varuni, the goddess of spirituous liquor. Gauri's festival is held on the new moon day in August. At bedtime, confections are eaten to ensure that the sweet grace of Gauri will be in the soul for a year. Compare Gauri to Manasa. *See also* Ardhanariswara; Devi; Durga; Kadru; Kali; Kasyapa; Parvati; Shiva; Sri; Varuna.

Gauri-Sankar (India)
    Mountain goddess of Mount Everest.

Gaut (Teutonic)
    "The Creator," or the "Great," an alternate name for Odin.

Gautama *Gotama* (India) *see* Ahalya; Buddha; Maitreya; Rishi; Sakyamuni.

Gavampati (Buddhist; India)
    This god of drought and wind is called upon for rain.

Gavidjeen (Celtic) *see* Cian.

Gawa (Africa) *see* Gamab; Kaang.

Gaya (India) "The Conquering." *See also* Durga.

Gaya Maretan (Zoroastrian; Persia)
    Also known as: *Gajomartan* ("Human Life"), *Gayomart* (Pahlavi dialect), *Gayomort, Kayumarth.*
    Passages from the *Avesta* refer to Gaya Maretan as the first to hear the thought and teachings of Ahura Mazda, and the first

to fashion the family of the lands. With the primitive bull, Gosh, all life was created. Gaya Maretan was Ahura Mazda's sixth creation according to the *Bundahish*. As the myth developed, Gaya Maretan was depicted as the prototype of all humans. In Iranian cosmological mythology, he was born from the sweat of Ahura Mazda's brow, and lived during the first three thousand years of creation as spirit. Ahura Mazda then made him corporeal. During his thirty years on the dark and demon-infested earth, he constantly battled the forces of evil. When the female demon, Jahi, convinced Angra Mainyu to poison him, Gaya Maretan became infected with disease and hunger. When he died, his body became brass, his limbs gold, iron and minerals. Spenta Armaiti preserved his golden sperm and forty years later Mashya and Mashoi, the first human couple, were created. In later times, Gaya Maretan, as Kayumarth, was known as the first Iranian king. His reign lasted thirty years. He was the father of Siyamek and grandfather of Hoshang. The epithet Gayomart was used in later times as the name of Gaya Maretan's heavenly counterpart. *See also* Ahura Mazda; Angra Mainyu; Hoshang; Jahi; Mashya; P'an Ku (China).

Gayatri (A) (India) *see* Sarasvati.

Gayatri (B) (India)
A sacred text of the *Vedas*. *See also* Savitri (A).

Gayomart (Persia) *see* Gaya Maretan.

Gayomort (Persia) *see* Gaya Maretan.

Gbaye-Gborun (Yoruba People, Africa) *see* Orunmila.

Gdugs-Dkar-Chan-Ma (Buddhist; India, Tibet) *see* Avalokitesvara; Sitatapatraparajita; Tara.

Ge (Fon People; Africa) *see* Gou.

Ge (Greek) *see* Gaea; Gou (Dahomey of Africa)

Ge Hinnom (Hebrew) *see* Gehenna.

Gea (Egypt) *see* Geb.

Geb (Egypt) Earth God
Also known as: *Gea, Keb, Kenken-Wer* ("The Great Cackler"), *Seb*.
The son of Shu and Tefnut, Geb became the spouse of Nut and father of Osiris, Set (Seth), Isis, and Nephthys. Geb was forcefully separated from his sister Nut by Shu. Geb followed Shu as ruler of the earth and was succeeded in turn by his son Osiris. Geb was one of the company of gods comprising the Ennead and was, according to the Pyramid Texts, one of the oldest of the deities. He is sometimes called Kenken-Wer or "the great cackler" because he laid the great egg from which the world sprang. He is generally depicted as a human with a goose on his headdress. Sometimes he is shown lying under the feet of Shu. Geb also appeared in the form of a crocodile. His gaping, dangerous mouth is symbolic of the primeval abyss. He is identified with the Greek god Cronus (q.v.). *See also* Atum; Gea; Isis.

Gebal (Greek) *see* Agrius (A).

Gebaliah (Greek) *see* Cybele.

Gefion *Gefjon, Gefjun* (Norse; Teutonic)
Also known as: *Diana* (Teutonic).
Fertility goddess. Gefion was promised as much land as she could plow in one day. To ensure that it would be a huge acreage, she married a giant and had four sons. She changed her four sons into oxen and with them, pulled part of the kingdom of King Gylfi down to the sea where it became Seeland. Gefion married Skiold who was one of Odin's sons and became the ancestor of the Danish race. It is possible that Gefion the virgin attendant of Frigg was the same as the Gefion described above. She presided over those who died unmarried. *See also* Freyja; Frigg.

Gefjon (Teutonic) *see* Freyja; Gefion.

Gefn (Teutonic) *see* Freyja.

Gegenees (Greek) The Argonauts killed these six-armed giants who lived in the mountains on the Mysian coast.

Gegeneis (Greek) "Children of the Earth" *see* Curetes.

Gehenna *Ge Hinnom* (Hebrew; possibly Egyptian origin, at least that of Dumah)
Also known as: *Jaahannam* (Arabic).
The underworld. Gehenna is sixty times as large as the world, and it would take a man 2,100 years to reach it. There are seven palaces in the place, each with 6,000 chambers, each of these having 6,000 boxes and in each box are 6,000 vessels filled with gall. The place is also said to be so deep it would take 300 years to reach the bottom of it. One legend tells of Gehenna being ruled by Dumah, a prince. He has 10,000 angels who help him judge sinners and decide their doom. A second prince, Arsiei, is in Gehenna. His job is to stop the righteous from praying for the wicked. *See also* Aahannam (Arabic); Hades (Greek); Hell; Rahabh (Hebrew); Tuat (Egypt).

Geirod *Geirrod, Geirrothr, Geruthus* (Norse; Teutonic)
Also known as: *Grimner, Grimnir*.
Some say he is the giant son of Hraudung and brother of Agnar. Others say he is the brother of the giant king Geirod who ruled Glasisvellir, a land where death does not exist. Geirod also goes under the name of Grimnir, a name used by Odin when he visited the hall of Geirod in disguise. Geirod was slain by Thor. *See also* Grimmir; Thor.

Geirrod (Teutonic) *see* Geirod.

Geirrothr (Teutonic) *see* Geirod.

Gekka-O (Japan)
God of marriage. He binds the feet of lovers with red silk thread.

Gelanor (Greek) King of Argos. *See also* Danaus.

Gelgia (Teutonic) *see* Fenrir; Gleipnir.

Gelgja (Teutonic) *see* Gleipnir.

Gello (Greek) *see* Gallu.

Gelou (Hebrew) *see* Gallu; Lilith.

Gendenwitha (Iroquois People, North America)
The Morning Star.

A mortal hunter named Sesondowah was captured by the dawn goddess but seeing a beautiful girl on earth, he changed into a bird and brought the girl back to heaven. Dawn was angry and tied him to a doorpost. He transformed the girl into a star and gave her the name, Gendenwitha, the Morning Star.

Genea (Phoenician)
Mother goddess of all mortals. *See also* Fire; Kolpia.

Genethlios (Roman) *see* Neptune; Poseidon.

Genie *Genii* (Persia) *see* Jinn.

Genius (Roman)
Also known as: *Iovialis*
God of life and being. The genius is the spirit residing in all humans and animals from birth to death. *See also* Daemon.

Genos (Phoenician) *see* Kolpia.

Gerd *Gerda, Gerdhr, Gerdr* (Scandinavian)
This beautiful giant daughter of Gymer and Aurboda is the frost goddess of the frozen earth and the goddess of light. After intense wooing, Freyr finally convinced her to marry him. They lived in the home of the gods, Asgard. *See also* Freyr.

Gere (Teutonic) *see* Geri.

Geri *Gari, Gere* (Norse; Teutonic)
Deified animal. Geri is one of the two wolves who lay at the feet of the great god Odin when he is on his throne. The other wolf is Freki.

Gerold Iarla (Irish) *see* Aine.

Gerra (Assyro-Babylonian)
An alternate spelling for Gabil, the god of fire.

Gerseme (Teutonic) *see* Freyja.

Gersimi *Gerseme* (Teutonic) *see* Freyja.

Geruthus (Teutonic) *see* Geirod.

Geryon (Greek)
King of Erythia. His parents are Chrysaor, the son of Poseidon and Medusa, and Callirrhoe, the Oceanid daughter of Oceanus and Tethys. His sister is Echidna, the half-nymph, half-snake, monster. The tenth labor of Heracles was to capture the many cattle owned by Geryon, who was killed in the process. *See also* Callirrhoe; Chrysaor; Echidna; Heracles; Oceanids; Tethys.

Geshtinnanna (Sumer) *see* Gestinanna.

Gestinanna *Geshtinnanna* (Sumer)
She is the daughter of the goddess Ninsun and the sister of the shepherd god Dumuzi. A seer, poet, scribe, and bookkeeper, she was known as "The Lady of Desolation," "The Lady of the Vine," "The Recorder of Hell," and "The Bookkeeper of Heaven." *See also* Dumuzi; Inanna; Ninsun.

Geuh Urvan (Persia)
He is an assistant to the Amesha Spenta Vohu Manah.

Gevar (Teutonic) *see* Miming.

Gewi (Bushman, Hottentot People, Africa)
Possibly a creator deity. He is the son of Cagn and brother of Cogaz. His mother is either Hyrax or Coti. *See also* Cagn.

Geyaguga (Cherokee People, North America)
Magical name of the Moon.

Ghaddar (pre–Islamic) *see* Jinn.

Ghanan (Maya People, Yucatan) *see* Yum Kaax.

Ghanta (Tibet) *see* Amrtakundali.

Ghantapani (Nepal) *see* Vajrasatwa.

Ghar-Jenti (India)
She is the house spirit of good fortune who walks around at night. Her presence can be detected by the sound of nails being pulled from wood.

Ghatotkacha (India) *see* Bhima (A); Karna; Kunti.

Ghede (Haitian)
Also known as: *Baron Cimetiere, Baron La Croix, Baron Piquant.*
God of the dead. Ghede is likely of African origin. He is associated with Baron Samedi. Children are protected by him. Ghede has healing powers. He is shown as a black man wearing a black coat, top hat and dark glasses. He carries a cane and is usually shown with a cigar or cigarette. His sign is a square cross on a low tomb. *See also* Mait' Carrefour.

Ghee (India) Sacrificial Butter. *See also* Agni.

Ghirdhima (Tibet) *see* Lu-ma.

Ghul (pre–Islamic) *see* Jin.

Gi (Greek) *see* Gaea.

Giane (Sardinia)
This woodland spinning spirit had breasts so long that she could throw them over her shoulder. Her singing attracts mortal males. When they respond, she has sex, the man dies, and she gives birth three days later.

Giant Eye, The (Eskimo) *see* Issitoq.

Giant Rabbit (Algonquin People, North America) *see* Michabo.

Giants (Greek)
The Greek giants were born when Gaea was impregnated by the blood of the castrated Uranus. The strongest were Alcyoneus and the leader of the group, Porphyrion. The others were Ephialtes, Eurytus, Clytius, Mimas, Enceladus, Pallas, Polybotes, Hippolytus, Gration, Agrius, Thoas, Aloeus, Antaeus, Anax, Hecatoncheiroi, Rhotetus, Thoon and Tityos. Many of the giants were killed during the war against the giants and the gods on Mount Olympus. Heracles and Dionysus were credited with a number of the deaths. It is possible that the Giants had snakes for feet. *See also* Alcyoneus; Antaeus; Erinyes; Eumenides; Gaea; Hecatonchires; Meliae; Themis; Uranus.

Gibal (Babylonia) *see* Gabal.

Gibil (Sumer, Assyria) *see* Gabil.

Gid-Kuzo (Finno-Ugric)
Protector of cattle from wild beasts and sickness.

Gidja (Australia)
Creator. Moon god. In the beginning there was only one sex, male. Nqunung-nqunnut or Mali the Bat, the older brother of Gidja, made the first woman by castrating Yalungur the Eagle-hawk. For another rendition, *see* Yalungur.

Gijigouai (Algonquin People, North America)
Messenger or sun deities. These supernatural beings are servants of Michabo. The name is both singular and plural. *See also* Michabo.

Gikuyu (Africa)
Also known as: *Kikuyu*.
First man. Founder of the race of people. God showed Gikuyu a beautiful country filled with fig trees and provided him with a mate named Moombi who was a creator deity. The two had nine daughters. God provided nine young men for these daughters. This began the Kikuyu race, named Moombi after the first woman. *See also* Kere Nyaa.

Gil (Babylonia) *see* Marduk.

Gilfaethwy (Celtic) *see* Gwydion.

Gilgamesh *Gilgamas, Gilgames, Gilgamish, Gilgamos, Gishgim-mash* (Hittite); (Mesopotamia)
Also known as: *Gizdubar* (Chaldean), *Izdubar*.
A super human, one-third man, and two-thirds god, he is sometimes described as a sun hero. He is variously called an ancient Sumerian king of Uruk and son of Ninmah, or the child of a peasant and his wife who was a daughter of Sakkhoras, a Babylonian king, or the son of Ninmah or Ninsun. The basic tale of Gilgamesh involves Enkidu, Ishtar, Utanapishtim, immortality and the flood. As the son of the goddess Ninsun and the god Lugalbanda (or Kullabu), he was known as the king of Uruk sometime before 2500 B.C.E. He built the city walls of Uruk and recruited all young men. Unhappy citizens, particularly the nobles, felt that he was acting in an arrogant and tyrannical manner, rather than in the role he was created for as a shepherd to the people. They prayed to the mother goddess Aruru for assistance. She created a rival hero, Enkidu. Wild and hairy, he had to be tamed by a harlot named Shamhat. She enticed him to shave and perfume himself. Once presentable, she led him to Erech to wrestle Gilgamesh. They were of equal strength so it was decided that a fight would be fruitless. Instead they became friends. They went in search of an opponent and found Khumbaba, the giant of the pine forest. With the aid of divine assistance, they killed him. Upon his return to Uruk, Ishtar, the goddess of love, fell in love with him. She made advances but he, aware of how many of her former lovers were residing in Hades, resisted. Insulted, the goddess complained to her father, the supreme god, Anu. He sent pestilence to Uruk in the form of a bull. Although it killed hundreds, Gilgamesh and Enkidu killed it. Ishtar was furious. Enkidu dreamed that either Gilgamesh or Enkidu would have to die. Enkidu fell ill and on the 13th day died. Gilgamesh was inconsolable. He knew of a man called Utanapishtim, the only survivor of the Great Flood, who has attained immortality and resides in paradise.

Gilgamesh went to seek this man for the secret of immortality. After a long, hazardous journey he reached the coast. Here he met Sifuri, who told him that Urshanabi (the Babylonian Charon, the ferryman on the Sea of Hades) was the only sailor who knew the sea. Gilgamesh instructed him to build a ship. When it was completed the sailor took Gilgamesh across the sea to the land where Utanapishtim lived. He was received graciously, and Utanapishtim told him the details of the great flood and how he was able to survive and achieve immortality. Before leaving, he gave Gilgamesh the plant of eternal youth. Gilgamesh returned to his own coast, but the plant, which grew only on the bottom of the sea, was stolen by a snake. He had lost his chance to become immortal. He did however, show his guide the walls of Uruk. In another myth, Gilgamesh is presented with the gifts of a magic drum and drumstick. Somehow his gifts disappeared into the underworld. Enkidu volunteered to retrieve them. He was cautioned by Gilgamesh to adhere to all rules in the underworld or he would be held forever. Enkidu ignored him and was seized. Gilgamesh appealed to Enlil and to Sin for assistance to rescue Enkidu but was ignored. It was Ea who instructed Nergal to make a hole in the ground. This opening allowed Enkidu's spirit to rise to the upperworld. Gilgamesh begged him for details about the underworld and was told by Enkidu that his body was full of worms and had turned to dust. This distressed Gilgamesh so, that he threw himself to the ground and wept. Gilgamesh is depicted with black, curly hair, and a beard. He wears fifty-pound armor and carries a four hundred–pound axe. His wrists are adorned with heavy gold bracelets, and he has two pet monkeys perched on his shoulders. *See also* Aruru; Enkidu; Ishtar; Khumbaba; Ninsun; Siduri.

Gilling (Norse; Teutonic)
This giant father of Suttung was murdered, as was his wife, by the drunk dwarfs Fjalar and Galar. *See also* Odraerir; Sattung.

Gilma (Babylonia) *see* Marduk.

Gilou (Hebrew) *see* Gallu; Lilith.

Gilvaethwy (Celtic) *see* Math.

Gimli *Gimle* (Teutonic)
This is the best of the good dwelling places in the afterworld. Righteous beings will be found there after the end of the world, known as Ragnarok (q.v.).

Ginnar (Teutonic) *see* Dwarfs.

Ginnunga-gap *Ginnungagap* (Teutonic)
Meaning "yawning chasm," Ginnunga-gap is the primeval abyss. In the frozen northern reaches of Ginnunga-gap, Niflheim, also known as the "Home of Fogs," the world of mist and darkness is located. Muspells-heim, the world of elemental fire, is located in the southern reaches of Ginnunga-gap. The powerful being known as Allfather resides in Ginnunga-gap. *See also* Audhumla; Elivagar; Muspells-heim; Nifl-heim; Ymir.

Ginnungagap (Teutonic) *see* Ginnunga-gap.

Gioll (Teutonic) *see* Gleipnir.

Giovava (Taino People, Antilles) *see* Cacibagiagua.

Gir (Sumer) *see* Irra.

Gira (Sumer) *see* Nergal.

Girau (Sumer, Assyria) *see* Gabil.

Girija (India) "From the Mountains" *See also* Parvati.

Girra (Sumer) *see* Irra; Nergal.

Girru (Sumer)
Girru is the god of fire, and of light, patron of civilization and messenger of the gods.

Gish Bar (Babylonia)
Sun god.

Gishnumunab (Babylonia) *see* Marduk.

Gishzida (Babylonia)
This god, along with Tammuz, intervened on behalf of Adapa, to convince the gods to grant him immortality. *See also* Adapa; Tammuz.

Gita (Tibet) *see* Lu-ma and Avalokitesvara.

Gitche *Kitshi* (Algonquian, Chippewa People, North America)
Also known as: *Gitchee Manito, Gitche Manitou, Great Hare, Kitcki Manitou, Kitshi Manito.*
High god. All-father. Great spirit. Master of Life. Chief of the Manitos (spirits). His second in command is Dzhe Manito (the good spirit). *See also* Manitou; Sedna (Eskimo).

Gitche Minito (Algonquian People, North America) *see* Gitche.

Gitchee Manitou (Algonquin People) *see* Gitche; Kitshi Manito.

Gitchy Monedo (North American Indians) *see* Gitche; Kitshi Manito.

Gizidu *Ningizzida* (Sumer) *see* Adapa; Ea.

Gjall (Teutonic)
Also known as: *Giallar Horn, Gjallar, Gjallarhorn, Ringing Horn.*
This is the horn left by Heimdall under the third root of the Yggdrasil tree. It will wait there until the apocalypse known as Ragnarok. Some say it was left in Mimir's spring. At the time of Ragnarok, Heimdall will sound the horn to awaken and summon all the gods from the nine worlds to meet in council. Gjall means resounding. *See also* Heimdall; Ragnarok.

Gjol (Teutonic) *see* Gjoll.

Gjoll *Gjol* (Teutonic) *see* Elivagar; Fenrir; Gleipnir; Niflheim; Thviti.

Glads-heim (Norse; Teutonic) *see* Gladsheim.

Gladsheim *Glads-heim* (Teutonic)
Gladsheim, located in Asgard, on the Plains of Ida, is the magnificent hall where Odin and the twelve high gods are seated. Vingolf, also located in Asgard, is the high seat of Frigga and the goddesses. Gladsheim, also Odin's zodiacal house, is one of his three palaces. His other abodes are Valaskjalf (where his throne was called Hlidskialf), and the grove Glasir. The

major hall in Asgard is Valhalla, the banquet hall of the Aesir, and the brave warriors are known as the Einheriar (also Einherjar). *See also* Aesir; Asgard; Breidablik; Einheriar; Frigga; Idawold; Odin; Sovabek; Valaskjalf; Valhalla.

Glasnir (Teutonic)
The name of the grove where one of Odin's sanctuaries is located. *See also* Gladsheim.

Glauce (Greek)
This is another name for Creusa. *See also* Creusa.

Glaucus (A) (Greek)
A minor sea god, he is the son of Poseidon and Nais, or perhaps Anthedon and Alcyone. Glaucus started out his life as a fisher. He did all right until he consumed a magic herb. The herb caused him to grow a tail. Whenever his catch fell on the tail, the fish came back to life. Glaucus developed a crush on Skylla. She rejected him and was turned into a monster by Circe, who was jealous that Glaucus preferred Skylla over her. Glaucus also assisted the Argonauts (q.v.). *See also* Circe; Poseidon; Skylla.

Glaucus (B) (Greek)
He is the son of Minos and Pasiphae. His siblings are Acacallis, Androgeus, Ariadne, Catreus, Deucalion, Euryale, Lycastus, Phaedra and Xenodice. Glaucus was smothered in a honey pot. Polyeidus resuscitated him.

Glaucus (C) (Greek)
Also known as: *Glaucus of Corinth, Taraxhippos.*
He was the king of Ephyra. His parents are Sisyphus and Merope. His siblings are Halmus, Ornytion and Thersander. He married Eurymede and became the father of Bellerophon and Deliades. His horses would only eat human flesh. When he refused to allow them to mate, he infuriated Aphrodite, who saw that his horses trampled him to death during the funeral games of Pelias. His ghost is known as Taraxhippos. *See also* Aphrodite; Bellerophon; Eurymede; Merope; Sisyphus.

Glaucus (D) (Greek)
He is the son of Antenor and Theano. His siblings are Acamas, Agenor, Archelous, Coon, Demoleon, Iphidamas, Laodamas, and Polybus. His half-brother is Pedaeus.

Glaucus (E) (Greek)
The son of Hippolochus, Glaucus was the co-leader of the Lycian army at Troy with Sarpedon (q.v.). When he found out that Diomedes' grandfather and his grandfather were friends, he exchanged his armor with Diomedes. While fighting for the corpse of Achilles, Glaucus was killed by Ajax the Salaminian.

Glaucus (F) (Greek)
He is the son of the king of Messenia, Aepytus.

Glauk-Opis (Greek) *see* Athena.

Gleipnir (Norse; Teutonic)
Also known as: *Gelgia, Gelgja, Gjol.*
The third and strongest chain that holds the wolf Fenrir. Made by the dwarfs, Gleipnir consists of six elements: the sound a cat makes when it moves, a woman's beard, the roots of a mountain, the sinews of a bear, the breath of a fish, and a bird's spittle. The other chains are named Laeding and Dromi. In some myths, Fenrir is bound by Gleipnir, then attached to the

rock Gioll, and then fastened to the black boulder, Thviti. In some versions Gjol or Gjoll is the name of one of the rivers flowing out of Nifl-heim. *See also* Dromi; Fenrir; Laeding; Nifl-heim; Thviti.

Gleti (Dahomey People, Africa)
Goddess of the moon.

Glispa (Navajo Indian)
Culture heroine. One of two sisters who married Bear and Snake. They were the creators of a particular dance which the shamans use for curing ills.

Gloin (Teutonic) *see* Dwarfs.

Glooscap (Algonquin) *see* Gluskap.

Glooskap (Algonquin, Penobscot Indians) *see* Gluskap.

Glunen (Celtic)
He is the son of the Gaulish culture hero Taran, and one of the seven survivors of the battle between Bran and Matholwch. *See also* Bran.

Gluskap *Glooscap, Glooskap, Glusgahbe* (Algonquin, Penobscot Indians, North America)
Representing good, Gluskap is opposed by his twin brother, Maslum, who represents evil. They created the solar system and mortals from their mother's body. He is a shape-changer but his normal form is a rabbit. Gluskap killed Malsum who then turned into a wolf. He was also involved in physical altercations with a group of powerful magicians known as the Kewawkqu, the sorcerer Medecolin, Pamola the evil spirit of the night, and another powerful sorcerer, Wimpe. He emerged the victor in each instance. Gluskap left in his birch-bark canoe after his work was finished, but he will return someday. Also *see* Nanabozho and Nichan regarding other Algonquin creation legends. *See also* Wimpe.

Gna *Gnaa* (Teutonic)
An attendant of Frigg (Frigga) and a messenger of heaven, when she mounted the steed, Hofvarpir (aka Hofvarpnir and Hofvarpner, also called Hoof-Tosser), who ran through air and water. The horse's sire was Hamskerpir. It is said she married King Rerir and bore him a son named Volsung who became a great hero. *See also* Frigg.

Gnaa (Teutonic) *see* Gna.

Gnome *see* Dwarfs.

Gnowee (Wotjabaluk People, Australia)
This sun goddess searches for her lost son every day by climbing the sky carrying a torch.

Go (Celtic) *see* Cian.

God of All Things (Greek) *see* Chaos.

God of Hanged Men (Teutonic)
A title for Odin.

God of Ravens (Teutonic)
A title for Odin.

God with Eight Banners, The (Japan) *see* Hachiman.

Godai-Myoo *Go Dai Myo-o* (Buddhist; Japan)
Also known as: *Godaison* (Japan), *The Five Kings*.
There are five Godai-Myoo, one for each of the five great Buddhas. They are known as the Five Kings, the Five Awesome Divinities, or the Five Great Ones with the Powerful Roar. Their function is to carry out the wishes of the Buddhas. They are represented as the terrible manifestation of the Buddha. Fudo-Myoo is the most important of the Godai-Myoo (Arya Achalanatha). He is the incarnation of Dainichi Nyorai (Maha-Vairocana). The other Godai-Myoo and Buddhas are Gozanze-Myoo (Trailokya-Vijaya-Raja), the incarnation of Ashuku (Akshobhyu); Gundari-Myoo, also known as Nampo Gundari Yasha and Kanro (Kundali), the incarnation of Hosho (Ratnasambhava); Dai Itoku-Myoo (Yamantaka), the incarnation of Mida (Amida, also known as Amitabha); and Kongo-Yasha-Myoo (Vajra-Yaksha), who is the incarnation of Fuko (Amoghavajra). Godaison is the popular name for the Godai-Myoo. There are two Myoo who are not considered Godai-Myoo; they are Kujaku-Myoo and Aizen-Myoo. *See also* Dai Itoku-Myoo; Dainichi Nyorai; Fudo-Myoo; Gozanze-Myoo; Kongo-Yasha-Myoo; Trailokyavijaya.

Goddess of All Things (Greek) *see* Chaos.

Goddess of Fantasy (India) *see* Maya (B).

Goddess of Illusion (India) *see* Maya (B).

Gode (Teutonic) *see* Bertha.

Godiva, Lady (England) *see* Epona.

Goemmason *Goemmson* (Japan) *see* Dai Itoku-Myoo.

Goewin (Celtic) *see* Gwydion and Math.

Gog and Magog (Celtic)
These giants are said to have been the sole survivors after Brut succeeded in destroying the giants of Britain. Brut installed them as porters at the palace gates of London. In Biblical lore, the term is generally interpreted to mean the enemies of God.

Gogopa (Greek) *see* Athena.

Gohone (Iroquois People, North America) *see* Adekagagwaa.

Goibniu *Goibhniu* (Irish, Celtic)
Also known as: *Govannon* (British, Welsh).
Goibniu is one of the Tuatha De Danann. Goibniu, Luchtaine, the carpenter, and Credne, the bronze worker, were responsible for making the weapons which were used to defeat the Fomorians. Goibniu also made the beer for the Tuatha de Dananns (q.v.). Compare Goibniu to Vulcan (Roman), and Tvastri (Vedic). *See also* Brigit; Credne; Dia'necht; Fomorians; Hephaistos (Greek); Ilmarinen (Slavic); Tvastri (Vedic).

Gokarmo (India) *see* Shakti.

Gokuraku Jodo *Gokuraku* (Buddhist; Japan)
Also known as: *Sukhavati* (India).
This is the Japanese Buddhist heaven, situated somewhere in the west. It has a pond filled with ambrosia, lotus flowers, and trees decorated with jewels. Birds of Paradise sing, and bells hanging from the trees play beautiful music. Sometimes it is known as one of three heavenly paradises: Gokuraku, Tosotsa

Ten and Royojusen. *See also* Amida; Amitabha; Chakravala (Buddhist Universe); Sukhavati.

Gold Mane (Teutonic) *see* Gullfaxi.

Golden Apples (Greek)
These apples grow in the Garden of Hesperides. One of Heracles' labors was to collect three of the Golden Apples from the garden. *See also* Eris; Heracles; Hesperides; Peleus; Thetis.

Golden Bells (Aztec)
A name for the moon goddess, Coyolxauhqui.

Golden Bough (Greek)
Deified object. On the advice of the Cumaean Sibyl, Aeneas plucked the golden bough. He gave it as a gift to Persephone, goddess of the underworld, and as a token to Charon the ancient ferryman so that he could be ferried across the river Styx to the Underworld. The golden bough was an oak branch covered in mistletoe that grew on a tree near Cumae. The golden bough was sacred to Persephone. *See also* Aeneas; Charon; Golden Apples; Golden Fleece; Persephone; Proserpina; Styx.

Golden Bristled (Teutonic) *see* Gullin-Bursti.

Golden Comb (Teutonic) *see* Gullinkambi.

Golden Fleece (Greek)
The sacred fleece of the ram was born of Poseidon and Theophane. It could speak and fly. The hide of the Golden Ram, entrusted by Phryxus to Aeetes, was guarded by Argus, the hundred-eyed monster. It was for the purpose of obtaining this fleece that Jason embarked on the Argonautic expedition. In another myth, Zeus as a young man discovered the great ram on Mount Ida. Supposedly it was the last of a breed of rams worshipped as deities during that time. He killed the ram but, distracted by a nymph, he left the carcass. A shepherd came upon it and kept the golden pelt. Wrapped around him he became powerful enough to end draughts. He made himself king, adorned the altar with the fleece and reigned for hundreds of years. In another legend, Poseidon rescued the children of Nephele from their wicked step-mother, Io. On the back of the ram they flew to Colchis. One child, Helle, fell off the ram and drowned. That part of the sea became Hellespont. His sister arrived safely and was welcomed by Aeetes, the king of Medea. The Golden Ram became the constellation Aries. *See also* Aeetes; Argonauts; Gaea; Golden Apples; Golden Bough; Ino; Jason; Medea; Phrixus; Poseidon; Zeus.

Goldfax (Teutonic) *see* Gullfaxi.

Golgos (Greek) *see* Adonis.

Gollveig (Teutonic) *see* Gullveig.

Gondemar (Teutonic) *see* Andvari.

Gondul (Teutonic) *see* Freyja.

Gonlod (Teutonic) *see* Gunnlod.

Good Striker, The (Celtic) *see* Sucellos.

Gopa (India) Cowboys. *See also* Radha.

Gopatshah (Persia) Deified half-man, half-ox. *See also* Srishok.

Gopel (India) The Cowherd. *See also* Krishna.

Gopinath (India) Lord of the Cowherds. *See also* Krishna.

Gopis (India)
They are the cowgirls, sometimes called milkmaids, with whom Krishna had affairs, or in some variations married. The *Purana* mentions 1,600 Gopis, though traditionally they number 16,108. Radha is the most famous of the Gopis (q.v.).

Gor (Pygmies of Africa)
Thunder deity. Elephant god whose loud voice is thunder.

Goranchacha (North Andes, South America) *see* Ramiriqui.

Gordius (Greek)
Gordius tied the Gordian Knot. An oracle proclaimed that whoever untied the knot would be the ruler of Asia. Alexander the Great untied the knot and became the ruler. Gordius and Cybele are the parents of King Midas. *See also* Cybele; Midas.

Gore (Slavic)
This god of misfortune can follow mortals into the grave.

Gorge (Greek)
She is the daughter of Oeneus and Althea. *See also* Althea; Calydonian Boar Hunt.

Gorgons (Greek)
Also known as: *Gorgo, Graeae, Graiae.*
Evil deities. They are the children of Ceto and Phorcys, though some say Gaea is their mother. The most popular Gorgon and the only mortal is Medusa ("cunning one"). The other Gorgons are Eurydale ("wide roaming") and Stheno ("strong"). They are the sisters of Echidna, Ladon, Scylla and the Graiae. They are described as three hideous wenches whose heads were covered with snakes instead of hair. To look into the eyes of a Gorgon meant one would turn to stone. It is possible that the Graiae guarded the cavern where the Gorgons lived. They have brass hands, wings of gold and tongues protruding between tusks, like those of a boar. It was Athene who gave Medusa her power and Perseus who killed her. *See also* Cyclops; Graiae; Harpies; Medusa; Pegasus.

Gorgopa *Grogopa* (Greek)
Goddess of death. She is an aspect of Athena in her form as a death goddess. *See also* Athena.

Gorgophone (Greek)
Gorgophone is the daughter of Perseus and Andromeda. Her siblings are Perses, Alcaeus, Mestor, Electryon, Sthenelus and Heleius. She married Perieres of Messene and became the mother of Aphareus, Borus, Icarius, Leucippus and Tyndareus. When Perieres died she married Oebaulus and became the first widow to ever remarry. Their children were Arene, Hippocoon and Peirene. She was buried in the market place at Argos close to the grave of the head of Medusa. *See also* Andromeda; Perseus.

Gorgyra (Greek)
She is the possible wife of the river god Acheron (q.v.).

Gorias (Celtic)
The Tuatha de Danann came from four cities. When they left

Gorias, en route to Ireland, they brought with them the treasure known as Lugh's Lance. The other three cities are Falias, Finias, and Murias. *See also* Tuatha de Danann.

Gortys (Greek)
He is the son of Rhadamanthus and Alcmene (qq.v.).

Gosh (Persia) *see* Dervaspa.

Gosirsa (China) *see* Niu-Y'ou.

Gotama (India) *see* Buddha; Gautama.

Gotterdammerung (German) *see* Ragnarok.

Gou (Fon People, Africa)
Also known as: *Ge, Ogun.*
God of the moon. Son of Mawu and one of the triad of Gou, Mawu, and Lisa. Lisa in her feminine form is the mother of Gou. Gou may be linked with Gu who is the god who supplied weapons and cutting edges and who is a thunder god. *See also* Gu; Lisa; Ogun.

Gouri (India) *see* Gauri.

Govannan (Celtic) *see* Don.

Govannon *Gobannon* (British)
Also known as: *Goibniu* (Celtic).
Govannon is the British equivalent of the Celtic god of smiths, Goibniu (q.v.).

Govinda *Govind* (India)
Herdsman or "Giver of Enlightenment." *See also* Krishna.

Gowree (India) *see* Devi.

Gozanze-Myoo (Buddhist; Japan)
Also known as: *Trailokya-Vijaya-Raja, Trailokyavijaya.*
Gozanze-Myoo is one of the five Godai-Myoo (Five Great Kings). He is an incarnation and an aspect of Akshobhya, the Dhyani Buddha, and some say Ashuku. As a protector of the Buddhist world, Gozanze-Myoo manifests the wishes of Buddha and protects the Buddhist world from its enemies. He lives in the region of the east. Gozanze-Myoo is depicted as a fierce, grotesque deity. He has four faces, a center eye, and bristles for hair. His eight arms, two joined at breast height, hold an assortment of attributes. In his left hands he has a stick, bow and lance. In his right hands he holds a sword, arrow, and a thunderbolt. His right foot is firmly planted on Jizaiten (also known as Mahesvara) and his left foot is lightly touching the hand of Umahi (also known as Uma), the wife of Jizaiten. *See also* Akshobhya; Dai Itoku-Myoo; Fudo-myoo; Godai-Myoo; Gundari-Myoo; Kongo-Yasha-Myoo; Trailokyavijaya; Uma.

Gozu Tenno *Gozu-Tenwo* (Buddhist; Japan)
Also known as: *Buto.*
Gozu Tenno is considered a deity of foreign import to Japan. Originally, he might have been the Chinese ox-headed deity named Niu Y'ou (Niu-t'ou). During the Middle Ages, Susano-wo was considered a god of the plague and because of purification rituals, he was confused with Gozu Tenno. He is depicted with the head of an ox. *See also* Buto (A); Niu-Y'ou; Susanowo.

Gozu-Tenwo (Japan) *see* Gozu Tenno.

Grace (Greek) *see* Graces.

Graces *Grace, Graeae, Gratiae* (Latin)
Also known as: *Charites.*
Good spirits who represented grace in giving, gratitude in receiving and grace in behavior. In early mythology the Graces were known as the Charites. The number of Graces varies but Hesiod indicated they were three in number, daughters of Zeus and Eurynome, or Zeus and Euphrosyne, or Zeus and Aphrodite, or Dionysus and Aphrodite, or Helius and Aegle. Though their parentage is questionable, they are generally said to be the children of Zeus and Eurynome. They were Euphrosyne (joy, festivity), Aglaea (radiant, splendor) and Thalia (the flowering, rejoicing). Homer, in the *Iliad*, adds Charis and Pasithea to the group and some say Charis was Grace herself. It is possible that Aglaea and Charis are one and the same deity. One of the Graces, possibly Aglaea or Charis, was said to be the mate of the fire god Hephaistos. They are known by the Greeks as Charites and by the Romans as Gratiae (there is a difference of opinion as to identifying the Roman Gratiae with the Graces and Charites) and are usually shown as Aphrodite's attendants, although it said that they also attended Apollo, Dionysus, Eros, and their half-sisters, the Muses. Their other half-sisters are the Horae (Hours). The people of Athens worshiped two of the Graces, Auxo ("increaser") and Hegemone ("leader"), and the Spartans, led by the founder of Sparta, king Lacedaemon, worshiped Cleta ("sound") and Phaenna ("brightness"). They were also worshiped at Boeotian Orchomenus in the form of stones that were evidently meteorites. The Graces spread happiness and harmony wherever they traveled and often provided entertainment at events on Mount Olympus. In what is known as their traditional attitude, they are three, standing naked, each with a shoulder draped over the other, the middle one facing the opposite way. They are often shown nude and dancing in a circle or partially clothed, holding hands. In ancient times, they were depicted in long tunics and crowns. The Graces are said to represent the rays of the sun. Gratiae. Compare to Eumenides. *See also* Aglaia (A); Anchises; Aphrodite; Charites; Helius; Hephaistos; Horae; Kathirat (Syria, Ugarit); Muses; Phorcys.

Gradivus (Roman)
Epithet of Mars (q.v.). *See also* Ares; Silvanus.

Graeae (Greek) *see* Graiae.

Graha (India)
They are evil male and female spirits who live in lakes. They cause eclipses of the moon and disease and are especially dangerous to children under the age of sixteen.

Grahapati *Grhapati* (Lord of the House) (India)
An aspect of Agni personifying the hearth fire. *See also* Agni.

Graiae *Graeae* (Greek)
The Graiae, Deino, Enyo and Pephredo, are the three daughters of Phorcys and Ceto. Sometimes they are found guarding the cavern of the Gorgons. They were born looking very old, ugly, and haggard. They shared one eye and one tooth between them. Their siblings are Echnidna, Ladon, Scylla and the Gorgons. *See also* Gorgons; Medusa; Perseus.

Grainme *Grainne* (Celtic)
Engaged to Finn, she fell in love with his friend Diarmait, the son of Corc. *See also* Finn.

Gram (Teutonic)
Also known as: *Balmung.*
Deified object. Mythical sword of Sigurd. *See also* Sigurd.

Gramadevata (India) *see* Gramadeveta.

Gramadeveta *Gramadevata, Ganv-devata* (pre–Aryan, Brahmanic; India)
Also known as: *Amma* (singular), *Ammanavaru* (plural; Mysore, India), *Dih, Dihwar, Ganv-devi, Gramdevati, Maramma* (Mysore), *Mariamma* (Mysore), *Thakurani* (Orissa, India).
They are guardian deities who are also known as household goddess and village deities. In some places, they are known as goddesses of smallpox or cholera. Although generally female, there are male Gramadevetas. All unusual events are attributed to their activities. As spirits of good and bad, who have various functions, they must be propitiated with offerings of rice, flowers, fruit, liquor, pigeons, goats, milk, camphor, and or incense. Hanuman is considered a Gramadeveta, as are Vishnu, Brahma, Aiyanar, Bhairon, Gansam Deo, and Mariamma. In some areas, the Gramadeveta are now considered to be avatars of Shiva and Vishnu. *See also* Bhairon; Brahma; Hanuman; Mariamma; Vishnu.

Gramanis (India) Fiends and goblins. *See also* Devas.

Gramdevati (India) *see* Gramadeveta.

Gramnnos *Gramnos, Grannos* (Gaulish, Celtic)
He is an ancient god of mineral springs. *See also* Borvo.

Gramnos (Celtic) *see* Gramnnos.

Grandfather Fire (Mexico) *see* Tatevali.

Grandmother (Maya) First woman to have sex. *See also* Ch'en.

Grandmother Growth (Mexico) *see* Takotsi Nakawe.

Grandmother of the Garudas (India) *see* Garudas; Kasyapa; Tamra.

Grandmother Toad (Huron People, North America) *see* Ketq Skwaye.

Grannos (Celtic) *see* Gramnnos.

Gratiae *Graeae, Graiae* (Greek) *see* Graiae.

Gration (Greek) *see* Giants.

Grdhra-Kuta (Japan) *see* Ryojusen.

Great Black Belt (Japan) *see* Daikoku.

Great Father (A) (Pawnee People, North America) *see* Tirawa.

Great Father (B) (Arawak People, South America) *see* Ifilici Wacinaci.

Great Hare (Native American) *see* Gitche; Michabo; Nanabozho.

Great Mother (A) (Greek) *see* Agdistis.

Great Mother (B) (Welsh) *see* Matronae; Modron.

Great Power (Pawnee People, North America) *see* Tirawa.

Great Rainbow Snake (Australia)
Creator. Some of the many names given this deity are Kunmanggur, Galeru, Ungur, Wonungur, Worombi, Wonambi, Wollunqua, Yurlunggur, Julunggul, Langal, Muit, Yero, Taipan, Mindi, Karia. He is usually shown with a large red knife.

Great Snapping Turtle (Fox People, North America) *see* Medi Kenagg.

Great Spider (Akoma, Koshairis People, North America) *see* Iatiku.

Great Spirit (Choctaw People, North America) *see* Aba.

Great Spirit of the Winds (Native North American People) *see* Ga-Oh.

Greek (Homeric) — Creation Legend *see* Oceanus; Pontus.

Greek (Olympian) — Creation Legend *see* Aegaeon; Gaea.

Greek (Orphic) — Creation Legend *see* Phanes.

Greek (Pelasgian) — Creation Legend *see* Cronus.

Green Taras (Tibet) *see* Amoghasiddhi; Arya Tara.

Grerr (Teutonic) *see* Freyja.

Grhapati (India) *see* Agni.

Grid (Teutonic)
Giantess wife of Odin. Her son, Vidar, slew Fenrir the wolf. Grid assisted Thor by lending him her magic gloves, girdle and staff to defend himself against the giant Geirod (q.v.). *See also* Fenrir; Odin.

Griffin (Scythia) *see* Gryphon.

Griffon (Scythia) *see* Gryphon.

Grihadevatas (India) *see* Devis.

Grimhild (Teutonic) *see* Sigurd.

Grimmir *Grimmr* (Norse; Teutonic), *Grimner, Grimnik*
Also known as: *Geirod, Odin.*
This is the name Odin assumed when he visited the hall of Geirod. He is generally shown with his face partially covered with a hood. *See also* Geirod; Odin.

Grimnikr (Teutonic) *see* Grimmir; Odin.

Grimnir (Teutonic) *see* Grimmir.

Grismadevi (Sumer)
Also known as: *Dbyar-Gyi-Rgyalmo* (Tibet).
Goddess of the seasons. She is red in color and shown with an animal head.

Grith (Teutonic)
She is the giant wife of Geirod, the giant, who tried to kill Thor.

Gritta (Teutonic) *see* Odin.

Gro-bdog (Buddhist; Tibet)
Also known as: *Di-do.*
Storm deities. Ten demon knife carriers.

Groa (Teutonic)
A sorceress, Groa was known for her medical skills and her abilities to use spells and incantations. When Sif was unsuc-

cessful in removing a stone fragment from Thor's forehead, she sent for Groa. On the verge of success, she became excited when Thor told her that she might once again see her lost child Orvandil. Her excitement caused her to forget where she had paused in her incantions. As a result, the stone remained in Thor's forehead. She is the wife of Aurvandil and mother of Svipdag. *See also* Aurvandil.

Grogopa (Greek) *see* Gorgopa.

Gromovit *Gromovnik* (Serbian)

Thunder or harvest deity. The Christians renamed him St. Iliya Gromovnik. *See also* Perun.

Gronw Pebyr (Celtic) *see* Blodeuwedd; Llew Llaw Gyffes.

Grudyen (Celtic)

He is the son of Muryel, and one of the seven survivors of the battle between Bran and Matholwch. *See also* Bran.

Grydat (Teutonic) *see* Odin.

Gryffon (Scythia) *see* Gryphon.

Gryphon *Griffin, Griffon, Gryffon* (Scythia)

Deified animal. These strong and vigilant beasts are transporters of deities. They destroy those who try to steal. They have the head of an eagle, the body of a lion and enormous wings. In ancient times they were associated with Nergal.

Gsin-rje gsed (Tibet) *see* Yama Kings; Yamantaka.

Gu *Gua* (Fon People, Africa)

He is a thunder god, and god of farming. Gu is the patron of blacksmiths. He gave the people all their tools and weapons. He is possibly the same or similar to Ge and Ogun. *See also* Gua.

Guabancex (Taino People, Haiti)

Goddess of storms, water, rain and wind. Her messengers are Coatrischie and Guantauva. Coatrischie collects water from the mountains. Some say these two are deities of darkness and light. In some versions, they have slightly different names: Coatrischie and Guatauva, who are also deities of darkness and light. One version associates her with Iermaogauacar, Apito, and Zuimaco. All are said to be mothers of Iocauna and Guamaonocon. *See also* Atabei; Iocauna.

Guabonito (Haiti; South America)

Spirit or sea nymph. She taught the medicine man Guagugiana how to use amulets of stones and gold. *See also* Orehu.

Guacarapita (Antilles, Haiti) *see* Atabei; Iella; Iocauna.

Guacas (Inca People, Peru) *see* Haukas.

Guachimines (Inca People, Peru) *see* Apocatequil; Guamansuri.

Gualicho (Patagonian People, South America)

An evil spirit.

Guamansuri (Inca People, Peru)

The first mortal, he was the father of the twins, Apocatequil and Piguero, posthumously. After seducing the sister of the Guachimines, he was murdered by them. *See also* Apocatequil.

Guamaonocon (Haiti, Taino People, Antilles)

Also known as: *Attabeira, Iocauna, Jocakuvague, Maorocon, Maorocoti, Vague, Yocahu.*

High god. "Father sky." Supreme being. His mother has five names. They are Attabeira, Mamona, Gaucarapita, Iella, and Guimazoa. According to legend the people pray to spirits called Zemes rather than directly to these deities. The Zemes are believed to be intermediaries who transmit the prayers of the people to the gods. There is a version where Guamaonocon is called by two names, Guamaonocon and Iocauna. Iocauna is sometimes referred to as a yucca spirit. *See also* Atabei; Iella; Iocauna; Zemes.

Guana (Africa) *see* Gamab.

Guantauva (Haiti) *see* Guabancex.

Guardian of the Fetus (Roman) *see* Alemona.

Guata (Teutonic) *see* Othin; Wotan.

Guatauva (Antilles) *see* Atabei; Guabancex.

Guayarakunny (Patagonian People, South America)

He is the creator of the world and the lord of the dead. Guayarakunny let men and beasts out of the underground caverns. The horns of the beasts frightened the people. They shut the caverns trapping all black cattle. Men and beasts return to the underground caverns after death.

Guaymi People, Costa Rica—Creation Legend *see* Nancomala

Gucumatz *Gukumatz* (Maya, Guatemala; Quiche People, Central America)

God of civilization. God of agriculture. A sky god, and a wind and rain deity, Gucumatz is also a god of farming and domestic life and is able to assume the shapes of many different animals. Gucumatz resembles Quetzalcoatl in many respects, and like the Aztec god, he was represented as a feathered serpent. He is primarily a Guatemalan deity. In the Mayan version, Gucumatz is one of thirteen creator deities. He is a shape changer and the son of the Sun and Moon. In some versions Gucumatz appears to be a co-creator with Huracan. In this same version three names are mentioned, Chipi-Caculha, Raxa-Caculha and Caculha Huracan. The first two may be thought of as the first men, while the third may be an aspect of Huracan. In the Quiche tradition, the gods Gucumatz, Tepeu, and Huracan created the ancestors of the Quiche people from maize. They were known as the Four Balams who were the gods of the north, south, east and west. Their names are Balam-Quitze (Smiling Tiger), Balam-Agab (Night Tiger), Iqi-Balam (Moon Tiger), and Mahucatah (Famous Name). Originally the Balams had the ability to see great distances. Nothing was hidden from them. Their creators became jealous. They blew mist over the eyes of the Balams leaving them with ordinary sight. The Quiche also had a jaguar god named Balam. *See also* Huracan; Kukulcan; Popol-Vuh; Tepeu.

Gudatrigakwitl (Wishosk People, North America)

A creator god. He first created fog, then realizing no one would be able to see his creation of men, changed the fog into all the beings on earth.

Gudrun *Grimhild, Gutrune, Krimhild* (Norse; Teutonic)

In the "Volsung Cycle," Gudrun is the daughter of Krimhild

and the mate of Siegfried. In the *Nibelungenlied*, she is known as Gutrune, the sister of Gunther (also known as Gunnar). In the third "Saga" she is known as Grimhild (or by the alternate spelling Krimhild). *See also* Sigurd.

Guecubu (Araucanian People, Chile)

An evil deity, his name means, "The Wanderer Without." *See also* Akanet.

Gueggiahora (Brazil)

Supreme being. Not worshiped as such, but said to be invisible and dwelling above the stars.

Guener (Irish) *see* Gwen.

Guesa (Chibcha People, South America)

Deified mortal. A sacrificial victim who was brought up for the sole purpose of being given to the god Bochica. He is shown as a boy with one eye, four ears and a long tail.

Guga (India)

Guga ia a serpent god sometimes shown with a human head.

Gugal (Babylonia) *see* Marduk.

Guha (India) *see* Karttikeya.

Guhkin-Banda (Sumer) The god and patron of goldsmiths.

Guhyaka (India)

Cavemen and treasure-keepers for Kuvera (q.v.).

Guimazoa (Antilles; Haiti) *see* Atabei; Iocauna; Zemes.

Guinevere *Gwynhwyvar* (British) *see* Arthur.

Gukumatz (Maya People, Yucatan) *see* Gucumatz.

Gukup Cakix (Maya People, Yucatan)

Also known as: *Vukub-Cakix.*

Evil deity. A giant. Husband of Chimalmat. Father of Zipacna and Caprakan. He pretended to be both sun and moon, but this vain, cruel, and clumsy deity was found out and punished by Hunahpu and Ixbalanque. *See also* Caprakan.

Gul-shes (Hittite) *see* Ullikummis.

Gula (Akkadian, Babylonia, Sumer)

Also known as: *Gatamdug, Gula-Bau, Ninhursag, Ninki.*

Mother or earth goddess. Goddess of vital heat. Defender of homes. Gula is a goddess who brings both illness and good health. She was believed, along with Nin-Karrak, to be the daughter of Anu. Some say she was the sister of Enlil. In some localities, Gula is said to be the wolf of Ninurta. A dog was her symbol. Under the name Mah or Belit-ili, Gula was a goddess of medicine. She is one of the brides of Samas. Gatamdug, a wise mother goddess, who was known for her ability to interpret dreams, eventually assimilated into Gula. She is shown seated and accompanied by a dog. Gula's emblem is the eight rayed orb. Compare her to Aa. She is possibly female counterpart of Damu (Tammuz). Gula is identified with the mother goddess, Mah (Belit-ili). She is sometimes identified with Ninmah, Ninki, Ninhursag, Ninurta and Aruru. *See also* Bau; Mah (B); Ninkarrak.

Gullfaxi *Goldfax* (Norse; Teutonic)

Also known as: *Gold Mane.*

Deified animal. He is the horse of the giant Hrungnir. The giant lost a race against Odin who rode the eight-legged steed, Sleipnir.

Gullin-Bursti *Gullinborst, Gullinbursti* (Norse; Teutonic)

Also known as: *Golden Bristled, Slidrugtanni.*

Magic boar. It was created by the dwarfs Brock and Sindri on direction of Loki, and given to Frey by Loki. In another version, this was the golden boar made for Loki to give to Freyr. It was made by the two dwarfs, Brokk and Eitri. *See also* Brock; Eitri; Loki; Sindri.

Gullinborst (Teutonic) *see* Gullin-Bursti.

Gullinbursti (Teutonic) *see* Gullin-Bursti.

Gullinkambi *Gullinkambe* (Norse; Teutonic)

Also known as: *Golden Comb.*

Deified bird. This cock will warn of the coming of Ragnarok. It will wake the Einherjar in Valhalla. Gullinkambi perches on the topmost branch of Yggdrasil and wakens the gods each morning.

Gulltoppr (Teutonic)

Heimdall's golden-maned horse. *See also* Heimdall.

Gullveig *Gollveig, Gulveig, Golveig-Heid, Gulveig-Hoder;* (Norse; Teutonic)

Also known as: *Angerboda, Angerbodha, Aurboda, East Wind Hag, Heid, Heidr, Ljod, Midgard, Orboda, Volva (the).*

Aspect. Evil goddess. Probably a form of Freyja. Her name means "Gold Might." One of the Vanir who was burned three times by the Aesir. She entered Asgard demanding reparation for an injury, was killed three times, yet lived. In another version she was a goddess of evil and ruler of Iarnvid. She is called the mother of the Varns. Although she is sometimes called an aspect of Freyja, some say she was an attendant of this deity. In one version she is the counterpart and ally of Loki. An evil, crafty, prophesying goddess, this giant caused misfortunes, sickness and death. She was pierced by spears, and burned in flames three times, but lives on. All but a part of her heart was destroyed. Loki found and swallowed it. Since the heart contained her evil soul, he became twice as evil. There are tales that she was the mother of werewolves, who infest the earth and murder men. Called the East Wind Hag, she is said by some to be the mother of Fenrir, Hel, and the Midgard Serpent. In some versions, Jormungandr was the Midgard serpent. Another name she calls herself is Ljod. She is associated with Freyja. *See also* Aesir; Angerboda; Fenrir; Hel; Jotuns; Loki; Midgard; Vanir.

Gulsa Goddesses *Gulses Goddesses* (Hittite)

In some renditions, the Gulsa goddesses assisted the mother goddess Hannahannas in her search for Telepinus (q.v.).

Gulu (Uganda, Africa)

A possible name for Heaven. The first man, Kintu, was supposed to have come from Gulu to earth along with his brothers (not named, possibly Kaikuzi), and married a woman named Nambi. In one version Gulu is the father of Walumbe. *See also* Kaikuzi; Kintu.

Gulveig (Teutonic) *see* Gullveig.

Gulweig-Hoder (Teutonic) *see* Angerboda; Gullveig.

Gumshea (Assyro-Babylonian) *see* Ishtar.

Gun (Fon People, Africa)
God of iron, war, and rain. Twin of Xevioso, and eldest son of Mahu and Lisa. *See also* Vodu.

Gunab (Africa) *see* Gamab.

Gunarh (Northwest Coast, Native North Americans)
Also known as: *Killer Whale.* Deified animal. Killer whale.

Gunarhnesengyet (Tlingit People, North America)
A great hunter hero.

Gundari-Myoo (Buddhist; Japan)
Also known as: *Amrita Kundika, Amrite Kundalin, Hosho, Nampo Gundari Yasha.*
Gundari-Myoo distributes celestial nectar to poor humans. He is one of the five myoo and a manifestation of Hosho. He is usually standing on a lotus with one foot raised. He is shown with three eyes, bristly hair and red body with eight arms. *See also* Dai Itoku-Myoo; Fudo-myoo.

Gundhary (India) *see* Gandhari.

Gundlad (Teutonic) *see* Gunnlod.

Gungner (Teutonic) *see* Gungnir.

Gungnir *Gungner* (Norse; Teutonic)
Magic spear of Odin. Gungnir was given to Odin by Loki. It was manufactured by the dwarf Brock or Sindri. In another version, on the day Odin exchanged his eye for the gift of memory, he commemorated the event by breaking a branch from the Yggdrasil tree and fashioned his beloved spear, Gungnir. *See also* Loki; Mimir.

Gunnar (Teutonic) *see* Gunther.

Gunnlod *Gonlad, Gonlod, Gundlad* (Norse; Teutonic)
Goddess and guardian of the mead of poetry. She is one of the wives of Odin and the mother of Bragi, the god of poetry, and Skadi and the nine giantesses who were the mothers of Heimdall. Some say Gunnlod was the daughter of the giant Sattung. She was in charge of the three jars of inspiration called Bodn, Odroror and Son, which Odin stole from her. *See also* Heimdall; Odin.

Gunnolth (Teutonic) *see* Odin.

Gunnthra (Teutonic) *see* Elivagar.

Gunther *Gunnar* (Teutonic) *see* Gudrun.

Gupta-Chara (India) *see* Bala-Rama.

Gur (Middle Eastern) *see* Bohu.

Guruhi (Gambia, Africa)
Evil deity. Worshiping this deity gave humans great power, but the god poisoned and tortured his opponents. He is represented as a stool on which stood an iron ball. Possibly the ball was originally a meteorite. He is similar to Famien.

Gushkinbanda (Babylon)
One of the gods created by Ea (q.v.).

Gutrune (Teutonic) *see* Gudrun.

Gwakko-Bosatsu (Japan)
Also known as: *Chandra-Prabha* (Sanskrit).
Moon deity. He is a companion of Nikko-bosatsu (an aspect of the sun). Shown as a youth, he has three knots in his long hair and is seated on a red lotus. His body is yellow and he holds a lotus-bud and a blue lotus in his left and right hands.

Gwawl (Celtic)
Deified mortal. Gwawl is a suitor of Rhiannon who was unsuccessful against his rival, Pwyll.

Gwen *Guener* (Irish)
Goddess of smiles. Sister of Jou and Sadurn. *See also* Venus.

Gwern (Celtic) *see* Bran; Branwen; Ogyrvan.

Gwidion (Celtic) *see* Gwydion.

Gwinn (Celtic; British)
Also known as: *Annwn.*
Underworld deity. One of the early Celtic gods of the underworld and ruler of the souls of slain warriors. The son of Lludd, he is the hunter of wicked souls. Since he abducted his sister Creudilad, he must now fight for her, forever. *See also* Achren; Annwn; Creudilad.

Gwri (Celtic) *see* Pryderi; Rhiannon.

Gwydion *Gwidion* (Celtic)
Gwydion, the god of civilization and arts is the son of Don the Enchanter and the brother of Gilfaethwy. A talented bard, Gwydion is also skilled in the arts, magic and battle. He gained entry into the court of King Pryderi. After mesmerizing the king with his poetry he demanded his prized pigs in payment. Pryderi refused. Gwydion tempted him with the offer of an exchange, the pigs for twelve magnificent horses and twelve purebred hounds. Pryderi accepted. The next day his acquisitions disappeared the same way they had appeared — by magic. The king had been swindled. Pryderi and his men pursued the villains, caught up with them, and a battle ensued. Gwydion killed Pryderi, and his brother Gilfaethwy raped Goewin, the virgin foot holder of their uncle, Math. Ostracized and without shelter, the brothers finally gave themselves up to Math. He turned Gwydion into various animal forms and under these guises the bard fathered numerous offspring. Their punishment lasted for three years. When released, Gwydion offered his sister, Arianrhod, as Math's new virgin foot holder, even though she wasn't a virgin. She failed the virginity test and subsequently gave birth to twin sons, Dylan and Llew. When Math found out that she was not a virgin, he threw Dylan into the sea where he became a water god. Gwydion was able to save Llew. He tricked his sister into naming him Llew Llaw Gyffes (Llew of the Skillful Hand) whom Gwydion raised as his own child. April Fool's Day originated with Gwydion as a result of the tricks he used to have his sister's "guise" removed from Llew. Llew's new name was Llew Llaw Gyffes. In earlier legends of Gwydion, his brother is Amathaon, and his mother is Anu. Amathaon, perhaps a patron of agriculture, fought with Gwydion against Arawn, the god of the underworld. He is similar to Wodan and the equivalent of Ogma (Ireland). *See also* Amathaon; Anu (A); Arianrhod; Blodeuwedd; Llew Llaw Gyffes; Math; Pryderi.

Gwyn Gohoyw (Celtic) *see* Pryderi.

Gwynhwyvar (British) *see* Arthur.

Gyane (Greek) *see* Aeolus (B).

Gyas (Greek)
He is the son of Melampus and brother of Cisseus. *See also* Melamous.

Gyges (A) (Greek)
One of the Hecatonchires. *See also* Chaos; Gaea; Hecatonchires.

Gyges (B) (Greek) A king of Lydia.

Gyhldeptis *Gyhledeptis* (Eskimo)
Also known as: *Hanging Hair.*
Princess. Vegetation spirit. She was responsible for destroying the dangerous whirlpool named Keagyihl Depguesk.

Gyhledeptis (Eskimo) *see* Gyhldeptis.

H

Ha (China) *see* Men Shen.

Ha-Mori (Japan)
God of leaves. Generally found with Ku-ku-no-chi, who is god of boles of trees. *See also* Kaya-no-hime-no-kami; Ku-ku-no-chi.

Ha-nui-o-rangi (Polynesia)
He is one of the sons of Rangi and Poko-ha-rua-te-po (qq.v.).

Ha-Sert (Egypt) *see* Aaru.

Ha-Tsiang (China) *see* Ha; Heng.

Ha Wen Neyu (Iroquois People, North America) Great Spirit.

Ha-Yama-Tsu-Mi (Japan)
God of the lower mountain slopes. *See also* O-Yama-Tsu-Mi; Sengen.

Hab'al *Habal, Hobal* (Arabia)
Possibly rain or fate deity. May have originally been called Ha-B'al (the lord) and later confused with Abel, the son of Adam. His consorts are Allat and Al-ozzah. Hab'al is said to have replaced the Arabic Khalasa. He is generally shown as a statue of red stone holding seven headless arrows in a gold right hand. The arrows were for divination purposes. He is sometimes shown as an old man with a long beard. Hab'al is said to have been destroyed by Mohammad.

Habal (Arabic) *see* Hab'al.

Habetrot (England) Goddess of spinning and healing.

Habil (Persian) *see* Abel.

Habl (Hebrew) *see* Abel.

Habone (Danish) *see* Fulla.

Hacavitz (Maya People, Yucatan) *see* Xumucane.

Hacha'kyum *Hachakyom* (Maya People, Yucatan)
God of real people. Hacha'kyum planted stars by sprinkling sand in the sky.

Hachakyom (Maya People, Yucatan) *see* Hacha'kyum.

Hachiman (Buddhist, Shinto; Japan)
Also known as: *God with Eight Banners (The), Hachiman Daibosatsu, Hachiman Taro, Yahata.*
War deity. He is a Shinto god of war, later adopted by the Buddhists. Hachiman is thought to be a deified mortal who was the Emperor Ojin, and son of the Empress Jingo. He is usually shown mounted on a horse and carrying a bow.

Hackeberg (Teutonic) *see* Odin.

Hactcin (Jicarilla Apache People, North America)
The Hactcin have always existed. They were the first beings. The Hactcin created the world, the underworld, and the sky. In another version, the Hactcin, children of the earth and sky, lived in the underworld. Their leader, Black Hactcin, created animals.

Ha'dad (Middle Eastern) *see* Hadad.

Hadad *Ha'dad, Haddad* (Phoenician, Semite, Syrian)
Also known as: *Adad, Addu, Aleyn-Baal, Baal, Martu* (Amorite), *Rimmon.*
Storm God. Originally, Hadad was a Syrian deity but in cuneiform text he was called Addu, who was a chief deity. Later, he was known as Rimmon, a thunder god of air and storm. He is said by some to be the son of Dagon. In one version, his mother/wife is Asherah. In another, he was said to be the father of the fate goddess Seimia. He possibly came from an ancient king who was an enemy of Solomon. The Syrians knew him as a god of lightning, rain, and fertility. The Nabataens worshiped Hadad as a thunder god. In later times he appeared in their cul-

ture under the guise of Zeus. Hadad resembled Reseph in his thunder god guise. Some say he is identical with Balmarcodes. *See also* Adad (A); Aleyn-Baal; Baal; Shaushka.

Haddad (Babylon) *see* Adad; Hadad.

Hades (Greek, Egypt)

Also known as: *Ades, Aides, Ais, Aldoneus, Charun* (Etruscan), *Dis, Duzakh* (Persia), *Dzokh* (Armenia), *Orcus, Pepi* (Egypt), *Pluto* (Roman), *Pluton, Tartarus.*

God of death. Giver of fertility. King of the Underworld. Hades is the son of Cronus the Titan god of the world and time and Rhea the mother of the gods. His siblings are Demeter, Hera, Hestia, Poseidon and Zeus. As a newborn, his father swallowed Hades, but Zeus was able to rescue him. Hades, Poseidon and Zeus shared as rulers of the universe. Hades made his home in Erebus, a realm never touched by light. Later, he abducted the goddess Persephone and forced her to become his spouse. He did show some compassion when her mother Demeter was overcome by grief. He told Persephone that she could leave the underworld if she had not eaten anything while there. Unfortunately, she had eaten the seeds of a pomegranate, so Hades decided to let her leave the abode of the dead for four or six months a year. Like a robber or thief, Hades dons his helmet of darkness that allows him invisibility and takes or snatches people from life. Their souls are whisked away for a fee by the boatman Charon to the dark, gloomy realm of Hades. Upon crossing the river Styx they are greeted by the horrifying three-headed guard dog, Cerberus. There are many caves and caverns to wind through before reaching the judges who will decide the soul's fate. The judges are Minos, Rhadamanthus, Aeacus, and Triptolemus. They weigh the good and bad deeds by placing them on the scales of Themis, the blindfolded, impartial goddess of justice. If the good outweighs the bad, the spirit is allowed to move to the Elysian Fields, if the reverse, the spirit is condemned to suffer in the fires of Tartarus. Other deities who make their home in Hades are the Furies and Hecate. In the Armenian Old Testament Hades is called Dzokh which came from the Persian Duzakh (Hell). The same document uses the word *ouydn* (Aidoneus) for the ruler of this hell. Hades is similar to the Egyptian Anubis, and Hades as Hell compares to the Egyptian Tuat. Compare Hades also to the Aztec Mictlan. Possibly the same as the Persian Santaramet. For Hades as a place of retribution, *see* Ixion, Sisyphus, and Tantalus. *See also* Aeacus; Cerberus; Charon; Cronus; Dis; Elysian Fields; Erebus; Gehenna; Hell; Minos; Persephone; Rhadamanthys; Rhea; Serapis; Styx; Tartarus; Themis.

Hadhayos (Persia) *see* Srishok.

Hadui (Iroquois People, North America)

This god of disease is a hunchback dwarf. According to legend he gave the secret of medicine, cure and the use of tobacco to Yoskeha (q.v.).

Hae-Sun (Korea) Sun goddess.

Haemon (A) (Greek)

His parents are Creon and Anioche or Eurydice. He died with his love, Antigone. *See also* Antigone; Eurydice (C).

Haemon (B) (Greek) He is the son of Thoas.

Haemus (Greek)

He is the son of Boreas, the north wind, and Oreithyia (who was raped by Boreas). He married the nymph, Rhodope. They called themselves Zeus and Hera and were subsequently turned into mountains. *See also* Boreas; Zetes.

Hafaza (Islamic)

The Hafaza are guardian angels who protect good souls after death.

Hafgan (Celtic) *see* Arawn; Pwyll.

Haftoreng (Persia) *see* Hapto-iringa.

Hag (Teutonic) *see* Jotuns.

Hagar (Hebrew) *see* Hajar (Islamic).

Hahai Wugti (Hopi People, North America)

The Spider Woman.

Hahgwehdiyu and Hahgwehdaetgah (Iroquois People, North America) *see* Taweskare and Yoskeha.

Hai (Hebrew) *see* Aai (Egypt); Ai.

Ha'iaka (Hawaii) *see* Pele.

Haidar (Persia) *see* Ali.

Haimavati (India) "Of the Himalayas." *See also* Parvati.

Haio Hwa Tha *Hayowentha, Hiawatha* (Mohawk People, North America)

God of law. Chief and Great Lawgiver.

Haitsi-Aibeb (Hottentot People, Africa) *see* Heitsi-Eibib.

Haiwa (Arabic) *see* Eve.

Hajar (Islamic) *Hagar* (Hebrew)

She is the Egyptian slave mistress or wife of Ibrahim. *See also* Zam Zam.

Hakahotu (Polynesia) *see* Fakahotu.

Hakaiki (Polynesia)

Hakaiki is one of a triad with Atea and Ono. *See also* Atea.

Hakea (Hawaii, Oceania) Goddess of the dead.

Haku (Japan) *see* Fuji.

Hala (India) The sacred ploughshare of Bala-Rama (q.v.).

Hala-Bhrit (India) *see* Bala-Rama.

Hala-Yudha (India) *see* Bala-Rama.

Halayudha (India) *see* Bala-Rama.

Haldja (Finnish) *see* Domovoj.

Halia (Greek)

Sea-woman. Halia is the daughter of Pontus, Poseidon or Uranus and Thalassa. She is the sister of the Telchines (q.v.).

Halirrhothius (A) (Greek)

He is the son of the sea god Poseidon and Euryte, the daughter of Hippodamas and wife of Porthaon. Halirrhothius raped Alcippe and was murdered by her father, Ares. Ares was the first man tried for murder. *See also* Alcippe; Ares; Hippodamas.

Halirrhothius (B) (Greek)
He is the son of Perieres and Gorgophone (q.v.).

Halitta (Arabic) *see* Alilat.

Hall of Many Seats (Teutonic) *see* Sessymir.

Hall of the Slain (Teutonic) *see* Valhalla.

Hallat (Sumer) *see* Allat.

Hallow Hills (Celtic) *see* Tuatha De Danann.

Hallows of Ireland (Celtic) *see* Manannan Mac Llyr; Tuatha De Danann.

Halmus (Greek)
The son of Sisyphus and Merope, he was the king of Boeotian Orchomenus. *See also* Chryse; Eteocles; Glaucus; Merope; Sisyphus.

Haltia (Finland)
Haltia is the name for the tutelary genius of each person. *See also* Domovoj.

Halys (Greek)
He is the river god son of Oceanus and Tethys. He courted Sinope, but was unsuccessful. *See also* Rivers; Sinope.

Hamadrades (Greek) *see* Hamadryads.

Hamadryad (Greek) *see* Hamadryads.

Hamadryads *Hamadryad, Hamadryades* (Greek)
Also known as: *Dryades, Dryads.*
Hamadryads were originally spirits of oak trees and later along with dryads became spirits of trees in general. Unlike the dryad, the life of the hamadryad lives in the tree and dies with the tree. The nymphs of fruit trees are known as maliades. Hamadryads are usually depicted as half-woman, half-tree. For other classifications of nymphs, *see* Nymphs. *See also* Dryads.

Hambaris *Hambarus* (Armenian but probably originally from Persia)
Also known as: *Jushkapariks, Pais, Vushkapariks.*
A type of Chimaera or spirit. They appear as mortal men who live and die, although they assume different forms, including the feminine. The Hambaris take up residence in deserted houses. They are mentioned in the Armenian version of the Christian Bible along with the Jushkapariks and Devs. In one version the Jushkaparik or Vushkaparik is similar to the Pairika, who was a female Dev (a Persian concept). The Hambaris sometimes appear as half-animal. *See* Chimaera; Devs.

Hambarus (Armenian) *see* Hambaris.

Hamedicu (Huron People, North America) High God.

Hamestagan *Hamistakan* (Persia)
This is an intermediate place between heaven and hell. Souls who have been judged to have performed an equal amount of good and bad during life wait here until the restoration of the world. The only punishment in Hamestagan is suffering from being hot or cold. *See also* Chinvat Bridge.

Hamhit (Egypt) *see* Poseidon.

Hamingja *Haminja* (Teutonic)
Goddess of fortune. She also acts as a guardian spirit. Hamingja stays with the mortal she chooses for life. Hamingja is particularly lucky for a child born with a caul (piece of membrane that surrounds a fetus and sometimes covers its head at birth). She is possibly one of the Lars. *See also* Fylgukona.

Haminja (Norway) *see* Hamingja.

Hammon (Egypt) *see* Amen.

Hammurabi *Khammurabi* (Babylonian)
Also known as: *Amraphel.*
Deified mortal. He is an ancient king who was said to have founded Babylon. He claimed to have been created by Dagon. *See also* Dagon; Marduk.

Hamsa (India) *see* Hansa.

Hamsapadika *Hamsavati* (India)
First wife of Dushyanta. *See also* Bharta (B).

Han-chung Li (China) *see* Arhats.

Han Chung-Li (China)
Also known as: *Chung-Li.*
One of the Eight Immortals. What little is known about him is that he was the master of Lu Tung-Pin and possibly Chang Kuo-lao. He is shown as a careless, corpulent old man. Han Chung-Li is dressed in a great mantle and he waves a feather fan. He is associated with Han Hsiang-Tzu. *See also* Arhats; Chung-Li-Ch'uan; Eight Immortals; Lu Tung-pin.

Han Hsaing-tzu (China) *see* Ho-hsien-ku.

Han Hsiang-Tzu *Han Siang-Tsi* (China)
One of the Eight Immortals (Pa Kung). He is the nephew of the great poet, Han Yu. The uncle indicated that his nephew had magical power, so he was possibly a god of magicians. He is shown as a boy with his hair tied in two small knots on either side of his head, carrying either a bouquet of flowers or a basket of peaches. He is associated with Lu Tung-Pin and Han Chung-Li. *See also* Eight Immortals.

Han Siang-Tsi (China) *see* Han-Hsiang-Tzu.

Hanan Cuzco (Inca People, Peru) *see* Tahuantin Suyu Kapac.

Hanata (Middle Eastern)
Ishtar as a warrior (q.v.). *See also* Anat.

Hanghepi Wi (Dakota People, North America)
Moon of the Night.

Hanhau (Maya People, Yucatan)
Also known as: *Ahpuch, Yum Cimil.*
Lord of death. He is the ruler of the cold underworld, Mitnal. *See also* Ahpuch; Mictlan; Mitnal.

Hani-Yasu-No-Kami (Japan) Goddess of clay and earth. *See also* Taki-Tsu-Hiko.

Haniyama-Himi (Japan) *see* Haniyasu-Bime-No-Kami.

Haniyasu-Bime-No-Kami (Japan)
Also known as: *Haniyama-Himi.*
Goddess of clay. She is one of the daughters of Izanami and the sister/wife of Pani-yasu-biko-no-kami. Haniyasu was created from Izanami's excrement. Other deities who came from the same source were Pani-yasu-biko-no-kami and Pani-yasu-bime-no-kami. She is probably the same as Toyo-uke-hime-no-himi (q.v.).

Haniyasu-Hime-No-Kami (Japan) *see* Izanagi.

Hannahannas (Hittite)
This mother goddess is associated with Telepinus and the Gulsa goddesses (qq.v.).

Hanpa (Sumer)
God of demons. Father of Pazuzu and lord of all demons. *See also* Pazuzu.

Hansa *Hamsa* (Hindu; India)
Originally a sacred goose, later a swan, Hansa became Brahma's mount. Hansa was sent by Shiva and Vishnu to awaken him to creative work. The ambrosia-filled gold or silver eggs laid by Hansa represent the sun and moon. Some say that it was Shiva in the form of Hansa who awakened Brahma. *See also* Brahma; Shiva; Vishnu.

Hanuman *Huniman, Hunooman* (Hindu; India)
Hanuman the flying monkey god is a healer, pharmacologist, grammarian, poet, warrior and builder. He is an extremely virile deity although he is completely chaste. He plays a prominent role in the *Ramayana.* Hanuman is the son of the wind god Vayu and the monkey queen, Angara. Dasaratha, Rama's father, held a ceremony to ensure that he would be granted sons. Each of his three wives received a cake. When Kaikeyi, the youngest wife, received her cake last she became highly agitated. Out of nowhere, a kite appeared and whisked her cake away. Angara, an Apsarases cursed to live as a monkey, who was the mate of the monster Kesari, was in the forest praying for a son. The kite found Vayu, who gave the cake to Angara. Suddenly, Shiva appeared and instructed her to eat the sweet. From the dessert, Hanuman was created to assist Vishnu in his avatar as Rama. Born with a ravenous appetite, his mother could not satisfy him. The sun appeared to the baby monkey like a piece of fruit. When he leapt after it, the sun in its chariot kept ahead of him. Before he knew it, Hanuman found himself in Indra's celestial territory. The great god whacked him with his thunderbolt and Hanuman fell to earth. Indra's action infuriated Vayu and he entered the deities' intestines and gave them all upset stomachs. To gain relief, Indra apologized to Vayu and then made Hanuman immortal. A loyal and faithful servant to Rama, he became the general in the army of the monkey king Sugriva, who attacked Lanka (Ceylon). In this capacity, he was the supervisor who oversaw the monkeys and bears as they built Rama's bridge from India to Sri Lanka. He killed Kalanemi and fought many battles against the Gandharvas and Rakshasas. Renowned for his intellect, his knowledge of homeopathic medicines was used to restore the wounded to health. When the king of the demons, Ravana, abducted Rama's mate, Sita, Hanuman assisted in her rescue. In size, he can appear as a giant, or as small as a thumb. He is worshiped by women who want children and by wrestlers. Eternally youthful, Hanuman is sometimes red or sometimes gold or yellow with a red face, a booming voice and an endless tail. In Nepal his images are usually covered with vermilion mixed with mustard oil and he is often dressed in a red cloth with a red or golden umbrella over his head. The tale of Rama and Hanuman is comparable to the story of Indra and the ape Vrishakapi. *See also* Angara; Apsarases; Bhima (A); Bhishma; Gandharvas; Gramadeveta; Indra; Jambavan; Kaliya (an incarnation of Kalanemi); Rakshasas; Rama; Ravana; Sugriva.

Haokah (Sioux People, North America)
Two-horned, meteor-throwing thunder god. His expression depicts half-cheer, half-grief. Haokah used the wind to beat the thunder drum. He cried when happy and laughed when sad. He also felt heat as cold and cold as heat.

Haoma *Homa* (Indo-Iranian)
Also known as: *Ephedra, Gaokerena, Sarcostemmaacidum, Soma, White Haoma, White Hom.*
This sacred plant of life when pressed yields a powerful stimulant said to give strength to men and gods. It was brought to the sacred mountain, Hara Berezaiti, by an eagle. In its natural state Vohu Manah gave it healing qualities. The first four men who pressed the sour milky juice of the haoma plant each received the boon of a great son: Vivanghvant had Yima, Athwya had Thraetaona, Thrita had Keresaspa and Pourushas had Zoroaster. In its supra-terrestrial form it is called White Haoma, also known as Gaokerena, and has within itself the seeds of all plant life. Haoma is known as the purifier of the Place of the Sacred Fire. Haoma has hallucinatory properties and is known to have inspired warriors and poets. It bestows religious insight, and gives husbands and children to women. It imparts immortality and can renovate the universe. Haoma is used in a lengthy ritual as part of the *Yasna* (sacred book) sacrifice. Incantations are used during the ritual to drive away evil and prepare for the coming of good. Though the forces of evil attempt to destroy the tree by forming a lizard, it is protected by ten *kar* (fish) who never stop swimming around it. Deified, Haoma is the son of Ahura Mazda (q.v.). Compare Hoama to Soma (Vedic), the Amrita (Hindu), Ambrosia (Greek), and Yggdrasil (Teutonic). *See also* Gandarewa; Thrita; Tree of Many Seeds; Vohu Manah; Yazatas; Yima.

Haoshyangha and Tahmouras (Persian) *see* Hushang.

Hap (A) (Egypt) Another name for Apis (q.v.).

Hap (B) (Egypt)
A variant spelling for Hapi, the god of the Nile.

Hapi *Hap* (Egypt)
Hap, the god of the Nile, lived under the rocks in a cave, guarded by snakes, near the First Cataract at Aswan. He is shown as a fat man (a sign of prosperity) with the breasts of a woman (some say one pendant breast is shown), which indicate his powers of fertility. Hap holds two plants, the papyrus and the lotus, or two vases, from which he pours water. He is also depicted carrying a tray of food. *See also* Tchabu.

Hapi-Ankh (Egypt) *see* Apis (A).

Hapi-Asar (Egypt) *see* Serapis.

Hapikern (Maya)

Hapikern is the evil serpent god who is the constant opponent of Nohochacyum, the creator (q.v.).

Hapinunu (Aymara, Quechua People, South America)

Flying female night spirits who catch people with their long pendulant breasts.

Hapto-iringa *Haftoreng, Haptok Ring* (Zoroastrianism; Persia)

Ursa Major. Hapto-iringa, the Great Bear, is chieftain of the north quarter of the sky. *See also* Aktar (The); Tishtrya; Yazatas.

Haptok Ring (Persia) *see* Hapto-iringa.

Hapy (A) (Egypt)

Hapy is one of the four sons and is shown with either a dog's head or an ape's head. His function was as a funerary deity in charge of protecting the small intestines (some say the lungs). The brothers were depicted on the urns used to store the organs of mummies. The other three brothers are Amset, Tuamutef, and Qebhsneuf. Associated with the four gods are the goddesses Nephthys, Neith, Isis, and Serquet.

Hapy (B) (Egypt) *see* Hapi.

Hapy-Wet (Egypt)

River god. God of the Nile in Heaven. When united with the sun god, Ra, Hapy-Wet is a form of the god Khnemu.

Har (A) (Teutonic)

"The High One," an alternate name for Odin.

Har (B) (Teutonic) One of the Dwarfs (q.v.).

Har (C) (Egypt) *see* Horus.

Har-End-Yotef (Egypt) *see* Horus.

Har-Pa-Neb-Taui (Egypt) *see* Horus.

Har-Sopdu (Egypt) *see* Sopdu.

Hara (Vedic; India)

"Universe Destroyer." This is another name for Rudra or Shiva (qq.v.). Harihara is the name for the deity formed by the combination of Shiva and Vishnu (qq.v.). *See also* Harihara.

Hara Berezaiti (Indo-Iranian)

This is a sacred mountain in the center of the earth. Roughly translated it means "Peak of the Law." *See also* Haoma.

Hara Gauri (Nepal) *see* Ardhanariswara.

Haraiti, Mount (Persian) *see* Hariati.

Harakhtes (Egypt)

Also known as: *Harakhte, Herakhty.*

The name is the Greek rendering, and means "Horus of the Horizon." Harakhtes represents the sun on its daily course. In time, Harakhtes became so closely associated with Ra that their characteristics and powers were inseparable, and Ra was known as Ra Harakhte or Ra Horaete. Harakhtes is depicted as a falcon. *See also* Horus; Khepri.

Harakhty (Egypt) *see* Ra-Harakhte.

Harates (Greek) *see* Aeneas.

Harbard (Teutonic)

This is the name Odin used while in disguise when he crossed the waters in a ferry. During the crossing, Harbard and Thor both bragged of their exploits. *See also* Odin; Thor.

Harendotes (Greek, Egypt)

Also known as: *Har-End-Yotef, Hartomes, Horus.*

Aspect of Horus. The name the Greeks gave Horus after he avenged his father, Osiris, by taking up arms against Set. *See also* Hartomes; Horus.

Hari (India) *see* Vishnu.

Hari-Hara (India) *see* Hara.

Hariati, Mount *Haraiti, Mount* (Persian, Iranian)

The site of the home of Ahura Mazda, which is situated on the highest peak. The home has one thousand pillars and is lit in and out by stars. Ahura Mazda is carried in a chariot drawn by four white horses with golden feet when he leaves the premises. *See also* Ahura Mazda; Alburz (Mount); Chinvat Bridge; Sraosha.

Harihara (Hindu; India)

Harihara represents the great gods Vishnu and Shiva as one. Vishnu appeared as a beautiful woman named Mohini. Shiva took one look at her and fell in love. Upon embracing her, he merged as one with her. At that moment, Vishnu assumed his "normal" form. In other interpretations, said to have developed in the ninth century A.D., Harihara has the combined attributes of Vishnu and Shiva. Shiva is the right side of the body, and Vishnu the left. The merging of the two great gods resulted from an attempt to reconcile the differences of the feudal lords who worshipped Shiva and Devi, and the followers of Krishna as the incarnation of Vishnu. The latter devotees were the smaller landowners. *See also* Shiva; Vishnu.

Harinagamesi *Harinaigameshin* (India)

A Brahmanic deer-headed fertility deity. *See also* Mahavira.

Harinaigameshin (India) *see* Harinagamesi.

Harini (India) *see* Apsarases.

Haripriya (India) *see* Lakshmi.

Harita (India) Divine Horses. *See also* Indra.

Hariti

Also known as: *Kishibojin* (Japan), *Men Brayut* (Bali), *Nanda* (Buddhist; India).

The goddess of smallpox and fecundity, Hariti, an ogress, is the mother of the Yakshas. Her name means "one who steals." She is the mate of Panchika and she either gave birth to or devoured five hundred demon children. In some accounts, she had five hundred healthy sons. Kuvera is also said to be her mate. She fed on human flesh and carried away a child daily. One of her sons, Pingala, was hidden by Buddha to teach her a lesson. This act made her realize the suffering that she had caused others and she was converted by Buddha. Her name was changed to Nanda, meaning "joy," and she then became the protector of all children. She is shown seated, with unkempt hair, and a child or cornucopia in her hand. *See also* Buddha; Kishimojin (Japan); Kuan Yin (China); Sitala; Yaksha and Yakshini.

Harits, The (India) Indra's Horses. *See also* Indra.

Harlot, The (Hebrew) *see* Lilith.

Harmachis (Egypt) *see* Horus; Ra-Harakhte; Sphinx.

Harmakis (Egypt) *see* Ra-Harakhte; Sphinx.

Harmonia (A) (Greek)
Also known as: *Hermione, Hermoine.*
Harmonia is the daughter of Ares and Aphrodite. In some versions of this myth she is said to be the daughter of Zeus and Electra, or a daughter of Atlas. As the offspring of Ares and Aphrodite, her siblings are Phobos, the god of panic; Pallor, the god of terror; Deimos, sometimes known as the god of dread; Enyo, goddess of war; Eros, the god of love; and Anteros, the god of passion. Harmonia married the sun hero Cadmus. Their children are Polydorus; Agave, who murdered her husband and went insane; Autonoe, who was also driven insane for torturing Semele; Ino, who murdered her children; and Semele, who died when Zeus revealed himself to her in his ethereal glory. When Harmonia and Cadmus were married the gods attended their wedding. The jealous fire god and smith, Hephaistos, who was the husband of Aphrodite, created a necklace and a veil or a robe as a wedding gift for Harmonia. The necklace was said to bring disaster upon all who wore it. It did. Their daughters endured horrendous tragedies. Finally Harmonia and her brilliant husband Cadmus were changed into snakes, or some say lions, by Ares and retired to the tranquil Elysian Fields, also known as the Islands of the Blessed. As snakes, Harmonia and Cadmus were depicted as black with blue spots. Harmonia is not to be confused with Harmonia, daughter of Menelaus and Helen. *See also* Anteros; Aphrodite; Ares; Cadmus; Hephaistos; Semele.

Harmonia (B) (Greek) *see* Helen; Semele.

Harmothoe *Harmathoe* (Greek)
Harmothoe and her husband, Panareus, were killed by the great god Zeus. She is the mother of Aedon, Cleothera and Merope. *See also* Aedon; Merope.

Haroeris (Egypt)
Also known as: *Hor Merti, Horkhenti Irti.*
A name by which Horus was called, the Greek form of Har Wer, and Egyptian name meaning "Horus the Elder" or "the Great."

Harops (Egypt) *see* Harpies.

Harpakhrad (Egypt)
An alternate name for Horus (q.v.). *See also* Banebdedet; Harpokrates.

Harpies *Harpiae, Harpy* (Greek)
Also known as: *The Hounds of Zeus, The Snatchers.*
Storm goddesses. Homer only named one Harpie, Podarge (also known as Celaeno), meaning "blackness," and Hesiod wrote of two, Kalaino, (also known as Aello, Aellopuus), meaning "howler," and Ocypetes, meaning "rapid." Their parents are Thaumas and the Oceanid Electra. In other myths their parents are said to be Poseidon and Gaea or Typhon, god of the storm winds and the sea monster Echida. As the daughters of Thaumas and Electra, their sister is Iris, the messenger of the gods. Podarge, impregnated by the West Wind, who is known as Zephyrus, or some say the North Wind, Boreas, gave birth to Achilles' famous horses, Xanthus and Balius. The Harpies earned their name "The Snatchers" when it was said that Hades had them bring living beings to him who were unwilling to die. It was also believed that the Harpies and other female bird-like creatures were ghosts who might snatch away mortals at whim. They also had a reputation for devouring corpses. Under the direction of the great Zeus they earned the name "The Hounds of Zeus" by "hounding" the ancient, blind soothsayer, king Phineus of Salmydessus, in Thrace. Zeus' problem with him was that he insisted upon revealing the future to mortals. Every time Phineus would sit down to eat, the Harpies would swoop down and steal his food, leaving excrement on the plate and a terrible stench behind as they flew off. Near death by starvation or suicide, the poor man was rescued by the Argonauts Zetes and Calais, sons of the North Wind, Boreas, and brothers of Cleopatra. In some legends, the Harpies are killed by the men and in others it is said they bargained with Iris or Hermes, who agreed to allow the Harpies to live if they would leave Phineus alone. The Harpies then retired to their cave on Mount Dicte in Crete. They are sometimes shown as vultures, or depicted as bird-like creatures with female heads, long claws and wings. The Harpies are similar to the Egyptian evil winds called the Harops which bring flies and locusts. They are also similar to Greek Cataclothes who were spinners of fate. *See also* Phineus for more details of his life. To compare to wind deities *see* Aegeon; Aello; Aeolus; Boreas; Eurus; Notus; Zephyrus; Zetes. *See also* Chimaera; Gorgons; Keres; Oceanids.

Harpina (Greek)
She is possibly the mother of Oenomaus by Alxion or Ares. *See also* Ares; Oenamnaus.

Harpokrates (Greek)
Also known as: *Harpakhrad, Heru-P-Khart, Heru-Pa-Khret.*
A name given to the child Horus by the Greeks, who looked upon him as the god of silence since he was depicted with his finger to his mouth. Generally shown nude with a sidelock of youth and the Double Crown. One hand touches his lips. Sometimes shown as a child, or a baby on his mother's knee. *See also* Horus.

Harpy (Greek) *see* Harpies.

Harpyiae (Greek) *see* Harpies.

Harsaphes *Arsaphes* (Greek)
Also known as: *Hershef* (Egypt).
A god of fertility and water, he was portrayed as ram-headed, he is the Greek form of the Egyptian Hershef. The chief center of his worship was at Heracleopolis Magna (The Great City of Heracles). He is identified with the Greek Hershef, the predynastic Egyptian Amon, and the Greek Heracles. *See also* Hershef.

Harsiese (Greek) *see* Horus.

Harsiesis (Greek)

Also known as: *Hor-Sa-Iset* (Egypt).

A Greek epithet of Horus, called Hor-sa-iset by the Egyptians, meaning "Horus, son of Isis," the infant who avenged his father, Osiris. He was conceived after his mother, Isis, had magically had intercourse with the dead body of Osiris. He is shown as hawk-headed, carrying instruments of death.

Hartomes (Egypt)

An epithet of Horus, meaning the "Lancer." He was depicted in bas-reliefs in the sanctuary at Edfu using his lance against his enemies, the armies of Set. *See also* Harendotes; Horus.

Haru-Yama-no-Kasumi-Onoko (Japan)

God of spring. Younger brother of Aki-Yama-no-Shitabi-onoko. He is the lover of Izushio-tome.

Haruspices (Etruria)

Deity of foretelling. An individual haruspex foretells events by interpreting abnormal meteorological events, unusual growths and births of deformed humans and animals.

Harut (Middle East; Islamic)

Harut is one of the two fallen angels. The other is Marut (q.v.).

Hasibwari (Melanesia, Solomon Islands) *see* Hatuibwari.

Hasisu (Phoenician) *see* Kusor.

Hasteseyalti *Hastseyalti* (Apache, Navajo, Papago People, North America)

Also known as: *Yebitsai, Yepitsai.*

Maternal Grandfather of the Gods, the Talking God, and creator. He belongs to a group of household and nature deities known as the Yei (q.v).

Hasteshogan *Hastsehogan* (Apache, Navajo, Papago People, North America)

Also known as: *Hastseltsi, Red Lord.*

God of racing. Known as the Red Lord, Hasteshogan is also a god of the evening and the west. He is also a household deity who belongs to a group of household and nature gods known as the Yei (q.v.). *See also* Ganaskidi; Hastseyalti.

Hastsehogan (Native North American) *see* Hasteshogan.

Hastseltsi (Native North American) *see* Hasteshogan.

Hastseoltoi (Apache, Navajo, Papago People, North America)
Goddess of hunting. Wife of war god.

Hastseyalti (Native North American People) *see* Hasteseyalti.

Hastsezini (Apache, Navajo, Papago, Pueblo People, North America)

A fire god. Called the "Black Lord." Originally four mysterious beings appeared before the first Pueblo people who were called Kisani. These four beings were Bitsis Lakai, Bitsis Dotli'z, Bitsis Litsoi and Bitsis Lizi'n. Bitsis Lakai was like the Navaho Hasteseyalti; Bitsis Dotli'z was like To'nenili, and Bitsis Lizi'n was like Hastesezini. The four mysterious gods created the first man and woman, Atsi Hastin and Aste Estsan.

Hastshehogan (Navajo People, North America) *see* Hasteshogan; Yei.

Hastsheyalti (Navajo People, North America) *see* Hasteseyalti; Yei.

Hat-Hor (Egypt) *see* Hathor.

Hat-Mehit (Egypt)

Dolphin goddess, wife of Ba-nab-djet, the ram of Mendes. *See also* Hathor; Neith.

Hathor *Athor, Athyr, Hat-hor* (Egypt, possibly Mesopotamia), *Hawthor.*

Also known as: *Hat-Mehit.*

Goddess of love, mirth and joy. Goddess of the sky and sun. Possibly a fertility goddess. Mortuary goddess. Hathor (hat-hor) means the "House of Horus." She protected infants and consoled the dead. In earlier times, as the sky goddess, she was regarded as the mother of the sun god, Horus, until she was replaced by Isis. It is thought that Hathor was given a bovine form because the concept of the sky as a cow was widespread in the Delta. In an ancient myth Hathor was said to have raised the young sun-god to heaven by means of her horns. She was known as "Hathor of the Horizon" and her animal was the wild cow. In later periods she was regarded as the solar eye. The sistrum, a musical rattle, was her attribute and fetish. There is reference to her as the mother of Ihy. The goddess Qadesh is thought to be an aspect of Hathor. Hathor was usually depicted in human form wearing a sun-disc flanked by cow's horns on her head. She was also represented as a cow or with the head or horns of a cow, and has been shown with two long ringlets similar to the style of Asherah. As the seven Hathors, they resemble the Fates and are possibly the same as Sekhet, or Bast. She could be associated with Bes. The ancient goddess Apt may be a form of Hathor. Also identified with Hathor is the goddess Ament. Another form of Hathor was the mother goddess Hat-Mehit, counterpart of Ba-neb-Tettu. She has been associated with Asherah and the Greeks identified her with Aphrodite. *See also* Amenhotep; Ament; Amentet; Amun; Astarte; Bes; Hat-Mehit; Horus; Isis; Ninhursag; Nut; Qadesh; Sekhmet.

Hati (Norse; Teutonic)

Also known as: *Gamr, Garm, Garme, Hati Hrodvitnisson, Maanegarm, Mana-garm, Manigarm* (Moon-hound), *Maragarme, Skoll.*

One of two gigantic wolves, in some myths known as werewolves, Hati is the brother of Skoll, and the son of Hrodvitnir. Skoll pursues the sun and Hati is always after the moon. Hati is also known as Garm, the watchdog of the dead, who is stationed at the entrance of Hel's domain. In some versions, the wolf Fenrir is called the father of Hati and Skoll. Hati and Skoll are known as the Varns. *See also* Fenrir; Garm; Ragnarok; Skoll.

Hati Hrodvitnisson (Teutonic) *see* Hati.

Hatmehit (Egypt) *see* Hat-Mehit; Neith.

Hatra (Mesopotamia) *see* Ba'al Shamin.

Hatuibwari *Hasibwari* (Melanesia, Solomon Islands)

Serpent deity. Supreme god. Creator god. He formed a woman from red clay and a man from the woman's rib. Hatuibwari is a winged serpent with a man's head and breasts of a woman.

Hau (Egypt) *see* Akeneh.

Hauillepenyi (Araucanian People, Chile)
This god of fog looks like a sheep with a calf's head and a seal's tail.

Haukas *Guacas* (Peru) Ancient sun deity.

Haumea (Hawaii)
(Hawaii; Maori People, New Zealand; Tahiti)
Also known as: *Haumea-ka-hanau-wawa* (Haumea giving birth noisily), *Ka-haka-ya-koko* (The Place of Blood), *Kame-haikana*, *Lau-mihi* (because she gathered crabs and seaweed), *Papa*, *Papa-hanau-moku* (Papa Giving Birth to Islands).
"Tree of Changing Leaves." Goddess of Childbirth. Goddess of Death. Mother Goddess. Mother of Pele. Sister of Kane and Kanaloa. This goddess introduced natural childbirth. Her own children were born from different parts of her body and were said to be "strange noisy creatures." Wildflowers were in her care but she could withhold their growth in times of need. Haumea, who had the power to transform herself from aged to young, and from young to aged, had many sons. When her oldest son came of age, Haumea died and was reborn so that she could marry him. In time, he died. Haumea again died and was reborn so that she could marry her youngest son. Later, she again died so that she could marry her great grandson. In all, she had six rebirths. Haumea owned an orchard with magical trees that gave the owner whatever he or she wanted. She gave some of her trees to earth children. She also had a spectacular fish tree. The tree had to be placed in the ocean for its fruits to become fish. She gave the tree to one of her sons who placed it in the sea (at that time the waters were without fish). He became the first fisher. His problem was that he was very greedy. Wanting all he could get, he shook the tree with such force that the fish fell from tree and swam away from him, instead of falling into his hands. That is why today one must fish for fish. Haumea also has the ability to disappear into trees. Once, when her husband was being chased for sacrifice, she grabbed him and they both entered into a tree for safety. *See also* Papa; Pele.

Haumia (Polynesia) *see* Haumia-Tikitiki; Hema; Hina; Tawhaki.

Haumia-Tikitiki (Polynesia)
Also known as: *Haumia.*
God of wild or uncultivated plants. He is the son of the sky god, Rangi, and mother earth, Papa. For a list of siblings, *see* Rangi. He is associated with Tawhiri, Tane, Tangaroa, and Tu. *See also* Haumea; Papa; Po; Rongo.

Haur (Teutonic) *see* Dwarfs.

Haurvatat and Ameretat
Also known as: *Khurdad and Amardad* (Pahlavi dialect), *Khurdadh, Khordadh* (Zoroastrian; Persia).
Associated with water and vegetation, these feminine deities are always together. Haurvatat is the goddess of health and Ameretat is the goddess of immortality. As Amesha Spentas they give wealth and herds of cattle. Their opponents are Hunger and Thirst. *See also* Ameshas Spenta; Daevas.

Havai (Polynesia) *see* Avaiki.

Havaiki (Polynesia) *see* Avaiki.

Havamal (Teutonic) *see* Fjalar; Loki.

Havfru *Havfrue* (Finno-Ugric)
Also known as: *Akkruva, Avfruvva.*
Goddess of fish and fishers. Protector of fishers. Havfru is often friendly to people. When a storm is eminent, she can be seen. She is a mermaid, half-fish and half-woman. The male version is bearded. Havfru is probably the same as Havfrue of the Danes. She is possibly the female counterpart of merman, Havmand, of the Danes.

Havgan (Celtic) *see* Arawn; Pwyll.

Havmand (Danish) *see* Havfru.

Hawaii — Creation Legend *see* Kane.

Hawaiki (Polynesia) *see* Avaiki.

Haweniyo (Iroquois People, North America)
Creator deity. Little known.

Hawiyah (Islam)
This is the seventh section in the Islamic Hell. Hawiyah is a bottomless pit reserved for hypocrites. *See also* Islamic Hell.

Hawwa (Babylonian) *see* Eve.

Hay Tau (Phoenician) *see* Adonis; Osiris.

Haya (Babylonian)
"Goddess of Direction." This is one of the titles of the goddess Ninlil (q.v.).

Haya-aki-tsu-hime (Japan) *see* Haya-akitsu-hime-no-kami.

Haya-akihiko-no-kami (Japan) *see* Haya-akitsu-hime-no-kami.

Haya-akitsu-hime-no-kami *Haya-Aki-Tsu-Hime* (Shinto; Japan)
Ruler of the Seas. Haya-akitsu-hime-no-kami (Rapid-Autumn-Princess Deity) is the daughter of Izanagi and Izanami and the sister/wife of Paya-aki-tu-piko-no-kami (also known as Haya-akihiko-no-kami, Rapid-Autumn-Lad-Deity). As the ruler of the turbulent seas she swallows all sins and catastrophes cast into the sea. Haya-akitsu-hime-no-kami was born after the creation of the eight islands of Japan. Haya-akitsu-hime-no-kami is one of the children of Izanagi and Izanami created to populate the terrain and become deities (kami) of the natural phenomena. There were thirty deities created during this time, gods of the seasons, the sea, earth, trees, winds, mountains, valleys and fire. Her brother/husband was the ruler of rivers. In some interpretations, they are the parents of the water, mountain, tree and wind deities and grandparents of fertility, fire, land and bird deities. Later, when Izanagi returned from Yomi (hell), other sea deities were created as he scrubbed the toxins from his body. The ruler of fish and all sea creatures, O-wata-tsu-mi, is the most prominent of the group. During periodical purification rituals, Se-oritsu-hime (Lady-Who-Descends-the-Rapids) is called upon to absolve followers of offenses. The heavenly offenses committed against the earth include pollution, removing water pipes, filling irrigation channels and sowing seed repeatedly. The earthly offenses include offenses committed in sexual relationships, such as bestiality,

the cutting of dead bodies, incest and leprosy. Haya-akitsu-hime-no-kami is also invoked. The god Ibukido-nushi (Breath-Blowing-Lord) blows the offenses to the goddess Haya-sasura-hime (Swift-Banishment-Lady), who lives in Yomi (hell). *See also* Izanagi and Izanami; Kaya-no-hime-no-kami (Ruler of the Grassy Plain); O-wata-tsu-mi.

Haya-ji (Shinto; Japan)
Also known as: *Haya-Tsu-muji-no-Kami.*

Whirlwind deity. Haya-ji is an ancient Shinto deity. When Ame-no-Wakahiko was killed by an arrow, the lamentations of his wife, Shita-teru-hime were heard in the heavens. The sympathetic sun goddess Amaterasu had Haya-ji take the body of Ame-no-Wakahiko back to earth for the funeral. In a variation of this myth, the gods sent the parents of Shita-teru-hime to earth for his funeral. In the Ryobu-Shinto tradition, Haya-ji is shown as an ugly man under the shape of a devil carrying a large bag across his shoulders from which he squeezes wind. For other early Shinto wind deities, *see* Amaterasu; Fu-jin; Shina-tsu-hiko. For additional details about Ame-no-Wakahiko *see* Ame no-oshido-mimi.

Haya-Sasura-Hime (Japan) *see* Haya-akitsu-hime-no-kami.

Haya-Tsu-muji-no-Kami (Japan) *see* Haya-ji.

Hayagriva (India)
Also known as: *Vishnu.*

"The horse-necked" god of learning, Hayagriva, is an aspect of Vishnu. As Hayagriva, his consort is the lion-headed goddess Shakti, Cha-dog-ma (also known as Vajra Shringkhala or Shringhala), who is associated with love. Hayagriva and Cha-dog-ma are the Door-Keepers of the West in the Bardo World. *See also* Ankusha; Shakti; Vajrapani; Vishnu; Yamantaka.

Hayasya (Buddhist; India) The Divine Mare.

Hayk *Hayik* (Ancient Armenia)
Also known as: *Hay.*

Sky-god. Culture hero. Possibly a god of wine and vegetation. Hayk, a culture-hero, overthrew Bel (also called Nimrod). Hayk is the father of Armenak, also a culture-hero and grandfather of Cadmus. He is a giant with curly hair, bright smiling eyes and a strong arm. Armenak may have been associated with the Teutonic hero Irmin and the Vedic Aryaman (qq.v.). *See also* Armenak.

Hayowentha (Native North American) *see* Haio Hwa Tha.

Hea (Chaldean) *see* Ea.

Heart of Heaven (Quiche People, Guatemala) *see* Huracan.

Heavenly Herdsman (Japan) *see* Kengiu.

Heavenly Spinster (China) *see* Chin Nu.

Hebat (Hittite) *see* Hepat.

Hebdomad (Gnostic; Chaldea, Egypt, Syria)
High gods. Sabaoth is one of the seven Hebdomad or Ogdoad deities coming indirectly from Sophia. *See also* Ogdoad; Sabaoth.

Hebe (Greek)
Also known as: *Ganumedes, Ganymeda, Juventas* (Roman).

Goddess of eternal youth. Hebe is the daughter of Zeus and Hera, sister of Ares, wife of Heracles and mother of Alexiares and Aniketos. She was a cupbearer to the gods until she indecently exposed herself. Ganymede replaced her. She restores youth and vigor by supplying Ambrosia and because of this she is sometimes called Ganymede. Iolaus restored Hebe's youth. *See also* Ares; Eos; Ganymede; Hera; Heracles; Juventas; Zephyrus.

Hecab (Greek) This is another name for Hecuba.

Hecate *Hekate* (Greek)
Also known as: *Aktiophi, Artemis* (possible aspect), *Brimo, Crantaeis* (possibly), *Diana, Enodia* (wayside goddess), *Proserpina, Selene* (possible aspect), *Trioditis* (goddess of the meeting of roads).

Underworld goddess. Goddess of night and darkness. Queen of ghosts. Queen of shades. Controller of the hidden things of nature. Possibly a moon goddess. Hecate is either the daughter of the Titan Perses and Asteria or Zeus and Asteria or Zeus and Demeter. Hecate presides over birth, life, death, streets and gates. Her priestess is Medea to whom she taught the art of magic. Hecate, often depicted with a torch, was only worshiped at night by torchlight. Dogs and black lambs were offered to her as sacrifices. She is sometimes shown as a triple statue at crossroads who has with her a pack of hounds. Sometimes she is shown with three heads: a dog, horse, and lion. Hecate is often confused with Artemis. She is similar if not the same as the Indian Ekata. Hecate is associated with Persephone and Pluto. Some think she was an aspect of both Selene and Artemis. The name Brimo was used for Hecate as well as for Persephone, Rhea and Demeter. Hecate as an epithet was used by Luna, Diana, and Persephone. *See also* Artemis; Demeter; Diana; Leto; Persephone; Rhea.

Hecaterus (Greek)
He is the possible father of the Curetes and the Satyrs. *See also* Curetes; Satyrs.

Hecatoncheires (Greek) *see* Hecatonchires.

Hecatoncheiroi (Greek) *see* Hecatonchires.

Hecatonchires *Hecatoncheires, Hecatontocheiroi, Hekatoncheires* (Greek)
Also known as: *Centimani, The Hundred-handed.*

Guardians. Hesiod wrote that the Hecatonchires are the three sons of Gaea (Earth) and Uranus (Sky). They are Briareus (also spelled Obriareus, and also called Aegaeon), Cotus (Cottus) and Gyes (Gyas or Gyges). Giants, each had fifty heads and one hundred arms. Their father was jealous of their great strength and hid them within their mother which filled her with pain. She tried to convince her youngest son, Cronus, to castrate Uranus. Instead, Cronus kept the giants imprisoned in Tartarus. She was more fortunate with Zeus. She convinced him to release her sons so that they could assist him in his battle with the Titans. When they had done so, he returned them to Tartarus and gave them the duties of watching over the Titan prisoners. Briareus was given leave by Thetis to once again assist Zeus in a squabble with opponents but he was returned to the dark section of the Underworld when his mission was accomplished. The monstrous siblings of the Hecatonchires are the Giants, the Cyclopes, and Typhoeus. *See also* Cronus; Cyclopes; Enceladus; Gaea; Giants; Hades; Tartarus; Typhon (A); Uranus.

Hecatontocheiroi (Greek) *see* Hecatonchires.

Hector (Greek)
He is the youngest son of Priam and Hecuba. He was killed by Achilles in the Trojan War. *See also* Achilles; Cassandra.

Hecuba *Hecab* (Greek)
After Troy fell, Hecuba was given to Odysseus as a slave. The sons of Polymnestor killed her youngest son, Polydorus. Seeking revenge, Hecuba blinded and killed the men. She was changed into a dog. *See also* Cassandra; Hector; Polydorus.

Hedj-Wer (Egypt) *see* Ape.

Heelios (Greek) *see* Helius.

Hefaidd Hen (Celtic) *see* Rhiannon.

Hefedha (Arabic)
Protector deity. Little known but this deity deters danger.

Hegal (Babylonia) *see* Marduk.

Hegemone (Greek) *see* Charities; Graces.

Heh *Hehu* (Egypt)
Also known as: *Hehet, Neheh.*
God of the immeasurable. God of eternity. He was part of the Ogdoad and by some accounts he mated with Hehut. Heh in numbers denotes a million. He is shown with the head of a frog and is also depicted kneeling and holding a notched palm rib in his hands. Heh was later identified with Shu. *See also* Maa-Nefert-ra; Neheh; Ogdoad.

Hehet (Egypt)
High god. One of the gods in the Pyramid Texts. *See also* Amun; Heh.

Hehuah (Christian, Hebrew) *see* Jehovah.

Hehui *Hehu* (Egypt)
High god. One of the eight ancient gods mentioned with Amen in the Pyramid Texts. In one version he is mated with Hehut. He has the head of a frog. Hehui is probably the same as Heh (q.v.). *See also* Amun.

Hehut (Egypt) *see* Maa-nefert-ra.

Heid (Teutonic) *see* Freyja; Gulveig.

Heidr (Teutonic) *see* Gulveig.

Heidrun (Teutonic)
Deified animal. Either Odin's or Valfather's she-goat. This animal feeds on the leaves and twigs of Lerad, Yggdrasil's topmost branch. Heidrun furnishes the food for the dead warriors in Valhalla. Heidrun is similar to Saehrimnir, the boar, who is also food for the gods. *See also* Saehrimnir; Valhalla; Yggdrasil.

Heilyn (Celtic)
He is the son of Gwynn the ancient, and one of the survivors of the battle between Bran and Matholwch. *See also* Bran.

Heimdall *Heimdal, Heimdallr* (Norse; Teutonic)
Also known as: *Heimdal-Rig, Rig.*
One of the Aesir. God who was the son of nine mothers, or brother of nine sisters. Some versions give the name of the father as Odin and the names of the mothers as Angeyja, Atla, Eistla, Eyrgjafa, Gjalp, Greip, Ind, Jarnsaxa, and Ulfrun. He visited three women, and had three different children. He is the watchman of the gods and guard of the bridge. He is the owner of the horn, Gjall, which can be heard all over the world. Heimdall is the only god who lived for a time among mortals. After he assumed the name Rig, he and a mortal woman produced Jarl. He may be the son of Odin. Heimdall needs very little sleep and can see a hundred miles, hear the grass grow and wool growing on sheep. The following is a list of the three women and their children. The race of Thralls: Edda the mate of Ai. By Heimdall she had Thrall who in turn married Thir (the drudge). Their sons are Fjosnir, Klur, Hriem, Kreggi, Kefsir, Fulnir, Drumb, Digraldi, Drott Leggjaldi, Lut and Hosvir. Their daughters are Drumba, Kumba, Okkvinkalfa, Arinnefja, Ambott, Eikintjasna, Ysjarughpja and Tronubeina. The race of Peasants: Amma the mate of Afi. From Heimdall she had Karl who married Snor. Their sons are Hal, Dreng, Hold, Thegn, Smit, Breid, Bondi, Bundinskeggi, Bui, Boddi, Brattskegg and Segg. The daughters are Snt, Brud, Svanni, Svarri, Sprakki, Fljod, Sprund, Vif, Feima, and Ristil. Heimdall's third woman was Mothir, the mate of Fathir. From Mothir, Heimdall had Jarl, who married Erna. Their children are the sons Bur, Barn, Jod, Athal, Arvi, Nid, Nidjung, Svein, Kund and Kon. The daughters are not named in legend; however, Heimdall's mothers are the daughters of Aegir and Ran. Heimdall has gold teeth so is known as "Gold Tooth." When Balder died, Heimdall rode Gulltoppr, his horse with the golden mane, to the funeral. Heimdall's home is called Himinbjorg. *See also* Aegir; Aesir; Balder; Freyja; Gjall; Gunlodd; Odin; Ran; Thor.

Heitsi-Eibib *Haitsi-aibeb* (Hottentot People, Africa)
Also known as: *Tsui-goab.*
Sorcerer god. Magician. He is the offspring of a cow or a virgin who ate a magic herb. A shape-shifter, Heitsi-Eibib eats special grass. He is the spirit of the bush and the hero of hunters. He dies and is reborn. His enemy is Gaunab (q.v.). *See also* Gaunab; Tsui'goab.

Hek (Egypt) *see* Heka.

Heka *Hek, Hekau, Hyk* (Egypt)
Serpent. God of magic. This serpent is mentioned in the magical formulae of Unas, King of the Fifth Dynasty. It is sometimes identified with Shu. *See also* Akeneh.

Hekate (Greek) *see* Hecate.

Hekatoncheires (Greek) *see* Hecatonchires.

Hekau (Egypt) *see* Heka.

Heke-Heke-I-Papa (Polynesia)
Earth goddess. One of the wives of Rangi. Of the many children of these two, the most well-known is Tama-nui-rangi. *See also* Rangi.

Heket *Hekt, Heqet, Heqt, Heqtit, Hequet* (Egypt)
The goddess who attends births. Heket attends Ra as he is

born again each morning. Along with other deities, she assists in forming children in the womb and presiding over births as a midwife. She is shown as a woman with the head of a frog. Sometimes, she is depicted as a frog at the end of a phallus. Heket is associated with Isis. She was the assistant to the goddess in bringing Osiris back to life. Heket is the female complement of Khnum, the ram-headed god. In some interpretations, she is known as his mother. *See also* Isis; Khnum.

Hekret (Egypt) *see* Akeneh.

Hekt (Egypt) *see* Heket.

Hel (Norse; Teutonic)
Also known as: *Hela, Hella, Urd, Urth.*

Goddess of the underworld. There is some confusion as who was really the deity of the underworld. Some say it is Odin. Hel, Hella, Hellawisi, Hellewite, Hellia, Helviti, Halvete, Helvede are the various names for the Underworld or "Place of Punishment." Hel is the daughter of Loki, and sister of Fenrir and Ifing. Hel's plate is called Hunger; her knife, Famine or Starvation; her bed was Sick Bed or Disease; and the bedhangings, Glimmering Misfortune or Misery. Hel is said to be the same as Helheim, one of the nine worlds of the dead. She is a woman whose upper body is alive and her lower body is half-dead and rotting. *See also* Balder; Garm; Gullveig; Hades; Hati; Hermod; Loki; Nifl-heim; Urd.

Hela (Teutonic) *see* Hel.

Helblindi (Teutonic)
He is the son of Farbuti, and brother of Loki. Helblindi is also a name given to Odin. *See also* Farbuti; Loki; Odin.

Heleius *Heleus* (Greek)
He is the son of Perseus and Andromeda. He ruled the Taphian Islands with Cephalus. *See also* Andromeda; Gorgophone; Perseus.

Helen (Greek)
Also known as: *Helen of Troy.*

Queen of Sparta. Helen is the daughter of Zeus and Leda or Nemesis. Her mortal step-father is Tyndareus. She is the half-sister of the Dioscuri (Castor and Pollux) and the sister of Clytemnestra. Early in life she was abducted by Theseus, the king of Athens and rescued by the Dioscuri. Renowned for her beauty, and pursued by various suitors, she chose Menelaus, but either eloped with or was abducted by Paris, a rich Trojan prince. This created the havoc that was said to have initiated the Trojan War. After his death she married Deiphobus, spent a number of years in Egypt and returned to Sparta with Menelaus after the fall of Troy. It is said that Menelaus originally wanted to kill her but melted at the sight of her beauty. Helen and Menelaus have a daughter, Hermione, and sons, Aethiolas and Maraphius. According to other sources, their children are Hermione, Pleisthenes and possibly Nicostratus. She also had three sons by Paris: Bunomus, Aganus and Idaeus, and a daughter, Helen. These sons are said to have died as infants under a collapsed roof in Troy. Helen is also the mother of Iphigeneia as a result of her relationship with Theseus. There are many versions of her death but it is likely that she was hung by the maids of Argive Polyxo who were avenging the death of

Tlepolemus at Troy. *See also* Acamas (A); Agamemnon; Ajax the Greater; Castor and Pollux; Hesione; Leda; Menelaus; Nemesis; Paris; Tyndareus.

Heleus (Greek)
He is the son of Andromeda and Perseus. His siblings are Alcaeus, Electryon, Gorgophone, Mestor, Perses and Sthenelus. *See also* Andromeda; Gorgophone; Paris; Perses.

Helheim (Teutonic) *see* Hel; Hell.

Heliades *Heliaads, Heliads* (Greek)
Deities of light. The Heliades are the daughters of the sun god Helius and the Oceanid, Clymene, and the sisters of Phaethon. Their names are Aegiale (also known as Phoebe), Aegle and Aetheria. They were changed into poplar trees and their tears became amber. The sons of Helius by Rhode are also called Heliades. A group of intelligent men, known for their interest in astrology, they are Actis, Candalus, Cecaphus, Macar, Ochimus, Triopas. *See also* Aegle (A); Clymene; Helius; Oceanids.

Helicaon (Greek)
He is the son of Antenor and Theano. *See also* Acamas (B); Agenor; Antenor; Archelous; Glaucus; Laodamas.

Helice (Greek)
She is the daughter of the king of Aegialus and wife of the king of Athens, Ion. *See also* Zeus.

Helios (Greek) *see* Helius; Sebek.

Helius *Heelios* (Ancient Greek), *Helios* (Greek; Roman)
Also known as: *Acamas* ("Untiring"), *Hyperion, Panderces* ("All-seeing"), *Sol* (Roman), *Terpimbrotos* ("He Who Makes Mortals Rejoice").

Sun god. Helius is the son of Hyperion and Theia. His siblings are the goddess of dawn, Eos, and the moon goddess, Selene. He married Perse and became the father of Perses, who is known for his brutality; Pasiphae, who by a bull became the mother of Minos; Aeetes, the cruel king of Colchis; and Circe, the sorceress. He is also thought to be the father of the Graces, by Aegle and the father of the Heliades, by other women. He may be the father of Aex, the Corybantes, and Augeias. He is also said to be the father of Achelous, by Gaea. He was loved by the nymph, Axibia. When Zeus apportioned the world, he neglected to give Helius a section. To keep him happy, the great god gave him the island of Rhodes. He drove a four or nine horse chariot named Quadriga through the sky during the day, accompanied by Eos. The names of his horses are Aethon, Astrope, Bronte, Chronos, Eous, Lampon, Phaeton, Phlegon, Pyroeis. Each night Helius returned from west to east on the river Oceanus, transported in a golden cup. Loyal to his children, he allowed his son Phaethon to borrow the sun chariot one day and it ended in disaster. He would take Circe and Aeetes on his rounds and he once loaned the chariot to his granddaughter Medea. Helius loaned the golden cup to Heracles twice; once for his journey to Erytheia and again in his search for the Garden of Hesperides. The giant Orion was healed of blindness by Helius. Aphrodite, furious at the all-seeing Helius for telling her husband that she was having an affair with Ares, got even by having him fall in love with the daughter of king

Orchamus, Leucothoe. He had to disguise himself to gain entry to her bedroom. A former love, the spiteful Clytie, inflamed with jealousy, told the king who punished his daughter by burying her alive. Overwhelmed with grief, Helius transformed her into a frankincense bush. The spurned lover died and became the flower, heliotrope, who turns its head to follow the sun each day. Some say the Colossus of Rhodes was a depiction of his form. Helius is also shown with a halo of rays and the attribute of a crocodile in his hand. Helius is often confused with his father, the Titan sun god, Hyperion. For additional offspring of Helius see Heliades. Compare Helius to the god of light, Apollo, to the Norse god, Sol, the Hindu sun god, Surya, the Slavonic god Dazbog, and the Roman Sol. See also Aeetes; Aegipan; Aegis; Aegle; Alcyoneus; Aphrodite; Ares; Clytie; Eos; Graces; Heliades; Medea; Oceanids; Orion; Pasiphae; Phaethon; Sebek; Selene.

Hell *Hel, Nifl-heim* (Teutonic from the root word Hel or Hol, possibly)
Also known as: *Amenti* (Egyptian), *Duzakh* (Persian), *Dzokh* (Armenian), *Gehenna* (Hebrew), *Hades* (Greek), *Irkalia* (Babylonian), *Kigal* (Akkadian), *Santaramet* (Iranian), *Sheol* (Hebrew), *Spenta Armaiti, Spentaramet, Tartarus*.
Underworld. Many versions of Hell describe it as being somewhere underground or below the earth. The Egyptians say it was Amenti with pits of flame and demons. The Norse say the Yggdrasil tree had its roots buried in Hell. The Akkadians call it Kigal. The Babylonians call it Irkalia. To some it is a place of the dead and of no return while some say it is just a stopover region. In traditional Western literature, the angel of Hell is Nasargiel. He oversees the torture of sinners. See also Amentet; Elysian Field; Gehenna; Hades; Hel; Helheim; Irkalla; Nifl-heim; Sheol; Spenta Armaiti; Spentaramet; Tartarus.

Hella (Teutonic) *see* Hel.

Helle (Greek)
Helle is the daughter of Athamas and Nepele, and the sister of Phrixus. The sister and brother escaped on the ram with the Golden Fleece. See also Golden Fleece; Ino; Nephele; Phrixus.

Hellen (Greek)
A Hero. King of Phthia. Hellen gave his name to the Hellenes, the Greek race. He is the son of Deucalion and Pyrrha, or possibly Zeus and Dorippe, or Prometheus and Clymene. With the nymph Orseis they are the parents of Dorus, Xuthus, and Aeolus. He is the grandfather of Ion and Achaeus. See also Achaeus; Aegimius; Aeolus; Deucalion; Ion; Xuthus.

Heloha (Choctaw People, North America)
The female Thunderbird.

Helunus (Greek) *see* Cassandra.

Hema (Polynesia)
He is the son of Kaitangata and Whaitiri, the cannibal goddess. His sibling is Punga. (In Hawaii, Kaitangata's wife is Hina-who-worked-in-the-moon and Hema's mother is the moon goddess Mahina.) Hema married the goddess Urutonga ("South-West"). They had two (some say three) children, Tawhaki, the god of thunder and good health, and Kariki. When

Hema inadvertently trespassed on the land of the goblins, he was put to death. His sons took revenge for his demise. See Haumea; Tawhaki.

Hemera (Greek)
"Day." She is the daughter of Erebus, who is the personification of the darkness of the Underworld, and Nyx, the personification of night. Her union with Cephalus, the son of the messenger of the gods, Hermes, and Herse, the personification of the dew, produced Phaethon, who was kidnapped by Aphrodite to watch over her shrine. See also Aither; Erebus; Hermes; Herse; Nemesis; Nox; Phaethon.

Hemsut (Egypt)
Deity of protection. Deity of destiny. Hemsut appears as the female counterpart of the "ka" (creative and preserving power of life). Hemsut wears an emblem and headdress of the shield. Above the shield are two crossed arrows. See also Ka.

Hemth (Egypt) *see* Akeneh.

Heneb (Egypt)
The god of grain and other land products, Heneb is the competitor of Osiris.

Heng (Huron People, North America)
Also known as: *De Hi No, Thunder.*
God of Thunder. Male fertility spirit. He is one of seven brothers, all atmospheric deities. See also Tsentsa; Yoskeha.

Heng and Ha (Buddhist; China)
Also known as: *Heng Ha Er Tsiang, Indra, Snorter and Puffer, Vajrapani.*
Heng and Ha are two forms of the Buddhist god Vajrapani, a name assumed by Indra when he was the bodyguard of Gautama. General Puffer is called Ha-Tsiang. General Snorter is called Heng-Tsiang. Heng is also known as Cheng Lung. See also Men Shen.

Heng-Ha-erh-Chiang *Heng Ha Er Tsiang* (China) *see* Heng and Ha; Men-shen.

Heng-O (China) *see* Chang-O.

Heng-Tsiang (China) *see* Heng and Ha.

Henga (Osage People, North America)
Deified bird. Sacred Eagle.

Henir (Norse; Teutonic) *Hoener, Hoeni, Hoenir, Hone, Honer, Honir.*
Also known as: *We* (possibly) or *Willi* (possibly).
"God of Silence." One of the triad, with brothers Odin and Lodur, or part of the trinity of Odin, Loki and Henir. Henir, was taken hostage to the Vanir in exchange for Niord. Known as the "God of Silence," he never spoke unless prompted by Mimir (also known as Memory). In some versions, Henir is part of the group that created the world from Ymir's body. See also Aesir; Loki; Midgard; Mimir; Odin; Ymir.

Henkhisesui (Egypt)
Wind deity. God of the east wind, shown as a snake-headed man with four wings.

Henmemet (Egypt) Lesser deities.

Heno (Iroquois People, North America) *see* Adekagagwaa; Hino.

Hentiu (Egypt)

Spirits of the twelfth sector of Tuat, the Henitiu are forms of Osiris.

Hentiu and Antiu (Egypt) *see* Antiu; Hentiu.

Hepa (Egypt) *see* Ap-taui.

Hepat *Hebat, Hepit* (Hittite, Hurrian)

Also known as: *Hepatu, Wurusemu.*

Hepat, the Hurrian goddess of beauty, fertility, and royalty, is the wife of the Teshub, the weather god. She is possibly the mother of Sharruma (also known as Sharma). In later times, she merged with the Hittite sun goddess, Wurusemu. She is shown standing on a lion or a panther, well-dressed, wearing a crown, jewels and ornate shoes. She was driven from her temple by Ullikummis (q.v.). *See also* Arinna; Teshub.

Hepatu (Hittite) *see* Hepat.

Hephaestus (Greek) *see* Hephaistos.

Hephaistos *Hephaestus* (Greek)

Also known as: *Mulciber, Ptah* (Egypt), *Vulcan* (Roman).

Divine artisan. Patron of crafts. Lord of artificers. Hephaistos is the son of Zeus and Hera, or by Hera by autogenesis. His siblings are the god of strife, Ares, the nymph, Arge, the goddess of strife, Discordia, Eleithyia, and Hebe, the goddess of eternal youth. Hephaistos is thought to have married either the youngest of the Graces, Aglaea, or the goddess of love, Aphrodite. He fathered the half-serpent Erichthonius either alone or with Athenia, Gaea or Attis; the Argonaut Palaemon by Lernus' wife; and possibly the outlaw Periphetes by Anticleia. He is also the father of Olenus, who was later turned to stone, and Tullius, the sixth king of Rome, by Ocrisia, a Roman slave. With Aetna he fathered the twin male Palici volcanoes although some feel they were the sons of Zeus and Thalia. He was also the father of Cerycon, king of Eleusis. In one version of his life, he was abused, rejected, and thrown out of heaven as a newborn by Hera because of his deformed legs. He landed in the Oceanus where he was rescued and raised by the Oceanid Eurynome and Thetis of the silver feet. In another version, Zeus threw him from heaven because of his deformity and he landed on the island of Lemnos where he was raised by the Sintians. He became an artisan in metal and created many fine and useful items. Pandora, the first female known to man was his creation. He also enabled Athena to issue forth from the head of Zeus by splitting it open with his hammer. His hot metal pellets killed the giant Mimas, he forged Achilles' magic armor, Heracles' magic shield, weapons for Aeneas and possibly fastened Prometheus to a cliff by chains to fulfill a request for Zeus. Multi-faceted, he designed Harmonia's necklace which is fatal to all who wear it, and built many beautiful palaces for the gods of Olympia. Hephaistos was helped in his craft by the dwarfs Sileni and Satyrs, the Cyclopes who did the heavy work, and his personal assistant and some say his son, the dwarf, Cedalion. Despite his abusive beginnings and the fact that he was unable to use his legs in the usual way, he used his upper body and his mind to create and to contribute to others. Hephaistos is some-

times shown as a stunted, bearded man, holding a hammer. He is sometimes shown with a conical hat. He is identified with but not the same as the Roman Vulcan. *See* Ares for information about Ares' affair with Hephaistos' wife Aphrodite. Compare Hephaistos to the Vedic Tvastri, the Slavonic Dazbog, the Celtic Goibniu, and the Egyptian Ptah. *See also* Acamas (D); Achilles; Aeetes; Aegis; Aeneas; Aglaia; Anteros; Ariadne; Athena; Cedalion; Credne; Curetes; Eurynome; Gaea; Graces; Harmonia (A); Hera; Mimas; Orion; Pandora; Prometheus; Ptah; Rivers; Stymphalian Birds; Thetis; Vulcan.

Hepit (Hurrian) *see* Hepat.

Hept-Shet (Egypt) *see* Assessors.

Heptet (Egypt)

Deity of death. This goddess assisted in the resurrection of Osiris. She has the body of a woman with the head of a bearded snake. On her head she wears a pair of horns surmounted by a solar disk, the Atef crown, and uraei with disks and horns. In each hand she holds a knife. *See also* Osiris.

Heqet (Egypt) *see* Heket.

Heqt (Egypt) *see* Heket.

Heqtit (Egypt) *see* Heket.

Hequet (Egypt) *see* Heket.

Her-Ba (Egypt) *see* Aai.

Her-Hequi (Egypt)

High gods. One of four deities in the fifth sector of Tuat.

Her-Pest (Egypt)

A form of the god Horus as victor over the great "male hippopotamus," the symbol of the god Set (Seth). *See also* Horus.

Her-T (Egypt) *see* Anhur; Hathor.

Her-Tchema (Egypt) *see* Horus.

Her-tesu-f (Egypt) *see* Ab-esh-imy-duat.

Her-Thertu (Egypt) *see* Tcheser-tep-f.

Hera *Here* (Greek)

Also known as: *Antheia* (Flowering One), *Argeia* (Argive Hera), *Juno* (Roman), *Karphophoros, Kourotrophos.*

Sky goddess. Queen of heaven. Goddess of women. Goddess of childbirth. Goddess of marriage. Goddess of wild things. Hera is the daughter of Cronus and Rhea. Her siblings are Demeter, Hades, Hestia, Poseidon, and Zeus. Zeus disguised himself as a cuckoo and seduced his sister. She became a jealous, exacting spouse. Hera visited severe vengeance upon the numerous females with whom her philandering mate Zeus became enamored, as well as upon their offspring. She became the mother of Ares, Arge, Discordia, Ilythia, Hebe, and Hephaistos. Typhon might also be her son. Hera's nurse is Euboea, her favorite handmaiden is Iris. Her attendants are the Charites and Horae. During the Trojan War she was on the side of the Greeks and assisted the Argonauts on numerous occasions. The name Antheia is used for Hera in her form as an adolescent. As an earth mother, goddess of wild things and child-rearer, she was known as Karpophoros. Hera's sacred fruits are the apple and pomegranate. Her sacred birds are the cuckoo, goose, and peacock. Hera is shown as a regal matron wearing a crown. She is calm in appearance and her eyes are wide-opened. *See also* Ares; Charities; Cronus; Demeter; Hades; Hephaistos; Horea; Medea; Jason; Juno; Poseidon; Zeus.

Heracles (A) *Herakles* (Roman) *Hercules* (Latin); (Greek).

Also known as: *Alcides* (name given at birth), *Criophorus, Melkarth* (Carthage), *Melqart, Monoecus.*

Hero. Heracles, the son of Zeus and Alemene (Alcmene), or Zeus and Alkmena, became the greatest of Greek heros, despite the obstacles he had to overcome. Hera, jealous of his birth by Zeus and a mortal woman, took her hostilities out on Heracles. Renowned for his strength, he strangled two serpents, which Hera had sent to destroy him, while he was still in the cradle. Zeus wanted him to live in the world and gain knowledge of the human condition so that the gods would have a greater understanding of mortals. He was known as Herakles or Hercules by the Romans, and Melqart by the Carthaginians. Driven mad by Hera, he accidentally killed his own children and his wife, Megara, daughter of Creon. On recovering he was so stricken with grief that he exiled himself and went to consult the oracle of Apollo at Delphi. He was commanded to serve Eurystheus for twelve years. During that period he performed twelve labors. The gods assisted him in his tasks, and he carried them out successfully. 1. Slaying the Nemean lion with his own hands. He was called Alcides after wearing the pelt of this lion. 2. To destroy the nine, or as some say, seven-headed Lernaean hydra which had ravaged the country of Lernae near Argos. The middle head was immortal and for every head lopped off by Heracles, two grew in its place. With the assistance of Iolaus, he burned away the heads and buried the immortal head under a great rock. He shot it with poisoned arrows and the wounds became incurable. 3. To capture the Arcadian or Cerynean stag which had golden horns and brazen hoofs. 4. To capture the Erymanthian boar in a net and carry him to Mycenae. Along the way he fought with the Centaurs, killing many of them and wounding his old friend Chirion, who died. 5. To clean the Augean stables which held three thousand oxen belonging to King Augeas of Elis. They had not been cleaned for thirty years and Heracles had to clean them in one day if he wanted the reward of one-tenth of the cattle. He accomplished this by turning the rivers Alpheus and Penus through the stables. Augeas then refused him the reward, and at a later time Hercules killed him. 6. To kill the Stymphalian birds which belonged to Ares and which had brazen claws and beaks. They used their feathers as arrows and preyed upon humans. 7. To capture the wild bull of Crete which King Minos of Crete had begged as a sacrifice from Poseidon. 8. To capture the man-eating mares of Diomedes, who fed his horses with human flesh. 9. To obtain the girdle of Hippolyte, queen of the Amazons, by making war on the Amazons and slaying Hippolyte. 10. To capture the oxen of Geryon. While there he erected the mountains in Spain and Africa, known as the Pillars of Hercules. 11. To fetch the three Golden Apples from the Garden of the Hesperides by sending Atlas to get them while he held up the heavens. 12. To bring Cerberus, the three-headed dog of Hades, to the Upperworld. Heracles was also known for his eight deeds: 1. Beating Antaeus in a fight. 2. Rescuing Alces-

tis from the Underworld. 3. Traveling as an Argonaut. 4. Rescuing Hesione. 5. Acting as a servant to Omphale. 6. Stealing the sacred tripos of Delphi after Apollo refused him purification. 7. The sacking of Troy. 8. His twelve labors. After performing the twelve labors Heracles was free from service to Eurystheus and returned to Thebes. He married Deianira, daughter of Oeneus of Calydon. When Nessus, a centaur, tried to abduct her, Heracles shot him with a poisoned arrow. The dying Nessus told Deianira to keep his blood since it would always preserve her husbands's love. Later, fearing that she was being supplanted by Iole, Deianira sent Heracles a garment soaked in the blood of Nessus, which poisoned him. After his death he was taken to Olympus, given immortality, and married Hera's daughter, Hebe. He was honored after his death with the task of guarding the Gates of Olympia. Heracles was characterized by brains, brawn, gluttony, drunkenness and sexual prowess. Although he slew many mythical monsters, he also drained swamps, built roads, and served the people. His earthiness and humor made him appealing to the common person. The name Criophorus (one who carries a ram) was given to Heracles after he carried a ram around the town three times to save the people of Tanagra from the plague. Compare Heracles to Krishna (India) and Arjuna (India). *See also* Abderus; Acca Larentia; Admete; Admetus; Aegimius; Aeneas; Agrius (A); Alcyoneus; Alpheus; Amazons; Antaeus; Ares; Calydonia Boar Hunt; Enceladus; Eos; Eurydice (C); Giants; Harsaphne; Helius; Hephaistos; Hera; Hesione; Hesperides; Hylas; Jason; Medea; Nereus; Pelops; Sarpedon (B); Scylla; Stymphalian Birds; Zetes.

Heracles (B) (Greek)

He is a Dactyl, who is the son of the nymph Anchiale or Rhea, the mother of the gods.

Herakhty (Egypt) *see* Harakhtes.

Herakles (Greek) *see* Heracles.

Heraktes (Egypt) *see* Ra-Harakhte.

Herb-Quelling (Japan) *see* Kusanagi.

Hercules (Greek) *see* Heracles.

Herdesuf (Greek) *see* Horus.

Herecgunina (Algonquin, Chippewa, Cree, Nascopie People, North America)

The power of evil.

Herfadir (Teutonic) *see* Odin.

Herhkhty (Greek) *see* Horus.

Heri-Seru (Egypt) *see* Assessors.

Herishef (Egypt) *see* Arsaphes.

Herjan (Teutonic)

This name, meaning "God of Battles," is an alternate name for Odin.

Herkeios (Greek) Zeus as the protector of the home.

Hermakhis (Egypt)

This is a title used for Horus. It means "Horus on the Horizon."

Hermanubis (Greek)

Also known as: *Anubis, Heru-em-Anpu* (Greek).

Aspect of Anubis. This name is used for the god Anubis in connection with his role as conductor of the souls of the dead, a function he shared in common with the Greek god Hermes. He is shown as a jackal-headed man, the same as Anubis (q.v.).

Hermaphroditos (Greek) *see* Hermaphroditus.

Hermaphroditus *Hermaphroditos* (Greek)

Also known as: *Atlantiades, Atlantius.*

Minor deity. Born as Atlantiades, the son of Hermes and Aphrodite was renowned for his beauty. His father had numerous children by other women but had long desired the goddess Aphrodite. She wasn't remotely interested in him until the great god Zeus intervened. He had his eagle swoop down and steal one of her slippers while she was bathing in the Achelous river. The eagle was instructed to deliver it to Her-me's home in the Egyptian city of Amythaonia. In return for the slipper, Aphrodite would have to satisfy Hermes' longing for her. She did, and of this union Atlantiades was born. (In some myths, a man named Anaplades and not Hermes played this role.) When Atlantiades was fifteen, the nymph Salmacis began to pursue him. An innocent, he rebuffed her advances, which infuriated her. When she spied him bathing in a fountain he jumped in and clung tightly to him while she prayed to the gods that they be united forever. Her prayers were answered in an unusual way. Atlantiades and Salmacis became one person physically sharing male and female attributes and he/she became known as Hermaphroditus. In another version of this myth it is said that whoever bathed in the fountain would lust after a person of the same sex. Compare Hermaphroditus to Hylas. *See also* Aphrodite; Hermes.

Hermeias (Greek) *see* Hermes.

Hermes *Hermeias* (Greek)

Also known as: *Agoneus* (Greek), *Mercury* (Roman), *Mercurius* (Roman), *Turms* (Etruscan).

Messenger of the gods. Hermes is the versatile god of commerce, and patron of travelers, shepherds, traders, and robbers. Early Egyptologists thought of him as a god of knowledge, and the Egyptians called him Mercury, Sebku or Sebek. In his aspect of Agoneus he is the patron of gymnastic exercises. He is the son of Zeus and Maia, and brother of Apollo. He fathered Autolycus, Cephalus, Ceryx, Myrtilus, and possibly Pan. His various loves are Herse, Deianeira (Persephone) and Penelope. A talented god, he is the inventor of the lyre and the pipes of Pan (both musical instruments). Hermes exchanged the pipes of Pan for the golden rod Apollo used to herd cattle. This rod became the caduceus which was Hermes' emblem. Many of his exploits turn upon thievery or mischief. He wears a winged cap and has wings attached to his ankles, enabling him to travel from place to place with the speed of the wind. He was originally a god of stones, stoneheaps, and boundaries. He was first shown as a mature bearded athlete. Later, he was depicted as a younger athlete carrying a caduceus and wearing winged sandals and a winged helmet. As Mercury his sacred animals are the goat, cock and the tortoise. The Greek people identified Hermes with the Egyptian god Thoth. *See also* Abderus; Acacallis; Aegisthus; Aether; Agraulos; Amphion; Ares; Argus (B); Autolycus; Calypso; Evander (A); Evander (B); Fates; Harpies; Hermaphroditus; Ino; Mercury (B); Oenamaus; Orion; Pelops; Perseus; Sebek; Semele; Thoth; Typhon (A); Zetes.

Hermin (Teutonic) *see* Irmin.

Hermione (A) (Greek)

She is also known as Harmonia. *See also* Harmonia (A).

Hermione (B) (Greek)

She is the daughter of Menelaus and Helen of Troy. *See also* Helen.

Hermitten (Tupi-Guarani People, Brazil)

In one of the Creation Legends, Hermitten and his two brothers, Coem and Krimen, escaped the Deluge by hiding in caves, or by climbing trees. In the legend, Guaracy, the sun, is the creator of all animals. The other creator gods are Jacy the moon, who created plant life, and Peruda who was concerned with human reproduction. *See also* Tawendore.

Hermod *Hermodr* (Norse; Teutonic)

The son of Odin, Hermod is a wind and war god. He acts as a messenger between the deities. When Balder suddenly died, Hermod volunteered to ride Odin's horse, Sleipnir, into the realm of Hel to search for him. He was unsuccessful in bringing Balder back from Helheim. He did bring the ring Draupnir back with him to give to Odin. Hermod and Bragi welcome dead war heroes into Valhalla. *See also* Balder; Bragi; Draupnir; Frigg; Hel; Odin; Sleipnir; Valhalla.

Hermoder (Teutonic) *see* Aesir.

Hero (Greek)

Hero is one of the Aphrodite's priestesses. Leander fell in love with her. Every night he swam across the Hellespont to see her. One night he drowned. Stricken with grief, the beautiful Hero drowned herself. *See also* Rivers.

Herok'a (Algonkian, Chippewa, Cree, Nascopie People, North America)

They are earth spirits known as "Those without Horns."

Herovit *Jarovit* (Slavic) God of the army.

Herse (Greek) "The Dew"

Herse is the daughter of Cecrops or Acteus and Agraulos. Her relationship with the messenger of the gods, Hermes, produced Cephalus and Ceryx. *See also* Agraulos; Cephalus; Ceryx; Hermes.

Hershef (Egypt)

Also known as: *Arsaphes* (Greek), *Harsaphes* (Egypt).

Known as "Terrible Face," this ram-headed god, adopted by the Greeks and known as Arsaphes or Harsaphes, was worshiped at Heracleopolis Magna. *See also* Harsaphes.

Hert-ketit-s (Egypt)

Underworld deity.

A lion-headed goddess, she presides over the pit Hatet, in the eleventh sector of Tuat. She belches fire on the wretched creatures who are then hacked to pieces by a large knife which she holds in both hands.

Hert-Nemmat-Set (Egypt)
Underworld deity.
A woman fiend in the fourth pit of the eleventh sector of Tuat who punishes the shadows and heads of the damned.

Hert-sefu-s (Egypt)
Underworld deity.
A woman fiend in the fifth pit of the eleventh sector of Tuat who does the same as Hert-Nemmat-Set.

Hertha *Nertha* (Norse; Teutonic)
Also known as: *Aertha, Aerth.*
Mother of the gods. Goddess of agriculture. She is specially worshiped at Shrove-tide when ploughs are carried in procession. *See also* Bertha; Nerthus.

Hertyr (Teutonic) *see* Odin.

Heru (Egypt)
A Hawk God. Probably an aspect of Horus. *See also* Aai; Ashenu; Horus; Unas.

Heru-ap-sheta-taui (Egypt) *see* Jupiter.

Heru-em-akbet (Egypt) *see* Harmachis; Sphinx.

Heru-em-Anpu (Egypt) *see* Hermanubis.

Heru Khent an Maa (Egypt) *see* Horus.

Heru-Khu (Egypt)
Also known as: *Heru-Khuti.*
Sun deity. One of four deities in the fifth sector of Tuat. Replaced by Amen and Amen-Ra. *See also* Mars.

Heru Khutti (Egypt) *see* Horus.

Heru Murti (Egypt) *see* Horus.

Heru-P-Khart (Egypt) *see* Harpokrates.

Heru-pa-kaut (Egypt)
Great Mother. She is the mother and counterpart of her son Ba-neb-tettu, the creator god. She is depicted with a fish, the symbol of plenty and fecundity, on her head.

Heru-Pa-Khret (Egypt) *see* Harpokrates.

Heru Sam Taui (Egypt) *see* Horus.

Heru-tuati (Egypt) *see* Ab-ta.

Heru Ur (Egypt) *see* Horus.

Heruka (Buddhist; Tibet)
Heruka is one of the numerous deities that emanated from Akshobhya. Also called the Great Heruka, he represents compassion, and his sakti, Nairatma, personifies knowledge. The worship of Heruka is said to confer Buddhahood on the worshipper. His mate in Bardo is Buddha Krotishaurima (the Mighty Wrathful Mother). Heruka appears with her on the Eighth Day in Bardo. She is embracing him, her right hand is clinging to his neck and with her left hand she is putting a blood-filled red shell to his mouth. Heruka is dark brown, with three heads, six hands and four feet. His middle face is dark brown, the right one is white and the left, red. He has nine eyes and protruding teeth. His hair is reddish-yellow. He wears garlands of severed heads and skulls, a tiger skin and snake ornaments. *See also* Akshobhya; Herukas; Shakti; Vajrapani.

Herukabuddhas (Tibet) *see* Herukas.

Herukas *Herukabuddhas* (Buddhist, Lamaism; Tibet)
The Herukas have three heads and six arms and represent the wrathful form of masculine energy and are known as knowledge-holding deities. The Herukas and their saktis are the manifestations of the Dhyanibuddhas and their saktis. Some say that the energy of Heruka manifests the wrathful manifestation of the Herukas who also have a peaceful manifestation. The Herukas are Kamaheruka, who is green; Ratnaheruka, who is yellow; Padmaheruka, who is red; Vairocana, white or a reddish-brown hue; and Vajraheruka, who is blue. *See also* Dhyanibuddhas; Heruka; Ratnasambhava.

Herunub (Egypt) *see* Horus.

Herusmatauy *Ahy* (Egypt)
He is the son of Horus of Edfu and Hathor.

Hery-sha-duat (Egypt)
Underworld deity. He is in charge of the fields of Tuat. He has nine sekhtiu (field laborers) to do the work.

Heryan (Teutonic) *see* Odin.

Hes (Egypt) *see* Bast; Horus.

Hesahet (Egypt) *see* Hesat.

Hesaret (Egypt) *see* Hesat.

Hesat (Egypt)
Also known as: *Hesahet, Hesaret.*
Deified animal. This divine cow nurses the children of the deities. She is reputed to be the mother of the Mnevis bull.

Hesione (Greek)
Hesione is the daughter of Laomedon, the king of Ilium, and Strymo, the daughter of the river god Scamander. Hesione's siblings are Astioche, Cilla, Hicetaon, Clytius, Priam, Lampus, and Tithonus. The third wife of Telamon, the king of Salamis, she became the mother of Teucer. One of Heracles' eight deeds was to rescue Hesione from the belly of a whale, or a similar near death experience. Her father had reneged on a promise to Poseidon who had sent a sea monster to plunder the land. An oracle told him that to save the land, he would have to sacrifice his daughter. As the oracle was about to be fulfilled, Heracles came upon the scene. He promised to rescue Hesione if Laomedon would give him two beautiful horses that had been gifts from Zeus. He did so. Heracles rescued Hesione but Laomedon again reneged in paying his debts. Heracles left to gather six ships full of warriors and he returned to Ilium. In retaliation, he ravaged the city and killed all of Laomedon's sons except Priam. He also abducted the beautiful Hesione and gave her to his friend Telemon. This occurred long before the Trojan War. At a later time, Hesione's nephew Paris went to Greece on the pretext of bringing his aunt back to her homeland. He went off course to Sparta, fell in love with Helen, and triggered the events

which led to the Trojan War. Not to be confused with Hesione who was perhaps married to Nauplius, or Hesione (also known as Asia or Axiothea), the wife of Prometheus. *See also* Astioche; Heracles; Priam; Scamander; Telemon.

Hespere (Greek)

One of the Hesperides, she is the possible daughter of Atlas and Pleione. *See also* Atlas; Hesperides; Pleione.

Hespereia *Hespere* (Greek) *see* Hespere.

Hesperia (Greek) *see* Hesperides.

Hesperides (Greek)

Also known as: *Daughters of the Evening, Hesperia.*

Guardians. The Hesperides are the daughters of Nyx and Erebus or Phorcys and Ceto or Atlas and Hesperis or Zeus and Themis. The number of Hesperides varies from three to seven. Names attributed to the deities are Aegle, Hespere, Erytheis, Arethusa, Hesperusa and Hespereia. The Hesperides, who loved to sing, and the hundred-headed dragon or serpent, Ladon, were appointed to guard the trees which bore the Golden Apples. When Hera married Zeus the apples were a gift from Gaea, who personifies the earth. The treasured apples were stolen by Heracles or by Atlas on behalf of Heracles and the Ladon was slain by Heracles. The Hesperides transmuted themselves into trees and in this form were helpful in directing the Argonauts to a spring in the desert created by Heracles. Athena recovered the sacred fruit in Eurystheus and returned it to the garden. In another version of this myth, it is the Garden of Hesperides where the four daughters of Hesperos (Vesperus), who became the Evening Star, sing while watching the tree of Golden Apples which is guarded by Ladon. The Garden of Hesperides has been compared to the Garden of Eden. *See also* Atalanta; Calypso; Golden Bough; Golden Fleece.

Hesperis (Greek)

She is the daughter of Hesperos and spouse of Atlas. *See also* Atlas; Hesperides.

Hesperos (Greek) *see* Hesperides.

Hesperus (Greek) *see* Hesperides.

Hesperusa (Greek) *see* Hesperides.

Hest (Egypt) Another name for Isis.

Hestia *Histia* (Greek) Also known as: *Vesta* (Latin).

Goddess of fire. Guardian of home and hearth. Hestia is the daughter of Cronus and Rhea and sister of Zeus, Poseidon, Hera, Hades and Demeter. She vowed to remain a virgin even though she had marriage offers from her brother Poseidon and the god Apollo. It is said that Hestia remained aloof from the squabbles on Mount Olympus, and was the representative of the public hearth in the city as well as in private homes. Hestia was the first deity to build a house. She is personified by the life-giving hearth fire. In a purifying ritual used by her worshipers, a virgin walks around the farm holding a cock in her hands to ward off weeds and injurious insects. Her emblem is fire. Compare Hestia to the Japanese goddess of fire, Fuji, and Agni of India. *See also* Apollo; Cronus; Demeter; Hades; Hera; Poseidon; Rhea; Vesta (Roman).

Hesus (Gaul) *see* Esus.

Het-Hert (Egypt) An alternate spelling for Hathor (q.v.).

Hetch-Abehu (Egypt) *see* Assessors.

Hetchuti (Egypt) *see* Aai.

Hetemet-bau (Egypt) *see* Aaru.

Hetet-sept (Egypt) *see* Aani.

Hetmehit (Egypt) *see* Banebdedet.

Hettsui-no-kami (Japan) *see* Inari.

Heumac (Mexico) *see* Quetzalcoatl.

Heve (Babylonian) *see* Eve.

Heveidd Hen (Celtic) *see* Rhiannon.

Heviosso (Africa) *see* Xevioso.

Hey-Tau (Egypt) *see* Adonis.

Heybajra (Buddhist) *see* Lhamo.

Heyoka (Dakota People, North America)

A group of deities known as the Oppositres.

Hgnss (Teutonic) *see* Freyja.

Hiawatha (Mohawk People, North America) *see* Haio Hwa Tha.

Hiceton (Greek)

He is the son of Laomedon and Strymo. Hiceton advised the Trojans to return Helen of Troy to Menelaus so that a war would not develop. *See also* Helen; Laomedon; Menelaus; Strymo.

Hidimba (India) *see* Bhima (A).

Hidimbaa (India) *see* Bhima (A).

Hieromneme (Greek)

Her father is the river god, Simoeis, and her sister is Astyoche. *See also* Anchises; Astyoche; Simoeis.

Higona (San Cristobal) *see* Figonas.

Hiisi (Finnish)

In early times, Hiisi was a sacred grove and its spirit. Later Hiisi became a forest demon who became the devil. Hiisi and cohorts, Lempo and Paha, directed the axe which cut Vainamoinen. Lempo turned the blade, Paha directed the blow, and Hiisi pushed it through the veins. In another version, Hiisi is identical with Lempo, and he is a love deity. *See also* Kalevala; Vainamoinen.

Hika-po-loa (Hawaii)

In later times, this ancient god was worshiped as the three gods, Kane, Ku, and Lono (q.v.).

Hikawa-hime (Japan) *see* Kushi-nada-hime.

Hiko-hohodemi-no-mikoto (Japan) *see* Hikohohodemi.

Hikoboshi (Japan) *see* Kengiu.

Hikohohodemi *Hoho-demi, Hohodemi, Hiko-hohodemi-no-mikoto* (Shinto; Japan)

Also known as: *Hoori, Ho-wori.*

Hikohohodemi (Prince-Fire-Subside), is the great-grandson of the sun goddess Amaterasu. His parents are Ninigi (Prosperity Man) and Kono-Hana-Sakuya-Hime (Blossoms-of-the-Trees-Blooming-Princess). In early recordings of this myth, Hikohohodemi's two brothers are mentioned, Hoderi and Hosuseri (Prince-Fire-Flash), also known as Ho-no-Susori. Later writing refers to one brother, Hosuseri. Hikohohodemi became a hunter and Hosuseri took up fishing. They did well in their chosen fields but for some reason decided to switch occupations for a time. The experiment was not successful. Hosuseri returned the bow and arrows to his brother and asked him to return his fishing equipment. Hikohohodemi had lost Hosuseri's fishhook, so he substituted a different hook, made from three parts of his sword. Hosuseri refused the substitute, as his original hook had magical qualities that allowed him to reel in large quantities of fish. The brothers quarreled. Grief-stricken, Hikohohodemi, weeping at the seashore, was found by the god Shiho-tsuchi. He suggested that Hikohohodemi visit the bottom of the sea and implore the assistance of the great sea god O-Wata-Tsu-Mi in his search for his brother's hook. Hikohohodemi made the journey and fell in love with the god's daughter, Toyo-Tama-Bime (Abundant-Pearl-Princess) and forgot his quest for the missing hook. They married and he stayed in the luxurious palace of the sea god for three years. Remorse overcame him when he remembered the reason for his trip. O-Wata-Tsu-Mi called an assembly of all the fish in the sea. One fish sent word that she could not attend due to illness. Her name is the "Red Woman" in one tradition and in another "The Kuchime" (mouth-female). Messengers were sent to assist her to the meeting. The magic hook, caught in her throat, was causing her illness. O-Wata-Tsu-Mi gave his son-in-law the hook along with a set of instructions to follow when he returned the hook to his brother Hosuseri. He also gave him two jewels that controlled the tides, the Kangi (Tide Ebbing Jewel) and the Mangi (Tide Flowing Jewel). Hikohohodemi mounted the back of a monster shark for the trip to Japan to return the fishhook to his brother. Toyo-Tama-Bime and O-Wata-Tsu-Mi have been depicted in combination human and dragon form. For the continuation of his adventure from this point, *see* Hosuseri. For information about his relationship with his wife, *see* Toya-Tama-Bime. For details of the birth of Hikohohodemi and his brothers, *see* Ninigi. For details about the undersea palace and other sea deities, *see* O-wata-tsu-mi. *See also* Hoderi; Sengen.

Hikuleo (Tongan People, Polynesia)
Goddess of Pulotu (the underworld).

Hildisvini (Teutonic) *see* Ottar.

Hill of Healing (Teutonic) *see* Lyfjaberg.

Himavan (India) *see* Ganga.

Himavat (India) "Owner of Snow." *See also* Ganga; Parvati.

Himavati (India) *see* Kali.

Himeropa (Greek)
A siren. She is the daughter of Achelous and Calliope, Melpomene, Terpsichore or Sterope. *See also* Achelous; Calliope; Sirens.

Hina (A) (Oceanic)
Also known as: *Hina-Hau-One* (Earth-formed maiden), *Hina-Keha* (Bright Lady), *Hina-Titama* (Dawn-maiden), *Hina-uri, Hine, Hine-nui-te-po, Hine-Te-Ngaru-Moana* (Lady-of-the-Ocean-Waves), *Hooho, Ina, Sina.*

Goddess of Darkness. Goddess of death. Dawn-maiden. Patron of travelers. Patron of arts and crafts. Goddess of the Moon. Hina was created by the god Kane to be his wife. In that role her name is Hine-Hau-One. She is also known as "Hine-the-mitigator-of-many-things," indicating her multi-functional roles. Hina became the goddess of darkness when she discovered that her father had committed insist with her under the guise of being her husband. She is closely associated with the moon and as Goddess of the Moon in her full phases, she is known as Hina-keha. She is also known by this name as a goddess of childbirth. When she is in her fish form she is known as Hine-Te-Ngaru-Moana. For an additional myth, *see* Tangaroa. *See also* Hine-nui-te-po; Ku and Hina.

Hina (B) (Polynesia) *see* Hine.

Hina-arauriki (Oceanic)
She is the wife of Turi-a-faumea. *See also* Faumea.

Hina-famed-in-story (Hawaii)
Skilled as a practitioner of magic, she was the sister/wife of Tiki (q.v.).

Hina-opuhala-koa (Hawaii)
Goddess of coral and spiny creatures of the sea. She can appear as a woman or as a coral reef. *See also* Ku and Hina.

Hina-ula-ohia (Hawaii)
Goddess of the ohia-lehua forest. In her home on the northern side of Oahu, we find her as the mate of Ku-ka-ohia-laka, the god of canoe builders, and mother of the voyager, Ka-ulu. On Maui she is the spouse of the god of lightning, Kaha'i, and mother of the god of comets, Wahieloa, and grandmother of the goddess of the dance, Laka. In her shape as the sacred ohia tree, she protects and shelters Hi'i-lawe, the child of Kakea, and Kaholo and also the daughter of Po-kahi, Lau-ka-ieie. *See also* Hina (A); Laka.

Hindu — Creation Legend *see* Brahma; Kurma; Shiva.

Hine-ahu-one *Hine-Hau-One* ("Earth formed Maiden"), (New Zealand; Polynesia)
Also known as: *Hina, Hina-Titama* ("Dawn Maiden"), *Hine, Hine-nui-te-po.*

First mother. After Tane had tried many times to make his mother Papa become his wife and as many times she refused but sent him to other females, he finally found Hine-ahu-one. This goddess gave birth to Tikitohua who became the ancestor of birds. Then she conceived Tiki-kapakapa, the first human child of Tane. In some versions she is sister-wife of Maui or created by Tane. *See also* Hine-tu-a-maunga; Papa; Tane.

Hine-nui-te-po (Polynesia)
Also known as: *Hine, Hine-ahu-one, Hine-hau-one, Hine-i-tau-ira.*

Goddess of the night. Goddess of the underworld. She is the ruler of all ten levels of the afterworld, although some say she only rules the upper four. Her father is Tane. Tane created Hine or, as some say, Hine-i-tau-ira (the first woman), from sand and clay, then had intercourse with her. When she realized what he had done, she fled to the underworld in shame. There she became Hine-Nui-Te-Po, the "Goddess of Night." In another rendition, she was created by Tane in the same manner but she was called Hine-hau-one and they had a child named Hine-titama who was the dawn maiden. She is described in some tales as having red eyes, sharp teeth, the body of a man, hair like seaweed and a mouth like a barracuda. *See also* Hina; Miru; Rohe; Tane.

Hine-tu-a-maunga (New Zealand; Polynesia)

Possibly a goddess of water or reptiles. In his second attempt to have his mother Papa as his wife, she refused again and sent him to Hine-tu-a-maunga (the mountain maid) to take as a wife. She conceived but instead of a child she brought forth rusty water and reptiles. *See also* Hine-ahu-one; Hine-nui-te-po; Mumuhango; Papa; Rangahore; Tane.

Hi'iaka *Hi'iaka-i-ka-poli-o-Pele* (Hawaii)

Supreme patroness of the hula. Sister of the goddess of fire and the goddess of dance, Pele. All chants for hula ceremonies are named under Hi'iaka, even those dedicated to Ku and Hina, the ancestral couple. Hi'iaka is the dear friend of the dancer Hopoe. *See also* Ku and Hina; Laka; Pele.

Hinlil (Assyria, Babylonia) Goddess of crops and grain.

Hino *Heno, Hinu, Hinun* (Iroquois People, North America)

Also known as: *The Thunderer.*

Sky and thunder god. Hino is the husband of the Rainbow and guardian of the Heavens. He is beneficial to humans but doesn't like them invading his domain. Among his many assistants are Oshadagea, the Dew Eagle, and Keneu, the Golden Eagle. Some say his brother is the West Wind. Hino's opponent is a great serpent. *See also* Adekagagwaa.

Hi'ona (San Cristobal) *see* Figonas.

Hinu (Iroquois People, North America) *see* Adekagagwaa; Hino.

Hinu-ua (Polynesia) *see* Atea.

Hinun (Iroquois People, North America) *see* Hino.

Hiordis (Teutonic) *see* Hjordis.

Hippasus (A) (Greek)

He is the father of Actor, the Argonaut. *See also* Actor (C).

Hippasus (B) (Greek)

Leucippe, the daughter of Minyas, is his mother (q.v.).

Hippe (Greek)

Hippe is the daughter of Cheiron and the mother of Melanippe. *See also* Aeolus (A); Aeolus (B); Cheiron; Melanippe.

Hippocoon (A) (Greek)

King of Sparta. He is the son of Oebaulus, king of Sparta, and Gorgophone, the widow of Oebalus' brother, Perieres, or Bateia. When Hippocoon refused to purify Heracles after he killed Iphitus, Heracles killed Hippocoon and his twelve sons. *See also* Gorgophone.

Hippocoon (B) (Greek)

He was the companion of Aeneas when he travelled to Italy.

Hippocrene (Greek)

Hippocrene, a deified fountain dedicated to the Muses, is located at the foot of Mount Helicon. It began to flow when the ground was struck by the hoofs of the winged horse, Pegasus. *See also* Muses; Pegasus.

Hippodamas (Greek) *see* Calydonian Boar Hunt.

Hippodameis (Greek) *see* Anchises.

Hippodamia (A) *Hippodameia* (Greek)

She is the daughter of Adrestus, the King of Argo, or Butes and Amphithea. Her siblings are Aegialeia, Aegialeus, Argeia, Cyanippus and Deipyle. She is the spouse of Peirithous and mother of Polypoetes. At her wedding a violent fight erupted between the Lapiths and the Centaurs. *See also* Adrestus; Centaurs; Cyanippus; Peirithous; Polypoetes.

Hippodamia (B) (Greek)

She is the daughter of Oenomaus and Evarte (who is the daughter of Acrisius and Eurydice). Her brother is Leucippus, who was killed when he dressed as a girl in an attempt to become acquainted with Daphne. Hippodamia became the spouse of Pelops, the king of Lydia and Pisa in Elis. She is the mother of Alcathous, Astydameia, Atreus, Chrysippus, Copreus, Lysidice, Nicippe, Pittheus, Thyestes and Troezen. Hippodamia had many suitors. Her father decided to hold a chariot race and give the winner the prize of his daughter. Hippodamia had other plans. She bribed the charioteer Myrtilus to fix the race so the winner would be Pelops. Hippodamia killed herself after murdering Chrysippus, thought to be the son of Pelops by Axioche or Astyoche. In other renditions it is offered Chrysippus' his half-brothers Atreus and Thyestes were responsible for the murder. *See also* Atreus; Chrysippus; Eurydice (C); Oenamaus; Pelops.

Hippodamia (C)

She is the daughter of Anchises, the king of Dardania who after being struck by Zeus' thunderbolt limped for the rest of his life. She is the sister of Aeneas and Lyrus (his father is Anchises but his mother is Aphrodite). Hippodamia is the wife of the valiant Alcathous, the son of Aesyetes, who was killed by Idomeneus in the Trojan War.

Hippodamus (Greek)

His parents are Agenor, the son of Pleuron and Xanthippe, and Epicasta, the daughter of Calydon and Aeolia.

Hippolochus (A) (Greek)

He is the son of Bellerophon and Philonoe and the father of Glaucus. *See also* Bellerophon; Glaucus.

Hippolochus (B) (Greek)

Hippolyte (A) (Greek)

Queen of the Amazons. She is the daughter of the god of war, Ares, and Otrera the Amazon queen. Her siblings are Antiope (Melanippe) and Penthesileia. She could be the mother of Hippolytus. One of Heracles' labors (his ninth) was to retrieve Hippolyte's magic girdle. It had been given to her by Ares. It is thought that after losing it, Hippolyte either died of a broken heart, or was murdered by Heracles. *See also* Acastus; Admete; Amazons; Ares; Frejya (Norse); Hippolytus (A); Penthesileia.

Hippolyte (B) (Greek)

Hippolyte is the daughter of Creteus. Her siblings are Amythaon, Pheres, and Promachus. She could have been the wife of Acastus. Hippolyte was attracted to Pelus but he rejected her advances. The spurned women lied to Acastus and said that Peleus had attempted to seduce her (*see* Acastus for details). There is a possibility that Peleus murdered Acastus. *See also* Acastus; Admete; Ares; Amazons; Peleus; Promachus.

Hippolytus (A) (Greek)

Also known as: *Auriga* ("The Charioteer" constellation), *Virbius*.

Deified mortal. He is the son of Theseus and possibly the Amazon queen Hippolyte. Phaedra, the daughter of Minos, the king of Crete, married Theseus, the hero king of Athens. Married or not, Phaedra was attracted to and fell in love with Hippolytus. He rebuffed her advances. She went to her husband and claimed that Hippolytus had attempted to seduce her. Theseus believed his spouse. Hippolytus had to flee the husband's wrath. Poseidon's sea-calves interrupted his flight, turned over his chariot, and caused his demise. When he reached heaven he was supposed to become the constellation Auriga. Instead, through Artemis' efforts he became the deity Virbius. *See also* Acamas (A); Adonis; Giants; Hippolyte (A); Phaedra.

Hippolytus (B) (Greek)

He is the giant son of the earth personified, Gaea. His giant siblings are Agrius, Alcyoneus (who stole the sun Helios' cattle), Gration (killed by Heracles during the battle of the Giants and the gods), Mimas (killed in the same battle), Polybotes (buried by the sea god Poseidon), Porphyrion (the leader of the Giants, killed by Heracles in the battle) and Thoon (killed in the same battle as his brothers). Hermes, the messenger of the gods, wearing his hat of invisibility, killed Hippolytus in the same war of the Giants and the gods. *See also* Agrius; Alyconeus; Gaea; Giants; Helios; Hermes; Polybotes; Poseidon.

Hippomachus (Greek)

His father is the militant Trojan, Antimachus, and his siblings are Hippolochus and Peisander.

Hippomedon (Greek)

One of the Seven against Thebes. He is the father of Polydorus by Evanippe. *See also* Adrestus; Evanippe; Polydorus.

Hippomenes (Greek)

He is the son or possibly the father of Megareus and Iphinoe. Either Hippomenes or Melanion married Atalanta of Boeotia, the daughter of King Schoeneus.

Hippona (Greek)

Goddess of horses.

Hipponoos (A) (Greek) *Hipponous, Hipponus* (Greek)

Another name for Bellerophon (q.v.).

Hipponoos (B) (Greek) He is the son of Priam.

Hipponoos (C) (Greek)

He was the last Trojan killed by Achilles before Achilles died.

Hipponoos (D) (Greek)

Astynome is his wife and Capaneus and Periboea, his children.

Hipponus (Greek) *see* Hipponoos.

Hippopotamus *see* Her-Tchema; Horus.

Hippotades (Greek)

This is an epithet for Aeolus, the god of the winds (q.v.).

Hiranya-kasipu *Hiranya Kasyapu, Hiranyakashipu, Ravana* (Brahmanic, Hindu; India)

Hiranya-kasipu, "gold eye," is a giant king of the demon Daityas and chief of the Asuras. He held a boon of invulnerability granted to him by Brahma. He was the brother of Hiranyaksha, the demon who drowned the earth. According to some, Hiranya-kasipu set himself up as the sole object of worship, in place of the gods, but his son Prahlada remained a fervent supporter of Vishnu, and all his father's attempts to do away with him were in vain. In disbelief at Prahlada's claim that Vishnu was omnipresent, Hiranya-kasipu kicked a pillar with his foot. When the pillar fell, Nara-Simha, the lion-headed human who was the fourth avatar of the god, appeared and tore him to pieces. Hiranya-kasipu's mate is Mahallika, who according to some sources is the daughter of Prahlada. His demonserpent son, Hrada, who practiced austerities, was known for stealing people's sacrifices from the gods. Vishnu was sent by the gods to lure him and his cohort demon friends away from the light of the Veda to the darkness of ignorance. *See also* Asuras; Brahma; Daityas; Diti; Hiranyaksa; Kalanemi; Mandodari; Nara-Simha; Prahlada; Ravana; Vamana; Vishnu.

Hiranyagarbha *Brahma, Narayana* (Vedic, Brahmanic; India)

He is the creator god of the heavens, earth, all that lives, and all the waters, including Rasa, the mythological river that encircles the earth and the atmosphere. His name literally means "Golden Germ." In one legend, he is the golden egg produced by the primal waters. From this egg the creator god Prajapati was born. In other legends Hiranyagarbha is formed in the first egg, and becomes the first male, Brahma (q.v.). *See also* Brahma; Pani (B); Prajapati.

Hiranyakashipu (India) *see* Hiranya-kasipu.

Hiranyaksa *Hiranyakasipu, Hiranyaksha* (Brahmanic, Hindu; India)

A Daitya. A giant demon who was helped by Brahma's strength and a protecting boon until he became ruler of the universe by toppling Indra from his throne, driving the gods from the heavens, and drowning the earth. Hiranyaksa, who was Ravana's first incarnation, was vulnerable only to the boar. In time, he was destroyed by the boar Varaha, Vishnu's avatar. *See also* Daityas; Diti; Hiranya-Kasipu; Ravana; Varaha.

Hiranyaksha (India) *see* Hiranyaksa.

Hiranyapura (India)

The city of the Daityas, Hiranyapura is sometimes located beneath the ocean. Other times, it breaks free and moves under the earth or sails through the air. *See also* Daityas.

Hiribi (Mesopotamia) *see* Hiribi.

Hirihbi (Mesopotamia; Syria, Ugarit)
He is referred to as a god of summer in some myths and a Sumerian king in other myths. *See also* Nikkal; Yarikh.

Hirnakess (India) A giant. *See also* Varaha.

Hiro (Polynesia, Tahiti)
Afterworld deity. In charge of the underworld of the Areoi priests. Similar to Urutaetae.

Hirugo (Japan) *see* Hiruko.

Hiruko *Hirugo* (Shinto as Hiruko, Buddhist as Ebisu; Japan)
Also known as: *Ebisu.*
Solar deity and god of the health of children. The background of Hiruko (meaning child leech) is debatable. In some traditions, he is the oldest child of Izanagi and Izanami and was born in the shape of a jellyfish. This would make him the first god (kami) born through intercourse. He would also be the brother of the great sun goddess Amaterasu, the moon ruler Tsuki-Yomi, and the storm god Susanawo. At birth, his parents were displeased with his form, so they placed him in a raft and let him drift away. His raft beached at Ebisu Shore, thus he became known as Ebisu. He was deaf and unable to hear the summons for the other deities to assemble and was the only deity not in attendance. Other scholars feel that Hiruko was a sun god who was ignored for political reasons by the followers of Amaterasu. In this capacity, he is the grandson of Amaterasu and the brother of Ninigi. In later interpretations as Ebisu, he was known as a god of fishermen. His father was Daikoku, the god of labor. Both became deities of the Shichi Fukujin (seven Japanese deities of happiness). *See also* Ebisu; Izanagi and Izanami; Ninigi; Shichi Fukujin; Tsuki-Yomi.

Hisa-me (Japan) *see* Shiko Me; Yomi.

Hisakitaimisi (Cree People, North America)
The Controller of Life.

Hischen (Maya People, Yucatan) *see* Chibirias; Icona.

Hiscilla (Greek)
She is the daughter of Myrmidon, the wife of Triopas and the mother of Erysichthon, Iphimedeia, Messene and Phorbas. *See also* Iphimedeia (A); Triopas.

Histia (Greek) *see* Hestia.

Hitchi (Hitchiti People, North America)
Deified plant. The first tobacco plant.

Hiuke (Norse; Teutonic)
Also known as: *Yuke.*
A moon god. Waxing moon. Hiuke, the waxing moon and Bil, the waning moon, always accompany Mani, the moon, on his rounds. *See also* Mani.

Hiyoyoa (New Guinea)
Land of the dead. Said to be ruled by Tumudurere and his wives and children.

hJamdpal (Tibet) *see* Manjusri.

hJig-rTen-Gsum-Rgyal (Tibet) *see* Trailokyavijaya.

Hjordis *Hiordis* (Teutonic)
In some myths, she is the second wife of Sigmund, the son of Volsung. He disposed of his first wife, Borghild, for killing his first son, Sinfiotli. Hjordis is a young princess daughter of Englimi, the King of the Islands. One of her suitors was king Lygni of the Hundling race. When she agreed to marry old Sigmund, Lygni declared war on Sigmund. Sigmund fought well but Odin interfered and shattered the sword Sigmund had pulled from the tree trunk. The defenseless Sigmund was wounded to the death by his enemies. Hjordis hid from Lygni, who wanted to claim her, and tried to save Sigmund. Sigmund knew it was Odin who indirectly killed him and all he wanted was for Hjordis to gather up the shattered sword and save the fragments. Hjordis and her maid were saved by Alf. Some say she became the wife of Alf and later bore a son, Sigurd. *See also* Alf; Borghild; Sigi; Sigmund; Sigurd.

Hkum Yeng (Burma)
A nat (spirit) who guards the villages of the Wa of Burma. He was propitiated by human heads from head-hunting excursions. *See also* Nats.

Hlamo *Hlamos* (Tibet) *see* Ganda; Shakti; Tara (B).

Hler (Teutonic) Underworld deity. *See also* Oegir; Ymir.

Hlidskialf (Teutonic) *see* Hlidskjalf.

Hlidskjalf *Hlidskialf, Hlithkjalf, Lidskialf, Lidskjalf* (Teutonic)
This is the throne where Odin sits when he surveys the world. *See also* Gladsheim; Odin; Sovabek; Valaskjalf.

Hlin *Hlina* (Teutonic)
The tears of mourners are kissed away by Hlin, the goddess of consolation. Hlin is also the second attendant of Frigga. *See also* Frigga; Fulla.

Hlithkjalf (Teutonic) *see* Hlidskjalf.

Hlodr (Teutonic) *see* Lodur; Loki.

Hlodyn (Teutonic)
This giant woman is sometimes known as the mother of Thor (q.v.). She is also known as Jord.

Hlooyn (Teutonic) *see* Jord.

Hlora (Teutonic) *see* Thor.

Hloride (Teutonic) *see* Thor.

Hloridi (Teutonic) *see* Thor.

Hlorrida (Teutonic) *see* Thor

Hlorridi (Teutonic) *see* Thor.

Hmin Nat (Burma)
This is a demon who causes intermittent fevers in travelers. The Hmin Nat also drives mortals insane. *See also* Hkum Yeng; Nats.

Hngss (Teutonic) *see* Freyja; Hnossa.

Hnikar (Teutonic) *see* Odin.

Hnitbjorg (Norse; Teutonic)
This is the mountain home of the giant Sattung where he hid the mead of poetry made from Kvasir's blood. He is associated with Fjlar and Galar. *See also* Sattung.

Hnos (Teutonic) *see* Hnossa.

Hnoss (Teutonic) *see* Hnossa.

Hnossa *Hngss Hnos, Hnoss,* (Teutonic) *see* Aesir; Freyja.

Ho-deri (Japan) *see* Hoderi.

Ho-hsien-ku *Ho-sien-ku* (China)
Also known as: *Damsel Ho, Kasenko* (Japan)
She is the only female in the group known as the Eight Immortals. Ho-hsien-ku went to heaven during daylight hours. A mortal damsel known in Taoist belief as Ho was said to have gone to heaven during daylight hours. One of the Eight Immortals, the god of barbers, Lu Tung-pin gave Ho-hsien-ku the peach of immortality. As Kasenko, she feeds on mother of pearls. Ho-hsien-ku is shown as an elaborately dressed woman with a lotus on her shoulder. Sometimes she is depicted as a girl wearing a lotus flower on her shoulder or with a Chinese lute. She is generally shown with Han Hsiang-tzu. *See also* Arhats; Eight Immortals; Lu Tung-pin.

Ho-masubi (Japan) *see* Kagu-tsuchi.

Ho-no-suri (Japan) *see* Hosuseri.

Ho-no-susori (Japan) *see* Hikohohodemi; Hoderi.

Ho Po (China)
Also known as: *Nine Songs.*
One of the nine heroes. God of the Yellow River. *See also* Nine Songs.

Ho Shen (China) God of Fire. *See also* Tsao Shen.

Ho-sien-ku (China) *see* Ho-hsien-ku.

Ho-suseri (Japan) *see* Hosuseri.

Ho-wori (Japan) *see* Hikohohodemi.

Hoa (Chaldean) *see* Aa; Aos; Ea.

Hoakils (Tierra del Fuego)
Hoakils is a spirit who grants power to the Yakamouch (shaman). *See also* Yakamouch.

Hoard Thoughts (Japan)
The universe was in darkness until Hoard Thoughts came up with a successful plan to woo the sun goddess, Amaterasu, from her cave. *See also* Amaterasu.

Hobal (Arabic, Indo-Persian) *see* Abel; Hab'al.

Hobnel (Maya People, Yucatan) *see* Hobnil.

Hobnil *Hobnel* (Maya People, Yucatan)
This food god and god of plenty, is one of a triad with Chac Mol and Ah-Kluic. *See also* Chac Mol.

Hocereu Wahira (Algonquin, Chippewa, Cree, Nascopi People, North America).
Disease-Bringer.

Hod (Teutonic) *see* Hodur; Odin.

Hod-Dpag-Med (Tibet) *see* Amida; Amitabha.

Hodar (Teutonic) *see* Hodur.

Hodd-Dropnir (Teutonic) *see* Mimir.

Hodd-Mimer (Teutonic) *see* Mimir.

Hoddmimir's Wood (Teutonic) *see* Yggdrasil.

Hoddrofnir (Teutonic) *see* Mimir.

Hoder (Teutonic) *see* Hodur.

Hoderi *Ho-deri* (Shinto; Japan)
Also known as: *Ho-no-susori.*
Hoderi is the son of Kono-Hana-Sakuya-Hime (Blossoms-of-the-Trees-Blooming-Princess) and Ninigi (Prosperity Man). His brothers are Hikohohodemi (Prince-Fire-Subside) and Hosuseri (Prince-Fire-Flash). In some early renditions the three brothers are referred to as triplets. In later myths, Hoderi was not included as one of Kono-Hana-Sakuya-Hime's sons. When the tales involve Hosuseri and Hikohohodemi they are called twins. Sometimes, Hosuseri is called the elder son. For details surrounding his birth, *see* Ninigi. In the Ninigi version, the three children are born at the same time. *See also* Hikohohodemi; Hosueri; Sengen.

Hodir (Teutonic) *see* Hodur.

Hodr (Teutonic) *see* Hodur.

Hodsrun (Tibet) *see* Kasyapa (B).

Hodur *Hod, Hodar, Hoder, Hodhr, Hodir, Hodr, Hotherus.* (Norse; Teutonic)
Also known as: *Bjorno-hoder.*
God of darkness. God of winter. The blind god of darkness and winter, Hodur accidentally killed Balder with an arrow made of mistletoe. The accident was instigated by the trickster Loki. In turn, in an act of revenge, Hodur was killed by Vali. (With innocent, pure Balder alive, evil could not prevail.) Hodur is one of the 13 major deities in the mythology of the "Eddas." The other deities are Odin, Thor, Njord, Freyja, Balder, Tyr, Heimdal, Bragi, Forseti, Vidar, Vali and Ull. Hodur will return at Ragnarok, the destruction of the universe. *See also* Balder; Boe; Ragnarok; Vali (A).

Hoener (Teutonic) *see* Henir; Loki.

Hoenir (Teutonic) *see* Henir.

Hofud (Teutonic)
This sword, used by Heimdall, is one of the treasures of the Aesir. *See also* Aesir; Heimdall.

Hofvarpir (Teutonic) *see* Gna.

Hofvarpnir (Teutonic) *see* Gna.

Hogni (Teutonic) *see* Sigrun.

Hoho-Demi (Japan) *see* Hikohohodemi.

Hohodemi (Japan) *see* Hikohohodemi.

Hoita (Mandan Indians, North America)
Spirit. Name for Spotted Eagle.

Hokewingla (Dakota Indian) The Turtle-man in the moon.

Holda *Holla, Hulda, Hulle* (Norse; Teutonic)
Also known as: *Frau Holle, Frau Venus.*

Goddess of weather. Probably the same as Frigga. In this case Holda is the dispenser of gifts and controllor of weather. She gave flax to mortals and taught them how to use it. This goddess lived in a cave and was then known as Frau Venus. She is ugly and long toothed, with long, shaggy hair. In her role as an evil deity, she is opposed by Bertha (q.v.). *See also* Frigga.

Holdja (Estonia) *see* Domovoi.

Holla (Teutonic) *see* Holda.

Holle (Teutonic) *see* Holda.

Holler (Teutonic) *see* Ull.

Homa *Haoma* (India)
A sacred drink similar to Soma, thought by some to be a dark beer or a port wine. *See also* Haoma; Soma.

Hometeuli (Mexico)
Creator. Known as the "First Cause," he created the universe. His residence is called Homeyoco (also known as Home-iocan) and is the place of the Trinity whose word created Cipatonal and Xumio, gods who lived before the deluge. *See also* Ciptonal.

Homosubi (Japan) *see* Kagu-tsuchi.

Homshuk (Maya) *see* Chalucas.

Homunculus (Greek)
Spirit. A tiny man, with miraculous power, he was manufactured rather than born. *See also* Dwarfs.

Homusubi (Japan) *see* Kagutsuchi.

Hone (Teutonic) *see* Henir.

Honga (Osage People, North America)
The Honga are earth people who live below the ground.

Honir (Teutonic) *see* Henir.

Honochenokeh (Iroquois People, North America)
Spirits of goodwill. Invisible Helpers.

Hoodmimir's Wood (Teutonic) *see* Ragnarok.

Hoof-Tosser (Teutonic) *see* Gna.

Hooho (South Sea Islands) *see* Hina.

Hoori (Japan) *see* Hikohohodemi.

Hopleus (Greek)
He is the son of Poseidon and Canace. For the names of siblings, *see* Canace.

Hor (Greek) *see* Horus.

Hor Bebdetite (Egypt) *see* Behdety; Horus.

Hor Behdetite (Egypt) *see* Behdety.

Hor Merti (Egypt) *see* Haroeris.

Hor-Nubti (Egypt) *see* Horus.

Hor-Sa-Iset (Egypt) *see* Harsiesis.

Hora-Galles *Tora-Galles* (Lapp) Thunder god.

Horae *Horai* (Greek)
Also known as: *Carpo, Dike, Eirene, Eunomia, Karpo, Thallo.*
Goddess of the seasons. These three sisters, Dike (justice), Eirene (peace) and Eunomia (lawfulness), are the daughters of Zeus and Themis. Their siblings are Astraea, the goddess of justice (also known as Dike), and the deities of destiny, the Moirai. As well as supervising the Olympic Games, the Horae guard the entrance to heaven and to Olympus. They are also Hera's attendants. *See also* Aristaeus; Hera, Moirai.

Horaematawy (Egypt) *see* Horus.

Horaios (Gnostic)
One of the seven ruling spirits created by the god Ophiomorphus, the serpent son of Ialdabaoth. They are called the Archons. *See also* Archons.

Horakhti (Egypt) *see* Horus.

Horakhty (Egypt) *see* Horus.

Horchia (Chaldea) *see* Aretia.

Horea (Egypt) She is the wife of Seth.

Horkhenti Irti (Egypt) *see* Haroeris.

Hormazu (Zoroastrian; Persia)
One of the alternative names for Ahura Mazda.

Hormerti (Egypt) *see* Horus.

Hormothoe (Greek) *see* Harmothoe.

Hormusda (Mongol) *see* Asuras (India).

Horn (Teutonic) *see* Aesir; Freyja.

Horn of Victory (India) *see* Shankha.

Hornbori (Teutonic) *see* Dwarfs.

Horomazes (Greek) *see* Ahura Mazda.

Horos (Greek) *see* Horus.

Horse-Face (China) *see* Ma-Mien; Nui-Y'ou.

Horseface (China) *see* Ma-Mien.

Horses of the Aesir (Teutonic) *see* Animals.

Horta (Etruscan) She is a goddess of agriculture.

Horus *Haroeris* (Greek), *Horos* (Egypt, Greek)
Also known as: *Aroueris, Aten, Har, Harocrates, Harpokrates* (Son of Horus), *Herdesuf, Herhkhty, Hermakhis* ("Horus on the Horizon"), *Heru Khent an Maa, Heru Khuti, Heru Murti, Herunub, Heru Sam Taui, Heru Ur, Hor, Horakhti, Hyperion* (Greek).
"Harpooner." A solar and sky-god. He is also a falcon god who protects the earth with his wings. Called Hor by the Egyptians and Horos by the Greeks, but known by the Latin form of his name, Horus is the son or sometimes the brother of Osiris and Isis. Isis, in the form of a hawk, is said to have conceived Horus as she fluttered above her husband's corpse in the swamps. He was called Harpokrates as a youth. Worshiped in different ways and places, he is always represented as a falcon or falcon-headed. Horus is one of the principle Egyptian deities.

The living king is always regarded as Horus incarnate. Horus is known by various other names. Her-tchema as a hippopotamus, Horaematawy, Horakhty, Hormerti, Hor-Nubti, Heru, Horus-Aah, Horus-Behdety, Horus Khenty En Maatyu, Heru-Pa-Khret, Har-End-Yotef, Har-Pa-Neb-Taui (the blind Horus) and many others. The cult of Horus originated either at Behdet or Nekhen. Behdet was located in the Western Delta near Imarut. In Behdet, Horus was presented as a war-like god with the head of a hawk (or falcon) who carried bows and arrows and was known as Horus of Behdet. In predynastic Nekhen, on the west bank of the Nile, the chief god was Nekheny ("the Nekhenite"), a falcon who wears two long plumes on his head. He later assimilated with Horus, who became Horus Nekhenite. Horus is the father of Imsety who was given androgynous features and was represented in the Middle Kingdom as a beardless man with the yellow skin color of a woman. Khenty-Khet, the crocodile god at Athribis, assumed the form and nature of Horus. Horus waged war against the murderers of his father (the forces of darkness). His uncle Seth, one of the villains, in the form of a black pig, injured Horus' eye. The "Eye of Horus" fought the enemies of light and was seen as fire. One of Horus' eyes is seen as the sun and the other as the moon. In another myth, Horus battles the hippopotamuses and crocodiles of Seth in defense of the sun god Ra. Seth rips out the eye of Horus. He retalitates by yanking off Seth's testicles, forcing him to return his eye. After the Fifth Dynasty, Horus was overtaken by the sun-god Ra. The falcon Horus is the emblem of royal authority. As a young man, Horus is shown with a side-lock of hair and his finger to his mouth. The spear of Horus is a weapon blessed by the goddess Neith and used by royalty. Replicas of the spear were often placed with the dead as protection en route to the next world. Horus is associated with Apollo. Compare Horus to the Vedic deities, Indra and Vishnu. *See also* Aamu; Ab-ta; Amen; Ament; Aten; Atum; Banebdedt; Bast; Bes; Hapy (A); Harakhtes; Harendotes; Harpokrates; Harsaphe; Harsiesis; Hartomes; Hathor; Her-Pest; Hera; Isis; Khenty-Khet; Min; Neith; Osiris; Qebhsneuf; Ra; Set; Sopdu; Thoth.

Horus-Aah (Egypt) *see* Horus.

Horus-Behdety (Egypt) *see* Horus.

Horus Khenty En Maatyu (Egypt) *see* Horus.

Horus-Pa-Kret (Egypt) *see* Horus.

Hoshang and Takhmoruw (Iranian, Persian)
    Also known as: *Haoshyangha and Tahmouras, Husheng and Tamuras, Husheng and Tamurath.*
    Hoshang is the grandson of Mashya and Mashyoi, the son of Siyamek and the father of Takhmoruw. Siyamek was killed by an evil Div (demon). Determined to avenge his father's death, Hoshang slayed two-thirds of the world's demons and proceeded to establish a peaceable kingdom. The art of blacksmithing is attributed to Hoshang. He also invented the axe, saw and hoe. He discovered a method to distribute water to fertilize the fields. He domesticated animals and made clothing from the hides of wild animals. His son, Takhmoruw, succeeded him after his death. (In the Avestic tradition, Takhmoruw, called Takhma Urupi, is not the son of Hoshang, but is his successor. In earlier texts, Takhmoruw is known as the son of Vivangh-

vant and a brother of Yima.) He taught his people to weave and spin. He cast a spell on the evil Ahriman, changed him into a horse and rode him around the world, some say for thirty years. While he was on tour, the evil Divs revolted. Takhmoruw returned with a massive club, and with the assistance of the good Divs, engaged in a short but dramatic battle. Takhmoruw tied up two-thirds of his enemies by magical means, hit the rest of them over the head with his club and tied them together. They begged for their lives and in return promised the king that they would teach him a beneficial art. He relented in order to learn their secret. They in turn taught him how to write and he became a learned man. Takhmoruw is also known as the "jailer of demons" (div-band). In other legends, Hoshang is known as the grandson of Gaya Maretan (q.v.). *See also* Ahriman; Daevas; Mashya; Yima (also known as a first king).

Hosho-Nyorai (Japan)
    The Buddha of goodness and beauty, he is also known as Ratnasambhava (q.v.).

Hosuseri *Ho-no-suri, Ho-suseri* (Shinto; Japan)
    Also known as: *Ho-deri.*
    Fisherman. Hosuseri (Prince-Fire-Flash) is the great grandson of the sun goddess Amaterasu. His parents are Ninigi (Prosperity Man) and Kono-Hana-Sakuya-Hime (Blossoms-of-the-Trees-Blooming-Princess). His brothers in early records are Hoderi and Hikohohodemi (Prince-Fire-Subside). Later myths generally do not mention Hoderi. Hosuseri was a famed fisherman and Hikohohodemi was a hunter. They decided to exchange occupations for a time. The experiment did not work to their advantage. Hosuseri returned his brother's bow and arrows. Hikohohodemi had lost his brother's magic fishhook. He broke his sword into three pieces and fashioned imitations. They were not acceptable to Hosuseri, for his magic fishhook had allowed him to catch large quantities of fish. The brothers quarreled, and Hikohohodemi was remorseful. A series of events led him on a lengthy undersea quest for the fishhook. Three years later, with the assistance of the sea god O-Wata-Tsu-Mi, the hook was retrieved. Hikohohodemi returned to the upperworld (Japan) to return it to his brother. The sea god had given Hikohohodemi two jewels that controlled the tides, known as the Kangi (Tide-Ebbing-Jewel) and Mangi (Tide-Flowing-Jewel). O-Wata-Tsu-Mi had advised Hikohohodemi that if his brother became angry and tried to attack him, to use the Mangi to swell the waters and drown him. He cautioned that if Hosuseri repented, he should use the Kangi to repeal the tide. Hosuseri was not satisfied. His rice fields had failed because his brother kept them flooded with the Mangi and Hikohohodemi's fields had prospered. Jealous, he continued to badger his brother. Finally, to cease the strife, Hikohohodemi utilized the Mangi and caused the waters to cover his brother completely. When Hosuseri promised to pay homage to his brother, Hikohohodemi used the Kangi to allow the tide to ebb and gave his brother his freedom. Kangi and Mangi symbolize divine authority and life force. For details about his inauspicious birth, *see* Ninigi. For details about the retrieval of the magic fishhook, *see* Hikohohodemi. *See also* Amaterasu; Hoderi; O-Wata-Tsu-Mi; Sengen; Toyo-Tama-Bime.

Hotar (India) "The Invoker." *See also* Agni.

Hotei *Hotei-Osho* (Buddhist; Japan)

Also known as: *Pusa.*

Hotei is one of the Shichi Fukujin (seven deities of happiness). A fat god of laughter and happiness, he often carries a bag of treasures which he bestows on those who never worry about troubles. He is of Chinese origin. Pusa is a common European appellation for Hotei. Hotei is usually shown with a large naked stomach, bald headed and with large ear lobes (symbol of omniscience). He holds a hand-screen and a large sack, and is often in the company of children. To the Zen believers, Hotei is depicted as a happy wandering monk who represents the carefree life of one who has found peace through the study of Zen. Comparable to Miroku-Bosatsu, the Japanese future Buddha, Pou-tai, the Chinese god of contentment, Mi-Lo Fu, the Chinese future Buddha, and Maitreya, the Sanskrit fourth or coming Buddha. *See also* Shichi Fukujin.

Hotei-Osho (Japan) *see* Hotei.

Hoth (Teutonic) *see* Loki.

Hothbrod (Teutonic) *see* Miming.

Hotherus (Teutonic) *see* Hodur.

Hotoru *Hoturu* (Pawnee People, North America)

Deified bird. Spotted Eagle Spirit. Sometimes, he is called a god of winds.

Hotu-papa (Polynesia) This is another name for Papa (q.v.).

Hotua Poro (Samoan) *see* Incubus (Medieval Europe).

Hou-Chi *Hou Ji, Hou-Tse* (China)

Also known as: *Prince Millet.*

Harvest deity. A hero of royal birth, Hou-Chi taught the Chinese people the principles of farming and became one of the immortals. Hou-Chi is considered to be the founder of the dynasty of Chou, which began in about the twelfth century B.C.E., the time of the beginning of the large feudal estates. He was believed to have been a miraculously born descendant of Huang Ti. Generally this deity was worshiped by peasants. Some say Celestial Prince Liu replaced Hou-tsi who was then either a god of soil or crops. He is depicted as an old man with millet stalks growing from his head. Hou-Chi was usurped by Liu (Celestial Prince Liu). *See also* Shen Nung (who resembles Hou-Chi).

Hou Ji (China) *see* Hou-Chi.

Hou-T'u

Also known as: *Hou-T'u nai nai* (China).

God of the soil. Earth mother. Her name was Hou-t'u nai nai before she was transformed into a goddess. Hou-T'u is probably the same as T'u-ti Shen (q.v.).

Hou-T'u Shen (China) *see* T'u-Ti Shen.

Hound of Culann (Celtic) *see* Cuchulain.

Hounds of Zeus (Greek) *see* Harpies.

Houris *Houri* (Islamic; India.)

Also known as: *Hurani* (Persia), *Huriyeh* (Arabic).

Heavenly maidens similar to the Apsaras. They welcome slain heroes back from battle as do the Valkyries of the Norse.

The Houris resemble white clouds. Compare them to the Valkyries and Apsaras.

Hours (Greek) *see* Horae.

How-Chu (China) God of the Air.

hPhags-skyes-po (Tibet) *see* Virudhaka.

hPhren-ba-ma (Tibet) *see* Mala.

Hra-f-ha-f (Egypt) *see* Assessors.

Hrada (India) *see* Hiranya-kasipu.

Hraesveglur (Teutonic)

He is a giant known as the Guardian of the Gates.

Hraesvelgr *Hrae-Svelger, Hraesvelg, Hraesvelgur* (Teutonic; Norse)

Also known as: *Jonakr* (possibly).

Winter god. Dressed in eagle plumes, Hraesvelgr the corpse-swallower directs the icy winds of Vasud to cause discomfort for mortals. He is possibly the same as Jonakr (q.v.). *See also* Vasud.

Hrafna (Teutonic) *see* Odin.

Hreidmar (Teutonic)

Also known as: *Hreithmarr, Reidmar.*

Magician. Hreidmar, also called King of the Dwarf Folk, is the peasant father of Ottar, who had been changed into an otter, Fafnir, Regin and three daughters. He is associated with Odin. *See also* Andarvi; Ottar; Regin.

Hreithmarr (Teutonic) *see* Reidmar.

Hreshtak (Armenian) Angels. *See also* Aramazd.

Hrid (Teutonic) *see* Elivagar.

Hrim-Faxi *Hrimfaxe* (Teutonic) *see* Aarvak; Alsvid; Dagr; Norns.

Hrim-Thurs *Hrimthursar* (Teutonic) *see* Bergelmir; Ymir.

Hrimfaxe (Teutonic) *see* Hrim-Faxi.

Hrimthursar (Teutonic) *see* Hrim-Thurs.

Hringhorn *Hringhorni, Ringhorn* (Teutonic)

Hringhorn is Balder's large ship, which was later used as his funeral pyre. The female giant Hyrrokin launched Hringhorn for Balder's funeral. *See also* Balder.

Hringhorni (Teutonic) *see* Hringhorn.

Hrodvitnir (Teutonic) *see* Fenrir; Hati; Skoll.

Hropt (Teutonic) *see* Odin.

Hrotik (Armenian) *see* Fravashi.

Hrsikesa (India) Lord of Senses. *See also* Krishna.

Hrungnir (Teutonic)

He is one of the giants who was slain by Thor. Hrungnir has a head and heart of stone, and is armed with a stone shield and a whetstone. Part of the whetstone is still buried in Thor's head. *See also* Thor.

Hsaing Chun (China)

He is the god of the waterways of Hsiang (Hunan) and one of the nine creator gods. *See also* Nine Songs.

Hsi-Ho (China)

Also known as: *Water Mother.*

Mother of the suns. Wife of Ti-suin. In ancient mythology there are ten suns and twelve moons. Hsi-ho controls the time each sun has a turn in lighting the world. There is a great tree in the Valley of the Lake which is the abode of the suns. While one climbs to the top to light the world, the others wait in the branches. Her worship is similar to that of Aphrodite or Venus.

Hsi-Hua (China)

Official residence for female fairies. This abode is under the control of the Fairy Queen, Hsi Wang Mu (q.v.). *See also* Hung-hua.

Hsi-Ling Shih (China) *see* Sien-tsan.

Hsi T'ien (China) *see* Amida.

Hsi-Wang-Mu *Hsi Wang Mu, Si Wang Mu* (China)

Also known as: *Wang Mu Niang-niang.*

Underworld deity. Goddess of Epidemics. Goddess of plague and pestilence. She is the Royal Mother of the Western Paradise. She possesses the Peaches of Immortality and governs the forces of plague and calamity. The list of the Immortals is kept by Hsi-Wang-Mu. Her residence is within a mountain of jade. Sometimes she is identified with Wang mu niang-niang (Lady Wang or Queen Mother Wang), the keeper of the Peaches of Immortality. In this manifestation, she is a tiger-toothed woman with a leopard's tail, who lives in a jade mountain to the west of Kun-Lun and rules over spirits of evil, sending plague and affliction to mankind. Later, as consort of Tung Wang Kung or as some say, Yu-ti, she resided with the Jade Emperor in the palace on Kun-Lun. Hsi-Wang-Mu is described as a gracious, young, and beautiful sovereign, the Queen of the West, and co-ruler along with Tung Wang Kung over San Hsien Shan (Isles of the Blest). One of her depictions is that of the tiger toothed woman. Another depiction shows her as a beautiful and gracious lady, sometimes winged, sometimes not. She corresponds in some respect to Ament the Egyptian goddess. *See also* K'un-lun; Shen t'ao; Wang-Mu-Niang Niang; Xi Wang Mu.

Hsiang Chun (China)

Hero deity of waterways. One of the Nine Heroes. He is god of the waterways of Hsiang (Hunan province). *See also* Hsiang Fu-jen; Nine Songs.

Hsiang Fu-Jen (China)

Two sisters who are part of the Nine Heroes. The sisters' names are Wo Huang and Nu Ying. *See also* Hsiang Chun; Nine Songs.

Hsing Shen (China) God of the Road.

Hsuan-T'ien Shang-Ti (China)

Deity of water. Supreme Lord of the Dark Heaven. He is sometimes called upon to remove demons and evil spirits. Like the god Kuan-ti, he also punishes evil doers. Hsuan-T'ien Shang-Ti is shown as a giant with naked feet, dressed in a black robe with a gold breast plate. He stands on a turtle which is surrounded by a snake. *See also* Cheng Wu; Kuan-ti.

Htamenmas *Pharmen-pa* (Tibet)

These animal and bird-headed goddesses are found in the Bardo World on the twelfth and thirteenth day holding skeletons and corpses. *See also* Kerimas.

Hu Ching-Te (China)

God of doors. One of the generals who has been deified as a god of the outer doors. He is usually paired with Ts'in Shu-pao, who is also a general. The two deities replaced Shen-t'u and Yu-lu. In another version, it is Ch'in Shu-pao and Yu ch'ih Ching-te who are the guards of the doors. Usually each deity is represented as a leaf on one-half of the outer door. *See also* Men-shen; Shen-t'u.

Hu-Shen (China)

Hail storms are averted by propitiating this local god.

Hu Sia (Egypt)

Also known as: *Hu and Sia; Saa.*

Hu is the god of sense of taste and also of the divine food on which gods and mortals feed. He is the force of creative will. Hu is said to have been born from the drops of blood from Ra when he mutilated his penis. In another version of this myth, it is related that Hu and Sia came into being from the drops of blood which fell when the great sun god Ra was circumcised. Hu appears at the Creation in the Boat of the Sun. Later, he appears at the Judgment of the Dead. Hu is portrayed as a human with a sign of his name above his head. *See also* Ra; Sia (who may be the same as Hu).

Hua Hsien (China) Goddess of flowers.

Huaaiti (Egypt) *see* Aai.

Huacas (Chincha People, Colombia)

Also known as: *Yamanamca Intanamca.*

Spirits or idols. One group of huacas is named Yananamca Intanamca. The Yananamca were destroyed by another huacas named Huallallo Caruincho who was apparently evil. He was called Lord and instructed the women to have only two children, one of which was to be sacrificed for him to eat. He in turn was overthrown by a hero deity named Pariacaca (q.v.). *See also* Coniraya Viracocha.

Huahuantli *The Striped One* (Aztec; Mexico)

An alternate name for Teoyaoimquit (q.v.).

Huaillepenyi (Araucanian People, Chile)

God of fog. He creates deformed children. Huaillepenyi lives on the banks of any watercourse. He is shown as a ewe with the head of a calf and tail of a seal.

Huallallo Caruincho (Andean, Peru)

Huallallo is an evil lord who ate the children sacrificed to him. *See also* Coniraya; Huacas.

Huan-T'ien Shang-ti (China) *see* Shang-ti.

Huana Cauri (Inca) *see* Tahuantin Suyu Kapac.

Huang, The (China)

Deity of good omen. As a male phoenix bird it is called Feng and the female is called Huang. The bird is said to sit only on the site of buried treasure.

Huang-Lao (China)

He is the first man, or creature created by the mixing of Yin and Yang. Huang-Lao was called "The Gold Colored One." He taught mortals the skills needed to exist on earth. *See also* P'an-Ku.

Huang-Ti *Huang Ti* (China)

Also known as: "Yellow Emperor." Inventor of the compass. Originator of bronze casting. His mother is Fu-Pao, a brilliant woman who bore him by miraculous conception and gave birth after being pregnant for two years. Huang-Ti's wife is Hsi-Ling Shih, who introduced the culture of silkworms. Hun-Tun is his son. One of his descendants is Hou Chi, a grain deity. *See also* Hou-chi; Hsi-Ling Shih; Hun-Tun.

Huang T'ien (China)

Also known as: *Shang Ti.*

Huang T'ien is the imperial heaven ruled by Huang T'ien Shang Ti. He rides on the back of a tortoise encircled by a serpent in the dark heaven or northern sky. *See also* Shang Ti.

Huang T'ien Shang Ti (China) *see* Shang Ti; Yu Huang.

Huasi-Camayac (South America) *see* Conopa.

Huasi-Camayoc (South America) *see* Conopa.

Hubaba (Middle Eastern) *see* Khumbaba.

Hubal (Persian)

He was the tutelary deity of Mecca until the advent of Islam, when his likeness was destroyed.

Hubar (Babylon)

Also known as: *Tiamat*

As Hubar, Tiamat is the personification of the underworld river of the same name. *See also* Tiamat.

Huchi Fuchi (Japan)

Goddess of fire. She is possibly a deity of the early inhabitants of Japan known as the Ainos.

Huecuvus (Araucanian People, Chile, South America)

The Huecuvus are shape-changing spirits of evil under the command of Pillan (q.v.).

Huehuecoyotl (Mexico) *see* Coxcoxtli; Xochipilli.

Huehueteotl (Aztec, Olmec; Mexico)

Also known as: *Old God, Xiuhtecuhtli.*

A fire god, he might have been the earliest deity discovered from the Teotihuacan period. It is quite possible that Huehueteotl was a volcano deity since this region is volcanic. Apparently worshiped for many centuries, he is shown as an old man sitting with his head bowed. The head and shoulders support an incense bowl. The name Huehueteotl is used sometimes for the Aztec god Xiuhtecuhtli (q.v.).

Huehuetonacacipactli (Aztec; Mexico)

Also known as: *Cipactli, Coxcoxtli*

Fish god. "Old Fish God of our Flesh." *See also* Cipactli; Coxcoxtli.

Huemac Possibly *Hueymac* (Aztec, Toltec People, Mexico)

Also known as: *Quetzalcoatl* (possibly).

God of earthquakes. Astrologer. In some myths Huemac rules with Quetzalcoatl, and in others he is an aspect of Quetzalcoatl. It is said that he was an astrologer priest and the first of the nine rulers. He died at the age of three hundred during the reign of the second ruler (or era). Huemac was said to have compiled a book of history and prophecy, and founded the city of Tollan. *See* Legend of the Four Suns; Topiltzin.

Hueymac (Mexico) *see* Huemac.

Hueytecpatl (Aztec People, Mexico)

Possibly a god of fire. He is associated with the flint stone and is one of the original quadruplets. *See also* Hueytonantzin.

Hueytonantzin (Aztec People, Mexico)

Mother goddess. She is the mother of the Lords of the Four Directions: Hueytecpatl, Ixuin, Nanacatltzatzi and Tentemic. Hueytonantzin was sacrificed each morning by her sons. *See also* Ixmacane.

Hugh (Celtic) *see* Aed.

Hugi (Norse; Teutonic)

Also known as: *Thought.*

Giant. Hugi outran Thor's human servant Thialfi in a race in Utgard-Loki's domain. The reason Thialfi could not beat him was because he was the embodiment of thought. *See also* Loki.

Hugin (Teutonic) *see* Huginn.

Huginn *Hugin* (Teutonic)

Huginn, "The News Gatherer," is one of Odin's ravens. *See also* Munin; Odin.

Huh and Hauhet (Egypt)

High gods. Huh (frog headed) and Hauhet (serpent headed) gods. Huh was the male and Hauhet the female. They are part of the Ogdoad, the eight gods who created the world. *See also* Ogdoad.

Huichilobos (Aztec) *see* Huitzilopochtli.

Huitzilo-Mexitli (Aztec) *see* Huitzilopochtli.

Huitzilo-Poktli (Aztec) *see* Huitzilopochtli.

Huitzilopochtli *Huitzilo-Poktli, Huitzilopoktli, Uitzilopochtli* (Aztec; Mexico)

Also known as: *Blue Tezcatlipoca, Curicaveri, Huichilobos* (name give by the Spanish), *Huitzilo-Mexitli, Hummingbird Left Hand, Mexitli, Mextli, Mixcoatl, Otontecutli, Tenochtitlan, Tezcatlipoca, Xocotl.*

Chief of the Aztec pantheon. God of war. Storm deity. God of lightning. Protector of travelers. Associated with the sun and fire. His name means "Hummingbird on the Left." The Aztecs were living in caves when they came upon a likeness of Huitzilopochtli. He became their leader; they saw themselves as children of the sun, and followed his directions. Often he led them in the form of a hummingbird. When he commanded that they leave Aztlan, their island home, they did. In time a number of followers split off and followed Huitzilopochtli's sister Malinalxochitl, a powerful woman who had amazing control over scorpions, snakes and spiders. Huitzilopochtli continued his way and led his people on an arduous journey lasting generations from Aztlan to Coatepec (Hill of the Serpent). It was here that he was reborn. Huitzilopochtli's mother Coatlicue was sweeping the temple one day when she tucked feathers into her blouse. When she finished her task and went to remove the feathers, they were gone. She knew she was pregnant. This divine impregnation was the god's beginning of his rebirth. His sister Coyolxauhqui and his 400 brothers known as the Centzon Huitznahuas, embarrassed and infuriated because of their mother's pregnancy, decided to murder her. They laid in wait and when she approached they decapitated the woman. Huitzilopochtli leaped from his mother fully grown and dressed in warrior's gear, flourishing Xiuhcoatl. In retaliation for their brutal act he dismembered his sister and killed all but a few of his brothers. His image was usually depicted in wood rather than stone. He is shown with a tuft of blue-green hummingbird feathers on his head, a golden tiara, a spear in his right hand and a shield in his left. He is often shown holding the smoking mirror common to Tezcatlipoca. Other depictions show him with hummingbird feathers on his left, holding a stick shaped like a snake. He is also depicted as being covered with gems, gold and pearls. His face is frequently painted with yellow and blue stripes, and he wears a black mask decorated with stars around his eyes. Human sacrifices were frequently made to Huitzilopochtli. According to some, various other tribal gods, such as Curicaveri (Tarascan), Mixcoatl (Chichimec), Otontecutli or Xocotl (Tepanec and Otomi people) are similar or identical with Huitzilopochtli. See also Centzon Huitznahuas; Chimalmat; Coatlicue; Coyolxauhqui; Hueytonantzin; Legend of the Four Suns; Otontecutli; Tezcatlipoca.

Huitzilopoktli (Aztec) see Huitzilopochtli.

Huitziton (Aztec) see Huitzilopochtli.

Huitznahua (Aztec)
   High gods. The Huitznahua are the remaining brothers of the war god Huitzilopochtli who were defeated but not deposed during the power struggle between the war god and his unfortunate sister, Malinalxochitl. See also Huitzilopochtli.

Huixtocihuatl (Aztec) see Uixtochihuatl.

Hulda (Teutonic) see Holda.

Huldra (Teutonic) see Bertha; Holda.

Huliamma (India)
   She is one of the Mutyalamma goddesses who are deities of the household. Huliamma is a tiger goddess. See also Mutyalamma.

Hulle (Teutonic) see Holda.

Hum-ba (Middle Eastern) see Khumbaba.

Humbaba (Middle Eastern) see Khumbaba.

Humhum (Middle Eastern) see Khumbaba.

Hummingbird Left Hand (Aztec People, Mexico) see Huitzilopochtli.

Hun-Apu (Quiche People, Guatemala) see Hun-cane.

Hun-cane Huncame (Quiche People, Guatemala)
   Hun-Cane and Vukubcame were co-lords of the cavern world of Xibalba. Hun-Cane and Vukubcame were destroyed by Hun-Apu and Xbalanque after they murdered Hunhun-Apu and Vuub-Hunapu. See also Xibalba.

Hun-Tun Hun Tun (China)
   God of chaos. The personification of chaos, a mythical emperor-god who held sway prior to the active forces, Yin and Yang. The emperor of the north (Hu) and the emperor of the south (Shu) met in the territory of Hun-Tun. Unfortunately, Hun-Tun lacked the necessary orifices for seeing, hearing and smelling. Because of his hospitality, Shu and Hu bored holes at the rate of one a day to give him orifices. On the seventh day, when they drilled the last hole, Hun-Tun died and at the same time the world was created. Sometimes Hun-Tun is the wicked son of Huang Ti. See also Shu-hu.

Hunab Ku (Maya) see Hunab-ku.

Hunab-Ku Hunab Ku (Maya People, Yucatan)
   Also known as: Kinebahan ("Mouth and Eyes of the Sun").
   Invisible Supreme God. Hunab-Ku is the great god without form, the chief of the Mayan pantheon. He is the father of Itzamna, and the spouse of the goddess of weaving Ixazalvoh (q.v.). Hunab-Ku is analogous to the Aztec god Ometeotl. See also Itzamna; Ometeotl.

Hunabku (Maya) see Hunab-Ku.

Hunahpu and Ixbalanque Hun-Ahpu (Maya People, Yucatan)
   Also known as: Alom, Cajolom, Hun-Ahpu and Xbalanque, Hunahpuguch, Hunahpuutiu, Qaholom.
   Demi-god. God of the hunt. Son of Hun Hunahpu and Xquiq. Twin brother of Ixbalanque ("little jaguar"), both born by miraculous birth. The twins have two other brothers, the talented monkey artisans, Hun Batz and Hun Chuen. Hun Batz and Hun Chuen caused their younger twin brothers a lot of grief. Years later when the twins were older and fed up with their brothers' constant abuse, they lured them into a tree with no escape. Hun Batz and Hun Chuen became monkeys. He and his brother attacked the great imposter of the sun, Gukup Cakix. During the battle, the evil giant pulled and ripped off Hunahpu's arm. With the help of an elderly couple, perhaps their grandparents, they punished Gukup, and Hunahpu retrieved his arm. The two brothers next destroyed two other evil beings, the sons of Gukup Cakix, Zipacna and Cabracan, a destroyer of mountains. The task was not easy. It demanded plotting, planning, and scheming, but the wins were successful. Next the hero twins set out to avenge the deaths of their father Hun Hunahpu and his twin, their uncle Vukub Aphu. They set out for the underworld and once there endured a series of trials and tribulations before achieving their goal. The brothers were then able to turn themselves to the task of creation. See also Alom; Camazotz; Caprakan; Gukup Cakix; Hunahpu-Guch; Qaholom; Zipacna.

Hunahpu-Guch Hunahpuguch (Maya)
   Also known as: Alom.
   Creator. Originally Alom (or Atonatiuh) of the four creator regents. He changed his name during the third attempt to create

men. *See also* Legend of the Four Suns. The name Hunahpu may be associated with both Hunahpu-guch and Hunahpu-utiu. There is a separate legend regarding Hunahpu (q.v.).

Hunahpuguch (Maya) *see* Alom; Hunahpu.

Hunbatz (Maya) *see* Hunhun-Ahpu; Xquiq.

Huncame (Quiche People, Guatemala) *see* Hun-cane.

Hunchouen (Central America) *see* Hunapu; Xquiq.

Hundred-Handed (Greek)
This is another name for the Hecatonchires (q.v.).

Hunhun-Ahpu and Vukub-Ahpu
Hunhun-Ahpu and Vukub-Ahpu had been lured to the underworld by the Xibalba people to compete in a ball game. The twin brothers lost the game and were sacrificed. Hun-hun-Ahpu's head was taken and hung from a barren calabash tree (likely as a warning to others). The tree began to grow fruit immediately. The story of the unusual tree spread rapidly. It attracted a young woman who went to have a look at it. Hun-hun-Ahpu's head spoke to her and enticed her to receive his saliva. Miraculously, she became pregnant with and gave birth to the hero twins Hunahpu and Ixbalanque (q.v).

Huniman (India) *see* Hanuman.

Hunooman (India) *see* Hanuman.

H'uraru (Pawnee People, North America)
Also known as: *Atira*.
Mother earth. Creator of all things. Earth spirit.

Hypnos (Greek) This is a name of Somnus, the god of sleep.

Hura-Kan (Central, South America) *see* Huracan.

Huracan *Huracan Hura-Kan, Hurakan, Hurucan, Hurukan* (Maya, Quiche People, Guatemala)
Also known as: *Caculha Huracan, Heart of Heaven* (Quiche), *Hurn*.
God of hurricanes; of summer storms; of whirlwinds. God of terror. Huracan and Gucumatz created all things including mortals who were originally formed from wood. The mortals displeased the gods so they decided to try again. This time the gods used maize to create men and formed women for the men. Huracan developed fire and gave it to mortals. Others believe the original creators are Gucumatz and Tepeu or Gucumatz and Qabauil. Huracan was especially revered in Guatemala. He is associated with the Aztec god Quetzalcoatl, and also with Gucumatz and Tepeu (qq.v). Huracan is associated with the Aztec god, Quetzalcoatl. *See also* Gucumatz; Quetzalcoatl; Tepeu.

Hurakan (Central, South America) *see* Huracan.

Hurani (Persia) *see* Houris.

Huriyeh (Arabic) *see* Houris.

Hurn (Central, South America) *see* Huracan.

Hurucan (Central, South America) *see* Huracan.

Huruing Wuhti (Hopi People, North America)
After creating everything else, this male/female deity made men and women out of clay. In other myths of the Hopi Cre-ation Legend, Huruing Wuhti are two mother goddesses. In some Hopi tales they are known as survivors of the Deluge and mothers of the ancestors of the tribe. Ragno, an old mother goddess, assisted the women during times of difficulty. Ragno is also a figure in the Pomo Indian Creation Legend. *See also* Ragno.

Hurukan (Central, South America) *see* Huracan.

Husbishag (Assyro-Babylonian)
Underworld goddess. She is the keeper of records of the time of death of individuals. Her spouse is the evil spirit, Namtar (q.v.).

Husheng (Iranian, Persian) *see* Hoshang.

Husheng and Tamuras (Persian) *see* Hushang and Takhmoruw.

Husheng and Tamurath (Persian) *see* Hushang and Takhmoruw.

Hutameh (Islam)
This is the third section in the Islamic Hell known as Daru el-Bawar. It is reserved for people of the Jewish faith. *See also* Islamic Hell.

Hutchaiui (Egypt)
Weather god. God of the west wind. He is depicted as ramheaded with four wings, or as a ram-headed beetle.

Huti Watsi Ya (Huron People, North America) The Pleiades.

Huve (Bushmen of Africa)
Also known as: *Huveane*.
Supreme God. After creating heaven and earth, Huve hammered some pegs into the sky and climbed back to heaven, removing the pegs as he climbed. He is possibly the same as Huveane of the Basuto people.

Huveane (Basuto People, Africa)
Creator. After creating heaven and earth, mortals caused Huveane great distress. He hammered pegs into the sky, climbed up them, removing them from below as he climbed higher and higher. Soon he was lost from sight and has not been seen since that time.

Huythaka (Columbia, South America) *see* Bochica; Chia; Cuchaviva.

Huzruwauqti (Pueblo People, North America)
Goddess of hard material. Her abode is located in the western home of the sun.

Hvar (Chaldean) *see* Hvare-khshaeta.

Hvaranah (Persia) *see* Khvarenanh.

Hvare-khshaeta *Hvarekhshaeta, Hvar* (Chaldean, Persian)
"The Brilliant Sun." In some legends he is one of the Yazatas and is known as the eye of Ahura Mazda. In Chaldean astrology he is associated with Tishtrya, known as the Dog Star, Mah the moon, and Anahita. He rides across the sky in a chariot drawn by swift horses. *See also* Ahura Mazda; Ameshas Spenta; Anahita; Tishtrya; Yazatas.

Hvarekhshaeta (Chaldean) *see* Hvare-khshaeta.

Hveheuteotl (Aztec) *see* Xiuhtecuhtli.

Hvergelmir *Hvergelmer, Vergelmir* (Teutonic)
Also known as: *Kvergjelme, Odraerir.*
This is an ever-flowing spring, well, or cauldron beginning under one root of Yggdrasil in the world called Nifl-heim. From Hvergelmir flowed ten, eleven, or twelve rivers known as the Elivagar. These streams hardened into ice blocks. *See also* Elivagar; Nifl-heim; Odraerir; Yggdrasil.

Hyacinth (Greek) *see* Hyacinthos.

Hyacinthos *Hyacinth, Hyacinthus, Hyakinthos* (Greek)
Deified mortal. Spring deity. Hyacinthos is the son of Pierus and the Muse Cleio, or Amyclas and Diomede. An extremely beautiful youth, loved by Apollo and Zephyrus, he was accidentally killed when Zephyrus, also known as the West Wind, blew Apollo's discus from its course. In another version, it was Phoebus who threw the discus and when Hyacinthos rushed to pick it up it bounced back and struck him in the face. From his blood sprang the hyacinth or in some legends, the lily. Three great goddesses, Aphrodite, Artemis and Athena, carried him to heaven. *See also* Aphrodite; Apollo; Artemis; Athena; Clytia; Muses; Zephyrus.

Hyacinthus (Greek) *see* Hyacinthos.

Hyades (Greek)
The Hyades are the five, or some say seven, daughters of Atlas and Pleione, Atlas and Aethra, or Oceanus and Tethys. Their siblings are Calypso, Hyas, the Hesperides and the Pleiades. *See also* Atlas; Calypso; Hesperides; Hyas; Naiads; Pleiades.

Hyagnis (Armenian, Greek)
Possibly a lightning god. Father of Marsyas-Masses. Some say Marsyas is a tribal variety of Hyagnis and Hyagnis is the Greek form of Vahagn. *See also* Marsyas; Vahagn.

Hyakinthos (Greek) *see* Hyacinthos.

Hyas (Greek)
He is the son of Atlas and Pleione. His siblings are Calypso, the Hyades, the Hesperides and the Pleiades. *See also* Atlas; Calypso; Hesperides; Hyades; Pleiades.

Hydra, Lernean (Greek)
Demon of draught and darkness. A nine-headed monster, Hydra is the son of Typhon and Echidna. For each head cut off, two would grow in its place unless the wound was cauterized. One of his nine heads is immortal. To fulfill his second labor, Heracles had to kill the Hydra. He burned away eight of its heads and buried the ninth under a rock. The Hydra caused Heracles' death. *See also* Cerberus; Chimaera; Crommyonian Sow; Echidna; Heracles; Iolaus; Sphinx; Typhon.

Hygeia *Hygea, Hygieia* (Greek)
Also known as: *Salus.*
Goddess of health. She is the daughter of the great healer, Asclepius, and Epione, the daughter of Merops. Her siblings are Acesis, Aegle, Iaso, Janiscus, Machaon, Panacea, and Podalirius. Hygeia is shown with a serpent drinking from a jar she is holding. *See also* Acesis; Aegle; Asclepius; Merops.

Hyk (Egypt) *see* Heka.

Hylas (Greek)
Deified mortal.

Hylas is the son of Theodamas, the king of the Dryopes, and the nymph Menodice, who is the daughter of the giant hunter, Orion. Heracles came upon Theodamas in his field and demanded either an oxen or a plough from him. When the king refused his request, Heracles, looking for an excuse to war with the Dryopes, murdered him and abducted the beautiful youth Hylas. He took the young man aboard the Argos as his attendant and lover. One day, while the ship was beached, Hylas went to draw water at a spring. Dryope and the nymphs of Pegae spied him. Entranced by his beauty, they lured him into the water. When an all night search party found only his water pitcher, Heracles went wild with despair. It is said that in his sorrow, Heracles made the waves sound his loved one's name as they pounded against the shore. Hylas was never heard from again. *See also* Argonauts; Hermaphroditus; Naiads; Nereids; Orion; Scylla; Sirens.

Hyllus (Greek)
He is the son of Heracles and Deianeira or Melite. *See also* Aegimius; Heracles.

Hylonome (Greek)
A centaur. She is the daughter of Ixion and Nephele. *See also* Ixion; Nephele.

Hymen (Greek)
Also known as: *Hymenaeus.*
God of marriage. A minor deity. Hymen may have been the son of Apollo and the muse Urania or a son of Dionysus and Urania, or Dionysus and Aphrodite. In some myths he is said to have been one of Aphrodite's attendants. The most romantic myth is that he was a poor musician who pined after a young woman who was forbidden to marry him because of his status. Pirates abducted the couple and sailed away with them. On board the ship, Hymen played enchanting music on his lyre and put the crew to sleep. Once asleep he threw them all overboard, and sailed the vessel back to Athens. Not only was he hailed as a hero, he was able to marry the woman of his dreams and sing at his own wedding. The song he sang was used thereafter at other nuptials and became known as the "hymenael." *See also* Dionysus.

Hymenaeus (Greek) *see* Hymen.

Hymir *Hymer* (Norse; Teutonic)
The sea giant Hymir is the son of Fornjot, and brother of Aegir. He became the father of Tyr. He is associated with Thor, who took Hymir's magic cauldron, used for brewing ale. Hymir also accompanied Thor on his fishing trip to hook the Midgard Serpent. *See also* Aegir; Fornjot; Midgard Serpent; Thor.

Hypate (Greek)
A Delphic Muse who personifies the high string of the lyre. Her sisters are Mese, the middle string, and Nete, the low string.

Hyperbius (Greek)
He is one of the fifty sons of Aegyptus. *See also* Adrestus; Aegyptus; Eteocles.

Hyperenor (A) (Greek)
He is one of the Sparti, the people who sprang from the soil when Cadmus sowed the teeth of the dragon. *See also* Cadmus; Chthonius; Echion.

Hyperenor (B) (Greek) Poseidon and Alcyone are his parents.

Hyperion (Greek)

Sun god. One of the Titans, son of Uranus and Gaea. His wife is his sister, Theia. Sometimes it is said that his wife is Euryphaessa. Hyperion is the father of Helios, the sun god, Selene, the moon goddess, and Eos, goddess of the dawn. He is depicted as a handsome man. Hyperion is sometimes confused with Helios (q.v.). *See also* Gaea; Oceanids; Uranus.

Hypermnestra (A) *Hypermestra* (Greek)

She is the eldest of the fifty daughters of Danaus. She refused to follow her father's instructions to all his daughters — to kill their husbands on their communal wedding night. She would not murder her husband, Lynceus, because he spared her virginity. She was tried and acquitted by the Argive judges. Later, she became the mother of Abas. After death, Hypermnestra, Lynceus and Aba were all buried in the same tomb at Argos. *See also* Danaus.

Hypermnestra (B) (Greek)

She is the daughter of Thestius and Eurythemis.

Hypnos *Hypnus* (Greek)

Also known as: *Somnus.*

God of sleep. His parents are Nyx and Erebus; his siblings: Aether, Cer, Dreams, Hemera, Momus, Moros, Nemesis and Thantos. Pasithea, one of the Charities, became his wife. Their children are Morpheus and the Dreams. *See also* Aether; Erebus; Keres; Morpheus; Nemesis; Nox; Sarpedon (B); Somnus.

Hypnus (Greek) *see* Hypnos.

Hyposouranios (Phoenician)

The giant son of Fire, Hyposouranios was the first to build towns. His brother Ousoos was the first to make garments from skins. *See also* Fire; Ousoos.

Hupseus (Greek)

King of the Lapiths. He is the son of Peneius and Creusa. His children are Astyagyia, Cyrene, Stilbe and Themisto. *See also* Creusa; Cyrene; Themisto.

Hypsipyle (Greek)

Queen of Lemnos. She is the mother of several children by Jason, the Argonaut. When the women of her father Thoas' kingdom attempted to kill him, Hypsipyle saved him. She was exiled to Lemnos. *See also* Jason.

Hyrieus (Greek)

King of Hyria. He is the son of Poseidon or Lycus and Alcyone. It is possible that Orion is his son. *See also* Orion.

Hyrmina (Greek)

She is the daughter of Epeius and Anaxiroe and the spouse of Phorbas. *See also* Actor (B).

Hyrrokin (Norse; Teutonic)

She is the female giant who at Odin's request, launched Balder's ship Hringhorn when he died. Because she performed this act without help, Thor became so angry that he tried to kill her. *See also* Balder; Hringhorn; Odin; Thor.

I

I (A) (China)

Also known as: *Excellent Archer.*

He is the god of bowmen. I shot down all but one of the ten suns because they heated the earth so much. He is the spouse of the moon goddess, Chang-o.

I (B) (Maya)

The goddess I is a water goddess who may be the same as Chalchiuhtlicue (q.v.).

I-Em-Hetep (Egypt) *see* Imhotep.

I Kaggen (Africa) *see* Cagn.

I-shi-ko-ri-do-me (Japan) *see* Ishikoridome-no-Mikato.

I-ti (China)

God of wine. I-ti is a former mortal who invented wine making. He is associated with Tu K'ang, the god of distillers.

Iacchus (A) (Greek)

Epithet of Bacchus. *See also* Bacchus; Dionysus.

Iacchus (B) (Greek)

He is the son of Demeter, Dionysus or Persephone.

Iaeuo (Greek) *see* Iao.

Iaevo (Hebrew) *see* Jehovah; Yahweh.

Iah (Egypt) (Hebrew) *see* Aa; Aah; Jehovah.

Iahweh (Chaldea) *see* Sabazios.

Iai (Egyptian) *see* Aah.

Iakchos (Greek) *see* Dionysus.

Ial (India)

Also known as: *Hari Hara-putra* (Vishnu, son of Shiva), *Ier.*

Son of a god. He is said by some to be a son of Shiva by Mohina (feminine Vishnu). *See also* Vishnu.

Ialdabaoth (Ophites; post–Christian Gnostics)

Spirit creator. One of seven ruling spirits created by the god

Ophiomorphus, the serpent son of Ialdabaoth. The first spirit is possibly Adonaeus or Adonai; the second, Ialdabaoth; third, Iao; fourth, Sabaoth; fifth, Astaphaios; sixth, Ailaios; seventh, Horaios. In some renditions, Ialdabaoth (conceived by Sophia) is the first ruler. *See also* Abraxas; Archons; Iao; Sophia.

Ialmenus (Greek)
An Argonaut. Co-ruler of Orchomenus with his brother Asclaphus. He is the son of Ares and Astyoche. Ialmenus and Asclaphus were both suitors of Helen of Troy. The brothers took thirty ships to Troy. *See also* Ares; Argonauts; Asclepius.

Ianus (Roman) *see* Janus.

Iao (Gnostic)
Also known as: *Iaeuo.*
Aspect or name for Yahweh or Jehovah. One of the Archons. Part of an invocation by an Hellenistic priest indicates this might be a god similar in nature to Yahweh; i.e., "I invoke thee.... Demon of Demons, God of Gods, The Lord of Spirits, the unwandering Æon, *Iao ouêi* [Jehovah?] hearken unto my voice... ." *See also* Abraxas; Jehovah; Yahweh; Zeus.

Iapetus *Iapetos* (Greek)
A Titan. He is the giant son of Uranus and Gaea. His siblings are Cronus, Pallas, Oceanus and the Titans. He married Clymene, one of the numerous ocean nymphs who are the daughters of Oceanus. Iapetus has four gigantic sons: Atlas, Menoetius, Prometheus (Forethought) and Epimetheus (Afterthought). *See also* Atlas; Clymene; Cronus; Epimetheus; Gaea; Prometheus; Uranus.

Iarnsaxa *Jarnsaxa* (Norse; Teutonic)
Also known as: *Iron Dirk, Sif* (possibly).
She is the giant mistress of Thor and mother of Magni, and in some renditions, Modi, and possibly Sif. She is not a member of the Asynjor. When he was three years old, Magni lifted the foot of the giant Hrungnir from the leg of Thor. *See also* Magni; Modi; Sif (B).

Iasion (Greek)
His parents are Zeus and Electra. Dardanus, his brother, is favored by Zeus. His children by Demeter are Philomelus, who invented the wagon, and Plutus, the god of agricultural riches. *See also* Dardanus; Demeter; Eirene; Electra.

Iaso (Greek)
Goddess of healing. Her name means "cure." She is the daughter of the great physician Asclepius and Epione, the daughter of Merops. Her siblings are Acesis, Aegle, Hygeia, Janiscus, Machaon, Panacea and Podalirius. *See also* Asclepius; Merops.

Iasus (A) (Greek)
He is the son of Lycurgus, the king of Arcadia, and Cleophyle or Eurynome. His wife is Clymene and their daughter is Atalanta. His siblings are Amphidamas, Ancaeus and Epochus. *See also* Atalanta; Clymene; Inachus.

Iasus (B) (Greek)
Son of Rhea and Anchiale. One of the Dactyli. *See also* Dactyli; Rhea.

Iasus (C) (Greek)
King of Argos. His parents are Argus Panoptes and Ecbasus or Triopas and Ismene. His siblings are Agenor and Pelasgus.

Iasus (D) (Greek) Aeneas killed Iasus during the Trojan War.

Iath (Celtic) *see* Eire.

Iatiju (Acoma People, North America)
Parent of the Katsinas who are food and rain deities. *See also* Pishumi; Shk.

Iatik (Native American) *see* Iatiku; Nautsiti.

Iatiku and Nautsiti *Iatik* (Akoma, Koshairis People, North America)
Creators. They are sisters who created man. The sisters were made by Iatik in some versions and in other versions it was the Great Spider (Sus'istinako) who created them. Iatiku is sometimes referred to as a corn mother.

Iaw (Hebrew) *see* Jehovah.

Ib (Egypt) *see* Ab.

Ibe Dji (Yoruba People, Africa)
The likeness of Ibe Dji is only involved in the ceremonies that commemorate the deaths of twin sisters.

Iblis *Eblis* (Islamic)
The Prince of Darkness. Chief of the Jinn. Originally he was the angel Azazel. *See also* Azazel; Jin; Satan.

Ibmel (Finno-Ugric) *see* Jumala.

Iboroquiamio (Orinoco People, South America)
Devil. Little known, but greatly feared deity.

Ibrahim (Islamic) *see* Abram.

Ibraoth (Middle East) *see* Sabaoth.

Ibukido-Nushi (Japan) "Breath-Blowing-Lord." *See also* Haya-akitsu-hime-no-kami.

Icarius (A) (Greek)
He is the son of Perieres and Gorgophone or Oebaulus and Bateia, the Naiad. *See also* Gorgophone; Hippocoon.

Icarius (B) (Greek)
This farmer taught other farmers how to grow grapes and produce wine as originally taught by Dionysus. One day, during a festival, the drunken farmers beat Icarius to death. Icarius and his daughter, Erigone, the harvest goddess, became the constellation Bootes (some say Erigone is the constellation, Virgo). *See also* Dionysus; Erigone.

Icarus (Greek)
In an attempt to escape from King Minos, Daedalus made wings held together by wax. His son, Icarus, flew too close to the sun and was killed. His body washed up on the island of Icaria. *See also* Daedalus; Minos.

Icheiri (Carib People, Antilles)
Spirits. Each cabin has a altar where food offerings are laid out for the Icheiri. They are generally thought of as intermediaries between humans and the celestial powers. There is a deity named Yris involved with the Icheiri. *See also* Lares; Penates.

Ichiki-Shima-Hime (Japan) *see* Benten.

Ichikishima-Hime-no-Mikoto (Japan) *see* Three Goddesses of Munakata.

Icona (Maya People, Yucatan)

Also known as: *Jesus.*

Creator. According to legends, the Spanish Christianized the people but the Mayans converted the Christian Jesus to Icona. Icona created all things and he and his wife, who is a virgin named Chibirias or Hischen, had a son named Bacab. The rest of the legend is similar to the crucifixion story of the Biblical God, Jesus, and the Holy Ghost. The Holy Ghost is called Echuac or Ekchuah. *See also* Christ; Jesus.

Ictinike (Sioux People, North America)

Known as the "Father of Lies," Ictinike was exiled from heaven by his sun god father.

Id (Aztec)

God of fire. This god of fire, both creative and destructive, holds a position of seniority among the gods. His dwelling place is the North Star.

Ida (A) (India) *see* Ida (B); Manu.

Ida (B) *Adda, Idavita, Ila* (India)

An earth goddess, goddess of devotion, speech and vital air, Ida is the daughter and perhaps spouse of Vaisavata. She is also called the instructor of Vaisavata, spouse of Budha, mother of Kuvera. *See also* Budha; Kuvera; Vaisavata.

Ida (C) (Greek)

She is the daughter of Corybas, spouse of Lycastus, and mother of Minos. *See also* Minos.

Ida (D) (Greek)

She is the daughter of Melisseus. She and her sister, Adrastia, fed Zeus when he was an infant in Crete. *See also* Adrastia; Amaltheia; Zeus.

Ida-Ten (Zen; Japan)

Also known as: *Wei-to* (China).

From a revelation of a Chinese monk, Tao Hsuan (also spelled Tao-Suan). Ida-Ten is the god who protects monasteries. Guardian of the law. He is regarded as having miraculous speed. Formerly, he was known as General Wei, who as a mortal was the first to be put in charge of protecting Buddhism and monks. Ida-Ten is depicted as a handsome young man wearing a Chinese-type helmet, breastplate, and holding a sword. He is associated with a demon named Sokushikki.

Idaea (A) (Greek)

She is one of the daughters of Dardanus (q.v.).

Idaea (B) (Greek) Idaea is an epithet of Rhea (q.v.).

Idaea (C) (Greek) She is the second wife of Phineus (q.v.).

Idaeus (Greek)

A herald for the Trojans. When Priam went to pick up his son Hector's body, Idaeus was his driver. *See also* Hector; Helen; Priam.

Idakru (Japan)

Idakru is sometimes referred to as a son of Susanowo, the Ruler of the Ocean and Mysterious Things. *See also* Susanowo.

Idas (A) (Greek)

An Argonaut. Member of the Calydonia Boar Hunt. His par-

ents are Aphareus and Arene or Poseidon and Arene. His siblings are Lynceus and Peisus. The two women in his life were abducted. Phoebe was abducted by Castor and Polydeuces. Marpessa was abducted by Apollo.

Idas (B) (Greek)

Also known as: *Acesidas.*

Idas is one of the Dactyli. One of his siblings is Heracles. *See also* Dactyli; Heracles.

Idavida *Ida* (India)

Idavida is the mother of the demon dwarf, Kuvera (q.v.).

Idavold (Teutonic) *see* Idawold.

Idavolir (Teutonic) *see* Idawold.

Idavoll (Teutonic) *see* Idawold.

Idawold *Idavold, Idavoll, Idavolir, Ithavoll* (Norse; Teutonic)

Place of the gods. Asgard is located on the Plain of Idawold. It is also the location of Odin's palace, and Vingolf, the palace of the goddesses. Gladsheim is located in Idawold. *See also* Asgard; Gladsheim; Vingolf.

Iddahedu (Babylon) *see* Nabu.

Ide (Northwest Coast Native North Americans) *see* Adee.

Idem-Kuguza (Finnish) *see* Orin-Murt.

Idi (Native North American People) *see* Adee.

Idim-Kuguza (Finnish) *see* Orin-Murt.

Idlirvirissong *Irdlirvirisissong* (Eskimo)

Sky deity. Demonic cousin of the Sun. In some versions she is the cousin of Aningan, the moon god. She is depicted as a clown. *See also* Alignak; Sedna.

Idmon (A) (Greek)

He is the son of Abas and Asteria or Cyrene, or Apollo and Asteria or Cyrene. *See also* Argonauts.

Idmon (B) (Greek)

He is one of the fifty sons of Aegyptus (q.v.).

Idmon (C) (Greek)

Arachne, the weaver, who hung herself and was turned into a spider by Athena, is his daughter.

Idomene (Greek)

She is the daughter of Pheres and Periclymene. Her siblings are Admetus, Lycurgus and Periopis. Her marriage to Amythao resulted in the births of Aeolia, Bias, Melampus and Perimele. *See also* Abas (A); Admetus; Aeolia; Melampus; Pheres.

Idomeneus (Greek)

King of Crete. He is the son of Deucalion, the brother of Crete, the husband of Medea and the father of a son, Idamante.

Idun *Iduna, Idunn, Idunna, Idhunn, Ithun, Y'dun* (Norse; Teutonic)

Idun, an Asynjor, is the goddess who guards the golden apples of eternal life for the gods. The Aesir needed the apples for their strength and health. Idun is the wife of Bragi, the god of poetry. Her brother is the giant Thjasse-Volund. When Loki was abducted by the giant Thiassi, he gained his release by promising to give Idun to him. Loki wooed Idun by telling her he knew where she could find better apples. They went into the woods together and Idun was taken by Thiassi. Without their apples, the Aesir grew old and dissipated. They threatened to punish Loki if he did not return Idun. Using Freyja's magic cloak, he flew into Thiassi's territory and rescued Idun. Thiassi chased them to the edge of Asgard, where he was killed by the Aesir. *See also* Aesir; Asynjor; Bragi; Loki; Sol (B); Thiassi.

Idyia *Eidyia* (Greek)
She is the daughter of Oceanus and Tethys, the spouse of Aeetes and the mother of Absyrtus and Medea. *See also* Absyrtus; Aeetes; Medea; Oceanus; Tethys.

Ie (Hebrew, Christian) *see* Jehovah.

Iegad (Pelew Islands)
Sun deity. The god who brought light to earth.

Iella (Antilles)
Mother goddess. Mother of the dual god Iocauna and Gaumaonocon. In legend she is a supreme being with five names. The other four names are Atabei, Mamona, Guacarapita, and Guimazoa. In another list, four names are given: Atabei; Gaumaonocan; Iocauna; Zemes.

Iemhetep (Egypt) *see* Imhotep.

Iermaogauacar (Antilles) *see* Iocauna.

Iesous (Greek) *see* Jesus.

Iesu (Hebrew) *see* Jesus.

Ieu (Hebrew) *see* Jehovah.

Ieui (Hebrew) *see* Jehovah.

Ifa (Yoruba People, Africa)
Also known as: *Fa* (Fon People), *Ifa-Eschu* (possibly), *Orunmila.*
God of wisdom and knowledge. Fire god. The name Ifa refers to the deity and to his oracle. There are conflicting legends pertaining to Ifa's origins. Some say that he came to earth with other deities at the beginning of time. His wisdom was necessary to establish order in the world. In early days, before the great division between heaven and earth, Ifa traveled frequently to consult with the supreme deity, Olodumare. One day on earth a family squabble developed and one of his eight children insulted him. He journeyed back to the celestial realm to live. His permanent departure left the earth in chaos and confusion. Food was scarce, disease was rampant and women became barren. The children were sent to beg their father's forgiveness. After an arduous trip they finally found Ifa ensconsed under a palm tree in heaven and he refused to budge. He gave his children each a kit containing sixteen palm nuts to be used for communication and divination. Through these tools he conveyed the desires of mortals to the deities and the will of the deities to the mortals. Ifa is also connected to Eshu. Eshu collected and read palm nuts from a miraculous palm tree, which was Ifa, thus satisfying the hunger of the gods. Sometimes Eshu is the servant of Ifa, to whom he is forced to surrender the art of divination; sometimes it is Ifa who has the art, and Eshu

forces Ifa to give him part of the knowledge. Eschu loves to test the character of people. Ifa, also known as a fire god, was worshiped under the emblem of the palm nut with sixteen stones, each stone had three or four eyes likely similar to the kits he gave his children. *See also* Eshu; Fa (A); Olodumare; Orunmila; Shango.

Ifgdrasil (Teutonic) *see* Yggdrasil.

Ifilici Wacinaci (Arawak People, South America)
Also known as: *Great Father, Wa Cinaci, Wa Murreta Kwonci.*
Probably a creator or culture hero. He may be the same as Wa Cinaci and Wa Murreta Kwonci. These names seem to mean "Maker" or "Great Father."

Ifing (Teutonic)
Ifing is a stream or river on the broad Plain of Idawold in Asgard in the upper sky where Odin set up his council. The water in this stream never froze. This is where Odin gathered together the twelve gods known as the Aesir and the twenty-four goddesses known as the Asynjor, to make a pact of harmony. Weapons and tools are made in Ifing. Ifing separates the realms between the giants and the gods. *See also* Aesir; Asgard; Asynjor.

Ifrit (Arabic) *see* Afrit.

Ifrits (Middle Eastern) *see* Jin.

Igaluk (Eskimo)
Sun deity. Alaskan name of the god of the Moon.

Iggdrasil (Teutonic) *see* Yggdrasil.

Igigi (Babylonian; Mesopotamia)
The Igigi, assistants to the chief of the gods, Anu, and other high gods, are the spirits of heaven who appear as stars. They are called upon before battles. With the Annunaki, they are the hosts of heaven and earth. Some writers do not differentiate between the Igigi and Annunaki. Others specify that the Annunaki are the spirits of earth. The Igigi and Anunnaki are the offspring of Anshar and Kishar, and Ellil (generally called Enlil) was their ruler. In other renditions, Ishtar is their leader. Marduk created the Anunnaki. *See also* Anshar; Anu; Anunaki; Apsu; Enlil; Ishtar; Kishar; Marduk.

Igirit (Hebrew) Ruler of Demons. *See also* Agrat Bat Mahalat.

Ignerna (British) *see* Arthur.

Ignis (Teutonic, Roman)
Deity of fire. Son of Manus, the mythical father of the Teutons. Associated with the Caberi and Vulcan (qq.v.).

Iha-haga-hime (Japan) *see* Kaya-No-Hime-No-Kami; Ninigi.

Iha-naga-himi (Japan) *see* Iwa-naga-hime.

Iha-no-hime (Japan)
Goddess of prosperity and long life. She is the very jealous wife of Nintoku.

Iha-tsutsu No Wo (Japan) *see* Izanami.

Ihasutsu-nome (Japan) *see* Izanami.

Ihi (Egypt)
Also known as: *Ahi.*

"The Sistrum Player." Deity of music. He is the son of Hathor and Horus. The sistrum is the musical instrument that is sacred to Hathor. *See also* Sistrum.

Ihi-yori-hiko (Japan)
Fertility deity. One of the four faces of Futa-na Island.

Ihoiho (Polynesia Society Islands)
Creator. Creator god who was followed by Timo-taata.

Ihuitimal (Toltec People, Mexico) *see* Mixcoatl.

Ihy (Egypt) *see* Hathor.

Ijaksit-Khoton (Siberia) *see* Ajysyt.

Ika-tere (Polynesia)
Father of fish. Brother of Tu-te-wehi and son of Tangaroa. *See also* Tangaroa; Tu-te-wehi.

Ikiti-simapine-no Mikoto *Ikiti-sima-pime-no-mikoto* (Japan) *see* Amaterasu; Three Goddesses of Munakata.

Iksion (Greek) *see* Ixion.

Ikto (Sioux People, North America)
He is the inventor of speech for mortals.

Iku-tu-pikone-nomikoto (Japan) *see* Amaterasu.

Il (Ugarit) *see* El.

Ila (A) (India) *see* Sarasvati.

Ila (B) (India) *see* Ida.

Ilabrat *Ili-abrat* (Babylonia, Sumer)
Also known as: *Ninsubur, Papsukkal, Papukkal.*
Ilabrat is the messenger sent by Anu to inquire why the south wind stopped blowing. This relates to the legend of Adapa breaking the wings of the southwest wind she-demon, Shutu. Some say he is shown with a staff or wand in his right hand. He is sometimes identified with Ninsubur. *See also* Adapa; Ninsubur; Papsukkal; Tammuz.

Ilah (Ugarit) *see* El.

Ilaheva (South Pacific)
The earth goddess spouse of the sky god Eitumatupua (q.v.).

Ilamatecuhtli *Ilamatecutli* (Aztec People, Mexico)
Also known as: *Old Mother, Tonantzin.*
This is a name for Tonantzin. In this form, Ilamatecutli is represented as the Earth Toad. She is a mother goddess, corn goddess, fertility goddess and the lord of the thirteenth hour of the day. The Earth Toad is shown swallowing a stone knife. *See also* Lord of the Day Hours; Tonantzin.

Ilancue *Ilancueitl* (Aztec People, Mexico)
Also known as: *The Old Woman.*
First goddess or Earth goddess. She is the wife, possibly first wife, of Ixtacmixcoatl. They are the ancestors of the People of Mexico. *See also* Chimalmatl; Ixtacmixcoatl.

Ilancueitl (Aztec) *see* Ilancue.

Ilat *Alilat* (Arabic)
She is an early mother goddess who has been likened to Aphrodite. *See also* Alilat.

Ilavida (India)
Ilavida is the mother of Kuvera and the spouse of Vishravas (q.v.).

Ildebaoth (Gnostic) *see* Abraxas.

Ile-gbigbona (Africa) *see* Sonponno.

Ile-titu (Africa) *see* Sonponno.

Ilem (Slavic) *see* Ilmarinen.

Ilhallubu (Babylon) *see* Adad.

Ili-abrat (Sumer) *see* Ilabrat.

Ilias (Arab) *see* Elijah.

Ilinbongasum (Saora People, India)
God of the rainbow. *See also* Adununkisum.

Ilithyia (Greek) *see* Ilythia.

Ilithyiae (Greek) *see* Ilythia.

Illa (Haiti) *see* Atabei.

Illa Ticci *Illa Tici* (Peru) *see* Viricocha.

Illillos (Sumer) *see* Enlil.

Illinus (Babylon) *see* Aus; Belus (B).

Illiyun (Islamic)
The seventh stage in Islamic Paradise. This is where the register of good deeds is kept.

Illuyankas (Hittite)
The storm god killed this giant serpent with the help of the goddess Inaras. She enlisted the assistance of a mortal named Hupasiyas. He agreed to aid her only if she slept with him, which she did to accomplish her goal. *See also* Inaras.

Illyrius (Greek)
He is the son of Cadmus and Harmonia. His siblings are Agave, Autonoe, Ino, Polydorus and Semele. *See also* Ino; Semele.

Ilma (Slavonic, Finnish)
God of the air. He is the father of Luonnotar who was the mother of Vainamoinen who in turn was a creator. Other references call Luonnotar the creator and the daughter of Ilma. *See also* Ilmarinen.

Ilmaka (Himyarite People, South Arabia)
War deity. Called the smiter.

Ilmaqah *Ilmuqah* (Semitic) Moon god. *See also* Allah; Elohim.

Ilmarinen *Ilmaris, Ismaroinen* (Finnish, Lithuanian, Slavic)
Also known as: *Ilem, Ilma, Inmar, Jen, Jumala, Jumla, Sangke.*
Smith god. Ilmarinen is the son of Ilmatar. He is the brother of Vainamoinen and Lemminkainen. His wife is Kildisin, the daughter of the sorcerer Pohja. Ilmarinen forged the sun. He also forged the magic mill known as Sampo with the point of a swan's feathers, milk from a sterile cow, a grain of barley and the wool of a ewe. There are stories about Ilmarinen and his brothers attempting to steal the Sampo and while doing so,

breaking it. In later versions of his myth we find that his spouse Kildisin has merged into Virgin Mary. Ilmarinen is associated with the hero, Vainamoinen. Compare Ilmarinen to the Vedic god Tvastri, and the Celtic god Goibniu. *See also* Ilma; Ilmatar; Jumala; Kalevala; Pohja; Sampo.

Ilmaris (Finland) *see* Ilmarinen.

Ilmatar (Finland)
Creator. Hero. This androgynous goddess (sometimes known as a hero) is the daughter of the god of air Ilma, mother of the creator of the sun Ilmarinen, the magician, Lemminikainen and the god of music Vainamoinen. In her female form she is a creator of all. (In some myths, Luonnotar is the mother of Vainomoinen.) *See also* Ilmarinen; Lemminikainen; Luonnotar; Vainamoinen.

Ilu (Ugarit) *see* El.

Ilumarru (Babylon) *see* Adad.

Ilus (A) (Greek) He is the son of Dardanus and Bateia (qq.v.).

Ilus (B) *Iulus* (Greek)
Also known as: *Ascanius*
He is the son of Aeneas and Creusa. His name links him with Ilium (Troy). It also links him with the Julian family of Julius Caesar and Caesar Augustus. *See also* Aeneas; Creusa.

Ilus (C) (Greek) Mermerus, the son of Pheres, is his father.

Ilus (D) (Greek)
The wrestler. Fourth king of Troy. His parents are Tros and Callirrhoe. His siblings are Assaracus, Cleopatra and Ganymede. He married Eurydice and became the father of Laomedon and Themiste. Ilus won fifty young men, fifty young women and a cow in the wrestling division of the Phrygian Games. Zeus gave Ilus the Palladium. A prophet told him to build a city on the spot where his cow would lay down. He named the city Ilion which was later changed to Troy. *See also* Anchises; Callirrhoe; Eurydice (C); Ganymede; Theano.

Ilyas (Islamic) *see* Elijah.

Ilyasin (Islamic) *see* Elijah.

Ilythia (Greek) *see* Eileithyia.

Im (Akkadian, Babylonian) God of storms. *See also* Rimmon.

Imana (Warundi People, Africa)
Supreme being. Chief of the Ancestral Spirits of the race.

Imaymana Viracocha (Inca)
Imaymana Viracocha is the son of the creator, Viracocha, and brother of Tocapo Viracocha. Viracocha sent his sons out to visit the people after the Great Deluge and the Creation. The brothers were to ensure that the people were still following the commandments they had been given. As they travelled, they named the different varieties of trees, bushes, plants, fruits, flowers and told the people which could be eaten or which would have curative powers and which varities were dangerous to their health. *See also* Manco Capac; Viracocha.

Imberombera (Australia)
Another name for the mother goddess, Waramurungundja (q.v.).

Imbrogeneis (Greek) *see* Curetes; Telchines.

Iment (Egypt) *see* Ament; Amenti.

Imgig (Sumer) *see* Zu.

Imhetep (Egypt) *see* Imhotep.

Imhotep *I-em-hetep, Iemhetep, Imhetep* (Egypt)
Also known as: *Imuthes* (Greek).
Deified mortal. God of learning, medicine and wisdom. God of builders. Imhotep was the architect of the Step Pyramid at Sakkara and an official of the pharaoh Zoser in the Third Dynasty. He was one of the few Egyptian mortals to obtain deification which in his case occurred two thousand years after his death. Memphis was the seat of his worship. Some say he was the scribe of Thoth. He is identified with the Greek Asclepius. *See also* Amenhotep, son of Hapu.

Imhursag (Sumer) *see* Ishkur.

Imi Kashiki No Mikoto (Japan) *see* Ama-no-minaka-nushi.

Immer (Sumer) *see* Ishkur.

Imra *Amra* (Kafir People, Afghanistan)
Also known as: *Dagun, Yamri.*
Supreme deity. Little known name for the supreme god by the Kafir people.

Imseti (Egypt) *see* Mesta.

Imsety (Egypt) *see* Horus.

Imuit (Egypt)
Deified object. Actually a fetish of one of the early gods, or possibly the name of one of the ancient deities. It is associated with Anubis and Osiris.

Imuthes (Greek) *see* Imhotep.

Imy-Hemef (Egypt)
"Dweller in His Flame." This serpent is fifty feet long. He lives on top of Bakhau, the Mountain of Sunrise.

In (Japan) *see* Yo.

In-shushinak (Elamite) *see* Adad.

Ina (Polynesia)
Also known as: *Hina, Hine, Sina.*
Heroine. Her spouse is Tinirau, and her sister, Rupe (also known as Ru). She has two children whose names are not mentioned. She is likely the same as Hina (q.v.). *See also* Tinirau.

Ina-gami Furu-kushi-nada-hime (Japan) *see* Kushi-nada-hime.

Ina-Init (Philippine)
Sun god. He is the husband of Aponbolinayen.

Inachus (Greek)
Also known as: *Inaclius.*
River god. In some myths Inachus is the son of Oceanus and Tethys, a river god of the river Inachus and the first king of Argos. In other versions, he is not a deity, but is the first king of Argos, who named the chief river of Argos after himself. As

the son of Oceanus and Tethys, he married his sister, the ash nymph Melia and they became the parents of Phoroneus and Aegialeus and a daughter, Io. Others say that Io's father was Iasus and that Argia was the mother of Io and Phoroneus. It is said that when Hera and Poseidon were quarrelling over who should receive the Argolis, Zeus intervened and asked the river gods Inachus, Cephissus and Asterion to make the decision. They decided in favor of Hera. This infuriated Poseidon who in retaliation dried up their river beds permitting them water only after the rains. Inachus was the first to worship Hera and his daughter Io became her priestess. It is said that the goddess Athena as Pallas Athena bathed in the waters of Inachus every year to restore her virginity. Hera also conducted a similar ritual in a spring known as Canathus. To compare to other river deities, *see* Achelous; Acheron; Alpheus; Asopus; Cephissus; Cocytus. *See also* Apsyrtus; Argus (B); Hera; Io; Meliae; Oceanids; Oceanus; Rivers; Tethys.

Inaclius (Greek) *see* Inachus.

Inadjet (Egypt) *see* Buto (A).

Inagami-Hime (Japan) *see* Kushi-nada-hime.

Inagi-Utasunhi (Cherokee People, North America)
Evil deity. The Dark Twin, a wild boy.

Inanna (A) (Sumer)
Also known as: *Annis, Ishtar* (Babylonian), *Tamar* (Hebrew).
Inanna, an earth goddess, grain goddess, goddess of date groves, and a goddess of wine and love, is also known as Queen of Battles. She is probably the daughter of Ningal, who is the wife of Nana. Inanna's sisters are Nanshe, Ninisinna, Ninmug, Nidaba, and Ereshkigal, and perhaps Anunit. Her brothers are Utu and probably Shamash. After the dilemma of making a choice between the shepherd god Dumuzi and the farmer god Enkidu, she decided to wed Dumuzi, although Utu thought that Enkidu would make the better mate. In some renditions, Inanna preferred Enkidu but Dumuzi was determined to wed her. During the summer month of either July or August, Inanna decided to travel to see her sister Ereshkigal, the Queen of the Underworld. In some versions of this myth, her reason for the descent is not clear. Other interpretations explain that she wanted to attend the last rites for Gulgallana, the husband of Ereshkigal. Before her departure, she instructed her vizar, Ninshubur, that if she did not return in three days, he should begin mourning rites for her. Further, she told him to inform the high gods, Enlil, Nanna and Enki, of her whereabouts and have them intercede on her behalf so that she would not be put to death. She had to pass through a series of seven gates. Neti, the gatekeeper, asked her why she was visiting the place of no return. After her explanation, he instructed her to leave a piece of clothing at each gate, as was the custom. Naked, she finally reached her sister and the seven judges, known as the Anunnaki. She was turned into a corpse and hung on a stake. She was informed that there was only one way out of the underworld: one could return to the upperworld if a substitute was provided. In the meantime, the three days had passed and Ninshubur approached the gods as he was instructed to do by Inanna. Enlil and Nana did not want to be involved. Enki performed magical rites and created two creatures from his fingernail. They

went into the underworld and sprinkled her corpse sixty times with the water and food of life. Revived, Inanna was allowed to leave accompanied by demons who were to return with her substitute. The demons claimed several substitutes whom Inanna refused to allow be taken: the vizar Ninshubur, Shara the god of Umma, and Latarak the god of Badtibira. Grateful for being spared, they humbled themselves before Inanna. Inanna and the demons traveled on to Dumuzi's domicile in Erech where he reigned as king. He was not at all upset that his wife had been in the underworld. Enraged, that he was not in mourning for her she instructed the demons to take him as her substitute. Later, relenting, she was able to make arrangements that Dumuzi and his sister Gestinanna would each spend six months in the underworld. In another myth about this ambitious goddess, she wanted the benefits of civilization to be conferred on the people in her city of Erech. Not only would it prosper the community, it would enhance her image politically. To accomplish this goal, she had to acquire the "Me," or decrees of civilization, which are similar to the Tablets of Destiny. The Me were in the custody of the god Enki in the Sumerian Eridu. She traveled to his domain in her ship, the *Boat of Heaven*. When she arrived, she was invited to join Enki at a banquet. Smitten by her, and later inebriated, he gave her the precious Me. She loaded over one hundred tablets on her *Boat of Heaven* and set sail for the voyage home. In the meantime, Enki, now sober, was informed by his messenger Isimud that he had given the tablets to Inanna. Upset, he sent Isimud and a group of sea monsters after the ship. When they reached Inanna, Isimud attempted to retrieve the tablets through civilized verbal communication. Inanna, determined not to relinquish her treasures, became furious that Enki had broken his word. She had Ninshubur rescue her, the tablets, and the ship. This was not to be the end of story. Enki was as determined to get his tablets back as Inanna was to keep them. Despite numerous additional onslaughts from the sea monsters, in the end, the victorious Inanna arrived in her port with her precious cargo, the Me. The ritual practices of Inanna and the Babylonian Ishtar were similar. Inanna was preceded by Belili (q.v.). Inanna has attributes similar to those of Ninhursag (q.v.). She is also identified with the Hebrew goddess Tamar. *See also* Anunnaki; Anunit; Dumuzi; Enki; Enkidu; Enlil; Ereshkigal; Gestinanna; Innini; Ishtar; Nana; Nanshe; Nidaba; Ninedinna; Ninsun; Shamash; Utu.

Inanna (B) (Babylonian)
Known as the "Mistress of Heaven," she is a mother goddess.

Inapatua (Australia) *see* Inapertwa.

Inapertwa *Inapatua* (Aborigine People, Australia)
Creators. The first rudimentary humans or incomplete men. Their form was indistinct, consisting of rounded shapes. The two highest gods (unnamed) came down and separated the various parts to make human beings. *See also* Numbakulla.

Inar (Hittite)
Destroyer of serpents. Inar once killed a great serpent and its family by feeding them so much food they could not get back in their holes.

Inaras (Hittite)
This goddess promised to sleep with the hero Hupasiyas if

he would kill the dragon Illuyankas and his offspring. Hupasiyas, with the help of the thunder god, killed the dragon, and Inaras kept her promise. *See also* Illuyankas.

Inari *Inari-m'yojim* (Japan)
Also known as: *Uka-no-kami, Httsui-no-kami*

Deity of rice, property and prosperity. Patron of sword-smiths and tradespersons. As Httsui-no-kami, deity of kitchen. An androgynous deity, Inari is also portrayed as goddess and often referred to as a vixen. As the goddess she is depicted as a fox and is often worshiped as a fox. Inari is associated with fire and smith-craft. As the god, he is depicted as a bearded old man with his attendants and messengers, two foxes. He is also shown sitting on a sack of rice or balanced on the back of a fox and holding two bags of rice. Inari's messenger is Kitsune, a bewitching fox, who is also the guardian of the rice crop. Geishas and prostitutes are sometimes spoken of as kitsune (foxes). The fox, of great magical importance in Japan, was feared for its malice. Depression and insanity are often attributed to the fox-spirit. In China, the fox is known as a sly companion of fairies. On the first day of the Horse (Hatsu-uma) in February, a major festival was held and Inari was a deity honored. On November 8, another festival, known as the Festival of the Goddess of the Kitchen Range, or the Feast of Bellows (Fuigo Matsuri) was held in Inari's honor. Here she is known as Httsui-no-kami. Other kitchen deities include Oki-Tsu-Hiko, Oki-Tsu-Hime and Kamado-no-kami. On this day, fires were lit to honor numerous deities, including Inari. The Romans had a goddess of ovens known as Fornax. The oven is a mother-symbol connected with food-producing and food-giving. The workings of witches and magic are connected with the kitchen and include the range, the oven or the hearth. The principal temple erected in honor of Inari is at Fushimi, near Kyoto. Inari is associated with and sometimes confused with Uke-mochi, the food goddess. *See also* Vesta.

Inari-m'yojim (Japan) *see* Inari.

Inca — Creation Legend (Peru) *see* Apocatequil; Coniraya; Irma; Mama Occlo; Mancho Capac; Pacari; Viracocha.

Incubi (Medieval European) *see* Incubus; Succubus.

Incubus *Incubi* (plural), *Succubus* (female) (Medieval European)

A supernatural being neither wholly good nor wholly evil. Known as the demon lover, an incubus fathered Merlin, Arthur's counselor. They are male spirits of evil dreams and nightmares. During the Middle Ages, it was believed that the incubus had intercourse with sleeping women. Unexplained pregnancies could conveniently be attributed to a virgin birth, and blamed on the incubus. Often the birth of twins, or babies born with birth defects were said to be the children of an incubus. These demons are often handsome, though smelly, with cloven feet. The incubus is comparable to the Celtic Dusii and Samoan Hotua Poro. *See also* Bhutas (Hindu); Demons; Jinn (Medieval Europe); Satyrs (Greek); Succubus.

Inda (India) *see* Indra.

Indech, King (Celtic) *see* Domnu.

Indra (Buddhist, Hindu, Vedic; India)
Also known as: *Aindri, Inda* (Buddhist), *Indra-nag, Indrani, Lord of the Gods and Destroyer of Their Enemies, Mahendra, Pakasasana, Parjanya* (Rain-bringer, name used in later myths), *Puramdara, Sahasramuska* (Thousand Testicled One), *Sakra, Satakratu, Skambha* (Support), *Taishaku* (Japan), *Vajrapani, Vritrahan* (Slayer of Vritra), *Vritrahana, Vrtrahanna.*

Indra is variously known as a supreme deity, a storm god and god of the atmosphere. In Vedic accounts, Indra is the son of the sky god Dyaus and the earth goddess Prithivi. Born from his mother's side, he was hidden and ignored at birth. His parents and the gods thought that his arrival would upset the universe and perhaps lead them to their doom. Hiding him was not the answer, for he made himself known from his earliest days. The chief of the Vedic gods, he is called the Mighty Lord of the Thunderbolt, Cloud-gatherer, and the Sender of Rain and its Fertility. In Hindu accounts, Indra is the son of Dyaus and Nistigri. It is also said the Mother of All Gods, Aditi, is either the mother of or the attendant to Indra. Some say his father was Tvashtri, the artisan deity who created the indestructible vajra. Energetic and impulsive, Indra was addicted to soma. It is possible that his first drink of the intoxicating nectar came from his mother's breast. Fortified by the beverage, he took his father's vajra (thunderbolt) and set out to battle the demons who plagued the land (*see also* Varcin). His consort is the jealous, lascivious Indrani, his son, Sitragupta. In some renditions, he is the twin brother of Agni. In one myth, he was ripped to pieces and reassembled by the gods. They were unable to find his penis and had to attach the member of a ram to Indra. He overcame the serpent Vritra with the advice and aid of Vishnu and fought against other demons. His home, Swarga (Vaijayanta), located between heaven and earth on Mount Meru was filled with dancers and musicians. His servants were demigods known as the Vasus. With Agni and Surya, he formed a triad of the major Vedic gods. Many Vedic hymns are in honor of Indra. He is the king of the gods, god of storms, slayer of demons, destroyer of fortresses and compeller of clouds. He befriended the outcast, the weak and the oppressed. After Indra killed the darkness and drought dragon, Vritra, he was looked upon with favor by the gods. Indra's assistants are the Maruts, subordinate, warrior-like storm gods who drink soma to fortify themselves for battle. Not always ethical, he was a treacherous fighter and could be unfair. A swaggering war god, he flew across the sky in his solar chariot wielding a thunderbolt. Yet, he exhibited human traits. The thunderbolt he used as a weapon was also used to bring the dead to life. Although he is a god, his conquests were not always accomplished alone. Often other deities intervened on his behalf. Indra is invoked to send rain during times of drought. He is often depicted with the vajra (thunderbolt) in his right hand and a bow in the other, or with a second pair of arms, holding lances. He is fair-complexioned, with ruddy cheeks, a red beard and shoulder length golden hair. He rides a horse and is depicted with his driver, Matali, in a flaming chariot drawn by two tawny horses with flowing tails and manes. Sometimes the horses are gold and red and are known as the Harits. Indra is symbolized by the bull. One of his symbols is the owl, indicating power. His vajra (thunderbolt) is the symbol of divine or mystic energy. It also symbolizes the male principle and the axis of the universe. His other weapons are the bow, net and hook (anka). It is said that Indra's long arms spanned the skies. In later times, he was depicted with a dog (*see* Yama). As a cattle-raider, he is associated with the horse and the bull. (The cattle are the clouds.) He is shown seated on his four-tusked elephant named Airavata (rain cloud). Airavata sprang from the churning sea of milk when the universe was created. Indra carries the elephant goad (lightning) and the vajra (thunder). He is sometimes depicted with seven arms holding a diadem, discus (chakra), elephant goad (ankusa), prayer beads, sickle, axe (tanka) and thunderbolt. Indra is said to be the personification of the great summer monsoon of north India. The Vedic horse is the symbol of the breath (Prana). To yoga practitioners, Indra's two horses can represent inhalation and exhalation. His chariot can symbolize the inner practice of yoga. Indra symbolizes the awakened life-force in yoga practice. The slaying of the dragon and the release of the seven rivers, symbolizes Indra as the pure life force that destroys the negative energy of disease and ignorance. Soma represents the fruit of the sacred tree or tree of knowledge. The magic arts, taught by Indra, are known as Indrajala. Another deity by the name of Indra is part of the Daeva group of deities. In ancient Persian mythology, Indra was a minor deity, known as Andra, a Daevas (evil spirit) who opposed Asha Vahista. (*See also* Devas.) As Andra, he waits on the bridge named Cinvat and heaves souls into hell. Indra is somewhat like Thor, the thunderer of Norse religion, and the Roman god of war, Mars (q.v.). As Indra-nag, he is depicted as a crowned king with a bow, attended by the serpent Nagas. Indra is equated with Varuna, who some say was ousted by Indra. In the Buddhist tradition, Indra is known as Inda and is subservient to Buddha. *See also* Kurma and Lokapalas regarding Airavata. Compare Indra with Horus (Egypt), Tiamat (Babylonia), and Verethraghna (Persian). Compare to Uranus and Cronus (Greek). *See also* Aditi; Adityas; Agastya; Ahalya; Arjuna; Asuras; Asvins; Bali (A); Bhishma; Brihaspati; Daityas; Deva (A), Deva (B); Dikpalas; Diti; Dyaus; Gandharvas; Garuda; Hanuman; Heng and Ha; Hiranyaksa; Indrani; Kamadhenu; Karna; Karttikeya; Krishna; Kunti; Loka; Lokapalas; Maruts; Meru Mountain; Mitra; Nagas and Nagis; Pandavas; Parjanyi; Parvati; Prithiva; Ratri; Ravana; Ribhus (The); Sakra; Samantabhadra; Shiva; Skambha; Soma; Surabhi; Surya; Surya-Bai; Swarga; Tvashtri; Ushas; Vach; Varuna; Vasus; Veda (The); Visvakarma; Vritra; Yama.

Indra-nag (India) *see* Indra.

Indrajala (India) Magic Arts. *See also* Indra.

Indrajit (India) Conqueror of Indra. *See also* Ravana.

Indranee (India) *see* Indrani.

Indrani *Indranee* (Nindu, Vedic; India)
   Also known as: *Aindra, Aindri, Paulomi-vallabha* (Lover of Paulomi), *Saci, Saki* (Sanskrit), *Shakrani* (Sanskrit).
   Indrani, the goddess of sexual pleasure, is the daughter of Puloman and is a reflection of her husband Indra. She is a highly sexual, eternally youthful, jealous, war-like woman. When Indra appeared to be spending too much time with the ape Vrishakapi, Indrani cast her burning eyes on him and he was filled with lust for her. Indra appeared and drove the ape away.

Later, Indra was caught by Vrishakapi in a comprising situation with Vrishakapi's wife. In time, Indra and Vrishakapi rekindled their friendship. Indrani had good reason for her jealousy. Her mate had a passion for women, particularly married women. He had another affair with the first woman created by Brahma, Ahalya, who was the wife of his teacher, Gautama. Indra and Indrani had a son, Sitragupta. Indrani owns the Kalpa, also known as the Parijata Tree. It is kept in Swarga, the celestial dwelling place of Indrani and Indra. Swarga is located between heaven and earth on Mount Meru. If the elderly gaze upon the magic wishing tree, they are reinvigorated. Other records indicate that Indrani was either married to or was the lover of Paulomi. Indrani is portrayed as a beautiful and sensual fair-complexioned woman. Compare Indrani to Lakshmi and the Greek Venus. Compare the Parijata Tree to Soma and Amrita (q.v.). *See also* Ahalya; Indra; Meru Mountain; Parijata; Ribhus; Satyabhama (third wife of Krishna); Swarga.

Indraprastha (India)
   Celestial palace. *See also* Pandavas; Visvakarma.

Inet (Egypt) *see* Aai.

Ingi (Teutonic) *see* Dwarfs.

Ingnersuit (Eskimo) *see* Inue; Tornaq.

Ingui-Frey (Teutonic) *see* Freyr.

Ingun (Teutonic) *see* Freyr.

Ingunar-Frey (Teutonic) *see* Freyr.

Ingvi-Frey (Teutonic) *see* Freyr.

Ini-Herit (Egypt)
   Also known as: *Onuris* (male).
   Goddess of mediators, diplomats, statesmen and conciliators. When the goddess Tefnut became angry and bore the sun away, it was Ini-Herit who sought after her, calmed her and returned the sun to the sky.

Ininguru (Australian)
   Goddesses of women. Possibly healing deities. Associated with the secret fertility rites of women. They travel across the desert to participate in the rites, and then return to the sky. They do appear now and then to see what is going on.

Inle (Yoruba People, Africa) *see* Olodumare.

Inmar (Finland) *see* Ilmarinen.

Innini (Sumer)
   Also known as: *Inanna, Ninanna, Ninhursag, Ninki, Ninsinna, Nintud.*
   Mother goddess. Although known in various aspects and different names, most say she was created by Anu and is his female counterpart. *See also* Astarte; Belit-ili; Dumuzi; Ereshkigal; Inanna; Ishtar; Ninhursag; Ninki; Nintud.

Innua (Eskimo) *see* Manitou.

Ino (Greek)
   Also known as: *Leucothea, Mater Matuta* (Roman), *The White Goddess.*
   Ino is the daughter of Cadmus of Thebes and Harmonia.

Her siblings are Agave, Autonoe, Illyrius, Polydorus and Semele. She married Athamas and became the mother of Learchus and Melicertes and the stepmother of Helle and Phrixus (their natural mother was Nephele). Ino and her sisters, Agave and Autonoe, spread rumors that Zeus was not the father of their dead sister's son, Dionysus. Nonetheless, Hermes persuaded her to raise Dionysus as a female to outwit the jealous Hera. Suffering from divine madness, Ino helped her sister Agave rip her son Pentheus to pieces. She also attempted to murder her stepchildren but they were able to escape on a winged golden ram. Hera was able to drive Ino and her husband insane and they killed their own children. Dionysus survived this madness because Zeus had Hermes take him to the nymphs of Nysa who resided on a mountainside near Helicon and there he stayed, possibly in the form of a lamb until manhood. In another version of her story, Ino was insanely jealous of Nephele, Athamas' first wife, and she took it out on her stepchildren by treating them cruelly. She fled to the sea with Athamas in pursuit and in a moment of madness she dove into the water with Melicertes. It is said that the Nereids accepted them as one of their own and Ino became the goddess Leucothea and Melicertes became Palaemon. As sea deities they came to the aid of sailors in distress and it is said that Leucothea once saved Odysseus from death. *See also* Dionysus; Harmonia (A); Mater Matuta; Nephele; Persephone; Portunus; Semele.

Inti *Intu* (Inca People, Peru)
Also known as: *Apu-Punchau.*
Inti or Apu-Punchau is the Peruvian name for the sun. In some legends, Inti is the sun god, father of Choun (also known as Viracocha), Pachacamac and Manco Capac. Other versions name him the brother/husband of Mama Quilla. Inti crosses the sky daily and plunges into the western sea. After swimming under the earth he reappears each morning. Eclipses are caused by his anger. He is depicted as a human with a bright face surrounded by rays and flames. Children and animals were sacrificed to Inti, Pachacamac, and Viracocha annually at a festival in their honor. In some legends he is associated with Tutujanawin (q.v.). *See also* Mama Quilla; Manco Capac; Pachacamac; Tupan; Virococha.

Intu (Inca People, Peru) *see* Inti.

Inua (Eskimo) *see* Manitou; Tornaq.

Inuat (Eskimo)
Also known as: *Inua, Inue, Tornaq.*
The spirit or doppelganger (sometimes called the "owner") of all living creatures, and everything in nature has this spirit, including non-living things. They live on after the death of the individual. Normally they are invisible, but sometimes can be seen as a light or fire, especially associated with foretelling death. *See also* Orenda; Tornaq.

Inue (Eskimo) *see* Inuat.

Io (A) (Greek)
Also known as: *Ida.*
Priestess of Hera. Cow goddess. Princess of Argus and daughter of Inachus (Inakhos). She was loved by Zeus who, to allay the suspicions of Hera, transformed her into a heifer. Hera was aware of the change and had the hundred-eyed Argus watch her. When Zeus had Argus killed by Hermes, Hera tormented Io with a gadfly, which drove her from place to place until she reached the Nile, where she recovered her human form and bore a son, Epaphus, by Zeus. The Greeks identified her with Isis. *See also* Adrastia; Apis (A); Apsyrtus; Golden Fleece.

Io (B) (Maori People, New Zealand; Polynesian)
Also known as: *Iho-Iho, Io-Mataaho, Io-Matua, Io-Matua-Te-Kora, Io-Nui, Io-Taketake, Io-Te-Toi-O-Nga-Rangi, Io-Te-Wananga, Io-Te-Whiwhi, Kore-Te-Whiwhia, Te-Io-Mate* (The God of Death), *Te-Io-Ora* (The Living God).
Supreme Being. All things flow from Io. The original creator, himself uncreated, he retains for himself the spirit and the life and the form. There is nothing outside or beyond him, and with him is the power of life, of death, and of godship. It is Io who selected Tane, the god of forests, to receive his secret knowledge. *See also* Papa; Rangi; Tane.

Io-Mataaho (Polynesia) *see* Io (B)

Io-Matua (Polynesia) *see* Io (B).

Io-Matua-Te-Kora (Polynesia) *see* Io (B).

Io-Nui (Polynesian) *see* Io (B).

Io-Taketake (Polynesia) *see* Io (B).

Io-Te-Toi-O-Nga-Rangi (Polynesia) *see* Io (B).

Io-Te-Wananga (Polynesia) *see* Io (B).

Io-Te-Whiwhi (Polynesia) *see* Io (B).

Iobates (Greek)
Also known as: *Amphianax.*
King of Lycia. He is the father of Philonoe and Stheneboea. When Bellerophon wanted to marry Stheneboea, Iobates sent him to fight the three-headed, fire-breathing Chimaera. When he safely returned, Iobates allowed him to marry Philonoe, not Stheneboea. *See also* Bellerophon; Chimaera; Proetus; Stheneboea.

Iocaste *Iokaste* (Greek) *see* Jocasta.

Iocauna (Taino People, Haiti)
Also known as: *Attabeira, Guamaonocon, Iermaogauacar.*
Supreme being. Iocauna is a supreme being known by two names, Iocauna and Guamaonocon. His mother has five names. They are usually listed as Iella, Atabei, Mamona, Guacarapita, and Guimazoa. In another list, four names are given: Atabei, Iermaogauacar, Apito, and Zuimaco. *See also* Atabei; Guamaonocon; Iella; Zemes.

Ioi (Chinook People, North America)
She is the sister of Blue-Jay (q.v.).

Iokaste (Greek) *see* Iocaste.

Ion (Greek)
Ion is the son of Apollo and Creusa (who was the wife of Xuthus). His is the brother of Janus, the Roman god of beginnings and endings. *See also* Achaeus; Creusa; Janus; Xuthus.

Iophossa *Chalciope* (Greek)
Another name for Chalciope, the daughter of Aeetes, king

of Colchis and Asterodeia. *See also* Aeetes; Asterodeia; Chalciope.

Iord (Scandinavian)
Goddess of earth. Daughter of Nott (Night).

Iormungandr (Teutonic) *see* Jormungandr.

Iouskeha (Native North American) *see* Ioskeha.

Iovialis (Roman) *see* Genius.

Iowahine (Hawaii)
First woman. Wife of Tiki. Both were formed from earth by Tane (q.v.).

Ipa Huaco (Inca) *see* Tahuantin Suyu Kapac.

Ipalnemoani *Ipalnemohuani* (Aztec People, Mexico)
Also known as: *Citlallatonac and Citalicue, Ometecutli and Omeciuatl, Tloque Nauaque, Tloquenahuaque, Tonacatecutli and Tonacaciutl.*
High god. One of the first Aztec gods. Called "He by Whom We Live," he was one of the unknown gods. In some versions, Ipalenemoani is a bisexual deity who is known by various names. *See also* Citlallatonac; Texcatlipoca; Tloque Nauaque; Tloquenahuaque; Tonacatecuhtli.

Ipalnemohuani (Aztec) *see* Ipalnemoni.

Iphianassa (A) (Greek)
She is the daughter of Proteus and Stheneboea (qq.v.). *See also* Iphinoe (A).

Iphianassa (B) (Greek) Another name for Iphigeneia.

Iphicles (Greek) *see* Argonauts; Eurydice (C).

Iphidamas (Greek) *see* Acamas (B).

Iphigenia *Iphigeneia* (Greek)
Also known as: *Chrysothemis, Iphianassa.*
Deified mortal. Daughter of Agamemnon and Clytemnestra. She was offered as a sacrifice to appease Artemis at the outbreak of the Trojan War. However, Artemis substituted her with a bear (some say a deer) and carried Iphigenia off to Tauris. She later became a priestess and saved the life of her brother Orestes when he was about to be sacrificed. Some say she is an aspect of Artemis and Helen. *See also* Achilles; Calchas; Orestes.

Iphimedeia (A) (Greek)
She is the daughter of Triopas, who is the son of Poseidon and Canace, and Hiscilla. Iphimedeia's siblings are Erysichthon, who sold his daughter into prostitution for food, and also descrated Demeter's grove, Messene, who married Polycaon, the first king of Messenia and Phorbas, the king of Thessaly, who fought Pelops (some say Phorbas is the son of Lapithus and Orsinome). Iphimedeia is the wife of her uncle, Aloeus and the lover of Poseidon. *See also* Aloeides; Aloeus; Erysichthon; Phorbas (A); Poseidon.

Iphimedeia (B) (Greek)
Her parents are Theseus, the hero king of Athens, and Helen of Troy. *See also* Helen; Theseus.

Iphinoe (A) (Greek)
She is the daughter of Proteus and Stheneboea or Anteia.

Her siblings are Iphianassa, Megapenthes and Lysippe. The god of wine, Dionysus, or the goddess Hera, drove her insane. *See also* Anteia; Dionysus; Hera; Lysippe; Proetus.

Iphinoe (B) (Greek)
Her father is Nisus, the king of Megara. Erymede and Scylla are her siblings. She married Megareus and became the mother of Evaecheme, Evippus, Hippomenes and Timalcus. *See also* Erymede; Evippus; Hippomenes; Scylla.

Iphinoe (C) (Greek)
She is the daughter of Alcathous and Evaecheme. *See also* Alcathous; Iphinoe (B).

Iphitus (Greek)
An Argonaut. Iphitus is the son of Eurytus and Antiope. He was killed by Heracles. *See also* Antiope; Argonauts (Names of); Heracles.

Iphtimis (Greek) *see* Nefertum (Egypt).

Ipila (Melanesia)
Creator. He carved the first human from wood and brought it to life by painting the face with sago milk. Although he carved more humans at a later time, his first human, Nugu, was punished by Ipila and made to hold the earth on his shoulders. Compare Ipila to Atlas. *See also* Nugu.

Iqi-Balam (Maya) *see* Xumucane.

Ir-Kalla (Akkadian, Babylonia) *see* Irkalla.

Ira (A) (Sumer) *see* Irra; Nergal.

Ira (B) (India) *see* Kasyapa.

Ira-Waru (Polynesian) *see* Maui.

Iraj (Persian) *see* Airya.

Iraja (India) *see* Kama.

Iravat (India)
He is the son of Arjuna and Ulupi. *See also* Arjuna.

Irawaru (Oceanic) *see* Maui.

Irdlirvirisissong (Eskimo) *see* Idlirvirisong.

Irene (Greek)
Also known as: *Eirene, Pax.*
Goddess of peace. *See also* Eirene.

Irin Mage (Tupi-Guarani People, Brazil)
In one version of the Creation Myth, Irin Mage, a powerful magician, caused a deluge to extinguish the great fire caused by Monan, the creator god. In another myth, the brothers Tawenduare, the god of day, and Arikute, the god of night, are the heroes of the deluge. *See also* Arikute; Monan.

Irinyes (Greek) *see* Erinyes; Eumenides.

Iris (Greek)
Goddess of the rainbow. Messenger of the gods. Iris is the daughter of Thaumas and Electra and sister to the Harpies. As the messenger of the gods, particularly Hera and Zeus, the rainbow is her path. She is shown as a beautiful robed woman carrying a staff. Sometimes she has wings. *See also* Electra; Harpies; Thaumas.

Irkalia (Babylonian) *see* Irkalla.

Irkalla *Ir-Kalla, Irkalia* (Babylon)
Underground or Hell. Counterpart of Island of the Blest. Land of "no return" beneath the earth. It is ruled by Nergal and his consort Ereshkigal. It is called the House of Dust and Darkness. Once entered, it can never be left. Some texts refer to Irkalla as an androgynous deity and as such a god or goddess of the underworld. *See also* Apsu; Dilmun; Hades; Hell.

Irkingu (Babylonia) *see* Marduk.

Irlek-Khan (Central Asia) *see* Erlik-Khan.

Irma (Inca People, Peru)
Also known as: *Pachacamac.*
He is a supreme deity who descended from the Sun and Moon. He quarrelled with Kon, a god of the Chimu people. After chasing the Chimu people into the sea he began a new race by creating three different eggs. A gold egg brought forth male nobles, a silver egg female nobles, and a copper for both sexes of the common people. Some mythologists say that Irma was probably a harvest god who was later renamed Pachacamac (q.v.).

Irmen (Teutonic) *see* Irmin.

Irmin *Ermine, Hermin, Irmen, Odin* (possibly); (Norse; Teutonic)
High god. Irmin was worshiped in parts of Germany. He may be the same as Odin. He uses a heavy chariot to ride the Milky Way which was called Irmin's Way. Compare Irmin to the Armenian Armenak. *See also* Odin.

Irnini (Babylonian) *see* Ishtar.

Iron Dirk (Teutonic) *see* Iarnsaxa.

Iroquois People — Creation Legends (North America) *see* Athensic; Enigorio and Enigohatgea; Itapalas.

Irra *Ira* (Assyro-Babylonian)
Also known as: *Gir, Girra, Nergal* (possibly).
Plague god. Underworld deity. God of pestilence. He is the cohort of An and he works for Nergal. *See also* Nergal.

Irsirra (Hurrite)
The son of Kumarbis. This spirit placed Ullikummis on Enlil's lap. *See also* Enlil; Kumbaris; Ullikummis.

Irus (A) (Greek)
Also known as: *Arnaeus.*
He was the attendant to Penelope's would-be lovers. Odysseus killed him in a boxing match. *See also* Odysseus; Penelope.

Irus (B) (Greek)
He is the son of Actor and Aegina. His siblings are Menoetius and Polymela. His children by Demonassa are Eurydamas and Eurytion. *See also* Eurydamas; Eurytion; Menoetius; Peleus; Polymela.

Isa (Hebrew) *see* Jesus.

Isakakate (Crow People, North America) *see* Isakawuate.

Isakawuate *Isakakate* (Crow People, North America)
Also known as: *Old Man Coyote, The Trickster.*
A trickster deity. Sometimes Isakawuate is the name used for the creator.

Isana (India)
"Ruler." A form of Shiva. *See also* Agni; Dikpalas; Shiva.

Isander (Greek)
His parents are Bellerophon, the son of Glaucus and Eurymede, and Philinoe, the daughter of Iobates. His siblings are Deidamia (who married Evander), Hippolochus (the father of Glaucus), and Laodamia (the wife of Sarpedon). *See also* Bellerophon; Evander; Glaucus; Sarpedon.

Isani (India) *see* Gauri.

Ischys (Greek)
He is the son of Elatus and Hippea. His siblings are Caenis and Polyphemus. He fell in love with Coronis but she was killed before their marriage. *See also* Caenis; Coronis; Polyphemus.

Isfenarmad (Persia) *see* Spenta Armaiti.

Ishi-kori-dome (Japan) *see* Ishikoridome-no-Mikoto.

Ishikoridome-no-mikoto *Ishi-kori-dome, I-shi-ko-ri-do-me* (Shinto, Japan)
Goddess of stone cutting and artisans. When the sun goddess Amaterasu withdrew into the depths of the cave named Ame-no-Iwato, darkness enveloped the earth. The deities convened and decided to commission the talented artisan Ishikoridome-no-mikoto to create a mirror that would entice Amaterasu from the cave. The goddess Ama-no-Uzume performed a frenzied dance known as the Karuga. The sun goddess, curious about the noise, peeked out of the cave, and attracted by her beautiful image in the mirror, was lured into the world. The darkness lifted and once again there was light. This famous mirror known as Kagami (also known as Yata-Kayami) became one of the three Insignia of the Throne. The goddess Ishikoridome-no-mikoto was later asked by Amaterasu to accompany her grandson Ninigi to earth when he took up his duties as the divine ruler of Japan. In Japan a mirror represents a woman's soul, knowledge, enchantment, history and principles. The mirror is an attribute of Amaterasu and Emma-O. The sacred mirror, Kagami is a symbol of purity. It is deposited in the goddesses' sanctuary at Ise. *See also* Ama-no-Uzume; Amaterasu.

Ishkhara (Babylonian, Hittite)
She is a goddess of love who is affiliated with Ishtar as a priestess. In another reference she is one of the deities who is called upon to listen to the believer (q.v.).

Ishkur *Iskur* (Akkadian, Hittite, Sumerian)
Also known as: *Adad, Enlil, Immer, Mer, Mermer, Mur.*
Wind god. Ishkur, who lives in the underworld known as Arallu, replaced Enlil as a god of the winds. In some renditions, he is known as a god of lightning who is the son of Enlil. He is sometimes identified with Adad and is possibly the same as Imhursag, the father of Ningirsu. *See also* Arallu; Enlil; Ningirsu.

Ishmael (Hebrew) *see* Ismail.

Ishtar *Istar* (Assyro-Babylonian; Akkadia, Chaldea, Semitic, Sidon, Sumer).

Also known as: *Absusu* (Sumerian), *Abtagigi* (She Who Sends Messages of Desire), *Agasaya, Ashtart, Ashtoreth, Athar* (Arabic), *Aya* (Babylonian), *Banitu* (possibly), *Belti* (Semite), *Bisi-Bisi, The Bride, Dilbar* (The War-provoking Evening Star), *Gamlat* (Babylonian), *Gumshea, Hanata* (Middle Eastern), *Inanna* (Sumerian), *Innini, Irnini* (possibly), *Kilili* (Queen of Harlots), *Meni* (possibly), *Minu-anni, Minu-ullu, Nin-kar-zi-da, Nin-khar-sagga, Nin-si-anna, Ninkarrak* (Sumerian), *Ninkasi, Ninlil* (Phoenician), *Sharis* (possibly an ancient name used by the Armenians), *Shaushka* (Hittite), *Shimti* (Akkadian; goddess of fate), *The Shrieker, Zanaru* (Lady of the Islands), *Zib* (evening star who stimulates sexual desire).

As a Babylonian goddess, Ishtar originally may have been a Sumerian or Akkadian goddess. A composite of numerous goddesses, she is generally thought to have originally been the earlier Sumerian goddess Inanna. Ishtar is a mother goddess, fertility goddess, the goddess of spring, a storm goddess, a warrior and goddess of war, a goddess of the hunt, a goddess of love, goddess of marriage and childbirth, goddess of fate, and a goddess who is the divine personification of the planet Venus. She is also an underworld deity. Her predominate aspects are as the mother goddess of compassion and the goddess of sex and war. She is invoked for protection against sickness and evil in her role as mother goddess. The sexual aspect of her persona is linked to the earth's fertility. She has a reputation for having numerous lovers who were killed when she was finished with them. As the daughter of Sin and sister of Shamash, the warlike side of her character is dominant. In her role as warrior, Ishtar rode into battle and sent the vanquished into the underworld. It is said that she once tore out the teeth of a lion. It is in this form that she was worshiped by the Assyrians, particularly at Nineveh and Erbil. She is the sister of the queen of the Underworld, Ereshkigal. Ishtar was worshiped at Uruk as the goddess of gentleness, love and desire. In this aspect, she is known as the daughter of the sky god Anu and the goddess Anat. Though not as violent, she was still demanding and had a bad temper. Ishtar's consort, and some say brother, is Tammuz, but she was also said to be the wife of Ashur, and the consort of many kings. In one of her numerous adventures, as Irnini, she was living in the huge Cedar Forest of the Amanus which were guarded by the giant Khumbaba. She had planned to build a table and chair from the wood of a huluppa tree that she had planted in her garden. Prevented from proceeding with her project by negative forces, Gilgamesh came to her aid. In return, she presented him with a magic drum and drumstick made from the huluppa tree. Their relationship was not always smooth. Ishtar once took revenge on Gilgamesh by sending a bull after him, when he spurned her advances. Enkidu saved Gilgamesh, but was rewarded for his bravery by being struck down with a fatal illness by Ishtar. In another tale, Tammuz was mortally wounded by a wild boar. He was cast into the underworld. Furious, she made a journey to the dark and dreary place. Aggressively she demanded entry and threatened to smash the doors down if refused. She also threatened to let the dead loose to wander among the living. The guardian of the gate gained permission from the ruler Ereshkigal to allow Ishtar through the gates. At each of the seven gates it was demanded that she leave an article of clothing or jewelry. Finally, naked, she appeared before the queen. In the meantime, the Upperworld mourned her absence. The vizier of the gods, Papsukaal, was tearing out his hair, and Shamash was in deep mourning. Her absence from the Upperworld caused the passions of all men and beasts to cease. The only way to return to normalcy was to persuade Ishtar to return. This, they knew, would be a difficult endeavor, as she would not consent to return without Tammuz. The great god, Ea, finally decided to create Asushunamir, a charming eunuch, to send to the Underworld to rescue Ishtar. With the use of magic incantations, which Ereshkigal could not resist, Ishtar was led from the Underworld by Namtar. She was part of the triad with Sin and Shamash. Ishtar as the goddess of love was irrestible. Her lovers were legion. Once tired of them, they were cast aside. When she descended to earth, she had a retinue of courtesans with her. Sacred prostitution formed part of her cult. Ishtar is identified with the Sumerian goddess Inanna and with Astarte of the Phoenicians and Babylonians. She has been identified with Ninlil. Ishtar corresponds to the Chaldean goddess Nintu (q.v.). Ishtar parallels the ancient Sumerian goddess Anunit in numerous ways (q.v.). The Hebrew goddess Tamar is equivalent to Ishtar. The Hittite goddess Shaushka is known as the Hurrian Ishtar. As Hanata, she is also a warrior. The Babylonian goddess Gamlat eventually assimilated into Ishtar, as did the Babylonian Aya (q.v.). The war goddess Agasya eventually became Ishtar as the sky warrior. The vegetation goddess Gumshea merged with Ishtar. Her titles of Minu-anni and Minu-ullu may link her with the Assyrian god or goddess, Meni (see Menu). Compare Ishtar to Isis (Egyptian), and the Inca goddess, Mama Allpa. Ishtar is depicted sometimes naked, with her hands clasping her breasts. Often she is bedecked in jewelry and has an elaborate hairstyle. She is also shown reclining, wearing a crowned crescent set with a shining stone on her head. Sometimes she is shown holding her symbol, the eight pointed star. In her battle stance, she carries a bow and is depicted standing on a chariot drawn by seven lions. The lion, bull, and dragon are Ishtar's emblems. The lion is her sacred animal and perhaps the dove. *See also* Abtagigi; Allat; Allatu; Anat; Anta; Anu (B); Arinna; Ashur; Astarte; Asushunamir; Atargatis; Athar (A); Aya; Belti; Boann (Celtic); Chemosh; Ea; Enki; Enkidu; Ereshkigal; Gilgamesh; Igigi; Inanna; Innini; Khumbaba; Kilili; Namtar; Ninkarrak; Ninkasi; Ninlil; Papsukaal; Ramman; Saltu; Sammuramat; Semiramis; Shamash; Sharis; Sin; Tammuz; Tiamat; Venus; Zerpanitum.

Ishum (Babylon) *see* Nergal.

Isimud (Sumer) *see* Inanna.

Isir (Babylon) *see* Tammuz.

Isis (Egypt; also worshiped in Pompeii, approx. 360 B.C.).

Also known as: *Ament, Ankhat* (Goddess of Land), *Anquat, Anquet* (Giver of Life), *Aset, Aust, Eset* (Giver of Life; Egyptian), *Hest, Isis Pharia* (Greek), *Kekhet* (Goddess of Harvest), *Khut* (Light Giver), *Methyer, Renenet* (Goddess of Food), *Satis* (Fertility), *Selene* (Greek), *Tcheft, Thenenet* (Power), *Usert* (Goddess of Tuat).

Patroness of loving wives and mothers. Goddess of the earth, protector of the dead. The Greeks called her Isis Pharia, the protector of seaman. She assimilated the functions of many other goddesses. Known as "the cunning one," Isis is the daughter of Geb and Nut, the sister-wife of Osiris and the sister of Seth and Nephthys. She is the mother of Horus. When Osiris was treacherously slain and dismembered by Seth, Isis and her sister Nephthys wandered the universe searching for the parts of his body to restore him to life. Isis wanted the same power that Ra held and she knew everything but his secret name. She tricked Ra by sending a serpent to poison him with its bite and made him reveal his name. By doing so her powers became greater. Isis, Osiris, and Horus formed the powerful Egyptian trinity. She was the principal goddess of ancient Egypt and identified with the moon by Plutarch although the ancient Egyptians regarded her as the "Eye of Ra." Isis is said to typify the female side of civilization in its struggle with barbarism as Osiris embodies the male aspect. The *Book of Breathings* was said to have been written by Isis for her dead husband (*see also* Shu). She is represented by having a solar disk between the horns of a cow. Horus and Isis were depicted as falcons when they were later worshiped in Gebtu. Isis is identified with Hathor. She was worshiped in Rome and Greece, and came to be identified with the goddess Demeter. She is also identified with Venus (Roman), Astarte (Phoenicia), Ishtar (Babylon), Diana of Crete, Proserpine of Sicilians, and Minerva of Athens. Compare Isis to Ishtar (Assyro-Babylonian), Marduk (Babylonian, who also used magic), and Freyja (Teutonic). *See also* Ab; Ament; Anquet; Anubis; Apis (A); Astarte; Atum; Geb; Hapy (A); Harsiesis; Heket; Horus; Io; Nephthys; Osiris; Qebhsneuf; Ra; Ranenet; Satis; Selene; Selket; Serapis; Serius; Set; Sothis; Usert; Wadjet.

Isis Pharia (Greek) *see* Isis.

Isis-Sothis (Egypt) *see* Sirius; Sothis.

Iskrychi (Poland) *see* Domovoi (Russia).

Iskrzychi (Slavic) *see* Domovoj.

Iskur (Babylon) *see* Ishkur.

Islamic Hell (Stages of)
   Known as Daru el-Bawar, the Islamic Hell is divided into seven stages:
   First: Jahannam (similar to purgatory).
   Second: Laza (reserved for Christians).
   Third: Hutameh (a fiery place reserved for Jewish people).
   Fourth: Sa'ir (reserved for Sabians).
   Fifth: Saqar (a fiery place reserved for the Magi).
   Sixth: Jahim (a hot fire of idol-worshipers).
   Seventh: Hawiyah (a bottomless pit reserved for hypocrites).

Islamic Paradise (Stages of)
   Known as Dar el-Jannah, Paradise is divided into eight stages:
   First: Jannatu el-Khuld, known as "The Garden of Eternity," and symbolized by green or yellow coral.
   Second: Daru el-Qarar, "The Dwelling of Peace," symbolized by white pearls.
   Third: Daru el-Salam, known as "The Dwelling which Abideth," symbolized by green chrysolite.

Fourth: Jannatu el-Adn, "The Gardens of Perpetual Abode," symbolized by large pearls.
   Fifth: Jannatu el-Ma'wa, "The Gardens of Refuge."
   Sixth: Jannatu el-Na'im, "The Gardens of Delight," symbolized by white silver.
   Seventh: Illiyun, where the register of good deeds is kept.
   Eighth: Jannatu el-Firdaus, "The Gardens of Paradise," symbolized by red gold.

Island of Flame (Egypt) *see* Ogdoad.

Island of the Blessed (Greek)
   On the western edge of Oceanus is the Island of the Blessed, an after-death land of happiness for those favored by the gods. *See also* Harmonia (A).

Ismail (Islamic) *Ishmael* (Hebrew)
   The son of Hajar and Ibrahim. *See also* Zam Zam.

Ismaroinen (Slavic) *see* Ilmarinen.

Ismenius (Greek)
   He is the father of Linus, the music teacher who taught Heracles, Orpheus and Thamyris how to play the lyre. *See also* Linus.

Ismenos (Greek)
   His parents are Amphion and Niobe. One of five sons and six daughters, they were all, except one, murdered. The males were killed by Apollo and the females (except Chloris) were killed by the goddess of the hunt, Artemis. *See also* Amphion; Amyclas; Artemis; Chloris; Niobe

Ismenus (Greek)
   He is the son of the river god Asopus and Metope. For the names of his siblings, *see* Asopus.

Isodaites (Greek) Another name for Dionysus.

Isong (Ekoi, and Ibibio People, West Africa)
   Also known as: *Eka Obasi, Obasi Nsi.*
   Goddess of fertility. She is called "The Tortoise-Shell Goddess."

Issitoq (Eskimo)
   Also known as: *The Giant Eye.*
   High god. The god who seeks out those who break the rules.

Istar (Assyro-Babylonian) *see* Ishtar.

Istaru (Assyria) *see* Astarte.

Istepahpah (Creek People, North America)
   A devouring monster.

Istio (Teutonic)
   Patriarchal deity. He is the son of Manus and the grandson of Tuisko.

Iswara (India) "Supreme Lord." *See also* Shiva.

Italapas (Chinook People, North America)
   Also known as: *Coyote.*
   In a Creation Legend, after the Deluge, Italapas ridded the

earth of water, and enabled mortals to begin a new life. He is also credited for establishing laws. *See also* Coyote.

Itchita (Yukut People, Siberia)

Tree goddess and healing deity. This goddess lives in birch trees. Her tiny assistants are spirits of grass and trees. They keep the spirits of sickness away from mortals.

Ith (Celtic) *see* Eire.

Ithavall (Teutonic) *see* Idawold.

Ithun (Teutonic) *see* Idun.

Iti (Egypt)

Also known as: *Ity*.

God of music. Son of the Bull of Ra and the goddess Hathor. He is also called the "Bull of Confusion." He is shown as a man with the double crown of Upper and Lower Egypt and the side-lock of youth.

Itoki (Nicaragua)

Creator deity. Great mother. Itoki is said to be a mother scorpion who dwells at the end of the Milky Way. She is responsible for sending the new souls of those recently born to their human life and she receives the souls of the newly dead. Her spouse is the great father Maisahana the founder of the Tauchca, Yusco, Sumo, and Ula people. Itoki is probably shown with many paps. *See also* Ituana; Maisahana.

Itom Ae (Yaqui People, South America)

Also known as: *Our Mother*.

Supreme Goddess. Not much known since this is a recent discovery.

Itsu-no-wo-ha-bari (Japan) *see* Ame-no-wo-ha-bari.

Ituana (Nicaragua) *see* Itoki.

Itylus (Greek)

He is the son of Zethus, the co-ruler of Thebes and Aedon, the "Nightingale." *See also* Aedon; Zethus.

Itys (Greek)

His parents are Tereus and Procne, who became a swallow after she accidentally killed Itys. *See also* Aedon; Procne.

Itza Mixcoatl (Mexico) *see* Mixcoatl.

Itzam-Kab-Ain (Maya People, Yucatan) *see* Ahmucen-Cab.

Itzama (Maya) *see* Itzama.

Itzamna *Itzmatul, Izamna* (Maya People, Yucatan)

Also known as: *Chichen Izta, Hunab Ku, Izamal, Izona, Kabil, Kabul, Kinich-ahau, Kinish-kakimo, Ytzmatul, Zamna*.

"Lizard House." Sky god. God of healing. God of drawing and letters. A chief god, he is the son of Hunab-Ku. He was the creator and father of both gods and men. He brought writing, and the use of maize and rubber. Squirrels were sacrificed and gifts were given to him. Itzamna kept the fields fertile for the people. Itzamna had the ability to restore the dead to life. He was sometimes called Kabul or Kabil. In some legends, he appears as a priest named Zamna. According to some writers,

Zamna, Izamal, and Itzmatul are modifications of the name Itzamna. He is shown with a red hand, to which the ill pray for healing. Itzamna is sometimes identified with Quetzalcoatl, sometimes with Tlaloc, and sometimes with Tonacatecutli. *See also* Cain; Kinich Ahau; Quetzalcoatl; Tlaloc.

Itzcoliuhqui *Itztlacoliuhqui* (Aztec People, Mexico)

God of darkness. He is responsible for earthquakes, volcanic eruptions, and disasters. Some say he is a god of cold and dryness. He is possibly an aspect of Quetzalcoatl. Itzcoliuhqui is sometimes identified with Texcatlipoca. *See also* Pillan.

Itzcueye (Honduras, Nicaragua, Central America)

Earth goddess. *See also* Ilancue.

Itzcuinan (Mexico) *see* Xochiquetzal.

Itzli (Aztec People, Mexico)

Itzli is a stone knife god, who is the Lord of the Second Hour of the Night. He is identified with Texcatlipoca (q.v.). *See also* Lord of the Night Hours.

Itzmatul (Aztec, Maya) *see* Itzamna.

Itzpapalotl (Aztec; Mexico)

Also known as: *Cihuatcoatl, Obsidian Butterfly, Tonantzin*.

Itztlacoliuhqui (Aztec) *see* Itzcoliuhqui; Quetzalcoatl; Tezcatlipoca.

Itztli (Aztec People, Mexico)

Also known as: *Texcatlipoca*.

Stone knife god. He rules the Second Hour of the Night. Itztli is usually depicted with Chalchiuhtlicue and Tlazolteotl (qq.v.). *See also* Texcatlipoca; Tonatiuh.

Iuchar (Celtic) *see* Cian; Dana.

Iucharba (Celtic) *see* Cian.

Iucharbar (Celtic) *see* Dana.

Iulus (Greek)

Also known as: *Ascanius, Ilus*.

Iulus is the son of Aeneas and Creusa (qq.v.).

Iuno (Etruscan) *see* Juno.

Iuppiter (Roman) *see* Jupiter.

Iusaas *Iusas* (Egypt)

Also known as: *Iusaaset, Nebt-Hetep*.

First deity. In later Egyptian mythology, she was believed to be the wife of Atum. Another wife of Atum was Nebhet Hotep. Iusaas sometimes appears as the sole parent of the first divine couple Shu and Tefnut. Other times, Iusaas and Nebhet Hotep are merely female aspects of Tem, who is bisexual in some accounts. Nebhet Hotep seems to have been a double of Iusaas, and is sometimes called "Mistress of the Gods." Iusaas is shown as a woman holding a scepter in her right hand and the ankh, in her left. She wears a vulture headdress surmounted by a uraeus, and a disk between a pair of horns. *See also* Atum.

Iusaaset (Egypt) *see* Iusaas; Shu.

Iustitia (Roman)
Another spelling for Justitia, the goddess of justice.

Iuturna (Roman)
Another spelling for Juturna, the goddess of springs.

Iuwen (Egypt) *see* Osiris.

Ivaldi (Norse; Teutonic)
Smith gods. They are two dwarfs called the sons of Ivaldi who made the three treasures for the gods. The golden hair for Sif, the ship Skidbladnir for Freyr, and the spear Gungnir for Odin.

Iving (Norse; Teutonic)
Deified river. The river that never freezes, it divides Asgard from Jotunheim. *See also* Asgard; Jotunheim.

Iwa (Polynesia, Hawaii) *see* Kupua.

Iwa-naga-hime *Iha-naga-himi* (Japan)
Fate deity. "The Lady of Rock-Perpetuity," and ugly sister of Ko-no-hana-sakuya-hime. When Ninigi chose the better looking of the two women, Iwa decreed that mankind would be short-lived like the flowers.

Iwasu-hime-no-kami (Japan) *see* Izanami.

Iweridd (British, Cymric, Irish)
She is the earth goddess wife of Llyr and mother of Bran and Branwen. Her name means "Ireland." *See also* Bran; Branwen; Llyr.

Ix (Maya)
In some myths, Ix is one of the four Becabs. He represents the west. His color is black. *See also* Becabs.

Ix-chel (Maya)
Also known as: *Chibilias.*
Goddess of childbirth. She is responsible for the fecundity of women. Ix-chel is also considered a guardian and a deity of medicine. Some say she is the wife of Izamna and mother of the Becabs.

Ix Tub Tun (Maya)
No function shown, but may be a rain deity. Her legend is that she spits out precious stones. She is shown as a snake.

Ixazalvoh *Ixzaluoh* (Maya People, Yucatan)
Ixazalvoh is the inventor and goddess of weaving, the goddess of healing, childbirth, prophecy, and sexuality. In some renditions, she is the spouse of the sun god Kinich Ahau. In other versions she is the spouse of Hunab-Ku (q.v.). *See also* Hunab-Ku; Ixchel; Kinich Ahau.

Ixbalanque (Maya)
Brother of Hunahpu (q.v.). *See also* Gukup Cakix.

Ixchel (Maya)
She is the goddess of healing, childbirth, prophecy, sexuality and weaving. *See also* Ixazalvoh.

Ixcocauhqui (Nahuatl People, Central America; Mexico)
God of fire and destructive lightning.

Ixcuin (Aztec) *see* Ixmacane.

Ixcuina (Maya) Goddess of pleasure. *See also* Ixmacane.

Ixcuiname (Mexico) *see* Ixmacane.

Ixion (Greek)
Also known as: *Iksion.*
Deified mortal. King of the Lapithae of Thessaly. Ixion is the son of Antion and Perimela (Perimele). There is a possibility that his father was not Antion but Phlegyas or Ares. He was the king of the Lapiths of Thessaly and he was married to Dia, the daughter of Eioneus. Some think that Zeus was the father of their child, Peirithous. He is also the father of Amycus and the Centaurs by Nephele. Ixion promised his father-in-law a valuable gift when he married Dia but he was unable to keep his word. Eioneus decided to take two of Ixion's horses until he could fulfill his promise. Furious, Ixion arranged to pay the debt but when Eioneus arrived he threw him into a pit of fire and killed him. This act stunned the populace and the deities for it was said to be the first time that a mortal had murdered a family member. After a long period of repentance, he was summoned by Zeus to Mount Olympus and placed at the table of the gods. But Ixion, unappreciative of his host's hospitality, tried to seduce Hera, the wife of Zeus. Zeus created a cloud named Nephele in the form of Hera; and Ixion, believing it was the goddess, was caught in the act of making love to her. Zeus punished him by chaining him to a fiery wheel which never ceased turning, either in the sky or in later mythology in the Underworld. In fairness to Ixion, Homer, in the *Iliad* said that Zeus was in love with Ixion's wife, Dia. Compare to the punishment of Sisyphus and Tantalus. *See also* Abas (C); Hades; Nephele; Peirithous.

Ixmacane *Ixcuin, Ixcuina, Ixcuiname, Ixmucane, Xmucane* (Maya)
Also known as: *Bitol, Teteoinnan, Tlazolteotl.*
Creator. One of the original four regents who tried to create mankind. He was changed into two gods by the fabricating gods Ajtzak and Ajbit. Before the change, his name was Bitol. This was also the time when the only female joined the group. She had the double name of Chirakan-Ixmucane, which links her with the creation deities. In another version, she is spoken of as Ixcuiname (four faces or four sisters) who represents the four ages of women. One of these sisters is Ixcuina, who is a goddess of pleasure. *See also* Bitol; Hueytonantzin; Ixpiyacoc; Teteoinnan; Tlazolteotl.

Ixmucane (Mexico) *see* Ixmacane.

Ixpiyacoc *Xpiyacoc* (Maya)
Also known as: *Tzakol.*
Creator. At the third attempt at creating mankind, Tzakol (one of the four original regents) was split into two gods, one of which was Ixpiyacoc. He and Tzakol were joined by the fabricating gods, Ajtzak and Akbit. In another version, Tzakol, Bitol, Alom and Qaholom (Cajolom) changed their names to Ixpiyacoc, Ixmucane, Hunahpuguch and Hunahpuutiu, then joined Ajtzak and Ajbit and one female deity named Chirakan-Ixmucane. *See also* Cipactonal; Ixmacane; Oxomoco.

Ixtab (Maya People, Yucatan)

Goddess of death. She is known as a goddess of those who hang themselves. Ixtab is shown as a limp body with a loop around the neck. She is related to Ahpuch, Yum Cimil and Hanhau, who are all deities of death. *See also* Mitlan.

Ixtaccihuatl (Aztec People, Mexico)

Also known as: *White Woman.*

Ixtaccihuatl is a sacred volcano in central Mexico. She is worshipped for earth, water, rain, and vegetation. *See also* Tlaloc.

Ixtacihuatl (Aztec) *see* Ixtaccihuatl.

Ixtacmixcoatl (Aztec People, Mexico) *see* Mixcoatl.

Ixtlilton (Aztec People, Mexico)

"Little Black One."

He is one of a group with Xochipilli and Macuilxochitl. They might be brothers. Ixtlilton, a god of healing, health and medicine, is associated with the Centzon Totochtin (q.v.). In some renditions, he is a god of maize or dancing. Ixlilton is associated with Centzontotochtin. *See also* Texcatlipoca.

Ixtliltou (Aztec) *see* Texcatlipoca.

Ixzaluoh (Maya) *see* Ixazalvoh.

Iyatiku (Crow, Pueblo People, North America)

Mother goddess. Corn goddess. She was instrumental in bringing mortals to the surface from the bowels of the earth. She made a ladder from a fir tree and after a woodpecker bored a hole in the rock above, mortals were able to climb into the next world. There were four worlds: white, red, blue, and yellow. Iyatiku helped the mortals from the red world to the blue world.

Izamal (Maya) *see* Itzamna.

Izamna (Aztec) *see* Itzamna.

Izanagi and Izanami *Izana-gi and Izana-mi* (Shinto; Japan)

Izanagi (Male Who Invites) and Izanami (Female Who Invites) were created by the celestial deities to create earthly manifestations. Izanagi and Izanami are the last of the seventh generation of the first deities born from chaos. Their first creation was the deity Hirugo, whom they set adrift to fend for himself. They created the eight Japanese islands (other islands came into being later) and the deities to inhabit the lands. (*See also* Izanami.) The last god, Kagu-tsuchi, the god of fire, burned the goddess and caused Izanani great pain and distress. From her bodily expulsions, the goddess Moaning-River was created and Izanami died. According to the *Kojiki*, her inconsolable husband Izanagi, beheaded the child with Ame-no-wo-ha-bari (Heavenly Point Blade Extended), his sacred sword. Blood from his sword fell to the ground and created eight more gods and from the body issued eight deities representing the mountains. In the *Nihongi*, Izanagi cut the serpent into three pieces, and each became a god. The drops of blood from his sword created the gods Kura-okami (Dragon god of the valleys), Kura-yama-tsumi (Lord of the dark mountains), Kura-mitsu-ha (Dark-water-snake or Valley-water-snake) and Taka-okami (Dragon-

god residing on the mountains). In the *Kojiki*, these deities issued from the blood between Izanagi's fingers. Izanagi then descended into Yomi (hell) to beg Izanami to return with him. Reluctantly, because she had tasted the food of Yomi, she approached the god of Yomi with her husband's request. Izanagi ignored her plea not to follow her into the castle and there he found Izanami rotting and full of worms, guarded over by the soldiers of Yomi and eight Thunder gods. He threw three peaches at the soldiers and managed to block the entrance to Yomi with a huge rock. Izanami, angry that he hadn't listened to her, chased after him and found herself barricaded by the rock in Yomi. She was so angry she caused one thousand people to die every day. In retaliation, he gave birth to fifteen hundred people to thwart her. After all they had been through, Izanagi and Izanami decided to part ways. After escaping the darkness of Yomi, Izanagi went to the sea to cleanse himself. This process created the terrestrial deities: a daughter Amaterasu (Heaven Illumining Goddess), the Ruler of the Realm of Light on Heaven and Earth; and two sons: Tsuki-yomi (also spelled Tsukiyomi-no-Mikoto), the Moon Ruler and Ruler of the Night, and Takehaya Susanowo, the Valiant Swift Impetuous Hero, who is the Ruler of the Ocean and Mysterious Things. For the Shinto creation myth, *see* Ama-no-minaka-nushi. For their creations between Hirugo and Amaterasu, *see* Kami and Haya-akitsu-hime-no-kami. The legend of Izanagi is similar to Pan-Ku of the Chinese. Compare to Orpheus (Greek). For additional information about thunder gods, *see also* Take-me-kazuchi. Izanagi created the first wind gods Shina-tsu-hiko, and O-Wata-Tsu-Mi. The peach, an attribute of Izanagi, symbolizes immortality and is used to ward off evil spirits and the plague. For more about the peach tree, *see* Yomi. *See also* Ame-no-wo-ha-bari; Hiruko; Izanami; Kaya-no-hime-no-kami; Kushi-nada-hime; Susanowa; Tsuki-Yomi; Yomi.

Izanami (Japan)

Also known as: *Izanami-no-kami.*

Creator. Izanami and Izanagi were given the function of creating the terrestrial deities. They were given a spear known as the "Celestial Jewel-spear." As they stood on Ama-no-uki-hashi, the "floating bridge of heaven" (also known as "Heavenly Stairs" or "Heavenly Rock Boat"), they fished around until they found the sea. They stirred the thick primeval waters, drew up the spear, and from its tip the island of Onogoro was formed. The original deities who sprang from chaos built a home for the couple with a central pillar. Izanami and Izanagi became man and wife by circling the pillar three times and meeting one another face to face. The first deity they created was the "leech child" Hirugo. Next they created the eight islands of Japan, known as their children. Others islands came into existence later. Once the islands had been created Izanami and Izanagi gave birth to the inhabitants which were the physical features of the terrain and the natural phenomena such as earth, sea, winds, trees, mountains, valleys, plains, seasons and fire. Thirty deities representing these elements are said to have been born. This included the goddess Iwasu-hime-no-kami (possibly the sand); a goddess, Haya-akitsu-hime-no-kami (Ruler of the Seas); Kaya-no-hime-no-kami (Ruler of the Plains and Goddess of Fields and Meadows); Ogetsu-hime-no-kami (Great Food Princess Deity, who is also known as Ogetsu-hime and

Oho-ge-tsu-himi). They also gave birth to the sea gods, likely snakes or dragons, known as Wata-tsumi (sea children) and the Miszuchi (water fathers), which are described variously as four-legged dragons, horned deities and large water snakes. These deities were not individually named but were appealed to when rain was needed during arid periods. The birth of her son the fire god, Kagu-tsuchi, seared and scorched Izanami. As she lay dying, additional deities were born from the expulsions of her body. These included Kanayama-hime (Metal-Mountain Princess Deity) and her brother; Haniyasu-bime-no-kami, the earth goddess and goddess of clay and her brother; Izunome-no-kami (Hallowed-Woman Deity) and her brother; Mitsuha-nome (also known as Mitsu-ha no-me), a water goddess variously described as a water snake or a producer of water, and her brother. Kuramitsuha-no-kami (Valley-Water-Greens Deity) is sometimes included in this group; however, according to the *Nihongi* this deity is said to have come from the body of their son, the fire god Kagu-tsuchi. Nakisawame-no-kami (Weeping-Marsh Woman Deity), described as a goddess dwelling at the base of the trees in the foothills of Mount Kagu, was formed from the tears of Izanagi who wept for his dead wife. Also listed is Ihatsutsu-nome, the wife of Iha-tsutsu no wo and mother of the god Tutsu-nushi no Kami, although according to the *Nihongi*, she may be of the following generation. They have been depicted hovering over the "ocean of chaos" just before the creation of the island of Onogoro. Izanami is shown as a woman with long hair. In the transla-tion of the *Nihongi* by Aston, she is shown with long hair, wearing an ornate robe and is facing Izanagi. Between them are two wagtails. The spear may be a phallic symbol. The pillar, a common symbol in many civilizations, is an object of honor in Japan. It is found in Shinto shrines and is known as Nakago no mibashira (Central August Pillar). The bridge, Ama-no-uki-hashi, is the connection between heaven and earth. In myth, the bridge collapsed into the sea one day as the gods were napping. From that time, it became necessary for the deities to have messengers travel back and forth. This bridge is also known as Ame-no-uki-hashi, Ama-no-hashadate, Ame-no-iha-fune, and Ukibashi. The bridge is symbolic of a transition from one state to another. Sometimes messengers are indicative of the union of heaven and earth. For additional details *see* Ama-no-minaka-nushi. *See also* Izanagi and Izanami for details of their relationship. *See also* Amaterasu; Ame-no-wo-ha-bari; Haya-akitsu-hime-no-kami; Kagu-Tsuchi; Kami; Kanayama-hime; Susanowo.

Izha (Indo-Iranian) Goddess of the sacrifice.

Izona (Maya) *see* Itzamna.

Iztac Ciuatl (Aztec) *see* Ixtaccihuatl.

Iztaccihuatl (Aztec) *see* Mixcoatl.

Iztacmixcoatl (Aztec) *see* Mixcoatl.

Izunome-no-kami (Japan) *see* Izanami.

J

Jaahannam (Arabic) The underworld. *See also* Gehenna.

Jabal (Sumer)
Patron of tents and flocks. *See also* Ea; Enki; Lumha.

Jacy (Tupi-Guarani People, Brazil)
Jacy is the moon, and the creator of plant life. *See also* Hermitten.

Jadapati (India) *see* Varuna.

Jade Emperor (China) *see* Yu Huang.

Jade Lady (China) *see* Yu Nu.

Jafnhar (Teutonic)
"Even as High," an alternate name for Odin.

Jagadgauri (India) Another name for Parvati (q.v.).

Jagadnatha (India) Another spelling for Jagannath (q.v.).

Jaganat (India) *see* Jagannath.

Jaganmatri (India)
"Mother of the World." *See also* Devi; Durga; Lakshmi.

Jagannath *Jagadnatha, Jaganat, Jagannath, Jaggurnath, Jayanat, Juggernaut*
Also known as: *Buddha, Krishna, Vishnu* (Hindu; India).
Jagannath, meaning "Lord of the World," is a title for Krishna, and a form of Krishna, who is worshiped for protection and removal of sins. One day, Krishna, in the form of an animal, was slain by a hunter. A pious king, Indradyumna, also known as Indrahumna, came upon his bones. Krishna instructed the king to have an image made of him and to place the bones inside. The great artisan Visvakarma agreed to create the idol, providing that the king would not look at it until it was finished. The impatient king kept pestering Visvakarma. Finally, after fifteen days he became so annoyed that he stopped his creation, leaving it without hands or feet. Some scholars believe that Jagannath was Buddha. During the festival of Snana-yantra, held in the month of Jyaishtha, the statue is bathed in milk.

During the following festival of Ratha-yatra, in the month of Ashadha (June-July), he is placed in his great car, accompanied by his brother Bala-Rama and his sister Jagannatha (also called Subhadra) and carried to his temple as part of a great procession. This ritual symbolizes regeneration. It is often said that worshipers dragging the car threw themselves under the wheels as an act of sacrifice. This is doubtful as the spilling of blood was considered a defilement. It is likely that the crushing crowds accidentally pushed believers under the car wheels. As Indradyumna retrieved the image before the hands and feet were completed, the statue is shown this way. The most primitive tribe in India, the Saora people, worship Jagannath as well as one hundred and twenty-six other deities. *See also* Bala-Rama; Buddha; Krishna; Subhadra; Vishnu; Visvakarma.

Jagannatha *Subhadra* (India) *see* Jagannath; Subhadra.

Jaggurnath (India) *see* Jagannath.

Jaguar God (Mexico; Aztec) *see* Tepeyollotl.

Jah (A) *Jeh* (Persia) *see* Jahi.

Jah (B) (Hebrew) *see* Jehovah.

Jahannam (Islam)
The first stage in Daru el-Bawar, the Islamic Hell (q.v.).

Jahi (Persia)
Also known as: *Jah* (Pahlavi dialect), *Jeh* (Pahlavi dialect).
She is the personification of female impurity in the *Avesta*. To defeat the evil that she has introduced into the world, the virgin Eredatfedhri is invoked. An evil harlot-demon, she aroused Angra Mainyu from his sleep and caused him to pour poison on the body of the first man, Gaya Maretan, which created world conflict. In the *Bundahishn* Jahi is the personification of sin. *See also* Ahura Mazda; Angra Mainyu; Drujs (female demons of deceit); Gaya Maretan.

Jahim (Islam)
The sixth stage in Daru el-Bawar, the Islamic Hell. It is reserved for idol-worshipers. *See also* Islamic Hell.

Jahve (Hebrew) *see* Jehovah.

Jahweh (Hebrew) *see* Jehovah.

Jaja (India) *see* Naga and Nagis.

Jakis (Japan) Malignant air spirits who cause illness.

Jala-Hastin (India) An aquatic spirit; a water-elephant.

Jala-Shayin (India) *see* Vishnu.

Jala-Turaga (India) An aquatic spirit; a water-horse.

Jaladhi-Ja (India) "Born in the Ocean." *See also* Lakshmi.

Jalandhara (India) *see* Asuras; Bali (B).

Jaldabaoth (Hebrew) *see* Jehovah.

Jalebha (India) An aquatic spirit, a water-elephant.

Jalpati (India) "Lord of the Waters." *See also* Varuna.

Jalu-Ketu (India) *see* Bhishma.

Jam (Persia) *see* Yima.

Jam-dbyans-mag-gi-rgyal-po (Tibet) *see* Manjusri.

Jam-pa-i-dbyans (Tibet) *see* Arpacanamanjusri.

Jam-pe-yang (Tibet) *see* Arpacanamanjusri.

Jam-pol (Tibet) *see* Manjusri.

Jam-yang-nge-gi-gya-po (Tibet) *see* Manjusri.

Jamadagni (India) *see* Parashur Rama; Rishi.

Jambavan *Jambavat* (Hindu; India)
Like Hanuman the monkey, Jambavan, king of the bears, was created by Vishnu to assist Rama, an avatar of Vishnu, in his fight against the evil demon Ravana. In return for his wise advise he was given the boon of being invulnerable to all except his father Vishnu. In the end, it was his father, in his avatar as Krishna, who killed him. For details about Jambavan's death, *see* Syamantaka the magic jewel. *See also* Hanuman; Krishna; Rama.

Jambavati (India)
Daughter of King of the Bears. *See also* Jambavan; Krishna; Syamantaka.

Jambha (Hindu; India) A demon killed by Vishnu.

Jambhala *Dsam-Bha-La* (Tibet), *Kuvera* (Sivaites) (Buddhist, Sivaites; India)
Jambhala, the god of wealth, walks on a person who vomits up jewels. He is an aspect of the protector of wealth, Kuvera. Jambhala is depicted as a golden corpulent young figure seated in Indian fashion. He holds a lemon (jambhara) and a mongoose (nakula). Another depiction of Jambhala shows him holding a trident and scepter, seated sideways on a horse dragon. Indonesian depictions often include him flanked by lions. The lemon's seeds are the seeds of the world. Compare Jambhala to god of the purse, Panchika. His Hindu counterpart is Kuvera. *See also* the goddess of wealth, Kurukulla.

Jambi (Africa) *see* Bumba.

Jambudvipa (Buddhist, Hindu; India)
Translated as Rose-appletree Island, Jambudvipa is the ancient mystical name for the continent of India. *See also* Meru Mountain.

Jamshid (Iranian)
The first Iranian mortal, Jamshid is the son of Vivanghvant, twin of a sister, Yimeh (also known as Yima), who was also his spouse, and brother of Spityura and Takma Urupa. *See also* Vivanghvant; Yima.

Jamuna River (India) Sacred River. *See also* Karna; Yami.

Jan *Jann* (Middle Eastern) *see* Jin.

Jana (Etruscan, Roman) Queen of Secrets. *See also* Janus.

Jana-Loka (India) *see* Loka.

Janaka (India) *see* Sita.

Janardana (India) *see* Vishnu.

Janguli (Buddhist; India)

An ancient serpent goddess who prevents and cures snake-bites. She is depicted playing a musical instrument or playing with a snake. She wears a snake necklace and ear adornments depicting coiled cobras. Her colors are white and gold. *See also* Tara (B).

Jann (Islamic) *see* Jinn.

Jannatu el-Adn (Islamic)

Meaning the "Gardens of Perpetual Abode," and symbolized by large pearls, this is the fourth stage in Islamic Paradise (q.v.).

Jannatu el-Firdaus (Islamic)

Meaning "The Gardens of Paradise" and symbolized by red gold, this is the eighth stage in Islamic Paradise.

Jannatu el-Khuld (Islamic)

Meaning "Garden of Eternity" and symbolized by green or yellow, this is the first stage in Islamic Paradise (q.v.).

Jannatu el-Ma'wa (Islamic)

Meaning "The Gardens of Refuge," this is the fifth stage in Islamic Paradise (q.v.).

Jannatu el-Na'im (Islamic)

Meaning "The Gardens of Delight," and symbolized by white silver, this is the sixth stage in Islamic Paradise (q.v.).

Janus (Etruscan, Roman)

Also known as: *Bifrons, Deus Clavigerus, Dianus, Gaelestis, Ianus, Janus Pater.*

High god. God of beginning and end. God of gates. He is an ancient Roman divinity. The Etruscans called him the father of the twelve gods, whose twelve altars belonged to twelve months. His consort was Jana (queen of secrets). He was loved by the virgin hunter and goddess of thresholds and door-pivots, Cardea. Some of his attributes were later transferred by the Christians to Peter. He was the god of beginnings and entrances; therefore, the first month of the year was named after him, and gates and doorways were under his protection. His temple at Rome was open in time of war and closed in time of peace. It was closed three times in Rome's first 700 years. Janus is represented with two faces turned in opposite directions. Sometimes with three or four heads, or one old face and one young. *See also* Cardea.

Jao (Hebrew) *see* Jehovah.

Japan — Creation Legend *see* Ama-no-mimaka-rushi; Izanagi and Izanami

Japara (Aborigine People, Australia) *see* Purukupali.

Japhet *Japheth* (Armenian)

God of the north. He is one of the triad consisting of Zervan, Titan, and Japhet. They are called "Princes of the Land." Japhet may either be Saturn's brother Iapetus, or Shem of the Book of Genesis. In Hebrew tradition he was the eldest of Noah's three sons, born 100 years before the flood. Some say he is identical with Iapetus (Greek). *See also* Zurvan.

Jappan (Aztec) Another spelling for Yappan (q.v.).

Jar-Sub (Turkey)

Home of gods. Jar-Sub is the general term for universe, ruled over by seventeen lords of land and sea. The term can mean any place inhabited by master-spirits.

Jara (India) Flesh-eating female demon. *See also* Jara-Sandha.

Jara-Sandha *Jarasandha* (Hindu; India)

Jara-Sandha is the son of King Brihadratha ("Big Carriage") and his two wives. Each wife had given birth to half-babies on the same day and threw them into the forest. A flesh-eating demoness, Jara, put the remains together (likely for a meal) and Jara-Sandha was formed. His wails alerted his father who ran to his rescue. When Jara-Sandha became king of Magadha, he was forced from the throne by demon Kansa. He was also forced to give Kansa two of his daughters for wives. Jara-Sandha was present with his demon army the day Rukmini and Krishna's cousin Sisupala were almost married. Jara-Sandha and his cohort, the demon Kalayavana, became Krishna's nemesis after the death of Kansa. During one episode in Krishna's life, Jara-Sandha imprisoned twenty thousand rajas. Krishna, and his cousins Bhima and Arjuna, both Pandavas, set out to rescue them. Jara-Sandha, who was renowned for his remarkable strength, was eventually killed in the resulting combat by Bhima, who, on the advice of Krishna, split him in half in a battle that lasted twenty-seven days. *See also* Arjuna; Bhima; Kansa; Krishna; Pandavas; Sisupala.

Jarah (Ugarit) *see* Eterah.

Jaralez (Armenian) *see* Arlez.

Jaras (India) *see* Krishna.

Jarasandha (India) *see* Jarha-Sandha.

Jari (Teutonic) *see* Dwarfs.

Jarl (Teutonic) *see* Heimdall.

Jarnsaxa (Teutonic) *see* Iarnsaxa.

Jarovit (Slavic) *see* Herovit.

Jashar (Middle East) *see* Adad (A).

Jason (Greek)

Also known as: *Diomedes.*

Leader of the Argonaut Expedition. Member of the Calydonia Boar Hunt. Jason (original name Diomedes) is the grandson of Aeolus, the son of Aeson (the Aeolian king of Iolcos), and Alcimede and the brother of Promachus. He is the father of Mermerus, Pheres, Alcimenes, Argus, Eriopis, Medeius, Thessalus, and Tisandrus, possibly by Medea. He is also the father of Euneus, Thoas and either Deipylus or Nebrophonus by Hypsipyle, queen of Lemnos. When Jason's uncle, Pelias, usurped the throne, his mother smuggled Jason, the rightful heir, to safety. She entrusted him to the care of Cheiron, the centaur, who changed Diomedes' name to Jason and reared him in a cave on Mount Pelion. When Jason turned twenty-one he made his way back to Iolcos to regain his father's kingdom. En route he stopped to help an old woman cross a stream and he lost a sandal. He never knew that the crone was Hera in disguise but she never forgot his kindness and remained his life-long ally. Previously, an oracle was revealed to Pelias warning him to beware of a man wearing one sandle. When Jason arrived wearing one sandal, Pelias decided to send him on a seemingly impossible venture to search for the Golden Fleece. The handsome young adventurer gathered together a renowned group of male and female heroes to assist him, including Peleus, the twins Castor and Polydeuces, and Atalanta, goddess of the hunt. Argos built the ship called the Argo and Orpheus joined them to sing and keep up their spirits. At one point, Heracles joined them for a short time to aid them in overcoming the numerous obstacles they encountered on their voyage. For details of these adventures *see* the Argonauts. When they finally reached Colchis, Jason met his preordained love, Medea, who assisted him with her magical powers in the next phase of his quest. *See* Medea for this portion of his life. In the end, Jason died alone and lonely. As he sat under the prow of the rotting Argo, it fell and killed him. Some myths say that he died by his own hand. There is also the possibility that he killed Aeetes, the father of Medea. *See also* Admetus; Aeetes; Apis; Apsyrtus; Argonauts; Argus (C); Calydonia Boar Hunt; Golden Fleece; Medea; Pheres (A); Phrixus; Sirens.

Jassuju (India) *see* Shuznaghu; Zumiang-nui.

Jatavedas (India) *see* Agni.

Jatayu (India)
He is the king of the eagles and son of Garuda (q.v.).

Javerzaharses (Armenian)
Nymphs. They are possibly female Kaches who were thought of as spirits of weddings, singing and rejoicing. They are also spirits of welfare, marriage and childbirth. The Javerzaharses are sometimes found on the river banks, prairies, and near the pines. *See also* Kaches; Torch.

Jayadratha (India) *see* Bhima (A).

Jayanat (India) *see* Jagannath.

Jeggua (Yoruba People, Africa)
Jeggua is the goddess of purity and virginity. *See also* Olodumare.

Jeh (Persia) *see* Jah.

Jehova (Hebrew) *see* Jehovah.

Jehovah *Jehova* (Hebrew)
Also known as: *Ahiah, Hehuah, Iah, Iao, Iaw, Ie, Ieu, Ieui, Jah, Jahve, Jahweh, Jaldabaoth, Jao, Jhvh, Jhwh, Jod-heh-vav-heh', Yahowah, Yahu, Yahveh, Yahweh, Yaw, Yehoveh, Yhwh.*

Supreme god. Originally a god of wrath. Generally pronounced Adonai or Elohim by the early Jewish people since the true name of the supreme being was never uttered. A creator deity, he made the earth, and all it contains in six days and established the seventh day as the sabbath. He created the first male and female, Adam and Eve. He appeared to only Abraham, Isaac, Jacob, and Moses in early versions of scripture. It is possible that Jehovah began as a deity of the vine. His symbols are a seven-branched candlestick or a hand emerging from a cloud. His only opponent was the serpent. When Jehovah appeared as a mortal on earth, he was known as Jesus. *See also* Jesus; Yahweh.

Jemdekhen (India) *see* Parashur Rama.

Jemshid (Persia) *see* Yima.

Jen (Finland) *see* Ilmarinen.

Jerah (Ugarit) *see* Elohim; Eterah.

Jeshodha (India) *see* Yasoda.

Jeshu (Hebrew) *see* Jesus.

Jesu (Hebrew) *see* Jesus.

Jesus (Hebrew)
Also known as: *Christ, Cristos, Iesous* (a corruption of the Hebrew Yehoshu'a, a common Jewish name; Greek), *Iesu, Isa, Jeshu, Jesu, Khrestos* (Greek), *Logos, Yesha.*

The Messiah. "Anointed One." Deified mortal. Very few historical records remain about his existence in the period associated with him, but one of the military aides of Moses was named Jehoshua, which was shortened to Jeshua. The Greeks replaced the "sh" sound with "s" which gave the name "Jesus." This name is mentioned several times in the original Greek New Testament, but various versions say he was the eldest of five sons of Joseph and Mary and in the biblical version he was divinely born of Mary, wife of Joseph, a carpenter. Early Coptic text (Pistis Sophia) tells of Jesus praying to his father by addressing him by various magical names: Aeeiouo, Iao, Aoi, and others. In another passage, Jesus addresses his god in the following names and words: Iao Iouo, Aoi, Oia, and others. It is believed by followers that Jesus is the supreme being in earthly form. *See also* Christ; Jehovah; Logos.

Jhoting (India)
This is the spirit of a dead lower caste Hindu who died dissatisfied. Jhoting is also the ghost of a dead man who never married and did not have relatives.

JHVH (*Jod-heh-vav-heh*) (Hebrew) *see* Jehovah; Yahweh.

JHWH (Hebrew) *see* Jehovah; Yahweh.

Jibb-Jang-Sangne (Dhammai People, India)
Jibb-Jange-Sangne and her brother, Sujang-Gnoi-Rise, are the mountain children of the sky god, Jongsuli-Young-Jongbu, and the earth goddess, Subbu-Khai-Thung. Their siblings, who were born as frogs, are Lujjuphu and Jassuju. *See also* Shuznaghu.

Jibril (Islamic) *see* Gabriel.

Jiburili (Arabic) *see* Gabriel.

Jicarilla Apache People — Creation Legend (North America) *see* Hactein.

Jig-ten-sum-gyal (Tibet) *see* Trailokyavijaya.

Jigoku (Buddhist; Japan).
Hell or Underworld. Jigoku is composed of eight hot sections known as To-Kwatsu and eight freezing sections known as Abuda. There are also sixteen sub hells, and four hells called Kimpen Jigoku. In Hell, an immense mirror reflects and exposes the crimes of the naked soul as it kneels before the table of three judges. The three judges are Kagu-hana, a decapitated head (nose); Emma-O, who sits in the middle; and Miru-me, also a decapitated head (eyes). When the sins have been weighed, the sinner is condemned to the appropriate hell. This fate can be avoided by the prayers of the living. Next, a Bodhisattva delivers the soul from the evils of hell and the transgressor is reborn in Paradise or on earth. There is a hell called Kodoku-jigoku which appears more like a spirit than a proper hell. Born a

prince who became a beggar monk, Kuya, through his writings and paintings, and Genshin, also known as Eshin Sozu, were well known for their dissertations on the ghastliness of hell. Depictions of the horrors of hell, pits of flame and ice, were common on screens toward the end of the Heian culture (late eighth and early ninth centuries). Compare Jioku to Hades (Greek), Tartarus (Greek), Tuat (Egypt), Yomi (Japan). For a complete description of the chief judge, *see* Emma-O; Oni. *See also* Gokuraku Jodo; Hell.

Jigs-Byed (Tibet) *see* Bhairava.

Jikoku (Japan) *see* Jikoku-Ten.

Jikoku-Ten *Jikoku, Jikokuten* (Buddhist; Japan)
"Land-bearer." Jikoku-Ten is one of the four Shi Tenno. Known as the four kings, these deities protect the four corners. Jikoku-Ten functions as the guardian of the east and protects his section from evil demons. Should a demon attempt to cross his path, he will be trampled. The four guards all wear uniforms and have ferocious facial expressions. Jikoku-Ten is depicted with a small container and holds a sword in his left hand. *See also* Bishamon-ten; Dhartarastra; Komoku-ten; Nio; Shi Tenno; Zocho-ten.

Jikokuten (Japan) *see* Jikoku-Ten.

Jimmu Tenno *Jimmu Tennu* (Shinto; Japan)
Also known as: *Kamu-yamato-ihare-biko, Kama-yamato-iware-biko, Toyo-mike-nu, Waka-mi-ke-nu-no-mikoto.*
First Emperor. Warrior. Conquerer. First Japanese demigod who was a human hero. Jimmu Tenno, the first emperor and founder of the Imperial Line of Japan, was born Kama-Yamato-Iware-Biko (also called Waka-mi-ke-nu-no-mikoto). He acquired the name Jimmu Tenno posthumously. He is the son of the sea princess Tama-Yori-Bime (Spirit-Medium-Princess, also known as Jewel-Good Princess) and her nephew Ama-tu-Piko-nagisa-take-U-gaya-puki-apezu-no-mikoto. Her nephew is the son of her sister Toyo-Tama-Bime (Lady Abundance Jewel) and Hikohohodemi (Prince-Fire-Subside). He was the youngest of four sons. In legend, Jimmu Tenno ascended the throne in the year 660 B.C.E. His seat of power was Yamoto in Honshu. He was said to have lived one hundred and twenty-seven or one hundred and thirty-seven years. In one myth, Jimmu and his brothers were attempting to bring peace to the land. They were guided by a three-legged, golden crow, which was eight feet long. It had been sent to them from the celestial realm. Jimmu had a sacred cross-sword and a fire-striker. To quell the raging storm his brothers jumped overboard. Tenno, the official title of the Emperor, has been kept to the present. It is thought to have been a word first used by Prince Shotoku when communicating with China. The name Jimmu means "son-of-heaven." Mythology and history entwined called the mythical Jimmu Tenno (Sun of Heaven) a great-grandson of the sun goddess Amaterasu. All following emperors dated from him and thus were called divine. In 1946, the emperor Hirohito renounced his divinity. The crow with three legs drawn within a solar disk is an early Chinese imperial emblem that represented the active life of the Emperor, his Yang. The three legs within the disk represent the main phases of the sun throughout the day: dawn, noon and dusk. The crow as messenger is also a common symbol. The sun goddess Amaterasu

has a crow as her messenger. It is also said that the crow symbolizes the isolation of the individual who lives on a higher plane. *See* Ama-no-minaka-nushi for the Shinto creation myth. *See* Amaterasu for details of divine emperors. *See also* Hikohohodemi; Ninigi; Toyo-Tama-bime.

Jimmu Tennu (Japan) *see* Jimmu Tenno.

Jina (India) *see* Buddha; Mahavira.

Jinimin (Aborigine People, Australia)
Also known as: *Jesus.*
He has black and white skin and will be the one who will give back the country to the original people.

Jinn *Jin* (Arabia, India, Indochina, Persia)
Also known as: *Ajnan* (Male), *and Jinniyah* (Feminine; Islamic), *Div, Djinn, Genie, Genii, Ghaddar* (pre-Islamic), *Ghul* (pre-Islamic), *Ifrits, Jann, Jinniyeh, Junun* (plural; Islamic), *Marid, Nar, Nara, Qutrub* (pre-Islamic), *Se'irim, Shaitan.*
Demons of evil and good. They live on the mountain Kaf and are ruled by King Suleyman or as some say, Azazel. Made of fire, they live, die and give birth much as humans do. However, they are extremely long-lived. Along with a sense of humor, they have supernatural powers. It is said that the Jinn assisted in the construction of pyramids. There are good and bad Jinn. They can appear as human. In the Arabic tradition, the plural is Jinn, the feminine Jinniyah, and the singular, Jinni. There are five types of Jinn: the Jann who have the least amount of power; the Jinn, usually evil; the Shaitan, who are usually imps or devils; the terrible Ifrit; and the Marid, who are the most evil and the most powerful. The leader and chief of the Jinn is Iblis. Usually the Jinn are invisible, but they can appear in any animal or human form. They frequently appear as snakes. In Persia a similar demon is called the Jann. Described as half-wolf, half-hyena. Jinn corresponds to Rephaim. There are many of these demons in all religions. The most common names are Divs, Damrukh Nara, Shelan Nara, Mardash Nara, Kahmaraj, Nara, Al, Akwan, Jann, Tarnush. *See also* Afreet; Al; Apsarases; Bhutas; Dalhan; Demons; Dusii; Genii; Iblis; Incubus; Lokapalas; Nagas; Rakshasas; Satyrs (Greek); Yakshas.

Jinniyeh (Middle Eastern) *see* Jin.

Jitoku (Japan) *see* Samantabhadra.

Jivaro People — Creation Legend (Andes, South America) *see* Cupara.

Jizaiten (Tibet) *see* Trailokyavijaya.

Jizo (Japan) *see* Jizo-Bosatsu.

Jizo-Bosatsu (Buddhist; Japan)
Also known as: *Jizo, Kshitigarbha* (India), *Ti-tsang Wang-p'u-sa* (China).
A god of mercy, and guardian of those in need, Jizo-Bosatsu will assist believers on all levels of existence. He protects the souls of little children and is propitiated by pregnant women and travelers. He carries a staff with six jingling rings that warn of his approach in case he should inadvertently step on a living creature. His statue is placed at crossroads. He is shown seated, bearing a jewel that grants wishes (the Cintamani) in his ring hand, and a staff in his left hand. *See also* Kshitigarbha; Ti-tsang; Yama Kings.

Jjuko (Bugand, Bantu People; Africa)
The spirit for fixing things. See also Balubaale; Kibuuka.

Joagh (Africa) Another spelling for Jocasta.

Joagh (Africa) see Juck.

Joca-Huva (Haiti) Sky god and possible son of Atabei (q.v.).

Jocakuvague (Antilles Islands, Haiti) see Guamaonocon.

Jocasta *Jocaste* (Greek)
Also known as: *Epicaste* (Homeric), *Iocaste, Iokaste*.
Deified mortal. Jocasta is the daughter of Menoeceus, the sister of Hipponome and Creon, and the wife of Laius and mother/wife of Oedipus. When Oedipus was older, the mother and son met. They did not recognize one another. A relationship ensued. She became the mother by Oedipus of the sons Eteocles and Polynices and daughters Antigone and Ismene. When she discovered that Oedipus was her son, she hung herself. Oedipus blinded himself. See also Antigone; Oedipus.

Jocaste (Greek) see Jocasta.

Jodo (Japan)
Also known as: *Ching-tu* (China).
Jodo is a heavenly western paradise ruled by Amita. It is similar to Kun-lun mountain. See also Ching-Tu.

Jogaoh (Iroquois People, North America)
The Jogaoh are fairy or dwarf people similar to the Pukwudjies of the Objiwa. There are three types: the Gahonga who inhabit rivers and rocks, the Gandayah who are in charge of grains, fruits and fish, and the Ohdowas who live underground. Their job is to keep control of the monsters who inhabit the underworld. See also Gahonga; Ohdowas; Pukwudjies.

Joghi (Africa) see Juck.

Jok (Acholi People, Africa) Juck.

Joli-Torem (Vogul People, Siberia)
Creator. His sister, Num, was the director of the the work involved in creation.

Jomali (Teutonic) see Jumala.

Jonakr (Teutonic)
Also known as: *Hraesvelgr*.
God of winter. Husband of Gudrun and father of Erp, Hamdir and Sorli. Possibly the same as another Winter God named Hraesvelgr (q.v.). See also Gudrun.

Jongsuli-Young-Jongbu (Dhammai People, India)
The sky god, Jongsuli-Young-Jongbu, and his earth goddess sister, Subbu-khai-Thung, were the first born children of Shuznaghu and Zumiang-nui, who existed above in a place where neither sky nor earth existed. The children were swallowed by the worm, Phangnalomang, and later rescued by another sibling. Upon release, Jongsuli-Young-Jongbu became the sky and his sister, Subbu-khai-Thung, became the earth. Together, they gave birth to the god Sujang-Gnoi-Rise and the goddess Jibb-Jang-Sangne, who became mountains. They also had a son, Lujjuphu, and daughter, Jassuju, who were born as frogs. The frogs mated and gave birth to the first mortals, Abugupham-Bumo and Anoi-Diggan-Juje. See also Shuznaghu.

Joogi (Africa) see Juck.

Jord *Jordh* (Norse; Teutonic)
Also known as: *Fjorgyn, Hlodyn, Jord Nerthus, Jorth.* (May be feminine version of *Njord* [also called *Erda*].)
Earth mother, or earth goddess. She is the mother of the human, Mannus. See also Aesir; Annar; Frigga; Odin; Thor.

Jordegumma (Swedish) see Madderakka (Lapp).

Jormungandr *Iormungandr* (Norse; Teutonic)
Also known as: *Midgard Serpent, Midgardsormen.*
Serpent. Jormungandr laid at the root of the tree of life, Yggdrasil, before Odin cast him into the sea. He is the offspring of Gulveig (or Loki) and brother of Fenrir and Hel. Jormungandr became so large he encircled the earth biting his own tail. He was killed by Thor, who in turn was drowned by the serpent's venom. See also Angerboda; Fenrir; Gullveig; Loki; Midgard; Nagilfar.

Jorojin *Ju-rojin, Jui, Jurojin* (Buddhist; Japan)
Jorojin, one of the Shichi Fukujin (seven deities of happiness), is the white-bearded god of longevity, wisdom and good luck. His origins stem from China. He is the controller of good health. Jorojin enjoyed drinking sake but was never considered a drunkard. A short god, he is accompanied variously by a tortoise, crane, or a black deer, all representing a happy old age. He sometimes appears dressed as a scholar, wearing a headdress and is also depicted leaning on a long staff. Sometimes he is holding a stick with a book on top. The book represents the life limit of every individual on earth. In Japan the crane is called *tsuru* and is a royal bird, symbolizing valor and loyalty. The deer is symbolic of Buddha's teachings and is one of the forms in which Buddha was born. In Japan the tortoise is the symbol of longevity (combined with the peach it signifies immortality). See also Fukurokujin; Shichi Fukujin.

Jorth (Teutonic) see Jord.

Jotun-heim *Jotunheim, Jotunnheim* (Teutonic; Norse)
Also known as: *Utgard*.
This is the snowy land of the giants who are known as Jotuns. The major city in Jotun-heim is Utgard. Jotun-heim is the home of Bergelmir, the only frost giant to survive the war between Odin and his family. Jotun-heim is one of the nine worlds which has a root of the Yggdrasil extending into it. In one myth the Jotuns were so cruel to mortals that the Aesir used the giant Ymir's eyebrows to make a great wall around the land of mortals, Midgard. See also Aesir; Baugi; Bergelmir; Jotuns; Midgard; Mimir; Odin; Utgard; Yggdrasil; Ymir.

Jotunnheim (Teutonic) see Jotun-heim.

Jotuns (Teutonic)
Also known as: *Jotun*.
These hostile ice giants were conquered by Odin. Three of the giants were female or perhaps one female giant born three times. Their names are Aurboda, Gullveig (also known as Gulvieg-Hoder), and Hag. They reside in Jotun-heim (q.v.). See also Gullveig; Mani (A); Odin; Thor; Utgard.

Joukahainen (Finland) *see* Vainomoinen.

Jouskeha (Native North American) *see* Ioskeha.

Jove (Etruscan, Roman)
Also known as: *Jupiter, Vediovis.*
Thunder god. Jove is another name for Jupiter. He is the Roman equivalent of Jehovah and Zeus. *See also* Jupiter; Mercury (A); Zeus.

Jubal (Sumer) Patron of music. *See also* Ea; Enki; Lumha.

Juck (Shilluk People, Africa)
Also known as: *Juok.*
Creator god. Although he created the world, he does not direct it. He is a very impersonal deity who is present in all things. In the beginning, he created the white man from white sand, the brown man from Nile mud, and the black man from black earth. *See also* Nyikang.

Juemel (Finno-Ugric, Slavic) *see* Jumala.

Juggernaut (India) *see* Jagannath.

Juichimen (Buddhist) God of mercy. *See also* Kuan Yin.

Juji-Yama (Japan) *see* Fuji.

Jukkui Ajayo (Inca People, South America)
Also known as: *Pipisao.*
Life force. It is believed this deity is a type of spirit responsible for the health of the body and mind. It leaves at night during sleep, but appears in dreams. It must return before the body awakens. If forced away by shock, the body is exposed to illness. *See also* Pachamama.

Juksakka (Lapp)
Goddess of birth. She had the primary function of changing the girl child into a boy child while still in the womb. Daughter of Maderakka.

Jukurokujin (Japan) *see* Fukurokujin.

Julunggul *Julunggl* (Maori People, Australia, New Zealand)
Rainbow snake (q.v.).

Jumala (Finno-Ugric, Slavic)
Also known as: *Ibmel, Ilmarinen, Jomali* (Teutonic), *Jemel, Jumla, Jumo, Mader-atcha, Ukko.*
Supreme god. God of the sky and thunder. God who decides how long mortals will live. He lives in the highest story of heaven in a house glistening with gold and silver. He has seven sons, and many assistant spirits who have wings. The Norse call him Jomali. Jumala was later replaced by Ukko. He is associated with Sangke. *See also* Ilmarinen; Ukko; Vainomoinen.

Jumla (Finno-Ugric, Slavic) *see* Jumala.

Jumna *Yami* (Hindu; India)
She is the goddess of the river of the same name (earlier known as Yamuna River), and the spouse of Varuna. Vasudeva crossed the Jumna when carrying the infant Krishna. *See also* Varuna; Yami.

Jumo (Finno-Ugric, Slavic) *see* Jumala.

Juno (Roman; may have been assimilated from the Etruscan deity Uni or Iuno)
Also known as: *Hera* (Greek), *Iuno* (Etruscan), *Juno Caelestis, Juno Lucina* (goddess of childbirth) *Juno Moneta* (goddess of finance), *Saturnia* (daughter of Saturn).
Goddess of marriage. Protector of women and of childbirth. Goddess of finance. Goddess of war. Originally, Juno was the goddess of the moon. Later, she assimilated to the Greek Hera. She is the daughter of Saturn and the wife of Jupiter. They are the parents of Mars. When Gaul assaulted Rome, her geese gave her warning and she saved the city. Her various epithets are Cinxia, Domiduca, Huga, Jugalis, Matrona, Pronuba, Unxia, Curitis (Quiritis), Lucina, Moneta, Regina, Sosphita, and Virginensis. Juno, the bitter enemy of Semele, was said to have struck Semele's son, the wine and fertility deity, Bacchus, with madness. Her sacred animal is the goat, and her sacred fruit, the fig. Juno's festival date is July 7. She is often shown as a stately woman holding a scepter with a bird on top in one hand and pomegranate in the other. She is associated with Jupiter and Minerva. *See also* Bacchus; Cupra; Hera; Semele; Tanit.

Juno Caelestis (Carthage) *see* Tanit.

Junun (Islamic) *see* Jinn.

Juok (Africa) *see* Juck.

Jupiter (The planet) *see* Brihaspati; Eurynome (A); Marduk; Tara (A).

Jupiter *Iuppiter, Juppiter.* (Roman; may have been a Syrian deity); (Jupiter of Doliche)
Also known as: *Heru-ap-sheta-taui* (Egypt), *Jove* (Etruscan), *Tina* (Etruscan), *Vediovis* (an early name), *Vedius, Vejovis* ("Little Jupiter"), *Zeus* (Greek).
Probably a war-god or fertility god. Air god. One of a triad of high gods; the other two are Mars and Quirinus. Jupiter was also part of the triad which included the goddesses Juno and Minerva. Different versions say he was son of Cronus and Rhea. Some say he was brother/husband of Juno. Some say he was husband of Antiope and father of Amphion and Zethus. Other consorts were Dione, Themis, and Europa. By Europa he was father of Minos, Rhadamanthus and Sarpedon. He was brother of Neptune, Pluto, Vesta, Ceres and Juno. In some legends his attendants were Victoria or Nice (Nike), Fama (goddess of flame), Fortuna, Hebe, or Juventas and Mercury. Jupiter was later assimilated to the Greek god Zeus. He was worshiped as Jupiter Feretrius (the smiter), Jupiter Elicius (lightning attractor), and Optimus Maximus (The Best and Greatest). He was first worshiped as a stone (Jupiter Lapis) when he came from Latium. He was worshiped by the Romans as a god of soldiers. He was called a patron of ironworkers. Oak trees were sacred to Jupiter. The name Vejovis, or Vedius, was used for Jupiter when he appeared without his thunder. Most legends of Jupiter parallel those of Zeus (q.v.). Compare to the Norse gods, Odin, Thor, and the Germanic Thunar. *See also* Aegis (Greek); Cronus; Dyaus (India); Jove; Juno; Mercury (A); Tina; Titans.

Jupiter-Ammon (Egypt) *see* Amen (B).

Jupiter Ammon (Greek) *see* Amen (B).

Jurapari *Jurupari* (Brazil)
Divine Protector. Guardian of tribal and family mores.

Jurasmat (Latvia)
"Mother of the Sea." High goddess. She follows mortals from birth to death. The other Lativian goddess who do the same are Laima (childbirth), Delka (the newborn), Laukamat (fields), Mezamat (wood), Lopemat (cattle), Darzamat (gardens), and Vejamat (winds).

Jurojin (Japan) *see* Jorajin; Shichi Fukujin.

Jurupari (Brazil) *see* Jurapari.

Jushkapariks (Armenian) *see* Hambaris.

Justice (Greek) An epithet of Themis, the goddess of justice.

Justice (Greek) Goddesses of justice. *See also* Dike, Themis.

Justice (Roman)
Goddesses of justice. *See also* Astraea, Justitia.

Justitia *Iustitia* (Roman)
Goddess of justice. She presides with Jupiter at a cult started by Augustus. Justitia is shown blindfolded, holding scales and a sword.

Juterna *Diuturna, Iuturna, Juturna* (Roman)
Goddess of healing springs, ponds, and rivers. In early times she was known as Diuturna. Her parents are Daunus and Venilia, and her brother is Turnus, the king of Rutulia. By Janus, she became the mother of Fontus. Jupiter seduced her, and later in compensation, he deified her. *See also* Janus; Jupiter.

Juturna (Roman) *see* Juterna.

Juventas (Roman)
Goddess of eternal youth. Patron goddess of the youth of Rome. She is similar to the goddess Hebe of the Greeks and is a symbol of the glory of Rome. *See also* Hebe; Jupiter.

Jvalamukha (India) *see* Amrtakundali.

Jwok (Africa) *see* Juck.

Jyotsna (India) Goddess of Twilight. *See also* Ratri.

K

K (Maya)
The god K is a wind god thought to be a form of Chac Mol (q.v.) *See also* "B."

Ka (Egypt)
The soul. Ka is created in mortals at the time of birth. The deity Khnum or an assistant made the mortal body on a potter's wheel and at the same time his or her double, Ka, was created. Ka stays within the mortal until the time of death when it splits into two and becomes a bird called the Akh. The bird flies into the Afterlife and becomes the Ka, or double of the mortal once again. Then the Ba, a human-headed bird, remains on earth in the body left behind by the Akh. In essence, Ka is the energy of every living thing. *See also* Ab; Ba; Fa.

Ka-Hemhem (Egypt)
Guardian. A lion god appearing in the sixth sector of Tuat.

Ka-onohi *Ka-onohi-o-ka-la* (Hawaii)
Conductor of the souls of dead chiefs. *See also* Lo-lupe.

Ka-onohi-o-ka-la (Hawaii) *see* Ka-onohi.

Kaang (Bushmen People, Africa)
Also known as: *Kho, Khy, Thora.*
The supreme god. As Thora, his adversary is Gawa, leader of the spirits of the dead who dwell in the sky. Sometimes Kaang is confused with Cagn. *See also* Cagn; Gawa.

Kaare (Norse; Teutonic)
Wind or storm giant. He is the son of Fornjotnr, the storm personified, the father of Iokul, the icicle personified, and the grandfather of Snaer, the snow personified. *See also* Fornjotnr.

Kaba *Kava* (Finno-Ugric, Russian)
Also known as: *Chuvash (Russian).*
Spirit of fate or providence. Father of the messenger, Puleh. The Russians call Kaba, Chuvash. *See also* Fates (Greek); Puleh.

Kabandha (Hindu; India)
Kabandha was a giant demon, the son of Devi Sri. During a fight with Indra, Indra's thunderbolt hit him and left him as a monster. As he wandered the forest he encountered Rama and begged him to destroy his body. From his ashes he was reborn as a good Gandharva. The appreciative demon assisted Rama in his fight against the demon king Ravana and his troops. He also advised Rama to become the friend of Sugriva, the king of the monkeys. He is headless with a large mouth and sharp teeth in his belly. His one large eye is centered in his breast. Legless, he moves around on eight arms. *See also* Gandharvas; Rama; Ravana; Sugriva.

Kabeiroi (Greek) Another spelling for Caberi (q.v.).

Kabibonokka (Algonquin People, North America) *see* Manibozho.

Kabil (A) *Kabul* (Maya) *see* Itzamna.

Kabil (B) (Arab, Persian) *see* Cain.

Kabirs (Greek) *see* Caberi.

Kabo Mandalat (Polynesia, New Zealand)
Demon of disease. This female spirit causes elephantiasis. She is depicted as a large hermit crab with legs like coconut trees.

Kaboi (Boliva, Brazil)
Possibly a bird deity. He is an ancient god who led his people from the lower world by a bird call.

Kabonian *Kaboniyan* (Tinguian People, Philippine Islands)
Culture Hero. Kabonian lives either in the sky or near Patok in a cave. In the first times he married a Tinguian woman. He gave the people rice and sugar cane and taught them to plant and reap. He also instructed the people how to perform ceremonies. Another important lesson he offered was how to rid themselves of evil spirits. Kabonian also entered the body of a woman to show her how to cure illness. Sometimes he is above the greatest of the deities, Kadaklan, in stature, and sometimes equal to him. *See also* Kadaklan.

Kaboniyan (Tinguian People, Philippine Islands) *see* Kabonian.

Kabta (Sumer) The god of bricks. *See also* Enki.

Kabun (Algonquin People, North America) *see* Kabibonokka; Manibozho.

Kacha (India) *see* Brihaspati.

Kaches (Armenian)
Similar to the Devs, the gluttonous, musical Kaches are benevolent spirits, and helpers of their god. They might be wind spirits. Compare the Kaches to Kobolds. *See also* Devs; Javerzaharses.

Kachinas (Zuni People, North America)
Kachinas are spirits of the dead who participate in the dancing and ceremonies along with the living. Their abode is at the bottom of a lake in an empty desert. They are generally represented as dolls.

Kachpikh (Tierra del Fuego)
Also known as: *Wild People.*
Evil spirits. These invisible spirits hate humans and can cause death and disease. They live in the forest or in caves.

Kadaklan (Tinguian People, Philippine Islands)
Creator. Kadaklan is not personalized. He is acknowledged as the creator of the earth, moon, stars, and sun. His wife is Agemem, and his two sons are Adam and Balujen. The sons and his dog Kimat, who is lightning, must see the Kadaklan's commands are obeyed. During storms Kadaklan amuses himself with his drum, which is the thunder. *See also* Kaboniyan.

Kadesh (Egypt) *see* Min; Qadesh.

Kadi (Sumer)
Kadi, the goddess of justice of Der, is a derivative of Kishar.

Kadomas (Tibet) *see* Dakinis.

Kadru (India)
The daughter of Daksha, mate of Kasyapa, mother of Nagas and Nagis, a daughter Manasa, and sons Sesha and Kapila. *See also* Daksha; Garuda; Gauri; Kasyapa; Manasa; Nagas and Nagis; Sesha.

Kafisi (Melanesia)
Creator goddess, she is the sister of Bunosi (q.v.).

Kagami (Japan) *see* Amaterasu.

Kagoro (Baziba People, Africa)
Kagoro is one of four sons of the father of gods, Wamara. His three brothers are Mugasha, god of water, Kazoba, god of the sun and moon, and Ryangombe, god of cattle.

Kaggen (Africa) *see* Cagn.

Kagu-Hana (Japan) *see* Jigoku.

Kagu-Tsuchi *Kagu-tsuchi, Kagu-Tsughi, Kagu-Zuchi, Kagut-suchi* (Shinto; Japan)
Also known as: *Ho-Masubi, Homusubi.*
Kagu-Tsuchi, the god of fire, is the son of Izanagi and Izanami. His birth scorched his mother and caused her death. The angry father drew his sacred sword and killed him. In the *Kojiki*, he is beheaded and in the *Nihongi* he is chopped into three pieces by Izanagi. Each dead body part created a deity and other deities sprang from his splattered blood. Kura-okami, Kura-yama-tsumi and Taka-Okami are other deities who were created during this episode. Some sources say that a total of eight deities were created from his death. Prayers are offered to Kagu-Tsuchi under the name of Ho-Masubi, who is known as the god who causes fire. In the Ryobu-Shinto tradition, Ho-Masubi is the god of Mount Atago. To protect one against fire, amulets of the wild boar were worn. The talisman of the wild boar was also used as protection against snakes in Japan. Complicated ceremonies were held to appease the fire god and to ensure the safety of dwellings from the devastation of fire. Kiri-Bi fire (pure fire) was obtained by the friction of pieces of Hinoki wood or by striking a hard stone with steel. The Emperor's food was prepared over Kiri-Bi fire and Shinto priests used it in their homes. The faithful had access to Kiri-Bi fire on New Year's day. It was obtained from the priests and carefully carried home. The home hearth would be lit from Kiri-Bi fire and the protection from fire would last throughout the year. Geishas and prostitutes could have Kiri-Bi fire struck over their heads to give them protection as they carried out their professional activities. For information about the *Kojiki*, the *Nihongi* and the Shinto creation myth, *see* Ama-no-minaka-nushi. One of Kagu-tsuchi's brothers is O-Yama-Tsu-Mi, the chief god and lord of the mountains. *See also* Atago-Gongen; Izanagi and Izanami; Kanayama-hime; Kura-okami; O-Yama-Tsu-Mi; Sengen.

Kagu-Tsughi (Japan) *see* Kagu-Tsuchi.

Kagu-Zuchi (Japan) *see* Kagu-tsuchi.

Kaguhana (Japan)
This deity locates those who do evil deeds. According to some he is shown on one side of Emma-O.

Kagura (Japan) *see* Amaterasu.

Kagutsuchi (Japan) *see* Atago-Gongen; Kagu-tsuchi.

Kah (Egypt) *see* Ba.

Kaha'i (Hawaii) God of lightning. *See also* Kariki; Tawhaki.

Kaharon (Greek) *see* Charon.

Kahil (Arabic) *see* Shahar.

Kahukura (Maori People, Polynesia)
God of war. Kahukura is a sacred deity of the early Maori people. His symbol is the rainbow.

Kai (Egypt)
One of the forms of Osiris in the sixth sector of Tuat.

Kai-n-Tiku-Aba (Samoa People, South Sea Islands)
"Tree of Many Branches." This sacred tree grows from the back of the father of the gods, Na Atibu. A man, known as Koura-Abi, who had a destructive disorder, came along and deliberately broke the tree down. The broken tree caused many people to be disruptive and even violent. The people scattered and sadness and sorrow became their companions. *See also* Nareau.

Kai-Tangata (Hawaii, Polynesia, New Jealand) *see* Kaitangata

Kaiaimunu (Melanesia)
The Kaiaimunu are powerful spirits who have individual names. Some legends say the Kaiaimunu were given to the tribe by Iko (also spelled Hido, Sido) a culture hero. The Kaiaimunu are generally made with wicker frames and depicted as monsters.

Kaikeyi (India)
One of Dasaratha's wives, she is the mother of Bharata. *See also* Bharata (A); Hanuman; Rama.

Kailasa (India)
Located on the sacred Mount Meru, Kailasa is the city of the gods Shiva, Kuvera, and Ganesha. *See also* Ganesha; Kuvera; Meru Mountain; Shiva.

Kaimai and Trentren (Araucana People, South America)
Two serpents who made the seas rise in a great flood to prove they had fantastic magic powers.

Kain (Hebrew, Moslem) *see* Cain.

Kaitabha (India) A giant demon. *See also* Durga; Kali.

Kaitangata *Kai-Tangata, Kattangata* (Polynesia)
Also known as: "*Man Eater.*"
Warrior deity. He is known for his prowess as a fighter. His wife is Whaitari, the cannibal chieftain from the sky, although a Hawaiian tale fashions the story differently, casting Hina-who-worked-in-the-moon as the wife of Kaitangata. They had two children, a son, Hema, and a daughter, Punga. Hema became the father of two sons, Tawhaki and Kariki. *See also* Hema; Tawhaki; Whaitari.

Kaizuki (Burganda People, Africa)
In some versions Kaizuki is the brother of Death. He is associated with the legend of Kintu, Gulu and Nambi.

Kaka-Guia (Africa) *see* Nyami.

Kakasians (Scythian) *see* Amazons.

Kakemono (Japan)
Carpenter gods. Kakemono of Fukurakuju is one of the seven gods of luck. He has a high domed head.

Kako (Greek, Roman) *see* Cacus, the fire-breathing giant.

Kala *Black Demon, Kala-Shiva* (Brahman, Hindu; India)
Kala is the god of time, death and destruction. When the universe is reborn after each destruction this deity insures that only those who are wise are not reborn but live on with him. He is usually identified with Shiva but sometimes with Yama, Brahma or Vishnu. Kala is also a name for Shiva as the spouse of Kali. *See also* Durga; Kali; Shiva; Yama.

Kala-Siva (India)
Double-sexed God of Time or Death. *See also* Kala; Shiva.

Kalacakra (Buddhist; Nepal, India)
Kalacakra turns the wheel of life. As Kalacakra is the title of a work in a division of the Kangyur, it is possible that Kalacakra is a personification of that work. He is usually depicted with four heads, each with three eyes. He has either twelve or twenty-four arms and two legs. His color is dark blue and he wears a tiger skin. He is always shown stepping to the left on two prostrate figures. The figure under his right foot holds a bow and arrow and the other figure holds a trident and the khatvanga (magic wand).

Kalachi (India) Yama's palace. *See also* Yama.

Kalaino *Celaeno* (Greek) *see* Harpies; Podarge.

Kalaipahoa (Hawaii, Polynesia)
Tree deity. She is the goddess who enters and poisons trees. Her two sisters, Kapo and Pua, are also poison trees.

Kalais *Calais* (Greek)
Another spelling for the wind god, Calais (q.v.).

Kalaka (India) *see* Daksha; Danavas.

Kalamahakala (India) *see* Mahakala.

Kalanemi (Hindu; India)
Kalanemi is the Rakshasa grandson of Hiranya-Kasipu, son of Virochana and nephew of the demon Ravana. His evil ways were extinguished when Vishnu killed him, but he was reincarnated as Kansa and Kaliya. *See also* Hiranya-kasipu; Kaliya; Kansa; Rakshasas; Ravana; Virochana.

Kalaratri (India)
This is a being created by Devi who was unsuccessful in his battle against the demons. *See also* Durga (B).

Kalasi-Suti (India) Son of a Jar. *See also* Agastya.

Kalayavana (India) A demon. *See also* Krishna.

Kalee (India) *see* Devi.

Kalevala *Kalewala* (Finnish)
The Kalevala, meaning "The Land of Heroes," is one of the world's great epics. Written in 1835, by Elias Lönnrot, it is a col-

lection of Finnish myths, legends and romances. It portrays Finland's superiority over Lapland, and the adventures of the deified heroes of Ilmatar. *See also* Ilmarinem; Leshy; Sampo.

Kali (Hindu; India)

Also known as: *Bairavi* (The Terrible), *Bhavani, Bhima-Devi* (Terrifying Goddess), *Black Mother, Camunda, Candi, Chamunda, Chandika* (The Burning or Fierce), *Chinnamastica, Devi, Devi-Kali, Durga, Himavati, Kali-Ma* (Black Mother), *Kalika, Kamakshi, Karali* (Terrible), *Karna-Moti* (With Pearls in Her Ears), *Khadga Jogini, Khadga Yogini, Krittivasas* (Clad in Hide), *Kumari, Maha-Kali* (Mighty Time), *Mahakalee* (The Great Black One), *Mahamya, Menakshi, Nitya-Kali* (Endless Time), *Parvati, Raksha-Kali* (Guardian Kali), *Rudrani, Sati, Shmashana-Kali* (Kali of the Burning Ground), *Shyama-Kali* (The Black One), *Syama* (Black), *Tara, Uma* (Light), *Vajrajogini.*

Kali the warrior goddess is also the goddess of fertility and time, the goddess of mysteries, and the goddess of destruction and death. She is generally thought to be an aspect of the great mother goddess Devi. Other scholars believe that she is a goddess in her own right and not an aspect or incarnation of prior goddesses. Initially, Kali was a minor goddess in Hindu mythology. She appeared with a noose to lead away the dead after the Kauravas raided the sleeping Pandavas in the battle at Kuruksetra. Devi, who is frequently referred to as Durga, overcame the demons Kaitabha and Madhu who were born of Vishnu during his cosmic sleep. Later, the demon brothers Sumbha and Nisumbha took over the celestial kingdom and ruled over the deities. The gods called upon Durga to subdue the evil spirits. She appeared to them in the form of the beautiful and composed goddess Parvati and assured the worried deities that she would handle the situation. Equipped with weapons supplied by the gods, she marched into battle as Durga, to confront the demons Canda and Munda. When she saw them approaching, her wrathful form overcame her. Furious, she furrowed her brow and Kali emerged in all her terrible magnificence. She leapt into the fight, armed with her sword and noose, decapitated the demons and presented their heads to Durga as a gift. Durga called upon Kali again when she confronted the nearly invincible Raktabija (also spelled Ratavija). Every time Durga pierced him with her sword, demons from his blood emerged in his likeness. Kali sprung into being again and solved the problem by opening her gigantic mouth and swallowing the despicable creatures. Next, she sucked the blood from Raktabija gaping wounds and killed him. And so, the heavens were once again free from evil. Kali, the goddess of fertility and time, is the personification of the opposing forces of creation and destruction. When Kali danced with Shiva her frenzy overtook them and the earth shook with their rhythm. As Shyama-Kali she allocates boons and dispels fear. As a protector, she is known as Raksha-Kali and is called upon in times of epidemics and natural disasters. Shamashana-Kali embodies the power of destruction. Kali is the patron goddess of the infamous Hindu Thugs also known as Thags or phansigar (strangler), an organization of murderers who were bound by vows of secret murder in the service of Kali. The goddess bares a slight resemblance to the earlier goddess of the night Ratri, the sister of the dawn goddess Ushas. She more closely resembles Nirriti the Vedic demon.

The differences are that Nirriti is presented clothed, with golden hair, and Kali, the female warrior is black. Nirriti's popularity waned as Kali's emerged. Both goddesses are associated with death and sorrow. Kottavei, a goddess of war who appears in the Tamil pantheon, corresponds with Kali. She is known as a sorceress who feeds on carnage. Kali's attendants are the Dakinis, female demons who feed on flesh and blood. In one depiction, a young Dakini is shown in a crouching position, with a vessel on her head. Kali is depicted as a skeleton type black or dark blue naked figure bedecked with skulls and serpents. Her eyes are red, and her tongue protrudes from her blood-smeared face. She wears earrings made of corpses, a garland of severed heads, and a girdle composed of severed hands. She has ten hands, each holding weapons. In a Tantric depiction, she is shown with a necklace of heads; in her two right hands, she holds the sword and the scissors of death. In her left hands, a bowl of food and the lotus of generation. In art, she is also shown dancing on Shiva's body, swinging a sword in one hand and his head in the other hand. She is often seen standing with one foot on the leg and the other on the chest of Shiva. Sometimes she is shown feeding on the entrails of her victims. A ritual thought by worshipers to fulfill desires and receive special powers is to invoke Kali by repeating some of her other names: Sati, Rudrani, Parvati, Chinnamastica, Kamakshi, Umak Menakshi, Himavati and Kumari. Her festival Durga Puja is celebrated in the autumn. Since the prohibition of human sacrifice, goats instead of human heads are presented as an offering to the goddess. Kali symbolizes the productivity of Nature. Her color is yellow and she is associated with the number five. Compare the awesome Kali to the irresistible Krishna. Compare Kali to Isis (Egypt). Kali and Durga resemble the goddess of smallpox, Sitala (q.v.). *See also* Agni; Bhavani; Dakinis; Devi; Devis; Durga; Gauri; Kala; Karttikeya; Kauravas; Khadga Jogini; Kumari; Lhamo (Tibet); Nirriti; Pandavas; Parvati; Ratri; Shiva; Tara; Ugra; Vishnu.

Kali-Durga (India) *see* Devi.

Kali-Ma (India) *see* Kali.

Kalia (Greek)

Goddess of vice. She tried to divert Heracles' attention from his studies with Cheiron, the immortal Centaur. *See also* Centaur; Cheiron; Heracles.

Kalika (India) *see* Devi; Karttikeya.

Kalinda-Kanya (India) *see* Yami.

Kalindi (India)

She is the daughter of Surya and wife of Krishna. *See also* Krishna.

Kaliya (Hindu; India)

Also known as: *Kalanemi* (an incarnation), *Kansa* (an incarnation).

Kaliya, an incarnation of Kalanemi, is a five-headed serpent who is depicted vomiting fire and smoke. His lives in the river Yamuna. It was from the river that he emerged to ravage the surroundings. As a child, Krishna dove from a tree into the water and the splash set the tree on fire. Kaliya and his troop of serpent demons attacked the young god, encoiled him and nearly killed him. Bala-Rama reminded Krishna that he was a god. Krishna then used his divine energy, overcame the serpent and danced on his head until he was left powerless. Krishna ousted him from his home and sent him to the sea but gave him his word that the Garuda, the enemy of serpents would not annihilate him. *See also* Bala-Rama; Garuda; Hanuman; Kala-nemi; Kansa; Krishna.

Kaliyuga (Hindu; India)

Part of the Kalpa cycle, Kaliyuga is the present age, known as "the age of iron." It began just over 5,000 years ago and will last for 400,000, some say 432,000 more years. It is the age of degeneration and is called the worst of the four great periods of world history. Virtue is becoming non-existent and mortals await the coming of Kalki the destroyer. Kalki is the tenth incarnation of Vishnu. He will arrive on his white horse to restore order to the world. Before he arrives there will be a drought lasting one hundred years, and seven suns will appear which will remove the last of the water. Fire will consume the earth, then twelve years of rain will submerge the world. Brahma will return at this point and the cycle will start again. *See also* Dwaparayuga; Kalki; Kalpa; Mahakala; Tretayuga; Vishnu.

Kalki *Kalkin* (Hindu, India)

Kalki is the tenth, future and final avatar of Vishnu. As Kalki, his mother is Awejsirdenee, the wife of Bishenjun. Upon his return he will appear as a giant man with a white horse's head, wielding a flaming sword, astride a white horse riding through the sky. His purpose will be to end evil and wickedness in the world. His appearance will take place at the end of our age, which is known as the iron age. When he arrives the wicked will be destroyed and the world will be created anew to enter an age of advancement. The day of Kalki's arrival is called the day of Pralaya. On this day Shiva will dance on the disintegrated world and Vishnu will sleep so that the world will be born anew. Compare Kalki to the Buddhist Maitreya. *See also* Kaliyuga; Shiva; Vishnu.

Kalkin (India) *see* Kalki.

Kallin-Kallin (Australia) "Chicken Hawk" *see* Yalungur.

Kalliope (Greek) *see* Calliope.

Kalma (Finnish)

Kalma, the goddess of death, is an underworld deity. Her companion is a monstrous animal who seizes and devours humans. Her name means "corpse odor." In other versions, Kalma is a male, known as a god of tombs. *See also* Kalevala; Manala.

Kalmashapada, King (India) *see* Parashara.

Kaloafu (Polynesia)

Kaloafu is one of the foster parents of Eel (Tuna). The other was Tuehie. Tuna was the lover of Hina. *See also* Hina; Tuna.

Kalpa *Brahma-Kapla* (Hindu; India)

This is a sub-cycle of Mahapralaya. One day in the life of Brahma is equal to 4,320 million years, or according to some, 4 billion human years. At this time Brahma awakens and three worlds are created: heavens, middle, and lower regions. The Kalpa is divided into 1,000 Great Ages (Mahayugas). Each Mahayuga is further divided into the four ages or Yugas: Krita,

Treta, Dwaparayuga, and Kaliyuga. In Jain mythology, Kalpa is one of the two uppermost levels of the universe; Kalpathitha is the other. In Kalpa, there are sixteen heavens known as Deval-okas. Each Devaloka has a name and its own inhabitants. In Kalpathitha there are fourteen abodes for the gods. Indrani, the wife of Indra, is the owner of the magic Kalpa Tree also known as the Parijata Tree. It is kept in Swarga, the celestial dwelling place of Indrani and Indra. If the elderly gaze upon this tree, they will regain their vigor. *See also* Dwaparayuga; Indrani; Kaliyuga; Kalpa; Mahapralaya; Parijata; Sesha.

Kalratri (Nepal) *see* Vajravarahi.

Kalseru (Australia) *see* Rainbow serpent.

Kalumba (Africa) *see* Kalunga.

Kalunga (Angola, Luba People, Zaire, Africa)

Also known as: *Kalumba, Kalunga-Ngombe.*

Kalunga is a god of death or a place of the dead. In a Luba tale he also appears as a Supreme Being. He created mankind, then realized Life and Death were coming along the road. He instructed a goat and a dog to guard the path. The dog fell asleep while on watch and allowed Death to enter. In Bahai, Brazil, Kalunga was known as a god of the sea, one of the gods in a pantheon of African deities worshiped by the Congo-Angola followers.

Kalunga-Ngombe (Africa) *see* Kalunga.

Kalupso (Greek) *see* Calypso.

Kalura (Australia)

Possibly a rain god or one who is associated with spirit children.

Kalypso (Greek) *see* Calypso.

Kam-Pala (India) *see* Bala-Rama.

Kama (A) (Buddhist, Hindu, Vedic; India)

Also known as: *Cama Ananga* (Bodiless), *Iraja* (Born in Water), *Kama Deva, Kamadeva, Pradyumna* (an avatar), *Rupastra* (Weapon of Beauty), *Samantaka* (Destroyer of Peace), *Samsara-Guru* (Teacher of the World), *Smara* (Memory).

The Vedas proclaim Kama as a supreme god and creator, who sprang from the cosmic waters. His first emanation was desire and his second, the power to achieve desire. He created Nara (waters) and threw a seed into them which became a golden egg. From this egg came Narayana, who is an aspect of Brahma, or the son of Krishna. When Brahma was acknowledged as the supreme god, it was said that Kama sprang from his heart. As a creative moral force he is said to be the son of Sraddha, the goddess of faith, and Dharma, the god of justice and virtue. In later times, as the god of sexual desire and love, his parents are Vishnu and Mayadevi (delusion), or Vishnu and the goddess of beauty and fortune, Lakshmi. His mate is Rati, the goddess of desire and passion. A reluctant Kama, painted green, was sent on a mission by the gods to rouse Shiva from his meditations, which had been ongoing for centuries. Irritated at being disturbed, Shiva turned Kama to ashes with the fire from his third eye. During this period, the earth was dry and arid. Unsettled, Shiva, who had been stung by Kama's arrow, was unable to return to his meditations until he married Parvati. The gods approached Shiva and requested that Kama, the god of love and sport, be returned to the world. He was restored as Pradyumna, the son of Krishna and Rukmini and was reunited with Rati. The beautiful, eternally youthful Kama rides on a parrot called Kameri, the wisest of all birds, or a peacock, the symbol of impatient desire. He carries a bow strung with bees, and five arrows pointed with flowers: the lotus, mango, asoka, muli and karunga, all emblems of desire. The blossoms of the damanaka tree which are associated with spring worship, are offered to Kama. His symbol is Makara, the monster fish, who is Varuna's vehicle. He is king of the love nymphs, the Aspara's, who dance around him. One nymph carries his red banner, bearing the emblem of Makara. Kama's adjunct is Vasanta, the deity who presides over the flower season, spring. Kama (love) ensures that creation in the universe will never cease. Kama is equated with the creative aspect of Agni (q.v.). He sometimes appears as an aspect of the Buddhist god of temptation and death, Mara (q.v.). Compare Kama to the Greek Eros. *See also* Asparases; Brahma; Dharma; Krishna; Lakshmi; Makara; Naryana; Parvati; Pradyuma; Priti; Rati; Shiva; Sraddha; Tapati; Vach; Vishnu.

Kama (B) (Hawaii, Polynesia)
High god. He is a powerful tutelar deity of all the islands.

Kama Deva (India) *see* Kama (A).

Kama-Dhenu (India) *see* Kamadhenu.

Kama-Yama-Hiko (Japan)
God of mountain minerals. *See also* O-Yama-Tsu-Mi; Sengen.

Kama-Yamato-Iware-Biko (Japan) *see* Jimmu Tenno.

Kamadeva (India) *see* Kama (A).

Kamadhenu *Camdhen, Kama-Dhenu, Kamdhain, Kamdhen, Kamdhenu* (Hindu; India)
Also known as: *Nandini, Savala, Surabhi.*
Kamadhenu, the "Cow of Desires," or the "Wish Cow," is one of the miraculous treasures churned from the sea by the gods. She has the ability to fulfill all wishes. In the form of a cow she belonged to Indra and to the sage Vasishtha. Kamadhenu produced the warriors who fought against the god of war, Arjuna. *See also* Parashur Rama for additional mythology. *See also* Kurma regarding the churning of the sea. Compare Kamadhenu to Audhumla (Teutonic). *See also* Arjuna; Nandi; Surabhi; Vasistha.

Kamado-No-Kami (Japan) *see* Inari.

Kamaheruka (Tibet) *see* Herukas.

Kamak (Iranian)
Drought demon. This gigantic bird holds back rain with its large wings. It was killed by Keresaspa (q.v.).

Kamakshi (India) *see* Devi.

Kamala (India) *see* Lakshmi.

Kamapua'a (Hawaii)
Also known as: *Kamapuaa.*

"The Great Boar." "Hog-child." Creator. He is the grandson of Kamaunua-niho (also spelled Ka-mau-nui, Kamaunu) the female sorcerer who was married to Humu (also spelled Aumu). In one of his numerous myths, he is newly born on the northern coast of Oahu. His older brother, Kahiki-honua-kele, tries to throw him away. His mother fresh from her purification bath finds him lying on her skirt in the form of a baby pig. His brother takes the infant pig to his grandmother's house. She recognizes her kupua grandson and raises him until he becomes of age. In another tale, Kamapua'a used his great snout to push up the earth from the bottom of the sea. This allowed the gods and people a place to live and land to cultivate. A protector of the gods and people, he was frequently in battle with their enemies. Kamapua'a also used his snout to dig wells. He was one of the many suitors of the great fire goddess, Pele. Initially, Pele looked upon him with disdain. However, in a contest, Kamapua'a won against his opponents by extinguishing all Pele's fires with mud. So it was that Kamapua'a and Pele were wed. He is described as a half-man and half-hog, but he is also a shapechanger. He covers the bristles on his back while in human form, often as a tall, handsome man, with sparkling eyes, by wearing a long cloak. Kamapua'a is also able to change himself into a fish or into plant life. *See also* Pele.

Kamapuaa (Polynesia, Hawaii) *see* Kamapua'a.

Kambel (Melanesia)
Sky deity and creator. Possibly a god of fire. Kambel cut down a palm tree which released humans.

Kamdhain (India) *see* Kamadhenu.

Kamdhen (India) *see* Kamadhenu.

Kamdhenu (India) *see* Kamadhenu.

Kame and Keri (Bacairi People, South America)
First men. They are twin brothers who after the Deluge became the creators of mankind, making men out of reeds. In another version, they created animals from a tree trunk. Kame and Keri stole balls of feathers from a vulture to make the sun and moon.

Kameri (India) Sacred parrot. *See also* Kama (A).

Kamehaikana (Hawaii)
Kamehaikana is the goddess Haumea's name when she is in human form. *See also* Haumea.

Kami (Japan, Egypt)
Also known as: *Ama, Chi-haya-buru, Kamit.*
Supreme force. Kami was created by Izanagi (Male Who Invites) and Izanami (Female Who Invites). Izanagi and Izanami were created by the triad produced from chaos. Their function was to create earthly manifestations. Their first creation was the Japanese archipelago followed by the creation of kami, followed by the divine rulers of the world. Kami represents all things produced. Kami is applied to all things from the lowest to the highest form of life, including the forces of nature. Kami means "beings more highly placed" and applies to everything that is revered. In the Shinto beliefs, all nature is venerated. By approximately C.E. 200 the religion of Shinto ("Way of the Gods") established that the Imperial Family had descended

from the sun goddess Amaterasu. This gave the emperor kami. He was not worshiped as a deity but the unquestionable religious position of the Imperial Line was thereafter called sacred. This lasted until 1946 when the emperor Hirohito renounced his divinity. Deities and spirits were also known as kami, though not all were worshiped. There are two groups of kami: those of heaven, Ama-Tsu-Kami and those of earth, Kuni-Tsu-Kami. In time, almost everything in nature and every locality had its kami, or spirit which were honored by shrines and sanctuaries. In early times Ama and Kuni (heaven and earth) were linked by stairs or some say a bridge called Ama-no-hashidate. This allowed the gods to communicate with earth by way of messengers. Some traditions say that kami was an early name for Egypt. For the Shinto creation myth, *see* Ama-no-minaka-nushi. Kami generally corresponds to the two souls of the gods. In some traditions, it corresponds to the gods and powerful mortals and in others the two souls exist in gods and mortals. The gentle, kind and happy one is nigi-mi-tama and the rough or violent one is ara-mi-tama. The opposite of Ama (heaven) was the underworld or kingdom of the dead called Yomi-tsu-kuni (land of darkness) or Ne-no-kuni (land of roots) or Soko-no-kuni (deep land). *See* Ama-tsu-kami for details of Ama (heaven). *See* Yomi for details about the underworld. For additional names applied to the bridge Ama-no-hashidate, *see* Izanagi.

Kami-mi-musubi (Japan) *see* Kami-mimusubi.

Kami-Mimusubi (Shinto, Japan)
Also known as: *Kami-mi-musubi* (Divine or Mysterious-producing), *Kami-musubi-mi-oya-no-mikoto*, *Kami-musubi-no-kami*, *Kamu-musubi.*
Mother goddess. Kami-mimusubi and her male counterpart Taka-Mimusubi are considered the secondary couple who followed the triad which sprung from primeval chaos. Her daughters are Yorodzu-hime (Taku-hata chi-hata hime), and probably Mi-ho-tsu hime. Her son is Suku-Na-Biko, who became the chief of the medicine deities. Another son may have been Omohi-kane no kami. When she heard the appeals of Okuni-nushino-mikoto's mother when he was killed, she returned him to life as a handsome young man. Kami-Mimusubi collected the seeds produced by the food goddess Ogetsu-hime-no-kami and used them for nutritional purposes. (Ogetsu-hime-no-kami is also known as Ogetsu-hime and Oho-ge-tsu-himi.)
In some traditions, Kami-Mimusubi represents Kami Romi. For information, *see* Ama-no-minaka-nushi. This listing will also give information regarding the Shinto creation myth and the *Kojiki*. Kami-Mimusubi is listed in the *Kojiki* as the third of the "Five Deities." Compare this myth to Amaterasu, who used goods produced by Ukemochi to produce a food supply. *See also* Okuni-Nushino-Mikoto; Suku-Na-Biko; Taka-Mimusubi; Ukemochi.

Kami-Musubi (Japan) *see* Kami-mimusubi.

Kami-musubi-mi-oya-no-mikoto (Japan) *see* Kami-mimusubi.

Kami-musubi-no-kami (Japan) *see* Kami-mimusubi.

Kami-nari (Japan) *see* Raijin; Take-mi-kazuchi.

Kami-rogi (Japan) *see* Ama-no-minaka-nushi.

Kami-romi (Japan) *see* Ama-no-minaka-nushi; Kami Mimusubi.

Kamiizanaginarisan (Japan) *see* Kami-Nari.

Kaminari Sama (Japan) *see* Raiden.

Kamit (Japan) *see* Kami.

Kammapa (Sesuto People, Africa)
The monster Kammapa devoured all mortals except one old woman. She gave birth to a child without the help of a man. She named the child Lituolene, who was born as an adult. In attempting to kill the monster, Lituolene was swallowed, and once inside he cut the monster open and released all the humans.

Kammus (Moabite) *see* Chemosh.

Kamo-hoalii (Polynesia, Hawaii) *see* Kamohoali'i.

Kamohoali'i (Polynesia, Hawaii)
Also known as: *Kamo-hoalii, King Moho.*
God of steam (vapor). Kamohoali'i is the son of the goddess of childbirth, Haumea. His sisters are Pele, the angry volcano goddess of Hawaii, and Hi'iaka. *See also* Pele.

Kamrusepas (Mesopotamia)
This goddess of magic and healing sent a bee to awaken Telepinus with its sting. He is the god of agriculture, fertility, and youth who had disappeared and brought all life to a standstill. Her actions were to remind him of his duty and to bring back the sun and life to mortals. *See also* Telepinus.

Kamsa (India) *see* Kansa.

Kamu-mimusbi (Japan) *see* Ama-no-minaka-nushi.

Kamu-mimusubi (Japan) *see* Ama-no-minaka-nushi.

Kamu-musubi (Japan) *see* Kami-mimusubi.

Kamu-yamato-ihare-biko (Japan) *see* Jimmu Tenno.

Kamus (Moabite) *see* Chemosh.

Kan-Xib-Yui (Maya People, Yucatan) *see* Ahmucen-Cab.

Kana (Hawaii, Polynesia)
Hero. Kupua (demi-god). Many of his legends tell us of his adventures as he traveled from island to island battling the evil Kupua. Often his impish brother Niheu (Sand Crab) accompanies him. Kana, born as a rope, is very, very tall. He can step from one island to another even though they may be 70 miles apart. He is variously known as the son of Hina and Hakala-nileo, Ku and Uli. Uli is sometimes his grandmother who raised him. One of Kana's most famous deeds was to travel to the entrance of the underworld to restore the stolen sun to his people. *See also* Ku; Kupua; Uli.

Kana-yama-biko-no-kami (Japan)
"Metal Mountain Prince Deity." *See also* Kanayama-hime; O-Yama-Tsu-Mi; Sengen.

Kana-yama-hime (Japan) *see* Kanayama-hime.

Kanaima (Arawak People, New Guinea) *see* Kenaima; Makonaima.

Kanakamuni (India) *see* Manushi-Buddhas.

Kanaloa (Hawaii, Polynesia)
    Also known as: *Milu, Tangaroa*
    God of the Underworld. God of the Squid. Teacher of magic. After earth was separated from heaven, Kanaloa became the leader of the first group of spirits placed on earth. It is said that the spirits had been "spit out" by the gods. Kanaloa led them in a rebellion but they were defeated and thrown into the underworld. People who are associated with canoes invoke Kanaloa and Kane. Kanaloa is called upon for the safe sailing of the canoe and Kane for canoe building. Kanaloa and Kane are also connected with fish ponds. There are numerous legends about the adventures of Kanaloa and Kane as they traveled throughout the islands establishing water springs and making certain that the springs were kept clean. Kanaloa appears in the shape of an octopus. *See also* Kane; Miru; Tanaoa; Tangaroa.

Kanati and Selu (Cherokee People, North America)
    The First Ancestors. The male, Kanati, and the female, Selu, were the first of the Cherokee people.

Kanayama-Hime (Japan)
    Also known as: *Kana-yama-hime.*
    Goddess of Metal. Kanayama-hime (Metal-Mountain Princess Deity) was created from the vomit of her mother, Izanami. Izanami had been seared and scorched by the birth of Kanayama-hime's brother, the fire god Kagu-tsuchi, and was deathly ill. Eight deities were born from her bodily emissions during this time. Kanayama-hime's brother/husband was Kana-yama-biko-no-kami (Metal-Mountain Prince Deity). *See* Sengen for other mountain deities. *See also* Izanami.

Kandu (India) *see* Pramloma.

Kane (Hawaii, Polynesia)
    Also known as: *Kane-Hekili* ("Thunderer"), *Tane.*
    God of Procreation. God of the Sea. In the first era, before heaven and earth, Kane dwelled alone in the darkness. Light was created in the second era. This is when the gods Ku and Lono, with Kane, created the earth and all that is on it. In the third era, they create man and woman, Kumu-honua (Earth Beginning) and Lalo-honua (Earth Below). In the fourth era, Kane, who had been living on earth, returned to live in heaven. The man, who had broken Kane's law, was then made immortal. In another rendition, Kane, Ku and Lono came out of po (night). They created three heavens. Kane's dwelling was the uppermost heaven, Ku's heaven came next and Lono's dwelling was in the lowest heaven. Then the gods fashioned the earth. Kane made the sun, moon and stars and placed them in the space between heaven and earth. He made the ocean salt. An image of man was formed from the earth, the head out of white clay brought from the north, south, east and west seas. Man's body came from red earth mixed with spittle. Man was formed after the image of Kane with Ku as the worker and Lono as the general assistant. Kane and Ku spat into his nostrils, Lono into his mouth and he became a living being. This first man is named Ke-li'i-ku-honua. He was given a splendid garden to live in and a wife, who was created from his right side. Her name is Ke-

ola-Ku-honua (or Lalo-hano). In ancient times, the three gods were worshiped as one under the name of Hika-po-loa. Kane is known as "the organizer." Kane is comparable to, and some say the same as, the Polynesian god Tane (q.v.). In Hawaiian mythology Kane is the father of the Goddess of Hawaii, Hi'i-aka (q.v.). As a culture god, Kane's name is often coupled with Kanaloa, god of the squid. *See also* Kanaloa; Ku; Ku-ka-ohia-laka; Lono.

Kane-Hekili (Hawaii, Polynesia) "Thunderer." *See also* Kane.

Kane Hoalani (Hawaii, Polynesia)
    Also known as: *Kane Milohai.*
    This ancient god, who is the father of Pele, owns a miraculous sea-shell. If the shell is placed on the ocean waves it turns into a spectacular sailing ship that will float the owner to any destination required almost immediately. *See also* Kane; Pele.

Kane-Kahili (Hawaii, Polynesia) One of the volcano deities.

Kaneapua (Hawaii, Polynesia)
    Fish god. Healer. Brother of the goddess Pele, Kaneapua and his brother Aukele-nui-aiku brought the first coconuts to Hawaii. They are planted at Kahaualea and Kalapana in the Puna district of the island. The akuhekuhe fish is one of Kaneapua's forms. *See also* Kupua-Huluena; Kuula; Laeapua; Pele.

Kangi and Mangi, The (Japan) *see* Hikohohodemi; Hosuseri; O-Wata-Tsu-Mi.

Ka'nini (Aborigine People, Australia)
    Spirit of the "Great Mother from the Water."

Kannon (Buddhist; Japan)
    Also known as: *Avalokitesvara, Bato Kannon, Fuku-kensaku Kannon, Ju-ichimen Kannon, Jundei Kannon, Kannon Bosatsu, Kuan Yin, Nyo-i-rin Kannon, Senju Kannon, Sho Kannon.*
    Goddess of mercy. She is one of the Bodhisattvas. Kannon Bosatsu is generally associated with Amida. *See also* Amida; Kuan Yin.

Kannuck *Kanook* (Haida, Kwakiutl, Tlingit, Tsimshian People; North America)
    Deified animal. Deity of darkness. The Wolf Spirit. Brother of Yehi. Kanook controls the waters and his brother, Yehi, is a spirit of light.

Kanook (Native North American) *see* Kannuck.

Kanro-O (Japan) *see* Amida.

Kansa *Kamsa* (Hindu; India)
    Also known as: *Kalanemi* (an incarnation), *Kaliya* (an incarnation), *Kenss.*
    During the second age of the world, Kansa, an asura (demon), was born as the son of Queen Pavanarekha and King Ugrasena. His real father is Drumalika, a demon, who assumed Ugrasena's form and raped Pavanareka. Their kingdom, Mathura, is an agricultural area and the populace is described as peace-loving. Eventually, Kansa deposed Ugrasena and ruled as a tyrannical king who oppressed his subjects. When he heard that his cousin Devaki would give birth to a son who would kill him, he murdered her sons and issued an order to have all male infants slaughtered. Devaki's infants Krishna and Bala-Rama

were spared through a ruse. Krishna was raised in the forest by the cowherds Yasoda and her mate Nanda. The goddess Devi transformed herself into the infant daughter of Yasoda and Nanda and told Kansa that Krishna had escaped and therefore Kansa would be made powerless. Kansa became the archenemy of Krishna and deployed multitudes of demons to obstruct him during his lifetime. The last plan he devised was to have Akrura, the head of his court, invite Krishna to Mathura for a sacrifice in honor of Shiva. He arranged to have Chanura, a wrestler, at the gates to overcome him. His backup plan was to have a huge elephant trample Krishna to death. What he did not know was that Akrura was a devotee of Krishna who went straight to Krishna and divulged the plan. A great brawl ensued with Krishna and Bala-Rama slaying Kansa and his eight brothers. *See also* Asuras; Bala-Rama; Devaki; Devi; Drumalika; Jara-Sandha; Kaliya; Krishna; Sisupala; Yadavas.

Kanthaka (India) Prince Gautama's horse. *See also* Buddha.

Kantoki-No-Ki (Japan)
Deified trees. Any tree struck by lightning is called Kantoki-No-Ki, which means "trees cloven by the god." They are never cut down.

Kanwa (India) *see* Shakuntala.

Kanya-Kumari (India) *see* Kumari; Shakti.

Kanzuras, Mount (Hittite, Hurrian) *see* Kumbaris.

Kapala (India) "Skull." *See also* Shiva.

Kapila (India) *see* Kadru; Manasa; Sagara.

Kapisha (India) Mother of the Pishachas (q.v.).

Kapohoikahiola (Hawaii, Samoa)
God of explosions. One of the volcano deities.

Kappa (Japan)
Water monster. River god. Kappa the dwarf was born from the mortals who had drowned in Japanese rivers. He has magic powers used to draw people, particularly children, to him. Like the evil Oni, he also rapes women. Since he is very polite, one can escape his clutches by bowing low to him. When he returns the bow, all the water leaks out from the hole in his head and he is rendered impotent. Although evil, he has a reputation for teaching mortals how to set broken bones and is also a trustworthy creature. If he compromises with a mortal, he will keep his end of the contract even to his own detriment. In some renditions Kappa is used in the plural. Kappa or the Kappa live in rivers, ponds or lakes and are vampires, feeding on their prey through the anus. Aside from blood, they like cucumbers and can be placated by tossing the vegetable into their dwelling places. Some think they originated with the early, semi-nomadic Ainu people. The mouths of streams and rivers have a deity known as Minato-no-kami. Kappa resembles a monkey without fur. Sometimes he is shown with fish scales or a tortoise shell instead of skin and is about the size of a small child. He is yellow-green, with an indentation on the top of his head. He is also depicted with the head of a monkey, body of a tortoise and legs and arms of a frog. *See also* Gaki; Oni; Shiko-me; Tengu.

Kapua (Hawaii) *see* Kupua.

Kara (Teutonic) *see* Valkyries.

Karala (India) "The Formidable." *See also* Durga; Parvati.

Karali (India) *see* Kali; Durga.

Kardama (India) *see* Varuna.

Karei *Kari* (Semang People, Malay Peninsula; Andaman Islands).
Creator. God of storms and thunder. Giver of souls. Recorder. Judge. His companion is Ple. He punishes wrong-doers for sins such as mocking tame or helpless animals, killing sacred birds, killing the sacred black wasp, and being too familiar with one's mother-in-law. When angry, he causes thunder. To atone, the sinner must gash shins, mix blood with water and toss it to the sky while calling out "Stop, stop."

Kari (Teutonic) Lord of the storm giants. *See also* Aegir; Ymir.

Karia (Australia) *see* Rainbow Snake.

Kariki *Karihi* (New Zealand, Hawaii, Polynesia)
Also known as: *Aliki* (Hawaii), *Kaha'i.*
Culture hero. He is the brother of Tawhaki, who is called the god of thunder by the Maori People, and son of Hema and the goddess Urutonga. His grandparents are Kattangata and the cannibal chieftain, Whaitiri. Kariki and his brother are involved in many adventures together as they search for their father who had been abducted by goblins, beaten to a pulp and thrown into a pit. *See also* Hema; Kaha'i; Tane; Tangaloa; Tawhaki; Whaitiri.

Karisini (India) *see* Lakshmi.

Karitay (Tamil People, India)
"Dark Mother." An ancient goddess of the forest who feeds demons from her beggar's bowl. *See also* Aiyai.

Kariteimo (Japan) *see* Kishimojin.

Karkotaka (India) *see* Nagas.

Karl (Norse; Teutonic)
God of Peasants. Karl is the son of Amma by Heimdall. He is the husband of Snor. He is the founder of the race of peasants. *See also* Heimdall.

Karlafberge (Teutonic) *see* Odin.

Karliki (Slavic)
The Karliki are various classes of spirits. *See also* Domovoi; Lyshie.

Karma Dakinis (India) *see* Dakinis.

Karma-Heruka (Tibet) *see* Karma-Krotishaurima.

Karma-Krotishaurima (Tibet)
She is found with her spouse Karma-Heruka in the Bardo World on the twelfth day. *See also* Padma Krotishaurima; Ratna Krotishaurima; Shakti.

Karma-Sakshi (India) "Witness of Deeds." *See also* Surya.

Karna (Hindu; India)
Also known as: *Anga-Raja, Radheya, Vasusena.*
The sage Durvasas gave Kunti a secret charm by which she

could become pregnant by the god that she loved over all others. The result was the virgin birth of Karna, the son of Kunti and the sun god Surya. He was born in a full coat of brilliant armor. Ashamed of his birth, Kunti abandoned the baby on the banks of the Jamuna River. Yami, the goddess of the river, gave him to the Ganges River and its goddess, Ganga. She arranged that Radha and her spouse, the charioteer Nandana (also called Shatananda), would find him and raise him. Indra was fascinated by the shining armor of the sun-child. In exchange for the armor, Indra gave him his magic spear. Karna gained immense strength from the weapon and became a great warrior. He was made the king of Anga (now Bengal), by Duryodhana. He was one of the contestants for the hand of Draupadi and although he won the event, she rejected him. Distressed, he joined her enemies, the Kauravas. During the war of the *Mahabharata* he killed Ghatotkacha and was later killed by Arjuna. After his death, Arjuna learned that Karna was his half-brother, the oldest son of his mother. His mother gave birth to other children by various gods but always remained virginal through the power of the sage, Durvasas. *See also* Arjuna; Bhima (A); Duryodhana; Ganga; Indra; Kauravas; Kunti; Radha; Surya; Yami.

Karna-Moti (India) "With Pearls in Her Ears." *See also* Kali.

Karora (Gurra People, Australia)
Supreme deity. Karora was born in darkness at the bottom of Ilbalintja (a dry pond or lake). After he left, the pond became filled with the juice of honeysuckle buds. He was the creator of many sons. In one myth, the sons injure the wallaby (Tjenterama) who became the first ancestor of the race. Karora is still asleep in Ilbalintja.

Karpios (Greek) *see* Dionysus.

Karpo *Carpo* (Greek) *see* Carpo.

Karpophoros *Kourotrophos* (Greek) *see* Hera.

Karsnik (Slavic) *see* Krsnik.

Kartavirya (India)
King with a Thousand Arms. *See also* Parashur Rama.

Kartika (India) *see* Karttikeya.

Kartikeya (India) *see* Karttikeya.

Karttekeya (India) *see* Karttikeya.

Karttikeya *Karttekeya, Kartika, Kartikeya* (Vedic, Hindu; India)
Also known as: *Agneya* (Son of Agni), *Ganga-ja* (Born from the Ganges), *Gangeya, Guha* (Secret), *Kumara, Mahasena, Scanda, Scanda, Sena-pati* (Army Commander), *Skanda, Subramanya*.
Karttikeya, the god of war and bravery and patron of thieves, in late Vedic myth was given life expressly to slay the demons who plagued the gods. There are numerous myths relating to his origins. We are told of Indra coming upon the beautiful Devasena when he was in the forest. The horse demon Keshin was about to rape her but fled when he saw Indra with his vajra (thunderbolt). Devasena asked Indra to find her a mate and protector. Noting that her name meant "Divine Array," he felt that

a warrior would be most suitable for her. He decided that Karttikeya would be appropriate. Strengthened by a mate with this auspicious name, this couple could lead the gods. In a variation of this story, Indra took Devasena to heaven to meet Brahma. Brahma decided that the god of fire Agni would be an appropriate mate for her. They became the parents of Karttikeya. In another version, when the gods were plagued by a demon, Shiva created six children by the flame of his third eye to combat it. His mate Parvati clasped them too tightly one day, and their bodies merged into one, but they retained six heads. He is also known as the son of Agni and the goddess of the river Ganges, Ganga. He was raised by the six Krittika sisters who received him from the Ganga. They all wanted to nurse him, so he developed six heads. Suaha, one of Daksha's numerous daughters, may have been his mother when she mated in disguise with Agni. He is also called the son of Daksha's daughter Parvati and Shiva, and the brother of Ganesha. He competed with Ganesha, the learned elephant god, for the hands of the goddesses of success, Siddhi and Buddhi, and Ganesha emerged the victor. Two goddesses, Bhadrakali and Kalika, who belonged to a group known collectively as the Matris or Divine Mothers, became Karttikeya's companions. They accompanied him when he went to slay the demon Taraka. These goddesses speak different languages, have different complexions, and wear various outfits. They live in trees, caves, crossroads, mountains and cremation grounds. (Kali was said to have belonged to this group.) In other renditions, Taraka was slain by Rama and Lakshmana. Karttikeya is depicted holding a bow and arrow as he rides Paravani, his peacock. Sometimes he is shown with six faces. Karttikeya is identified with the planet Mars. He may have been derived from an ancient war god named Muruhan. Karttikeya is sometimes said to be the spouse of the goddess Shashthi (q.v.). *See also* Agni; Asuras; Bana; Bhisma; Brahma; Daksha; Devi; Ganesha; Ganga; Indra; Kali; Parvati; Rama; Taraka; Vach; Visvakarma.

Karu (Greek) *see* Car.

Karus (Greek) *see* Car.

Kasa-Nagi (Japan) *see* Susanowo.

Kasa Sona (Melanesia)
First beings. These deities were on earth long before mankind and were born with the sun.

Kasandra (Greek) *see* Cassandra.

Kasenko (Japan) *see* Ho-hsien-ku.

Kashijotem (Japan) *see* Kichijo-Ten.

Kashiko-ne No Mikoto (Japan) *see* Ama-no-minaka-nushi.

Kashyapa (India) *see* Kasyapa.

Kasin (Mayan) *see* Nohochacyum.

Kassandra (Greek) *see* Cassandra.

Kastiatsi (Acoma People, North America)
The Rainbow. *See also* Katsinas; Shruistha.

Kastor and Polydeukes (Greek) *see* Castor.

Kasyapa (A) *Kashyapa* (Brahmanic, Hindu; India)
Also known as: *Kasyapa Marica, Kesava.*
Kasyapa is the progenitor of all living things on earth. Mating with the self-formed goddess Aditi, they became the parents of the Adityas and the god Vivasvat. The *Vishnu Purana* states that Vishnu is also their son. He mated with Danu, the daughter of Daksha, and her sisters: Ira, mother of earthly vegetation; Surasa; Diti, with whom he was the father of the Daityas; and Surabhi the cow goddess. With Vinata the underworld goddess he became the father of the Garudas. With Kadru, another of Danu's sisters, he became the father of the Serpent Race, known as the Nagas and Nagis. According to some renditions, he married all thirteen of Daksha's daughters. He was also the mate of the grandmother of the Garudas Tamra, and Sumati, the daughter of Vinata. He had another daughter, Saudamani, and was also the father of the Pisashas, Rakshasas and Yakshas. Kasyapa is one of the seven great rishis (sages) and an arch-priest for Rama. Kasyapa is sometimes identified with Prajapati (q.v.). *See also* Aditi; Agni; Andhaka; Aruna; Asuras; Daityas; Daksha; Diti; Gandharvas; Garuda; Gauri; Kadru; Krodha; Manasa; Marichi (B); Nagas and Nagis; Pisasha; Rakshasas; Rishi; Sagara; Sumati; Surabhi; Vishnu.

Kasyapa (B) (Buddhist; India)
Also known as: *Hodsrun* (Tibet), *O-sung* (Tibet).
Known as the luminous protector, Kasyapa is the third Manushi-Buddha who lived on earth for 20,000 years preceding Gautama Buddha. *See also* Manushi-Buddhas.

Kathar (Ugarit)
Also known as: *Kathar the Clever.*
God of architects, artisans, and weapon makers. Kathar built the palace of Baal. Kathar is identified with Hephaistos (q.v.).

Kathar-Wa-Hasis (Ugarit) *see* Khasis.

Kathirat, The (Syria, Ugarit)
They are known as the wise goddesses and have been compared to the Greek Graces (q.v.). They are depicted as swallows who are associated with maternity. *See also* Yarikh.

Katkochila (Wintun People, North America)
In the Creation Legend, Katkochila set fire to the earth after someone stole his magic flute. A great flood doused the fire.

Katonda (Luganda People, Africa)
Creator. This is a creator god. His name was used by the Christians and Muslims for their god.

Katsinas (Acoma People, North America)
Also known as: *Katcinas.*
Rain and food deities. Younger children of Iatiju, with powers to bring rain and food. Probably the same as Katcinas of the Pueblo People. *See also* Iatiju; Kastiatsi; Mayochina; Pishumi; Shk; Shruistha; Tsichtinaka; Uchtsita.

Kattangata (Polynesia) *see* Kaitangata

Katyayani (Southern India)
This goddess uses a tiger as her vehicle. The tiger's skin is used by worshipers of Shiva and by sannyasins.

Kauhausibware (San Cristobal)
Creator. Similar to Kafisi.

Kaukabhta (Syrian) *see* Astarte.

Kaukas (Lithuanian) *see* Krukis.

Kaukis (Prussia) Household dwarf spirits.

Kaukomielli (Finnish) *see* Ahti; Lemminkainen.

Kaulu (Hawaii, Polynesia)
Also known as: *Kana.*
Voyager. Trickster. God of cultivated foods. Kaulu is one of three brothers, one evil, one good. Born on Oahu, he is the youngest son of Ku-ka-ohia-laka and Hina-ula-ohia. His older brother, Kamano, threatened that Kaulu would die upon birth. Fearing to take human form, Kaulu chose to be born in the form of a rope. Another brother, Kaeha (or Kaholeha), put him on a shelf and cared for him. Kaeha was taken to the sky lands of Kane and Kanaloa. Kaulu went in search of him. The obstacles were many, but because of his two exceptionally strong hands, he was able to overcome them. When strong waves presented themselves, he broke them up. (As a result, we now have surf.) His troubles were far from behind him when he reached Kaeha. He had to trick and deceive the gods and the chief of sharks, Ku-kama-ulu-nui-akea (or Kalake'e-nui-a-a-Kane), who had swallowed Kaeha. When Kaulu finally retrieved his brother, they returned to Papakolea in Moanalua. Kaula went to Kapalama where he killed the goddess of fertility and guardian of cultivated plants, Haumea, and on to Kailua, where he killed Lono-ka-eho, who had eight foreheads and ruled the north side of Oahu, and his dog, Kuilioloa. In another adventure under the guise of a small weakly man, he was told by the gods Kane and Kanaloa to take all he could from their vegetable plot. *See* Kana, who was also born in the shape of a rope. *See also* Haumea; Hina-ula-ohia; Kupua; Kupua-Huluena.

Kauravas, The *Kurus.* (Hindu; India)
In the *Mahabharata*, the Kauravas are despicable scoundrels who are the enemies of their cousins, the five noble Pandavas. The Kauravas are the one hundred sons of the blind king Dhritarashtra and Gandhari. The eldest son, Duryodhana, became the leader of the Kauravas in the great war of the *Mahabharata*. When Dhritarashtra was offered the gift of sight by a magician, he refused because he did not want to see his people killed. In one episode, the Kauravas and Pandavas fought for possession of his kingdom. A public contest of strength was held between the cousins. Arjuna, a Pandava, was the winner who received the princess Draupadi as a prize. She became the wife of the five Pandavas. A gambling match took place and the Kauravas defeated the Pandavas by cheating and drove them into exile. It took thirteen years for the Pandaras to overcome the Kauravas. The Kauravas are also called Kurus, after their ancestor, Kuru. The Kauravas symbolize the forces of darkness, draught or winter, and the Pandavas symbolize fertility and growth. *See also* Arjuna; Bala-Rama; Bhishma; Duryodhana; Kali; Karna; Kunti; Pandavas; Tapati.

Kausalya (India) *see* Rama.

Kaushalya (India) Mother of Rama. *See also* Rama.

Kausiki (India) *see* Durga.

Kaustubha (India)
Vishnu's sacred jewel. *See also* Kurma; Vishnu.

Kauveri (India) *see* Kuvera.

Kauyumari (Huichol People, Mexico)
Also known as: *Wolf.*
Trickster deity. Most of the tales about this deity show him as a foil of the Moon. The Moon causes him a great deal of trouble such as having him cut down a honey tree only to find the honey turned to stones or lifting the tail of a donkey which is supposed to shower him with coins, but instead showered him with manure. There are many other tales of this deity and in some he appears to be involved in legends of creation. He is also said to be one of the survivors (along with a dog) of the flood caused by the earth mother, Nakawe.

Kava (A) (Iran, Persia)
Mythical smith deity. He and King Faridun were responsible for the capture and imprisonment of the evil Zahhak. *See also* Faridun; Zahhak.

Kava (B) (Finno-Ugric) *see* Kaba.

Kawa-no-kami (Japan)
River god. Although most important rivers have their own deities, Kawa-no-Kami is said to be king of all.

Kawelo (Polynesia, Hawaii) A trickster spirit. *See also* Kupua.

Kaya-no-hime-no-kami *Kaya-no-mi-oya-no-kami, Kaya-nu-himi, Kayanu-hime-no-kami* (Shinto; Japan)
Also known as: *Ko-no-hana-sakuya-hime* (Lady-who-makes-the-trees-bloom), *Nu-zuchi, Nuzuchi.*
"Ruler of the Grassy Plains." Vegetation goddess. Goddess of herbs. Protector of fields and meadows. Kaya-no-hime-no-kami is the daughter of Izanagi and Izanami. She became the wife of Opo-yama-tu-mi-no-kami and the mother of four daughters and four sons who were of the third earthly generation. As the daughter of Izanagi and Izanami, she was created after the eight islands of Japan. Other inhabitants created were the deities of the wind, sea, seasons, trees, mountains, valleys and fire. She is called one of the separated spirits of the goddess of food, Toyo-uke-bime, and the god of the boles of trees Kuku-no-shi (Kukunochi-no-kami). As Kuku-no-shi, this deity is associated with the god who protects the leaves of the trees, Ha-mori, and the god of the soul of the tree, Ko-dama (the Echo). One of her daughters, Kono-Hana-Sakuya-Hime (Blossoms-of-the-Trees-Blooming-Princess) married Ninigi (Prosperity Man). Kaya-no-hime-no-kami is associated with the goddess of fields, No-no-kami. The deification of vegetation is to encourage the regeneration of life and is connected with fertility and fecundity. Herbs are indicative of nature and health and are connected to food. As a symbol of natural forces, they can be medicinal or poisonous. In many civilizations, the tree is a manifestation of life. In Japan it was believed that trees were endowed with speech, known as the echo. The echo, Ko-dama, is the soul of the tree. *See also* Haya-akitsu-hime-no-kami (goddess of the sea); Izanagi and Izanami; Kuku-no-shi; Ninigi; O-yama-Tsu-Mi; Sengen (goddess of Mount Fuji); Toyo-uke-hime-no-himi; Ukemochi (goddess of food).

Kaya-no-mi-oya-no-kami (Japan) *see* Kaya-no-hime-no-kami.

Kaya-nu-himi (Japan) *see* Kaya-no-hime-no-kami.

Kayanu-hime-no-kami (Japan) *see* Kaya-no-hime-no-kami.

Kayumarth (Persia) *see* Gaya Maretan.

Kayurankuba (Zulu People, Africa) Storm spirit.

Kazoba (Baziba People, Africa)
Kazoba is the god of the sun and moon. His father is the father of gods, Wamara. He has three brothers: Kagoro; Mugasha, the god of water; and Ryangombe, the god of cattle.

K'daai Maqsin (Yakut People, Siberia)
Also known as: *Kudai-Bakshy.*
Spirit of blacksmiths. This underworld deity gives blacksmiths their skill. In some renditions, K'daai Maqsin is the name of the afterworld for the souls of blacksmiths.

Keagyihl Depguesk (Native North American)
The spirit of the whirlpool.

Keb (Egypt) *see* Geb.

Kebehsenuf (Egypt) *see* Qebhsneuf.

Kebehut (Egypt)
Goddess of freshness. Daughter of Anubis. *See also* Anubis.

Kebhsnauf (Egypt) *see* Qebhsneuf.

Keckamanetowa (Fox People, North America)
Also known as: *Ketchimanetowa.*
Deified animal. The Gentle Manitou. In some versions this is also the name of a creator.

Ked *Ket* (Celtic)
Also known as: *Annis.*
Malevolent deity. An evil mother goddess, she hides in caves or under rocks. She tries to catch children to suck their blood.

Keelut (Eskimo)
Evil spirit. Depicted as a hairless dog, this spirit who lives in the earth.

Kefi (Egypt) Kefi is a guardian of the tenth sector of Tuat.

Kehkeh (Egypt) *see* Aani; Utennu apes.

Kei-Kung (China, Taoist)
Also known as: *Lie-kung, T'ien-chu.*
Thunder god. Husband of T'ien Mu. *See also* Lie-kung; T'ien Mu.

Kek (Egypt)
Also known as: *Emen, Keku, Kekui.*
God of Darkness. He is the husband or mate of Kekut (Keket). Kek is probably a male version of Keket.

Keket *Kekuit* (Egypt)
Goddess of Darkness. Another name for Isis. One of the deities mentioned in the Pyramid Texts. She is the wife or mate of Kek or Kekui. *See also* Amun; Kekui.

Kekhet (Egypt) *see* Isis.

Kekri (Finno-Ugric)
Cattle deity. Kekri increase the number of cattle.

Keku (Egypt) *see* Kek.

Kekui (Egypt) *see* Kek.

Kekuit (Egypt) *see* Keket; Kekui.

Kelpie *Kelpy* (Scotland)

This one-eyed, ill-tempered water-sprite lurks in lakes, rivers and the sea. He rushes to his victims with a terrible roar, snatches them and drags them beneath the surface. In another version of this myth, he appears in the form of a horse on the banks of a river and intices travelers to mount him. Once mounted, he takes his rider into the deep water to drown. He is sometimes referred to as a god of lakes and rivers.

Kelpy (Scotland) *see* Kelpie.

Kematef (Egypt) *see* Amen (B).

Kemosh (Moabite) *see* Chemosh.

Kenaima *Kanaima* (Orinoco region, South America)

Also known as: *Orehu, Yauahu* (Arawak People).

The Kenaima are generally considered as greatly feared spirits of human origin. They are both malevolent and vengeful. The exception is the Orehu, water-sprites who appear as mermaids. They can be benevolent at times. The Yauhahu are usually the familiars of shamans or medicine men. The Kenaima usually appear in animal form. *See also* Makonaima; Orehu.

Kenemti (Egypt) *see* Assessors.

Keneu (Iroquois People, North America)

Also known as: *Kineun*.

Deified bird. This golden eagle assists Hino, the Thunderbird. In the legends of the Menominee Indians he is called Kineun. *See also* Hino.

K'eng-san-ku (China)

Also known as: *San-ku, Tsi-ku, Ts'iku*.

Deity of the Privy. Originally, she was a deified mortal named Lady Ts'i. She was killed by Lady Ts'ao by being thrown into privy-pit. She is usually shown as a large ladle with the bowl forming the head with a human face. Twigs and cloth make up her body.

Kengiu (Japan)

Also known as: *Ch'ien Niu* (China), *Ching Yuh* (Korea), *Hikoboshi*.

Cattle god. Known as the "Heavenly Herdsman," Kengiu was romantically involved with the weaver Shokujo (q.v.). *See also* Chin Nu (China); Shokujo.

Kenken-Wer (Egypt)

"The Great Cackler," a name for Geb (q.v.).

Kenos (Tierra del Fuego)

First man. Kenos was sent to Earth by the supreme god and told to bring order to the world. He fashioned male and female organs from peat, and from them, created mortals, the first of which was the ancestor of the Onas. He returned to the sky to become a constellation.

Keoloewa (Hawaii)

Ancient sorcery god. His image is made of wood dressed in native tapa, with the head and neck of wicker-work covered with red feathers to make it look like a birdskin. He wears a native helmet hung with human hair. His mouth is large and distended. This figure was placed in the inner room of the temple at the left of the door, with an altar before it. *See also* Uli.

Kenss (India) *see* Kansa.

Kent Sehet (Egypt) *see* Anubis.

Kentauros (Greek) *see* Centaurs.

Kentaurs (Greek) *see* Centaurs.

Ker (A) (Greek) *see* Keres.

Ker (B) (Pelasgian) Another spelling for Car or Q're, the solar god of ancient Syria.

Ker-Neter (Egypt) *see* Aaru; Ament; Amentet.

Kerberos (Greek) *see* Cerberus.

Kere Nyaa (Africa)

Home of a god. The mountain called Mount Kenya. This was the resting place of the god who made the first people. He created three sons: Kamba, Masai and Kikuyu. These were the founders of the three races by the same names.

Keremet (Russia)

Possibly a god of harvest. A powerful, mischievous god. His spouse is the Earthwife goddess Mukylcin.

Keres (Greek)

Also known as: *Cer, Ker*.

Death Spirits. The Keres were grim spirits who carried the dead to their fate. Often quoted in plural, they were said to be the daughters of Nyx and the sisters of Moros (doom), Momus, Hypnos, Dreams, Aether, Nemesis, Charon and Thanatos. They embodied the inevitability of death and are identified with the Fates (bringers of death). Their function and appearance is similar to the Erinyes although in general they lacked the retributive qualities of the Erinyes. *See also* Erinyes; Fates; Harpies.

Keresaspa (Zoroastrian; Persian)

Also known as: *Garshasp, Sama Keresaspa Naire-manah* (name in early times).

As he is a heroic warrior and not a god, Zoroastrians do not worship him. He is the son of Thrita and as Sama he became the grandfather of Rustam and, as Nariman, the great grandfather of Rustam. He captured Yima's Khvarenanh (glory) which gave him the strength to rid the earth of many demons. He killed Gandarewa (also known as Kundrav), the dragon of the cosmic ocean Vourukasha, as well as Srvara, Vareshava, Pitaona, Arezo-shamana, the sons of Nivika and of Dashtayani, the nine sons of Pathana, Snavidhka, the nine sons of Hitaspa and the murderer of his brother Urvakhshaya. When he originally died, Keresaspa's soul was not admitted to Garotman (heaven). It was thought that he lacked respect for fire and that he had little interest in religion. Khnathaiti, a witch whom he wed, was said to have robbed him of his spiritual interests. After lengthy petitioning by Zoroaster, the angels, and the animals, he gained entry. When the monster Azhi Dahaka breaks free from Mount Demavand at world's end, he will create demonic havoc in the world. Keresaspa will be resurrected to kill the monster. With his magic club, he will also slay Angra Mainyu, who represents evil creation, and Druji who represents falsehood. Keresaspa will thus save the earth. He is depicted as a youthful warrior with sidelocks. *See also* Angra Mainyu; Gandarewa; Kamak; Srvara; Yima.

Keri and Kame (Bacairi People, South America) *see* Kame and Keri.

Keridwen *Ceridwen, Cerridwen, Kerridwen* (British, Celtic, Welsh)

An early British fertility goddess, Keridwen evolved into a goddess of poets and a goddess of inspiration and knowledge. A shape changer, her abode is in an underwater Elysium. She is the daughter of Ogyren, the mate of Tegid Voel, and the mother of three children. Her daughter Creirwy was a very beautiful child and her son Avagdu was extremely ugly. Keridwen developed a magic potion for her son that would ensure inspiration when drunk. She used six plants to develop the potion which was placed in Amen, the magic cauldron. The process took a year and a day. Gwion Bach was placed in charge of stirring the brew. One day, three drops splashed on his fingers. He sucked his fingers to stop the pain and was immediately possessed of all knowledge. He stole the cauldron and ran away. Keridwen pursued him. He changed into a hare to escape her. She changed into a greyhound. He then became a fish and she became an otter. He became a bird, and she became a hawk. Finally he became a kernel of corn. She became a hen and swallowed him. From the kernel of corn, she became pregnant. The child she gave birth to became Taliesin, the most famous of bards. Keridwen is the equivalent to Irish Bridget.

Kerimas (Tibet)

Also known as: *Keyuri.*

These goddesses, also known as the Eight Wrathful Ones, appear in human form in the Bardo World on the twelfth and thirteenth day. They haunt cemeteries and cremation grounds. Each one carries a different part of the human body. *See also* Htamenmas.

Kerkios (Greek) *see* Castor.

Kerlaug (Teutonic) *see* Kerlaung.

Kerlaung *Kerlaug, Kerlogar* (Norse; Teutonic)

Rivers of the dead crossed by the bridge Bifrost. Thor must swim or walk across these rivers as his weight would not be sustained by the bridge Bifrost. *See also* Bifrost; Thor.

Kerlogar (Teutonic) *see* Kerlaung.

Kerres (Roman) *see* Ceres.

Kerridwen (Celtic) *see* Keridwen.

Kerub (Roman, Semite) *see* Cherub.

Kerwan and Katcina Mana (Hopi People, North America)

Maize deities. The Sprouting Maize Spirits.

Kesare (India) *see* Kesari.

Kesari *Kesare* (India)

He is the monster husband of the monkey queen Angara. *See also* Hanuman.

Kesava (India)

"Having Fine Hair." Another name for Kasyapa (q.v.). *See also* Daksha; Kasyapa (A); Krishna; Vishnu.

Keshi (India) *see* Keshin.

Keshin *Keshi, Kesin* (India)

A horse-shaped demon. *See also* Karttikeya; Krishna.

Kesin (India) *see* Keshin.

Kesini (India)

She is the daughter of Vidharba, mother of Asamanjas and one of the spouses of Sagara (q.v.).

Kessiepeia (Greek) *see* Cassiopeia.

Ket (Celtic) *see* Ked.

Ketchimanetowa (Fox People, North America)

Supreme god. The Great Spirit.

Ketq Skwaye (Huron People, North America)

Also known as: *Grandmother Toad.*

She is a creator goddess.

Kettu *Kittu* (Babylonian)

Deity of justice and truth. He is the son of Shamash and brother of Misor (q.v.).

Ketuiti (Egypt) *see* Aai.

Keturah (Hebrew) *see* Abram.

Keuakepo (Hawaii, Polynesia)

God of fire. One of the volcano deities. He brings the night rain, or rain of fire.

Kewawkgu (Algonquin People, North America)

A tribe of powerful magicians. *See also* Gluskap.

Keyuri (Tibet) *see* Kerimas.

Kha (Egypt) *see* Ba.

Kha-a (Egypt)

Underworld deity. He is an archer in the tenth sector of Tuat.

Khadau and Mamaldi (Amur People, Siberia)

First mortal. They are the first humans, or parents of the first shamans. They are also masters of the underworld or creators. After Mamaldi created the continent of Asia she was killed by her husband. Khadau continued to create shamans, but his wife gave them souls.

Khadga Jogini *Khadja Jogina, Khadga Yogini* (Buddhist; Tibet)

Also known as: *Blue Tara, Kali, Ugra Tara, Vajrajogini, Vajra Tara.*

Khadga Jogini as the Blue Tara is the most important of the three fierce Manifestations of Tara (Blue, Yellow, Red). She is short and fat with round, red eyes. Her forked tongue protrudes through her teeth. She is draped in a tiger skin, wreathed with human skulls, has four to twenty-four arms and dances on human corpses. *See also* Agni; Kali; Tara.

Khadga Yogini (India) *see* Khadga Jogini.

Khadhomas (India) *see* Dakinis.

Khadja Jogina (Tibet) *see* Khadga Jogini.

Khadomas *Khahdoma* (Tibet)

The Khadomas, fairy-like female goddesses, are particularly helpful, when called upon, by followers of Yoga. One of the Khadomas is the goddess Yeshe-Khahdoma, who wears a tiara. *See also* Dakinis; Remati.

Khados (Tibet)

The chief of the Khados is Sangye Khado also known as Buddha Dakini. *See also* Dakinis.

Khahdoma (Tibet) *see* Khadomas.

Khaibit (Egypt)

Shadow of a man, similar to Ka and Ba. Able to move about freely when separated from the body. *See also* Ba; Ka.

Khaldi (Armenian, Iranian)

Also known as: *Bag-Mashtu* (possibly), *Bag-Mazda*.

Supreme God. Khaldi is an ancient supreme or moon deity of the Armenian Urartian population who called themselves Khaldians. This god was associated with a weather or storm god called Theispas and a sun-god called Artinis. All might have been derived from the Babylonian deities or conversely the Babylonians might have developed their triad of Sin, Shamas and Ramman from these gods. Some think Khaldi was identified with Bag-Mashtu (also known as Bag-Mazda) who was a sky god that later became the Iranian Ahura Mazda. *See also* Ahura Mazda; Artinis; Bag-Mashtu; Khaldi; Sin; Theispas.

Khalil (Arabic, Hebrew) *see* Abram.

Khalisah (Arabic) Goddess of Purity.

Khammurabi (Babylon) *see* Hammurabi; Marduk.

Khandro (India) *see* Sarasvati.

Khandros (India) *see* Dakinis.

Khang Fei (China) *see* Chang Fei.

Khar (Iranian) *see* Khara (A).

Khara (A) *Khar* (Iranian)

Khara is a gigiantic three-legged ass with two normally situated eyes, two eyes on the top of his head and two eyes on his hump. He has nine mouths, and one horn. He stands in the cosmic ocean Vourukasha and assists in world management. His sharp eyes enable him to overcome evil. *See also* Vourukasha.

Khara (B) (India) *see* Nikasha; Shurpanaka.

Kharchheri (Buddhist; Nepal)

Also known as: *Avalokitesvara, Six Syllabled Lokeswara*.

Kharchheri, the deity of wisdom and knowledge, is an aspect of Avalokitesvara known as the Six Syllabled Lokeswara. The six syllables are "OM MANI PADME HUM," which is constantly chanted by devotees. White in color, Kharchheri is four-armed and wears many ornaments. He carries the rosary in his right hand and a full blown lotus in the left. The other two hands are raised to his chest in the gesture of prayer holding the jewel, the symbol of knowledge. *See also* Avalokitesvara.

Khasa (India)

Possibly one of Daksha's sixty daughters and possibly the mother of the Rakshasas (q.v.).

Khatwanga (India) Shiva's Sacred Club. *See also* Shiva.

Khaya (India) *see* Chhaya.

Khebieso (Ewe People of Dahomey Group, Africa)

Also known as: *So*

God of lightning. *See also* Bo.

Kheiron (Greek) *see* Cheiron.

Khema (Hebrew) *see* Af (C).

Khemi (Egypt) *see* Assessors.

Khen-pa (Tibet)

Dressed in white garments, he has white hair and rides a white dog. Khen-pa controls the sky demons. *See also* Khon-ma.

Khenemu-Shu (Egypt) *see* Shu.

Khensu *Khonsu* (Egypt)

Also known as: *Aa, Chespisichis* (Greek), *Chons, Chunus, Khensu-Nefer-Hetep, Khensu-Pa-Khart, Khensu-Ra, Khons, Khons Hor, Khuns*.

An early moon god of healing and regeneration, Khensu is considered to be the divine child of Amen and Mut. His name means "traveler," and he crosses heaven as the moon-god. He was well known as a healer during the reign of Ptolemy IV. He may be a form of Amen and Ptah. He is represented as a young man in the form of a mummy with bound legs bearing the moon's disc and crescent on his head. He is also represented as wearing a crescent moon and disk surmounting a skullcap. In later periods he is shown standing on crocodiles. He is associated with Thoth (q.v.). *See also* Aa; Aah; Amen (B); Ptah; Thoth.

Khensu-Nefer-Hetep (Egypt) *see* Khensu.

Khensu-Pa-Khart (Egypt) *see* Khensu.

Khensu-Ra (Egypt) *see* Khensu.

Khenti-Amentet (Egypt) *see* Amentet; Osiris.

Khenti Amenti *Khentamenti, Khentamentiu* (Egypt)

Also known as: *Ophois, Up-uaut*.

Underworld deity. He is a wolf-god of Abydos with whom Osiris was sometimes identified in his capacity as Ruler of the Dead. The name, meaning "Ruler of the West," may have been given to Upuaut in connection with his worship as lord of the dead, especially at Abydos. He is described as jackal-headed. Khenti is sometimes identified with Ophios, Upuaut, and Osiris. *See also* Osiris; Up-uaut.

Khenti-Amenti (Egypt) *see* Aai.

Khenti-qerer (Egypt) *see* Aai.

Khentimentiu (Egypt)

God of destiny. The god who rules the destiny of the dead.

Khenty-Amentiu (Egypt) *see* Ap-uat.

Khenty-Khet (Egypt) *see* Horus.

Khepera (Egypt) *see* Khepri.

Kheperi (Egypt) *see* Aai; Khepri.

Khepi (Egypt) *see* Aai.

Kheprer (Egypt) *see* Aai.

Khepri *Chepera, Khepera, Kheprer, Kheperi, Khoprer* (Egypt)
Also known as: *Chafura.*
Creator. Khepri is one of the gods of the "Ennead." He was believed to have been born of Nunu. Khepri is identified with Ra as the morning sun, born again each day. He is often depicted with the face of a scarab, or with a scarab surmounting his head, a symbol, as was the sun, of creation and rebirth and everlasting life. He is one of the original creation gods and is said to be self-created, since he copulated with his own shadow. From his semen came Shu and Tefnut. In one version, Khepri is the creator of Nun. Harakhtes is also a winged beetle-god representing the morning sun. Khepri is usually shown as a human with the head of a scarab-beetle. The sun beetle was a popular amulet, a symbol of new life thought to give light and warmth. It was often placed in the tomb with the deceased. *See also* Ab; Ab-ta; Amen (B); Harakhtes; Khepera; Nun; Ptah; Shu; Tefnut.

Kher-Aha (Egypt) *see* Aaru.

Khert Neter (Egypt)
Also known as: *Tuat.*
Another title for Tuat, the underworld. *See also* Tuat.

Khesef-haa-heseq-neha-hra (Egypt)
Underworld. The name of the Seventh Hour of Tuat. This is the hidden abode of Osiris. The name of the city he passes through is called Tephet-shetat, and the names of the serpents and deities are Mehen, Neh-har, Ab-she, Serqet, Her-tesu-f; the goddesses: Temtith, Tenity, Nakity and Hetemitet. Also mentioned are Ankh-aru-tefehau, Ankhtith, Hekenth, Af-Tem and the crocodile, Ab-sha-am-Tuat. *See also* Tuat.

Khesfu (Egypt)
God who carries a spear in the Tenth Sector of Tuat.

Khetaka The sacred club of Bala-Rama (q.v.).

Kheti (Egypt)
A large serpent in the eight sector of Tuat, Kheti belches fire to punish those who have gone against the rites with Osiris. On his back stand seven gods. *See also* Osiris; Tuat.

Khetrpal (India) *see* Bhumiya.

Khi-Dimme-Azaga (Babylonia)
Mother goddess. She is possibly the daughter of Ea. Some say she is identical with Belit-Sheri. *See also* Ea.

Khnem-Renit (Egypt) *see* Ap-taui.

Khnemiu (Egypt)
The Khnemiu are four deities wearing red crowns, found in the Eleventh Sector of Tuat.

Khnemu (Egypt) *see* Khnum.

Khnoumis (Greek, Egypt) *see* Khnum.

Khnum (Egypt)
Also known as: *Amen-khum, Amun-kneph, Chnemu, Chnoumes, Chnoumis, Cnuphis, Ef, Khnemu, Khnoumis* (Greek), *Khnumu, Kneph, Knephis, Knepth, Kueph.*
Creator deity. At Elephantine, Khnum was called "Lord of Elephantine" and "the maker of heaven and earth and the underworld, and of water and of the mountains." He fashioned men out of clay on a potter's wheel and breathed life into them. As the "Father of Fathers" and the "Mother of Mothers," he assisted Heket, the birth goddess, at births. He was also regarded as protector of the source of the Nile. He had three consorts: Heket, Anukis and Satis. Khnum was part of a triad with Anukis and Satis. In another version his wives were Anqet and Satet and he was said to guard the waters coming from the lower world. Khnum could also be addressed as Neith (the goddess), thus acknowledging his feminine side. Khnemu represented the gods of the four elements: earth, air, fire, and water. He is depicted as a ram or with a ram's head (some say as a serpent's head). He has been represented with four heads. Khnum later merged with the god Min. *See also* Aani; Abu; Anubis; Heket; Min; Neith; Ptah; Satis.

Khnumu (Egypt) *see* Khnum.

Kho (Bushmen; Africa) *see* Kaang.

Kho-Dumo-Dumo (Basuto People, Africa)
Evil demon. He swallowed everything on earth but missed one woman. This woman had a son named Ditaolane who killed the demon and released all it ate. Ditaolane became chief and eventually allowed himself to be killed. At death his heart changed into a bird and flew away.

Khoda (Persia) Supreme spirit.

Kholumolumo (Bantu People, Africa)
Monster cannibal that eats everybody and everything.

Khon-ma (Tibet)
Also known as *"Old Mother."*
She is in charge of the earth demons. Her face has eight wrinkles, she wears yellow robes, carries a golden noose, and rides on a ram. Her counterpart is Khen-pa (q.v.).

Khons (Egypt) *see* Aah; Khensu; Thoth.

Khons Hor (Egypt) *see* Khensu.

Khonsu (Egypt) *see* Khensu.

Khonus (Egypt) *see* Khensu.

Khonvum (Pygmy People, Africa)
Supreme deity. He is the supreme god, worshiped as a sky god, who controls celestial phenomena. He resurrects the sun each morning by throwing broken pieces of the stars at it. He carries a bow made of two serpents that become the rainbow.

Khoprer (Egypt) *see* Khepri.

Khordadh (Persia) *see* Ameratat; Haurvatat.

Khoromozitel (Slavic)

Also known as: *Domovik, Domovoi, Uboze.*

Domestic deities. This is possibly another name for the Domovoi (q.v.).

Khors (Slavic)

He is the god of health and hunting who is depicted in the form of a stallion. Khors is associated with Dazbog and Perun (qq.v.).

Khosadam (Siberia)

Evil deity. She is the wife of the high god Ec. After she was driven out of heaven for being unfaithful to Ec, she became a devourer of souls.

Khoser-et-Hasis (Ugarit)

Also known as: *Bn-Ym.*

He is the son of the sea. *See also* Bod-Baal.

Khoton (Yakut People, Siberia) *see* Khotun.

Khotun *Khoton* (Yakut People, Siberia)

Also known as: *Kubai-khotun.*

Khotun is the goddess of birth and nourisher of people. She lives in a lake of milk, although some say that she lives in the Zambu tree. The milk from her large breasts are the origin of the Milky Way. *See also* Ajysit.

Khou *Khu* (Egypt)

God of light. Khou is similar to the Ka or Ba which is the essence of the soul. Khou is depicted as a crested bird. *See also* Ka.

Khovaki (Tungus People, Siberia)

Also known as: *Savaki.*

Either creator god or spirits that protect shamans.

Khrestos (Greek) *see* Jesus.

Khristos (Greek) *see* Christ.

Khronos (Greek) *see* Cronus.

Khshasthra Vairya *Khashthra* (Zoroastrian; Persia)

Also known as: *Shahrevar, Shahriver* (Pahlavi dialect).

An Amesha Spentas, Khshasthra Vairya is a god of metal and protector of the poor and weak. He personifies Ahura Mazda's sovereignty and his triumph over evil on earth. His opponent is the arch-demon Sauru. In the court of heaven his associates are Mithra, Asman, and Aniran. He is associated with the stream of molten metal that will test all men at the end of the world. Through Ahura Mazda, Khshasthra allots the final rewards and punishments to the dead. His flower is the royal basil. *See also* Ahura Mazda; Amesha Spentas; Daevas; Sauru; Shahapet; Vohu Manah; Yazatas.

Khshathrapati (Persia) *see* Shahapet.

Khu (Egypt) *see* Ba; Bia; Khou.

Khudjana (Africa) *see* Ribimbi.

Khulater (Siberia) Ruler of the dead.

Khumbaba *Hubaba, Humbaba* (Akkadia, Babylon, Sumer)

Also known as: *Hum-ba, Humhum, Huwawa.*

Monster. Wicked demon. A monster and lord of the Mountain of Cedars (Lebanons), also known as the Cedar Forest of the Amanus. After Enkidu dreamed he was hurled into the underworld, Gilgamesh made offerings to the god Shamash, who told him to overcome Khumbaba, the giant of the cedar forest. The two friends made the long journey and succeeded in their task. Khumbaba is said to have had breath like a hurricane and a voice like a storm. A giant, he took the shape of a dragon who spits fire. One of the local deities of the Elamites was named Humba or Hubaba and was said to be an earth god. Connected to Tammuz. Ishtar, as the goddess Irnini, lived in the forest for a time. *See also* Gilgamesh; Ishtar.

Khumban (Sumer)

High god. Husband of Kiririsha. He is a god of Elam who corresponds to the Babylonian god Marduk.

Khun (China, Mongol)

A white dragon horse who is a protector against demons. *See also* Kun (B).

Khun-Lun (China) *see* Kun-Lun.

Khuno (Peru)

God of storm and snow. A certain group of Indians set fire to a forest in order to clear the land for crops. The smoke from the fire offended Khuno and he sent down terrible rain and hail, destroying their villages and some of the land. When it was over the people found a plant with bright green leaves which they put in their mouths to stay their hunger. This was the beginning of the use of the cacao plant.

Khuns (Egypt) *see* Khensu.

Khuran-Nojon (Buriat)

Rain god. He owns nine barrels of rain. When he opens one barrel it rains for three days.

Khurdad and Amardad (Persia) *see* Ameratat; Haurvatat.

Khurdadh (Persia) *see* Ameratat; Haurvatat.

Khuri Edzhin (Buriat)

God of music. Deity of musical instruments who teaches mortals the art of music.

Khusor (Semite) God of navigation and of incantations.

Khut (Egypt) *see* Isis.

Khuzwane (Lovedu People, Africa)

Creator. Little is known about Khuzwane, but he left his footprints on the rocks.

Khvarenanh *Hvaranah, Khwarenah* (Persia)

Often called "Glory" and literally meaning "light or luster," the Khvarenanh is the substance that makes gods and mortals powerful, and influences the planets. It is found in cosmic space, the sea, milk, or the reeds. *See also* Ba; Ka; Yima.

Khy (Bushmen, Africa) *see* Kaang.

Khyati (India) *see* Lakshmi.

Ki (Chaldea, Sumer)

Also known as: *Kishar* (the Earth).

The earth, personified as the goddess Ki, is the daughter of Nammu and the mother of Enlil, and possibly the goddess Damkina. *See also* An; Damkina; Enlil; Kishar; Nammu; Ninhursag; Ninki; Ninmu (A).

Ki-gulla (Babylon) *see* Kulla.

Ki-No-Mata-No-Kami (Japan) *see* Kappa.

Kian (Celtic) *see* Cian.

Kianto (Maya) God of foreigners and diseases.

Kiara (Africa) *see* Mbamba.

Kibalso (Africa) *see* Kibuuka.

Kibu (Melanesian)
Kibu, the land of the dead, is an island located in the west.

Kibuka (India) Aryan war god.

Kibuuka *Kibuka* (Bantu, Buganda People, Africa)
Also known as: *Kibalso*.
Storm spirit. Founder of the Buganda. A spirit who some say was formerly a human king. One of the Balubaale, he is the brother of the great god Mukasa. Compare Kibuuka to the Yoruba deity Shango. *See also* Balubaale; Mukasa.

Kichigonai (Quiche People, Guatemala)
Deity of light. Creator of the day.

Kichijo-Ten (Japan)
Also known as: *Kashijotem*.
Goddess of good fortune. Goddess of beauty. She is sister of Bishamon and the rival of the jealous Benten. Kichijo-Ten is usually shown holding the sacred gem in her left hand. *See also* Benten; Bishamon.

Kicva (Celtic) *see* Pryderi.

Kiehtan (Massachusetts People, North America)
Supreme Being. *See also* Gitchi.

Kien Niu (China) *see* Chin Nu.

Kien t'an (China) *see* Chang.

Kigal *Ki Gal* (Akkadian) *see* Hell.

Kigatilik (Eskimo) A Fanged Demon.

Kihe-Wahine (Hawaii) Goddess of demons and lizards.

Kiho (Tuamotuan Archipelago; Polynesia)
Also known as: *Kiho Tumu*.
A supreme god, Kiho dwells beneath the foundations of Avaiki. Though he created all things, he does not have a mate. *See also* Atea; Avaiki; Io; Po; Rua.

Ki'i (Hawaii) *see* Tiki.

Kii (Polynesia) *see* Tiki.

Kikimora *Kikimoras* (Slavic)
Also known as: *Mora*.
Part of the Domovoi spirit group, this household deity is said to live in the cellar or in the ovens. She helps around the house, but she dislikes laziness and will break items and spoil food if the house isn't kept clean. She can also disturb sleeping people. Kikimora is ageless and is depicted with chicken's legs and a long nose. In some legends, she is the wife of Domovoi. *See also* Domovoi; Zduh.

Kiku-jido (Japan)
He is an eternal youth and god of the chrysanthemum. *See also* Sennins.

Kikuyu (Africa) *see* Gikuyu; Kere Nyaa.

Kildisin (Finnish, Slavic)
Goddess of birth. Wife of Ilmarinen. Daughter of the sorcerer Pohja. She is prayed to by those who desire children. *See also* Ilmarinen.

Kili (Teutonic) *see* Dwarfs.

Kilili (Assyria, Babylon)
Also known as: *Absusu, Abtagigi, Ishtar*.
Deity of Harlots. One of the Babylonian and Assyrian aspects of Ishtar as queen of the harlots. Her title means "One who Leans Out," or "Queen of the Windows." Some say she is an evil spirit. She is similar to the Sumerian Abtagigi and Absusu. *See also* Abtagigi; Ishtar.

Killer Whale (Northwest Coast Native North Americans) *see* Gunarh.

Kilyikhama (Brazil, Peru)
This is the name of a class of demons. One Kilyikhama is a boy who has lights on each side of his head. Another is called the "White Kilyikhama." He rides and whistles in his little boat in the swamps. One Kilyikhama is the most dangerous of all. He is described as being very tall and thin, with eyes that look like balls of fire. His very appearance signifies instant death. The Kilyikhama ride on the Milky Way in the form of white birds. They wait for the right moment to descend into the bodies of men. Another demon of this class is called Aphangak who are ghosts of men. Little is known of their characteristics although they are greatly feared. *See also* Demons.

Kimat (Tinguian People, Philippine Islands)
Kimat is the lightning personified as the dog of the creator Kadaklan (q.v.).

Kimbu-Sangtung (Dhammai People, India)
Kimbu-Sangtung is one of the children of the first mortals, the brother and sister, Abugupham-Bumo and Anoi-Diggan-Juje. *See also* Shuznaghu.

Kimpen Jigoku (Japan) *see* Jigoku.

Kimpurushas, The (India)
These spirits are followers and servers of Kuvera (q.v.).

Kinebahan (Maya) *see* Hunab-ku.

King Moho (Polynesia, Hawaii) *see* Kamohoali'i.

King Yama (India) *see* Yama; Yama Kings.

Kingmingoarkulluk (Eskimo)
This diminutive Eskimo is a benevolent land spirit who sings when approached by humans.

Kings of Hell (China) *see* Diamond Kings; Kshitigarbha.

Kings of Tara (Irish) *see* Banbha.

Kingu *Kingugu* (Babylon, Sumer)
Chief of monsters. Battle leader for Tiamat. One of the sons of Apsu, the primeval sea god of fresh water and Tiamat, the dragon personification of the salt sea. He is sometimes called husband-son of Tiamat. Tiamat made Kingu commander of the monsters she created to form an army that would free Apsu from the captivity imposed upon him by Ea. She endowed Kingu with the "Tablet of Destinies," which Marduk retrieved after overcoming him. In some versions, Marduk bound him in the underworld and took the tablets of fate, after which he burned Kingu and used his blood to create man. The "Tablet of Destinies" was said to be placed on Kingu's head or breast by Tiamat. When Marduk gained possession of the tablet, he placed it on his breast. The tablet may be an amulet. *See also* Apsu; Ea; Marduk; Tiamat.

Kinharigan (Dasun People, Borneo)
Creator. He and his wife, Munsumundok, killed one of their children and planted the pieces. From these came plants and animals to feed mankind.

Kinich Ahau (Maya People, Yucatan)
Also known as: *Kinish-Kakimo.*
Sun god. God of healing and medicine. Husband of the goddess of weaving, Ixazalvoh. His name means "the Lord of the Face of the Sun." Kinich Ahau may be the same as the Maya god "G" (q.v.). *See also* Itzamna; Ixazalvoh.

Kinilau (Polynesia) *see* Tinirau.

Kinish-Kakimo (Mexico) *see* Itzamna.

Kinkini-Dhari (Tibet)
Also known as: *Til-bu-ma* (Tibet).
This Shakti is the serpent-headed Door-Keeper of the North, along with her spouse, Amritahari, in the Bardo World. They are associated with stern justice. *See also* Ankusha; Chadog-ma; Shakti; Zhag-pa-ma.

Kinma (Babylon) *see* Marduk.

Kinnaras, The (India)
They are the horse-headed male musicians in Kuvera's heaven. *See also* Kuvera.

Kintu (Africa)
First man. Kintu was found by the sons of heaven (in some versions heaven is called Gulu) and their sister Nambi. He and Nambi became the ancestors of the human race. *See also* Gulu; Ngai.

Kipu-Tytto (Finnish)
Goddess of illness. Daughter of Tuonetar and Tuoni. She lives in Tounela (hell). *See also* Manala; Tounela.

Kiririsha (Sumer)
Queen of the gods. A goddess of Elam who is the wife of the high god Khumban.

Kirke (Greek) *see* Circe.

Kirnis (Slavic) God of ripening cherries. *See also* Lawkapatim.

Kiron (Greek) *see* Cheiron.

Kisani (Navaho People, North America) *see* Atse Estsan; Atse Hastin.

Kishar *Kissare* (Assyro-Babylonian)
Also known as: *Ki* (the Earth).
"Whole Earth." Mother goddess. She is the sister and wife of Anshar, by whom she was the mother of Anu and Ea. Her parents are Lahmu and Lahamu (according to others, Tiamat and Apsu). When associated with Nergal, Kishar is one of the watchmen of Ereshkigal. It is not known if this representation is male or female. The names Anshar and Kishar mean "host of heaven," and "host of earth." She is probably a winged dragon like her parents. Kishar is associated with Anshar as a pair of deities. She is similar to the Greek Lache and Lachos. *See also* Anu (B); Apsu; Ea; Igig; Kadi; Lahamu and Lahmu; Tiamat.

Kishibojin (Japan) *see* Kishimojin.

Kishijoten (Japan) *see* Bishamon.

Kishimogin (Japan) *see* Kishimojin.

Kishimojin *Kishimo-jin, Kishibojin* (originally from India, on to China and later Japan)
Also known as: *Hariti, Kariteimo.*
Demon goddess. Goddess of children. Kishimojin was a demon goddess who devoured children in the town of Rajagriba while Buddha Sakyamuni lived there. He promised her that if she maintained her peaceful aspect, he would insure that the villagers would leave offerings for her. The once evil demon became a protector of children and women in childbirth. She is shown seated, surrounded by children, or standing and holding a baby. Sometimes she holds the Flower of Happiness in her hand. *See also* Hariti; Sakyamuni; Sitala.

Kisimbi (Congo, Africa) *see* Nymphs.

Kisin (Maya) *see* Nohochacyum.

Kissare (A) (Assyro-Babylonia) *see* Kishar.

Kissare (B) (Babylonian Creation Legend of Damascisu) *see* Anu (C); Belus (B).

Kistna (India) *see* Krishna.

Kitchaka (India) *see* Bhima (A).

Kitchi Manito (Native North American) *see* Kitshi Manito.

Kitcki Manitou (Algonquian and Sioux People, North America) *see* Kitshi Manito.

Kitimil and Magigi (Pelew Islands)
First people. Only known as the survivors of the deluge.

Kitshi Manito *Gitchee Manitou, Gitchy Monedo, Kitcki Manitou* (Algonquian, Chippewa, Oglala, Sioux People, North America)
Also known as: *Gitche, Tanka, Wakan, Wakonda.*
Supreme beneficial spirit. He is opposed by Mitshi-Manitou (Mudje-Monedo), a bad spirit. *See also* Gitche; Tirawa; Wakonda.

Kittu (Sumer) The personification of justice. *See also* Kettu.

Kiun (Hebrew) *see* Chiun; Rephaim.

Kivutar (Finnish)
Goddess of disease. Daughter of the Tuoni and Queen of the Underworld, Tuonetar. Sister of Loviatar, Kipu-Tytto, Kivutar, and Vammater. They live in the underworld known as Manala (q.v.). *See also* Tuonetar; Tuoni.

Kiyamat-Saus (Finnish) *see* Kiyamat-Tora.

Kiyamat-Tora (Finnish)
Also known as: *Tamek-Vui, Touni.*
He is a prince or judge of the dead who is assisted by Kiyamat-saus.

Kkhrafstras (Persia)
Evil spirit. This creature, who is linked with decay and corpses, lives on dead matter.

Kla (Ashanti People, Africa)
Also known as: *Sisa.*
Goddess of goodness. Her counterpart, the male Kla, is the essence of evil. The Kla survives death and is then called Sisa. The name is both male and female.

Klehanoai (Navaho People, North America)
Also known as: *Bekotshidi.*
Moon carrier. He is the husband of Yolkai Estsan. He lives in the east. *See also* Ahsonnutli; Yolkai Estsan.

Klotho (Greek) *see* Clotho.

Knaritja (Aborigine People, Australia)
Great Father or Eternal Youth. His skin is "reddish," and he is emu-footed. His wives have dog feet.

Kneph (Egypt) *see* Khnum.

Knosu (Egypt) *see* Aah.

Ko-Dama (Japan) *see* Kay-no-hime-no-kami.

Ko-no-hana-sakuya-hime (Japan) *see* Kaya-no-hime-no-kami.

Kobine (Oceanic) *see* Nareau.

Kobolds (Teutonic)
Originally, Kobold was a dwarf miner in Teutonic myth. Later, Kobolds were known in German myth as benevolent earth spirits who usually haunt houses. Compare Kobolds to Kaches.

Kodoku-Jigoku (Japan) *see* Jigoku.

Koevasi (Melanesian)
Creator. She is a snake goddess who is the ancestor of all the people of Florida Island in the Solomons. Similar to Kafisi (q.v.).

Kohin (Australia) *see* Baiame.

Koin (Australia) *see* Baiame.

Kojiki, The (Japan) *see* Ama-no-minaka-nushi.

Kojin *Kojin-Sama* (Japan)
This androgynous kitchen deity always keeps the kitchen stocked with food.

Kokko (Zuni People, North America)
Spirits. The Kokko, a group of deities led by Koloowisi, appeared in human form. *See also* Palulukon.

Kokuzo-Bosatsu *Kokuzo* (Buddhist; Japan)
Also known as: *Akasagarbha.*
The deity Kokuzo-Bosatsu possesses the virtues of wisdom and compassion; indestructible, without beginning and without end. He is shown seated on a lotus which in turn is placed on a lion. In his hands, he carries a lance and a jewel.

Kokytus (Greek) *see* Cocytus.

Koloowisi (Hopi, Zuni People, North America)
Also known as: *Palulukon* (Hopi).
He is the chief of a group of rain and lightning spirits called Kokko by the Zuni. *See also* Palulukon.

Kolpia (Phoenician)
He is the wind who is the spouse of Baau and father of Aion and Protogonos in the "Creation Legend of Philo Byblos." Baau may be the same as the Babylonian goddess Ba'u. Aion (meaning "life") and Protogonos were the first to discover edible fruits. They became the parents of Genos and Genea, the first to worship the sun. Genos and Genea were the parents of Light, Fire and Flame. *See also* Air (A) for the Phoenician Creation Myth of Damascisu; Fire.

Kombu (Bantu People, Africa) Either a spirit or a creator god.

Komoku (Japan) *see* Komoku-ten.

Komoku-ten *Komoku* (Buddhist; Japan)
Also known as: *Virupaksha* (India)
Komoku-ten ("Wide-gazing") is one of the four Shi Tenno guardian kings. In some renditions he is the guardian of the west and in others the south. He is shown holding a lance or brush in his hand and in his other hand he holds the sheath of his sword, or his hand is on his hip. *See also* Bishamon-Ten; Jikoku-Ten; Nio; Shi Tenno; Virupaksha; Zocho-Ten.

Komorkis (Blackfoot People, North America)
The moon goddess. *See also* Apisirahts.

Kompira (India) *see* Kuvera.

Kompira-Daigongen (India) *see* Kuvera.

Kon (A) (Teutonic) *see* Heimdall.

Kon (B) (Chimu People, South America) *see* Irma.

Kondoy (Mixe People, Mexico) *see* Chalucas.

Kongara-Doji (Japan) *see* Fudo-Myoo.

Kongo-Yasha-Myoo (Buddhist) Japan
Also known as: *Vajra-Yaksha* (Sanskrit).
Guardian. A Godai-Myoo. Kongo-Yasha-Myoo is one the Five Great Kings, known as the Godai-Myoo. They are incarnations and manifestations of the five great Buddhas and the protectors of Buddhism. Kongo-Yasha-Myoo is the wrathful incarnation of Fuku who is also known as Amoghasiddhi and Amoghavajra in Sanskrit. Kongo-Yasha-Myoo is depicted with three heads, bristling hair and six arms. He stands on two lotus blossoms with his left leg raised and is surrounded by flames.

His front head has five eyes. He is the only deity with this distinguishing feature. In his lowest right hand, he holds an arrow. In the right hand near his breast, he holds the vajra (thunderbolt) and in his uplifted third hand, a sword. In his left hands he holds a wheel, bow and bell. He is also shown with one head and four arms. *See also* Amoghasiddhi; Dai Itoku-Myoo; Fudo-Myoo; Godai-Myoo; Gozanze-Myoo; Gundari-Myoo; Shi Tenno.

Kongorikishi (India) *see* Vajrapani.

Konjo (China) *see* Tara (B).

Konkara (Japan) *see* Fudo-Myoo.

Kono-Hana-Sakuya-Hime (Japan) *see* Hikohohodemi; Hoderi; Hosuseri; Ninigi; Sengen; Toyo-Tama-Bime.

Konohana-Chiru-Hime (Japan) *see* Kushi-nada-hime.

Koo-chul-inn (Celtic) *see* Cuchulain.

Koodjidnuk (Eskimo)
Spirit of healing. A good spirit who came from creation as a large bird with a hooked beak, a black head, and a white body.

Koppa-Tengu (Buddhist; Japan)
The Koppa-Tengu, goblins who have mouths like beaks and bodies with small wings, are the inferiors of the Tengu (q.v.).

Kooshelta (India) *see* Rama.

Kooshelya (India) *see* Rama.

Kootamoinen (Finnish) Another name for Kun, the moon.

Koran *Qur'an* (Islamic)
The sacred text of Islam, known as the *Koran*, is divided into 114 chapters, or suras. Revered as the word of God, the *Koran* is said to have been dictated to Muhammad by the archangel Gabriel. The *Koran* is accepted as the foundation of Islamic law, religion, culture, and politics. *See also* Muhammad.

Kore (Greek)
Kore is an epithet of Persephone. *See also* Demeter; Persephone.

Kore-Te-Whiwhia (Polynesia) *see* Io (B).

Korka-kuzo (Finno-Ugric) *see* Domovoi; Dvorovoi.

Korka-murt (Finno-Ugric) *see* Domovoi; Dvorovoi.

Korobona (Arawak People; Carib)
A great female warrior and culture heroine, Korobona is said to have been seduced by a water demon. In the Carib Creation Legend, the first Carib was born as a result of their union. *See also* Mama Nono.

Korraval (Tamil People, India)
Korraval, the goddess of victory, is the wife of Silappadikaram, the name used for Bala-Rama by the Tamil People. *See also* Silappadikaram.

Korred (Celtic) Fairies. *See also* Korriganes.

Korriganes (Celtic)
Fairies. It is generally said that there are nine Korriganes.

They are shape changers who are spirits of the wind. They can cause death with their breath, but can also cure diseases and heal wounds. The Korriganes are less than two feet high and have long hair. They usually wear a white veil.

Korubantes (Greek) *see* Corybantes.

Korybantes (Greek) *see* Corybantes.

Koshchei (Slavic)
Immortal evil snake. This serpent carries off princesses and the mother or wife of the hero. He is killed by a magic death-egg thrown or broken by the hero.

Koshi (Japan)
An eight-headed dragon. *See also* Kushi-nada-hime; Susanow.

Koshin (Japan)
Also known as: *Koshin-Sama.*
Road deities. Monkey gods. In some versions, Koshin is a god of the roads. In others this is the collective name of the three monkeys who portray see, speak, and hear no evil. The individual names are Mizaru, Kikazaru, and Iwazaru.

Kotan-Shorai (Japan) *see* Buto (B); Susanowo.

Kotari (India) *see* Devi.

Kothar and Khasis *Kathar, Kathar the Clever, Kathar-Wa-Hasis, Kothar-u-Khasis* (Ugarit)
They are two gods of architects, artisans, and weapon makers. Sometimes they are referred to as one deity, Kothar-u-Khasis. The magic weapons "Yagrush" (Chaser) and "Aymur" (Driver) were made by Kothar-u-Khasis, as was Baal's abode. Once while attending a feast at the home of King Danel, the king noticed Kothar's bow and arrows. King Danel persuaded him to give them to him. He in turn gave them to his son, Aqhat. When the goddess Anath saw the weapons, she coveted them. She offered Aqhat a large amount of gold and silver, but he would not part with his prized possessions. He even refused the gift of immortality from her. Anath devised a plan and sought and obtained permission from the great god El to implement it. She changed the minor deity Yatpan into a vulture and asked him to fly over Aqhat while he was eating, knock him over, and fly off with the bow and arrows. Unfortunately, Yatpan killed Aqhat and carried off the bow which subsequently was lost. Anath mourned Aqhat's death which had caused famine to fall over the earth. She promised to return him to life if he would give her the bow and arrows, so that she could return once again make the earth fertile. Aqhat's sister, Paghat (sometimes called Pughat), and her father the king attempted many measures to restore fertility, to no avail. The famine lasted for seven years. When they heard the news of Aqhat's death, Danel vowed vengence. His prayers to Baal were answered and he was permitted to examine all the vultures to see which one killed his son. Paghat had designed her own plan. Unbeknown to her, she employed her brother's murderer, Yatpan to help her find the killer. During this period, Danel found the remains of his son in the stomach of the mother of the vultures, Sumul. After cursing three cities in the area where his beloved son died, he returned home and mourned for seven years. Compare Kothar to Hephaistos (Greek). *See also* Anath; Baal; El; Yam-Nahar.

Kothar-u-Khasis (Ugarit) *see* Khasis; Kothar.

Koti (Creek People, North America)
Animal spirit. A water-frog, a helpful spirit.

Koto-Shiro-Nushi (Japan)
Okuni-Nushino-Mikoto, who is one of the Shichi Fukujin (seven gods of happiness), could be the father of Koto-Shiro-Nushi. *See also* Okuni-Nushino-Mikoto; Take-Minakata.

Kotoshironushi-No-Mikoto (Japan) *see* Ebisu.

Kottavei (India)
A goddess of war, Kottavei feeds on carnage. *See also* Kali.

Kottos (Greek) *see* Cottus; Hecatoncheires.

Kou-Hun-Shih-Che (China) *see* Wu-Ch'ang.

Kouretes (Greek) *Korubantes* (Crete) *see* Curetes; Telchines.

Kouros (Greek) *see* Curetes.

Kourotrophos (Greek) *see* Karpophoros.

Kox (Aztec) *see* Coxcoxtli.

Kozoba (Baziba People, Africa)
God of the sun and moon. He is the son of the father of the gods, Wamara, and the father of Hangi. *See also* Wamara.

Krakuchanda (India) *see* Manushi-Buddhas.

Kratos (Greek)
"Power." He is the son of the Titan, Pallas and the Oceanid, Styx. His siblings are Bia ("Force"), Nike ("Victory") and Zelos ("Zeal"). *See also* Nike; Pallas; Styx.

Kravyad (India) "Flesh Eater." *See also* Agni.

Kresnik (Slavic) *see* Krsnik.

Kricco (Slavic)
God of fruits of the fields. *See also* Lawkapatim.

Krimen (Tupi-Guarani People, Brazil) *see* Hermitten.

Krimhild (Teutonic) *see* Gudrun.

Kripa (India)
He is the husband of Drona and the father of Ashvatthaman. *See also* Duryodhana.

Krishna *Kistna, Kristna, Krsna* (Hindu, Vaishnava; India)
Also known as: *Acyuta* (Immovable), *Arisudana* (Slayer of Enemies), *Gopel* (The Cowherd), *Gopinath* (The Lord of Cowherds), *Govind, Govinda* (Herdsman or Giver of Enlightenment), *Hrsikesa* (Lord of the Senses), *Janardana* (Liberator of Men), *Juggernaut* (Lord of the World), *Kesava* (Having Fine Hair), *Madhava* (Husband of Laksmi), *Madhusudana* (Slayer of Madhu), *Mathuranath* (Lord of Muttra), *Vasudeva, Yadava* (Descendent of Yadu).
Krishna, the eighth avatar of Vishnu, is known as a god of vegetation, love, and erotic delight. Vishnu assumed the form of Krishna to overcome Kansa, the tyrannical king of Mathura. The *Mahabharata*, the main source for Krishna's legend, records that Vishnu plucked two hairs from his head, one white and one black. The strands were placed in the wombs of Rohini, and

Devaki. Rohini bore Balarama from the white hair and Devaki gave birth to Krishna from the black hair. According to the *Purana*, the sage Narada told Devaki's uncle Kansa that her son would kill him. Kansa then put Devaki's six children to death. Balarama, the seventh was transferred to the womb of Rohini, the second wife of Vasudeva, and she subsequently gave birth to Krishna. He was born in Vrindavana, a wood in Vraja. Krishna was exchanged for the newborn daughter of the cowherd Nanda. In time Kansa discovered the truth and on numerous occasions tried to kill Krishna. As a child, Krishna was spontaneous and impetuous, a little rascal. He loved sweets and butter and would steal them whenever he could. Obedient when near his mother, once out of her sight, he was constantly getting into mischief. During his youthful period, his playfulness continued. He loved sports and flirting with the cowgirls (*gopis*). Kansa, his evil uncle, continued to send his retinue of monstrous demons to kill Krishna. Putana, the demon daughter of the demon king Bali, arrived disguised as a beautiful woman. She attempted to suckle Krishna with her poison-filled breasts. Krishna sucked the life from her. Sakta-Sura flew in and tried to crush Krishna but was crushed by him. Trinavarta, the "Whirlwind," blew in and swept up the young god. Krishna increased his weight and held on to his neck until he was so heavy that the exhausted demon fell to the ground and shattered. Other demons followed: Vatsasura, the female demon in the shape of a cow; Bakasura disguised as a raven (or some say a giant crane); Aghasura, the younger brother of Putana; and Batasura, in the form of a huge snake. All were killed by the young god. Dhenuka appeared in the form of a giant ass, and was killed by Bala-Rama. The demon bull-fiend Arishta (also called Arista) was so powerful that his movement shook the earth. He attempted to crush Krishna, but ended up being choked to death. Krishna had a major battle with the many-headed serpent Kaliya. The serpent had been polluting the waters, stealing the cows, and preventing the women from fetching water. Kansa had the monster in a position of defeat but when Kaliya's fish-tailed wives begged the god to spare him, he consented on the condition that he remain in the sea and he was warned that he would be destroyed by the serpent-eagle Garuda, if he ever appeared on land. Indra, overcome by jealousy of the popular god, tried to destroy mortals by sending floods. To protect the cowherds and the cattle, Krishna held Govardhana mountain for seven days with his little finger. In time, Indra's anger turned to admiration for the strong, determined young god, who had become a friend and the charioteer for his son, Arjuna. Krishna's action-filled adventures were far from over. He killed Kansa's father-in-law Jarasandha and brother Sunaman. He carried off the daughter of the king of the Gandharvas, conquered Saubha, the city of the Daityas, and overcame Varuna. He killed Panchajana and confiscated his conch shell, stole the magic Parijata tree from Swarga, Indra's heaven, and planted it in his celestial home Dvarka (meaning "City of Gates"). He took Agni's fiery discus (chakra) and with Arjuna's help, he burned the Khandava forest. Krishna's travails were not over. Next came the demon Keshin in the shape of a horse. Krishna thrust his fist down the beast's throat and caused him to explode. Kuvalayapida, the demon, appeared in the shape of an elephant. Other demons harassed him, notably Shankha-Sura and Kalayavana. Krishna's consort during this period was

Radha, an incarnation of the goddess Lakshmi, who was the faithful wife of Vishnu. During the battle between the Pandavas and the Kauravas, Krishna fought with Arjuna and his army fought on the other side with Duryodhana because Krishna was related to both sides. Rukmini, who was Krishna's wife, and also an avatar of Lakshmi, had a son who was an avatar of Kama the god of love. They named him Pradyumna. The demon Sambara abducted the child and he was raised by Sambara's spouse or housekeeper, Mayadevi. When Pradyumna grew older, his son, Aniruddha, was abducted by the Usha, a Daitya. Krishna arrived on the scene with Pradyumna and Bala-Rama. They engaged in a ferocious battle with Usha's father Bana and his troops of Daityas. Krishna and company emerged the victors and his grandson was rescued. Krishna also killed Kansa and then went to the lower regions to retrieve his six brothers, killed before his birth. The hunter Jaras mistook Krishna for a deer and accidentally shot him in his only vulnerable spot, his heel. Krishna's jewelled abode of Dvarka disappeared under water seven days after he died. Pradyumna was killed during a brawl in Dvarka and Bala-Rama died under a tree. During his lifetime, the irresistible Krishna married Kalindi and Madri, the daughters of the sun god Surya; Jambavati, the daughter of Jambavan, king of the bears; and Satyabhama, the daughter of Satrajit. His wrathful wife was Bhama. The *Purana* gives Krishna 16,100 wives and 180,000 sons. Krishna's companion was Yudhishthira, the eldest of the five Pandavas. In the Vedic tradition, Krishna gave the *Bhagavad Gita* to Arjuna to encourage him on the battlefield in his fight for truth. Krishna's period marks the end of the Vedic era. Krishna is generally shown with black skin, symbolizing wisdom and eternity and sometimes with four arms, possibly denoting the four directions. He is also shown in slate-blue color, often wrestling with a serpent or playing his flute, which is known as "Call-of-the-Infinite." The sound of his music is irresistible to all who hear it. He is traditionally shown clothed in a jewelled sari with a high conical crown. His consort Radha is red or pink in color. During the first full moon of spring, Phalguna (February–March), a celebration known popularly as the Holi festival celebrates Krishna's life as a cowherd. Colored water and powders are offered to Krishna and Radha. The Rasa and the Hallisa dances celebrate Krishna's life. Krishna-Janmashtami is the celebration of Krishna's birthday. He was born at midnight on the eighth day of the dark fortnight of Bhadrapada (August–September). A twenty-four hour fast is observed. Temples are decorated in his honor, bells are rung and conches blown. Another ceremony, Jhulanayatra, known as the Ceremony of Swinging the Lord Krishna, is held during the eleventh to the fifteenth days of the bright fortnight of Sravana (July–August). Krishna killed the serpent Kaliya by dancing on his head and trampling him to death, symbolizing the triumph of good over evil. Krishna's weight is the weight of the earth. His mantra is "*Om Namo Bhagavate Vasudevaya*." His numerous wives represent the stars. Pradyumna represents love and Aniruddha, egotism. The hunter Jaras represents cold or old age. The demoness Putana is depicted as about fifteen feet tall. Krishna is associated with the tamala tree. It has dark bark and dark leaves and is an object of veneration by Vaishnava devotees. For Kansa's background *see* Drumalika. Compare Krishna's vulnerability to the vulnerability of Achilles. Compare Krishna to Heracles and Osiris. *See also* Aditi; Arjuna;

Bala-Rama; Bali; Bana; Bhima (A); Daityas; Devaki; Devi; Drumalika; Duryodhana; Gopis; Jambavan; Juggernaut; Kama (A); Kansa; Lakshmi; Pandavas; Parijata; Parikshit; Pradyumna; Radha; Sankhasura; Satyabhama; Sisupala; Soma; Subhadra; Swarga; Syamantaka; Vishnu; Visvakarma; Yadavas.

Krishna Dwaipayana (India) *see* Vyasa.

Kristna (India) *see* Krishna.

Krita (Hindu; India)
Also known as: *Kritayuga.*
Part of the cycle of Kalpa, Krita is the golden age which lasts 1,728,000 years. Virtue is 100 percent, and Dharma, god of justice and duty, walks on four legs and is colored white. *See also* Dwaparayuga; Kalpa.

Kritanta (India) The god of death. *See also* Yama.

Kritayuga (India) *see* Krita.

Krittika Sisters *Kirteka* (India) *see* Karttikeya; Rishi; Vasistha.

Krittikas (India) *see* Vasistha.

Krittivasas (India) "Clad in Hide." *See also* Kali.

K'ro-bo-mi-gyo-ba (Tibet; Japan) *see* Acala.

Krodha (India)
Her name means "anger." She is the daughter of Daksha, the spouse of Kasyapa, and the mother of all four-footed predators and birds of prey. *See also* Bhutas; Daksha; Kasyapa; Shiva.

Kronos (Greek) *see* Cronus.

Krotishaurima, Buddha (Tibet) *see* Heruka.

Krsanu (India) "The Archer." *See also* Soma.

Krsna (India) *see* Krishna.

Krsnik *Karsnik, Kresnik* (Slavic)
Protector deity. A benevolent god, he protects the family from werewolves and vampires. He battles Vlkodlak, the werewolf.

Krukis (Slavic)
Also known as: *Kaukas* (Lithuanian), *Pukys.*
Household spirits. The Krukis along with Peseias are protectors of domestic animals. The Krukis were also the patrons of blacksmiths. They are part of the Domovoi group (q.v.).

Kruth, The (Cambodia) *see* Garuda (India).

Ksama (India) *see* Lakshmi.

Kshiti-Apsarases (India) *see* Apsarases.

Kshiti-garbha (Central Asia) *see* Kshitigarbha.

Kshitigarbha *Ksitgarbha, Kshiti-garbha* (India; Buddhist; Central Asia)
Also known as: *Jizo* (Japan), *Ti-Tsang* (China), *Ti-Tsang Wang-P'u-sa* (China).
Kshitigarbha was not known in Indian Buddhism and Lamaism. Throughout Central Asia (beginning in China), he was a an old god of the earth representing fertility and growth, a Bodhisattva, and a patron of travelers. He regulates the six

paths (gati) taken by the souls of mortals, deities, animals, demons, and asuras after being judged by the ten Kings of Hell. In paintings by Yueyen-Kwang, the ten kings are depicted clustered around Kshitigarbha. Kshitigarbha's head is shaved and sometimes he wears a wreath or a traveler's shawl. In his right hand he carries a ringed stick known as a *Khakkara*, and in his left hand, a pearl known as *Cintamani*, the wish-granting gem. The Cintamani is also the emblem of Mahakala, Ratnapani, Ratnasambhava, and Samantabhadra. He is related to the air god, Akasagarbha. Kshitigarbha is similar to the chief of the Yama Kings (q.v.), and the same as Jizo Bosatsu of Japan (q.v.). *See also* Akshobhya; Chu-kiang; Dhyanibodhisattvas; Pien-ch'eng; Ratnapani; Ratnasambhava; Samantabhadra; Sung Ti; Ti-Tsang; Wu Kuan; Yama Kings; Yen-lo.

Ksitigarbha (Central Asia) *see* Kshitigarbha.

Ktesios (Greek) Zeus as the guardian of property.

Ku and Hina (Hawaii)
Ku, the first male creative force, and Hina, the first female creative force, are invoked as inclusive of the total ancestral line, past, present and future. Ku presides over all male deities and Hina presides over all female deities. Ku as Master of the Universe is called Ku-Kau-Akahi (Ku Standing Alone). Many of the early gods were given Ku names. A few examples: Ku as god of the forest would be Ku-moku-hali'i (Ku spreading over the land), Ku-olono-wao (Ku of the deep forest). Ku as god of war would be Ku-nui-akea (Ku the supreme one), Ku-kaili-moku (Ku snatcher of land). Ku is a god of war and a sorcery god. *See also* Hi'iaka; Hika-po-loa; Hina; Kane; Ku-ka-ohia-laka; Ku-mauna; Lono.

K'u-ch'u K'iao (China)
Also known as: *Bridge of Pain.*
Underworld bridge. Once the soul is given the Broth of Oblivion by Lady Meng (Meng-p'o) they must cross this bridge where they are confronted by two demons. *See also* Meng (A); Ti-yu.

Ku Gods (Hawaii) *see* Ku and Hina.

Ku-ka-ohia-laka (Hawaii)
God of the hula dance. God of canoe builders. He is the husband of Hina-ula-ohia (q.v.). In the temples he is depicted as a feather god and worshipped with Kanaloa, Kane, Ku-nui-akea and Lono. *See also* Hiiaka; Laka (A).

Ku-Kali-Moku *Kukalikimoku* (Hawaii, Polynesia)
God of war. God of sorcery. He is the most famous of the Ku gods. His cries are heard over the deafening sounds of battle. Ku-Kali-Moku was also the most famous god of sorcery, until the advent of Ka-lei-pahoa, the sorcery god of Molokai. Ku-Kali-Moku is shown with a head of blood-red bird feathers. Upon his head, he wears a Roman-type helmet. *See also* Ku and Hina; Uli.

Ku-Kau-Akahi (Hawaii)
Ku, the first male creative force, is called Ku-Kau-Akahi ("Ku Standing Alone"), as the Master of the Universe. *See also* Ku and Hina; Ku Gods.

Ku-mauna (Hawaii)
Ku of the Mountain. He is one of the forest gods who was banished by the goddess of fire Pele, for refusing to destroy prince Lohiau when she asked him to do so. He was overcome in her fire and died. Later, he was worshipped as a local rain god.

Ku-ula-kai (Hawaii)
God of abundance in the sea. He is one of the gods of fishers, and some say the chief of all the gods of the sea. He built the first fishpond. At death, he bequeathed the objects he used to control the fish to his son Aiai. He also taught him how to address the gods and how to set up fish altars. The four objects were Pahiaku-kahuoi, a decoy stick, Leho-ula, a cowry, Manai-a-ka-lani, a hook and a stone called Kuula. When dropped into the pond this stone drew fish. Many myths involve Ku-ula-kai and his son Aiai. *See also* Ku and Hina.

Ku-waha-ilo (Hawaii)
One of the conductors of the souls of dead chiefs. *See also* Lo-lupe.

Kua Tsi-i (China) God of happiness. *See also* Fu-Shen.

Kuai (Arawak People, Amazon, Brazil)
Hero and fertility spirit. Very little is said of this deity except he was considered to be the one who introduced the mask dances. He still dances in the sky-world. Kuai is possibly related to the Katchinas of the Zuni and Pueblo Indians.

Kuan Jung (China) *see* Kuan-Ti.

Kuan-Ti (China)
Also known as: *Kuan Jung, Kuan Yu.*
A war hero who became a personal god of war, Kuan-Ti had been a loyal and faithful general and scholar named Chang-sheng, Shou-chang or Yun-chang (Yen Ch'ang). He was raised to the status of a god after his death. As a patron of the people, he protected them by preventing rather than making war. Kuan-Ti predicts the future for his followers. He sometimes plays the part of a judge who is called upon to punish those who do evil to others. In this case he sends his attendant, Shou-t'sang, to give out the punishment. Kuan-Ti is said to have a son named Kuan P'ing. In some versions he is also a god of literature. As Kuan or Kuan Yu he was associated with Liu Pei and Chang Fei, all were warriors and according to some were from eight to nine feet tall. He is said to have been one of three generals of the Han dynasty who swore brotherhood. He is depicted with a red face and green clothing. Sometimes he is shown as a giant nine feet high with a beard two feet long. He is usually carrying weapons and is sometimes on horseback. His festival day is May 13. His name is similar to the Buddhist goddess of mercy, Kuan Yin. *See also* Hsuan-T'ien Shang Ti.

Kuan-yin (China) *see* Kuan Yin.

Kuan Yin *Kuan-yin, Kwan-yin* (China)
Also known as: *Avalokitesvara* (India), *Juichimen, Kannon* (Japan), *Kwan-she-yin, Kwannon, Nyo-i-rin Kwan-on* (Male), *Po-i Ta-shi, Sung-tzu-niang-niang.*

She is the goddess of mercy and fecundity, protector of women, bringer of rain, and savior of sailors. Her titles are The All Merciful, Bodatsu, Bodhisattva, Buddha, The Divine Voice of the Soul, Goddess of Fertility, Goddess of Mercy and Knowledge, Great Bodhisattva, The Melodious Voice, The Merciful Mother, The Mother, Of the Hundred Hands, The Prostitute, The Saviouress, The Triple, Wife and Daughter. Some say that she was originally an Indian Bodhisattva known as Avalokitesvara, or, some say, the Buddhist god of mercy, Juichimen. She was clearly masculine and portrayed with a fine line mustache. She parallels the goddess Vach (India). She was also said to have eleven heads and was called Sung-Tzu-Naing-Naing. Kuan Yin is possibly a form of Kunti or Parvati. In some legends, she is a goddess of prostitutes, also called public girls. Kuan Yin is generally clad in a white dress and holding a lotus flower, or, seated on a lotus and carrying a child. Her different aspects are shown in different dress and with two, four, six, and as many as a thousand arms. Some think she is a form or aspect of Tara (B) (q.v.). *See also* Avalokitesvara; Hariti; Nijuhachi-bushu; P'an Chin-Lien; Parvati, Ti-Sang.

Kuan Yu (China) *see* Kuan-Ti.

Kuang Mu (China) *see* Mo-li Hung.

Kubaba (Kish)
Deified mortal. Mother of Puzur-Sin, first king of the Fourth Dynasty of Kish. The goddess herself, a former barmaid, reigned as queen of the Third Dynasty for 100 years.

Kubebe (Greek) *see* Dionysus.

Kubele (Greek) *see* Cybele.

Kubera (India) *see* Kuvera.

Kubira (India) *see* Kuvera.

Kudai (Siberia) A Sky God. *See also* Ameshas Spenta.

Kudai Bai-ulgon (Altaic, Tartars) *see* Bai Ulgan.

Kudai-Baksy (Siberia) *see* K'daai Maqsin.

K'uei-Hsing *K'uei-Sing, Kuei-Sing* (China)
The god of examinations. He fulfills an important function as assistant to the god of literature, Wen Ch'ang (Wen-ti). Although very ugly, he is well liked, since it was he who selects the successful examination candidate. He is usually depicted standing on a turtle. When turned down by the emperor because of his appearance, K'uei-Hsing attempted to drown himself. The turtle Ao rescued him. He carries a bushel basket to measure the talents of the candidates presented to Tung Wang Kung (also known as Yu-ti), the Jade Emperor. The bushel basket represents his function as a god of the constellation Big Dipper. The Chinese call the Big Dipper "Bushel." K'uei-Hsing is associated with Wen Ch'ang.

Kuei-Hui (China)
Kuei-Hui is a bottomless pit in the Eastern Sea into which all the waters of this world and of the Han flow. Mortals call the Han the Milky Way. The Five Islands of the Immortals once floated in the Kuei-Hui but a giant sank two of them. The other three islands are lost. *See also* Milky Way.

Kueph (Egypt) *see* Khnum.

Kuetzal-Koatl (Mexico) *see* Quetzalcoatl.

Kuhu (India)
She is the moon goddess daughter of Angiras and possibly the sister of Agni.

Kui (Maori) This blind storm goddess eats human flesh.

Kujaku-Myoo (Japan)
Also known as: *Mahamayuri.*
Protector from calamity. An aspect of a Bodhisattva. Kujaku-Myoo is one of the more gentle myoo who dwells in the Tushita heaven. Shown seated on an eight-petalled lotus, usually with four arms, holding a flower, fruit and a peacock feather, Kujaku-Myoo has a white body and wears white transparent garments.

Kujum-Chantu (Thompson People, Pacific Northwest, North America)
The Earth. Creator deity. She is seen as the whole earth. The first humans lived on her fat belly. Because she worried about the humans falling off she died of her own accord and the valley of her chest became the area where the Apa-Tanis live. Her eyes became the sun and moon and from her mouth came Kujum-Popi, who directed the sun and moon to shine. *See also* Kujum-Popi.

Kujum-Popi (Thompson People, Pacific Northwest, North America)
Born from the mouth of Kujum-Chantu (earth), this deity created or sent the sun and moon into the sky. *See also* Kujum-Chantu.

Kukalikimoku (Hawaii, Polynesia) *see* Ku-Kali-Moku.

Kuko-no-shi (Japan) *see* O-Wata-Tsu-Mi.

Kuksu (Maidu, Pomo People, North America)
In the Maidu legends, Kuksu, a culture hero, is the first man. The Pomos call him the elder brother of the creator god Marumda. *See also* Marumba; Ragno.

Kuku-no-shi *Ku-ku-no-shi* (Shinto, Japan)
Also known as: *Kukunochi-no-kami* (possibly).
God of mountains. God of the boles of trees. One of the children of Izanami and Izanazi. Kuku-no-shi is the brother of Oho-wata-tsu-mi, Shima-Tsu-Hiko, and Oho-yama-tsu-mi. In some traditions, the food goddess Toyo-uke-hime-no-himi separated herself into the god Kuku-no-shi and the goddess of grasses and herbs, Kaya-no-hime-no-kami. *See also* Ha-mori; Izanami and Izanagi; Kaya-no-hime-no-kami; Toyo-uke-hime-no-himi.

Kukulcan *Cuculcan* (Maya People, Yucatan)
Also known as: *Cezalcouati, Gucumatz, Quetzalcoatl.*
Patron of artisans. Inventor. An early serpent god, Kukulcan is the Mayan form of the Mexican god, Quetzalcoatl. It is said that he instituted a system of laws, and numerous inventions, among them the calendar. His place of worship was the city of Quirigua. *See also* Gucumatz; Quetzalcoatl.

Kul (Finnish)
Also known as: *Kul-Uasa, Vasa, Vodyanoi, Vodyanoy.*

Nymphs. The Kul are selfish water sprites who dislike sharing their fish with mortals. They also inflict sickness on mortals. *See also* Vodyanoi.

Kulla (Babylon)

God of temples. Anu or Ea created this god to restore temples.

Kulmu (Etruscan)

God of tombs. He is shown with shears and torches.

Kumara (India) *see* Karttikeya.

Kumarbis *Kumbari* (Hurrian)

Kumarbis, a sky god and weather god, became the father of the gods by castrating and swallowing his father's testicles. (Anus, his father, had achieved his position by ousting his father Alalus from the throne.) Anus told Kumarbis that he had swallowed three mighty gods: the river god Aranzahas, Tashmishu, who may have been a rain god, and a god whose name cannot be deciphered from ancient tablets, but who is thought to be a storm god. Kumarbis spit them out on Mount Kanzuras. Kumarbis plotted to create a rival storm god. He fathered the god Ullikummis after having union with a rock three miles long, according to some myths. Others say that how the birth came about is unclear. Ullikummis grew to monstrous proportions and assisted his father in his struggle against the storm, thunder, and rain god Teshub, who was also the son of Kumarbis, and his brother Tashmishu. Eventually, Kumarbis was deposed by Teshub. *See also* Alalus; Anu (B); Anus; Teshub; Ullikummis.

Kumari (Hindu, India)

Also known as: *Devi, Kali, Kanya-Kumari* (Daughter-virgin).

Kumari, meaning "the maiden," is a virgin goddess worshiped by virginal, young women. She is called the "Living Goddess." Kumari is an aspect of Devi and Kali (qq.v.).

Kumbari (Hittite, Hurrian) *see* Kumarbis.

Kumbhakara *Kumbhakarna* (India)

Kumbhakara is a giant monster who sleeps for six months and wakes up for a day. Nikasha is thought by some to be the mother of Kumbhakara; Ravana; Khara; Vibhishana, a good natured demon; and a daughter, Shurpanaka, who is a giant she-demon. *See also* Kuvera; Nikasha; Ravana; Shurpanaka; Vishravas.

Kumbhakarna (India) *see* Kumbhakara.

Kumbhandas (India) *see* Dhartarastra.

Kummiya (Hittite, Hurrite)

He is the storm god who battled Ullikummis (q.v.).

Kumudavati (India) *see* Kumunda.

Kumund (India) Elephant guard. *See also* Lokapalas.

Kumunda (India) *see* Dikpalas; Nagas and Nagis; Rama.

Kumush (Modoc People, North America)

A creator god. After the world was destroyed, he returned to the land of the dead with his daughter, who was also dead.

Kumush wearied of dancing with spirits at night who became skeletons by day, and taking a basket of bones, he returned to earth and created a new race of people. He is described as being a beautiful blue color.

Kun (A) (Peru) God of the Desert.

Kun (B) *Khun* (China, Mongol)

The Sovereign God turned to Kun for help following a devastating, lasting flood. In very remote times the world was flooded. Kun worked nine years in an attempt to dam the water. He was not successful. The price he paid for his labors was high. Either Yao or Shun, his successor, executed Kun. They ordered his son Yu to carry on with his father's work. Yu stole soil that had magical properties from the Lord. The soil known as the "swelling mold" kept swelling in size. He hoped it would hold the water back. It did not. The Lord, enraged with Yu for stealing the "swelling mold," had him executed in a dark place without sun in the north, known as Feather Mountain. Yu's body lay for three years without decomposing. Eventually someone came along and sliced his stomach open. His son Yu emerged. Later Yu had a son named Ch'i (q.v.). Kun is possibly the same as Khun of the Mongols, a white dragon horse that was a protector against demons. Kun is associated with Fu-hsi. There are many legends based on Kun's experiences. In some of them, Kun is successful in his attempts to close the dam, and is rewarded with the throne. Often, it is said that Kun was born from a stone that had been split open, and he turned into a bear.

Kun (C) (Finnish)

Also known as: *Kootamoinen.*

A god who is the moon.

K'un-Lun (China) *see* Kun-Lun.

Kun-Lun Mountain *K'un-Lun, Khun-Lun* (China)

Also known as: *Ching-Tu.*

The Lord of the Sky's capital on Earth. The mountain abode of the celestial lords. The Queen Mother, Hsi Wang Mu, cultivates and keeps the Peaches of Immortality on Kun-Lun Mountain. She acts as a hostess when the feasts of immortality are given for the gods. Her husband Tung-wang-kung and the other immortals also live on Kun-Lun Mountain. Kun-Lun is located in the extreme west, extending to the heights of the sky and depths of the earth. It is the dwelling place on earth of the Lord of the Sky, Tung Wang Kung. In later mythology, it took on the features and quality of a heavenly paradise. Kun-Lun is probably the same as Jodo of the Japanese people. *See also* Feng-tu; Hsi Wang Mu; Nu Kua; Tiyu; Yama Kings.

Kun-Rig (India) *see* Vairocana.

Kunapipi (Australia) *see* Waramurungundja.

Kunapipi-Kalwadi-Kadjara (Australia) *see* Ngaljod; Rainbow Snake; Waramurungundja.

Kund (Teutonic) *see* Heimdall.

Kundalini (India)

Also known as: *Bhujangi* (Serpent).

She is the Supreme Power in the body, located at the base of the spinal column, in the area called the lowest chakra or bodily center. She has the form of a coiled and sleeping serpent and is often represented coiled around a lingam (the phallus as a mystical object).

Kundrav (Persian) *see* Gandarewa.

Kung Kung (China)

A dragon or horned monster who struck down the pillars of the firmament with his head, causing tremendous earthquakes and the resulting great Deluge when the vault of heaven collapsed and fell.

Kuni-no Sa-tsuchi No Mikoto (Japan) *see* Ama-no-minaka-nushi.

Kuni-toko-tachi-no-mikoto (Japan) *see* Ama-no-minaka-nushi.

Kuni-Tsu-Kami (Shinto; Japan)

Earthly deities. Kuni-Tsu-Kami is the name given to earth deities. These deities lived on the islands of Japan. They could go to Ama (heaven) and the gods of heaven, known as Amatsu-kami could also move to earth. The Ama in heaven could only find out what was happening on earth if a messenger came to the celestial realm with news. These deities could see into the future without the use of divination. For the Shinto creation myth, *see* Ama-no-minaka-nushi. *See also* Kami.

Kunmanggur (Australia) *see* Rainbow Snake.

Kunti *Pritha* (Hindu; India)

Queen Kunti, also known as Pritha, is the daughter of a nymph and King Sura of Mathura. She is the sister of Vasudeva and the wife of Pandu. When she was very young, the sage Durvasas granted her the opportunity to bed with five gods. She chose four and permitted Madri, Pandu's other wife, to choose the fifth deity for herself. As a result of Kunti's activities, she became the virgin mother of a son Karna by the sun god Surya and three of the Pandavas: Yudhisthira, by Dharma; Bhima, by Vayu; and Arjuna, by Indra. Karna was born in full armor. Kunti, worried about the wrath of the community, hid the child in the river Aswa. He was cared for by a series of foster river-goddesses, including Yami and Ganga, who saw that he was discovered. Nandana, the charioteer to the blind King Dhritarashtra, raised him. When Indra saw his shining armor, he traded it for a spear that never missed. It was Karna who first fell in love with and was rejected by the beautiful goddess Draupadi because of his lowly station in life. A spirited woman, she was the daughter of the king of the Panchalas. Later, she was won as a prize by Arjuna at an archery contest. At Kunti's insistence, she became the shared wife of the Pandavas. In some versions, it was Karna who won Draupadi and then was rejected by her. Angered, Karna joined the enemies of the Pandavas, the Kauravas, and fought against his half-brothers. He killed Ghatotkacha but later was killed by Arjuna. After his death, the Pandavas discovered that Karna was their brother. Indra invited Kunti and her family to reside in his celestial city, Swarga. *See also* Bhima (A); Dharma; Gandhari; Indra; Karna; Kauravas; Krishna; Pandavas; Prithivi; Radha; Surya; Swarga; Vishnu; Yudhisthira.

Kuntu-bzang-mo (Tibet) *Samanta-Bhadra* (India)

Divine Mother and Shakti, she is the mate of Samantabhadra (q.v.). *See also* Shakti.

Kuo Shang (China)

One of the nine heroes. Kuo Shang appears as thick, dark clouds.

Kupala (Slavic)

Water deity. Goddess of joy. Primarily a goddess of water, Kupala was also worshiped in fire rites. She is involved in magic and healing herbs. Kupala is shown as a straw figure dressed in a woman's gown and adorned with ribbons and jewelry. Sometimes she has wooden arms. Similar in nature to Yarilo (q.v.).

Kupua *Kapua* (Hawaii; Polynesia)

Trickster spirits. Demi-gods. Shape-changers. The Kupua are born in non-human form, either as an egg or a plant, although there are exceptions. Someone, often a maternal grandparent, recognizes the Kupua's divinity and raises him. He is gifted, intelligent, and has a huge appetite. In Kupua stories, we are often told that the kupua has been offered the daughters of the chief as gifts. Then the kupua is sent off to overcome a dangerous hellion who is petrifying the land. Kupuas are known under various names. Kawelo is a spear-thrower and fisher; Iwa is a master thief; Ono is a fisher who was born as an egg; Kana, born in the shape of a rope, was brought up by his grandmother, Uli. Maui is classed as a kupua. *See also* Kamapua'a; Kana; Ku; Kupua-Huluena; Mafuike; Uli.

Kupua-Huluena (Hawaii)

He is a well known kupua who is credited for bringing vegetable foods to the islands. *See also* Kanea; Kaneapua; Kaulu; Kupua.

Kur (Sumerian)

Underworld deity. He is a monster who throws stones. He is the villain who is depicted as the empty place between the sea and the earth's crust. In some legends, he carries Inanna to the underworld. He is associated with Inanna and possibly with Ninurta.

Kura-Mitsu-Ha (Japan)

"Dark Water Snake." Kura-Mitsu-Ha and his brothers, Kura-yama-tsumi and Kuru-okami, were born from the blood of their brother, the fire god Kagutsuchi, when he was killed by their father, Izanagi. *See also* Izanagi and Izanami; Kagutsuchi; Kura-Okami; Taki-tsu-hiko.

Kura-Okami (Shinto) Japan

Rain and snow god. Weather deity. In the *Nihongi* (*Chronicles of Japan*), Kura-Okami was created from the blood of the upper part of a sacred sword belonging to Izanagi when he killed his son, the fire god Kagu-tsuchi. Two other deities born at the same time are Kura-yama-tsumi (Lord of the Dark Mountains) and Kura-mitsu-ha (Dark-water-snake). In another section of this document, the deity Taka-Okami (Dragon-god-residing-on-the-mountains) was born from the pieces of the Kagu-tsuchi's body. In the *Kojiki*, Kura-Okami, Kura-yama-tsumi and Kura-mitsu-ha were created from the blood that leaked between Izanagi's fingers when he killed Kagu-tsuchi. Kura-Okami (Dragon god of the valleys) is said to be a snake or dragon god who controls the rain and snow. Kura-Okami is shown as a dragon or serpent. For the Shinto creation myth and information about the *Kojiki* and the *Nihongi*; *see* Ama-no-minaka-nushi. *See also* Izanagi and Izanami; Taka-okami; Taki-tsu-hiko.

Kura-Yama-Tsumi (Japan)

"Lord of the Dark Mountains." *See also* Izanagi and Izanami; Kura-okami; Taki-tsu-hiko.

Kuramitsuha-no-kami (Japan) *see* Izanami.

Kurangara (Aborigine People, Australia)

Spirits. The Kurangara have long flexible limbs forked on the ends. They are usually depicted with a long muzzle, and exaggerated genitals.

Kuretes (Greek) *see* Curetes.

Kurke (Prussia; Slavic)

Also known as: *Curche.*

Deity of agriculture. Also the name of a weevil. A cult prayed to Kurke to control this weevil.

Kurma (Brahmanic, Hindu; India)

Kurma the tortoise is the second avatar of Vishnu. When the gods were losing their strength after a Rishi laid a curse on Indra, Vishnu took charge. He instructed the Daevas to join with the Asuras to churn the sea of milk, using Mount Mandara as the churning stick, and Vasuki king of the snakes and Seshu the endless serpent as the churning rope. The endeavor took a thousand years. The reason for this action was to bring to the surface all solid objects including the miraculous cup containing soma which had been lost during the Great Deluge. Soma, the beverage of immortality would revitalize the deities. Vasuki consented to assist only if he would be given a share of soma. The rapid motion and the weight of the churn threatened the sea and the earth below. Only Vishnu, assuming the form of Kurma the giant tortoise could save them. He dove to the bottom of the ocean to serve as a base for Mount Mandara. The efforts of the gods on one side of the churn and the demons on the other, at last, brought forth from the churning the treasures of the Vedic tribes lost in the Deluge. During these efforts, Vasuki vomited up halahala, a poison also called Visha, which emitted toxic fumes that could have killed everything, including the gods and demons. Shiva, who was watching over the project, caught the poison and swallowed it. The only ill-effect he suffered was a scalded gullet, which left a bluish trace, the result of his mate strangling him to save him. This incident gave him the surname Nilakantha (blue-throat). When Dhanvantari, the physician of the gods, rose from the sea, he held the cup of soma in his hands. After Vishnu retrieved it from the asuras, the gods were restored to their former vitality and sovereign authority. In the *Satapatha Brahmana*, Kurma is an avatar of Prajapati. Some records indicate that many of Prajapati's exploits were tranferred to Vishnu. Numerous treasures were churned from the sea. Soma, mentioned above, was the first item; the divine physician was next, followed by the goddess of beauty, Lakshmi; Sura, the goddess of wine; Chandra, the moon; Rambha, the beautiful Asparas nymph; Uchchaihsravas, the moon-colored horse; Vishnu's jewel, the Kaustubha; the magic tree, Parijata; Kamadhenu, the miraculous cow; Airavata, Indra's milk-white elephant; Shankha, a large shell, and the warrior who could blow it; Dhanus, the bow that always struck its target; Visha, a substance that could be healing or poisonous; the god Dhanvantari, who is said by some to hold a cup of sparkling soma in his hand; and Varuni, queen of Varuna

and goddess of spiritous liquor. The number of items retrieved varies from fourteen to thousands, as does the sequence of the item retrieved. Some of the treasures caused battles between demons and gods and others saved countries. *See also* Amrita; Apsarases; Asuras; Chandra; Daevas; Indra; Kamadhenu; Lakshmi; Matsya; Parijata; Prajapati; Rambha; Savarbhanu; Sesha; Shiva; Soma; Surabhi; Varaha; Vasuki; Vishnu.

Kuru (India)

Kuru is the common ancestor of the Kauravas and their cousins the Pandavas. *See also* Kauravas; Pandavas; Tapati.

Kuruksetra, Battle of (India) *see* Kali; Pandavas.

Kurukshetra (Hindu; India)

The sacred battlefield where the *Mahabharata* war was fought.

Kurukulla (Buddhist; East Asian)

Also known as: *Red Tara.*

Goddess of wealth. She is reddish in color and has four arms. The upper two arms are in a threatening position and the lower arms in a soothing position. *See also* Jambhala; Kuvera; Tara (B).

Kururumany (Arawak People, South America)

Creator. Kururumany is the husband of Kulimina. He created males and she created females. He returned to earth one day to check on his creation and found the people corrupt. As punishment he deprived them of immortality and left various serpents, lizards and vermin behind to make their life uncomfortable. In other legends, Kururumany has two wives. One wife is Emisiwaddo, who is possibly connected with ants, and the other wife is Wurekaddo, who is only known as one who works in the dark. There is mention of a higher god than Kururumany named Aluberi or Amalivaca, but little is known about these deities other than they may be tricksters. *See also* Makonaima; Purrunaminari.

Kurwaichin (Polish, Slavic)

Deity of animals. His primary duty is to watch over the lambs, while Kremara takes care of pigs. He is similar to Makosh, who took care of small domestic animals; to Walgino, who took care of cattle; and Zosim, who was in charge of bees. Another god who takes care of pigs is Priparchis.

Kusanagi (Japan)

Also known as: *Ame-no-murokumo-no-tsurugi* (Sword-of-black-clouded-heavens), *Herb-Quelling.*

Deified object. The Kusanagi is the remarkable sword Susanowo drew from the tail of an eight-headed serpent he slaughtered after his arrival in Izumo province. He gave the sword to his sister Amaterasu, who gave it to her grandson, Ninigi, when she sent him to reign on earth. She also gave him the other two treasures, the jewel and the mirror. The Kusanagi is known as the famous Herb-Quelling and is one of the three symbols of imperial sovereignty. The name Herb-Quelling originated from the period when the sword was in the possession of the warrior Yamato-Takeru. When he was ambushed, he was able to cut down burning bushes with the weapon. The divine sword is the symbol of courage. Compare Kusanagi to the sword Ame-no-wo-ha-bari. The Kusanagi is comparable to the

Arthurian Excalibur, the magic sword of King Arthur. For details about the Excalibur, *see* Vivian. *See also* Ame-no-wo-ha-bari for additional sword symbolism. For details of the three sacred treasures, *see* Amaterasu; Kushi-nada-hime; Ninigi; Susanowo.

Kusha (India)

Kusha is the son of Rama and Sita, the twin brother of Lava, the spouse of Kumudavati, and the father of Kushamba. *See also* Kumunda; Rama; Sita.

Kushi-nada-hime *Kushinada-Hime* (Wondrous Inada Princess); (Shinto; Japan)

Also known as: *Ina-Gami Furu-Kushi-Nada-Hime* (True-hair-touching-princess), *Inagami-Hime*.

Rice goddess. Kushi-nada-hime is the youngest of eight daughters. Her parents are Asi-na-duti, an earthly deity, and Tenazuchi-no-kami (Hand-Stroking-Elder). Every year an eight-headed snake from the Koshi district would slither into Izumo and feast upon one of the young women. When Susanowo, the son of Izanagi, arrived in the area, the parents of Kushi-nada-hime told him of their travails. Kushi-nada-hime was their only daughter alive, and the snake was due for his annual visit. Susanowo had a solution. He changed the young woman into a comb and stuck it into his hair. He filled eight bowls with saki and waited. Koshi, the snake, arrived and was bewitched by the aroma wafting up from the bowls. Each head lapped up the rice wine and the inebriated snake fell off to sleep. Susanowo, ready to take advantage of the situation, chopped the greedy villain into pieces. To his delight, he found a remarkable sword in the middle of the snake's tail. He presented the weapon to his sister, the sun goddess Amaterasu. It later became known as Kusanagi. Susanowo, ready to settle down, married Kushi-nada-hime. He built her a wedding palace and composed what is known as the oldest Japanese poem. They became the parents of Okuni-Nushino-Mikoto, who became Lord of Izumo. The *Kojiki* lists six generations of the descendants of Kushi-nada-hime. The female deities, their fathers, husbands and children are Konohana-chiru-hime (Blossoms-of-the-Trees Falling-Princess). Her father was Opo-yama-tu-mi-no-kami. She married Ya-sima-zinumi-no-kami and was the mother of a son, Pupa-no-modi-kunusunu-no-kami. Hikawa-hime, daughter of the wife of Okami-no-kami, married Pupa-no-modi-kunusunu-no-kami and had a son, Puka-buti-no-midu-yare-pana-no-kami. Amenotsudoe-chine-no-kami married Puka-buti-no-midu-yare-pana-no-kami and became the parents of a son, Omidu-nu-no-kami. Futemimi-no-kami, the daughter of Punoduno-no-kami, married Omidu-nu-no-kami and became the mother of a son, Ame-no-puya-kinu-no-kami. Sashikuni-waka-hime, the daughter of Sasi-kuni-opo-no-kami, married Ame-no-puya-kinu-no-kami and became the mother of Okuninushi (Okuni-Nushino-Mikoto) and eighty other sons. The snake and sword are frequently a part of the myths of Susanowo. In early Japan, the thunder god was a snake. The comb could signify male dominance or masculinity. For details about the sword, *see* Kusanagi; for details about the hero's life and the sacred treasures, *see* Susanowo; for his early life, *see* Izanagi; for his relationship with his sister, *see* Amaterasu. For information about the Shinto creation myth, the *Kojiki*, and the *Nihongi*, *see* Ama-no-minaka-nushi. *See also* Izanagi and Izanami; Okuni-Nushino-Mikoto.

Kushinada-hime (Japan) *see* Kushi-nada-hime.

Kusor (Phoenician)

God of the seasons. God of divination. God of mechanical devices. Inventor. God of sailors (possibly). Kusor and his brother, Hasisu, were involved in the construction of windows in the temple of Baal. The god Aleyn did not want windows, so they installed a skylight instead. Kusor was in charge of letting rain fall on earth through the skylight. As god of mechanical devices, he invented the fishing boat, fishing hook, fishing lines, navigation and iron-working. Kusor and Hasisu are sometimes known as one god, Kusor-Hasisu. He is identified with the Greek Hephaistos.

Kusug (Assyro-Babylonia) *see* Ea.

Kuu (Finnish)

Kuu is the name for the moon. Her daughter was named Kuutar.

Kuula (Hawaii, Polynesia)

God of the sea. God of fishing. His counterpart is Aiaiaku-ula, the goddess of fishers. *See also* Kaneapua.

Kuvalayapida (India) A demon. *See also* Krishna.

Kuvanna (India) A Yakshini. *See also* Yaksha.

Kuvera *Kubera, Kubira* (Hindu, Brahmanic, Buddhist, Vedic; India)

Also known as: *Dhana-Pati* (Lord of Wealth), *Dhanada* (Giving Wealth), *Kompira* (Tibet), *Kompira-Daigongen* (Tibet), *Namu-tho-se-ser-chhen* (Tibet), *Namu-Zozusen, Nara-Raja* (King of Men), *Ratna-Garbha* (Jewel-Belly), *rNam-t'os-sras-gsir-ch'en* (Tibet), *Takshaka, Vaisravana*.

Kuvera, known as the chief of evil beings during the Vedic period was elevated to the position of god of wealth and lord of treasures of the earth by the Hindus. He is the hideous dwarf son of Visravas and Idavida (Ida), and is considered by some to be an aspect of Shiva. He inherited Sri Lanka from his father but was ousted by his evil half-brother Ravana. Kuvera owns the earth's gold, silver and jewels. Pushpaka, the flying chariot was a gift to Kuvera from Brahma. This magic vehicle, devised by the divine architect Visvakarma, could contain a whole city. Kuvera moved into the palace of Lanka, also built by Visvakarma for the Rakshasas. They had deserted it when they were expecting an attack by Vishnu. Later, when the situation had settled, they decided they wanted their city of wealth back. The daughter of one of their leaders was sent to seduce Kuvera's father. From that union, the demon Ravana and two sons were born, the monster Kumbhakarna and Vibhishana, the good-natured demon. Kuverva was driven from his home along with the Gandharvas, Rakshasa, Kimpurushas and Yakshas. They settled in Alaka, the wealthiest city in the universe, located in the Himalayas. In other interpretations, his home was in a superb palace in Kailasa or on Mount Meru. On Mount Mandara, he maintains a beautiful garden known as Chaitraratha. Kuvera is chief of the Yakshas and Guhyakas and the ruler of the North; the location of the mineral rich mountains. His attendants are known as the Kinnaras and his chief attendant is Manibhadra (also known as Manivara). Kuvera's mates are Yakshi, Charvi or Kauveri, a Danava, the daughter of Mura, and Rambha, who was also sexually involved with Ravana. He has three sons and a daughter, Minakshi (also called Minakshidevi), the "fish-eyed goddess." Minakshi and her husband Sundara are thought by some to be incarnations of Parvati and Shiva. Minakshi and Minakshidevi are sometimes included as a name for the mother goddess Devi. He is also said to have mated with Hariti, who gave birth to five hundred demons. Kuvera is usually accompanied by two fiends, Yaksha and Yakshi. White in color, he is shown as a fat dwarf with three legs, eight teeth and one eye. He is also seen as a pot-bellied, ugly, black, heavily jewelled man, sitting cross-legged and holding a purse. In some depictions, he is golden-yellow, astride a white lion with a green mane, holding the banner of victory in his right hand and the mongoose under his left arm. His daughter Minakshi is described as having lustrous eyes and a beauty that subdued all earthly and heavenly beings. She had three breasts, but when she met Shiva, one of her breasts disappeared. Kuvera is a fertility deity, god of wealth, tutelary household spirit, protector of sailors and god of the dead. He has a jar of honey that revitalizes the elderly, restores sight to the blind and ensures immortality to all tasters. His non-tantric symbol is the caitya (*see* Stupa). The Kinnaras are musicians as well as Kuvera's attendants. They have human bodies and horses' heads and are said to have been born at the same time as the Yakshas. For Kumbhakarna and Vibhishana, *see* Ravana. Kuvera is associated with the goddess of wealth Kurukulla. (*See also* Panchika, god of the purse.) *See also* Abheda; Brahma; Devi; Dikpalas; Gandharvas; Hariti; Ida (B); Jambhala; Lokapalas; Maitreya; Mandara Mountains; Parvati; Rakshasas; Rama; Rambha; Ravana; Shiva; Takshaka; Virudhaka; Visvakarma; Yaksha and Yakshini.

Kvasir *Kvaser* (Teutonic)
A wise giant, Kvasir was killed by the dwarfs Fjalar and Galar. His blood, when mixed with honey, and distilled in the magic cauldron Odherir, became the source of an intoxicating beverage that gave wisdom and inspiration to poets. Odin favored this drink. In some accounts, Kvasir was created from the spittle of the Aesir and the Vanir. Compare Kvasir to Soma (India). *See also* Aesir; Baugi; Dwarfs; Odraerir; Vanir.

Kvergjelme (Teutonic) *see* Hvergelmir; Nifl-heim.

Kwammang-a (Bushmen, Africa)
Creator of the moon. He is sometimes described as grandson of Cagn. Cagn made Eland from Kwammang-a's discarded shoe. Eland was killed by Kwammang-a, and when he burst the gall the fluid blinded him. He wiped his eyes with a feather, which he then threw into the sky. It became the moon. Some call Kwammang-a a rainbow lord. Associated with Cagn (q.v.).

Kwan-on (Japan) *see* Kuan Yin.

Kwan-she-yin (China) *see* Kuan Yin.

Kwangiden *Kwangiten* (Japan)
Protector deity and god of good fortune. In Buddhist mythology the two devas Ganapati and Vinayaka are joined to become the Japanese Kwangiden. Kwangiden is shown in several forms, but usually as elephants when male and female deities. In male form he is sometimes shown as a man with a human body and an elephant's head. Normally he has four hands and four legs. Sometimes he is shown with two or six arms.

Kwangiten (Japan) *see* Kwangiden.

Kwannon (Japan) *see* Kannon; Kuan Yin.

Kwarenah (Persia) *see* Khvarenanh.

Kwetzal-Koatl (Mexico) *see* Quetzalcoatl.

Kwoth (Dinka, Neur People, Africa)
Also known as: *Kuth* (plural).
These spirits, known singularly as Kwoth, are divided into those above (kuth nhail) and those below (kuth piny).

Ky-Klopes (Greek) *see* Cyclops.

Kyala (Nyakyusa People, Tanzania)
Sky god. He was promoted from a local god to chief god, then to supreme god. At that time he was no longer worshiped, being too far above for petty worries of mortals.

Kybebe (Greek) *see* Cybele.

Kybele (Hittite) *see* Cybele.

Kyklopes (Greek) *see* Cyclops.

Kypris (Greek) *see* Aphrodite.

Kyrene (Greek)
Another spelling for Cyrene, the nymph queen of Libya.

Kyrgys-Khan (Altaic, Tartars)
With his brother Sary-Khan, he is a god of happiness. They are the grandsons of Bai Ulgan (q.v.).

L

L (Maya)
Aspects of known as: *"The Old Black God."*

He is shown toothless, with black paint covering one-half of his face. L may be the same as the Aztec Tepeyollotl (q.v.).

La Strega (Roman) *see* Befana.

La Vecchia (Roman) *see* Befana.

La'a Maomao (Polynesian) God of winds.

Labartu (Assyrian)
They are female demons who live in marshes and mountains. At one time it was thought that they kidnapped children. Later, they were considered benevolent. *See also* Lamassu.

Labosum (Saora People, India)
This earth god is offered rice and wine when a new home is built. He is implored to keep ants from eating the wood. Adununkisum, the sun god, is then offered a mango leaf filled with rice to keep the house safe from fire. *See also* Adununkisum.

Labyrinth (Greek)
The Labyrinth was built by Daedalus for king Minos to contain the Minotaur. *See also* Daedalus; Minos; Minotaur.

Lacedaemon (Greek)
Founder and king of Sparta. He is the son of Zeus and Taygete (q.v.).

Lachesis (Greek)
"Caster of Lots." She is one of the Fates (q.v.).

Lachmu (Babylon)
Also known as: *Lache.*
Deity of darkness. He is the husband of Lachama (Lachos). Some say Lachmu and Lachama are the parents of Anshar and Kishar. *See also* Anshar; Apsu; Kishar; Tiamat.

Lada (Romanian, Slavic)
Goddess of spring. Lado is the sun god spouse of Lada. In later times, Lada was venerated as an aspect of the Virgin Mary and was worshiped during the Christmas season.

Lado (Slavic) Husband of Lada (q.v.).

Ladon (A) (Greek)
Ladon, the son of Oceanus and Tethys, is the god of the river Ladon. *See also* Oceanus; Rivers; Tethys.

Ladon (B) (Greek) He traveled with Aeneas from Troy to Italy.

Ladon (C) (Greek) The name of a dog belonging to Actaeon.

Ladon (D) (Greek)
He is the hundred-headed and hundred-voiced dragon son of Phorcys and Ceto, or possibly Typhon and Echidna. Ladon and the Hesperides protected the garden where the Golden Apples were kept. When Heracles came to get the apples, he killed Ladon. Ladon became the constellation Draco. *See also* Ceto; Echidna; Evander (A); Heracles; Hesperides; Medusa; Phorcys; Typhon.

Ladru (Irish) *see* Cessair.

Lady Meng *Lady Ming* (China)
Goddess of Hell. *See also* Meng (A).

Lady of Heaven (Middle Eastern) *see* Anat.

Lady of Kazailu (Mesopotamia) *see* Martu.

Lady of Ninab (Mesopotamia) *see* Martu.

Lady of Sati (Egypt) *see* Anoukis; Anquet.

Lady of the Bed (China) *see* Ch'uang-Mu.

Lady of the Lake (Arthurian) *see* Vivien.

Laeapua (Hawaii, Polynesia)
God of fishers. He is the local god of Lanai who is associated with Kaneapua, who is also a god of fishers.

Laeding *Leding* (Teutonic)
Fenrir was first bound by a chain called Laeding, made of strong iron links. The second chain was called Dromi. The last and strongest chain was named Gleipnir. *See also* Fenrir; Gleipnir.

Laerad (Teutonic) *see* Ledrad.

Laertes (Greek)
King of Ithaca. Argonaut. Member of the Calydonia Boar Hunt. He is the son of Arceisius and Chalcomedusa, or Cephalus and Procis. He married Anticleia who may have already been pregnant by Sisyphus. His children are possibly Odysseus and Ctiemene. Laertes was one of Penelope's suitors. *See also* Anticleia (A); Argonauts; Sisyphus.

Laga (Teutonic) *see* Odin; Saga.

Lagamal (Sumer)
Son of a god. A deity of Elam who was believed to be the son of Ea.

Lagi (Polynesian) *see* Rangi.

Lahamu and Lahmu *Lachama and Lachmu, Lakhamu and Lakhmu.*
Also known as: *Asakku* (Assyro-Babylonian).
The dragons Lahamu and Lahmu were the first forms of life created by Apsu and Tiamat. Lahamu is the female, and Lahmu is the male. From their union, Anshar and Kishar were created. Lahamu is invoked when a building is completed. They are described as "hairy," or "muddy." They have three pairs of curls and are naked except for a triple sash. *See also* Anshar; Apsu; Kishar; Marduk; Tiamat.

Lahar (Sumer)
Created by Enlil (Ea in Babylonian mythology) and sent to earth by Enki, Lahar is the god of cattle. *See also* Ashnan; Ea; Enki; Enlil.

Lahmu *Lakhmu* (Assyro-Babylonia) *see* Lahamu.

Laima (Latvia)
Goddess of childbirth. Laima is one of the deities who accompany Latvians from birth to death.

Laius *Laios* (Greek)
King of Thebes. He is the son of Labdacus (who is the son of Polydorus and Ncyteis). Laius married Jocasta (also known as Epicasta), the daughter of Menoeceus. He is the father of Oedipus. *See also* Jocasta; Oedipus; Polydorus.

Lajnan (Micronesia) *see* Rigi.

Laka (A) (Hawaii)
Laka, the goddess of the wildwood, is the sister of Lono (q.v.).

Laka (B) (Hawaii) He is the ancestor of the Menehune people.

Lakchos (Greek) *see* Bacchus.

Lakemba (Polynesia) *see* Lothia; Miru.

Lakhamu *Lakhmu* (Sumer)

Huge serpents, the first deities to be born of Apsu and Tiamat. They in turn gave birth to Anshar and Kishar. *See also* Lahmu.

Lakhamu and Lakhmu (Assyro-Babylonian) *see* Lahamu.

Lakhe (Babylon) *see* Belus (B).

Lakhmu (Babylon) *see* Lahamu.

Lakhus (Babylon) *see* Belus (B).

Lakshmana (India)

He is the son of King Dasartha and Queen Sumitra, twin of brother Shatrughna, and faithful brother of Rama. *See also* Agastya; Bharata (A); Karttikeya; Rama; Ravana.

Lakshmi *Laksmi, Laxmi* (Buddhist, Jain, Hindu; India)

Also known as: *Devi Sri* (Noble Goddess), *Dharani* (an avatar), *Haripriya* (Beloved of Vishnu), *Jaganmatri* (Mother of the World), *Jaladhi-Ja* (Born in the Ocean), *Kamala* (an avatar), *Karisini* (One Possessing Dung), *Ksama* (Earth), *Lala, Luttchmeen, Mama Lakshmi, Matrirupa* (Mother of All Living Things), *Padma* (Lotus Goddess), *Phra Naret* (Siam), *Radha* (Lotus goddess), *Rohini* (an avatar), *Rukmini* (an avatar), *Shakti, Shri, Sita* (an avatar), *Sree, Sri, Varahini* (an avatar), *Vriddhi* (Goddess of Growth).

In early times, (pre–Vedic) Lakshmi was an earth goddess. Later, in the *Rig-Veda* she is known as Sri and Lakshmi. In the *Ramayana* she is a beautiful goddess of fortune and prosperity, one of the treasures born of the churning of the sea of milk. She emerged holding a lotus and proceeded to bestow blessings upon the universe. The deities were dazzled by her brilliance, and each one wanted her for a partner. She decided upon Vishnu as her mate, and in each of his ten avatars she is there as her avatar to join him in his activities. Her avatars as Vishnu's mate are Kamala or Padma, mate of Vamana (Vishnu's dwarf avatar); Dharani (meaning the Earth), mate of Parashur Rama; Sita, mate of Rama; Varahini, mate of Varaha; Radha, mate of Krishna; and some say Rukmini, another of Krishna's consorts. In some tales, Vishnu and Lakshmi are the parents of the god of love, Kama, and the goddess Tisnavati. In the *Purana*, Lakshmi is the daughter of Brighu and Khyati. Prior to her relationship with Vishnu, she was the consort of Agni and the mother of the three Agnis (fires). Lakshmi is a culmination of the aspects of the three great goddesses of Indian rivers, Ganga, Yamuna and Sarasvati. She is one of a Hindu Triad with Sarasvati and Devi. In this representation, she is known as the Red Goddess. As Karisini, she is the fertility goddess who gives soil, crops and animals. In some areas, aside from being the goddess of glory and prosperity, she is the goddess of rice. She is known to people who fish for a living as Empress of the Sea. Sacrifices are made to her for a good catch and a safe journey home. Lakshmi is approached by the faithful who desire children, fame, fortune, health, horses, cows, and by men who desire sons. She is also a favorite goddess of business people. She does not have temples, but is worshiped in the home. Lakshmi, the symbol of Vishnu's creative energy, is usually depicted seated and holding a pink or blue lotus. In some depictions, she has four hands; two hands are in the protective gesture (abhaya mudra), and in her other hands, she holds a mirror and a vermillion pot. Shown beautifully dressed, she is often accompanied by two dwarfs. She is also depicted seated or standing on her symbol, the lotus. Her complexion is golden and she sometimes has two arms. She is associated with the elephant, especially the white elephant known as Sri-gaja, who symbolizes rain and fertility. In Buddhist art, she is shown with two elephants. Her vehicle is the owl. This could be because the owl feeds on rodents which damage crops. As her companion, she is able to keep watch over owls and ensure agricultural prosperity. Lakshmi appears on the Parijata tree as a flower. A winter festival is held for Lakshmi and Kali, called Diwali (feast of lamps). During this period, the new moon in late October or early November (Kartik), bankers and merchants count their wealth. In Nepal an annual celebration takes place on the new moon night in November to celebrate Lakshmi. As the goddess of growth and charity, she is also celebrated on the Friday before the full moon in Sravana (July–August), in a festival known as Lakshmi-Vrata. In Sanskrit, the word lakshana means a "lucky sign," and the word laksha, "a luck mark." In the *Rig-Veda*, the word Lakshmi is used for "good luck." In the *Atharva Veda* there are two Lakshmis, one for good and one for bad luck. The Hindu reverence for the cow is based on the worship of Lakshmi, the beautiful goddess of material and spiritual prosperity. Lakshmi is comparable to Kishijoten, sister of Bishamon (Japan) (q.v.). She is also comparable to Vasundhara. Compare Lakshmi to Indrani and the Greek Venus. The Greeks compared Lakshmi to Artemis (q.v.). Lakshmi may be the same as or is associated with Ardhanariswara (q.v.) Sometimes, Lakshmi is said to have assisted Soma (q.v.). For other treasures retrieved from the churning of the sea of milk, *see* Kurma. *See also* Agni; Andhaka; Brighus; Devi; Ganga; Garuda; Kama (A); Krishna; Kurma (the tortoise avatar of Vishnu); Parashur Rama; Parijata Tree; Radha; Rama; Sarasvati; Shakti; Sisupala (regarding Rukmini); Sita; Soma; Sri; Tulasi; Vaikuntha; Vamana; Varaha; Varuna; Vishnu; Yami.

Lakshmi-Vrata (India) Festival. *See also* Lakshmi.

Laksmi (India) *see* Lakshmi.

Lala (Etruscan) *see* Diana; Lakshmi.

Lamashtu (Middle Eastern) *see* Anat; Lamassu.

Lamassu *Lamashtu, Lamastu, Lammea* (Babylonia, Hebrew, Sumer)

Also known as: *Labartu, Labasi, Lamme* (Sumerian).

Demoness. Forerunner of Lilith. She is probably a child-slaying demon similar to Lilith of the early Hebrews. Originally Lamassu was the Sumerian deity Lamme. She is said to be the daughter of the god of heaven, Anu. She attacks pregnant women and children. The mere mention of her name can strike terror in people. She has a violent temper and when she is on a rampage she will chase domestic animals and accost them with her bare hands. She can slide in and out of houses at will, terrifying the inhabitants. She might be shown as a winged animal.

She has also been depicted standing on the back of a wild ass, a serpent in each hand and suckling a wild pig and a jackal. Some say that she resembles a leopard and has the face of a lion. She is shown with wild hair and bare breasts. *See also* Abyzy; Labartu; Lamia; Lilith; Sedu.

Lambodara (India) *see* Ganesha.

Lamech (Sumer) *see* Lumha.

Lamhf hada (Celtic, Irish, Welsh) *see* Lugh.

Lamia (A) *Lamma, Lamiae* (Greek)
Lamia, the daughter of Belus and possibly Libya. She fell madly in love with the great god, Zeus. The ever-jealous Hera turned Lamia into a snake with the head and breasts of a woman. Hera killed all but one of Lamia's children. This drove Lamia insane. When she saw a child in its mother's arms she would seize the infant, tear it to pieces and devour it. She terrorized people until she was slain, possibly by Eurybatus, the son of Euphemus. *See also* Alcyoneus; Hera; Lamassu; Scylla; Sirens; Zeus.

Lamia (B) (Greek)
Lamia, the daughter of the sea god Poseidon, and Zeus are the parents of Sibyl Herophile.

Lamia (C) (Greek)
She was the monster of Crissan who roamed the land killing and eating humans at random. This ended when the Delphic Oracle recommended that mortals be sacrificed to her. The first person chosen was Alcyoneus, who with his brother Porphyrion were the strongest of the Giants. Before Alcyoneus was devoured, Eurybatus killed her.

Lamia (D) (Greek)
Lamia is a god who was worshipped at Eleusis.

Lamiae (Akkadian, Greek) *see* Lamia.

Lamis (Greek) *see* Agenor (A).

Lamma (Akkadian, Greek) *see* Lamia.

Lamme (Sumer) *see* Lamassu.

Lampethus *Lampetie* (Greek)
One of the Heliades, daughter of Helios or Apollo and Neaera. Lampethus and her sister, Phaethusa, were so devastated at the death of their half-brother Phaethon that they were turned into poplar trees and shed tears of amber. *See also* Aegle (A); Heliades; Helius; Phaethon (A).

Lampetie (Greek)
Another spelling for Lampethus, one of the Heliades (q.v.).

Lampon (Greek) *see* Helius.

Lampus (Greek)
He is the son of the king of Troy, Laomedon, and Leucippe, Placia or Strymo. *See also* Astyoche; Hesione; Priam.

Lamus (Greek)
His parents are Heracles and the queen of Lydia, Omphale. Heracles was Omphale's slave for three years. Lamus' siblings are Agelaos and Alcaeus. *See also* Heracles; Omphale.

Lan-ts'ai-ho (China)
Patron of Gardeners. *See also* Arhats; Eight Immortals.

Land of the Setting Sun (Egypt) *see* Ament.

Land of Women (Irish) *see* Tir na mBan.

Langal (Australia) *see* Rainbow Snake.

Langali (India) *see* Bala-Rama.

Langi (Polynesian) *see* Rangi.

Langit (Polynesian) *see* Rangi.

Lao-Tien-Yeh (China) *see* Yu Huang.

Lao-Tzu (Taoism; China) *Lao Tzu*
Also known as: *Shen Pao, T'ai-Shang Lao-chun.*
High god. Lao-Tzu is said by some to have lived in the first part of the 6th century B.C.E. and is thought to be the founder of Taoism. Other scholars debate his existence. In the Taoist tradition, Lao-Tzu became an immortal after death. He appeared in spirit form to Zhang Dao Ling about two centuries later and gave him the authority to establish the dogma and tenets of *Tao jiao*, or religious Taoism. His movement was known as the "Way of the Celestial Masters" *(Tien Shi)*. Lao-Tzu is the ruler of the third heaven (T'ai Ch'ing) and the teacher of kings and emperors. Once a mortal named Laotse or Lao Tze, he was later deified as Shen Pao and was associated with the San Ch'ing (The Pure Ones). In some versions he was connected with Confucius. He is possibly the same as Cheou-lao, the god of longevity. *See* Chang Tao-ling regarding the founders of existing Taoism. *See also* Shang Ch'ing; T'ai Ch'ing; Yu Ch'ing.

Laocoon (A) (Greek)
He is the son of the Trojan seer, Antenor, and a priestess of Athena, Theano. For the names of his siblings, *see* Theano. *See also* Acamas (B); Argonauts, Laodamas (A).

Laocoon (B) (Greek)
The son of Capys and Themiste, who is also the cousin of Capys, Laocoon is the brother of Anchises and husband of Antiope. *See also* Anchises; Antiope.

Laocoon (C) (Greek)
An Argonaut, Laocoon, the son of Oeneus, sailed on the Argo to protect his half-brother Meleager (q.v.).

Laocoon (D) (Greek)
The son of Priam and Hecuba, he was the Trojan priest of Apollo and the sea god Poseidon. It was Laocoon who warned his colleagues that there were soldiers in the Wooden Horse. *See also* Priam.

Laodamas (A) (Greek)
He is the son of the Trojan seer Antenor and Theano, who was a priestess of Athena at Troy and who also founded Padua after the fall of Troy. For a list of his siblings, *see* Theano. *See also* Acamas (B); Apsyrtus; Laocoon (A).

Laodamia (A) (Greek)
She is the daughter of Bellerophon and Philonoe. Her hus-

band (who may be her son by Zeus) is Sarpedon, and their child is Evander. *See also* Bellerophon; Evander (B); Sarpedon (A); Sarpedon (B).

Laodamia (B) (Greek)
She is the daughter of Acastus, the Argonaut king of Iolcus, and Astydameia, the daughter of Pelops and Hippodameia. Her siblings are Sterope and Sthenele. She has brothers who are unnamed. *See also* Acastus; Sterope; Sthenele.

Laodice (A) (Greek)
Also known as: *Electra.*
She is the daughter of Agamemnon and Clytemnestra. Her siblings are Chrysothemis, Iphigeneia and Orestes. *See also* Acamas (A); Agamemnon; Electra.

Laodice (B) (Greek)
The daughter of Priam and Hecuba. After the fall of Troy, she was swallowed by the earth. *See also* Hecuba; Priam.

Laodice (C) (Greek)
Cinyras, the king of Paphos in Cyprus, is her father.

Laomedon (Greek)
King of Troy. He is the son of Ilus, the wrestler and the fourth king of Troy and Eurydice. Laomedon contracted with Apollo and Poseidon to build the walls of Troy. When they had finished the project, Laomedon refused to pay them. The two gods sent a sea monster after him. Laomedon bribed Heracles to kill it. Again, Laomedon refused to pay for the services rendered. Furious, Heracles sent eighteen ships to Troy. Laomedon and all his sons except Priam were killed. *See also* Astyoche; Eurydice (C); Hesione; Poseidon; Priam.

Lapithae *Lapiths* (Greek)
The Lapithae were Thessalians ruled by Peirithous. They were constantly fighting with the Centaurs. *See also* Centaurs; Hippodamia (A).

Laphystios (Greek) *see* Dionysus.

Lara (A) (Roman)
Also known as: *Mania.*
Evil deity. A nymph. Mother of the Manes. She was too talkative so her tongue was cut out by Jupiter. *See also* Manes; Mania.

Lara (B) (Greek)
She is the wife of the messenger of the gods, Hermes, and the mother of the household gods, the Lares, according to some sources.

Larentia (Roman) *see* Acca Larentia.

Lares *Lars* (Etruscan, Roman, Greek)
Also known as: *Lar* (Singular), *Penates.*
Ancestor spirits. Gods of the home. The Lares are two ancient Etruscan gods, embraced by the Romans. Originally, they were thought to be spirits of the field. In later times, they represented deified spirits of ancestors, and their function was to shield descendants against harm. Each state had Lares and each household kept a Lar, likely in the form of a statue. Lares were orignally found in fields and later at intersections. The Lar of the household was acknowledged upon departure from

and arrival to the home, and at meals. Their queen may have been the earth or mother goddess, Acca Larentia. She was either the wife of Carutius or Faustulus and in either case was the nurse of Romulus and Remus. The household Lar is often depicted as a young man holding a drinking horn and cup. Their sacred animal is the dog. Some say the parents of the Lares are Hermes and Lara. Compare the Lares to Domovoi. *See also* Acca Larentia; Lupa; Romulus.

Larunda (Greek) *see* Muses.

Larvae (Roman)
This is another name for the ghosts known as Lemures (q.v.).

Lasema *Lasya, Sgeg-mo-ma* (Tibet)
Goddess of beauty. *See also* Akshobhya; Mamaki; Ratnasambhava.

Lasthenes (Greek)
He helped Eteocles defend the city of Thebes along with the Thebans, Actor, Hyperbius, Melanippus, Megareus, and Polyphontes. *See also* Adrestus; Eteocles; Melanippus.

Lasya (Tibet) *see* Lasema.

Lat (A) (Egypt) *see* Leto.

Lat (B) (Arabic) *see* Allat.

Latarak, God of Badtibira (Sumer) *see* Inanna.

Latmikaik (Pelew Islands, Micronesia)
Latmikaik, a sea goddess, rose from the waves. She brought forth fish, which built a tower that became earth. With her husband Tpereakl, she shared in governing the earth. She had two sons and it is possible mankind resulted from the joining of these to fish.

Latona (Roman)
She is the Greek Leto. *See also* Diana; Leto; Sekhmet.

Laufey (Teutonic)
Laufey is the giant mother of Loki and possible spouse of Farbauti. *See also* Loki.

Laukamat (Latvia)
Birth and death goddess. Goddess of fields. She accompanies Latvians from birth to death. *See also* Laima.

Laukosargas (Prussia)
God of fields and grain. He is similar to Lawkapatim (Polish).

Laume (A) (Prussia)
Goddesses of protection. They, along with Kaukis (small dwarfs and gnomes) protect the home. *See also* Kaukis.

Laume (B) (Lithuanian)
A supernatural hag, Laume rides around in her iron wagon, carrying a whip. She was once caught stealing from Perun's garden. *See also* Perun.

Laurin (Teutonic) *see* Andvari.

Lausus (A) (Greek)
"Scorner of the Gods." Lausus was a close friend of the Lord of Darkness, Turnus. He was killed by Aeneas. *See also* Abas (A); Aeneas; Turnus.

Lausus (B) (Greek) He is the brother of Rhea Silvia.

Lava (India) *see* Kusha.

Lavania (Greek) *see* Aeneas; Turnus.

Laverna (Roman) Goddess of thieves.

Lawgiver of Society (Nigeria; Africa) *see* Ala (B).

Lawkapatim (Polish, Slavic)

Field spirit. Her primary job is to preside over the tilling of the field. She is similar to Datan and Tawals and the Slavic gods, Kricco (fruits of the field) and Kirnis (god of ripening cherries). *See also* Datan; Laukosargas.

Laxmi (India) Another spelling for Lakshmi.

Laza (Islam)

The second stage in Daru el-Bawar, the Islamic Hell, Laza is reserved for Christians. *See also* Islamic Hell.

Learchus (Greek)

He is the son of Athamas and Ino. His father accidentally killed him. *See also* Ino.

Lebe (Dogon People, Africa)

One of the first people. Lebe is the oldest of the eight ancestors who came from heaven. He represented "word" or "speech." In a complex legend Lebe died or was swallowed by the seventh ancestor (a snake), but "word" remained as stones, so, in a sense, Lebe or language is represented by a stone. Lebe is associated with the Nummo spirits (q.v.).

Leda (Greek)

Her parents are Thestius and Eurythemis. Three of her siblings are Althaea, Hypermnestra and Plexippus. Leda's mortal husband is King Tyndareus, by whom she had Clytemnestra and Castor. She is the mother of Helen and Polydeuces by Zeus. For details to compare to other women who were seduced by Zeus in other forms: *see* Aegina; Antiope; Danae; Europa. *See also* Althea; Castor; Helen; Nemesis.

Leding (Teutonic) *see* Laeding.

Ledrad *Laerad* (Teutonic)

The upper bough of the Yggdrasil tree (q.v.).

Legba (Dahomey, Fon People, Africa)

Also known as: *Eschu*.

An individual's personal god, a god of the crossroads, and a trickster. The Legba statue represents the master of the house and placed in front of him are pots, which are members of his family. Numerous myths revolve around Legba. It is said that in the beginning Legba lived on earth with his supreme god. He only did what he was instructed to do by his god. When he did something harmful to fulfill his orders, the people blamed him, and eventually came to hate him. Finally, Legba approached his god and asked why the people should hate him as he was only fulfilling god's will? God responded that the ruler of a kingdom should be acknowledged and thanked for all good and his servants for all that is bad. This may be why Legba is sometimes considered to be a devil. In some versions Legba is a messenger of the twin deities, Mawu and Leza (Lisa), and generally associated with Eshu, Fa, and the thunder god Heviosso. Legba is shaped like a mound of clay with a molded phallus and covered with protective cover of thatch. *See also* Eshu; Fa (A); Leza.

Legend of the Four Suns (Aztec)

Also known as: *Legend of the Five Suns*.

First earths. There are several versions of this legend. 1. There were four eras before our own. The first era, known as Nahui Ocelotl, ruled by Tezcatlipoca, was called Tiger Sun, which lasted 676 years. Then inhabitants of the planet Earth were eaten by tigers and the sun vanished. The second sun (Nahui Ehecatl), ruled by Quetzalcoatl, was called the "Four Wind." At the end of 364 years mortals were swept away by fierce winds and the survivors changed into monkeys. The third sun, Nahui Quiahuitl, ruled by Tlaloc, was called "Four Rain." At the end of 312 years a terrible fire shower destroyed most of mankind, and all remaining mortals were changed into birds. The Fourth Sun, Nahui Atl, ruled by the goddess Chalchihuitlicue, was destroyed by a great flood after 676 years, and only a man and a women survived. The Fifth Sun, which is our current era, is called Nahui Ollin, or 4 Motion. Ruled by Xiuhtecuhth, it will end in earthquakes. 2. The name of the First Sun is Chalchuihutonatiuh; the Second Sun, Tletonatiuh; the Third Sun, Yohualtonatiuh; and the Fourth Sun, Ehecatonatiuh. 3. The names of the regents of the suns are Atonatiuh, the First Age; Tlalchitonatiuh, the Second Age; Ehcatonatiuh, the Third Age; and Tlatonatiuh, the fourth age. In this legend Quetzalcoatl appeared in the third sun age. 4. In this version, Tonacatecutli and Tonacaciuatl dwell in the thirteenth heaven. Four gods are born from them: Camaxtli, Tezcatlipoca, Quetzalcoatl, and Huitzilopochtli. From them came Oxomoco and Cipactonal (first man and woman). They created Mictlantecutli and Mictlanciuatl to be in charge of hell. Their next creation was Cipactli, a sea monster they used to shape the earth, and Tlaloctecutli and his wife Chalchiuhtlicue to have dominion over the sea. Oxomoco and Cipactonal had a son who married a woman formed from a hair of the goddess Xochiquetzal. This pair created a half sun which gave so little light the gods made another half sun which became Tezcatlipoca. In another version the various deities were named: Quetzalcoatl, Atonatiuh, Ocelotonatiuh, Quiyauhtonatiuh and Ecatonatiuh. The ancient belief of the people of Yucatan also has four ages of the world. Saiyamkoob were the first people who lived in darkness. They were followed by the Tsolob, who were destroyed by flood, then followed the Mayan civilization. *See also* Atonatiuh; Chicomoztoc; Nata; Tlazolteotl.

Lei-Kung (China)

Also known as: *My Lord Thunder*.

The god of thunder. Lei-Kung carries out punishment against the guilty who have escaped the law or whose crime was not discovered. At times, he solicits the aid of humans, rewarding them for furthering his work. He is depicted as an ugly man with claws and wings and a blue body, wearing nothing but a loin cloth and carrying a mallet. At his side hang his drums. He is associated with Tien Mu (Mother Lightning) Yu-tzu (Master of Rain), Yun-t'ung (Cloud God), and Feng-po (God of Winds). Sometimes Feng-po is replaced by the goddess Feng-p'o-p'o (Goddess of Winds). *See also* Kei-Kung.

Leipt (Teutonic) *see* Elivagar.

Leiriope (Greek)

The river god Cephissus and Leiriope are the parents of the beautiful, vain god, Narcissus. *See also* Cephissus; Narcissus.

Leische (Russian)

Spirit of the woods. He is worshiped in a circle of birch trees. One must face east and bend down and look between the legs and call for Uncle Leische to grant a wish or bargain for the soul.

Lelex (A) (Greek)

King of Megara. He is the son of the sea god, Poseidon, and Libya. His brothers are the twins, Agenor, the king of Phoenicia, and Belus, king of the Egyptians. *See also* Agenor (A); Belus (B).

Lemminikainen (Finnish)

Also known as: *Ahti, Ahto, Kaukomielli.*

Magician. His mother is the goddess, Ilmater, who is also a magician. He is the hero brother of Vainamoinen and Ilmarinen. In an attempt to kill a swan he was thrown into a river and drowned. His mother restored him to life. In another version of the myth, he is the consort of Wellamo or Vellamo. They live deep under the sea in a place called Ahtoia. He is holder of the treasure Sampo. Some say Lemminikainen bore the epithet Ahti so he could be both god and hero. *See also* Ahti; Ilmarinen; Louhi; Vainomoinen.

Lempo (Finnish) *see* Hiisi.

Lemures (Roman)

Also known as: *Larvae, Remuria.*

Spirits of the dead. They are evil spirits who return to wreak mischief and terror among the living. One of the Lemures is said to be the ghost of Remus.

Lenaeus (Greek)

"He of the Winepress." An epithet of Dionysus (q.v.).

Leodegrance (Celtic) Another name for Bran (q.v.).

Leodocus (Greek)

He is the Argonaut son of Bias, king of Argos, and Pero. For a list of siblings, *see* Pero.

Leprechaun *Lepracaun, Leprachaun, Leprecawn, Leprechawn, Lubrican* (Celtic, Irish)

Spirit. A small fairy who goes around looking like an old man. Leprechauns are known for their fine leather work; the shoes they craft are among the finest known. It is said that a leprechaun will divulge the location of his life savings if captured by the commanding glare of a mortal gaze. However, when bullied and threatened by thieves, leprechauns can be disagreeable. They are associated with the Cluricaune, who haunt cellars. *See also* Dana; Dwarfs.

Ler (Celtic) *see* LLyr.

Lerad (Teutonic)

Deified tree. The Lerad is topmost branch of the Yggdrasil tree. *See also* Yggdrasil.

Lernus (Greek)

He is the possible father of the Argonaut Palaemon. *See also* Hephaistos.

Leshacikha (Slavic)

She is the wife of the forest-dwelling shape changer, Leshy.

Leshonki (Slavic)

They are the children of Leshy and Leshacikha.

Leshy *Leshies* (plural), *Lesiy, Lesiye, Lyeshy, Lesovik* (Slavic)

Also known as: *Miehts-Hozjin.*

Forest faun or satyr. A shape changer of the wild areas. Some say he is the offspring of a mortal woman and a demon. Although not evil, he enjoys misdirecting mortals and kidnapping young women. He wears his shoes on the wrong feet. Leshy is the protector of all birds and animals in the forest. His protector is a bear. Humans can thwart him by putting their clothes on backwards. Leshy has a wife called Leshacikha and children known as the Leshonki. His shape is human, but his blood and skin tone are blue and he does not have a shadow. His eyes and beard are green. Often he appears like the devil, with horns, goat's feet and finger-claws. He is similar in nature to the field spirits known as Polevik (q.v.). *See also* Domovoi; Kalevala.

Lesiy (Slavic) *see* Leshy.

Lesovik (Slavic) *see* Leshy.

Lethe (Greek)

Deified river. This river, one of five in Hades, is known as the river of forgetfulness. When the soul travels this river all pain and anguish from the past is forgotten. The soul is prepared from this trip to enter the etheral Elysian Fields. The name of the river's nymph is also Lethe, the daughter of Eris (strife). The other four rivers in Hades are Acheron, the river of woe; Cocytus, the river of wailing; Phlegethon, the river of fire, and Styx. *See also* Acheron; Cocytus; Elysian Fields; Eris; Hades; Styx; Tartarus.

Leto (Greek)

Also known as: *Lat* (Egypt), *Latona* (Roman).

Goddess of light. Leto is the daughter of Ceos and Phoebe, sister of Asteria and mother by Zeus of the twins Apollo (the sun) and Artemis (the moon goddess and goddess of the hunt). Leto is identified by the Romans as Latona or Queen Lat and by the Egyptians as Lat, a fertility goddess of the date-nut and olive. Persecuted by the jealous Hera, who sent the serpent Python to harass her, she wandered the land searching for a safe place to give birth. Hera kept the goddess of birth, Ilythia, away from Leto, who suffered horribly for nine days. Iris, the messenger of the gods was able to locate Ilythia and guide her to Leto who had finally found solace on the desolate rock called Delos, which floated on water and was tossed about by waves. This rock was really Asteria, Leto's sister, who had resisted the sexual overtures of Zeus and was turned into a quail and then a rock. Even here Leto had to promise that with the birth of Apollo the land would become fertile and worshippers would come from afar to honor the birth of the sun deity. Now Zeus, who had originally abandoned Leto because of his fear of Hera, came forth in appreciation and anchored Delos to the floor of the sea. Poseidon has also been credited with this deed. Out of deference to Hera, who swore that Leto would not give birth where the sun shone, he erected a dome over the rock and four pillars that reached the bottom of the sea. Other myths are easier on Zeus. They say that he altered Leto's appearance from a woman to a quail, which allowed her to escape Hera's wrath and fly to Delos. Leto was also called the personification of darkness. Niobe, the wife of Amphion, the king of Thebes, and the mother of fourteen children made facetious remarks to Leto for only having two children and further insulted her by saying that her female child, Artemis, was masculine and her male child, Apollo, was feminine. Enraged, Leto sent Apollo to murder the sons of Niobe and Artemis to murder the woman's daughters. Apollo spared Amyclas and Artemis spared Meliboea. *See also* Aeneas; Amphion; Apollo; Artemis; Ceos; Hera; Ilythia; Iris; Niobe; Zeus.

Leucippe (A) (Greek)

The daughters of Minyas, Leucippe, Alcithoe and Arsippe were driven insane by Dionysus when they refused to honor him. While in a music-induced frenzy, the three sisters killed Hippasus, Leucippe's son. *See also* Alcithoe; Calchas; Dionysus; Minyas.

Leucippe (B) (Greek)

She is the daughter of Thestor and Megara.

Leucippus (A) (Greek)

He is the son of Oenomaus and Evarete and the brother of Hippodameia. *See also* Gorgophone; Hippodameia (B); Oenomaus.

Leucippus (B) (Greek)

His parents are Perieres and Gorgophone. *See also* Borus; Gorgophone; Icarius.

Leucopeus (Greek) *see* Calydonian Boar Hunt.

Leucosia (Greek) One of the Sirens (q.v.).

Leucothea (Greek)

Also known as: *Ino, Mater Matuta, White Goddess.*

Leucothea is the name given to Ino by the Nereids after she drowned and was made into a sea goddess. *See also* Ino; Nereids.

Leucothoe (Greek)

She is the daughter of the king of Persia, Orchamus, and Eurynome. Her father buried her alive when he heard about her love affair with Apollo. She turned into a frankincense bush. *See also* Apollo; Clytia; Eurynome; Helius.

Leviathan (Gnostic; Babylon, Ugarit.)

Also known as: *Livyathan* (Hebrew), *Nakhash, Rahabh, Tannin.*

This serpent was slain by Gabriel with the assistance of Yahweh. Gabriel made a tent from the skin of Leviathan to cover the walls of Jerusalem. Compare Leviathan to Tiamat and Mot. In some renditions, Leviathan is the same as the dragon Lotan (meaning "covering") of the Ugarites, who was slain by Baal. *See also* Apepi; Rahabh.

Leza *Lisa* (Bantu People, Africa)

Also known as: *Chilenga, Lubumba, Reza, Rezha.*

High god. Leza is generally thought of as being a god of lightning or rain. It seems that different names denote different functions of this god. The name may supersede Mpambe, Chiuta, and the early Leza of the Yaos of Africa. Some say Leza is a god-

dess and as such is either the wife or mother of Mawu. Some also say she is one of a triad along with Mawu and Ge. When associated with Mawu she is an androgynous deity called Mawu-Lisa. In some versions both Leza and Mawu are the twins of Nana Buluku who was the female creator of everything. Leza is shown as chameleon. *See also* Lisa; Mahu.

Lha-mo (Tibet) *see* Dakinis.

Lhamo *Lha Mo* (Buddhist, Hindu; India)

Lhamo, a defender goddess is an important goddess to the Tibetans. She is often found in a corner behind a curtain in monasteries. The only feminine divinity of the Dharma Palas (Eight Terrible Ones), and the only defender goddess of the Mahayana school. She was outfitted with weapons by the gods. To determine the fate of mortals, she has two die given to her by Heybajra. Brahma gave her a peacock feather fan and Vishnu gave her a lion which she wears in her right ear. In her left ear hangs a serpent, given to her by Nanda, the serpent. Vajrapani gave her a hammer. Other gods presented her with a mule covered by the skin of a demon, with reins of venomous serpents. Lhamo is depicted seated side-saddle on her mule. Her expression is fierce and she has a third eye. Covered in a tiger skin, she wears a long garland of heads. In her right hand, which is raised, she carries a scepter and in her left, a skull cup which is held at her breast. *See also* Brahma; Kali; Nanda, Vajrapani; Vishnu.

Li (China) *see* T'ieh-Kuai.

Li Hun (China)

Hero or god of ceremonies. One of the nine heroes, Li Hun is worshiped as a god of ceremonies. *See also* T'ieh-kuai Li.

Li T'ieh-Kuai (China) *see* T'ieh-Kuai.

Lia Fail (Celtic)

Deified object. The Stone of Destiny. It was brought to Ireland by the Tuatha De Danann and was placed at the Hill of Tara. Upon this stone are crowned the kings of Ireland. The voice of the stone will groan its mighty approval when a worthy king rides across it. It will remain silent if the ruler is unworthy.

Liaksit (Yakut People, Siberia)

Another spelling for Ajysyt, goddess of childbirth and domestic animals.

Libanza (Upotos People, Congo, Africa)

Evil deity. Supreme god. He is probably associated with the moon, since he allowed the moon to die only twice each month, but because mortals did not obey his wishes they had to die permanently.

Liber (Roman)

Also known as: *Bacchus.*

Fertility god. Liber is the Roman equivalent of the Greek god of wine, Bacchus. He is the husband of Libera, goddess of wine, who is identified with the Greek Persephone. Liber and Libera are worshiped with Ceres. *See also* Agdistis; Bacchus; Dionysus.

Liber Pater (Roman) *see* Dionysus.

Libera (Roman) Goddess of wine. She is the wife of Liber.

Libertas (Roman) Goddess of liberty.

Libitina (Roman)
Goddess of death. Underworld goddess. She is worshiped in a similar way to Persephone.

Libya (Greek)
Libya is the daughter of the son of Zeus and Io, Epaphus, and Memphis, the daughter of the river god, Nile. She married Triton, the son of the sea god Poseidon, and Amphitrite, goddess of the sea. Libya is the mother of Lelex and by Poseidon, the twins Agenor and Belus. There is a possibility that she is the mother of Lamia by her son, Belus. See also Agenor (A); Belus; Lamia; Lelex.

Lidskialf (Teutonic) see Hlidskjalf.

Lidskjalf (Teutonic) see Hlidskjalf.

Lie-Kung (China) see Kei-Kung

Lif (Norse; Teutonic)
Also known as: Life.
Lif is the mortal who will survive after Ragnarok by hiding in the tree of life, Yggdrasil. He will father the new race of humans. His mate is Lifthrasir (meaning "eager for life"). In some versions of this myth, Lif is female and Lifthrasir is male. See also Ragnarok; Yggdrasil.

Life (Teutonic) see Lif.

Lifthrasir (Teutonic) see Lif; Ragnarok.

Ligeia (Greek)
She is the daughter of Achelous and Calliope and is one of the Sirens. See also Sirens.

Light (Phoenician) see Kolpia.

Light Bearer, The (India) see Ushas.

Lightning Man (Australia) see Mamaragan.

Ligoapup (Micronesia) see Ligobund.

Ligobund (Micronesia, Caroline Islands)
Also known as: Luk.
He is a creator god who made earth habitable, then gave birth to three children who were the first humans. In another rendition of this myth, it was Luk who did this, and it was his daughter (Ligoapup) and her daughter's son (who was made from the rib of this son) who married Ligoapup and started the human race. Another version tells that Ligoapup bore a girl first, then from her arm came a boy and from her eye another boy, then from her other eye another girl. In some versions Luk is thought to be the highest deity, and his wife is Inoaeman. He is also said to have a sister named Rat. Some legends say he is the lord of all who are evil and deceitful. Possibly Ligoapup is the same as Ligoububfanu from the island of Truk. She is the wife of Anulap and a creator deity. See also Ligoububfanu; Luk; Nareau; Yelafaz.

Ligoububfanu (Island of Truk, Micronesia)
Creator. The wife of Anulap who was possibly a creator also.

Similar to, or may be the same as, Ligoapup of the Caroline Islands. See also Ligobund.

Likho (Slavic)
"Evil One." She has one eye and is the personification of evil. See also Lyeshy.

Liknites (Greek) see Dionysus.

Lil (Sumerian) see Enlil.

Lilavati (India) "Charming Woman." See also Devi.

Lilis (Hebrew) see Lilith.

Lilith *Lillity* (Hebrew)
Also known as: Ailo, The Harlot, Lilis, Queen of the Demons.
First woman. Queen of demons. As the first wife of Adam, she was rejected because she was not quite human. The ancient Hebrew people said that she refused to submit to Adam. She learned the sacred name "Yahveh" and therefore received wings and flew to Paradise. Her curse was that every child she had would die in infancy. After she tried to kill herself, the supreme god gave her power over all infants until they were eight days old, unless they were protected by the angels Sanoi, Sansenoi, and Sanmangalaph. In order to protect their new children, the early Hebrews hung an amulet around the child's neck, with "Sen, Sam, San," written on it. She has special power over illegitimate children, and she catches youths with her kisses. She is similar in nature to the Sumerian demon Alu under the guise of Ailo. She is also similar to the Babylonian deity Lamashtu. The word "lil" means a spirit of the same kind as the afreets (unclean spirits) of the Arabic People of the present day. Lillity, a feminine form, is a female evil spirit with the habits of a vampire in the demonology of the Jewish People. These gods or spirits rule the world of the night, darkness and evil and are hostile to humans. The only protection from them is through the use of magic spells and incantations. See also Agrat Bat Mahalat; Alu; Gallu; Gelu; Lilu.

Lilithu (Sumer, Baylonia) see Lilu.

Lilitu (Sumer, Babylonia) see Lilu.

Lilli (Sumer, Babylonia) see Lilu.

Lillith (Akkadian) see Lamassu; Lilith.

Lillity (Semite) see Lilith.

Lillu (Babylonia, Sumer) see Lilu.

Lilu *Lilithu, Lilitu, Lilli* (Babylon, Sumer)
Also known as: Lilith (possibly).
Demon. This spirit of lasciviousness entices women in their sleep. He is the counterpart of Lilli and may be related to Lilith of the Hebrews. Lilu is associated with the Babylonian demons Alu, Gallu, Lamashtu, Utukku.

Limnades (Greek)
The Limnades are dangerous nymphs who reside in lakes and swamps. See also Naiads.

Ling-Pao T'ien-Tsun (China)
Also known as: Tao Chun.
High god. Ruler of T'ai Ch'ing, the second heaven of the San

Ch'ing, Ling-Pao is the Guardian of the Sacred Books and the god of keeping time. *See also* San Ch'ing; Yu Ch'ing.

Lingodbhava (India) *see* Shiva.

Linus (Greek)
He is the son of Ismenius. Heracles, Orpheus and Thamyris were taught to play the lyre by Linus. Heracles, in a rage, killed his teacher with the lyre. *See also* Heracles; Orpheus.

Liomarar (Island of Yap, Micronesia)
Creator deity. She threw sand to create the island of Ulithi. Her daughter, Lorop, had three sons, one of whom is Motiki-tik (q.v.).

Lion with the Steady Hand (Celtic) *see* Llew Llaw Gyffes.

Liosalfar (Teutonic) *see* Alfar.

Lipaurus (Greek)
He is the father of Cyane who married Aeolus and became the mother of six sons and six daughters who married each other. *See also* Aeolus (B).

Lir (Irish)
Also known as: *Llyr* (Wales)
Lir is a well known local sea god who lived on the coast of Antrim. One of his children (by Penardun) who became notable is Manannan (Manawydan Ap Llyr). He is also the father of Bran by Iweridd. Some say that he is the father of Creiddylad or Cordelia. *See also* Creiddylad; Llyr; Manannan Mac Llyr.

Lisa *Leza, Lissa* (Dahomey, Fon People, Africa)
Also known as: *Chilenga, Mawa-Lisa* (androgynous), *Mawu, Mawu-Lisa, Reza, Rezha.*
Sky deities. Twins born to Nana Buluku. Lisa, the male, is god of the sun, sky and power, and is called the Chameleon. Mawu, the female is goddess of earth, moon and fertility. In some aspects this is an androgynous deity known as Mawu-Lisa. In male form, Mawu was a creator and part of the trinity Lisa, Ge, and Mawu. In another version Lisa is a mother goddess whose sons were Mawu (the sun) and Gou (the moon). *See also* Leza; Mahou.

Lit (Teutonic) *see* Dwarfs.

Little Cat (Egypt) *see* Bast.

Liu-Hai (China)
God of wealth. Liu-Hai is shown as a boy holding a string of gold cash over his head. A large tree-footed, money-distributing toad is biting the string.

Liu Pei (China) God of basket makers and straw shoe makers.

Livyathan (Hebrew) *see* Leviathan.

Ljod (Teutonic) *see* Angerboda; Gullveig.

Ljosalfaheim (Teutonic) *see* Alfheim.

Llampallec (Andean) *see* Naymlap.

Llaw Erent (Celtic) *see* Llud.

Llaw Gyffes (Celtic) *see* Llew Llaw Gyffes.

Llawerein (British) *see* Llud.

Llediaith (Celtic) *see* Llyr.

Lleu (Celtic) *see* Llew Llaw Gyffes.

Lleu Llaw Gyffes (Celtic) *see* Llew Llaw Gyffes; Lugh.

Llew (Celtic) *see* Arianrhod.

Llew Llaw Gyffes *Lleu Llaw Gyffes* (Celtic)
Also known as: *Llaw Gyffes, Lleu, Llew, Lugus.*
Llew Llaw Gyffes, a sun deity and corn divinity, is the son of Arianrhod and possibly her brother, Gwydion. His twin brother, Dylan, was thrown into the sea by Arianrhod or his uncle Math, where he became a sea deity. Gwydion saved Llew, disguised him as a shoemaker and raised him. Arianrhod placed a "guise" on her son which ruled that he would never have a name, a mortal wife, nor weapons. Gwydion, through the use of trickery was able to revoke the "guise." Gwydion and Math made a beautiful wife for Llew Llaw Gyffes from a tree and an assortment of blossoms. Her name is Blodeuwedd. She was born without a soul and soon betrayed her husband by sleeping with the lord of darkness, Gronw Pebyr. In order to kill her husband she had to trick him into revealing the secret of his vulnerability. He was only vulnerable when he had one foot on a cauldron, the other on a buck (or billy-goat), with his hair tied to an oak branch. In other versions, the setup is similar but the spear used to kill him had to be forged on a specific day a year before death. The scene was finally set and Gronw Pebyr aimed the weapon and struck Llew Llaw Gyffes in the groin. His hair tied to the oak branch saved him from touching the ground. He turned into an eagle. Gwydion tended his wound and with his magic returned the man to his mortal form. Llew Llaw Gyffes returned to his home and killed Gronw Pebyr. In other renditions, Llew Llaw's vulnerable spot, like Achilles, is his heel. Llew Llaw means "Lion with the Steady Hand." He is associated with the eagle. Compare Llew to the Irish Lugh. *See also* Arianhod; Blodeuwedd; Gwydion; Math.

Llud *Lud, Ludd* (British)
Also known as: *Argetlam* (Celtic; "The Silver Handed"), *Ereint, Llaw Erent* (Gaul), *Llawerein* (British; "The Silver Handed"), *Llud Llaw, Nodens, Nuada, Nud, Nudd* (Welsh).
The city of London was named in honor of the river god Llud. The city's original name was Caer Ludd, and the temple of Llud was atop Ludgate Hill. It is thought by some researchers that Llud displaced the earlier goddess of the Thames, Tamesis. Llud has an artificial silver hand. Compare Llud to Nuada.

Llud Llaw (Celtic) *see* Llud; Nuada.

Llwch Lleu (Celtic, Irish, Welsh) *see* Lugh.

Llyr *Ler* (Wales), *Lir* (Irish)
Also known as: *Llediaith, Llyr Marini.*
Llyr is the same as the Irish sea god, Lir. *See also* Bran; Branwen; Manwydan Ap Llyr.

Lmahuika (Polynesia)
Underworld deity. This goddess rules the edges of the underworld. She may be same as Locha, Lothia, and Miru.

Lmylitta (Babylon) Goddess of fertility. Goddess of childbirth.

Lnyiko (Cameroon)

God of divination. He is the son of Nyokon and Mfan who was driven from heaven by his father.

Lo Ching Hsin or T'ien Pao (China) *see* Yu Ch'ing; Yuan-shih T'ien-Tsun.

Lo-lupe (Hawaii)

Also known as: *Olo-pue, Ololupe.*

God of Maui. Conductor of the souls of dead chiefs. He is invoked in the rite of deification of the dead and resurrection of the dead. Warriors greatly fear this god. Lo-lupe is depicted in the form of a lupe (kite) shaped like a sting ray. Other conductors of the souls of dead chiefs are Ka-onohi, also called Ka-onohi-o-ka-la (the eyeball of the sun) and Ku-waha-ilo (Ku of the maggot-dripping mouth). *See also* Ku and Hina.

Loa (Polynesia, Marshall Islands)

Creator. Loa created everything with the aid of a seagull who wove the dome of heaven.

Locana (India)

"Buddha Eye." *See also* Akshobhya; Dhyani Buddhas; Maitreya.

Locha (Polynesia) *see* Lmahuika; Lothia; Miru.

Lodar (Teutonic) *see* Loki.

Lodbrok (Teutonic) *see* Ragnar Lodbrog.

Lodder (Teutonic) *see* Loki.

Lodur (Teutonic) *see* Loki.

Lofn (Norse; Teutonic)

Goddess of love. Some say she is the goddess who smiles on illicit unions and sparks passionate love. Others say her task is to remove obstacles from the path of lovers. In some versions, she is an attendant of Frigg. *See also* Frigg.

Loge (Teutonic) *see* Logi.

Logh (Celtic) *see* Aesar (B).

Logi *Loge* (Norse, Finnish; Teutonic)

Also known as: *Flames.*

He is the giant fire god who beat Loki in an eating match in the court of Utgard-Loki. Logi is identified with Loki (q.v.).

Logos (Egypt, Alexandria)

Also known as: *Jesus.*

Gnostic version of the son of god. Aspect of Jesus. Arius of Alexandria attempted to revive Sabellianism about 318 C.E. He said that god's son, Logos, created the world. Logos is generally regarded as meaning "reason." Logos is associated with Sophia (reason and wisdom). *See also* Jesus; Sarasvati.

Loha-Mukha (India)

A race of iron-faced male cannibals who each have one leg.

Loka (Buddhist, Hindu; India).

In Tibetan Buddhism, Loka is one of the three divisions of the universe. In Hinduism, there are three or seven Lokas, heaven, earth and hell, often called Tri-Loka (Triloka), and Sapta-Loka, the seven-world universe. There is mention of an eight-world universe and also detailed descriptions that mention fourteen Lokas, seven that rise above the earth and seven that descend from the earth. The seven worlds of Sapta-Loka are the earth known as Bhur-Loka; the abode of the Munis and Siddhas, located between the earth and the sun and known as Bhuvar-Loka; Indra's heaven, located between the sun and the pole-star, known as Swarga or Svar-Loka; the abode of Bhrigus and other saints, Marar-Loka; the abode of Brahma's children, Jana-Loka; the abode of the Vairajas (also known as Vairagis), the ascetics, known as Tapa-Loka and Pitri-Loka; Brahma's abode, known as Satya-Loka, where he resides with other immortals. Other realms are Soma-Loka, the abode of the moon and planets, Gandharva-Loka for heavenly spirits, Rakshasa-Loka for demons and Pishacha-Loka for imps. The Lokaloka mountains, located beyond the farthest of the seven seas, divides the visible world from the infinite darkness beyond. *See also* Gandharvas; Meru Mountain; Naraka (B); Pretas; Swarga; Vaikuntha; Yama.

Lokaloka Mountains (India) *see* Loka.

Lokamatri (India) *see* Gauri.

Lokanatha (India) *see* Samantabhadra.

Lokapalas, The (Brahmanic, Buddhist, Hindu, Vedic; India)

Also known as: *Great Kings,* (Buddhist), *Jig-rten-skyon* (Tibet).

This is a name given to the Vedic deities who became protective spirits under Brahmanism. They are the guardians of the eight quarters of the world. In the Buddhist world, they live around Meru Mountain and guard the entrance to the Buddhist paradise of Sukhavati. The Lokapalas are also known as the eight Hindu gods and their elephants. They guard the eight main points of the compass. Indra and his elephant Airavata (in the *Ramayana,* "Virupaksha") guard the east. Yama and his elephant Vamana (in the *Ramayana,* "Mahapadma") guard the south. Agni and his elephant Pundarika guard the southeast. Sometimes Kuverva is substituted for Agni. Surya or Nirriti and the elephant Kumuda guard the southwest. Varuna and his elephant Anjana (in the *Ramayana,* "Saumanasa") guard the west. Vayu and his elephant Pushpa-danta guard the northwest. Kubera and Savabhauma (in the *Ramayana,* "Himapandara") guard the north and either Soma or Prithiva or Shiva and Supratika guard the northeast. The demon Ravana claims that he is the guardian of the fifth world, the center. Compare the Lokapalas to the male guardians of the gates of Bardo, *see also* Amrtakundali. *See also* Agni; Chakravala (Buddhist Universe); Dhartarastra (regarding the Four Great Kings); Dikpalas; Gandharvas; Ganesha; Indra; Niritti; Prithiva; Ravana; Shiva; Soma; Sukhavati (Paradise); Surya; Takshaka; Varuna; Vasuki; Vayu; Virudhaka; Virupaksha; Yama.

Loke (Teutonic) *see* Fjalar; Loki.

Lokeswar (Nepal) *see* Lokeswara.

Lokeswara *Lokeswar* (Buddhist; Nepal, India)

Also known as: *Avalokitesvara.*

Lord of the world. There are said to be one hundred and eight forms of Lokeswara, who is a form of Avalokitesvara. This form was assumed when the Buddhist pantheon incorporated

Shiva. One form is Chintamani Lokeswara, the Lokeswara of the wishing gem, who is said to dispense jewels and wealth to his devotees. Chintamani is richly ornamented. He wears a sacred thread of jewels and earrings and a full blown lotus at each shoulder. *See also* Avalokitesvara; Shimhanada Lokeshara; Sristikanta Lokeswara.

Loki (Norse; Teutonic)

Also known as: *Fjalar, Loder, Lodur, Loke, Lokkju, Lopter, Lopti, Sagloki, Suttung, Thok* (possibly), *Utgard-Loki.*

In some legends Loki appears evil and in others a faithful ally of Odin and other gods. He is known as a culture hero, and one of the Aesir. In other myths, he is a fire and strife demon, and a trickster. As Utgard-Loke, he was first conceived a fire demon, who also caused earthquakes and optical illusions. He may also have originated as a giant, though other myths indicate he was related to the dwarfs. He is said to be the father of Neri (Norine). In some myths Loki has a brother named Byleipt, Byleipter, or Byleist, although Loki was called Lopter at the time. In some versions, as Loder, he was the brother of Odin and Hoener. His mother is Laufey and his father Farbauti, who is also known as the father of Bleifstr, and Helblindi (a name given to Odin). He became the god of strife and the spirit of evil, possibly because he swallowed the half-burned heart of Gullveig. Myth has it that after doing so, he gave birth to the wolf Fenrir, the Nithog serpent and Hel, mistress of the underworld, all considered monsters. He caused the death of Balder by convincing the blind Hoth to throw mistletoe at him, the only thing said to have been able to kill him. Balder would have been allowed to leave Hel if every living thing would weep for him. When Loki heard of this edict, he took on the form of a woman and became the one exception and would not weep for him. He is said to have originally obtained Thor's hammer from the dwarfs and is also credited with the invention of the fishing net. Once, in the form of a mare he enticed away the horse of the giant who was building the walls of Asgarth in order to make him break his contract. In this legend he gives birth to Othin's eight-legged horse, Sleipnir. He has been called the Sly One, the Trickster, the Shape Changer, and the Sky Traveler and is said to have flown around in Freyja's falcon feathers. He was finally chained to a rock, where a serpent dripped venom on him and where he is to remain until the Twilight of the Gods (also known as Ragnarok). His wife, Sigyu stays with him and catches the poison in a dish. In the holocaust at the end of the world, Loki will lead the forces of Midgard. Midgard is the part of the world inhabited by men, imagined as a fortress encircled by a huge serpent, built by the gods around the middle region of the universe. *See also* Aeigir; Aesir; Balder; Fafni; Farbuti; Fenrir; Fjalar; Fornjotnr; Freyja; Gullin-Bursti; Gullveig; Gungnir; Heimdall; Hel; Helblindi; Henir; Huehuecoyotl (Aztec); Hugi; Idun; Jormungandr; Logi; Midgard; Neri; Nott; Odin; Ragnarok; Ran; Thok; Thor; Vili; Ymir.

Lola (India) Goddess of fortune.

Lone Man (Native North American) *see* Maninga.

Longo Rongo-Ma-Tane (Polynesia) *see* Lono; Rongo.

Loni (Teutonic) *see* Dwarfs.

Lono (Polynesia, Hawaii)

Also known as: *Longo Rongo-Ma-Tane, Ono, Rongo*

God of thunder, rain and darkness. God of fertility. God of agriculture. God of singing (in the Marquesas). One of the triad with Kane and Ku. He is associated with cloud signs and the phenomena of storms. He is offered first fruits in Polynesia. His sister is Laka, the goddess of the wildwood. In Hawaiian mythology the tale is told that one day, Lono came down to a rainbow in search of a wife. He found her and they lived happily together until he heard that she had been unfaithful. He beat her to death. Later, he felt very sorry that he had killed her. To assuage his heaviness of heart, he initiated games and feasts in her honor. Lono climbed into his canoe (filled with provisions) and sailed away, promising to return one day with a bountiful island. So it was that it became a tradition to hold an annual festival of five days full of feasts, processions, fun and sports. In a variation, Lono sent his two brothers from island to island in search of a wife for him. They came upon a beautiful woman known as Ka-iki-lani who lived with the birds in a breadfruit grove. Lono descended on a rainbow and took her as a wife. She became the goddess Ka-iki-lani-ali'i-o-Puna. They lived a blissful life and often surfed together. An earth chief made love to Lono's woman and the pardisical environment was destroyed. Infuriated, he beat her to death even though she proclaimed her innocence. In this rendition, as in the prior one, he feels sorry, initiates games in her honor, hops into a canoe and sails away. Prayers are offered to Lono for rain, abundant crops, or escape from illness and travails. His symbol is a straight wooden post ten to fifteen feet long with approximately a ten-inch circumference. It is topped by a knob, which some say represents a bird. Near the top a cross-piece about sixteen feet long is tied. Feather wreaths hang from it and at each end lengthy streamers of white tapa cloth hang. This representation is called Lono-makua (Father Lono). Lono is identified with Rongo (q.v.). *See also* Hika-po-loa; Hina-ula-ohia; Kane; Ku.

Lopamudra (India) *see* Agastya.

Lopemat (Latvia) Creator and goddess of cattle.

Lopter (Teutonic) *see* Loki.

Lord Nose (Aztec) *see* Yacatecuhti.

Lord of Elephantine (Egypt) *see* Khnum.

Lord of the Bed (China) *see* Ch'uang-Kung.

Lord of the Dance (India) *see* Nataraja.

Lord of the Gallows (Teutonic) A title for Odin.

Lord of the Land of Tehennu (Egypt) *see* Ash.

Lord of the Land of the Olive Tree (Egypt) *see* Ash.

Lord of the Magic Tooth (Maya) *see* Ahau-Chamahez.

Lord of the Regent of Death (Mexico) *see* Miclantecutl.

Lord of the Winds (China) *see* Yu Shih.

Lords of the Day Hours (Aztec)

The hours of day and night are ruled by gods. There are thirteen Lords of the Day. The Lords of the Day are (1) Xiuhtecuhtli, (2) Tlaltecuhtli, (3) Chalchihuitlicue, (4) Tonatiuh, (5) Tlazolteotl, (6) Teoyaoimquit, (7) Xochipilli, (8) Tlaloc, (9) Quetzalcoatl, (10) Tezcatlipoca, (11) Mictlantecuhtli, (12) Tlauixcalpantecuhtli, and (13) Ilamatecuhtli. *See also* Lords of the Night Hours, and individual deities listed.

Lords of the Night Hours (Aztec)

There are nine Lords of the Night Hours. They are (1) Xiuhtecuhtli, (2) Itzli, (3) Piltzintecutli, (4) Cinteotl, (5) Mictlancihuatl, (6) Chalchihuitlicue, (7) Tlazolteotl, (8) Tepeyollotl, and (9) Tlaloc. *See also* Lords of the Day Hours, and individual deities listed.

Lorop (Micronesia)

She is the daughter of the creator, Liomarar. Lorop has three sons, one of whom is Motikitik, the hero god. *See also* Lowa; Motikitik.

Lorride (Teutonic) *see* Thor.

Lorridi (Teutonic) *see* Thor.

Lotan (Ugarit) *see* Baal; Leviathan.

Lothia (Loyalty Islands, Polynesia.)

Also known as: *Lakemba, Locha.*

Deity of the afterworld. Lothis is the goddess who rules the afterworlds. She might be same as Miru, or Lmahuika. *See also* Hiro; Miru; Rohe; Urutaetae.

Lothurr (Teutonic) "The Fighter." *See also* Thor.

Loucetius (British, Celtic) *see* Cocidius; Tuetates.

Louhi (Finnish; Lapland)

Goddess of evil. Louhi is a sorceress who rules the land of Pohja. According to some she bargained with Vainamoinen the magician and musician to exchange the talisman sampo for her daughter. She reneged on her bargain and allowed her daughter to marry the smith Ilmarinen, who made the magic sampo. In the Lapland version of this tale, she is the mistress of Pohjoa the sorcerer and a goddess of fog and wind. *See also* Lemminkainen; Pohja; Sampo; Vainomoinen.

Louquo (Carib People)

First man. He came down from the sky and after creating humans from his body, returned to heaven.

Loviatar (Finnish)

Goddess of disease. She is the wife of the wind and mother of nine monsters of disease. She is the daughter of the Lord of Tuonela (the underworld), who is also the god of death, Tuoni, and Tuonetar, and the sister of Kivuatar, Kipu-Tytto and Vammater. They live in Manala. Loviatar is described as having a large face and wrinkled skin. *See also* Manala; Tuonela; Tuonetar; Tuoni.

Lowa (Micronesia)

Creator god. It is not certain whether Lowa came from the sky or the sea. He created the Marshall Islands by emitting the sound "Mmmm." The first humans, a boy and a girl, issued forth from a blood blister on his leg. *See also* Lorop; Tangaloa.

Loxias (Egypt) *see* Apollo.

Loz (Babylon)

With Nergal and Ninmug he ruled Meslam, the underworld. *See also* Nergal.

Lu-Hsing (China)

The god of salaries. Born mortal, Lu-Hsing was deified and given immortality. He is associated with the gods of happiness and long life. His symbol is the deer, Lu, on which he is often mounted.

Lu-ma *Gita, Ghirdhima* (Tibet)

Goddess of music and song. *See also* Gita.

Lu Pan *Lupan* (China)

God of carpenters. His two wives are the goddesses of lacquer-workers. One wife is red and the other wife is black. Once, Lu Pan made a wooden falcon that was able to fly.

Lu Tung-Pin *Lu-Tung-Pin* (China)

Also known as: *Ancestor Lo, Lu Tsu, Lu Yen.*

One of the Eight Immortals. God of Barbers. In many legends about Lu Tung-Pin, he plays the role of punishing the wicked and rewarding the good. In some versions, as Ancestor Lo he is a god of barbers. Lo is either a substitute for Lu-Tung-Pin or an addition. Ancestor Lo is credited for shaving the head of an emperor whose skin was sensitive. He is usually shown as a young man in robes, carrying a fly-chaser and a sword. *See also* Arhats; Eight Immortals; Han Chung-Li; Ho-hsien-ku.

Lubrican (Celtic) *see* Leprechaun.

Lubukhanlung (Dhammai People; India)

Lubukhanlung, Sangso-Dungso and Kimbu-Sangtung are the children of the first mortals, Abugupham-Bumo and Anoi-Diggan-Juje. Their grandparents are the brother and sister frogs, Lujjuphu and Jassuju. *See also* Shuznaghu.

Lubumba (Africa) *see* Leza.

Luchta (Irish) *see* Credne.

Luchtaine (Irish) *see* Credne; Goibniu.

Lucifer (Latin)

Name of the morning star. The name is also used for Satan. Luciferians are fallen angels. *See also* Kanaloa; Satan.

Lucina (Greek, Roman)

Also known as: *Juno.*

This goddess of light is Juno. As Lucina she presides over the birth of children. *See also* Diana; Eileithyia; Juno.

Lud *Ludd* (Celtic) *see* Llud; Nuada.

Ludd (Celtic) *see* Don; Lud.

Ludjatako (Creek People, North America)

Deified animal. The Giant Turtle.

Lug (Celtic) *see* Lugh.

Lug Lonnbemnech (Celtic) *see* Lugh.

Lugal-Banda *Lugalbanda* (Sumer)

He was the god and shepherd king of Uruk, where he was worshipped for over a thousand years. Some say he was the third king of Uruk after the Deluge. One of his tasks was to protect

Gilgamesh. The adventures of Lugal-Banda are similar to those of Gilgamesh. He was said to have conquered the Dragon Zu. Lugal-Banda is possibly the same as Lugalmeslam. *See also* Gilgamesh; Zu.

Lugalabdubur (Babylonia) *see* Marduk.

Lugaldimmerankia (Babylonia) *see* Marduk.

Lugaldurmah (Babylonia) *see* Marduk.

Lugallanna (Babylonia) *see* Marduk.

Lugalmeslam (Sumer) *see* Nergal.

Lugalugga (Babylonia) *see* Marduk.

Lugas (Celtic, Irish, Welsh) *see* Lugh.

Lugeilan (Caroline Islands)
God of knowledge. Son of Aluelop (also known as Luk). First teacher of mortals. He taught the arts of tattooing and hairdressing. He also taught people how to cultivate crops.

Lugh *Lug* (Celtic, Irish, Welsh)
Also known as: *Find* ("Fair-haired One"), *Lamhfhada* ("of the Long Arm"), *Lleu Llaw Gyffes, Llwch Llawwynnawc* (Welsh), *Lug Lonnbemnech* (Many Blows), *Lug Samildanach* ("Many-skilled"), *Lugas*.
God of sorcery, poetry, history, and carpenters. Solar deity. Lugh "of the many skills" is the grandson of the Tuatha De Danann Dia'necht and also the grandson of the Fomosian Balor, whom he eventually killed. He is the son of Cian, a Tuatha De Danann, and the Fomorian moon goddess, Etlinn. He is also the brother of Dagda and the divine father of the hero Cu Chulain. He was raised by the sea god, Manannan Mac Llyr. Lugh is the custodian of the magic spear, one of the four talismans of the Tuatha De Dananns. The spear has a mind of its own, and it strikes the enemy of its own will. Along with the spear, when in battle, Lugh wears a helmet and carries a shield that magically protects him from being wounded. Lugh was the first person to engage in battle on horseback. He rides a horse named Enbarr, a gift from his foster father. Lug appeared at King Nuada's court with a company of fairies and offered to assist the Tuatha De Danann's in their battle to overcome the evil giants, the Fomorians. As one had to have a skill to be a Tuatha De Danann, he was admitted only after he recited his talents and accomplishments. It followed that he led the group to victory in the Second Battle of Magh Tuiredh, and after the death of Nuada he became the king of the Tuatha De Danann. In some versions of this story, Nuada relinquishes the throne to Lugh prior to the battle. Constantly fighting darkness, he avenged his father Cian's death and also killed his demonic grandfather Balor, using a slingshot. Lugh is depicted as a handsome, youthful, athletic man and is associated with the eagle, his horse, Enbarr, and his dog, Failinis. Lugh is thought by some to be the Romano-British Mercury. He is equivalent to the Welsh Lleu Llaw Gyffes. Lugh is associated with Arianrhod. Compare Lugh to Odin and Varuna. *See also* Balor; Bress; Cailleach Bheare; Cian; Cu Chulain; Dagda; Dia'necht; Manannan Mac Llyr; Mercury (A); Mercury (B); Tuatha De Danann.

Lugus (Gaul, Celtic)
Llew Llaw Gyffes was known as Lugus in Lyons. His festival

Lugnasad, was held on the first of August. *See also* Llew Llaw Gyffes.

Lujjuphu (India) *see* Shuznaghu; Zumiang-nui.

Luk (Caroline Islands, Micronesia)
Also known as: *Lugeilan, Luke-Lang, Lukelang, Lukelong, Yelafath, Yelafaz.*
Creator god of all things. God of knowledge. His wife is either Inoaeman or Ligoapup, who could also be his sister. His son by one of the women is Olifat. Luk took trees and plants from heaven and set them on the barren earth. He also taught mortals to cultivate crops. Luk is particularly associated with the coconut palm. *See* Ligobund; Lukelong; Nareau; Olifat; Yelafaz.

Luke-Lang (Micronesia) *see* Luk.

Lukea (Greek) *see* Artemis.

Lukelang (Micronesia) *see* Luk.

Lukelong (Micronesia)
The goddess Lukelong existed in the beginning. She created the heavens and then the earth. *See also* Luk.

Lullu (Babylon) First Man. *See also* Mami.

Lumauig (Oceanic) *see* Maui.

Lumha (Sumer)
Also known as: *Ea, Enki, Lamech.*
Patron of singers. Under the name of Enki, Lumha is the father of Jabal, the patron of tents and flocks, Jubal, patron of music, and Tubal-cain, patron of the forge. *See also* Ea; Enki.

Lumimu-Ut (Oceanic)
Creator. At first there was only the ocean and a rock. From the rock came a crane, then a female deity who was created from the sweat of this crane. From a place called "Original Land" she took two handfuls of earth. She spread it on the rock and created the world. Then she created plants and trees. From her union with the wind she conceived a son, and through incest with this son she bore all the gods. The Samoan and Melenesian legends have a similar story of everything coming from a stone, and the belief that gods and men were born from incest between mother and son. *See also* Tane.

Luna (Roman)
Also known as: *Artemis.*
Goddess of the moon. *See also* Artemis; Selene.

Lung (China)
Also known as: *Lung-Wang.*
Serpent dragon and one of the Ssu-ling. It can become invisible or change color and size. Lung is usually shown bearded, his head with horns, a scaly body, and claws. Sometimes he is shown as a human. Lung could be part of, or the same as, the Dragon Kings (q.v.). He is similar to the Nagas (q.v.).

Lung-Wang (China) *see* Dragon Kings; Lung.

Luojatar (Finnish) *see* Luonnotar.

Luonnotar *Luojatar* (Finnish)
Also known as: *Synnytar.*

Nature deity. She is the daughter of Ilma, god of the air. Luonnotar created earth and the heavens from the eggs of a duck. One half of the eggs became the earth, the other half, the heavens. The yolks became the sun and the whites the moon. Her son Vainamoinen remained in her womb until he became bored, thirty years later. She has two other sons, Ilmarinen and Lemminkainen. *See also* Ilma; Vainamoinen.

Lupa (Roman)

Also known as: *Acca Larentia.*

Lupa, meaning "wolf," is a nickname for the goddess Acca Laurentia (q.v.).

Lupan (China) *see* Lu Pan.

Lusin (Armenian)

This is an ancient name for the Armenian moon goddess.

Luttchmeen (India) *see* Lakshmi.

Lycaon (Greek)

King of Arcadia. His parents are Pelasgus and either Meliboea or Cyllene. His siblings are Maenalus, Nyctimus, Pallas, and forty-six other brothers. *See also* Acamas (B); Maenalus.

Lycaste (Greek)

She is the daughter of the last king of Troy, Priam, and the wife of the Argonaut Polydamas.

Lycastus (Greek)

He is the grandson of Zeus and Europa. His parents are Minos, king of Crete, and Pasiphae, who mated with a bull and became the mother of the Minotaur. His siblings are Acacallis, Androgeus, Ariadne, Catreus, Deucalion, Eurydale, Glaucus, Phaedra and Xenodice. Lycastus wed Ida. Some say Lycastus' son Minos II was really the son of Lycastus' father Minos. *See also* Acacallis; Ariadne; Minos; Pasiphae.

Lycean (Egypt) *see* Apollo.

Lycius (Greek) This is an epithet of Apollo, the wolf god.

Lycotherses (Greek)

King of Illyria. He was the second wife of Agave, who murdered him so her father Cadmus could take over the throne. *See also* Agave; Cadmus.

Lycrus (Greek)

He is the son of the renowned warrior Abas. *See also* Abas (A); Anchises.

Lycurgus (A) *Lycus* (Greek)

He is the son of Pheres and Periclymene (Clymene). His maternal grandfather, Minyas, was said to have built the first treasury. His siblings are Admetus, Idomene, Lycurgus, and Periopis. Lycurgus was resurrected after death by Asclepius. *See also* Admetus; Ino; Minyas.

Lycurgus (B) (Greek)

King of Arcadia. For lineage details *see also* Iasus (A).

Lycurgus (C) (Greek)

He is the son of Heracles and Praxithea, one of the fifty daughters of Thespius. Forty-eight of Praxithea's sisters slept with Heracles in one night.

Lycurgus (D) (Greek)

King of the Edonians of Thrace. His great enemy was Dionysus. When he refused to give him shelter, the great god Zeus blinded him and drove him insane. In his insanity, Lycurgus committed several atrocities. He killed his son, attempted to rape his mother, and cut off his own legs. The cause of his death is unknown. He might have killed himself, or he was thrown to the wild animals.

Lycurgus (E) (Greek)

He is the son of Pronax and brother of Amphithea.

Lycurgus (F) (Greek) An Athenian orator.

Lycus (A) (Greek)

King of Thebes. He is the possible son of Poseidon and Celaeno, and the husband of Dirce. *See also* Amphion; Antiope; Epopeus; Zetes.

Lycus (B) (Greek)

One of the fifty sons of Aegyptus. *See also* Aegyptus; Danaids.

Lycus (C) (Greek) He is the Centaur son of Ixion and Nephele.

Lycus (D) (Greek) King of Libya. His daughter is Callirrhoe.

Lycus (E) (Greek) He is the son of Ares.

Lyeshy *Lyeshie* (Slavic) *see* Leshy.

Lyfjaberg (Norse; Teutonic)

Also known as: *Hill of Healing.*

Hill of healing. Every woman who climbs this hill will be cured. It is also the hill where Menglad rules with her attendants. Her hall is called Lyr.

Lykeious (Greek) *see* Apollo.

Lynceus (Greek)

A son of Aegyptus, whose life was saved by his wife Hypermnestra when her sisters murdered all his brothers. He became king of Argos. *See also* Abas (A); Aegyptus; Argonauts; Danaus; Perseus.

Lyngvi (Norse; Teutonic)

The island on Lake Amsvartnir where Fenrir is bound and waiting for Ragnarok. *See also* Fenrir; Ragnarok.

Lysippe (A) (Greek)

She is one of the fifty daughters of Thespius.

Lysippe (B) (Greek)

Her parents are Proetus and Stheneboea or Anteia. She married Melampus. *See also* Proetus; Melampus.

Lyr (Irish) *see* Manannan Mac Llyr.

Lyrus (Greek) *see* Aeneas.

Lysianassa (Greek)

Her father is Polybus, the son of the messenger of the gods, Hermes, and Chthonophyle. *See also* Adrestus; Hermes; Polybus.

Lysidice (Greek)

Her parents are Pelops and Hippodameia. She became the

mother of Hippothoe by Mestor, the son of Andromeda and Perseus. *See also* Pelops.

Lysimache (Greek)

Lysimache is the daughter of Abas. She is the possible wife of Talaus, the Argonaut. *See also* Abas (B); Adrestus.

M

M (Maya)

He is the god of travelers who corresponds to Yacatecuhtli (q.v.).

Ma-Bellon (Roman) *see* Arinna.

Ma-Hina (Hawaii) *see* Hina.

Ma-Mien *Mamien, Ma-Vien* (China)

Also known as: *Asvamuttakha* (India), *Bach-Ma* (Indo-China), *Horse-Face*.

"Horse-Face." Protector deity. With his companion Niu-t'ou, meaning "Ox-head," he conducts people to hell. Ch'eng-Huang, the god of walls and ditches, controlled Ma-Mien. In some versions of this myth it is the two Wu-ch'ang who conduct the souls to hell. (*See* Wu-ch'ang.) In some versions Ma'mien and Niu-t'ou are demons. Ma-Mien is shown in the form of a white horse. He is opposed by the Door Guards. *See also* Men Shen; Niu-Y'ou; Yama Kings.

Ma-Mo (Tibet)

Female disease spirits who are often the spouses of malignant demons.

Ma-Negoategeh *Ma Negoategeh* (Iroquois People, North America)

Evil deity called the "The Evil Twin."

Ma-Ngee (Africa) *see* Ngewo-wa.

Ma-p'am-pa (Tibet) *see* Ajita.

Ma-Riko-Riko (Maori)

First woman. She was created by Arohi-rohi (Mirage) from the warmth of the sun.

Ma-tshiktshiki (Oceanic) *see* Maui.

Ma-Tsu (China) *see* Ma-zu

Ma-tsu-p'o (China) *see* T'ien-hou.

Ma-vien (China) *see* Ma-mien.

Ma-Zu (China)

Also known as: *Ma-Tsu*.

Goddess of fishermen and sailors. Ma-zu began her life as a devout young woman in the eleventh century C.E. She is still popular in Hong Kong and Taiwan.

Maa (A) (Egypt) *see* Ap-Taui.

Maa (B) (Egypt) *see* Maat.

Maa-an-f (Egypt) *see* Assessors.

Maa-Nefert-Ra (Egypt)

The name of the Twelfth Hour of Tuat. The city is called Khepert-kekui-khaat-mest and the pylon Then-neteru. This place is where the god is reborn in the form of Khepera, Nu, Nut, Hehu and Hehut. The deities mentioned are Ka-en-Ankh-neteru, Af, and Amkhiu. The god is accompanied by twelve unnamed goddesses and twelve gods who praise Ra. Other gods mentioned are Hehu, Hehut, Nehui, Ni, Nesmekhef, Nu, Nuth. *See also* Tuat.

Maa-thet-f (Egypt) *see* Aaru.

Maa-uat (Egypt) *see* Aai.

Maahes (of Nubian origin; Egypt)

This lion-headed god who was worshiped in Egypt, may be the son of Ra and Bast. He is shown as a lion or lion-headed man.

Maan-Emoinen (Finnish) *see* Rauni.

Maanda (Africa) *see* Ngewo-wa.

Maanegarm (Teutonic) *see* Hati.

Maat (Egypt)

Also known as: *Maa, Maet, Maht, Mat, Maut*.

Goddess of truth and justice. Weigher of souls. Maat is the daughter of the sun god Ra and the female counterpart and perhaps wife of Thoth. When Ra created the world, he brought truth and justice, in the embodiment of Maat, to mortals. As well as being the regulator of the path of the sun, she represents the order which rules the worlds through balance. The foundation of Egyptian religion was based on the necessity of practicing Maat to preserve truth, justice and social order. Maat led the dead souls to the Hall of Judgement to appear before Osiris. Her symbol is the feather, used to counterbalance the hearts of the departed. In her hall there are forty-two judges or assessors (regarded as priests), each of whom the dead must convince that he or she is "maaty" and has not committed any one of forty-two unacceptable acts. Maat's opinion is taken into consideration in making the decisions. The god Anubis places the departed one's heart on one pan of the scale and the feather on the other pan. Next, the god Thoth reads the verdict while the monster Amit stands in attendance ready to chew up the hearts of the guilty. This is not the end of the ordeal for the departed soul. The next step is to name the parts of the door which open into the region of the blessed, followed by other questions. Maat is shown in human form wearing a headdress with an ostrich plume. She is also depicted with a feather taking the place of her head. The feather of Maat symbolizes truth. Maat is associated with Amen-Ra. *See also* Aati; Ament; Amentet; Amit; Anubis; Apet; Mafdet; Negative Confession; Osiris; Ra; Thoth.

Maati (Egypt) *see* Aati.

Maati-f-em-tes (Egypt) *see* Assessors.

Maaty (Egypt) *see* Aati.

Mab (Celtic) *See* Maeve.
Mabinogion, the (Celtic). *See also* Arianrhod.

Mabon (British, Celtic, Irish, Welsh)
Also known as: *Mabonagrain, Mabuz, Maponos* (Wales).
God of music. Possibly a god of hunters. Mabon, "the divine youth," is the son of the river-goddess Modron. The tale is told that he was kidnapped from his mother when he was three days old. It took many adventures before his rescuers found him (inside a salmon) and released him from the Otherworld. *See also* Angus; Matrone.

Mabonagrain (Celtic) *see* Mabon.

Mabuz (Celtic) *see* Mabon.

Mac Cecht (Irish) *see* Banbha.

Mac Cuill (Irish) *see* Banbha.

Mac Greine (Irish) *see* Banbha.

Mac Ind Og (Celtic, Irish) *see* Angus.

Mac Oc (Celtic) An alternate name for Angus (q.v.).

Mac Og (Celtic, Irish) *see* Angus.

Macar (Greek) *see* Aeolus (A); Heliades.

Macareus (Greek)
He is one of six brothers and seven sisters who are the children of Aeolus of Magnesia, who was the ancestor of the Aeolians and Enaret. Macareus committed suicide after having an incestuous relationship with his sister Canace. *See also* Canace (for the names of his other siblings).

Macha (Celtic)
Fertility goddess and goddess of war. Macha is an early fertility-goddess of Ireland, the eponym of Ulster's capital. She is also a warrior-goddess, who paralyzed the enemy troops because they made fun of her. Macha is comparable to Epona and Rhiannon. She is associated with the Morrigan. *See also* Epona; Mab; Morrigan; Rhiannon.

Machaon (Greek)
He was a surgeon and a co-ruler of parts of Thessaly. His parents are the healer Asclepius and Epione, the daughter of Meropes. His siblings are Acesis, Aegle, Hygieia, Iaso, Janiscus,

Panacea, and Podalirius. He married Anticleia and became the father of Alexanor, Gorgasus and Nichomachus. He was one of Helen of Troy's numerous suitors. Machaon fought and died in the Trojan War. *See also* Asclepius; Helen; Hygieia.

Machchael *Marocael* (Taino Indians; Antilles)
Guardian. He watches the entrance of the cave where the first people emerged. Once he was late in returning to the cave and was turned into a stone. *See also* Marocael.

Machulas (Aymara People, South America) *see* Achachilas.

Macris (Greek)
She is the daughter of Aristaeus, the instructor of bee-keepers, and Autonoe and the sister of Actaeon. When Dionysus was hiding in a cave to escape his mother's murderous wrath, Macris brought him honey (likely from her father's hives) to eat. *See also* Actaeon; Aristaeus; Dionysus.

Macuilxochitl (Aztec; Mexico)
Also known as: *Five Blossoms, Xochipilli.*
Deity of music and dancing. One of the attendants of the high gods. The name is a synonym of Xochipilli (q.v.).

Mada (Hindu; India)
Mada is the demonic monster god of drunkenness or intoxication. Mada is also the god of liquor, women, dice, and hunting. In the *Mahabharata*, it is written that the Asvin twins rejuvenated the aged and wealthy sage Chyavana. Chyavana was the son of Bhrigu. He married the youthful Sukanya, the daughter of Saryata, and rued his aging physique. Delighted with his newfound youth, he told the Asvin twins of a soma get-together in the heavens, hosted by the gods. They decided to attend but were barred from entering by Indra because of their humble origins. It was said that the twins spent too much time with mortals to be pure. Chyavana decided to make a sacrifice to the Asvins and infuriated Indra. Armed with a thunderbolt and a mountain Indra proceeded to attack Chyavana. Chyavana conjured up the monster Mada, who was powerful enough to swallow the universe and the heavens. Indra yielded and permitted the Asvins to imbibe soma with the other deities. Mada symbolizes thought. *See also* Asvins; Soma.

Madderakka (Lapp)
Also known as: *Jordegumma* (Swedish).
Goddess of women. Goddess of childbirth. Creator of the infant. She is the mother of three daughters, Juksakka, Sarakka and Uksakka.

Mader-Akka (Finnish) *see* Akka.

Maderakka (Lapp) *see* Juksakka.

Madhava (India)
Husband of Laksmi. *See also* Krishna; Vishnu.

Madhu (India)
An extremely evil demon. Madhu and his followers were slain by the gods. Their marrow or "meda" covered the earth, who has since been called Medini. *See also* Durga; Kali.

Madhupriya (India)
"Friend of the Wine." *See also* Bala-Rama.

Madhusudana (India) Slayer of Madhu. *See also* Krishna.

Madhyama (India) *see* Vach.

Madira (India) "Of Spiritous Liquour." *See also* Devi.

Madivi *Mandavi* (India) *see* Bharata.

Madri (India)
She is the mother of two of the Pandu Princes, the twins Nakula and Sahadeva. *See also* Asvins; Krishna; Kunti; Pandavas.

Maeander (Greek)
River god. His parents are Oceanus and Tethys (qq.v.). *See also* Rivers.

Maenads (Greek)
Also known as: *Bacchae, Bacchantes, Bassarides.*
Possibly storm spirits. Female followers of Dionysus. He inspired them to ecstatic frenzy and they carried out his orgiastic rites. The first Maenads were the Nymphs. The Maenads are depicted naked or wearing thin veils. Wreaths of ivy crown their heads. They carry a two handled urn. Sometimes they are playing a flute or tambourine as they frenetically dance. In some versions they are attendants of Bacchus (q.v.). *See also* Dionysus.

Maenalus (A) (Greek) Father of Atalanta.

Maenalus (B) (Greek) Pan's sacred mountain in Arcadia.

Maenalus (C) (Greek)
The oldest of the fifty sons of the king of Arcadia, Lycaon. He made the mistake of serving the great god Zeus human flesh. Zeus hurled a thunderbolt at him and he died. Not to be confused with Lycaon, also an Arcadian king, who deliberately cut his son to pieces and offered him as a sacrifice to Zeus.

Maenawr Penardd (Celtic)
Fertility god. Magician. He owns a magic rod and a carrion eating sow. The sow is said to be Keridwen in disguise.

Maeoe (Celtic) *see* Maeve.

Maet (Egypt) *see* Maat.

Maeve *Meave, Mave* (Celtic)
Also known as: *Maeoe, Meadhbh, Mebhdh, Medb.*
Goddess of war. Originally, Maeve was the goddess of Ireland's sovereignty, the goddess of Tara, the island's magical center. In later versions, she was demoted in myth, as Irish culture changed under Christian influence, to an ordinary mortal queen. The original was definitely not a queen. Her name meant in Celtic "intoxication" or "drunken woman." Legend says she ran faster than horses, slept with innumerable kings whom she discarded, and carried birds and animals across her shoulders and arms. Maeve is the central figure of the most important remaining old Irish epic, the *Tain Bo Cuillaigne*, or *Cattle Raid of Cooley*. After comparing possessions with her consort, King Aillil (Ethal Anbual), she found he had a magic bull which she did not possess. She used her army to steal the magic bull of Cooley. After a great battle with the hero Cuchulain, she finally took the bull, but it in turn had to fight with Aillil's bull and they tore each other to pieces. *See also* Cuchulain; Mab.

Mafdet (Egypt)
Mafdet was worshipped in the earliest times as a goddess of judicial authority. Her name also stood for an apparatus used for executions. It was a pole, curved at the top with a coil of rope around the shaft and a projecting blade. Mafdet is also known as a snake fighter. She is represented as a feline predator and is shown running up the execution pole. In the Late New Kingdom she is shown in scenes from the judgment hall of the beyond. *See also* Maat.

Mafuike (Polynesian)
God or goddess of the underworld and of fire. One of the ancestors of Maui who tricked her into giving him her fingers which he quenched in a stream. In her anger she set the world on fire but Maui called on rain, sleet and snow to put it out. *See also* Kupua; Maui.

Magatama (Japan)
The Magatama are curved ornamental jewels belonging to the goddess of light, Amaterasu. They are one of the three insignia depicting Imperial power. The jewels symbolize the benevolence of the sun goddess' soul. *See also* Mi-kura-tana-no-kami; Susanowo.

Magh Tuiredh First Battle of (Celtic) *see* Credne.

Maghayanti (India) A Krittika sister. *See also* Rishi.

Magic Thunderbolt (India) *see* Tvashtri; Vajra.

Magna Mater (Greek)
Magna Mater, "Mother of the Gods," is an epithet for Rhea. *See also* Cybele; Rhea.

Magnes (Greek)
Magnes, the son of Aeolus and Enarete, was a human magnet, the nails in his shoes caused his feet to become magnetized to the ground. *See also* Aeolus (A); Argus (E).

Magnesia (Greek) *see* Canace.

Magni *Magne* (Norse; Teutonic)
Also known as: *Might, Thrud.*
God of strength. Son of Thor and the giantess Iarnsaxa, he lifted the giant Hrungnir's foot from his father when he was only three nights old. He and his brother Modi will inherit the hammer Mjollnir after Ragnarok. *See also* Iarnsaxa; Mjollnir; Modi; Ragnarok; Thor.

Mah (A) (Persia) *see* Ameshas Spentas; Hvare-khshaeta; Yazatas.

Mah (B) (Persian, Semitic, Sumerian, Akkadian, Chaldean)
Also known as: *Aruru, Belit-Ili, Gula, Mama, Mami* (Sumerian), *Ninmah.*
God of the moon. Queen of gods. Creation goddess. Assistant to Vohu Manah of the Amesha Spentas. Mah has been given the task of regulating time and tide. In her Semitic role of Belit-ili she is a deity of animals. As Mah or the Akkadian goddess Mami she is credited with creating seven women and seven men from clay and blood. As Gula, she is a goddess of medicine. In her creation role she is thought of as being Aruru. Mah is possibly androgynous since some versions call this deity a god. In Chaldean astrology, she is associated Hvare-Khshaeta, the sun;

Tishtrya, the Dog Star; and Anahita, who is associated with the planet Venus. In later times, the Roman goddess of war, Bellona became known as Mah-Bellona. Mah is sometimes identified with Ninlil. She was associated with Anu after the flood. *See also* Aruru; Belit; Bellona; Ninmah; Tishtrya.

Mah Asruna (India) *see* Avalokitesvara.

Mah-Bellona (Roman) *see* Bellona.

Maha Isvari (India) "Great Potentate." *See also* Devi.

Maha-Kali (India) *see* Kali.

Maha-Maya (India) *see* Devi.

Maha-Pita (India) "The Great Father." *See also* Brahma.

Maha Sambara (Nepal) *see* Sambara (A).

Maha-Vairochana Tathagata (India) *see* Dainichi-nyorai.

Mahabharata (Hindu; India)
The *Mahabharata* is a long epic poem about the struggle between the Pandavas and their cousins the Kauravas (qq.v.).

Mahachandrarosana (Nepal) *see* Chandamaharoshana.

Mahadeo (India) *see* Parvati.

Mahadeva (India)
"Great God"; a praise name for Rudra-Shiva. *See also* Rudra; Shiva.

Mahagauri (India) *see* Gauri.

Mahakala (Hindu, Buddhist; India, Tibet)
Also known as: *Dharmapala Kalamahakala, Dharmapala Sitamahakala, Shiva.*
Mahakala is a title used for Shiva as the god of irrevocable time. In this aspect, Shiva is shown with an axe in one hand and a human body in the other hand. The Buddhist use this as a title for the deities Dharmapala Kalamahakala and Dharmapala Sitamahakala, the black and white protector spirits. In Tibet, Mahakala, the "Power of Devoring Time," keeps evil away. He wears a fierce expression on his face, a knife in his headdress and in one hand he holds a skull formed into a cup that is full of blood. *See also* Shiva.

Mahakalee (India) "The Great Black One." *See also* Devi; Kali.

Mahakali (India) *see* Devi; Gauri.

Mahakaruna (India) *see* Avalokitesvara.

Mahalaxmi (Hindu; India)
Mahalaxmi is an aspect of the mother goddess Durga. She is one of eight mother goddesses who rides a lion and carries many weapons, though she is not a menacing figure. Seated on her lion, she is shown with sixteen arms, carrying assorted weapons, as well as a book, rosary, bell and lotus. *See also* Durga.

Mahallika (India) *see* Hiranya-kasipu.

Mahamaya (India) *see* Maya (A).

Mahamayuri (Japan) *see* Kujako-Myoo.

Mahamya (India) *see* Kali.

Mahapadma (India) *see* Lokapalas.

Mahaprajapati (India) *see* Prajapati (B).

Mahapralaya (Hindu; India)
Mahapralaya is the complete cycle of universal time as represented by the one hundred year life of Brahma. At the end of this time, the entire universe, including Brahma and all the other gods, is destroyed in the Great Cataclysm (Mahapralaya). Following Mahapralya there will be one hundred years of chaos, then another Brahma is born, along with a new cycle. *See also* Kaliyuga; Kalpa.

Maharajni (India) "Great Queen." *See also* Devi.

Mahasena (India) *see* Karttikeya.

Mahasiddhas (Buddhist; India)
Tantric saints. *See also* Padma Sambhav; Samantabhadra.

Mahasthamaprapta (Nepal)
She is a Dhyanibodhisattva who is often seen standing to the right of an important deity with her colleagues, Akasagarbha, Avalokitesvara, Kshitigarbha, Mahasthamaprapta, Maitreya, Manjusri, Sarvanivaranaveskambhin, Trailokyavijaya. Vajrapani or Samantabhadra are sometimes substituted for one of the eight Dhyanibodhisattvas. *See also* Dhyanibodhisattvas; Samantabhadra.

Mahavira (Jains; India)
Also known as: *Jina, Vardhamana.*
The Mahavira, meaning "Great Man," was the twenty-fourth and last tirthankara ("keeper of the fords") of the Jains. He left his celestial abode to live on earth to alleviate human suffering. He chose to be an embryo in the womb of Devananda, the wife of Rishabhadatta, a Brahman who lived at Kundapura. Devananda was given fourteen (some say sixteen) favorable signs in a dream. The omens were an elephant, a bull, a lion, the goddess Sri, a garland, the moon, the ocean, a celestial abode, jewelry, a banner, a vase, a lake of full of lotuses, and an eternal flame. Her delighted husband was certain that this was an indication that their son would be a great Brahman scholar and religious leader. Sakra, the king of gods in Heaven had different plans. He decided that it would be more favorable for Mahavira to be the son of a Kshatriya. He ordered the gods' messenger and leader of the heavenly infantry, Harinagamesi, meaning "the-Man-with-the-antelope's-head," to transfer the embroyo from Devananda's womb to the womb of Trisala (also known as Priyakarini), the wife of the Kshatriya Siddhartha. Now she was given the fourteen signs that Devananda had received. From that time they enjoyed good fortune in all aspects of their lives. Twenty-five hundred and niney years ago, the child was born and given the name Vardhamana, meaning "he-who-grows, he-who-develops." He grew up as a prince in Bihar and married Yasoda. They became the parents of a daughter Riyadarshana (also known as Priyadarsana). (The Digambaras, a magor Jain group, do not believe that he ever married.) Vardhamana's parents, who were followers of the twenty-third Jain savior Lord Parsva's doctrine, decided to leave the world and did so by starving themselves to death. Vardhamana, in his thirtieth year, was granted permission by his brothers and authorities of the kingdom to give away his wealth. He spent

the next twelve years as an ascetic and gained enlightenment. At this time he became Jina, the Victor. As Jina he taught for thirty years. His followers were known as Jainas or Jains after their master. He formed them into four groups: monks, nuns, laymen and laywomen. The number of disciples is given as fourteen thousand in some documents and in others forty-two hundred. At the end of this period, he was "kevalin" (omniscient) and he was ready to die. He had himself carried to a hall brightened by heavenly light, and was placed on a throne of diamonds. He preached for many hours and in the still of the night, when his followers had fallen asleep, he died. The year was 485 B.C.E. Many lamps were lit, but his soul had already departed for heaven. This incident is commemorated by the Jains in a festival known as Divali. *See also* Buddha; Sakra; Siddhartha.

Mahayogi (India) "Great Yogi." *See also* Shiva.

Mahayuga (India) *see* Dwaparayuga.

Mahendra (India) *see* Indra.

Mahesvara (India)
"Great Lord." *See also* Shiva; Trailokyavijaya; Uma.

Mahi (India) Mother of the planet Mars. *See also* Bhumi.

Mahina (Hawaii) *see* Hina.

Mahisa (India) *see* Mahisasura.

Mahisasura (India) "Buffalo Monster." *See also* Devi; Durga.

Mahisha (India) *see* Mahisasura.

Mahishamardini (India) *see* Durga.

Mahlaima (India) *see* Mala.

Maho Penekheka (Mandan)
The Evil Power. *See also* Maho Peneta.

Maho Peneta (Mandan) The Great Spirit.

Mahomet (Turkish) *see* Mohammed.

Mahou (Dahomey People; Africa) *see* Mahu.

Mahre and Mahrianag (Ancient Persian)
Adam and Eve. *See also* Adam.

Mahrkusha (Iranian, Persian)
"Destroyer." The demon who will destroy all mortals by frost and snow. *See also* Yima.

Maht (Egypt) *see* Maat.

Mahu *Mawu* (Dahomey, Fon People; Africa)
Also known as: *Mawa, Sogbu.*
Mahu is the daughter of Nana Buluku, and twin sister of the male deity Lisa. She is the mother of Dan. A creator goddess, she is associated with the sun and the moon. Mahu was transported by the great serpent Aido Hwedo as she moved around creating the earth and mortals. She is known as the mother or the twin sister of Lisa in some myths. As a male deity of metal working Mawu is also called Gu, which is also the name of the metal used in making swords. Either she or Nana Buluku is the creator. Sometimes a part of a trinity with the chameleon god Lisa and Ge the moon god. Some writers say Mawu is the chief creator deity of the Dahomey people, but still associated with Lisa and Ge. In this same version Mawu is called the father of Lisa or that Lisa was the mate of Mawu. She is considered androgynous when linked with Lisa as Mawu-Lisa. In this relationship, Lisa a male deity is associated with the sun and Mawu is the sky god and chief of all deities. *See also* Agbe; Aido Hwedo; Leza; Mahu.

Mai (Turkey) *see* Umai.

Maia (A) (Roman)
Dawn goddess. Goddess of fertility. Plant goddess. Maia, an ancient Roman goddess of fertility, could have been the consort of Vulcan. The consort of the Romano-British deity Mercury was known as Maia, as was the goddess worshipped in Rome with Mercury. Maia is associated with Fauna, the goddess of animals, farming and nature. *See also* Mercury (A); Mercury (B).

Maia (B) (Greek)
Maia is one of the Pleiades, the seven daughters of the Greek god Atlas and Pleione (also known as Aethra). She is the mother of the messenger of the gods, Hermes, by Zeus. *See also* Calypso; Pleiades.

Maia (B) (India) *see* Maya (A).

Maidere (Tartar) *see* Maitreya.

Maijunga (Aborigine People, Australia)
God of the Southeast Wind. *See also* Bara.

Mainda (India) Monkey Child. *See also* Asvins.

Maira Ata *Maira* (Tupi-Guarani People, Brazil)
Also known as: *Sommay.*
Culture hero. He was able to predict the future with the help of spirits. His children are the twins Ariconte and Timondonar. Some say only one son was Maira Ata's and the other was the son of a mortal named Sarigoys. The story is that the twins had to pass tests before Maira Ata recognized them as his sons. Ariconte and Timondonar opposed one another. During an argument, Timondonar stamped his foot on the ground and caused the great deluge. The only survivors were Timondonar, Ariconte and their wives. *See also* Ariconte; Maire-Monan.

Maire-Monan (Tupinambas People, Brazil)
Also known as: *Transformer.*
Culture hero and teacher. Maire-Monan came after Monan, who was the creator of mankind. Maire-Monan had the power to change men and animals into other forms in order to punish them for misdeeds. He taught men governing and agriculture. Men killed him because of his changes. He is probably the same as Maira Ata since the legends are similar. *See also* Ariconte; Maira Ata.

Maisahana (Nicaragua, Central America)
Great father or first man. Maisahana and his wife Itoki were the first people. They were the founders of the Mosquito, Tuachca, Yusco, Sumo and Ulua people. There is no indication that Maisahana and Itoki were worshiped as deities. *See also* Itoki.

Mait' Carrefour (Haitian)
God of crossroads and moon deity. He is the brother of

Ghede (Baron Samedi) and possibly came from the Kalfu Indian religion. Some say he is a patron of magicians. Mait' Carrefour is generally shown with his arms in a cross-like position. *See also* Ghede.

Maitreya (Buddhist; India)

Also known as: *Ajita, Byamspa* (Tibet), *Champ-pa* (Tibet), *Maidere* (Tartar), *Metteya, Mi-Lo Fu* (China), *Miroku-Bosatsu* (Japan).

Known as the loving one, Maitreya is the fourth and future Buddha. His given name is Ajita. He resides in Tushita heaven and is expected to appear on earth in human form four thousand years after the disappearance of Gautama Buddha. In some traditions, it is said that it will be five thousand years after Gautama Buddha's disappearance that Maitreya will appear. He is also worshiped as a Dhyanibodhisattva. He is the only Bodhisattva worshiped by the Hinayanist and the Mahayanist Buddhists. In Bardo, the Tibetan Buddhism after-death state, Maitreya appears with Akshobhya and his sakti Locana. Maitreya is sometimes depicted standing, adorned with ornaments and holding a lotus stalk in his right hand. If he is represented seated as a Buddha, his legs are either interlocked or dangling. His color is yellow and sometimes his images bear the figures of the Dhyani Buddhas. His vahanas (vehicles) are the lion, or the lion throne, or the symbol of divine wisdom, a white elephant. His emblem is the caitya (the stupa that holds sacred relics). Compare Maitreya to the Kalki (Hindu) and Hotei (Japan). *See also* Abheda; Ajita; Akshobhya; Buddha; Dhyani Buddhas; Dhyanibodhisattvas; Kuvera; Manushi-Buddhas; Mi-Lo Fu; Miroku-Bosatsu; Samantabhadra; Stupa; Tushita; Vairocana.

Makali (Hindu; India) *see* Parvati.

Makanaima (Arawak People; New Guinea) *see* Makonaima.

Makara (Hindu; India)

Makara is a sea monster known as the mount of Varuna, the symbol of Kama (the god of love), and the vehicle of Ganga. A source of life and death, Makara dispenses the water of life to the good and death to the evil. Makara carries a priceless pearl in his mouth. If a man is courageous enough to retrieve it, it is assured that the woman of his dreams will fall in love with him. In early Indian art, the Makara resembled a crocodile. It evolved into a composite fish elephant and is depicted variously as a dolphin, a crab, a crocodile or a shark. In Central Java, it usually has a monster's head, gaping jaws, large teeth, and an elephant's trunk. Sometimes another mythical animal emerges from the trunk, and from its jaws, figures of deities, lions, or birds emerge. The Makaras are associated with darkness and water. In the Hindu zodiac, Makara represents Capricorn. *See also* Ganga; Kama (A); Varuna.

Makara Sisters (Aborigine People, Australia)

Deified birds. Originally the Makara Sisters were Emu women, but because of the unwelcome advances of the Dingo men called the Wanjin, they flew away. To capture them the Dingo men set fire to their hiding place, a fire which ruined the Makara's wings, but because they had to step so high over the flames their legs became elongated. Now the Emu cannot fly, but they can outrun people. The Emu are beautiful women with long, honey colored hair, and bodies covered with icicles. The icicles falling from their bodies cause frost in late winter. Sometimes the Maraka sisters are called the Seven Sisters and are compared to the Pleiades.

Makemake (Easter Islands, Hawaii)

Patron of the Bird Cult. Makemake is a local god of the Hawaiians who took the place of Tane. He drove the birds to an island to protect them from egg stealers. There are indications that Makemake was later adopted by the Easter Island People. Makemake possibly developed from the Tahitians' giant bird who swallows mortals, named Matu-'u-ta'u-ta'ua.

Makh (Hittite) *see* Ullikummis.

Makila (Pomo People, North America)

Father of Dasan (q.v.).

Makkal (Middle Eastern) *see* Moloch.

Makonaima *Makanaima, Makunaima* (Arawak People, New Guinea; Caribbean; South America)

Also known as: *Kanaima, Kenaima.*

One who works in the night. His work is done under the darkness of night. In early times, all creatures could speak and all lived in harmony. At that time, his son, Sigu, ruled over all animals. Makonaima created a tree bearing many fruits, but Sigu (who is an apparent trickster) cut down the tree. The stump of the tree was filled with fish of every kind, but for some reason the stump began to overflow. Capped by Makonaima with a basket, the flow was stopped. A monkey (also a trickster) removed the basket and a deluge followed. Makonaima saved the animals by placing some in a cave and others in a tree. At daybreak the waters had receded, but the animals were completely changed. Thus began our present world. In another tale, Makonaima, a creator, is the twin brother of Manape. He pulled down the "Tree of Life" against the opposition of the rodent, Agouti. This brought about the flood that destroyed mankind. After the tree had fallen, it spread plants all over the earth. Makonaima appears to belong to a class of avengers known as Kenaima (q.v.). He is possibly analogous to Wakanda and Manito. *See also* Aimon Kondi; Kururumany.

Makunaima (Caribbean, South America) *see* Makonaima.

Mala (India) *see* Ratnasambhava.

Malah (Babylonia) *see* Marduk.

Mali (Australia) "The Bat" *see* Gidja.

Malik (Sumer) *see* Nergal.

Malinalxochitl (Aztec)

She is the sister of Huitzilopochtli (q.v.).

Malsum (Algonquin People, North America)

The Destructive Force. He is the brother of Gluskap.

Mama (Sumer) *see* Ama; Mah (B); Mami.

Mama Allpa (Inca; Peru)

An Incan earth deity and goddess of the harvest. Mama Allpa is known as the "great nourisher of mankind." The Carib earth-goddess, Mama Nono, is comparable to Mama Allpa, as are

Artemis and Ishtar. Mama Allpa is described as having numerous breasts. *See also* Artemis; Ishtar; Mama Nono.

Mama Cocha (Inca; Peru)

Also known as: *Mother Sea.*

Mother goddess. Sea Mother. Mama Cocha is the sister and wife of Viracocha, the creator of mortals. She is a goddess of rain and of water, associated especially with Lake Titicaca. Fishers worship her. *See also* Copacati; Mama Pacha.

Mama Cora (Inca; Peru)

Corn goddess. She is the daughter of Pirrhua. *See also* Manco Capac; Pirrhua.

Mama Coya (Inca) *see* Tahuantin Suyu Kapac.

Mama Huaco (Inca) *see* Ayar Aucca.

Mama Ipacura (Inca) *see* Ayar Cachi.

Mama Lakshmi (India) *see* Lakshmi.

Mama Nono (Carib People, Antilles)

She was the earth mother goddess of this now extinct tribe. Korobona was another female figure known as a cultural heroine, and mother of the first Carib. *See also* Korobona; Mama Allpa.

Mama Occlo *Mama Ocllo* (Inca; Peru)

Also known as: *Mama Oella, Mama Ogllo.*

First woman. She is the sister and wife of Manco Capac who made the trek with him in search of Cuzco. Mama Occlo instructed the Inca women in the domestic arts. *See also* Manco Capac; Viracocha.

Mama Ocllo (Inca) *see* Mama Occlo.

Mama Oella (Inca) *see* Mama Occlo.

Mama Ogllo (Inca) *see* Mama Occlo.

Mama Oullo Huaca (Inca) *see* Mama Occlo.

Mama Pacha (Inca) *see* Pachamama.

Mama Quilla (Inca; Peru)

Moon goddess. Inti, the sun, is her brother/husband. With the exception of Venus, the planets and stars were her attendants. As the moon goddess of the ancient Peruvians, she presided over the births of children. Mama Quilla was represented as a disk of silver with the face of a human. She is associated with Cuycha the rainbow, Catequil the thunder god, and Chasca, the planet Venus. Mama Quilla is comparable to the Roman goddess Diana. *See also* Cuycha; Inti.

Mama Raua (Inca; Peru) *see* Ayar Uchu.

Mama Zara *Zaramama* (Inca; Peru)

Grain Mother. She is an ancient corn or grain goddess.

Mamaki (Buddhist; Tibet)

Known as the shakti of Akshobhya, Ratnasambhava and Vajrasatwa, this goddess is a Dhyanibuddhasaktis. She appears in the Second Day in Bardo embracing Vajrasatwa, attended by the female Bohisattvas Lasema and Pushpema, and the male Bodhisattvas Say-nying-po and Champ-pa. Her asana (position) is lalita; one leg pendant sometimes supported by a lotus and the other leg in the position of a Buddha. Her mudras are varanda, also called vara, the gift bestowing mudra; the arm is pendant, all fingers extended downward, and the palm turned outward, and vitarka, which signifies argument; the arm is bent, all fingers extend upward, except the index finger which touches the tip of the thumb, with the palm turned outward. She is shown holding three mayurapiccha (peacock feathers) at shoulder level. Her color is yellow. Her emblems are the kapala (human skull cap), karttrika (chopper), mayurapichha (peacock feather), and ratna (jewel). *See also* Akshobhya; Dhyani Buddhas; Maitreya; Ratnasambhava; Shakti; Tara (B); Vajrapani; Vajrasatwa.

Mamaldi (Siberia) *see* Khadau.

Mamandabari (Aborigine People; Australia)

They are important Dreamtime spirits who rose out of the ground. Sometimes they are said to be two brothers or a father and son. They are responsible for teaching various rituals.

Mamaragan (Aborigine People, Australia)

Also known as: *Lightning Man.*

Storm god. He lives at the bottom of a waterhole in the dry season and rides the top of thunder clouds in the wet season. The Lightning Man is shown with stone axes on his joints. He is similar to Daramulun.

Mama'sa'a (Fox People, North America) The First Man.

Mamers (Roman) *see* Mars.

Mami (Akkadian, Babylon, Chaldea, Sumer)

Also known as: *Ama, Aruru, Mah, Mama.*

Mother goddess. She is variously called the Mother-Womb, the Bearing One, the Mother Goddess, the Creator of Destiny, The Creator of Mankind, the Mistress of All the Gods. Goddess of childbirth. The goddess who, according to the beliefs held at Eridu, molded man out of clay, softened by the blood from a god slain by Ea. Mami aided mothers in childbirth. In the *Poem of Creation,* Mami created the first man, whose name was Lullu. *See also* Ama (A); Aruru; Mah (B).

Mami-Ngata (Aborigine People; Australia) *see* Bunjil.

Mamien (China) *see* Ma-Mien.

Mammitu (Assyro-Babylonian).

Also known as: *Mammetu, Mammetum.*

Mammitu plots the destiny of the newborn child's life. She also decrees the fate and future of men.

Mamona (Antilles) *see* Atabei; Iella; Iocauna.

Mamu (Aborigine People; Australia)

Spirit animal. Mamu is a large spirit Dingo who captures and eats the spirit of any child who wanders away from camp. *See also* Mopaditis.

Man Eater (Polynesia) *see* Kaitangata.

Man-la (India) *see* Bhaishajyaguru.

Mana-garm (Teutonic) *see* Hati.

Mana-heim *Manheim, Mannheim* (Teutonic)

Also known as: *Midgard.*

Mana-heim is the part of Midgard inhabited by human beings (rather than giants or dwarfs). Some do not differentiate between Mana-heim and Midgard (q.v.).

Manabozho (Native North American) *see* Nanabozho.

Manabush (Algonquin People, North America) *see* Nanabozho.

Manaf (Arabic)

This ancient god, called by some a sun god, was caressed by women, except during their menses, when it was forbidden.

Manala (Finnish)

Also known as: *Tounela, Tuomela.*

The underworld. It is inhabited by giants of various races as well as those mortals who are dead and awaiting rebirth. The giants know quite a bit about medicine and can often provide remedies for illnesses. The inhabitants of Toumela have as their queen, Tuonetar, who has as her husband, Tuoni. Their daughters, who are described as very ugly, included Kipu-Tytto (goddess of illness) and Loviatar (source of evil and goddess of disease), who in turn is the mother of nine monsters of sickness. There is also Kivutar and Vammatar, who are goddesses of disease, and finally the god of death, Kalma. The giants are associated with Vainamoinen. *See also* Hell; Kalma; Kipu-Tytto; Kivutar; Loviatar; Tuonetar; Tuoni.

Manannan (Irish) *see* Manannan Mac Llyr.

Manannan Mac Lir (Irish) *see* Manannan Mac Llyr.

Manannan Mac Llyr *Manannan Mac Lir* (Celtic, Irish)

Also known as: *Manannan, Manawydan Ap Llyr* (Celtic) *Manawyddan.*

Manannan Mac Llyr is a sea god, god of the capes of the sea, god of storms and waves, god of fishers, god of war and shape changer. He is the son of Lyr. He married Fand who was later given to Cuchulain. In time she was returned to her husband. To insure that the lovers would never meet again, he shook his magic cloak between them. He became the father of Mongan by Caintigerna, the wife of Fiachna. This was accomplished by one of his favorite pastimes; he assumed the form of her husband and climbed into bed with her. Aside from frolicking with women, he also had serious responsibilities. An ancient deity, he prepared the Sidhe for the Tuatha de Danann. He was the guardian of the Blessed Islands and the guardian of the Hallows. With Pryderi, the son of the goddess Rhiannon, he was also the guardian of the Grail. His life was made easier with a ship that could follow his command without sails; a cloak that made him invisible; a helmet that consisted of flames; and a sword that could not be swayed from its mark. It was said that he fed the Tuatha De Danann pigs for food. The pigs constantly came to life cooked and ready to be eaten the next day. Manannan Mac Llyr became the foster father of the great deity Lugh, whom he received in payment from Lugh's father, Cian. He was also the foster father of numerous other deities. The Blessed Islands have been identified with the Isle of Man and the Isle of Arran. One of Manannan's consorts may have been Aoife, the woman warrior or perhaps another woman with the same name. She was punished and changed into a crane for stealing the secret alphabet of knowledge from the deities. Her intent was honorable. She intended to give it to mortals. She used her new shape to her advantage and made a bag from her skin, which she used to hold the alphabet and accomplish her mission. Not to be confused with Manawydan Ap Llyr (Manawyddan), the stepfather of Pryderi. Manannan and Manawyddan have common attributes. *See also* Aine; Aoife (B); Cian; Cuchulain; Fand; Lugh; Tuatha de Danann.

Manasa *Manassa.* (Hindu; India).

Also known as: *Manasa-Devi, Shakti, Vaishnavi* (wife of Vishnu).

Manasa, the snake goddess, is the daughter of Kadru and Kasyapa and sister of Sesha, Kapila, and the Nagis and Nagas. The Shivalas, followers of Shiva, maintain that Shiva is her father. With Shiva, her mother is said to be Gauri. She is a demanding goddess and anyone who encounters her cannot turn away from her. A wealthy merchant named Chand had been given certain powers by Shiva because of his devotion. Manasa was angry and demanded that Chand worship her. When he refused, she made his life hell on earth. First, she ripped up his prize garden. Next she appeared to him in the form of an enticing young woman and promised to marry him if he would transfer his powers to her. Beguiled, he did as asked. She transformed herself back into her goddess form and demanded his worship. He thought that the fatal attraction was over and again, he refused. Furious, she set out to make life impossible for him. His garden was once more uprooted, she bit his six sons to death, and his ships containing all his wealth were sunk. He was left stranded on a desert island and almost starved to death. Still, he would not give in to her demands. He survived and eventually made his way home and attempted to rebuild his life. Manasa had not forgotten him. Although he had taken elaborate precautions to protect himself from her, she still managed to harass him. He married and had a son, Lakshmindra. His son married Behula and on his wedding night, a snake slipped into the bed and bit him to death. The new bride put her husband's body on a raft and sailed the rivers for six months hoping that a doctor would be able to revive him. Eventually, she came upon a washerwoman who led her to Manasa. Lakshmindra was restored to life only on the condition that Chand be made to worship her. The couple journeyed home and related Manasa's proposition. Finally, on the eleventh day of the second half of the moon, Chand relented and worshiped the serpent goddess. The Shivalas believe that the worship of cobras will keep them safe. Manasa is invoked for protection against snakebites. She is known to inspire women, and those who are sterile invoke her for fertility. During worship, Manasa and her serpent family are appeased by various items, including milk. She is a protector of animals, and is also worshiped by hunters. Compare Manasa to Gauri. *See also* Devi; Kadru; Kasyapa; Nagas and Nagis; Sesha; Shakti; Shiva; Takshaka; Vishnu.

Manasa-Devi (India) *see* Manasa.

Manasa-Putra (India) "Brain Born." *See also* Rishi.

Manasi (India) *see* Asparases.

Manassa (India) *see* Manasa.

Manat (Arabic) *see* Menat.

Manawddan (Irish) *see* Manannan Mac Llyr.

Manawydan Ap Llyr *Manawyddan, Manawydan Son of Llyr* (Celtic)

Also known as: *Manannan Mac Llyr* (Celtic, Welsh).

Deified mortal. Manawydan Ap Llyr, frequently referred to as Manawyddan, is the son Llyr. He was one of seven survivors who took Bran's head to London. Manawydan was the second husband of the goddess Rhiannon and the stepfather of Pryderi. He was known as a teacher, craftsman, and a dependable man who was always able to make a living. A bright and cunning individual, he rescued Rhiannon and Pryderi from a magic castle. Manawydan Ap Llyr is often called the Welsh counterpart of Manannan Mac Llyr and has attributes similar to Pwyll. *See also* Bran; Branwen; Pryderi; Rhiannon.

Manawydan Son of Llyr (Celtic) *see* Manawydan Ap Llyr.

Manawyddan (Celtic) *see* Manawydan Ap Llyr.

Manco Capac *Manco-Capac, Manco, Manko-Kapak* (Inca; Peru)

Also known as: *Ayar Manco, Pirrhua-Manco, Tahuantin Suyu Kapac.*

Solar god. Teacher of religion, agriculture, weaving and civilization. In the beginning, Manco Capac and his three older brothers, all children of Inti, the sun, emerged from the Paccari-Tambo (Inn of Origin) caves. The eldest son proclaimed the earth belonged to him. Manco Capac was so furious that he trapped his brother in a cave and sealed it with huge boulders. He also pushed his second eldest brother over a precipice. While falling to his death, he was changed to stone. The acts were witnessed by the remaining brother, who decided that the best thing for him to do was to flee. He was never heard from again. Manco Capac went on to establish the city of Cuzco, where he was worshiped as the Son of the Sun. In another version of the origins of the Incas, caves are again the point of emergence. The three caves are the same name as in the previous myth, Paccari-tambo or sometimes Tambotocco (Place of the Hole). In the beginning, four brothers and four sisters emerged from the middle cave. Their names and numbers vary from myth to myth. While searching for habitable land for a settlement, one of the brothers, Ayar Cachi, incurred the wrath of his siblings. A strong, boastful, show-off, Ayar was finally tricked into returning to the Cave of Origin under the pretext of gathering items they had left behind. Once inside, his brothers on the outside sealed the wall so he could not escape. The brothers set up temporary housing at Tambu Quiru and while there were visited by the spirit of Ayar Cachi, the brother sealed in the cave. He persuaded them to proceed on their journey and to found the city of Cuzco. Ayar Cachi stayed behind on Huanacauri, a hill. There he turned himself into stone where he became the object of veneration for a later Inca cult. (In another rendition, it was another brother, Ayar Uchu, who after teaching Manco Capac certain rituals, turned himself into stone.) In a variation, the sun god felt compassion for mortals who were at that time living in a barbaric state. He sent his son, Manco Capac and his daughter, Mama Ocllo, to earth to instruct the mortals in the ways of civilized living. They traveled many miles before they found a place where the long golden rod they were carrying could be buried in the earth. When they finally reached a place where the earth accepted the rod, it was Cuzco. Over time they gained the native people's confidence and taught them the art of civilization. They also established the worship of the sun. Manco Capac is associated with Pachacamac. *See* Tahuauntin Suyu Kapac for another version. *See also* Mama Occlo; Pachacamac; Viracocha.

Mandara Mountain (Hindu; India).

A sacred mountain range in the Himalayas, Mandara mountain is the home of Durga. It was this mountain that was used as a pole in the churning of the ocean of milk. *See also* Deva (A); Durga; Kuvera; Loka; Meru Mountain.

Mandavi (India) *see* Madivi.

Mandishire (Siberia) *see* Manjusri.

Mandodari (Hindu; India)

The daughter of Maya the architect, Mandodari is the eldest wife of Ravana and also the wife of his brother Bihishan. Some say that she is a later avatar of the Daitya Hiranya-kasipu. *See also* Hiranya-kasipu; Maya (C); Ravana.

Mane (Teutonic) *see* Nat.

Manes (Roman)

Spirits of the dead. *See also* Dis; Dis Pater; Orcus; Pitri; Pluto.

Mangadevatas (India) *see* Devis.

Mangaia Island — Creation Legend (Polynesia) *see* Vari (A).

Mangala (A) (India) "The Auspicious One." *See also* Devi.

Mangala (B) (Mande People, Africa)

Creator. Supreme being. Mangala created seeds and mankind from an egg. He also created Pemba and Faro as the twins. *See also* Faro; Pemba.

Mangi and Kangi, The (Japan) *see* Hikohohodemi; Hosuseri; O-Wata-Tsu-Mi.

Manheim (Teutonic) *see* Mana-heim.

Mani (A) *(Mane)* (Teutonic)

Mani, the moon, and Sol, the sun, are the offspring of the giant, Mundilfari. *See also* Aarvak; Muspells-heim; Odin; Sol (B).

Mani (B) (Brazil, South America)

Food deity. There are several versions relating to this god. Most appear to be connected with the advent of missionaries. In one, the "Good Spirit" came down and introduced the plant manioc to the people and taught them how to prepare it as a food. He didn't teach them how to reproduce the plant. Later, a young virgin was seduced by a young man who was really a metamorphosed version of Manioc. The daughter of this union led the people, and showed them how to plant and cultivate manioc. In another version it was a pale son who was born from the union and he was named Mani; but he died without any signs of sickness after one year. He was buried and a odd plant grew on his grave. Because birds became intoxicated after eating the fruit from the plant, the people opened the grave and found the manioc root which they called Mani-oka. In other versions Mani lived to a ripe old age, teaching the people many things. Among the most important was the method of planting and using the manioc root. *See also* Tupan.

Mani (C) (Polynesia)

Mani is accompanied on her rounds by the waxing moon, Hiuki, and the waning moon, Bil. Mani is able to bring the god of darkness, Tangaroa, back to life by shaking his hands in a coconut shell. *See also* Tangaroa.

Mani (D) *Manes* (Manichaeism; Babylon)

Mani, a native of Babylonia, took up his cause in approximately C.E. 242. His beliefs were combined with Zoroastrianism, the dualism of Mazdaism and the Gnostic tradition borrowed from Christians of John the Bapist and the Mandaeans. The combination formed the basis for his dualistic religious philosophy. He was the self-proclaimed highest spokesperson of Christ. The Christians denounced Manichaeism as a heresy.

Mania *Maniae* (Etruscan, Greek)

Goddess of the dead. The Greeks called her "Daughter of Night." She was thought to be responsible for causing moonsickness. In ancient days, children were sacrificed to her. In Etruscan mythology she is an underworld deity and consort of Mantus. *See also* Lara.

Manibozho (Indian People, North America) *see* Nanabozho.

Manigarm (Teutonic) *see* Hati.

Manik (Maya People, Yucatan)

Manik is the god of sacrifice. He is similar to Xipe Totec (q.v.)

Maninga (Mandan)

Water spirit. The Flood Spirit. Lone Man defeated Maninga but Maninga later returned and made the water rise. Lone Man planted a sacred cedar tree then had his people build a high stockade of willow planks, which was called the Great Canoe. When the water started to overflow the walls Lone Man threw precious shells that were favorites of Maninga. The deity caused the water to recede to pick up the shells and the people created a magic turtle drum which drove Maninga away forever.

Manitou *Mandio, Manito* (Native North American People; various groups)

Also known as: *The Great Spirit or Manitos.*

Supreme deity. The spirit or spirits that rule all things. The masters of life. In one version Gitche-Manito means a good spirit and Matche-Manito is a bad spirit. Similar to the Eskimo Inuat. Manitou is similar to the Iroquois Orenda. *See also* Gitche.

Manju Bara (India) *see* Manjusri.

Manjughosa (India) *see* Manjusri.

Manjughsha (India) *see* Manjusri.

Manjunghose (India) *see* Manjusri.

Manjushree (India) *see* Manjusri.

Manjushri (India) *see* Manjusri.

Manjusri *Manjushree, Manjushri* (Buddhist; India, Tibet)

Also known as: *Arpacanamanjusri, Dharmacakra* (Soft-voiced Lord of Speech; one of four manifestations), *hJamdpal* (Tibet), *Jam-dbyans-mag-gi-rgyal-po* (Tibet), *Jam-pol* (Tibet), *Jam-yang-nge-gi-gya-po* (Tibet), *Mandishire* (Siberia), *Manju*

Bara, Manjughosa (Pleasant Voice), *Manjughsha, Megh Sambara* (Nepal), *Monju* (Japan), *Monju-Bosatsu* (Japan), *rNamsnan-mnon-byan* (Tibet), *Siddhaikaviramanjughos* (White One with Soft Voice; a manifestation), *Simhanadamanjusri* (Lion-voiced Charming Splendor; a manifestation), *Tiksnamanjusri* (Charming Splendor; a manifestation), *Vagisvara, Vagiswara, Vajrahara, Varanga, Wen-shu* (China), *Yamantaka* (Manjusri's fierce form), *Yamari* (Foe of Yama).

Manjusri, the god of learning, speech, science, and wisdom, was born from a lotus, without parents. In Sanskrit, his name means "Great Fortune" or "Deep Virtue." At birth, a tortoise sprang from his face. He lived on Mount Panchashirsha (five peaks) in the Himalayas. Manjusri arrived in the area riding on his lion and with one swipe of his sword drained the water of Lake Nagavasa which filled the valley. In some traditions he is considered to be the founder of culture and learning in Nepal. Others venerate him as the founder of the universe and the god of agriculture. They dedicate the first day of the year to him. One of the Dhyanibodhisattvas, he forms a triad with Avalokitesvara and Vajradhara. He is single, but is often involved with the wives of his Hindu friends, Vishnu and Brahma. He is portrayed as yellow, or of a golden hue, sometimes seated in a posture of teaching. He is generally shown sitting on a blue lion surrounded by clouds representing ignorance. He holds either a lotus, a sword or a book in his hands. His delusion-cutting sword, known as the "Sword of Wisdom," indicates the ability to obliterate the clouds of ignorance. Sometimes he bears small figures of the Dhyani Buddhas in his hair. He also appears in a feminine appearance. In Japan, Manjursri is paired with Fugen-Bosatsu (in Sanskrit, Samantabhadra). He is shown seated on a lotus and riding an elephant. In his fierce form as Yamantaka or Yamari, he celebrates his victory over the demon of death, Yama. He has three or six faces and mutiple hands; he carries a sword, thunderbolt, axe and noose and is usually shown with a necklace of skulls. Megh Sambara, who is the angry aspect of Manjusri in Nepal, is known as the god of protection against enemies. He is depicted with a buffalo head and is in the company of a female. *See also* Arpacanamanjusri; Avalokitesvara; Brahma; Dhyani Buddhas; Dhyanibodhisattvas; Monju-Bosatsu; Prajnaparamita; Samantabhadra; Sambara; Sarasvati; Vishnu; Yamantaka.

Manko-Kapak (Inca) *see* Manco Capac.

Manmatha (India) This is Vishnu as the god of love (q.v.).

Mannheim (Teutonic) *see* Mana-heim.

Manru (Babylonia) *see* Marduk.

Mantchu-Muchangu (Shongo People, Africa)

God of dressmakers. He taught humans how to make clothes and cover their bodies.

Mantis People — Creation Legend (Bushman Group, South Africa) *see* Cagn.

Mantius (Greek) *see* Abas (B).

Mantradevatas (India) *see* Devis.

Mantus (Etruscan) *see* Mania.

Manu (Hindu; India)

Manu is one of fourteen patriarchs. Each patriach ruled or

will rule the world for one period of its history. Each period of time, known as a Manvantara or Manu interval, is equal to 4,320,000 years. Each interval is named for its own Manu and ends with a great flood. We are now considered to be in the seventh interval and the Manu for this period is Vaivasvata, the son of the sun god Vivasvat. The first Manu, "The Intelligent," who emanated from Brahma was Svayam-bhuva and as Brahma's son was the progenitor of mortals. His wife, Satarupa, emanated from the goddess of knowledge Sarasvati. Svayam-bhuva was the father of the ten Prajapatis and the seven, and later ten Maharishis. Svayam-bhuva created the *Manu-sanhita*, the Book of Hindu Laws. In the *Satapatha Brahmana*, it is said that Manu came upon a small fish on the bottom of his wash bowl. The fish begged to be saved and in return promised to save Manu from certain destruction when the Great Deluge flooded the land. Manu saved the fish until it grew so large that it had to be taken to the ocean. That day, the fish instructed Manu to build a ship. When the flood arrived, Manu boarded the ship and was towed around for years by the fish. Finally, Manu and the ship arrived on Mount Himalaya. When the waters subsided, everything on earth had perished except for Manu. Manu offered a sacrifice of whey, cream and ghee (the sacrificial melted butter), and was given a woman, who was called his daughter. Manu turned himself into a bull to avoid the act of incest. Ida, his daughter turned herself into a she-goat and Manu turned into a he-goat. This went on until the earth was populated with animals. Manu is one of "the seven sages" who shine in Saptarshi (the Great Bear constellation). A similar myth is told in the *Mahabharata* involving the seventh Manu, Vaivasvata, and Matsya, the fish avatar of Vishnu. For details, *see* Matsya. Compare to the creation myth of Brahma. *See also* Daksha; Pishachas; Prajapati; Rishi; Sanja; Sarasvati; Varaha; Vasistha; Vishnu; Vivasvat.

Manuai (Admiralty Islands)
He is the first man, who created woman from the trunk of a tree, mated with her and became the founder of the people. *See also* Takaro.

Manusha-Rakshasis (Hindu; India)
Female demons in human form. *See also* Rakshasas.

Manushcithra (Persia) *see* Faridun.

Manushi-Buddhas *Manusibuddha* (Buddhist; India)
The Manushi-Buddhas appear in the form of a human to live on earth and teach the doctrine of Buddha. The seven Manushi-Buddhas are Vipasyin, Siokhi, Vishvabhu, Krakuchanda, Kanakamuni, Kasyapa and Sakyamuni (Gautama). The last four belong to our present Kalpa. (A Kalpa is four billion human years and is the same as one day for Brahma.) In another list, five Manushi-Buddhas are given: Krakuchandra, Kanakamuni, Kasyapa, Sakyamuni, and Maitreya, the future Buddha. Another reference lists seven: Dipankara, Vipasyin, Sikhin, Visvabhu, Krakuchanda, Kanakamuni, and Kasyapa with Maitreya, the eighth and future Buddha. They are Buddhas of compassion and are depicted wearing monastic garments and have bare heads and usually long-lobed ears. *See also* Dhyani Buddhas; Dipankara; Kasyapa (B); Maitreya; Sakyamuni; Samantabhadra; Vajrapani.

Manusibuddha (India) *see* Manushi-Buddhas.

Manyu (Persia) *see* Angra Mainyu.

Manzan Gormo (Burait)
Mother goddess. Said to have created the Milky Way from her excess milk. *See also* Ajysyt; Khotun; Milky Way.

Maorocon (Antilles) *see* Guamaonocon; Iocauna.

Maorocoti (Antilles) *see* Guamaonocon; Iocauna.

Maou (Africa) *see* Mahou.

Maponos (Wales) *see* Mabon.

Mar (Aborigine People, Australia)
Also known as: *The Cockatoo-man.*
Fire deity. He was the only one who knew how to make fire until little bird-man Takkanna stole the secret. A fight developed and all were changed into birds and Takkanna became the robin, his red feathers reminding all that he had given fire to the people.

Mara *Namuci* (Buddhist, Lamaist; Hindu; India)
Mara, the god of lightning, seduction, temptation, physical love and death, was the father of three beautiful daughters known as the Lust goddess, the Thirst goddess and the Delight goddess. Mara sent them to distract Buddha from his meditations as he sat under the Bo Tree. Their sensual dances failed to sway the devout Buddha. Mara hurled mountains at Buddha and they were transformed into flowers and celestial chariots. Mara is the ruler of the sphere of the pleasures of sense and the commander of an army of demons. His function is to delay the coming and preaching of the Law. Said to be homeless, Mara wanders the earth to catch the souls of the dying. His demons are described as having grimacing faces, and distorted bodies, some with a second face in their stomachs. They are shown on foot or riding elephants brandishing various weapons. Mara is sometimes depicted as a vulture. In the Hindu tradition, Mara personifies evil and death. Mara is the same as the Hindu death demon Mrtyu. Compare Mara to Garuda (Hindu). *See also* Akshobhya; Buddha; Kama.

Marakayikas (Japan) Also known as: *Ma.* Goblins.

Maramma (India) *see* Gramadeveta; Mariamma.

Marapa (Melanesia)
Afterworld. Some Solomon islanders believe that those with idle souls become the nests of white ants. All the dead can become ghosts in human or animal form.

Maraphius (Greek) *see* Helen.

Marar-Loka (India) *see* Loka.

Marareus (Greek) *see* Aeolus (A).

Mararisvan (Hindu; India)
Lightning and thunder deity. The messenger of Vivasvant. The one who brought fire to mortals.

Marassa (Haitian)
They are twins gods who are likely harvest deities. *See also* Lisa.

Marathonian Bull (Greek)

As his seventh labor, Heracles had to capture this bull who had ravaged the land. It was finally killed by Theseus. *See also* Heracles; Theseus.

Marawa (Melanesia)

Death god. After Qat created mortals, Marawa tried to follow suit by fabricating humans from a tree. He breathed life into them, but instead of burying them for three days like Qat, he covered them for seven days. They were badly decomposed. As a result man lost immortality. Marawa is a malicious opponent of Qat (q.v.).

Marcra Shee (Irish) *see* Sheehogue.

Mardall (Teutonic) *see* Freyja.

Mardoll (Teutonic)

"Shining One Over the Sea," Mardoll is another name for Freyja (q.v.). *See also* Aesir.

Marduk *Aleyn-Baal, Amaruduk, Asar, Asarri, Ashur* (Assyrian), *Bel Marduk, Belos, Enlil* (Sumeria), *Merodach;* (Akkadia, Assyria, Babylonia, Sumer)

Also known as: *Addu, Agaku, Agilma, Aranunna, Asaru, Asaruali, Asarualim Nunna, Asaruludu, Asharu, Barashakushu, Bel Matati, Dumuduku, Enbilulu, Epadun, Exizkur, Gibil, Gil, Gilma, Gishnumunab, Gugal, Hegal, Irkingu, Kinma, Lugalabdubur, Lugaldimmerankia, Lugaldurmah, Lugallanna, Lugalugga, Malah, Manru, Marukka, Marutukku, Mummu, Namtillaku, Nari, Nebiru, Papalguenna, Shazu, Sirsir, Suhgurim, Suhrim, Tuku, Tut, Zahgurim, Zahrim, Ziku, Zisi, Ziukkinna, Zulum.* (The preceeding forty-nine names are from the "Hymn of the Fifty Names of Marduk.")

King of the gods, supreme god, and god of storm and lightning, Marduk was also known as a sun god, fertility god and patron god of Babylon, which he founded. He is the son of Enki, or Ea and Ninki, or Ea and Damkina. Some say that Marduk was born of Apsu, the Ocean. With the goddess Zerpanitum, he became the father of Nabu, the god of speech and language. Marduk who had invincible courage, became lord and ruler of the gods, a reward for fighting Tiamat and her assistants; a viper, a dragon and the Lahamu. When the moon god Sin was threatened by evil spirits, it was Marduk who fought off his oppressors and routed them, restoring Sin's light. The goddess of evil, Tiamat, arranged a campaign to have her followers of darkness, led by her son Kingu, attack the gods. The deities found out about it and endowed Marduk with the abilities of a magic cloak and the abilities of a magician. The talking cloak gave instructions to Marduk on how to appear and disappear. The deities, impressed to find that Marduk's words were powerful gave him the sceptre, throne and the magic weapon to slay Tiamat. (His father, Ea had killed Apsu with the aid of magic incantations.) After slaying the monster Tiamat, Marduk secured the Tablets of Destiny from the demon Kingu (some say Zu). He used one-half of the skin or body of Tiamat to cover the earth. In other accounts, half of Tiamat's body was placed above the earth as the sky. He kept the sky in place with bars and charged guards with the responsibility of not letting Tiamat's waters escape. Marduk became the chief god of the Babylonian pantheon, and took on the characteristics of Enlil, as well as the attributes and functions of other gods. Marduk constructed Esharra (patterned after Apsu, Ea's abode) as an abode for the great gods. When Marduk went to battle Ea, aside from his magic weapons, he carried an amulet in the form of an eye in his mouth, and herbs in one hand to ward off evil influences. His next step in the creation of the universe was to establish the order of the months according to the moon's changes. From this came the calendar. He also instituted the three celestial ways. In the northern heavens was the way of Enlil, Anu in the zenith, and Ea in the south. The celestial order was under the charge of the planet Jupiter. Next came the creation of mortals to service the gods. Ea suggested that this be done by slaying the demon Kingu and using his blood to fashion the mortals. In other accounts he created mortals with the aid of the goddess Aruru, from clay. Marduk's temple, Esagila was built for him by the gods as a token of their appreciation. Officially he had fifty great names, received by proclamation by command of Anu. Marduk, as Merodach was also the mate of the Chaldaea, Sumer goddess of compassion, Shala. He was often called Bel-Marduk, god of Accad and Sumer after Hammurabi came into power. Some say the word amour came from Amaruduk which was an early form of Marduk. In his role of Tammuz, Marduk later disappeared, according to some research. Marduk is said to be the same as Telepinus, the son of Teshub of the Hattic people. Marduk is the same as Bel of the Babylonian and Assyrian religion (q.v.). Compare Marduk's myth to the myth of Yam-Nahar (Ugaritic). *See also* Aleyin; Anu (B); Anunnaki; Apsu; Aruru; Ashur; Damkina; Ea; Enki; Enlil; Igigi; Isis (Egyptian, who also used magic); Kingu; Lahamu; Nabu; Nebo; Nimrod; Ninki; Rahabh; Sin; Telepinus; Tiamat; Zerpanitum; Zi; Zu.

Mare Goddess (Celtic) *see* Rhiannon.

Maree (Celtic)

Also known as: *Mari* (Crete), *Mouri.*

Maree, the goddess of wells, trees and stones was worshiped in ancient Scotland. There is a record of an ancient goddess of the same name from the Minoan people who was a mother deity. It is remotely possible they are connected. *See also* Mari (India).

Margarme (Teutonic) *see* Hati.

Mari (Hindu; India)

Mari is the goddess of death and diseases found in valleys, or hills. She is worshiped by the Koramas of India and is said to be the same as the Great Mother, Devi. The Koramas also worship Shiva and Vishnu and venerate holy stones, trees and isolated areas, where they believe demons and spirits dwell. Mari is depicted with four hands, holding a trident, skull, rope and a drum. She is possibly the same as the ancient goddess of Crete with the same name. *See also* Bhavani; Devi; Maree (Celtic); Shiva; Vishnu.

Mariamma *Maramma, Marimata* (Gramadeveta) (India)

The goddess of smallpox, and other diseases. It is thought by some researchers that she is not an ancient deity and may have been named after the Virgin Mary. However, there is a group of ancient deities, the Gramadeveta, who are known in Mysore as Mariamma and Maramma. *See also* Gramadeveta.

Marica (Roman)

The name for the Greek sorceress, Circe (q.v.).

Marichi (A) *Marici, Marishi.* (Buddhistic Hinduism; India)

Also known as: *O-zer-chem-ma* (Tibet), *Tou Mu* (China), *Ushas.*

She is the ray of dawn comparable to the Hindu Ushas except that Marichi is frightening. Some say she that she is a terrible goddess who emanates from Vairocana. Others feel that she is a forerunner of Vairocana. In some references she is called the mother of Gautama Buddha. She is portrayed with three faces, one is a boar's snout, and a frontal eye. She has ten threatening arms, her head is crowned with skulls and wreathed in flame. She is depicted variously with a hook, thunderbolt, a bow and arrow, a needle and a cord. Her car is drawn by seven pigs. Marichi is usually accompanied by Rahu, the demon of eclipses and ruler of meteors. *See also* Buddha; Chandi; Marishi-ten (Japan); Maya (A); Tou Mu (China); Ushas; Vairocana.

Marichi (B) (Hindu; India)

The son of Brahma and the father of Kasyapa, Marichi was the chief of the Maruts and a Rishis. *See also* Brahma; Kasyapa (A); Maruts; Rishi.

Marid (Arabic) *see* Jin.

Marimata (India) *see* Gramadeveta; Mariamma.

Marinette (Haitian)

Earth goddess. Wife of Ti-Jean Petro. *See also* Ti-Jean Petro.

Maris (Greek) *see* Ares.

Marisha *Marsha* (Hindu, India)

An Asparasa and goddess of the dew, she is the daughter of the Pramlocha, spouse of Prachetas (Prachetases) and mother of Daksha. *See also* Asparases; Daksha; Pramloka; Urvasi.

Marishi-Ten (Japan)

Also known as: *Marichi-Bosatsu, Marichi-Deva.*

God or Goddess of warriors. Goddess of first light. She is invisible and rules the light that appears in the sky before the sun. She guards warriors against the weapons of their enemies. In some versions Marishi-Ten is a male with the same attributes. She is depicted either standing or sitting on one or seven galloping boars. She has two, six or eight arms and holds various weapons including a bow and a sword. Her image was often found on warrior's helmets. Marishi-Ten wears a costume of a Chinese lady and holds a fan. Compare her to Ushas the Vedic goddess of dawn and Eos, the Greek goddess of dawn. *See also* Aurora; Marichi (A).

Marocael (Taino People, Antilles) *see* Cacibagiagua; Machchael.

Marri (Babylon) *see* Adad; Mari.

Marru (Babylon) *see* Adad.

Marruni (Melanesia)

Creator. Earthquake deity. Called the "earthquake." He cut pieces from his tail to create people and creatures of the land. Has a human body ending in a snake's tail. Similar to Bunosi (q.v.).

Mars (Roman)

Also known as: *Ares* (Greek), *Heru-khuti,* (Egypt), *Mamers, Mavors* (Roman).

God of war. God of agriculture. God of prophecy. Patron of husbandmen. Patron god of the city of Florence. Mars is one of a triad of high gods with Jupiter and Quirinus. He is the son of the weather god, Jupiter, and Juno, the goddess of marriage, or Juno and a mystical flower, or Juno alone. His spouse was the minor goddess Nerio. Mars became the father of Romulus and Remus by Rhea Silvia, and the father of Amor by Venus. His sacred shield, the Ancile, was guarded by his priests, the Salii. His sacred bird is the vulture. As the god of prophecy he is attended by Picus, the woodpecker. In time, Mars assimilated to the Greek god Ares, but unlike his counterpart, was extremely popular. Compare Mars to the Vedic Indra, and Norse Thor. *See* Ana-Purna; Ares, Discordia; Esus; Picus; Silvanus. Compare Mars to the Vedic Indra and the Norse Thor. *See also* Ana-Purna; Ares; Discordia; Esus; Silvanus.

Mars the planet (Greek) *see* Eurynome (A).

Marsalai (Melanesia)

Malevolent guardian spirits of the hunting grounds, they inhabit rocks, pools, and holes. The Marsalai are dangerous to child-bearing women and can cause miscarriages and stillbirths. They can also cause earthquakes, winds, landslides and floods. These spirits are generally depicted as a striped or two-headed snake or lizard.

Marsyas (Asia Minor, Greek)

Also known as: *Marsyas-Masses* (Armenian).

River deity. Son of Hyagnis, the lightning god. A Seleni (woodland satyr) who was flayed to death by Apollo for playing one of Athena's cast-off flutes. As Marsyas-Masses he is also a flute-playing river god. He is probably shown as a satyr. He could be a tribal god similar to Hyagnis, then changed to Vahagn by the Phrygians. *See also* Hyagnis; Vahagn.

Marsyas-Masses (Armenian) *see* Marsyas.

Martanda *Marttanda Savita, Surya, Vivasvan, Vivasvant, Vivasvat* (The Bright One); (Brahman; India)

Martanda, one of the Adityas and the eighth son of Aditi, emerged from an egg as a shapeless lump. His mother took one look at him and threw him away. The divine moulder took the compound and created the god Martanda. The excessive material fell to earth and became elephants. In early times, Martanda was an attribute of the sun, and later became a sun god. Some legends indicate he was the forerunner of Vishnu and Pushan. Martanda, the personification of the setting sun, daily crosses the sky. His chariots are drawn by seven red or white horses. *See also* Aditi; Adityas; Varuna; Vivasvat. He is associated or identified with Vishnu and Pushan (qq.v.).

Marttanda (India) *see* Martanda.

Martu (Mesopotamia; Sumer)

A relatively minor god. He is associated with the god Numushda (god of the city, Kazailu). His wife is the daughter of this god. The daughter is unnamed, but is referred to as the Lady of Ninab, or the Lady of Kazailu. There was a tribe of nomadic Semites living to the west of Sumer, who were called the Martus.

Martummere (Australia) *see* Nurrundere.

Maru (North Island Maori, Polynesia)
Also known as: *Tu Matauenga.*
Commander of the Heavenly Hosts. War God. On the South Island, Maru is known as Tu Matauenga. Maru is called upon by war leaders to be with them during battle and to ensure that they will emerge as victors. He has a huge fire that is used to burn the demons he has vanquished.

Marukka (Babylon) *see* Marduk.

Marumda (Pomo People, North America)
With his brother Kuksu, Marumda created the world. First they attempted to destroy their creation by fire and then by water. They were rescued by the mother goddess Ragno (q.v.). *See also* Kuksu.

Marunogere (Melanesia)
God of females. He created the first female sex organs by boring holes into women.

Marut (India) *see* Vayu.

Maruta (India) *see* Vayu.

Maruts (Vedic, Hindu; India)
Also known as: *Rudras, Rudriyas, Sons of Rudra.*
The fast-flying Maruts, storm spirits, gods of the hurricane and warriors are the sons of Rudra and Prisni, the cow goddess, who is also known as the goddess of the dark season. Some sources name the goddess Diti, also known as Danu, the mother of the giant Daityas, as the mother of the Maruts. The Maruts were all born at the same time in the form of a lump. Rudra-Shiva took the lump and shaped it into the attractive youths. In other renditions, Shiva as a bull, fathered them with Prithivi, who was in the shape of a cow. They were said to have been separated in the womb by Indra. Vayu the wind god is another deity named as the father of the Maruts. Rodasi, the wife of Rudra is a companion of the Maruts. She frequently rides in their chariot across the sky. They are known as cohorts of the war gods and constant companions of the storm god Indra. They are usually numbered at forty-nine but some sources say there are twenty-one Maruts. In the *Rig-Veda*, there are said to be twenty-seven, or one hundred and eighty Maruts. Their weapons are used to penetrate the cloud-cattle and cloud-rocks, releasing torrents of rain. In some accounts, they assisted Indra in his battles with the dragon Vritra. The Maruts are companions and allies of Indra and they reflect his personality. Storm gods, they ride on whirlwinds, flashing lightning and creating thunderous sounds. They incorporate playful and war-like aspects at the same time. In ancient texts, they are known as the Rudras and were considered duplicates of Rudra, the god of the dead. In later times, when Rudra became a celestial being, the Maruts became gods of the atmosphere. The Maruts are depicted as gay youths and alternately fearsome warriors. They wear bright skins, golden helmets and breastplates. Their ankles and wrists are adorned with gold bracelets. Cleanliness is important to the Maruts. They delight in scrubbing one another clean. Their weapons are bows, arrows, axes and gleaming spears. They ride in a golden-wheeled chariot drawn by three deer. Maruts is not to be confused with the singular Marut or

Maruta which refers to Vayu. Compare the Maruts to the Greek Curetes. *See also* Aditi; Adityas; Daityas; Devi; Diti; Indra; Marichi (B); Prithivi; Ribhus (the); Rudra; Swarga; Varuna; Vasus; Vayu; Vedas (the).

Marutukku (Babylon) *see* Marduk.

Marzyana *Marzann* (Slavic)
Earth mother or grain goddess. She is identified with Ceres. *See also* Datan.

Masa-katu-a-katu-kati-paya-pi-ame-no-oso-po-mimi-no-mikoto (Japan) *see* Amaterasu.

Masaka-yama-tsu-mi (Japan)
God of the steep mountain slopes. *See also* Naka-Yama-Tsu-Mi; O-Yama-Tsu-Mi; Sengen.

Masan (Hindu; India)
Deity of disease. Masan comes from the ashes of the funeral pyre and causes illness in children by throwing ashes over them. He is sometimes shown as a child or a bear and is generally black in color.

Masauwu (Hopi People, North America)
God of death. Some say he is a god of fire and war.

Masaya (Aztec People; Nicaragua)
Underworld goddess. She rules the volcanos and causes earthquakes. Bad souls go to her domain. She shares the underground with Mictanteot.

Masewi and Oyoyewi (Acoma People, North America)
War Spirits. The Twins. For other Acoma deities, see Iatiju; Kastiatsi; Katsinas; Pishumi; Shk; Shruistha.

Mashkhith (Hebrew) *see* Af (C).

Mashtu (Babylon)
She is the goddess of the moon, brother of Mashu, and daughter of Nannar.

Mashu (Babylon)
Moon god. Brother of Mashtu the goddess of the moon. Both are children of Nannar. Some say they resemble Hyuki and Bil of the Teutonics. See Nana (B).

Mashya and Mashyoi *Masha and Mashyoi* (Persia, India, Iran)
First humans. They are the two humans who were from the seed of Gaya Maretan. They in turn gave birth to Fravak and Fravakain and Siyamek and Siyameki (sometimes called Siyakmak and Nashak). They are the ancestors of the human race. Mashya and Mashyoi grew up under the form of a tree. (The Greek Corybantes were born as trees; Attis was born from an almond tree and Adonis from a myrtle tree.) Their mythology is comparable to legend of Adam and Eve. *See also* Ahura Mazda; Angra Mainyu; Drujs; Gaya Maretan; Hushang.

Masli (India) *see* Parvati.

Maslum (Algonquin People, North America) *see* Gluskap.

Massim-Biambe (Mundang People; Africa)
Creator deity. The son of Phebele (male principle) and Mebeli (female principle) received the soul (tchi) and life from

Massim-Biambe. This son was called Man. Since Massim-Biambe is invisible he can only be contacted through objects called Grigris.

Mat (Egypt) *see* Maat.

Matali (India) Indra's celestial chariot driver. *See also* Indra.

Matarisvan *Atharvan* (India)
A demigod, Matarisvan is the author of the fourth Veda. He is sometimes listed as a Rishi. *See also* Agni; Rishi.

Mater Matuta (Roman)
Also known as: *Leucothea* (Greek).
Goddess of birth. Mater Matuta is said to be a dawn goddess also known as the Greek Leucothea, the White Goddess, a goddess of the sea. She began her life of tragedy as Ino, the daughter of Cadmus and Harmonia. *See also* Cadmus; Dionysus; Harmonia; Hera; Ino; Semele.

Mater Turrita (Greek) *see* Cybele.

Math (Celtic)
Also known as: *Math Hen* (old math or ancient), *Math Mathonwy* (Welsh).
God of sorcery. Benevolent deity. Shape shifter. Math is an ancestor of the House of Don, the son of the sky deity Mathonwy and the brother of the goddess Don. He is the uncle of Arianrhod, Gwydion and Gilvaethwy. A skilled magician, he taught his art to his nephew Gwydion. It is said that he was so sensitive that he could hear the slightest sounds of the world. Math's feet were extremely important for they held the key to his vulnerable spot, perhaps in his heel. When he wasn't in battle it was necessary for him to have a footholder. This task, considered an important position, entailed having his feet held in the lap of a virgin female. When his footholder, Goewin, was raped by his nephew Gilvaethwy, he married her in an attempt to eradicate her shame. He was known for his beneficence to those who had suffered and his fairness in meting out punishment without being vindictive. Compare Math to Dagda. *See also* Arianrhod; Don; Gwydion; Llew Llaw Gyffes.

Math Hen (Celtic) *see* Math.

Math Mathonwy (Celtic) *see* Math.

Matholwch (Celtic) *see* Bran; Branwen.

Matholwych (Celtic) *see* Bran; Branwen.

Mathuranath (India) Lord of Muttra. *See also* Krishna.

Matuka (Polynesia)
He is the giant cannibal killed by Rata, the hero-god. *See also* Rata.

Mati-Syra-Zemlya (Russian, Slavic)
Also known as: *Mother Earth Moist.*
Earth goddess. The ancient Slavic People and Russians worshiped Earth as a divinity. She was possibly a deity of foretelling the future or a deity of justice.

Matlalcueje (Aztec; Mexico)
Rain goddess. Companion of Chalchiuhtlicue.

Ma't'outt Naing (China) *see* Ts'an Nu.

Matri Mother (India) *see* Devi.

Matrikas (India) *see* Ganda.

Matris, The (India) *see* Ganda; Karttikeya; Shakti.

Matrona (Celtic) River goddess. *See also* Sequana.

Matronae (Celtic)
Also known as: *Matres, Matres Britanne* (Roman), *Modron*.
Mother goddesses. They are the three mother-goddesses who oversee fertility. The Matronae are lovers of peace, tranquility and children. In one version the Romans gave them the name Matres and considered them goddesses of fate. In another version Modron was the wife of Urien who was an underworld deity. She was also the mother of Mabon. As Modron, the Welsh "Great Mother," she is comparable to Dana. *See also* Mabon.

Matrs (India) Female Demons. *See also* Ganda.

Matsya (Hindu; India)
Matsya the fish is thought by many to be the first avatar of Vishnu. However, in the *Bhagavata-Purana*, Matsya is the tenth incarnation of twenty-two. He came as tiny fish into the hands of Manu Vaivasvata, the seventh Manu. Matsya begged to be allowed to live, and promised Vaivasvata in return to save him from the impending Great Deluge. Matsya grew so swiftly that Vaivasvata thought he would be happier in the ocean. Once in his natural surroundings, Matsya was able to give instructions to Vaivasvat for building the ship to save himself. On board was the seed of all plant life and pair of all living creatures. When the flood came, only a great horned fish, Matsya, the avatar of Vishnu, could be seen. Manu Vaivasvata moored his ship on Matsya's horn and was saved. Vishnu, in his form as Matsya is credited with teaching Manu the law. A Manu (Father) is one of fourteen patriarchs, each of whom was a ruler of the earth for one period of its history. The first Manu, an emanation of Brahma was Svayam-bhuva. In another episode, Brahma is asleep during a period of universal chaos. The sacred Veda slips from his mouth, and the demon Hayagriva absconds with it. Matsya comes to the rescue, slays the demon and restores the Veda. In a later version of this myth, recorded in the *Mahabharata*, the fish responds that he is Brahma Prajapati, the creator of the Brahmanas. Some researchers liken Vaivasvata to Noah. This myth, recorded in the *Mahabharata*, is similar and often confused with the myth from the *Satapatha Brahmana*. For details, see Manu. *See also* Kurma (Vishnu's avatar as a tortoise); Prajapati; Vasuki; Vishnu.

Matsyendranatha (Nepal)
He is a "god-saint" who brought salvation to Nepal. Identified with Avalokitesvara, his followers practice a blend of Buddhism, Hinduism and popular religion. He is propitiated as the god of salvation and rain.

Matu-'u-ta'u-ta'ua (Tahiti)
A giant bird that swallows men. *See also* Makemake.

Maturang (Oceanic)
He is the possible son of the creator spider god, Nareau (q.v.).

Mau (A) (Egypt)

Meaning "mew," Mau is an alternate name for the fire and cat goddess Bast (q.v.).

Mau (B) (Oceanic) *see* Maui.

Mau-aa (Egypt) *see* Aai.

Maudgalyayana (India)

He is the equivalent to the Chinese Mu-lien, who is the assistant to Ti-tsang-wang-pu-sa, the god of mercy.

Maui *Mowee* (Polynesia, New Zealand, Samoa, Hawaii, New Hebrides).

Also known as: *Amoshashiki, Ma-tshiktshiki, Mau, Maui-tikitiki, Maui-tukituki, Milu, Mosigsig, Motikitik* (Micronesia), *Rupe, Tiitii* (Samoa).

Sun god, later a culture hero. Inventor of fishing and sailing ropes. Inventor of the fish basket. Inventor of kite-flying and dart-throwing. Creator of the dog. A Kupua (trickster spirit). Son of Mahuika or Ta-ranga, and Ru. The number of brothers he has depends on the legend. Sometimes he does not any siblings. Other times he has three, four or six brothers. In the Maori tradition, his father is Makea-Tutara, the chief of the underworld and his mother is Taranga. Within this family structure he is the youngest and ugliest of five sons. His brothers are Maui-Taha, Maui-Roto, Maui-Pae, and Maui-Whao. It happened that Maui came into the world prematurely as his mother was walking along the beach. His body had not yet taken form. She wrapped him with her hair and put him into the sea. Sea fairies came upon him and nursed and cared for him, until a terrible storm came along and routed him from his hiding place in the kelp. He was thrown back onto the beach. An ancestor, Tama-Rangi, happened upon him and through his tales and songs of Maui's people awakened him to life. Maui then began his travels and eventually found his family. His adventures were many as befits a culture hero. Once, deciding that the days were too short and the nights too long, he starved his grandmother to death so he could have her magic jawbone. Maui used the jawbone to beat the sun into slowing its daily travels. The benefit for mortals was longer hours of light for work. He also used the magic jawbone as a hook for fishing. On one ocassion, his catch was a huge fish. He instructed his brothers not to touch it until he returned from giving thanks. They ignored his request and cut the fish raggedly in two sections. It jerked and squirmed and threw itself around. The fish was the island of New Zealand. Maui, who was mortal because his father forgot to bestow immortality upon him, also controlled the winds and arranged the stars. Many tales illustrate how he managed to get fire. Usually it was by trickery, fighting for it, or stealing it. Often the goddess of fire, Nahui-Ike, who resided in the Underworld is the individual who is tricked into giving him fire. The fire went from him as a gift to his people. There was a time when Maui was highly perturbed with his wife for not feeding him on time. She was involved romantically with someone named Ri. Maui turned Ri into a dog. It could have been avoided if he had been fed on time. There are myths where Maui's brother-in-law Ira-waru was changed into a dog. In this instance Maui has a sister, Hina-uri. Some call him the eight-headed Maui. He was variously known as Maui-of-a-thousand-tricks, Maui-tupua-tupa, Maui-the-wise, Maui-tikiti-ki-a-

Taranga, Tama-nui-a-te-ra. Maui is associated with Atea, Ru, Tane, and Hina. He was said to have defeated Tuna. Sometimes Maui is associated with Mokoroa the shark, and he is even said to be the son of Tangaroa. Sometimes he is similar to Lumauig, Matuarang, and Qat. Many of the feats credited to Maui also appear in legends of Tangaroa. Maui is likened to the Greek Ulysses (q.v.) *See* Hina; Kupua; Mafuike; Motikitik; Nareau; Qat; Tuna.

Maui-tikitiki (Polynesian) *see* Maui; Motikitik.

Maui-tukituki (Polynesia) *see* Maui.

Mauna (Native North American People) "The Earth Maker."

Maut (Egypt) *see* Apet; Maat.

Mauti (Egypt) *see* Aai.

Mave (Celtic) *see* Maeve.

Mavors (Roman) *see* Mars.

Mawa-Lisa (Africa) *see* Lisa.

Mawu (Africa) *see* Mahu.

Mawu-Lisa (Africa) *see* Lisa.

Maya (A) *Maia* (Buddhist; India)

Also known as: *Mahamaya, Mayadevi, Shakti.*

Maya was the spouse of Rajah Suddhodana (sometimes called Sedowdhen or Siddown). He was the chief officer of the Sakyas, a small Aryan tribe. They lived in Kapilavastu, the capital of Shakya, about one hundred miles northeast of Benares and thirty to forty miles south of the Himalayas. Maya was chosen as the mother of Gautama Buddha. The Bodhisattva appeared in a dream, entering her womb (or right side) in the form of a pure white, six tusked elephant. It was predicted that the child's destiny would lead him to the life of an ascetic or universal ruler. After his birth a huge ceremony was held to name him. Eighty thousand relatives, and one hundred and eight Brahmins attended. Gautama had one hundred godmothers. Maya died of joy seven days after her son's birth and he was raised by her sister Prajapati. When he renounced the world to live as a monk, Gautama became known as Sakyamuni and Siddartha. Maya is generally depicted as lying on her left side. Sometimes she is shown sitting on a lotus. Two elephants sprinkle her from waterpots they hold with their trunks. Marichi is also said to be the mother of Siddartha. In Ceylon, the goddess Avany is known as the mother of Sakyamuni. For additional details of Gautama's birth see Buddha. *See also* Indra; Kadru; Lokapalas; Marichi (A); Maya (B); Nagas; Sakyamuni; Sesha; Shakti; Sri.

Maya (B) (Hindu; India)

Also known as: *The Goddess of Fantasy, The Goddess of Illusion, Maya-Devi* (Powerful Goddess), *Maha-Maya, The Universal Mother, The Universal Shakti.*

The daughter of Anrita and Adharma, Maya is the spouse of Brahma and the mother of a daughter, Sumaya. In later times, she was identified with Kali-Durga. *See also* Adharma; Anrita; Maya (A).

Maya (C) (Hindu; India)

He is the father of Mandodari who married the demon Ravana. Maya, an architect, built a palace for the Pandavas. *See also* Mandodari; Pandavas; Ravana.

Maya People — Creation Legend (Yucatan) *see* Ahmucen-Cab; Ajtzak; Xumucane.

Mayadevi (A) *Mayavati* (India)

Mother/wife of Pradyuma, she is identified with Rati. *See also* Kama (A); Krishna; Pradyuma; Rati.

Mayadevi (B) (India) *see* Maya (A).

Mayauel *Mayahuel* (Nahua People, Aztec People, Mexico)

Goddess of pulque and childbirth. A mortal woman, Mayauel discovered the intoxicant pulque from a mouse who was drinking from an agave plant. Her discovery led to her deification. In another version she was a many-breasted goddess who was transformed into the maguey (agave) plant becaused of her fruitfulness. Some legends say she suckles a fish. The agave plant is regarded as the Tree of Life by the Nahua people. It is believed that Xolotl nursed the first man and woman created by the Aztec gods from its milk. Mayauel is sometimes shown sitting on a cactus plant with a looped cord to show that she helped women in childbirth. Night is her special time. Mayauel is possibly shown as a white fox or coyote. She is frequently depicted with four hundred breasts, seated on or in front of the agave plant. Mayauel is sometimes associated with Quetzalcoatl. *See also* Xolotl.

Mayavati (India) *see* Mayadevi (A).

Mayochina (Acoma People, North America)

Deity of summer. The Summer Spirit. For other Acoma deities, *see* Katsinas.

Mayon (Tamil People, India)

He is an ancient god comparable to Krishna.

Mba (Babua People, Eastern Sudan) *see* Bele.

Mbamba *Mbambe, Mpambe* (Wakonde People, Africa)

Also known as: *Kiara*.

A supreme god, Mbamba lives above the sky. He is associated with Leza and Nyambe who represent the sun. Mbamba is shown in human form and is white and shining.

Mbambe (Africa) *see* Mbamba.

Mbir (Guarayu People, South America)

Also known as: *Miracucha*.

Creator. Mbir is a worm, generally shown in human form, who created and shaped the world. He could be the same as Mbere, the creator god of the Fans.

Me (Sumer) *see* Nabu.

Me-phem-pa (Tibet) *see* Ajita.

Me-tog-ma (Tibet) *see* Pushpema.

Meabel (Celtic) *see* Dagda.

Meadhbh (Celtic) *see* Maeve.

Meave (Celtic) *see* Maeve.

Mechaneus (Greek) "Manager and Contriver." An epithet of Zeus.

Mecisteus (Greek)

One of the Seven Against Thebes. His parents are Talaus and Lysimache or Lysianassa. His son is Euryalus. Mecisteus was killed by Melanippus. *See also* Adrestus; Astynome; Pronax.

Mecurius (Roman) *see* Hermes; Mercury (A).

Mede (Greek)

Mede is another name for Periboea, the wife of Icarius and the mother of Penelope.

Medb (Celtic) *see* Maeve.

Medea *Medeia, Medeias, Medeius, Medus* (Greek)

Sorceress. Medea is the daughter of Aeetes and Eidyia, sister of Absyrtus and half-sister of Chalciope. A sorceress, taught by her aunt Circe, she could use her powers for good or evil. Jason of Ioclus, the handsome leader of the Argonauts, arrived in Colchis in quest of the Golden Feece. Medea met him and fell in love. Unknown to her, this arrangement had been preordained by the goddesses Hera and Athene, who had personal agendas. King Aeetes agreed to relinquish the Golden Feece under seemingly impossible conditions. Medea agreed to assist Jason in his quest if he promised to take her with him on the Argos and marry her. He swore to do so. Medea used her powers to lull the dragon who guarded the fleece so that Jason could steal it and then fled Colchis with him. King Aeetes, who never intended to part with the fleece threatened to burn the Argos and massacre the crew and he set out in pursuit of them. Under false pretenses, Medea arranged a secret meeting with her brother Apsyrtus, who met her on an island where he was killed, chopped up and thrown into the sea. (*See* Apsyrtus.) Medea and Jason moved to Corinth, had sons (Alcimedes, Argus, Eriopis, Medeius, Mermerus, Pheres, Thessalus and Tisandrus) and lived quietly for ten years. The Golden Fleece was hung in the temple of Zeus at Orchomenus. The ambitious Jason, renowned for his early adventures, accomplished only because of Medea's powers, decided to divorce her and marry Glauce (also called Creseusa and Creusa), the daughter of the King of Corinth. Infuriated, Medea made Glauce a magnificent wedding gown. When she tried it on it burned her flesh away and she died in agony. Her father also perished while trying to save her. Medea also killed her sons (except possibly Thessalus), either out of revenge or to save them from living in exile. Again, accounts of her adventures differ; she was said to have had two sons whom she murdered. She escaped from Corinth on a sky-borne chariot driven by two dragons, a gift from her grandfather, Helius. She fled to Thebes hoping for protection from Heracles, whom she cured from the insanity that caused him to kill his children. He was too involved with his labors to be of help so she went on to Athens. The aging King Aegeus promised her protection if she would give him the children he had been denied. He did have a son, Theseus, but at the time he was unaware of his existence. He married Medea and they had a son, Medus (Medeias, Medeius). Eventually, Theseus turned up at the court. Medea, fearful that he would claim the throne tried to have him killed. (*See* Theseus.) Aegeus discovered that Theseus was his first son, and it was he who convinced his father to exile Medea. (*See* Medus). According to some renditions, after her death Medea became a consort of Achilles in the Elysian Fields. Others say that she was worshipped as a goddess.

See also Aeetes; Apsyrtus; Argonauts; Ariadne; Golden Fleece; Helius; Jason; Medus; Pheres (A); Theseus.

Medecolin (Algonquin People, North America)
A sorcerer. *See also* Gluskap.

Medeias *Medeius, Medus* (Greek)
He is the son of Jason or Aegeus and Medea. *See also* Medea; Medus; Pheres (A).

Medeius (Greek) *see* Medea; Medus.

Medha (India)
She is possibly one of Daksha's daughters and the spouse of Dharma. *See also* Daksha; Dharma.

Medi Kenaga (Fox People, North America)
Deified animal. The Great Snapping Turtle.

Medica (Roman)
An epithet of the goddess Minerva as the patroness of physicians.

Medicine Buddhas (Buddhist; Tibet)
Also known as: *Abheda, Mi-che-pa* (Tibet), *Mi-p'yed* (Tibet).
The Medicine Buddhas are usually found in two groups, one of eight and one of nine, seated in a meditative pose. They wear monastic robes without ornaments. They wear the sign of insight on their foreheads (urna), their hair is styled in a high chignon (usnisa), the symbol of supernatural wisdom, and they usually have long ear lobes. *See also* Abheda.

Medini (India) Mother of the planet Mars. *See also* Bhumi.

Medus (Greek)
Also known as: *Medea, Medeias, Medeius.*
Medus is thought to be the son of Medea and Aegeus, king of Athens. Hesiod claimed that Jason was Medus' father and that Cheiron raised him. After Medea attempted to murder Theseus, whom she suspected would inherit the throne, she and Medus were driven from Athens and went to Colchis. Aeetes, her father the former king of Colchis, was by some accounts killed by his brother Perses. Perses had been warned that a descendent of Aeëtes would seek revenge, so when he heard of the arrival of Medus he imprisoned him. Medea, impersonating an ancient priestess promised to end the plague in the area if she could have Medus to use in her sacrifical rites. Perses agreed and was slaughtered by the sword of Medea given to Medus, thus avenging his grandfather. Other accounts say that it was Medea who killed her father Perses. Medus went on to conquer the land to the east and named it Media although some believe that Medea named it in honor of herself. *See also* Aeetes; Medea; Perses.

Medusa (Greek)
Also known as: *Medousa.*
A Gorgon. Medusa is the daughter of Phorcys and Ceto. Her lover, who is possibly her husband, Poseidon, is the father of her children, Pegasus and Chrysaor. She is also to be the mother of Caca and Cacus by Vulcan. Her siblings are Echiodna, Euryae, Stheno, Scylla, Ladon and the Graiae. The goddess Athene, enraged that she had slept with Poseidon in one of her temples, changed the once beautiful Medusa into a Gorgon monster. Perseus, jealous of her affair with Poseidon, decapi-

tated her. Some think that Athene guided his sword. From the blood of her body her twin sons, Pegasus the winged horse and Chrysaor the warrior-giant, were born fully grown. Not only did Athene wear Medusa's head in the center of her aegis but she is said to have given two vials of Medusa's blood to Asclepius the healer. With the blood from her left side he was said to be able to raise the dead and with the blood from her right side he could destroy instantly. Other myths say that she divided the blood and Asclepius used his share to save people while Athene used her share to kill and instigate wars. Medusa's gaze turned men to stone and her blood populated the Libyan desert with snakes. Her body was buried in the marketplace of Argos. As a Gorgon, Medusa is depicted with wings, glaring eyes, huge teeth, a protruding tongue, and claws. Her hair is full of serpents. *See also* Aegis; Athene; Caca; Ceto; Chrysaor; Gorgons; Graiae; Oceanids; Pegasus; Perseus; Poseidon; Scylla; Vesta.

Megaera *Megaira* (Greek)
One of the three Furies. She is the daughter of Gaea. Her siblings are Alecto and Tisiphone (qq.v.) *See also* Calchas; Erinyes; Eumenides; Eurydice; Furies; Heracles.

Megaira (Greek) *see* Megaera.

Megara (A) (Greek)
Megara is the daughter of the king of Thebes, Creon, and Anioche or Eurydice. Her siblings are Enioche, Haemon, Menoeceus and Pyrrha. She married Heracles. *See also* Creon; Pyrrha.

Megareus (Greek)
Ruler of a portion of Boeotia. He married Iphinoe and became the father of Evaecheme, Evippus, Hippomenes and Timalcus. *See also* Adrestus; Evippus; Hippomenes.

Megh Sambara (Nepal) *see* Manjusri.

Megin-giord *Megingiord* (Norse; Teutonic)
Also known as: *Megingjardir.*
This is Thor's magic belt. His strength is doubled when he wears Megin-giord.

Megingiord (Teutonic) *see* Megin-giord.

Megingjardir (Teutonic) *see* Megin-giord.

Meh-Urt (Egypt) *see* Amen (B).

Mehen (Egypt)
Mehen, a great serpent deity, is responsible for protecting Ra from the monster Apophis on his journey to Tuat. Mehen is mentioned in the First Division (First Hour) of Tuat, in the Seventh Hour, and in the Eighth Hour. The gods pulled the sun boat of Ra at Mehen's command. When the sun god is depicted traveling across the night sky he appears with a cabin around him and the serpent coiled protectively around the cabin. She is mentioned as a serpent goddess in the ancient "Hymn to Amen-Ra." *See also* Ab-esh-imy-duat; Akeneh; Apepi; Apophis; Nekhbet; Shepes.

Mehendra (India) *see* Indra.

Mehit (Egypt)
Supreme goddess. Mehit, the wife of Anhur, is identified

with Tefnut. She is depicted with the head of a lioness. *See also* Anat; Anhur.

Mehu (Philippines) *see* Finuweigh.

Mehueret (Egypt) *see* Neith.

Meiden (Lithuania) God of animals and forests.

Meido (Japan) *see* Yomi.

Meilanion (Greek) *see* Melanion.

Meili (Teutonic) *see* Odin.

Meilichios (Greek)
Meilichios is the name of Zeus when he is in serpent form.

Meion (Greek) He could be the father of Cybele (q.v.).

Mekel (Sumer) *see* Nergal.

Melampus (Greek)
A talented mortal who could speak to and understand animals, Melampus became known as the greatest of all prophets. He was unable to cure Iphinoe, a follower of Bacchus, the Greek god of wine, of insanity. Her sister, Lysippe, became the wife of Melampus. His children are Abas, Antiphates and Mantius. *See also* Abas (B); Argonauts; Bacchus; Iphinoe; Lysippe; Proetus.

Melanesia — Creation Legend *see* Agunua.

Melanion (Greek)
His father is Amphidamas and his brother is Antimache. Either Melanion or Hippomenes married Atalanta. When Melanion and Atalanta were caught having sex in a sacred place they were turned into lions. *See also* Atalanta; Hippomenes.

Melanippe (A) (Greek)
Also known as: *Arne*
Her parents are Aeolus, the son of Hellen, and Hippe, the daughter of Cheiron, the immortal Centaur. Her children by Poseidon, Aeolus II and Boeotus were taken from her by Aeolus, when they were very young. Aeolus also blinded Melanippe. Initially they were cared for by a cowherd, but later they were adoped by Theano, the wife of Metapontus, who already had two sons. The four young men fought and Theano's sons were killed by Melanippe's sons. Her heart heavy with grief, Theano comitted suicide. Poseidon cured Melanippe's sight and she married Metapontus. *See also* Aeolus (B); Ares; Arne; Theano.

Melanippe (B) (Greek)
This is another name for the Amazon queen, Antiope.

Melanippus (A) (Greek)
He is the son of Astacus of Thebes. *See also* Acamas (A); Adrestus.

Melanippus (B) (Greek) The son of Ares.

Melas (Greek)
Melas is the son of Licymnius and Perimede and the brother of Argeius and Oeonus. While assisting Heracles in a fight against Eurytas, he was killed. It was Eurytas who taught Heracles to use a bow. When Eurytas would not give Heracles his wife Antiope, Heracles killed him. *See also* Calydonian Boar Hunt; Eurytus; Phrixus.

Melatha (Choctaw People, North America)
Deified animal. Male Lightning Bird.

Meleager (Greek)
He is the Argonaut son of Ares or Oeneus and Althea. He married Cleopatra, the daughter of Idas, and became the father of Polydora. It was Meleager who killed the Calydonian Boar. When the Curettes attacked the Calydonians, Meleager was killed. The goddess of the hunt, Artemis, changed him into a guinea-fowl. *See also* Aeetes; Althea; Ares; Argonauts; Artemis; Calydonian Boar Hunt.

Melech (Middle Eastern) *see* Moloch.

Melekh (Middle Eastern) *see* Moloch.

Melesians (Irish) *see* Amergin.

Melete (Greek)
Melete is the Boeotian muse of practice. Her sisters are Aoide, the muse of song, and Mneme, the muse of memory. *See also* Gaea; Mneme; Uranus.

Melgart (Carthage) *see* Heracles.

Melia (Greek)
She is the daughter of Oceanus and Tethys. She is the sister/wife of Inachus and the mother of Aegialeus, Io and Phoroneus. She became the mother of Ismenius by Apollo. *See also* Apsyrtus; Inachus; Io; Meliae; Oceanus; Tethys.

Meliae (Greek)
Ash nymphs. The Meliae, nymphs of manna ash trees, the Giants and the Erinyes sprang from the blood of the castrated Uranus. The ash tree is said to be a sacred tree which was originally used in rain-making ceremonies. The Three Fates dispensed justice under the ash tree and it is said to be one of the goddesses of retribution's (Nemesis') seasonal disguises. One of the meliae, Melia married her brother, the river god Inachus, and became the mother of Phoroneus the first king of Argos; Aegialeus, who some think was the founder of Sicyon; and Io, who was changed into a cow. She may have been the mother of Mycene (eponym of Mycenae). Some say Melia is the daughter of Oceanus and that Argia is the mother of Phoroneus and Io. *See also* Aegialeus; Erinyes; Eumenides; Fates; Gaea; Giants; Inachus; Io; Mycene; Nemesis; Phoroneus; Uranus.

Meliboea (A) (Greek)
Also known as: *Chloris.*
She is the daughter of Amphion and Niobe. Artemis, goddess of the hunt, spared her life and killed her five sisters. Apollo killed her five brothers, sparing Amyclas, according to some. *See also* Amphion; Amyclas; Apollo; Artemis; Chloris; Leto; Niobe.

Meliboea (B) (Greek)
She is the Oceanid daughter of Oceanus and Tethys. Her marriage to the king of Arcadia, Pelasgus, produced a son, Lycaon. *See also* Lycaon; Oceanus; Tethys.

Melicertes (Greek)
Also known as: *Palaemon, Portunas, Portus.*
God of ports and harbors. Melicertes is the son of Athamas and Ino. His mother drowned him and he became the god Palaemon. *See also* Athamas; Ino; Melkart; Palaemon; Portus; Sisyphus.

Melie (Greek) *see* Amycus.

Melissa (Greek)

Melissa is the daughter of Melissus, the king of Crete. With her sister Amalthea she nursed the infant Zeus. *See also* Adrastia; Amalthea.

Melisseus (Greek)

He is the father of Adrastia and Ida, the nursemaids of the infant Zeus. *See also* Adrastia.

Melissus (Greek)

King of Crete. He is the father of Amalthea and Melissa, the nursemaids of the infant Zeus.

Melkart *Melcarth, Melkarth, Melqart, Melquart* (Ammonite, Phoenicia, Tyre)

Also known as: *Aleyn-baal, Baal, Melicertes, Milcom, Moloch, Palaemon, Palaimon, Palamon.*

Originally a solar deity, but later became god of travelers, sailors, and of the city of Tyre. Melkart, like the phoenix, is regenerated by fire. He is associated with both Baal and the Greek Heracles. Some Greek versions say Melkart's father was named Demarus, the son of Uranus who married his sister and mother, Ashtart (Astarte). Some writers say the Greeks adopted this god and gave him the name Melicertes or Palaemon. As Melicertes, he was the son of Athamas and Ino. Later he became the sea god Palaemon. He was also said to be an opponent of Yahveh. He is sometimes shown carrying an axe or spear in one hand and a shield in the other. He is also shown riding a sea horse. The Egyptians show him with the head of a gazelle. There are those who say he is identical with Moloch. Compare him to the Greek fire god and smith, Hephaistos. *See also* Agrius (A); Aleyn-Baal; Astarte; Attis; Heracles; Tammuz.

Melkarth (Carthage) *see* Heracles; Melkart.

Melpomene (Greek)

Muse of Tragedy. Her name means "singing." She sang mourning songs for dead poets and people of accomplishment. One of the nine Muses, Melpomene is the daughter of Zeus and Mnemosyne (Memory). With Achelous, the river god, she became the mother of the Sirens. She is usually shown with a tragic mask, the buskin (a laced half boot with thick soles worn by actors in Greek and Roman tragedies), sometimes with a lyre or scroll and wearing a crown of leaves. *See* Achelous; Mnemosyne; Muses; Sirens; Zeus.

Melquart (Canaan) *see* Astarte; Melkart.

Memnon (Egypt, then to the Greeks)

King of Ethiopia. He is the son of Tithonus (who was turned into a grasshopper when he grew old) and the goddess of the dawn, Eos. Memnon killed Antilochus, a close friend of Achilles during the Trojan War. Achilles in turn killed Memnon. In fact, he died many times and in many places. Zeus made him one of the Immortals. Hephaistos made his bright armor. Birds (souls) flew from his funeral pyre. Memnon is also a name of one of the gigantic statues of Amenophis III located in Thebes. *See also* Antilochus; Eos; Hephaistos; Priam.

Memphis (Greek)

Her grandparents are Oceanus and Tethys, her father is the river god Nile and her sister is Anchinoe. Memphis married Epaphus, king of Egypt and became the mother of Libya and Lysianassa. *See also* Agenor (A); Apis (A); Libya; Nile.

Memphis Triad (Egypt)

This triad consists of Ptah, Sekhmet, and Imhotep. Sometimes Nefertum replaces one of the three gods.

Men *Min* (Egypt)

Aspect of Khem. He is shown with a thyrsus in his right hand and a pine cone in the left. *See also* Min.

Men Brayut (Bali) *see* Hariti.

Men Shen *Men-Shen* (Buddhist; China)

Also known as: *Ch'en Ch'i, Ch'in Ch'iung, Cheng Lung, Ha, Heng, Heng-Ha-erh-Chiang, Hu Ching-te, Shu Yu and Yu Lei, Snorter and Blower, T'ai-Tsung, T'ien Wang.*

Door guards. Men Shen is the collective name for door guards in early mythology. Shen-t'u and Yu-lu were the right and left deities. One has a red face, the other is black. These were later replaced by Yu-ch'ih Ching-te and Ch'in Shu-pao, who were deified mortals. They were replaced with Heng-Ha-erh-Chiang (Sniffing and Puffing Generals) or T'ien Wang (The Heavenly Kings). It is the job of the door guards to be certain all papers are in order when Ox-head (Niu-t'ou or Gosirsa) and Horse-face (Ma-mien) or the Wu-ch'ang (Mr. White and Mr. Black) come to conduct the souls to hell. In one version the names of two mortal marshals in the military are given. These are Cheng Lung and Ch'en Ch'i, later to become known as Heng (Cheng Lung) and Ha (Ch'en Ch'i) or "Snorter and Blower" respectively. They are generally shown in military garments, holding weapons. The door guards are associated with the Jade Emperor. Sometimes a third door guard is associated with them. He is known as Wei Cheng. *See also* Celestial Kings; Heng and Ha; Ma-Mien; Shen-T'u.

Men-Ur (Egypt)

Deified animal. A sacred bull of Memphis. *See also* Mnevis.

Men-urt (Egypt) *see* Amen (B).

Mena (A) (India) Mother of Parvati. *See also* Devi; Parvati.

Mena (B) (Roman)

She is the goddess of menstruation who presides over the months.

Menaka (Hindu; India)

An Asparasa who was sent by the gods to interrupt the spiritual practices of the maharishi Vishvamitra. *See also* Asparases; Marisha; Urvasi.

Menakshi (India) *see* Devi.

Menat *Manat* (Arabic)

This goddess of destiny was venerated in northern Arabia. Followers prayed to her for rain and for victory over enemies. She is associated with Allat and Al-Uza (qq.v.). *See also* Gad; Menu; Unsas.

Mendean Triad (Egypt)

The triad of Banebdedet, Hermehit, and Harpakhrad. *See also* Banebdedet.

Mendes (Egypt)

Sacred animal. A ram in whose form Osiris was sometimes incarnated. The ram is a symbol of virility.

Mene (Greek) Another name for Selene, goddess of the moon.

Menelaus (Greek)

Menelaus, the king of Sparta is the son of Atreus and Aerope. His siblings are Agamemnon and possibly Pleisthenes and Cleolla. With the assistance of Odysseus, he married Helen of Troy. Menelaus was in the Wooden Horse. He never died but went directly to the Eden-like Elysian Fields. *See also* Agamemnon; Elysian Fields; Helen.

Menerva (Etruscan) *see* Minerva.

Menestratus (Greek)

He saved his lover Cleostratus from being eaten by the dragon who appeared every year in Thespiae.

Menesthius (Greek)

He is the son of the river god Spercheius, and Polydora. His mother and her husband Borus raised him.

Menfra (Roman) *see* Minerva.

Meng (A) *Meng-P'o, Meng-Po Niang-Niang* (China)

Also known as: *Lady Meng, Lady Ming.*

Guardian. She prepares the broth of oblivion (Mi-Hung-T'ang) for those who return from judgment. She lives just outside of hell. After she gives souls the broth they must cross K'uch'u k'iao (the Bridge of Pain). *See also* Ti-yu; Yama Kings.

Meng (B) (Celtic) *see* Dagda.

Meng-T'ien (China)

God of the writing brush. He is a mortal from the military who was deified for inventing the writing brush. *See also* Ts'ai Lun; Ts'ai Shen.

Menglad *Menglod* (Norse; Teutonic)

Also known as: *Freyja.*

Goddess of healing. Her home is on Lyfjaberg, the hill of healing. In the form of Menglod she is said to be a spouse of Svipdag. She is possibly a form of Freyja.

Meni (Babylon) *see* Menu.

Mennon (Teutonic) *see* Thor.

Menodice (Greek)

She is the daughter of Orion and the mother of Hylas. *See also* Hylas; Orion.

Menoeceus (A) (Greek)

He is the father of Creon, Hipponome and Jocasta.

Menoeceus (B) (Greek)

He is the son of Creon and Anioche or Eurydice.

Menoetius (A) (Greek)

He is the son of Iapetos and Clymene or Asia. His siblings are Atlas, Epimethius ad Prometheus. During the battle between the Giants and the gods, Menoetius was torpedoed into Tartarus by one of the great god Zeus' thunderbolts. *See also* Abderus; Epimethius; Iapetus; Oceanids.

Menoetius (B) (Greek)

An Argonaut. His parents are Actor and Aegina. He married either Sthenele or Periopis and became the father of the hero, Patroclus. *See also* Actor; Aegina; Patroclus.

Menra (Roman) *see* Minerva.

Menrfa (Etruscan) *see* Minerva.

Menrva (Etruscan) *see* Minerva.

Menthe *Mentha, Mintha* (Greek)

Menthe, a nymph of the river Cocytus in the underworld, was the secret lover of Hades until Demeter found out about the affair. Either Demeter or Persephone beat Menthe brutally and changed her to dust. From Menthe as dust came the mint plant. *See also* Cocytus; Demeter; Hades; Persephone.

Menthu (Egypt, Greek) *see* Buchis.

Mentu (Egypt, Greek) *see* Buchis.

Menu *Meni* (Chaldean) (Assyro-Babylonian, Chaldean)

Menu is variously called a mother goddess, a goddess of fate, and a goddess of good luck. She is also known as Meni, the Babylonian goddess of love. Some say that Menu is male, and that he is a moon deity. Menu may be associated with Gadda (q.v.), and possibly is the same deity Manat (q.v.). *See also* Ishtar; Min.

Menuis (Egypt) *see* Ra.

Menur (Egypt, Greek) *see* Mnevis.

Mer (Babylon, Sumer) *see* Ishkur; Rimmon.

Mer-en-aaui-f (Egypt) *see* Ap-taui.

Mer-ur (Greek) *see* Apis.

Mercurius (Gallo-Roman) *see* Mercury (B).

Mercury (A) (Roman)

Aspects or known as: *Mercurius, Vialis* (Roman)

The protector of roads, and travelers, the deity of commerce, patron of merchants, thieves, scoundrels, and astronomers, Mercury is also the messenger of the gods.

He is the Roman version of the Greek Hermes. He was worshipped in Rome (approx. 495 B.C.) along with a goddess who appears to be Hermes' mother, Maia (also known as Rosmerta), the daughter of Atlas. The Latin poet Ovid, who wrote of Mercury's friendship and adventures with the god Jupiter, described him as a humorous and shrewd deity. Mercury's original name has not been discovered but many believe him to be the Irish Lugh. The name of Vialis was used because Mercury presided over the making of roads. Mercury is shown as a youthful male standing on tip-toe, wearing a winged hat and winged sandals. He is also depicted with coins or a purse and sometimes with a golden chain. This depiction is almost identical to the description of Hermes, except that Hermes is not shown with a purse. His attributes are the sword, chalice and harp. The cock was his sacred bird and the tortoise and goat were his sacred animals. His symbol was the four-horned serpent (quadricornutus serpens). He was often depicted holding a caduceus (a staff with two serpents entwined), and a purse. The staff is his attribute as it is for Asclepius, Dionysus and Hermes. He also appears in Gaulish dress, bearded, with his sacred animals, the cock, goat and tortoise. *See also* Hermes; Lugh (guardians of roads and travelers). *See also* Acca Larentia; Esus; Pitho.

Mercury (B) The planet. *See also* Budha (India); Eurynome A (Greek).

Meriones (Greek) *see* Acamas (B).

Merlin (British) *see* Arthur; Vivien.

Mermer (Sumer) *see* Ishkur.

Mermerus (A) (Greek)
Mermerus was well known for his ability to concoct poison. He is the son of Pheres (q.v.).

Mermerus (B) (Greek)
His parents are Jason the Argonaut and Medea, the seer and magician. *See also* Jason; Medea.

Merodach (Babylon) *see* Marduk.

Merope (A) (Greek)
Another name for Eriboea (q.v.). *See also* Aepytus; Oceanids; Orion; Pleiades; Sisyphus.

Merope (B) (Greek)
She is the daughter of Erechtheus, the 6th or 7th king of Athens.

Merope (C) (Greek)
One of the Pleiades. She is the daughter of Atlas and Pleione. Because she married the mortal Sisyphus, she is not visible in the night sky. *See also* Alcyone; Atlas; Electra; Pleiades; Pleione.

Merope (D) (Greek)
Also known as: *Clytie.*
She is the daughter of Pandareus and Harmothoe. When the great god, Zeus, killed her parents, she and her sister, Cleothera were raised by Athena. When the Harpies kidnapped the sisters, they were forced to be servants to the Erinyes. *See also* Athena; Erinyes; Harmothoe; Harpies.

Merops (A) (Greek)
King of Percote. His father is also known as Merops. Merops, the younger, became the father of Arisbe, Adrastus, Amphius and Cleite. He taught Aesacus how to interpret dreams. *See also* Aesacus; Cleite; Oceanids.

Merops (B) (Greek) He is the husband of Clymene.

Merops (C) (Greek)
He traveled with Aeneas from Troy to Italy.

Mers (Greek) *see* Ares.

Mertseger (Egypt)
Also known as: *Mert-sekert, Merseger.*
Funerary goddess. This Theban goddess, who represents silence, is closely associated with Osiris. Mertseger is the Greek name of the Egyptian snake goddess, Mert-sekert. She is depicted as a snake with the head of a woman, often surmounted by the solar disk, or with the head of a vulture and a snake on either side of her human head.

Meru Mountain (Brahmanic, Hindu, Jain, Buddhist; India)
Also known as: *Deva-Parvata, Kailasa* (Buddhist), *Ratnasanu, Sumeru.*
The sacred mountain of Mount Meru is placed in the Himalaya range. A mystical range, the cosmic center is both interior and exterior. It has three luminous peaks each composed of gold, silver and iron. Often called the golden mountain, it is located on the round, flat, continent of Jambudvipa, known as the world's center, where the cities of the gods are located. Mountains, separated by oceans, surround Mount Meru, which acts as a pivot for the three worlds. The sun, moon, stars, and all heavenly bodies revolve around it. Meru is Brahma's heaven (known as Brahmapura), and home to numerous other deities. Indra's heaven, Swarga (or third heaven), is located on the summit, which is said to be 84,000 *yojanas* (leagues) high. His site, built by the divine architect Tvashtri, is portable and can be moved anywhere. Vishnu's paradisical Vaikuntha is on its slopes. The Gandharvas reside in the foothills and demons live in the valleys. The Buddhist religion has a similar mountain called Kailasa. Meru is the center of the world lotus and the axis of the human spinal column. Jambudvipa, the ancient esoteric name for India, is located around Meru. Meru corresponds to the Mt. Olympus of the Greek mythology. Mount Mandara, which became the home of the earth goddess Durga, is another sacred mountain. *See also* Bhishma; Brahma; Durga; Indra; Indrani; Kurma (Vishnu's avatar as a tortoise); Loka; Patala; Swarga; Tvashtri; Vaikuntha; Visvakarma.

Merur (Egypt) *see* Ra.

Merwer the Bull (Egypt) The sacred animal of Atum (q.v.).

Mese (Greek)
One of the Delphic Muses, she personifies the middle string of the lyre. Her sisters are Hypate, the high string, and Nete, the low string.

Mesede (Melanesian)
God of archery. When his bow is drawn it causes fire. He is associated with the goddess Abere.

Meshkhent (Egypt) Another spelling for Meskhenit.

Meshlamthea (Greek) *see* Neral (Sumer).

Meskhenit *Meshkhenet, Meskhent, possibly Meshkhent* (Egypt)
Also known as: *Hathor*
Goddess of childbirth. Meskhenit determines the "ka" of the child while still in the womb. At birth, she determines the infant's destiny. Four Meskhenits appear as servants of Isis in the circle of Abydine gods. Meskhenit is identified with the birth brick, which is used for squatting when the woman is about to give birth. According to the *Rind Papyrus*, Thoth carved the time of one's death into birth bricks. Meskhenit is identified with Hathor in her role of mother goddess. She is sometimes shown as a woman with a headdress of palm-shoots or as a brick with a woman's head. *See* Isis; Ka.

Meskhti (Egypt) *see* Ap-taui.

Meslam (A) (Babylon)
This is another name for Aralu, the underworld.

Meslam (B) (Egypt) *see* Amset.

Mesperit-Arat-Maatu (Egypt)
The name of the Sixth Hour of Tuat. *See also* Osiris; Tuat.

Messene (Greek)
She is the daughter of Triopas and Hiscilla, and the wife of the first king of Messenia, Polycaon. *See also* Hiscilla; Iphimedeia; Triopas.

Messibizi (Algonquin People, North America) *see* Michabo.

Messon (Algonquin People, North America) *see* Michabo.

Messou (Native North American) *see* Nanabozho.

Mesta (Egypt) *see* Amset.

Mestha (Egypt) *see* Amset.

Mesti (Egypt) *see* Amset.

Mestor (Greek) *see* Andromeda; Gorgophone.

Metapontus (Greek)
He might be the son of Aeolus and brother of Melanippe. Theano had two sons when Metapontus married her. He assumed they were his children. They had two more sons before he found out that the first two children were not his. He killed Theano and her two sons. (Theano founded Padua after the fall of Troy.) *See also* Theano.

Metharme (Greek)
She is Pygmalion's daughter. *See also* Adonis; Pygmalion.

Methyer (Egypt) *see* Isis.

Metidice (Greek)
He is one of Adrestus' children. *See also* Adrestus.

Metis (Greek)
Metis is the daughter of Oceanus and Tethys and the first wife of the great god Zeus. When she became pregnant with their daughter, the goddess Athena, Zeus swallowed her. He was fearful that a second child would be a son more powerful than he. Athena was born from Zeus' brain, through his head. Metis was known for her infinite wisdom. It is said that she knew more than all the gods. *See also* Athena; Cronus; Eurynome (A); Oceanids; Zeus.

Metope (Greek)
She is the wife of the river god Asopus, and the mother of twenty daughters and three sons. For a partial list of their names, *see* Pelasgus (B). *See also* Aegina; Antiope; Asopus; Rivers.

Metropator (Gnostic) *see* Demiurge.

Metrope (Greek) *see* Phaethon.

Metteya (India) *see* Maitreya.

Metu-khut-f (Egypt) *see* Aai.

Metztli (Aztec) *see* Meztli.

Meuler (Araucanian People, Chile)
Wind god.
God of all winds, waterspouts and typhoons. He is represented as a lizard who is disappearing underground.

Mexitli *Mextli* (Aztec) *see* Huitzilopochtli.

Mezamat (Latvia) Goddess of Forests.

Mezavirs (Latvia)
Also known as: *Mezadevs.*
God of Forests. Probably the same as Mezamat.

Meztli *Metztli* (Aztec; Mexico)
Also known as: *Coyolxauhqui, Tecciztecatl* (Male), *Yohualticitl* (the Lady of the Night).
Moon goddess. Goddess of darkness. Agricultural goddess. Meztli was burned in flames, symbolic of the consuming of night and the birth of the light of day. Meztli is the same as the Yohualticitl. *See also* Coyolxauhqui; Tecciztecatl; Tezcatlipoca; Yohualticitl.

Mi-che-pa (Tibet) *see* Abheda; Medicine Buddhas.

Mi-Ho-Tsu Hime (Japan) *see* Kami-Mimusubi.

Mi-Hung-T'ang (China)
Also known as: *Broth of Oblivion, Mi-Hun-T'ang.*
Broth of oblivion. Lady Meng gives the broth to all mortals who pass through the doors of hell. The drink causes them to forget their past.

Mi-Kura-Tana-no-Kami (Japan)
The sun goddess Amaterasu's sacred jewels. *See also* Amaterasu; Susanowo.

Mi-Li (China) *see* Mi-Lo Fu.

Mi-Lo Fu
Also known as: *Ajita* (the invincible), *Byamspa* (Tibet), *Chem-pa* (Tibet), *Maitreya* (India), *Mi-Li, Miroku-Bosatsu* (Japan), *Pou-T'ai* (China); (Buddhist; China).
He is the last teacher and savior of our world period. In India he is known as Maitreya and in Japan, Miroku-Bosatsu. He is pictured as a fat, jovial figure with a mountainous stomach. Mi-Lo Fu is comparable to the Pou-tai (Chinese). Compare him to Hotei (Japan). *See also* Ajita; Maitreya; Miroku-Bosatsu.

Mi-Oya-no-Kami (Japan) *see* Fuji.

Mi-p'yed (Tibet) *see* Abheda; Medicine Buddhas.

Miach (Celtic)
He is the physician son of Dia'necht, and the brother of Airmid. *See also* Airmid; Dia'necht.

Michabo (Algonquin People, North America)
Also known as: *Giant Rabbit, Great Hare, Messibizi, Messon, Missabos, Missiwabun.*
Supreme deity. Creator of the human race. He was a shape changer who created man by mating with a muskrat. One of his messengers is Gijigouai. In some versions his opponent is Kabun, his father. In other versions, it is his brother Chokaniok who is his opponent. *See also* Kitcki Manitou; Nanabozho.

Miclantecutli *Mictlantecutli, Mictlantecuhtli* (Mexico, Aztec)
Also known as: *Acolnauactl, Tzontemoc.*
Lord of Chicunauhmictlan, the region of Death. Lord of the eleventh hour of the day. Patron of the north. Miclantecutli cares for the souls that arrive in his domain. His spouse is

Miclancihuatl, the goddess of death and lord of the fifth hour of the night. The couple live in a windowless house in Chicunauhmictlan. Quetzalcoatl and his twin brother, Xolotl, stole the bones of the previous generation from him. In anger, Miclantecutli sent quails in pursuit, but the two managed to get away with the bones. (The bones fell and broke during the escape. These broken bones became a race of mortals of various heights and weights.) Miclantecutli's symbol is the skeleton god of the dead. He appears as a skelton of bleached bones splattered with blood spots. Often he is decorated with owl feathers, and head adornments and banners made from paper. He wears a neck piece of extruded eyeballs. *See also* "A"; Chicunauhmictlan; Legend of the Four Suns, Lords of the Day Hours; Lords of the Night Hours; Omeyocan; Quetzalcoatl.

Micronesia — Creation Legend *see* Areop-Enap; Nareau.

Mictanteot (Aztec People, Nicaragua)
Underworld deity. God of the underground where dead souls go. Good souls go to join Tamagostad and Zipaltonal. One of the major gods of the underground is Masaya the goddess of volcanos. Similar to Mictlantecuhtli (Mexico). *See also* Masaya.

Mictecacihuatl (Aztec People, Mexico) *see* Mictecaciuatl.

Mictlantecutli (Aztec) See Micantecutli.

Mictlantecuhtli (Aztec) *see* Miclantecutli.

Miclancihuatl (Aztec)
Lady of the Region of Death. See also Miclantecutli.

Mictlan (Aztec)
A commonly used abbreviation for Chicunauhmictlan.

Micux (Natchez People, North America)
A heroine. The human daughter of a cannibal spirit.

Mid-gard (Teutonic) *see* Midgard.

Midas (Greek)
King of Phrygia. Discoverer of white and black lead. His parents are Gordius of the "Gordian Knot" fame and Cybele. King Midas entertained Silenus, the king of Nysa, and in return Silenus gave him the "golden touch." One day as he bathed in the river Pactolus he lost his touch. He is shown with the ears of an ass, given to him by Apollo. *See also* Cybele; Gordius.

Middle Earth (Teutonic) *see* Midgard.

Mider *Midir, Mithr.*
Also known as: *Aileili* (Celtic).
A chief god of the underworld. He is the son of Dagda and Boann and the brother of Angus. Mider was raised as the foster son of Manannan mac Lir. When he grew up, he in turn fostered Angus of the Brugh. Mider owned a magic cauldron that was stolen from him by Chchulainn. He had two abodes. He lived in a castle on the Isle of Man where he kept three exceptional cows and a magic cauldron. The castle was guarded by three cranes. Whenever a stranger passed, the cranes would croak loudly. His other residence was at the sidh (burial mound) of Bri Leith (in County Longford). As Aileili, he is Etain's lover. *See* Angus; Blathnat; Boann; Etain (A).

Midewiwin (Algonquin People, North America)
Sacred dance. It is the "Great Medicine Dance" which guards

the tribe in matters of safety, health and wealth. The Chippewa Indians used the name for their society of shamans.

Midgaard (Teutonic) *see* Midgard.

Midgard *Mid-gard, Midgaard, Midgarth* (Norse; Teutonic)
Also known as: *Mana-heim, Middle Earth.*
Midgard is the earth, the abode of man; it is one of the nine worlds of Norse mythology. Midgard, meaning middle abode, is located halfway between Nifl-heim and Muspells-heim. Midgard was fashioned from the body of the evil frost giant Ymir who was slain by Odin, Vili, and Ve. The skull of Ymir became the vault of heaven over Midgard. The four corners of heaven were held up by four strong dwarfs, one stationed in each corner: Nordri, Sudri, Austri, and Westri. The light for Midgard was supplied by sparks from Muspells-heim. The sun and moon were also created from this source. Ymir's flesh became the land, his blood the sea, his bone the mountains, and his hair the trees. Ymir's eyebrows were used to encircle Midgard to protect it from the evil Giants. Jormungandr, also known as the Midgard Serpent, encircles the whole earth. Midgard is where Odin, Vili and Ve, or in some versions Odin, Henir, and Loki found the ash and elm trees or two blocks of wood from which they manufactured the first man and woman, Ask and Embla. Odin gave them souls, Henir gave them motion and senses, and Loki gave them blood and complexions. After Midgard was created, other gods came to assist Bor's sons in fashioning a dwelling place for the gods. It is known as Asgard (q.v.). *See also* Asgard; Ask; Bor; Dwarfs; Gullveig; Henir; Jormungandr; Jotun-heim; Loki; Mana-heim; Muspells-heim; Nifl-heim; Odin; Sudri; Ve; Vili; Westri; Yggdrasil; Ymir.

Midgard Serpent (Teutonic) *see* Jormungandr; Midgard.

Midgardsormen (Teutonic) *see* Jormungandr.

Midgarth (Teutonic) *see* Midgard.

Midir (Celtic, Irish) *see* Mider.

Miehts-Hozjin (Lapp) *see* Leshy.

Mielikki (Lapp)
Forest spirit. He is the husband of Tapio and possibly a god of hunters. *See also* Tapio.

Mig-mi-bzan (Tibet) *see* Virupaksha.

Might (Teutonic) *see* Magni; Thrud.

Mighty Striker, The (Celtic) *see* Sucellos.

Mihir (Persia) *see* Mitra.

Mihr (Armenian; Iranian)
Also known as: *Mithra.*
Probably a god of light, air, war, and contracts. Possibly an underworld or fire deity. Although called the son of Aramazd and brother of Anahit and Nane, he seems to have been a different god than Mithra. He was of the triad of Aramazd and Anahit of the Armenians. In Persia, he was said to represent the sun and was a child of Ormazd. Later, he was replaced by the god Vahagn. As god of fire he was associated with Hephaistos of the Greeks. *See also* Anahita; Aramazd; Mithra; Vahagn.

Mihtajan (Persian) Mithra's festival. *See also* Mitra.

Mii-no-kami (Japan) *see* Kappa.

Mikak'e (Osage People, North America)
Star deities. The Star People.

Mikal (Middle Eastern) *see* Moloch.

Mikura-Tana-no-kami (Japan) *see* Amaterasu.

Milanion (Greek) *see* Melanion.

Milaraspa *Mila-Raspa* (Buddhist)
Born early in the twelfth century, Milaraspa spent his life wandering through Tibet converting people to Buddhism. He was a mendicant poet who is said to have written over one hundred thousand poems. Milaraspa is depicted as seated on a lotus petal covered with a gazelle skin. He has short, curly hair, holds his right hand behind his ear as though listening to something. In his left hand he holds a begging bowl.

Milcom (Middle Eastern) *see* Moloch.

Milesians (Irish) *see* Amergin; Tuatha De Danann.

Miletus (Greek)
He is the son of Apollo and possibly Acacallis. He loved Sarpedon, the son of the great god, Zeus. *See also* Acacallis; Minos; Sarpedon (A).

Milk (Gilyak People, Siberia) Devils.

Milky Way *see* Breathmaker (North America); Chin Nu (China); Irmin (Teutonic); Itoki (Japan); Ituna (Central America); Khotun (Siberia); Kilyikhama (South America); Kuei-Hui (China); Manzan Gormo (Middle Eastern); Muludaianinis (Australia); Vahagn (Armenia).

Milomaki (Amazon People, Brazil)
Food deity. According to myth, a little boy came from the sun and was gifted with a voice that charmed all the people. They called him Milomake or Son of Milo. In the legend, shortly after hearing the boy sing the people ate some fish that killed many of them. Thinking the boy was the cause of the deaths, they killed and burned him. From his ashes came a long blade of grass which quickly developed into a giant Paziuba palm. The men make flutes from this palm which they play when the fruit is ripe. Only men can play or look on the flutes for women and children will die if they so much as glimpse the instrument. He could be related to Tupan.

Milu (Oceanic) *see* Maui.

Mim (Teutonic) *see* Mimir.

Mimar (Teutonic) *see* Mimir.

Mimas (Greek) *see* Ares; Giants; Hephaistos.

Mime (Teutonic) *see* Mimir.

Mimer-Nidhad (Teutonic) *see* Mimir.

Mimi *Mini* (Aborigine People, Australia)
Spirits. These spirits are responsible for teaching the people to paint. They are usually shown dancing, fighting, running, or hunting. Their bones are so brittle they refuse to go out in the wind. Their diet consists of people and yams.

Miming (Teutonic)
In a Danish version, drawn from Norse sources, regarding the death of Balder, it is necessary for Hodur to gain possession of Miming's sword to wound Balder. Miming is a forest troll who is the son of Hothbrod, and the foster son of Gevar. In the same version, Hodur is not a blind god, but a god distinguished for his strength and prowess. In another version, Miming's sword was creted by the clever smith Volund for his son Heime. *See also* Balder; Hodur; Volund.

Mimir *Mim, Mimar, Mime, Mimer-Nidhad* (Norse; Teutonic)
Also known as: *Baugreginn Jotunn* (King of the Gold Rings), *Hodd-Dropnir, Hodd-Mimer* (Treasure-Mimer), *Hoddrofnir* (The Treasure-dropping One), *Naddgofugr.*
Chief of smiths. God of prophecy and wisdom, god of waters, ponds, and a god of knowledge, the giant Mimir is sometimes called a water demon. He is the keeper of the well of wisdom which also mirrors the future. Mimir's Well flows from the root of the tree of life, Yggdrasil in Jotun-heim. Mimir drinks from the well daily. When the war between the Aesir and the Vanir ended, Henir and Mimir were given to the Vanir as hostages. Henir, a handsome man was thought to be chieftain material and was given a position of leadership in Vanaheim. When the Vanir realized that Henir was incompetent without Mimir, they killed Mimir and sent his head to the Aesir. Odin embalmed the head and used his magic to cause the head to talk. Mimir's talking head was able to answer Odin's questions and tell him secrets of life that were hidden from others. Odin asked Mimir for a drink of the magic beverage from his spring or well. Mimir agreed but demanded in return one of Odin's eyes, which Mimir later used as a cup. Odin never regretted exchanging his eye for wisdom. He was also given the ability to see the future which saddened him. In commeration of that day, Odin broke a branch from the Yggdrasil tree and created his cherished spear Gungnir. Odin's eye may symbolize the all-seeing sun, which sinks into the sea in the evening and from which the "keeper of the sea" appears to be drinking at sunrise. Mimir is the son of Ymir and was formed from the sweat from under Ymir's left arm. Mimir is Odin's uncle, and Bolthorn's brother. Compare Mimir's story to the tale of the Celtic god Bran. *See also* Aesir; Bestla; Bolthorn; Gungnir; Henir; Jotun-heim; Mimir's Well; Odin; Vanaheim; Vanir; Yggdrasil.

Mimir's Well (Norse; Teutonic)
Well of wisdom. The god Mimir is in charge of the magic spring of wisdom that bubbles up from the root of the Yggdrasil tree. Odin gave an eye for a drink from this well. Mimir's head was cut from his body by the Vanir gods, but was restored to life by Odin. It still protects the well. *See also* Mimir; Odin; Yggdrasil.

Min *Men, Menu, Minub* (Egypt)
Also known as: *Amen* (possibly), Amsu.
God of fertility, vegetation, procreation. God of those who travel in the desert. God of hunters and miners. One of the most ancient gods of Egypt, he was called Min of Koptos. The original gods of this area, Rahes and Min, were depicted as falcons. It appears that Min replaced this god and may have been associated with the Canaanite/Phoenician deity of war, Reshep. Both had the same consort who was the Syrian goddess of love,

Quadesh. The cult of Min celebrated the god's festival at harvest time by sacrificing a white bull. He is variously shown as an ithyphallic bearded man, a storm god wielding thunderbolts, a bull, and later as a falcon when he became identified with Horus the Elder as a sky god. He was worshipped in the form of a sacred white bull. Lettuce (considered an aphrodisiac) was one of his most important attributes and was offered to him during ceremonies and is shown with him in many reliefs. He is also depicted in human form with his legs tight together, an erect phallus, a club or stick above his arm, which was raised stiffly with his hand extended to one side, wearing a skullcap with two plumes and two streamers hanging down the back. His personal fetish represented the cigar-shaped cuttle-fish. He is identified with Amen-Ra and with the Greek god Pan. *See also* Aahes; Amen (B); Amsu; Khnu; Nephthys; Quadesh; Reshep.

Min-Amen (Egypt) *see* Amsu.

Minabozho (Algonquin People, North America)
Sea deity. He is the god who fell into the sea and caused it to overflow.

Minakshi (India) "Fish-Eyed." *See also* Devi; Kuvera.

Minakshidevi (India) *see* Devi; Kuvera.

Minato-no-kami (Japan) *see* Kappa.

Mindi (Australia) *see* Rainbow Snake.

Minerva *Menerva, Menrfa, Menrva* (Etruscan, later, Roman)
Also known as: *Athena* (Greek), *Medica.*
Keeper of the city of Rome. Goddess of war. Patroness of physicians. Goddess of intellectual activity, particularly schools. Goddess of wisdom. Patroness of arts and crafts. Patron and goddess of craftspeople. She is the daughter of Jupiter and one of the triad of Jupiter, Juno and Minerva. She has the same qualities as the Irish Brigit and may be the same as the Celtic Belisama. Minerva's sacred animal is the antelope. Thought to be a prophetic animal, its eyes are associated with sharpness of vision. *See also* Aegis; Ana-Purna; Athena; Bellerophon; Brigantia; Brigit; Cupra; Isis; Juno; Tina.

Minga Bengale (Shongon People, Africa)
God of hunters. God who taught humans how to make nets.

Minibozho (Native North American) *see* Nanabozho.

Minipat (Africa) see Muluku.

Minos (Greek)
King of Crete. Law-giver. Shipbuilder. Minos is the son of Zeus and Europa and the brother of Rhadamanthys and Sarpedon. Rhadamanthys was the king of Crete before Minos. His brother Sarpedon went into exile when Minos became the ruler. Minos married Pasiphae the daughter of Helius. He is the father of Acacallis, Androgeus, Ariadne, Catreus, Deucalion, Euryale, Glaucus, Lycastus, Phaedra and Xenodice. Europa married Asterius, the childless king of Crete who adopted her sons by Zeus: Minos, Sarpedon and Rhadamanthys. Upon his death the brothers quarreled either over the estate or over the love of a beautiful young man named Miletus or Atymnius. When the young man declared his preference for Sarpedon, Minos drove his brothers from the kingdom. To quell other rivals and to

illustrate his divine heritage he prayed to Poseidon to send him a bull which he promised to sacrifice. Poseidon honored his desires and sent a stunning beast up from the sea. When Minos saw it, he couldn't bear to part with it and nefariously sacrificed a substitute. Enraged, Poseidon decided to follow through with a bullish plan. At this time, Minos was married to Pasiphae, the moon goddess. They had a large family: Catreus, who was killed accidentally; Deucalion, the Argonaut; Androgeus, the Panathenaic athlete who was killed by the Marathonian bull; Acacallis, who, pregnant by Apollo, was banished to Libya by her father; Glaucus, who as a baby drowned in a large jug of honey; Ariadne, who fell in love with Theseus and helped him escape from the Labyrinth; Phaedra, who married Theseus and eventually committed suicide; and Xenodice. Poseidon with the assistance of the well known inventor and craftsperson Daedalus arranged to have Pasiphae fall in love with the bull that Minos would not sacrifice. The result of this union was the monstrous deity of darkness, Minotaur, a half-human, half-bull creature. Minos took care of the situation and continued to look after his kingdom. He was a well-liked monarch who established laws handed down by Zeus. His wife grew weary of his multitudinous affairs, detailed in another section. His exact cause of death is not certain but it has been said that Minos was killed by the daughters of King Cocalus of Camicus who drowned him in boiling water. After death he became a judge in the Underworld along with his brother Rhadamanthys and Aeacus who was a son of Zeus and the king of Aegina. For details of the impact that Minotaur had on the lives of Athenians, *see* Minotaur. For details of Minos' extramarital affairs, *see* Britomaris. Some researchers write that Minos as judge of the underworld was not the Minos described above. They name him the son of Lycastus and Ida or sometimes the son of some other Minos. The judges who sit with him in the underworld are Rhadamanthys and Sarpedon. *See also* Acacallis; Aeacus; Aegis; Europa; Helius; Orion; Pasiphae; Perse; Rhadamanthys; Sarpedon (A); Styx; Theseus.

Minotaur *Minotaurus* (Greek)
Also known as: *Asterion, Asterios, Asterius.*
Deified animal. Deity of darkness. Minotaur, meaning Bull of Minos, was the half-bull, half-human creature who was the offspring of Pasiphae, the wife of Minos, and a bull. His name was Asterius, meaning "star," but he is usually called the Minotaur. Minos had the inventor Daedalus construct the famous Labrinyth to contain and hide the monster. Minos felt that Aegeus, the king of Athens, was responsible for the death of his son Androgeus and in retribution he demanded that seven young men and seven young women, all Athenians, be sacrificed to the beast annually or every nine years in some versions of the myth. Theseus the hero, always looking for a stupendous obstacle to overcome, decided to conquer the Minotuar. Ariadne, the daughter of Minos, had seen Theseus and fallen in love with him. She knew that if he entered the Labrinyth it would be a one way path to certain doom. She approached Daedalus the builder of the maze for assistance. It was decided that Theseus would take a large ball of twine and tie one end of it to the entrance of the Labrinyth and unwind it as he made his way to the beast. When he found Minotaur, he beat him to death with his fists, followed the twine back to the entrance and exited to

safety. In other versions of this legend, this beast was the offspring of Europa, the mother of Minos. Depicted as either a monster or bull with the head of a man or vice versa. *See also* Aeetes; Daedalus; Minos; Pasiphae; Theseus.

Minotaurus (Greek) *see* Minotaur.

Mintha *Minthe* (Greek)
Other spellings for Menthe, the nymph of the Cocytus river in Tartarus, the underworld. *See also* Menthe.

Minthe (Greek) *see* Menthe.

Minu (Egypt) *see* Min.

Minu-anni (Assyro-Babylonian) *see* Ishtar.

Minucihr (Persia) *see* Faridun.

Minyas (Greek)
Minyas built the first treasury. He is the maternal grandfather of Admetus and the son of Aeolus, Chryses or Poseidon. He is the father of Alcithoe, Arsippe, Clymene, Leucippe and Periclymene. His daughters Alcithoe, Arsippe and Leucippe were driven mad by Dionysus and turned into bats. *See also* Admetus; Dionysus.

Minyas, The (Greek)
They are the daughters of Minyas. *See also* Admetus; Argonauts.

Miolnir (Teutonic) *see* Mjollnir.

Mir (Sumer) *see* Ishkur.

Mirabichi (Ottawa People, North America) God of the water.

Mirage (New Zealand) *see* Arohi-rohi.

Miralad *Miralaidj* (Australia) *see* Djanggawuls.

Miralaidj (Australia) *see* Miralad.

Miroku-Bosatsu *Maitreya* (India), *Mi-Li* (China); (Buddhist; Japan)
Miroku-Bosatsu is the future Buddha who lives in the Tosotsa-Ten (heaven). He will come down to earth 5,670 million years after the entry of the Buddha into Nirvana. He is shown standing on one foot with the other on his left knee, and his right hand on his chin. Sometimes he is depicted standing or seated on a lotus and sometimes he is shown sitting. *See also* Arrida; Maitreya; Mi-Lo-Fu; Tushita.

Mirsi (Sumer) *see* Mirsu.

Mirsu *Mirsi* (Sumer)
Also known as: *Tammuz.*
After creating gods of the sea, Anu created land gods. As a land god, Mirsu was the god of irrigation. Mirsu is also a title of Tammuz (q.v.). *See also* Anu.

Miru (A) (Polynesia)
Also known as: *Locha, Lothia.*
Goddess of the underworld. She shares her responsibilities with Hakea of Hawaii, Lothia or Lakemba of Loyalty Island, or Locha of the same island. Some say Miru ruled only the last three of ten levels of the afterworld. Demonic in the worst sense

of the word, she seduces men to drunkenness on her "kava" which she stocks abundantly in her cellar. Next she cooks her victims in her large, eternally lit oven. When the bodies are ready, she eats the souls. *See also* Hine-nui-te-po; La'i-la'i; Lmahuika; Rohe.

Miru (B) (Polynesia)
Miru, the god of the dead, collects souls in his cave. Large lizards, who are nourished by the flies in the underworld, are his servants.

Miru-me (Japan) *see* Jigoku.

Misambwa (Luganda People, Africa)
They are spirits connected with the clan and with natural objects. The Misambwa may be related to Massim-Biambe of the Mundang people of the Congo. *See also* Massim-Biambe.

Misca (Aztec People, Nicaragua)
God of traders. Misca shared in creation with Ecalchot, Ciaga, Quiateot, Chiquinau, and Vizetot. All were ruled by Tamagostad and Zipaltonal. *See also* Chiquinau; Ciaga; Ecalchot; Quiateot; Vizetot.

Misharu (Sumer)
Also known as: *Misor.*
This deity of law and order could be the same as Misor.

Misor (Semite, Phoenician)
Also known as: *Misharu.*
Creator of salt. Culture hero. Misor may be the god of the autumn sun. He is sometimes referred to as a god of righteousness. Misor is usually mentioned in connection with Sydyk. He could be indirectly related to Kettu and Misharu. *See* Sedeq; Sydyk; Zatik.

Misrakesi (India) *see* Asparases.

Missabos (Algonquin People, North America) *see* Michabo.

Missiwabun (Algonquin People, North America) *see* Michabo.

Mistelteinn (Teutonic)
In some myths, this is the magic weapon used to kill Balder (q.v.).

Mistress of all the Gods (Middle Eastern) *see* Mami.

Mistress of Heaven (A) (Middle Eastern) *see* Nane.

Mistress of Heaven (B) (Babylonia) *see* Inanna (B).

Mistress of the Gods (Middle Eastern) *see* Anat.

Miszuchi (Japan) *see* Izanami.

Mit (Egypt) *see* Nut.

Mithr (Celt) *see* Mider.

Mithra (Persia) *see* Mitra.

Mithras (Roman) *see* Mitra.

Mitnal (Maya People, Yucatan)
Underworld or hell. Ruled by Hanhau or Ahpuch. Mitnal is sometimes identified with Mictlan, the Aztec underworld. *See also* Hanhau; Ixtab.

Mitoshi-no-kami *Mitosh-no-kami, Mitoshino* (Japan)

The god of the harvest. He is sometimes known as a deity of food. He is probably the same as Miketsu-oho-kami.

Mitra *Mithra, Mithras* (Roman); (Aryan, Mazdean, Mithric, Hindu, Vedic, Zoroastrian; Babylonia, India, Persia, Greece, Rome)

Also known as: *Dharmaraha* (India), *Mihir* (Persia), *Mihr* (Pahlavi dialect), *Shamash, Surya* (India), *Yama* (India).

Sun god. Fertility god. Corn god. Mitra is a Babylonian sun and fertility deity and known as an aspect of Shamash. As a Vedic sun god and a Hindu solar deity, Mitra, one of the Adityas, is represented as ruler of the day and Varuna, the moon, as ruler of the night. He is the son of the self-formed goddess Aditi. His siblings are Varuna, Aryaman, Indra, Savitri, Bhaga, Ansa, Vivasvat, Daksha and perhaps Surya. Mitra is one of the triad with Varuna and Aryaman, or some say Agni (fire), and Vayu (wind), or a dyad with Varuna. In the latter instance he is co-guardian (with Varuna) of the laws by which the universe is maintained and nature is made fruitful. He guards over contracts and friendships and Varuna presides over oaths. Together they are known as "supporters of justice." As an aspect of Yama he rules over departed souls. The goddess Danu is sometimes said to be the mate of Mitra-Varuna. Some ancient texts identify Mitra as a sky-goddess. Dharmaraha is said to be a form of Mitra. In some legends, Mitra is identified as the joint father of Agastya, with Varuna by the Apsarasa Urvasi. In pre–Zoroastrian times, he was the giver and guardian of cattle, and a god of light who personified loyalty and obedience. In Zoroastrianism, Mitra is known as Mithra. Mithra, with Sraosha and Rashnu are the judges of dead souls on Chinvat Bridge. In Zoroastrianism, Mithra was armed with a knife and a torch when he was born from a rock in the sphere between heaven and hell. His birth was witnessed by shepherds and the Magi. All animals and herbs were born from the blood of the primeval ox, known as Geusha Urvan that Mithra attacked and killed. This ox went to heaven where it remained as the protector of animals. Bulls were sacrificed to Mithra as part of covenants or pacts between two nations. Thus, he is known as the god of the contract. He is the protector of truth and the enemy of lies. After the death of Zoroastra, Mithra and Anahita were incorporated into Zoroastrianism along with the concept of astralism, possibly by the Magi. Mithra's feast, Mihrajan, takes place on approximately September 7 and lasts for six days. His birthday is December 25. He is one of twenty-eight Izeds (spirits, or angels) surrounding the throne of Ahura Mazda. He has ten thousand eyes and ears, is all-seeing, all-hearing, and never sleeps. Nothing escapes his notice. He watches over family life, and detests the darkness of lies and deceptions. His chariot is drawn by four horses. Mithra is generally shown with a dog, serpent and crow. The dog is his venerated companion. He is also depicted as a lion-headed man with a serpent twined around his body, standing on a globe. India adopted Mithra as Mitra and in later times, he was worshiped in Rome as the patron of soldiers and merchants. Reliefs of a young god attired in a Persian costume and wearing a conical hat were found in Mithraic sanctuaries which are known singularly as the Mithraeum. He is kneeling on a bull and plunging a dagger into its neck. The bull's genitals are being attacked by a scorpion, a serpent drinks the blood and a dog springs from the wound. Ears of wheat emerge from the bull's tail. The bull represents the life force. The scorpion implies the lower world defeating its life-giving purpose. The serpent symbolizes the earth made fertile by sacrificial blood. The Mithraeum was generally found in a cave but if one was not available it was built in a subterranean crypt. At one end a relief was fashioned showing Mithra killing a bull. The Mithraic Mysteries excluded women but permitted men from all economic stratas to become members. Though prevalent in Greece, it was far more popular in Rome where it was established in approximately 67 B.C.E. The worship of Mithra in Rome became extremely important and was valued for its mystery and its ethical system. A depiction known as the Vatican Mithra shows him killing the bull with the assistance of the dog, serpent and a scorpion. Mithra's sacred animals are the ox, bull, cock, and lion. The raven is his sacred bird and the sunflower his sacred flower. The violet is consecrated to Mithra. In the Mithraic doctrine, he was often worshiped in caves. Cakes and the sacred Haoma beverage were offered to him. In the Mazdean legends, the supreme being, Ahura Mazda created Mithra to assist him in battle against his twin brother, Angra Mainyu, the personification of darkness and evil. Mithra, as the male principle, brought forth the moon and the sun, from his light and heat. He also brought forth the female principle in the form of the goddess of waters, Anahita. *See also* Aditi; Adityas; Adon; Agastya; Agni; Ahura Mazda; Alburz (Mount); Anahita; Angra Mainyu; Aryaman; Bhaga; Chinvat Bridge; Daksha; Danu; Haoma; Indra; Mihr; Parvati; Rashnu; Savitri (A); Shamash; Sraosha; Surya; Urvasi; Varuna; Vasistha; Vayu; Vivasvat; Yama; Yazatas; Yima.

Mitshi-Manitou *Mudje-Monedo* (Chippewa People, North America)

Evil spirit. He is the opponent of Kitshi Manito (q.v.).

Mitsu-ha No-me (Japan) *see* Izanami.

Mitsuha-nome (Japan) *see* Izanami.

Mixcoatl *Mixkotl* (Aztec, Huejotzingo People, Tlaxcalan People; Mexico)

Also known as: *Camaxtli* (known by this name as principal god of the Huejotzingo and Tlaxcal people), *Huitzilopochtli, Iztac Mixcoatl, Red Tezcatlipoca, Totepeuh.*

"Cloud Serpent." God of hunting. Associated with war and fire. Identified with the stars. Mixcoatl is the son of Tonacatecuhtli and Tonacacihuatl. He has three siblings. He is the father of 400 sons known as the Centzon Huitznahua. Mixcoatl became the father of Quetzalcoatl with one of the five females he created to service the sun. Once, Tezcatlipoca assumed Mixcoatl's identity. As Tezcatlipoca-Mixcoatl he brought fire to mortals. Mixcoatl's festival, Quecholli (the "small bird"), takes place during the first 18 days of November. A male and a female were sacrificed to him. It was the time to produce and service weapons for war. Mixcoatl wears a black mask, sometimes with white dots symbolizing stars surrounding it. The god of the Morning Star, Tlahuizcalpantecuhtli also wears the same eye gear. Mixcoatl's body is painted with red and white stripes. He is sometimes shown with a bow and arrow and a basket to carry his hunter's catch. *See also* Camaxtli; Huitzilopochtli; Quetzalcoatl; Tezcatlipoca.

Mixkotl (Mexico) *see* Mixcoatl.

Miysis (Egypt) God of the slaughter. *See also* Bast.

Mizimu (Luganda People, Africa)
Also known as: *Muzimu.*
Spirits of the dead.

Mjollnir *Miolnir, Mjolnir* (Norse; Teutonic)
Deified object. Magic hammer of Thor. Regardless of distance, the hammer always returns to the hand of Thor. The hammer is so red-hot, Thor wears the magic glove or gauntlet, Iarn-greiper, to hold it. It was made by the dwarfs Brokk and Eitri.

Mka-gro-ma (Tibet) *see* Dakinis.

Mkah Hgroma (Buddhist; Tibet)
Blessings and esoterical knowledge are the boons received from believers in Mkah Hgroma, who is a type of mother goddess. She is similar to the Hindu dakinis (q.v.).

Mmoatia (Twi People, Africa)
Also known as: *Aboatia* (singular).
Spirits. The Mmoatia are little people of the forest, or "fairies."

Mmokos (Slavic)
Also known as: *Mokusa.*
Goddess of sheep. Goddess of those who spin wool.

Mnemosyne (Greek)
Goddess of memory. She is the Titan daughter of Uranus and Gaea, and mother, by Zeus, of the Muses, goddesses of the arts. *See also* Ceos; Cronus; Gaea; Melpomene; Muses; Themis.

Mneuis (Egypt) *see* Mnevis.

Mnevis *Mneuis* (Egypt)
Also known as: *Menur, Mer-ur, Wer-mer.*
Sacred bull. He is the sun god Ra, incarnated as a bull. He is depicted as a black bull with the sun-disk between the horns. *See also* Apis (A); Buchis; Osiris.

Mo-hi-hai (China) God of water.

Mo-li (China) *see* Tien-Wang.

Mo-li-chi (China) *see* Chandi; Tou Mu.

Mo-li Ch'ing (Buddhist; China)
Also known as: *Tseng Chang.*
Protector deity. God of happiness. One of the Diamond Kings (Ssu Ta Chin-kang). Mo-li Ch'ing is the brother of Mo-li Hung, Mo-li Hai and Mo-li Shou. He can create wind, smoke or serpents. This god is twenty-four feet tall with a beard like copper wire. He wears a jade ring on his finger, carries a spear and a magic sword. *See also* Mo-li Hai; Mo-li Hung; Mo-li Shou; Ssu Ta Chin-kang.

Mo-li Hai (China)
Protector deity. God of happiness. Brother of Mo-li Ch'ing, Mo-li Hung and Mo-li Shou. One of the Diamond Kings. He is probably a storm or weather deity. Mo-li Hai is shown holding a four-string guitar. *See also* Diamond Kings; Ssu Ta Chin-kang.

Mo-li Hung (China)
Also known as: *Kuang Mu.*
Protector deity. God of happiness. One of the Diamond Kings (Ssu Ta Chin-kang). Brother of Mo-li Ch'ing, Mo-li Hai and Mo-li Shou. He can cause darkness with his magic umbrella. When he turns it upside down it produces storms, thunder, wind, and earthquakes. Mo-li Hung is shown holding an umbrella. *See also* Ssu Ta Chin-kang.

Mo-li Shou (China)
Also known as: *Ch'ih Kuo.*
Protector deity. God of happiness. One of the Diamond Kings. Brother of Mo-li Ch'ing, Mo-li Hung, and Mo-li Hai. This deity is in charge of an animal that is similar to a white rat. When turned loose from the panther-skin bag which keeps him in check, he turns into a white winged elephant that devours men. Mo-li Shou also can bring forth a snake or other man-eating creatures. He is shown with two whips and a bag made of panther skin. *See also* Diamond Kings; Ssu Ta Chin-kang.

Moaalii (Hawaii, Polynesia)
Moaalii is a local shark god of Molokai and Oahu. He is similar to Ukanipo.

Mode (Teutonic) *see* Modi.

Modgud (Norse; Teutonic)
Guardian. She is the woman who guards the bridge over the river Gjoll in Jotunheim.

Modi *Mode* (Norse; Teutonic)
God of wrath or courage. Wind deity. Son of Thor and the giant female Iarnsaxa. Modi and his brother Magni will inherit the hammer Mjollnir after Ragnarok. *See also* Iarnsaxa; Magni; Mjollnir; Ragnarok; Thor.

Modron (Welsh) "Great Mother." *See also* Matronae.

Modsogner *Modsognir* (Norse; Teutonic)
Also known as: *Mimir* (possibly).
Creator of dwarfs. Chief of all artists. Modsogner is one of the dwarf creator gods who existed before creation. He was assisted in the task of creating dwarfs resembling man, by Durin. Some say Modsogner and the rest of the dwarfs were created by Odin and his brothers from the maggots found in the flesh of Ymir. There is reference to Modsogner as an aspect of Mimir. *See also* Durin; Mimir; Ymir.

Moerae (Greek) *see* Moirai.

Moertholl (Teutonic) *see* Freyja; Moertholl.

Mohammed *Muhammad* (Arabic), *Mahomet* (Turkish).
Also known as: *al-Amin* ("Honest"; Islamic).
The son of Abd-allah and Amina and the grandson of Abd-el-Muttalib, Mohammed was born in Mecca in Common Era (A.D.) 570 and died in 632. Some say that his birth date is not certain and place it between 568 and 572. His father died before his birth. During his teens, he was known as al-Amin. He is the last of the divine messengers sent to warn mortals. Married several times, his first wife, a widow fifteen years his senior, was Khadija. During their happy marriage of twenty years, they had two (some say three) sons who died and four daughters, Zainab,

Ruqaiyah, Umm Kulthum, and Fatimah. Mohammed is the founder of Islam and the author of the *Koran*, the *Hadith* and the *Sirah*. The Word of God was revealed to Mohammed through the Angel Jibril (also: Gabriel). His message appealed to people of the lower socio-economic strata and posed a threat to the ruling classes. He was accused of being insane, being possessed by evil spirits and of being a magician. Mohammed and his small band of followers were persecuted incessantly. In the year 620, Mohammed had a vision that became known as the "Night Journey" or "Ascension." On the winged horse Burag, guided by Jibril, he was taken from the Ka'ba at Mecca to the Temple in Jerusalem. He climbed the ladder of light to the foot of the heavenly throne. In the world, conditions grew worse for him. Eventually he left Mecca and went to Yathrib, later known as Medina. Mohammed's flight in 622, known as the Hegira (or hijra), marks the beginning of the Islamic calendar. The majority of the Medinans accepted Islam. The Jewish colony resisted his message and numerous battles resulted. It was during this period that the jihad or "holy war" was born. His armies were victorious throughout the area and when they returned to Mecca peaceful arrangements were made with his former enemies. A few years later, feeling that death was eminent, the Prophet led ninety thousand believers into Mecca. On sacred Mount Arafat, where Adam and Eve had met, Mohammed gave his final sermon. It was accompanied by rites still practiced by muslims. The prophet's favorite fruit was the date. Mohammed denounced the characterization of Jesus as the Son of God, but referred to him as another prophet. *See also* Abraham; Gabriel; Jesus; Koran.

Mohini (India) She is the female incarnation of Vishnu.

Moira (Roman) Goddess of fate. *See also* Eumenides; Fates.

Moirae (Greek) *see* Moirai.

Moirai *Moerae, Moira, Moirae* (Greek)
Also known as: *Atropos, Fates* (Roman), *Parcae* (Roman).
Deities of destiny. Clotho (the spinner), Lachesis (the caster of lots), and Atropos (the unbending) are the three daughters of Zeus and Themis. They control the actions and destinies of mortals. They were known to the Romans as the Fates. (In an ancient Babylonian legend the Moira were seven goddesses of fate.) The Moirai are depicted as three old women, one with a distaff, one with a spindle, and one with shears. *See also* Eumenides; Fates; Fortuna; Themis; Tyche.

Moiragetes (Greek)
As guides of the Moirai, Apollo and Zeus are known as the Moiragetes. *See also* Fates; Moirai.

Mokusa (Slavic)
Another name for Mmokos the goddess of sheep.

Molc (Middle Eastern) *see* Moloch.

Molech (Middle Eastern) *see* Moloch.

Molione (Greek)
She is the wife of Actor and the mother of Eurytus and Cteatus, possibly by the sea god, Poseidon. *See also* Actor (B).

Molionides *Molionidae* (Greek)
The twin sons, who were possibly joined, of Actor and

Molione. Their names are Cteatus and Eurytus. *See also* Actor (B).

Moloch *Malik, Melech, Melekh, Molc, Molech, Mollac, Molloch, Molokh, Mulac* (Ammonite, Canaanite, Semite)
Also known as: *Agni, Makkal, Mikal, Milcom*.
This ancient sun god represents the negative aspects of the sun's heat in some renditions. He was thought to bring plagues. At one time, followers assuaged him by the sacrifice of newborn children. The Canaanites thought of Moloch as a god of wealth. His name probably came from the word "melech" which means "king." In Hebrew writings the term "bosheth" (meaning shame) was used as a reference to an idol, but when the diacritical marks were inserted Melech became Molech, then Moloch. *See also* Agni; Nergal; Yahweh.

Molokh (Middle Eastern) *see* Moloch.

Molpe (Greek) She is one of the Sirens (q.v.).

Molus (Greek)
Molus is the son of Ares, who is the only son of Zeus and Hera, and Demonice, the daughter of Agenor and Epicasta, or possibly Alcippe. *See also* Ares.

Mommu (Assyro-Babylonian) *see* Mummu.

Momo (A) (Hopi People, North American)
Deified insect. The Honeybee.

Momo (B) (Celtic) *see* Eire.

Momona (Antilles) *see* Atabei.

Momus (Greek)
The Fault-finder. God of ridicule. He is the son of Nox and Erebus and the brother of Aether, Cer, Charon, Dreams, Hemera, Hypnos, Moros, Nemesis and Thanatos. Momus' big mouth, always spewing sarcastic and ridiculing remarks, had him ousted from Olympus. He also made sarcastic remarks to the god of fire, Hephaestus, and the goddess of love, Aphrodite. *See also* Erebus; Keres; Nox.

Monan (Tupi-Guarani People, Brazil)
Also known as: *Maire-Monan*.
An ancient creator god, Monan created mortals. He later attempted the destruction of the world by fire as punishment for their evil ways, but a great flood saved it. He was later replaced by Maire-Monan (q.v.). *See also* Ariconte; Irin Mage.

Mondamin (Chippewa People, North America)
Corn Spirit. *See also* Nokomis; Onatah.

Moneta (Roman) *see* Juno.

Mongan (Irish) *see* Manannan Mac Llyr.

Monju (Japan) *see* Monju-Bosatsu.

Monju-Bosatsu *Monju*.
Also known as: *Manjusri* (Buddhist; India; Japan)
A very popular deity of old Japan, he is a deity of education, enlightenment and transcendental wisdom. Among the Bodhisattvas he is paired with Fugen. He is shown seated on a lotus supported on a lion, or sometimes cross-legged and sometimes with one leg on the ground. He often has a scroll in one hand

and a scepter in the other. Sometimes he is depicted with a sword in his hand which is used to cut down the obstacles of enlightenment. Monju-Bosatsu is said to be identical to the Manjusri (India). *See also* Amida; Bodhisattva; Manjusri; Samantabhadra.

Mono (Japan) *see* Oni.

Monoecus (Greek) An epithet of Heracles.

Monogenes (Gnostic) *see* Nous.

Mont (Egypt)
Also known as: *Menthu, Mentu, Month.*
A war god of Thebes. He lived in Hermonthis in Upper Egypt. For a short time, he was adopted by Amon and Mut and called their son. Some writers say he was a supreme deity until demoted by the god Amun or Antum. In some versions, in his aspect of Mentu or Menthu, he was the god of the rising sun. Mont is depicted as falcon-headed or sometimes as a bull-headed man. *See also* Amen; Buchis; Menthu.

Month (Egypt) *see* Mont.

Moon-hound (Norse; Teutonic) *see* Hati.

Mopaditis (Aborigine People, Australia)
Spirits of the dead. They look like people but no one ever sees them. They are invisible by day, white in the light of the moon, and black when it is dark.

Mopsus (A) (Greek)
He was a well known seer who won a contest against Calchas to see who was the better prophet. *See also* Calchas.

Mopsus (B) (Greek)
He is the Argonaut son of the seer, Ampycus, and Chloris. Mopsus was also present on the Calydonian Boar Hunt. He died from a snake bite in Libya.

Mora (Slavic) *see* Kikimora.

Morave (Melanesian) *see* Abere.

Mordred (Arthurian) *see* Adder.

Morgan Le Fay (British, Celt) *see* Arthur; Morrigu.

Morganes (Celtic, Welsh)
Also known as: *Morgan, Morgens* (British).
Female water spirits. Mermaids. In the singular form, Morganes is a lake spirit who is possibly connected with Morgan Le Fay.

Morirai (Greek) *see* Eumenides.

Morityama (Acoma People, North America)
The Spring Spirit. See also Katsinas; Mayochina.

Morkul-Kua-Luan (Aborigine People, Australia)
Known as the "Spirit of the Long Grass," Morkul-Kua-Luan is probably a food spirit. He is shown with half-closed eyelids and a beak-like nose.

Mormyrus Kannume (Egypt) *see* Oxyrhynchus.

Morning Star (Pawnee People, North America) *see* Tirawa.

Moros (Greek)
Goddess of destiny. Moros is the daughter of Nox and Erebus. She is not a well known deity but is thought to have been invisible and all-controlling. *See* Erebus and Nox for the names of her siblings. *See also* Aether; Keres; Oneiroi.

Morpheus (Roman)
God of dreams. He is the son of Somnus or Hypnos. Morpheus has 999 brothers. His uncle is the god of death, Thanatos. Morpheus, one of the Oneiroi, who represent dreams, is generally represented a chubby, winged child, holding poppies in his hand. *See also* Hypnos; Somnus; Thanatos.

Morrigan (British, Celt) *see* Morrigu.

Morrigu (Arthurian)
Also known as: *Badb Catha* (possibly), *Macha, Morgan Le Fay, The Morrigan, Morrigu-Morrigan, Nemain.*
"Great Queen." Goddess of war. Queen of ghosts. Possibly a sea deity. Morrigu is known as the forerunner of Morgan Le Fay. She dwells in Avalon along with King Arthur. Morrigu is sometimes called Arthur's sister. She has eight sisters. Others say she is mistress of Guingamore, wife of Uriens (king of Gore), and mistress of Sir Accolon. In one version, she is one of the forms of Badb, and one of a triad with Macha and Nemain, who are also cruel goddesses of war. This triad is often called Morrigu. Unable to charm the hero Cuchulain, her passion soon turned to hatred. A shape-changer, she used the identity of an eel, a wolf, and a red-eared heifer to attack him when he was extremely vulnerable fighting off other enemies. His injuries were severe and Badb also wore war wounds from the encounter. Later, as he was walking along a road, he encountered an old woman milking her cow. He begged for a drink. When he finished the beverage, he bestowed his blessing upon the woman. A short time passed and he realized that the woman was Morrigu, in disguise. His blessings had healed her. Morrigu can appear as a seductive young woman, or as a lame, swarthy hag with a big mouth. *See also* Badb Catha; Banbha; Cuchulain; Dagda; Macha; Nemain.

Mors (Roman)
Also known as: *Thanatos.*
God of death. Mors is the personification of death. *See also* Somnus.

Morta (Roman)
Morta is an epithet of Parca, the goddess of childbirth. *See also* Parca.

Moschel (Latvia) God of cows.

Mosigsig (Oceanic) *see* Maui.

Mot (Ugarit)
God of the netherworld. God of the season of crops or god of aridity and death. He dies by the scythe at the hands of Anat at harvest time and is reborn in spring. From the works of Philo, Mot was produced from a self-created being called Desire. This "breath" was sometimes thought to be slime or other rotting water-based substances. From it came the germs that were the origin of everything. Baal or Aleyin, the son of Baal, was Mot's opponent. Some say Mot is El's favorite son. Once, Mot devoured Baal and was forced to regurgitate the god by Baal's

sister Anat with the aid of Shapash. He is sometimes confused with the god Yam. Deities associated with Mot are the dragon Tannin and the serpent Loran. *See also* Anat; Asherah; Astarte; Baal; Yamm.

Mother Earth (Greek) *see* Chaos.

Mother Earth Moist (Russian, Slavic) *see* Mati-Syra-Zemlya.

Mother of All Things (Pawnee People, North America) *see* Tirawa.

Mother of the Mind (Maya) *see* Alaghom Naom.

Mother Scorpion (Central America) *see* Ituana.

Mother Sea (Inca) *see* Mama Cocha.

Mother Womb (Middle Eastern) *see* Mami.

Mothir (Norse; Teutonic)
Goddess of the nobly born. Heimdall as Rig slept between Fathir and Mothir and from his union with Mothir was born Jarl. *See also* Heimdall; Jarl.

Motikitik (Micronesia)
Creator. He is the son of Lorop. There are similarites between him and the Polynesian deities Maui-tikitiki, Motikitik, and the Melanesian god Maui.

Mountains (Greek) Goddess of mountains. *See also* Gaea.

Mouri (Celtic) *see* Maree.

Mowee (Oceanic) *see* Maui.

Moymis (Babylon) *see* Belus (B).

Mpambe (Africa) *see* Mbamba.

Mridani (India) *see* Devi.

Mrigavyadha (India) "Piercer of Deer." *See also* Rudra.

Mritya (India) "Death." *See also* Yama.

Mrtyu (Hindu; India)
Also known as: *Mara* (Buddhist).
Mrtyu is a death demon and the messenger of Yama, the god of death. *See also* Mara; Yama.

Mtanga (Africa) *see* Mulungu.

Mu-King (China)
Also known as: *Mu Kung, Yu Huang.*
He is the god and ruler of the immortals. Mu King was the first living creation, born of primeval vapor. He is the same as Yu Huang.

Mu Kung (China) *see* Mu-king.

Mucalinda (Buddhist; India) *see* Muchilinda.

Muchilinda *Mucalinda* (Buddhist; India)
Muchilinda is a Naga serpent king who protected Buddha by making a seat from his body for the master and protecting him with his hood. *See also* Buddha; Nagas.

Mudhead (Hopi People, North America) The clown. *see* Tehabi.

Mudungkala (Aborigine People, Australia)
She is a blind creator goddess who rose from the ground long before the creation of hills and before there was sunrise. Mudungkala brought forth three children, a boy and two girls, and they became the first people.

Mueragbuto (New Hebrides) *see* Takaro.

Mugasha (Baziba People, Africa)
God of water. He is the son of Wamara, the father of gods.

Muhammad (Arabic) *see* Mohammed.

Muit (Australia) *see* Rainbow Snake.

Mukasa (A) (Bantu People, Uganda, Africa)
Supreme deity. Oracle. This deity is the "spirit of the lake." He is also the spirit of plenty and fertility. His symbol is a stone pillar. He was senior among the Balubaale (*see* Baluballe). The people of Uganda people call him the highest god of all the pantheon. Mukasa is said to be son of one of the higher gods, possibly Musisi, the earthquake god. His mortal mother is Nambubi. In some legends, Mukasa has three wives. *See also* Balubaale; Bumba; Gulu; Katonda; Kibuuka; Kintu.

Mukasa (B) (Vedic; India)
Mukasa is a kind and peaceful god of plenty.

Mukunda (Buddhist; India) Goddess of the Drum.

Mukuru (Africa) *see* Omumborombonga.

Mul-lil (Akkadian, Semitic) *see* Adar (B).

Mulac (Middle Eastern) *see* Moloch.

Mulciber the Smelter (Roman) Epithet of Vulcan. *See also* Hephaistos; Vulcan.

Muliebris (Etruscan, Roman) *see* Fortuna.

Mulius (Greek)
Mulius, the husband of Agamede, was killed in the Trojan War by Achilles or Nestor. *See also* Actor (C); Nestor; Poseidon.

Muludaianinis (Aborigine People, Australia)
Gods of sleep. Muludaianinis are the women whose men had affairs with other men's wives. This caused a fight and all of them went into the sky. The men became the Milky Way and the women the stars. At dusk the Muludaianinis men travel across the sky to visit their wives. When they are finished they wipe the perspiration from their bodies. It falls onto mortals below and makes them sleepy.

Muluku (Macouas People, Africa)
Chief creator deity. After Muluku made the earth he dug two holes and from these brought forth a man and a woman. Because the two were too stupid to use the tools he supplied, he took the tails from two monkeys (who knew how to use the tools) and placed them on the humans. This made monkeys human and humans monkeys. His opposition is Minipa.

Mulungu (Yao People, Malawi; East Africa)
Also known as: *Mtanga, Umlungu* (Zulu).
Supreme god. Mulungu could be a name for the white man, or just a name for the white man's god. He may be a forerun-

ner of Mpambe, Chiuta, and Leza. He caught two tiny people in his fish net and created the human race from them. In some legends, he went to heaven on a spider's web. Mulungu may also be the same as Mtanga of the Yao People. *See also* Leza; Unkulunkulu.

Mumham (Celtic) *see* Eire.

Mummu (Assyro-Babylonian; Sumer)

Mummu personifies the waves of the ocean, created from the union of Apsu and Tiamat. In Babylonian mythology, Mummu is Apsu's vizier. Tiamat and Apsu consulted with him when the younger gods became so rowdy they wanted to destroy them. Tiamat had second thoughts, but Mummu and Apsu devised a plan. Somehow, the gods caught wind of the scheme, and the wise Ea decided upon a counter-move. After casting a spell on Apsu, he killed him. He bound Mummu up and put a cord through his nose. Ea then constructed a sacred chamber where he could rest in peace. It was in this chamber that Marduk was born. *See also* Apsu; Marduk.

Mummu-Tiamat (Sumer) *see* Tiamat.

Mumuhango (Polynesia)

The ancestor of Tane. Tane wanted to create a woman for a mate and asked his mother Papa to be his wife. She refused and sent him to Mumuhango. The result of his union with Mumuhango was a tree, not a woman. *See also* Hine-tu-a-maunga; Papa; Tane.

Munda (India) A Demon. *See also* Chunda (B); Durga; Kali.

Mundilfari *Mundilfaer, Mundilfore, Mundilare* (Norse)

He is the giant father of Mani, the moon, and Sol, the sun. *See also* Mani; Sol.

Munga Munga (Oceania) *see* Mungamunga.

Mungamunga *Munga Munga* (Aborigine People, Australia)

Goddesses of women. They are generally shown as a pair of fairy-like creatures who are associated with secret fertility rites of women. They are attractive goddesses who are sometimes invisible.

Mungan-Ngaua (Aborigine People, Australia)

Mungan-Ngaua lived on earth a long time ago. He taught the secret rites of an initiation ceremony. His son, Tundum, conducted the first rites. Tundum and his wife were turned into porpoises after a cosmic cataclysm in which almost the whole human race perished.

Mungu *Mungo* (Giryama People, Africa)

Rain deity. Among the Pygmies, Mungu is a creator god who sometimes seems to be a first ancestor and sometimes a culture hero. He may have five or six other names. Mungu is the possessor of the totality of mana. A goat and chicken are offered in sacrifice to him.

Muni (India) *see* Gandharvas.

Muninn and Huginn (Norse; Teutonic)

Also known as: *Memory and Thought.*

Deified birds. Information gatherers. Muninn and Huginn are Odin's ravens. They perch on his shoulders until morning when they head out for the world. At nightfall, they return and report the world news to Odin. *See also* Odin.

Munis (India) Sages. *See also* Brahma; Loka.

Munitus (Greek)

He is the son of Acamas and Laodice. *See also* Acamas (A).

Munon (Teutonic) *see* Thor.

Munsumundok (Borneo) *see* Kinharigan.

Muntalog (Indonisian) *see* Wigan.

Muntu (Egypt) *see* Buchis.

Mur (Sumer) *see* Ishkur.

Murtaza (Persia) *see* Ali (B).

Muruhan (India) *see* Karttikeya.

Muryoju (Japan) *see* Amida; Dnichi-nyorai.

Muryoka (Japan) *see* Amida.

Musa (Africa) Spirit of the forest. Protector of hunters.

Musala (India) The sacred pestle of Bala-Rama (q.v.)

Musagetes (Greek)

An epithet of Apollo as the patron of the Muses.

Musali (India) *see* Bala-Rama.

Musellsheim (Teutonic) *see* Muspells-heim.

Muses (A) (Greek)

Spirits of inspiration. The nine Camenae Muses are the daughters of Zeus and Mnemosyne (Memory). Their names are Clio, also spelled Cleio (the personification of history), Euterpe (lyric poetry), Thalia (comedy), Melpomene (tragedy), Terpsichore (choral dance and song), Erato (erotic poetry), Polyhymnia, also spelled Polymnia (religious poetry and sound), Urania (astronomy), and Calliope (epic poetry). The talented and inspiring group sang for deities and mortals at weddings, funerals, and other commemorative occasions. The Muses were companions of Apollo in his aspect as Apollo Musagetes, the god of music. *See also* Aloeides; Fates; Graces; Hyacintos; Melpomene; Sirens.

Muses (B) (Greek)

The Boeotian Muses are the three daughters of Uranus and Gaea. They are Aoide, the muse of song; Melete, the muse of practice; Mneme, the muse of memory.

Muses (C) (Greek)

The Delphic Muses are the personifications of the high, middle and low strings of the lyre. Their names are Hypate, Mese and Nete. They were discovered by the youthful giants Otus and Ephialtes on Mount Helicon.

Muses (D) (Vedic; India) They are Bharati, Ila and Sarasvati.

Mushdamma (Sumer) "The Great Builder." *See also* Enki.

Muspel (Teutonic) *see* Muspells-heim.

Muspelheim (Teutonic) *see* Muspells-heim.

Muspellheim (Teutonic) *see* Muspells-heim.

Muspells-heim *Muspelheim, Muspellheim, Muspellsheim* (Norse; Teutonic)

Also known as: *Muspel.*

Located in the southern section of the primeval abyss known as Ginnunga-gap, Muspells-heim is the world of elemental fire. From the rivers of Muspells-heim flowed waters of bitter poison which in time became solid masses that filled a vast central space. The ice from Nifl-heim, located in the north of Ginnunga-gap rolled down into contact with these deposits and formed thick coatings of hoar-frost. The warm air of Muspells-heim blew in and melted the hoar-frost. The continual action of cold and heat, and according to some, the will of the powerful Allfather, created Ymir (also called Orgelmir), the first ice giant. Muspells-heim is guarded by the flame giant Surtr. In some myths it was Surtr's flaming sword that melted the hoar-frost. *See also* Aarvak; Austri; Ginnunga-gap; Mani; Midgard; Nifl-heim; Surtr; Svalin; Ve; Vigrid; Vili; Ymir.

Musso Koroni *Mousso Koroni* (Bambara and Mande People, Africa)

Also known as: *Koundye.*

Goddess of disorder. She is the wife of Pemba and daughter of the Voice of the Void. In the Mande stories, she is the twin of Pemba. She came to earth in the ark. *See also* Faro; Mangala.

Mut *Muut* (Egypt)

Mother goddess. Queen of heaven. Goddess of feminine arts. Mut is the wife of Ammon, Amon, Amun or Amenand. She is the mother of Khensu. Mut could be an androgynous deity, since she was believed to have both male and female reproductive organs. She is depicted as a lioness or vulture headed. One depiction shows her with a phallus. She is also represented as a woman wearing a vulture skin on her head with the Upper Egyptian crown on top. Mut is the counterpart of Amen-Ra. She is identified with Bast and Sekhmet. *See also* Adonis; Amen; Ament; Ammon; Bast; Khensu; Khonso; Nut; Sekhmet.

Muta (Roman) Muta is the goddess of silence. *See also* Lares; Larunda.

Mutuhei (Polynesia) *see* Atea; Tanaoa.

Mutunus (Roman)

Also known as: *Priapus* (Greek).

Deity of flocks and fruitfulness. He is similar to the son of Dionysus and Aphrodite, Priapus, the fertility god.

Mutyalamma (India)

House deities. The pearl goddesses. They are Chinnintamma, the goddess who is head of the house; Callalamma, who presides over the buttermilk; Yaparamma, who presides over business transactions; Gangamma, the water-goddess. There is Balamma, who presides over household carts; Huliamma, the tiger goddess; and one more widely worshipped, Ankamma, the goddess of cholera, or sometimes of disease in general. These goddesses are from a small village on the east coast in the Telugu country. Some villages have goddesses that are called by no special name, but simply, Uramma or Gramadeveta, meaning "village-goddess" or Peddamma, meaning "Great Mother." The suffix "amma" indicates "feminine."

Muy'ingwa (Hopi People, North America)

Underworld deity. He is the god who gave the Indians maize.

Muyscaya People — Creation Legend (South America) *see* Chimini-Pagus.

Mwambu and Sela (Kenya, Africa)

First man and woman. God created them so his new sun had people to shine upon.

Mycene (Greek)

She is the daughter of Inachus and Meliae. *See also* Meliae.

Myersyats (Slavic)

The moon personified as a goddess. *See also* Dazbog.

Myesyats (Russian, Slavic)

The moon. Two versions of Myesyats are told. In one Myesyats is the wife of Sun (Dazhbog) and when they fight an earthquake results. In another it is the Sun who is the wife and Myesyats is the husband and their children the stars. The sun is also called Dazhbog in Slavic mythology.

Mygdon (Greek)

He is the son of Poseidon and Melie and the brother of Amycus. Mygdon became the King of Phrygia. *See also* Amycus.

Mylitta (Babylon, Chaldean)

Also known as: *Belit.*

Goddess of fertility and childbirth. She is the same as Belit. *See also* Ashtoreth; Astarte.

Mylitti (Assyro-Babylonia) *see* Belit.

Myo-Ken (Japan) *see* Amatsu-Mikaboshi.

Myrmidons (Greek)

They are the Thessalian people who were allies of Achilles during the Trojan War. *See also* Aeacus; Aegina.

Myrrha (Greek)

Also known as: *Smyra.*

Myrrha is the daughter of the king of Paphos, Cinyras, in Cyprus and Cenchreis. Some say she was the daughter of the king of Assyria, Theias. Aphrodite was angry with Myrrha either because her mother boasted that the young woman was more beautiful than Aphrodite, or possibly because Myrrha did not honor the great goddess properly. Aphrodite punished her by giving her incestous feelings for her father. When he was intoxicated, Myrrha slept with him for twelve nights and as a result became pregnant. When her father found out, he chased after her with a sword. She prayed to the gods to make her invisible so he could not harm her. They changed her into a myrrh tree and it is said that her tears became the gum from the tree. Cinyras killed himself. Nine months later, the infant Adonis emerged from the split tree. *See also* Adonis.

Myrtilus (Greek)

He is the son of Hermes and Clytie. *See also* Hippodameia; Oenamaus; Pelops; Sisyphus.

Mysinger *Mysing* (Iceland)

Sea deity. According to legend he commanded Fenja and Menja to grind out salt or ice from Frothi's Mill (also known as the World mill) in order to hold up his ship. Unfortunately no one told them to stop, so they are still grinding out ice.

N

N (Maya)
God of the end of the year.

Na-Arean (Micronesia) *see* Nareau.

Na Atibu (Oceanic)
This is another name for the first human, De Babou. *See also* Nareau.

Na-naki-me (Japan) *see* Ame no-Oshido-Mimi.

Na Reau (Micronesia) *see* Nareau.

Na Rena (Micronesia) *see* Rigi; Riiki.

Naaki (Finnish)
Water spirit. A dangerous shape changer who pulls people under the water. He is one of the attendants of Ahti (q.v.).

Naarayan (India) *see* Narayana (A).

Naareau (Gilbert Islands) *see* Nareau.

Nabu *Nebo* (Mesopotamia)
Also known as: *Nabug, Tigranes* (Iranian).
Nabu, the son of Marduk, is the god of wisdom, intelligence, and justice, the patron of writers and writing, and a messenger and scribe of the gods. The "Tablets of Fate" were in his charge, and he inscribed the judgments made by the gods. He was Bel's messenger. His vessel is a ship named Iddahedu. Nabu is the spouse of Tashmetrum (Tashmetu), or in some versions, either Nisaba (goddess of the harvest) or Nana. He was thought of by some worshipers as a higher god than Marduk. His temple was at Borsippa (the site was later assigned to the Tower of Babel). Nabu may have originally been the ancient Sumerian deity known as Me, or Sa, or even more ancient, the gods Ur and Dubbisag. Nabu is said to be the same as the angel Pravuil or Vretil of the Hebrews. He is represented, as is Marduk, with a dragon and also with the tools of engraving. His counterpart is the grain goddess, Nidaba. In some legends Nabu is connected with Dilmun (q.v.). Compare Nabu to Thoth (Egypt). *See also* Nana; Nebo; Nisaba (A); Nusku; Puleh; Sin; Tablets of Fate; Tashmetrum; Tiur (Armenian).

Nabudi Women (Aborigine People, Australia)
Evil, malicious spirits, the Nabudi Women send invisible barbs into people who travel alone and make them ill.

Nabug (Assyrian) *see* Nabu.

Nachash *Nchsh* (Hebrew)
Serpent. Nachash is said by mystics to be the serpent who tempted Eve. He is similar to the Naga and Nagis (India).

Nacht (Teutonic) *see* Nott.

Nacon (Maya People, Yucatan) War god.

Naddgofugr (Teutonic) An alternate name for Mimir.

Nadi-Devata (Buddhist; India) River goddess.

Nadija (India) *see* Bhishma.

Nadimmud (Babylon) *see* Ea; Enki; Nudimmud.

Nag (India) *see* Naga Naga Knaya.

Naga Knaya (India)
They are the daughters of the Naga Naga Knaya.

Naga Naga Knaya *Nag* (Buddhist, Hindu; India)
The Naga Naga Knaya are the part-human, part-serpent guardians of the law of Buddha. They are rain deities, guardians of the water and guardians of wealth. A priceless jewel is carried in their foreheads or throats. Their daughters are known as Naga Knayas. Two Naga kings, Nanda and Upananda, were said to have given Buddha, in his mortal form as Gautama, his first bath. Buddha's almsbowl was a gift from the Nagas. Another version of the Naga mythology states that the Hindu gods Indra and Brahma received their first baths from the Nagas. One Naga king is Virupaksha, one of the Four Great Kings who guard the entrance to the Buddhist paradise of Sukhavati. The upper portion of the Naga Naga Knaya is human and the lower part is a snake. The Naga serpents are represented as two entwined serpents, symbolic of chthonic transcendence. As guardians, their images represent the life force and are often found at the portals of Buddhist and Hindu shrines. Regarding the Four Great Kings, *see* Dhartarastra. *See also* Brahma; Buddha; Chakravala (Buddhist Paradise); Indra; Nagas and Nagis (the); Sukhavati; Virudhaka; Virupaksha.

Naga-pasa (India) Brahma's arrow.

Naga-Teka (India) Snake Killer. *See also* Garuda.

Nagarjuna (India) *see* Abheda; Dainichi-nyorai; Stupa.

Nagas and Nagis (Hindu, Jain; India)
Also known as: *Bhogavati* (for Nagis), *Bhogini* (for Nagis), *Bhujagas, Jaja, Nagas and Naginis, Nagas and Nagunis, Nagnis, Naia, Naja, Naje, Pannagas, Uragas.*
The Nagas and Nagis, a race of serpents, were the one thousand sons and daughters of Kadru (the daughter of Daksha) and her mate, the sage Kasyapa. Minor deities, their purpose was to populate Patalas (the underworld) where they live in luxurious palaces. The females are always well dressed and known to be clever. When they appear as nymphs, mortal men fall in love and sometimes marry them. Some of their daughters appear as beautiful women, such as Ulupi, who became the mate of Arjuna. Padmavati is a Nagi queen who was the mate

of Dharanendra. Sesha, Vasuki, and Ananta are well known Nagas. The Nagas harm mortals only when they are mistreated. Although their venom is deadly, they also carry the elixir of life and immortality. The Naga kings are Takshaka (his mate is Manasa) and Vasuki. Vishnu sleeps on a bed provided by the body of the Naga Sesha while the three, five, seven or nine hooded heads of this snake give him shade. The giant bird-like Garudas, their mortal enemies, enjoying feeding on them. The Nagas are associated with weather, particularly rain and in times of drought pictures of the Nagas are worshiped. In later Hindu times, Karkotaka was known as the king of the Nagas who control weather. The Pancha-muke, a five-faced Naga, spreads his five hoods over many gods. Another Naga king, Paravataksha, lived under a lake shaded by a holy tree. His sword caused earthquakes and his roar caused thunder. The Nagas and Nagis are often shown in three forms: fully human with snakes on the heads and necks; the upper body in human form with the lower region in snake form or as common snakes. The Nagas carry a precious jewel in their heads. The cobra Capella is called a Naga and elephants are often referred to as Nagas because of their long trunks. An historical dynasty of kings in India were known as the Naga-Dwipa. *See also* Arjuna; Bhutas; Daksha; Kadru; Kasyapa; Kumunda; Manasa; Muchilinda; Naga Naga Knaya; Sarpas; Sarpis; Sesha; Takshaka; Vajrapani; Vasuki; Vishnu; Vrita.

Nagelfare (Teutonic) *see* Nagilfar.

Nagilfar *Naglfar, Naglefar, Naglefare, Naglfari* (Norse; Teutonic)
Ship of death. This ship was manufactured from nail parings of the dead whose relatives neglected to pare the nails before the deceased was laid to rest. Iormungandr (the Midgard snake) will create a giant wave that will release the ship from its mooring in the outer regions of Nifl-heim. Piloted by Loki, it will set sail for the conflict of Ragnarok.

Naglefar (Teutonic) *see* Nagilfar.

Naglefare (Teutonic) *see* Nagilfar.

Naglefari (Teutonic) *see* Nagilfar.

Naglfar (Teutonic) *see* Nagilfar.

Naglfari (Teutonic) *see* Nagilfar.

Nagnis (India) *see* Nagas.

Nagua (Aztec) *see* Nahual.

Nagual (Native North American) *see* Nagua.

Nah-Hunte (Sumer)
Sun-god. The sun-god of the Elamites, he was also a deity of law and order and of light.

Nahochacyumchac (Maya) *see* Nohochacyum.

Nahual (Aztec)
Also known as: *Nagua, Nagual, Nahual.*
The Nagual is a person's personal spirit. It accompanies one through life. The Nagual is generally in the form of a bird or beast which makes it presence known in various ways. *See also* Ba; Ka.

Nahualpilli (Aztec) *see* Tlaloc.

Nai (Egypt) *see* Akeneh.

Nai-nai Niang-niang (China) *see* Sheng mu; T'ien Hou.

Nai-nai-miao (China)
Goddess of children. The devotees of Nai-nai-miao pray to become pregnant. She is generally associated with Sheng mu and is related to T'u-shan.

Nai-No-Kami (Japan) *see* Take-mi-kazuchi.

Naia (India) *see* Nagas.

Naiades (Greek) *see* Naiads.

Naiads (Greek)
Also known as: *Naiades.*
Water deities. Healers. The Naiads are divine but not immortal, fresh-water nymphs, who live in brooks, fountains and lakes. They are the daughters of Zeus or daughters of Oceanus and Tethys. Healers, they are the attendants of Athena and nurses of Adonis, Dionysus, and Zeus. (In another tradition, it is the Hyades who nursed Dionysus.) The ever youthful and lovely nymphs had the gift of prophecy and lived on the food of the gods, ambrosia. According to the Greek philosopher Plutarch (C.E. 46?–120?), nymphs never lived over nine thousand six hundred and twenty years. Generally kind, they could be menacing as in the case of the Russian nymphs known as the Rusalki. Other types of nymphs are the Crenae and Pegae who live in springs, the Potamids who live in rivers and streams and the Limnads who live in stagnant waters. Other nymphs are Cassotis and Castalia of Parnassus, and Hago, the ruler of a fountain on Mount Lycaeus. *See also* Aganippe; Calypso; Daemon; Hylas; Nereids; Nymphs; Oceanids; Rusalki.

Naids (Greek) *see* Nymphs.

Naiga-Mesha (India) *see* Nejamesha.

Nairatma (Tibet) *see* Heruka.

Nairitya *Nairrita* (Nepal)
God of Dread. *See also* Dikpalas; Rakshasas.

Nairrita (India) *see* Nairitya.

Nairrita (India) *see* Devi.

Nairyosangha (Iranian)
God of fire. Messenger of Ahura Mazda. Devotees bring Nairyosangha offerings for sacrifice. He is similar to the Narasamsa.

Naivedya (India) *see* Nidhema.

Naja (India) *see* Nagas.

Najade (Slavic) Water nymphs.

Naje (India) *see* Nagas.

Nak (Egypt)
Serpent. He is an ancient serpent fiend who was defeated by Amen-Ra who is mentioned with another fiend called Sebau.

Nakawe (Mexico) Earth Mother. *See also* Kauyumari.

Naka-yama-tsu-mi (Japan)
God of mountain slopes. One of the eight sons of Ho-Masubi. See Sengen for other mountain deities. *See also* Ho-Masubi; O-Yama-Tsu-Mi; Sengen.

Nakhash (Semite) *see* Rahabh.

Nakime (Japan) *see* Ame no-Oshido-Mimi.

Nakisawame-no-kami (Japan) *see* Izanagi.

Nakiu-Menat (Egypt) *see* Aai.

Nakshatras (India) *see* Vasus.

Nakula (India)
He is the fourth of the Pandu Princes and the twin of Sahadeva. *See also* Asvins; Madri; Pandavas.

Nakula and Sahadeva (India) *see* Asvins.

Nala (India) The Ape. *See also* Visvakarma.

Nam-kha-ing-kya-wang-chug-ma (Tibet)
Also known as: *Akasha Dhatu Isvari.*
"Divine Mother of Infinite Space." *See also* Shakti; Vairocana.

Nam-tho-se-ser-chhen (Tibet) *see* Kuvera.

Namandjolk (Aborigine People, Australia)
He is a malevolent spirit being.

Namarakains (Aborigine People, Australia)
Arnhem Land. They are evil spirits who steal the spirits of sick people.

Namargon (Aborigine People, Australia)
Also known as: *Lightning Man.*
Storm spirit. Husband of Barginj. He is responsible for storms and thunder. He uses his head, knees and elbows to strike the clouds and produce lightning. Namargon is depicted with stone axes emerging from his head.

Namasangiti (Buddhist; Tibet).
Also known as: *Vairocana.*
Namasangiti is an emanation of Vairocana and is thought to be the deification of the Namasangiti literature of the Buddhist pantheon. Namasangiti, white in color, sits in the meditative pose on the lotus with his eyes half-closed and a smile on his face. He has one head, twelve arms and wears numerous ornaments. Namasangiti is associated with Prajnaparamita (q.v.). *See also* Vairocana.

Namcui (India) *see* Mara.

Namios (Greek) *see* Apollo.

Nammu (Chaldea, Sumer)
Also known as: *Aruru, Ki, Ningal, Ninhursag, Ninmah, Nintu.*
In Sumerian cosmogony, Nammu is the eternal primeval sea; the mother of all the gods and the one who gave birth to heaven personified as the god An, and earth, who is personified as the goddess Ki. Their union created the air god Enlil, which made Nammu his grandmother. Enlil separated from An and Ki (heaven and earth), and the universe was created as heaven and earth separated by air. In one myth, Nammu is depicted as the mother of the god of wisdom, Enki. As he slept in the deep, the other gods, who expected his help, were clamoring for food. They complained to the mother goddess Nammu who roused him. He instructed Nammu and her daughter Ninmah, the goddess of birth, to create mortals. They would be fashioned from clay for one purpose. Their existence would free the gods from working. The mortals would till the fields and grow the food. Enki was delighted with this innovation and decided to give a banquet to celebrate. Enki and Ninmah drank too much and became inebriated. Ninmah took clay from "over the abyss," and fashioned six types of mortals. Only two are clearly defined. One is a barren woman and the other a eunuch. Enki decided that the fate of the eunuch would be to stand before the king. He then proceeded to create a physically and mentally deficient mortal. When he saw his creation, he asked Ninmah to do something for the pathetic being. There was nothing that she could do. Angry, she cursed Enki for his creation. Compare Nammu to the Assyro-Babylonian goddess Tiamat. *See also* An; Aruru; Ea; Enki; Enlil; Ki; Ningal; Ninhursag; Ninlil; Ninmah; Ninmu; Nintu.

Nampo Gundari Yasha (Japan) *see* Gundari-Myoo.

Namtar (Assyro-Babylonian, Sumer)
Also known as: *Namtaru.*
Chief of seven devils. Evil spirit. He brings plagues to mortals and carries out the destructive plans of Nergal. Namtar has sixty plagues under his control. His spouse is Husbishag, the record-keeper who records the fate of all in the kingdom of Arallu. Namtar acts as the messenger of Ereshkigal. When Ishtar sought Tammuz in the underworld, Namtar was ordered to strike her with a disease. He restored her to health upon her release. *See also* Arallu; Ereshkigal; Husbishag; Ishtar; Nergal.

Namtaru (Sumer) *see* Namtar.

Namtillaku (Babylonia) *see* Marduk.

Namu-tho-se-ser-chhen (Tibet) *see* Kuvera.

Namu-Zozusen (India) *see* Kuvera.

Nana (Greek)
She is the daughter of Sangarius and the mother of Attis. *See also* Agdistis; Attis; Sangarius.

Nana *Nina* (Akkadia, Sumer)
Also known as: *Anna-Nin, Belit-Sheri* (possibly).
Mother goddess. She is the sister of Tammuz and wife of Nabu. Some say she is a moon goddess, or goddess of flocks and rivers. *See also* Anahita; Belit-Sheri; Nanai; Ningal; Ninsun.

Nana Buluku (Fon People, Africa; Haiti).
Supreme deity. God of herbs and medicine. Father of twins Mahu and Leza. He could be androgynous as some renditions refer to Nana Buluku as the primordial mother of the twins. *See also* Lisa; Mahu.

Nanabojo (Native North American) *see* Nanabozho.

Nanaboojoo (Native North American) *see* Nanabozho.

Nanabozho *Nanabojo, Nanaboojoo* (Algonquin, Chippewa, Cree, Fox, Memomin, Ojibwas, Ottawa, Potawatomi, Sauk People, North America)

Also known as: *Great Hare, Kabibonokka, Manabhozho, Manaboojoo, Manabozho, Manabush, Messou, Michabo, Minibozho, Winabojo, Wolverine.*

Trickster. Transformer. Cultural hero. The myths about Nanabozho abound. He takes many forms among Native North Americans. In the Potawatomi tradition he is the eldest of quadruplets. Nanabozho and the second eldest, a boy, have human form. The third brother is a magician of reknown and a White Hare. The youngest quadruplet, Flint, killed their mother at birth. When Nanabozho grew up, he in turn killed Flint. Nanabozho lived with his second brother, until the jealous supernaturals drowned him. This caused Nanabozho to war against the supernaturals. They tried to assuage Nanabozho by initiating him into Midewiwin, the sacred medicine society. His drowned brother returned and was sent to preside over dead souls. The Cree and Ojibway tell of Nanabozho searching for his brother. When he locates him running with a pack of wolves, he joins him. The brothers shared many adventures. Eventually, Nanabozho is sent from the pack with one wolf as a companion. The companion is seized by underwater beings, and rescued by Nanabozho. A deluge followed, but Nanabozho was able to escape on a raft. Muskrat dived from the raft to take a small piece of earth so that Nanabozho could recreate the world. In another myth, as a creator god he flooded the universe to put out the fire started by his enemies. From the mud, he formed the earth and mortals. Nanabozho taught his creation how to survive. In the Algonquin tradition, he is one of five gods. The other four gods are Kabibonokka (north wind), Kabun (west wind), Shawano (south wind), and Wabun (east wind). He is said to live on an island named Michilimakinak. He has a brother, Chibiabos, and a grandmother, Nokomis (similar to Kitchki Manitou). In other myths, he is a creator god who placed four beneficial spirits at the four corners of the heavens. Their fuction is to hold up the heavens and contribute to the happiness of the human race. In one rendition, the four spirits are his brothers Shawano, Kabun, Kabibonokka, and Wabun. In the Algonquin legend Kabibonokka was god of the north. The other brothers are Shawano (south), Kabun (west), and Wabun (east). In the Algonquin creation legend, Manibozho is known as a culture hero, though some say he is a sun god. He was hunting when the great lake flooded and the world was covered with water. He sought safety on a mountain. Before descending, he sent a raven, a muskrat, and an otter to ensure the waters had receded. Known as the "Great Hare," he married the muskrat and became the ancestor of the tribe. In most legends these deities were born from the earth mother, who died giving them life. Though many names are used by the different Native North Americans for Nanabozho, the similarity of the legends may indicate it is the same deity.

Nanahuatzin *Nanauatzin* (Aztec People, Mexico)

Deity of light. This pimple-faced little god was chosen to be the light of the world. Although the world existed, there was no sunshine. The god Tecciztecatl offered his service, but even though he offered splendid tribute, he was unsuccessful. Little Nanahuatzin had little to give, so he threw himself into the sacred fire and was chosen to be the sun. *See also* Meztli, Tecciztecatl, Yohualticitl.

Nanai (Japan) *see* Ame no-Oshido-Mimi; Nana (Babylon)

Nanan-Bouclou (Africa; Haiti) *see* Nana Buluku.

Nanauatzin (Mexico) *see* Nanahuatzin.

Nancomala (Guaymi People, Costa Rica)

As the great flood ebbed, Nancomala came upon the water maiden Rutbe. They became the parents of the Sun and Moon, who were the twin ancestors of humans.

Nanda (A) *Nund* (India) *see* Devaki; Devi; Kansa.

Nanda (B) (India) *see* Lhamo; Naga Naga Knaya.

Nanda (C) (India) Protector of children. *See also* Hariti.

Nandaka (India) Vishnu's divine bow. *See also* Vishnu.

Nandana *Shatananda* (India) *see* Karna; Kunti.

Nandi (Hindu; India)

Nandi, the white bull, is Shiva's mount and guardian of all four-footed animals. He is also the guardian of Shiva's temples. He is the calf of the Cow of Plenty, Surabhi. The Rishi, Vasistha owned him. Nandi's form is most often seen lying down at the entrance or inside of the temple. His testicles, symbolizing the source of life, are touched by followers as they enter the place of worship. *See also* Badari; Kamadhenu; Nandini; Shiva; Vasistha.

Nandini (India)

She is the female aspect of Shiva's bull Nandi. Nandini is a wish-fulfilling cow. *See also* Kamadhenu; Nandi.

Nandisha (Hindu; India)

Also known as: *Shiva.*

Nandisha, a dwarf with a monkey face, is an aspect of Shiva. He confronted the demon Ravana in Skanda's forest. Ravana ridiculed and taunted him. Nandisha warned the demon that he would be killed by monkey-faced beings. Incredulous, Ravana lifted a mountain to throw at the dwarf. Nandisha put his toe in the mountain and crushed the demon's hands. Ravana had to spend the next thousand years singing hymns of praise to Shiva in order to placate the god. *See also* Ravana; Shiva; Skanda.

Nandisvara (India) *see* Shiva.

Nane (Armenia, Babylonia, Sumer)

Also known as: *Anahita, Hanea, Nana.*

Goddess of the Evening Star. Mistress of Heaven. Originally a goddess of the Sumerians, it is likely that she is the same as Nana. Some say she was the daughter of Aramazd. Later, Nane was identified with Athene and Nana. *See also* Anahita; Athene; Ishtar; Nana.

Nang-sal-ma (Tibet) *see* Aloka.

Nanih Waiya (Choctaw People, North America)

First place or creator. The name means "Bending Hill" or the place of emergence. At a later date used as name for the Christian creator.

Nanna (A) (Norse; Teutonic)

Moon goddess. Nanna is the wife of Balder and the mother

of Forseti. She saw her husband killed by the mistletoe thrown by Hoder. Overcome, she threw herself on his funeral pyre. *See also* Balder; Hoder; Forseti.

Nanna (B) *Nannar* (Assyro-Babylonia)
Also known as: *Sin.*
Moon god and god of divination and astronomy. The moon god of the Sumerians, he is the counterpart of the Babylonian god Sin. Nanna is worshiped in the form of an elderly man. His symbol is the crescent. *See also* Mashu; Sin.

Nannan (Celtic) *see* Eire.

Nannar (A) (Babylonia)
She is a moon goddess and the twin sister of Shamash (q.v.).

Nannar (B) (Sumer) *see* Nanna (B).

Nanook (Eskimo)
Also known as: *Nanuq.*
The Bear. The Pleiades.

Nanshe (Sumer)
A goddess of the waters of springs who had the ability to interpret the dreams sent by Zaqar. A daughter of Ea, she was, like her father, worshiped at Eridu and at Lagash, where a yearly festival was held in her honor.

Nantosuelta *Nantosvelta* (Celtic)
Also known as: *Winding River.*
Fertility goddess. Nantosuelta, a Gaulish fertility goddess, is the consort of Sucellos (Silvanus in southern Gaul). She is frequently shown with Sucellos and is often seen holding a pole topped by the replica of a small house (perhaps a bird house). The goddess is accompanied by a raven. *See also* Silvanus; Sucellos.

Nanu (Celtic) *see* Anu (B); Eire.

Nanuq (Eskimo) *see* Nanook.

Naonghaithya (Persia) *see* Naonhaithya.

Naonhaithya *Naonghaithya, Naosihaithya* (Persia)
A Zoroastrian archdemon. *See also* Daevas; Darvands.

Naosihaithya (Persia) *see* Naonhaithya.

Napaeae (Greek)
They are shy but merry nymphs who live in wooded areas and are often found as members of Artemis' entourage. *See also* Artemis; Nymphs.

Napi (Blackfoot People, North America)
During a great disaster, Napi, the founder of the tribe, led his people to the safety of Nina Stahu, a great cave. *See also* Apisirahts.

Na'pi (Blackfoot People, North America)
Also known as: *Old Man.*
Creator deity. A god who created man and woman from clay.

Nar Nara (Pakistan) *see* Jin.

Nara (India) *see* Narayana (A); Nari.

Nara-Raja (India) *see* Kuvera.

Nara-Simbha (India) *see* Nara-Simha.

Nara-Simha *Nara-Simbha, Narashinha, Narasimba, Narasimbha, Narasinha* (Man-Lion) (Brahmanic, Hindu; India)
Also known as: *Nara simhavatara.*
Nara-Simha is the fourth avatar of Vishnu. The tyrant Haranya-kasipu, who is one of the Daityas (demons), was furious when his son Prahlada refused to worship him and instead declared his belief that Vishnu was the only true god. Brahma had given immunity from harm to Haranya-kasipu. There were a few provisions. He could not be killed by day or night, by animal or man, nor could he be killed inside or outside of his home. When his son would not obey him Haranya-kasipu cursed and kicked a pillar and challenged Vishnu to come forth if he was truly omniscient and omnipresent. Vishnu appeared as Nara-Simha the half-man, half-lion and ripped his adversary to pieces. Haranya-kasipu was killed between day and night, at dusk, neither in nor out, but in his doorway, and not by an animal nor a man but by a half-beast, half-man. Prahlada took over his father's position, but reigned with kindness and wisdom. His grandson was the demon Bali who left Sutala in Patala, a region under the world by Vishnu. Nara-Simha is described as red, with a thick bristling mane dripping blood. He wears a garland made from the entrails of his enemy. This myth appears to be symbolic of the struggle between light and darkness. *See also* Bali; Daityas; Hiranya-kasipu; Matsya; Prahlada; Vamana (Vishnu's avatar as a dwarf); Varaha (Vishnu's avatar as a boar); Vishnu.

Narada (Hindu; India)
Also known as: *Brahma-deva.*
A rishi (sage), Narada sprang from Brahma's forehead. He did not get along well with Daksha, so Daksha decreed that Narada would be born from one of his daughters. This happened and the father was Brahma. As only gods are born twice of the same father, Narada became Brahma-Deva. Narada, a friend of Krishna, invented the lute and taught the Gandharvas to play it. *See also* Brahma; Daksha; Gandharvas; Pradyuma.

Narah (India) *see* Narayana (A).

Naraka (A) *Narakasur, Naraka-asura* (Hindu; India)
A vile and powerful giant demon, Naraka was king of Pragiyotisha. The personification of darkness, he conquered all the kings on earth and became an arch enemy of the gods. He stole Aditi's earrings and wore them himself in his fortress castle. He took Indra's canopy and abducted sixteen thousand one hundred young women from earth and the celestial realm. In the form of an elephant he raped the daughter of the divine architect Visvakarma. Krishna went after him with a vengeance. He battled the demon and his army, including Muru, the five-headed demon, and his seven sons. After defeating Naraka, the palace was open to reveal countless treasures and the female prisoners. When Krishna saw the young women, it was love at first sight. He whisked them off to his heavenly abode and married them. *See also* Aditi; Sita; Vasundara; Yama.

Naraka (B)
Also known as: *Dmyal-wa, Naraloka* (Tibet); (Buddhist, Hindu; India).
The lowest Hindu world, where the wicked are punished

after death. The home of goblins and sorcerers, it has twenty-eight divisions. (*See* Patala). In the Buddhist tradition, it is one of the six paths or conditions of existence and is also called Nara. The six conditions are divided into eight classes: birth, old age, sickness, death, misfortunes and punishments, offensive objects and sensations, separation from loved ones, ungratified wishes, and the struggle for existence. *See also* Loka.

Naraloka (India) *see* Naraka (B).

Narasamsa (India)
"Praise of Men," a title of Agni. *See also* Agni.

Narashinha (India) *see* Nara-Simha.

Narasimba (India) *see* Nara-Simha.

Narasimbha (India) *see* Nara-Simha.

Narasimhavatara(India) *see* Nara-Simha.

Narasinha *Man-Lion* (India) *see* Nara-Simha.

Narayana (A) *Nara, Narah, Naarayan, Satya-Narayana, Satyapir* (Hindu; India)
A thousand-eyed being greater than Brahma, Narayana is the creator, preserver and destroyer of worlds. He is the eternal male who bore even Brahma in his indestructible body. He lay for ages on the primeval waters, known as Nara, floating on a banyan leaf while sucking his toe. When he decided to create everything from his body, speech was born from his mouth, the Vedas from his body, amirita from his tongue, the firmament from his nose, heaven and sun from his eyes, temples from his ears, clouds and rain from his hair, lightning from his beard, rocks from his nails, and mountains from his bones. His toe-sucking position symbolizes eternity. In another version he created Purusha. As Satya-Narayana he was originally Satyapir, the combination Hindu and Muslim deity. Satya-Narayana is worshiped once a month at dusk. Among his elaborate offerings is a delicacy made with sugar, flour, milk, and banana. Narayana is also a name that became associated with Buddha in later times. Compare Narayana to Purusha. *See also* Brahma; Kama; Naryana (B); Parvati; Vishnu.

Narayana (B) (Hindu, Muslim; India)
Also known as: *Vishnu.*
Narayana, "Moving Waters," is an epithet of Vishnu. When Brahma began creating the world, he awakened Vishnu, who was asleep on the serpent Sesha on the ocean's floor. When Narayana is used as a mystic name of Vishnu, it recalls Purusha. *See also* Brahma; Narayana (A); Purusha; Sesha; Vishnu.

Narayana (C) (Hindu; India)
He is a Rishi, the son of the deity Dharma and Ahimsa. He practiced his penance with an intensity that alarmed the gods. *See also* Dharma; Rishi.

Narayana (D) (Hindu; India)
The son of the first man, Nara, who is identified with Vishnu. *See also* Narayana (A); Narayana (E); Nari (B); Vishnu.

Narayana (E) (Hindu; India) An epithet for Brahma.

Narcissus (Greek)
Deified mortal. A beautiful youth, he is the son of the river god Cephissus and the nymph Leiriope. To avenge Narcissus' rebuff of the nymph Echo's love, Aphrodite, who regarded the incident as a rebuke to herself, caused Narcissus to become enamored of his own reflection in the waters of a stream. Unable to embrace or kiss the image, he pined away until he was changed into a flower, the narcissus. *See also* Aphrodite; Cephissus; Echo.

Nare (Teutonic) *see* Narve.

Nareau *Na Reau, Naareau, Nareua, Narleau, Naruau, Nauru* (Oceanic)
Also known as: *Areop-Enap, Na-Arean, Tekikinto, Tekikitea, Tekitekite.*
Spider. Creator-trickster god. Nareau and his daughter Kobine came from Te Bo Ma, the primeval darkness, and Te Maki (meaning "Cleaving Together") and created heaven and earth. Next, they created the first humans, De Babou and De Ai (also known as Na Atibu and Te-Po-ma-Te-Maki). Riiki the eel or Rigi the worm, who are sometimes credited with the creation of all, perhaps assisted Nareau. Nareau sent De Babou and De Ai with instructions to tend the earth. They disobeyed his orders not to have offspring and gave birth to the sun, moon, and sea. Because they pleaded for forgiveness he allowed them to remain and they began the human race. Some say Nareau has a son named Maturang who fished upland to form the islands. Nareau is possibly the same as Tabakea, the turtle, who was called "the Father of All Things." Nareau, who is shown as a spider is somewhat similar to Qat. *See* Riiki and Rigi for a different creation story. *See also* Areop-Enap; Kai-n-Tiku-Aba; Ligobund; Luk; Lukelong, Qat; Yelefaz.

Narfe (Teutonic) *see* Narve.

Narfi (Teutonic) *see* Narve.

Nari (A) (Teutonic) *see* Narve.

Nari (B) (India)
Nari is the "Mother of the Earth," the primordial woman, spouse of Nara and, according to some, the mother of Viraj. *See also* Viraj.

Nari (C) (Babylonia) *see* Marduk.

Narleau (Gilbert Islands) *see* Nareau.

Naru (Teutonic) *see* Narve.

Naru-kami (Japan)
Also known as: *Kami-nari.*
God of thunder. Same as Kami-nari. Symbolizes thunder and lightning. *See also* Kami-nari.

Naruau (Gilbert Islands) *see* Nareau.

Narve *Nare, Narfe, Narfi, Nari, Narvi* (Norse; Teutonic)
He is the son of Loki and his third wife, the loving, faithful Sigyn. His brother, Vali, was named after the Vali who avenged Balder. The gods turned Vali into a wolf expressly to rip Narve's body apart. His intestines were used by the gods to tie up his father. *See also* Loki; Sigyn; Vali.

Narvi (Teutonic) *see* Narve.

Nasamon (Greek)
Nasamon is the grandson of Apollo and Acacallis and the

son of the Libyan chieftain Amphithemis (also known as Garamas) and Tritonis. His brother is Caphaurus, also known as Cephalion. *See also* Acacallis.

Nasargiel (Hebrew) A fallen angel who rules in Hell.

Nasatyas and Dasra (India)

The "Wonder Workers," Nasatyas and Dasra are the twin healing deities known as the Asvins. In later times, the Asvins declined in mythological status and became the Zoroastrian archdemon Naonghaithya. *See also* Asvins.

Nasilele (Zambia, Africa)

Moon goddess. Wife or mate of Nambi or Nyambe. *See also* Nyambe.

Nasrah (Arabic) The Hewer.

Nastrond (Norse; Teutonic)

Also known as: *Shore of Corpses.*

Underground. In this section of Hel the dragon Nidhod gnaws on the corpses of evil doers. *See also* Hel; Nidhod.

Nasu (Zoroaster; Persia)

This female demon, one of the Drujs, is able to enter a corpse in the shape of a fly. The glance of a dog is able to drive her away, in a funeral rite known as sag-did ("dog-sight"). Should she invade a living body, a nine day purification ceremony known as Barashnum will rid the person of her impurities. *See also* Angra Mainyu; Drujs.

Nat (A) (Greek) *see* Sol (B).

Nat (B) (Teutonic) *see* Nott.

Nat-thami (Burma)

They are the eleven maiden nats (spirits) who guard eleven royal umbrellas in Mandalay. *See also* Nats.

Nata and Nena (Aztec People, Mexico)

Survivors of the flood. Nata and Nena were warned by Tezcatlipoca about a coming flood. They took refuge in a hollowed log. Tezcatlipoca warned them not to eat anything except a single ear of maize. They disobeyed the god and ate roasted fish they had caught. Tezcatlipoca punished them by changing the fish into dogs. Similar to tale of Noah and that of Coxcox and Xochiquetzal (q.v.). Nata and Nena are associated with Citlallatonac (q.v.). *See also* Legend of the Four Suns; Tezcatlipoca.

Natagai (Mongol)

Also known as: *Nogat.*

A little food is placed in the mouths of these images at each meal. They are considered gods of prosperity and weather. They preside over earth, house, cattle and corn. The images are generally made of felt material. They are possibly the same as the health deity, Tangri (Mongol). *See also* Ahura Mazda (Persian); Tangri.

Nataraja *Nataraja Siva* (Hindu; India)

Also known as: *Natesha* (Lord of the Dance), *Shiva*, *Sudalaiyadi* (Dancer of the Burning Ground).

Nataraja, the master of rhythm and dancing, is an emanation of Shiva. His cosmic dance, Nadanta, consists of five movements: creation, preservation, destruction, reincarnation or illusion, and nirvana. Separately, these movements represent the activities of Brahma, Vishnu, Rudra, Mahashvara and Sadashiva. Nadanta is performed in the golden hall of Chidambaram in the center of the universe. When Shiva dances, a halo surrounds his head and legions of spirits surround him. He plays his own drum, Damaru, and as he whirls he keeps the stars and planets in orbit. His dance symbolizes the constant movement of the universe. When he dances in cemeteries, the unclean spirits heed his call and are brought into his circle of power. The serpent Sesha saw Shiva's performance and was so enthralled that he renounced his life style in hope of seeing it again. When attacked by the demon Muyalaka, Shiva pressed his toe on him and broke his back as he continued his cosmic dance. Shiva invented the Tandava dance to please "Uma" the mother. Another dancer in Shiva's court is Tandu the god of dancing. Shiva, shown with his right leg raised in dance, is known as Natesha. *See also* Sesha; Shiva; Uma.

Natesha (India) "Lord of the Dance." *See also* Nataraja; Shiva.

Nats (Buddhist; Burma)

Spirits of air, sky, earth, forest, hills, rivers, streams, wind, and rain, nats are also household ghosts and ghosts of cultivated fields. Agricultural nats are known as Saba-Leippya. *See also* Hkum Yeng; Hmin Nat; Nat-thami; Sa-bdag (Tibet); Thein.

Natu-no-me-no-kami (Japan) *see* Ukemochi.

Natu-taka-mi-no-kami (Japan) *see* Ukemochi.

Nature (Greek) *see* Chaos.

Nau (Egypt) *see* Nut.

Nau and Naut (Egypt) *see* Nau and Nen.

Nau and Nen (Egypt)

Also known as: *Nau and Naut, Nau-Shesma* (possibly).

Probably creator deities. Nau, the monster serpent, has seven serpents on his seven necks. He is usually associated with his consort, Nen, but little is known about either except that they are mentioned in the Pyramid Texts along with Amen and Ament. Nau and Nen may be one deity with dual names. *See also* Amen.

Nauholin (Aztec)

Sun god. Nauholin was worshiped by Early Aztec warriors or knights.

Nauisithous (Greek)

He is the son of the sea god, Poseidon, and Periboea. It was Nauisithous who purified Heracles after he murdered his children. *See also* Calypso; Heracles; Nauplius; Poseidon.

Naunet (Egypt) *see* Ogdoad (the); Ptah.

Nauplius (A) (Greek)

Astromoner, sailor. He is the husband of Clymene.

Nauplius (B) (Greek)

Nauplius is the son of Poseidon and Amymone and the half-brother of Nauisithous. He is a sailor and a navigator. *See also* Argonauts; Hesione; Poseidon.

Nauroz (Persian) A Persian festival. *See also* Yima.

Nauru (Gilbert Islands) *see* Nareau.

Nausinous (Greek)

He is the son of Odysseus and Calypso. Nausinous and Nausithous share the same mother, Calypso, who was broken-hearted when Odysseus left her. *See also* Calypso; Odysseus.

Nav (Slavic)

Spirits. Spirits of mortals who died tragically and too soon.

Nava-ratri (India) Hindu Festival. *See also* Durga-puja.

Navagrahas (Nepal) *see* Dikpalas.

Navasard (Armenian)

Navasard is a New Year's celebration in honor of Aramazd (q.v.).

Nayanezgani and Thobadzistshini (Navajo People, North America)

Also known as: *Atseatsan and Atseatsine* (possibly).

Culture heroes. Possibly sun and sea deities. Slayers of the Alien gods and Child of the Waters. They cleaned the world of the man-devouring giants, except those of cold, hunger, old age, and poverty. *See also* Anaye.

Naymlap (Andean People, South America)

Also known as: *Llampallec.*

Supreme deity. Possibly a sea deity. Legend indicates that he was either a mortal chieftain or a deity of great renown. Long ago Naymlap and his wife, Ceterni, and a group of assistants came from the north. These people reigned for a long time, then given wings by his power, rose to the sky and disappeared. His followers attempted in vain to search for him but he left no trace except for an idol carved from green stone, which they called Llampallec. Naymlap was followed by Cium, who perished of hunger in a below ground chamber. According to myth he wanted to appear immortal. After nine different kings, the king named Tempellec followed and attempted to move the statue, but a demon who appeared as a beautiful woman seduced him. Shortly after this it began to rain for thirty days, followed by a severe famine. Tempellec's people threw him into the sea and he was followed by a change in the form of government. The original group of people who came with Naymlap were Pitazofi (a trumpeter), Ninocolla (warden of the throne), Ninagentue (cup-bearer), Fongasigde (spreader of shell dust on the water), Ochocalo (head of the food preparing), Xam (in charge of face paints), and Llapchilulli (in charge of vestments and plumes).

Nazi (Semitic, Sumerian)

One of the goddesses created by Ninhursag. In one version, Nazi is a deity who heals the phallus. *See also* Ninhursag.

Nchsh (Hebrew) *see* Nachash.

Ndengei *Ndengi* (Fiji Islands)

Creator. He is the divine serpent god with stone flesh who hatched mortals from a bird's egg. His son, Rokomoutu, is also a creator, but only of land. In one story, Ndengei hatched two eggs, one a boy and one a girl. They became the ancestors of the human race. In a different rendition, a great bird laid the two eggs which were hatched by Ndengi. One became a boy, the other a girl. He is also a god and judge of the underworld. It is difficult for the soul to reach him, as the way is barred by a giant

wielding an axe. If the soul is wounded, it cannot appear in the place of judgment. Whenever Ndengei turns over, there are earthquakes. *See also* Figonas; Kafisi.

Ndengi (Fiji Islands) *see* Ndengei.

Ndjambi Karunga (Herero People, Southwest Africa)

He is the omnipresent supreme being known for his kindness.

Ndrianahary (Africa) *see* Ndriananhary.

Ndriananahary '*Ndriananahary, *'*Ndrianahary* (Madagascar, Africa)

Supreme deity. He sent his son, Ataokoloinona, to earth to see if it was suitable for inhabitation. The son never returned, so he sent his servants who are dead people to search for him, but they never returned to earth. *See also* Andriamanitra.

Ne (Egypt)

One of the principal gods mentioned in the Pyramid Texts.

Ne No Kuni (Japan) *see* Ne-No-Kuni.

Ne-No-Kuni (Japan) *see* Yomi.

Naenia (Roman) Goddess of funerals.

Neaera (A) (Greek)

She is the wife of Strymon, the Thracian river god, and the mother of Evadne. *See also* Argus (A); Strymon.

Neaera (B) (Greek)

She is one of the six daughters of Amphion and Niobe.

Neb-Abui (Egypt) *see* Assessors.

Neb-baui (Egypt) *see* Aai.

Neb-Hrau (Egypt) *see* Assessors.

Neb-Maat (Egypt) *see* Assessors.

Neb-senku (Egypt) *see* Aai.

Neb-Ti (Egypt) *see* Nephthys.

Neba-per-em-khetkhet (Egypt) *see* Assessors.

Nebhet Hotep (Egypt) *see* Nebt-Hetep.

Nebiru (Babylon) *see* Marduk.

Nebmerutef (Egypt)

Deity of writing. A scribe, he was inspired by Thoth, the patron god of writing and record keeping.

Nebo (Hebrew, Sumer)

Also known as: *Ak, Marduk, Merodach* (Akkadian).

Nebo is a name for Marduk when he is the "God of Trading." In this form he is also called a teacher and writer. As Ak, he has traits similar to Mercury in that he is called a messenger and a recording angel. *See also* Marduk; Nabu; Namtar.

Nebrophonus (Greek)

He is possibly the son of Jason and Hypsipyle. *See also* Jason.

Nebt-het (Egypt) *see* Aai.

Nebt-Hetep (Egypt) *see* Iusaas.

Nebt-Hetep *Nebhet Hotep* (Egypt) *see* Atum; Iusaas.

Nebt Ushau (Egypt)

Nebt Ushau is the name of the Eighth Hour of Tuat. The name of the pylon guarding the entrance is Aha-en-urt-nef. The city Osiris passes through at this hour is Tebat-neteru-s. Only gods and spirits who have been mummified and buried appropriately occupy this place. Four ram forms of the god Tathenen guard Osiris. The other gods mentioned during this section of the sun god's trip are Affi, Aranbfi, Ba-neteru, Horus, Isis, Ka-Amentet, Khatri, Khepera, Nut, Osiris, Rem-neteru, Seb, Sebeq-hra, Shu, Ta, Tefnut, and Tem. The doors in the Circle, Shesheta, are Hetemet-khemiu, Tes-aha-Ta-thenen, Tesermen-ta, Tes-khem-baiu, Tes-neb-terer, Tes-sekhem-aru, Tes-sept-nestu, Tes-sheta-em-thehen-neteru, Tes-sma-kekui. *See also* Tuat.

Nebthet (Egypt) *see* Nephthys.

Nechtan (Celtic, Irish) *see* Boann.

Neda (Greek)

Neda was one of the infant Zeus' nurses. *See also* Zeus.

Nedu (Sumer) *see* Arallu.

Nef-em-baiu (Egypt) *see* Aai.

Nefer Hor (Egypt) A son of the god Thoth.

Nefer-Tem (Egypt) *see* Assessors.

Nefertem (Egypt) *see* Nefertum.

Nefertum *Nefer-Tem, Nefertem* (Egypt)

Also known as: *Iphtimis* (Greek), *Horus.*

God of the sun. God of perfumes. Nefertum is the son of Ptah and Sakhmet. He is one of the triad of Memphis which is composed of Ptah, Sakhmet and Nefertum. Nefertum and Horus (child of the sun) united to become a single entity. He is sometimes shown with a lion's head or as a youth seated on a lotus blossom. He wears a crown of either a lotus with two feathers or with one lotus alone. He is often depicted standing on a recumbent lion. One of his attributes is a saber. Nefertum is identified with Thoth and Horus. *See also* Ptah; Sekhmet.

Negafok (Eskimo) The cold weather spirit.

Negative Confession (Egypt)

Negative Confession is a rite that takes place before the Weighing of the Heart. There are forty-two Negative Confessions from the Eighteenth Dynasty. They are 1. I have not done iniquity. 2. I have not robbed with violence. 3. I have not done violence to any man. 4. I have not committed theft. 5. I have slain neither man nor woman. 6. I have not made light the bushel. 7. I have not acted deceitfully. 8. I have not purloined the things which belong to God. 9. I have not uttered falsehood. 10. I have not carried off goods by force. 11. I have not uttered vile or evil words. 12. I have not carried off food by force. 13. I have not acted deceitfully. 14. I have not lost my temper and become angry. 15. I have invaded no man's land. 16. I have not slaughtered animals which are the possessions of God. 17. I have not laid waste the lands which have been ploughed. 18. I have not pried into matters to make mischief. 19. I have not set my mouth in motion against any man. 20. I have not given way to

wrath without due cause. 21. I have not committed fornication, and I have not committed sodomy. 22. I have not polluted myself. 23. I have not lain with the wife of a man. 24. I have not made any man to be afraid. 25. I have not made my speech to burn with anger. 26. I have not made myself deaf unto the words of right and truth. 27. I have not made another person to weep. 28. I have not uttered blasphemies. 29. I have not acted with violence. 30. I have not acted without due consideration. 31. I have not pierced my skin, and I have not taken vengeance on the gods. 32. I have not multiplied my speech beyond what should be said. 33. I have not committed fraud, and I have not looked upon evil. 34. I have never uttered curses against the king. 35. I have not fouled running water. 36. I have not exalted my speech. 37. I have not uttered curses against God. 38. I have not behaved with insolence. 39. I have not been guilty of favoritism. 40. I have not increased my wealth except by means of such things as are mine own possessions. 41. I have not uttered curses against that which belongeth to God and is with me. 42. I have not thought scorn of the god of the city. (This list was compiled from the reference book *Who's Who in Egyptian Mythology*, by Anthony S. Mercatante.) *See also* Amit; Maat; Osiris; Thoth.

Negoogunogumbar (Pygmy People, Africa)

He is a monster ogre who swallows children.

Neha-Bra (Egypt) *see* Serqet.

Neha-Hau (Egypt) *see* Assessors.

Neha-Hra (Egypt) *see* Ab-esh-imy-duat.

Nehallennia (Norse)

Goddess of plenty. She is a local deity who appears to be connected with the sea or with sailors. According to some she was a deity worshiped only on Walcheren Island in the North Sea. The cornucopia is her symbol.

Neheb-Kau (Egypt) *see* Assessors; Nut.

Neheb-Nefert (Egypt) *see* Assessors.

Nehebkau *Neheb-kau* (Egypt)

Serpent deity. Mother goddess. She is one of the principal deities mentioned in the Pyramid Texts. Nehebkau is generally thought of as an underworld deity. In some versions this goddess is associated with food. She is shown as a serpent with human legs.

Neheh (Egypt)

Also known as: *Heh.*

Deity of eternity. This god is the personification of eternity, representing unending time and a long, happy life. He is shown as a squatting man carrying a symbol of life and wearing a curved reed on his head. *See also* Heh.

Nehelennia (Teutonic)

Fertility goddess. Nehelennia is depicted standing on a boat. *See also* Nerthus.

Nehesu (Egypt) *see* Aamu.

Nehi (Egypt) *see* Aai.

Nehmauit (Egypt)

A wife of Thoth. Her name means "Uprooter of Evil."

Neht (Egypt)

One of the principal gods mentioned in the Pyramid Texts.

Neit (Egypt) *see* Neith.

Neiterogob (Masai People, Africa) Goddess of Earth.

Neith *Neit* (Egypt)

Also known as: *Mehueret* (her name as the Celestial Cow), *Net, Nit, Nut, Nyt, Pallas Athene* (Greek), *Tehenut* (the Libyan).

Mother of the gods. Goddess of hunting. Mistress of the cow. Sky goddess. Warrior goddess. Mortuary goddess. Protector of the city of Sais (capital of Egypt in the seventh century A.D.). Protector of marriage. Weaver. Patron deity of the arts of domestic life. Arbitrator. In early times she was worshiped as two crossed arrows either on a shield or an animal skin. Later, she had the attributes of a woman. She wore a crown and held a bow and arrows. Later still, she appeared with her attribute, the weaver's shuttle. Around the 7th century C.E. she became the mother of the gods, and a sky goddess. Neith existed before the beginning and it was she as Mehueret, the Celestial Cow, who gave birth to the sky. Renowned for her skills and her wisdom, she was the weaver of the world. When conflict arose between Horus and Set over the vacancy left by Osiris' death, the god called upon Neith to act as the arbitrator. She is shown with Isis offering bread and water to the dead when they reach the otherworld. She is often seen with Selket, the goddess who protects the canopic vase holding the intestines of the dead. Neith is one of the deities who welcomes the dead at the gates of the otherworld. Sometimes she is replaced by Ament, Hathor, Maat, or Nut. When Osiris died, she watched over his coffin with Isis, Nephthys, and Selket. The practice of placing weapons around funeral biers in ancient times may have been connected to her. It was said that mummy wrappings were the gifts of Neith and they allowed the dead to partake of her divine powers. Neith dwells in Acacia. She is often depicted with a shield and arrows or with a bow and arrows. Sometimes as a cow with stars on its belly. The Nile perch was sacred to Neith. The goddess Hatmehit wore a fish (perhaps a dolphin) on her head and was revered as the "first of the fishes." As personification of the sky, she could be identified with Nut. Neith is the female counterpart of Anubis. She is identified with the Greek Athena. Sometimes, Neith is called the mother of Ra. Her association is with Khnum, Sobek and Amunet, Thoth and Horus. Her name is associated with the hunting goddess, Sais. *See also* Ament; Amentet; Anubis; Athena; Chaos; Hathor; Hapy (A); Horus; Khnum; Nut; Selket; Set.

Nejamesha (Jains; India)

Also known as: *Naiga-Mesha, Nemeso.*

God of children. He has wings and the head of a goat.

Nekhbet (Egypt)

Also known as: *Eileithya* (Greek), *Nekhebet, Nekhebit.*

Goddess guardian of Upper Egypt. Her epithet is "she who binds the nine bows." The Greeks called her Eileithya (the city of Eileithyiaspolis) and as such was the goddess of childbirth.

Known as the vulture goddess, Nekhbet became a national goddess and represented Upper Egypt. Lower Egypt was represented by Wadjet of Buto (also known as Edjo), the snake goddess. The vulture and the snake represented the two halves of the country. Symbols of the animals became embodiments of the two crowns and the two uraei surrounding the solar disc were often thought of as Nekhbet and Wadjet. Nekhbet is also one of the principal deities mentioned in the Pyramid Texts. She is depicted as a serpent or a vulture protecting the pharaoh as she hovers over his head with her wings outstretched or as a woman wearing a vulture skin over her head. Nekhbet is the counterpart of Buto. *See also* Wadjet.

Nekhebet (Egypt) *see* Nekhbet.

Nekhen (Egypt) *see* Assessors.

Nekheny (Egypt) *see* Horus.

Nekhibit (Egypt) *see* Nekhbet.

Neleus (Greek)

King of Pylos. Neleus is the son of the sea god, Poseidon, and Tyro, who was the second wife of Cretheus, the founder and first king of Iolcus. Neleus is the twin of a brother, Pelias. The twins were abandoned at birth and raised by a keeper of horses. Pelias carried the imprint of a hoof on his face from being kicked by a horse when he was an infant. Pelias usurped Neleus from the throne to prevent Aeson, the eldest son of Cretheus and Tyro, from becoming king. Neleus married Chloris and became the father of twelve sons. He refused to purify Heracles after he murdered Iphitus during a bout of insanity. Angry, Heracles killed all Neleus' sons, except Nestor. *See also* Cretheus; Iphitus; Heracles; Pelias; Pyro.

Nemain *Neamhan, Neman* (Celtic)

Goddess of panic. War goddess. Might be same as Morrigu Morrigan. Possibly part of the triad of Neman, Morrigu and Macha that made up Badb. *See also* Badb; Morrigu.

Neman (Celtic) *see* Nemain.

Nemcatacoa (Chibcha People, Bogata, South America)

God of weavers and dyers. His history is similar to the rainbow god Chuchaviva. Both of these deities have the unusual task of guarding drunkards. *See also* Chuchaviva.

Nemeds (Irish) *see* Banbha; Tuatha De Danann.

Nemesco (India) *see* Nejamesha.

Nemesis (Greek, Persian)

Also known as: *Adrasteia.*

Goddess of retributive justice. Nymph-goddess. Nemesis, the daughter of Erebus and Nox, who relentlessly meted out just punishment to evildoers, lawbreakers, the proud and haughty, is known as Daughter of the Night. She was also known and worshipped as the beautiful daughter of Oceanus because as the nymph-goddess with the apple-bough she was also the sea-born Aphrodite, sister of the Erinyes. It is possible that her Greek origin transpired when the Persians, conquered after invading Greece, left behind a block of marble from which the Greeks carved a statue of Nemesis. It is said that in attempting to avoid Zeus, she changed herself into a goose but failed to escape when Zeus became a swan. Her egg, hatched by Leda, became Helen of Troy (the cause of the Trojan War). She has been shown as a regal woman seated in a chariot drawn by griffons. (The griffon was the symbol of retributive justice.) The ash tree was one of Nemesis' seasonal disguises. She is also depicted with an apple-bough in one hand, and a wheel in the other, wearing a silver crown embellished with stags. *See also* Adrastia; Aether; Erebus; Eumenides; Helen; Keres; Meliae; Nox.

Nemeso (India) *see* Nejamesha.

Nemo-kuni (Japan) *see* Yomi.

Nemon (Celtic)
Also known as: *Nemontana.*
She is a war goddess who served under Morrigu (q.v.).

Nempterequeteva (Chibcha People, Bogata South America) *see* Bochica.

Nemquetcha (Muyscaya People, South America) *see* Chia.

Nemquetheba (Chibcha People, Bogata, South America) *see* Bochica.

Nen (Egypt) *see* Nau; Nen.

Nenaunir '*Nenaunir*. (Masai People, Africa)
An evil storm god, Nenaunir is in opposition to Ngai. He may be linked to a flood myth about the rainbow swallowing the earth. The Masai attacked the rainbow and forced it to give back the earth. *See also* Ngai.

'**Nenaunir** (Masai People, Africa) *see* Nenaunir.

Neno-Katatsu-kuni *Ne-no-kuni* (Japan)
"Land of Roots." Another name for Yomi, the underworld realm of the dead. *See also* Yomi.

Neolya (Russia) *see* Dolya.

Nephele (Greek; possibly Semitic)
Zeus created a cloud named Nephele to look like Hera. Ixion, the king of the Lapiths of Thessaly, embraced her cloud form and they became the parents of the Centaurs and Amycus. She married Athamas and became the mother of Phrixos and Helle. Athamas' second wife, Ino, was so jealous of Nephele that she attempted to murder Phrixos and Helle. They were able to escape her fury on a winged golden ram. *See also* Abas (C); Athamas; Ino; Ixion; Phrixus.

Nephthys *Nephythys* (Egypt)
Also known as: *Nebthet, Neb-Ti.*
Goddess of the dead. Mistress of the palace. Guardian (with Hapy) of embalmed lungs. She is the daughter of Geb (the earth) and Nut (the sky). She was the wife of her brother Set the god of thunder. Commitment did not stop her from getting her other brother Osiris intoxicated and then seducing him. Anubis, the god of embalming was the son of their union. When Set murdered Osiris, she left him. With Isis, another protector of the dead, the goddesses embalmed Osiris. To mourn Osiris, they turned themselves into kites. Nephthys and Isis are shown with winged arms. Nephthys is the female counterpart of Set and Min. *See also* Anubis; Atum; Geb; Hapy (A); Isis; Nut; Osiris; Selket; Set.

Nephythys (Egypt) *see* Nephthys.

Nepra (Egypt) God of corn. *See also* Tchabu.

Nepri (Egypt) *see* Renenet.

Nept-Uns (Roman) *see* Neptune.

Neptune (Roman)
Also known as: *Nethunus* (possibly Etruscan), *Poseidon* (Greek).
God of the waters. Husband of Salacia, goddess of streams. *See also* Aello; Harpies; Poseidon.

Neptunus (Roman) *see* Neptune.

Nereides (Greek) *see* Nereids.

Nereids *Nereides* (Greek)
Nymphs of the sea and ocean. Shape shifters. The Nereids are the fifty daughters of Nereus and Doris. The Greek authors Homer, Hesiod, Hyginus and Apollodorus all named them, but the number of Nereids and their names were not in accord. Actaea, Agave, Doto, Dynamene, Galateia, Panope (Panopae in Hyginus' list), Pherusa, Speio, and Thetis are in all four recordings. Other Nereids who developed individual myths are Ceto (also called the daughter of Oceanus and Gaea), Amphitrite and Doris. They were said to dwell at the bottom of the Mediterranean with Nereus and they could be the prototypes of the mermaid. Kind to sailors, they assisted the Argonauts as they navigated their ship past Charybdis and Scylla, who guarded the entrance to the straits of Messina. The beautiful, gentle nymphs are attendants of the sea-goddess Thetis. *See* Naiads, the deities of lakes and fountains, for comparison to other water deities. *See also* Acis; Amphitrite; Andromeda; Ceto; Charybdis; Doris; Hylas; Irra; Nereus; Nymphs; Reshep; Scylla; Thetis.

Nereus (Greek)
Also known as: *Phorcus, Phorcys, Phorkus, Phorkys, Proteus.*
Sea god. Shape shifter. Nereus is a sea divinity, son of Oceanus and Gaea, or Pontus and Gaea. His siblings are the "fair-faced" Ceto; the sea god Phorcys; Thaumas, also a sea god; Eurybia, the "flint-hearted;" and Crius. He married the sea goddess Doris, with whom he had fifty daughters, called the Nereids. Nereus, known as "the old man of the sea," was a shape shifter, gifted with prophecy and lived in the Aegean Sea. He was captured by Heracles who forced him to disclose the location of the Garden of Hesperides. Nereus, like most sea gods, is depicted with seaweed for hair. *See also* Actaea; Amphitrite; Ceto; Doris; Gaea; Nereids; Oceanus; Thaumas.

Nergal *Nirgalu* (Assyro-Babylonia, Phoenicia, Sumer; possibly of Egyptian origin).
Also known as: *Enmesarra, Gira, Girra, Ira, Irra, Lugalmeslam, Malik, Mekel, Meshlamthea, Reshef, Reshep.*
God of the underworld. Lord of fires. Supreme ruler and judge of Arallu, the land of the dead. God of midsummer sun, war, pestilence, the chase, and a protector deity. He is also a god of flocks and foaling. In earlier myths, he was a god of war. He is the brother and counterpart of Ninurta. Nergal led a company of evil spirits (possibly seven gods) who were ruled by Narudu, into the underworld, forcing its queen, Ereshkigal, to marry him and appoint him sovereign of her kingdom as the price of peace. In the form of Irra, his messenger is Ishum. He is associated with Marduk and is sometimes identified with Shamash. Nergal's attribute is a sword or the head of a lion. He

is possibly shown as a winged lion. *See also* Allatu; Arallu; Ereshkigal; Irra; Naruda; Ninurta; Satan.

Neri (Norse; Teutonic)

Also known as: *Norine.*

He is the ruddy faced sky or morning god, who is the son of Loki and Nott (qq.v.).

Nerig (Babylon) *see* Ninib.

Nerivik *Nerrivik* (Eskimo People, Greenland)

Also known as: *Arnarquagssaq, Sedna.*

Sea goddess. Nerivik was a mortal woman who was snatched up by a petral (sea-bird). Her relatives attempted to save her but were also attacked so they threw her into the sea. She grabbed the side of their boat and they chopped off her fingers. The fingers became seals and whales. Nerivik sank to the sea's floor, was transformed into a sea goddess and became the ruler of the food for the living and ruler of the souls of the dead. She is guarded by a ferocious dog. She is sometimes called the "Food Dish." Nerivk is comparable to Sedna (q.v.) *See also* Adlivun, the home of Sedna.

Nerrivik (Greenland) *see* Nerivik.

Nerta (Egypt) *see* Ap-taui.

Nertha (Teutonic) *see* Nerthus.

Nerthus *Nertha* (Norse; Teutonic)

Also known as: *Hertha, Iron Lady* (German), *Njord, Terra Mater* (Roman).

A goddess of water, fertility, death and peace. Earth deity. She is the sister or wife of Njord. As a deity of death and fertility, the Teutons carried Nerthus around on a wagon to fertilize the fields. Her symbol is a boat. *See also* Bertha; Hertha; Njord.

Nesaru (Arikara People)

"The Power Above." Supreme deity. He created Mother Corn from an ear of corn. She led the people from the underworld to the light of day.

Nesert (Egypt)

One of the principal gods mentioned in the Pyramid Texts.

Nesr (Arabic) Vulture God.

Nesreca (Serbian) *see* Sreca.

Nessus (Greek)

His parents are Ixion and Nephele. A Centaur, he attempted to rape Deianeira and was slain by her husband, Heracles. The blood and semen of Nessus, left on his coat and given to Heracles by Deianeira caused his death. After death, Nessus became the ferryman of the river Evenus, in the underworld. *See also* Centaur; Deianeira; Heracles; Ixion; Nephele.

Nestor (Greek)

King of Pylos for three generations. He was possibly married to Anaxibia. A wise and honorable man, Nestor had ninety ships that sailed to the Trojan War. Remarkably, they all returned safely. *See also* Antilochus; Eurydice.

Nesu (Sumer) *see* Aruru; Ninhursag.

Net (Egypt) *see* Amen (B); Ament; Neith.

Netch-baiu (Egypt) *see* Aai.

Netchesti (Egypt) *see* Aai.

Nete (Greek)

One of the Delphic Muses, she personifies the low string of the lyre. Her sisters are Hypate, the high string, and Mese, the middle string. *See also* Muses (Delphic).

Neter (Egypt)

Also known as: *Neteri, Netra, Nutar.*

The Neter is a sacred symbol in the form of an axe. It is one of the earliest representations of a divinity. There is argument as to its meaning, but some think that it means divine, strong, or mighty.

Neter-Khertet (Egypt) *see* Tuat.

Neter Mut (Egypt)

Also known as: *Theotokos* (Christian).

Aspect of Isis. A very old and common title of Isis. The Christian Fathers translated this name as Theotokos, or Mother of God. *See also* Isis.

Neter-Ta (Egypt)

Heaven. In an old document or hymn to Amen-Ra, Neter-Ta is described as the Divine Land.

Neteri (Egypt) *see* Neter.

Netetthap (Egypt)

One of the principal gods mentioned in the Pyramid Texts.

Nethert (Egypt) *see* Aai.

Neti (Sumer) *see* Arallu; Inanna.

Netra (Egypt) *see* Neter.

Neuri (Slavic)

The Neuri are a race of sorcerers who change into wolves for several days once each year. They are possibly connected with the name Vlkodlak which was the vampire or werewolf.

Ng Ai (Africa) *see* Ngai.

'Ng Ai (Masai People, Africa) *see* Ngai.

Nga (Yurak People, Siberia) God of the underworld and death.

Ngahue (Polynesia, New Zealand)

Afterworld deity. He is probably the head of the underworld as is Tawhaki. Ngahue is similar to the Tahitian, Hiro and Uru-taetae.

Ngai *Ng Ai, 'Ng Ai, 'Ngai* (Masai Group; Kikuya People, East Africa)

He is a High God, the creator of all things. His abode is in the sky but when he visits earth, always invisible, he stays in the mountains. His visits are made to achieve a general overview of his people. He distributes rewards and punishments as he deems necessary. He is called upon during times of disasters, and prayed to during rites of passage, and special functions, such as marriage. He is also known as a sky god, and god of rain and clouds. Ngai found the first mortal Dorobo, or Kintu.

With the first mortal, he found an elephant and a serpent. Ngai places a guardian angel beside every man to defend him against dangers. Ngai's opponent is the evil deity Nenaunir (q.v.). *See also* Kintu.

'Ngai (Masai People, Africa) *see* Ngai.

Ngakola (Banda People, Africa)
Creator. Brother of Tere. He breathed life into mortals. *See also* Tere.

Ngalijod (Australia) see Rainbow Serpent.

Ngaore (Polynesia, New Zealand)
Goddess of grass (probably). Tane tried for a fourth time to make his mother Papa become his wife, but she again refused and sent him to Ngaore (meaning "tender one"). Instead of children, his new wife conceived rush type grasses. After many other attempts, Tane finally found a wife who would bear a human child. She was Hine-ahu-one (q.v.). *See also* Hine-ahu-one; Mumahango; Papa; Rangahore; Tane.

Ngaru (Mangaia Island, Polynesia)
A culture hero, Ngaru caused a deluge to keep the female demon Miru from cooking him. He also overcame the sky demon Amaite-Rangi. *See also* Miru.

Ngewo (Africa) *see* Ngewo-wa.

Ngewo-Wa *Ngewo* (Mende People; West Africa)
Also known as: *Maanda, Ma-Ngee.*
Creator of everything. He was called by the humans he created Maanda (grandfather), Ma-ngee (grandfather-take-it) and Ngee-wolo-nga wa-le (grandfather-take-it-is-spread-wide). The first name was given him because he gave humans whatever they asked for. The second name was given him after he disappeared.

Ngunyari (Australia) *see* Walangala.

Ngurunderi (Australia) *see* Bunjil; Daramulun; Nurrundere.

Ngurvilu (Araucanian People, Chile)
God of water, lakes, and seas. He is the cause of boat and swimming accidents. Ngurvilu is shown in the form of a cat with a long claw on the end of its tail.

Ngworekara (Fan People, Africa)
An evil demon king, he rules over the kingdom of evil spirits who were souls of the dead. Ngworekara and his spirits are depicted with dirty ears, droopy noses resembling elephant trunks and, long straggly hair.

Nhangs (Armenian, Persian)
Evil river spirits. They can appear as women, mermaids, seals, crocodiles and even sea monsters. They drag swimmers under water and drown them. *See also* Devs.

Ni (Inca People, Peru)
Also known as: *Ocean.*
Sea deity. Little is known about Ni, but he or she was worshiped as a provider of fish. *See also* Si; Vis.

Nibelung *Nibelungen, Niblungs, Niflungar, Niflungs* (Norse; Teutonic)

High gods. Nibelung is the brother of Schilbung. They were slain by Siegfried with the sword Balmung. In the plural, the Nieblungs are dwarfs who came from a land of mist where Giuki and Grimhild ruled. The rulers have three sons: Gunnar, Hogni, Guttorm, and one daughter, Gudrun. *See also* Dwarfs; Gudrun; Siegried; Sigurd.

Nibelungen (Teutonic) *see* Nibelung.

Niblungs (Teutonic) *see* Nibelung.

Nicahtagah (Maya) *see* Xumucane.

Nice (Greek) *see* Nike.

Nichan (Gros-Ventre Group of Algonquin People, North America)
He is a creator god who first destroyed the world by fire and later water. *See also* Gluskap; Manibozho.

Nicippe (Greek)
Also known as: *Amphibia.*
Her parents are Pelops and Hippodameia. She married Sthenelus and had three children: Alcino, Eurystheus and Medusa (not to be confused with the Gorgon, Medusa). See Hippodameia (B) for the names of Nicippe's siblings. *See also* Pelops.

Nick (Teutonic) *see* Nix.

Nicor (Teutonic)
They are malignant water monsters who drown people. *See also* Nixie.

Nicostratus (Greek)
Helen of Troy was driven from Sparta by Nicostratus and his brother, Megapenthes, when the king of Troy, Menelaus, died. *See also* Menelaus; Helen.

Nidaba (Babylon)
Corn goddess. Counterpart of Nabu. In old legends she was, like Nabu, a patron of letters. Nidaba is associated with Adad and Enlil. Some believe she was a form of Ishtar. She is depicted with serpents springing from her shoulders. *See also* Nabu.

Niddhogge (Teutonic) *see* Nidhod.

Nidhema *Naivedya Sal-za-ma* (Tibet) *see* Amoghasiddhi.

Nidhod (Teutonic)
Also known as: *Niddhogge, Nidhogg, Nidhoggr, Nidhug, Nighhoggr, Nithogg.*
A winged dragon, Nidhod flies around Nifelhel. He is one of several monsters who try to injure the roots of the world-tree, Yggdrasil. Nidhod chews on the corpses of evil people. *See also* Nastrond; Yggdrasil.

Nidhogg (Teutonic) *see* Nidhod.

Nidhoggr (Teutonic) *see* Nidhod.

Nidhug (Teutonic) *see* Nidhod.

Nidim (Assyro-Babylonia) *see* Ea.

Nidra (India)
She is the goddess of sleep, and the daughter of Brahma.

Nifelheim (Teutonic) *see* Nifl-heim.

Nif'fleheim (Teutonic) *see* Nifl-heim.

Nifl-heim *Nif'fleheim, Nifelheim, Nifhel, Niflheim, Nivlheim.* (Norse; Teutonic)

Also known as: *Hel, Hell, Realm of the Mist.*

Nifl-heim, the world of mist, ice and darkness, is situated in the north section of Ginnunga-gap, the primeval abyss. Within Nifl-heim is a spring known as Hvergelmir (also called Kvergjelme). From the spring ten, eleven, or twelve rivers known collectively as the Elivagar flowed and turned to ice by the cold wind from Ginnunga-gap. The goddess Hel became the queen of Nifl-heim where the tree of life, Yggdrasil tree, has roots. Nifl-heim is known in some myths as the lowest of nine worlds and the abode of those who die of old age or disease. *See also* Bifrost; Elivagar; Ginnunga-gap; Gleipnir; Hel; Hell; Hvergelmir; Midgard; Muspells-heim; Surtr; Yggdrasil; Ymir.

Niflheim (Teutonic) *see* Nifl-heim.

Niflhel (Teutonic) *see* Nifl-heim.

Niflung (Teutonic) *see* Nibelung.

Niflungar (Teutonic) *see* Nibelung.

Niflungs (Teutonic) *see* Nibelung.

Nig (Teutonic) *see* Nix.

Nighhoggr (Teutonic) *see* Nidhod.

Night (A) (Greek) *see* Chaos; Fates; Nyx.

Night (B) (Norse; Teutonic)

Goddess of night. Daughter of Narvi. Mother of Day. She rides her horse around the world. *See also* Nott.

Night Gods (Aztec) *see* Lords of the Night Hours.

Night Journey (Islamic) *see* Mohammed.

Nightingale (Greek) *see* Aedon.

Nigi-mi-tama (Japan) *see* Susanowo.

Nigishzida (Mesopotamia) *see* Anu (B).

Nihongi, The (Japan) *see* Ama-no-minaka-nushi.

Nii-no-ama (Japan) *see* Suitengu.

Nijuhachi-bushu (Japan)

Protectors. They are the servants of the goddess of peace, Kuan-Yin. Twenty-seven of the servants' names are Hibakara-o, Sanshi-taisho, Mansen-o, Kompira-O, Karura-o, Kinnara-o, Konshiki-kujaku, Komoku-ten, Kendatsuba, Konda-o, Gob-ujo, Misshakukongo, Bishamon-ten, Daibon-ten, Teishaku-ten, Toho-ten, Zocho-ten, Shakara-o, Magora-o, Nandaryu-o, Daibenszit-ten, Makeshura, Shimmo-ten, Naraen, Basosennin, Mawara-ten, and Manzenshao.

Nik (Teutonic) *see* Nix.

Nikasha (India)

She is thought by some to be the mother of Ravana, Khara, Vibhishana, Kumbhakarna and a daughter, Shurpanaka. *See also* Kuvera; Ravana.

Nike *Nice* (Greek)

Also known as: *Athena, Victoria* (Roman).

Goddess of victory. Nike is the daughter of the river nymph Styx and the Titan, Pallas. Her sisters are Bia, the personification of violence or force, Zelus, jealousy or zeal, and Cratus, strength. As Nice, not to be confused with Nice, mother of Nicodromus, or Athena as Athena Nice. She is shown as a winged woman holding a wreath. She is also depicted raising a trophy or leading the horses of heroes. *See also* Pallas; Styx.

Nikkal (Mesopotamia)

Goddess of the fruits of summer. Some think that she is the youngest of the Kathirat (q.v.). *See also* Yarik.

Nila Tara (India) *see* Tara (B)

Nila-Vastra (India) *see* Bala-Rama.

Nilakantha (India) "Blue Throat." *See also* Shiva.

Nilavarahi (Nepal) *see* Varahi.

Nile (Greek)

He is the river god son of Oceanus and Tethys. His children are Anchinoe, who married Belus, king of the Nile and Memphis, who married Epaphus, king of Egypt. *See also* Agenor (A); Anchinoe; Belus; Epaphus.

Nimah (Sumer) *see* Ninmu (A).

Nimrod (Hebrew)

Early deified king of Babel. Nimrod, grandson of Ham and son of Cush, is generally thought of as the first mortal ruler of the world. He is sometimes identified with Marduk. Nimrod ordered the building of the Tower of Babel. *See also* Marduk.

Nimsimug (Babylon)

She is the daughter of Enki and Ninmu. Her daughter is the goddess Utto by her father, Enki.

Nimue (Arthurian) *see* Vivien.

Nimurta (Sumer) *see* Ninurta.

Nin-Ib (Akkadia, Assyro-Babylonia, Sumer)

Also known as: *Adar, Nerig, Nin-ib, Nineb, Ninurta, Nirig, Reshep.*

God of spring sun and morning sun. He is usually shown as an eagle. *See also* Adar; Ninib; Ninurta.

Nin-Ip (Babylon) *see* Ninib.

Nin-kar-zi-da (Assyro-Babylonia) *see* Ishtar.

Nin-karrak (Assyro-Babylonia) *see* Ninkarrak.

Nin-khar-sagga (Assyro-Babylonia) *see* Ishtar.

Nin-kharak (Assyro-Babylonia) *see* Ninkarrak.

Nin-Khursag (Sumer) *see* Ninhursag.

Nin-Ki (Sumer) *see* Ninki.

Nin-Lil (Semitic) *see* Adar; Ninlil.

Nin-si-anna (Assyro-Babylonia) *see* Ishtar.

Nin-Si-Anna (Middle Eastern) *see* Ishtar.

Nina (A) (Mexico) *see* Xochiquetzal.

Nina (B) (Sumer)

Also known as: *Ninetta, Ninevah.*

Mistress of the Goddesses. Nini is a local goddess. She is a daughter of Ea and goddess of the city of the same name, later called Ninevah. She uttered oracular responses from the temple at Nina, dedicated to her brother Ninurta. Her sister is the architect goddess, Nisaba. With Imhursag, she became the mother of a son, Ningirsu. *See also* Belit-sheri; Ea; Ishtar; Nana.

Ninagal (Assyro-Babylonia) *see* Ea.

Ninanna (Babylonia) *see* Innini; Nintud.

Ninatta and Kulitta (Babylonia)

They are goddesses of music who are Ishtar's attendants.

Ninazu (Sumer)

Sun god. He is the grandfather and possible father of Tammuz.

Ninbubu (Assyro-Babylonia) *see* Ea.

Nindubarra (Assyro-Babylonia) *see* Ea.

Nindulla (Semitic) One of the deities created by Ninhursag.

Nindurra (Sumer) *see* Ninkurra.

Nine Songs, The (China)

Creators. 1. Tung Huang T'ai I was worshiped as the Eastern Emperor. 2. Yun Chung Chun, god of the clouds. 3. Hsaing Chun, god of the waterways of Hsiang (Hunan). 4. Hsiang Fu-Jen, two daughters of Emperor Yao, Wo Huang, the older, and Nu Ying, the younger. 5. Ssu Ming, arbiter of life and death, protector of virtue and enemy of evil. 6. Tung Chun, god of the sun rising in the East. 7. Ho Po, god of the Yellow River. 8. Shui Shen, god of the fishes. 9. Yu Po, Feng I and Shui I, gods of the waters. *See also* Dragon Kings; Ho Po; Yu Shih.

Nineb (Babylon) *see* Ninib.

Ninedinna (Babylon)

She is the Goddess of the Records of the Dead. She may be the same as the Sumerian goddess Ninisinna, a sister goddess of Inanna (q.v.).

Nineishizda (Sumer, Babylon) *see* Ningishzida.

Ninella (Assyro-Babylonian) *see* Damkina.

Ninetta (Sumer) *see* Nina.

Ninevah (Sumer) *see* Nina.

Ningal (Semitic, Sumer, Babylon)

Also known as: *Aruru, Ninhursag, Ninmah, Nintu.*

Sun goddess. She is the wife of Sin, and mother of Shamash. Ningal is identified with the Summerian goddess, Ki. *See also* Aruru; Ianna; Nammu; Nana; Ninhursag; Ninlil; Ninmah; Nintu.

Ningirda (Sumer) *see* Ereshkigal.

Ningirsu (Sumer)

Also known as: *En-Mersi, Ninurta* (possibly).

Deity of irrigation and fecundity. God of the city of Lugash.

He is the son/husband of Bau. In later times, he became a war god. Ningirsu is shown as a goat, a lion-headed eagle, or a lion with a branch in his front paws. Possibly he is the same as Ninurta (q.v.). He may be an aspect of Tammuz.

Ningishzida (Babylon, Sumer)

Also known as: *Nineishizda, Unummuzida.*

Guardian or tree god. Created by Anu. Some say he is the father of Tammuz, with whom he guarded the gate of Anu's dwelling place. The mother of Tammuz is either Etuda or Ereshkigal. The Sumerians called Ningishzida a companion of Tammuz. In one poem he seems to be connected with Arallu, the underworld. This is substantiated by his mother being a ruler of Arallu. The title Unummuzida may be one of Tammuz or possibly a completely different deity. He could be an aspect of Eshmun or Tammuz. He is associated with Adapa. Ningishzida is represented as bearded and with a serpent springing from each shoulder. *See also* Arallu; Tammuz.

Ningizzida (Sumer) *see* Gizidu.

Ningursu (Sumer) *see* Ningirsu; Ninurta.

Ningyo (Japan)

Mermaid spirit. Ningyo, sometimes seen by earthly eyes, has long hair and the body of a fish. Pearls are said to be her tears. A woman who eats the mermaid spirit's flesh gains perpetual youth and beauty.

Ninharsag (Sumer) *see* Ninhursag.

Ninhursag *Nin-Khursag, Ninharsag, Ninkhursag.* (Sumer, Accad)

Also known as: *Aruru, Bau, Belit, Belit-Illi, Belitis, Ga-tum-dug, Gula, Innini, Ki, Nammu, Ningal, Ninkarrak, Ninki, Ninlil, Ninmah, Nintu, Ninurta.*

Earth goddess. Mother goddess. Fertility goddess.

As Ninhursag, she is called Earth Mother, queen of the cosmic mountain and queen who gives birth. As wife or sister of Enlil, she created the deities Nindulla, Ninsu-utud, Ninkasi, Nazi, Dazima, Nintil and Enshagme. She created men from clay. In one legend she is the mother of Egime and Lil (also called Nesu). In another legend, as the wife of the water god Enki, she became the mother of Ninmu, the plant goddess, the grandmother of Ninkurru and the great grandmother of Uttu the goddess of plants. She is also worshiped under the name of Ninlil. *See also* Aruru; Belit; Beltis; Damkina; Enki; Enlil; Ga-Tum-Dug; Gula; Innini; Ki; Namma; Nammu; Ningal; Ninki; Ninlil; Ninmah; Ninmu; Ninti (one of the eight healing goddesses created by Ninhursag to heal the eight areas of disease in Enki); Nintu; Ninurt; Uttu.

Niniane (Arthurian) *see* Vivien.

Ninib (A) (Japan) *see* Ninigi.

Ninib (B) (Sumer) *see* Ninurta.

Ninigi (Shinto; Japan)

Also known as: *Ninib, Ninigi-no-mikoto* (The Heavenly Grandchild), *Piko-po-no-ninigi.*

God of prosperity. Founder of the imperial house. Ninigi's full name translated is His-Augustness-Heaven-Plenty-Earth-Plenty-Heaven's-Sun-Height-Prince-Rice-Ear-Ruddy-Plenty.

Ninigi, also known as Prosperity Man, was sent to earth by his grandmother, the sun goddess Amaterasu, and other deities to become the divine ruler of Japan. He replaced Okuni-nushino-mikoto's sons. To insure strong leadership, Amaterasu gave Ninigi the three symbols of power. In later years, the items, a mirror, jewels and a sword, became the Imperial emblems of power. Ninigi settled in a palace on Cape Kasasa in the province of Hyuga. He met and married a woman noted for her beauty, Kono-Hana-Sakuya-Hime (Blossoms-of-the-Trees-Blooming-Princess), also known as Sakuya-hime. She is the daughter of the mountain god O-Yama-Tsu-Mi (also spelled Opo-yama-tu-mi-no-kami) and Kaya-no-hime-no-kami (meaning Ruler of the Grassy Plains) and the sister of Iha-haga-hime. The princess is an ancestor of the Emperor Jimmu Tenno. Ninigi, a jealous husband did not believe that she was faithful to him because she conceived the night of their wedding. His attitude infuriated her. She built a muro, a small dwelling without doors, and at the moment of birth, she set fire to it. She told Ninigi that if she were not telling the truth, the child would die. As the flames soared around her, she gave birth to three sons, Hoderi, Hosuseri and Hikohohodemi. The new mother and children emerged unharmed from the inferno. Later writing mentions only two sons, Hosuseri and Hikohohodemi. Ninigi's wife Kono-Hana-Sakuya-Hime had a divine rice field named Sanada. From her rice she made "heavenly" sweet sake, according to the early Shinto recordings in the *Nihongi*. She initiated the annual festival which was later known as Nihi-nahe (also nihi-name) celebrated November 23rd. On this day the season's new rice was offered to the gods and to the Emperor. When her sons were born she severed their umbilical cords using a bamboo knife. Bamboo represents courage and steadfastness and is considered a lucky symbol. Cherry trees surround the shrine dedicated to Kona-Hana-Sakuya-Hime, O-Yami-Tsu-Mi and Iha-haga-hime. O-Yama-Tsu-Mi is venerated as Father Mountain and Iha-haga-hime as Rock Princess. For events prior to Ninigi's descent to earth, *see* Izanagi. For details of the sacred treasures, *see* Susanowo. *See also* Ama-no-Uzume; Amaterasu; Ame-no-Oshido-Mimi; Hikohohodemi; Hiruko; Hosuseri; Ishikoridome-no-Mikoto; Kaya-no-hime-no-kami; Kusanagi (the sacred sword); Okuni-Nushino-Mikoto; Sengen; Susanowo; Take-mi-kazuchi; Toyo-Tama-Bime.

Ninigi-no-mikoto (Japan) *see* Ninigi.

Ninigiku (Sumer)
Also known as: *Ea*.
This name, meaning "King of the Sacred Eye," was given to Ea because of his omniscience and wisdom.

Ninildu (Babylon) God of construction. *See also* Ea.

Nininni (Babylon) *see* Nintud.

Ninisinna (Sumer) *see* Inanna; Ninedinna.

Ninkarrak *Nin-karrak, Nin-kharak, Ninkarraka* (Assyro-Babylonia, Sumer)
Also known as: *Gula* (possibly), *Ishtar, Ninhursag, Ninki.*
Babylonian and Sumerian goddess of medicine and healing, Ninkarrak nursed sick humans. She is the daughter of Anu, sister of Gibal, the fire-god, and is sometimes given the role as the consort of Ninurta. The dog, as a protector of homes is asso-

ciated with her. Ninkarrak is also an epithet of Ishtar (q.v.). *See also* Adapa; Anu; Daminka (B); Gula; Ninhursag; Ninki.

Ninkarraka (Assyro-Babylonia) *see* Ninkarrak.

Ninkasi (Semite)
God of the vine. Ninkasi is one of the deities created by Ninhursag. He is sometimes shown as a goddess. She (or he) helped Lugalbanda or Ninurta in rescuing the "Tablets of Fate" from the nest of Zu. Ninkasi is similar to Dionysus.

Ninkhursag (Sumer) *see* Ninhursag.

Ninki *Nin-Ki* (Sumer)
Also known as: *Bau, Belit-Illi, Belitis, Damgalnunna, Damkina, Ga-Tum-Dug, Gashan-Ki, Gula, Innini, Ki, Ninhursag, Ninkarrak, Ninlil, Ninmah, Ninmu, Nintu.*
It is possible that she is a goddess of fresh water and one of Enki's wives. She was honored at the funeral ceremony for Gilgamesh. *See also* Beltis; Damkina; Ea; Enki; Gula; Ki; Marduk; Ninhursag; Ninkarrak; Ninlil; Ninmah; Ninmu (A); Nintu.

Ninkilim (Sumer) *see* Ninurta.

Ninkurra *Nindurra* (Sumer) *see* Enki; Ninmu; Uttu.

Ninlil (Assyro-Babylonian; Sumer)
Also known as: *Beltis, Haya* ("Goddess of Direction"), *Ninhursag, Ninki, Ninlilla, Nisaba.*
Ninlil is a mother goddess, air goddess, goddess of fertility, and goddess of sailors. She is the daughter of Nunbarshegunu, a goddess said to have lived in Nippur before the creation of mortals. Known as the Sumerian virgin mother, Ninlil was considered to be Enlil's consort or sister/wife. In one interpretation of this myth, Ninlil was raped by sky god Enlil as she was sailing. He was condemned by a council of gods to live in the underworld for his despicable deed. In another version, Ninlil deliberately disobeys her mother and bathes by the river so that Enlil will see her. In yet another variation, it is her mother, Nunbarshegunu, who is determined to arrange a marriage between Ninlil and Enlil. In both versions, the result is similar. He seduces the goddess and leaves her. She follows him and although he keeps turning up in disguise, they are again intimate. On the boat that is crossing the river to the underworld, she submits to him once more, and their child Nanna (also known as Sin) is conceived. She fell so deeply in love with him that she followed him to the underworld. The gods decided that she had to postpone this trip until she gave birth as the child was to be Nanna the moon god and they didn't want him born under the earth. After Nanna's birth, he was left in heaven and Ninlil descended to join Enlil. They had three more children who were minor underworld deities. In some renditions, the three children are born first. They are the substitutes who must be left in the underworld so that Nanna may be born in heaven. Ninlil and Enlil became the grandparents of Nanna's offspring by Ningal, who is the sun god Utu. Ninlil assisted Enlil in bestowing kingship on earthly monarchs. She was one of a trinity with Anu and Ea. This myth may be connected with an early belief in the impregnating powers of water. *See also* Anu; Aruru; Beltis; Ea; Enlil; Ishtar; Nammu; Nanna (B); Ningal; Ninhursag; Ninki; Nisaba; Utu.

Ninlilla (Assyro-Babylonian) *see* Ninlil.

Ninma (Sumer) *see* Ninmu.

Ninmah (Middle Eastern) *see* Mah (B).

Ninmah (Sumer)

Also known as: *Aruru, Mah, Ningal, Ninhursag, Ninki, Ninmu.*

Ninmah is one of the most important aspects of the goddess Mah. Mah has forty-one other names and aspects. *See also* Aruru; Mah (B); Nammu; Ningal; Ninhursag; Ninki; Ninmu; Nintu.

Ninmu *Ninma* (Sumerian)

Also known as: *Ki, Ninki, Ninmah, Ninsar.*

Ninmu the goddess of plants is the daughter of the water god Enki and the goddess Ninhursag. Through incest with Enki, she became the mother of Ninkurra. Ninkurra later mated with her grandfather Enki, and Uttu, the goddess of plants, was born. In a variation of this myth, Nintu and Enki became the parents of Ninmu and Ninkurra. Enki committed incest with Ninkurra and became the father of Uttu goddess of plants. There is a possibility that Ninmu is also a sea goddess. She is associated with the Sumerian goddess, Nammu (q.v.) and identified with the goddess Ki (q.v.). *See also* Enki; Ninhursag; Ninki; Ninmah; Uttu.

Ninmug (Sumer) *see* Inanna.

Ninsar (Sumer) *see* Ea; Ninmu.

Ninshubur (Sumer) *see* Inanna.

Ninsinna (Babylon) *see* Innini; Nintud.

Ninsu-Utud (Akkadian, Babylonian, Sumerian)

Goddess of Healing. She is one of the deities created by Ninhursag. One of her specialities is to heal aching teeth. Ninsu-Utud is the spouse of Ninazu. *See also* Ninhursag.

Ninsubur (Akkadian, Babylonian, Sumerian)

Also known as: *Ilabrat, Ili-Abrat, Ninurta, Papsukkal.*

Messenger. In one legend Ishtar sent Ninsubur to get a description of her rival Saltu. The name is also an early title of Ninurta. Ninsubur is identified with Papsukkal and Ilabrat, who are also messengers. *See also* Ilabrat; Ninurta; Papsukkal; Tammuz.

Ninsun (Chaldea, Sumer)

Also known as: *Situr.*

She is the goddess of the city of Uruk and mother of the multi-talented goddess Gestinanna and the shepherd god Dumuzi. She may also be the mother of Gilgamesh. Depicted as a cow, she was considered omniscient. She is identified with Aruru. *See also* Dumuzi; Gestinanna; Gilgamesh.

Ninth Division of Tuat (Egypt)

This division of Tuat is guarded by the monster serpent Ab-ta (q.v.).

Ninti (Sumer)

She is one of the eight goddesses of healing who was created by Ninhursag to heal corresponding diseased parts of Enki's body. Her specific healing area was the rib. *See also* Enki; Ninhursag.

Nintil (Akkadian, Babylonian, Sumerian)

One of the goddesses created by Ninhursag. *See also* Ninhursag.

Nintu (Sumerian)

She is a mother goddess and goddess of birth who corresponds to Ninhursag and Ishtar (qq.v.). She also parallels Mami, Aruru and Ninmah. She is linked with Enki in some myths. *See also* Enki; Nammu; Ningal; Ninhursag; Ninki; Ninmu; Nintud.

Nintud *Innini, Ninanna, Nininni, Ninsinna, Nintu* (Akkadia, Babylon, Sumer)

Also known as: *Belit, Belit-Ilani.*

Earth goddess. Goddess of childbirth. Possibly the sister of Enlil. As Innini she is a mother goddess who was created by Anu. Her children are Nergal and Ninurta. In her form of Nintud her husband/son was Dumuzi (Tammuz). *See also* Aruru; Belit; Belit-ili; Belit-Illi; Ereshkigal; Innini; Ishtar; Ki; Nammu; Ningal; Ninhursag; Ninki; Ninmah; Nintu; Nintud.

Nintue *see* Aruru

Ninurash (Sumer) *see* Ninurta.

Ninurta *Nimurta* (Akkadia, Canaan, Sumer)

Also known as: *Ennammasht, Ningirsu, Ninhursag, Ninib, Ninkilim, Ninsubur, Ninurash.*

War god. Irrigation god. Patron of hunters. Fertility deity. God of copper and coppersmiths. South Wind personified. The son of Enlil, and Belet-Ili. In some myths his mother is the earth goddess Ninman. There is reference to the pig being sacred to Ninurta and thus he had two other titles, Ennammasht (lord of swine) and Ninkilim, who was killed by a wild boar. The name Ninsubur was an early title of Ninurta although Ninsubur was a god in his own right. In one Sumerian myth, Ninurta instructed by his weapon, Sharur, destroys the underworld demon Asag. The Kur waters rose up and prevented irrigation waters from reaching the fields. A famine followed, but Ninurta was able to circumvent its severity by constructing a great wall made from piles of rocks in front of Sumer and over the Kur. He then directed the waters back into the Tigris. His mother, Ninmah came to visit and was made queen of the stone mound and given the name Ninhursag. Ninurta's symbol is an eagle. He is sometimes shown as lion-headed. He is associated with Ningursu. Ninhursag was possibly Ki, queen of the cosmic mountain, fertility and earth goddess (Sumerian). *See also* Abu; Ningursu; Ninhursag; Ninkasi; Ninsubur.

Ninzadim (Assyro-Babylonia) *see* Ea.

Nio (Buddhist; Japan)

Protectors of Buddhism. Guardian deities. The Nio are spirits who prevent evil from entering monasteries. Their functions include the protection of children and prevention of theft. They receive offerings of straw sandals from followers. The Nio, considered minor deities, were originally derived from Hinduism and incorporated into the Buddhist pantheon. The Nio are represented as two statues of Vajrapani. They are usually red in color and draped in simple garments. Two Nio exist at the right and left of the portals at Great South Gate of Todai-ji. They were carved in 1203 by Unkei and Kaikei. They are twenty-six feet high and although discolored, the pigment reveals red skin, brown hands and multi-colored garments. There is a glaring expression on their faces and they have muscular bodies. *See also* Bishamon-Ten; Jikoko-Ten; Komoku-Ten; Shi Tenno; Zocho-Ten.

Niobe (A) (Greek)

Niobe is the daughter of Tantalus and Dione and the sister of Pelops and Broteas. Her intense pride in her children was the cause of their destruction. Because she had seven sons and seven daughters, she boasted of her superiority to the goddess Leto who had only two children, her twins Apollo and Artemis. To punish her arrogance, Apollo killed all of Niobe's sons and her husband Amphion, and Artemis killed all her daughters. In other versions one son, Amyclas, and one daughter, Meliboea, were spared. Niobe wept until she was transformed into marble from which streamed incessant tears. Euripides and Apollodorus place the number of her children as fourteen, seven daughters and seven sons. Sappho said there were eighteen; Homer said twelve; Hesiod, twenty; and Herodotus wrote that she had only four children. *See also* Aedon; Amphion; Apollo; Argus (A); Artemis; Leto; Pelops; Satyrs; Tantalus (A); Zethus.

Niobe (B) (Greek)

First mortal woman to be loved by a deity. Niobe is the daughter of Phoroneus, the first king of Argos, and either Cerdo known as Cerdo the wise, Peitho, possibly the goddess of persuasion, or Teledice. Her siblings are Car, the king of Megara (his mother was likely Cerdo), and Apis, the ruler of Apia, who was killed by Telchis and Thelxion. Niobe and Zeus are the parents of Typhon, Pelasgus, Argus and Osiris. *See also* Apis (B); Car; Niobe (A).

Niord (Teutonic) *see* Aegir; Njord.

Niparaya (Pericu People, Native North American)

Supreme deity. Husband of Amayicoyondi and father of three sons, Quaayayp (man), Acaragui, and although the other is not named, he may be Wac or Tupuran. The children were likely virgin births as Niparaya did not have sexual relations with his wife and he does not have a visible body. The Pericu People had only a few deities associated with Niparaya. Cucumunic, who created the moon, and Puratabui, who created the stars.

Nipin and Pipoun (Algonquin, Montagnais People, North America)

Also known as: *Nipinoukhe and Pipounoukhe.*

They are the spirits of summer and winter who divide the world between themselves. Nipin brings the heat of summer and the beauty of the world, but when he changes places each year with Pipoun, then winter returns, and so returns the cold and bitterness of this season. Nipin might be the same as the god Niparaya of the Pericu People.

Nipinoukhe and Pipounoukhe *see* Nipin and Pipoun.

Nir-Jara (India) *see* Amrita.

Nirba (Akkadian)

He is a creator deity and a god of harvest.

Nireus (Greek)

The sea god Poseidon and Canace are his parents. *See also* Aloeus; Canace; Epopeus.

Nirgalu (Babylon) *see* Nergal.

Nirig (Babylon) *see* Ninib.

Nirrita (India) *see* Nirriti; Rakshasas.

Nirriti (Hindu, Vedic; India)

Nirriti, the daughter of Surabhi, the cow goddess and goddess of plenty, protects the weary, down-trodden, and those born into crime as long as they are ethical. She is presented as elderly, tired and emaciated. Dressed in black, her hand is always out to receive alms. Her name means "misery." In other depictions, she is the Vedic goddess of death and spouse of Nirrita, the guardian deity of the Southwest. She is the mother of the Rakshasis and Rakshasas. *See also* Kali; Lokapalas; Rakshasas; Surabhi.

Nirruti (India)

Mentioned in the *Rig-Veda*, the god Nirruti is depicted on a lion surrounded by Rakshasas and nymphs. *See also* Rakshasas.

Nirvana (India)

Heaven. A place of perfect rest. Some believe the name means death. *See also* Aaru; Amida; Elysian Fields.

Nisaba (A) (Sumer)

Goddess of architecture. Patron of letters. *See also* Nabu; Nina (B); Ninlil.

Nishatha (India) Son of Bala-Rama (q.v.).

Nisis *Nisus* (Greek)

Deified mortal. He is the king of Megara, whose lock of purple hair (on which his life and fortune depended) was snipped off by his daughter, Scylla, and presented to King Minos, with whom she had fallen deeply in love. Nisus was transformed into a sea eagle, and his daughter into a sea bird.

Nisroch (Assyrian)

Possibly a sky god. May be the same as Nisr-uku, an eagle-headed deity of the Assyrians. Possibly associated with Anu.

Nissyen (Celtic) *see* Bran.

Nistigri (India) *see* Indra.

Nisumbha (India) A Demon. *See also* Durga; Kali.

Nisus (Greek) *see* Nisis.

Nit (A) (Egypt) *see* Neith.

Nit (B) *Niti* (India) *see* Devaki.

Nitatui (India) A Krittika sister. *See also* Rishi.

Nithog (Teutonic) *see* Loki.

Nithogg (Teutonic) *see* Nidhod.

Niti (India) *see* Devaki.

Niti-ghosha (India) *see* Brihaspati.

Nitwatakawaca (India)

The indestructible demon. *See also* Arjuna.

Nitya-Kali (India) *see* Kali.

Niu (Egypt) *see* Amen (B).

Niu-T'ou (China) *see* Niu-y'ou.

Niu-Y'ou *Niu-t'ou* (Buddhist; China).

Also known as: *Gozu Tenno* (possibly Japan), *Horse-Face, Ox-Face, Ox-Head.*

He is one of the T'u-ti, gods of place. With his companion Ma-Mien, he is the assistant to the Yama kings and Ch'eng-Huang, the god of walls and ditches. Niu-Y'ou and Ma-Mien are the deities who retrieve the souls for the Yama Kings, although in some versions, it is the two Wu-ch'ang who pick up the souls. Niu-Y'ou may have been imported to Japan where he is known as Gozu Tenno. He is opposed by the Door Guards. *See also* Goganze-Myoo (Japan); Gozu Tenno (Japan); Ma-Mien; Yama Kings.

Nivlheim (Teutonic) *see* Nifl-heim.

Nixe (Teutonic) *see* Nixie.

Nixie *Necar, Necks, Nick, Nig, Nik, Nixe, Nixie, Nixy, Nokel,* (Teutonic)

Also known as: *Stromkarls.*

Lesser water divinities. The Nixie belong to a group of kind, loving male water spirits along with the Stromkarls and the Necks. The female water spirits are the Undine. The Undine, Necks, Nixie and Stromkarls sometimes leave the water to attend village dances. The only way they can be detected is by seeing the damp hem of their clothing. They are described with fish tails. They often sit by the water combing each other's long green or blonde hair or playing the harp and singing. The Undines also have green teeth. *See* Nugal.

Nixy (Teutonic) *see* Nixie.

Njord *Niord, Njorth* (Norse; Teutonic)

Also known as: *Nordur.*

Originally a Vanir, this giant is the god of riches, dispenser of wealth, and a fertility, harvest, fire, and weather god. When called upon by those at sea he assures good fortune. He brings on sunset by quenching the fires of day. When the war between the Vanir and the Aesir ended, and a treaty was being agreed upon, each race gave hostages to the other. Njord and his son Frey were given to the Aesirs. In exchange, the Aesirs gave Odin's brother Henir and the wise Mimir to the Vanir. Njord became one of the main gods of the Aesir. Njord met and married Skadi, the beautiful, giant daughter of Thiassi. In some accounts Skadi is the mother of Frey. In other accounts she is called the stepmother of Frey and Freyja. Njord's first spouse was the earth goddess Nerthus who may also be his sister. Njord, the personification of summer, loved his home, Noatun, which is near the sea. His spouse Skadi, who personifies winter, preferred the mountains. She tried to live with him part of the time. It did not work out, so she left him to return to the mountains. One of the strange tales of Njord was that he was Saturnus, the father of Jupiter, Neptunus, and Plutus. Jupiter wasn't satisfied with the gift of heaven from the god Saturnus and made war on him. Saturnus hid in Italy and changed his name to Njord. Njord is depicted as a handsome man dressed in a short green tunic. Sometimes he wears a crown of seaweed and shells. He is also shown wearing a brown brimmed hat decorated with eagle or heron feathers. *See also* Aesir; Balder; Freyja; Jord; Nerthus; Skadi; Vanir.

Njorth (Teutonic) *see* Njord.

Nkosi Yama'kosi (Ndebele People, Zimbabwe, Africa)

Supreme being. This name applies to both a god and to leading mortals.

Nkulnkulu (Africa) *see* Unkulunkulu.

No-no-kami (Japan) *see* Kaya-no-hime-no-kami.

Noah (Hebrew)

Hero. Survivor of the deluge. According to legend, he was the second founder of the human race and his original name was Menachem. He was saved from a great flood by building an ark of gopher wood and sheltering his family and a pair of every living thing. Some versions say they lived in the ark for forty days and nights and other versions say the flood lasted a year. *See also* Abram; Cessair.

Noatun (Norse; Teutonic) Dwelling place of Njord in Asgard.

Nodens (Celtic) *see* Llud.

Nodotus (Roman) Roman god of knots in the straw.

Noesarnak (Eskimo People)

One must carefully approach Noesarnak, the land spirit. She is depicted as a woman with spindly legs who is dressed in deer skins and carries a deer skin mask.

Nogamain *Nogomain* (Aborigine People, Australia)

Creator. He is described the same as Djamar, but he, like Atnatu, made himself out of nothing. He doesn't have any family according to some. According to others, he has a wife and son, who is described as a hunting spear. Nogamain is sometimes called the man in the moon. He was possibly replaced by Kunmanggur and Kukpi by other tribes. *See also* Djamar.

Nogat (Mongol) *see* Natagai.

Nogomain (Australia) *see* Nogamain.

Nohochacyum (Maya People, Yucatan)

Also known as: *Kasin, Nahochacyumchac, Nukuchyumchakob.*

"Grandfather." God of creation. Opponent of the evil god Hapikern. He is the son of two flowers and brother of the gods Yantho, meaning "good"; Usukun, meaning "bad"; and Uyitzin, meaning "neutral." They are associated with Xamaniqinqu, "the spirit of the north," and Kisin, "the earthquake." Nohochacyum is a single great father and chief god. His servants are the spirits of the east, ruled by Usukun, thunder, and the constellations. At the end of the world he will wrap the serpent Hapikern around his body who will draw people to him to be killed. *See also* Usukun; Xamaniqinqu; Yumchakob.

Nokel (Saxon) *see* Nixie (Teutonic).

Noken (Teutonic) *see* Nugal.

Nokomis (Algonquian People, North America)

Also known as: *Ethinoha, Grandmother* (Iroquois), *Wenonah.*

Earth Mother or Earth Goddess. Her daughter is the corn spirit, Onatah. She is the grandmother of Nanabozho. In one legend, Nokomis fell to earth and became Wenonah, the wife of Hiawatha. *See also* Mondamin; Nanabozho.

Nommo (Dogon People, Sudan, Africa)

Also known as: *Nummo.*

Twin gods. The supreme god, Amma, fertilized earth with rain and produced the twins, Nommo, a male and female. They are heavenly blacksmiths, who created copper. The first fire was stolen from them. They are generally thought of as water or spirits of water. *See also* Amma (A); Yuragu.

Nomus (Greek) *see* Aristaeus.

Noncomala (Central America)
Supreme deity. In this story Noncomala was angry at the local province of Guaymi so he flooded it. Nubu, another local god, held on to the seed of man, which he expelled during his dreams. Once his anger abated, he planted the seeds. From the good seeds came man and woman and from the bad seeds came monkeys. *See also* Nubu.

Nona (Tahiti)
Also known as: *Haumea* (Hawaii)
Ancestor of the Tafa'i People. She is comparable to Haumea, the Hawaiian goddess of childbirth and cultivated plants. *See also* Haumea.

Nono *Nona* (Greek) She is one of the three Fates (q.v.).

Nootaikok (Eskimo)
He is the spirit of icebergs and possibly a god of seals.

Nor (Teutonic) *see* Aarvak; Nordri; Norvi.

Nordi (Teutonic) *see* Aarvak; Austri.

Nordre (Teutonic) *see* Nordri.

Nordri *Nordre* (Norse; Teutonic)
He is one of four dwarfs who support the heavenly vault (made from the skull of Ymir) on their shoulders. The others are Sudri, Austri, and Westri. From their names came the North, South, East and West.

Nordur (Teutonic) *see* Njord.

Norea (Coptic)
One of the first mortals, she is the sister of Seth and wife of Noah.

Norine (Teutonic) *see* Neri.

Norn (Teutonic) *see* Norns.

Nornir (Teutonic) *see* Norns.

Norns (Norse; Teutonic)
Also known as: *Nornir.*
Goddesses of destiny. There are a number of Norns both good and evil. The three prominent goddesses are Urd (fate), Skuld (personification of the future), and Verdandi (necessity). They reside under and care for Yggdrasil, the tree of life, near Urd's well. The Norns control the unchanging universal laws and the fate of mortals and the Aesirs. Urd and Verdandi were beneficial, but Skuld was said to undo the good work of the other two. The Norns didn't appear until the end of the Golden Age. Their main purpose was to weave the web of fate. The Norns dress themselves in swan plumage from the two swans they care for in the waters from Urd's Well. Compare the Norns to the Fates. *See also* Aesir; Fylgia; Urd's Well; Yggdrasil.

Norse — Creation Legend *see* Ginnunga-gap.

North Wind (Greek) *see* Boreas; Chaos; Eurynome (A).

Norve (Teutonic) *see* Norvi.

Norvi (Norse; Teutonic)
Also known as: *Narvi, Nor, Norve.*
Norvi is the giant father of Nott (Night) and the ancestor of the Norns. *See also* Norns; Nox.

Notos *Notus* (Greek)
Also known as: *Auster, South West Wind.*
He is the son of Astraeus and Eos. *See also* Astraeus; Boreas; Eos; Notus.

Nott (Norse; Teutonic)
Also known as: *Nacht, Nat.*
Nott, the goddess of night, is the daughter of the giant Norvi (or some say Mimer) and sister of Dagr (day). She rides in a dark chariot drawn by the sable horse, Hrim-faxi. The mane of the horse drips dew and hoarfrost onto the earth below. She has been married three times. Her first husband was Naglfari, with whom she had a son, Aud. Her second husband was Annar, with whom she had a daughter, Jord, and her third husband was Dellinger (Delling), by whom she had a son, Dag. *See also* Aarvak; Dag; Nat (B); Night.

Notus *Notos* (Greek)
Also known as: *Auster, South West Wind.*
God of wind. Notus, the son of the Astraeus (the starry sky) and Eos the goddess of dawn, is called the South West Wind. He is the dispenser of rain and of sudden and heavy showers. His siblings are Boreas (North Wind), Zephyrus (West Wind) and Eurus (South East Wind). Notus is generally shown as an old grey haired man with a gloomy face. His head is covered with clouds, he has dark wings and wears sable. Compare Notus to Fu-jin (Japan). *See also* Boreas; Chimaera; Eos; Zephyrus.

Nous (Valentinus sect, Post-Christian Gnostics)
Also known as: *Monogenes.*
First deity. Nous (possibly with mate, Sige) was the first perfect being who came from the Unknowable Father. Because he was too great to act directly, he and his partner Aletheia produced the perfect number of offspring: Logos and Zoe and their children, Bythios, Mixis, Ageratos, Henosis, Autophyes, Hedone, Akinetos, Synerasis, Monogenes, and Macaria who acted in his place. Logos and Zoe, in turn, produced another set that consisted of an imperfect number of aeons: Anthropos and Ecclesia, Paracletos and Pistis, Patricos and Elpis, Metricos and Agape, Ecclesiasticus and Macariotes, Theletas and Sophia. The offspring acted on matter in place of Nous. *See also* Dionysus.

Nox (Greek)
Also known as: *Nyx.*
Nox, the goddess of night, is pictured as a "Great Black Bird," the Greek personification of Night, who was born out of the primordial Chaos. From her egg came Eros and from her shell Oranos and Gaia (Heaven and Earth), who are called the parents of the Titans. In another myth, she is the daughter of Chaos and the wife of her brother Erebus. She became the mother of Thanatos (Death), Moros (Destiny), Hypnos also known as

Somnus (god of sleep), Momus the fault finder, Nemesis (goddess of retributive justice), Aether (Sky) and Hemera (Day), Oneiroi (Dreams), Cer (goddess of violent death), Charon (ferryman of the dead) and possibly Hesperides and Old Age. She has also been identified as the mother of Fraus (divinity of treachery) by Orcus (Pluto). She is represented as winged, or sitting on a chariot, clothed in black, surrounded by stars. For the development of creation on earth at this time, *see* Cronus. Compare Nox to the Vedic goddess of the night, Ratri. *See also* Aether; Aither; Erebus; Fates; Furies; Keres; Nemesis.

Nu (Egypt)

Water deity. This god and his counterpart goddess, Nut, were water deities and the most ancient gods of the Egyptians. They are part of a company of gods, usually four pairs called Paut. *See also* Hehu; Hehut; Kekui; Kekuit; Kerh; Kerhet. Others say the eight gods were Ament, Nu, Nut, Hehui, Hehet, Kekui, Keket, and Hathor. As mentioned in the "Papyrus of Nesi-Khensu," Nu appears to be a deity of time or possibly a god of potters. He is also mentioned in relationship with Khensu. In the Chinese mythology the name is associated with Chih Nu. Nu is the counterpart of the goddess Nut. He is associated with Amen. Sometimes, he is identified with Hapi. *See also* Aai.

Nu-Kua *Nu Kua* (China)

Also known as: *Nu Wa Naing Naing.*

Creator of the human race. Nu-kua is the wife and sister of the renowned sage Fu-hsi and mother of the ten spirits. Her recipe for creating mortals began with yellow mud. She dipped a rope into the mud and then trailed the rope around; the drops that dripped from the rope became men and women. In another rendition, like many other creators she fashioned mortals from lumps of clay. When evil giants set fire and flame loose upon the world, Nu-Kua restored everything by replacing the overturned poles of the world with the feet of a giant turtle which repaired the widespread damage that came after the catastrophic flood and fire. She also melted stones of five colors to repair a rip in the sky. In some versions her name has two parts. Nu was the brother and Kua the sister, and they were the first human pair. She is shown as a woman from the waist up, and a dragon's tail below. She holds a pair of compasses. *See also* Fu-hsi; Kun-Lun Mountain.

Nu Wa Naing Naing (China) *see* Nu-Kua.

Nu-Zuchi (Japan) *see* Kaya-no-hime-no-kami.

Nuada *Nuadhu* (Celtic)

Also known as: *Argetlam* ("the Silver Handed"), *Llud, Llud Llaw Ereint, Lud, Nuada Argentlam, Nuadha Airgedlamh, Nud Nodens.*

Nuada is the chief of the Tuatha de Danann who lost his hand or arm in battle. The hand or arm was replaced by one of silver created the smith and healer, Dia'necht. Compare Nuada to the British Llud, the Vedic and Hindu deity Savitri, and to the Norse deity Odin. *See also* Airmid; Bress; Credne; Dagda; Dia'necht; Llud; Lugh; Tuatha De Danann.

Nuada Argentlam (Celtic) *see* Nuada.

Nuadha Airgedlamh (Celtic) *see* Nuada.

Nuadhu (Celtic) *see* Nuada.

Nuba (Sudan)

Sky god. Nuba sent the god Su to earth down a bamboo-shoot with some peas. Su dropped some on the way which struck the drum he was supposed to have beaten for Nuba to bring him up. Nuba pulled up the bamboo, causing Su to fall and break his leg. *See also* Wantu Su.

Nubti (Egypt)

Also known as: *Set.*

Epithet of Set. Known as the "Golden One," he shoots his arrows at the noon-day sun.

Nud (Celtic) *see* Llud; Nuada.

Nud Nodens (Celtic) *see* Nuada.

Nudd (Celtic) *see* Llud.

Nudimmud *Nadimmud* (Babylon)

Also known as: *Ea, Enki.*

Creator. Nudimmud, as Ea, created the Apsu-Ocean, and some say, the other gods. He is the son of Anu and one of a triad with Anshar and Kishar. *See also* Apsu.

Nuga (Melanesia)

Creator. A great crocodile, Nuga created rivers by the lashing of his tail. He is associated with the creator Ipila (q.v.).

Nugal (Teutonic)

Also known as: *Noken.*

Deified animal. Nugal is a dapple-grey horse or a brown ass. He uses his fiery tail to lead people astray. Nugal is often associated with the Nixies. *See also* Nixie.

Nuit (Egypt) *see* Amunet.

Nujalik (Eskimo)

Goddess of the land-hunt.

Nuktelios (Greek) *see* Dionysus.

Nukuchyumchakob (Maya) *see* Nohochacyum; Yumchakob.

Nuliajuk (Netsilik Eskimo People)

She is the mistress of land and sea and the mother of animals. Her power gives her the ability to cause storms and to make animals visible or invisible. She rules through spirits. One spirit is responsible for recording the violations of taboos. When she was a young human female, she was grossly abused. Once while on the sea, her knuckle joints were cut off one by one. They fell to the bottom and became sea animals. She sank to the bottom and became the mother of the sea animals. There are numerous variations of this myth. Nuliajuk is comparable to Sedna (q.v.).

Num (Samoyd)

Also known as: *Ec* (Yenisei), *Num-torem, Numi-torem, Torum* (Ugrain).

Supreme god. The Vogul people say he lives in the seventh heaven which contains the water of life. The sun and moon are his eyes. In some myths, he is a thunder or sky god. *See also* Ec; Torum.

Numbakulla (Aborigine People, Australia)

First deity (both plural and singular). Born out of nothing

or always existing. He, or as some say, these two created everything. After inserting a pole into the earth, Numbakulla climbed
it and left the planet forever. In some renditions, Numbakulla
created humans from amorphous creatures from Inapatua
(q.v.).

Nummo (Africa) *see* Nommo.

Numokh Mukana (Mandan) The First Man.

Numphe (Greek) *see* Nymphs.

Nun (Egypt) *see* Atum; Khepri; Nu; Ptah; Ptah.

Nun and Naunet (Nunet) Egypt. *See also* Nun.

Nunam-shua (Eskimo People, Pacific Region)
She is the owner of all the land animals, and mistress of land
and mountain forests. She wears a coat made of the furs of all
animals and beams with radiant light. *See also* Sedna.

Nunbarshegunu (Assyro-Babylonian) *see* Ninlil.

Nund (India) *see* Nanda.

Nunet (Naunet) (Egypt) *see* Nun.

Nunu (Egypt) *see* Khepri; Nun; Thoth.

Nunyunuwi (Cherokee People, North America)
His name means "dressed in stone." He is a destructive cannibal spirit.

Nurelli (Aborgine People, Australia)
High god. According to myth this deity created all things.
Once he completed the task he gave men laws then returned to
the sky. His story is related to Bunjil's story.

Nurra (Assyro-Babylonia) *see* Ea.

Nurrundere *Nurundere, Nurunderi* (Aborigine People, Australia)
Also known as: *Baiame, Bunjil, Daramulun, Martummere,
Ngurunderi, Pun-gel.*
Creator gods. Some say it was Nurelli who created everything. Others say Bunjil, Daramulun, or Mungan-ngaua were
the supreme creators. In one version, Nurrundere is a culture
hero who taught crafts and skills. In most versions of his myths,
Nurrundere left for Wyrra-warre, the sky.

Nurunderi (Australia) *see* Martummere; Nurrundere.

Nusku (Assyro-Babylonian, Sumer)
A messenger of the gods, Nusku is also the god of fire, light,
and civilization. He is referred to variously as the first born of
Enlil, the moon god Sin, or Anu. He was known to have burned
sacrificial offerings to the gods. Nusku is the minister and vizier
of Enlil, and he sometimes acted as a god of justice. His symbol is the lamp. He is equated with Nabu and Gabil (qq.v.). *See
also* Anu; Enlil; Nabu; Sin.

Nusmatlizaix (Bella-Coola People, North America)
Deified bird. When the world was first populated, the rivers
and people were imprisoned in the cave called Nusmatlizaix. A
huge rock barred the entrance. The Eagle was unable to break
in, but the Raven succeeded and freed the human race.

Nut (Egypt)
Goddess of the sky. Nut is one of the Ennead, a group of
eight deities. She is the child of Shu, dryness, and Tefnut, water.
Her male counterpart or husband is Nu. She is the mother, by
her brother, Geb, of Osiris, Isis, Seth and Nephthys. It was Nut,
in the form of a cow, who called Ra to the heavens where Nut
became the support of the sky. In the *Book of the Dead*, there is
a reference that Nut is the mother and Seth the father of Osiris.
Nut was caught being unfaithful by her husband. He cursed her
so that she could only give birth on the days which were not on
the calendar. Nut sought counsel from Thoth. In a board game
with the moon god, Thoth won a part of each day which
amounted to five days during which Nut could give birth. This
was the mythical origin of the five additional days which the
Egyptians annually inserted at the end of every year in order to
establish harmony between lunar and standard time. During
these five days Orsiris was born on the first, the elder Horus on
the second, Set (Typhon) on the third, Isis on the fourth and
Nephthys on the fifth day. According to Heliopolitan theology
Nut was the mistress of the heavenly bodies which were said to
be all her children who entered her mouth and emerged from
her womb. She was called "the female pig who eats her piglets."
It is said that as the mother of the sun-god Re, she swallowed
him in the evening and gave birth again in the morning. She is
represented bearing a vase on her head, and is usually depicted
with her hands and feet planted on the earth and her body arch-
ing up to form the vault of heaven. She is sometimes shown
with the head of a uraeus topped with a disk, and with the head
of a cat. Nut is also shown as a woman bearing a vase of water
on her head. She is also represented as a suckling sow. The
sycamore tree was a manifestation of Nut. The leaves shielded
the dead Osiris and the branches were said to have restored his
soul. She was comparable to the Greek god Rhea. She was also
comparable to Hathor in that both were cow-goddesses. She
has been identified with Hathor, Mut, Nit and Neith. The
Greeks compared Nut and Seb to Cronus and Rhea. She is mentioned as a form of the goddess Neheb-Kau and counterpart of
the serpent god Nau. *See also* Aai; Ament; Amentet; Amun;
Atum; Ennead (the); Hathor; Isis; Nephtys; Osiris; Ra; Sopdu;
Thoth.

Nutapa (South America) *see* Dyai.

Nutar (Egypt) *see* Neter.

Nu'umea (Polynesia)
Heaven. Goddess of uncultivated plants. As a goddess, she
is the wife of Wakea. She was killed when Kaulu tossed her into
the net of Maoleha. Nu'umea is associated with the trickster
Kaulu. *See also* Haumea; Wakea.

Nux (Greek) *see* Nix; Nox.

Nuzuchi (Japan) *see* Kaya-no-hime-no-kami.

Nyalic (Africa) *see* Nyalitch.

Nyalitch (Dinka People, Africa)
Also known as: *Nyalic.*
Supreme god. Lord of spirits. God of sky and rain. See also
Abuk.

Nyambe (Nigeria, Africa)
Also known as: *Bumba, Nyambi.*

Nyambe is the sun as a supreme deity. He punishes those who try to climb up and kill him. Once, when Nyambi lived among mortals, he gave them a magic tree which would give them immortality. The mortals treated Nyambe with disrespect. He pulled up the tree and disappeared. In a tale from Zambezi, Nyambe is the spouse of Nasilele, who appears to be a moon goddess. Nyambe is used as a name for the Supreme Being in the western tropics of Africa. It may be the same as Nyame. *See also* Bumba.

Nyambi (Africa) *see* Nyambe.

Nyame *Nyami* (Ashanti, Twi People, Africa)
Also known as: *Kaka-Guia, Nyame and Asase, Onyame.*
Androgynous Creator. Funerary deity. Possibly a storm god or goddess. Father and mother god. As a goddess, she is Nyame or Nana or Nyankoipon (Ashanti, Africa). Her husband is Asase Yaa, god of rain, wind, sun, moon, night and sleep. Nyame's female name-day is Thursday. To open a new field or to dig a grave one must have her permission. As Kaka-Guia he was considered a male deity and a funerary god who brought souls to the supreme deity. In the Mande version Nyame is the vital force and is associated with Pemba and Faro. Sometimes Nyame is personified as the moon. Nyame is similar to or the same as Nyankopong. *See also* Abonsam; Asase Yaa; Nyambe.

Nyame and Asase (Africa) *see* Nyame.

Nyamia (Africa) *see* Nyamia Ama.

Nyamia Ama (Senegal, Africa)
Also known as: *Nyamia.*
Storm deity. Nyamia Ama, often called an invisible sky god, controls storms, rain and lightning. He is said to be a white child with large ears. Nyamia Ama is associated with Evua (the sun), Kaka-Guia (god of the soul) and Guruhi (god of evil). *See also* Nyame.

Nyankopon (Africa) *see* Nyankopong.

Nyankopon Kweku (Africa) *see* Nyankopong.

Nyankopong (Ashanti People, Africa)
Also known as: *Nyankopon, Nyankopon Kweku, Onyankopon, Onyankopong.*
Nyankopong once lived on earth, but moved to the sky because an old woman kept hitting him with her pestle as she pounded grain. Similar to Nyame, he may be her forerunner. *See also* Nyame.

Nyasaye (Maragoli People, Kenya, Africa)
He is the chief of spirits and is generally shown as a pole surrounded by a pile of stones.

Nyceteus (Greek)
Nyceteus is the son of the sea god, Poseidon, and Celaeno. He is also referred to as the son of Chtonius or Hyrieus and Clonia. When he found that his daughter Antiope was pregnant by Zeus, he committed suicide. *See also* Antiope.

Nyctimene (Greek)
Raped by her father, Epopeus, the king of Lesbos, she was subsequently changed into an owl by Athene.

Nyikang (Shilluck People, Africa)
Deified ancestor. God of agriculture. God of rain. He instituted the tradition of marriage between siblings, and ritual murder. Ancestor god of the Shilluck, who is the intermediary between the people and Juck. Nyikang is believed to be either the father of Omara (the first man) or the descendant of the first cow, or crocodile. He created his subjects by changing wild animals to people, or he fished men out of the water, or brought them out of a calabash. Although he dies by strangling himself or disappears in a whirlwind, he always returns. He must, or the Shilluck people will all die. *See also* Juck.

Nyktelios (Greek) *see* Dionysus.

Nymphs *Numphe*
Also known as: *Aegle* (the name of more than one nymph); (Greek)
Spirits. Nymphs are attractive female divinities who inhabit certain objects or places in nature. The Oceanids and Nereids are the sea nymphs: Naiads are fresh-water nymphs of fountains and lakes; Dryads and Hamadryads are tree nymphs; and the Oreades are mountain nymphs. The worship of nymphs was extensive and their places of worship were usually situated near springs, woods or caves. There are also dangerous water nymphs, known as Bisimbi, in the Congo (Africa). They live at the mouths of rivers, and in wells or ponds and are thought to be spirits of the dead. These nymphs are made of water and can only be seen at dawn rising like wisps of dew. Nymphs represent different aspects of nature. They are usually depicted as young, beautiful, often naked and promiscuous. *See also* Aegle; Dryads; Naiads; Napaeae; Nereids; Oceanids.

Nyokon (Cameroon People, Africa)
Supreme god. His first son, Nyiko, the spider of divination, became the lover of his mother, Mfam. Nyokon drove him away. Nyiko still holds the secrets of divination of his father.

Nyx (Greek) *see* Nox.

Nzambi (Bantu People, Africa)
Also known as: *Mpungu, Nzambi, Nzame.*
Androgynous creator deity. Supreme god, and invisible god of creation. He created the first man, Fam, who became vain, so Nzambi buried him in a hole, but Fam still caused mankind misfortune. Nzambi then created a second man, Sekume. Sekume created a wife from a tree (Mbongwe) and they became the ancestors of the human race. Nzambi came down to earth and fell in love with Mboya, a mortal girl, and had a son, Bingo, who has a legend of his own. As Nzambi Mpungu this deity is a goddess who had several other legends. *See also* Bingo; Bumba; Nzame.

Nzambi Mpungu (Africa) *see* Nzambi.

Nzame (Fon People, Africa)
Also known as: *Nzambi.*
High god. Nzame has many wives and three sons, Whiteman, Blackman, and Gorilla. He is probably the same as Nzambi although the legends differ. *See also* Nzambi.

Nzamgi (Bakongo People, Lower Congo, Africa)
He is the supreme god, creator of all things. Inaccessible, he is not worshiped. Nzamgi intervenes in the creation of every child. Those who violate his laws are punished.

O

O-kuni-Nushi (Japan) *see* Okuni-nushino-Mikoto.

O-mi-t'o Fo (China) *see* Amida.

O-pa-me (Tibet) *see* Amida.

O-sung (Tibet) *see* Kasyapa (B).

O-Wata-Tsu-Mi *Oho-Wata-Tsu-Mi, O-Wata-Tsumi* (Shinto; Japan)

Also known as: *Shio-zuchi* (Old Man of the Tide).

God of the sea. Ruler of all sea creatures. When Izanagi stepped into the great sea to cleanse himself of the pollutants of Yomi (hell), numerous sea deities were created. Among them are O-Wata-Tsu-Mi, the ruler of fish and all sea creatures; Shima-Tsu-Hiko, god of the wind; Kuko-no-shi, god of the trees; and Oho-yama-tsu-mi, god of the mountains. O-Wata-Tsu-Mi is considered the most important god of the group. Another sea god is Shiho-tsuchi. O-Wata-Tsu-Mi lives in a palace with his family on the sea floor. The palace has a great gateway flanked by towers of coral. The curved, sloping roof is made of lapis lazuli tiles. A huge cassia tree with fanning branches grows in front of one of the towers. The interior exudes wealth. Inside, there are rugs of sealskin and silk. Delicacies from the eight corners of the sea are served at meals. O-Wata-Tsu-Mi has two messengers, a monster shark and a crocodile. Hikohohodemi, the son of Ninigi, once stayed with O-Wata-Tsu-Mi for three years while looking for his brother's fishhook. He married the sea god's daughter Toya-Tama-bime and O-Wata-Tsu-Mi gave him two jewels of the tides known as Kangi (Tide Ebbing Jewel) and Mangi (Tide Flowing Jewel). With the advent of Ryobu-Shinto, a new sea god was created, named Sui-tengo, who is associated with the Hindu god Varuna. Sui-tengo is the protector of sailors and sick children. Sui-tengo is depicted in the shape of a woman holding a child in her arms. The woman represents Nii-no-ama and her grandson, the infant Emperor Antoku. Antoku and his nurse drowned in Dan Bay near Shimonoseki in the year 1185. O-Wata-Tsu-Mi and Toya-Tama-bime are depicted as a combination of human and dragon form. *See also* Haya-akitsu-hime-no-kami; Hikohohodemi; Hosuseri; Izanagi and Izanami; Toyo-Tama-Bime; Yomi.

O-Wata-Tsumi (Japan) *see* O-Wata-Tsu-Mi.

O-Yama-Tsu-Mi (Japan)

Chief god and lord of the mountains. He is appealed to before trees are cut down, particularly trees used to construct temples. He is the brother of the fire god, Kagu-tscuhi. His wife is Kaya-no-hime-no-kami (Ruler of the Grassy Plains). One of their daughters, Kono-Hana-Sakuya-Hime (Blossoms-of-the-Trees-Blooming-Princess) is the wife of Ninigi and the mother of Hoderi. *See also* Hoderi; Ninigi; Sengen.

O-zer-chem-ma (Tibet) *see* Marichi (A).

Oado (Persia) Kushana wind god.

Oak of Mughna (Celtic) *see* Abellio.

Oak of Two Greens (Celtic) *see* Dagda.

Oannes *Onnes, On* (Babylonian, Chaldean, Sumerian, Greek)

Also known as: *Aos, Dagon, Ea* (Semitic).

Earth deity. Oannes is the Greek name for Ea, the god of wisdom, who taught agriculture, irrigation and shipbuilding to the Babylonians. In Sumerian myth, Oannes came from the sea to bestow knowledge of the arts, sciences, and culture upon the people. At the end of each day, he returned to the sea. He is depicted as half-fish, half-man monster, or goat. In Syrian myth, his mate is the sea goddess Ataryatis Derketo (also known as Atargatis), and he is the father of Semiramis, who became the Queen of Babylon. *See also* Aa; Aeacus; Aos; Atargatis; Ea; Poseidon; Semiramis.

Oarion (Greek) *see* Orion.

Oath (Teutonic) *see* Var.

Oba (A) (Yoruba People, Africa)

River goddess. Goddess of wisdom and culture. Oba is Shango's favorite of his three wives. He won her from his brother, Ogun. An excellent cook, she followed her sister Oschun's advice and cut off her own ear and put in the soup she was cooking for him, in order to assure herself of her husband's affection. When he found the flesh, he became angry and sent her away. She became the river Niger. *See also* Ogun; Olodumare; Shango.

Oba (B) (Africa)

He is the traditional king of the Edo People.

Oba-Orun (Yoruba People, Africa) *see* Olodumare.

Obagat (Pelew Islands)

Creator deity. Wanted to give mankind immortality, but Rail gave them disease and death instead. Possibly the same as Lukeland (q.v.).

Obasi Nsi (West Africa) *see* Isong.

Obassi (Africa) *see* Obassi Osaw.

Obassi Osaw *Obassi* (Hausa People of the Niger, Africa)

Creator diety or high god. He gave mortals everything but fire which had been stolen by a boy.

Obastet (Egypt) *see* Bast.

Obatala (Yoruba People, Africa)

Also known as: *Orish-nla, Orish-oko, Orisha-ijaye, Orisha-ogiyan, Orisha-popo*.

First creation of the supreme being, Olodumare. His original name was Orish-nla. Sky god or earth deity. God of peace and order, representative of purity and law. Protector of town entrances. He is known as the sculptor god because he shapes babies while in they are in the womb. He makes barren women fertile. Obatala is asked by other deities to intervene on their behalf to Olodumare. His lineage varies; he is the son of Olodumare (who is also known as Olorun), the supreme being, and Olokun, the sea. His brother is Oduduwa. Or, he is the son of Oduduwa and brother/husband of Yemoja. Or, he is the father of Aganju and Yemoja who gave birth to Orungan who impregnated his mother. His mother gave birth to Dada, Schango, Ogun, Ochossi and Schankpannan. Obatala is the god of the north. Sometimes he is known as the master of the sky. We are also told that he was sent down to the waters by Olodumare to fashion earth. He drank some palm wine and was unable to finish his task. His replacement was Oduduwa. Obatala, who loves cleanliness, is depicted as an elderly man with white hair, dressed in white robes, in white surroundings. Sometimes he is accompanied by his spouse, Yemoja. For the Yoruba creation myths, see Oduduwa, Orish-nla and Olodumare. See also Aganju; Ogun; Shango; Yemoja.

Obe (Africa) see Obi.

Obeah (Africa) see Obi.

Oberon (Anglo-Franco) see Alfheim.

Obi (Africa; West Indies)
Also known as: *Obe, Obeah.*
Obi is a form of witchcraft which is often used for antisocial behavior. However, in the hands of the proper person, it can be a powerful source of good.

Obosom (Africa) see Abosam.

Obriareus (Greek)
He is one of the Hecatonchires. Known to mortals as Aegaeon and to the gods as Obriareus, he is also known as Briareus. See also Aegaeon; Hecatonchires.

Obsidian Butterfly (Aztec) see Itzpapalotl.

Obtala (Yoruba People, Africa) see Orish-nla; Shango.

Ocaleia (Greek)
Ocaleia is the wife of Abas and the mother of the twins Acrisius and Protetus. See also Abas; Acrisius; Proetus.

Ocean (Greek) see Oceanus.

Oceanic — Creation Legend see Areop-Enap; Lukelong; Lumimu-Ut; Nareau; Riiki.

Oceanides (Greek) see Oceanids.

Oceanids *Oceanides* (Greek)
Nymphs. Guardians of youth. The Oceanids are the children of Oceanus and Tethys. They have three thousand sons known as the Rivers and three thousand daughters known as the Oceanids. Not all lived in the sea. Some had the gift of prophecy and others were shape changers. The eldest daughter, Styx, is the only offspring who is a river deity. Metis is a goddess of wisdom and prudence. Europa and Asia became land masses, and

Calypso is an island nymph. Doris became the mother of fifty daughters, nymphs known as the Nereids. Eidyia (Idyia) married Aeetes, king of Colchis. Electra with Thaumas became parents of the Harpies and Iris. Callirrhoe and Medusa's son Chrysaor became the parents of a three-headed creature named Geryon. Perseis (Perse) became the mother of Circe, Pasiphae, Aeetes and possibly Perses. Clymene became the mother of Menoetius, Prometheus, Epimetheus and Atlas, according to Hesiod. Ovid called her the mother of Phaethon by Helius, though she was married to the king of Egypt, Merops. The Heliades are her children. To compare to other water deities, see Achelous; Naiads; Nereids; Rivers; Sirens; Styx. See also Achelous; Alpheus; Asopus; Cephissus; Chrysaor; Clytia; Cocytus; Europa; Harpies; Heliades; Inachus; Nymphs; Oceanus; Titans.

Oceanus *Okeanos* (Greek)
Also known as: *Ocean.*
A Titan and a sea deity. Oceanus is the lord of Ocean, the unending river that encircles the world, including the rivers of Hades. He is one of the Titans, son of Uranus and Gaea, brother of Cronus, and the brother and husband of Tethys. He is the god of all waters, including those of the underworld and a contributor to the formation of the universe. He is the father of three thousand river gods, known as Rivers, and three thousand water nymphs, known as Oceanids, as well as various other children. Oceanus is sometimes referred to as the father of Triptolemus, the prince of Eleusis. He may be the father of Acmon and Passalus by Theia. Oceanus and Gaea are also the parents of Crius, Eurybia, Nereus, Phorcys and Thaumas. He is also said to be the father of Thetis, Eurynome and Perse. Either Oceanus, Apollo or Perses is the father of Cariclo, the wife of Cheiron. Oceanus and Tethys raised their sister Rhea's daughter Hera. In old age, Oceanus' tide came in with the advent of the Olympians reign and he was replaced by Poseidon. In the Pelasgian creation myth, Oceanus and Tethys were the rulers of the planet Venus. (See Eurynome.) Oceanus is depicted reclining with an oar and sea animals. See Oceanids and Rivers for additonal names of his children. Compare Oceanus to the Assyro-Babylonian, Apsu. See also Achelous; Aeetes; Alpheus; Amphitrite; Apsyrtus; Asopus; Cephissus; Ceto; Chaos; Clytia; Cocytus; Cronus; Eurynome (A); Gaea; Inachus; Meliae; Naiads; Nemesis; Nereids; Nereus; Pontus; Poseidon; Rhea; Styx; Themis.

Ocelotonatiuh (Mexico) see Legend of the Four Suns.

Ocepta *Ocypete* (Greek) She is one of the Harpies (q.v.).

Ochimus (Greek)
He is one of the Heliades and the father of Cydippe. See also Heliades.

Ochren (Celtic) see Achren.

Ochun (Africa) see Oschun.

Ocirvani and Tsagan-Sukuty (Mongol)
Ocirvani and Tsagan-Sukuty descended from heaven to the Primordial Ocean. Tsagan-Sukuty was asked by Ocirvani to dive to the depths and return with mud. They spread the mud over a turtle and fell asleep. Sulmus, the deity of evil, tried to drown the two gods, but everytime he rolled over them the earth expanded.

Ockabewis (Chippewa People, North America)
Messenger of the gods. Teacher of mankind.

Ocleia (Greek) *see* Aglaia.

Ocrisia (Greek)
She was a Roman slave who was the mistress of Hephaistos
(q.v.).

Octli (Aztec People, Mexico)
Also known as: *Centzontotochtin.*
Gods of intoxicating drink. A general name for pulque
deities. *See also* Centzon Totochtin; Colhuatzincatl; Ometochtli; Patecatl; Texcatzoncatl.

Ocypete (Greek) She is one of the Harpies (q.v.).

Od (Norse; Teutonic)
Also known as: *Oder, Odin, Odnir, Odur, Othur, Svipdag.*
Some say Od is Freyja's lost husband, while others say it is
another name for Odin. *See also* Freyja.

Od-Dpag-Med (Tibet) *see* Amitabha.

Od-Hroerir (Teutonic) *see* Odraerir.

Oddua (Africa) *see* Oduduwa.

Odem (Hebrew) *see* Adam.

Oder (Teutonic) *see* Od or Odin.

Odherir (Teutonic) *see* Odraerir.

Odhinn (Teutonic) *see* Odin.

Odhroerir (Teutonic) *see* Odraerir.

Odin *Odhinn, Othin, Othinn, Othinus, Ouvin, Votan, Votan,
Wodan, Wode, Wodemus, Woden, Wodhen, Wodin, Wotam,
Woutan, Wuotan* (Norse; Teutonic)
Also known as: *Allfather, Baleyg* ("One with Flaming Eyes"),
Biblindi, Bileyg ("One with Evasive Eyes"), *Bilflindi, Bolverk*
("Evil- Doer"), *Bolverkin, Breit-Hut,* ("Chooser of the Slain"),
Farma-Tyr, Fjolnir, Gagnrad ("He Who Determines Victories"),
Galgavaldyr, Gangler, Gaut ("The Creator") *God of Hanged
Men, God of Ravens, Grimmr, Grimnikr, Grimnir, Habard,
Hackeberg, Hakoi-berent, Hanga-tyr, Har* ("The High One"),
Harbard, Helblindi, Herfadir, Herjan ("God of Battles"), *Her-
tyr, Heryan, Hnikar, Hrafna, Hropt, Jafnhar* ("Even as High"),
Karlafberge, Lord of the Gallows, Od (possibly), *Odr, Omi, Oski,
Rafnagud, Roptatyr, Sidhottr, Sigfadir* ("The Father of Battle or
of Victory"), *Sigtyr, Skidskegg, Thudr, Uggerus, Vafud, Vale,
Valfadir, Valfather, Valkjosandi* (Scandinavian), *Vegtam, Vid-
forull, Wild Huntsman, Woden, Ygg* ("The Awful"), *Yggr.*
There are many legends associated with Odin, the supreme
deity, and god of war, intelligence, and poetry. Odin so thirsted
after knowledge that he sacrificed an eye to his uncle, the giant
Mimir, for a drink of the beverage of wisdom from Mimir's
Well. Considered to be the wisest of all deities, other gods
sought advice from him. One of his abodes, named Gladsheim,
is located in Asgard. From his throne, known as Hlidskialf, in
Valaskjalf, Odin is able to see and know all throughout the
world. His dietary habits are sparse; at his banquets he drinks
only wine. The meat set before him is given to his wolves, Geri

and Freki. A handsome man, his sexual appetite is robust. Some
say he is a polygamist. Among his spouses are Jord, Frigga, Rind,
Saga, Grid, Gunnlod, and Skadi. Some say he had only two
wives, Gritta and Grydat, but numerous affairs with mortal
women, female giants, and supernatural beings. In an ancient
legend, Odin's sons are named Weldegg, Beldegg, Sigi, Skiold,
Saeming, and Yngvi. They are reputed to have been mortal
kings. In another ancient legend, Odin and Frigga have seven
sons who are said to have founded the Anglo-Saxon heptarchy.
Yet another rendering couples Odin with Jord, with whom he
had a son Thor, with Frigg a son Balder, with Grid a son Vidar,
with Rind a son Vali, and other sons Heimdal, Hod, Bragi, Tyr,
Meili, and Hermod. Odin is known as a magical sovereign with
a vast knowledge of the runes, a magical method of divination,
later used in the formation of an alphabet. The runes gave him
the power to kill enemies, cure illness, and compel women to
sleep with him. His magical powers give him the ability to
assume many guises. He prefers the identity of the traveler so
that he can wander the earth observing the actions of people.
His ravens, Huginn, who personifies thought, and Muninn,
who personifies memory, lift from their perches on his shoulders each day and fly to various places in the universe. When
they return they tell Odin of all they have seen. Odin travels
wherever he desires on his eight-footed horse, Sleipner, the
fastest horse in the world. In one legend, Odin appeared to the
giant Gunnolth in the form of a snake and spent three nights
with her. During this time, she gave him a few drinks of the
beverage of poets, Odraerir. Odin also bragged that he had slept
with seven sisters. As a warrior, he encourages his men to fight
like dogs and wolves. Two warriors, Sigmund and Sinfjotli, are
characterized as werewolves. The cult of the berserkir, warriors
dedicated to Odin, dressed in wolf or bear skins fight like wild
animals. In some legends, Odin is thought of as a horse and
horses were sacrificed to him. Odin is also thought of as a death
demon in Teutonic folklore. He told Aun or On, the king of
Sweden, that he could live as long as he sacrificed one of his sons
every ninth year. The king followed the instructions but when
it came to his tenth son the Swedes would not allow him to be
sacrificed, so the king died and is said to be buried in Upsala.
There is an interesting myth that tells of Odin being exiled by
the other gods who were unhappy with his transgressions. They
provided a substitute, the crafty wizard Oller who ruled for ten
years and was expelled from his throne when Odin returned.
Oller moved to Sweden and was slain as he attempted to rebuild
his fortunes. In one myth Odin is known as the god of wisdom,
agriculture, poetry and war. He is the god of death and battle,
originally one of three brothers born of Bor at the beginning of
time. In that version the three created a man and woman, Ask
and Embla, from two trees. Odin gave them breath and life, his
brother Vili gave them understanding, and his other brother Ve
gave the warmth and human characteristics. In another version, it is Odin who created the progenitors of the human race
and all living things including the first mortals, Ask and Embla.
His brothers are Vili and Ve. Odin's sons with Frigga are Balder,
Hodur, a blind god, and Boe. Boe is sometimes called his son
by Rind. Odin had Boe kill the slayer of his father, Balder. Other
sons of Odin are Ty, Brage, and possibly Heimdall and Vidar.
In legends of Thor, Odin was said to be his father and Jord or
Fjorgyn, his mother. Odin is also thought of as a death demon

in Teutonic folklore. Wednesday in the English and Scandinavian language comes from Odin's name. He collects fallen warriors known as einherjar. They will assist him in the foretold battle of Ragnarok at the end of time. Men were hung as sacrifices to Odin. Odin voluntarily hung himself from the tree of life, Yggdrasil, for nine nights without food or beverage. By carefully observing everything around him, he noticed magic runes beneath him. With great effort he was able to lift them, and was immediately set free. He was rejuvenated by his experience of self-sacrifice. Odin is pictured as a grey-bearded, one-eyed man in a blue cloak and a broad-brimmed hat who usually carries his magic spear, Gungnir, and wears the ring Draupnir. His symbol is the eagle, and sometimes the wolf, or raven. In most versions, his two ravens, Huginn and Muninn, are perched on his shoulders, and his two wolves, Geri and Freki, lay at his feet. In nearly every respect Odin is similar to Jupiter (Roman) and Zeus (Greek). Odin is the same as the Wodan (German). Compare Odin to Nuada (Celtic), Lugh (Celtic), Savitri (Hindu), Varuna (Hindu) and Esus (Gaul). See also Aesir; Ask; Audhumla; Balder; Baugi; Bergelmir; Bestla; Boe; Bor; Buri; Embla; Frigga; Gladsheim; Grid; Gunnlod; Harbard; Heimdall; Helblindi; Hermod; Hlidskjalf; Hoder; Huginn; Jord; Jotun-heim; Jotuns; Loki; Mimir; Mimir's Well; Muninn; Odraerir; Ragnarok; Rind; Saeming; Saga; Sigi; Sigmund; Sinfjotli; Skadi; Sleipnir; Sokvabek; Ull; Ve; Vidar; Vili; Yggdrasil; Ymir.

Odnir (Teutonic) see Od or Odin.

Odraerir *Od-Hroerir, Odherir, Odhroerir, Odrerer, Odrorir, Odrovir, Othrevir, Othroerir* (Norse; Teutonic)

Also known as: *Eldhrimir* ("Firefrost"), *Hvergelmer, Hvergelmir.*

Odraerir is one of the vessels of magic mead. In this myth the gods created the god of wisdom, Kvasir, from their saliva. Two dwarfs, Fjalar and Galar, slew him and drained his blood into three vessels. Two of the vessels were crocks named Son and Boden. The third vessel was the kettle named Odraerir. They mixed the blood with honey, and anyone who sipped from this mixture became a great poet and singer. After killing the giant Gilling and his wife, Fjalar and Galar were captured by Gilling's brother Sattung. In return for their lives they traded the mixture to Sattung who put it in charge of his daughter, Gunnlod. In some myths, Odraerir is guarded by Bolthorn's son. Odin in one of his adventures found the magic mead and drank all three vessels, thus becoming the greatest of all poets and singers. In his haste to empty all he had taken Odin emptied his mouth into a vessel the people of Asgard prepared, but spilled a few drops. This allowed the mortals who lapped it up the great power of poetry. Odraerir was called Eldhrimir when it was used to boil the flesh of the wild boar. See also Baugi; Bolthor; Fjalar; Gilling; Gunnlod; Hvergelmir; Kvasir; Niflheim; Odin; Sattung; Son (A).

Odrerer (Teutonic) see Odraerir.

Odrorir (Teutonic) see Odraerir.

Odrovir (Teutonic) see Odraerir.

Odu-Duwa (Africa) see Oduduwa.

Odudua (Africa) see Oduduwa.

Oduduwa *Odudua, Odu-Duwa* (Yoruba People, Africa)

Androgynous earth deity. "Self-existent ruler who created all beings." Often Oduduwa is known as the goddess wife of Obatala. Together they are credited as the creators of earth. Sometimes it is Obatala who created mother earth from his spouse Oduduwa. Oduduwa has a son, Ogun, who became a renowned warrior. Creator of dry land. King of Ife. In some creation myths, Oduduwa was sent to finish the job of creation after Obtala fell into a drunken sleep. Some say Oduduawa as a god is the father of Aganju and Yemaja. In another version his son is Oranyan. In a version of the creation myths of the Yoruba people, Olodumare, the supreme being created the earth from a celestial gaseous mass. It was formed in what became known as the cities of Oyo, Ife and Ibadan in Nigeria. The first divine spirit who was created, known as an Orisha, was Oduduwa. He was given the spirit of Olodumare and could act as Olodumare. He was the highest authority on earth and the foremost ruler. He filled a deep abyss with gasses left from the creation of the earth and created water. From water the next Orisha was formed in the likeness of Oduduwa and as Oduduwa but with opposite qualities. Yembo, the mother of water followed and became the spouse of Oduduwa. From Yembo all the waters of the world were created. The marriage of Oduduwa and Yembo represented the union of the sea and the earth. From this union came the creation of other Orishas. For other versions of the creation myth of the Yorubas, see Orish-nla and Olodumare. See also Ajanju; Ife; Obtala.

Odur (Teutonic) see Od; Odin.

Odysseus (Greek)

Also known as: *Ulixes* (Latin), *Ulysses* (Roman).

Deified mortal. Son of Laertes or possibly Sisyphus, and Anticleia. King of Ithaca Husband of Penelope. The wiliest of the Greek leaders at Troy, he was the inventor of the wooden horse. His wanderings on the way home from Troy, which form the subject of Homer's *Odyssey*, lasted twenty years. Finally he reached home and killed the suitors by whom Penelope had been surrounded during his absence. Achaemenides, a companion of Odysseus, was abandoned by him in Sicily and saved by Aeneas. See also Aeneas; Aeolus (B); Ajax the Greater; Ajax the Lesser; Anticleia (A); Argus (F); Calypso; Ino; Sirens; Sisyphus.

Oebaulus (Greek)

King of Sparta. He is the husband of Gorgophone, who was first married to his brother, Perieres. She was the first Greek woman to remarry. See also Gorgophone.

Oedipus *Oidipous, Oidipodes* (Greek)

Deified mortal. King of Thebes. Son of Laius (Laios) and Jocasta, who, fulfilling a prophesy of the oracle at Delphi, unwittingly killed his father and married his mother. Laius, attempting to thwart Fate, ordered his infant son to be killed. Jocasta had the child carried to Mount Cithaeron where he was raised by a shepherd. Unaware of his lineage, he killed a stranger who turned out to be his father on the road to Thebes years later. He was rewarded with the hand of his mother, the Queen of Thebes, for ridding the city of the dangerous Sphinx by guessing its riddle. When she discovered her son's identity, Jocasta committed suicide and Oedipus, tormented by the Erinyes, blinded himself. He left Thebes with his daughter Antigone, and died at Colonus near Athens comforted by the hero Theseus. *See also* Adrestus; Antigone; Eteocles; Jocasta; Polyneices; Theseus.

Oegir (Teutonic)

Also known as: *Hler.*

Sea deity. Consort of Ran (the robber, or tempest). As Hler, he is the ruler of the underworld. Hler and Ran raised up the fierce waves called Kolga. Hler's consort is the goddess Hela. *See also* Hel.

Oegishailm (Norse; Teutonic)

Magic Helmet. Helmet of darkness worn by Fafnir.

Oenamaus *Oenomaus* (Greek)

Oenamaus is the son of Ares or Alxion by Harpina, who is the daughter of the river god Asopus, or possibly the Pleiad Asterope. In some traditions, Asterope is the wife of Oenamaus and not his mother. He married Evarete, the daughter of Acrisius, and became the father of Hippodamia and Leucippus, who dressed as a female to befriend Daphne and was killed by her friends. Oenamaus, the king of Pisa, was told by an oracle that he would be killed by his future son-in-law. In order to negate the prophecy he devised chariot races offering Hippodamia as the prize. Certain that he would never be defeated because he had been given a pair of winged horses and special armor by his father Ares, he was able to eliminate twelve or thirteen suitors who lost the races and their lives in the treacherous contest. Each participant was instructed to take Hippodamia in his chariot and dash off toward Corinth. If Oenamaus overtook him, he was beheaded and his head was nailed to the palace door. Pelops, the son of Tantalus, had heard of Hippodamia's great beauty and of her father's wealth. Determined to emerge the victor, he prayed to Poseidon for guidance and he became friendly with Myrtilus, a son of Hermes, who was in charge of maintaining Oenamaus' chariot. Pelops bribed the man by offering him a night in bed with Hippodamia and half the kingdom if he would leave the linchpin out of the king's chariot wheel. Some writer's believe that Hippodamia bribed Myrtilus, who was said to be in love with her. Pelops emerged the victor of the race when the wheel of the king's chariot flew off and he was hurled to the ground. As he was dying, Oenamaus cursed Myrtilus for betraying him and declared that his once trusted assistant would die at the hands of his new friend, Pelops. *See also* Acrisius; Ares; Daphne; Hippodamia (A); Leucippus; Pelops.

Oenarus (Greek) *see* Ariadne.

Oeneus (A) (Greek)

He is the son of the god of war, Ares, and Demonice or possibly Alcippe. His siblings are Evenus, Molus, Pylus and Testius. *See also* Alcippe; Ares.

Oeneus (B) (Greek)

King of Calydon. Oeneus is the son of Porthaon and Euryte. His siblings are Alcathous, Agrius, Melas, Sterope and Leucopeus. His first marriage was to his niece, Althea. He was the father of Deianeira, Gorge (who was later turned into a guinea fowl by Artemis) and Toxeus. Some say Meleager is also his child. Althea felt responsible for the death of Meleager, so she hung herself. After Althaea's suicide, Oeneus married Periboea. Their children are Olenias, Perimede and Tydeus (some say he is the son of Oeneus' daughter Gorge). Oeneus has a son, Laocoon, by a member of his household staff. It was the custom of the land owners to pay homage to the goddess of hunting, Artemis. Oeneus forgot to pay his dues. The infuriated goddess sent the Calydonia Boar to plunder his land. Oeneus killed Toxeus for jumping a ditch that was to protect Calydon. Oeneus was also killed, possibly by his brother Agrius' sons. *See also* Althea; Ares; Artemis; Athena; Calydonian Boar Hunt; Heracles; Laocoon; Meleager; Periboea.

Oengus (Celtic, Irish) *see* Angus; Dwyn.

Oengus of the Bruigh (Celtic, Irish) *see* Angus.

Oenomaus (Greek) *see* Oenamaus.

Oenone *Oinone* (Greek)

Oenone is the daughter of the river god Cebren. A nymph, she married Paris, who later abandoned her for Helen. Oenone and Paris had two children, Corythus and Daphnis. Corythus either found his father in bed with Helen and killed him or Paris killed his son because the young man fell in love with Helen. Oenone attempted a reconciliation, but was not successful. Though she had the gift of healing, she could not heal her inner anguish. When Paris, wounded in battle at Troy, appealed to her to heal him, she refused. Stricken with remorse, she acquiesced but it was too late. He died. She hung herself. *See also* Helen; Nymphs; Paris.

Oenopion (Greek)

He is the son of Dionysus and Ariadne or Theseus and Ariadne. Dionysus taught him the art of cultivating the vine. He married the nymph Helice and became the father of a daughter, Merope, and several sons. When Orion raped Merope, Oenopion blinded him. *See also* Ariadne; Dionysus; Merope; Orion; Pleiades; Theseus.

Ogdoad, The (Egypt)

Also known as: *Island of Flame, Primordial Hill.*

Heaven. The "Island of Flame" or "Primordial Hill" was the first body to appear. Upon it, in turn, appeared an Ogdoad of eight divinities who created Atum. They are Nun and Naunet (also spelled Nunet), god and goddess of the ocean; Heh and Hehet (also called Huh and Huker), god and goddess of the immeasurable who created the sun; Kek and Keket (also called Kuk and Kuket), god and goddess of darkness which enables the sun to shine; Amun and Amunet (also called Nui and Nuit), god and goddess of mystery who are made of air and, as Nui and Nuit, invisible. The head of this pantheon is Thoth, who found the ancient deities instated in Khemenu, "the town of eight," along with Wenet, the goddess-hare and a baboon. It is said that the great sun god Ra rested there when he rose for the first time. The male halves of the Ogdoad were frog-headed and the female halves were serpent-headed. *See also* Amen; Ament; Ennead; Hebdomad; Huh and Hauhet; Isle of the Blessed; Thoth; Wenet.

Ogetsu-Hime *Ogetsu-Hime-No-Kami* (Japan) *see* Izanami; Kami-Mimusubi; Ukemochi.

Oggun (Yoruba People, Africa) *see* Ogun.

Ogham (Celtic) *see* Ogma.

Ogma (Celtic, Gaul, Irish)
Also known as: *Ogham, Ogmios.*
Deity of eloquence and language. When he spoke, Ogma wore a lion skin. He had fine gold chains attached to his tongue. The gold chains indicated the gift of speech was precious. *See also* Boann; Dagda.

Ogmios (Celtic) *see* Ogma.

Ogoni (Slavic) God of Fire. *See also* Agni.

Ogoun (Africa, Haitian) *see* Obatala; Ogun.

Ogrigwabibikwa (Pygmy People, Africa)
Dwarf shape changer. A dwarf who changes into a reptile.

Ogue (Yoruba People, Africa) *see* Olodumare.

Ogun *Oggun* (Dahomey, Yoruba People, Africa; Caribbean; Central America; South America)
Also known as: *Gu* (African), *Ogoun* (Haitian).
God of iron. God of warriors, surgery (including circumcision). God of hunting. God of blacksmiths, goldsmiths and butchers. In some traditions Ogun is the second son of Oddua and Yembo. He came into the world from a volcano as it was erupting and brought with him the ability to forge weapons and tools. He has a warlike nature, and a persona that demands respect. Presently, he is popular with hunters and owners of cars and trucks. In the past, humans were sacrificed to him, now he is offered dogs in some areas. In early times, when the earth was a marsh, Ogun came from the celestial realm on a spider's web to hunt. Later, when the supreme deity Odolumare had the Orishas organize the earth, Ogun was the only one with an iron machete. He cut through the impenetrable thorn bushes and made access easier for the deities. His reward was a crown. He preferred the life of the warrior and hunter and left to live alone on a hilltop where he could pursue his passions. After many years, he returned wearing unacceptable blood stained clothing and was refused entry by the gods. Ogun made new clothing from the bark of a palm tree and found another place to live. In the Voodoo belief he is associated with rum. He is sometimes associated with the Haitian goddess Erzulie. Ogun is comparable to the Fon deity of metal, Gou. *See also* Aganju; Oba (A); Obatala; Yemoja.

Ogyges (Greek)
King of Athens. His parents are Poseidon and Gaea. Antaeus and Charybdis are his siblings. He married Thebe. *See also* Antaeus; Charybdis; Thebe.

Ogyrvan (Celtic)
Ogyrvan is a magic cauldron. It is also listed as one of the treasures of Britain. Another magic cauldron listed as one of the treasures of Britain is Gwigawd.

Oh-Kuni-Nushi (Japan) *see* Okuni-Nushino-Mikoto.

Oh-kuninushi (Japan) *see* Okuni-Nushino-Mikoto.

Oh-magatsumi (Japan) *see* Okuni-Nushino-Mikoto; Susanowo.

Oh-Yama-Tsumi (Japan) *see* Fuji.

Ohdowas (Iroquois People, North America)
Evil spirits.
They are dwarfs who live underground and control all the monsters. *See also* Dwarfs (Teutonic); Gahongas; Gandayaks; Jogaoh.

Oho-ge-tsu-himi (Japan) *see* Ogetsu-hime-no-kami.

Oho-hiru-me No Muchi (Japan) *see* Amaterasu.

Oho-iwa Dai-myo-jin (Japan)
Also known as: *Oiwa Daimyojin*
"Great God of the Rock." *See also* Taki-Tsu-Hiko.

Oho-Kuni-Nushi-No-Kami (Japan) *see* Okuni-Nushino-Mikoto.

Oho-to-mahe No Mikoto (Japan) *see* Ama-no-minaka-nushi.

Oho-to-nochi No Mikoto (Japan) *see* Ama-no-minaka-nushi.

Oho-yama-tsu-mi (Japan) *see* O-Wata-Tsu-Mi.

Ohonamochi (Japan) *see* Taki-Tsu-Hiko.

Ohouris (Egypt) *see* Anhur.

Ohoyo Osh Chishba (Choctaw People, North America)
Deity of corn. Her name means "Unknown Woman," the name of the Corn Mother.

Ohrmazd *Ormuzd* (Persia)
Also known as: *Ahura Mazda.*
The first creator. He created the Immortals, followed by the Yazatas, followed by everything else. He is both mother and father of all. *See also* Ahura Mazda.

Oidipodes (Greek) *see* Oedipus.

Oidipous (Greek) *see* Oedipus.

Oileus (Greek)
Oileus, the king of Locris, is an Argonaut. He married Eriopis and became the father of Ajax the Lesser. At one time, Oileus and Apollo were lovers. *See also* Ajax the Lesser; Argonauts.

Oinone (Greek) *see* Oinone.

Oiwa Daimyojin (Japan)
Another name for the "Great God of the Rock," Oho-iwa Dai-myo-jin. *See also* Taki-Tsu-Hiko.

Okami-no-kami (Japan)
She is a descendant of the rice goddess, Kushi-nada-hime (q.v.).

Oke (Yoruba People, Africa) *see* Olodumare.

Oke Hede (Mandan) Evil deity. The Evil Twin.

Okeanos (Greek) *see* Oceanus.

Oki (Huron People, North America) *see* Orenda.

Oki-tsu-hiko (Japan)
Kitchen god. *See also* Ch'an Tzu-fang (China); Inari; Tsao Chun (China); Tsao Wang (China).

Oki-tsu-hime (Japan)
Kitchen god. *See also* Ch'an Tzu-fang (China) Inari; Tsao Chun (China); Tsao Wang (China).

Okikurumi (Ainu People, Japan)
Also known as: (Male) *Aeoina Kamui, Ainu-rak-kur, Pon Okikurumi.*
Sea goddess. Androgynous deity. Husband of Turesh. When the world was new and too hot for people to walk, Okikurumi did their fishing for them, sending his wife to deliver his catch. One Ainu disobeyed the order that none should see her face and caught her by the hand. Immediately, she turned into a sea monster. As punishment, Okikurumi no longer fished for the people. That is why the Ainu are very poor. In some legends, Okikurumi is the first man and was born from the goddess Chikisani and a sun god. *See also* Chikisanti; Fuji.

Okitsushima-Hime-no-Mikoto (Japan) *see* Three Goddesses of Munakata.

Oklatabashih (Choctaw People, North America)
First woman. Her name means "Mourner of the People." She is the survivor of the Flood.

Oko (Yoruba People, Africa)
Oko, the god of agriculture, is the son of Yembo.

Okolner (Norse; Teutonic)
Home of deities. A hall named Brimer in Okolner is where the giants will convene to consume ale after the end of the world known as Ragnarok.

Oku-Thor (Norse; Teutonic)
Also known as: *Thor.*
Oku-Thor is the name used for Thor when he journeys in thunderstorms.

Okuni-Nushino-Mikoto (Shinto; Japan)
Also known as: *O-Kuni-Nushi, Oh-Kuninushi, Oho-Kuni-Nushi-No-Kami, Okuninushi, Yachihoko-no-Kami* (God of Eight Thousand Spears).
God of medicine and sorcery. One of the Shichi Fukujin (seven gods of happiness). Storm god. God of marriage. God of wealth. God of fishing. God of sericulture. Okuni-Nushino-Mikoto (Great Land Master) is said in most legends to be the son of the Valiant Swift Impetuous Hero, Susanowo, and Kushi-nada-hime. Okuni-Nushino-Mikoto, his father and brothers are the rulers of Izumo. They are the rulers of mysterious and evil happenings. His father, also a storm god, can be gentle and kind or wild and unruly. He is either the chief or an associate of the spirits of the underworld. Okuni-Nushino-Mikoto, as a medicine man and sorcerer works for the welfare of the people. His close associate is the dwarf god Suku-na-biko (Small Prince of Renown), who is the chief of the medicine men. One of Okuni-Nushino-Mikoto's eighty brothers is Oh-Magatsumi (Great Evil-doer). During times of natural disasters and pestilence, the people directed their prayers to these deities. The logic was that one appealed to the instigators of evil to avert evil. When Susanowo descended into Yami (hell), Okuni-Nushino-Mikoto took over as the ruler of Izumo. In this capacity, he is the overseer of the ghosts of old rulers, known as Ujikami. Some say that his overlord was the evil deity Ama-tsu-mika-hoshi. Okuni hated suffering, so he prevented evil spirits from injuring mortals. Once he came upon the skinned hare of Inaba who was in great pain. The brothers of Okuni-Nushino-Mikoto had advised the hare to bathe in the salty sea and dry his body in the wind. This procedure intensified his misery. Okuni-Nushino-Mikoto prescribed a fresh water dip and a roll in the sedge. Sedge is a type of plant similar to grass but the stems are solid rather than hollow. The procedure cured the hare and in thanks he offered Okuni-Nushino-Mikoto the princess Yakami, which enraged Okuni's brothers. Through various underhanded methods, they killed him. His mother appealed to the goddess Kami-Musubi, who returned her son to life as a strong, young man. To protect him from the wrath of his jealous brothers, he was sent to Susanowo's realm in the underworld. In his new location, he met and fell in love with Suseri-Hime, the daughter of Susanowo. He abducted her, a bow and arrow, a sword and a harp, all prized possessions of his benefactor. He was captured and sentenced to numerous labors. In this myth he was duped by his brothers and burned to death by a hot, rolling stone. It was not to be his end. He was reborn as a beautiful youth and named Yachihoko-no-Kami. It is said that he rode a bronze horse once a year and all who saw him turned into dogs. In time, Ninigi, the grandson of his aunt, the sun goddess Amaterasu, overthrew him and took over the throne. In some versions, Okuni-Nushino-Mikoto was the son-in-law and successor, rather than the son of Susanowo. Other renditions say that it was Onamuji, the brother of Okuni-Nushino-Mikoto, who was forcibly removed from the throne. Okuni-Nushino-Mikoto has a daughter named Shita-teru-Hime who married Ame-no-Wakahiko, the renowned warrior god. He may have been the father of two sons, Koto-shiro-nushi and Take-minakata. With Daikoku, Okuni-Nushino-Mikoto became one of the Shichi Fukujin (Seven Gods of Happiness), representing wealth. In some traditions, Okuni-Nushino-Mikoto is said to worship the deity Omiwa. *See* Kushi-nada-hime for alternate lineage. *See also* Amaterasu; Ame-no-Oshido-Mimi; Daikoku; Kami-Mimusubi; Kushi-nada-hime; Ninigi; Shi Tenno; Shichi Fukujin; Suku-na-biko; Susanowo; Take-mi-kazuchi; Yomi.

Okuninushi (Japan) *see* Okuni-Nushino-Mikoto.

Ol-Okun (Africa) *see* Olukun.

Ol-Orun (Yoruba People, Africa) *see* Olodumare.

Ola'li (Maidu People, North America) *see* Coyote.

Old Age (Greek) *see* Nox.

Old Black God, The (Maya) *see* "L."

Old Coyote (Mexico) *see* Huehuecoyotl.

Old God (Mexico) *see* Huehueteotl.

Old Woman Earth (Ashanti People, Africa) *see* Asase Yaa.

Oldherir (Teutonic) *see* Odraeirir.

Olelbis (Wintun People, North America)

Also known as: *Earth-Maker*.

Creator deity. The god Olelbis lives with two old women. His home is in Olelpanti in a beautiful sweat-house that grew until it was the largest paradise and most beautiful place in the world. When the world was destroyed by a great fire, Olelbis called upon Kahit (the wind) and Mem Loimis (the waters) to put out the fires. After, he restored the earth and created a new race of people. He is similar to Taikomol of the Yuki tribe, Yimantuwinyai of the Hupa and K'mukamtch of the Klamath People.

Olelpanti (Wintun People, North America)

Olelpanti, the home of the god Olelbis, is described as being on the upper side of the highest place. *See also* Olelbis.

Olenias (Greek) *see* Calydonian Boar Hunt.

Olenus (Greek)

Hè is the brother of the divine artisan, Hephaistos (q.v.).

Oler *Oller, Uller* (Norse; Teutonic)

Another name for Ull, the god of winter (q.v.).

Olifat *Olofat* (Caroline Islands; Micronesia)

Also known as: *Iolofath, Obagat, Orofat, Wolphat, Yelafath*.

Trickster deity. Messenger. Son of the god Luk and a mortal female. He emerged as an adult from his mother's skull. Olifat traveled between heaven and earth. He is a trickster god, who waged war on the other gods. Once he was put to death but his father revived him. Olifat became the messenger between Luk and mortals, and brought fire to them. In some legends it is Olifat who decreed that mankind would not be immortal. He is similar to Nareau, and is associated with Luk (qq.v.).

Oller (Teutonic) *see* Odin; Oler; Ull.

Ollerus (Teutonic) *see* Ull

Oloddumare (Yoruba People, Africa) *see* Olodumare.

Olode (Africa) *see* Sonponno.

Olodumare *Oloddumare* (Yoruba People, Africa)

Also known as: *Olofi, Olofin-Orun* (Supreme King), *Olorun* (Lord of Heaven or Owner of Heaven).

Creator deity. Olodumare, the supreme deity of the Yoruba, is the creator of everything in heaven and on earth. Born of the primordial heaven Olokun, he is the highest deity in the Yoruba pantheon. Olodumare knows the innermost thoughts and feelings of all mortals. He is said to be an impartial god who controls the destiny of each individual. Other deities in the pantheon are known as Orishas (spirits, also called divine beings) and are generally identified with, or are manifestations of, the forces of nature and patrons of occupations. Orishas have the power to be in different places at the same time. Orishas according to rank following Olodumare are Obatala, who represents purity and law; Eleggua, the ruler of all paths and opportunities in life; Ogun (also called Oggun), deity of iron; Oshosi, the hunter and judge; Ozun or Osun, the communicator; Asogguano, who represents epidemics and health matters; Orisha-Oko, Dada, the goddess of the brain and its senses; Ogue, Oke, Inle, Meyi, Argayu, the sun deity and god of the desert; Shango, the thunder deity; Jeggua, the goddess of purity and virginity;

Oba, the goddess of wisdom and culture; Oya, the goddess of the air we breathe and the deity of water; Yemaya, who represents salt water; Orula and Oshun, who represents sweet water. The priests in the Yoruba religion are considered prophetic and act as intermediaries between mortals and the orishas. Some tradionalists think that Olodumare is one of a trinity rather than the supreme deity of the Yoruba. Some also say he created men, but others say it was Orisha-Nla (also spelled Orishanla, the great orisha), or that Olodumare and Orisha-Nla are one and the same being. Another opinion is that the female deity Oduduwa was the creator. In the United States, the names Olodumare, Olorun or Olofi are used by followers of the Yoruba faith. Symbols or images of Olodumare are not made, nor are temples dedicated to him, though prayers are offered to him and thanks given to him for every part of life and existence. It is said that Olodumare's favorite color is white. Some scholars treat the name Olorun as a vulgarization of Olodumare. The creation myths of the Yoruba vary in different locales. For two versions, *see* Oduduaw and Orish-nla. *See also* Eshu; Ifa; Ogun; Olorun; Orish-nla; Oschun; Shango.

Olofad (Micronesia) *see* Olifat.

Olofat (Micronesia) *see* Olifat.

Olofi (Yoruba People, Africa) *see* Olodumare.

Olofin-Orun (Yoruba People, Africa) *see* Olodumare.

Olokun *Ol-Okun* (Benin, Yoruba People, Nigeria, Africa)

"Owner of the Sea." "Lord of the Great Waters." "Lord of the Undertow." God of wealth and commerce. Provider of children. Olokun is the son of Osanobua, the creator god, or one of the children of Aganju and Yemaya. He is the father of the sky god, Olorun (also known as Olodumare). (Others say that Olorun and Olokun are rivals not relatives and that Olorun created the world and mortals.) He is the primeval sea and it is from him that the supreme deity Olodumare came forth. Olokun's splendid palace is underwater. He is a cultured god who loves beauty in all its forms. His wife, Yemaya, the goddess of salt water, represents the surface of water. More women worship him than men. Sailors pray to him for safety on their journeys. His attendants are both human and fish-like. Olokun is depicted as having mudfish as legs. In another depiction, he wears a cylindrical hat, a ceremonial apron covers his pants and he is bare-footed. *See also* Olodumare; Olorun; Orunmila.

Olorun (Benin, Yoruba People, Africa)

Also known as: *Olodumare*.

"Owner." Sky god. Creator of the world and mortals. *See also* Olodumare; Olokun.

Olu-Igbo (Africa)

Jungle deity. Owner of the bush and jungle.

Oluksak (Eskimo)

A god of lakes, he lives on the banks of the water. Only an Angakok (shaman) can talk to him.

Olumbe (Africa)

Also known as: *Orumbe*.

A god of death. Ruler of the kingdom of the dead, Magombe. Similar to the Basumbwa people's god of death named Lufu or Lirufu.

Olusi (Yoruba People, Africa) *see* Eshu.

Oluwa (Yoruna People, Africa) *see* Olodumare.

Olympian Creation Myth (Greek) *see* Aegaeon; Gaea.

Olympus (Greek)

Home of the gods. A lofty mountain on the border between Macedonia and Thessaly, which is the abode of the gods.

Omacatl (Aztec People, Mexico)

Also known as: *Two Reeds*

God of festivity and joy. Omacatl was worshiped primarily by the rich. At his festivites bountiful feasts and orgies were offered. He is represented as a black and white squatting figure. On his head he wears a paper coronet. Around his shoulders hangs a flower-fringed cloak. He carries a spectre, a symbol of royalty. *See also* Tezcatlipoca.

Ometecutli and Omeciuatl (Aztec, Toltec People, Mexico)

Also known as: *Ometeotl, Tonacatecutli and Tonacaciuatl* ("Lord and Lady of our Flesh").

"Lords of Duality." "Lords of the Two Sexes." They are the father and mother of mortals and have existed from the beginning. As a bisexual deity the names represent the supreme god Ometeotl. They dwell in Omeyocan and from there the souls of babes are assigned their role in life and sent to the surface of earth. They are identified with the ancestral couple, Cipactonal and Oxomoco. *See also* Ipalnemoani; Ometeotl; Tloque Nahuaque; Tonacaciutl.

Ometeotl *Ometeuctli, Ometecuhtli, Omeciuatl* (Aztec, Toltec People, Mexico)

Also known as: *Ometecutli and Omeciuatl, Tloque Nahuaque.*

"Two God." Ruler of Omeyocan, the "Place of Duality." Supreme being and creator of the universe. Ometeotl as Ometecutli and Omecuiatl is the embodiment of two persons, both god and goddess, representing dualistic, opposite forces within one deity. Ometeotl corresponds to Hunab-ku, the principal god of the Maya People. *See also* Citlanlinicue; Hunab-ku; Quetzalcoatl; Tloque Nahuaque.

Omeyocan (Aztec People, Mexico)

Home of the gods. Dwelling place of Ometeotl. The souls of babies are kept in Omeyocan until given to the mortal world. *See also* Chicunauhmictlan.

Omi (Teutonic) *see* Odin.

Omi-tsu-nu (Japan)

Earth deity. "Beach-Field-Master." Grandson of Susanowo, the storm god. He enlarged the country by tying a rope to various places and having the people pull on it.

Omicle (Phoenician) *see* Air (A); Aura.

Omidu-nu-no-kami (Japan) *see* Kushi-nada-hime.

Omito (China) *see* Amida.

Omit'o-fo (China) *see.* Amida.

Omito-Fu (China) *see* Amida; O'Mi-To-Fu.

Omiwa (Japan) *see* Okuni-Nushino-Mikoto; Suku-Na-Biko.

Omohi-kane No Kami (Japan) *see* Kami-Mimusubi.

Omorka *Omoroka* (Babylon, Chaldea)

Supreme deity. Moon or sea goddess. In one version this ruler was cut in two by Bel and one half became the sky, the other the earth. Some say she is identical with Tiamat (q.v.). *See also* Bel.

Omoroka (Babylon) *see* Omorka.

Omphale (Greek)

Omphale, the queen of Lydia, made Heracles her slave for three years. They had three children, Agelaos, Alceus and Lamus.

Omumbo-Rombonga (Africa) *see* Omumborombonga.

Omumborombonga *Omumbo-Rombonga* (Herero People, Africa)

Also known as: *Mukuru.*

Deified object. The sacred tree of life from which everything sprang. The people of the district called it Mukuru or Father Mukuru. Some versions associated this deity with Cagn (q.v.).

On (Chaldea) *see* Oannes.

Ona (Tierra del Fuego) *see* Alakaluf.

Onamuji (Japan) *see* Okuni-nushino-mikoto; Susanowo; Take-mi-kazuchi.

Onar (Teutonic) *see* Anar.

Onatah (Iroquois) *see* Onatha.

Onatha *Onatah* (Iroquois People, North America)

Goddess of wheat. She is the daughter of Eithinoha, who was called "Our Mother." Abducted by a demon of the underworld, Onatha was rescued by the sun.

Oneiroi (Greek)

The Oneiroi are the children of the god of sleep, Hypnos, or Nox, the personification of night. They represent dreams. *See also* Dreams; Ereus; Hypnos; Nox.

Oneus (Greek)

A wine connoisseur, Oneus is the host of the gods and celebrities. *See also* Calydonian Boar Hunt.

Oni (Buddhist; Japan)

Devils. These devils, often giant size, can fly. They have been known to be comic, cruel, malicious and lecherous. The function of the Oni of hell is to hunt down, capture and deliver the souls of the accused to the judges in Jigoku via a flaming chariot. The earth Oni are shape changers and can become a living being or an inanimate object. There are invisible Oni who whistle, speak or sing. The Oni who dress in red are responsible for diseases and epidemics. Some say the ancient name for these demons was Shiko-Me and Mono, and that they possibly came from China or India. Like the Kappa, the Oni have a reputation for raping women. These colorful demons are red or green with heads of oxen or horses if they are the Oni of hell. The earth Oni can be pink, blue, red, or grey in color. They have horns and sometimes three eyes, three toes and three fingers. Sometimes they carry a mallet or an iron spiked rod, and wear a loin cloth of tiger skin. They are similar to the Gaki demons. *See also* Kappa; Shiko-Me; Tengu.

Oni-tsu-nu (Japan) *see* Susanowo.

Onlar (Turkey) *see* Cin.

Onnes (Chaldea) *see* Oannes.

Onnophris (Egypt) *see* Onophris.

Ono (Hawaii; Polynesia)
Also known as: *Lono* (Hawaii), *Rongo* (Marquesas).
Ono is the son of the god of darkness, Tanaoa, and brother of Atea, the god of light. In some myths, Ono is a Kupua (trickster spirit) and fisher, born of an egg. He is one of a triad with Atea and Hakaiki. In the Marquesas, Ono as Rongo is a patron of singing. He is also associated with cultivated foods. *See also* Atea; Kupua; Rongo.

Onoophris (Egypt) *see* Aa Nefer.

Onophris (Egypt)
Also known as: *Onnophris, Onuphis, Osiris, Unnefer.*
Onophris, meaning "Good One," is a name for Osiris as god-ruler of Egypt. *See also* Osiris; Unnefer.

Onoruame (Tarahumara People, South America)
Also known as: *Our Father.*
Supreme deity. Nothing known at present. Recent discovery.

Onouris (Egypt) *see* Anhur.

Onuphis (Egypt) *see* Aa Nefer; Buchis; Onophris.

Onuris (Egypt) *see* Anhur; Ini-herit.

Onyame (Akan People, Africa)
Another spelling for Nyame.

Onyankopon *Onyankopong* (Ashanti People, Africa) *see* Nyankopong.

Onyankopong (Africa) *see* Nyankopong.

Ooyarrauyamitok (Eskimo)
A food deity. Ooyarrauyamitok sometimes resides on earth and sometimes in heaven. He can help humans procure meat.

Ope (Norse; Teutonic) Demon of torture or hysteria.

Opet (Egypt) *see* Apet; Taueret.

Ophiomorphus (Gnostic)
He is the creator serpent god, who is the son of Ialdabaoth. *See also* Archons; Horaios.

Ophion (Greek)
At one time, Ophion, the Titan, ruled Olympus with his wife, Eurynome. He was unseated from the throne and thrown into the sea or the underworld by Cronus, the god of the world, and his sister/wife Rhea, the mother of the gods. *See also* Chaos; Cronus; Eurynome (A); Rhea.

Ophois (Egypt) *see* Ap-aut; Khenti Amenti.

Ophois Wepwawet (Egypt) *see* Ap-uat.

Opian Menoetius (Greek) *see* Abderus.

Opis (Greek)
Opis is an attendant of the goddess of hunting, Artemis. *See also* Orion; Rhea.

Opita (Haiti)
The Opita are spirits of the dead who once peopled the world. They live on the island of Coaibai. They only go out at night. If you fight with an Opita, you will die.

Opo (Ashanti People, Africa)
Spirit of the ocean. A child of Nyame.

Opo-Kuni-Nusi (Japan) *see* Three Goddesses of Munakata.

Opo-yama-tu-mi-no-kami (Japan) *see* Kushi-nada-hime; Segan.

Opochtli (Aztec)
He is the god who presides over the catching of birds and fish.

Ops (Roman)
Also known as: *Rhea.*
Harvest deity. Originally, Ops was an ancient goddess of plenty who was replaced by Rhea. *See also* Cybele; Eire (Celtic); Rhea.

Oranos (Greek) *see* Nox.

Oratal (Greek) *see* Bacchus.

Orboda (Teutonic) *see* Gulveig.

Orchomenus (Greek)
He is the father of Elara, who with Zeus became the parents of the giant Tityus. Tityus was killed by either Zeus or Apollo and Artemis after he attempted to rape Leto. *See also* Apollo; Artemis; Leto; Tityus.

Orcus (Roman) *see* Dis Pater; Hades; Nox; Pluto.

Oreades (Greek) *see* Oreads.

Oreads *Oreades* (Greek)
Mountain nymphs. Oreads are the nymphs who inhabit caves and mountains. Pan, who was raised by nymphs after his mother abandoned him, enjoyed frolicking with the lithe spirits. When the goddess Artemis goes hunting, the Oreads are her attendants. They are shown as graceful women dressed in hunting costume. *See also* Artemis; Echo; Nymphs.

Orehu (Arawak People, South America)
Evil spirits. Nymphs. The Orehu are similar to mermaids who drag men and their canoes down to the bottom of rivers and lakes. In one legend they appeared to be beneficial since they gave a medicine man some unusual power. They are similar to the Yauhahu, and the Haitian Guabonito.

Oreithyia (Greek)
Oreithyia is the daughter of Erechtheus and Praxithea. She is the mother of the twins Calais and Zetes, Chione (who threw her son Eumpolus into the ocean), Cleopatra (who married Phineus), and Haemus (who was changed into a mountain). Boreas, the north wind carried Oreithyia away and raped her. *See also* Boreas; Calais; Zetes.

Orenda (Iroquois People, North America)
Also known as: *Otgon, Otkon.*
Supernatural force. The in-dwelling spirit of all things. The opposite spirit is Otgon, thought to be "bad magic." *See also* Inuat; Manitou; Oki; Wakanda.

Orendil (Teutonic) *see* Aurvandil.

Orestes (Greek)
Deified mortal. Orestes is the son of Agamemnon and Clytemnestra. He killed his mother and her lover, Aegisthus, to avenge their murder of his father. Thereafter, he was hunted by the Furies and fled from country to country. When, by Apollo's command, he submitted to trial before the Areopagus at Athens, he was acquitted and returned to Argos to ascend the throne. His spouse is Hermoine (q.v.). *See also* Aegisthus; Agamemnon; Eumenides.

Orgelmir (Teutonic) *see* Ymir.

Ori-hime (Japan) *see* Amatsu-Mikaboshi.

Orihime (Japan) *see* Amatsu-Mikaboshi.

Orin-Murt (Finnish)
Also known as: *Idem-Kuguza.*
Barn spirit. Considered a spirit of the threshing barn.

Orion *Oarion, Urion* (Greek)
Hunter. Constellation. Orion, a famous giant and hunter, was the son of the sea god Poseidon or Hyrieus, king of Hyria, and Euryale, the daughter of Minos. He became the father of the nymph Menodice. In a later account of his birth it is said that Hyrieus, king of Thrace or of Boeotian Hyria, who had been a gracious host to Poseidon, Hermes, and Zeus, was asked by the gods how they could repay him. He asked for a child. They urinated on the hide of a bull and buried it. After nine months, Orion grew up on the spot and was named Urion by his father. Orion married Side, who bragged that she was more beautiful then Hera. It is possible that this did not sit well with the jealous goddess, for Side died young and was sent to the Underworld. Orion met Merope, the daughter of Oenopion, king of Chios, and asked for her hand in marriage. As the price of betrothal Oenopion set the task, which Orion quickly accomplished, of clearing his island of wild beasts. Impatient, Orion did not wait for the wedding, he raped his fiancée and reaped the wrath of her father, who blinded him and threw him out on the beach. Orion, who had the power to walk on water, found his way to Lemnos. Out of pity, the god of fire and metalworking, Hephaistos, offered him the services of his servant, the dwarf Cedalion, who mounted on the shoulders of the giant guided him to the sun where his eyesight was restored by the sun god Helius (some say Apollo). His eyesight restored but his judgement still cloudy, he chased the daughters of Atlas, the Pleiades and possibly their mother, Pleione (whom he didn't recognize as his great grandmother), around for years until they became exhausted. To give them relief, Zeus placed them among the stars. Orion and his dog Sirius joined the moon goddess Artemis for the more traditional type of hunting. Old habits die hard; it is said that she shot him either for raping her or her attendant Opis, or out of jealousy because he slept with Eos, the goddess of dawn. In another less dramatic version, he was stung by a monster scorpion sent by the goddess Gaea (earth) and died. After death Orion became the brightest constellation in the sky along with Sirius, his faithful dog. *See also* Acacallis; Artemis; Helius; Hephaistos; Hylas; Pasiphae; Pleiades.

Orish-nla Orishanla (Yoruba People, Africa)
Also known as: *Obtala.*
Creator. The Yorubas have many rich creation myths that vary from locale to locale. Orish-nla was an Orisha (divine being), some say the first created by the supreme deity, Olodumare. He was sent to what became the city of Ife. He received a little earth in a snail shell, a hen with five toes and a pigeon. With this cache he was instructed to reorganize the primeval watery mass that was to become the earth. The birds scratched the earth, the hen scattered the dirt, and the earth spread out. In other versions, the Orisha Orunmila was with him and together they created the physical nature of the planet. Other Orishas joined them, rain began to fall and the creation of mortals followed. In a variation, Orisha-Nla was instructed to create mortals and the Olodumare would give them life. In an important variation of the creation myth pertaining to Orish-nla, he was sent to earth to create. Instead he fell into a drunken sleep from ingesting palm wine. The Orisha Oduduwa came from the celestial realm to investigate and upon seeing Orish-nla's condition, he fulfilled the creation command. This rendition explains why the followers of Orish-nla are forbidden to drink palm wine. In a variation of this myth, it is not Oduduwa who is the divine messenger but a chameleon. He gave Eshu, his servant of long standing, the gift of a plot of land to develop. The servant, himself a god of fate, was jealous and wicked and hated his function as a caregiver. He placed a huge boulder on a hill overlooking the land. When Orish-nla stopped by to see how the garden was growing, the wicked servant pushed the boulder over the ledge. It fractured Orish-nla into many pieces. The Orisha Orunmila collected the parts of Orish-nla's body and distributed them to different locations. It is said that Orish-nla had one wife. At some point, Orish-nla became the Orisha Obatala. This may be because at one time the name Orish-nla encompassed all Orishas. *See also* Obatala. Like Olodumare, Orish-nla favors the color white. He also likes snails cooked in butter. The distribution of his body parts indicates that his spirit is found in all living things. After the distribution of his body parts, the number of Orishas (gods), became four hundred and one, considered to be a sacred number to the Yoruba people. The number of Orishas in the pantheon varies with other sources, there are said to be up to twelve hundred. The chameleon as the divine messenger is also used in the myths of the Bantu and Pygmies. To compare to other creation myths of the Yoruba, *see* Olodumare. *See also* Eshu; Fa (A); Obatala.

Orish-Oke (Yoruba People, Africa) *see* Olodumare.

Orish-Oko *Possibly Orish-oke* (Yoruba People, Africa)
God of agriculture, patron of farmers.

Orisha-Oko (Yoruba People, Africa) *see* Olodumare.

Orishanla (Africa) *see* Orish-nla.

Orishas (Yoruba People, Africa) Divine spirits. *See also* Obatala; Oduduwa; Olodumare; Orish-nla; Orunmila.

Orithyia (Greek) *see* Orethyia.

Orko (Basque) God of thunderstorms.

Ormazd (Iranian) *see* Ahura Mazda.

Ormet (Norse; Teutonic)
The dead must cross this river in Helheim. *See also* Hel; Thor.

Ormizd (Armenian) *see* Aramazd.

Ormuz (Iranian) *see* Ahura Mazda.

Ormuzd *Ormazd, Ormuz* (Persia) *see* Ahura Mazda.

Ornytion (Greek)
He is the son of Sisyphus and Merope. *See also* Sisyphus.

Oro (Polynesia, Tahiti)
Also known as: *Oro-of-the-laid-down-spear.*
God of War. Oro was worshiped as one of the gods of the Polynesian priests or entertainers called Ka'ioi or Arioi. Some say he is a god of the afterlife. In the Maori version he is a peace god and the son of Ta'aroa. He is similar to Urutaetae and Hiro of the Areoi people of Tahiti. Oro is sometimes associated with the god Tane. *See also* Roma-Tane; Ta'aroa; Tane.

Orokannar (Africa) *see* Amagandar.

Oromazez (Iranian) *see* Ahura Mazda.

Oromila (Benin People, Africa)
He is a spirit of divination who might be same as Orunmila of the Yoruba People.

Oromuco (Aztec) *see* Omeciutal; Oxomoco; Xmucane.

Orpheus (Greek)
A famous lyrist, he is the son of Apollo and the musical Muse Calliope, and husband of Eurydice. He received his lyre from Apollo and played upon it so exquisitely that all things, animate and inanimate, were charmed. He is one of the heroes of the Argonaut expedition. His music enabled his shipmates to avoid being lured by the enchanting voices of the evil serpents known as the Sirens and thus they avoided certain death. On her wedding day, Eurydice, the new wife of Orpheus, was trying to escape the romantic overtures of Aristaeus, the beekeeper, said by some to be her husband's half-brother. A swarm of his bees chased her and she was bitten by a snake and died. Orpheus followed her to Hades and begged Pluto to allow her to accompany him back to earth. His request would be granted, he was told, if he would not look at his new bride until the borders of Hades had been passed. The temptation was too great. He looked — and lost her forever. In grief for her he spurned the Thracian women, who became incensed and tore him to pieces during the celebration of Dionysus. Compare Orpheus to Izanagi and Izanami (Japan). *See also* Adonis; Aeneas; Aristaeus; Cerberus; Eurydice (A); Hymen; Jason; Muses; Sirens.

Orphne (Greek)
She is called by some, the wife of Acheron. *See also* Acheron.

Orry (Celtic) *see* Ouri.

Orseis (Greek)
She is the nymph wife of Hellen. *See also* Aegimius; Aeolus (A).

Orsilochus (Greek)
Alpheus, the river god, is his father. *See also* Alpheus.

Ort (Finnish)
Also known as: *Urt.*
The name of the soul.

Ortheis (Greek) *see* Aeolus (A).

Orthrus (Greek) *see* Typhon (A).

Orula (Africa) *see* Olodumare.

Orumbe (Africa) *see* Olumbe.

Orun-Mi-La (Africa) *see* Orunmila.

Orunmila *Orun-Mi-La* ("Heaven Knows Who to Save"), (Yoruba People, Africa)
Also known as: *Fa,* (The Sky Knows Who Will Prosper), *Gbaye-Gborun* (He Who Lives on Earth and in Heaven), *Ifa.*
Sky deity. God of the oracle. God of knowledge. Messenger of the gods. God of healers. Orunmila is the eldest son of Olorun. A creation myth applied to Orunmila is similar to one told about Orish-nla. Orunmila received soil in a snail shell, a hen and a pigeon and was ordered to go to a primeval mass and create earth. In a variation, he assisted Orish-nla in creating the physical nature of the earth. A deity of divination, he served as the intercessor between the gods and mortals. As a divine messenger, knowledgeable of all languages on earth, he used a rope to commute between heaven and earth. He decided to stay in heaven but had to return to earth when Olokun, the Owner of the Sea, created havoc and made the planet uninhabitable. As Ifa, he is a physician who taught the use of herbs, attended women giving birth, and set up health clinics in many areas. While dwelling on earth, he chose sixteen disciples to study his methods of healing. His favorite food is the rat. For Orunmila's role in creation, *see* Orish-nla. Compare to the Yoruba creation myth pertaining to Oduduwa. *See also* Ifa for another aspect of his life. The Fon people of Dahomey call a similar deity Fa. Orunmila is similar to the Greek Hermes. *See also* Olokun; Olorun; Orish-nla.

Orvandel (Teutonic) *see* Aurvandil.

Osanyin (Africa)
God of curative medicine and divining.

Oschun *Oshan, Oshun* (Yoruba People, Africa)
Queen of the Sweet Water. Lady of Charity. Goddess of the river Osun. Goddess of food. She is the daughter of Oba Jumu and Oba Do. She is one of Shango's mates. Together they had human children. Their descendants still live along the river banks. Oschun is turned to in times of need. She will provide what is needed, and make the way a little easier. In later times, Oschun became popular in Cuba and Trinidad. *See* Oba (A); Olodumare; Shango.

Oshadagea (Iroquois People, North America)
God of the West. He fights the fire demons who destroy vegetation by flying with a load of water on his back and dropping it on the crops. He is known sometimes as the assistant to Hino.

Oshadi-Pati (India) Supervisor of Herbs. *See also* Soma.

Oshan (Africa) *see* Oschun.

Oshosi (Yoruba People, Africa)

He is known as the hunter and the judge. *See also* Olodumare.

Oshun (Africa) *see* Shango.

Osiris (Egypt)

Also known as: *Af-Osiris, An, Anzety, Apis, Asar, Asartait* ("The Swathed One"), *Asir, Asiri, Ausar* ("Highest of All Powers"), *Ausiri, Bull of the West, Iuwen, Onnophris, Onophris, Ptah-Sokar-Osiris, Uasir, Unnefer, Wennefer* ("The Eternally Good Being").

Osiris is one of the chief Egyptian gods and the first king of the Nile. He is the son of Seb and Nut. His siblings are Elder Horus, Set (also known as Typhon), Isis, and Nephthys. He married his sister Isis and became the father of Horus. He was given rule of the earth by his father. His station allowed him to civilize mortals by giving them laws, agriculture and religion. He also introduced viticulture and received the name Wennefer ("the eternally good being"). His wife Isis discovered wheat and barley growing wild and he introduced cultivation to the people. His vegetable aspect is symbolized by corn and many effigies made of corn husks and corn-stuffed images bandaged like mummies have been located. Osiris is thought to have been the first mummy. Like the corn, he was first trodden in the earth (burial), then rested in the dark and the new seed germinated (resurrection). Osiris was also a tree spirit. In the hall of Osiris at Denderah, the coffin containing the hawk-headed mummy of Osiris is depicted as enclosed within a tree. He is also known as "God of the Flood" and the Nile was called the "efflux of Osiris." In his aspect as a moon god he was known as Iuwen. He was referred to as a ram god. He was regularly identified with the bull of Apis of Memphis and the bull Mnevis of Heliopolis. His name may mean "place of the eye" which would correspond to his written sign. In early times, Osiris merged with Anedjti, the royal god of Bursiris. Osiris adapted his insignia of the rule, crook and flail. The phoenix, although the "ba" of Ra, the sun god, is also a manifestation of Osiris according to the *Book of the Dead*. The phallus, another manifestation attributed to the dead Osiris, is a symbol of the life forces overcoming death. Osiris's brother Set (the power of darkness and evil) was so jealous of his brother's attributes that he murdered him. The method employed varies from myth to myth. In one tale, Set enticed Osiris into a wooden box and threw him into the water where he was washed up by the sea at Byblos and discovered by Isis. She placed his remains in a coffin that Set tore open and then ripped his body into fourteen parts. Isis searched for him and wherever she found a remnant of his body, she built a shrine. (*See* Isis.) In another version of his death, Set assumed the shape of a wild boar and ripped Osiris limb to limb. A variation of this tale has Set hunting a boar and coming across the mangled body of his brother. Yet another version gives Set an accomplice, Thot. They trap Osiris, tear his body to pieces and throw him into the water. After death, Osiris became Lord of the Underworld and Judge of the Dead. He represents the sun who is overcome by night but who rises again the next morning. Reincarnated he was known as Apis. After the beginning of the Middle Kingdom all transfigured dead became Osiris, who is a symbol of resurrection. His mythical resurrection was ascribed to Anubis' knowledge of embalming, to Isis who gave him breath by flapping her wings above him and Horus who gave him the eye of Horus (gouged out by Set). Under Osiris the Egyptians were persuaded to give up cannibalism. He taught them farming, the pleasures of music and framed a legal code for them. The major cult shrine was at Abydos where an important temple was erected by Seti I in the Nineteenth Dynasty. The Greeks associated him with Dionysus and Hades. He is usually shown as a man with a beard, bound around with the clothes used in mummification but with his two hands free enough to hold a shepherd's crook and a whip, both of them symbols of authority. Osiris is sometimes joined with other gods, and depending on the god he wears a different costume. For example, Osiris-Aah is portrayed with a crescent moon or full moon on his head. The color of his skin is depicted as white (like mummy wrappings), black (the realm of the dead) or green (resurrection). There are over one hundred and fifty names or aspects of Osiris; i.e., Af-Osiris, an aspect of Osiris meaning the "flesh of Osiris." He is named Iuwen in his aspect as moon-god. Osiris is associated with Adonis (Greek), Eshmun (Phoenicia), and Tammuz (Babylon). *See also* Aani; Aaru; Aati; Ab-esh-imyduat; Adonis; Ament; Amentet; Anubis; Apis (A); Apis (B); Atum; Dionysus; Horus; Isis; Mnevis; Niobe (B); Onophris; Serapis; Set; Styx (Greek); Typhon (A); Wenenu.

Osiris-Apis (Egypt) *see* Apis (A); Serapis.

Osiris-Hapi (Egypt) *see* Apis (A).

Oski (Teutonic) *see* Odin.

Osorapis (Egypt) *see* Apis (A); Serapis.

Ossa (Greek)

Ossa is a sacred mountain in Thessaly, upon which the Giants piled Mount Pelion in order to climb to the heavens. *See also* Olympus.

Ostra (Teutonic) *see* Eastre.

Osun (Africa) *see* Oschun.

Ot (Mongolia)

She is a fire queen and goddess of marriage who is associated with Umai (q.v.).

Otafuku (Japan) *see* Ame-no-uzume.

Oter (Teutonic) *see* Ottar.

Otgon (Iroquois People, North America) *see* Orenda.

Othin (Teutonic) *see* Odin.

Othinn (Teutonic) *see* Odin.

Othinus (Teutonic) *see* Odin.

Othrevir (Teutonic) *see* Odraerir.

Othroerir (Teutonic) *see* Odraerir.

Othur (Teutonic) *see* Od or Odin.

Oti (Africa) *see* Cagn.

Otkon (Iroquois People, North America) *see* Orenda.

Otontecutli (Aztec) *see* Huitzilopochtli; Xocotl.

Otos (Phoenician) *see* Air (A); Aura.

Otr (Teutonic) *see* Ottar.

Otrera (Greek)

Otrera was one of the Amazon queens. She married Ares and became the mother of Antiope, Hippolyte and Penthesileia. *See also* Antiope, Ares; Hippolyte.

Otshirvani (Central Asia)

In this myth, the creator god Otshirvani and his assistant, Chagan-Shukuty, came down from heaven. They saw a turtle (some say frog) diving in the water. Otshirvani caught the turtle and placed it on its back. Shukuty dove in and brought up some earth from the bottom. The earth was placed on the turtle's stomach. Shulmus, the devil, climbed on the stomach with them in order to drown them. Otshirvani, trying to escape, caused the earth to increase to its present size. *See also* Vajrapani (India).

Ottar *Oter, Otr, Ottarr, Otter* (Norse; Teutonic)

Sea deity. Son of Hreidmar and brother of Fafnir and Regin. A fisherman, he changed into an otter. He was murdered by Loki. *See also* Andarvi; Fafnir; Hreidmar; Sigurd.

Ottarr (Teutonic) *see* Ottar.

Otter (Teutonic) *see* Ottar.

Otua (Polynesia) *see* Atea.

Otus (Greek)

Otus and his twin brother, Ephialtes, are known as the Aloeides. They are the sons of the sea god Poseidon or possibly Aloeus and Iphimedeia. Otus was the first to worship the Muses. *See also* Aloeides; Muses.

Oulapatou (Tierra del Fuego)

Also known as: *Wild Men of the West.*

The Oulapatou are dangerous spirits of the dead. They are invisible except when cutting the throats of sleeping people and eating their limbs. Although invisible most of the time, they are able to imitate the sounds of birds and animals. The Oulapatou are generally thought of as the dead who return to earth as evil spirits. *See also* Taquatu.

Oulomos (Phoenician)

Born by Ether and Air, he produced Chousorus, according to the Creation Legend of Mochus. *See also* Air (C).

Ouranos (Greek) *see* Uranus.

Ourea (Greek) *see* Gaea.

Ouri (Celtic)

Also known as: *Orry.*

An early sun god.

Ousoos (Phoenician)

He was the first to use skins for garments. His brother Hyposouranios was the first to build towns. *See also* Fire.

Ouvin (Teutonic) *see* Odin.

Ovinnik (Slavic)

Barn spirits. The Ovinnik are mischief-making spirits who live in barns. They have been known to set barns on fire. If there is a large, ragged black cat wandering around the property, it is likely an Ovinnik. They are one of the Domovoi spirits and are similar to the Bannik. *See also* Bannik; Domovoi.

Ox-Face (China) *see* Niu-Y'ou.

Ox-Head (China) *see* Ma-Mien; Men Shen; Niu-Y'ou.

Oxlus (Greek)

He is the son of Ares and Protogeneia. *See also* Ares.

Oxomoco *Oromuco, Oxomuco* (Aztec People, Mexico)

Also known as: *Piltzintecutli* (probably), *Xmucane* (Maya).

First man. Oxomoco and his wife, Cipactonal, were created by the four first gods. These gods were Camaxtli, Tezcatlipoca, Quetzalcoatl and Huitzilopochtli. The son of Oxomoco and Cipactonal married a woman made from the hair of the goddess Xochiquetzal. In some legends of the Hopi and Zuni Indians, Tamagostad and Cipattoval are identical with Oxomoco and Cipactonal. In some Mayan legends Oxomoco and Cipactonal are similar to Xpiyacoc and Xmucane. *See also* Camaxtli; Cipactonal; Legend of the Four Suns; Tamagostad; Xmucane.

Oxomuco (Aztec) *see* Omeciutal; Oxomoco.

Oxyrhynchus (Egypt)

Also known as: *Mormyrus Kannume.*

Deified fish. The Oxyrhynchus was worshipped in the Egyptian city of the same name and renounced in other sections as it was the fish said to have eaten the phallus of Osiris after he was chopped to pieces by the evil god Set. *See also* Osiris; Set.

Oya (Yoruba People, Africa)

Goddess of violent rainstorms. Chief wife of the three wives of Shango. The others are Oschun and Oba. Shen, her husband, disappeared, she turned into the River Niger. *See also* Olodumare; Oschun; Shango.

Ozun (Yoruba People, Africa) "The Communicator." *See also* Olodumare.

P

Pa (China)
Goddess of Drought. *See also* Huang Ti.

Pa-cha *Pa Ch'a* (China)
Pa-cha is a local god who is a protector against locusts. He began life as a mortal who became a general under the name of Liu Meng-tsaing-kun or Liu T'ai-wei. After death he was deified. Pa-cha is shown as a soldier with an eagle's beak or as a man with a bird's beak and feet, wearing a petticoat. He has unusually long fingernails.

Pa Hsien (China)
Also known as: *Eight Immortals, Pa Kung.*
See also Eight Immortals.

Pa Kung (China) *see* Pa Hsien.

Pa-yama-to-no-kami (Japan) *see* Ukemochi.

Pacari (Inca People, Peru)
The four brothers and sisters who founded the four religions of Peru are said to have come from Pacari, the Cave of Refuge. The first brother was Pachacamac, the second unnamed, the third was Viracocha, and Manco Capac was the fourth. In another version of this myth, two brothers, Apocatequil and Piguerao, with the help of Atagucho, cut their way out of the cave. *See also* Apocatequil; Inca Creation Legends.

Paccari Tampu (Inca People, Peru)
House of the gods. The House of the Dawn. It is a cave south of Cuzco on the Vilcamija River where Manco Capac and his brothers first appeared on earth.

Pachacamac *Pacha-Camak* (Pre-Inca, later incorporated into Inca)
Also known as: *Pacharurac* (Maker), *Viracocha* (possibly).
Supreme god. Creator. Earth god. All things emanate from Pachacamac. He is the son of the sun, Inti, and brother of Manco Capac and Viracocha. His spouse is the earth mother Pachamama. His greatest rival is Viracocha ("Foam of the Lake"). Pachacamac has the attributes of a culture hero, for he taught useful arts and crafts to the people. He is affiliated with Coniraya (q.v.). *See also* Bachue; Manco Capac; Pacari; Pachayachachic.

Pacharurac (Peru) *see* Pachacamac.

Pachayachachic (Peru)
Creator and possible director of the universe. He was brought into being in the later Inca times. *See also* Pachacamac.

Pachamama *Pacha-Mama* (Pre-Inca, Peru)
Earth mother. Some call her the wife of Pachacamac and others the wife of the sun god, Inti. Animals, particularly llamas were offered to her as sacrifice. Pachamama is still worshipped in Peru, where some identify her with the Christian Virgin Mary. *See also* Pachacamac.

Padma (India) Lotus Goddess. *See also* Lakshmi.

Padma Dakinis (India) *see* Dakinis.

Padma Krotishaurima (Tibet)
She is found in the Bardo World on the eleventh day offering a red shell full of blood to Padmaheruka (q.v.). *See also* Karmakrotishaurima; Ratna Krotishaurima; Shakti.

Padma-pam (India) *see* Padmapani.

Padma Sambhav (Tibet) *see* Samantabhadra.

Padmaheruka (Tibet) *see* Herukas; Padma Krotishaurima.

Padmapani *Padma-pam* (India)
An epithet of Avalokitesvara.

Padmavati (India) *see* Nagas and Nagis.

Paeon (A) (Greek)
He is the son of Nestor and Eurydice. One of his siblings is Antilochus (q.v.).

Paeon (B) (Greek) Another name for Apollo's son Asclepius.

Paeon (C) (Greek)
Possibly a son of Poseidon and Helle. Brother of Edonus. They are part of the Edoni tribe.

Pagoda (Buddhist) *see* Bishamon; Diakoku; Stupa.

P'ags-skyes-po (Tibet) *see* Virudhaka.

Pah (Pawnee People, North America)
He is the moon god spouse of Shakura, the sun, and father of one child. He was placed in the west by the creator god, Tirawa (q.v.).

Paha (Finnish) *see* Hiisi.

Pahulu (Hawaii)
An ancient goddess of sorcery who ruled Lanai, Molokai and a sect of Maui.

Pai (Egypt)
Guardian. He guards the twelfth sector of Tuat.

Pai Mu-tan (China)
Also known as: *White Peony.*
A courtesan, Pai Mu-tan is called upon to distract practicing ascetics. She fell in love with Lu Tung-pin, who accompanied her to the bridge leading to Paradise. As "White Peony,"

she is the symbol of wealth, honor, love and female beauty. *See also* Apsarases (India); Pramlocha (India).

Paia (Polynesia) *see* Rangi.

Pairikas *Pairika* (Zoroastrian; Persia)
Also known as: *Paris.*
These female demons are spirits of seduction who cast spells on everything. They are known to cause shooting stars and meteors. They are the counterparts of the Yata. *See also* Ameshas Spenta; Angra Mainyu; Drujs; Yata.

Pairimaiti (Persia) *see* Spenta Armaiti.

Pais (Armenia) *see* Hambaris.

Paisacha (India) *see* Pishachas.

Pakadringa (Aborigine People, Melville Island, Australia)
A thunder god. He was the son of Quork-quork. He, along with Tomituka, the monsoon rain goddess, and Bumerali, live in Tuniruna, the upperworld, during the dry season, but at the end of the season they travel together. Tomituka brings the rain, Bumerali brings lightning, and Pakadringa brings thunder. Some say it is Bumerali's voice that makes the thunder. *See also* Tomituka.

Pakasasana (India) *see* Indra.

Pakhet (Egypt) *see* Sekhmet.

Pakheth (Egypt) *see* Pakht.

Pakht *Pakheth* (Egypt)
Also known as: *Bast.*
Pakht, a goddess with the head of a lioness, is identified with Bast. She guards the entrance to dwellings and tombs. *See also* Bast.

Palaechthon (Greek)
He is the son of the earth, Gaea. He became the father of the king of Argos, Pelasgus.

Palaemon (Roman)
Also known as: *Melicertes* (Greek), *Portunus* (Latin).
Palaemon is the Roman god of ports and harbors. The Isthmian Games were founded in his honor. He could be connected with Janus, the god of beginnings and endings. *See also* Melkart.

Pales (Roman)
Pales is an ancient rustic god (he is both male and female), who may have been a god of cattle. He is possibly connected with the Greek Palikoi, who are twin sons of Zeus and Thalia (qq.v.). There is also a pastoral goddess named Pales. Each spring during her celebration, known as Parilia, fires of straw were lit and people passed through them to be purified.

Palici (Greek)
The Palici are the twin male Sicilian volcanoes born from the bowels of the earth. Their parents are said to be either Zeus and his daughter Thalia, or Hephaistos and Aetna. *See also* Hephaistos; Thalia.

Palladium (Greek)
Deified object. The Palladium is a wooden image of Pallas Athene at Troy, on which the safety of the city depended. (Some say it was a metal image.) It was stolen by Odysseus, the king of Ithaca, and Diomedes, the king of Aetolia, and rescued by Aeneas, known as the founder of the Roman race.

Pallantia (Greek)
Her parents are Evander (also known as Evandrus) and Deidamia, the daughter of Bellerophon and Philonoe. Her siblings are Pallas, the founder of the Pallanteum in Italy, Roma and Sarpedon II. Her son by Heracles was named after her brother, Pallas. *See also* Deidamia; Evander; Pallas; Sarpedon (B).

Pallas (A) (Greek) An epithet of Athene (q.v.).

Pallas (B) (Greek)
He is the giant son of Uranus and Gaea who was skinned alive by Athena during the battle of the gods and Giants. *See also* Athena; Gaea; Giants; Uranus.

Pallas (C) (Greek)
Evander and Deidamia are his parents. His siblings are Pallantia, Roma and Sarpedon. He was associated with Aeneas. *See also* Aeneas; Evander (B); Pallantia; Sarpedon (B).

Pallas (D) (Greek)
The son of Crius and Eurybia, his siblings are Astraeus and Perses. His marriage to the Oceanid, Styx, the ruler of the underworld river, produced Bia, Kratos, Nike and Zelos. *See also* Astraeus; Crius; Nike; Styx.

Pallas (E) (Greek)
Heracles and Pallantia are his parents.

Pallas (F) (Greek)
He is the son of Lycaon and Cyllene. He became the father of Chryse (q.v.).

Pallas (G) (Greek)
His father is Megamedes and his children are possibly Eos, Helios, and Selene.

Pallas (H) (Greek)
The daughter of Triton (who is the son of Posedion and Amphitrite), she was accidentally killed by her friend the goddess of war, Athena.

Pallas Athena (Greek) *see* Pallas.

Pallas Athene (Greek) *see* Pallas.

Pallor (Greek)
Pallor, the god of terror, is the son of the god of war, Ares, and his sister, the goddess of love, Aphrodite. His siblings are Anteros, the god of passion; Deimos, the god of fear; Enyo, the goddess of war; Eros, the god of love; Harmonia, who was later turned into a snake by her father; and Phobos, the god of fear and terror. *See also* Anteros; Ares; Deimos; Eros; Harmonia (A); Phobos.

Palmyra (Mesopotamia) *see* Ba'al Shamin.

Palta (Greek) *see* Rhea.

Paltar (Teutonic) *see* Balder.

Palulop (Micronesia)
God of Navigators. God of knowledge. In some myths, he

is the son of Alulei. He is the father of Rongerik and Rongela-panp or Alulei. He is also said to be the father of Big Rong, Little Rong, and Faravai. *See also* Alulei; Rongerik.

Palulukon (Hopi People, North America)

He is the Great Serpent, considered the master of rain and lightning. Palulukon is the same as Koloowisi of the Zuni People. *See also* Kokko.

Pamola (Algonquin People, North America)

He is an evil spirit of the night. *See also* Gluskap.

Pamphylus (Greek)

Aegimius, the king of the Dorians, is his father and his brother is Dymas, the Trojan who disguised himself as a Greek during the Trojan War. *See also* Aegimius.

Pan (Greek)

Also known as: *Aegipan, Consentes, Faunus* (Roman).

The god of woods, fields, and wildlife. God of flocks. Patron of hunters, shepherds. Inventor of the panpipes (syrinx). Pan's parents are Hermes and Dryope or Hermes and Penelope, or Zeus and Callisto, or Zeus and Hybris, or Apollo and a wood nymph. Pan was abandoned by his mother and raised by nymphs. He was very fond of music, enjoyed dancing with the nymphs and mischievously frightening people who walked through forests at night. When Hermes took Pan to Olympus, the gods were pleased with his delightful music and impish countenance. He is represented as having two small horns, a flat nose, and the lower limbs of a goat. He is often depicted wearing the ears of an ass, an emblem of acute perception. Apollo gave the ears of an ass to Midas for enjoying Pan's music. In this instance, it was to ridicule the king. Compare Pan to Bacchus and Silenus to whom the ass was a sacred animal. The Greeks identify him with the Egyptian god Ba-neb-djet, also a ram-god. Pan is sometimes confused with the Satyrs. *See also* Acis; Aegipan; Aegis; Evander (A); Min; Silvanus.

P'an Chin-Lien *P'an Kin-Lien* (China)

She is a goddess of fornication and patroness of prostitutes. When she was a young widow, her brother-in-law caught her with her lover and killed him. In other legends she is a mortal widow killed by her father because of her bad habits. After death, she was deified. *See also* Hariti; Kuan Yin.

P'an Kin-Lien (China) *see* P'an Chin-Lien.

Pan-Ku (Chinese) *see* Chaos.

P'an Ku (Taoist; China)

Also known as: *Yuan-shih T'ien-wang.*

P'an Ku is sometimes called the creator of the universe, which he formed with a hammer and chisel. His creation took eighteen thousand years. Each day he grew six feet taller than the day before. When his project was completed, he died so that creation could live. He is called the giant who became the world. His voice is thunder, his breath the wind and his tears (some say his blood), the rivers. His limbs are the four quarters of the world, the soil was formed from his flesh, and the constellations from his beard. Herbs and trees were produced from his skin and teeth. His bones and marrow gave us precious stones, metals and rocks. His perspiration produced the rain. Insects crawling across his body became mortals. In other variations,

he is said to have been born in the egg of chaos. It is also said that he was born from Yin and Yang, the dual forces of nature. He is described as having a body four times the size of that of an ordinary mortal. Two horns project from his head, and two tusks from his upper jaw. His body is thickly covered with hair. He is also depicted as a small man, dressed in bearskin or leaves. He holds a hammer in his right hand and a chisel in his left hand (sometimes the tools are reversed). Sometimes he holds the moon in one hand and the sun in the other hand. He is often shown with a dragon, unicorn, phoenix and tortoise. In some legends, he is depicted with the body of a serpent and the head of a dragon. *See also* Adam; Adhibuddha; Buddha; Gaya Maretan; Purusha; Ymir.

P'an-T'ao *Fan T'ao* (China)

Also known as: *Shen-T'ao.*

Divine fruit. The P'an-T'ao are the peaches of the orchard of heaven (Huang t'ien) that ripened only once in three thousand years and bestowed immortality. To the Chinese, the peach became the symbol of long life, as did the tortoise. There is some confusion whether the peaches or the tree that bears them are named P'an-T'ao or Shen-T'ao. These peaches were the property of Queen Mother Hsi Wang Mu (Wang-mu-niang-niang) and Yu-huan-shang-Ti (the Jade Emperor). *See also* Hsi-Wang-Mu.

Panacea (Greek)

She is the goddess of health, daughter of Asclepius and Epione. *See also* Asclepius.

Pancasirsha, Mount *Pancaskiki, Mount* (Nepal) *see* Manjusri.

Panch Buddhas (Nepal) *see* Dhyani Buddhas.

Pancha-muke (India) *see* Nagas.

Panchajana (India)

Panchajana was originally a sea demon who lived in a conch shell under the ocean. He kidnapped Sandipani's son. Krishna, infuriated, dove into the water, killed him, and took his shell to use as a trumpet. When the horn is blown sinners are annihilated. During ceremonies a small shell, the symbol of Krishna's conch shell, is used to pour holy water over the image of Krishna. Worshipers often have an image of the conch shell branded on their arms. *See also* Krishna.

Panchali (India)

Another name for Draupadi (q.v.).

Panchashirsha, Mount *Pancaskika, Pancasirsha* (Nepal) *see* Manjusri.

Panchika (Buddhist; India)

He is the son of the ogress Hariti, and possibly Kuvera, the chief of the Yakshas. In Nepal, Panchika is known as the god of the purse. He is depicted with Hariti and his symbol is the pike. Panchika is similar to Jambhala and Kuvera (qq.v.). *See also* Hariti; Yaksha.

Pandara *Pandaravasani* (Buddhist; India)

Pandara, known as the "White-clad One," is the sakti (consort) of Amitabha. In an ancient legend, it is said that Pandara wore clothing made of stone, which could only be cleaned by fire. She is depicted as a beautiful woman, wearing flowers in her hair, many ornaments, holding two lotus flowers and seated on a lotus. She symbolizes the all-consuming essence of fire which is also purifying and leads to compassion. Her color is rose, her position (asana) is lalitasana (one leg pendant, the other in the position of a Buddha). Her emblems are the cakra (Buddhist wheel), kapala (altar object), padma (lotus), and utpala (blue lotus). Her mudras are varada (her arm pendant with fingers and palm extended outward) and vitarka (her arm bent, fingers extended upward, except the index finger, which touches the tip of the thumb, the palm outward). The varada signifies gift-bestowing or charity and the vitarka signifies argument. *See also* Amitabha; Dhyani Buddhas.

Pandaravasani *Pandaravasini* (Tibet) (India) *see* Avalokitesvara; Pandara.

Pandareus (Greek)

The son of Merops of Miletus and a nymph, Pandareus became the king of Miletus in Crete. He married Harmothoe and became the father of Aedon, who became a nightingale after trying to commit suicide and Cleothera and Merope, who were kidnapped by the bird-like monster sisters the Harpies and forced to serve the Erinyes. Pandareus and Merope were killed by Zeus after stealing the statue of a golden dog made by Hephaistos, the god of fire. *See also* Aedon; Cleothera; Merope; Zethus.

Pandavas, The (Hindu; India)

The noble Pandavas were the heirs of Pandu, the son of Ambalika and Vyasa. Fertility gods and guardians of crops, they were born of virgin birth by their mothers, Kunti (also known as Pritha) and Madri. The eldest Pandava, Yudhisthira, the son of the god Dharma, known for his integrity, is Krishna's companion. The others are Bhima, a fiery-tempered giant, the son of the wind god Vayu; Arjuna, the son of Indra, known as chivalrous; and Nakula and Sahadeva, wise and beautiful twins who are the sons of the Asvins. The Pandavas shared the beautiful goddess Draupadi as their wife. When they were exiled for thirteen years by the Kauravas, who represent the winter or drought, the earth was not fertile. The struggle between the Pandavas and their jealous cousins, the one hundred Kauravas, is known as the "Great Battle of Kurukseta." It lasted eighteen days and is described in the *Mahabharata*. The five Pandavas are symbolic of the five senses and the five elements. *See also* Arjuna; Asvins; Bala-Rama; Bharadvaja; Bhima (A); Bhishma; Brihaspati; Dharma; Duryodhana; Indra; Jara-Sandha; Kali; Kauravas; Krishna; Kunti; Madri; Maya (C); Pandu; Satyavati; Tapati; Visvakarma; Vyasa; Yudhisthira.

Panderces (Greek) "All-seeing." *See also* Helius.

Pandora (Greek)

First woman. Zeus, enraged at the theft of the celestial fire by Prometheus, had Hephaistos, the god of fire, mould a woman from clay whose beauty would cause strife among the human race. The gods gave her various gifts: charm, beauty, the art of healing, eloquence, skills in woman's work and the ability to sing. In one myth, Zeus gave her the beautiful box and forbade her to open it. Her curiosity overcame her and when she opened it every human ill and plague escaped into the world, leaving only "hope" (Elpis) in the box. Another myth states that

Epimetheus had the box in his house and Pandora found it when they married, opened it against his warnings and all human sorrows and sufferings were let loose except hope. "Pandora's Box," therefore, has come to mean something that appears valuable, but is, in truth, a curse. There is a parallel to the story of the Vedic deity Vishnu (q.v.) *See also* Epimetheus; Hephaistos.

Pandrosos *Pandrosus* (Greek)

She is the daughter of Acteus and Agraulos or Cecrops and Agraulos. Her siblings are Agraulos, Erysichthon and Herse. *See also* Acteus; Agraulos.

Pandu (India) *see* Arjuna; Bhishma; Duryodhana; Kunti; Pandavas; Vyasa.

Panhellenius (Greek)

"God of all Greeks." An epithet of Zeus.

Pani *Panis* (Hindu; India)

The Pani are devious aerial dwarf demons who live on the other side of the River Rasa and are Indra's enemies. They inspire foolish acts and encourage slander and disbelief. Compare the Pani to the Darbas and the Pishachas. *See also* Hiranyagarbha.

Pannagas (India) *see* Nagas; Nagis.

Panopae (Greek) *see* Nereids.

Panope (Greek)

Panope is one the the fifty daughters, known as the Nereids, of Nereus and Doris. *See also* Doris; Nereids; Nereus.

Panpati (India) *see* Ganesha.

Panther, The (Iroquois People, North America) *see* Dajoji.

Papa (A) *Fakahotu, Hakahotu, Papa-tu-a-nuku, Tu-metua.* (Polynesia; New Zealand)

First goddess. Goddess of earth and fertility. The female element. Opposite of Te Tumu. Her spouse is Wakea, Vatea or Rangi. Her origins vary in different myths. With Rangi, the sky as her spouse, we find them so entwined that light cannot shine through their entities. The gods, highly annoyed, talked of killing them. Finally, Rongo, Tangaroa, Haumia, and Tu tried to pry them apart, but were not successful. Papa and Rangi's son, Tane, after great effort, was able to separate his parents. Another son, Tawhiri, the god of winds, worried that his parents would be injured, created storms in an attempt to stop Tane. The storms created havoc and many creatures from the sea fled to the swamps. Tangaroa lost many of his subjects. This caused a rift between the brothers who have been enemies since that time. In another legend Papa is the goddess Tu-metua, who is the daughter of Timatekore (Tima-te-kore), and his wife Tamaiti-ngava-ringavari. Papa is the consort of Vatea. They had five children: Tangaroa, Rongo, Tonga-iti, Tangiia, and Tane. In another version, a sky god named Rehua was one of the sons of Rangi and Papa. In one legend Papa-tu-a-nuku (who was probably Papa) was the unfaithful wife of Tangaroa. She had a alliance with Rangi which resulted in a fight between Tangaroa and Rangi. *See* Adam; Maui; Rangi; Tangaroa; Tawhaki; Vatea.

Papa (B) (Mexico) *see* Topiltzin.

Papa-Tu-Anuku (Polynesia) *see* Papa (A).

Papa-tu-a-nuku (Polynesia)

Earth deity. One of the wives of Rangi. Their children are Rehua, Tane, Paia, Tu, Rongo and Ru. One version relates that Papa-tu-a-nuku was the wife of Tangaroa. She left him for Rangi, which caused a fight between the two gods. *See also* Rangi.

Papalguenna (Babylonia) *see* Marduk.

Papsukkal *Papukkal, Papsukal* (Mesopotamia)

He is the chief minister of the gods of heaven. *See also* Ilabrat; Ishtar; Ninsubur; Tammuz.

Papukkal (Sumer) *see* Papsukkal.

Paqok (Mexico) *see* Shtabai.

Par (Egypt)

Par is a form of the god Amen-Ra, called the "Lord of the Phallus," "Lofty of Plumes," and "Lord of Transformation, whose Skins are Manifold," The goddess Sekh-met-Bast-Ra is the female counterpart of Par. She is the "Phallus Goddess." *See also* Amen.

Para (India) *see* Vach.

Parae (Greek) *see* Fates.

Parameshthin Prajapatya (India) *see* Agni; Indra; Prajapati; Soma.

Parashara (Brahmanic, Hindu, India)

He is a Brahmin, a Rishi (arch-priest) and poet, son of Adrisyanti and King Kalmashapada who turned into the demon, Shaktar. Parashara later became the spouse of Satyavati and as a result of embracing her, the father of Vyasa. A section of the Himalayas was burnt when he performed a sacrifice. *See also* Satyavati; Rishi; Vyasa.

Parashur Rama *Parasu-Rama, Parasuraman, Purrishram, Pursurama* (Brahmanic, Hindu, India)

"Rama with an Axe." Parashur Rama is the sixth avatar of Vishnu. In this avatar, he returned to earth in human form as a Brahmin, the youngest of the five sons of the sage Jamadagni (also known as Jemdekhen) and Renuka (also spelled Runeeka). The Kshatriyas, a class of warriors, had gained power in the world. The gods felt that the power should be placed in the hands of the priests instead of the warriors and possibly the Vaishya, who were farmers, merchants, and tradespeople. The rationale was that learned men would provide an honest and peaceful environment. They dispatched Vishnu to earth as Parashur Rama to rectify the problem. Parashur Rama was taught the art of weaponry by Shiva, who gave him the battle axe known as Parashu. Parashur Rama in turn instructed Arjuna how to use weapons. Jamadagni and Renuka entertained the king with a thousand arms, Kartavirya. When he left their dwelling, he helped himself to a calf. This was not an ordinary calf. It was Kamadhenu, the Cow of Plenty, who could grant all desires. Parashu Rama killed the king and the king's sons in turn killed Jamadagni. Incensed, Parashur Rama eliminated all Kshatriyas from the earth. At a later time, the sea god Varuna gave Parashur Rama a tract of land that had previously been under water. Parashur Rama called it Malabara and opened it for settlement to all the Brahmins. In another legend, Parashur Rama is disguised as a monk. Indra had left his cow, Kamad-henu, the Cow of Plenty, in the care of the monks to keep the Kshatriyas from abducting her. Parashur Rama took care of the threat by killing the enemies. Their dead bodies cluttered the earth, leaving no room for the Brahmin. Parashur Rama appealed to Varuna who agreed to give him as much land as his arrow could cover when shot from his bow. Yama overheard this discussion and took the shape of an ant so he could nibble at the bow and insure that the arrow would not cover an extensive territory. His plot worked. Parashur's arrow merely glided to Malabara. Originally Parashur Rama was not an avatar of Vishnu. He did, however, have Vishnu's bow. His wife was Dharani, the Earth. In time, he was incorporated as one of the less important avatars of Vishnu. Compare the ant myth to a similar myth pertaining to Vishnu's death (q.v.) *See also* Kamadhenu; Lakshmi; Vamana (Vishnu's avatar as a dwarf); Vishnu; Yama.

Parasu-Pani (India) *see* Bhavani.

Parasu-Rama (India) *see* Parashur Rama.

Parasurama (India) *see* Parashur Rama.

Parasuraman (India) *see* Parashur Rama.

Paravani (India) Sacred peacock. *See also* Karttikeya.

Paravataksha (India) *see* Naga.

Parbati (India) *see* Devi; Parvati.

Parca (Roman)

Also known as: *Morta.*

Parca is the goddess of childbirth. She is one of the Parcae. *See also* Fates.

Parcae (Roman)

Roman name for the Fates. *See also* Fates; Moirai; Parca.

Parganya (India) *see* Parjanya.

Pariacaca (Inca People, Peru)

Creator deity. He was one of five eggs hatched by a falcon. Pariacaca was the creator while the other four eggs became the four winds. Later, all became men. *See also* Coniraya; Huacas; Pacha-Camac; Yananamca Intanamca.

Pariae (Greek) "Ancient Ones." *See also* Fates; Graces.

Parijata Tree *Kalpa Tree, World Tree* (Hindu; India)

The Parijata Tree is the Hindu tree of the universe. It is owned by Indrani, the wife of Indra, and is planted in Swarga, the celestial dwelling place of Indrani and Indra. The Parijata Tree was found at the bottom of the Ocean of Milk when the waters were churned. At one point, Krishna's wife demanded it for herself. A battle issued between Krishna and Indra and Krishna emerged the victor. The Parijata was taken to Dvarka until Krishna died and it was returned to Indrani, though some say that Krishna returned it of his own accord. Swarga is located between heaven and earth on Mount Meru. If the elderly gaze upon the magic wishing tree, they are reinvigorated. The Parijata Tree is said to yield all objects of desire. *See also* Andhaka; Indra; Indrani; Krishna; Kurma, Lakshmi; Satyabhama; Swarga.

Parikshit (Hindu, India)

The king of Hastinapura and patron of poetry, Parikshit is the grandson of the warrior Arjuna and the son of Abhimanya and Uttara. He was killed before birth by Ashvatthaman and brought back to life by Krishna. *See also* Abhimanya; Arjuna; Ashvatthaman; Krishna.

Paris (A) (Greek)

He is the second son of the king of Troy, Priam, and his queen, Hecuba (daughter of the Trojan river god, Cebren). His siblings are Aesacus, Cassandra, Creusa, Deiphobus, Hector, Helenus, Polyxena and Troilus. Paris mated with the water nymph Oenone and they became the parents of two boys, Corythus and Daphnis. When Hecuba was pregnant with Paris, she had a terrible nightmare about giving birth to a firebrand that destroyed Troy. When Paris was born Priam forced his chief herdsman, Agelaus, to take the infant to Mount Ida and to leave him there exposed and alone. He was suckled by a she-bear for five days. Agelaus returned to rescue the baby and to raise him as his own son. Later, Paris reconciled with his birth parents. During his youth, he became an excellent herdsman, archer, and musician. A handsome man, he had also developed an eye for beauty. During the marriage festivities for Peleus and Thetis, the goddess of discord Eris arrived in an angry mood. She was the only deity not invited to the affair. She tossed a golden apple bearing the inscription "For the Fairest" among the guests. Three beauties claimed it: Aphrodite, Athene, and Hera. Paris was called upon to decide which goddess was "the fairest." He choose Aphrodite. Athene and Hera were furious with him. He abducted Helen from the event and took off for Greece. When he refused to return Helen, the Greeks marched against Troy, and so the Trojan War began. When Troy was captured Paris was hit by a poisoned arrow belonging to Heracles, but shot by Philoctetes. Wounded, he returned to his wife Oenone to be healed. Understandably, she rejected him and departed. Overcome with guilt, she returned to find him dead. She hanged herself. *See* Atalanta who was also exposed and suckled by a she-bear. *See also* Achilles; Agamemnon; Ajax the Greater; Cassandra; Eris; Helen; Hesione.

Paris (B) (Persia) *see* Pairikas.

Parjanya *Parganya, Parjanya-vata* (Rain and Wind); (Vedic; India)

Parjanya, an Aditya, is the third on the list of the twelve names or forms of the sun god Surya. He may have been the husband of the earth goddess Prithiva. Parjanya abides in the clouds and with his rays sends water to earth. He could be the same as Perkunis (Armenian) and Perun (Slavonic). *See also* Adityas; Indra; Prithiva; Soma; Surya; Varuna.

Parjanya-vata (India) *see* Parjanya.

Parnasavari (India) *see* Tara.

Parnassus (Greek)

Deified mountain. A mountain in Phocis, dedicated to Apollo, Dionysus and the Muses.

Parthenia (Greek) An epithet of the virgin goddesses Artemis, Athena and Hestia.

Parthenopaeus (Greek) *see* Adrestus; Ares.

Parthenos (Greek) *see* Athena.

Partholanians (Irish) *see* Partholon.

Partholon *Partholan* (Irish)

Master of all crafts. Partholon, the leader of his people, the Partholanians, arrived in Ireland via Spain. They encountered the Fomorians, an evil race of giants. *See also* Banbha; Beltine; Cessair.

Partholonians (Irish) *see* Partholon.

Parusha (India) *see* Purusha.

Parvata (India) *see* Parvati.

Parvati *Parbati, Parvata, Parwati, Purbutty* (Hindu; India)

Also known as: *Adrija* (Mountain-born); *Ama; Amba* (Mother); *Ambika* (Mother); *Bagavati; Bhairavi* (Terrible); *Bhavani; Bhowani; Devi; Durga* (Inaccessible); *Gauri* (The Yellow); *Girija* (Mountain-born); *Haimavati* (Of the Himalayas); *Jagadgauri; Karala; Kausiki* (She of the Sheath); *Makali; Minakshi; Minakshidevi; Sali Kanya* (Mountain Maiden); *Sati* (Virtuous); *Skandaganani* (Mother of Skanda); *Uma* (Light).

Parvati, the mountain goddess, is an aspect of the great mother goddess Devi. As Parvati, the daughter of Mena, who is married to Himavat, the god of the Himalayans, she is known as the great virgin. She is the sister of the goddess Ganga, who is the personification of the sacred river Ganges. Parvati's relationship with Shiva followed Shiva's relationship with Sati. When Sati died, the gods wanted Shiva to remarry and decided that Sati should return as Parvati. Shiva was a practicing ascetic so absorbed in his practice that he never noticed the beautiful young woman. After several years, the gods sent the god of love, Kama, to intervene. He struck the chord of desire within Shiva, but Shiva, annoyed at the interruption, reduced him to ashes with his third eye. He was later returned to life. It took several years before Shiva acted on his passions. During this period, Parvati engaged in asceticism and continued to hope that their relationship would be consummated. Finally, she married Shiva and many more years passed before she became the mother of Karttikeya, the god of war and patron of thieves, and Ganesha, the elephant god of wisdom. In some legends, Karttikeya's mother is said to be Ganga and Ganesha's status is also disputed. Shiva had an ongoing feud with his former father-in-law, Sati's father, Daksha. Parvati noticed from her home on Mount Kailasa that Daksha was holding festivities to celebrate a great sacrifice in honor of Vishnu. Once again, he had neglected to invite Shiva. When Parvati informed her husband, the *Mahabharata* tells us that he became so furious that he rushed to the scene of the activities and caused an uproar that made the whole universe shake. In his rage, he attacked the gods. He knocked out Pushan's teeth and blinded Bhaga. He struck Narayana with his trident and Brahma had to intervene. In the *Puranas*, we are told that when Shiva found out that he had not been invited to the sacrifice, he was so livid that he created a terrifying being called Virabhadra, the monster of destruction. He also created thousands of similar demigods whom he dispatched to the air. During the ensuing melee, nature was in chaos. Indra was trampled, Yama's staff was broken, the goddess of literature, Sarasvati had her nose cut off, Mitra was blinded, Agni's hands were cut off and Chandra was badly beaten. Finally, Daksha admitted Shiva was the supreme god, or Vishnu, who had Shiva by the throat, forced Shiva to acknowledge Vishnu's supremacy. Parvati and Shiva spent many harmonious periods together but they also had their share of marital woes. Once while Shiva was pontificating on the Veda, she fell asleep. Enraged, he threw her out of heaven and she spent some time on earth as the human daughter of a fisherman. He also had a bad habit of intruding on her bath, even though she had made her desire for privacy clear to him. (*See* Ganesha.) Parvati was also Shiva's consort or wife as Devi, and other aspects of Devi: Sati, Durga, Gauri, Kali and possibly as Bishen and Mahadeo. In the Bengali tradition, as Kali, she is the mother of Brahma, Shiva and Vishnu. Parvati is usually shown holding weapons in her ten hands. Her animal is the lion and she is associated with music. This mountain goddess is associated with Annapurna mountain, as is the goddess of daily bread, Ana-Purna (q.v.). For Minakshi, *see* Kuvera. *See also* Agni; Andhaka; Ardhanapriswara; Asuras; Avalokitesvara; Bhavani; Brahma; Daksha; Devi; Devis; Durga; Ganesha; Gauri; Indra; Kali; Kama (A); Karttikeya; Mitra; Pushan; Ratri; Rudra; Sarasvati; Sati (A); Shiva; Trailokyavijaya; Uma; Virabhadra; Vishnu.

Parwati (India) *see* Devi; Parvati.

Pasa (India) *see* Amrtakundali.

Pashadhari (India, Tibet) *see* Ankusha; Zhag-pa-ma.

Pasht (Egypt) *see* Bast.

Pashupa (India) *see* Shiva.

Pashupati (A) (India) *see* Pasupati.

Pashupati (B) (Nepal)
Also known as: *Gu-lang* (Tibet).
This goddess is propitiated by mothers of children, particularly in Tibet.

Pashupati (C) (India)
"Lord Protector of Animals." *See also* Shiva.

Pashyanti (India) *see* Vach.

Pasi (India) *see* Varuna.

Pasiphae (Greek)
She is the daughter of Helios and Perse. Her siblings are Aeetes, Circe and Perses. She married Minos and became the mother of Acacallis, Androgeus, Ariadne, Catreus, Deucalion, Eryale, Glaucus, Lycastus, Phaedra and Xenodice. In the form of a cow, built for her by Daedalus, she slept with a bull and became the mother of the Minotaur. (Some writings call Pasiphae the daughter of Callirrhoe and Chrysaor.) *See also* Acacallis; Aeetes; Ariadne; Daedalus; Deucalion; Helios; Minos; Minotaur; Oceanids; Orion; Perses.

Pasithea (A) (Greek)
One of the Graces, Pasithea married Hypnos (sleep) and became the mother of Morpheus. *See also* Graces.

Pasithea (B) (Greek)
A Nereid, she is the daughter of Nereus and Doris.

Passalus (Greek)
One of the Cercopes, who are two-tailed gnomes, Passalus is the son of Oceanus and Theia. *See also* Oceanus.

Patagonian People — Creation Legend (South America)
see Guayarakunny.

Pasupata *Pinka* (India) Shiva's Sacred Trident. *See also* Pinka.

Pasupati *Pashupati* (India)
Also known as: *Shiva.*
Shiva as "Lord Protector of Animals" is known as Pasupati. He is described as the five-faced herdsman who wanders through the forests naked. *See also* Prajapati; Rudra; Shiva.

Patala *Patalas* (Hindu; India)
This is the lowest region of the underworld, lying beneath Mount Meru. Patala is 70,000 yojanas below the earth. It is the dwelling place of the semi-divine Asuras, which includes the Daityas, Danavas and Yakshas and is guarded by the Nagas. Vishnu left Patala to Bali, the grandson of Prahlada and great-grandson of the demon Hiranya-Kasipu. It is also the collective name for the seven (sometimes eight) infernal regions. Beneath Patala are the hells and the serpent Sesha who holds the world upon his hood. The beauty of Patala equals that of the seven upper regions. *See also* Arjuna; Asuras; Bali; Daityas; Gandharvas; Loka; Meru Mountain; Nagas and Nagis; Nara Simha (Vishnu's avatar as half-male); Naraka; Prahlada; Sagara; Sesha; Vamana (Vishnu's avatar as a dwarf); Vasuki; Vishnu.

Patalas (India) The Underworld. *See also* Patala.

Patecatl (Aztec People, Mexico)
Pulque deity. He is one of the Centzon Totochtin group (four hundred rabbits who are the gods of inebriation) and discoverer of the peyote plant from which liquor is made. He is probably a son of Cinteotl. In some legends, he is the husband of Mayahuel. *See also* Centzon Huitznahuas; Centzon Totochtin; Colhuatzincatl; Mayahuel.

Pathalavati (India) *see* Durga.

Patol (Gnostic) *see* Alaghom Naom.

Patroclus (Greek)
He is the son of Menoetius (the son of Actor and Aegina) and Periopis or Sthenele. During the Trojan War, he was a leader, along with Achilles, of the Myrmidons. The two heroes were close friends. When Patroclus died his bones were mixed with the bones of Achilles. The funeral games of Patroclus were held in his honor. *See also* Abderus; Achilles; Actor (A); Ajax the Lesser; Sarpedon (B).

Paulomi-Vallabha (India) Lover of Paulomi. *See also* Indrani.

Pautiwa (Hopi People, North America) The Sun.

Pav (India) *see* Agni.

Pavaka (India) *see* Agni.

Pavamana (India) *see* Agni.

Pavana (India) *see* Vayu.

Pavanareka, Queen (India) *see* Kansa; Yadavas.

Pax (Roman)
Also known as: *Eirene, Irene.*
Goddess of peace. *See also* Eirene; Plutus.

Paya-aki-tu-piko-no-kami (Japan)
Also known as: *Haya-akihiko-no-kami.*

"Rapid-Autumn-Lad-Deity." *See also* Haya-akitsu-hime-no-kami.

Payatamu (Zuni People, North America)
Deity of flowers. When he plays his flute, flowers bloom and butterflies follow him. *See also* Pan.

Payetome (Brazil, South America)
He is a white-bearded agriculture deity.

Paynal *Painal, Paynalton* (Aztec People, Mexico)
Also known as: *Huitzilopochtli.*
Paynal is the name of the of Huitzilopochtli's stand-in rather than substitute or impersonator at many of his festivals and when he spends part of the year in Hades. He wears Huitzilopochtli's attributes during these periods. Paynal is sometimes considered a messenger. *See also* Huitzilopochtli.

Pazuzu (Sumer)
Wind deity. Pazuzu is the son of Hanpa, the king of evil demon spirits. Pazuzu rages like a whirlwind bringing disease to mortals. He has four wings, a half-human, half-animal head, with ram's horns and his hind feet are talons. His body is covered with scales or feathers. He has the tail of a scorpion and his phallus terminates in a snake's head. *See also* Hanpa.

Peaches of Immortality (China) *see* Hsi-Wang-Mu; Kun-Lun Mountains; P'an-T'ao; Wang-Mu-Niang-Niang.

Pedaeus (Greek)
Pedaeus is the son of Atenor and an unknown woman. For a list of his siblings, *see* Atenor. He was raised by his father's wife, Theano. *See also* Acamas (B).

Pedsi and Pehor (Egypt)
Pedsi and Pehor were Egyptian brothers who drowned in Nubia and were deified in the Late Period. They became the focus of an important local cult. They may have been buried in a concealed chamber in a small temple at Dendur. This temple has been reconstructed in the Metropolitan Museum of Art in New York. Unlike Greece, the deification of mortals was rare in Egypt. *See also* Amenhetep; Imhoteph.

Pegae (Greek)
The nymph, Pegae, fell in love with Hylas, the Argonaut. She sacrificed him by drowning him. *See also* Hylas; Naiads.

Pegasos (Greek) *see* Pegasus.

Pegasus *Pegasos* (Greek; earlier, Assyrian, Hittite)
Also known as: *Pegasus of the Wells.*
Deified animal. Pegasus is the winged horse offspring of the sea foam of Poseidon and the blood of his mother Medusa. Medusa, pregnant by Poseidon, was beheaded by her husband Perseus. Pegasus and his brother, the warrior Chrysaor, were said to have sprung from her neck fully grown. Favored by the Muses, he stamped his hoof and produced the sacred Hippocrene spring on Mount Helicon and the Hippocrene spring at Troezen. Pegasus played a prime role in the tribulations of Bellerophon. Pegasus was stung by the gadfly sent by Zeus and it sent Bellerophon reeling. Pegasus continued to Olympus where he carried thunderbolts for Zeus. He was also said to be the steed of Eos and Athene. Pegasus is shown as a winged white horse. The Hippocrene Well means the "Horse's Well" and was horse-shaped. The name Pegasus means "springs of water." The foot of the horse is said to represent the penis and the horseshoe the vagina. The hoof as a life-creating symbol symbolized the reproductive organs of the male and female. *See also* Aarvak; Bellerophon; Chimaera; Eos; Gorgons; Medusa.

Pehor and Pedsi (Egypt) *see* Pedsi.

Pei-Chi-Chen (China) *see* Cheng Wu.

Peiras (Greek)
Some think there is a possibility that Peiras is the father of the eternally youthful, mortal monster Echidna by Styx, the river goddess. *See also* Argus (A); Echidna; Styx.

Peirene (A) (Greek) She is the daughter of Gorgophone.

Peirene (B) (Greek) Her father is the river god, Achelous.

Peirithous (Greek)
King of the Lapiths. Member of the Calydonian Boar Hunt. His parents are Ixion or Zeus and the Lapith, Dia. Hippodameia is his wife and the golden-haired Polypoets is their son. After an attempt to kidnap Persephone, Peirithous was sent to Hades for eternity. *See also* Calydonian Boar Hunt; Ixion; Persephone.

Peisander (Greek)
He is the son of the Trojan Antimachus and the brother of Hippomachus.

Peisidice (Greek)
She married Myrmidon and became the mother of Actor, Antiphus and Eupolemeia. For a list of her thirteen siblings *see* Canace. *See also* Aeolus (A); Antilochus.

Peisinoe (Greek) She is one of the three Sirens (q.v.).

Peisistratus (Greek)
He is the son of Nestor and Eurydice or possibly Anaxibia. *See also* Antilochus; Perseus; Polycaste.

Peitho (Greek)
Peitho is the goddess of persuasion. Her parents are the messenger of the gods, Hermes, and the goddess of love, Aphrodite. *See also* Aphrodite; Car; Hermes; Niobe (B).

Pekoi (Hawaii) A trickster deity. *See also* Kapua.

Pelasgian Creation Myth (Greek) *see* Eurynome (A); Pelasgus (A).

Pelasgus (A) (Greek)
First mortal. In the Pelasgian creation myth, Pelasgus was the first mortal, who rose up from the Arcadian soil and taught his followers, the Pelasgians, how to build huts, how to nourish themselves with acorns and clothe themselves with sheep or pig-skin clothing. *See also* Eurynome (A).

Pelasgus (B) (Greek)
He is the son of the river god, Asopus, and Metope. His two brothers are Ismenus and Pelagon. He has twenty sisters, some of whom are Aegina, Antiope, Chalcis, Salamis, and Thebe. *See also* Aegina; Asopus.

Pelasgus (C) (Greek)
First king of Arcadia. He is the son of Zeus and Niobe (said

to be the first mortal to be loved by a god) or Gaea (Earth). His siblings are Argus, who was the first son of Zeus' by a mortal; Isis; Typhon; Osiris (Serapis), who married his sister Isis and was murdered by Typhon. He married Cyllene and was the father of Lyacaon who was his successor to the throne. See also Argus (A); Asopus; Eurynome (A); Niobe (B); Typhon.

Pelasgus (D) (Greek)

His parents are Triopas and Sois. His siblings are Agenor, Iasus and Xanthus. Pelasgus built a temple dedicated to Demeter at Argos. He reinforced the city and renamed it Larissa, after his daughter.

Pelasgus (E) (Greek)

His parents are the sea god Poseidon and Larissa (the daughter of Pelasgus). See also Pelasgus (D).

Pele (Hawaiian, Polynesian)

Also known as: Ai-laau (Wood Eater), Hina-ai-ka-malama (her name as a woman on earth), Hina-hanaia-i-ka-malama (the Women who Worked in the Moon), Ka-ula-o-ke-ahi (The Redness of the Fire), Pele-ai-honua (Eater of the Land), Pele-honua-mea (Pele of the Sacred Earth), Pele-Ulu (possibly).

Mother goddess. Fire Goddess. Goddess of the Kilauea volcano. Goddess of Dance. Pele, the goddess of the Kilauea volcano on Hawaii, erupts when she is angry. She is the daughter of Moemoe (Moemoe-a-aulii) and Haumea. She has seven brothers and five sisters, or five brothers and seven sisters. One sister, whom she tucked under her armpit in her travels, is Hi'i-aka-i-ka-poli-o-Pele (in the armpit of Pele) who was born in the shape of an egg. There are several versions of her arrival in Hawaii: she was expelled from her distant homeland; she was driven to the island by a flood; she was driven out of Kahiki (Tahiti) by her sister; she went in search of her brother Kamo-hoali'i; or that she simply loved to travel. It is said that she caused the flood when sea water poured from her head while searching for the husband who deserted her. One of her forms is as the goddess Pele-ulu. Pele travels with the great gods Ku and Lono and some minor deities including her friend Hopoe. She is comparable to the goddess of fire or the underground of the Maoris, Pare or Parewhenua-mea. She is associated with the god of hogs, Kamapaua'a. Pele's myths revolve around her establishment of a home at the volcano and sending for her lover Lohiau to share her home. Compare to Fuji (Japan), Agni (India), Hestia (Greek), Vesta (Roman). See also Haumea; Kamohoali'i.

Pele-Ulu (Hawaii) One of the forms of Pele (q.v.).

Peleus (Greek)

King of Myrmidons. An Argonaut. Member of the Calydonian Boar Hunt. Owner of a sword made by the fire god, Hephaistos. Peleus is the son of Aeacus, who was the king of Aegina (and after death a judge of the dead in Hades), and Endeis the daughter of Cheiron and Chariclo (the daughter of Apollo). Peleus is the brother of Telamon and half-brother of Phocus. Phocus was murdered by Peleus and Telamon. Actor absolved and purified Peleus of the murder, gave him one-third of his kingdom, and either Antigone or Polymela for a spouse. (Some say Polymela was his daughter.) Astydameia, the daughter of Pelops and Hippodameia, fell in love with Peleus. When he rejected her advances she went to Polymela with a fabricated story. Polymela was so devasted that she hung herself. (Peleus might have murdered her and cut her body to pieces in retaliation.) After Polymela died Peleus married Thetis (daughter of Nereus and Doris). (Zeus wanted to be Thetis' lover but heard the prophesy that the son of Thetis would be more illustrious than his father, so he gave her to Peleus.) At their wedding, the goddess Eris rolled the Golden Apple. They became the parents of Achilles. See also Acastus; Achilles; Actor (A); Aeacus; Aegina; Argonauts; Calydonia Boar Hunt; Creteus; Eris; Hephaistos; Hippolyte (B); Jason; Paris.

Pelias (Greek)

Pelias, the king of Iolcus, is the son of the sea god Poseidon and Tyro, who was married to her uncle Cretheus. Pelias is the twin brother of Neleus. Abandoned by his mother at birth, he carried an imprint on his face from a horse who had kicked him. He usurped his brother's throne and prevented Aeson, the eldest son of Cretheus and Tyro, who was next in line, from becoming king. See also Admetus; Cretheus; Jason; Neleus.

Pelion (Greek)

Deified mountain. Mount Pelion is located in Central Magnesia in Thessaly. In their wars against the gods, the Giants placed Mount Pelion on Mount Ossa in order to scale the heavens with greater ease. The Centaur, Cheiron, reared a number of Greek princes in his cave on this mountain. It was on Mount Pelion that Acastus attempted to have Peleus killed. Material to build the Argos came from the wooded range. See also Acastus; Argos; Cheiron; Giants; Peleus.

Pelios (Greek) see Acastus.

Pelopia (Greek) see Aegisthus; Ares.

Peloponnesus (Greek) A peninsula in southern Greece. See also Achaeus.

Pelops (Greek)

Descendant of the gods. Deified mortal. Pelops is the son of the king of Sipylus, Tantalus, and Dione (the daughter of Atlas) or possibly one of the other Pleiades. Pelops siblings are Broteas and Niobe. Broteas carved his mother's image in a rock and when he wouldn't do the same for Artemis, she drove him insane and he burned himself to death. Niobe was eventually turned to stone. Through nefarious maneuvers Pelops married Hippodamia, the daughter of Oenamaus. Pelops fathered numerous children: Alcathous, the Megarian king; Astydameia, who was chopped to death by Peleus; Atreus, king of Mycenae; Copreus, who was killed by Heracles; Lysidice; Nicippe, also known as Amphibia, who married Sthenelus; Pittheus, the king of Troezen; Thyestes, the king of Mycenae who raped his brother Atreus' wife, Aerope; Troezen, who co-ruled Troezen with Pittheus; and possibly Epidaurus and the robber Sceiron (Sciron). He was also the father of Chrysippus by either Astyoche or Axioche. Chrysippus was murdered by his half-brothers, Atreus and Thyestes, or by his stepmother Hippodamia. Pelops had an unusual beginning in life. His father, Tantalus, chopped him up and served him as a meal to the deities. All but the goddess of agriculture, Demeter, realized what Tantalus had done. Demeter ate Pelops' left shoulder. The gods restored the infant to life and Demeter gave him an ivory shoulder. He was so beautiful that the sea god, Poseidon, fell in love with him and took him to Olympus. In time, he was returned to earth, some say because of his father's crimes. When he married Hippodamia he became the king of Pisa and proceeded to acquire surrounding areas as well. Under the pretense of friendship he became acquainted with King Stymphalus of Arcadia and then brutally murdered him to procure his land. Before his marriage, he had made promises to Myrtilus, a son of Hermes, that he did not intend to keep. Myrtilus kept reminding him of his debt which included the privilege of sleeping with Hippodamia for one night and half of the kingdom. Finally, Pelops killed Myrtilus by throwing him into the water, possibly near Elis harbor. This act manifested a curse put on Myrtilus by Oenamaus as he was dying. Now, as Myrtilus saw his death fast approaching, he cursed the house of Pelops. Some say that Pelops murdered Myrtilus the same day that Pelops won Hippodamia's hand. In the end it was thought that Pelops realized his wife and or his sons were guilty of murdering Chrysippus and she either committed suicide or went to live with her sons. Nothing is known about Pelop's death although his great-grandson, Heracles, established a shrine in his name at Olympia. (Not to be confused with Pelops, the twin of Teledamas, children of Cassandra and Agamemnon who were murdered as infants or Pelops the son of Amphion and Niobe.) For the devious method employed by Pelops to win Hippodamia's hand, *see also* Argus (A); Astydameia; Demeter; Eurydice (C); Hippodamia (A); Oenomaus; Tantalus (A).

Pelus (Greek) *see* Actor.

Pemba *Pembu, Pembo* (West Africa)
Supreme being or creator. He was born from the Cosmic Egg but found the world was incomplete so Pemba returned to retrieve seeds from the egg. Those seeds were impure, so Pemba's twin, Faro, was sacrificed to purify the earth. In another version, as Pembo, he is a god of water, agriculture, and wisdom. He is the son of the Voice of the Void, husband of Musso Koroni. *See also* Faro; Mangala (B).

Penates (Etruscan, Roman)
Gods of the household. The Penates are usually in groups of two or three. They were honored at mealtimes by families as gods of storerooms. They are shown most often in a dancing attitude. These gods share the hearth with Vesta and the Lar. The Romans connected them with the Terminalia and Janus. *See also* Lares; Janus.

Peneius (Greek)
Peneius is the river god son of Oceanus and Tethys. *See also* Oceanus; Rivers; Tethys.

Peneleos (Greek) *see* Argonauts.

Penelope (Greek)
Deified mortal. Wife of Odysseus. She was besieged by more than a hundred suitors during her husband's absence at Troy. She firmly believed that Odysseus would return and therefore delayed a decision as long as possible. Finally she promised to make a choice when she had completed a certain robe which she was then weaving. By undoing at night what she had woven

during the day, she was able to put off the suitors until Odysseus returned. *See also* Calypso; Odysseus.

Peneus (Greek)
River deity. A river god in Thessaly and father of the nymph Daphne, who was pursued by Apollo.

Penglai (Taoist, China)
A magic island, home of immortal beings who possess the secrets of eternal life.

Penthesileia (Greek)
Queen of the Amazons. She is the daughter of Ares and Otrera and the sister of Antiope (also known as Melanippe) and Hippolyte. An ally of the Trojans, she was killed at Troy by Achilles (q.v.). *See also* Amazons; Ares; Antiope; Hippolyte (A).

Pentheus (Greek)
King of Thebes. His grandfather is Cadmus, who introduced the alphabet to the people. His parents are Echion, who is one of the Sparti, and Agave. Pentheus was ripped to pieces by his mother and his aunts. For details, *see* Agave, Ino. *See also* Cadmus.

Peparethus (Greek)
He is the son of Dionysus and Ariadne. *See also* Ariadne; Dionysus.

Pepi (Egypt) *see* Apep; Apepi; Apophis; Hades; Rahabh; Tiamat.

Per Uadjit (Egypt) *see* Uatchet.

Percht (Teutonic) *see* Bertha.

Perchta (Teutonic) *see* Bertha.

Perdix (A) (Greek)
Also known as: *Calus, Talus.*
Inventor. He is the son of Perdix. Perdix worked as an assistant to his uncle, Daedalus. Daedalus, jealous of his nephew's inventions, murdered him.

Perdix (B) (Greek)
She is the mother of Perdix (A) and sister of Daedalus and Sicyon.

Pereplut (Slavic) Goddess of drink and changing fortunes.

Pereus (Greek)
He is the son of Elatus and Laodice and the father of Neaera, the wife of Aleus.

Peri (Persia)
The Peri are beautiful, good spirits who guide mortals to the Land of the Blessed. They are opponents of the evil daevas.

Perialces (Greek)
He is possibly the son of the king of Argos, Bias, and his wife, Pero. *See also* Pero.

Periboea (A–F) (Greek)
(A) Daughter of Hipponous, second wife of Oeneus. Mother of Tydeus. (B) Sometimes known as Merope. Spouse of Polybus of Corinth. Foster mother of Oedipus. (C) Daughter of Alcathous and Euaechme or Pyrgo. Second wife of Telamon.

Mother of Ajax. She rejected the love of Minos. (D) Mother of Nausithous by Poseidon. (E) Mother of Pelagon by Axius. (F) Periboea who is also known as Asterodia, Dorodoche and Mede. She is the spouse of Icarius. Some of her children are Iphthime, Penelope and Perileus.

Periclymenus (A) (Greek)
He is the shape-changer son of Neleus and Chloris. *See also* Argonauts; Chloris; Neleus.

Periclymenus (B) (Greek)
The sea god Poseidon is his father. His mother is Chloris.

Perieres (Greek)
King of Messenia. His parents are Aeolus and Enarete. He has six brothers and seven sisters. For a list of their names *see* Canace. *See also* Enarete; Gorgophone.

Perigune (Greek)
She is the daughter of Sinis and the mother of Melanippus by Theseus. *See also* Acamas (A).

Perikionios (Greek) *see* Dionysus.

Perimede (A) (Greek)
She is the daughter of the king of Calydon, Oneneus. *See also* Calydonian Boar Hunt; Jason.

Perimede (B) (Greek)
Her parents are Oeneus and Periboea. She married Phoenix.

Perimede (C) (Greek) Her sister is Amphitryon (q.v.).

Perimela (Greek) She is the mother of Ixion (q.v.).

Perimele (A) (Greek)
Her parents are Admetus and Alcestis. Some say she is the mother of Magnes. *See also* Alcestis; Admetus; Magnes.

Perimele (B) (Greek)
Perimele is one of six daughters of Aeolus and Enarete. She has seven brothers. For a list of their names, *see* Canace. Achelous seduced Perimele. Two children were born of the affair, Hippodamas and Orestes. Her furious father threw her into the sea. Poseidon changed her into an island. *See also* Achelous; Aeolus (A); Aeolus (B); Hippodamas; Orestes; Poseidon.

Periopis (Greek)
She is the daughter of Pheres and Periclymene. Her siblings are Admetus, Idomene and Lycurgus. *See also* Admetus; Pheres.

Periphetes (Greek)
Also known as *Corynetes*. He had a bad leg and carried a club to kill travellers. *See also* Anticleia (D); Hephaistos.

Perit (Egypt)
Afterworld deity. One of twelve goddesses in the ninth sector of Tuat. She utters words of power causing the life and strength to arise in Osiris. The other goddesses are Aat-aatet, Aat-khu, Hent-nut-s, Nebt-mat, Nebt-setau, Nebt-shat, Nebt-shef-shefet, Netert-en-khentet-Ra, Sekhet-metu, Shemat-khy (or khu), and Tesert-ant.

Perkaunas (Lithuanian) *see* Perkunis; Perun.

Perkuna Tete (Armenian, Lithuanian)
Thunder and lightning goddess. She bathes the sun at the end of the day. *See also* Perkunis.

Perkunas (Armenian) *see* Perkunis.

Perkunis *Perkunas, Pehrkon, Perkun, Perkuns* (Armenian, Lithuanian, Slavic)
Also known as: *Armat, Erkir.*
God of heaven and thunderstorms. Weather deity. The names Perkunas, Erkir, or Armat of the ancient Armenians are associated with the earth. Perkunis and Erkir may be a female version of one of these gods. In another version the Lithuanians had a goddess of thunder and lightning. Her name was Perkuna Tete. Oak trees were holy to Perkunis and when Christian missionaries cut them down the people complained that their forest deities were being destroyed. During times of draught animal sacrifices were made to Perkunis deep in the woods. Perkunis resembles Zeus. Compare Perkunis to Parjanya (India). *See also* Jupiter; Perun; Thor.

Permessus (Greek) *see* Aganippe (A).

Pero (Greek)
Pero is the beautiful daughter of Neleus and Chloris. She married Bias, the king of Argos, and became the mother of the Argonaut Areius; the Argonaut Leodocus; Talaus, also an Argonaut. She could also be the mother of a daughter, Alphesiboea, and another son, Perialces.

Peron (Slavic) *see* Perun; Pyerun.

Peroun (Slavic) *see* Perun.

Perse *Perseis* (Greek)
She is the Oceanid daughter of Oceanus and Tethys. Some of her siblings' names are Clymene, Doris, Electra, Meliboea, and Proteus. She has numerous other siblings who are rivers, streams, and fountains. Perse married Helius and became the mother of Aeetes, Circe, Pasiphae, and Perses. *See also* Aeetes; Circe; Electra; Helius; Minos; Oceanids; Oceanus; Pasiphae.

Perseis (Greek) Another spelling for Perse.

Persephone *Persephassa, Proserpina* (Roman), *Proserpine* (Roman); (Greek; possibly from Asia)
Also known as: *Brimo, Core, Despoina* (Arcadian) *Kore, Proserpina* (Roman).
Goddess of corn and the underworld. Daughter of Demeter and Zeus, commonly referred to as Kore or Core. Hades carried her off and married her in the lower world. (*See* Demeter.) Persephone could not leave Hades permanently since she had eaten a pomegranate in the lower world. They struck a compromise by which Persephone would spend one-third of the year with Hades and two-thirds with Demeter. Now when Persephone is in Hades, the earth is barren; when she is with Demeter, the earth blossoms. The name Brimo is also used for Demeter, Hecate, and Rhea. Her attributes are the bat, the narcissus and the pomegranate. Some legends associate her with Adonis. *See also* Admetus; Adonis; Baubo; Cocytus; Demeter; Hades; Hecate; Rhea; Sirens; Styx; Zeus.

Perses (A–D) (Greek)
(A) Son of Perseus and Andromeda. (B) Son of Helios and Perse. (C) Son of Crius and Eurybia, siblings Astraeus and Pallas, spouse of Asteria, father of Hecate. (D) Possibly the father of Chariclo.

Perseus (Greek)

Also known as: *Eurymedon* (Called this name by his mother, *Pterseus*.)

Perseus is the grandson of Acrisius, son of Zeus and Danae (Dahana) and husband of Andromeda, or possibly Persika or Aurigena. Raised by Polydectes, king of Seriphos, he was sent by him to fetch the head of Medusa. Guided by the deities Athene and Hermes, he stole the single eye and tooth shared by the Graiae, sisters of the Gorgons, which he refused to return until they directed him to the nymphs who had the magic helmet, wallet, and winged sandals of Hades. The exchange was made and he was also given a mirror from Athene and a sickle from Hermes. He found the Gorgons and used the mirror to look at Medusa while he beheaded her, for it was said if a man looked directly at her, he would turn to stone. He placed the head in the wallet, the helmet which made him invisible on his head, and fled. (For a variation of this myth *see* Medusa.) In some versions of this myth he is said to have stopped at the palace of the Titan Atlas to rest. His reception was not hospitable so he turned Atlas into a mountain (Mount Atlas). This portion of the myth is in dispute because Atlas is alive generations later in other tales. He then flew on to Chemmis in Egypt to visit his ancestors, Danaus and Lynceus. (During Herodotus' day these were the only Egyptians to worship Perseus.) As he passed over the Ethiopian colony of Joppa, on the coast of Syria, he saw Andromeda, a naked damsel in distress and rescued her from a sea-monster. He stayed with her for a time and they had a son, Perses. (*See* Andromeda.) He returned to Seriphos to find his mother a fugitive from Polydectes. He rescued her by turning Polydectes and his court to stone with the head of Medusa. He then made Dictys (the seaman who originally rescued him when he was an infant) the king of Seriphos. His battles over, he returned the weapons to Hermes and gave the head of Medusa to Athene and set sail for Argos with his mother, his wife, and some say, a party of Cyclopes. He convinced his grandfather Acrisius that he was not seeking revenge for his illtreatment of him and his mother when he was born. During a celebration in honor of his return (according to other sources the funeral games of the father of Tentamides of Larissa), he threw a discus (said to be his invention), and accidentally killed Acrisius thus fulfilling the oracle which had haunted Acrisius for so many years. Perseus is said to have traded the kingdom of Argos for Tiryns where he established the city of Mycenae and fortified Midea with the assistance of the Cyclopes who built walls around both cities. After death, Athene had Perseus and Andromeda placed among the stars. It has also been written that Dionysus came to Argos to punish Perseus who retaliated by inflicting madness on the women of Argive who then began to devour their children. Perseus realized his mistake and placated Dionysus by dedicating a temple to him. This tale is similar to the story related about Perseus' grandfather's twin brother, Proetus. For details of Perseus' birth *see* Acrisius. *See also* Aegis; Antilochus; Athene; Chrysaor; Danae; Dionysus; Medusa; Pegasus.

Pertunda (Roman)

Goddess of marriage.

Perun *Peron, Peroun, Piorun, Pyerun* (Polish, Russian, Slavic)

Also known as: *Perkunas* (Armenian).

War God. God of thunder. Lord of the universe. His weapon is the thunderbolt. It is thought by some that Perun may be the same as or associated with the Vedic god Parjanya who in turn was an aspect of Indra. He was the chief deity of the warrior class. It is said that at Novgorod an image of Perun in the likeness of a man stood with a thunder-stone in his hand. Elsewhere, a fire of oak wood burned in his honor and if it went out the attendant paid with his life. He was invoked by early Russian monarchs before going to war. He is shown with three heads surrounded by flames. He is similar to Zeus, Jupiter and Thor. Analogous to Svantovit (q.v.). Compare to Parjanya (India). *See also* Dazbog; Gromovit; Khors; Perkuna Tree; Perkunis; Volos.

Pesedjet (Egypt) *see* Ennead of Heliopolis.

Peseias (Slavic)

Protectors of domestic animals. *See also* Krukis.

Pesthi (Egypt)

Afterworld deity. An archer in the tenth sector of Tuat.

Petesuchos (Egypt) *see* Sebek.

Petra (Egypt)

Afterworld deity. A god in the eleventh sector of Tuat. He has a disk on his head and stretches his arms to keep apart the wings of the serpent Tchet-s.

Phae (Greek)

She is the daughter of the destructive whirlwind, Typhon, and the monster, Echidna.

Phaedra (Greek)

Phaedra is the daughter of Minos and Pasiphae and the second wife of Theseus. She has a step-son, Hippolytus, and two children, Acamas and Demophoon. Phaedra ended her life by suicide. *See also* Acacallis; Acamas (A); Adonis; Ariadne; Demophoon; Minos; Pasiphae; Theseus.

Phaenna (Greek) *see* Graces.

Phaethon (A) (Greek)

Sun deity. Phaethon is the son of Helius (the sun) and the Oceanid, Clymene. He could be the son of Clymenus by Metrope, which would make him the grandson of Helius. In an effort to prove that Helius was his father he drove the sun chariot Quadriga through the sky for one day. It was his last day. He lost control of the horses and was flung from the vehicle into the Eridanus river and became a swan. His grief-stricken sisters, the Heliades, were transformed into poplar trees. Others say that he was killed by Zeus when he drove his father's chariot too close to earth and almost set the world on fire. Some consider Phaethon the constellation Aurigia, known as the Charioteer. *See also* Aegle (A); Apsyrtus; Eos; Heliades; Helius; Oceanids; Phaethusa; Rivers.

Phaethon (B) (Greek) Another name for the Argonaut Absyrtus, king of Colchis. *See also* Aither.

Phaethon (C) (Greek)

He is the son of Cephalus, (the son of Deion and Diomede) and the goddess of dawn, Eos, or Tithonus, the brother of Phaethon and Eos. Aphrodite kidnapped him to be a guard at her shrine.

Phaethusa (Greek)

She is a Heliad. The death of her half-brother, Phaethon, grieved her so deeply that she turned into a poplar tree. *See also* Aegle (A); Heliades.

Phaland (Teutonic) *see* Volund.

Phalerus (Greek) One of the Argonauts (q.v.).

Phallus Goddess (Egypt) *see* Par.

Phan-Ku (China) *see* Chaos.

Phanes (Greek)

Also known as: *Ericepauis; Eros; Fan; Phanes-Dionysus; Protogenus Phaethon; Protogonos.*

Orphic Creation Legend. Light or the god of light. In the Orphic creation myth, the awesome goddess, black-winged Night was impregnated by Wind and laid a silver egg protected by the womb of darkness. From this egg, Eros, known as Phanes, emerged and created the earth, sky, sun and moon. He lived in a cave with Night, who called him Protogenus Phaethon, and Ericepauis. She represented herself to him as the triad of Night, Order, and Justice. Before the cave sat the goddess Rhea, who beat on a drum so that mortals would heed the oracles of the triple-goddess who ruled the universe. In time, her scepter was passed to Uranus. Although the name Eros is associated with Phanes it is not the god of love, but rather is influenced by the mystical doctrine of love. Double-sexed, with four heads, golden wings and the heads of a ram, bull, snake and lion. Compare to the Pelasgian creation myth, *see* Cronus. Compare to the Homeric creation myth, *see* Oceanus; Pontus. Compare to Olympian creation myth *see* Aegaeon; Gaea. To compare to Hesiod's creation myth, see Pontus. *See also* Chaos; Eurynome (A); Gaea.

Phanesphoebe (Greek) *see* Rhea.

Phangnalomang (Dhammai People, India)

Phangnalomang is the worm who devoured the earth goddess Subbu-Khai-Thung and her brother, the sky god, Jongsuli-Young-Jongbu. For details, *see* Shuznaghu.

Phanus (Greek)

Phanus is the Argonaut son of the god of wine, Dionysus, and possibly Ariadne. *See also* Argonauts; Ariadne; Dionysus.

Pharmen-ma (Tibet) *see* Htamenmas.

Pheme (Greek)

Also known as: *Fama* (Roman).

Goddess of rumors.

Pheres (A) (Greek)

He is the son of the Argonaut Jason and Medea, the priestess of Hecate. His siblings are Alcimenes and Thessalus, who are twins; Argus, who was murdered, possibly by his mother; a sister, Eriopis; Medeias, who was exiled from Athens; Mermerus, who was possibly killed by his mother; Tisandrus. He was either killed by Medea when he was a child, or he was stoned to death by the Corinthians. *See also* Jason; Medea.

Pheres (B) (Greek) He is the father of Antigone, the wife of Cometes (q.v.).

Pheres (C) (Greek)

His son is Mermerus who was known for his poison-making abilities.

Pherusa (Greek)

She is one of the fifty daughters of Nereus and Doris, known as the Nereids.

Philandros (Greek) *see* Acacallis.

Philomelus (Greek)

Inventor of the wagon. His parents are Iasion and Demeter and his brother is Plutus, the god of agricultural riches. *See also* Demeter; Eirene; Plutus.

Philemon (Greek)

Philemon and his wife of many years, Baucis, were kind to Zeus and Hermes. They received special boons from the gods. At the end of their lives, Philemon was changed into an oak tree and Baucis was changed into a linden tree. *See also* Baucis.

Philinoe (A) (Greek)

She is the daughter of Iobates, the king of Lycia, and the wife of Bellerophon, who originally wanted to marry Philinoe's sister, Stheneboea. *See also* Anticleia; Bellerophon; Stheneboae.

Philinoe (B) (Greek)

Her parents are Tyndareus, the king of Sparta, and Leda. Her siblings are the Dioscuri (known as the "Gemini Twins"), Phoebe, Timandra (there is a possibility that Phoebe and Timandra are the same person), Clytemnestra and their half-sister Helen of Troy. *See also* Clytemnestra; Dioscuri; Helen; Leda.

Philippines — Creation Legend *see* Finuweigh.

Philyra (Greek)

Philyra is one of the many daughters of Oceanus and Tethys. She changed into a horse to mate with Cronus who was also in horse form. The union produced Cheiron, the immortal Centaur. *See also* Cheiron; Cronus.

Phineus (A) (Greek)

Soothsayer. Phineus is the son of the king of Tyre, Agenor and Telephassa or Argiope. His siblings are Cadmus, Europa, Phoenix, Cilix, Demodoce, Electra, Thasus and possibly Argus. He is also said to be the son of Agenor's son Phoenix, or, of Poseidon. He is a blind soothsayer and the king of Salmydessus, in Thrace. In some legends it is said that Zeus blinded him and sent the Harpies to constantly punish him for revealing the future to mortals. Other legends say that Poseidon blinded him for telling Phrixus which route to take to Colchis or Phrixus' sons the best way to reach Greece. Yet other versions say that the North Wind, Boreas, and the Argonauts blinded him because he had blinded his sons who were Boreas' grandsons. Phineus' first marriage was to Cleopatra, the daughter of Boreas and Oreithyia. They had two children who may have been Pandion and Plexippus. His second marriage was to Idaea, the daughter of king Dardanus of the Scythians. They also had two children, Mariandynus and Thynius. Idaea told Phineus that his sons by Cleopatra had raped her. Enraged, he blinded and tortured them. The Argonauts rescued the men and convinced them not to kill their step-mother. Instead, she was sent back to her father, who sentenced her to death for her apparent untruths. In variations of this myth, it is Cleopatra's brothers,

Zetes and Calais, who save Phineus from the Harpies. Or another version is that the Harpies swooped him up and carried him to the land of the Scythians, his second wife Idaea's father's territory. *See also* Aello; Boreas; Calchas; Harpies; Zetes.

Phineus (B) (Greek)

Coward. Phineus is thought to be the son of Belus, king of the Egyptians, and Anchinoe, a daughter of the Nile. His siblings are Cepheus, king of Ethiopia; Aegyptus, king of Egypt; Danaus, king of Libya; and a sister, Thronia. He was engaged to his niece, princess Andromeda, the daughter of king Cepheus. She was chained to a rock and about to be devoured by a sea monster and Phineus would not attempt to rescue her. Perseus killed him, turned him to stone, rescued the maiden and married her. *See also* Agenor (A); Andromeda; Perseus.

Phlegethon (Greek)

Phlegethon is the river of fire in the underworld, Hades. There are four other rivers in Hades: Acheron, the river of woe; Cocytus, the river of wailing; Lethe, the river of forgetfulness; Styx *see* Acheron; Cocytus; Lethe; Tartarus; Styx.

Phlegon (Greek) *see* Helius.

Phlegyas (Greek)

He was the king of Orchomenus, who was suceeded by Chryses. His parents are Ares and Chryse, or Ares and Dotis. His children are Coronis and possibly Ixion. Enraged when his daughter was raped by Apollo, he burned down the great god's temple at Delphi. In retaliation, Apollo murdered Phlegyas, sent him to the underworld, Hades, and hung a large stone over his head. (Some say he was killed by Lycus and Nycteus.) *See also* Apollo; Ares; Chryse; Coronis; Hades; Ixion.

Phobos (A) (Greek)

God of fear and terror. He is the son of Ares and Aphrodite. For a list of his siblings *see* Anteros. *See also* Ares; Harmonia (A).

Phobos (B) (Greek)

Phobos (meaning terror) is one of the four horses belonging to Ares. The other three horses are Aithon (meaning fire), Conabos (meaning tumult), Phlogios (meaning flame).

Phocus (A) (Greek)

He is the son of either Ornytion, who is the son of Sisyphus and Merope or the sea god Poseidon. His brother is Thoas. After curing Antiope of insanity, he married her. *See also* Antiope; Merope; Poseidon; Sisyphus.

Phocus (B) (Greek)

Phocus is the Argonaut son of Caeneus and brother of Priasus, who were also Argonauts.

Phocus (C) (Greek)

The son of Aeacus and Psamathe, he married Endeis, the daughter of the Centaur, Cheiron, and Chariclo and became the father of Crisus, Naubolus and Panopaeus. He was murdered by his half-brother, Peleus, his brother, Telamon, and his wife Endeis.

Phoebe (A) (Greek)

Phoebe is an epithet of the moon goddess, Artemis.

Phoebe (B) (Greek)

Phoebe, the Titan, is the daughter of Gaea and Uranus. She is sister/spouse of Coeus and the mother of Asteria and Leto. Her grandchildren are Artemis and Apollo. Her epithet is Phoebus (meaning, shining).

Phoebe (C) (Greek)

Phoebe is a half-sister to Helen and sister to the Dioscuri and Clytemnestra.

Phoebe (D) (Greek)

She was engaged to Lynceus, kidnapped by Polydeuces and married Castor.

Phoebe (E) (Greek) A Heliad, she is also known as Aegiale.

Phoebus (Roman)

Aspects or known as: *Apollo, The Bright One.*

Sun god. Phoebus was the Roman title for Apollo. He was the son of Jupiter and Latona and the brother of Diana. Apollo was not originally a sun deity but a god of medicine, music, and prophecy. In the 5th century B.C.E. he was adopted by the Romans, who hoped that his influence would help the people avert the plague. The healing rays of the sun could be considered a symbol for Apollo as Phoebus. *See also* Apollo.

Phoenician — Creation Legend (from Philos Bybios) *see* Aer; Arura; Baau (B); Chaos; Dagon (B).

Phoenix (A) *Phenix, Phoinix* (Egypt)

The Phoenix bird, the symbol of immortality, lives for five hundred years, burns in its nest, becomes ashes and is reborn, in a continuous cycle. The bird eventually ended up in Phoenicia, which was said to have been named for him. The Phoenix is possibly the same as Bennu Bird of the Egyptians (q.v.).

Phoenix (B) (Greek)

King of the Dolopians. He is the son of Amyntor and Cleobule. When his father found out that Phoenix had seduced his (the father's) concubine, he blinded him. Peleus asked Cheiron to restore his sight. *See also* Cheiron; Peleus.

Phoenix (C) (Greek) He is a lieutenant who served Achilles.

Phoenix (D) (Greek)

He may be the father of Adonis by Alphesiboea.

Phoenix (E) (Greek)

Phoenix, the son of Agenor, may be the same as Phoenix (D). *See also* Agenor (A).

Phorbas (A) (Greek)

King of Thessaly. He is either the son of Lapithus and Orsinome and brother of Periphas, or the son of Triopas and Hiscilla and brother of Erysichthon, Iphimedeia and Messene. Phorbas is the father of Actor, Augeias and possibly Tiphys. (Tiphys, the pilot of the Argo, could be the son of Hagnias.) Phorbas fought Pelops. *See also* Actor (B); Iphimedeia (A); Pelops; Tiphys.

Phorbas (B) (Greek)

A renowned boxer, Phorbas was killed by Apollo.

Phorbas (C) (Greek)

Phorbas was the lover of the god Hermes. He was a cattle rancher who led the Phrygians against the Greeks in the Trojan War. *See also* Apollo; Hermes.

Phorbas (D) (Greek)
The son of Argus, he later became the king of Argolis.

Phorbus (Greek)
The father of Pronoe who married Aetolus, his grandchildren are Calydon and Pleuron.

Phorcys (Greek)
Also known as: *The Old Man of the Sea.*
Phorcys, an ancient sea god, is the son of Pontus (Sea) and Gaea (Earth). His siblings are Ceto (Keto), Nereus, Thaumas, Crius, and Eurybia. Married to his sister, the sea monster Ceto, he became the father of monstrous serpent Ladon, the Gorgons, and Graiae. Ladon has also been said to be the offspring of Typhon and Echidne or self-conceived by Gaea. He was also the father of the nymph Thoosa by an unknown woman. Thoosa is the mother of the famous Cyclops, Polyphemus, by Poseidon. Phorcys may have been the father of the barking monster Scylla, by Ceto, Crataeis or Hecate and was possibly the father of monster Echidna and the Hesperides. *See also* Ceto; Cyclops; Gaea; Hesperides; Medusa; Nereus; Oceanus; Polyphemus (B); Pontus; Skylla.

Phorkos (Greek) *see* Sirens.

Phoroneus (Greek)
First king of Argos. Inventor of fire. Oracular hero. Phoroneus is the son of the river god Inachus and the ash nymph Melia and the brother of Aegialeus and Io. In some legends, Argia is said to be his mother as well as the mother of his sister, Io. He married either Laodice, Peitho or Cerdo and was the father of Niobe, Apis and Car. Niobe, who was the first mortal woman whom Zeus loved, became the mother of twelve children, eleven of whom were murdered. Phoroneus' son, Apis, by the nymph Teledice (Cinna) was killed by Telchis and Thelxion. Car became the king of Megara and inaugurated the worship of the goddess of agriculture, Demeter, in his kingdom. Phoroneus was the first person to bring a group of people together and form a marketplace. He was also the first to erect an alter to Hera in Argolis although his father Inachus was said to be the first to worship the goddess. The Argives claimed that he was the first to discover the use of fire and bring it to mortals and not Prometheus as claimed by other mythologists. They also credit Phoroneus with making Hera's armor. After death Phoroneus was retired to the Elysian Islands. Compare to the metal and bronze smith, Hephaistos. Phoroneus is said to be the counterpart of the Celtic Bran. *See also* Apis (B); Apsyrtus; Argus (A); Car; Curetes; Hera; Inachus; Meliae; Niobe (B); Prometheus.

Phra (Egypt) *see* Re.

Phra In Suen (Siam) *see* Shiva.

Phra Narai (Siam) *see* Vishnu.

Phra Naret (Siam) *see* Lakshmi.

Phra Noreai-Narayana (Cambodia) *see* Vishnu.

Phrixos (Greek) *see* Phrixus.

Phrixus *Phrixos, Phryxus* (Greek)
Deified mortal. Phrixus is the son of Athamas and Nephele,
who with his sister, Helle, escaped from their wicked stepmother Ino on the back of a winged, golden ram and flew to Colchis. Only Phrixus survived. He married Chalciope, the daughter of Aeetes, the cruel king of Colchis, and became the father of Argus (who convinced Aeetes to give the Golden Fleece to Jason), Cytissorus (who helped the Argonauts capture the Golden Fleece), Melas, Phrontis and some writers mention Presbon. In some accounts, Phrixus lived a long and happy life and others say that his father-in-law Aeetes killed him to protect himself, having learned from an oracle that he would die by the hands of a foreigner. *See also* Aeetes; Argus (D); Athamas; Golden Fleece; Ino; Jason; Nephele.

Phrontis (Greek)
He is the brother of the deified mortal Phrixus (q.v.).

Phryxus (Greek) *see* Phrixus.

Phtha (Egypt) *see* Ptah.

Phuca (Celtic) *see* Puck.

Phuphlans (Etruscan) *see* Bacchus; Fuflans.

Phyag-na-rdo-rje (Tibet) *see* Vajrapani.

Phyag-na-rin-chen (Tibet) *see* Ratnasambhava.

Phyderi (Celtic) *see* Pryderi.

Phylacides (Greek) *see* Acacallis.

Phylacus (Greek)
Phylacus, the former king of Phylace, is the son of Deion and Diomede. He wed Clymene, the daughter of Catreus, the partial ruler of Crete, and became the father of Alcimede, who became the mother of the hero and Argonaut Jason and Iphiclus, also an Argonaut. *See also* Actor; Clymene; Diomede.

Phyllis (Greek)
Phyllis is the daughter of one of the kings of Thrace: Lycurgus, Phyleus or Sithon. She married Demophoon and had an affair with Acamas. For details, *see* Acamas (A).

Phylodameia (Greek) *see* Danaus.

Phylomache (Greek)
Phylomache is the daughter of Amphion and Niobe. *See also* Acastus; Amphion; Niobe.

Phyrra (Greek) *see* Eurydice.

Phytalmios (Greek) *see* Dionysus.

Phyxios (Greek) God of Escape. An epithet of Zeus.

Pi-hia Yuan-kun (China) *see* Sheng-mu.

Pi-hsia-yuan-chun (China) *Pi-hsia*
Also known as: *Kuan Yin* (Buddhist), *Princess of the Streaked Clouds, Shen Mu, Sheng-mu, Yuan-kun.*
Goddess of childbirth and women with children. She had two attendants, one who brought children, the other ensured good eyesight for them. She is the daughter of the Great Emperor of the Eastern Peak, Tung Huang T'ai I. Pi-hsia-yuan-chun is shown as a woman wearing a headdress adorned with the wide-winged birds. Pi-hsia-yuan-chun is indirectly associated with

the Jade Emperor (Yu-ti). She is the same as the Buddhist deity, Kuan Yin. *See also* Tung Huang T'ai I.

P'i-Lu-Cha-Na (China)

P'i-Lu-Cha-Na is a god of light who is the same as Vairo-cana (q.v.). *See also* Vajrasatwa.

Pi-yusha (India) *see* Amrita.

Picus (Roman)

Demigod. Prophet. His parents are the god of agriculture, Saturn, and the nymph Venilia or Sterculus, the King of Latium (who is often identified with Saturn) and Venilia. Some say he is the twin of the ancient god of agriculture Pilumnus. The women in Picus' life are Pomona, the goddess of fruit trees and gardens, and the nymph Canens. Circe, the sorcerer with the wonderful hair fell madly in love with Picus. When he rejected her, she turned him into a woodpecker. Canens searched for him for six days. Grief-stricken when she could not find him, she dissolved in her own tears and died. Picus is the companion of Mars in his role as god of prophecy. Picus could be an aspect of Saturn. *See also* Circe; Fanus; Mars; Saturn.

Pidray *Pidrai* (Canaan, Syria, Ugarit)

She is the daughter and perhaps wife of the god of rains, Baal, and the sister of two sisters, Tallai and Arsai. Her name means "mist," and she is a nature goddess who symbolizes light. Her sister Tallai symbolizes dew and rain, and Arsai symbolizes the earth. *See also* Baal.

Pien-ch'eng (Central Asia)

One of the Ten Kings of Hell. Supervised by King P'ing-teng Tushi, he beats the guilty souls. *See also* Kshitigarbha.

Pierus (Greek) *see* Muses.

Piko-po-no-ninigi (Japan) *see* Ninigi.

Pillan *Pilan* (Araucanian People, Chile, South America)

Weather god. Thunder god. After death, tribal chiefs, assuming the form of volcanoes, were met by Pillan. Pillan's activities cause lightning and earthquakes. Pillan has many spirits of evil, known as Huecuvus, under his command, who bring drought, disease, and other disasters to mortals. The Huecuvus are shape changers. The other spirits under Pillan are the Cherruve, who look like snakes with human heads. *See also* Auchimalgen.

Piltzintecutli *Piltzintecuhtli-Tonatiuh* (Mexico, Aztec)

Also known as: *Oxomoco* (probably).

He married a woman who was made from one of the hairs of the goddess, Xochiquetzal. (This legend is the same as that attributed to Oxomoco.) Some say he was connected with Tonatiuh Metztli and Tezcatlipoca. His hair is golden. During festivals he is represented by young men climbing poles in contests. Piltzintecutli is the planet Mercury. *See also* Legend of the Four Suns; Oxomoco; Tonatiuh; Xochipilli; Xochiquetzal.

Pilumnus (Roman) Ancient god of agriculture. *See also* Picus.

Pinaka (India) Shiva's sacred bow.

Pinau (Inca) *see* Ayar Auca; Manco-Capac; Tahuauntin Suyu Kapac.

Ping-ten Tush (Central Asia) *see* Kshitigarbha; Peen-Ch'eng.

Pinga (Caribou Eskimo People, North America)

She is the guardian of animals, the goddess of souls, guardian of the souls of the living, and a healing deity. She instructs the moon-god Alignak when to return the souls of the dead to earth to be reborn. *See also* Alignak; Sedna.

Pingala (India) *see* Hariti.

Pinka *Pasupata* (India)

Pinka is Shiva's sacred trident which symbolizes his primary functions of creation, preservation, and destruction. *See also* Shiva.

Piorun (Slavic) *see* Peron; Perun.

Pipisao (South America) *see* Jukki Ajayo.

Pirrhua-Manco (Peru) *see* Manco Capac.

Pisakas (India) *see* Pishachas.

Pisasha (India) *see* Pishachas.

Pishacha-Loka (India) *see* Loka.

Pishachakis (India) *see* Pishachas.

Pishachas *Paisacha, Pisakas, Pisasha, Pishachakis* (female), *Pishachi* (female); (Brahmanic, Hindu; India)

Also known as: *Pishags* (Celtic).

The Pishachas are vicious, flesh-eating demons who are usually found hanging around burial grounds. The males are known to seize sleeping, drugged or insane women, which results in illegitimate births. Manu condemned these acts. These bloodthirsty monsters are believed to be the souls of mortals who have died violent or untimely deaths. Others say they emanate from Shiva in his angry form as Rudra. In the *Mahabharata*, they were created by drops of water from Brahma and they live in Northern India. The demon Pishacha, a daughter of Daksha, is the mother of the Pishachas and Pishachis. These demons, like the Apsaras, who originally haunted rivers and holy pools, are described as pious. The Asapishachikis are female demons who are another kind of Pishachis (female Pishachas). The Pishachas are similar to the Rakshasas but more malevolent. *See also* Apsarases; Bhutas; Darbas; Dasyus; Panis; Pratas; Rudra.

Pishachi (India) *see* Pishachas.

Pishags (Celtic) *see* Pishachas (India).

Pishumi (Acoma People, North America)

The Spirit of disease. *See also* Katsinas; Mayochina.

Pisinoe (Greek) *see* Sirens.

Pistis Sophia

(Post-Christian Gnostic. Possible remnants of worshipers associated with Marcion and Valentinus)

Also known as: *Pistis, Sophia.*

Supreme deity. Known as the "Virgin of Light," Sophia resembles the characteristics of the Asiatic goddess Astarte or the Greek Aphrodite. The doctrine of the Gnostics differs from Christian doctrine in many ways, particularly in their concepts of the life and death of Jesus. Pistis Sophia appears to follow a great deal of the Egyptian beliefs. Their version of heaven consists of a series of spheres, one above the other. Hell follows that of the Egyptian Tuat in that there are halls with governors corresponding to the travels of Osiris through Tuat. The governors are Enkhthonin, Kharakhar, Arkharokh, Akhrokhar, Markhour, Lamehamor, Lonkhar, Arkheokh, Xarmarokh, Rhokhar, and Khremaor.

Pitamaha (India) "Grandfather." *See also* Brahma.

Pitar (India) *see* Pitri; Prajapati.

Pitri-Loka (India) *see* Loka.

Pitripati (India) *see* Yama.

Pitris (Hindu; India)
Also known as: *Pitar.*
Semi-deified, the Pitris are the souls of ancestral spirits. The living give offerings to insure that the Pitris will reside in paradise with their ruler Yama. Svadha ("Sacrifice") is their mother. Compare Pitris to Fravashi; Manes. *See also* Daksha; Prajapati.

Pitriyana (India) Path of the Fathers. *See also* Yama.

Pittheus (Greek)
King of Troezen. He is the son of Pelops and Hippodameia, the father of Aethra and the grandfather of Theseus. For a list of his siblings, *see* Pelops. *See also* Hippodameia; Theseus.

Piye-Tao (Mexico) *see* Coqui-Xee.

Place of Reeds (Aztec People, Mexico) *see* Aztlan.

Plain of Two Mists (Celtic) *see* Achren.

Plains of Ida (Teutonic) *see* Gladsheim.

Plat-eye (West Indies)
An evil spirit or ghost that often appears in the shape of a dog with captivating eyes that can envelope the victim. Sometimes only eyes are visible and the longer you stare at them the larger they become. The Plat-eye is usually seen on the night of the new moon.

Pleaser of Brethern (Egypt) *see* Qebhsneuf.

Pleiades (Greek)
Deified mortals. They are the seven daughters of Atlas and Pleione or Atlas and Aethra, who being pursued by Orion, appealed to the gods for help. Zeus transformed them into doves and placed them among the stars. Their sisters were the Hyades. One of the Hyades, Sterope, disappeared after marrying a mortal. The other Pleiades are Alcyone, Celaeno, Electra, Merope, Maia and Taygeta and possibly Calypso. *See also* Calypso; Maia; Merope; Orion; Pelops.

Pleione (Greek)
Also known as: *Aethra* (Greek).
She is the Oceanid daughter of Oceanus and Tethys. *See also* Calypso; Orion; Pleiades.

Pleisthenes (Greek) *see* Agamemnon; Helen.

Pleuron (Greek)
Pleuron is the son of Aetolus, the king of Elis, and Pronoe. His brother is Calydon (who married Aeolia). Pleuron and Xanthippe married and became the parents of Agenor (who married Epicaste) and three other children.

Plexippus (Greek) *see* Althea.

Plouton (Greek) *see* Pluton.

Pluto (A) *Plutos* (Greek)
Also known as: *Dis Pater* (Roman), *Hades* (Greek), *Mantu* (Etruscan), *Orcus* (Roman), *Pluton* (Giver of Wealth).
Underworld deity. The taciturn brother of Zeus, who placed him in charge of all the Lower World. Zeus gave him the scepter of Tartarus. *See also* Cerberus; Dis Pater; Fabruus; Hades; Serapis.

Pluto (B) (Greek)
Pluto is the daughter of Cronus, lover of Zeus and mother of Tantalus.

Plutodotes (Greek) *see* Dionysus.

Pluton *Plouton* (Greek)
An epithet of Hades as the "Giver of Wealth."

Plutus (Greek)
Also known as: *Plouton, Ploutos.*
God of agricultural abundance. He is the son of Iasion and Demeter. The goddess of peace, Pax, raised him. He was blinded by Zeus for bestowing his gifts on good and noble mortals only. Since that time his gifts are distributed indiscriminately. *See also* Demeter; Eirene.

Pneuma (Egypt) *see* Shu.

Po (Samoan; Oceanic)
Also known as: *Ao-Pouri.*
Pre-existent darkness. Po is the son of Ilu (the Firmament) and Mamao (Space). Po's sister/mate is Ao (day). With Ao, Po created two children, Rangima (Bright Sky) and Rangiuri (Night Sky). Together Po's parents were the sky. Tagaloa the Ocean god (known in Polynesia as Tangaroa) placed high rocks in strategic positions to hold the sky in place. *See also* Ta'aroa.

Po-i Ta-shi (China) *see* Kuan Yin.

Podarge (Greek)
Also known as: *Celaeno* ("blackness").
Podarge is one of the Harpies and the mother, by Boreas, the north wind, of Achilles' immortal steeds, Xanthus and Balius. Her parents are Thaumas and Electra. Her siblings are Aello and Ocypetes. *See also* Aello; Celaeno; Harpies; Xanthus; Zephyrus.

Poeas (Greek) One of the Argonauts.

Pohja *Pohjola* (Finland)
Located beyond a great whirlpool, north of Finland in the Arctic Ocean, Pohja is the home of the dead. It is ruled by Louhi, the evil sorceress. *See also* Ilmarinen; Louhi; Vainomoinen.

Pohjola (Finland) *see* Pohja.

Poko-ha-rua-te-po (Polynesia)
Night wind. One of the wives of Rangi. Their children are Ha-nui-o-rangi, Ta-whiri-ma-tea, and many wind deities. *See also* Rangi.

Pole Star (Pawnee People, North America) *see* Tirawa.

Polevik (Russian, Slavic)

Also known as: *Polevoi, Polevoy.*

Spirit of the field. If you are drunk and fall asleep in a field, a Polevik may attack and murder you. A Polevik is usually dressed in white. He may have grass in place of hair. He could appear as a dwarf with two different color eyes. The female version may be Poludnitsa, who is not as vicious. Sometimes shown in white. *See also* Leshy.

Polias (Greek) *see* Athena.

Pollux (Roman)

Pollux is the Roman name for the Greek Polydeuces. *See also* Castor; Dioscures; Leda; Polydeuces.

Polotu (Polynesia, The Tongan people)

The Underworld. Ruled by the goddess, Hikuleo.

Poludnitsa (Russian, Slavic)

Also known as: *Polednica, Poludnica, Prez-Poludnica.*

Goddess of the fields. Although she is probably related to the Polevik, she is not a murderer. Like the Leshy, she loves to misguide travelers. She particularly likes to make children get lost in corn fields. Poludnitsa is described as a lovely woman dressed in white.

Polybotes (Greek)

He is a giant son of Gaea, who is associated with the sea god, Poseidon. *See also* Gaea; Giants.

Polybus (A) (Greek)

His parents are Antenor and Theano. *See also* Acamas (B); Argus (C).

Polybus (B) (Greek)

He is the son of the messenger of the gods, Hermes. He married Periboea.

Polybus (C) (Greek)

King of Corinth. Polybus is the son of the sun god Helios. He married Merope. Oedipus is his foster child. *See also* Helios; Merope; Oedipus.

Polycaste (Greek)

She is the youngest sister of Antilochus (q.v.).

Polycaon (Greek)

First king of Messenia. He is the husband of Messene (q.v.). *See also* Iphimedeia (A).

Polydamas (Greek)

Polydamas is the son of Antenor and Theano. An Argonaut, he married Lycaste, the daughter of Priam, the last king of Troy. Father and son were accused of being traitors in the Trojan War. *See also* Acamas (B); Antenor; Priam; Theano.

Polydectes (Greek)

Polydectes is the son of the human magnet, Magnes, and a Naiad (fountain and spring spirits). The fisherman who turned king, Dictys, is his only sibling. Polydectes was supposed to be guarding Danae and her son, Perseus. He attempted to rape Danae but was stopped by Dictys. His life ended when he was turned to stone by Perseus. *See also* Acamas (B); Acrisius; Dictys; Perseus.

Polydeuces (Greek)

Also known as: *Pollux* (Roman).

One of the Dioscuri. His famous parents are Zeus and Leda and his sister is Helen of Troy. Polydeuces is the famous warrior brother (some say friend) of Castor. *See also* Amycus (A); Argonauts; Castor; Helen; Jason; Leda; Zeus.

Polydora (A) (Greek)

Polydora is the daughter of the Argonaut who killed the Calydonian Boar, Meleager, and Cleopatra, the daughter of Idas and Marpessa. *See also* Meleager.

Polydora (B) (Greek)

Her parents are Peleus and Antigone or Peleus and Polymela. Achilles is her half-brother.

Polydore (Greek)

She is one of the fifty daughters of Danaus, forty-nine of whom murdered their husbands on their joint wedding night. Her husband was Dryops. *See also* Danaus.

Polydorus (A) (Greek)

He is the son of the king of Thebes, Cadmus, and Harmonia. His parents were turned into beautiful snakes. *See also* Cadmus; Harmonia (A); Ino.

Polydorus (B) (Greek)

His parents are Priam and Laothoe or Priam and Hecuba. He could not participate in the Trojan War because of his youth. Instead, he was given a treasure to transport to Polymnester, the king of Thrace. The king murdered Polydorus for the treasure. Hecuba in turn, killed Deipylus, the son of Polymnester and Ilione (the daughter of Priam and Hecuba and is the woman who raised her brother Polydorus), and blinded Polymnester. *See also* Hecuba; Priam.

Polyeidus (Greek)

Polyeidus is a prophet. He once died and was brought back to life by Glaucus, the son of Minos. *See also* Acacallis; Bellerophon; Glaucus; Pasiphae.

Polyhymnia *Polymnia* (Greek)

She is the Muse of song. *See also* Muses.

Polyidus (Greek) *see* Polyeidus.

Polymede (Greek)

She is the daughter of the thief Autolycus and the mother of the Argonaut hero Jason (q.v.).

Polymela (A) (Greek)

Polymela, the daughter of Actor and Aegina, committed suicide when she thought her husband, Peleus, had abandoned her. *See also* Actor; Peleus.

Polymele (B) (Greek)

She is the daughter of Peleus and Polymela. *See also* Jason; Polymela.

Polymnia (Greek)

Another spelling for the Muse of song, Polyhymnia.

Polynices *Polyneices* (Greek) *see* Polynices.

Polynesia — Creation Legend *see* Ta'aroa; Vari (A); Vatea.

Polynices (Greek)

Polynices is the son of Oedipus and Jocasta (some say Euryganeia could be his mother). He agreed with his brother, Eteocles, to be the king of Thebes on alternate years. Eteocles reneged on the agreement. The brothers fought and killed each other. Their deaths caused Adrestus to lead the Seven Against Thebes. *See also* Adrestus; Antigone; Eteocles; Oedipus.

Polypheme (Greek) *see* Jason.

Polyphemus (A) (Greek)
Giant. He is the one-eyed giant son of Poseidon and nymph Thoosa (some say the son of Uranus and Gaea) and most renowned of the Cyclops. He rivaled Acis for the affections of Galatea. When she rebuffed his overtures, he killed Acis. He captured Odysseus and twelve members of his crew, and ate two crew members a day. The remaining crew members were able to escape, after Odysseus blinded Polyphemus, by tying themselves to the underside of goats and sheep. He lived on the island of Sicily. *See also* Acis; Cyclops; Odysseus; Phorcys; Poseidon.

Polyphemus (B) (Greek)
First king of Cius in Mysia. He is the Argonaut son of Elatus of Arcadia and Hippea. His siblings are Caenis (who was born female and changed her sex to male) and Ischys, the lover of Coronis (the Thessalian princess who was unfaithful and who was subsequently killed). Polyphemus fought against the Centaurs but was later abandoned by his colleagues, the Argonauts, because he was an old man. *See also* Argonauts; Caenis; Centaurs; Coronis; Polyphemus.

Polyphontes (Greek)
He was one of the Thebans defending the city against the Seven Against Thebes. His colleagues were Actor, Hyperbius, Lasthenes, Melanippus, and Megareus. *See also* Adrestus; Megareus; Melanippus.

Polypoets (A) (Greek)
He is the blonde son of Peirithous and Hippodameia. With Leonteus, he took forty ships to the Trojan War. He was also the winner of the iron ball throwing contest at the funeral games of Patroclus. *See also* Hippodameia (B).

Polypoets (B) (Greek) His parents are Apollo and Phthia.

Polypoets (C) (Greek)
He is the son of Odysseus and Callidice.

Polytechus (Greek) *see* Aedon.

Polyxena (Greek) *see* Achilles; Cassandra.

Polyxo (A) (Greek)
She could be the mother of Deipylus (q.v.) *See also* Antiope.

Polyxo (B) (Greek)
She is the wife of Nycteus and the possible mother of Antiope.

Polyxo (C) (Greek) One of Apollo's priestesses.

Pomona (Roman)
Goddess of fruit trees and orchards. She was pursued by many suitors, including Vertumun, the god of the season. She rejected all of them. Vertumun disguised himself, returned to her and was accepted as her husband. Pomono's sacred month

is September. She is comparable to the goddess of plenty, Ophs (q.v.).

Pon Okikurumi (Japan) *see* Okikurumi.

Pontos (Greek) *see* Pontus.

Pontus *Pontos* (Greek)
Also known as: *Oceanus.*
Sea deity. According to Hesiod, Pontus (the sea), Uranus (Sky), and Ourea (Hills) were created by Gaea (Earth) when time began. He is without personal attributes and is thought to be a personification of the vastness and deepness of the sea. Pontus and his mother Gaea became the parents of the sea monster Ceto, Crius, and the sea gods Nereus, Eurybia, Thaumas and Phorcys. These offspring are also attributed to Oceanus and Gaea. *See also* Ceto; Chaos; Gaea; Nereus; Oceanus.

Popol-Vuh (Maya)
"The Collection of Written Leaves." This early book compiles myths, including the creation myth, psuedo-history and later pure history of the Quiche People. It is a source of the names of many of the Mayan deities. Among the creator gods mentioned are Ajbit, Ajtzak, Alom, Bitol, Cabaguil, Chirakan-Ixmucane, Gukumatz, Hunahpu-guch, Hunahpu-utiu, Ixmucane, Ixpiyacoc, Qaholom, Tepeu, and Tzakol. Each of these deities have their own entry.

Porphyrion (Greek)
He is one of the giant sons of Uranus and Gaea. He died at the hands of Heracles. *See also* Alcyoneus; Giants.

Porthaon (Greek)
First king of Calydon. He is the son of Agenor and Epicaste and the father of Alcathous, Agrius, Melas, Oeneus and Sterope by Euryte. *See also* Agrius; Oeneus; Calydonian Boar Hunt; Sterope.

Portunus (Roman)
Also known as: *Melicertes* (Greek), *Palaemon.*
Portunus is the Latin name for the Roman god of harbors and ports, Palaemon.

Porus (Roman) God of plenty.

Poseidon (Greek; possibly Indo-European origin)
Also known as: *Aegeus, Genethlios, Hippios, Neptune, Neptunius* (Roman), *Neptuns* (Etruscan).
Poseidon is the Greek god of the sea. God of rivers (in Thessaly). Patron of horse racing. One of the twelve great Olympians. Poseidon is the son of Cronus and Rhea, brother of Zeus, Hades, Hera and Hestia. Swallowed at birth by his father, he was later set free by Zeus. Zeus, Hades and Poseidon drew lots and Poseidon received the sea as his domain. He took up residence in a palace in the depths of the Aegean Sea. Daily Poseidon rides through the ocean in a chariot led by sea-horses. Called the patron of horse racing, he is said to have created the horse by a blow of his trident on a rock. In classical times, Poseidon was known as Hippios, taken from *hippo,* meaning "horse." In his horse form he coupled with Demeter in her form as a mare and created many horses as offspring. The Romans called him Neptune. As Neptune he is the husband of Salacia (goddess of salt water), who was similar to Amphitrite. He was thought to have

ruled the earth but was replaced by Zeus. Don was one of the twelve great Olympians. In one myth, Laomedon asked Poseidon to assist in building the walls of Troy, and later refused to pay him. In retaliation, Poseidon sent a sea monster to devour Laomedon's daughter, but it was killed by Heracles. He desperately wanted the privilege of naming the city as did Athene. After arguing over it, they agreed that the one who could bestow the most useful gift upon the city would have the right to name it. Poseidon struck his trident into the ground and a well of water appeared (another myth says a horse appeared) but Athene summoned the olive tree to spring from the ground. She won the contest. He was an ally of the Greeks in the Trojan War. Like Zeus, he had many lovers and offspring. One of his lovers was Agamede, the wife of a sterile husband, Mulius. Agamede and Poseidon had three sons: Actor, Belus and Dictys. He is usually depicted seated in a chariot as he is drawn across the sea by horses, holding a trident in his hand (used for creating earthquakes). On his head sits a crown of marine shells and aquatic plants. An attribute of Poseidon is the destructive whirlwind, which twirls around to the left. (A whirlwind which twirls to the right has a quiet center.) The great fish Ceto was sacred to Poseidon. Some say Aegeus is a form of Poseidon. For a list of his offspring by his spouse Amphitrite (q.v.) Compare Poseidon to Sedna (Eskimo People). Compare to Varuna (India). *See also* Actor (B); Actor (C); Aegis; Aello; Aeolus (A), Aeolus (B); Agenor (A); Ajax the Lesser; Aloeides; Althea; Amycus (A); Andromeda; Antaeus; Ares; Athene; Bellerophon; Belus; Calydonia Boar Hunt; Ceto; Cronus, Curettes; Dictys; Europa; Eurydice (C); Gaea; Golden Fleece; Harpies; Hestia; Inachus; Lamia; Medusa; Minos; Oannes; Oceanids; Oenomaus; Orion; Paeon (E); Pasiphae; Pegasus; Pelasgus; Pelias, Pelops; Periboea (E); Periclymenus (B); Perimele (B); Phineus (A); Phocus (A); Phorcys; Polybotes; Polyphemus; Sarpedon (B); Scylla.

Poshaiyangkyo (Zuni People, North America)

Father of all Medicine. First Man.

Postverta *Postvorta* (Roman)

Also known as: *Carmenta, Carmentis.*

She is the goddess of the past and a prophet. Her sister, Antevorta (the future), is also a prophet. At one time, the sisters were one. Postverta is also the goddess of women's ailments and childbirth. *See also* Antevorta; Carmentis.

Postvorta (Roman) *see* Postverta.

Potamids *Potameides* (Greek)

The Potamids are nymphs who live in fountains, springs and rivers. *See also* Naiads; Napaeae; Nymphs; Oceanids; Oreades.

Potos (Phoenician) *see* Air (A); Aura.

Pou-Tai (China) *see* Hotei (Japan); Mi-Lo Fu.

Poudan (German) *see* Odin.

Pourushas (Persian) *see* Haoma.

Prabhasa (India) *see* Vasus.

Pradyumna (Hindu; India)

Also known as: *Kama* (an earlier avatar).

Sambara, the draught demon, abducted Pradyumna, the week old son of Rukmini and Krishna, and threw him into the water where he was swallowed by a fish. Sambara's housekeeper, Mayadevi, found the child inside the fish and raised him. In some renditions, the sage Narada, upon seeing the infant, informed Mayadevi that he was a god. In other accounts, it is said that when he was of age, Mayadevi told him that she was not his real mother and that she loved him. An affair ensued, they killed Sambara, and Pradyumna whisked her off to Dvarka, his father Krishna's celestial kingdom. They became the parents of Aniruddha. Pradyumna came to his end in a drunken brawl and returned to life once again as Kama. Mayadevi is an avatar of Ratri, Kama's love in his earlier life as Pradyuma, god of love. *See also* Aniruddha; Dvarka; Kama (A); Krishna; Mayadevi; Narada; Ratri; Rukmini; Sisupala (one of Krishna's demon enemies).

Prah Prohm (Cambodian) *see* Brahma.

Prahlada (Hindu; India)

Prahlada is the son of the demon king, Hiranya-kasipu. To his father's chagrin, Prahlada was devoted to the god Vishnu. This devotion caused consternation and anger to the evil demon Hirany-kasipu, who tried to kill his son and failed. Vishnu, in his avatar as Nara-Simha, the half-man, half-lion, finally killed Prahlada's father. Vishnu left the region of Patala to Prahlada, who was a kind and just king. He became the grandfather of the virtuous king of Mahabalipura, Bali. *See also* Bali (B); Daityas; Hiranya-kasipu; Nara-Simha; Patala; Vamana (Vishnu's avatar as a dwarf); Vishnu.

Prajapati (A) *Dhata, Dhatr, Pasupati* (Lord of Cattle), *Pitar, Pitri, Rudra* (Vedic, Brahmanic, Hindu; India)

In the *Rig-Veda X*, Prajapati (the Golden Embryo) is the supreme god, and creator of all. As the creator and the life force of all the gods he is the first of all gods. In the *Satapatha Brahmana*, Prajapati is produced in the form of a golden egg. When he burst from the egg, the gods Agni, Indra, Soma and Parameshthin Prajapatya were created from his breath. From his downward breath the Asuras were created, bringing forth darkness. From the tears he wiped away came the air, from the tears that fell into the primordial waters came the earth, and the tears he wiped upward became the sky. He then created all else. In one version he was created from the primeval waters and was born in one year, and said to have a life span of one thousand years. From his first words came the seasons and the worlds. He is said to have created the Asuras. By Ushas, the goddess of the dawn, he was the father of Rudra, the storm and wind deity. Prajapati's epithet "Lord of Creation" or "Lord of Creatures" was used for Brahma and occasionally Indra. The son of Brahma, Manu, was later given this title as were the seven archpriests known as Rishis: Angiris, Bhrigu, Narada, Daksha, Kasyapa, Visvamitra and Vasishtha. Prajapati worshiped the lingam and drove the chariot of Rudra in the form of Arjuna. Prajapati is associated with and possibly the same as the god Visvakarma. *See also* Agni; Arjuna; Asuras; Brahma; Brighus; Brihaspati; Daksha; Hiranyagarbha; Indra; Kama; Kasyapa; Krishna; Kurma; Manu; Purusha; Rama; Rishi; Rudra; Sarasvati; Skambha; Soma; Surya; Vach.

Prajapati (B)

Also known as: *Mahaprajapati* (India)

She is the sister of Maya, and Siddartha's aunt.

Prajapatis (India)

The Prajapatis are the children of Brahma who were created from his mind. They are usually considered to be the same as the Rishis and Manus. *See also* Manu; Rishi.

Prajna (India) *see* Prajnaparamita.

Prajnaparamita *Prajna* (Buddhist; India)

Also known as: *Ses-rab-kyi-pha-rol-ta-phyin-pa* (Tibet). Prajnaparamita, the goddess of knowledge and transcendental wisdom, is usually associated with Manjusri. In some versions, the effigy of Akshobhya resides inside her gown. The teachings of Prajnaparamita formed the foundations of Mahayana Buddhism. Her color is white or yellow and she is shown seated on a lotus making the gesture of teaching, sometimes holding a book or a pink lotus. Her emblems are the Buddhist rosary known as a mala, a Buddhist non-tantric symbol called the pustaka, which is made of long palm leaves, and tied with a string, and utpala, a blue lotus. In an East Java Andes site carving, she is seated on a round lotus cushion. Her hands are in the dharmacakra-mudra (raised in front of her chest). This position symbolizes the "Turning of the Wheel of the Law." A lotus stalk rises from the pedestal, and winds around her left shoulder. On the top of the lotus flower rests a book, the *Sutra of Transcendental Wisdom*. She wears a profusion of numerous necklaces and bracelets and a conical headdress. The lower part of her body is covered with a patterned *kain*. In other depictions she is shown with four arms. *See also* Akshobhya; Manjusri; Namasangiti; Sarasvati.

Prakriti (Brahmanic, Hindu; India)

She is the mother of Brahma as the personification of nature. *See also* Purusha; Shakti.

Pralamba (Hindu; India)

Pralamba is an Asura who in the shape of a giant elephant was killed by Bala-Rama. *See also* Asuras; Bala-Rama.

Pramadvara (Hindu; India)

Pramadvara is the wife of Ruru, a giant Danava (q.v.).

Pramantha (India) Hindu fire god.

Pramati (India) *see* Agni.

Pramlocha (India) *see* Pramloka.

Pramloka *Pramlocha* (Hindu; India)

Pramloka, an Asparasa, was sent by Indra or Kama to distract the sage Kandu from his practice. She became pregnant and gave birth to the goddess of dew, Marisha. After being with Pramloka for nine hundred and seven years, six months and three days, which seemed like one day to Kandu, she left him. Pramloka spent the rest of her time swinging from tree to tree as a tree nymph. *See also* Asparases; Indra; Kama (A); Marisha.

Pramzimas (Lithuania)

Supreme deity. Pramzimas sent the giants Wandu (the wind) and Wejas (the water) to destroy mankind because of its wickedness. There were still a few pious mortals living, so he repented and saved them in a nut shell.

Prasena (India) *see* Syamantaka.

Prasetas (India) "Supremely Wise." *See also* Varuna.

Prasni (India)

Prasni is a cow goddess who is known as the "Goddess of the Dark Season." *See also* Maruts.

Prasuti (India)

She is the daughter of Manu who married Daksha, the early Vedic god. *See also* Daksha.

Pratas (India) *see* Pishachas.

Pratyusha (India) *see* Vasus.

Pravuil (Hebrew) *see* Nabu.

Praxidice (Greek)

Goddess of justice. *See also* Dike; Themis.

Praxithea (A) (Greek)

She is one of the fifty daughters of Thespius. She and forty-eight of her sisters slept with Heracles in one night. Praxithea became the mother of Lycurgus as a result of her union with Heracles. One sister remained a virgin.

Praxithea (B) (Greek)

Erichtonius is her husband and Pandion, the king of Athens who died heartbroken when his daughters turned into birds, is her son.

Precht (Teutonic) *see* Bertha.

Preng-ta-ma (Tibet) *see* Mala.

Presbon (Greek)

Presbon is the son of Phrixus (who is the son of Athamas and Nephele) and Chalciope (the daughter of Aeetes, the king of Colchis and the nymph Asterodeia). Presbon is the father of Clymenus, who became the king of Boeotia. *See also* Phrixus.

Preta-Loka (India) *see* Loka; Pretas.

Preta-Raja (India) King of the Ghosts. *See also* Yama.

Pretas *Yi-dvag* (Tibet); (Hindu, Buddhist; India, Tibet)

The Pretas, spirits of dead persons, often called hungry ghosts, inhabit Preta-Loka, the realm of tortured spirits also known as the ghost world. They committed wrongful deeds in a former life and have been sentenced to the circle of perpetual hunger. The Pretas are sometimes said to be goblins who travel in groups and who haunt graveyards. Comparable to the Gaki (Japan). *See also* Bhutas; Loka; Yaksha; Yakshinis.

Priam (Greek)

Also known as: *Podarces*.

"Ransomed." The father of fifty sons, and twelve daughters (some say he had fifty daughters), he was the last king of Troy. Too aged to fight during the Trojan War, he was killed by Pyrrhus. *See also* Acamas (A); Achilles; Amazons; Cassandra; Hesione.

Priamus (Teutonic) *see* Thor.

Priapos (Greek) *see* Priapus.

Priapus (Greek)

Also known as: *Fecundus, Mutunus, Priapos*.

Fertility god. God of fruitfulness. God of gardens, bees, vines, sheep and goats. Priapus is the son of Dionysus and Aphrodite, although some say his father is Hermes. Despite the beauty of his parents, he was born ugly and deformed. He became obsessed with Lotis, the daughter of Poseidon. He chased her until she was changed into a lotus tree. Priapus is identified with Hermes and Pan. His sacrificial animal is the lamb. Statues of Priapus are usually made of red painted wood. He is shown with unusually large sexual organs. *See also* Adonis.

Priapus (B) (Greek)

He is the son of Caeneus and brother of Phocus. The three men are Argonauts.

Primigenia (Etruscan, Roman) *see* Fortuna.

Primordial Hill (Egypt) *see* Ogdoad, The.

Prince Cataract (Japan) *see* Taki-tsu-hiko.

Prince Millet (China) *see* Ho-Chi.

Prishni (India) *see* Prisni.

Prisni *Prishni* (India)

She is the Cow Goddess also known as the Goddess of the Dark Season. *See also* Maruts; Rudra.

Pritha (A) (India)

Mother of the Pandavas. *See also* Kunti; Pandavas.

Pritha (B) (India) *see* Kunti; Prithiva.

Prithi (India) *see* Prithiva.

Prithiva (Hindu, Vedic; India) *Pritha, Prithi, Prithive, Prithivi,* (Earth), *Prthivi.*

Also known as: *Dyaus-Pita* (Sky Father), *Dyaus-Pitri, Dyava-Matar* (Earth Mother), *Dyavaprithivi, Dyavaprthivi* (Sky and Earth).

In the Vedas, Prithiva, the earth and personification of fertility, is the wife of Dyaus (heaven or the sky) and the mother of the great storm god Indra and Agni, the god of fire. Her daughters are the goddess of dawn Ushas and Ratri. She may have been the daughter or wife of the sage Prithu, and possibly the wife of the rain god Parjanya. When Indra was born miraculously from her side, the heavens and earth shook in fear. Prithiva and the other gods were also frightened. Fearing that Indra would be the harbinger of great changes in the divine order and possibly the cause of their destruction, Prithiva hid him away and ignored him. Prithiva and Dyaus were invoked separately or as a couple known as Dyavaprithivi. (*See* above for variations of the name.) They are thought of as the parents of the gods and of mortals. The Vedic gods, considered close to nature, are represented by astronomical bodies and the weather. They are divided into gods of the sky, gods of the atmosphere and gods of the earth. Examples of sky gods are Mitra and Varuna; gods of the atmosphere, Indra and the Maruts; gods of the earth, Agni and Soma. It is thought by some writers that Prithiva was either male or androgynous. In this case, she would be addressed or invoked by the name Dyaus-Pita (Sky-Father). Prithiva is depicted as a cow and Dyaus as a bull. In Vedic cosmology, heaven and earth represent a dual world, known as

Rodasi. Between heaven and earth is Antariksha, the atmosphere, where gods and demons struggle for supremacy. Apas, the celestial waters, lay beyond Antariksha, as does the Sun world, Swar. The great heaven of the gods is known as Rochana. Prithiva is associated with the solid state of matter. Her colors are orange-red and yellow. In some traditions, her color is yellow and her symbol is a yellow square. Prithiva corresponds closely to the earth goddess Bhumi (also known as Bhu, Bhumidevi, Bhu-devi), said to be a wife of Vishnu (q.v.). She is comparable to the sow and earth goddess Sukarapreyasi. Compare to Gaea (Greek). *See also* Agni; Devas (A); Dharti Mai Parjanya; Dyaus; Indra; Kunti (also known as Pritha); Lokapalas; Maruts; Ratri; Soma; Ushas; Varuna.

Prithive (India) *see* Prithiva.

Prithivi (India) *see* Prithiva.

Prithu (India) *see* Prithiva.

Priti (India)

She is thought to be one of Daksha's daughters and is one of the spouses of the god of love, Kama. *See also* Daksha; Kama; Rati; Vishnu.

Priyadarsana *Riyadarshana* (India) *see* Mahavira.

Prodromes (Greek)

After death, the twins Zetes and Calais, sons of the north wind, Boreas, and the river nymph Oreithyia, were turned into the Prodromes, winds from the northeast. *See also* Zetes.

Proetus (Greek)

Proetus is the son of either Abas and Aglaia or Ocaleia, and he was the twin brother of Acrisius. Proetus and Acrisius began quarrelling before birth. Abas gave his sons the kingdom of Argos but during a bitter dispute Acrisius expelled Proetus, who fled to Lycia and married the daughter of Iobates, Antea (also called Stheneboea). With the assistance of Iobates, during a bitter battle at Epidaurus, Proetus regained his share of Argos. Shields were thought to have been used for the first time during this conflict. The goddess Hera was said to have cast a spell causing insanity on Proetus' daughters, Lysippe, Iphinoe and Iphianassa. The infliction was passed to the other women of the kingdom. Proetus offered Melampus, a Messenian seer, a large portion of his kingdom to cure them. He sent a group of strong men who created loud noises and chased the women to Sicyon. During the chase all the women were healed except Iphinoe who died. Proetus' wife fell in love with Bellerophon, who had come to Proetus to be purified, but he declined her advances. Scorned, she told Proetus that Bellerophon had attempted to seduce her and demanded that her honor be defended. Proetus had Bellerophon deliver a sealed letter to Iobates asking him to slay Bellerophon. *See also* Abas (A); Acrisius; Aglaia; Aristaeus; Bellerophon; Danae; Iobates; Iphinoe; Lysippe; Melampus; Perseus; Stheneboea.

Promachus (Greek)

His parents are Aeson and Alcimede (or possibly Polymede). He is the brother of Jason, the Argonaut, who was killed by Pelias, the king of Iolcus. *See also* Jason; Hippolyte (B); Pelias.

Prometheus (Greek)

Creator. Seer. Inventor of architecture, astronomy, medicine, writing, metal-work. He is the Titan son of Iapetos and Clymene (also known as Asia) or Gaea and brother of Atlas and Epimetheus, (some say Menoetius). His wife is Hesione, though others say she was Pandora or Pyrrha. Hesione or Pronoea became the mother of his son Deucalion. This son and his wife Pyrrha survived the great nine day Deluge that extinguished all others on the earth. Prometheus stole sacrificial fire from the heavens to give to mortals. When Zeus found out, he chained Prometheus to a rock on Mount Caucassus. Daily, an eagle or a vulture would stop by and feed on his liver, which fortunately regenerated. Finally, Heracles rescued him. In other renditions, Prometheus stole the fire from the hearth of Zeus, or the workshop of Hephaistos, or from the fiery chariot of the sun. He is sometimes credited as being the artist who shaped men and beasts from clay. According to Hesiod, Clymene was the mother of Prometheus, Menoetius, Epimetheus and Atlas. *See also* Achaeus; Aeolus (A); Deucalion; Epimetheus; Hephaistos; Oceanids; Pandora; Themis.

Pronax (Greek)
He is the son of Talaus and the father of Amphithea and Lycurgus. *See also* Adrestus; Amphithea; Talaus (for a list of siblings).

Prontis (Greek) *see* Phrixus.

Proserpina *Proserpine* (Roman)
Also known as: *Persephone* (Greek).
Queen of the underworld. *See also* Demeter; Hecate; Isis (Egypt); Persephone.

Proserpine (Egypt) *see* Proserpina.

Proteus (A) (Greek)
King of Egypt. He was the second husband of Psamathe and the father of Cabeiro, Theoclymenus and Theonoe. There is a possibility that he is the same as Proteus, known as the Old Man of the Sea.

Proteus (B) (Greek)
Old Man of the Sea. His parents are Oceanus and Tethys. He is a prophet and shape-changer who herded sheep for Poseidon.

Protogeneia (A) (Greek)
She is the daughter of Aeolia and Calydon. *See also* Aeolus (A); Ares.

Protogeneia (B) (Greek)
Deucalion and Pyrrha are her parents. She became the mother of Opus by Zeus.

Protogonos (A) (Greek) *see* Phanes.

Protogonos (B) (Phoenician) *see* Kolpia.

Prthivi (India) *see* Prithiva.

Pryderi (Celtic)
Also known as: *Phyderi*.
Originally a fertility lord. Later, ruler of the dead. Pryderi began life as Gwri, the son of Rhiannon and Pwyll. When he was an infant, he was grabbed from his cradle by an otherworldly monstrous claw. The household staff made it appear as though his mother was responsible. She was severely punished. One evening as Teirnyon Furf Liant was attending his mare who was about to give birth, the same claw attempted to snatch the foal. Teirnyon was able to drive it away. Pryderi, hiding in the stable, cried out to Teirnyon. The man saved the child and raised him as his own. In later years, he realized that the young man looked like his natural father and so returned him to his birth parents. Eventually, he married Cigfa (Kicva), the daughter of Gwyn Gohoyw. One day while hunting with his stepfather he managed to get stuck to a golden bowl and was spirited-away to the Otherworld. In a variation of this myth, he is with his mother and they enter a magic castle and are both trapped. In each case, his stepfather, Mananwydan ap Llyr, an ingenious man, rescues him. Pryderi also accompanied the giant Bran when he went to rescue his sister Branwen. He was one of the seven who survived the battle. Gwydion, the son of Don the Enchanter, stole Pryderi's pigs. A fight followed and the thief killed Pryderi who then became a lord of the Underworld. Compare to Zeus and Romulus, both taken from their mothers as infants (as was Moses). *See also* Gwydion; Mananwydan ap Llyr; Rhiannon.

Psamathe (Greek)
Psamathe is the Nereid daughter of Nereus and Doris. She changed the amorous Aeacus, king of Aegin and son of Zeus, into a seal when he would not stop pursuing her. They had a child, Phocus. Aeacus died and became a judge in the otherworld. Psamathe remarried Proteus, the king of Egypt. *See also* Aeacus; Phocus; Proteus.

Psedjet (Egypt) *see* Ennead, The.

Psyche (Greek)
Psyche is a nymph who personifies the human soul and immortality. Eros, the god of love, married her. He visited her nightly, concealing his features from her and leaving before dawn. Contriving to see him, she lighted her lamp one night and was enraptured by his beauty. When he was awakened by a drop of oil which fell on his face from the lamp, he fled, and she wandered in search of him. The goddess of love, Aphrodite, was furiously jealous and tried to thwart the lovers. Eros' prayers to the gods were answered and Psyche ultimately joined him on Mount Olympus. Compare Psyche to the Indian Urvasi. *See also* Aphrodite; Eros.

Ptah *Phtha, Pthah* (Egypt)
Also known as: *Naunet, Nun.*
Ptah was known as "the Ancient One." He is the son of Nun, husband of Sekhmet and the father of Nefertem. At Memphis, he coalesced with Ta-tanen and Sokar. Ptah was an important god, and his name was sometimes combined with other gods. Ptah-Osiris, Ptah-Seker, Ptah-Seker-Osiris, Ptah-Seker-Tem, Ptah-Hap, Ptah-Nun, and Ptah-Tatenn (or Tenen). One of the Triad of Memphis which consisted of Ptah, Sakhmet and Nefertum. His masculine aspect was Nun, and Naunet was his female aspect. The invention of the arts are attributed to him. In the Pyramid Age he was a creator god. His creative power was said to have been manifested in every heartbeat and every word. Like Khnum he was said to have created all beings on a potter's wheel. In the Late Period, he became a composite deity, Ptah-Sokar-Osiris, having incorporated the nature of Osiris and

Sokar. Short of stature, he is often mistaken for a child. He is sometimes shown as a bearded man with a tight cap and garments with the Menat (weight) hanging from the back of his neck. Depictions of the Late Period often show him with female breasts and he has been represented as a standing mummiform figure with tall plumes on his head. His holds a scepter. Compare Ptah to Hephaistos (Greek). *See also* Apis (A); Astarte; Khnum; Khonsu; Naunet; Nun; Osiris; Sekhmet.

Ptah-il-Uthra (Gnostic) *see* Abathur.

Ptah-Sokar-Osiris (Egypt) *see* Osiris; Ptah; Sokar.

Ptous (Greek)
He is the brother of Athamas and Themisto (qq.v.)

P'u-hien (China) *see* Samantabhadra.

P'u-hsien (China)
Also known as: *Pushan.*
The name P'u-hsien was given to the Vedic sun-god Pushan in Chinese mythology. *See also* Kuan-yin; Pushan; Ta-Shih-Chih.

Pu-sa (China) *see* Bodhisattvas.

Puchan (India) *see* Pushan.

Puck (Celtic)
Also known as: *Phouka, Phuca Pwakas, Pwalso.*
A spirit. The Irish Phuca is an evil spirit who appears as a demon horse. The British Puck is a mischievous elf. The Pwakas are good natured trolls. All analogous to the Pixy or Fairy.

Pueblo People — Creation Legend (North America) *see* Awonawilona; Sussitanako.

Pueo-nui-akea (Hawaii)
Owl god. Guardian. He is an owl god who brings life to the souls who are wandering on the plains.

Puka-buti-no-midu-yare-pana-no-kami (Japan) *see* Kushi-nada-hime.

Pukkeenegak (Eskimo People, North America)
Goddess of childbirth and clothing. Pukkeenegak procures food for her worshipers. She appears with her face tattooed, big boots on her feet, clad in a pretty dress.

Pukku (Babylon)
The sacred drum given to Gilgamesh by Ishtar.

Pukwudjies (Ojibwa People, North America)
Fairy people who inhabit the forests.

Pukys (Slavic) *see* Krukis.

Pulah (Finnish) *see* Puleh.

Pulastya (India)
He is the grandfather of the demon Ravana. *See also* Rakshasas; Ravana.

Puleh *Pulah* (Finno-Ugric, Russian)
Messenger. Puleh is the son of the writer of fate, Kaba. He is similar to Nabu and Thoth. *See also* Kaba.

Pulinda and Pulini (India)
Children of Kuvanna the Yakshini. *See also* Yakshini.

Puloma (India) *see* Daksha; Danavas.

Puloman (India) *see* Indra.

Pun-Gel (Australia) *see* Bunjil.

Puna (Polynesia) *see* Tii Tokerau.

Punchau (Inca People, Peru)
He is a sun god who is depicted as a warrior armed with darts. He is comparable to Epunamun (Araucanian).

Pund-Jel (Australia) *see* Pundgel.

Pundarika (India) *see* Dikpals; Lokapalas.

Punoduno-no-kami (Japan) *see* Kushi-nada-hime.

Punyajana (India) "Friendly Folk." *See also* Yaksha; Yakshini.

Pupa-no-modi-kunusunu-no-kami (Japan) *see* Kushi-nada-hime.

Puramdara (India) *see* Indra.

Purandhi (India) Goddess of Plenty.

Purbutty (India) *see* Devi; Parvati.

Puripais (Greek) *see* Dionysus.

Purohita (India)
The family priest of the gods. *See also* Brihaspati.

Purrishram (India) *see* Parashur Rama.

Purrunaminari (Maipuri, Orinoco People, South America)
Creator deity. According to myth Taparimarru, the wife of Purrunaminari bore a son named Sisiri by virgin birth. Purrunaminari has the title of "He Created Men." *See also* Kururumany.

Purukupali (Aborigine People, Australia)
Creator god and god of death. Angered because his wife Bima had allowed his son Jinini to die, he beat her and her lover, Japara. With Jinini, he walked into a whirlpool to die. He decreed that all must die because of this incident. Japara partially escaped the decree by changing himself into the moon. The scars of the beating he received still show on his face. He still has to die for three days, but is returned to life each month. For another version of the moon myth, *see* Alinda.

Purusa (India) *see* Purusha.

Purusha *Parusha, Purusa* (Brahmanic, Vedic; India)
Also known as *Ambika, Brahma, Viraj.*
In the Vedic tradition, Purusha, the "Primal Man," is a cosmic giant with a thousand heads who was sacrificed by the gods to create the universe. His heads became the sky, his feet the earth, his navel the air. His limbs produced mortals. Later, in the Brahmanic tradition, Purusha, meaning "person," was known as the first man and was the physical manifestation of Brahma. After floating on the primeval waters for a thousand years, he broke out of the golden cosmic egg. Fearful and lonely, the lord of the universe divided himself into a male and female half and created Ambika (also known as Viraj) and proceeded to create offspring. Next in the form of a pair of cattle, they created cattle and the cattle created offspring. The same steps were followed to create all living creatures in the universe. He

destroyed all sins by fire. Purusha is described as having a thousand eyes and a thousand feet which encompass the earth on every side. Symbolically, Purusha lives in the heart of every individual and Purusha fills the cosmos. Purusha represents the male force which is opposed to but unites with Prakriti, the female force (Nature), to form creation. Purusha as the grand sacrifice, who was sacrificed by the gods to create the world, stresses the importance of sacrifice as a creative event. Compare Purusha to Narayana. This creation myth is from the *Rig-Veda* X. For another creation myth from the same source, *see* Prajapati. *See also* Adam; Adhibuddha; Brahma; Buddha; Narayana (B); P'an Ku (China); Sarasvati.

Purvachitti (India) *see* Apsarases.

Purvadevatas (India) *see* Devis.

Pusa (European) *see* Hotei (Japan).

Pusait (Lithuania, Prussia)
Spirit. Pusait is a wood spirit who hides under lilac-bushes. Little dwarfs called "kaukis," bring him food from the house.

Pusan (India) *see* Pushan.

Pushan *Puchan, Pusan* (Hindu; India)
He is the son of Aditi and lover of his sister, the sun goddess Surya. A solar deity, Pushan was known in later times as an Aditya. A god of growth, he is the restorer of what is lost, guardian of roads and of cattle, and guardian of the dead. He presides over love and marriages and protects travelers. Known as a wonder-worker, Pushan motivates, invigorates and provides abundance, including food for all living things. He was the discoverer of soma, the elixir of the gods, according to some renditions and the husband of Rohini. He drives a chariot drawn by male goats, carries a golden lance, awl or goad. Because he does not have teeth (they were kicked out by Shiva), he eats offerings of mush. Pushan shares traits similar to the Asvin twins (q.v.). Compare to Thor (Norse) and Dagda (Celtic). *See also* Aditi; Adityas; Daksha; Martanda; Parvati; Savitri (A); Soma; Surya.

Pushpa (India) *see* Pushpema.

Pushpa-danta *Pushpadanta* (India)
Elephant guardian of the northwest. *See also* Dikpalas; Lokapalas; Vayu.

Pushpadanta (Nepal) *see* Pushpa-danta.

Pushpaka (India)
The celestial chariot. *See also* Kuvera; Ravana.

Pushpema *Me-tog-ma* (Tibet), *Pushpa* (India)
She is a goddess personifying blossoms. *See also* Mamaki.

Puspa (Tibet) *see* Akshobhya.

Putan (Micronesia)
Putan and his sister created everything from parts of their bodies. Some say it was Putan who instructed his sister to create everything from his body after he died.

Putana (India)
A fifteen foot female demon with poisonous breasts. She is

the daughter of Bali and sister of Bana. *See also* Bali (B); Bana; Krishna.

Pwalso (Celtic) *see* Puck.

Pwyll (Celtic)
Also known as: *Pwyll Pen Annwn* (Welsh).
Pwyll, who inadvertently insulted Arawn, the ruler of Annwn, the underworld, changed bodies with him for a year. During this period, he overcame Arawn's enemy, Hafgan, and was rewarded with the title "Lord of Annwn." In a lengthy epic, Pwyll married Rhiannon, a fertility goddess. They had a son originally named Gwri, later known as Pryderi. Tragedy visited their home and life changed drastically for the happy couple. Regarding his marriage to Rhiannon, *see* Rhiannon. For information about the relationship between Pwyll and Arawn, *see* Arawn. *See also* Achren; Annwvyn; Pryderi.

Pwyll Pen Annwn (Celtic) *see* Pwyll.

P'yag-na-rdo-rje (Tibet) *see* Vajrapani.

Pyerun (Slavic, Russian, Polish) *see* Perun.

Pygmalion (Greek)
Sculptor. King of Cyprus. Although Pygmalion was a misogynist, he created the statue of a beautiful woman and fell in love with it. Aphrodite took pity on him for the way he loved the statue, named Galatea, so she gave it life and they became parents of a son Paphos. Pygmalion also has a daughter, Metharme.

Pylades (Greek)
He is the son of Strophius and Anaxibia. He married Electra (also known as Laodice), the daughter of Agamemnon and Clytemnestra, and became the father of Medon and Strophius II. *See also* Aegisthus.

Pylus (Greek)
Pylus is the son of the god of war, Ares, and Demonice, who is the daughter of Agenor and Epicasta. *See also* Ares.

Pyracmon (Greek) *see* Acamas (D); Cyclops.

Pyrene (Greek)
Pyrene could be the mother of Cygnus by Ares (q.v.).

Pyriphlegethon (Greek) *see* Phlegethon.

Pyroeis (Greek) *see* Helius.

Pyrrha (A) (Greek)
Achilles was named Pyrrha when he lived as a woman. *See also* Achilles; Deucalion; Epimetheus.

Pyrrha (B) (Greek)
Pyrrha was the first woman. She is the daughter of Epimetheus and Pandora. *See also* Epimetheus.

Pyrshak-Khan (Altaic, Tartars) *see* Bai Ulgan.

Pythagoras (Greek) *see* Abaris.

Pythia (Greek) *see* Artemis.

Python (Greek)
Python is the famous serpent of the cave of Mount Parnassus, slain by Apollo. *See also* Apollo; Leto.

Q

Qabauil (Central, South America) *see* Huracan.

Qadesh *Kadesh, Quedesh, Qetesh* (Hittite, Semitic)
Aspects or known as: *Hathor* (Egypt), *Qadishtu, Qodshu.*
Fertility goddess. Goddess of love. She was the consort of Amurru (Reshef). She is thought to be of Syrian origin and as Kadesh, the ancient Hittite goddess, she is an aspect of Astarte and is known as the patroness of prostitutes and the holy one. Sacred prostitution rites were carried out in her cult. As the Egyptian Qetesh, she is depicted nude, holding flowers, standing on the back of a lion, sometimes facing the viewer. As Qadesh (the "holy"), called Anat, she is shown naked, standing on a lion and holding a weapon, between the Egyptian fertility god, Min, and the Canaanite god Resheph. Qadesh is comparable to the Persian Anahita and the Phoenician Anat (who is also called Quadesh). *See also* Aleyin; Allat (patroness of prostitutes); Amurru; Anahita; Anat; Astarte; Hathor; Min; Resheph.

Qadishtu (Egypt) *see* Qadesh.

Qaholom (Maya People, Yucatan) *Cajolom*
Also known as: *Hunahpu, Hunahpuutiu.*
Creator. One of the four original regents who created earth. At the time of the third creation attempt, he was made into two gods, Qaholom and Hunahpu. They were joined by the fabricating gods Ajtzak and Ajbit. *See also* Alom; Hunahpu; Popol-Vuh.

Qahootze (British Columbia, Native North American)
A supreme deity.

Qamaits (Bella Coola People of North America)
Also known as: *"Afraid-of-nothing," "Our Woman."*
Sky deity. A goddess of one of the upper heavens. Some think she is a goddess of war. She rarely visits earth and when she does sickness and death result. The Bella Coola pray to her subservient gods, Senx (the sun, called "Our Father") and Alkuntam, who created man.

Qasavara (Melanesia)
Evil spirit. Spirit opponent of Qat. A cannibal ogre who kills and stores Qat's brothers in a chest. Qat burns Qasavara in his home, and revives his brothers by blowing through a reed in their mouths. *See also* Qat.

Qat (Melanesia)
Also known as: *Quat* (New Hebrides).
A creator spirit. He created three men and three women from a tree, then hid them for three days. He gave them life by dancing and drum beating. In another tale, he created men from clay and women from plaited fronds of sago-palms. He is also credited with creating various animals and purchasing night from I'Qong (Night) who also taught him how to make dawn.

His evil counterpart is Marawa. Qat has eleven brothers all named Tangaro. In some tales Qat is opposed by his brothers. In some it is Marawa who is his opposition. Some feel Qat is the counterpart of the Polynesian deity, Maui. More likely he is closer to Nareau. *See also* Marawa; Maui.

Qeb (Egypt) *Geb, Keb.*
Also known as: *Qebeb, Qebk, Seb.*
High god. He is the husband of Nut and father of Isis, Nephthys, Osiris, and Set. Qeb is known as the "Great Cackler" who laid the solar egg. He is shown with the head of a goose. The Greeks identified Qeb with Cronus. *See also* Isis; Nephtys; Osiris; Set.

Qebehsennuf (Egypt) *see* Qebhsneuf.

Qebh-sennuf (Egypt) *see* Qebhsneuf.

Qebhet (Egypt)
Also known as: *Qebhut.*
Qebhet, the goddess of cool water, is the daughter of Anubis.

Qebhsnauf (Egypt) *see* Qebhsneuf.

Qebhsneuf *Kebehsenuf, Kebhsnauf, Qebehsennuf, Qebehsenuf, Qebh-sennuf, Qebhsnauf, Qebsnuf* (Egypt)
He is one of four divine sons of Horus and Isis. A hawk-headed god, he guarded the intestines, specifically the liver and gall bladder, in the Canopic vases. He was also the guardian of the west. His name means "Pleaser of Brethren." *See also* Amset; Hapy (A); Horus; Isis; Tuamutef.

Qebhut (Egypt) *see* Qebhet.

Qebsnuf (Egypt) *see* Qebhsneuf.

Qebui (Egypt)
God of the north wind. He is shown as a four-headed ram with four wings, or as a man with four ram heads.

Qeften (Egypt) *see* Aani.

Qererti (Egypt) *see* Aai.

Qerhet (Egypt)
Goddess of nomes. She is a serpent goddess, who is the patron of the eight nomes of Lower Egypt.

Qerti (Egypt) *see* Assessors.

Qetesh (Egypt) *see* Qadesh.

Qodshu (Egypt) *see* Qadesh.

Q're (Pelasgian)
Another spelling for Car, the ancient solar god of Syria. *See also* Car.

Qu-ba (Egypt) *see* Aai.

Quaayayp (Pericu People, Native North American)
Also known as: *Man.*
Teacher. Son of Niparaya and Amayicoyondi. Brother of Acaragui. Known as a great teacher who had many servants. It is said that he was murdered. Although dead, he still bleeds. He doesn't speak so an owl speaks for him. Quaayayp is opposed by Wac or Tupuran, who was evil.

Quadriga (Greek)
Quadriga is the name of the chariot driven by Helios, the sun, as he traverses the sky daily. *See also* Helios; Phaethon.

Quajaip (Mexico)
Also known as: *Possibly Metipa.*
Culture hero. Little information, but may have been a Christianized version of Jesus, since he was killed by the people and a wreath of thorns was placed on his head. May be related to another dying deity named Metipa.

Quakuinahaba (Mojave People, Native North America) *see* Cathen.

Quartiana (Roman) *see* Febris.

Quechua People—Creation Legend (Bolivia, Souther America) *see* Dohitt.

Quedesh (Egypt) *see* Qadesh.

Queen of Battles (Sumer) *see* Inanna (A).

Queen of the Dead (Nigeria; Africa) *see* Ala (B).

Queen Mother of the West (China) *see* Hsi Wang Mu.

Queen Mother Wang (China) *see* Wang-mu-niang-naing.

Quetzal-Coatl (Mexico) *see* Quetzalcoatl.

Quetzal-Cohuatl (Mexico) *see* Quetzalcoatl.

Quetzal-Koatl (Mexico) *see* Quetzalcoatl.

Quetzalcoatl *Kuetzal-Koatl, Kwetzal-Koatl, Quetzal-Coatl, Quetzal-Cohuatl, Quetzal-Koatl,* (Mexico, Aztec, Toltec, Maya)
Also known as: *Ce Acatl Quetzalcoatl* "One-reed Quetzalcoatl," *Ehecatl, Itztlacoliuhqui, Kukulcan* (Maya), *Omecutli-Omeciuatl, Ometecutli, Quetzalcoatl-Ehecatl, Quetzalcoatl-Xolotl, Tlahuizcalpantecuhtli, Tlauixcalpantecuhtli, Tohil-Heumac, Yolcuatl.*
"Feathered Serpent." Supreme deity. God of air, clouds and wind. God of medicine and the healing arts. God of fertility and wealth. God of thieves. God of gambling. God of fishermen. Messenger of the gods. Patron of farmers, planters, gardeners and others who work with the soil. Patron of stone engravers and cutters and of builders. Patron of gold and silversmiths and of all who work with metal. Inventor of books and writing. Inventor of the calendar. Of Toltec origin, he is the son of Ometecuhtli and Omeciuatl. Quetzalcoatl and Xolotl, his raggedy-eared dog and double and sometimes called his twin, journeyed down to the underworld, known as Mictlan, to steal the bones of mortals from a previous generation. Although Mictlantecutli, "Lord of the Sojourn of the Dead," sent quails to pursue them, Quetzalcoatl and Xolotl succeeded in their task. He sprinkled his own blood on the bones to create the present generation. The Toltec People believed that

Quetzalcoatl was sent to earth by the supreme god to be an earthly king. He was a decent ruler until he fell under the spell of a witch goddess. Tezcatlipoca, in his form of the Blue Hummingbird, Huitzilopochtli, was the instigator of this scenario. He would later become the patron of the Aztecs. The witch had under her control a magic mushroom. It was given in beverage form to the king, who innocently drank it. He became highly intoxicated. While in this state, he had sex with the witch, breaking a sacred tradition. His only choice was to leave Mexico. He took his dwarfs and other creatures who would die on the journey and sadly departed. Quetzalcoatl reached the sea coast, embarked in a raft made of serpent skins and sailed toward the sunrise. The fire of the rising sun ignited his raft. His heart arose from his body and joined the sun. It can still be seen shining in a solar eclipse. This event took place on C.E. July 16, 750, according to a painting in the ancient Mexican sacred book, *Codex Vindobonensis Mexic.I.* Nine Toltec rulers followed the first ruler, each called Quetzalcoatl. Quetzalcoatl is linked to Venus as the Morning Star. His double, or twin, Xolotl is the Evening Star. Quetzalcoatl is offered fruit and flowers. He is sometimes represented as a serpent clothed in the green feathers of the quetzal bird. Sometimes he appears as an aged bearded man with fair or black hair, large eyes and a high forehead. He is dressed in a long robe. *See also* Ehecatl; Huemac; Kukulcan; Legend of the Four Suns; Ometecuhtli; Tezcatlipoca; Xolotl.

Quetzalpetlatl (Mexico) *see* Quetzalcoatl.

Quiateot (Aztec People, Nicaragua)
Rain god. He belongs to a group of creation deities ruled by Tamagostad and Zipaltonal. Quiateot is associated with Ecalchot, Ciaga, Quiateot, Misca, Chiquinau and Vizetot. *See also* Chiquinau; Ciaga; Oxomoco.

Quiche People—Creation Legend (Guatemala) *see* Gucumatz.

Quilaztli (Aztec) *see* Cihuatcoatl.

Quinametzim (Tlaxcala, Toltec People, Mexico)
Giants. The Quinametzim are giants who inhabited the earth in the distant past, as mortals count it, and warred against mortals. According to legend, these giants ruled the second of four or five worlds (or eras). Their era is called the Sun of the Earth. When the human races of the Olmecs and Xicalancas ruled the third world called the Wind Sun, they completely destroyed the rest of the giants. At this time, the gods Quetzalcoatl or Huemac came into being. When the humans refused to obey the god's teachings the world was destroyed by high winds and the people were turned into monkeys. *See also* Legend of the Four Suns; Sun of Fire; Tloque Nahaque.

Quineuhyan (Aztec)
Emergence myth. *See also* Chicomoztoc)

Quinkan (Australian Aborigines)
Underground spirits. Dangerous and powerful spirits living in caves and crevices.

Quires (Gallo-Roman) *see* Silvanus.

Quirinus (Roman)
Also known as: *Mars, Romulus, The Spear God.*
Initially, Quirinus was an independent god worshipped by Sabine settlers on Quirinal Hill. He had a priest, the Flamen

Quirinalis. His spouse was Horta Auirini or the spouse of Romulus, Hersilia. It is possible that the Sabines borrowed Quirinus from one of the Roman names for Mars. Eventually, in the later period of the Republic, Quirinus merged into Mars. When Romulus was referred to as a god, the name Quirinus was used. Quirinus is also an epithet of Mars. Quirinus is the name of either an associate of Bellona's, or a spouse, or son. *See also* Mars.

Quiyauhtonatiuh (Mexico) *see* Legend of the Four Suns.

Quork-quork (Aborigine People, Australia)
He is the father of the thunder god, Pakadringa (q.v.).

Qur'an (Islamic) *see* Koran.

Qutrub (pre–Islamic) *see* Jin.

R

Ra *Re* (Egypt)
Also known as: *Atchet* (his female aspect), *Atum, Khepra, Phra.*
God of the sun. King of gods and mortals. In the beginning, Ra was alone, embraced by Nun, the primeval waters, protected only by a lotus. He impregnated himself and bore the air, Shu, and the moisture, Tefnut, by spitting them out of his mouth. Shu and Tefnut came together and the earth, Geb, and the sky, Nut, were born. Geb and Nut mated and produced Osiris, Isis, Set, and Nepthys. They became the nine major deities of Egypt. Collectively, with Ra at the helm as the principal deity known as Ra-Horakte, they are known as the Ennead of Heliopolis. The world came into being when Nut, transforming herself into a cow, transported Ra to the heavens on her back, and he received the title of "Lord and Creator of the World." Ra, as the sun, travels across the sky in his bark boat which he changes in the morning and evening. In the morning he boards his morning boat, Matet, and then as a falcon-headed man wearing the coiled cobra and the sun disk (uraeus) he boards his evening boat, Semktet (also called Mesektet), for his trip through the rivers of the Underworld. Ra created mortals from his tears. In time, seeing that his mortals were deceitful and unfaithful, he ordered the goddess Hathor to rid the earth of them. She was so enthusiastic about her task that only after major efforts he was able to get her to cease and desist. When Ra's eye (the sun) began to wander and could not be found at night, he sent either Anhur or Thoth to retrieve it. What they found was that the sun's place at night had been taken over by the moon. An uproar ensued that did not quiet down until Ra found suitable places and times for his eye and the moon. Many times we find Ra's name attached to another god. This gives the priest additional power. At one time, there were as many as seventy-five forms of Ra. Ra's cult symbol is the obelisk. His personal symbol is the sun. He is depicted as a hawk-headed mortal, wearing the sun's disk and uraeus, holding a scepter with a grey-hound's head. As Khepra, Ra is a dung beetle (q.v.) Additional myths pertaining to Ra are found under Isis and Nut. *See also* Aani; Amen; Astarte; Aten; Atum; Hapi; Horus.

Ra-ateni (Egypt) *see* Aai.

Ra-Harakhte (Egypt)
Also known as: *Harakhty, Harmachis* (Greek), *Heraktes, Ra-Horakhty.*
Supreme deity. Ra-Harakhte is a composite name given to the sun as ruler of Egypt and chief of the gods of Heliopolis. His name means "Horus of the Horizon." He is shown with the head of a falcon and wearing the solar disk wreathed by the Uraeus. The Greeks know him as Harmachis. *See also* Horus.

Ra-Heru-Khuti (Egypt) *see* Aaru.

Ra-Horakhty (Egypt) *see* Ra-Harakhte.

Ra-Jin (Japan)
Spirit of weather. This spirit of the thunder and wind is similar to the Oni. He has a round frame behind his back, on which are fastened small drums.

Ra-Tem (Egypt) *see* Atum; Sopdu.

Raashiel (Semitic) Earth god.

Rabisu (Mesopotamia; Babylonian)
A Mesopotamian demon who appears in nightmares; a Babylonian ghost who set bodies on end.

Rada (Haitian People, Dahomey origin, Africa)
Rada is the name for a pantheon of Haitian deities of the *vodun* cult. Other Haitian pantheons are the Petro, Congo, and Ibo gods. *See also* Agbe.

Radha (Hindu; India)
Also known as: *Lakshmi.*
Radha, an avatar of Lakshmi, is celebrated in Indian poetry and art as the pretty cowgirl who pined for Krishna while he danced and flirted with other women. The women, known as gopi or cowgirls, were irresistibly drawn to Krishna by the strains of his flute. Their dance, known as the "Rasalia" or play of delight, lasted for six months. Their spouses, known as the gopa or cowboys, were left behind while the women frolicked. The men were not jealous for they did not realize the passage of time or the absence of their mates. After a period of extensive foreplay Radha and Krishna finally fulfilled their love for

one another. Their union, as man and wife, represents the world coming into existence. Radha is associated with the earth and the west. She is not to be confused with Radha the wife of Adhiratha (Dhritarashtra's charioteer), who adopted Karna, the son of Kunti and Surya. *See also* Karna; Krishna; Kunti; Lakshmi; Surya; Vishnu; Yami.

Radheya (India) *see* Karna.

Rafnagud (Teutonic) *see* Odin.

Rafu-sen (Japan) Goddess of the plum blossom.

Raga (India) A musical melody personified as a deity.

Raga-Vidyaraja (India) *see* Aizen-Myoo (Japan).

Ragnar Lodbrog (Norse; Teutonic)
Sun hero. It is possible that he was a mortal named Ragnar. He killed the winter serpents and was given the name Lodbrog. Ragnar was the husband of Thora, who died. He married Aslog and became father of Ingvar and Ubbe, who were mortal men. According to the tale, he could only be killed by a viper.

Ragnarok *Ragnarokr* (Norse; Teutonic; Icelandic)
Also known as: *Gotterdammerung* (German), *Twilight of the Gods.*
Ragnarok is the apocalyptic final battle between the gods and the giants, involving all creation. It is the world's end when all life will be destroyed, including the gods. The nine worlds will be submerged. After the war, two humans named Lif and Lifthrasir will emerge from Hoodmimir's Wood. They will propagate the new human race. According to Norse myth, Ragnarok is the day when Loki and his followers will break their bonds and meet the gods for their final battle. All will be killed and there will be total destruction followed by regeneration. A new earth will arise, peopled by sons of Odin, Thor, Balder, and Hodur. They will live in harmony with mortals in the new world created by Alfadur (All Father). Compare Ragnarok to Armageddon. *See also* Balder; Fenrir; Garm; Hati; Hodur; Lif; Loki; Nagilfar; Odin; Skoll; Thor; Vigrid.

Ragnarokr (Teutonic) *see* Ragnarok.

Ragno (Hopi, Maidu, Pomo People, North America)
An old mother goddess, Ragno appears in the Pomo Indian Creation Legend associated with the brothers Kuksu and Marumda (qq.v.). In the Hopi Creation Legend, she is associated with the Huruing Wuhti (q.v.). *See also* Marumda.

Rahabh (Semitic)
Also known as: *Nakhash, Tannin.*
Serpent. The early Hebrews believed in a monster nature serpent called Rahabh, Tannin or Nakhash. God (Yahweh) was called on to "break the heads of Leviathan and of the dragons in the waters." He was created on the fifth day of the week of creation, and was killed by Gabriel with the assistance of Yahweh. *See also* Leviathan; Pepi.

Rahes *see* Min.

Rahu *Bhangi* (Cambodia; Hindu; India)
Originally a Daitya, this monster demon, known as "The Grasper," causes eclipses by eating the sun. He is the son of Simhika, one of Daksha's numerous daughters. Jealous of the gods who were drinking the elixir, soma, he changed himself into a god to join them. While Vishnu was creating the world, he seized the elixir and drank enough to fill a river. Surya the sun and Soma the moon were watching, and they told Vishnu. He threw his discus named Sudarshana at him and sliced off his head. His body fell to earth with the force of an earthquake but his head remained alive. It devours the moon monthly and the sun occasionally. He is depicted with a dragon's head, four arms and a tail like a comet. His chariot, drawn by eight black horses (representing night clouds), carries him through the sky. He gained immortality by drinking the sacred soma. Followers worship him by walking over hot cinders. He can be frightened away by bathing in holy waters during an eclipse, by the piercing cries of female bathers, the sounds of the conch shell, and devotional songs. *See also* Daityas; Daksha; Marichi; Savarbhanu (for a variation of this myth); Soma; Sudarshana; Surya.

Rahula (A) (Buddhist; Nepal).
Rahula is known as the Dharma Protector and is said to have arisen from the land of fire and infinite ferocity. He is grey, has nine heads, four arms and one thousand flaming eyes.

Rahula (B) Son of Gautama and Yasodhara. *See also* Buddha.

Raiden *Raijin, Kaminari Sama* (Japan)
This demon god of thunder likes to nibble on navels. The goddess Uzume caught him in her bath. He has claws and usually carries a string of drums. The only protection from him is to hide under a mosquito net. *See also* Take-mi-kazuchi.

Raijin (Japan) *see* Raiden.

Rainbow Snake *Great Rainbow Snake* (Australia)
Also known as: *Angamunggi, Galeru, Julunggul, Kalseru, Karia, Kunapapi Langal, Kunmanggur, Mindi, Muit, Ngaljod (female), Taipan, Ungud, Wollunka, Wollunqua, Wonambi, Wonungur, Worombi, Yero, Yurlunggur.*
Sky deity. He shaped the land and produced spirit children. The Rainbow Snake is sometimes identified as a mother goddess, sometimes a god, sometimes both. As Kunmanggur, he is associated with Tjinimin, the Bat.

Raja of Kasi (India) *see* Bhishma.

Rajarishis (India) *see* Rishi.

Rajyadidevatas (India) *see* Devis.

Raka (Polynesia) *see* Raki.

Raki *Raka* (Polynesia; Maori People, New Zealand)
Also known as: *Rangi.*
High god or creator. Storm deity. Most of the legend of Tane and Raki is similar to that related in Rangi. The only difference is that Tane decided to clothe Raki with stars, but they only made Raki look good at night. Some think the sun and moon were Rangi or Raki's children and later placed for eyes in the sky. In some versions of this mythology, Raka (trouble) presided over the basket of winds which he received from Vari-ma-te-takere. She also gave him the land called Moana-Irakau. *See also* Rangi; Vatea.

Raksasa (India) *see* Rakshasas.

Raksha-Kali (India) see Kali.

Rakshas (India) see Rakshasas.

Rakshasa-Loka (India) see Loka.

Rakshasas, The *Manusha-Rakshasis* (female demons in human form), *Raksasa, Rakshas, Rakshasi* (female Rakshasa), *Yakshas* (Hindu; India)

The Rakshasas, semi-divine evil spirits, are the foes of gods and mortals. They have magic powers and can take on any form at will. According to the *Ramayana*, they were created from Brahma's foot to protect the primeval waters. Their king was the demon Ravana. In other sources, they are said to be descendants of the sage Pulastya or the children of Nirriti, the Vedic goddess of death and guardian of the southwest, and her mate Nirrita, or the children of Khasa, who may have been one of Daksha's sixty daughters. As shape changers, they can appear as animals, especially dogs, vultures and owls. When the monkey god Hanuman went to their home in Sri Lanka in search of Sita, he saw that they came in every conceivable shape and form. They can appear as monstrous humans, old women or beautiful men and women. Their colors are yellow, green, or blue. Their eyes are usually vertical slits and they have matted hair and large bellies. Their fingers are set on backwards and they each have five feet. Their diet is made up of human flesh and food that has been sneezed on or contaminated by insects. If touched by their poisonous fingernails one can die. They love to hang out in cemeteries, destroy sacrifices and enter humans through their food, causing illness and insanity. Occasionally, a Rakshasas can be kindly. Vibhishana, the younger brother of Ravana, is an example. His character and behavior were unacceptable to Ravana, so he exiled him. Vibhishana went on to join Rama and became the viceroy of Lanka. Visvakarma, the divine architect, built the dwelling place of the Rakshasas. A Rakshasa known as Nairitya, the god of dread, was transformed into a guardian deity of the eight directions. His post was the southwest. A ninth century sculpture from Central Java thought to be Nairitya shows a man seated on a rectangular pedestal with the right leg folded on top of the left. He is dressed in a loincloth and wears a high headdress and elaborate jewelry. His hair is long and falls over his shoulder. He carries a sword with a curved blade in his right hand, which rests on his right knee. His left hand is placed on the right foot and he holds a small oval shield. His heavenly status is indicated by a pointed, petal-shaped halo. In a later depiction, he is seated on his mount, a bhuta (demon). Many Rakshasas were cruel humans in their previous life. If one is frightened or pestered by a Rakshasas, address it as "Uncle" and it will disappear. They represent the forces of evil and the human aspects of greed, deceit, lust and violence. See also Agastya; Agni; Asuras; Bhima (A); Bhutas; Brahma; Daitya; Hanuman; Kalanemi; Kasyapa; Kuvera; Nirriti; Pishachas; Rama; Ravana; Sita; Vasistha; Visvakarma; Vritra; Yaksha.

Rakshasi (India) see Rakshasas.

Rakshodhidevatas (India) see Devis.

Raktabija (India) A Demon. See also Kali.

Raluvhimba (Venda People, Northern Transvaal, South Africa)

The Supreme Being. Creator of All. Raluvhimba is offered prayers and sacrifices particularly during times of drought.

Rama (Hindu; India)

Also known as: *Rama-candra* ("The Embodiment of Righteousness"), *Rama-Chandra, Ramachandra, Vishnu.*

Ramachandra, often called Rama, was the Prince of Ayodhya and the seventh avatar of Vishnu. His mission in this form was to defeat the giant demon Ravana and to teach morals by setting an example. Rama, the eldest son of King Dasaratha (also known as Dasarata) and Kaushalya (also spelled Kausalya and Kooshelya) and grandson of Aja of the Solar Race. He was born as a result of Dasaratha performing a "horse sacrifice" known as the Ashvamedha. After the sacrifice, Dasaratha's three wives, Kausalya, Kaikeyi and Sumitra, spent the following night next to the beast's carcass as part of a rite thought to impart the animals potent fertility spirit to them. Vishnu appeared to Dasaratha in his celestial form after the sacrifice and gave him a nectar, a divine essence of itself, to be shared among the women. Kausalya received half and the other women each received a quarter of the total amount. Sumitra divided her portion into two. Kausalya gave birth to Rama, Kaikeyi to Bharata, and the youngest wife Sumitra gave birth to the twins, Lakshmana and Satrughna. Each son had within him the percentage of Vishnu's essence equal to the amount of nectar ingested by his mother. Kaikeyi, the second wife of Dasaratha and the mother of Rama's half-brother Bharata, wanted Rama exiled for fourteen years and wanted her son to become the king. Dasaratha had promised to fulfill any wish for his wife and it was with great pain that he told his dear son Rama of the agreement. Rama, his wife Sita, and his brother Lakshmana, abiding by Dasaratha's wish, went into exile. Sita was then abducted by the evil giant Ravana, king of the island of Lanka. Rama enlisted the assistance of the flying monkey gods Hanuman, Sugriva, and their troops to rescue her. Eventually, he returned to his home to reign but his life was fraught with struggles against Ravana and the demon Rakshasas. Throughout his life, Rama remained courageous and virtuous. The *Ramayana*, an epic poem divided into seven books, thought to have been composed in the third century by Valmiki, recounts the episodes of Rama's life. It is said that the reading of the *Ramayana* will remove all sins. Another famous epic, known as the *Tulsi Das*, written by Tulasi Dasa, servant of Lakshmi, in the late medieval Hindi period (1541–1605), also celebrates his life. Lakshmana, a partial representation of Vishnu represents perfect loyalty. Sita, an avatar of Sri, a wife of Vishnu, represents female purity and fidelity. Her name means "furrow," and symbolizes the fertile earth. Rama, thought also to be a vegetation deity, symbolizes the fertilizing function of the sky. Ravana represents evil and Lanka represents Ceylon. The Ashvamedha or "horse sacrifice" was a ritual performed by ancient Vedic kings. They sacrificed the finest stallion in hopes of producing a son. The queen was then required to spend the night next to the dead beast and to perform certain sexual rites. Of all the domestic animals, the horse was the most honored. It was believed that if a ruler would sacrifice a hundred stallions, he would become ruler of the world. In later times, the rites were modified. The horse was symbolically used during the ritual and then released to roam for a year. If the horse was found in another king's domain, the king would either accept that the horse's owner was his superior, or he would fight. The following year the horse was sacrificed. Under cover of the horse's robe, the queen would perform ritual acts thought to endow her with the animal's fertility power. The horse was then offered to the Lord of Creation, Prajapati. Kausalya is described as a virtuous woman; Kaikeyi, as young, beautiful, and proud; and Sumitra is said to have been sweet and loving. The story of Rama and Hanuman is similar to the story of Indra and the ape Vrishakapi. *See also* Agastya; Ahalya; Bali (A); Ganesha; Hanuman; Indra; Jambavan; Karttikeya; Kasyapa; Kumunda (regarding Kusha; another of Rama's sons by Sita); Kuvera; Lakshmi; Parashu Rama; Prajapati; Rakshasas; Ravana; Sampati; Sita; Soma; Sugriva; Vishnu; Visvakarma.

Rama-candra (India) *see* Rama.

Rama-Chandra (India) *see* Rama; Vishnu.

Ramachandra (India) *see* Rama.

Rambha (Hindu; India)
   The most beautiful of the Asparas, with an amiable disposition, Rambha is the spouse of Kuvera, who was raped by the demon Ravana. She was one of the treasures rescued by Kurma (Vishnu's avatar as a tortoise) from the Churning of the Ocean of Milk. Indra sent her to tempt the ascetic Visvamitra who did not submit to temptation but turned her into a stone. *See also* Apsarases; Kurma; Kuvera; Ravana; Rishi.

Ramiriqui (Muzo People, Colombia)
   Ramiriqui and his nephew, Sogamozo, created men and women. Men were created with yellow clay and women from an herb. Later Ramiriqui became the sun and Sogamozo became the moon.

Ramman (Armenia)
   Also known as: *Adad.*
   Weather or storm god. One of the early triad of Khaldi, Theispas and Artinis. He could be a forerunner of one of the Babylonian triads, Sin, Shamas, and Ramman. *See also* Adad; Khaldi.

Rammanu (Sumer) *see* Adad.

Rammon (Sumer) *see* Adad.

Rampanohitaolana *Rampanahoditra, Rampanaohozatra, Rampanaora see* Rampanelombelona.

Rampanelombelona (Madagascar).
   Creator deities. Five of the Zanahary gods who created mortals.

Ran (Norse; Teutonic)
   Ran, the goddess of the sea, is the mate of the sea deity, Aegir. She pulls drowning men down with her net. She is the mother of nine daughters who represent the waves. One of her daughters is the water goddess Angeyja. *See also* Aegir.

Ranan (Egypt) *see* Renenet.

Ranga-Hore (Polynesia) *see* Rangahore.

Rangahore *Ranga-Hore* (Polynesia, New Zealand)
   She is probably a goddess of stones. In the third attempt by

Tane to make his mother Papa his wife she refused again an sent him to his ancestor Rangahore to be his wife. This woman conceived stones instead of a child. *See also* Hine-ahu-one; Hine-tu-a-maunga; Ngaore; Papa; Tane.

Rangda (Bali; India)
   Rangda is a goddess of fertility connected with paddy fields. She is depicted with large breasts and with flames spewing from her mouth. She is also known as a witch.

Rangi (Polynesia; New Zealand)
   Also known as: *Atea, Atea Rangi, Raki, Rangi-Nui, Te Tumu.*
   Rangi is the sky god father/spouse of Papa, mother earth. In the darkness before anything began, known as Ao-pouri, beings called Po (representing the Primeval Void) wanted to create light. In some versions, these beings were the children of Rangi and Papa, while other versions say they were offspring of Po. (*See also* Po for description of the children.) The children argued about tearing Rangi and Papa apart, killing them if necessary, to make light and darkness. Finally, the god of forests, Tane, succeeded in separating the two, and found hidden, the human race. His brother, the storm god Tawhiri, was extremely upset at the separation of his parents. He acted out by creating upheavals from hurricanes and storms, uprooting his brother Tane's forests. He established his power by dominating the authority of the sky. Another brother, the god of war, Tu, did not want to submit to the power of Tawhiri. A struggle ensued between the brothers which signified the beginning of warfare. The islands of the Pacific Ocean were formed by their struggle. In the meantime, Tangaroa set the sun and moon in place and created the first woman, Hine. Hine and Tane united and created the children, who were the first Polynesian people. Tane, who symbolized fish of all species assigned Rongo the position of the god of cultivated food, Haumia-tikitiki the god of wild food, Tawhiri-ma-tea the god of winds and storms, and Tu-matauenga the god of man. In another version of this myth, Rangi is replaced by Raki and the brothers are named Tane, Takaroa, Paia and Rehua. In this scenario, it is Tane and Paia who lifted Rangi from Papa. In another version, Rua and a group of night and day gods assisted him in raising the heavens. According to some legends, Rangi had a series of other spouses and children. Four of the six wives mentioned are Poko-ha-rua-te-po, Papa-tu-a-nuku, Heke-heke-i-papa, Hotu-papa and the fifth and sixth are not described. Most of the children of these unions of Rangi and his various wives are listed as gods and goddesses in their own right. A brother, Akatauire, the husband of Ruange, is mentioned in some myths as a co-ruler, with Rangi, of Mangaia island. Rangi was known as Atea Rangi by Tuomotuans. *See also* Atea; Heke-heki-i-papa; Hotu-papa; Papa (A); Po; Poko-ha-rua-te-po; Raki; Rehua; Rongo; Rua; Tane; Tangaroa; Tawhiri-ma-tea; Tu; Tu-matauenga; Vatea.

Rangi-Nui (Polynesia) *see* Rangi.

Rangidimaola (Madagascar)
   A jester deity. He was summoned by Zanahary to be the companion of his son Razanajanahary. When Rangidimaola became vain and offensive, Zanahary sent him to earth as punishment. Razanajanahary visited his friend and gave him three pieces of wood, which Rangidimaola sculpted into human form. Razanajanahary then breathed life into them.

Ranno (Egypt) *see* Renenet.

Raphael (Semitic) God of air.

Rapithwin (Zoroastrian; Persia)

God of the noon day heat and of the summer months. When the demon of winter arrives, Rapithwin retreats below the earth and keeps the subterranean waters warm so plants and trees do not die. In Zoroastrian teaching, Ahura Mazda performed the sacrifice that resulted in the creation of the world, during Rapithwin's time of day. When the time of the renovation of the world occurs, it will also take place during Rapithwin's time of day. *See also* Ahura Mazda; Tishtrya; Yazatas.

Rasa (Brahmanic, Vedic; India)

The Rasa is the mythological river that encompasses the earth and the atmosphere. *See also* Hiranyagarbha; Pani (B).

Rashnu *Rasn* (Pahlavi dialect), *Rasnu* (Zoroastrian; Persia)

Along with Mithra and Sraosha, the angel Rashnu passes judgment of the souls of the dead on Chinvat Bridge. He holds the golden scales. *See also* Ahura Mazda; Ameshas Spenta; Chinvat Bridge; Mithra; Sraosha; Yazatas.

Rasoalao (Madagascar)

Underworld deity. She is one of two daughters of a Vazimba woman (one of the dead). The other daughter is Ravola. Before the mother died she bequeathed the gift of wild animals to the oldest daughter, Rasoalao, and to the younger daughter, Ravola, the tame animals.

Rat (Egypt)

Also known as: *Rat-Taiut.*

She is called "Mother of Gods." She could be the wife of the sun god Ra, or perhaps the name Rat is a feminized version of Ra's name. She is sometimes shown wearing a headdress of a disk with horns and the uraeus and sometimes with two feathers on the disk.

Rat-Taiut (Egypt) *see* Rat.

Rata (Polynesia)

Also known as: *Laka, Ratu-nui.*

Hero-god. As Laka he is the grandson of Tawhaki. In some legends, he is the son of Tokerau and Wahieroa. He is the possible son of the eel-woman Faumea. The tales of Rata are sometimes confused with those of Tawhaki and of Hina. Rata is credited with killing the cannibal giant Matuku. *See also* Faumea.

Ratana Sambhav (Buddhist; Nepal) *see* Dhyani Buddhas.

Ratatosk (Norse; Teutonic)

Also known as: *Ratatpslr.*

Deified animal. Ratatosk is the rabbit or squirrel who runs up and down the Yggdrasil tree promoting strife between the eagle on top and the serpent, Nidhogg, at the roots. *See also* Nidhogg; Yggdrasil.

Ratatpslr (Teutonic) *see* Ratatosk.

Ratavija (India) A Demon. *See also* Kali.

Ratha-yatra (India)

A festival for Krishna in his form as Jagannath, "The Lord of the World."

Rati (Hindu; India)

Also known as: *Maydevi; Mayavati* (Deceiver).

She is the soul mate of the god of love, Kama. When he was consumed by Shiva's third eye, she appealed to Parvati to use her influence to have him restored to life. Her request was fulfilled and he was incarnated as Pradyumna. As Mayadevi, she protected him as he grew up in this incarnation. *See also* Brahma; Kama; Parvati; Pradyuma; Priti; Shiva; Vishnu.

Ratna Dakinins (India) *see* Dakinis.

Ratna-Garbha (India) "Jewel-Belly." *See also* Kuvera.

Ratna Krotishaurima (Tibet)

This goddess, who also has the title Shakti, is found in the Bardo World on the tenth day, offering Ratnaheruka a red shell filled with blood. *See also* Karma-Krotishaurima; Padma Krotishaurima, Ratnaherukca; Shakti.

Ratnaheruka (India) *see* Herukas; Ratna Krotishaurima, Ratnasambhava.

Ratnapani (India) *see* Dhyani Buddhas; Dhyanibodhisattvas; Kshitigarbha; Ratnasambhava, Samantabhadra, Vajrapani.

Ratnasambhava (Buddhist; India)

Also known as: *Chak-na-rin-chhen* (Tibet), *Hosho-Nyorai* (Japan), *Phyag-na-rin-chen* (Tibet), *Ratna Sambhav* ("Born of a Jewel"), *Ratnaheruka* (Yellow Heruka Buddha), *Ratnapani, Rin-chen-bhyun-idan* (Tibet).

Ratnasambhava, the Buddha of goodness and beauty, is the third of the Dhyani Buddhas or Buddhas of Meditation. The central figure of the Ratna family, Ratnasambhava symbolizes wealth and dignity and the cosmic element of sensation. His negative aspect is the exploitation of wealth, and in Nepal, the embodiment of slander. His female counterpart is Mamaki, who is also said to be the consort of Akshobhya and Vajrasatwa. Ratnasambhava is accompanied by two female bodhisattvas on the third day in Bardo. The goddesses are Mala, the goddess of ornamentation, and Dhupa, the goddess who carries incense. Mala is also known as hPhren-ba-ma (Tibet), Preng-Ta-Ma and Mahlaima. Dhupa is also known as Dhupema, Dug-Po-Ma and bDug-spos-ma (Tibet). She is one of the Eight Mothers of Buddhism. Bardo, the Tibetan Buddhism after-death state, is considered the place of transition between death and rebirth. Ratnasambhava, yellow in color, always faces the south. He is seated in the gift-bestowing position (varada mudra). His symbols are the pearl (cintamani) and ghanta (bell). The horse throne is his vehicle. It represents intelligence and beauty of form. His yellow color symbolizes the wealth or fertility of the earth. The pearl or wish-fulfilling gem, which he always wears, indicates the absence of poverty. The pearl (cintamani) is also the symbol for an object used as a point of concentration when meditating. Ratnasambhava is also depicted embracing Mamaki. She symbolizes the water required as fertilizer by the earth. She is also depicted in the lalita asana (one leg pendant, often supported by a lotus. Her mudras (poses) are varanda and vitarka. The varada is the gift-bestowing gesture. The arm is pendant, all fingers are extended downward, and the palm is extended outward. The vitarka signifies argument. The arm is bent, the index finger touches the tip of the thumb, the other fingers extend upward. The goddess Mala brings out the beauty of the earth. Peaceful in demeanor, she is usually depicted dancing (arhaparyankasana). Mala has two or four arms and holds a Buddhist rosary. Dhupa represents clean air and space for vegetation to grow and waters to run clearly. Dhupa is also shown dancing, has two or four arms and holds an incense vase. *See also* Amrtakundali; Dhyani Buddhas; Herukas; Hosho-Nyorai; Kshitigarbha; Mamaki; Vairocana; Vajrapani; Vajrasatwa.

Ratnasanu (India)
Sacred Mountain. *See also* Meru Mountain.

Ratri *Ratridevi* (Hindu, Vedic; India)
Ratri is the benevolent goddess of the starlit night, darkness and sexual passion. She is the daughter of the earth goddess Prithiva and the sister of the dawn goddess Ushas, the fire god Agni and the storm god Indra. She may have been the spouse of Dyaus, who is also the husband of Prithiva. Although Ratri is said to have given birth to beings of darkness, she is not to be feared. She is invoked for protection against robbers and other perils of the night. Ratri is associated with the goddesses of twilight, Jyotsna and Sandhya, and the twin Asvins. When Ratri, dressed in dark clothes adorned with gleaming stars, retires, her sister Ushas, the goddess of dawn returns. She is depicted as a beautiful woman, sometimes shaking a cymbal. Compare to the Greek goddess of the night, Nox. *See also* Agni; Asvins; Dyaus; Indra; Prithiva, Sandhya.

Ratridevi (India) Goddess of the Night. *See also* Kali; Ushas.

Ratu-nui (Oceanic) *see* Faumea; Rata.

Rau (Egypt)
Afterworld deity. Rau carries a spear in the tenth sector of Taut.

Rauni (Finnish)
Also known as: *Akka, Maan-Emoinen.*
Thunder god. Rauni and his wife are deities of fertility. Some writers say Ukko was a supreme god and Rauni or Akka was his wife. One version uses the name Maan-Emoinen in place of Rauni and calls her an earth goddess. In this version she is the consort of Jumala or Ukko. Rauni is the wife of the thundergod Ukko of the Finns. The Lapps have a goddess named Ravdna to whom they sacrifice reindeer as they do to the thundergod. Analogous to Freyr and Freyja. *See also* Jumala; Ukko.

Ravana (Hindu; India)
Also known as: *Hiranyaksha, Hiranyakshipu, Indrajit* (Conqueror of Indra), *Sisupala.*
Ravana, a giant demon, was king of the Rakshasas in the island kingdom of Lanka. Given a protective boon by Brahma for the austerities he practiced over thousands of years, Ravana could not be killed by the gods, demons or Gandharvas. He was only vulnerable to men and beasts. He had three incarnations as Vishnu's archenemy, the first, in the form of Hiranyaksha; the second, Ravana; and the third, Sisupala. He is the grandson of Pulastya and the son of Visravas and a Rakshasi. (Some say his mother was Nikasha.) His sister is the she-demon giant Shurpanaka meaning "she who has nails like winnowing baskets," who acted as a spy for her brother. He has two brothers and a half-brother, the dwarf god of wealth, Kuvera. His brother Kumbhakarna is a giant monster who would sleep for six

months and wake up for a day. The younger brother, Vibhishana, although a demon, is of good character, much to Ravana's displeasure. After being exiled by Ravana, he was invited to join forces with Rama and eventually became the viceroy of Lanka. His eldest wife was the slender-waisted Mandodari who also mated with Bibhishan, said by some to be Ravana's brother. Ravana's mistress Rambha was also sexually involved with his half-brother Kuvera. A formidable, flying foe, able to assume any form, he could create tremendous storms, break mountains in half, and with his hands stop the sun and the moon. Even the great god Indra was unable to overcome him. Ravana overtook Swarga, Indra's heaven, captured Indra and made him a lowly servant. He was in good company; the great god Agni was the cook, Varuna the water carrier, and Vayu the sweeper. Ravana seized Lanka from his brother Kuvera and forced him to supply money. In desperation, the gods approached Vishnu for assistance in overcoming the demon. Vishnu came to earth as Rama to battle the evil and havoc personified as Ravana. One of Ravana's despicable actions was raping women. In the forest of Dandaka, Sita, her husband Rama and his faithful brother Lakshmana were living in exile. The demon Ravana dressed as a priest, made his way to the hermitage and attempted to seduce Sita. When she rejected him, he abducted her and carried her to Lanka. Rama organized Sugriva and Hanuman and their troops of monkeys and bears who were created by the gods to assist in overcoming Ravana. After building a bridge to Lanka they engaged in many battles. The lengthy attacks ended when Rama shot an arrow created by Brahma and given to him by the sage Agastya, through Ravana's chest. The arrow flew into the ocean, purified itself and returned to Rama. So it was that the creator who had protected evil incarnate ultimately destroyed it by his creation. Ravana is depicted with ten heads, twenty arms, copper color eyes and long, sharp teeth. In some carvings he is shown as a human being. His mount is the flying chariot Puspaka, which he confiscated from Kuvera. His attributes when disguised as a priest are a gourd on a strap, and a jingling staff known as a khakkhara in Sanskrit. *See also* Agastya; Agni; Bali (A); Brahma; Daityas; Gandharvas; Hanuman; Hiranya-kasipu; Hiranyaksha; Indra; Kalanemi; Kuvera; Lokapalas; Mandodari; Maya (C); Nandisha; Nikasha; Rakshasas; Rama; Rambha; Sampati; Shurpanaka; Sisupala; Sita; Sugriva; Swarga; Varuna; Vayu; Vishnu.

Raven (North American Indian) *see* Yehl.

Ravola (Madagascar) *see* Rasoalao.

Razanajanahary (Madagascar) *see* Rangidimaola.

Razeka (Arabic) Tribal god of food.

Rbhus (India) *see* Ribhus (The).

rDorge-sems-dpa (Tibet) *see* Vajrasatwa.

rDorje-P'ag-mo (Tibet) *see* Dorje Phagmo.

Re (Egypt) *see* Ra.
Realm of the Mist (Teutonic) *see* Nifl-heim.

Red Lord (A) (Native North American) *see* Hastseltsi.

Red Lord (B) (China) *see* Ch'i-ti, and Shang Ti.

Red Man (Cherokee People) *see* Asgaya Gigagei.

Red Woman (Cherokee People) *see* Asgaya Gigagei.

Rediyas (Semitic) God of water.

Regin *Reginn* (Norse; Teutonic)
Regin is probably a god of wisdom or a celestial smith, though some say he is a god of sowing and reaping. Known as a master smith, Regin taught Sigurd the art of the warrior. Regin is the youngest son of Hreidmar, the king of the dwarfs. His other sons are Fafnir and Otter. In the end, Regin was killed by Sigurd. He is usually shown with a forge. *See also* Fafnir; Sigurd.

Reginn (Teutonic) *see* Regin.

Rehua (Polynesia) *see* Maui; Rangi.

Reia (Greek) *see* Rhea.

Reidi-Tyr (Teutonic) *see* Tyr.

Reidmar (Teutonic) *see* Hreidmar.

Rekhi (Egypt) *see* Aai.

Rem (Egypt)
God of weeping. Rem is the personification of the sun god Ra's tears. His name means "to weep."

Remati (Tibet)
This tutelary goddess is chosen by certain yogis because she is associated with Tantric secret doctrines. *See also* Yeshe-Khahdoma.

Remi (Egypt)
God of fish. Known as the "Fish God." Remi is sometimes identified with the god Rem. *See also* Aai.

Remphan (Hebrew) *see* Rephaim.

Remus (Roman) *see* Romulas and Remus.

Renen (Egypt) *see* Renenet.

Renenet (Egypt)
Also known as: *Ernutet, Isis, Ranan, Ranno, Renen, Renenit, Renenutet, Thermuthis.*
Goddess of children. Goddess of fertility and the harvest. Lady of the granaries and fertile land. Renenet feeds the newborn infant and names her. She will attend her when she is judged after death. One of the months of the Egyptian calendar is named for Renenet. As Renenet, Isis is the goddess of the harvest. As Thermuthis, offerings are made to her when the corn is harvested and the grapes are pressed. She is portrayed sometimes as lion or snake-headed. She is also depicted as being crowned with the uraeus and with two ostrich feathers. As Renenet, she is also shown carrying Nepri, the young god of corn. Renenet has some of the same functions as Shai (q.v.). She is associated with Meshkhent (q.v.). *See also* Isis.

Renenit (Egypt) *see* Renenet.

Renenutet (Egypt) *see* Renenet.

Renniu (Egypt)
Afterworld deities. Four bearded gods in the eleventh sector of Tuat.

Renpet (Egypt)
Renpet is the goddess of the eternity of time. She is a deity of the springtime of life and of the early calendar. She is shown wearing a long palmshoot curving above her head.

Renuka (India) *see* Parashur Rama.

Rephaim *Rephan, Rephain, Remphan* (Hebrew)
Also known as: *Anakim, Chiun, Kiun.*
Giants. Old Testament ghosts of darkness or giant demons of Canaan. Two well-known giants are Goliath and Og. Some think they represent the souls of the dead in Sheol. Rephaim is probably the same as Remphan, who is the Satan of the ancient Israelites. Some say Chiun (a goddess of plenty) is also the name of an idol worshiped in ancient times. *See also* Chiun; Jinny.

Rephain (Hebrew) *see* Rephaim.

Rerek (Egypt)
Aspect of Set. Rerek is a form of the monster serpent taken by the god Set to oppose the sun god Ra from appearing daily in the East. Rerek is identified with Apophis.

Rerit (Egypt) *see* Taueret.

Rerir (Norse; Teutonic)
Rerir, who is probably a drought aspect of the sun, is the grandson of Odin and the son of Sigi. Rerir desperately wanted a son. Frigga (Freyja) sent her messenger Gna (or Liod, Ljod) with a miraculous apple which she dropped in his lap. He and his unnamed wife ate the apple and in due time their beautiful son, Volsung, was born. Shortly afterward Rerir and his wife died. *See also* Volsung.

Rert (Egypt) *see* Taueret.

Rerti (Egypt) *see* Assessors.

Rertu (Egypt) *see* Taueret.

Reshef (Syrian) *see* Reshep.

Reshep *Reshef, Resheph, Reshepu, Reshpu* (Egyptian)
Also known as: *Aleyin, Apollo, Nergal* (Babylonia), *Ninib.*
As an Egyptian deity, Reshep is a warrior god and is the same as the Semitic Aleyin/Amurru. He is depicted with a crown of gazelle horns, carrying a shield, spear and a club. *See also* Aleyin; Amurru; Min; Nergal; Qadesh.

Resheph (Babylonia) *see* Reshep.

Reshepu (Babylonia) *see* Reshep.

Reshpu (Babylonian) *see* Reshep.

Rest-F (Egypt) *see* Ap-taui.

Revanta (India) *see* Sanja.

Revati (India) Wife of Bala-Rama (q.v.).

Reza (Africa) *see* Leza, and Lisa.

Rhadamanthus *Rhadamanthys* (Greek)
The great god of thunder, Zeus, in the form of a white bull, had intercourse with Europa, the daughter of Agenor, and Rhadamanthus and his brothers Minos and Sarpedon were conceived. He married the widow Alcmene after the death of her

husband Amphitryon, who was killed fighting Erginus, the king of Boeotian Orchomenus. The ruler of Crete, Rhadamanthus was ousted from the throne by his brother Minos. Rhadamanthus married Alcmene and became the father of Erythus and Gortys. A lover of justice on earth, at death he was appointed one of the three judges of the dead in Hades along with Aeacus and Minos. In the Cretan tradition, Rhadamanthus is known as the son of Phaestus. For more information on his early family life, *see* Minos; Sarpedon (A). *See also* Aeacus; Europa; Styx.

Rhadamanthys (Greek) *see* Rhadamanthus.

Rhea (Greek)
    Also known as: *Acrea, Bona Dea, Brimo, Cybele, Idaea, Magna Mater, Opis, Ops, Reia, Tellus, Tera, Titaea.*
    Rhea is the oldest Greek goddess historically connected to the earth. She is known as the daughter of Phanesphobe, and wife of Cronus, who is also her brother. Other legends write that she is the daughter of Uranus and Gaea and mother of Zeus, Demeter, Hades, Hera, Hestia, and Poseidon. A syncretistic goddess, she was worshiped by many names, and had as many different attributes as she had adherents. She is well known for saving the life of Zeus by substituting a stone for him at birth which Cronus swallowed thinking it was Zeus. Rhea was particularly popular in Phrygia as Cybele, where she was regarded as a goddess of forest and wild animals. As the protectress of civic commerce she wore a symbolic castellated crown. Sacred dances were held in her honor in forests and on mountains, by her priest, the Corybantes. In the Pelasgian creation myth, Rhea and Cronus were the rulers of the planet Saturn. The name Brimo is used for Rhea as well as Demeter, Hecate and Persephone. She is shown in a carriage drawn by lions. *See also* Acamas (A); Adrastia; Cocytus; Corybantes; Cronus; Cybele; Demeter; Eurynome (A); Gaea; Hecate; Hestia; Nut; Oceanus; Ops; Persephone; Zeus.

Rhea-Silvia (Gallo-Roman) *see* Silvanus.

Rhene (Greek) *see* Ajax the Lesser.

Rhiannon (Gaul, Celtic)
    Also known as: *Mare Goddess.*
    Deity of horses. Moon goddess. Rhiannon is the daughter of Hefaidd Hen, Lord of the Underworld. Pwyll glimpsed Rhiannon galloping on her white mare. Entranced, he attempted to follow her but was unable to match her speed. He asked her father for her hand in marriage but was manipulated into making it possible for her former love to wed her. Rhiannon devised a way for Pwyll to outsmart them and the lovers were married. In time, they had a son, Gwri, later called Pryderi. Tragedy struck one night as the infant lay sleeping. Otherworld forces snatched him away. His nurses and attendants, fearful of being blamed, killed puppies and smeared the blood on Rhiannon's face while she was asleep. Rhiannon was found guilty of devouring her son. Her punishment was to carry every visitor to the court on her back (like a horse) and tell them of her wickedness. Years later Pryderi was returned by Teyron and Rhiannon was acquitted. When her husband died she married Manawyddan. Her tribulations were not over. She followed her son to an otherworldly castle where he became stuck to a golden bowl. Perhaps in an attempt to aid him, she also became stuck. Mother and son served a lengthy term in the Otherworld until Manawyddan was able to devise a plan to set them free. Her magic birds awoke the dead and put the living to sleep. In a number of sculptures, Rhiannon is accompanied by birds. The magic birds of Rhiannon sang to the beheaded Bran's head so he would not realize the passing of time. Compare Rhiannon to the Arthurian Vivien. Rhiannon is thought to be a later version of the great Celtic fertility queen, Rigatona. She is comparable to the continental "Horse Goddess," Epona, and has the attributes of the Greek goddess, Despoina. For information about Pryderi's absence, *see* Pryderi. *See also* Despoina; Epona; Manawydan Ap Llyr; Pryderi; Pwyll; Rhiannon.

Rhibus (India) *see* Ribhu.

Rhind (Teutonic) *see* Rind.

Rhode (Greek)
    Rhode is the daughter of the sea god, Poseidon, and the sea goddess, Amphitrite. *See also* Amphitrite.

Rhodope (Greek)
    Rhodope is the nymph who married Haemus. They called themselves Zeus and Hera and were changed into mountains. *See also* Haemus.

Ri (Akkadian) Goddess of light or water.

Ribhu (India) *see* Ribhus (The).

Ribhuksan (India) *see* Ribhus (The).

Ribhus, The *Rbhus* (Vedic; India)
    Arbhu (in early times), *Rbhus, Rhibus, Ribhu* (singular), *Ribhuksan.*
    Initially, Ribhus was an early Vedic sun deity. Later he became a wind deity and still later he became one of three artisan elf deities, known collectively as the Ribhus. The Ribhus, also called Ribhuksan, are Vaja and Vibhvan (also called Vibhu). They are the sons of Indra and the goddess of the morning light, Saranyu, who is the daughter of Tvashtri. In some legends, they are the sons of Sudhanvan, the "good archer." The Ribhus, artisan elves, learned their skills from their grandfather, Tvashtri. Cosmic chariots and horses for Indra and other deities were created by the Ribhus. They improved upon Tvashtri's creation of the miraculous bowl that held soma by making it into four cups. Their innovation made Tvashtri jealous and caused him to hide himself. The magic cow of plenty that could bestow all blessings was accredited to the Ribhus' skills. Elderly parents were revitalized by their powers. They assisted Indra in creating and holding up the heavens in some renditions. They made grass, herbs, and passages for streams. Renowned for their kindness, occasionally they engaged in overt rivalry with their grandfather Tvashtri. These actions may have reflected the animosity between Indra and Tvashtri during certain periods. Presented in human form, therefore of humble origins, they were refused entry into heaven. After death they were recognized for their magical contributions to the gods and their powers over nature and were granted immortality. As a creator, Indra is sometimes called a Ribhu. As a group, the Ribhus appear as stars or rays of the sun. The Adityas, Maruts and Vasus are

depicted in the same manner. Sudhanvan the archer is thought to represent the sun's rays. The magic cow symbolizes a cloud. The horses and chariots are the winds and sun. The four cups represent the four quarters of the moon. The elderly parents are the sky and the earth. Compare to Indrani's Kalpa Tree. Compare the Ribhus to the Asvins. *See also* Adityas; Indra; Maruts; Saranyu; Tvastri; Vasus.

Rig (Norse; Teutonic)

Also known as: *Heimdall, Riger, Rigir.*

Aspect of Heimdall. This is the name of the god Heimdall when he created the three races of men. He is generally shown as a stately old man. *See* Heimdall.

Rig-Veda (India) An ancient book of creation myths.

Rigatona (Celtic) *see* Rhiannon.

Riger (Teutonic) *see* Rig.

Rigi (Micronesia) *see* Riiki and Rigi.

Rigir (Teutonic) *see* Rig.

Riiki and Rigi (Micronesia)

Also known as: *Lajnan (Female), Na Rena.*

Creators. Either of two eels or worms who raised the sky on the orders of Nareau. There are several versions of this worm, eel, or grub. In one Rigi helped Yelafaz raise the upper half of a mussel shell. In another, Rigi was a butterfly that helped Tabuerik separate the heavens from the earth. One strange version from the Marshall Island area is that Rigi or Na Rena came out of a rock. *See also* Lukelong; Nareau; Yelafaz.

Rima (Inca People, Peru)

Also known as: *Rimac.*

War god. Little information is available about Rima. He was called "He Who Speaks" and was consulted by chiefs before going into battle. He could be an oracle. *See also* Pachacamac.

Rimmon (Assyro-Babylonia)

Also known as: *Adad Rammon, Barku (Syrian), Mer (Akkadian), Tessub (Cassite).*

God of storm and lightning. He is similar to Adad, Adonis, Teshub. He is identified with Hadad or Addad. *See also* Hadad.

Rin-chen-bhyun-idan (Tibet) *see* Ratnasambhava.

Rind (Norse; Teutonic)

Also known as: *Rhind, Rinda, Rindar, Rinde.*

The giant goddess, Rind is the personification of the hard and frozen earth. She is the mistress or one of the wives of Odin and mother of Vali. *See also* Boe; Odin.

Rinda (Teutonic) *see* Odin; Rind.

Rindar (Teutonic) *see* Rind.

Rinde (Teutonic) *see* Rind.

Ringesum (Saora People, India)

God of the wind. *See also* Adununkisum.

Ringhorn (Teutonic) *see* Hringhorn.

Ringing Horn (Teutonic) *see* Gjall.

Ririt (Egypt) *see* Taueret.

Rishi *Rishis* (plural), *Rsi, Rshis.* (Brahmanic, Hindu, Vedic; India)

Also known as: *Angiras, Angiris, Prajapatis, Saptarshi* (collective title).

The Rishis were born from Brahma's mind. These sages, poets and priests preserved and handed down the knowledge imparted from the Vedas (sacred Sanskrit scriptures). The names and number of Rishis varies depending on the tradition. Some say there are seven and others ten or fourteen Rishis. The oldest list of seven rishis includes Atri, Bharadvaja, Gautama, Jamadagni, Kasyapa, Vasistha and Visvamitra. Together, the seven Rishis form the constellation of the Great Bear. A more common list includes Agastya, Angiras, Atri, Bhrigu, Kasyapa, Vasistha and Visvamitra. Matarisvan, said to be the author of the fourth Veda (also known as Atharvan, and is sometimes listed as a Rishi), brought the fire god, Agni, to a semi-divine patriarchal Rishi, named Angiras. His duties were to act as priest of the gods and lord of the sacrifice. He was a poet, astronomer and law-giver. In some accounts, he is said to be the son of Agni's daughter, Agneyi. Other renditions call him the father of Agni, Brihaspati and Utathya. Another patriarch mentioned is Manasa-Putra. There are three classes of Rishis, the Rishis of the gods, known as Devarishis, the priestly sages known as Brahmarishis, and the Rishis of royal origin known as Rajarishis. The spouses of the seven Rishis are known as the Krittika sisters, six of whom became the Pleiades. As the nurses of Karttikeya, only six sisters are usually mentioned. The seventh is sometimes mentioned as being a small star, dark or hidden near the Great Bear. The list of their names varies. One list mentions Abrayanti, Amba, Arundhati, Chupunika, Dula, Maghayanti, Nitatui, and Varshayanti. The Rishis are said to be the most visible stars of Ursa Major. *See also* Agastya; Agni; Brahma; Brighus; Brihaspati; Daksha; Karttikeya; Kasyapa (A); Kurma (Vishnu's avatar as a tortoise); Marichi (B); Manu; Narayana (C); Prajapati; Rambha (regarding Visamitra); Surabhi; Vasistha, Vedas; Visvakarma.

Rishis (India) *see* Rishi.

Rishtu (Assyro-Babylonian) *see* Apsu.

Rissalka (Slavic) *see* Rusalki.

Rivers (A) (Greek)

River deities. Guardians of youth. Oceanus and Tethys were reputed to have had three thousand daughters, known as the Oceanids, and three thousand sons, known as the Rivers. Some of the River deities are Achelous, the oldest and most famous, a shape changer and father of the Sirens; Acheron, whose heritage is attributed to Oceanus as his father and either Tethys, Gaea or Demeter as his mother; Alpheus, famous for his pursuit of Arethusa; Asopus, who attempted to rescue the kidnapped Aegina; Asterion, who helped Inachus and Cephissus judge between Poseidon and Hera to see who would be the patron deity of Argos; Achelous (Axius), the healing river deity who cured Alcmeon of insanity; Cebren, father of Oenone, Paris' first wife; Caecinus, possibly the father of Euthymus, the Olympic boxer who fought the ghost Hero to death; Cephissus, thought to be the father of Narcissus; Cocytus, deity of a river in Hades said to flow with tears of the dead; Crimisus, the father of Acestes; Eridanus, the deity of a mythical river which could be the Po (Phaethon was said to have fallen from the sky into this river, leaving a lingering noxious odor which the Argonauts were able to smell some time later as they passed the area); and Halys, an unsuccessful contender in his pursuit of the virgin Sinope. Inachus was one of the referees asked to decide whether Hera or Poseidon should have possession of the Argolis. Ladon is noted for its beauty; the deity may be the father of the nymph Daphne, who disliked men, and Metope, who married her uncle Asopus; his brother Peneius has also been called their father. Other river deities include Maeander, the circuitous river and the deity Maeander, the father of Samia who married the king of the island Samos; Scamander, who became infuriated when Achilles filled his river, also named Scamander, with the bodies of dead Trojans and flooded the plain. In retaliation, the fire god Hephaistos dried the river. *See also* Achelous; Acheron; Acestes; Aegina; Alpheus; Cephissus; Cocytus; Hephaistos; Inachus; Oceanids; Oceanus; Phaethon; Pontus; Sinope.

Rivers (B) Sacred rivers of India. *See also* Byas; Ganga; Yami.
Rivers of Hvergelmir in Nifl-heim (Teutonic) *see* Elivagar.

Riyadarshana (India) *see* Mahavira.

rNam-parsnon-sras (Tibet) *see* Vairocana.

rNam-snan-mnon-byan (Tibet) *see* Manjusri.

rNam-t'os-sras-gsir-ch'en (Tibet) *see* Kuvera.

Robigus (Roman)
God of rust or mildew. A red or rust colored dog was sacrificed to Robigus, every April.

Robur (Celtic) Oak tree god. *See also* Abellio.

Rock-Sene (Gambia, Africa)
High god. Rock-Sene is generally considered the creator of the sun and moon and also a deity of the harvest and of thunderstorms. He is both kind and destructive.

Rod and Rozanitsa (Slavic)
Deities supplanted by Perun. *See also* Perun.

Rodasi (India)
She is the spouse of the storm god Rudra. *See also* Maruts; Rudra.

Rodu (Sumer) God of fruitfulness.

Rogo-tumu-here (Oceanic)
Also known as: *Rogo.*
Demon octopus. He once abducted Tangaroa's daughter-in-law while she was surfing. Tangaroa rushed to the rescue in his canoe. After a bitter struggle, Tangaroa overcame the octopus and saved his daughter-in-law. *See also* Faumea.

Rohe (Polynesia; New Zealand)
Along with Hine-nui-te-po, Rohe ruled the afterworld. He rules three of the ten levels. *See also* Hine-nui-te-po; Miru.

Rohini (India) *see* Bala-Rama; Krishna; Pushan; Rudra; Soma.

Roma *Rome* (Greek)
Goddess of war. Roma (meaning strength), the eponym of Rome, is the daughter of Evander and Deidamia. Her siblings are Pallas, Pallantia, Sarpedon and possibly Dyne (meaning power). She is depicted as a tall woman with a noble air about her. She wears a helmet and a long robe and resembles Athena. *See also* Evander (B); Sarpedon (B).

Roma-Tane (Polynesia)
God of Paradise. He was worshiped by the Arioi, who were priests or entertainers on the islands around Tahiti. *See also* Oro; Tane.

Romulus and Remus (Roman, assimilated to Greek)
Also known as: (Romulus) *Quirinus.*
Culture heroes. They are twin brothers who are the sons of Mars and the vestal virgin Sylvia (Rhea Silvia). Their mother, condemned to be buried alive, set the twins adrift on the Tiber. They were rescued and suckled by a she-wolf. Later Romulus killed Remus and founded the city of Rome, which he named after himself, and became its first king. Builders from Etruria were called to construct the city. They taught him the written rules and sacred ceremonies to be observed. A round pit was dug where the Court of Assembly now stands. Each worker brought along a small piece of earth from his area. It was thrown into the pit along with symbolic fruits of the earth. With a plow drawn by a bull and a cow, Romulus drew the boundary of the city in a circle. Romulus also killed King Acron after the rape of the Sabine women. The pit was called the "mundus," which also means "cosmos." It was covered by a huge stone known as the "soul stone." It is said that on certain days the stone was removed and the spirits of the dead rose from the center of the pit. Rome was known as the square city, yet is was built in a circular shape. Many refer to this design as an architectural mandala. Compare to other infants taken from mothers. Pryderi; Rhea Silvia; Zeus.

Rona (Polynesia)
"Tide Controller." She is the daughter of Tangaroa, the sea god. One night as she carried a bucket of water home to her children, clouds had slipped across her path, making the way dark. Rona slipped and hurt her foot against a root. Annoyed, she said unkind things about the moon. The moon overheard her and put a curse on the Maori People. Today, one can see Rona on the moon. When Rona upsets her bucket, it rains.

Rongerik and Rongelap (Marshall Islands)
Heros. They are two brothers who are a part of the family of Palulop. *See also* Palulop.

Rongo (Polynesia)
Also known as: *Lono* (Hawaii), *Lono Rongo-Ma-Tane, Ono, Orongo, Rono.*
God of cultivated food. He is also called a god of night. He is the twin brother of Tangaroa or Haumia-tikitiki and the son of Papa and Tangaloa or Vatea, depending on the legend. In one version, as the child of Papa and Vatea, he is known as the brother of Tangaroa, Tonga-iti, Tangiia, and Tane. Other versions say he is known as the son of Rangi and Papa and the brother of Haumia. He was known as Ono in the Marquesas and Lono in Hawaii. In one myth, he descends on a rainbow to find a mortal wife. In a Mangaia Island myth, Rongo, an underworld war god is the son of Papa-Tu-Anuku (often called Papa),

the great mother of the gods, and Vatea. With his mother's help, his twin brother Tangaroa was driven from his position as king of the island, and Rongo took his place. Later, the island was submerged after a natural disaster. Eventually it surfaced along with a new king called Rangi who said he was the grandson of Rongo. *See also* Haumia; Hotu-papa; Lono; Papa (A); Po; Rangi; Tangaroa; Tane; Tawhiri; Tu; Vari (A); Vatea.

Rono (Polynesia) *see* Rongo.

Roptatyr (Teutonic) An alternate name for Odin.

Rose-Apple Land (India) *see* Jambudvipa.

Roskva (Norse; Teutonic)

Roskva, a servant girl and her brother, Thialfi, were given to Thor by a peasant in payment for a mischievous deed of Loki. Little is said of Roskva, but Thialfi lost a race with Hugi in one of Thor's adventures. Some say Roskva is the daughter of Orvandel.

Rosmerta (Gallo-Roman) *see* Mercury (B).

Rshis (India) *see* Rishi.

Rsi (India) *see* Rishi.

Ru (Polynesia) *see* Rua; Rupe.

Ru-piny (Africa) *see* Woko.

Rua (Polynesia)

Also known as: *Ru, Rua-Haka, Rua-Haku.*

God of the ocean. God of craftsmen. Rua is the Abyss who brought forth the octopus Tumu-ra'i-feuna that held heaven (Atea) and earth together causing darkness. It is Rua who caused the great flood because a fisherman's hook became entangled in his hair. Even though angry, Rua forgave the fisherman but took revenge by flooding the world. Only the fisherman, a friend, a hog, a dog, and several hens were allowed to live until the waters returned to the proper level. Rua is possibly the same as the ocean deity, Tinirau. Rua might be the same as Ruahatu of Tahiti. *See also* Tinirau.

Rua-Haka (Polynesia) *see* Rua.

Ruad Ro-Fhessa (Celtic) *see* Dagda.

Ruad Rofhesa (Celtic) *see* Dagda.

Ruadan (Irish) *see* Brigit.

Ruange (Polynesia) *see* Rangi.

Rudra (Brahmanic, Hindu, Vedic; India).

Also known as: *Araga* ("the burning midsummer sun"), *Bhutapati* (Prince of Demons), *Mahadeva* ("Great God;" a praise name for Rudra-Shiva), *Mrigavyadha* (Piercer of the Deer), *Pasupati* (Lord of Cattle), *Prajapati, Siva, Tryambaka* (Three-Mothered or Three-Eyed).

Rudra is the deity of storms and winds, the divine physician, lord of cattle and wildlife, lord of song and sacrifices, God of the dead and the underworld, and the deity of robbers and beggars. An early Vedic god, he is the son of the goddess of dawn Ushas and Prajapati. Rudra is the father of the Maruts, also known as Rudras by the cow goddess Prisni or perhaps Rodasi

or Diti. His other consorts are Rudrani, the cruel goddess of bloody sacrifices, also known as Devi-Uma-Kali; Ambika, an aspect of Devi; Durga also an aspect of Devi; Parvati, another aspect of Devi; Uma Haimavati and Suaha, the daughter of Daksha. His spouse Sati, known as the virtuous wife, committed suicide when Rudra died. Suaha is also called the wife of Agni and perhaps the mother of Karttikeya. In the *Rig-Veda*, Rudra is portrayed as compassionate and generous. Later, in the *Brahmanas*, with Rudrani, the storm goddess who spreads disease and death, as his wife, he is a grotesque and dreadful god. Known as the "God of Storms" and the "Lord of Time and Death," he is the red god of storms, winds and mountains. He is also a deity of the dead and a demon skilled in archery, who brought disease with his arrows. When appeased, he is a healer and creator of life, and protector of god of cattle and wild life. Under the name Mrigavyadha (piercer of the deer), he wounded Prajapati who had committed incest with his daughter, Rohini, who changed herself into a gazelle or deer. To save himself from Rudra's wrath, Prajapati promised he would make Rudra king of animals, which is how Rudra became known as Pasupati "Lord of Cattle." There are other records indicating that the Mother of the Gods, Aditi, is the mother of the Rudras. In later times, in the Puranas, Brahma was sacrificing to the fire made from his own effulgence. He wiped perspiration from his forehead with a piece of wood and cut himself. A drop of blood fell into the fire. From the blood, by the will of Shiva, sprang Rudra, who separated himself into eleven beings. Rudra chose not to adore Brahma but instead sought Shiva. In his terrible aspect, Rudra is described as a wild tempered, murderous man, with a swarthy build, who spits like a beast. He rides a boar, and shoots the arrows of disease and death at mortals and gods alike. He is also described as having a red face and a blue neck. Sometimes he is shown with red hair. His animal is the mole and his home, the crossroads. In his beneficent aspect he is thought to be as dazzling as the sun. He is also depicted with brown skin and braided hair. His name, Tryambaka, is used when accompanied by the three mother-goddesses and indicates descent from three mothers which may symbolize the triple division of the universe, or the mystical third eye. When he emerged from Brahma's blood, he had five heads, ten hands, and fifteen eyes. For remedial purposes he used cow urine and possibly leeches. For other Vedic healers, *see also* Agni, Asvins, Diti, Indra, Soma. (Of this group, Rudra is the only one who did not partake of soma.) Compare Rudra to the Greeks Hermes and Typhon. Rudra shares the characteristics of Agni (q.v.). *See also* Aditi; Brahma; Brihaspati; Daksha; Devi; Diti; Durga; Kasyapa; Maruts; Parvati; Pishachas; Sati (A); Shiva; Ushas; Vajrapani; Vedas.

Rudra-Shiva (India) *see* Agni; Rudra; Shiva.

Rudrani (India)

Goddess of bloody sacrifices. *See also* Devi; Kali; Rudra.

Rudriyas (India)

They are the sons of Rudra (q.v.). *See also* Maruts.

Rugevit (Slavic)

Also known as: *Rugievit.*

God of war. He has seven faces, wears a bull's head on his

chest and a swan with spread wings on his curly hair. He is similar to Radigast, Svantovit and Yarovit.

Rugievit (Slavic) *see* Rugevit.

Ruha D'qudsha (Mandean Gnostic)

Rukma (India) Brother of Rukmini. *See also* Sisupala.

Rukmini (India)
Mother of Bhadracharu by Krishna. *See also* Jara-Sandha; Kama (A); Krishna; Lakshmi; Satyabhama; Sisupala.

Ruma (India) Queen of the Apes. *See also* Sugriva.

Rumar (India) *see* Aruna.

Rumia (Polynesian)
Rumia is the shell that existed in the primeval darkness known as Po. The inner shell of Rumia is known as Timi-iti. Within Timi-iti is Ra'a-ti, the place where the supreme god, Ta'aroa created himself. *See also* Po; Ta'aroa.

Rumina (Roman) She is the goddess of nursing mothers.

Rumor (Greek)
The spreader of rumors, she is the last daughter of mother earth, Gaea.

Runeeka (India) *see* Parashur Rama.

Runes (Norse; Teutonic)
The Runes is a system of writing said to be invented by Odin. It was reputed he cut the magic writing on the teeth of his horse, Sleipnir, with the sword Gungnir. Odin had the gift of wisdom and runes. As a talisman it is used for protection. Today, the Runes are used as a method to foretell the future.

Rupastra (India) *see* Kama.

Rupe (Polynesia)
Also known as: *Ru*.
He is the winged hero, brother of Hina. *See also* Hina; Maui.

Ruqaiyah (Islamic) *see* Mohammed.

Ruru (India) "Hound." *See also* Shiva.

Rusa (Semitic) *see* Allat.

Rusalkas (Slavic)
Rusalki, Rusalky, Rissalka (singular).
Also known as: *Vili*.
Winged female spirits of the water and woodland. In some myths, the Rusalkas are the spirits of women who die before marriage and then become water sprites. In other myths, they are the unbaptized souls of dead children, or the spirit of any mortal youth who died by drowning. The Rusalkas possess eternal youth, have beautiful voices and unusual powers. Rusalkas in the south are soft and gentle, those in the north are frigid and stern. In summer they reside in forests and in winter they live in water. Some believe the Rusalkas live in certain green trees which some believe are the homes of the dead. The Rusalkas sometimes send storms and rain. They can be charming allies or harmful enemies. In their beautiful form, they have a reputation for enticing men to succumb to them and then they drag them into the sea. They hate absinthe, so if one holds a leaf of it in one hand the Rusalkas can be overcome or defeated. They have long green hair which enables them to tickle mortals to death. They are shown as beautiful maidens or very ugly, pallid young women with dishevelled hair. Compare to the Greek Naiads and Sirens. *See also* Nymphs for Greek classes of nymphs.

Rusalki (Russia) *see* Rusalkas.

Russalka (Russia) *see* Rusalkas.

Rustam (Persia)
Deified king. He is the father of Zal who exposed his son on a mountain top where the vulture Simurgh rescued him. The legend of Rustam, Sam, and Zal is a long tale of the various kings of ancient Persia. *See also* Sam; Simurgh; Zal.

Rutali, The (Greek) *see* Evander (B).

Rutbe (Guaymi People, Costa Rica) *see* Nancomala.

Ruwa (Kilimanjaro, Djaga People, Africa)
Supreme deity. He broke open the pot which held mortals prisoners. Ruwa then planted a yam called Ukaho which was forbidden to all humans. In a tale similar to Adam and Eve, the mortals ate the yam which made them vulnerable to disease.

Ryangombe (Baziba People, Africa)
God of cattle. Ryangombe is the son of Wamara, the father of gods (q.v.).

Ryojusen (Japan)
Also known as: *Grdhra-Kuta*.
Japanese Buddhist heaven.

Ryu-Wo (Buddhist; Japan)
Also known as: *Ryujin*.
King of dragons. Sea king. Ryu-Wo is the dragon king of the Ryujins, and the guardian of Buddhas's religion. Ryu-wo has a human body, though he wears a serpent on his crown. His retainers are serpents, fish and other marine monsters.

Ryujin (Japan) *see* Ryu-wo.

S

Sa (A) (Egypt)

Life Preserver for travelers on the river. The hippopotamus goddess, Tauret, is shown standing upright with her hand on the life preserver, Sa, which is made of papyrus. *See also* Tauret.

Sa (B) (Sumer) Ancient Sumerian god. *See also* Nabu.

Sa-bdag (Tibet)

The Sa-bdag are spirits known as earth-movers who live in soil, lakes, springs, and houses. The image of the local Sa-bdag is placed inside the outer gateway. It is offered wine and bloody sacrifices. *See also* Nats (Burma).

Sa-Yori-Bime-No-Mikoto (Japan) *see* Amaterasu; Three Goddesses of Munakata.

Saa (Egypt) *see* Sia.

Saa-Set (Egypt)

Serpent in afterworld. Huge serpent that stands on his tail. He is in the first sector of Tuat. *See also* Akeneh.

Saba-Leippya (Burma)

Agricultural nats (spirits). *See also* Nats.

Sabala (India) "Heavenly Hound." *See also* Yama.

Sabaoth (Chaldea, Syria)

Also known as: *Iahweh Sabaoth, Iao-sabaoth, Ibraoth, Lord Sabaoth, Sabaoth the Adamas.*

Possibly an underworld deity. Archon and ruler of the fifth sphere. One of the seven Hebdomad or Ogdoad deities coming indirectly from Sophia. Sabaoth is the grandson of Ialdabaoth and the son of Ialdabaoth. He is the guard of the gate called Portal of Life which opens into the lower zone of heaven. There are Gnostic texts that associate Sabaoth with the god Osoronnophris who might have been an Egyptian deity during the time of Moses. He has a chariot with a four-faced cherub and angels. *See also* Archons; Barbelo; Ialdabaoth; Ogdoad; Pistis Sophia; Tuat.

Sabaoth Adamas (Gnostics) *see* Adamas.

Sabazios (Gnostic) *see* Sabizios.

Sabazius (Greek)

Sabazius is an epithet of Dionysus (q.v.). *See also* Cybele.

Sabines (Gallo-Roman) *see* Silvanus.

Sabitu (Babylon)

This goddess rules the land along the sea of death. *See also* Siduri.

Sabizios (Armenia, Chaldea, Phrygia, Syria, Thrace)

Also known as: *Iahweh Sabaoth* (possibly), *Sabazios, Zagreus.*

Sabizios is possibly a serpent creator deity or a serpent god of the underworld. He might have been one of the deities of the Valentinus Gnostic sect. Sabizios is sometimes associated with the goddess Barbelo who was said to be his mother. He is is also identified with Jehovah. Some say he was worshiped under the name of Zagreus by the Thracians and Phrygians. *See also* Barbelo; Ialdabaoth; Sabaoth.

Sacharis (Egypt) *see* Seker.

Sachi (India) *see* Sagara.

Saci (India) *see* Indra; Indrani.

Sacontala (India) *see* Shakuntala.

Sacred Tooth (Buddhist)

The tooth of Guatama Buddha which is enshrined in Kandy, Sri Lanka.

Sacti (India) *see* Shakti.

Sacy-Perere (Brazil) Happy forest spirits.

Sa'd (Arabic) *see* Allat.

Sadurn (Irish) She is the sister of Gwen, the goddess of smiles.

Sadwes (Persia) *see* Hapto-iringa.

Sae-no-Kami (Japan)

God of roads. *See also* Chimata-no-Kami; Sanzu-no-Kawa.

Saehrimni (Teutonic) *see* Saehrimnir.

Saehrimnir *Saehrimni* (Teutonic)

Saehrimnir is the divine boar who daily is killed, boiled by the cook, Andhrimnir, in the cauldron Eldhrimnir. He provides the food for the gods. No matter how much is eaten at each meal, the supply never runs out. Each morning the boar comes to life again.

Saeming (Teutonic) *see* Odin; Seming; Thor.

Saena (Persia) *see* Simurgh.

Saga (Teutonic)

Also known as: *Laga.*

Goddess of history, legend and song. She is one of the wives and daily drinking partner of Odin. He visits her in the crystal hall of Sokvabek. *See also* Odin.

Sagar (Islam)

A fiery place reserved for the Magi in the fifth section of the Islamic Hell (q.v.).

Sagara (Hindu; India)

The grandson of Bahu, and son of Sachi, the king of Ayodhya, Sagara spent seven years in his mother's womb before birth. His father, driven from his throne by the Haihayas, died in exile in the jungle before he was born. When Sagara was old enough, Aurva, the sage, gave him a magic weapon known as the Agneyastra that allowed him to exterminate most of his father's enemies and reclaim the throne. Aurva's powers allowed Sagara's spouse Sumati, the daughter of Kasyapa, to give birth to sixty thousand sons. His other spouse, Kesini, the daughter of Vidharba had one son, Asamanjas. This son was troubled and Sagara eventually abandoned him. The other sixty thousand sons also had behavioral problems. The gods complained to the great god Vishnu and the sage Kapila about their behavior. During his thirty thousand year reign he constantly attempted to bring the Ganges River down from the celestial realm, without success. In an attempt to usurp Indra, he decided to perform the horse sacrifice to signify his claim to universal dominion. When Indra caught wind of the plan, he assumed the disguise of a demon and drove the horse to the underworld. Infuriated, Sagara sent his sixty thousand sons, who had been responsible for guarding it, in search of the animal. They dug a deep pit and ended in Patala, the underworld, where they found the horse and Kapila. When they accused the sage of stealing their father's horse, he reduced them to ashes with the powerful rays of his eyes. Anshumat, the son of Asamanjas and the grandson of Sagara searched for his uncles. Eventually he came upon their ashes, Kapila, and the horse in the pit. This huge hole was named Sagara which means "ocean." Kapila told Anshumat that his uncles could only be purified by the waters that ran through Vishnu's feet. He did permit the grandson to return the horse to Sagara. It was the grandson of Anshumat, Bhagiratha, who dug the bed for the river of heaven that cleanses the sins of all sinners, the Ganges. Her waters reached the underworld and purified the ashes of Sagara's sons so that they could enter Swarga. *See also* Ganga; Kasyapa (A); Patala; Sumati; Swarga; Vishnu.

Sagbata (Dahomey, Fon People, Africa)

Smallpox deity. Associated with the god Dan, they are a group of four Vudus, consisting of Sagbata, the earth god who spread smallpox among mortals; Xevioso, god of thunder; Gun, god of iron; Avlekete (also known as Agbe), god of the sea. Sagbata is thought by some to be the son of Mawu. *See also* Agbe; Mawu; Vodu; Xevioso.

Sahadeva (India)

He is a Pandu prince and the twin of Nakula. *See also* Asvins; Madri; Pandavas.

Sahaganya (India) *see* Apsarases.

Sahar (Middle Eastern) *see* Elohim.

Sahasrabhuja (Buddhist; Nepal)

Sahasrabhuja is an aspect of Avalokitesvara. He has eleven heads and one thousand arms. The basic image of Avalokitesvara is depicted with eleven heads and eight arms. The other arms form a mandala and are sometimes marked with eyes. The eleventh head at the top is said to be that of his parent, Tathagata. The heads have a peaceful countenance with the exception of the tenth head which looks angry. His main hands are held against his chest; the upper hands hold the rosary and the full blown lotus. The other four hands display a jewel on the right and a pot and bow and arrow on the left. *See also* Amoghapasa Lokeswar; Avalokitesvara; Tathagata.

Sahasramuska (India)

Thousand Testicled One. *See also* Indra.

Saho-yama-hime (Japan) The goddess of spring.

Sai-no-Kami (Japan) *see* Sanzu-no-kawa.

St. Bridget (Celtic) *see* Brigantia; Brigit.

Saint Brigit (Irish) *see* Brigit.

St. George *see* Anat; Anhur.

Sa'ir (Islam)

This is the fourth state in the Islamic Hell. It is reserved for Sabians (people from Saba, an ancient Arab state).

Sais (Egypt) *see* Neith.

Saites (Greek) *see* Sapi.

Saiva (Lapp) Protective Deity.

Saiyamkoob (Maya People, Yucatan)

Also known as: *The Adjusters.*

First people. Dwarfs built the now ruined cities in total darkness long before there was light from the sun. At that time a living bloody rope came from the sky and brought them food. Once the sun appeared the people turned to stone. The rope was cut or broken and it divided the earth and sky. At this time a flood visited earth and destroyed the people. The second people, known as the Tsolob (The Offenders), were also destroyed by flood. The Maya lived in the third world and they were also destroyed by a flood. The present world is an admixture of all the races of the Yucatan. There was no indication of how this world will end. *See also* Legend of the Four Suns.

Sak (Egypt)

Composite animal. The Sak is an animal with the front of a lion, the rear part a horse, the head of a hawk, and a tail that terminates in a lotus-like flower. She is shown with a collar around her neck and with bars and stripes on her body, which has eight breasts.

Saka-no-mi-wo-no-kami (Japan)

God of the mountain slope. *See also* Naka-Yama-Tsu-Mi; Sengen.

Sakarabru (Guinea, Africa)

God of darkness. God of medicine, justice and retribution. Sakarabru, represented as a ball of maize, can be a demon or a healer. He appears during the changes of seasons and the new moon.

Sakhmis (Egypt) *see* Sekhmet.

Saki (India) *see* Indrani.

Sakko (India) *see* Sakra.

Sakra *Sakko* (Buddhist, Jain; India)

Sakra is the divine spirit who received Buddha (Brahma) in a golden bowl at birth. He is the chief Deva, and when Buddha was born, he ordered ten thousand sankhas to be blown. The shank or conch shell *(Concha Veneris)*, was used as a "sounder" to drive away demons. He is referred to as one of the twelve Adityas. In the Jain tradition, Sakra, the "King of Gods in

Heaven," decided that the fetus of Mahavira should be transferred from the womb of Devananda to the womb of Trisala. The name Sakra is also an epithet for Indra and a name for India. *See also* Adityas; Buddha; Indra; Mahavira.

Sakta-Sura (India) A demon. *See also* Krishna.

Sakti (India) *see* Shakti.

Saktis (Hindu) *see* Astamatrikas.

Sakunadevatas (India) *see* Devis.

Sakuni (India) A demon. *See also* Duryodhana.

Sakuntala (India) *see* Apsarases.

Sakya-t'ub-pa-dam-g-Nas-brtan (Tibet) *see* Sakyamuni.

Sakyamuni (Buddhist; India)
Also known as: *Buddha, Gautama, Gotama, Sakya-t'ub-pa-dam-g-Nas-brtan* (Tibet), *Sha-kya-tup-pa* (Tibet), *Shih-chia-mou-ni* (China), *Siddartha* (He Who Has Fulfilled the Object of His Earthly Coming), Tathagata.
Born Siddartha, son of Maya by divine birth, he became the monk Gautama, also called Sakyamuni, when he renounced the world. He was a member of the Sakya tribe belonging to the Gautama clan. Sakyamuni means "the sage of the Sakya tribe." He is the third Buddha and the fourth Manushi-Buddha, lord of the present world cycle. His asana (position) is dhyana (meditative). He sits on a red lotus. His mudras (positions) are dhyana bhumisparsa (the right arm pendant over the right knee with the hand and palm inward with all fingers touching the lotus throne), dharmacakra (the left hand covering the right hand against the breast), or varada (arm pendant, fingers extended outward and palm turned outward), or vitarka (arm bent, palm outward and all fingers extended upward, except the index finger which touches the tip of the thumb). His mount is a lion throne and his color is gold. His emblem is a patra (begging bowl). *See also* Akshobhya; Buddha; Kishimojin; Manushi-Buddhas; Maya; Samantabhadra; Vajrapani.

Salachia (Roman) *see* Salacia.

Salacia *Salachia* (Roman)
Also known as: *Amphitrite* (Greek).
Goddess of salt water and springs. *See also* Amphitrite; Neptune; Nereids; Poseidon.

Salagrama (Hindu; India)
The Salagrama are small rounded stones that symbolize the living presence of Vishnu. They are the objects of daily worship. Their river-worn shell is flint-like ammonite and they are different colors but generally black. They have one or more holes in the side. They are usually found in the Gandaki River, one of the tributaries of the Ganges.

Salamis (Greek)
She is the daughter of Asopus and Metope and sister to twenty-one siblings. Salamis was once kidnapped by Poseidon. *See also* Aegina; Asopus; Metope; Pelasgus; Thebe.

Salema and Sakia (Arabic)
Gods of rain and of health. Sakia is an ancient Arab god who was worshiped as the provider of rain and Salema is a health provider.

Sali Kanya (India) Mountain Maiden. *See also* Parvati.

Salii (Roman)
They are the priests of Mars who guard his sacred shield, called the Anchile.

Salkis (Egypt) *see* Selket; Serqet.

Salm (Persia) *see* Cairima.

Salmacis (Greek)
Salmacis is the name of the nymph of the fountain of the same name. All men who drink from its waters become effeminate. *See also* Hermaphroditus.

Salmon (Babylon) *see* Saramana.

Salmoneus (Greek)
King of Elis. His parents are Aeolus and Enarete. They have seven sons and seven daughters. (For a list of their names, *see* Enarete.) Salmoneus' wife Alcidice died giving birth to a daughter, Tyro. His next wife, Sidero, imprisoned Tyro, but she was rescued by her sons, Neleus and Pelias. Sisyphus threw Salmoneus out of Thessaly. When he started imitating thunder and lightning, it did not strike the great god Zeus as humorous. He killed Salmoneus and sent him to the underworld. *See also* Aeolus (A); Canace; Enarete; Sisyphus.

Salmoxis (Greek) *see* Bacchus; Dionysus.

Saltu (Babylon)
This deity of discord was created by Ea as an opponent or rival of Ishtar. *See also* Ea; Ishtar.

Salus (Roman)
Goddess of health, prosperity, and public welfare.

Sam (Persia)
High god. Deified King. Sam exposed his son Zal on a mountain top where the vulture Simurgh rescued him. *See also* Rustam; Simurgh.

Samana (India) The Leveller. *See also* Yama.

Samanta-Bhadra (India) *see* Samantabhadra.

Samantabhadra (Buddhist; India) *Samanta-Bhadra*
Also known as: *Fugen Bosatsu* (Japan), *Fugen En-myo* ("Indestructible Existence," Japan), *Jitoku* (Japan), *Lokanatha, P'u-hein* (China), *Zuntu-zang-po* (Tibet).
Samantabhadra, the deity of universal goodness and happiness, is one of the five Buddhist creators of the universe. The other four are Avalokitesvara, Ratnapani, Vajrapani, and Visvapani. Samantabhadra is the head of one of the three groups of boddhisattvas. Each group contains sixteen boddhisattvas. The other two groups are lead by Buddha Maitreya (Future Buddha). Samantabhadra is a member of a group of eight Buddhas known as Dhyanibodhisattva. The other Buddhas in this group are Akasagarbha, Avalokitesvara, Kshitigarbha, Mahasthamaprapta, Maitreya, Manjusri, Sarvanivaranaveskambhin, and Trailokyavijaya. Sometimes Samantabhadra or Vajrapani substitute for one of the eight. The Dhyanibodhisattva evolved from the meditations of the Dhyani Buddhas. The mortal manifestations of the Dhyanibodhisattva are known as Manushi-Buddhas. They come as teachers and live on earth for a short

period. Samantabhadra's consort is Dharmavajra. In Tibet, in the Red Cap sect, known as Mying-ma-pa, Samantabhadra is the same as Adibuddha. The Red Cap tradition was founded in the ninth century C.E. by Padma Sambhav. An ancient guru, and perfected being, he is the most important of the Mahsiddhas (Tantric saints). In Tibet, the wife of Samantabhadra is the goddess Kuntu-bzang-mo, the Divine Mother. In Japan, Samantabhadra is known as Fugen Bosatsu and he is considered one of the most important boddhisattvas. Fugen Bosatsu, also called Jitoku, personifies wisdom, compassion, cordiality and constancy. He is known as the "Sweeper of Pine Needles." Fugen is paired with Manjursi among the boddhisattvas. Fugen, the god of compassion and bestower of longevity, understands the motives and actions of all mortals. He is often shown wearing a crown, seated on a lotus with his legs crossed. In his left hand he holds a lotus surmounted by a sword surrounded by flames. His right hand is slightly raised, the palm turned outward and the fingers stretched outward, except the fourth and fifth fingers, which are bent. He is also depicted with multiple arms. In one depiction he has twenty arms, each holding an object. As a youth he is shown seated on a lotus, sometimes holding a manuscript. The lotus is upheld by one or more elephants, the symbol of longevity. Samantabhadra is depicted as blue or green. He is shown nude, without ornaments with and without his consort Dharmavajra. His mudra is vajrahumkara (his wrists are crossed at the breast and he is holding ghanta and vajra, a bell with a thunderbolt handle), the symbol of the supreme and eternal Buddha. A vajra is also the thunderbolt of Indra. In his form of Lokanatha, he is yellow, carries the jewel on a lotus and makes the gesture of charity known as the varada mudra. The arm is pendant, all fingers extended downward and the palm turned outward. As Lokanatha he is known as the assistant of Avalokitesvara. *See also* Adibuddha; Amrtakundali; Avalokitesvara; Dam-c'an-r-do-rje-legs-pa; Dhyani Buddhas; Dhyanibodhisattvas; Kshitigarbha; Kunto-Bzang-mo; Maitreya; Manjusri; Manushi-Buddhas; Sakyamuni; Trailokyavijaya; Vajrapani.

Samantaka (India) *see* Kama (A).

Samantamukha (Buddhist; Nepal)
Samantamukha is a manifestation of Avalokiteswara. Known as the "All Pitying One" or the "All Sided One," he looks in all directions to protect all creatures. His numerous heads and eyes enable him to concentrate on the most auspicious way to redeem mortals. The three tiers of heads indicate that he looks down on the three worlds: the world of desire, the world of form and the world of non-form. He is shown with eleven heads on three tiers, eleven brains and twenty-two eyes. *See also* Avalokitesvara.

Samantapancaka (India)
Brahma's sacred altar. *See also* Brahma.

Samas (Northern Semitic) Sun god. *See also* Sams; Shamash.

Samavurti (India) The Impartial Judge. *See also* Yama.

Samaya-Tara (India) *see* Amoghasiddhi.

Samba (India) *see* Krishna.

Sambara (A) *Shambara* (India)
Draught demon. *See also* Krishna; Pradyuma.

Sambara (B) (Buddhist; Nepal)
Also known as: *Chakra Sambara, The Great Defender.*
Maha Sambara, the deity of supreme bliss, has seventeen heads in five rows, four in each row and one at the top. All his faces have bulging eyes, gaping mouths and fangs. He has two sets of seventeen and eighteen arms, for a total of seventy arms. He has four primary arms which hold the goddess of bliss, Vajravarahi (Nepal). Each of his feet has six toes and he stands in the alidh asana posture (stepping to the left with the right leg straight and the left leg bent). He is also described with twelve arms and four heads, each with three eyes. He holds various symbolic objects and is shown embracing Vajrabarahi. Sambara is used in spiritual exercises; meditation and yoga practices. *See also* Chakra Sambara; Dorje Phogmo (for Vajravarhi); Pradyuma; Varahi.

Sambo-kojin (Japan)
Kitchen god, with three faces and two pairs of hands.

Samdhya (India) Goddess of Twilight. *See also* Ratri.

Samdya (India) *see* Sandhya.

Samgna (India) *see* Sanja.

Samhitas, The (India)
The Samhitas is the name given to the four sacred books: the *Rig-Veda, Sama-Veda, Yajur-Veda, Atharva-Veda,* of the Vedas that are generally considered to form a unit.

Samia (Greek)
She is the daughter of the river god Maeander and the wife of of the Argonaut, king of Samos, Ancaeus. *See also* Ancaeus; Maeander; Rivers.

Samildanach (Celtic) *see* Lugh.

Samjuna (India) *see* Sanja.

Sammunus (Roman)
Probably an epithet of Hades (q.v.). *See also* Tina.

Sammuramat (Armenia)
Also known as: *Ishtar, Semiramis* (Syria).
See Atargatis; Ishtar; Semiramis; Sharis.

Samnati (India) *see* Devaki.

Sampati (Hindu; India)
The son of Garuda and the assistant to Rama, Sampati is a gigantic speaking eagle. He was instrumental in locating Rama's spouse, Sita, who had been abducted by the evil demon, Ravana. *See also* Garuda; Rama; Ravana; Sita.

Sampo (Finland)
Sampo is the magic mill that grinds out prosperity. It is held by a wicked giant, and there are many battles over its possession. It was forged by Ilmarinen. *See also* Louhi; Vainamoinen.

Sampo-Kwojin (Japan) *see* Susanowo.

Sampsa Bellervoinen (Finland)
God of the sowing season. He flees to the North each year and must be brought back.

Sams (Southern Semite)

She is a sun goddess who is equal to the Northern Semite sun god Samas. She is also comparable to Allat (q.v.).

Samsara-Guru (India) *see* Kama (A).

Samvarana (India) *see* Tapati.

San Ch'ing *Sang Ch'ing* (Taoism; China)

Also known as: *The Three Heavens.*

The residence of the three supreme gods. The first heaven, located in the Jade Mountain, is called Yu Ch'ing and is ruled by Yuan-shih T'ien-tsun, or Lo Ching Hsin or T'ien Pao depending on the source. Both gods are the source of all truth. The second heaven is called Shang Ch'ing and is ruled by Ling-pao T'ien-tsun or Tao Chun. He is in charge of the sacred books. The third heaven is called T'ai Ch'ing which is ruled by Lao Tzu. He is also called Shen Pao, T'ai-shang Lao-chun or Cheou-Lao, and is considered the teacher of emperors and kings and a god of longevity. Comparable to the Buddhist three heavens. *See also* Ling-Pao T'ien-Tsun; San Hsien Shan; San Kuan; San Yuan; T'ai Shang San Kuan.

San Hsien Shan (China)

Also known as: *San Kuan.*

Home of the gods. "The Three Isles of the Blest" (P'eng-lai, Fang-chang, and Ying-chou) are the most desirable residence for the Immortals. (*See* Chiu Kung.) This is the location of the Peach Tree of Immortality (P'an-T'ao or Shen-T'ao). A similar heaven is called San Ch'ing (Three Pure Ones) and San Kuan (Three Agents) (q.v.). Similar to the Taoist San Ch'ing.

San Kiai Kung (China) *see* San Kuan.

San-ku (China) *see* K'eng-san-ku.

San Kuan (Taoist; China)

Also known as: *San Kiai Kung* (Lords of the Three Worlds), *San Kuan Ta Ti* (Three Great Emperor Agents), *San Yuan* (Three Origins), *T'ai Shang San Kuan* (Three Supreme Agents).

Spirits. The San Kuan are the three agents who rule over heaven, earth and water. The Agent of Heaven is T'ien-kuan. He is a god of happiness. The Agent of Water, Shui-kuan, wards off misfortune. Ti-kuan is the Agent of Earth and grants remission of sins. They are usually shown sitting or standing together holding tablets in their hands. Sometimes only T'ien-kuan is shown. He is standing and holding an unfolded scroll in his hands. The Three Agents are similar to the Japanese Shichi Fukujin. *See also* San Ch'ing.

San Kuan Ta Ti (China) *see* San Kuan.

San Yuan (China) *see* San Kuan.

Sandacos (Greek, Persia)

Sandacos, said to be the father of Adonis, the Greek god of love, is a local god of the city of Celenderis. He could be the same as Sedeq (q.v.).

Sandakos (Phoenician) *see* Adonis.

Sandhya *Samdhya* (Hindu; India)

Sandhya, originally a nature goddess and later a goddess of twilight, is said to be the shy daughter of Brahma. Once when drunk and in the form of a stag, Brahma had incestuous desires and chased her through the sky. He was apprehended by Shiva, who cut his head off with a bow and arrow. From that time, it is said that Brahma paid homage to Shiva. Sandhya is also the period that precedes a Yuga, one of the four Hindu ages of the world. The four ages are Krita, Treta, Dvapara and Kali. Sandhyavandona was originally the Hindu morning and evening prayer (twilight worship). *See also* Brahma; Ratri; Shiva.

Sandili (India) Possibly the mother of Agni or Brahma.

Sang-gyeman-gyila-beduryr-o-chi-gyal-po (Tibet) *see* Bhaishajyaguru.

Sangarius (Greek)

He is one of the river god sons Oceanus and Tethys and the father of Nana. His grandson is Attis. He could be the father of Hecuba by Metope. *See also* Attis.

Sangay Chanma (Tibet) *see* Shakti.

Sangke (Slavic) *see* Ilmarinen.

Sango (Africa) *see* Shango.

Sangreal (Greek) *see* Holy Grail.

Sangso-Dungso (Dhammai People, India)

Sangso-Dungso, Kimbu-Sangtung and Lubukhanlung are the children of the first mortals, the brother and sister, Abugupham-Bumo and Anoi-Diggan-Juje. Their grandparents are the brother and sister frogs, Lujjuphu and Jassuju. *See also* Shuznaghu.

Sangye Khado *Buddha Dakini* (Tibet) *see* Khados.

Sanhara (India) "Destruction." *See also* Shiva.

Saning Sari (East Indies, Java, Sumatra) "Mother of Rice."

Sanja *Samgna, Samjna, Samjuna, Sanjna* (India)

In Puranic mythology, Sanja is the daughter of Visvakarma, the sister of the goddess Barhishmati, and the spouse of the sun, Surya. In some renditions, they became the parents of Manu and the twins, Yama and Yami. When she could no longer endure Surya's brilliance, she had her assistant, (some say her sister) Chhaya or "Shade" take her place and she transformed herself into a mare and galloped off into the forest. After a time, Surya discovered that his mate had disappeared. He became a stallion, and when he found her they came together sexually and became the parents of the Asvin twins and Revanta. After this reconciliation, they lived together for a time as horses but eventually returned to human form. In order to make her living conditions at home more tolerable, she had her father shave away an eighth of Surya's rays. In some renditions, Sanja is said to be the spouse of Soma (q.v.). The mythology of Sanja and Saranyu are similar and they are often considered to be the same deity. *See also* Asvins; Manu; Saranyu, Surya; Tapai; Visvakarma; Yama.

Sankara (India) Healer. *See also* Shiva.

Sankashana (India) *see* Bala-Rama.

Sankhasura (Hindu; India)

Sankhasura was a Yaksha (demon) in the employ of Kansa,

Krishna's archenemy. One night when Krishna and his half-brother Bala-Rama were frolicking with the cowgirls, Sankhasura mingled among them and attacked some of the women. When Krishna heard their screams, he pursued the demon and beheaded him. *See also* Bala-Rama; Krishna; Yaksha.

Santanu (India) *see* Bhishma.

Santaramet (Iranian, Persian)
Santaramet is a type of hell referred to in the Armenian Old Testament. The inhabitants are evil spirits called Santaram-etakans. Santaramet is also the name of an ancient Armenian goddess of the underworld, who was the Persian Spenta Armaiti (q.v.). *See also* Dzokh; Hades; Hell; Spantaramet.

Sanumati (India) *see* Apsarases.

Sanzu-no-kawa (Japan)
Also known as: *Chimata-no-kami* (singular), *Sai-no-kami*, *Yachimata-hiko* (singular).
Divine river. Deities of the roads and highways. "The River of Three Routes." The soul must go to one of three places, toward the hells, toward the beast life, or toward the realm of the "hungry ghosts." There are judges on all three roads where the soul is examined. Other names associated with the Sanzu-no-kawa: Chimata-no-kami, the god of the road; Yachimata-hiko, god of countless roads. The deities were created by Izanagi to protect travellers. Possibly the collective name of the judges is Sai-No-Kami. *See also* Chimata-no-kami.

Sapi (Egypt)
Also known as: *Saites* (Greek).
Afterworld deity. In the fifth nome in the Nome-Lists the name is associated with the goddess Nit or Neith.

Sapling (North America) *see* Yoskeha.

Sapta-Loka (India) *see* Loka.

Saptarshi (India) The seven Rishis. *See also* Rishi.

Saptungtongsum (Saora People, India)
The god of dancing. *See also* Adunukisum; Krishna.

Sar-Akha (Finnish) *see* Akha.

Sarah *Sarai* (Hebrew) *see* Abram.

Sarai (Hebrew) *see* Abram.

Sarama (India) Heavenly Hound. *See also* Yama.

Saramana (Assyro-Babylonia)
Also known as: *Salmon, Selamanes, Shulmanu, Sulman*.
He is a war god shown with a battle axe. Saramana is sometimes identified with Reshep.

Sarameya (India) Heavenly Hound. *See also* Yama.

Saranya (India) *see* Saranyu.

Saranyu *Saranya, Sharanyu* (Vedic, Hindu; India)
Saranyu, goddess of the clouds and morning light, is the daughter of the sun Tvashtri, possibly the twin sister of a brother Trisiras, the spouse of Vivasvat and perhaps the mother of the twins Yami and Yama, the Asvin twins and the artisan elves known as the Ribhus. She lived up to her name, which means the "fleet running one." Shortly after a magnificent wedding, attended by all the gods in the world, she disappeared. Her husband's brilliance had become unbearable. She was gracious enough to create a look-alike, Sarvana, to stay behind in her place. In time, when Vivasvat realized what had happened, he went to find her. What he found was his spouse disguised as a mare. They agreed to a reconciliation under the conditions that he would have some of his brightness shaved away so that she could have a little shade in her life. Her father performed the operation and she helped him reshape the shavings from his rays into weapons for the gods. Compare Saranyu to Sanja. Saranyu corresponds with dawn goddesses Aurora (Roman); Ausera (Lithuanian); Aya (Chaldean); Eos (Greek); Ushas; Zorya Utrennyaya (Slavic). *See also* Asvins; Ribhus; Trisiras; Tvashtri; Visvakarma; Vivasvat; Yama; Yami.

Sarapis (Egypt, Greek) *see* Serapis.

Sarasvati *Saraswati* (Buddhist; Chinese)
Also known as: *Arya Sarasvati* (Tibet), *Benten* (Japan), *Brahmani, Brahmi, Dakini Ye-she-tsho-gyal* (Victorious One of the Ocean of Wisdom), *Gayatri* (Singer), *Khandro, Logos* (The Word), *Prajnaparamita, Satarupa* (She of a Thousand Shapes), *Savitri, Shata-et, Shata-Rupa, Vac, Vach, Vach-Sarasvati, Vajra-vina, Viraj, Yang-Chen*.
Originally, Sarasvati was the Vedic goddess of the Sarasvati river and was associated with fertility and prosperity. Her holy waters flowed west from the Himalayas into the sea. The sage Utathya cursed the waters when Varuna stole his spouse and now the river water ends in the desert. Later, Sarasvati became the goddess of speech, learning, the cultural arts and science. She is credited with bringing the Sanskrit language to the people. In some traditions, it is believed that she discovered soma, the elixir of the gods. Sarasvati was born of Brahma's self, and it was for her love that he created the world. She was his daughter and became his spouse. Sarasvati, Lakshmi and Ganga were also mates of Vishnu. The strife in their relationship caused him to suggest that she marry Brahma. One day when she was to play a role in a sacrificial function Brahma sent word for her. She replied that she was involved with her grooming and that he could wait. Angry, he decided not to wait. He married a second wife, the goddess Gayatri. Incensed with his actions, she cursed him and declared that he should only be worshiped once a year. Sarasvati is known as the "White Goddess" when she is one of a trimurti with the goddesses Lakshmi and Devi. She is one of the goddesses of the Jaina pantheon along with Lakshmi and the Apsarases. As Satarupa, she is the mother of Manu Svayam-bhuva, the first Manu. She is considered the female aspect of Viraj created from the substance of Purusha or Prajapati. The three Vedic muses are the goddesses Bharati, Ila and Sarasvati. In the Buddhist pantheon, Sarasvati is the goddess of poetry and music and the spouse of Manjusri Jampal, the god of learning. Sarasvati is shown as beautiful and graceful young woman often smiling, white in color, wearing a crescent moon on her brow. She has two or four arms and is usually shown holding a book, a lyre or a drum, a rosary, and a lotus. Sometimes she holds a container of Soma and the Vidya, emblem of knowledge. Her mount is the peacock, which is shown with its tail spread. She is also depicted seated on a swan and sometimes on a lotus petal. Sarasvati is also shown as an attendant or con-

sort of the fire god, Agni. As Vajravina, she holds a stringed instrument known as the vina, in her right hand. As Arya Sarasvati, she is bright red in color and has three faces, six arms and an aggressive attitude. Sarasvati merged with the goddess of highest wisdom, Prajnaparamita (Prajna), and is shown with three eyes, the moon in her crown, holding a book and a lotus. Sarasvati's festival, Dawat Puja, or "worship of the inkstand," is held in the month of Magh (January-February). On her day, the only writing instrument that may be used is a pencil. Following the festival, new pens and ink must be used. In Bengal, followers worship pens, ink and account books in her honor. Twigs and blossoms of the mango tree are among offerings given to this goddess. Offerings to Sarasvati cleanse the liar immediately. Sarasvati is intellectually compatible with Vach, the goddess of sound and almost identical to the goddess Benten of Japan. *See also* Agni; Andhaka; Apsarases; Brahma; Dakini Ye-she-tsho-gyal; Devi; Ganga; Lakshmi; Logos; Manu; Parvati; Prajnaparamita; Savitri; Shakti; Soma; Sri; Varuna; Vishnu; Yami.

Saraswati (India) *see* Sarasvati.

Sarbanda (Babylon, Syria) A goddess of war or the bow.

Sarika (India) *see* Durga.

Sarna Burhi (India) Bengali tree goddess.

Sarnga (India)
Sarnga is Vishnu's divine bow. *See also* Vishnu.

Sarpanit (Assyro-Babylonian) *see* Zerpanitum.

Sarpas and Sarpis (India)
They are semi-divine serpents who dwell in heaven, in the air, on earth, and in the lower regions. Unlike the Nagas and Nagis, they do not walk or run.

Sarpedon (A) (Greek)
King of Lycia. Sarpedon is the son of Zeus and Europa. His siblings are Minos and Rhadamanthus. He was raised by Asterius, the king of Crete who had married Europa. Later he married Laodamia and was the father of Evander. As a youth he was exiled from Crete with Rhadamanthus by his brother Minos when Minos found out that a beautiful young man, either Miletus or Atymnius was in love with Sarpedon. His son Evander married Deidamia, the daughter of Bellerophon, and inherited his father's kingdom. In some legends they became the parents of Sarpedon named after Evander's father. In other legends, both Sarpedon (A) and Sarpedon (B) are thought to be the same man. Sarpedon's brothers Minos and Rhadamanthus became judges in the underworld after death. *See also* Asterius; Europa; Evander; Minos; Rhadamanthus; Sarpedon (B); Zeus.

Sarpedon (B) (Greek)
Warrior. Sarpedon was the son of Zeus and Laodamia, daughter of Bellerophon, or of Evander and Deidamia. As the son of Evander and Deidamia his siblings were Pallas who was later killed by Turnus, Roma (the eponym of Rome) and Pallantia (the eponym of the Palatine Hill, the highest of the seven hills of Rome). As the son of Zeus and Laodamia he was a brave warrior who commanded the Lycian troops and was slain by Patroclus. His dear friend Glaucus could not bear to see the

Achaeans desecrate his body, nor could the dead man's father, Zeus. He sent Apollo to purify the corpse and had Hypnos (Sleep) and Thanatos (Death) transport it to Lycia for burial. Sarpedon is thought to represent the creeping light of heaven. In later traditions, Sarpedon is named as one of the sons of Zeus and Europa. There was another Sarpedon who was thought to be the son of Poseidon who was killed by Heracles for torturing visitors to his home. *See also* Evander (B); Glaucus; Sarpedon (A).

Sarume, The (Japan) *see* Ama-no-Uzume.

Saruta-Biko-No-Kami (Japan) *see* Ama-no-Uzume.

Saruto-Biko (Japan) *see* Ama-no-Uzume.

Sarva (India) The Destroyer. *See also* Agni; Shiva.

Sarvaga (India) *see* Bhima (A).

Sarvamangala (India)
"Universally Auspicious." *See also* Devi.

Sarvana (India) *see* Saranyu.

Sarvani (India) *see* Devi; Tapati.

Sarvanivaranaveskambhin (India) *see* Amoghasiddhi; Dhyanibodhisattvas; Samantabhadra.

Sarvanivaranviskambin (India) *see* Amoghasiddhi.

Sarvari (India) Water goddess.

Sarvavasini (India) *see* Devi.

Sary-Khan (Altaic, Tartars)
A god of happiness. *See also* Bai Ulgan.

Saryata (India) *see* Mada; Sukanya.

Sasabonsam (Africa)
An evil spirit. He lurks in the branches of the trees and jerks up unwary travelers by hooking his toes under their armpits. His legs are long and can be uncurled to go longer; his feet point backward. He has a pointed beard and horns and has thin lips. His arms are outstretched, and skinny wings, like those of a flying fox, join his arms to his legs.

Sashikuni-waka-hime (Japan) *see* Kushi-nada-hime.

Sasi-kuni-opo-no-kami (Japan) *see* Kushi-nada-hime.

Sasilekha (India) *see* Apsarases.

Sata-rupa (India) *see* Vach.

Satakratu (India) *see* Indra.

Satan *Sathanas, Sathan* (Akkadia, Babylon, Sumer, Persia)
Also known as: *Arya Sarasvati, Belial, Charun, Devil, Eblis, Iblis; Irra* (possibly, Babylon), *Nergal.*
Underworld deity of evil. Satan is possibly Irra of the Babylonia pantheon. He is one of the demons recognized by Jesus. In one version of his mythology, he is the twin brother of the archangel Michael and ruler of the evil deities, Azazel, Beelzebub, Belial, Chemos, Dagon, Moloch, Rimmon and Thammuz. In one description he is depicted (as Charun), with horse-ears and a hooked nose, his flesh is blue as if decaying, and he carries

a mallet to strike down his victims. Charun is believed to have influenced the medieval concept of Satan. Satan is similar in nature to Lilith. *See also* Azazel; Charon; Devil; Nergal.

Satarupa (India) *see* Sarasvati; Shiva; Manu.

Satavaesa (Zoroastrian; Persia)
An unidentified star or constellation and one of the Yazatas (q.v.).

Satet (Egypt) *see* Khnum; Satis.

Sathan (Babylon) *see* Satan.

Sathanas (Babylon) *see* Satan.

Sati (A) *Ambika, Amvika, Devi, Parvati, Suttee, Uma* (Brahmanic, Hindu; India)
Sati, one of the numerous daughters of Daksha, is an early aspect of the great mother goddess Devi. As Sati, the "good wife," she committed suicide by burning herself to death when her mate Shiva in his aspect as Rudra the storm god was killed. Sati is depicted with a calm face and dressed in a girdle and necklace. She is also shown with a child on her knee. The practice of burning a wife on her husband's funeral pyre is known as sati or suttee. *See also* Ardhanariswara; Daksha; Devi; Durga; Kali; Parvati; Rudra; Satis (Egypt); Shiva; Uma.

Sati (B) (Egypt) *see* Satis.

Sati, Queen (C) (India)
Queen Sati is the mate of the Brahmin and Maharishi King Visvamitra.

Satis (Egypt)
Also known as: *Isis, Isis-Satis, Isis-Sothis, Satet, Sati, Satis.*
River deity. Satis was the first wife of the creator god, Khnum. An archer-goddess, she assisted her spouse in protecting the upper Nile and the Cataracts. Arrows were the symbols of the swiftness of the Nile's course. Satis presented water to the deceased for purification. When Khnum identified with the sun god Ra, Satis became the "eye of Ra." She is sometimes confused with Satet. She is depicted in human form wearing on her head the white crown of the South with two horns and holding a bow and arrow. There is a similarity between Satis and the Hindu goddess Sati. She is sometimes identified with the goddess Ament. There is a possibility that as Sati she is a form of Isis (q.v.). *See also* Anukis; Khnum; Sati (A).

Satrajit (India)
A Yadava. *See also* Satrajit; Satyabhama; Yadava.

Satrughna (India) *see* Rama.

Sattung *Suttung* (Norse; Teutonic)
Also known as: *Fjalar, Loki, Utgard-Loke.*
Sattung is the giant son of Gilling or Surtr. He is the brother of Baugi and the father of Gunlodd. Sattung captured the Mead of Poetry from the two dwarfs, Galar and Fjalar, but lost it to Odin in his guise of Bolverk. *See also* Fjalar; Kvasir.

Saturn *Saturnus* (Roman)
Also known as: *Cronus* (Greek), *Heru-ka-pet, Heru-p-ka* (Egypt).
God of agriculture. God of workers and the vine. Responsi-

ble for prosperity and abundance. His spouse is Ops and they are the parents of Jupiter. Saturn is also the father of Juno and Picus by the nymph Venilia and possibly Sterculus, the king of Latium. Once the ruler of the world, he was removed from his position by his son Jupiter. *See also* Cronus; Jupiter; Ops; Sterculus.

Saturn the Planet (Greek) *see* Eurynome (A).

Saturnus (Roman) *see* Saturn.

Satya-Loka (India) *see* Loka.

Satya-Narayana (India) *see* Narayana (A).

Satyabhama (Hindu; India)
Satyabhama, the daughter of Satrajit, is generally thought to be Krishna's third wife. She claimed that a jewel that once belonged to her father was rightfully hers. When Satyabhama heard that Krishna had given his other wife, the beautiful goddess Rukmini, a flower from the magic Parijata Tree, she became indignant and demanded that he bring her the whole tree. Krishna went to Svarga, Indra's celestial dwelling place, with Aditi's earrings (Indra's mother) and Indra's canopy and requested the tree. When Indra refused to oblige him, Krishna uprooted the tree and left, pursued by Indra and his forces. Krishna kept the tree for a year and then willingly returned it to Indra. Krishna was involved with Jambavan, the King of the Bears who had a precious jewel that belonged to Krishna. *See also* Indrani; Jambavan; Krishna; Parijata Tree; Syamantaka.

Satyapir (India) *see* Narayana.

Satyavan (India) "Possessing Truth." *See also* Savitri (B).

Satyavati (Brahmanic, Hindu; India)
Satyavati, meaning "the Truthful One," is the daughter of the Asparasa Adrika who lived in the shape of a fish and the king of Chedi, the mate of the rishi Parasara, and the mother of a son Vyasa. At a later time, she became the mate of king Shantanu of Hastinapura, the mother of two more sons, Chitrangada and Vichitravirya, and the grandmother of the Pandavas. *See also* Asparases; Bhishma; Pandavas; Parashara; Vyasa.

Satyrs (Greek)
Also known as: *Fauns.*
Deities of the woodland. The Satyrs, woodland deities, are descendants of Hecaterus and Apis, Niobe or Car. They were addicted to sensual pleasure and associated with the worship of Dionysus and Bacchus. They loved and overindulged in the "nectar of the gods," music, dancing and frolicking with women. When the Satyrs age, they are known as the Sileni. The Satyrs are ruled by Silenus, the king of Nysa, an expert musician, who resembled the Satyrs in appearance. The Satyrs are depicted as ugly, with a pug-nose, goat ears, budding horns and a short tail. *See also* Bacchus; Bhut (India); Corybantes; Dionysus; Hephaistos; Incubus (Medieval Europe); Jinn; Silenus.

Saubhadra (India) *see* Abhimanyu.

Saudamani (India) *see* Apsarases; Kasyapa; Yakshini; Yaska.

Saumanasa (India) *see* Lokapalas.

Saunanda (India) The sacred club of Bala-Rama (q.v.).

Saurasa (Hindu, India)

A giant female Rakshasa, Saurasa opened her mouth to swallow the monkey general Hanuman as he flew through the air. He had enlarged himself to the size of a mountain but when she caught him, he reduced himself to the size of a thumb. Once he was inside of her, he enlarged himself again, she burst open and he escaped. *See also* Hanuman; Rakshasa.

Sauromatai (Scythian) *see* Amazons.

Sauru (Zoroastrianism; Persia)

Sauru is the arch-demon who personifies the mismanagement of government and inebriation. He opposes Khshasthra Vairya (q.v.). *See also* Daevas; Darvands.

Savabhauma (India) *see* Lokapalas.

Savaki (Siberia) *see* Khovaki.

Savala (India) *see* Kamadhenu.

Savarbhanu (Hindu; India)

He began life as a Daitya with four arms and a tail. When soma, the elixir of the gods was being passed around, at the churning of the sea of milk, he slipped between Surya and Chandra and managed to gulp a portion. He was apprehended by Vishnu who sliced him in two with his discus, Sudarshana. The powerful effects of the soma gave each part immortality and Savarbhanu became Ketu and Rahu and was placed in the stellar sphere. Ketu appears as a dragon's tail carried through the sky in a chariot drawn by eight swift red horses. The dragon-headed Rahu rides in a chariot drawn by eight black horses. He despises the sun and the moon and is constantly pursuing them. Occasionally, he catches the planets and an eclipse occurs. *See also* Chandra; Daitya; Kurma (regarding the Churning of the Sea of Milk); Rahu (for a variation of this myth); Soma; Sudarshana; Surya.

Savita (India) *see* Martanda; Sita; Vivasvat.

Savitar (India) *see* Savitri (A).

Savitr (India) *see* Savitri (A).

Savitri (A) *Savitar, Savitr* (Heaven), *Surya, Vach, Vach-Sarasvati* (Vedic, Hindu; India)

Originally, Savitri and Vivasvat were attributes or names of the sun. Later, they became deities. Savitri is the son of Aditi and one of the Adityas. He became the king of heaven, the giver of life, the father of the sun goddess Surya and possibly the Asvins. He is represented by universal movement, seen in the course of the sun and the motion of the winds and seas. Known as the "Generator," "The Stimulator," "The Inspirer" and "The Life-giver," it is Savitri who calls for the night to approach. Savitri dispels disease and give mortals longevity and gods immortality, for he puts all to rest. He is invoked for the remission of sins. Savitri has golden eyes, hands and tongue. As the personification of the rising and setting sun, he rides through the heavens in a chariot drawn by glittering horses with white hoofs. In sacrifices, he cut off his hand but the attendant priests restored it. His hand represents the sun's rays and the new hand is the lights of dawn. In the Hindu tradition, if the mantra of the *Gayatri* (a sacred text of the Vedas) is chanted upon rising, the magical powers of the text are exorcised on behalf of the reciter. The mantra "Om" is the basis of the *Gayatri*. Savitri is an aspect Surya, the sun god, and was later identified with Vishnu, whom he most resembles. In the *Upanishads,* Savitri appears as Purusha, "The Golden Person." Compare him to the Norse god Odin's lost eye and the Celtic deity Nuada's silver hand. *See also* Aditi; Adityas; Asvins; Daksha; Mitra; Pushan; Sarasvati; Savitri (B); Surya (A); Surya (B); Vach; Varuna; Vishnu; Vivasvat.

Savitri (B) *Deva-Kanya* (Hindu; India)

Savitri, the daughter of Asvapati, choose the exiled prince Satyavan to be her husband. She was not thwarted by the warnings of the court sages that her loved one only had one year to live. The year passed and the god of death, Yama appeared to escort Satyavan to the land of the dead. Savitri followed them until her feet bled. She pleaded with Yama to release her spouse. Impressed by her willingness to follow her mate to death's doorstep, the god agreed to allow Satyavan to return to her so that they could have many children together. Savitri is a name applied to many goddesses and is a common female name. A celebration is observed yearly by women in honor of Savitri, who did not allow death to conquer love. Savitri as a sun goddess could represent the sun and her husband the setting or dying sun. Another Savitri was the daughter of the sun and the wife of Brahma. Compare Savitri to the Greek goddess Alcestis. *See also* Sarasvati; Savitri (A); Yama.

Say-nying-po (Tibet) *see* Mamaki.

Sayori-bime-no-mikoto (Japan) *see* Three Goddesses of Munakata.

Scamander (Greek)

Also known as: *Xanthus.*

River god. His parents are Oceanus and Tethys. During the Trojan War, he assisted the Trojans, who were fighting with the Greeks, by flooding his river. He is the maternal grandfather of Cilla (q.v.). *See also:* Callirrhoe; Hesione; Rivers.

Scamandrus (Greek) *see* Rivers.

Scanda (India) *see* Skanda.

Scarab (Egypt)

Deified insect. A representation of a beetle, the sacred symbol of everlasting, eternal transformation and of immortality. The scarab is associated with the god Khepri and was often used as a seal, or an amulet worn for protection against evil. *See also* Amulet.

Scarphe (Greek) *see* Jason.

Scathach (Celtic)

Goddess of the sky. Sorceress. *See also* Aoife.

Sceiron (A) (Greek)

He is the son of Pelops or Poseidon who was killed by Theseus. *See also* Pelops.

Sceiron (B) (Greek)

Sceiron is the northwest wind. His parents are the Titan, Astraeus and Eos, the goddess of dawn.

Schoeneus (Greek)

He is the king of a section of Boeotia. His parents are Athamas and Themisto. *See also* Atalanta; Athamas.

Scrat (Teutonic) Wood demon. *See also* Dus (Celtic).

Scylla *Skylla* (Greek)

Sea-monster. Although her lineage is murky, the legends of Scylla are clear. She was either the daughter of Phorcys and Hecate or Phorcys and Crataeis, or Typhon and Echidna, or Poseidon. In other legends, she is the daughter of the queen of Libya, Lamia, whom Zeus adored. When the jealous Amphitrite found out about Scylla's affair with Poseidon she had the enchantress Circe turn the beautiful nymph into a sea-monster. In another version, Circe, angry that Scylla would not respond to the romantic overtures of Glaucus, poured poison into her bathing pond. Scylla stepped in to cleanse herself and turned into a monster. The jealousy of another woman also created havoc in Lamia's life. Scylla and Charybdis harassed sailors in the Straits of Messina; it was impossible to avoid the danger of one without encountering the other. When Heracles was navigating his oxen through the straits of Sicily, Scylla reached out, grabbed one of the animals and gorged herself. Incensed, he killed her. Phorcys, her father, was able to revive her. Little is known about Charybdis except through the writing of Homer. He tells us that she lived in the sea under a rock on which a fig tree grew. She swallowed the angry waves of the sea three times a day and then regurgitated them. He called her the daughter of Poseidon and the Earth (Gaea). He wrote that the angry Heracles hurled a thunderbolt at her when she stole his oxen and thus changed her into a sea monster. Scylla barked like a dog and had twelve feet, six necks and six heads, each with three rows of teeth. *See also* Calypso; Ceto; Circe; Giants; Gorgons; Hylas; Lamia; Medusa; Nereids; Poseidon; Sirens.

Se-oritsu-hime (Japan)

Lady-Who-Descends-the-Rapids. *See also* Haya-akitsu-hime-no-kami.

Seb (Egypt) *see* Aai; Geb; Nut.

Sebak (Egypt) *see* Sebek.

Sebek *Sebak, Sebeq, Sebku Sobek* (Egypt, Greek)

Also known as: *Helios* (Greek), *Petesuchos, Sebek-Hetep, Sobk, Sobk-Re, Suchos, Sukhos* (Greek).

Sebek was a local god at the city of Arsinoe (called Crocodilopolis by the Greeks), in Faiyum. He was an early fertility god and later a god of death. A crocodile, believed to be the incarnation of a god, he is a protector of reptiles. Sebek prevents decay of the body in the tomb and provides speech and sight to the dead. He is associated with the pharaohs of the Thirteenth Dynasty. He is depicted as a crocodile or a crocodile-headed man. As Helios (Greek) he is depicted with a halo of rays and the attribute of a crocodile in his hand. There are depictions of crocodiles which carry a falcon's head adorned with the double crown indicating the relationship between Suchos and Horus. In the *Book of the Dead*, Sebek assists in the birth of Horus. *See also* Horus; Sukhos (Greek).

Sebek-Hetep (Egypt) *see* Sebek.

Sebeq (Egypt) *see* Sebek.

Sebi (Egypt)

Sebi is a monster serpent who guards the entrance to the twelfth sector of Tuat.

Sebuit-nebt-uaa-khesfet-sebau-em-pert-f (Egypt)

Afterworld name. The name of the Eleventh Hour of Tuat. The city of Re-qerert-apt-khat which Osiris passes through has the pylon Sekhen-tuatiu. The deities who accompany the god or soul on the journey are Fa, Ermenu, Athpi, Netru, Shepu, Reta, Amu, Ama, Shetu, Sekhenu, Semsem, Mehni, Sem-shet, Sem-Nebt-het, four forms of Neith, Aper-hra-neb-tchetta, Tepui, Shetu, Tchet-s, Petra, Temu, Shetu, Nebt-ankhiu, Nebt-khu, Nert, and Hent-neteru. There are pits in this place. They are Hatet, guarded by Hert-ketit-s; another unnamed pit guarded by Hert-Hantua; another guarded by Nekenit; and two others guarded by Hert-Nemmat-Set and Hert-sefu-s. Three other goddesses are included in this journey: Pesi, Rekhit, Her-sha-s, and Sait and another god, Her-ut-f. *See also* Tuat.

Sechmet (Egypt) *see* Sekhmet.

Sedeq (Ancient Hebrew; Canaan; Persian; Syrian.)

Also known as: *Melchi-sedeq, Sydyk.*

Sun deity. Sedeq, a chief deity of the Palestinians, is the father of the seven Kabirs (great gods). He is usually associated with the god Misharu and called Melchi-sedeq. Under the names of Sydyk and Misor, they are the sons of Shamash and as culture heros, are the discoverers of salt. *See also* Misor; Zatik.

Sedit (Wintun People) *see* Coyote.

Sedna (Eskimo People)

Also known as: *Ai-willi-ay-o, Arnaknagsak, Arnarquagssaq, Avilayoq, Nerivik, Nerrivik.*

Sea goddess. Mother of all sea creatures. Sedna is the daughter of Anguta or Angusta. In one myth, Sedna fell in and out of love with a bird spirit. During her father's attempt at rescuing her from the spirit he became frightened and threw her from the boat. She tried to climb back in and he cut off parts of her hand which became seals and other sea creatures. There are many variations on this theme. Another myth tells us that her nameless parents were giants. She had a voracious appetite and one night began nibbling on her mother and father. Horrified, they managed to throw her into the sea. She clung to the side of the boat and they chopped off her fingers which turned into sea creatures. She sank to the bottom, set up housekeeping, and became the ruler of all sea creatures and the dictator of storms. The Angakok (shaman) would visit her in a trance. He was received by the ruler in a luxurious tent in Adlivun under the sea furnished with the skins of various sea animals. The great lady would watch him dance and amuse her and then would give him a message for the people, generally regarding the food supply; if it was to be abundant they should stay, if sparse, they should move on. The toxic matter thrown into the sea (representing sins) tangles her hair. Her hair also tangles when land and sea meat are cooked together. Hunters who do not hunt with respect for the hunted caused her terrible pain. When Sedna is treated with honor, gentleness and honesty she provides food for humans, hence is called the "Food Dish." She is also called the "Great Sea Mother." It is Sedna who initiated taboos. She particularly dislikes dirty women. When a taboo is broken, she takes the women's sewing articles and covers over the seals, so that they cannot be hunted. The shaman is called to bring her to him with his magic songs. When she possesses him, other men hold him tightly. During this period, the men are able to confess all breaches of taboos. Her hair becomes smooth again and she returns to her home in the sea. Her lights are turned up, the storms subside, and the animals are once again free to be hunted. However, the hunters must wait for four days before proceeding with the hunt. During this period, women do not sew. In some descriptions, Sedna is fat, hideous, and ill-tempered. She is also depicted as a giant with one eye. In another description, her hands are like seal's flippers. She is the counterpart of the Pacific Eskimo goddess Nunam-shua (q.v.), and comparable to Nerivik. Compare Sedna to the Greek sea god, Poseidon. *See also* Adlivun; Anguta; Aningan; Nerivik; Tornaq.

Sedrat (Arabic)
Deified tree. Sedrat is the lotus tree that stands on the right-hand side of the throne of Ali. Countless angels rest in the shade of this tree and two rivers run from its roots.

Sedu *Shedu* (Babylon, Semitic, Hebrew)
Also known as: *Alad.*
Benevolent, obtuse demons. Door or gateway guardians (possibly). They are shown as winged animals, probably cows or bulls. Associated with the Lamassu. *See also* Lamassu.

Seeta (India) *see* Sita.

Sefer (Egypt)
Deified animal. A animal with the winged body of a lion and the head of an eagle.

Sefkhet-Aabut (Egypt) *see* Seshat.

Seger (Egypt) *see* Seker.

Segesta (Greek)
Segesta is a nymph and the possible mother by the river god, Crimisus, of the Trojan War hero, Acestes. *See also* Acestes.

Segetia (Roman)
Also known as: *Tutilina.*
Agricultural deity. Corn deity. Segetia protects the fruits and vegetables of the harvest. In some locales, she specifically protected the grown corn. Segetia may be an aspect of Ops and is comparable to the Greek goddess of corn, Seia. The difference is that Seia protects the corn before it sprouts.

Segomo (Celtic)
Another name for the god of war, Cocidius (q.v.).

Sehetch-khatu (Egypt) *see* Aai.

Seia (Greek)
Corn deity. Goddess of corn before it sprouts. *See also* Ops; Segetia.

Seilenos (Greek) *see* Silenus.

Seiren (Greek) *see* Sirens.

Se'irim (Middle Eastern) *see* Jin.

Seitaka Doji *Seit Ka-doji* (Japan)
He is the servant and messenger of Fudo-myoo. In one hand, he holds a stick. *See also* Fudo-myoo.

Sekem Taui (Egypt) *see* Ap-uat.

Seker (Egypt)
Also known as: *Sacharis, Seger, Socharis, Sokar, Sokare, Sokaris.*
Early god of vegetation. Deity of the necropolis of Memphis. He is closely affiliated with Osiris. Seker is shown as a seated hawk-headed man holding sovereignty emblems in his outstretched hand. He is sometimes shown with the head of man holding a knife in each hand. *See also* Amentet; Osiris; Ptah.

Sekhait (Egypt) *see* Sekhmet.

Sekhauit (Egypt) *see* Sekhmet.

Sekhautet (Egypt) *see* Sekhmet.

Sekhem (Egypt) The soul or vital power. *See also* Sekhmet.

Sekhem Em Pet (Egypt)
Also known as: *Anubis.*
Sekhem Em Pet is the name for the god Anubis as a son of Osiris. *See also* Sekhem Taui.

Sekhem-hra (Egypt) *see* Aai.

Sekhem Taui (Egypt)
Also known as: *Anubis.*
Sekhem Taui is another name for the god Anubis as a form of his father, Osiris.

Sekhemus (Egypt)
Afterworld deity. The name of the Fourth Hour of Tuat. The boat of Ra arrives at the Circle called Ankhet-kheperu (*see* Aat) which has a pylon called Ament-sthau. Ra is guided along the hidden path called Re-stau and the winding road of the Amme-het to the land of Seker, which is filled with fearsome snakes. Along the way Osiris is merged with Seker and becomes Osiris Seker. Re-stau has three doors called Mates-sma-ta, Metes-neheh, and Metes-mau-at. Osiris Seker passes through the door guarded by the goddess Am-mut who consumes souls with fire from her mouth. Thoth and Horus go in front of Osiris and they pass through the serpents, Hetch-nau, Seker, Amen, Hekent, Menmenu, Neheb-kau and the scorpion Ankhet. *See also* Taut.

Sekhen-ba (Egypt) *see* Aai.

Sekheper-khati (Egypt) *see* Aai.

Sekher-remu (Egypt) *see* Aaru.

Sekhet (Egypt) *see* Bast; Hathor; Ra; Sekhmet.

Sekhet-aaru (Egypt) *see* Aaru.

Sekhet-hetep (Egypt) *see* Aaru.

Sekhmet (Egypt) *Sakhmet, Sechmet, Sekhem*
Also known as: *Bast, Mut, Sekhait, Sekhauit, Sekhautet, Sekhem-bast-ra, Sekhet.*
Warrior goddess. Goddess of childbirth, fire, heat. Punisher of mortals for sins. Protector of the righteous (in later times). Sekmet was created by Ra from the fire in his eyes to punish mortals for their sins. Sekhmet became the wife of Ptah, though often described as his mother, and mother of Nefertem. Together they made up the Memphite Triad. Her name means

the "Mighty One" and she is known to spread terror. She is a fearless warrior who uses arrows. The hot desert winds are her breath and a fiery glow emanates from her body. Sekhmet, the negative aspect of Bast, is well known for her knowledge of magic and sorcery. The local goddess Mut merged with Sekhmet when Thebes became the royal residence. She is depicted with the head of a lioness or as a lioness. She is also shown with a solar disk, crowned with the poisonous uraeus-serpent. As Sekhem-bast-ra she is worshiped with Bast and Ra as a compound deity. In this form, she is the consort of Ptah-seker-ausar. Sekhmet is identified with Hathor who took the shape of a lioness and did battle for Ra against those mortals who were rebellious against him. She is also identified with Mut and Pakhet. The Greeks called her Sakhmis, Latona, and Artemis. See also Bast; Mut; Sakhmet; Ra.

Sekhmet-Bast-Ra (Egypt)
Strange deity portrayed as a male head on the body of a woman with a phallus.

Selamanes (Babylon) see Saramana.

Selene *Selena, Selina* (Greek)
Also known as: *Artemis, Diana, Mene, Luna* (Roman), *Phoebe.*

Goddess of the moon. Selene is the daughter of Hyperion or Pallas and Euryphaessa or Theia. Her siblings are the sun god Helius and the goddess of dawn, Eos. Selene had a long term affair with a beautiful, younger man, Endymion. She kept him in a somnolent state and every night paid him a visit. Over time, she had fifty daughters by Endymion. With Zeus she had three children, Pandia, Ersa and Nemea. The shepherd god Pan turned himself into a white ram and had sex with her. A very beautiful goddess, sometimes shown with wings, she rides across the skies in a chariot pulled by two white steeds. See also Artemis; Diana; Eos; Helius; Isis.

Selk (Egypt) see Selket.

Selket (Egypt) see Serqet.

Selkis (Greek) see Selket.

Selkit (Egypt) see Selket.

Selqet (Egypt) see Selket.

Selquet (Egypt) see Selket.

Selsabil (Islamic)
Water the flavor of ginger flows from this fountain in Paradise.

Semaahut (Egypt) see Aai.

Semele (Greek)
Also known as: *Thyone.*

Semele is the daughter of the king of Thebes, Cadmus, and Harmonia. Her siblings are Agave, who later murdered her husband and went insane and then murdered her son; Autonoe, who was driven insane for her treatment of Semele; Ino, who raised Dionysus and later went insane; and two brothers, Illyrius and Polydorus. Semele was loved by Zeus and became the mother of Dionysus. The jealous Hera appeared to Semele in the form of Beroe, her nurse, and persuaded her rival to ask Zeus to appear to her in all the splendor of his divinity. Semele, unable to endure the brilliance of Zeus in his divine form, was burnt to ashes, but Hermes rescued her unborn child Dionysus, and sewed him into the thigh of Zeus from which he was later born. Her jealous sisters, Autonoe, Ino and Agave, spread vicious rumors about Semele and were punished throughout their lives by Zeus or Dionysus. In another version of this legend, Persephone was the mother of Dionysus and he was snatched away and eaten by the Titans. Zeus saved the child's heart and served it to Semele in a drink from which she became pregnant. In later years, Dionysus went to the underworld, Hades, and took Semele to Mount Olympus where she became immortal under the name of Thyone. Some think Semele (or Persian Zamin) was Zemelo, an ancient earth goddess of the Phrygians. The Greeks identified her with the mother of the Egyptian Osiris. See also Actaeon; Bagos Papaios; Cadmus; Dionysus; Hera; Ino; Juno.

Semi (Egypt)
Deified object. Semi is a large winged uraeus standing on its tail. It is found in the tenth sector of Tuat.

Semiramis (Assyria)
Also known as: *Sammuramat.*

A goddess of love and war, she is the daughter of Ataryatis Derketo of Ascalon, the Syrian fish goddess (also known as Atargatis), and Oannes the god of wisdom. Ishtar's dove fed her as a newborn until she was found by the shepherd Simmos, who raised her. She wed Menon, who was a general of King Ninus of Assyria. After his death, she married Ninus and became the Queen of Babylon. After his death, she became the ruler of Assyria. She led mighty war campaigns against Persia, Egypt, Libya and Ethiopia, and conquered the eastern world. She was also noted for building Babylon and its famed hanging gardens. See also Atargatis; Oannes.

Semit-her-abt-uaa-s (Egypt)
The name of the Fifth hour of Tuat. Osiris must pass through Semit-her-abt-uaa-s, the capitol city of Seker. The pylon and circle of the city are called Aha-neteru and Ament, respectively. Within the city are the souls called Baiu amu Tuat who are hidden beings. The boat of Osiris is towed by seven gods and seven goddesses, and he is accompanied by the gods Her-khu, An-hetep, Her-hequi, and Hetch-met. See also Tuat.

Sena (India) see Karttikeya.

Sena-pati (India) see Karttikeya.

Senenahemthet (Egypt)
Serpent demon. It is mentioned in a magical formula of Unas, a king of the Fifth Dynasty. See also Akeneh.

Sengen (Japan)
Also known as: *Asama, Kono-hana-sakuya-hime* (The Princess Who Makes the Blossoms of the Trees to Flower), *Sengen-Sama.*

The goddess of Mount Fujiyama. Although many shrines have been dedicated to Sengen, an important one has been established on the summit of the sacred Mount Fuji. Pilgrimages are made to her sanctuary during the summer months and worshipers honor the rising sun. Based on this practice, there could be a connection between Sengen and the sun goddess Amaterasu. In her role the similarity between the short lives of mortals and the short lives of blossoms is illustrated. (*See* Sakuya-hime.) Many shrines are erected on mountains, as they are considered sacred. Additional mountain deities are O-Yama-Tsu-Mi, chief god and lord of the mountains. This deity was appealed to before trees were cut down, particularly trees used to construct temples. He was born from the blood of his brother, the fire god Kagu-tsuchi. O-Yama-Tsu-Mi married Kaya-no-Hime-no-Kami (Ruler of the Grassy Plains). One of their daughters, Kono-Hana-Sakuya-Hime (Blossoms-of-the-Trees-Blooming-Princess), married Ninigi and became the mother of Hoderi, Hosuser and Hikohohodemi. Other mountain deities are Naka-Yama-Tsu-Mi and Saka-no-Mi-Wo-no-Kami, gods of the mountain slopes; Masaka-Yama-Tsu-Mi, god of the steep mountain slopes; Ha-Yama-Tsu-Mi, god of the lower mountain slopes; Shigi-Yama-Tsu-Mi, god of the mountain foot; Kama-Yama-Hiko, god of mountain minerals; the goddess Kanayama-hime (Metal Mountain Deity); her brother Kana-yama-biko-no-kami (Metal Mountain Prince Deity). *See also* Amaterasu; Fuji; Hikohohodemi; Hoderi; Hosuseri; Izanagi; Izanami; Kagu-Tsuchi; Kanayama-hime; Kaya-no-Hime-no-Kami; Ninigi; O-Yama-Tsu-Mi.

Sengen-Sama (Japan) *see* Sengen.

Senk-hra (Egypt) *see* Aai.

Senki (Egypt) *see* Aai.

Sennins *Sennin* (Japan)
Also known as: *Weiwobo.*

Sometimes known as one god, sometimes as more than one god with various attributes. High god. Tobo-saku. Known variously as the "Prime Man of the East," and Weiwobo, the "Queen Mother of the West." The Prime Man of the East is an old man who never grows any older. His immortality is symbolized by a peach in his hand. The Queen Mother lives on a plateau, close to Heaven, far to the west of China. Rafu-sen is the female deity of the plum-blossom. Kinko Sennin rides on a pure white crane and plays his harp while flying through the air. Kiku-jido, deity of the Chrysanthemum, is an eternal boy who lives somewhere in the mountains. Most of the Sennins are shown as a man seated on a chair with a staff in his hand. *See also* Izanagi (for peach symbolism).

Senx (Bella Coola People, North America)
The sun. Senx is called "Our Father." *See also* Alkuntam.

Sepa (Egypt) *see* Centipede.

Sepes (Egypt)
A deity who lives in the persea tree at Heliopolis.

Sept (Egypt) *see* Aaru.

Septu (Egypt) *see* Sopdu.

Seqeq (Egypt) *see* Sebek.

Sequana (Gallo-Roman)
Sequana, an early deity, is the river and earth goddess of the Seine and its valleys. Relics from her sanctuary were found in

marshes near the source of the Seine River. Her sanctuary was thought to be a healing center, based on the found objects, which included human and animal figures, torsos, heads, limbs, and internal organs. The items may have been offerings to the deity. During her festival, the Celts pulled an image of a duck with a berry in its bill along the river. Other Celtic river goddesses are Belisama, Clutoida of the Clyde, Devona of the Devon, Matrona of the Marne, and Verbeia of the Wharfe. *See also* Belisama.

Sequinek *Seqinek* (Eskimo)
Aspect. Another name for God of the sun.

Ser-Kheru (Egypt) *see* Assessors.

Seraa (Egypt) *see* Aai.

Serafili (Muslim) *see* Gabriel.

Seraphim (Hebrew) *see* Angels.

Serapis *Sarapis* (Greek)
Also known as: *Apis, Asar-Apis, Asar-Hap, Asar-Hapi, Asarhap, Hapi-Asar, Osiris-Apis, Usur-Api.*

The Greeks derived the name Serapis from a combination of Osiris-Apis. During the Ptolemaic period Serapis was the Egyptian state god under the Greek rulers. In Greece, Serapis, a god of the underworld, was worshiped as god of the Ptolemies in the Serapeum temple in Alexandria. It was in Alexandria that the funeral cult of the dead bull was celebrated. Many of the myths attached to Serapis are similar to those of Osiris because in Memphis, Serapis was confused with Osorapis (Osiris Apis), the Greek name for Apis, and was worshiped with Osorapis. Serapis is shown as a bull-headed man wearing the solar disk and the uraeus between his horns. He is also shown wearing a corn modius on his head. In Greece and Rome he was usually represented as a figure similar to Pluto or Hades. Serapis is sometimes identified with Zeus, Asclepius, and Dionysus. *See also* Amentet; Apis (A); Argus (A); Onophris.

Serekhi (Egypt) *see* Assessors.

Serpent Lady (Aztec People, Mexico)
A name for Coatlicue. She is also variously called the Serpent Petticoated and Serpent Skirt. *See also* Coatlicue.

Serpents (Egypt)
Also known as: *Dragons.*

Sacred magical formulae. In the text of *Unas*, there are a series of short magical formulae, many directed against serpents. The following serpents are included: Ufa, Nai, Heka, Hekret, Setcheh, Akeneh, Amen, Hau, Antaf, Tcheser-tep, Thethu, Hemth, and Senenahemthet. The Nagas, Azi-dahak, Ahji are a few of the serpents of India. Kou-lung is a serpent from China. Even in Christianity St. George had his dragon.

Serqet *Selket, Selqet, Selquet Serket* (Egypt)
Also known as: *Salkis.*

Underworld deity. Protector of the dead and living. Scorpion goddess. With her winged arms widespread, she protects the mummy and guards the canopic jars containing the viscera. With the goddesses Neith, Isis and Nepthys, Serqet, the daughter of the sun god Ra, watches over the body of Osiris. During the Seventh Hour of Ra's journey to Tuat, Serquet confronts, seizes, and ties up the evil serpent, Neha-bra, who attempts to prevent Ra's boat from moving ahead. Serquet is depicted as a woman with a scorpion on her head and also as scorpion with the head of a woman. She is a companion of Isis and once sent seven of her scorpions to protect Isis from Set. She also protected Qebhsenuef. Worshipers of Serqet will never feel the scorpion's sting. *See also* Ab-esh-imy-duat; Hapy (A); Isis; Neith; Nephthys; Tuat.

Serqi (Egypt) *see* Aai.

Ses-rab-kyi-pha-rol-ta-phyin-pa (Tibet) *see* Prajma-paramita.

Sesa (India) *see* Sesha.

Sesha *Sesa, Sesha, Seshu, Shesha* (Brahmanic, Hindu; India)
Also known as: *Ananta* (Endless), *Anata, Anata-Sesha, Sesanaga, Virupaksha.*

Sesha, the world serpent, and Vasuki, one of the three kings of the Nagas, were used by the gods as a rope, in the churning of the Ocean of Milk. Sesha forms the couch where Vishnu rests on the primal sea. With his thousand hooded heads, he provides shade for his master. He is one of the Nagas kings who rule in Patala, the underworld. He is the son of Kasyapa and Kadru and the brother of Manasa. Sesha came into being when he sprang from the mouth of Bala-Rama as he was dying. His name, given to him by Brahma, means "eternal." Earthquakes are caused when he moves one of his heads. At the end of each kalpa (1,000 ages), he destroys the world with fire. Sometimes he is represented as a man in the form of Bala-Rama. As a serpent, he is depicted with a thousand heads, dressed in purple, and holding a plow and pestle. He symbolizes Time. Sesha is sometimes identified with Vrita. *See also* Bala-Rama; Kadru; Kalpa; Kurma (for churning of the ocean of milk); Manasa; Nagas and Nagis; Narayana (B); Nataraja; Patala; Vasuki; Virupaksha; Vishnu; Vrita.

Seshat (Egypt)
Also known as: *Sefkhet-Aabut, Sesheta.*

Deity of builders. Goddess of writing. Seshat is closely linked to Thoth as the patroness of writing and literature and the recorder of historical events. She is a helpmate to Thoth in his work and is the wife most often mentioned in connection with him. Her epithet is "She Who Is Foremost in the House of Books." She is also known as "Lady Builder." Seshat is a deity of the stars and to builders by aiding them in the stellar alignment of new structures, especially temples. She is depicted wearing a crescent and star with two plumes on her head or a headdress resembling a seven-pointed star crowned by a bow or a crescent. She usually wears a panther skin over her dress and holds a palm leaf in her hand. *See also* Sefkhet-Aabut; Thoth.

Sesheta (Egypt) *see* Sefkhet-Aabut; Seshat.

Seshetai (Egypt) *see* Aai.

Seshmu (Egypt)
God of perfume. Perfume deity and provider. Seshmu is mentioned from the Old Kingdom onward as the god of perfume and a provider, perhaps of material goods. Fragrance, aside from the olfactory advantages, was said to be infused with the power for immortality.

Seshu (India) *see* Sesha.

Sesi (Egypt) see Aai.

Sessrumnir (Norse; Teutonic)
Sessrumnir is the hall of the goddess Freyja in Asgard. *See also* Asgard.

Sessrymner (Teutonic) *see* Freyja.

Set *Seth, Seti, Sut* (Egypt)
Also known as: *Sutekh, Typhon.*

God of evil and darkness. Weather deity. Known as a born plotter. Set is the son of Geb and Nut, brother of Osiris, Isis and brother/husband of Nephthys. Sometimes he is known as the father of Anubis. In ancient times, he was the patron deity of Lower Egypt. When Upper Egypt overtook Lower Egypt, he became known as the god of darkness and the evil opponent of his nephew, Horus. During the Hyksos period he was worshipped as the chief god. During the Nineteenth and Twentieth Dynasties Set was known as a benevolent god who restrained the forces of the desert. He was the patron of the Ramessides. His good standing did not last long and by the Twenty-first Dynasty, he was once again the god of evil. He was insanely jealous of his brother Osiris, and numerous myths relate how he slaughtered him. In one tale, he tricked his brother Osiris by having a chest made that could only fit Osiris. When Osiris got in the chest, it was sealed and tossed into the Nile. The chest was found by Isis, but later came back to Set, who cut Osiris' body to pieces. Isis found all of the body except the penis and scrotum and restored Osiris to life. Set was slain in vengeance by Horus and thrown into the desert to live forever. Set is represented as having a hyena-like body, the muzzle being pointed and the ears high and square. In his aspect as Akherkh, he is a griffin-like animal. Set is represented as darkness and has been compared to a destructive, cruel sea, while Osiris, his direct opposite, is compared to light and the river Nile for his life-giving attributes. Set has many animal aspects: the antelope, donkey, ass, crocodile, and sow. The ass, often thought of as slow and stubborn, was an insignia of Set. It symbolized lust and cruelty. In Greece, as an animal sacred to Silenus and Bacchus, it represents wisdom and prophetic powers. Set is identified by the Greeks as Typhon. *See also* Ab-ta; Akherkh; Anat; Atum; Bast; Horus; Isis; Osiris; Seth; Sopdu; Typhon (A).

Set-Hra (Egypt)
A monster serpent who guards the entrance to the eighth sector of Tuat.

Set-Kesu (Egypt) *see* Assessors.

Set-Qesu (Egypt) "Crusher of Bones." A demon.

Seta-Ta (Egypt)
Guardian. Seta-Ta is a mummified god standing at the end of the corridor in the fourth sector of Tuat.

Setana (Celtic) *see* Cuchulain.

Setanta (Celtic) *see* Cuchulain.

Setcha (Egypt)
Setcha is an animal having the body of a leopard and the head and neck of a serpent.

Setcheh (Egypt)

Serpent demon used in the magical formula of *Unas.*

Setchet (Egypt) *see* Akeneh.

Setem (Egypt)

God of hearing. He is depicted with an ear above his head.

Seth (Egypt) *see* Set.

Setheniu-Tep (Egypt)

Afterworld deities. Four divine beings wearing white crowns found in the eleventh sector of Tuat.

Sethu (Egypt)

Also known as: *Setu.*

Sethu is a monster serpent god who guards the entrance to the tenth sector of Tuat. He carries a spear.

Seti (Egypt) *see* Set.

Setu (Egypt) *see* Sethu.

Seven Against Thebes (Greek)

They attempted to conquer the city of Thebes, unsuccessfully. Their sons, the Epigoni, successfully made the same attempt on the city of seven gates, ten years later. For details *see also* Adrestus.

Seven Generation Deities, The (Japan) *see* Ama-no-minaka-nushi.

Seven Snakes (Aztec)

A name for the maize goddess, Chicomecoatl.

Sgeg-mo-ma (Tibet) *see* Lasema.

Sgrib-pa-rnam-sel (Tibet) *see* Amoghasiddhi.

sGrol-mas (Tibet) *see* Tara.

Sha (Egypt)

Sha is a deified composite animal who has long square ears and a tail that looks like an arrow. It resembles the animal of the god of evil and darkness, Set.

Sha-kya-tup-pa (Tibet) *see* Sakyamuni.

Shadrapha (Phoenicia)

Also known as: *Shed the healer.*

God of Healing.

Shahapet (Armenian, Iranian, Slavic)

Also known as: *Khshathrapati, Shavod, Shoithrapaiti, Shvaz, Zd.*

Known as an Armenian lord of the land, he appears as a man or a serpent. He is a good spirit, unless he is angered. When found in houses, he is called Shavod, and is known as a lazy household guardian. On the last day of February he is forced out of the house to take up his duties in the field. The householders bang on the walls of the houses with old clothes, sticks and bags to arouse him. As a spirit of graveyards or fields, he is known as Shavz. Shahapet, Shvod, and Shavz are used in combination to frighten children. Similar to Iranian Khshathrapati. *See also* Shvaz; Shvod.

Shahar and Shalim (Canaan, Syria)

Also known as: *Ab, Amm, Kahil, Wadd, Warah.*

"The Gracious God." Twins sons of El. Shahar ("dawn") is the god of dawn, and Shalim ("peace") the god of sunset. South Arabians had many names for the moon god: Warah (the Wanderer), Kahil (the Old One), Wadd (the Loving) and Ilmuqah, which has no meaning, but may follow in the same vein as Ab (father) or Amm (ancestor or uncle) Associated with the Canaanite Shemesh, a sun god, and Yareah, god of the moon. *See also* Alilah; El; Elohim; Il; Ilah.

Shahpet (Armenian) *see* Shvaz.

Shahr (Mesopotamia) see Ba'al Shamin.

Shahrevar *Shahriver* (Persia) *see* Khshasthra Vairya.

Shahriver (Persia) *see* Shahrevar.

Shai (Egypt)

Also known as: *Shait.*

"Fate." The god Shai accompanies each human from birth to death, decreeing the course of his life, and appearing with the soul of the dead when it is tried and judged before Osiris. Sometimes Shai is coupled with the goddess Renenet ("Fortune"). She stands near the pillar of Balance where the dead are judged. *See also* Aai; Osiris; Renenet.

Shait (Egypt) *see* Shai.

Shaitan *Shetan* (Islamic)

An evil spirit. In the Arabic tradition, Shaitan are one of five types of Jin. *See also* Azazel; Devil; Jin.

Shakrani (India) *see* Indrani.

Shaktar (India)

The demon who was originally King Kalmashapada. *See also* Parashara.

Shakti *Sacti, Sakti* (Pre-Vedic, Hindu, Saktism, Tantraism, Tantric Buddhism, Mahayana Buddhism; India)

Also known as: *Aditi, Asa Poorna, Buddha Krotishaurima* (Tibet), *Cha-dog-ma* (Tibet), *Chak-yu-ma* (Tibet), *Devi, Durga, Gokarmo, Hlamos, Kanya-Kumari* (Daughter-virgin), *Kunto-bzang-mo* (Tibet), *Lakshmi, Mamaki* (Tibet), *Manasa, Matris (the), Maya, Nam-kha-ing-kya-wang-chug-ma* (Tibet), *Padma Krotishhaurima* (Tibet), *Prakriti, Ratna Krotishaurima* (Tibet), *Sangyay Chanma* (Tibet), *Sarasvati, Til-bu-ma* (Tibet), *Varuni, Yasodhara.*

Shakti is the Mother Goddess. She personifies the creative and destructive aspects of Divine Power. The Mother Goddess has come into the world in many forms to destroy evil and strengthen good. In the *Tantra,* there is one Universal Power, one Supreme Being, the Divine Mother. From herself, she created herself and her male aspect. In Hindu and Budhhist traditions, she is the consort of the god and represents his female aspect. Each member of the Hindu Trimurti has his Shakti. Shakti is also an epithet for many Indian and Tibetan goddesses. *See also* Ankusha; Devi; Durga; Ganesha; Hayagriva; Heruka; Kinkini-Dhari; Kuntu-bzang-mo; Lakshmi; Mamaki; Maya (A); Purusha (regarding Prakriti); Ratna Krotishaurima; Soma; Vairocana; Vilva (sacred tree); Zhag-pa-ma.

Shakuntala *Sakuntala Sacontala* (Hindu; India)

Raised by the sage Kanwa, this nymph became the mate of Dushyanta and mother of Bharata (q.v.).

Shakura (Pawnee People, North America) *see* Pah; Tirawa.

Shakuru (Pawnee People, North America)

Also known as: *Atius, Atius Tirawa.*

High god. Shakuru is the messenger between earth and the sky spirit, Tirawa. Some say he is a god of health and strength. *See also* Atius Tirawa.

Shal-za-ma (Tibet) *see* Nidhema.

Shala (Chaldea, Sumer)

An ancient Sumerian goddess of compassion, Shala was later included in the Chaldean Pantheon. She is the consort of Adad, or some say Marduk as Merodach, Dumuzi and Ramman. *See also* Dumuzi; Marduk; Ramman.

Shalem (Canaan, Syria) *see* Shahar and Shalim.

Shamas (Babylon) *see* Shamash.

Shamash *Chemosh, Shamas, Shemesh* (Mesopotamia) *Shamshu, Samsu or Sham-shu* (Arabia), *Chemosh, Shemesh.* (Probably of Sumerian origin, then adopted by the Akkadian people along with the entire Sumerian pantheon.)

Also known as: *Babbar, Shahan* (possibly), *Shullat, Utu* (possibly).

Sun god. In the regions of Sippar and Larsa, a god of divination. Possibly a deity of fire under the name of Shahan and a god of prophecy. Shamash is the son of Sin the moon god, or some say Enlil. He is the twin brother/spouse of the passionate goddess Ishtar. (Some say Aya is his spouse.) He is the father of Kittum ("truth") and Mesharum ("justice"). Originally a Semitic deity, Shamash was brought to Mesopotamia by the Akkadians. With his father, Sin, the moon-god, and his twin sister, Ishtar, Shamash forms an important triad. Elsewhere, he is one of a Babylonian triad with Sin (the moon) and Ramman (weather god). Shamash has the ability to deliver oracular responses of prophecy. His chief sanctuary was in Babylon, and he was also worshiped, possibly as Utu or Babbar at Sippar and Larsa or Ellasar. Scorpion men open his vast palace door every morning. (He lives in the mountains somewhere in the east.) His driver Bunene waits in the chariot for Shamash armed with his saw to mount the vehicle. They set out on their daily journey. At day's end they enter through another vast door in the mountains of the west and travel through the earth to their starting place. The sun and moon were represented by a crescent and disk by the South Arabians from the ninth to second century. His Sumerian counterpart is Utu. Shamash is associated with Gilgamesh. *See also* Aa, Aah, Ba'al Shamin; Mithra; Mitra; Shamash; Sin.

Shamashana-Kali (India) *see* Kali.

Shambara (India) *see* Sambara.

Shamshu (*Samsu*) (Arabic) *see* Shamash.

Shan Kuei (China)

Demon of the mountains. One of the nine heroes.

Shang Ch'ing *San Ch'ing* (China)

Supreme god of the "Superior Heaven." *See also* Lao-tien-yeh; San Ch'ing; Yu-huang-shang-ti.

Shang-di *Shang-ti* (China)

Ruler on High. Shang-di is the highest god of the Shang dynasty. He was later equated with Tian and was important in state rituals.

Shang Ti (China) *Shang-Ti*

Also known as: *Huan-T'ien Shang-Ti, Huang-Ti, Ti.*

Supreme god. Shang dynasty. The ancients knew him as the "Lord of the Dark Heaven," who was supreme over five deities. Each god had a sector of the sky. Ts'ing-ti, called the Green Lord, was in charge of the East. Ch'i-ti was over the South and was called the Red Lord. The god of the West was Po-ti, who was called the White Lord. Huan-ti, god of the North, was called the Dark Lord and the Center was under the rule of the Yellow Lord, Huang-ti. Shang Ti is represented as a man ten feet tall, surrounded with a halo, his long hair hanging over his back, generally clothed in a black robe. He is sometimes depicted as sitting on the back of a tortoise which is circled by a serpent. *See also* Chen Tsung; Huang T'ien; Lao-tien-yeh; T'ien; Yu-huang-shang-ti.

Shango (Yoruba People, Africa)

Earth god. God of thunder and lightning. Storm god. God of the east. God of war. God of justice and fairness. Shango is the earth born son of Obtala and brother of Ogun. He was the mortal king of Oya as well as a doctor who lived in a palace with several wives, including Oya, Oshun and Oba. His wife Oya had the reputation for being a very fierce woman who had an abundant beard. Shango had a bad temper and when he was angry he could kill by breathing fire. However, his wives apparently caused him great despair, for he committed suicide by hanging and now rules from the celestial realm. There, he acts as a god of justice. He punishes liars, thieves and those who work sorcery for negative means. The axe, representing the thunderbolt, is his weapon. When alive he carried a double-headed axe of stone said to have fallen from heaven. His altar is a three-forked tree that contains a basin with stones that also fell from heaven. In early days, if lightning caused fire, it was not extinguished even if a dwelling was burning because of the fear one had that Shango might retaliate. When Shango disappeared, his wife Oya changed into the river Niger. Shango is depicted with a double-headed axe similar to Thor's hammer. Shango represents thunder and the sound of thunder is said to be his bellowing. His sacred animal is the ram, and he is often shown with a ram's head and horns. From early times the Yorubas have been renowned for their bronze casting and their stone carving. Carved figures representing the Shango cult wore the double-axe insignia, often on the head or carried in their hands with a ram's head carved on the top. The Ashanti storm god is their supreme deity, Nyame. The Dinka People have the deity Deng, who has the aspects of a storm god. The Buganda war god Kibuka has storm god characteristics. Compare Shango to Zeus and Ammon-Ra. *See also* Ifa; Oba; Obtala; Olodumare; Oschun; Oya.

Shani (India) *see* Tapati.

Shankha-sura (India) A demon. *See also* Krishna.

Shantanu (India) King of Hastinapura. *See also* Vyasa.

Shap (Syria, Ugarit) *see* Shaphash.

Shaph (Ugarit) see Shaphash.

Shaphash *Shap, Shapsh* (Syria, Ugarit)
She is the sun goddess often called "Torch of the Gods," who helped Anath bind and carry the body of Baal to the top of Mount Tsaphon. There she assisted in his burial and the accompanying feast. Later, when he was resurrected but could not be found, Shaphash went to find him. She was successful and Baal once again sat on the throne in Zaphon. A fight took place between Baal and Mot. Shaphash arrived on the scene, separated them, intimidated Mot, and paved the way for a reconciliation. *See also* Anath; Baal; Mot.

Shapsh (Syria, Ugarit) see Shapash.

Shar (Sumer) see Anshar.

Shara (Armenian) God of food. Son of Armais.

Shara of Umma (Sumer) see Inanna; Shara.

Sharabha (India) see Shiva.

Sharanyu (India) see Saranyu.

Sharira (Buddhist) see Stupa.

Sharis (Urartian People of Armenia)
Mother goddess. She could be the forerunner of Ishtar as some of the Babylonian deities migrated to Armenia. Some place Sharis in the same category as Sammuramat, a name that is an epithet of Ishtar. There may even be some relation to the Armenian goddess, Semiramis.

Sharma (Hittite, Hurrian) see Sharruma.

Sharruma *Sharma* (Hittite, Hurrian) see Hepat.

Shasnli *Shakanli* (Choctaw People, North America)
Animal monster.

Shasti (A) (Bengal, India)
A protector of children, known as the Mother-Sixth, Shasti is worshiped on the infant's sixth day of life. Sometimes she is worshiped with Karttikeya as her spouse and she is considered to be his Divine Army. Shasti is depicted as riding a cat. She could be an aspect of Uma.

Shasti (B) (Hindu; India)
Shasti is the female form of the elephant-headed god, Ganesha.

Shastradevatas (India) see Devis.

Shata-Rupa (India) see Sarasvati.

Shatananda *Nandana* (India) Karna.

Shatarupa (India) "She of a Thousand Forms." *See also* Vach.

Shatrughna (India) Twin brother of Lakshmana (q.v.).

Shaumya (India) see Shiva.

Shaushga (Hurrian, Hittite) see Shaushka.

Shaushka *Shaushga* (Hurrian, Hittite)
Known as the Hittite Ishtar, Shaushka is the sister of three brothers, Teshub, Tashmishu and Hadad the storm god. Ishtar's name is usually used in the texts of the period in place of her own name. *See also* Ishtar; Teshub.

Shavod (Slavic) see Shahapet.

Shawano (Algonquin) see Manibozho.

Shaya (India) see Chhaya.

Shazau (Babylonia) see Marduk.

She-Chi *She, She-Tse* (China, Taoist)
Also known as: *Thu, Tu.*
Spirits of earth and grain, respectively. Possibly a single spirit with the same attributes. Also called gods of soil and crops. According to some this deity was originally an official under the rule of the Yellow Emperor.

She-Tse (China) see She-Chi.

Shedu (Babylon) see Sedu.

Sheehogue and Deenee Shee (Irish. Called the "Gods of the Earth" in the *Book of Armagh*)
Also known as: *Marcra Shee* (fairy cavalcade), *Slooa-shee* (fairy host).
Fairies. The Sheehogue and Deenee Shee are fallen angels, not good enough to be saved, but not bad enough to be lost. At one time, they were the giants of the Tuatha De Danann, but became smaller as they were no longer worshiped. Among them are the Pookas and Fir Darrigs, who are bad fairies. The other fairies are mischievous, but not bad. Sheehogue (sidheog) is singular, Deenee Shee (daoine sidhe) is plural. *See also* Banshee; Leprechaun; Tuatha De Dannan.

Shehbui (Egypt)
Shehbui, the god of the south wind, is portrayed as a lion-headed man with four wings.

Shelartish (Urartian People, Armenia)
Shelartish is possibly a local god or one of the less important moon deities. He is associated with the goddess Sharis. There is a possibility that he was part of an early Urartian pantheon along with either Khaldi and Theispas or Shamas and Ramman.

Shelf of the Slain (Teutonic; Norse) see Valaskjalf.

Shelva (Toltec People, Mexico)
Shelva is the giant who escaped the Great Deluge by climbing the mountain belonging to the god of water. When the waters subsided, Shelva built the pyramid of Cholula.

Shemerthi (Egypt)
God of bowmen. He is an archer god in the tenth sector of Tuat.

Shemesh (Mesopotamia)
Sun god. Little known deity, but he might have been a twin of Yareah who was a moon deity. He is associated with Shahar and Shalem who are deities of dawn and sunset. *See also* Shahar and Shalem; Shamash.

Shemsu Heru (Egypt)
They are lesser deities who are the assistants to the god Horus. They also aid the dead.

Shemti (Egypt) *see* Ab-ta.

Shen Nung (China) *see* Shen-nung.

Shen-Nung *Shen Nung* (China)

God of Agriculture. Deified mortal. Shen-Nung's son is the spirit of grain, Chu. Shen-Nung, the emperor of the third millennium B.C.E., brought the skills of agriculture to his people. After his death he was deified.

Shen Shu (China) *see* Shen-T'u.

Shen-T'ao (China) *see* P'an-T'ao.

Shen-T'u (Taoist; China)

Also known as: *Men-Shen, Shen Shu.*

Guardian. They are the original door guards of the early Chinese. Along with Yu-Lu and Shen Shu (or Shu Yu) the two gods guard the gates to hell. They were later replaced by the Sniffing General and the Puffing General. Men Shen is the collective name for the door gods. *See also* Hu Ching-te; Men Shen; Ts'in Shu-pao.

Sheng-Mu *Sheng-mu* (Taoist; China)

Also known as: *Nai-nai Niang-niang, Pi-Hia Yuan-Kun, T'ai-Shan Niang-Niang, T'ien-Hou.*

Mother goddess. Goddess of women and children. Her family name is Ch'en. Sheng-Mu is the daughter of T'aiyuehtati, the Emperor of the Eastern Peak. She is the wife of Mao Ying. She is a personal god (one who did great deeds during her lifetime). The daughter of a fisherman, she has the ability to cast out demons. She is the patron of farmers and fishers as she used her gift to aid them during her lifetime. She died at twenty-one. She keeps two of the demons she tamed with her. They act as messengers. Sheng Mu is shown wearing a headdress made of three birds with outspread wings. She is usually associated with the goddess of healing, Sung-tsi niang-niang (q.v.).

Shennda Boaldyn (Isle of Man) *see* Beltine.

Sheol (Hebrew)

Also known as: *Hell.*

Underworld. The grave or dwelling place of the dead. A place of darkness. The early Israelites pictured Sheol as a dim, underground world where all the souls of the dead were sent. It is a place without torture, but Sheol is also without joy. Sheol is similar to Arallu, Gehenna, Hades, Hell and Tuat.

Shepes (Egypt)

Aspect of Thoth. Shepes is a form of the god Thoth who appears in the seventh sector of Tuat. He is depicted seated with three headless figures, enemies of Osiris, kneeling before him. Their hearts have been ripped out and their bodies chopped up. There are other interesting figures in various positions around him: the god Af-Asar, the serpent Ankhtith, Hekenth the lion-headed goddess, and three hawks wearing double crowns on their human heads. The god Af-Tem sits regally nearby on a serpent shaped like a throne. Horus, whom Shepes in the form of Thoth once cured, also appears during this period with a retinue of gods and the goddesses of the twelve hours. *See also* Abesh-imy-duat (for other supportive members and enemies of this hour); Horus; Thoth.

Shepi (Egypt) *see* Aai.

Shesat Maket Neb-s (Egypt)

Afterworld deity. The name of the second hour of the night in Tuat. Osiris or the dead pass through the country called "Urnes" using the boat of Ra, proceeded by four other boats. The gods who minister to the dead in the second hour are Isis, Khnemu, Seb, Thoth, Afu, Ketuit-ten-ba, Kherp-hu-khefti, Heru-Tuat, Seben-hisq-qhaibit, Benth (two ape gods), Aana, Horus-Set, Mest-en-Asar, Met-en-Asar, Sesenet-khu. Following are the seven goddesses: Mest-tcheses, Amam-mitu, Hertuaiu, Sekhet of Thebes, Amet-tcheru, Ament-nefert, Nit-tep-Ament. Then there are Nebui, Besabes-uaa, Nepr, Tepu, Hetch-a, Ab, Nepen, Ar-ast-neter, Amu-aa, Heru-khabit, Anubis, Osiris-Unnerfer, Khui, Horus and Set, Hen-Heru, Hun, Hatchetchu, Nehr, Makhi, Renpti, Afu, and Fa-trau. *See also* Tuat.

Shesemtet (Egypt)

She is the lion-headed sky goddess consort or wife of Shesemu.

Shesemu *Shesmu* (Egypt)

Underworld or afterworld deity. God of the wine press. Shesemu is the lord of the last hour of the night and consort or husband of Shesemtet. As the god of the wine press he pushes the head of transgressors into the wine press and crushes their skulls. He is shown as a human with lion or ox head. *See also* Tcheser-tep-f; Tuat; Unas.

Shesera (Egypt)

Afterworld deity. A god that appears in the tenth sector of Tuat. He is depicted armed with arrows and with a solar disk for a head.

Shesha (India) *see* Sesha.

Shesmu (Egypt) *see* Sesemu.

Shesshes (Egypt) *see* Ab-ta.

Shet-Kheru (Egypt) *see* Assessors.

Sheta-Ab (Egypt)

Guardian of the sixth sector of Tuat. His name means "Secret heart."

Shetan (Islamic) *see* Shaitan.

Shetu (Egypt)

A serpent monster. He has the unusual ability to disappear into his own body when Ra ceases to speak. He appears in the eleventh sector of Tuat.

Shi-pa Lo-han *see* Arhats.

Shi Tenno, The *Shitenno* (Buddhist; Japan)

Guardians. The Shi Tenno, said to be five hundred years old, are guardians of the four cardinal points of the compass. They function as protectors of the world against the demons. Their names and directions are often given as guardian of the north, Bishamon, also known as Tamon; of the south, Zocho; of the west, Komoku; and of the east, Jikoku. Another list gives the north to Bishamon; the south to Komoku; the east to Jikoku; and the west to Zocho. The Shi Tenno are often located at temple gates to ward off evil spirits. The Nio serve a similar function. These and other guardian figures are known as Kongo Rikishi, or the strong men who hold the thunderbolt. The guardian figures are often depicted as "foreigners" with long curly hair, bulging eyes and fierce expressions on their faces. *See also* Bishamon; Godai-myoo; Jikoku-Ten; Konko-Yasha-Myoo; Nio; Shichi Fukujin.

Shi-tien Yen-wang (China) A name for the ten Yama Kings (q.v.).

Shi-wang (China) *see* Yama Kings.

Shichi Fukujin, The (Buddhist; Japan)
The Shichi Fukujin are the seven deities of luck, a group of six gods and one goddess. Their names are Benten the goddess of love; Bishamon the god of war; Daikoku the god of prosperity; Ebisu the god of workers and fishing; Fukurokujin the god of health and longevity; Hotei the god of good luck and generosity; Jorojin the god of wisdom. These deities have come together from different origins. Benten, as Benzaiten and Bishamonten (a male and female), is originally Hindu. Fukurokujin, Jorogin and Hotei are of Chinese origin. The name Pusa is a common European rendition for Hotei. The healer and sorcerer, Okuni-Nushino-Mikoto combined with Daikoku, became one of the Shichi Fukujin or Seven Gods of Happiness in later mythology. The images of the Shichi Fukujin were worn as charms. Benten is shown with a lute; Bishamon holds a weapon with an ax-like blade and a steel spike mounted on the end of a long shaft (similar to a halberd); Daikoku holds a mallet and sits on two rice bales; Ebisu holds a fishing rod and a plate of fish; Fukurokujin is depicted with a stork, a cane and a book of fate; Hotei has a large belly, a big smile and holds a bag containing desirable items; Jorojin is accompanied by a deer. Bishamon was also one of the guardians of the four points of the compass known as the Shi Tenno. *See also* names of individual deities for additional information and various spellings of names. *See also* Hiruko; Okuni-Nushino-Mikoto.

Shidure (Sumer) *see* Siduri.

Shidurri (Sumer) *see* Siduri.

Shigi-yama-tsu-mi (Japan)
God of the mountainfoot. *See also* O-Yama-Tsu-Mi; Sengen.

Shih-chia-mou-ni (China) *see* Sakyamuni.

Shiho-Tsuchi (Japan) *see* Hikohodemi; O-Wata-Tsu-Mi.

Shiko-Me *Shikome* (Terrible Woman); (Japan)
Also known as: *Gogo-me, Gogome, Hisa-me, Hisame, Yomo-tsu-shiko-me* (Ugly-Female-of-the-World-of-the-Dead).
Devils. Evil female spirits. Storm deities. The Shiko-Me are grotesque, evil, female deities who reside in Yomi, the underworld. Izanami was chased by a crowd of these demons along with eight attendant thunder demons and fifteen hundred assistant devils, as he fled from Yomi. Some say the Shiko-Me were an early form of the devil deities, the Oni. *See also* Gaki; Izanagi; Izanami; Kappa; Oni; Tengu; Yomi.

Shikome (Japan) *see* Shiko-me.

Shilup (Choctaw People) *see* Shilup Chito Osh.

Shilup Chito Osh (Choctaw People, North America)
Also known as: *Shilup.*
The Great Spirit or the name of a ghost.

Shima-tsu-hiko (Japan) *see* O-wata-tsu-mi.

Shimhanada Lokeswara (Buddhist; India)
Healer. Shimhanada Lokeswara is an aspect of Avalokitesvara and is regarded by the Mahayanist Buddhist as a healer of all diseases. He appears in many forms which vary slightly from one another. Shimhanada Lokeswara is depicted with a white complexion, three eyes, and a crown of matted hair (Jatamukuta). He wears a tiger skin and sits on a lion. A white trident with a white snake wrapped around is held in his right hand. In his left hand, he holds a burning sword on a lotus. *See also* Avalokitesvara; Lokeswara.

Shimmei (Japan)
Shimmei is a name used for the goddess Amaterasu, who is a sun goddess, the founder of sericulture, the guardian of agriculture, the deity of peace and order and the ancestor of the ruling family. *See also* Amaterasu.

Shimti (Akkadian) Goddess of Fate. *See also* Ishtar.

Shin-je-she-chi-chyil-khor (Tibet) *see* Yamantaka.

Shina-to-be (Japan) *see* Shina-tsu-hiko.

Shina-tsu-hiko (Shinto) Japan
Wind god. Shina-tsu-hiko and Shine-tsu-hiko (Shina-to-be) were born of Izanagi's breath. They hold up the sky and fill the void between heaven and earth. They are the superiors of the minor wind deities Tatsuta-hiko and the goddess Tatsutsa-hime. Prayers are offered to Shina-tsu-hiko, Shine-tsu-hiko, Tatsuta-hiko and Tatsutsa-hime when a plentiful harvest is desired. These deities are also invoked by fishermen and sailors. Amulets are worn to protect believers from the ill-effects of the wind and protection against storms. Tasuta-hiko and Tatsutsa-hime are named after the sanctuary where they are worshiped. *See also* Amaterasu; Fu-jin (god of winds); Haya-ji (whirlwind deity); Izanagi.

Shine-tsu-hiko (Japan) *see* Shina-tsu-hiko.

Shining One, The (Greek) *see* Aglaia.

Shinto Creation Myth (Japan) *see* Ama-no-minaka-nushi.

Shio-Zuchi (Japan)
"Old Man of the Tide." Shio-Zuchi is another name for the god of the sea and ruler of all sea creatures, O-Wata-Tsu-Mi (q.v.).

Shiri-Kume-na-Nawa (Japan)
"Don't Retreat-Rope." This rope was tied across the entrance to the cave known as Ame-no-Iwato, where the light of the world, personified as the goddess Amaterasu, had sequestered herself. *See also* Amaterasu.

Shishupala (India) *see* Sisupala.

Shita-teru-Hime (Japan)
She is the daughter of Okuni-Nushino-Mikoto, the god of medicine and sorcery. Ame-no-Oshido-Mimi, the son of the

sun goddess, Amaterasu, fell in love with her. *See also* Ame-no-Oshido-Mimi; Haya-ji; Okuni-Nushino-Mikoto.

Shitala (India) *see* Sitala.

Shitenno *Shi Tenno* (Japan)
Guardians. The four guardian kings. Zocho (in India, known as Virudhaka), Jikoku (in India, known as Dhritarashtra), Komoku (in India, known as Virupaksha) and Tamon (in India, known as Vaisramana). They protect the East, West, North and South regions of the sky. The Shitenno are assisted by eight generals, who are also protecting deities. *See also* individual gods.

Shiu-Mu Naing-Naing (China)
Water mother. *See also* Hsi-Ho and T'ien-Hou.

Shiva *Siva* (Hindu; India).
Also known as: *Ananda* (Joy, Happiness), *Ardhanari-Ishvara* (The Lord Who Is Both Male and Female), *Ardhanariswara* (Nepal), *Asitanga* (With Black Limbs), *Badari* (Lord of Badari Shrine), *Baidya-isvar*, *Bhaga* (The Divine), *Bhadra Vira*, *Bhairab*, *Bhairava* (The Destroyer), *Bhutesvara* (Lord of Spirits and Demons), *Dakshina-Murti* (Facing South), *Digambara* (Clothed in Space, Dressed in Air), *Garudi* (Shiva's secret form as female bird of prey), *Hara* (Universe Destroyer), *Isana*, *Iswara* (Supreme Lord), *Kala-Siva* (Double-sexed god of time or death), *Kapala* (Skull), *Krodha* (Anger), *Mahadeva* ("Great God," a praise name for Rudra-Shiva), *Mahakala* (God of Irrevocable Time), *Mahayogi* (Great Yogi), *Maheshvara* (Great Lord), *Nandisha* (Lord of Nandi), *Nandisvara*, *Nataraja Siva* (King of the Dance), *Nataraja* (Cosmic Dancer), *Nilakantha* (Blue Throat), *Panchamukhi-Maruti*, *Pashupa*, *Pashupati*, *Pasupati* (Lord Protector of Animals), *Phra In Suen* (Siam), *Rudra* (Storm), *Ruru* (Hound), *Sanja*, *Sankara* (Healer), *Sarva* (The Destroyer), *Sanhara* (Destruction), *Sharabha*, *Shaumya* (a peaceful aspect), *Sudalaiyadi* (Dancer of the Burning Ground), *Sundara*, *Sundareshwar*, *Syama* (Black), *Tryambaka* (Three-mothered or Three-eyed), *Unmatta* (Raging), *Vaidya-nath* (Lord of the Knowing Ones or Lord of the Physicians), *Virabhadra* (Monster of Destruction), *Vishvanatha*, *Visnanatha* (Vishna's name as the presiding deity of the sacred city of Benares); (Brahmanic, Hindu, Vira-Shaivaisma, Vedic; India)
Shiva has one thousand and eight names and epithets. He is a creator god, moon god of the mountains, god of agriculture, fertility god, lord of the cosmic dance, god of the arts and learning, god of truth, god of luck, god of the rivers, god of the forests, god of death, of yoga, of cremation grounds, and the lingam. He was a god of a primitive Hindu religion, later adopted into the Brahmanic pantheon. In this capacity, he embraced the destructive qualities of his Vedic predecessor Rudra, the storm god of the *Rig-Veda*. Shiva's attributes are truth, energy, and darkness. It is said that he does not have incarnations, although some followers declare that he has twenty-eight. His celestial abode is Kailasa where the faithful hope to arrive after death. Shiva stands beneath the sacred river Ganges which flows from the Himalayas in great torrents. The water flows through his matted hair and divides into the seven holy rivers of India. Frequently he is called upon to assist other gods in their fight against evil. During the Churning of the Ocean of Milk, when the serpent demon Vasuki was used as a churning rope, he vomited poison. The toxin threatened pollution of the ocean and the death of the other deities. Shiva quickly caught the noxious spill in his throat. His wife Parvati sprang to his aid and strangled him to keep him from swallowing it. He survived and was left with the legacy of a blue throat. Shiva has eight terrifying aspects: Asitanga, Bhairava, Kapala, Krodha, Rudra, Ruru, Sanhara, and Unmatta. His consorts are aspects of the Great Mother Goddess Devi who appears as Gauri, Sati, Parvati, Uma, Durga and Kali. He is the third member of the Hindu Trinity and he represents the destroyer but has aspects of regeneration. The other two members are Brahma, who represents the principle of creation, and Vishnu, who is the preserver. As Ardhanari, Shiva represents Shiva with Parvati or Durga and is both male and female. Agni is identified with Shiva as Rudra-Shiva, his destructive aspect. The followers of Shiva maintain that Brahma created the universe and was outside of the universe. He was awakened by Shiva, in the form of Hansa the goose. From Brahma's head sprang Angira (memory), from his breast Dharma (very loosely translated as "the ultimate conduct of all things"), from his body, mind and matter. He then proceeded to divide his body in half, the right half being Manu, the first perfect man, and the left half female, Satarupa, who is Maya or "illusion." In the *Mahabharata*, it is written that Krishna worshiped Shiva. The Buddhist Shingon sect consider Fudo-Myoo an aspect of Shiva. Shiva, as the ascetic, is often depicted with white matted hair, and an ash-smeared body. He is seated on the skin of a tiger, elephant or deer, covered by a snake canopy. This position symbolizes that he has overcome aggression and greed. On each side of his third eye he has three horizontal gold stripes, known as *tiku*, his caste mark. (Vishnu has three converging vertical strokes). Around Shiva's blue neck, he wears prayer beads, and the writhing cobra Vasuki. The crescent moon is depicted on his forehead, the symbol of the sovereignty given to him at the Churning of the Ocean. His mount, the white bull Nandi, is nearby and his son with the elephant head, Ganesha, is at his feet. Nandi, the guardian of all quadrupeds, provides the music for the dance of Shiva Nataraja known as the Tandava. Nandi's symbol is the crescent moon and his consort is Nandini, the cow who could fulfill all desires. The elephant symbolizes strength, power, wisdom and knowledge. Shiva's emblems are the lingam (phallus) and the footprint. Worship of the lingam celebrates his creative power. He usually has four faces, three eyes and ten arms. He rules with his eastward face, rejoices with his northward face, delights in all creation with his westward face, and with his southward face he shows his angry and destructive side. Shiva is also shown with five faces, three eyes and four arms, wearing snakes as ornaments and a string of skulls around his neck. Sharabha is a form of Shiva who appears as a black monster with eight legs and tusks and long claws. He lives in the Himalayas and is said to be over a hundred miles in length. As the god of music, Shiva Nataraja has his hourglass drum and frequently a stringed instrument known as the *vina*. He is sometimes pictured as a type of Dionysus or a Bacchus, drunk with wine and dancing madly on the mountains. As Bhutesvara, he dances in Smashana, the cemetery where the dead bodies are purified. He wears a necklace of skulls, and is garlanded with serpents. In Smashana, visitors must avoid the Vetala, an evil spirit who sneaks into corpses and makes them act like zombies who commit unspeakable crimes. In other depictions Shiva carries

a trident named Pasupata or Pinaka, created by the divine smith, Visvakarma, a bow named Ajagava (some call the bow Pinaka), an arrow, and a noose. He also has a club with a skull on the end named Khatwanga. His other attributes are the elephant and the rat. His sacred plant is the Asoka ("Calotropis Gigantea"). The Bilva (sacred fruit) and the Nirgundi, a three-leaved plant, are also his emblems. The leaves of the sacred Vilva (bel) tree are used in cermonial worship of Shiva and Shakti. Red China roses are essential in worshiping Shiva. In his manifestation as Nandisvara, he is shown in a ca. 9th century sculpture from Central Java as a slender prince dressed in royal attire, guarding the entrance to a shrine. He wears a crossed sacred thread, two girdles and two sashes, tied at the hip. His head, slightly inclined, is framed by an oval halo. His face shows a three-quarter profile. Behind his right shoulder is his traditional attribute, a trident. As Ardhanari-Isvara, he is represented with one female breast, depicting his male and female nature. During the moon-month Phalaguna the wedding of Shiva and Parvati is celebrated with a feast known as Shivaratri. Shiva represents the totality of all being and he aids all who worship him. If his name is repeated with devotion, faith and concentration, the heart is cleansed from sin and in rebirth the worshiper will live a happy life. *See also* Kurma regarding Shiva as Nilakanth. Compare Shiva and Nandi to Ptah and Apis (Egypt). Shiva corresponds to Vishnu (q.v.). Compare to the creation myth of Brahma. *See also* Andhaka; Ardhanariswara; Arjuna; Badari; Baidya-nath; Bana; Banalingas (sacred stones); Bhaga; Bhairab; Bhairava; Brighus; Daksha; Dakshina-Murti; Devi; Durga; Fudo-Myoo (Japan); Gramadeveta; Hanuman; Hara; Indra; Kala; Kali; Kalki; Kama (A); Krishna; Kuvera; Lokapalas; Mahakala; Manasa; Manu; Meru Mountain; Nandi; Nandisha; Nataraja; Panchamukhi-Maruti; Parashur Rama; Parvati; Pasupati; Pinka; Pushan; Ratri; Rudra; Sandhya; Saranyu; Sati (A); Sitala; Soma; Tara (A); Trailokyavijaya; Vasuki; Virabhadra; Visvakarma; Vritra; Yaksha and Yakshini.

Shivaratri (India) Celebration Feast. *See also* Shiva.

Shiwanni and Shiwanokia (Zuni People, North America)
When Awonawilona created clouds and the air, the sky deities, Shiwanni and his wife Shiwanokia, decided to be creative. Shiwanni spit on his hand, slapped it, and formed yucca suds. His floating suds became the stars and constellations. Shiwanokia's suds fell to earth and became Awitelin Tsita, the Earth Mother. *See also* Awitelin Tsita; Awonawilona.

Shk *Shakak* (Acoma People, North America)
The Winter Spirit. *See also* Iatiju.

Shoden (Japan) *see* Ganesha (India).

Shoithrapaiti (Slavic) *see* Shahapet.

Shojo (Japan)
The Shojo are denizens of the deep, who look something like orangutangs. They are merry deities and as they drink heavily, they are known as gods of sake, a rice wine. Their faces are red, and they have long red hair. They carry a dipper and wear gaudy dresses of red and gold.

Shokujo (Japan) *see* Amatsu-Mikaboshi.

Shony (Celtic) *see* Son.

Shore of Corpses (Teutonic) *see* Nastrond.

Shou (Egypt) *see* Shu.

Shou-hsing *Shou-Sing, Shouhsing* (China)
Also known as: *Lao-Jen, Nan-Chi, Shou-Lao.*
Shou-hsing is the god of long life, wealth and happiness. He is highly revered for his power to give mortals the gift of longevity. He records the destined date of a person's death, but could sometimes be persuaded, by honor and sacrifice, to alter his figures favorably. He is closely connected with the god of long life and salaries Lu-hsing (or Lu-sing) and the god of happiness Tsu-hsing, who were often depicted with him. This group is known as Fu-shou-lu. Shou-hsing is also known as Nan-chi lao-jen or Shou-lao (Old Man of the Southern Pole). Shou-hsing is generally depicted carrying a staff and holding a peach of immortality. He is an old white-bearded man with a bulbous bald head who is sometimes shown with a turtle or stork. Shou-hsing is part of a triad with Fu-hsing and Lu-hsing. He is associated with the god of happiness, Fu Shen, and the god of wealth and happiness, Ts'ai Shen.

Shou-lao (China)
Old Man of the Southern Pole. *See also* Shou-hsing.

Shou-Shen (China) *see* Shou-hsing.

Shou-Sing (China) *see* Shou-hsing.

Shou-Ts'ang (China)
Servant deity. Shou-Ts'ang executed justice on the orders of Kuan-Ti. He was also the squire and groom for the god of war.

Shouhsing (China) *see* Shou-hsing.

Shraddha (India) *see* Sraddha.

Shri (India) *see* Sri.

Shru (India) *see* Sri.

Shruisthia (Acoma People, India) The Autumn Spirit.

Shu *Shou* (Egypt at Nay-ta-hut; Libyan)
Also known as: *God of Air.*
God of atmosphere. God of dry winds. Shu and his sister/wife Tefnut were the first couple of the *Ennead* of Heliopolis. When his father Ra (the sun) ordered Shu to separate Geb and Nut from their embrace so light could come through, he did so. He held Nut up to form the sky. After the reign of Ra, Shu became the ruler of the world until he was overtaken by Apep's children. Weakened by the melee he gave the throne up in favor of Geb. The heavenly hosts threw a major farewell party that lasted for nine days. When it was over, Shu graciously retired to heaven. Shu and Tefnut were known as the "Twin Lion Gods." Overall, Shu personified the atmosphere which divides the sky from the earth. The goddess Isis wrote a book entitled *Book of Breathings* for her dead husband Osiris. It was concerned with the necessity of breathing in the underworld, of living after death. To do so, the deceased had to identify with the god Shu. Shu is usually depicted with one or more ostrich (or feather) plumes on his head and sometimes as the support of the vault of heaven. Shu's name means "dry," "empty." *See*

also Aai; Amun; Anat; Anhur; Geb; Heh; Isis; Khepri; Khnemu; Ra; Seb; Tefnut.

Shu-Hu (China)

Lightning. Shu, the northern god, and Hu, the southern god, created the world from the body of Chaos (Hun-tun). After the creation of the world, their names were combined and became the lightning that struck Chaos and allowed the world to emerge. *See also* Hun-tun.

Shu Yu and Yu Lei (China) *see* Men Shen.

Shualu (Babylon) *see* Aralu.

Shui Chun (China) *see* Shui Shen.

Shui I (China)

God of the waters. *See also* Nine Songs; Shui Shen.

Shui Jung (China)

Also known as: *Ch'eng Huang.*

As Shui Jung, he is one of the Pa Cha (Eight Spirits). As Ch'eng Huang, he is the god of walls and ditches. *See also* Ch'eng Huang.

Shui-kuan (China)

Also known as: *Shui Shen.*

Water deity. He belongs to the triad known as San Kuan. They are the Three Supreme Agents, or Three Origins. With Shui-kuan is T'ien-Kuan, the agent of heaven, and Ti-Kuan, the agent of earth. It is Shui-Kuan's job to defend men from evil. He rides his horse through water and is followed by fish. He is identical with Shui Shen. *See also* Nine Songs; San Kuan.

Shui Shen (China)

Also known as: *Shui Chun, Shui I, Shui-kuan.*

God of the waters. He is one of the Nine Songs, the nine creator gods. Shui Shen is similar to Yo Po and identical with Feng I. *See also* Nine Songs; Shui-Kuan.

Shukra *Sukra* (India) *see* Asuras; Brighus; Brihaspati.

Shullat (Sumer) *see* Shamash.

Shulmanu (Babylon) *see* Saramana.

Shura (Japan)

The Shura, male reincarnations of warriors who died in battle, are furious spirits who live in the sky where they fight one another.

Shurpanaka *Surpanaka* (India)

Shurpanaka is a Rakshasi (giant female demon) who is probably the daughter of Nikasha and sister of Ravana, Kumbhakarna, Khara, and Bihishan. *See also* Nikasha; Ravana.

Shutu (Mesopotamia)

South West Wind demoness. *See also* Ilabrat.

Shuznaghu and Zumiang-nui (Dhammai People, Northeast India)

Shuzanghu and Zumiang-nui lived above in a place were neither sky nor earth existed. Zumiang-nui gave birth to the earth goddess Subbu-Khai-Thung and the sky god Jongsuli-Young-Jongbu. The children fell from their space and were swallowed by the worm Phangnalomang. Zumiang-nui had another child and the worm came to devour it. Shuzanghu trapped him, split his stomach open and rescued his children who took their positions as the earth and the sky. They united and gave birth to the goddess Jibb-Jang-Sangne and the god Sujang-Gnoi-Rise, who became mountains, followed by a son, Lujjuphu, and daughter, Jassuju, who were born as frogs. In turn, they mated and gave birth to the first mortals, Abugupham-Bumo and Anoi-Diggan-Juje. They became the parents of Lubukhanlung, Sangso-Dungso and Kimbu-Sangtung. Abugupham-Bumo and Anoi-Diggan-Juje are described as being covered with hair. *See also* Agni; Brahma; Prajapati; Purusha.

Shvaz (Armenian)

Also known as: *Shahpet.*

Shvaz is a spirit or ghost of the fields who appears in the spring of the year. He may be identified with Shahapet (q.v.). *See also* Shvod.

Shveta Tara (India) "White Tara." *See also* Tara (B).

Shvod (Armenian)

This house guardian appears to mortals once yearly. He is beneficent unless he is angered. He may be related to Shahapet (q.v.). *See also* Shvaz.

Shyama-Kali (India) "The Black One." *See also* Kali.

Si-Wang-Mu (China)

Si-Wang-Mu is a name for Hsi-Wang-Mu, the goddess of epidemics, plagues and pestilence. *See also* Hsi-Wang-Mu.

Sia (Egypt)

Also known as: *Saa.*

God of the sense of touch or feeling, and of knowledge and understanding. Sia was born from the drops of blood that flowed when the sun god Ra mutilated his penis. He was subsequently invoked as a protector of the genitals of the deceased. Sia also is one of the gods who watch the heart of the deceased being weighed at the great judgment. *See also* Hu; Ra.

Sia People — Creation Legend (North America) *see* Sussistinnako

Sibhol (Celtic) *see* Eire.

Sibu (Andean People, Peru)

Creator. Sibu created rocks on which a monster bat defecated. From this material sprang trees and grasses. The bat could travel to the underworld (Nopatkuo) where he fed on the blood of Benu, the earth. Benu is the daughter of Namaitami who in turn is the daughter of Namasia. When the inhabitants of the underworld found out what the bat was doing they made a snare that cut the monster in half. Sibu healed the bat but required it to always keep its head down so its innards would not fall out. Now, the bat must always stay in this position. There are other stories about Sibu, one of which involves a flood myth. *See also* Sura (A).

Sibyl (Greek)

Also known as: *Sibylla, Sibylle, Sif.*

Prophet. There are numerous women in ancient mythology from various civilizations known as Sibyl. They are almost all prophets who also act as intermediaries between mortals and the gods. The original Sibyl is thought to be the Greek Sibyl, daughter of Dardanus and Neso. When Apollo asked her what she wanted, she asked to live as many years as the number of grains of sand she held in her hand. But she forgot to ask for youth and consequently shrivelled to a tiny size. When children asked her, "Sibyl, what do you want?" she could only answer with the words, "I want to die." *See also* Amaltheia; Golden Bough; Sif.

Sibyl Herophile (Greek) *see* Lamia.

Sibylla *Sibyl* (Greek) *see* Sibyl.

Sibyls (Greek)
Deified mortals. Women with the gift of prophecy who interceded with the gods on behalf of human supplicants. The Sibyls are usually very young or very old. They reside in and around caves. *See also* Sibyl.

Sibzianna (Babylonian) *see* Tammuz.

Siddhaikaviramanjughos (India) *see* Manjusri.

Siddhartha *Siddartha* (Buddhist, Jain; India)
Also known as: *Buddha.*
Siddhartha is the father of Mahavira. Siddhartha is an epithet for Buddha and a praise name for saints. The name is also used to depict one who has accomplished total enlightenment and self-control, or who has accomplished his reason for being on earth. *See also* Buddha; Mahvira; Sakyamuni.

Siddhas, The (Hindu, Jain; India)
Also known as: *Siddhanganas* (male), *Siddhanjanas* (female).
The Siddhas, demi-gods with great occult powers, reside in eternal bliss in Sidda-Sila, a region above the Kalpas in the zenith of the universe. There are 88,000 holy beings, all manifestations of Vishnu. *See also* Loka.

Siddhi (India)
Goddess of success. *See also* Ganesha; Karttikeya.

Side (Greek) *see* Orion.

Sidero (Greek)
"The Iron One." She is the second wife of Salmoneus and stepmother of Tyro. Tyro's twin sons, Neleus and Pelias, rescued their mother when Sidero had her imprisoned, and then murdered Sidero. *See also* Cretheus; Salmoneus.

Sidhe, The (Celtic) *see* Tuatha De Danann.

Sidhi-Data (India) *see* Ganesh.

Sidhottr (Norse; Teutonic) *see* Odin.

Sido (Melanesian)
Also known as: *Hido, Iko.*
Hero god. He is a trickster and shape changer. His wife is Sagaru. In death he planted crops to feed the souls of the dead.

Siduri *Shidure, Shidurri, Siduru* (Assyro-Babylonian)
Also known as: *Ishtar, Siduri-Sabitu.*
Sea deity. She is described as a beautiful goddess who lives by the sea in the midst of a beautiful garden strewn with gems. When she could not deter Gilgamesh from his desire to find Uta-Napishtim, Siduri directed him to elicit the help of Urshanabi. Siduri is shown as a serpent. Others describe Siduri as a veiled barmaid who is a manifestation of Ishtar. Her home is on the seashore not far from the Land of Life where the deified mortal Utnapishtim lives. *See also* Ishtar; Sabitu; Utnapishtim.

Siduri-Sabitu (Sumer) *see* Siduri.

Siduru (Sumer) *see* Siduri.

Sie-king T'ai (China)
Magic mirror. Sie-king T'ai is the mirror used by Ts'en-kuang to judge the dead before he assigns them to one of the ten hells of Ti-yu. *See also* Ti-yu; Ts'en-kuang-wang.

Siegfried (Teutonic) *see* Sigurd.

Sien-tsan (China)
Also known as: *Hsi-ling Shih.*
Goddess of weaving silk. The goddess and patroness of the art of silk cultivation. In her mortal life, she had been the wife of the emperor Shen-Nung, who was also deified. There is a similar version where Hsi-Ling Shih was the wife of Huang-ti and introduced the silk worm to the Japanese. *See also* Huang-ti; Toyo-Uke-Hime-no-Himi; Ts'an Nu.

Sieroji Zemele (Lithuania) *see* Zemina.

Sif (A) (Greek) Sif is an alternate name for Sibyl.

Sif (B) (Teutonic; Norse)
Sif is the wife of the thunder god, Thor. Her golden hair, cut off by Loki, was replaced by hair spun from gold by the dwarfs. She is the mother of Lorride and a daughter, Thrud. Sif is the owner of the jewel-dropping ring, Draupnir. *See also* Iarnsaxa; Sibyl; Thor; Thrud.

Sig-Tyr (Teutonic) *see* Tyr.

Sige (A) (Teutonic) *see* Sigi.

Sige (B) (Sumer) *see* Zi.

Sigfadir (Teutonic) *see* Odin.

Siggeir (Norse; Teutonic)
Siggeir is possibly a lord of darkness. He is the husband of Signy, who is the daughter of Volsung. *See also* Sigmund; Signy; Sinfiolti.

Sigi (Norse; Teutonic)
Also known as: *Sige.*
Deified mortal. King of Franconia. Sigi is one of the sons of Odin. He is the father of Rerir and grandfather of Volsung. He is usually depicted as a wolf. *See also* Odin; Volsung; Zi (Babylon).

Sigidi (Africa) *see* Eshu.

Sigird (Teutonic) *see* Sigurd.

Sigmund (Norse; Teutonic)
Sun hero. Sigmund is the eldest of the ten sons of Volsung and Liod. With his twin sister Signy they were the parents of Sinfiotli (Sinfjotli). Sigmund's first wife Borghild murdered Sinfiotli. His second wife Hiordis is the mother of Sigurd. Sigmund furnished swords to the fallen warriors in Valhalla. He, alone, was able to pull Gram, the magic sword, from the oak tree where Odin had thrust it. Siggeir, the husband of Sigmund's sister Signy, was so jealous of Sigmund's ownership of the Gram the sword that he had all the Volsungs slain. Only Sigmund escaped and hid in a cave. After a long series of events Sigmund

and Sinfiotli avenged the deaths of the Volsungs, but Signy perished in the flames that killed Siggeir. *See also* Arthur; Odin; Signy; Volsung; Volsung Saga.

Sigmund and Sinfjotli (Teutonic) *see* Odin.

Signy (Norse; Teutonic)
Dawn goddess. She is the only daughter of Volsung and Liod. Her brother, Sigmund, is the eldest of ten brothers. With Sigmund she became the mother of Sinfiotli. Signy and her son killed Siggeir (her former husband) to avenge the death of Volsung. *See also* Sigmund; Volsung.

Sigoo (Arawak People, New Guinea)
Sigoo took the animals and birds to the high mountains so that they could survive the Great Flood.

Sigrdrifa (Teutonic) *see* Brynhild.

Sigrun (Teutonic)
Also known as: *Kara.*
She is the daughter of Hogni. Sigrun was reincarnated as Kara, who is one of the Valkyries (q.v.).

Sigtyr (Teutonic) *see* Odin.

Sigu (Arawak People, New Guinea)
Ruler of the animals. *See also* Makonaima.

Siguna (Teutonic) *see* Sigyn.

Sigurd (Norse; Teutonic)
Also known as: *Siegfried, Sigird.*
He is the handsome hero of the Volsunga saga. He was born after his father Sigmund's death. His mother, Sigmund's second wife, was Hiordis. Sigurd, encouraged by Regin, killed Fafnir so he could have the treasures stolen from Andarvi. Sigurd was in love with a Valkyrie woman, Brynhild. He went to Giuki's kingdom, the land of the Nibelungs. Grimhild, the wife of Giuki, gave Sigurd a magic love potion. He completely forgot his longing for Brynhild and fell in love with Gudrun, the daughter of Giuki and Grimhild, whom he married. Later, Sigurd went to Brynhild and wooed her for his brother-in-law Gunnar. Later still, Brynhild, understandably jealous, played a role in having Sigurd murdered. *See also* Andarvi; Fafnir; Sigmund.

Sigyn (Norse; Teutonic)
Also known as: *Siguna.*
Earth goddess. Sigyn sits by her husband Loki's side collecting the poison that drips on his face. This is his punishment for misdeeds. She will stay with him until Ragnarok. Sigyn is the mother of Narve and Vali. *See also* Loki; Narve; Ragnarok; Vali.

Sigyu (Teutonic) *see* Loki.

Sikhin (India) *see* Manushi-Buddhas.

Silappadikaram (Tamil People, India)
Bala-Rama is worshipped under this name by the Tamil people. His spouse is the goddess of victory, Korraval. *See also* Bala-Rama.

Silas (Roman) *see* Silvanus.

Silenus *Seilenos, Seilenoi, Selenus* (Greek)
Also known as: *Seilenus* (plural), *Sileni* (plural).
King of Nysa. A jovial old deity, Silenus, a talented musician, has the gift of prophecy. He is a companion, teacher and protector of Dionysus. He also appears as a guardian of the drunken Bacchus. Silenus is the son of either the shepherd god Pan, or Hermes, the messenger of the gods, or the earth mother goddess, Gaea, and possibly the father of the Centaur Pholus by an ash nymph. Silenus killed the monster Enceladus during the war against the Giants. Woodland gods known as Sileni gave king Midas the "golden touch." Silenus is depicted as a burly intoxicated old man riding an ass or with the ears of an ass. The Sileni are often confused with the Satyrs. Both were represented as animals, either horses or goats. *See also* Bacchus; Enceladus; Hephaistos; Midas; Satyrs.

Silik-mulu-khi (Akkadian)
The god of light and protector of mortals, Silik-mulu-khi is the son of Ea. *See also* Ea.

Silili (Babylon, Chaldea)
The Divine Mare; she is the mother of all horses.

Silvanus *Sylvanus* (Roman)
Also known as: *Callirius* (Woodland King), *Gradivus, Quirinus, Silas, Sylvan.*
Agricultural god. Silvanus, the protector of farmers in the Narbonnaise (southern Gaul) area, is affiliated with the ancient earth goddess Aeracura and was once thought of as a god of war. One of his consorts was the Celtic goddess Nantosuelta. His consort Rhea-Silvia is a priestess of Vesta. Their offspring, the Sabines, are also called Quires. Silvanus is depicted with a scythe or a mallet with his foot resting on a cask. It is thought that his animal is the stag. He is the same as the Celtic hammer or thunder god Sucellos. He is also identified with the vegetation god, Sylvain. He is sometimes identified with Mars and sometimes with Pan. *See also* Aeracura; Cernunnos; Nantosuelta; Sucellos; Vesta.

Simbi (Haitian)
Also known as: *Simbi en Deux Eaux.*
God of fresh water, rain and magicians. He is shown in snake form.

Simbi en Deux Éaux (Haitian) *see* Simbi.

Simhanadamanjusri (India) *see* Manjusri.

Simharatha (India) *see* Durga.

Simhika (India)
She is one of Daksha's daughters and the mother of Rahu. *See also* Daksha; Rahu.

Simoeis (Greek)
He is the son of Oceanus and Tethys and the father of Astyoche and Hieromneme. *See also* Astyoche.

Simurgh (Persia)
Also known as: *Garuda* (India), *Saena.*
Simurgh is the vulture who saved Zal, the father of Rustam. He gave Zal one of his feathers and told him to throw it into a fire whenever he needed help. Compare Simurgh to Garuda (India). *See also* Rustam; Sam.

Sin *Sinu* (Sumer, Babylon, Akkadian)

Also known as: *Nanna, Nannar.*

Moon god. Sin, the early god of the moon, is the son of Enlil and husband of Ningal, father of Nusku. He has the reputation of being a wise god who shared his wisdom with other deities every month. Marduk placed Sin in charge of marking monthly time by his waxing and waning. With his light, his enemies, the evil beings, could be watched. When the Utukku (spirits) with Ishtar and Shamash extinguished his light, Marduk came to the rescue and battled the attackers. He was successful in bringing back the light from the eclipse. Sin is known as Nanna in Sumer, where he was worshiped in the form of an elderly man. His symbol is a crescent. He is also believed to be the father of Nusku. *See also* Enlil; Ishtar; Marduk; Nanna; Ningal.

Sin-Nanna (Babylon) God of the Moon. *See also* Sin.

Sina (Polynesia) *see* Ina.

Sindre (Teutonic) *see* Sindri.

Sindri (Norse; Teutonic)

Also known as: *Sindre.*

Master smith. The dwarf Sindri resides in his palace located in a hall in the Nida mountains. He and his brother Brokk and perhaps others are known as the Sons of Ivaldi. The mischievous Loki had cut off all of Thor's faithful wife Sif's golden hair. Enraged, Thor said he was going to crush Loki to death. Loki, a trickster, was able to talk his way out of the situation by promising to have hair for Sif made of gold that would grow like her own hair. He went to the Sons of Ivaldi. They fufilled Loki's promise and at the same time fashioned the ship Skidbladnir and the magic spear, Gungir. Loki put his head on the block and made a wager with Brokk that Sindri would not be able to fashion three other items as precious as the hair, ship and spear. Sindri and Brokk set about their task. Sindri placed a hog in the forge and instructed Brokk to blow the bellows without stopping until he returned. Meanwhile, a pesky fly kept annoying Brokk. He ignored it even when it settled on his neck. When he lifted the hog from the forge it had turned into a boar with golden thistles. The boar came to be known as Gullin-Bursti. He kept on working. When Sindri returned he lifted the magic gold ring Draupnir from the forge. Next Sindri laid iron in the forge and instructed Brokk to keep the bellows blowing or the work would be ruined. The pesky fly was still flitting around. This time it landed between Brokk's eyes and stung him. It was so bad that blood poured down his face and blinded him. At that point, Sindri returned, reached into the forge and took out Mjollnir the magic hammer. He sent Brokk off go to Asgard to collect the payment of Loki's head to settle the wager. Settled in their places of judgment, the Aesir decided that Odin, Thor and Frey were to judge between Loki and Brokk. Loki gave Odin the spear, Thor the golden hair, and Frey the magic ship. Brokk gave Odin the magic ring, Frey the golden boar, and Thor the magic hammer. The Aesir decided that Brokk had won the wager. Loki wanted to reclaim his head, but Brokk would not hear of it. Loki, wearing his magic shoes, took giant steps over land and sea. Brokk asked Thor to assist him. He did and Loki was apprehended. The dwarf was ready to chop off Loki's head when Loki said the wager was for his head only and not his neck. Not to be thwarted, Brokk sewed together Loki's lips.

The name Sindri is also the hall with the red roof in the world to come after Ragnarok. *See also* Dvalin; Loki; Odin; Ragnarok; Sif; Svart-alfa-heim; Thor.

Sinfiotli (Norse; Teutonic)

Also known as: *Sinfjotle, Sinfjotli.*

A werewolf. He is the son of Sigmund and his sister Signy, and half-brother of Siggeir. Sigmund and Sinfiotli in werewolf guise murdered people and when there were not any candidates available, they attacked one another. Sinfiotli was killed, but was brought back to life and together they avenged the death of the Volsungs. Sinfiotli also helped his mother murder Siggeir. *See also* Siggeir; Sigmund; Signy; Volsung.

Sinfjotle (Teutonic) *see* Sinfiotli.

Sinfjotli (Teutonic) *see* Sinfiotli.

Sinfjotli and Sigmund (Teutonic) *see* Odin.

Singhini (Nepal) Female guardian demon.

Sinilau (Polynesia) *see* Tinirau.

Sinivali (Hindu; India)

Goddess of fecundity and easy birth. Sinivali is thought to be one of Vishnu's spouses. *See also* Dharti Mai; Vishnu.

Sinon (Greek)

Sinon, the son of Sisyphus and Anticleia (the daughter of Autolycus and wife of Laertes), was a Greek spy during the Trojan War. He could be the brother of Odysseus. *See also* Sisyphus.

Sinope (Greek)

Virgin deity. Sinope, the daughter of Asopus, was whisked off by Zeus, who promised to grant her any wish if she would submit to his ardent advances. Her wish was to remain a virgin and according to most myths, her wish was granted despite the pursuits of Apollo, the river-god Halys, and Zeus. She lived on an island, happy with her solitude. Diodorus Siculus claimed that Apollo finally deflowered her and that she became the mother of Syrus. *See also* Amentet; Apollo; Asopus.

Sintians, The (Greek)

In some myths, Hephaistos was raised by the Sintians on the island of Lemnos. *See also* Hephaistos.

Sinu (Sumer) *see* Sin.

Sio Calako (Hopi People, North America) A giant.

Sio Humis (Hopi People, North America) The Rain Spirit.

Siokhi (India) *see* Manushi-Buddhas.

Sioux People — Creation Legend *see* Wakataka.

Sipendarmidh (Persia) *see* Spenta Armaiti.

Sippara (Egypt) *see* Aah.

Sipylus (Greek) *see* Aedon.

Sirat (Islamic)

The Sirat is the bridge that spans hell, known as Daru el-Bawar. It is similar to the Zoroastrian Chinvat Bridge (q.v.).

Sirdu (Chaldean) *see* Aa.

Sirens *Seiren, Syren* (Greek)

The Sirens are evil nymphs who lived on various islands off the coast of southern Italy. The islands named are Cape Pelorus, the Isle of Anthemusa, Capri, and the Siren Islands. They are the daughters of the river god Achelous and the muse of tragedy, Melpomene or Terpsichore, the muse of dance. Other writers name Achelous the father and Calliope, the muse of poetry, or Sterope (also known as Asterope) as their mother. They have also been called the daughters of the ancient sea god Phorkos and the sisters of the demon Skulla. Homer named two Sirens but other writers say there were three, four or eight. Their names are given variously as Leucosia, Ligeia and Parthenope, or Aglaopheme (meaning brilliant voice), Aglaope, Molpe (meaning song), and Thelxiepeia (meaning enchanting words), or Himeropa and Peisinoe (Pisinoe), meaning the persuasive. The Sirens once witnessed Persephone being raped by Hades. Intent upon revenge, they were given wings by Zeus. In another legend, it is related that Aphrodite punished them with strange bodies because they never fell in love. Their greatest love was for their perceived talent. They challenged the Muses to a musical competition and lost. The Muses' crowning glory is the tiaras they made from the Siren's feathers. Their melodious voices enchanted sailors and lured them to their deaths. The only mortals known to survive the dangerous route past their island was Jason and the crew of the Argos, who had taken great precautions, and at another time, Odysseus. When Odysseus sailed by their island unscathed, the Sirens felt their loss of power and flung themselves to their deaths. Represented as birds with wings and the head and breasts of a woman. Compare the Sirens to the Russian Rusalki and Russalka. *See also* Achelous; Aello; Calydonian Bear Hunt; Fates; Gorgons; Graiae; Harpies; Hylas; Jason; Lamia; Muses; Odysseus; Orpheus; Scylla.

Siris (Assyro-Babylonia) *see* Ea; Zu.

Sirius (Egypt)

Also known as: *Sirius the Dog-star, Sothis.*

Sirius, known as the brightest star, marked the beginning of the sacred Egyptian year. The Egyptians called it Sothis and considered it the star of Isis. Visible just before sunrise about the time of the summer solstice, Sirius signified the beginning of the sacred Egyptian year. In female form, Sothis represented the goddess of love and life, who comes to wake her lover from the dead. *See also* Aktar; Hapto-iringa; Isis; Orion; Tishtrya; Sothis.

Sirona *Dirona* (Gaul, Celtic) *see* Borvo.

Sirrida (Chaldean) *see* Aa.

Sirrush (Sumer)

Sirrus, who has four feet and long legs with talons on his hind paws, is a dragon sacred to Marduk. The long neck of his scaly body ends in a large-eyed snake-head with straight vertical horns and a split tongue darting forward.

Sirsir (Babylonia) *see* Marduk.

Sirsootee (India) *see* Devi.

Sisa (Ashanti People, Africa) *see* Kla.

Sistrum (Egypt)

Sacred object. The Sistrum is a rattle used in the worship of Isis, Hathor, and Min. It is usually depicted as having a handle with the top shaped like the head of Hathor with cow's ears, and a horseshoe-shaped metal frame with loose cross-bars that rattle when shaken. Sometimes there were metal disks along the strings. The sound frightened away demons. *See also* Ihi.

Sisupala *Shishupala* (Hindu; India)

Also known as: *Ravana.*

Sisupala, the King of Chedi, is the third avatar of the demon Ravana. When he was an infant, Krishna was visiting and noticed his deformities. He took the child on his knees, and his third eye and two extra arms disappeared. Sisupala's hatred of Krishna grew into an obsession and he could barely sleep without thinking about him. In later years, he was engaged to Rukmini, the daughter of the King of Vidarbha, Bhishmaka. The engagement and impending wedding were arranged by her brother Rukma, who was a friend of the evil Kansa, who had been killed by Krishna. Rukmini, an avatar of the goddess Lakshmi, was in love with Krishna. She wrote to him and begged to be rescued from the ceremony. He arrived on the scene and pulled her into his chariot and they sped away pursued by Sisupala, Jara-Sandha and Rukma. Rukma tried to kill Krishna, but was apprehended by Krishna's half-brother Bala-Rama. Rukmini interceded for him and her brother was spared. Krishna ensconced her in his celestial dwelling place, Dvarka, and in time they produced ten sons, including Pradyumna, and a daughter, Charumati. Sisupala, who never forgave Krishna for interfering with his relationship with Rukmini, harassed him whenever he had the opportunity. Krishna tolerated him because he had promised Sisupala's mother that he would forgive him a hundred wrongs. On the hundred and first incident, Krishna threw Sudarsana, his magic discus, at him and split him in half. His soul burst into flame, bowed before Krishna and was absorbed into his feet. The discus Sudarsana is formed like a wheel with an extremely sharp edge. It lives in the sky and by rotation comes to Vishnu's hand. It emits fire sparks and lightning and can burn down cities. Vishnu and his avatars used it in battle to slay demons. *See also* Bala-Rama; Jara-Sandha; Krishna; Lakshmi; Pradyuma; Ravana.

Sisyphos (Greek) *see* Sisyphus.

Sisyphus *Sisyphos* (Greek)

The underworld deity Sisyphus is the son of Aeolus and Enarete. He became the king of Corinth and married the Pleiad Merope and became the father of Thersander, Glaucus, known as Glaucus of Corinth, Halmus (Almus) the king of Boeotian Orchomenus, and Ornytion. Sisyphus discovered that the renowned thief Autolycus was responsible for stealing his cattle. In retribution, he seduced Autolycus' daughter Anticleia, who was married to Laertes, and he became the father of Sinon and possibly Odysseus. Sisyphus and his brother Salmoneus despised one another and Sisyphus wanted him killed. He consulted an oracle and following the advice he had an affair with his brother's daughter, Tyro. They had two sons but when she learned about the oracle, she felt that Sisyphus hated his brother more then he loved her, so she murdered the children. Sisyphus discovered the dead bodies and falsely accused Salomoneus of the deaths and had him expelled from Thessaly. It is felt that Sisyphus committed a heinous act at this time and was condemned to Hades to roll a huge rock uphill which, upon reaching the top, always rolled to the bottom. Some think that Zeus, angry with Sisyphus for divulging that he had abducted Aegina, the daughter of Asopus, ordered Hades to punish him. When Sisyphus reached Tartarus, he managed to manipulate Hades into allowing him to return to the world, and promised that he would return. He broke his promise and had to be dragged back by Hermes. Sisyphus, known as a cunning and avaricious man, also had another side. He discovered the dead body of his nephew Melicertes on the Isthmus of Corinth, which had been brought ashore by a dolphin. He buried him at that location and founded the Isthmian games in his honor. His son Glaucus was murdered by Pelops and his ghost was known as Myrtilus. For the genealogy of Sisyphus, see Aeolus (A). Sisyphus is similar to Ixion. For another explanation for his severe punishment in Hades, see Aegina. Compare his punishment to that of Ixion and Tantalus. See also Anticleia (A); Asopus; Autolycus (A); Bellerophon; Canace; Erinyes; Hades; Pelops; Salomoneus.

Sita Seeta (Hindu; India)

Also known as: Bhumija, Lakshmi.

Sita is described in some renditions as self-formed as a seed furrow in the soil. In this form she is known as Bhumija and is said to have sprung from the earth where she was discovered by King Videha while he was ploughing. Other legends proclaim that she is either the daughter of the earth Bhumi or the earth goddess and goddess of wealth Vasundhara and sister of her brother Naraka. A beautiful sister, Urmila, the daughter of Janaka, is also mentioned. In another version, she is the daughter of Savita who personifies the sun and the lover of Soma the moon. Sita is a fertility goddess and goddess of agriculture. She is an incarnation of Lakshmi who follows Lakshmi's incarnation as Dharani. Sita was extremely beautiful and attracted many suitors. A competition was held to see who would have the privilege of being her mate. The winner of the event had to bend the bow that Shiva had been given by Janaka. Rama, Vishnu's seventh avatar, was the victor as was predestined. Sita followed him into the forest when he was exiled. One day, while Rama was hunting, Sita was abducted by the demon Ravana and carried off to Sri Lanka. He tried to seduce her but she resisted his overtures. A battle to gain her back developed and she was rescued by Rama, his devoted brother Lakshmana and Hanuman and his troop of monkeys. Rama would not believe that Sita did not have sex with Ravana. Finally, in desperation to prove herself, she threw herself onto a burning pyre. The god of fire Agni knew that she was pure and did not burn her. Still her spouse did not believe her. He insisted that she go off to live in the forest even though he knew that she was carrying his child. She lived with the sage Valmika and gave birth to twin sons, Kusha and Lava. When the children were about fifteen Rama first saw them and knew instantly that they were his children. He wanted his family back, but Sita, who was heartbroken, returned to the womb of the earth, her birth place. Sita symbolizes the resourceful earth and the pure and faithful spouse. See also Agastya; Bharata (A); Bhu-Devi; Bhumi (regarding Bhumija); Hanuman; Kusha; Lakshmi; Rama; Ravana; Sampati; Soma; Sugriva; Vasundara.

Sitala Shitala, Sitla (Hindu; India)

Sitala is the black goddess of smallpox. She was thrown out of Shiva's paradise, Kailasa, for throwing her gold necklace at the great god, which gave him ulcers. Kicked by a cow, she cursed all cows to lives of heavy labor. Her curse gave all cows one teat for the calf, one for the gods, one for the king, and one for the owner. It was further decreed that the animal's hide would be used for shoes and drums. She also cursed the mango tree, causing it to be devoured by insects and used for burning the dead. Sitala, who dispenses and cures smallpox, is invoked for protection against the disease. She has eight faces studded with eyes and teeth like boar's tusks. Her hair is made of peacock feathers and two elephants hang from her ears. In her hands are a sword, dagger, trident, cup, wheel, rope and an ape. Her clothes are serpents. She is also depicted wearing red robes, carrying reeds to chastise her victims and riding an ass. The milk from an ass is thought to be a cure for smallpox. Sitala is worshiped in spring and summer and during times of illness. During this time, the patient is surrounded by neem leaves. She is sometimes identified with Devi in her aspects of Durga and Kali (q.v.). See also Hariti; Kishimojin (Japan); Shiva.

Sitamahakala (India) see Mahakala.

Sitatapatraparajita (Tibet) see Avalokitesvara; Gdug-dkar-chan-ma; Tara (B).

Sitatara (India) see Tara (B).

Sith (Teutonic)

Harvest deity. One of the wives of Orvandel. Mother of Ull and stepmother of Svipdag. Legend says she prepared the food of wisdom from the fat of three serpents.

Sitla (India) see Sitala.

Siton (Phoenician)

An alternate name for Dagon. See also Dagon (B).

Sitragupta (India) Son of Indra. See also Indra.

Sittung (Teutonic) see Fjalar.

Situr (Sumerian) see Ninsun.

Siudleratuin (Inuit, Eskimo) Spirits of the dead.

Siva (India) see Shiva.

Siyamek (Persian) see Hushang; Takhmoruw.

Sjofn (Teutonic)

She is a messenger goddess who inspires human passion. Sjofn is also an attendant of Frigga.

Skad (Teutonic) see Odin.

Skade (Teutonic) see Skadi.

Skadhi (Teutonic) see Skadi.

Skadi (Norse; Teutonic)

Also known as: Skade, Skadhi, Skathi.

Goddess of winter. Goddess of the chase (possibly). Skadi is the daughter of Hrim-thurs or Thiassi. Because of the death of Thiassi, the gods allowed her to choose a husband from the gods. Blindfolded, she could only see the gods' feet. She wanted to be the wife of Balder but her blind choice was Niord. For a time, she spent part of the year with Niord and part of the year in her wintery home. Later, the two separated and she became the wife of Odin. They had a son, Saeming, who became the first king of Norway. Later still, she married the winter god, Uller. Some say Freyja was her daughter. Skadi was the one who fastened a serpent over Loki's head so venom dripped on his face, but Loki's wife Sigyn held a cup to catch the venom. When she had to take a moment to empty the cup, the venom caused Loki such pain that his agonized movements caused earthquakes. Skadi wears silvery armor, a short white hunting dress, white fur leggings, broad snowshoes and holds a spear and arrows. She is usually accompanied by wolves or dogs. *See also* Balder; Loki; Njord; Sigyn.

Skambha (Hindu; India)

"The Supporter." Skambha is an axis deity who sustains the worlds. He is sometimes identified with Brahma. Skambha is also an epithet of Agni, Indra and Soma.

Skanda *Scanda* (Hindu; India)

Skanda is another name for the war god Karttikeya (q.v.). *See also* Bana; Devi; Durga; Kumara; Nandisha; Visvakarma.

Skandaganani (India) *see* Parvati.

Skandas, The Five (Buddhist)

The five cosmic elements. *See also* Dhyani Buddhas.

Skathi (Teutonic) *see* Skadi.

Skidbladner (Teutonic) *see* Skidbladnir.

Skidbladnir *Skidbladner* (Norse; Teutonic)

Skidbladnir is Frey's ship. It can be folded like a napkin and put into a pocket. It was presented to Frey by Loki. The ship was probably fashioned by a dwarf, either Brokk, Ivaldi or Sindri.

Skidskegg (Teutonic) *see* Odin.

Skin-Faxi (Norse; Teutonic)

Also known as: *Skinfaxe, Skinfaxi.*

Skin-Faxi is the steed who draws the chariot of Dag through the heavens. His name means "shining mane." *See also* Dag; Hrim Faxi.

Skinfaxi (Teutonic) *see* Skin-faxi.

Skiold (Teutonic) *see* Odin.

Skirner (Teutonic) *see* Skirnir.

Skirnir *Skirner* (Norse; Teutonic)

Also known as: *Shining.*

Skirnir is the messenger of Freyr who won the giantess Gerda for him. He was awarded Frey's magic sword.

Skjold (Teutonic) *see* Thor.

Skogsfru (Scandinavian)

A woodswoman, Skogsfru is considered unlucky to hunters because she lures them away from their fires in the forests.

Skoll (Norse; Teutonic)

Skoll, a giant wolf, may be a god of eclipses and sunsets. Skoll pursues the sun daily, and will swallow it before Ragnarok. His brother, the more forbidding of the two, is the giant wolf

Hati. He pursues the moon. Skoll is thought by some to be the son of Hrodvitnir. Others say he is the son of the wolf Fenrir. Skoll and Hati are known as the Varns. *See also* Fenrir; Hati; Ragnarok.

Skoyo *Soyoko* (Hopi, Sia People, North America)

The Devouring Monsters. The Hopi Indians call them Soyoko.

Skrymer (Teutonic) *see* Skrymir.

Skrymir *Skrymer* (Norse; Teutonic)

Also known as: *Utgard-Loke, Utgard-Loki.*

Giant. Thor, Loki and Thialfi were traveling through the forest en route to Utgard, the land of the giants. They met the giant Skrymir who joined them. Over the days as they moved along, the giant placed them in strange conditions. At one point, angry and frustrated, Thor attempted to kill him with his magic hammer Mjollnir, but could not. The giant would not die. Later they discovered that Skrymir was Utgard-Loki who is Loki in disguise using his magic powers. *See also* Loki.

Skuld (Teutonic) *see* Norns.

Skulla (Greek) *see* Sirens.

Sky (Greek) *see* Chaos; Gaea.

Skyamsen (Tlingit) Thunderbird.

Skyites (Greek) *see* Dionysus.

Skylla (Greek) *see* Scylla.

Sleipner (Teutonic) *see* Sleipnir.

Sleipnir (Norse; Teutonic)

Also known as: *Sleipner.*

Odin's horse. Sleipnir is the offspring of Svadilfari and the trickster of Asgard, Loki, who had taken the shape of a mare to consummate the union. The eight-footed Sleipnir has supernatural strength. When Balder died, Hermod (Odin's son) rode Sleipnir to Hel to try to gain his release. *See* Asgard; Balder; Hel; Loki; Odin; Runes.

Slid (Norse; Teutonic)

Deified river. Slid is one of the rivers or streams coming from Hel. It consists of nothing but water and naked swords or daggers and spears. *See also* Hel; Hvergeilmir.

Slidrugtanni (Teutonic) *see* Gullin-Bursti.

Slooa-Shee (Irish) *see* Sheehogue.

Smaj (Serbia)

Protector of the Serbian nation. These divinities resemble winged male mortals and have been known to shoot fire while flying.

Smara (India) "Memory." *See also* Kama (A).

Smashana (India)

Smashana is the cemetery where dead bodies are burnt for purification. *See also* Shiva.

Smok (Slavonic) *see* Zmek.

Smyra (Greek) *see* Myrra.

Smyrna (Greek) *see* Adonis; Myrrha.

Snana-yantra (India) Festival for Jagannath (q.v.).

Snatchers, The (Greek) *see* Harpies.

Snor (Teutonic) *see* Heimdall

Snorta (Teutonic) *see* Snotra.

Snorter and Blower (China) *see* Heng and Ha; Men Shen.

Snorter and Puffer (China) *see* Heng and Ha; Men Shen.

Snotra (Norse; Teutonic)
Also known as: *Snorta.*
She is the goddess of virtue and knowledge and Frigga's attendant. *See also* Frigga.

So (Ewe People, Dahomey, Africa) *see* Khebieso.

Sobek (Egypt) *see* Neith; Sebek.

Sobk (Egypt) *see* Sebek.

Sochos (Egypt) *see* Sebek.

Sogamozo (Colombia) *see* Ramiriqui.

Sogbo (Dahomey People, Africa)
Sogbo, also known as Mahu, the earth and fertility goddess, is the mother of the god, Agbe, whom she placed in charge of world affairs. *See also* Agbe; Mahu.

Sojobo (Japan) *see* Tengu (The).

Sois (Greek)
Sois is the wife of Triopas and the mother of Pelasgus. *See also* Pelasgus (D).

Sokar *Sokari, Sokaris* (Egypt) *see* Seker.

Sokare (Egypt) *see* Seker.

Sokari *Seker* (Egypt) *see* Osiris.

Sokaris (Egypt) *see* Seker.

Sokkvabek (Teutonic) *see* Sokvabek.

Soko-no-kuni (Japan)
"Deep Land." Another name for Yomi, the underworld realm of the dead. *See also* Yomi.

Sokotsu-kuni (Japan)
"Bottom Land." Another name for Yomi, the underworld realm of the dead. *See also* Yomi.

Sokushikki (Japan)
Sokushikki is a demon who is associated with the protector of monasteries, Ida-Ten. *See also* Ida-Ten.

Sokvabek *Sokkvabek* (Norse; Teutonic)
The home of the gods. Odin and Saga met at Sokvabek daily to drink the waters of the river. *See also* Breidablik; Gladsheim; Hlidskjalf; Odin; Saga.

Sol (A) (Roman)
Also known as: *Helius* (Greek).

Sol is the Roman god of the sun, identified with the Greek god, Helius. *See also* Helius; Sol (B).

Sol (B) (Norse; Teutonic)
Also known as: *Nat, Sun.*
Sol and Mani are the giant children of Mundilfari. He named Mani after the moon, and Sol after the sun. (The orbs had been newly created.) Sol, the sun maid, is the spouse of Glaur (glow). Sol and Mani were transferred to the sky where they daily accompany their horses through the heavenly course. Sol is protected from the sun's hot rays by the magic cooling shield Svalin. *See* Aarvak; Idun; Nott, Sol (A).

Solal (Caroline Islands)
Ancient deity. Supreme being. Solal, the oldest of gods, planted a tree on the rock from which the world is made. He climbed the tree, and halfway up he created earth, then he climbed to the top where he created the sky for the dwelling place of his brother, Aluelop.

Solang (Micronesia)
God of canoe builders or carpenters. He appeared to Longorik in the shape of a bird and with the assistance of the ants, helped him build the first canoe. He is associated with Alulei (q.v.).

Solomon (Semite) *see* Chemosh.

Solymi (Greek) *see* Bellerophon.

Solymians (Greek)
The Solymians are Lycian warriors who fought Bellerophon and lost. *See also* Bellerophon.

Soma (Hindu, Vedic; India; Persia)
Also known as: *Amrit* (Water of Immortality), *Amrita, Chandra, Haoma* (Persian), *Indu* (The Moon), *Oshadhi-pati* (Supervisor of Herbs), *Skambha* (Support), *Soma Pavamana* (Self-Purifying Soma), *Syenabhrita* (Eagle-borne).
In the Vedic texts, Soma is coupled with Agni. With the rise of Hinduism, and the advent of the deities Vishnu, Shiva, Shakti and later, Krishna, the stature of Soma and Agni fell to a lower rung. The deity Soma is a moon god, a god of the flowing waters, a god of inspiration, ecstasy and riches. In later times, he became a god of herbs and healing. Soma means "The Joyous One." Soma, the beverage of the gods, is a sacred plant and the juice extracted from it gives strength, wisdom, and immortality to those who drink it. The moon is said to contain this celestial nectar, which reputedly also grew on earth. In one legend, the archer Krsanu shot at the eagle that carried Soma. A feather from the bird fell to earth and created the growth of the plant; Soma the god is the personification of soma juice. He took various shapes, and shared many of Indra's characteristics. Many myths surround the origins of soma the golden nectar and Soma the deity. Some feel that Soma is Indra and that it was Indra who discovered soma in the Himalayas; yet other versions claim the goddess Sarasvati found Soma in the Himalayas and brought it to the other deities. Other myths are Indra first tasted soma from his mother's breast; the goddess of waters Vach, who was one of Indra's wives, gave soma to the half-bird, half-man, celestial spirits known as the Gandharvas. Later, they were charged with caring for the plant. Other vari-

ations are that Soma is the son of Parjanya; Soma is the son of the sage Atri (the son of Brahma) and Anasuya; Soma married the Vedic maiden of the sun, Surya. He had twenty-seven wives, who are the daughters of Daksha. When he ignored all the women except Rohini, his father-in-law placed a curse on him. Soma was afflicted with leprosy, and when he lost strength, so did all earthly creatures. When Daksha lifted the curse, he declared that Soma's realm, the moon, would wax and wane each month. Rohini (Red Cow or Red Deer) is also known as the wife of the moon god Chandra. A goddess named Diksha, about whom little is known, is also mentioned as a wife of Soma. The etymology of her name is roughly, "solemn preparation." In later times Soma was known as the embodiment of the moon. Later still, he became known as a god of herbs and healing. It is thought that medicinal herbs derive their healing properties from the ambrosia, Soma. Without leaves or branches, the beverage was produced by crushing the stem. The yellow juice of the plant and the sound it made as it passed through the sieve represent thunder and lightning. The resulting liquid, described as being the color of golden nectar, symbolizes the rain, or in other interpretations, semen. The beverage also symbolizes liberation, inspiration, and immortal life. Soma the plant had a real and a mythical existence. It was used in ritual ceremonies. Soma the deity has been described as a celestial bull, a bird, and a giant of the waters. He is also depicted as a youth, brown, active and wise, adorned in gold. The twenty-seven daughters of Daksha represent the twenty-seven lunar stations. Soma's symbol is a silver crescent. He rides through the heaven in Indra's three-wheeled chariot pulled by ten brilliant white horses, the steeds of Vayu (the wind). His celestial bow, later owned by Arjuna, is named Gandiva. Soma and fire were the two major *Rig-Veda* sacrifices. The goddess Amritika, a celestial being, is mentioned as the goddess who poured soma, the intoxicant, love potion, or hallucinogen. She represents the feminine as a vehicle of transformation. The moon, known as Shasha, means "hare," which explains why the hare is considered by some to be a moon deity. Soma the beverage is similar to the Indo-Iranian Haoma, the ambrosia of the Greeks, and Manna of the Israelites. Varuna is referred to as the keeper of Soma. His daughter by Varunari is Varuni, the goddess of spirituous liquor. Soma is comparable to the Greek Dionysus (q.v.). Soma and the Sumerian deity Tammuz are said to be counterparts as each is associated with the waning and waxing of the moon. The renowned imbibers of Soma are Indra and Agni (q.v.). Sometimes the goddess Lakshmi (q.v.) assists Soma. Compare Soma to the Parijata Tree kept by Indrani. For other healing deities, *see* Asvins; Rudra. *See also* Arjuna; Brihaspati; Chandra; Daksha; Gandharvas; Garuda; Hoama; Kurma (Vishnu's avatar as a tortoise); Loka; Lokapalas; Prithiva; Rahu; Savarbhanu; Sita; Skambha; Surya; Surya-Bia; Tara (A); Vach; Varuna; Vasus; Yama.

Soma-Loka (India) *see* Loka.

Somavati (India) Moon Goddess. *See also* Soma.

Sombol-Burkan (Buryat)

As he rested on the Primordial Ocean, Somboi-Burkan, a creator god, asked a water bird to dive to its depths. The bird returned with mud from which the god created the earth. In a variation of this myth, Sombol-Burkan created man from the same substance.

Somin-Shorai (Japan) *see* Buto (B); Fuji.

Somnus (Roman)

Also known as: *Hupnos, Hypnos* (Greek), *Hypnus* (Greek).

Roman god of sleep. Father of one thousand sons. He wears black garments covered with golden stars. A crown of poppies adorns his head. In his hand, he holds a goblet of poppy juice. Some say has wings. *See also* Erebus; Hypnos; Nox.

Somo (Buddhist) *see* Tara (A).

Son (A) (Norse; Teutonic)

Also known as: *Blood*.

Deified object. One of the jars that holds the mead of poetry brewed from Kvasir's blood. *See also* Kvasir.

Son (B) (Celtic)

Also known as: *Shony*.

Sea god. He is offered whiskey for good fishing and kelp. He is superseded by Brain-uil (St. Brendan).

Son of Self (India) *see* Agni; Tanunapat.

Son of Svarog (Slavic) "Son of the Sky." *See also* Dazbog.

Sonponno (Africa)

Also known as: *Ile-Gbigbona, Ile-Titu, Olode*.

Deity of smallpox and related diseases. He is also called Olode (Owner of the Public), Ile-Gbigbona (Hot Ground), and Ile-Titu (Cold Ground).

Sons of Mil (Irish) *see* Amergin.

Soora (India) *see* Sura (B).

Sopd (Egypt) *see* Sopdu.

Sopdu *Septu, Sopd* (Egypt)

Also known as: *Har-Sopdu*.

Earth deity. God of the frontier. Sopdu is one of the gods of the four quarters of the earth, along with Horus, Set, and Thoth. When the goddess Nut, in the form of a cow, was on her way to heaven with Ra-Tem on her back, her legs began to shake. The gods of the four quarters were called to steady her. Each god took one of her legs, and the god Shu supported her belly. In the Pyramid Texts, Sopdu is mentioned in connection with the teeth of the deceased. His link to Horus in the Middle Kingdom led to the name Har-Sopdu in the New Kingdom. He is depicted as a crouching falcon. In human form he is shown with a crown of two falcon feathers and a shemset girdle. *See also* Horus; Nut; Set; Thoth.

Soped (Egypt)

God of the roads. A hawk-headed god who protected the roadway that led out of Lower Egypt.

Sophax (Greek) *see* Antaeus.

Sophia (Gnostic) *see* Pistis Sophia.

Sophia-Prunikos (Gnostic)

One of the Aeons, Sophia-Prunikos, who personifies wisdom, is the mother of Ialdabaoth. She is similar to Ennoia. *See also* Alaghom Naom Tzentel; Barbelo; Ennoia; Pistis Sophia.

Sopt (Egypt)

Spirit of the twilight or light of dawn. As Horus-Sopt he is the light of dawn.

Soramus (Roman) Roman name for Apollo.

Soteira (Greek)

An epithet of Athena, Artemis and Persephone. *See also* Athena.

Soter (Greek) "Father and Savior of Man." An epithet of Zeus.

Sothis (Egypt)

Also known as: *Isis-Sothis, Sirius.*

Sothis is the female form, deified as a goddess, of the dog star Sirius. The name Sothis is the Greek form of the Egyptian word for Sirius. She was later associated with Isis. Sothis is depicted as a woman with a star on her head and is also portrayed as a large dog. Shown riding side-saddle on the dog, she is known as Isis-Sothis. Sothis was frequently represented among the Greeks and Romans as a cow. *See also* Isis; Sirius.

Sotshirvani (Siberia) *see* Vajrapani.

South West Wind (Greek) *see* Notus.

Soyoko *Skoyo* (Hopi, Sia People, North America)

Soyoko is the generic name for monsters. The Sia Indians call them Skoyo.

Spantaramet *Spentaramet* (Armenian, Iranian, Persian)

Also known as: *Amesha Spentas, Santaramet, Spenta Armaiti.*

A goddess of vineyards, Spantaramet is similar in aspect to the Persian Spenta Armaiti, and Dionysos of the Greeks. She was possibly known as Santaramet by the Armenians but later they used the name of Aramazd in her place. The name Santaramet was then associated with the underworld. The evil spirits who dwell in Santaramet are called Santarametakans. *See also* Amesha Spentas; Dionysos; Hades; Hell; Santaramet; Spenta Armaiti.

Sparte (Greek) *see* Acrisius; Sparti.

Sparti *Sparte* (Greek)

Also known as: *Sown-men.*

The Sparti are dragon-men who sprouted from the dragon's teeth which were planted in mother earth by Cadmus (q.v.).

Spear of Lugh, The (Celtic) *see* Tuatha De Danann.

Speio (Greek)

A Nereid, Speio is one of the fifty daughters of Nereus and Doris. *See also* Doris; Nereids; Nereus.

Spenishta (Iran)

One of the five sacred fires. It burns before Ormazd and eats but does not drink. *See also* Ahura Mazda.

Spenjaghrya (Iran)

A demon, Spenjaghrya represented winter or darkness. He was slain by Vazishta who represents lightning.

Spenta Armaiti (Zoroastrian; Persia)

Also known as: *Armaita, Armaiti, Armati, Asfandarmad, Isfenarmad, Santaramet, Sipendarmidh, Spantaramet* (Armenia), *Spendarmad* ("Bounty").

An Ameshas Spenta, she is the daughter of Ahura Mazda and sits at his left hand. Known as the guardian of the earth, and keeper of the vineyards, she is the personification of faithful obedience, religious harmony and worship. She also ensures pasture for cattle. Robbers, evil men and irreverent wives distress her. The archdemons opposed to Spenta Armaiti are Taromaiti, who personifies presumption, and Pairimaiti, who personifies crooked-mindedness. She appeared to Zoroaster visibly. In ancient Armenia, she was known as Spantaramet, the goddess of the underworld. *See also* Ahura Mazda; Ameshas Spenta; Asvins (India); Daevas; Gaya Maretan; Hell; Spantaramet; Zoroaster.

Spentaramet (Persia) *see* Spantaramet; Spenta Armaiti.

Spercheius (Greek)

River god. His parents are Oceanus and Tethys. He became the father of Menesthius by Polydora. Menesthius saved his lover, Cleostratus, from being eaten by the dragon who attacked Thespiae once a year.

Sphinx (Greek, Egypt, Asia Minor)

Also known as: *Harmachis, Harmakis, Heru-em-akbet.*

The Egyptian Sphinx is a spirit guardian of entrances. The most famous is known as Sesheps. A sphinx represents vigilance and is often depicted as a devourer. It can appear as a ram-headed lion, a hawk-headed lion and human-headed lion. The sphinx was often created from stone and shown in a crouched position, wearing the headdress of a pharaoh. The Greek Sphinx is the daughter of Typhon and Echnidna, or Orthus and Chimaera. Her siblings are the Caucasian Eagle, Cerberus, Chimaera, Crommyonian Sow, Hydra, Orthus, Nemean Lion, and an assortment of vultures. She guarded the road on the way to Thebes and asked all those who passed to solve a riddle. The riddle was "What goes on four feet, on two feet, and on three?" She killed those who failed to answer the question correctly. When Oedipus finally solved her riddle, she killed herself. The answer to the riddle is Man. The mortal as a child crawls, as an adult, walks upright and in old age is supported by a cane. The Greek Sphinx is depicted with the upper part as a female, her torso part dog, the tail of a snake, wings of a bird, and lion paws. She spoke in a human voice. Greek sphinxes are either female or androgynous and are winged. Iconographically, the sphinx is often said to be the female equivalent of the Centaur. The difference is the sphinx is depicted immobile and the centaur in movement. Sphinxes all like riddles. *See also* Cerberus; Chimaera; Eurydice (C); Sesheps; Typhon (A).

Spider Woman (Zuni People, North America) *see* Ahayuta Achi.

Spiniensis (Roman)

Agricultural deity. A god who helped clear a field of thorns.

Spinning Damsel *Weaver Damsel* (China) *see* Chin Nu.

Spirit of the Long Grass (Australia) *see* Morkul-Kua-Luan.

Spor (Slavic) The spirit of growth.

Sraddeheva (India) *see* Yama.

Sraddha *Shraddha* (Hindu; India)

Sraddha, the goddess of faith, is the mate of the god of justice Dharma and the mother of the god of love, Kama. Sraddha is also a sacred word meaning faith, belief or trust and a practice of giving a meal to the deceased. *See also* Dharma; Kama.

Sraddhadeva (India) God of Funeral Directors. *See also* Yama.

Sraosh (India)

Also known as: *Srosh*.

Messenger. God of obedience and devotion. A mediator or divine messenger between gods and mortals. Usually combined with Mithra and Rashnu as guardian angels. They will be judges of the otherworld. *See also* Amshaspands; Fravashis; Mithra; Rashnu; Yazatas.

Sraosha *Sros* (Pahlavi dialect); (Zoroastrianism; Persia)

With Mithra and Rashnu, Sraosha ("the obedient") greets the soul at death and presides over judgment of the soul. He conveys prayers to heaven, feeds the poor, and is the destroyer of evil. His opponents are Aeshma, the embodiment of fury, and the leader of the demons, Angra Mainyu. The guardian angel of the world, he lives on the highest peak of Mount Hariati in a self-lit house with a thousand pillars. Four horses with golden feet draw his chariot. *See also* Aeshma; Ameshas Spenta; Angra Mainyu; Chinvat Bridge; Daevas; Hariati (Mount); Mitra; Rashnu; Yazatas.

Sreca (Serbia)

The genius of good fate, Sreca is the opposite of Nesreca, the genius of evil fate. *See also* Dola; Dolya.

Sri *Shri, Shru* (Hindu; India)

Sri is the name of Lakshmi when she was incarnated as the wife of Rama, an avatar of Vishnu. In Northern India, the coconut is sacred to her. It is called Sriphala, or fruit of Sri. Her mount is a white elephant named Sri-gaja. *See also* Lakshmi; Sarasvati. She is comparable to Kishijoten, sister of Bishamon (q.v.) (Japan).

Sri Dewi (Javanese) Goddess of Rice.

Sri-gaja (India) The white elephant of Sri (q.v.)

Srin-po (Tibet) Ghouls or vampires the color of raw flesh.

Sringatpadini (India) A Yakshini (q.v.).

Srinmo (Tibet)

Female demon of death.

Sriphala (India) The sacred coconut of Sri (q.v.).

Srishok *Hadhayos* (Persia)

Mortals rode the back of this heavenly bull to pass from the central portion of earth, Khwanirath, to the surrounding six portions, the Keshvars. Srishok will be the last animal offered in sacrifice at the renovation of the world. Because of his importance, he is protected by Gopatshah, the half-man, half-ox. *See also* Vourukasha.

Sristikanta Lokeswara (Buddhist; Nepal)

An aspect of Avalokitesvara, he is depicted with one face, two arms and stands on a lotus. Amitabha appears over his head. His right hand is held in the gesture of charity (varada) and his left hand is placed near his navel. Numerous four-armed gods emanate from his body. *See also* Amitabha; Avalokitesvara; Lokeswara.

Srnkhala (India) *see* Amrtakundali.

Srosh (Persia) *see* Sraosh.

Srvara (Persia)

This horned dragon had teeth as long as an arm, eyes as large as three wheels, huge ears and a horn as high as the evil Dahhak. Keresaspa jumped onto his back and stayed there for a half-day until he finally clubbed him to death. *See also* Gandarewa; Keresaspa.

sSin-rje-gsed-kyi-dkyil-kor (Tibet) *see* Yamantaka.

Ssu Ling (China)

Four spiritual animals. Ch'i-lin or Pai Hu, the unicorn, is the chief of the animals; the Phoenix, Feng-huang or Chu Ch'ieh, is the chief of all birds; the tortoise, Kuei Shen, is the chief of all mollusks; the dragon, Lung, is the chief of all scaly animals. *See also* Kuei Shen.

Ssu Ming (China)

Arbiter of life and death, and protector of virtue. One of the Nine Heroes. He is divided into two beings and is sometimes confused with Shang T'ai and Wen Ch'ang. *See also* Nine Songs.

Ssu Ta Chin-kang (Buddhist; China)

Also known as: *Diamond Kings of Heaven, Kings of Hell, T'ien-wang*.

The Ssu Ta Chin-kang are four brothers, protector deities who are gods of happiness. Their names are Mo-li Ch'ing or Tseng Chang; Mo-li Hung or Kuang Mu; Mo-li Hai or To Wen; and Mo-li Shore or Ch'ih Kuo. They represent "pure, vast, sea, and age." Generally, they are considered to be mortal generals who were deified. *See also* Diamond Kings; Mo-li Ch'ing; Mo-li Hai; Mo-li Hung; Mo-li Shou.

Staphylus (A) (Greek)

An Argonaut. He is the son of Dionysus and Ariadne or Theseus and the husband of Chrysothemis and Ariadne. *See also* Argonauts; Ariadne.

Stellar Goddess (China) *see* Chin Nu.

Stenele (Greek) *see* Danaus.

Sterculius (Roman) *see* Stercutius.

Stercutius (Roman)

Also known as: *Sterculius*.

Agricultural deity. His father is Fanus, the inventor of herding, hunting and husbandry, and he is the possible father of Picus, the prophet who was turned into a woodpecker by the goddess Circe. Stercutius oversees the manicuring of the fields. He invented many agricultural tools and was the first to use manure. *See also* Acis; Fanus; Picus.

Sterope (A) (Greek)

She is the daughter of Acastus, the King of Iolcus and son of Pelias and Astydameia or perhaps Hippolyte. She is the sister of Laodamia and Sthenele.

Sterope (B) (Greek)

Also known as: *Asterope.*

She is the Pleiad daughter of Atlas who was turned into stone and Pleione (also known as Aethra). Her siblings are Alcyone, Celaeno, Electra, Maia, Merope and Taygete. She is either the wife or mother of Oenomaus.

Sterope (C) (Greek)

She is the daughter of the King of Tegea and Argonaut, Cepheus, and the sister of Aerope and possibly Echemus.

Sterope (D) (Greek)

She is the daughter of Porthaon, the first king of Calydon and Eurtye, the daughter of Hippodamas. Her siblings are Agrius, Alcathous, Melas, Oeneus and Leucopeus. She could be the mother of the Sirens.

Steropes (Greek)

"Lightning."

He is the Cyclops son of Uranus and Gaea, brother of Arges and Brontes. *See also* Acamas (D); Aegaeon; Cyclops; Gaea.

Sthalidevatas (India) *see* Devis.

Stheneboea

Also known as: *Antea* (Greek)

She is the daughter of Iobates (also known as Amphianax), the King of Lycia and the sister of Philonoe. Stheneboea married Proetus and became the mother of Iphinoe, Iphianassa, Lysippe and Megapenthes. Bellerophon made it clear that he wanted Stheneboea as his wife. Her father, Iobates, sent him to fight Chimaera, the fire-snouting three-headed daughter of Echidna and Typhon. After slaying Chimaera, Bellerophon returned and was given the hand of Stheneboea's sister, Philonoe. Stheneboea was in so in love with Bellerophon that she committed suicide. *See also* Antea; Bellerophon; Iobates; Proetus.

Sthenelaus (A) (Greek)

He is the son of Actor who was killed while fighting the Amazons with Heracles.

Sthenelaus (B) (Greek)

He is the son of Androgeus, the famous athlete who is the son of Minos and Pasiphae. His brother is Alcaeus, King of Thasos, with whom he shared the throne.

Sthenelaus (C) (Greek)

His parents are Capaneus and Evadne. He was one of Helen of Troy's numerous suitors.

Sthenelaus (D) (Greek)

He is the son of Perseus (who is the son of Zeus) and the beautiful Andromeda. His siblings are Alcaeus, Gorgophone, Heleus, Mestor, Perses and Electryon. *See also* Alcaeus; Andromeda; Electryon; Gorgophone; Heleus; Mestor; Perses; Perseus.

Sthenele (Greek)

She is the daughter of Acastus, who is the King of Iolcus, and Astydameia, who is the daughter of Pelops and Hippodameia. Her siblings are Laodamia and Sterope. She wed Menoetius, the son of Actor and Aegina, and became the mother of Patroclus who was a close friend of Achilles with whom he shares burial grounds on White Island. *See also* Acastus; Laodamia; Patroclus; Stercutius; Sterope (A).

Stheno (Greek)

Stheno is one of the Gorgons. *See also* Gorgons; Medusa.

Stone of Fal (Celtic) *see* Tuatha De Danann.

Stratius (Greek)

He is the son of Nestor and Eurydice, or possibly Anaxibia. His siblings are Antilochus, Artetus, Echephron, Paeon, Peisidice, Peisistratus, Perseus, Polycaste and Thrasymedes. *See also* Antilochus; Nestor; Perseus.

Straw Mirror (Mexico) *see* Texcatzoncatl.

Strenia (Roman)

Goddess of fruits. She presides over New Year festivals. Strenia corresponds to the goddess of health, Salus.

Stribog (Slavic)

God of the wind. Slavic mythology has several gods of the wind and storms which may be related. They are Dogoda the west wind, Varpulis, the noise of the storm, and Erisvorsh, the deity of the holy tempest. They are all related to Perun (q.v.). *See also* Varpulis.

Stromkarl (A) (Sweden)

Fresh water spirit.

Stromkarl (B) (Norway)

"River Man." He is a talented musician who is a spirit of a waterfall. If a white kid or black lamb is sacrificed to him on a Thursday, he will teach the believer one of the eleven tunes he knows. If the student dares to play the eleventh tune, men, women, infants, cups, plates, chairs and tables must dance wildly.

Strymon (Greek)

River god. His parents are Oceanus and Tethys. He is the father of Evandne. *See also* Argus (A); Hesione.

Stupa (Buddhist)

Also known as: *Caitya, Dagoba, Pagoda, Sharira, Tope.*

A chief symbol of Buddhism, the stupa is a mound that is found in many forms and ranges from the size of an amulet to several hundred feet. A sacred object, it is revered because it is thought to preserve relics of Gautama Buddha. The sacred Indian world mountain Sumeru is known as a Stupa. When covering the remains of other Buddhas or holy men it is called sharira. It is known as a tope when it is erected as a memorial to a priest. *See also* Abheda; Amida; Buddha; Kuvera; Maitreya (the stupa is his emblem); Nagarjuna; Yamai.

Stymphalian Birds (Greek)

As his sixth labor, Heracles had to rid the Stymphalian lake in Arcadia of these birds. They were able to wound all who approached them with their arrow-like feathers. Hephaistos, the god of fire, made a bronze rattle that Athene gave to Heracles. The sound frightened the birds away. They flew to the island of Ares in the Euxine Sea, and it was there that the Argonauts encountered them. *See also* Athene; Hephaistos; Heracles.

Stymphalus (Greek)

King of Arcadia. The son of Laodice. Stymphalus was killed by Pelops. *See also* Aeacus; Laodice; Pelops.

Styx (Greek)

River deity. A Titan, the nymph Styx is the daughter of Oceanus and Tethys or Uranus and Gaea. She married the Titan Pallas, the son of Crius and Eurybia. They became the parents of Zelus (Zelos), meaning jealousy or zeal; Nike, meaning victory; Cratus (Kratos), meaning strength; and Bia, meaning force or violence. Their offsprings exhibited the attributes of Zeus. In some renditions of this legend it is thought that Styx was the mother of Persephone by Zeus, though it is usually Demeter who is named as her mother. When Zeus rebelled against Cronus and was attacked by the Titans, Styx deserted her brothers and with her children became one of the first deities to assist the great god. In gratitude, Zeus gave her the river Tartarus which bordered the lower regions of the underworld. She also ruled over her river, the Styx, one of the rivers of the underworld that separates the boundaries of the world between the living and the dead. It flows around the infernal regions nine times. The supreme judge Minos and his associates, Rhadamanthus and Aeacus, were located on the far bank of the Styx. Charon, the ferryman, also took dead souls across this river as he did on other rivers of the Underworld. Zeus agreed that all important oaths uttered by the Immortals would be sworn on the waters of the Styx. The messenger of the gods, Iris, would fly down to Tartarus for a vial of water from the river and return it to the oath sayer to drink, thus making the oath sacred. If the oath was broken, the person would go into a coma for one to nine years depending on the version of the myth. If the oath sayer regained consciousness and still did not abide by the oath, he or she was expelled from the company of the Olympians forever. It is said that when Hera swore by Styx from the peaks of Olympus, she could touch the earth with one hand and with the other could reach the seas. Thetis plunged her son Achilles into the Styx at birth to make him invulnerable. Only his heel remained dry. The mythology of the Styx is said to have originated in Egypt and legend has it that Isis buried Osiris on its banks. *See also* Acheron; Cocytus; Gaea; Golden Bough; Hades; Lethe; Mino; Oceanids; Oceanus; Rhadamanthus; Tartarus; Tethys; Uranus; Zeus.

Suaha *Suada, Svaha, Swaha* (Hindu; India)

Also known as: *Agnayi.*

Suaha is one of the numerous daughters of the early Vedic god, Daksha. He gave Suaha to Agni to be his wife. She is also reputed to be one of the wives or consorts of the great god of winds and storms, Rudra. *See* Agni; Daksha; Karttikeya; Rudra.

Suadela (Roman) *see* Aphrodite.

Suasuthur (Teutonic) *see* Summer.

Subbu-Khai-Thung (Dhammai People, India)

She is the earth goddess daughter of Shuznagu and Zumiang-nui who existed before the sky and earth. Her sky god brother, Jongsuli-Young-Jongbu, was born at the same time. The children were swallowed by the worm Phangnalomang. For details, *see also* Shuznaghu.

Subhadra *Jagannatha* (Hindu; India)

She is the daughter of Vasudeva and Devaki, sister and spouse of Arjuna and mother of Abhimanyu (also known as Saubhadra) by Krishna. *See also* Abhimanyu; Arjuna; Devaki; Krishna.

Subramanya (India) *see* Karttikeya.

Succubus *Succuba* (Middle Ages)

The Succubus is a female demon from the class of demons known as Incubi. The Succubus comes to men in the night. When the male awakens, the proper prayers must be recited to prevent pregnancy from the union, for if children are produced they are considered demonic. *See also* Incubus.

Sucellos (Celtic)

Also known as: *The Good Striker, The Mighty Striker.*

God of death. God of fertility. Thunder god. Known as Silvanus in southern Gaul, Sucellos is a charitable underworld deity who is thought by some to be connected with Dis Pater and has been equated with Cernunnos. His consort is the fertility goddess, Nantosuelta. Sucellos is shown as a heavy-set man, with long hair and a beard, wearing a long, belted tunic, sometimes with tights and sometimes bare-legged. He holds a long-handled mallet in one hand (indicating creativity) and a drinking vessel (fertility) in the other. He is frequently shown with Nantosuelta and is often accompanied by a dog. Compare Sucellos to Thor and Dagda. *See also* Cernunnos; Dis Pater; Nantosuelta; Silvanus.

Suchos (Egypt) *see* Sebek.

Suci (India) *see* Agni.

Sudalaiyadi (India)

"Dancer of the Burning Ground." *See also* Nataraja; Shiva.

Sudarsana (India) *see* Sudarshana.

Sudarshana *Sudarsana* (Hindu; India).

Sudarshana, Vishnu's magic discus, lives in the sky. Shaped like a wheel with edges sharp enough to cut off the heads of demons and tops of mountains, it spits fire and causes lightning. Sudarshana always returns to Vishnu. *See also* Rahu; Savarbhanu; Sisupala.

Suddhodana, Rajah (India)

Putative father of Gautama Buddha (q.v.).

Sudhanvan (India) "The Good Archer." *See also* Ribhus.

Sudjaje (Slavic) Goddesses of destiny.

Sudre (Teutonic) *see* Sudri.

Sudri *Sudre* (Norse; Teutonic)

Sudri is one of the four dwarfs who supported the heaven's vault, made from the skull of Ymir, on their shoulders. His name became South. The other dwarves are Nordri, Austri and Westri. *See also* Aarvak; Dwarfs; Nordri; Ymir.

Sudyumna (India) Son of Vaivasvata (q.v.).

Suetiva (Colombia) *see* Chia.

Suffete (Ugarit)

A beast who is the Lord of the River. *See also* Bod-Baal.

Sugriva *Sukrip* (Hindu; India)

The son of Surya, Sugriva was the honorable ruler of the Vanavasas, who are forest dwellers. His powerful half-brother

Bali ousted him from his throne. He did not regain his position until Rama killed Bali. In return, Sugriva, his commander-in-chief Hanuman, and his army of monkeys aided Rama in his battle against the demon Ravana and the rescue of Rama's mate, Sita. Sugriva is the spouse of Ruma, Queen of the Apes. See also Bali (A); Hanuman; Kabandha; Rama; Ravana; Sita; Surya; Tara (A); Yadavas.

Suhgurim (Babylon) see Marduk.

Suhiji-Ne No Mikoto (Japan) see Ama-no-minaka-nushi.

Suhiji-ni No Mikoto (Japan) see Ama-no-minaka-nushi.

Suhrim (Babylonia) see Marduk.

Sui-tengo Suitengu (Japan)
Suitengo is the protector of sailors and sick children. She is depicted in the shape of a woman holding a child in her arms. See also O-Wata-Tsu-Mi.

Suilap (Altaic, Tartars) see Bai Ulgan.

Suitengu (Japan) see O-Wata-Tsu-Mi; Sui-tengo.

Sujang-Gnoi-Rise (Dhammai People, India)
He is the mountain son of Shuznaghu and Zumiang-nui. His siblings are a sister, Jibb-Jang-Sangne, who is also a mountain; another sister, Jassuju, and a brother, Lujjuphu, who were born as frogs. See also Shuznaghu.

Sukan-Bikona (Japan) see Suku-na-Biko.

Sukana-Biko (Japan) see Susanowo.

Sukanthi (India) see Apsarases.

Sukanya (India)
She is the daughter of Saryata and wife of Chyavana. See also Mada.

Sukapreyasi (India)
Sow and earth goddess. See also Prithiva; Varaha.

Sukarasya (Buddhist; India) The Divine Cow.

Sukati (Egypt)
Afterworld deity. A minor god found in Tuat. If the deceased is able to recite a certain formula and keep it secret from the god, he is allowed to drink from the deepest and purest part of the celestial stream, and eventually to become "like one of the stars in the heavens."

Sukhavati (Buddhist; India)
Also known as: Go-Kuraku-Jodo (Japan), The Happy Realm of Sukhavati, Hsi T'ien (China), Red Western Realm of Happiness, Si-Fang Ki-Lo Shi-Kiai, Ts'ing-tsing T'u.
Sukhavati is the western paradise of Amitabha. A place of perfection located an incalculable distance from earth, this is where the soul is invited to be born again. The blessed are surrounded by jewel-laden trees, beautiful gardens and serene waters. They bathe in water that is always the right temperature, without fear of drowning. Apparel is provided to the specifications of the blessed. One need only think of the food, aroma, and music most loved and it is provided. Apsarases (nymphs) attend every need. In Sukhavati, souls are conceived in lotus hearts. The soul develops and is nourished by the teach-

ings of Buddha. The flowers ripen by the rays (fingers) of Buddha and the soul comes forth. It is in Sukhavati that the souls are judged. The bad souls are judged by Ch'eng-huang and the good souls by Kuan-yin. After judging they are sent to Tung-yo ta-ti who is called the Emperor of the Eastern Peak. Sukhavati is generally represented by a square structure of bamboo covered by sheets of paper. See also Amida; Amitabha; Apsarases; Chakravala (Buddhist Universe); Dhartarastra (Guardian in the Heaven of the Four Great Kings); Gokuraku; Lokapalas; Naga Knaya; Tushita; Yidak.

Sukhos (Egypt) see Sebek.

Suko (Dahomey People, Africa) Supreme god.

Sukra (India) see Shukra.

Sukrip (India) see Sugriva.

Suku-na-Biko Sukan-bikona, Sukuna-biko, Sukuna-bikona, Sukuna-biko-na-no-kami (Shinto; Japan).
Chief of medicine deities. Suka-na-Biko (Small Prince of Renown) is the dwarf son of the goddess Kami-Mimusubi. When Okuni-Nushino-Mikoto was murdered by his brothers, Kami-Mimusubi was called upon by his mother and she resurrected the woman's son. Suku-na-Biko mysteriously arrived by boat to assist Okuni-Nushino-Mikoto, the son of Susanowo, in establishing his kingdom. Suku-na-Biko is a medicine god who wears moth wings with small feathers. One day he climbed a millet plant when it was ripe. His weight made the plant bend and he was flung to the heavens, where he remains to this day. Okuni-Nushino-Mikoto, who acutely felt the loss of his colleague, called out to the heavens in despair. A blinding light appeared over the sea and a voice announced itself as the protecting deity and instructed the distraught man to worship him on Mount Mimoro. His name was Omiwa. For additional details see Kami-Mimusubi; Okuni-Nushino-Mikoto.

Sukuna-biko (Japan) see Suku-na-Biko.

Sukuna-biko-na-no-kami (Japan) see Suku-na-Biko.

Sukuna-bikona (Japan) see Suku-na-Biko.

Sul (Celtic, British) Goddess of warm springs.

Sulman (Babylon) see Saramana.

Sulmus (Mongol)
Deity of evil. See also Ocirvani; Tsagan-Sukuty.

Sulochana (India) A Yakshini. See also Yaska.

Sumati (India)
Sumati is the daughter of Vinata and Kasyapa and the mate of Sagara. She gave birth to a giant gourd containing sixty thousand sons. See also Garuda; Kasyapa; Sagara.

Sumatra — Creation Legend see Batara Guru.

Sumaya (India) see Maya (C).

Sumbha (India) A demon. See also Durga; Kali.

Sumeru (India)
Sacred Mountain. See also Meru Mountain; Stupa.

Sumitra (India) A Yakshini. See also Rama; Yaska.

Summano (Etruscan) *see* Uranus.

Summer (Teutonic)
God of the Season. Descendent of Svasud and one of the rulers of the seasons. The god Summer is the enemy of Winter. *See also* Winter.

Summer Spirit (Acoma People) *see* Mayochina.

Sumul (Ugarit) Mother of the Vultures. *See also* Khasis; Kothar.

Sumuqan (Assyro-Babylonian)
"King of the Mountain." Sumuqan is a cattle god who lives in Ereshkigal's court in the underworld. *See also* Enki; Ereshkigal.

Sumur (Central Asia) The world mountain. *See also* Abyrga.

Sun (Norse; Teutonic)
Also known as: *Sol.*
The sun. Sun is the daughter of Mundilfari. She drives the sun on its course through the heavens. *See also* Helius; Mundifari; Ra; Surya.

Sun Hou-tzu (China)
Ruler of the monkeys. Sun Hou-tzu is a monkey or a fairy who carries a magic wand. When he was taken in chains, to the land of the dead, Sun Hou-tzu found and tore up the page on which his name was recorded, stating he was no longer subject to death. The king, Yen-Lo-Wang, conceded to his declaration.

Sun-pin (China)
Sun-pin is the mortal who invented shoes to cover his feet after his toes were cut off in a war.

Sunaman (India) *see* Krishna.

Sunda (India) *see* Arjuna.

Sundara (India) *see* Kuvera; Shiva.

Sundareshwar (India) *see* Shiva.

Sung Chiang *Sung Kiang* (China)
God of thieves. Once a renowned bandit, Sung Chiang was later deified. The more ancient mortal bandit named Chi is also worshiped as another god of thieves.

Sung Kiang (China) *see* Sung Chiang.

Sung Ti (Buddhist; Central Asia)
Sung Ti is one of the Kings of Hell who after the sinners are judged guilty, tortures them with hot water and fire. *See also* Kshitigarbha.

Sung-tsi (China) *see* Avalokitesvara; Kuan-yin.

Sung-tsi Kuan-yin (China) *see* Avalokitesvara; Kuan-yin.

Sung-tsi Niang-niang (China) *see* Sung-tzu Naing-naing.

Sung-tzu-Naing-naing *Sung-tsi Niang-niang* (China)
Goddess of Fecundity and Healing. Goddess of newborn children. She likes incense, firecrackers and rattles. She is one of six deities who are in the train of Sheng mu. Sung-tzu Naing-naing is shown with an infant in her arms. She is usually associated with Sheng mu.

Sung-tzu-niang-niang (China) *see* Kuan Yin.

Sunstone, The (India) *see* Syamantaka.

Suntra (Hindu; India) Fertility goddess.

Supai (India) *see* Supay (A).

Supai (Inca) *see* Supay (B).

Suparnas (Hindu, India)
Winged supernatural beings who dwell in the Simbali forest under the rule of Garuda. They are invoked at the daily presentation of water to deceased ancestors. *See also* Garuda.

Supay (A) (India) God of air.

Supay (B) (Collao, Inca People, Peru)
Also known as: *Supai.*
God of the dead. Evil spirit. Lord of minerals. Supay rules over those spirits that did not go to the Land of the Sun and are confined within the dark earth. Supay demanded human sacrifices, especially children, to populate his kingdom. He has the ability to transform himself into an animal and to make animal sounds. He can also appear as a charming mortal and when the confidence of his victim has been won he is said to enter the body and cause epilepsy or madness. Silver can be transformed to gold by this god of the dead. Supay, who emits a sulfuric odor, is sometimes depicted with a lion's body, ram's horns, and tiger's teeth. *See also* Anchancho; Ekkekko.

Support (Polynesia) *see* Tango.

Suprabha (India) *see* Arjuna.

Supratika (India) *see* Dikpalas; Lokapalas.

Sura (A) (Andean People, Peru)
Supreme deity. Maize seed was given to Sura by Sibu, another supreme god. While planting the seed it was stolen by Jaburu who is an evil god. Given a cup of chocolate by Sibu, Jaburu swelled so much he blew up. The seed was then returned to Sura.

Sura (B) *Soora* (India) Goddess of Wine. *See also* Kurma.

Surabhi (Dravidian, Hindu; India)
Known as "the fragrant one," Surabhi the cow goddess and goddess of plenty is one of Daksha's daughters. Born from the churning of the ocean, she descended to earth with Indra. Later she became one of the mates of the sage Kasyapa and the mother of cows, buffaloes and the goddess Nirritti. She symbolizes Nature's productive power and is closely connected with "Cow of Desire," Kamadhenu. She is associated with the Rishi (q.v.). *See also* Daksha; Indra; Kamadhenu; Kasyapa; Kurma; Nirritti.

Surabhidatta (India) *see* Apsarases.

Suradevi (India) Goddess of wine and spirits.

Surapamsula (India) *see* Apsarases.

Suras (Persian) *see* Aditi.

Surasa (India) *see* Kasyapa.

Suris (Persian) *see* Aditi.

Surisi (India) *see* Devi.

Surisvari (India) "Divine Lady." *See also* Devi.

Surpanaka (India) *see* Shurpanaka.

Surt (Teutonic) *see* Surtr.

Surter (Teutonic) *see* Surtr.

Surtr (Norse; Teutonic)

Also known as: *Black Surt, Surt, Surter, Surtur.*

Fire god. Surtr is a flame giant who guards Muspells-heim (Muspell). His sword sent sparks which partially melted the great ice-blocks coming from the streams of the Elivagar. He is the father of Sattung (or Glaur) and grandfather of Gunlodd. At the apocalyptic final battle of Ragnarok, Surtr will lead his band consisting of army of Hel, Liki, Garm, Fenris and Iormungandr against the Aesir and Vanas. Surtr will kill Frey and proceed to end the world with his fiery sword. *See also* Audhumbla; Elivagar; Fjalar; Ginnunga-gap; Gunlodd; Hvergelmir; Sattung; Sol; Vigrid.

Surtur (Teutonic) *see* Surtr.

Surya *Surja* (Brahmanic, Hindu, Vedic; India)

Also known as: *Dina-Kara* (Day-Maker), *Divine Vivifier, Karma-Sakshi* (Witness of Deeds), *Surya-Bai* (female aspect of Surya), *Surya Narayana* (Surya's title as a divine incarnation of Vishnu).

Surya, the sun god and god of fate, is variously described as one of three sons of Dyaus, or the son of Aditi or Brahma. In early times, as the son of Dyaus, he was one of a triad, with his brothers, Indra and Agni. He was also a part of a triad with Agni and Vayu. As the power of the sun, in a fixed universe, he is the god of everything, both moving and static. He removes darkness, heats the world, and is the nourisher and stimulator of mortals. His light cures darkness, leprosy, and poverty. He became the husband of Sanja, who is the daughter of the divine artificer, Visvakarma. Surya is also represented as the father, husband or lover of the beautiful Ushas, goddess of the dawn. As in the mythology of Vivasvat, Surya married and was later left alone by his mate, who could not tolerate his dazzling light. Surya's spouse Sanja, the daughter of Visvakarma, bore three children before her departure. She arranged for the shade goddess Chhaya to take her place. In some renditions, the substitute mate is Aswini who is said to be the mother of the Asvin twins. It was several years before Surya realized that Chhaya was not his wife. In the form of a stallion, he searched for and found Sanja, who had disguised herself as a mare. They were reunited only after her father shaved away an eighth of his rays. Surya is called the father of the Asvin in some legends and the father of the twins Yama and Yami in other renditions (as is Vivasvat) or the father of both sets of twins. He is the father of the goddesses Kalindi and Madri who became wives of Krishna. The goddess Kunti, also known as Pritha, chose Surya as one of her five lovers. Surya is said to be the source of amrita which he passes to Soma the moon god to dispense to the gods. As with Soma, a hostile atmosphere exists between Surya and the demon Rahu, who sometimes swallows him. In the Purana, Surya is celebrated as the supreme soul in all the Vedas. He is given names and epithets corresponding to the major deities; Indra, Dhata (or Dhatr, a synonym of Prajapati) known as the Creator of All Things, Parjanya, Tvashtri, Pushan, Aryama, Vivasvat, Vishnu, Ansuman (who keeps the vital organs functioning properly), Varuna, and Mitra. The deities Savitri and Vivasvat were absorbed by and became aspects of Surya. This god was widely worshiped during the Vedic and Puranic periods. He is often referred to as the eye of Varuna (the moon) and Mitra (the sun). As a fate deity, Surya sees all and notes all. He bestows immortality on the gods and presides over the length of a mortal's life. He is invoked to cure illness and to eradicate evil spirits, for his radiance destroys darkness. Surya is depicted as a goat or horse, sometimes as an eagle in flight, or as a short or legless man. He is also shown as a dark red man with three eyes and four arms. Two of his hands hold water-lilies, the third is in an attitude of blessing, and the fourth is shown in an attitude of encouragement. He is sometimes shown with gleaming, golden hair and arms, riding in a golden chariot drawn by seven red mares, or one mare with seven heads. This could represent the seven constituent colors of the sun's rays. He is preceded by his twin sons, the Asvins, who ride in a golden chariot. Surya's symbol was the swastika, which during this period was a symbol of generosity. Rahu swallowing Surya is the sun darkened by an eclipse. Orthodox Brahmans repeat the Gayatri mantra three times a day, to receive the sun god's blessing. The sun is praised in the form of Brahma in the morning, Vishnu at noon, and Shiva in the evening. For the Hindus, the celebration worship day for the sun god is on the seventh day after the new moon in the month which corresponds to January-February (Magha). Red lotuses are used during the worshiping of Surya. Compare Surya to Helius (Greek) and Sun (Teutonic). *See also* Adityas; Agastya; Agni; Aruna; Asvins; Bali; Brahma; Ganesha; Indra; Krishna; Lockapalas; Martanda; Mithra; Mitra; Parjanya; Prajapati; Pushan; Radha; Rahu; Sanja; Savarbhanu; Savatri; Soma; Sugriva; Surya-Bai; Syamantaka; Tapati; Urvasi; Ushas; Varuna; Vasistha; Vedas (The); Vishnu; Visvakarma; Vivasvat.

Surya-Bai *Savitri, Surya* (Male aspect of Surya-Bai); (Vedic, Hindu; India)

Surya-Bai, the sun goddess, is the female representative of the sun. She is the daughter of the sun god Savitri. Surya is the wife of Soma the moon god. In some legends she appears as the spouse of the twin gods of light, the Ashvins. She has been called the lover of the moon god Chandra. In Vedic mythology, as Surya-Savitri, representing the sun at winter solstice, she is the wife of Pushan and the Asvins. Surya is depicted in a three-wheeled car accompanied by the Asvins. This group of three, in their three-wheeled car, symbolizes the morning, noon and evening light. As Surya Savitri, the goddess represents the dawn. There is a connection between Surya-Bai and the Persian fire goddess Anahita (q.v.). *See also* Asvins; Chandra; Savitri (B); Soma; Surja; Surya; Ushas.

Surya Narayana (India) "Moving in Waters." *See also* Surya.

Suryabhauma (Nepal) *see* Dikpalas.

Suryi (India) *see* Yami.

Susa-no-wo (Japan) *see* Susanowo.

Susa-noo (Japan) *see* Susanowo.

Susano (Japan) *see* Susanowo.

Susano-o-no-Mikoto (Japan) *see* Susanowo.

Susanoo (Japan) *see* Susanowo.

Susanowo *Susa-no-wo, Susano, Susanoo, Susa-noo* (Shinto; Japan)

Also known as: *Atago-Gongen, Buto, Susano-o-no-Mikoto* (His Brave Swift Impetuous Male Augustness), *Taka-haya-susa-no-wo, Take, Takehaya Susanowo.*

God of water. God of storms. God of the sea. God of forests. Ruler of the ocean and mysterious things. God of love and marriage (in later times). Susanowo is one of a trinity with Amaterasu and Tsuki-yomi. He is the son of Izanagi (Male Who Invites) and Izanami (Female Who Invites). His sister Amaterasu is the sun goddess and ruler of the light in Ama (heaven) and on earth. The moon god and ruler of the night, Tsuki-yomi, is his brother. Susanowo is variously called Swift-Impetuous-Deity, the Impetuous Male, and the Valiant Swift Impetuous Hero. When Izanagi escaped from Yumi (hell) where he had unsuccessfully attempted to persuade Izanami to return with him, he felt tainted by death's grasp. He plunged into the powerful sea to cleanse himself of the pollutants that had adhered to his being. From his discarded clothing, the dirt and grime of the underworld was released into the water. This act liberated many evil spirits from the darkness to the light. He threw in his stick and the God-set-up-at-the-crossroads was created. When he cleansed his body, two deities who created ills were produced. To counterbalance their manifestations, he created two deities to set the ills right. He then dove into the sea and all the sea deities were created. When he washed his left eye, his daughter, the beautiful sun goddess Amaterasu, came forth. From his right eye, her brother, the moon god, Tsuki-yomi was born. When he washed his nose, Susanowo was created. Izanami gave them definite realms and functions. Amaterasu was to be the sun goddess and ruler of the realm of light on heaven and earth. Tsuki-yomi was the moon ruler and ruler of the night. To Susanow, Izanami gave the domain of the ocean and other mysterious things. The sun goddess and the moon goddess followed their father's command and took up their duties. Susanow alone was recalcitrant. He insisted that he wanted to be with his mother Izanami, who was now the genius of death in the underworld. Finally, his father drove him away. Before departing, he went to bid his sister Amaterasu farewell. En route to the celestial sphere he caused a major uproar. Mountains shook and the earth groaned and quaked in upheaval. The alarmed sun goddess, fearing a confrontation, prepared her bow and arrows. Susanow assured her that his visit was without malice. To prove his intent, he suggested that they each create children. The sun goddess took her brother's sword and broke it. She masticated the three pieces, blew a mist from her mouth and created three goddesses. The storm god asked Amaterasu for Mi-kura-tana-no-kami, her strand of jewels. He split them between his teeth, blew a mist from his mouth and created five male deities. Amaterasu decided that these were her children as they had evolved from her jewels. Excited with his accomplishments he lost control. A rampage evolved and destruction ensued. He roared through the land and obliterated the rice fields and irrigation systems his sister had developed. He sul-

lied the sacred observances of the rules of purity that she had instituted by piling excrement in her sacred places. Unwilling or unable to deal with his unexpected outburst, Amaterasu secreted herself in a cave and the world was immersed in darkness. (*See* Amaterasu.) For his impetuousness he was punished by the gods. His beard was shaved, his nails were ripped from his fingers and toes and he was ousted from heaven. When Susanowo was controlled by Ara-mi-tama, his wicked soul, his nature was evil. When Nigi-mi-tama, his beneficent soul, was in charge, Susanowo was gentle and kind. On one occasion, the life of the rice goddess Kushi-nada-hime was endangered. The eight-headed dragon Koshi was making his annual visit and she was his next victim. Susanowo tricked the monster and chopped him into pieces. Susanowo and Kushi-nada-hime were married. He gave the sword Kusanagi that came from the tail of the dragon to his sister Amaterasu. Susanowo is the father of Okuni-Nushino-Mikoto (Great Land Master). His son is a healer and sorcerer, who works for the welfare of the people. It is often said that he is the only descendant of Susanowo. In other traditions, another son is mentioned: Oh-Magatsumi (Great Evil-doer), who was the source of all evils. Idakru is also mentioned as a son. Oni-tsu-nu is said to be the grandson of Susanowo. In one legend, Susanowo, dressed in rags, made his way to the home of a wealthy man, Kotan-Shorai. It was a wild and stormy night and the Susanowo asked for lodging. Kotan-Shorai, who did not recognize him, refused him entry. Susanowo chopped the inhospitable man into five pieces and offered him as a sacrifice. This complicated deity was eventually banished to the place of exile, Izumo. There, with his sons, they ruled the land and continued to rebel against the solar deities for a time. In the province of Izumo, as an ancestor of the Izumo tribe, Susanowo was reputed to have planted the forests on the coasts of Korea. He also created the mountains on the southern side of Japan (in the province of Kii). These remarkable locations sprang from the hairs on his head and beard. As instruments for mysterious and sometimes evil happenings, Susanowo was thought to be the chief of spirits in Yomi-tsu-kuni (land of darkness) or the underworld. Susanowo, Oh-Magatsumi, Okuni-Nushino-Mikoto and Suku-Na-Biko (the chief of the medicine men) were called upon by the Izumo followers whenever disease ravaged the land or a major disaster occurred. Susanowo's attribute is the ox. The killing of the dragon is an aspect of Susanowo as a warrior. The myths of Susanowo are related primarily to water, thunder and the snake. In early Japan, the snake was considered the god of Thunder. The sword, known as Kasanagi, a symbol of courage, is one of the three insignia depicting Imperial power. (*See* Kasanagi.) A mirror known as Kagami, also called Yata-Kayami, the symbol of purity, is another insignia. The third of the insignia is the curved ornamental jewels that symbolize the benevolence of the soul of the sun goddess Amaterasu. The jewels is known as Magatama. It is thought that originally they came from the claws of a tiger or the tusk of a boar. The Chinese believed that the claws of a tiger or the tusks of a boar possessed magical qualities. The Magatama however is characteristically Japanese. Kotan-Shorai literally means inhospitable. *See also* Buto (B). In many ancient cultures, to be inhospitable to friends, strangers and in some cases enemies was a grievous infraction of social mores and sometimes a crime. (*See* Fuji.)

For the Shinto creation myth, *see* Taka-mi-musubi. Susanowo might be the same as Shina-Tsu-Hiko. He is identified with Buto, Emma-O, Sampo-Kwojin and Tsuki-yomi. Other personifications of the warrior are Futsu-nushi (Sharp-Cutting-Lord) and Take-mika-zuchi (Valiant-August-Thunder). These gods, following the command of the sun goddess, went to vanquish the unruly deities in Izumo. For the return of the world from darkness to light, *see* Amaterasu; Hiruko; Izanagi and Izanami; Okuni-Nushino-Mikoto; Yomi. Compare Susanowo to Andromeda who was saved from the sea monster by Perseus (Greek). The tale of Susanowo and Kotan-Shorai is comparable to the myth of Buto, the ox-headed king, who is an aspect of Susanowo. *See also* Atago-Gongen; Buto (B); Kushi-nada-hime; Ninigi (who became the ruler following Okuni-Nushino-Mikoto's sons); Suku-Na-Biko; Three Goddesses of Munakata; Ukemochi.

Suseri-bime (Japan) *see* Okuni-Nushino-Mikoto.

Suseri-hime (Japan) *see* Okuni-Nushino-Mikoto.

Susetka (Russia) *see* Domovoi.

Sus'istinako *Great Spider* (Akoma, Koshairis People, North America). *See also* Iatiku; Sussistinnako.

Sussistinnako (Sia People, North America)
First creature. The Great Spider Sussistinnako was the first of all living creatures. It was not until he shook his magic rattle and sang that the other living creatures came forth. He created two women: Utset (mother of Indians), and Nowutset (parent of other men). Another version says he created the two women from the east and west points of the lower world. The cosmogony of the Sia is similar to that of the Navajo.

Sussitanako (Keres, Pueblo People, North America)
Sussitanako, the spider woman, created her daughters Ut Set and Nau Ut Set from her singing as she spun. Ut Set became the Mother of the Pueblo people and Nau Ut Set became the mother of all other people. From turquoise, abalone and natural colored rocks, her goddess daughters created the moon and the sun.

Sut (A) (Islamic)
He is the demon of lies. His father is Iblis and his brothers are Awar, Dasim, Tir and Zalambur. *See also* Azazel.

Sut (B) (Muslim) Lord of lies. Son of Eblis.

Sutalidihi (Cherokee People, North America)
The sun. Sutalidihi is the name given to the sun, Unelanuhi.

Sutekh (Egypt) *see* Set.

Suttee (India) *see* Sati (A).

Suttung (Teutonic) *see* Loki; Sattung.

Sutty (India) *see* Devi.

Suvetar (Finnish)
Goddess of the South Winds. She heals with honey dropped from clouds.

Suvinenge (Dahomey People, Africa)
Suvinenge is a messenger between sky and earth. He has the body of a vulture with a bald man's head.

Svadha (India) *see* Pitri.

Svadilfare (Norse; Teutonic)
Also known as: *Svadilfari*.
Deified animal. Svadilfare belongs to the giant who offered to build the wall around Asgard if given the goddess Freyja. The god Loki, in mare form, lured Svadilfari away from his work of hauling stones. From Loki's union with Freyja the great stallion Sleipner was born. The wall was unfinished so Freya was saved. *See also* Loki.

Svadilfari (Teutonic) *see* Svadilfare.

Svafnir (Teutonic) *see* Odin.

Svaha (India) *see* Suaha.

Svald (Teutonic) *see* Idun.

Svalin (Norse; Teutonic)
Svalin is a cooling shield made by the gods to protect the horses who draw the sun chariot, Aarvak and Alsvid. *See also* Aarvak; Alsvid; Muspells-heim; Sol (B).

Svanhild (Teutonic) *see* Swanhild.

Svantevit (Slavic) *see* Svantovit; Svetovid.

Svantovit *Svantevit* (Slavic)
Giant warrior god. God of plenty. Local deity. Svantovit is called the father of the sun and fire. His white horse was used for divination by the priests in later times. He is generally shown holding a bull's horn in his right hand. Hanging beside him are a sword, saddle and bridle. He is similar to the war-gods Rugievit, Yarovit, or Radigast. He is analogous to Pyerun (q.v.). *See also* Svetovid.

Svantrovit (Slavic) *see* Svetovid.

Svar-Loka (India) *see* Loka.

Svarga (India) *see* Swarga.

Svarof (Slavic) God of fire.

Svarog (Slavic)
Also known as: *Svarozits*.
God of the atmosphere, or high god. Svarog is the father of Dazhbog (the sun) and Svarogich (fire). He is identified with Perun (q.v.).

Svarozic (Slavic)
Svarozic is an ancient god of fire. He is the son of Svarog (q.v.).

Svarozits (Slavic) *see* Svarog.

Svart-Alfa-Heim (Teutonic)
Also known as: *Alfar, Svartalfaheim*.
Home of the evil spirits. When Ymir was killed, a host of maggot-like creatures were breeding in Ymir's flesh. These creatures became Dwarfs, Gnomes, Kobolds, and Trolls. Because of their evil ways they were sent down to Svartalfaheim, the underground home of the black dwarfs, where they must remain. If they come forth during the day they will be turned to stone. It is reputed these creatures have a great store of gold, silver and precious gems. Their opposite creatures are Fairies and Elves who are good and reside in Alf-heim (Alfheim). *See also* Ymir.

Svartalfaheim (Teutonic) *see* Svart-Alfa-Heim.

Svart-Alfar (Norse; Teutonic)
Also known as: *Svartalfar.*
Dwarfs. Maggot-like creatures who came from the flesh of Ymir. They were pictured as black dwarfs or dark elves. They had to stay underground or be turned to stone. They were intelligent and knew the past and future. Homely, dark-complexioned beings with green eyes, large heads, short legs, and crow's feet. *See also* Svartalfaheim.

Svartalfar (Teutonic) *see* Svart-Alfar.

Svasud *Svosud* (Norse; Teutonic)
Also known as: *Svasuthr.*
Possibly a god of the summer sun. He is the giant father of Summer. *See also* Summer; Vasud.

Svasuthr (Teutonic) *see* Svasud.

Svayam-Bhuva (India)
The First Manu. *See also* Manu; Matsya.

Svetovid (Slavic)
Also known as: *Svantevit, Svantovit, Svantrovit.*
Chief of the gods. God of fate, fertility and war. He is possibly the same as Svasud (Teutonic). *See also* Svantovit.

Sviagod (Teutonic) *see* Freyr.

Sviagris (Scaldic)
The Scaldic name for the goddess Freyja's necklace, Brisingamen.

Svipdag (Teutonic) *see* Odin or Od.

Svipday (Teutonic) *see* Aesir.

Svosud (Teutonic) *see* Svasud.

Swaha (India) *see* Suada.

Swanhild (Teutonic; Norse)
Also known as: *Svanhild.*
She is the daughter of Sigurd and Gudrun. After Sigurd's death she married Jormunrek (Ermenrich). When Swanhild was accused of adultery with her stepson, Randwer, Jormunrek had Randwer hanged and Swanhild trampled to death by horses. Swanhild was so beautiful the horses could not trample her without a cover over her. She was avenged by Sorli and Hamdir (two of the three sons of Gudrun) who cut off the hands and feet of Ermenrich. Odin (in his one-eyed form) interfered before they killed him, but bystanders still stoned him to death. *See also* Gudrun; Odin; Sigurd.

Swarga *Svarga, Svarga Loka* (Hindu; India)
Vaijayanta, Indra's celestial home and its great city, Amaravati, which means "Full of Ambrosia," is located on the sacred Meru Mountain. It was built by the architect of the gods, Tvashtri. Swarga, guarded by the white elephant Airavata, is a portable dwelling place and can be moved anywhere. It is here that the faithful await their next birth on earth. Indra presides over Swarga accompanied by his wife, Indrani. The Maruts and other major deities attend their needs. The Apsarases and Gandharvas provide entertainment. The healing twin deities, the Asvins, are the physicians of Swarga. In this capacity they are known as Nasatya collectively or sometimes Dasra and Nasatya. *See also* Amaravati; Andhaka; Apsarases; Arjuna; Asvins; Indra; .ndrani; Krishna; Kunti; Loka; Maruts; Meru Mountain; Parijata; Ravana; Sagara; Tvashtri; Vaikuntha; Visvakarma; Yama.

Swayambhu (Nepal) *see* Adibuddha.

Swetavarahi (Nepal) *see* Varahi.

Sword of Nuada, The (Celtic) *see* Tuatha De Danann.

Syama (India)
"The Heavenly Hound." *See also* Kali; Shiva; Yama.

Syamantaka (Hindu; India)
A magic jewel also known as the Sunstone, Syamantaka protected its owner from all harm providing the owner was of good character. If the wearer was evil, it brought evil and ultimately destruction to the person. Each day, this stone produced eight loads of gold. Surya, the sun god, originally gave the jewel to the Yadava, Satrajit, as a gift for his dedicated worship. Krishna coveted it and was riled when Satrajit refused his request. Satrajit's brother Prasena borrowed the jewel one day when he went hunting. Although he was immortal, he was wicked and when he was attacked by a lion, it swallowed the gem and killed him. Krishna was a prime suspect when Satrajit found that Syamantaka was missing. However, Jambavan, the king of the bears, saw the incident from his home in a cave. He killed the lion and secured Syamantaka. In defense of his honor, Krishna set out to find out what had happened to the jewel. His detective work led him to Jambavan. A lengthy and vicious battle followed in the cave. After seven days, Krishna's party assumed the worst and they returned to his celestial home, Dvarka, with news of his death. Back in the cave, the great god was still engaged in combat with Jambavan that lasted for another fourteen days. Finally, Krishna struck a mortal blow to the giant bear. Jambavan realized before death that his battle had been with a god. He turned the jewel over to the conqueror, begged for forgiveness, and gave Krishna his daughter Jambavati as a spouse. Krishna returned the jewel to its rightful owner, Satrajit. Grateful for Krishna's honorable behavior, Satrajit gave Krishna his daughter Satyabhama. He did not retain ownership of the Sunstone for long. He was murdered and Syamantaka was stolen. For some reason, the thief gave the jewel to Krishna's uncle Akrura. Unaware of this transaction, Krishna and Bala-Rama set out, found the culprit and murdered him. But he did not have the jewel. Bala-Rama, who loved Krishna, was convinced that he had stolen the jewel and his accusation led to a serious rift in their friendship. Uncle Akrura finally admitted that he was in possession of Syamantaka. Krishna, Bala-Rama and Satyabhama each claimed ownership but in the end, Akrura was allowed to keep it. *See also* Bala-Rama; Jambavan; Krishna; Surya; Syamantaka; Yadavas.

Syamatara (India) *see* Tara.

Syavana (India) *see* Mada.

Sydycos (Phoenicia) *see* Sydyk.

Sydyk (Phoenicia, Syria, Greek, Babylon)
Also known as: *Sedeq, Sydycos.*

High god. He is the father of the seven or eight Kabirs (Cabiri) who were "great gods," and of Eshmun (Asclepius). He might be related to the Syrian hero-god Sandacos. He could be one of the Phoenician twin deities Sydyk and Misor. *See also* Astronoe; Cabiri; Sedeq.

Syenabhrita (India) "Eagle-Borne." *See also* Soma.

Syenovik (Russian) *see* Domovoi.

Syga-Tojon (Yakut) *see* Ulu Tojon.

Sylain (Gallo-Roman) *see* Silvanus.

Sylg (Teutonic) *see* Elivagar.

Sylvan (Roman) *see* Silvanus.

Sylvanus (Roman) *see* Silvanus.

Symaetis (Greek) *see* Acis.

Symoethis (Greek) *see* Acis.

Syn (Norse; Teutonic)
Also known as: *Synia.*
Goddess of tribunals and trials. Syn is Frigga's attendant. She guards the door of Frigg, and acts for defendants at trials.

Synia (Teutonic) *see* Syn.

Synnytar (Finland) *see* Luonnotar.

Syr (Teutonic) *see* Freyja.

Syren (Greek) *see* Sirens.

Syrus (Greek) *see* Sinope.

T

Ta (Egypt) *see* Ba.

Ta-Djesant (Egypt) *see* Tuat.

Ta-Fan (China)
Ta-Fan is the same as the god Brahma (India).

Ta-Ret (Egypt) *see* Assessors.

Ta-Sent-Nefert (Egypt)
She is the wife of Haroeris, who is a form of Horus. Ta-Sent-Nefert was worshipped with their son P-neb-taui.

Ta-Shih-Chih (China) *see* Tammuz (q.v.).

Ta-Shih-Chih (Buddhist; China)
A Dhyanibodhisattva. Ta-Shih-Chih is the same as the goddess Mahasthamaprapta (Nepal). She is a companion of the goddess of peace, Kuan-yin; the god of learning, Wen-shu; the god of happiness, P'u-hsien. *See also* Dhyanibodhisattvas; Manjusri; Pushan; Samantabhadra.

Ta-Tanen (Egypt) *see* Tanunen.

Ta-Tchesert (Egypt) *see* Tuat.

Ta-urt (Egypt) *see* Taueret.

Ta-uz (Babylonian) Festival Assessors.

Ta'aroa *Taaroa* (Polynesia)
Also known as: *Tangaroa, Te Temu, Tii-Maaraatai.*
Supreme deity. Creator. In the beginning, Ta'aroa developed himself. He existed in Fa'a-ti, the place within the shell named Timi-iti. The outer portion of this shell, named Rumia, existed before creation, in a primeval void of darkness named Po. Eons

passed before Ta'aroa slipped from his shell. He was alone. He proceeded to create a new shell for himself and retreated once again. Time passed. Finally, Ta'aroa used the new shell for a foundation and the original one for the top of the sky. He identified himself as the "Source," Te Tumu, the creator of all things. Ta'aora's spine became a mountain ridge, his vitals, the clouds, his arms and legs, the earth. The enormous effort he used to create the universe caused a vast amount of perspiration to accumulate, from which the oceans were created. He also created the god Atea, the light, who in turn began all life. Ta'aroa is associated with Tumu-ra'ifeuna (the Great Octopus). *See also* Atea; Io (B); Maui; Tane; Tangaroa; Po.

Taaroa (Polynesian) *see* Ta'aroa.

Taaroa Kanaloa (Hawaii) *see* Tanaoa (Polynesia).

Taatoa (Oceanic) *see* Tangaroa.

Tabakea (Oceanic)
"The Turtle." He is called the "Father of All Things." *See also* Nareau.

Tablets of Fate (Sumer)
Also known as: *Dup Shimati.*
The destiny of the world is written on the sacred Tablets of Fate. They were called Dup Shimati. The god who had the tablets in his possession became all-powerful. They were given to Kingu to mark his power.

Tabu-Eriki (Polynesian) *see* Tabuerik.

Tabuerik *Tabu-Eriki* (Oceanic)
Creator deity. In legends similar to those of Yelafaz, Nareau

and Lukelang made Tabuerik, the lightning and thunder god, who in the form of a bird had Rigi, a butterfly who flew around and separated heaven from earth. *See also* Lukelang; Nareau; Riiki; Tangaroa; Yelafaz.

Tacatecutli (Aztec People, Mexico)

God of merchants and adventurers. Tacatecutli opened the way for the other gods. He also opened paths for the imperial armies.

Tachen (Polynesia) *see* Take (B)

Tacita (Roman) Deity of silence.

Tafa'i (Polynesia; Tahiti) *see* Tawhaki.

Tages (Etruscan)

Tages, a small demon who is the son or grandson of Jove, rose from a ploughed furrow and immediately began to predict the future and the signs sent from the gods. He was the first of the Etruscan prophets.

Taguacipa *Taquacipa* (Inca)

"The Deceiver." An evil deity, Taguacipa is in opposition to Viracocha. He undoes the good that Viracocha creates. *See also* Pachacamac; Viracocha.

Tahuantin Suyu Kapac (Inca People, Peru)

Also known as: *Ayar Aucca, Ayar Manco, Ayar Uchu, Ayars, Colla, Cusco Huanca, Hanan Cuzco, Huana Cauri, Manco-Capac, Urin Cuzco.*

Earth gods. The Tahuantin Suyu Kapac are four brothers who are sons of the Sun. Ayar Cachi (also known as Colla) is ruler of the east, Ayar Aucca (also known as Pinau) is ruler of the south, Ayar Manco (also known as Manco) is ruler of the north and Ayar Uchu (also known as Tocay) is ruler of the west. They are similar to Becabs and Acatl. *See also* Acatl; Becabs; Manco-Capac; Texcatzoncatl; Viracocha.

T'ai Ch'ing (China) *see* Ling-Pao T'ien-Tsun; San Ch'ing.

T'ai Ching (China) *see* Yu-Huan-Shang-Ti.

T'ai I (China) *see* T'ai Shan.

T'ai Shan (China)

Also known as: *T'ai-yo Ta-to, T'aiyo Tato, Tung Huang T'ai I.*

God of life. God of fate. God of destiny. God of death. The Great Emperor of the Eastern Peak, the god of T'ai-shan, a mountain in northern China, delegated by the Jade Emperor, Tung Wang Kung, to oversee the lives and activities of mortals and all creatures on earth. He determined the course of men's lives, assisted by a large bureaucracy to handle the details, records, and statistics. In time, T'ai Shan assumed control over life and death. A large splendid temple for this god is in Peking. He is known under different names in other legends. He is said to be the father of Sheng-mu.

T'ai-Shan Niang-Niang (China) *see* Sheng-mu.

T'ai Shang San Kuan (China) *see* San Kuan.

T'ai-Tsung (China) *see* Men shen.

T'ai-yo Ta-to (China) *see* T'ai shan.

Tailtiu (Celtic)

She is the earth goddess wife of Eochaid mac Eire, the king of the Fir Bholg.

Tain Bo Cuailnge (Celtic) Welsh divine bulls.

Taipan (Australia) *see* Rainbow Snake.

Taishaku (Japan)

Taishaku is the Japanese name of the Vedic god Indra.

Tait (Egypt)

Goddess of linen weaving. She is associated with Isis and the swathing of Osiris' body for burial.

T'aiyo Tato (China)

T'aiyo Tato is another name for T'ai Shan, the god of fate, destiny, life and death. *See also* T'ai Shan.

Tajikaroo (Japan) "Prince Mighty Power." *See also* Amaterasu.

Taka-haya-susa-no-wo (Japan) *see* Susanowo.

Taka-Mimusubi *Takami-Musubi, Taka-mi-Musubi* (Shinto; Japan)

Creator deity. Taka-Mimusubi (High Producing) and Kami-Mimusubi (Divine or Mysterious Producing) are the secondary deities who formed the triad that sprang from Chaos. The head of the triad is Ama-no-minaka-nushi, the Eternal Land Ruler. In some traditions, Taka-Mimusubi represents Kami-rogi, the Divine Male, and Kami-Mimusubi represents the Divine Female, Kami-romi. *See* Ama-no-minaka-nushi for the Shinto creation myth. *See also* Amaterasu; Kami-Mimusubi.

Taka-okami (Japan)

Taka-okami is a rain god who dwells in the mountains. *See also* Izanagi; Izanami; Kagu-tsuchi; Kura-okami; Taki-tsu-hiko.

Taka-pime-no-mikoto (Japan)

She is the daughter of one of the Three Goddesses of Munakata, Takiri-bime-no-mikoto, who is also known as Okit-sushima-hime-no-mikoto (Mist-Princess-Godddess) and possibly Opo-kuni-nusi. Her brother is Adi-siki-taka-pikone-no-kami. *See also* Three Goddesses of Munakata.

Takama-no-hara (Japan)

Also known as: *Ama.*

Heaven. Takama-no-hara (abode of the gods) is often called Ama (heaven). The ruler of Ama is the radiant sun goddess Amaterasu. Ama is described as a beautiful spot with terrain the same as Japan's and geographically not far away. In early times a bridge named Ama-no-hasidate connected earth to Ama (heaven). This allowed the deities to move back and forth with ease. One day, as the gods were napping, the bridge collapsed. Now there are the celestial deities, known as Ama-tsu-kami, who reside in Takama-no-hara or Ama, and the earthly deities, known as Kuni-tsu-kami, who reside on the islands of Japan. The deities are not confined to their locales. There are times when the Takama-no-hara will settle on earth and the Kuni-tsu-kami will move to the celestial realm. However, the heavenly deities do not know what is transpiring on earth unless news is brought to them by messenger. The opposite of

Takama-no-hara or Ama is Yomi, the underworld realm. *See also* Ama-no-minaka-nushi; Amaterasu; Yomi.

Takami-Musubi (Shinto) Japan. *See also* Taka-Mimusubi.

Takaro (New Hebrides) *see* Tangaroa.

Take (A) (Japan) *see* Susanowo; Take-mi-kazuchi.

Take (B) (Polynesia)
Also known as: *Tachen*.

Take is the point below Vari in the creation tale. It is the stem of the coconut (Avaiki) which is the universe. The god Tamaa was said to have planted the first coconut tree. Take is also a general term the Polynesians use for god. *See also* Avaiki; Vari.

Take-mi-kazuchi *Take-mika-zuchi, Take-mikazuchi* (Shinto, Japan)

The great general Take-mi-kazuchi (Valiant August Thunder) was appointed by the sun goddess Amaterasu and other deities to travel to earth on a mission. He was given a companion for his journey, the god of fire, also known as the genius of weapons, Futsu-nushi (Sharp Cutting Lord). The task of the thunder deity and the fire deity was to force the submission and abdication of Onamuji, or some say, Okuni-Nushino-Mikoto from the throne of Izumo province. It had been decided that Ninigi, the grandson of Amaterasu, was to be the new ruler. Take-mi-kazuchi's brother, Aji-suki-takahikone, was also a thunder deity. As an infant, he had to be carried up and down a ladder and put in a boat that sailed around the islands to subdue his screaming and hollering. He later became the father of the rain god Taki-tsu-hiko (Prince Cataract). Another god widely worshiped was Kami-Nari, also known as Raiden, the god of rolling thunder. An earthquake god appeared in later times (approximately C.E. 599) named Nai-no-kami. The boat and the ladder represent the connection of thunder between heaven and earth. An earthquake could be depicted as thunder under the earth. Kami-Nari is described as having horns on his head and tusks in his wide mouth. A tree split by lightning was venerated and could not be cut down. *See also* Amaterasu; Izanagi; Ninigi; Okuni-Nushino-Mikoto; Raiden; Susanowo; Taki-tsu-hiko.

Take-mi-musubi (Japan) *see* Takami-musubi.

Take-mika-zuchi (Japan) *see* Take-mi-kazuchi.

Take-mikazuchi (Japan) *see* Take-mi-kazuchi.

Take-Minakata (Japan)

It is possible that Okuni-Nushino-Mikoto, who is one of the Shichi Fukujin (seven gods of happiness), is the father of Take-Minakata and Koto-shiro-nushi. If so, they would have a sister, Shita-teru-Hime, who married Ame-no-Wakahiko, the renowned warrior god. *See also* Okuni-Nushino-Mikoto.

Takehaya Susanowo (Japan) *see* Susanowo.

Takemiskazuchi no Mikoto (Japan)
He is a warrior god represented by the deer.

Takhma Urupi (Persia) *see* Hoshang.

Takhmoruw (Persia) *see* Hoshang.

Taki-mi-Mushubi (Japan) *see* Ame-no-Oshido-Mimi; Taka-Mimusubi.

Taki-tsu-hiko (Shinto; Japan)
Also known as: *Prince Cataract*.

God of waterfalls. Taki-tsu-hiko, the son of the thunder god Aji-suki-takahikone and nephew of the thunder god Take-mi-kazuchi, dwells on the mountains and is the god of waterfalls. West of the Kaminabi mountain there is a stone that became the soul of Taki-tsu-hiko. Taka-okami, a rain deity, also dwells in the mountains. In some renditions, he also produces snow. Another rain god, who produces snow and dwells in valleys, is Kura-okami (dragon god of the valleys). Kura-okami and his two brothers, Kura-yama-tsumi and Kura-mitsu-ha, were born from the blood of their brother, the fire god Kagu-tsuchi, when he was slaughtered by their father Izanagi. Another deity, Oho-iwa Dai-myo-jin also known as Oiwa Daimyojin, was known as the great god of the rock. There is also a goddess of clay and earth known as Hani-Yasu-no-Kami and a god of earth, Ohonamochi. Taki-tsu-hiko was said to be in the shape of a rock. Prayers are sent to him for rain in times of drought. In some depictions the deities appear as serpents or dragons. *See* Kura-okami for details of his origins. In early times, red, black or white horses were sacrificed to bring rain and red horses to stop rain. *See also* Take-mi-kazuchi.

Takiri-bime-no-Mikoto (Japan) *see* Amaterasu; Three Goddesses of Munakata.

Takitsu-hime-no-Mikoto (Japan) *see* Three Goddesses of Munakata.

Takitu-pime-no-Mikoto (Japan) *see* Three Goddesses of Munakata. *See also* Amaterasu.

Takkanna (Australia) *see* Mar.

Takoroa (Polynesia) *see* Rangi.

Takotsi Nakawe (Huichol People, Mexico)
Also known as: *Grandmother Growth*.

Earth goddess. Agricultural goddess. Takotsi Nakawe is the giver of long life. She is the mother of the armadillo, peccary and bear.

Takshaka *Kuvera, Vaisravana* (Hindu; India)

Takshaka is the king of the serpents known as Nagas and Nagis. He and the other serpents were instrumental in protecting the other gods and mortals. They forbid spiritual truths to those not worthy and grant them to the deserving ones. The sage Astika, son of the serpent goddess Manasa, intervened to save Takshaka from death. Injury or death from a snake bite can be avoided if the person remembers to utter Astika's name when bitten. *See also* Kuvera; Lokapalas; Manasa; Nagas; Yakshas.

Taku-hata Chi-hata Hime (Japan) *see* Ama-no-minaka-nushi; Kami-Mimusubi.

Takuskanskan (Dakota People, North America)
"The Moving God" who is the wind and a trickster.

Talaus (Greek)
Talaus is the Argonaut son of the king of Argos, Bias, and

Pero, who is the daughter of Neleus and Chloris. His children are Adrestus, who became the king of Argos, the leader of the Seven against Thebes and the leader of the Epigoni; Aristomachus, Astynome, Eriphyle, Hippomedan, Mecisteus, Metidice, Parthenopaeus and Pronax. *See also* Abas (B); Adrestus; Bias.

Taliesin (British) *see* Amergin; Bran.

Talisman
A talisman is an object usually engraved with figures and generally worn as a charm. The talisman is thought by believers to possess magical powers. *See also* Ab; Benten; Buto; Ilmarinen; Kagu-tsuchi; Runes; Tuatha De Danann; Vainamoinen.

Tallai (Canaan, Syria, Ugarit)
She is the daughter of Baal who symbolizes dew and rain. Her sisters are Arsai, who symbolizes the earth, and Pidray, a nature goddess who symbolizes light.

Talus *Talos* (Greek)
Talus is the son of Perdix and the brother of Daedalus, the inventor. Jealousy led him to kill his brother Daedalus. He was then turned into a partridge by the goddess of the hunt, Athena. *See also* Daedalus.

Tama-Yori-Bime (Japan) *see* Jimmu Tenno; Toyo-Tama-Bime.

Tamagostad (Aztec People, Nicaragua)
Also known as: Possibly *Oxomoco.*
Creator. He is the husband of Zipaltonal (also known as Cipattonal). They are the ruling deities of Ecalchot, the wind god; Ciaga, the water god; Quiateot, the rain god; Misca, the god of traders; Vizetot, the god of famine. The gods were part of creation. They live in the heaven of good souls. Some writers say Tamagostad and Zipaltonal or Cipattonal are the same as Oxomoco and Cipactonal. On the other side of heaven is the realm of Mictanteot ruled by the goddess of volcanoes, Masaya. *See also* Oxomoco.

Tamanduare (Tupi-Guarani People, Brazil) *see* Timondonar.

Tamar (Hebrew)
She is equivalent to Ishtar (q.v.). *See also* Inanna.

Tamats (Mexico)
Also known as: *Elder Brother.*
God of wind and air. He is a messenger of the gods and the conqueror of the underworld people. A shape changer deity, he sometimes appears as a wolf, a deer or even a pine tree.

Tamazcalteci (Aztec)
A name for Cihuatcoatl and Tonantzin. *See also* Tonantzin.

Tamek-Vui (Finnish) *see* Kiyamat-Tora.

Tamendonar (Tupi-Guarani People, Brazil) *see* Timondonar.

Tammus (Greek) *see* Harpies.

Tammuz (Assyro-Babylonia)
Also known as: *Ab-u, Adonai, Damu-zi-abzu* (Tammuz of the Abyss), *Dao, Daonus* (the instructor of agricultural arts), *Dumuzi, Enlil* (sometimes), *Es-u, Isir, Sibzianna* (shepherd and hunter), *Tamoza, Thammuz.*
Possibly a tree god, originally. Vegetation god. God of the spring sun. God of crops. Tammuz is the son of Ningishzida and Etuda. He is the brother/lover of Ishtar in their youth. Tammuz became the ruler of Uruk. The mythology of Tammuz and Ishtar is closely related to the earlier mythology of the Sumerian Dumuzi and Inanna. A major difference occurs when Dumuzi descends into the underworld: it is because an angry Inanna allowed the demons to take him there as her substitute. In the Tammuz tale, a grieving Ishtar attempted to rescue Tammuz from his descent into the underworld. More aggressive than her earlier counterpart, Inanna, Ishtar threatened to let the dead free to terrorize the living if she was not allowed to enter the underworld. When she was admitted, she did not return immediately. Papsukkal, the vizier of the great gods, earlier made it clear what would happen if Ishtar did not return to the upperworld. He appealed to Ea for her release. Ea created the eunuch Asushunamir to enter the lower realm to persuade Ereshkigal, ruler of the underworld and sister of Ishtar, to give him the life-water bag. He charmed the goddess, who then ordered her vizier Namtar to give him the bag. During the yearly summer solstice, it was Ishtar who had Tammuz torn to pieces and thrown into the sea. His absence caused a barren earth, and her grief. Finally, Ishtar agreed that Tammuz would spend six months of the year in Arallu (the underworld) with her sister Ereshkigal, who was the queen of the region, and six months with her (Ishtar) in the upperworld. In the end, with his father Ningishzida, he guarded the gate of Anu, in the city of the gods. His festival is the Ta-uz. Sometimes he appears in goat form. The cock is sacred to Tammuz. Compare to: Aa, Abu, Adon, Adonis, Angus, Cybele, Asushunamir and Gula. Tammuz is known as the counterpart of the Vedic deity Soma (q.v.). Both deities are associated with the waxing and waning of the moon. As a harvest god, Tammuz died each winter and was reborn each spring. Compare the agricultural myth of Tammuz to the Hittite god Telepinus. Compare to Boann and Dagda (Celtic). Tammuz is associated with Adonis (Greek), Eshmun (Phoenicia), and Osiris (Egypt). *See also* Aa; Anu (B); Arallu; Damkina; Dumuzi; Ea; Enlil; Inanna; Ishtar; Marduk; Mirsu; Namtar; Ningishzida; Papsukkal.

Tamoanchan (Aztec People, Mexico)
Paradisiacal place of origin. It was to the mythical city of Tamoanchan that Quetzalcoatl brought the "precious bones" from which the first men were made by Quetzalcoatl, and the goddess Quilaztli. This is the place of origin of the "Mother of the Deities," Teteoinnan. Itzpapalotl, the "Obsidian Butterfly," is a goddess of Tamoanchan. Tamoanchan is represented by a tree in blossom emitting blood. *See also* Ciuateteo; Itzpapalotl.

Tamon (Japan) *see* Bishamon.

Tamon-Tenno (Japan) *see* Bishamon.

Tamontennu (Japan) *see* Bishamon.

Tamoza (Babylonian) *see* Tammuz.

Tamra (India)
Grandmother of the Garudas. *See also* Garudas; Kasyapa.

Tan (Egypt) *see* Ament; Amentet; Amenti.

Tanabata Hime (Japan) *see* Amatsu-Mikaboshi.

Tanabata Tsume (Japan) *see* Amatsu-Mikaboshi.

Tanaoa (Polynesia)

Also known as: *Taaroa Kanaloa* (Hawaii), *Tangaroa*.

A god of darkness or hell, or a god of thunder. He came from Chaos and produced Ono. In another version of his legends, he and Mutuhei (darkness and silence) ruled Po, the primeval abyss. Atea, the god of light, is in constant opposition to Tanaoa. *See also* Atea; Ono; Qat; Rangi; Ta'aroa; Tangaloa.

Tandu (Hindu; India)

Tandu is one of Shiva's principal attendants. He is primarily a teacher of mimicry and dancing.

Tane (New Zealand, Polynesia)

Also known as: *Kane* (Hawaii), *Tane, Tane-mahuta, Tawhiri, Tawhiri-ma-tane, Ti'i*.

Creator. God of forests and creatures of the forest. Tane is the son of Rangi, the sky father, and Papa who is mother earth. His siblings are Olo, Oro (or Koro), and some say Tu. Others say Rangi and Papa were his children, and that he was the god of darkness or the underworld. Still others say his children were twin boys (Tonga-iti and Tangi-ia) and that his consort was Tangia. Some say his wife was Hine (Hine-hau-one) who later became Po, the goddess of darkness. Tane and the goddess Vatea produced the triad of Tangaroa, Rongo, and Tane or the pair Tangaroa and Tiki. In one myth, we find Tane, after many trials with various female deities that gave unsatisfactory results, mating with Hine-ahu-one, who gave birth to the egg, known as Tikitohua, that resulted in the bird ancestor of all birds. Her next child was Tiki-kapakapa who was the mother of the first human child. Another legend relates that when Tane went to heaven, he left the rainbow as a reminder of his presence on earth. Man was created from red earth and the spittle of Kane. He was also said to be part of the triad of Ku and Lono. The three breathed life into man and made woman from his bones. The name they gave man was Tiki or Tiki-aw-a-ha and the woman Iowahine. One other version tells of Tane shaping a woman out of earth and mating with her, producing Hine-itau-ira with whom he also mated. When she found out he was her father she killed herself and went to the underworld where she became Hine-nui-te-po, the great goddess of the night (q.v.). Tane is sometimes associated with the war god Oro. Compare to Kane (Hawaii). *See also* Hine; Maui; Papa; Rangi; Ta'aroa; Tawhiri-ma-tane; Tu.

Tane-mahuta (Polynesia) *see* Tane; Tawhiri-ma-tea.

Tanen (Egypt) *see* Tanunen.

Tangaloa (Polynesia, Samoa)

Also known as: *Lowa, Tangaroa*.

Pre-existent creator. Sea god. He lived in the Void with his messenger, the bird Tulli. Tulli flew over the vast expanse of waters searching for a place to rest. Tangaloa threw down a rock which became one of the Samoan Islands, Manu'a. Tangaloa created other islands, including Tonga and Fijii. Tulli complained that he needed shade on the islands, so Tangaloa sent the "Peopling Vine." It was from this plant that the first man

was made. In another version, Tangalo was born from his mother's head or he came from the Po (The Void). His sons were Vaka (Laka) and Ahu (Tupo). Called "god on high" he was the deity of fair-haired people, and light and plenty. He is a god who re-created the earth after it was destroyed by the flood. Elsewhere, we read of Tangaloa as a messenger between the high gods; Tama-poulialamafoa (King of Heaven), Tangaloa-eiki (Celestial Chief), Tangaloa-tufuga (Celestial Artisan), and Tangaloa-atu-logo-logo (Celestial Messenger). In this case he created the earth on orders from those above. In one of the Samoan legends there was a great flood that covered the earth. Only two mortals (Seve and Pouniu) temporarily saved themselves by swimming. Tangaloa saw their plight and sent two men down with hooks. They drew Samoa from under the sea for the mortals' refuge. Tangaloa is also credited for raising the sky. *See* Tangaroa, Timo-taata, Ihoiho, Taaroa and Tiki, all creator gods of Polynesia and the surrounding islands. The deity, Lowa of the Marshall Islands, may have been a cognate of Tangaloa. *See also* Laka; Po; Qat; Takaro; Tane; Tangeroa; Qat.

Tangara (Greek)

She is the daughter of Enarete and Aeolus of Magnesia, who is the son of Hellen and Ortheis. *See also* Aeolus (A); Canace; Enarete; Salmoneus.

Tangaroa (Polynesia, Samoa, Tahiti, Society Islands, Marquesas, New Zealand)

Also known as: *Kanaloa, Taaroa, Tabu-eriki, Tabu-Eriki, Tanaoa, Tangaloa, Ta'oroa, Te Temu, Tonga-iti, Tongaiti, Upao, Vahu*.

Creator. God of the ocean and of fishers. God of house builders and carpenters. One myth tells of this deity creating earth by throwing rocks into the sky, or throwing a rock from heaven to earth; the other version is that he created earth by breaking the primordial egg into two halves which become earth and sky. A third version said that he was son of Rangi and Papa (or Vatea and Papa), and brother of Rongo, and god of fish and reptiles. Also the father of Tu-te-wehi (Tu-te-wanawana) and Ika-tere, whose mother was Punga. In some legends Rangi and Papa were once known as a pair, Kane and Kanaloa. One story associates him with a maiden named Vinmara, who in turn resembles the Malaysian sky maiden, Widadari. The name Vinmara might be associated with the Sanskrit Vindhyadara. In one legend Papa (Papa-tu-a-nuku) was the wife of Tangaroa, but was unfaithful and went to Rangi for solace. This caused a fight between Rangi and Tangaroa. Tangaroa is sometimes confused with Tane. He is possibly related to Roma-Tane, the Polynesian god of paradise. He is similar in some respects to Qat of Melanesia and to Tagaro and Takaro. *See also* Faumea; Maui; Tane; Tangaroa.

Tangere (Tartars of the Volga) *see* Tangri.

Tango (Polynesia)

Also known as: *Support*.

One of the children of Vari-ma-te-takere, the great mother. His land is called Enua-kura. *See also* Vatea.

Tangri (Altaic)

Also known as: *Tangere* (Tartars of the Volga), *Tengeri* (Buryats), *Tengri* (Mongols and Kalmyks), *Tingir* (Beltirs).

This celestial, omniscient god was not worshipped in temples. It is generally thought that he was not represented in the form of a statue. He was offered prayers and sacrifices. All natural disasters were thought to be signs of his discontent. Later, the Mongols and Buryats referred to numerous gods by the name Tangeri. The Tangeri were gods who ate the fruits of the World Tree. *See also* Bai Ulgan.

Tanit *Tanith* (Carthage, Phoenicia)
Also known as: *Caelestis, Juno Caelestis, Tlanit Pene Baal.*
A celestial or lunar goddess. Tanit is the wife or consort of Baal Hammon. She is identified by some with Juno Caelestis (Juno) of the Romans. Her symbol is a circle inside a crescent supported by a blunt cone, similar to Hathor's symbol. She is sometimes linked with Ishtar, Ashtart and Astarte. Sometimes, she is associated with Artemis.

Tanith (Carthage) Chief goddess of Carthage.

Tanka (Oglala People, North America) *see* Kitcki Manitou.

Tanngniostr (Teutonic) *see* Tanngnost.

Tanngnost (Norse; Teutonic)
Also known as: *Tanngniostr, Tooth Grinder.*
Deified animal. Tanngnost is one of the two goats who pull Thor's chariot. The other goat is named Tanngrisni.

Tanngrisni (Norse; Teutonic)
Also known as: *Gat Tooth, Tanngrisnr.*
Deified animal. One of the goats that pulls Thor's chariot. The other is called Tanngnost.

Tanngrisnr (Teutonic) *see* Tanngrisni.

Tannin (Semite) *see* Leviathan; Rahabh.

Tano (Ashanti People, Africa)
God of rivers and thunder. Tano is the son of Asase Ya and Nyame. His brother and rival is Bia. He is often described as being an antelope when he is associated with his opponent, Death. *See also* Abosom; Asase Yaa; Bia; Nyame.

Tantalus (A) *Tantalos* (Greek)
Sun deity. Tantalus, king of Lydia, is the son of Zeus and Pluto. He married Dione and became the father of Pelops, Niobe and Broteas. A wealthy king, he had a banquet for the deities and decided that he would test their powers and reveal a few of their secrets. He cut his infant Pelops into pieces and served him for dinner. All but Demeter realized what he had done. His angry father punished him in Tartarus, the lowest region of the underworld, with a raging thirst for eternity. Standing under a loaded fruit tree in water up to his chin, Tantalus could never quite either grasp the fruit or drink from the water. Compare his punishment to the punishment of Sisyphus and Ixion. *See also* Amphion; Demeter; Erinyes; Niobe; Oenamaus; Pelops; Tantalus (B).

Tantalus (B) (Greek)
Also known as: *Tantalos.*
Tantalus is the son of Amphion and Niobe.

Tantalus (C) (Greek) He is the son of Thyestes and Aerope.

Tantalus (D) (Greek)
He was married to Clytemnestra and was killed by Agamem-

non. Tantalus (C) and (D) are different versions of the same person. *See also* Aerope; Agamemnon; Clytemnestra.

Tanunapat (India) "Son of Self." *See also* Agni.

Tanunen (Egypt)
Also known as: *Ta-tanen, Tanen, Tathenen, Tenen, Tetenen.*
Local god of Memphis. Tanunen is sometimes identified with Ptah, who has a human form and wears two ostrich feathers and two ram's horns on his head. He could be an aspect of Ptah as an earth god. *See also* Ptah.

Tao (China)
Tao is the universal energy and primeval cosmic force. *See also* T'ien.

Tao Chun (China) *see* Ling-Pao T'ien-Tsun.

Ta'oroa (Polynesia) *see* Tangaroa.

Tapa-Loka (India) *see* Loka.

Tapati (Hindu; India)
Tapati, meaning "The Hot One," is the daughter of Chhaya the shade, and Surya the sun. Surya did not know that his wife Sanja had left him and had used Chhaya as a substitute wife. A lovely golden colored nymph, Tapati lived in the celestial realms. She has two brothers, Shani and Savarni. Her father arranged that king Samvarana would get lost in the forest and seemingly come upon Tapati accidentally and fall in love with her. The events transpired accordingly with help from the love god Kama. Tapati, however, vanished when the king spoke to her of his romantic feelings. Thoroughly smitten, he went in search of his heart's desire. She appeared to him in a vision and told him that she could not be his mate without her father's permission. He worshipped the sun for twelve days before his request was granted. Surya had a sage escort his daughter to earth and she married the king. Leaving his kingdom behind, he took his bride to the mountain forests where they lived for twelve happy years. While away, anarchy spread throughout his realm and the couple was forced to return to restore harmony. Tapati and Samvarana were the parents of Kuru, an ancestor of the Pandavas and Kauravas. *See also* Kama; Kauravas; Pandavas; Sanja; Surya.

Tapio (Finnish)
Called the "Golden King," he is a woodland lord. His family is composed of his wife, Mielikki, and children Nyyrikki and Tuulikki. His home is called Tapiola. Tapio is an old man with a brown beard, wearing a high hat of fir cones and a coat of tree moss.

Taqiacopa (Inca) *see* Taguacipa; Virococha.

Taquatu (Tierra del Fuego)
Also known as: *Yaccy-Ma* (possibly).
Taquatu is an invisible giant spirit. He travels in his canoe over the water and in the air. If you are idle and not alert, he could take you aboard his canoe and carry you far from home. *See also* Yaccy-Ma.

Tar-Ata (Middle Eastern)
Tar-Ata is a name for the goddess Atargatis (q.v.).

Tara (A) (Brahmanic, Hindu; India)

Also known as: *Kali, Taraka.*

Tara, a stellar deity, is the mate of Brihaspati who represents Jupiter, or Soma (the moon), and the mother of Buddha (Mercury). In some legends, she married her brother Sugriva. She is a furious destroyer and slayer of evil beings. On one occasion, the god Soma (the moon), intoxicated with power, abducted Tara (the star). Brihaspati, a learned man who instructed the gods, attempted to rescue his wife unsuccessfully. Soma would not relinquish the goddess even when instructed to do so by the great Brahma. A war, known as the Tarakamaya, erupted with Tara leading the gods and Soma the demons. In some interpretations, Brihaspati formed the party of the gods and fought against Soma. During this encounter, Shiva slashed Soma's face in half with a trident. The goddess appealed to Brahma for assistance and finally Soma gave his captive her freedom. Pregnant, she returned to her husband. He refused to accept her until after the child was born. A miraculous birth occurred immediately. The male infant was so beautiful that Soma and Brihaspati both claimed to be the father. Brahma asked the goddess who was the father of the child and she replied that it was Soma. Soma, as the lord of constellations, embraced his son and named him Buddha. Buddha later became the founder of the lunar dynasties. (This Buddha is not Gautama, the great Buddha of the Buddhist tradition.) Tara is not to be confused with Rama's monkey general's wife of the same name. Tara is a gracious and lovely figure, but when she is depicted as an aspect of Kali, the wife of Shiva, she appears as a dark goddess wearing skulls. *See also* Brahma; Brihaspati; Kali; Shiva; Soma; Sugriva.

Tara (B) (Buddhist, Jainist, Lamaist; Country of origin, India)

Also known as: *Bhrkuti* (Yellow Tara), *Bribsun* (Green Tara), *Dol Jyang* (Green Tara, Tibet), *Dolma* (Tibet), *Ekajata* (Blue Tara), *Hlamo* (Tibet), *Januli, Konjo* (White Dolma, China), *Kurukulla* (Red Tara), *Kwan-Yin* (China), *Mamaki, Nila Tara* (Blue Tara), *Parnasavari, sGrol-mas* (Tibet), *Shveta Tara* (White Tara), *Sitatara, Syamatara* (Green Tara), *Tara-Amba, Tara-Dharani, Tara Utpala* (Green Tara), *Tara White* (Nepal), *Taraka, Wen-Ch'en* (White Tara, China).

In early times, Tara, a stellar goddess, was invoked for safe passage across the seas. Later she became the protector of all mortals as they crossed the ocean of existence. She is the destroyer of fears, remover of obstacles and bestower of boons. She is the wife and female counterpart of Avalokitesvara in his role as the Savior from the Eight Perils. As Tara White and Tara Green she is the spouse of Avalokitesvara and shares his qualities. She is the three-eyed goddess of daytime depicted with a wheel on her chest, playing a lute. She is usually shown seated but occasionally, she is in a standing or dancing position, dressed and crowned like a boddhisattva. As Tara White and Tara Green she is kind and gentle. As Tara Yellow, Red and Blue she is threatening. Tara was born from tears which fell from Avalokitesvra's eye as he gazed with pity upon the suffering world. As Tara Utpala (Green Tara), she helps her believers through the night. Utpala is the most popular aspect of Tara in Tibet. Sometimes she is shown with a rosary and a book. Often her right hand is in the varada mudra which is the charity pose, with the arm pendant and all fingers extended outward. Her left hand is in the vitarka or argument mudra with the arm bent and all fingers extended upward, except the index finger, which touches the tip of the thumb. Sorrow is relieved in her aspect as Tara-Dharani. As Tara-Amba she represents the "Mother." As Nila Tara she is the consort of Akshobhya, the second Dhyani Buddha. She holds a half-closed water-lily or lotus, often blue, in her left hand. As the consort of Amoghasiddhi her mount is a roaring lion and her emblems are the kapal and visvavajra. Tara has one hundred and eight names. She is comparable to Kuan Yin (China). Princess Konjo was one of two princesses who are thought to have introduced Buddhism to China. She is said to be an incarnation of the White Dolma and is named Wen-Ch'en. She married the King of Tibet, Srong-btsangombo (also spelled Srong-tsan-gampo). *See also* Amoghasiddhi; Avalokitesvara; Chandamaharoshana; Dhyani Buddhas; Khadga Jogina; Vairocana.

Tara (C) (India) *see* Bali (A).

Tara-Amba (India) *see* Tara (B)

Tara-Dharani (India) *see* Tara (B).

Tara Utpala (India) *see* Tara (B)

Tara White (Nepal) *see* Tara (B).

Taraka (India)

Taraka is a she-demon who lives in a forest near the Ganges River. She feasts upon travelers. *See also* Karttikeya; Tara (B).

Tarakamaya *Taraka-Maya* (India)

A divine war. *See also* Brihaspati; Tara (A).

Taramis (Celtic) *see* Taranis.

Taranga (Polynesia)

Taranga is the mother of the trickster-god, Maui. When he was an infant, she cradled him in a top-knot of her hair. *See also* Maui; Tu-matauenga.

Taranis *Taramis* (Celtic)

"The Thunderer." God of thunderstorms. The enemies of Taranis were put in a cage and burned according to one source. It is thought that this may be an exaggeration, although it has been said that this ritual was practiced by the Gauls in the first century B.C.E. The attribute of Taranis is the wheel. *See also* Esus; Jupiter; Odin.

Tarapaca (Peru) *see* Virococha.

Taraxhippos (Greek)

Taraxhippos is the name of the ghost of Glaucus of Corinth. *See also* Glaucus.

Tareya-Wagon (Mohawk People, North America)

Supreme deity. The god who liberated the Kaniengehaga, better known as the Mohawks, from confinement beneath the surface of the earth. He then led them to the Valley of the Mohawk on the surface of the planet.

Tarhuhyiawahku (Iroquois People, North America)

High god. Name of the giant holder of the heavens.

Tari-penu (India) *see* Bura-penu.

Tarik (Persian)

Tarik is one of the evil demons created by Ahriman to be his assistant. *See also* Darvands.

Tariki (India) "Delivering." *See also* Devi.

Taromaiti (Persia) *see* Spenta Armaiti.

Tartaros (Greek) *see* Tartarus.

Tartarus *Tartaros, Tartus* (Greek)

Also known as: *Erebus, Hades, Hell.*

Underworld. Tartarus, the final stop for the souls of wicked mortals, is the deepest part of the underworld, a dark and abysmal place often referred to as Hades' kingdom. It is surrounded by black rivers, a bronze fence and iron gates. The guards are either the Hecantonchires, who are three giants, each with fifty heads and one hundred arms, or Cerberus, the multiheaded dog who never sleeps. Originally Tartarus was a prison for gods who had been ousted from Olympus and many Titans who were the enemies of Zeus ended up in this hell. One must cross the rivers Acheron, Cocytus, Phlegethon, Lethe and Styx under the employ of Charon, the ancient ferryman, to reach this destination. There are several points of entry to the final stop: Epirus, Heraclea Pontica, and Colonus. Erebus, also a place where souls go to die, is frequently used as a synonym for Tartarus. The personification of Tartarus, also known as Tartarus, was born out of Chaos, as were Gaea (the earth personified) and Eros (love personified). By his sister Gaea, Tartarus became the father of Typhoeus and possibly the immortal monster Echidna. Compare Tartarus to Jigoku and Yomi (Japan) and Tuat (Egypt). *See also* Acheron; Aither; Cerberus; Charon; Cocytus; Dis; Enceladus; Erebus; Gaea; Hades; Hecatonchires; Hell; Lethe; Phlegethon; Pluto; Styx; Typhon (A).

Tartus (Greek) *see* Tartarus.

Tarutius (Etruscan) The wealthy spouse of Acca Larentia.

Tashmetrum (Sumer)

Goddess of writing. She is the wife of Nabu, the god of writing.

Tashmetum *Tashmetu* (Sumer) *see* Nabu.

Tashmishu *Tasmisu, Tasmisus* (Hurrian, Hittite) *see* Shaushka; Teshub.

Tasmisu (Hurrian, Hittite) *see* Tashmishu.

Tasmisus (Hurrian, Hittite) *see* Tashmishu.

Tathagata (Nepal) *see* Buddha; Dhyani Buddhas; Nyorai; Sahasrabhuja; Sakyamuni.

Tathagata Mahavairokana (India) *see* Dainichi-nyorai.

Tathenen (Egypt) *see* Tanunen.

Tatjenen (Egypt)

Tatjenen is an early god of the Memphite region who was later identified with Ptah of Memphis. He is shown as a bearded man wearing a crown with two feathers and a solar disc above a pair of ram's horns. *See also* Ptah.

Tatsuta-Hiko (Japan) *see* Tatsuta-Hime.

Tatunen (Egypt)

"One, the Maker of Mankind." Creator. Tatunen is the same as Tanen (q.v.).

Tatzitzebe (Choco People, Columbia, South America)

High god. *See also* Caragabi.

Taueret *Ta-urt, Tueris* (Egypt)

Also known as: *Apet, Opet, Rerit, Rert, Rertu, Ririt, Theoris* (Greek), *Tuart.*

Hippopotamus Goddess. Goddess and Protector of Childbirth. Goddess of Vengeance. Underworld Goddess. Protector women and their offspring during their infancy. During the New Empire worship of Taueret was so popular in Thebes that children were named after her. Her images were found in many homes. She is portrayed as a hippopotamus with large udders who is standing upright on her hind feet. One hand is on the Sa (life preserver). As the goddess of vengeance, she has the body of a hippopotamus and the head of a lioness. She brandishes a dagger. Sometimes she carries a huge crocodile with open jaws on her shoulders. Taueret is associated with Bes (q.v.) *See also* Apet; Sa; Theoris.

Taurt (Egypt) *see* Taueret; Theoris.

Tauru (Persia) *see* Taurvi.

Taurvi *Tauru* (Zoroastrian; Persia)

The archdemons Taurvi and Zairishi are the opponents of the goddesses Haurvatat and Ameretat. *See also* Daevas; Haurvatat; Zairishi.

Taus (Middle Eastern) *see* Azazel.

Tauthe (Babylonia) *see* Apsu; Belus (C); Tiamat.

Tawals (Polish) *see* Datan; Lawkapatim.

Tawendonare (Brazil) *see* Tawenduare.

Tawenduare *Tawendonare* (Tupi-Guarani People, Brazil)

God of daylight. Tawenduare is the constant foe of his brother Arikute, god of night and always the victor in their struggle. *See also* Arikute.

Taweskare (North America) *see* Yoskeha and Taweskare.

Tawhaki (Hawaii, Polynesia, New Zealand)

Also known as: *Kaha'i* (Hawaii), *Tafa'i* (Tahiti).

Maori god of thunder and lightning. Tawhaki is the grandson of the fighter Kaitangata and the cannibal chieftain from the sky, Whaitiri. He is the son of Hema and a goddess. His brother is Kariki (known as Aliki in Hawaii). Many stories of Tawhaki revolve around the adventures he shares with Kariki as they search for their father. Hema had been abducted by the goblins, beaten unmercifully and thrown into a pit for trespassing on their property. Tawhaki and his wife are the parents of Wahieroa, who in turn had a son, Rata. Tawhaki caused the great flood either by stamping on the floor of heaven which cracked allowing the waters to flood the earth, or by causing his mother's excessive weeping by his actions. Another version says Tawhaki caused the flood as revenge on an attempt to kill him. There is a version that tells of Tawhaki and his brother searching for their father, Hema, in the sky where they ran into

Whaitiri, the cannibal cheiftain, who is his grandmother in many myths. Kariki was killed by falling from the spider web that leads to heaven. Some versions say Tawhaki found his wife in the upperworld and stayed there as a deity of lightning. Others say he brought his wife (unnamed) to earth where she bore him a son, Wahieroa, who in turn married and fathered Rata. In a mixed up tale, Wahieroa was killed by Matuku (a cannibal giant) before Rata was born. There are numerous comments about the attractive, gleaming red skin of Tawhaki. He was irresistible to women. He is sometimes shown as bird. His exploits are similar to those of Maui and Tane. In Maori myth, Tawhaki is the youngest son of the goddess Urutonga ("South West") and Hema. *See also* Kaitangata; Rata; Wahieroa.

Tawhiri (Polynesia) *see* Tane; Tawhiri-ma-tea.

Tawhiri-ma-tane (Polynesia) *see* Tawhiri-ma-tea.

Tawhiri-ma-tea *Tawhiri-ma-tane* (Polynesia)
Also known as: *Tane, Tawhiri.*
A god of winds, hurricanes and storms, he is the son of Rangi, the sky father, and mother earth, Papa. His brothers are Tu and Tane. He opposed the separation of his parents, Rangi and Papa, by Tane, to create the world. To show his displeasure, Tawhiri caused huge storms and vicious whirlwinds which destoyed his brother Tane's forests. This in turn caused the perpetual war between Tane and Tangaroa. Tawhiri-ma-tea might have caused the destroying deluge. He is the father of thirteen children, two who are strong winds and eleven who are clouds. Some of the children's names are A-Kahiwahiwa (Fiery Black Clouds), Ao-Kanapanapa (Glowing Red Clouds), Ao-Nui (Dense Clouds), Ao-Pakakina (Wildly Drifting Clouds), Ao-Potango (Dark Heavy Clouds), Ao-Pouri (Dark Clouds), Ao-Roa (Thick Clouds), Ao-Takawe (Scurrying Clouds), Ao-Whetuma (Fiery Clouds), Apu-Hua (Fierce Squalls) and Apu-Matangi (Whirlwind). *See also* Ao-Pouri; Ao-Toto; Papa; Rangi; Tane; Tangaroa.

Tawiscara *Taweskare, Tawiskaro, Tawiskorong* (Huron, Iroquois People, North America) *see* Yoskeha and Taweskare.

Tawiskaro (North America) *see* Yoskeha and Taweskare.

Tawiskorong (North America) *see* Yoskeha and Taweskare.

Taygete (Greek)
She is one of the Pleiades and one of the great god Zeus' innumerable lovers. From their union, she had a son, Lacedaemon (q.v.). *See also* Pleiades.

Tchabu (Egypt)
Tchabu, the god of drink, is mentioned in a hymn to Hapi, the god of the Nile, along with the god of corn, Nepra and Ptah. *See also* Hapi; Ptah.

Tcheft (Egypt)
Tcheft is a title for the goddess Isis as the goddess of food that is offered to the gods.

Tchemtch-hat (Egypt) *see* Aai.

Tcheser-Tep *Teheser-Tep-f* (Egypt)
A serpent demon mentioned in the magical formula of Unas. *See also* Assessors; Shesemu; Shesmu.

Tchet-s (Egypt)
A winged monster serpent in the eleventh sector of Tuat. Probably the same as Tcheser-Tep.

Tcolawitze (Hopi People, North America)
Either a god of fire or fire itself.

Te-aka-ia-oe (Polynensia) *see* Avaiki; Vatea.

Te-manava-roa (Polynesia) *see* Avaiki; Vatea.

Te-Po-ma-Te-Maki (Oceanic)
This is another name for one of the first people. *See also* De Babou and De Ai; Nareau.

Te-tangaengae (Polynesia) *see* Avaiki; Vatea.

Te Tumu *Te Temu* (Polynesia) *see* Rangi; Ta'aroa; Tangaroa.

Te-vaerua (Polynesia) *see* Avaiki; Vatea.

Tebati (Egypt) *see* Aai.

Tebi (Egypt) A name given to one of the solar gods.

Tecciztecatl *Teccuciztecatl, Teciztecatl* (Aztec People, Mexico)
Also known as: *Coyolxauhqui, Meztli* (Female or Male), *Tezcatlipoca, Yohualticitl* (the Lady of the Night).
Moon god. Tecciztecatl offered to light the sun, but because of fear of the sacred fire refused to enter the flames. Nanahuatzin entered the flames and became the sun. Because of Tecciztecatl's cowardice the gods threw a rabbit into the moon and thus Tecciztecal became the moon. He is shown as an old man with butterfly wings. He is the same as Meztli. Tecciztecatl was replaced by the goddess Coyolxauhqui. *See also* Coxcoxtli; Coyolxauhqui; Meztli; Nanahuatzin; Yohualticitl.

Teccuciztecatl (Mexico) *see* Tecciztecatl.

Tecmassa (Greek)
Tecmassa was either the wife or mistress of Ajax the Greater.

Tecpatl (Aztec People, Mexico)
God of the north. One of four year-bearers or year gods. Tecpatl is in charge of region of the north, and of the destiny of the person who is in this point of space and time. The other year gods are Acatl, Tochtli and Calli. *See also* Acatl; Calli; Tochtli.

Tectamus (Greek)
King of Crete. He is the brother of the king of the Dorians, Aegimius, and the father of Asterius. (Some say Minos and Pasiphae are Asterius' parents.) *See also* Aegimius.

Tecuciztecatl (Aztec) *see* Tecciztecatl.

Tecumbalam (Central America) *see* Xecotcovach.

Tefenet (Egypt) *see* Tefnut.

Tefnut *Tefenet* (Egypt)
Goddess of rain, dew and mist. She is the daughter of Atum, the sister-consort of Shu and the mother of Geb and Nut. Shu and Tefnut were the first couple of the Ennead of Heliopolis. Tefnut is depicted as a woman with a lioness' head or as a lioness. Tefnut and Shu were created by the self-copulation of

the sun god Ra or Tem, or were born from his spittle. After Thoth criticized her for having abandoned Egypt and leaving the country desolate, she wept great tears, but her tears soon turned to anger. She changed into a ferocious, bloodthirsty lioness, and her mane smoked with fire as her face glowed like the sun. She roamed drenched in the blood of her enemies. Shu and Tefnut may be associated with the underworld. Tefnut is represented as a lioness or lioness-headed. Sometimes, she is seen in human form wearing a sun's disk encircled by a cobra on her head. In Buto, Tefnut and Shu were worshipped in the form of flamingo-like children (symbolic for the sun and moon). She is identified with Nehemauit, Menhit, Sekhet, Apsit, Khepri, Ra, Atum, Anat, Amun, Aai, Anhur and Shu. *See also* Atum; Ennead; Geb.

Tegeates (Greek)
He was the lover of Acacallis and is possibly the father of Cydon. *See also* Acacallis.

Tehabi (Hopi People, North America)
"Mudhead, the Clown." Trickster deity.

Teharonhiawagon (North America) *see* Yoskeha.

Tehenut (Egypt) *see* Neith.

Teheser-Tep-f *Tcheser-Tep, Tcheser-Tep-f.* (Egypt)
A deified being or possibly a god. He is one of the forty-two judges in the Hall of Maati. He examined the bodies of the dead gods after they were captured by Am-kehun. If they were found fit, the bodies were bound by Her-thertu and their throats were cut and intestines removed by the god Khensu, then Shesemu butchered and cooked them for the deified king Unas. *See also* Unas.

Tehuti (Egypt)
Also known as: *Aah Tehuti, Djehuty, Thoth.*
"The Measurer." Tehuti is a title of Thoth. As Tehuti, he has the power to grant life to the deceased for millions of years. *See also* Aah; Ape; Thoth.

Teiresias (Greek) Another spelling for Tiresias, the great seer.

Teirnyon Furf Liant (Celtic) *see* Pryderi.

Teka-Hra (Egypt)
A monster serpent who guards the entrance to the Fifth Division or Fifth Hour of Tuat. *See also* Aau.

Tekhi (Egypt)
Tekhi is the goddess of the first month of the year. In some cases she is considered the female counterpart of Thoth. She is shown wearing a pair of high feathers.

Tekikinto (Micronesia) Another name for Nareau.

Tekikitea (Micronesia) *see* Nareau.

Tekitekite (Micronesia) *see* Nareau.

Tekkeitsertok (Eskimo People)
God of earth. He is a high hunting god who owns all the deer.

Telamon (Greek)
King of Salamis. An Argonaut. Member of the Calydonia Boar Hunt. He is the son of the king of Aegina, Aeacus, and Creusa (some say Endeis, who is the daughter of Cheiron and Chariclo). His brother is Peleus and his half-brother is Phocus. Telamon had three wives: Glauce, who burned to death at her wedding; Periboea, who went to Greece as a sacrifice for the Minotaur; and Hesione, who was rescued from a whale's stomach by Heracles. *See also* Aeacus; Ajax the Greater; Glauce; Hesione; Peleus; Periboea; Phocus.

Telavel (Lithuania)
The god of smiths and iron, Telavel, forged the sun and put it in the sky.

Telchines (Greek, Crete, Boeotia; Phoenicia)
Also known as: *Korubantes* (Crete) *Kouretes.*
Sorcerers. Rain-bringers. The Telchines are sons of the sea god, Poseidon, and Thalassa or possibly sons born from the blood of Uranus. Some of their names are Antaeus, Lycus, Megalesius, and Ormenos. They have five other brothers and a sister, the sea-woman Halia. When they mixed water from the River Styx with sulphur they ruined the harvest and killed the flocks. They are similar to the Caberi (q.v.). *See also* Corybantes; Dactyls; Poseidon; Styx.

Telchis *Telchin* (Greek)
With Thelxion, seized the throne of Apis. *See also* Apis (B); Niobe (B).

Teledamas (Greek)
Teledamas is the twin brother of Pelops. Their parents are Agamemnon and Cassandra. *See also* Agamemnon; Cassandra; Pelops.

Teledice (Greek)
She is the possible mother of Apis, Car and Niobe. *See also* Car; Niobe (B).

Teledyne (Greek) *see* Apis (B).

Telegonus (Greek)
He is the son of Odysseus and Circe. His siblings are Ardeas (who was later changed into a heron), Agrius and perhaps Latinius. Telemachus is his half-brother. Unknowingly, Telegonus killed his father Odysseus. Later, he married Penelope, his father's wife. He is not to be confused with Telegonus the spouse of Io, or Telegonus the son of Proteus. *See also* Calypso; Circe; Odysseus; Telemachus.

Telemachus (Greek)
He is the son of Odysseus and Penelope. His half-brother is Telegonus. Odysseus had disappeared from Troy for twenty years. During a part of that period Telemachus was taught by Athena. When old enough he left in search of his father. He met up with him in Eumaeus' hut. The three men killed all of Penelope's suitors. Telemachus also killed his father's consort, the sorcerer Circe, and then he fled to Italy. *See also* Calypso; Odysseus; Penelope; Telegonus.

Telephassa (Greek)
Also known as: *Argiope* (possibly).
She is the spouse of king Agenor and the mother of Cadmus, Cilix, Demodoce, Europa, Phineus, Phoenix, Thasus and possibly Argus. She went with her sons in search of Europa, who

had been kidnapped. There is a possibility that Telephassa and Argiope are two different women. *See also* Agenor (A); Europa.

Telepinus *Telepinu* (Hittite)
Also known as: *Marduk* (possibly).

Telepinus, the son of Teshub, is the god of youth, agriculture, and fertility. Occasionally he would leave the area. His absence created numerous difficulties. The land would become blighted and famine would abound. Angry one day, he disappeared again. Finding him was imperative. Hannahannas, the queen of heaven, sent a bee to search for him. The bee found him asleep in a meadow and stung him. He was so infuriated that he destroyed everything around him. The queen sent an eagle to return him to her. With the assistance of beautiful young women (possibly the Gulsa goddesses), the goddess of healing Kamrusepas, who brought along sesame and nectar, he was cleansed of his negativity. Then all good things were restored to earth. Compare to the Ugaritic Baal. *See also* Kamrusepas; Marduk; Teshub.

Telexiepeia (Greek) *see* Sirens.

Telipinu (Hittite) *see* Telepinus; Teshub

Telkhis (Greek) *see* Apis (B)

Tellus (Roman)
Also known as: *Gaea* (Greek); *Tellus Mater.*
Earth goddess. A pregnant cow was sacrificed to her. Associated with Pales. *See also* Gaea; Rhea.

Tellus Mater (Roman) *see* Tellus.

Telpochtli (Mexico) *see* Texcatlipoca.

Tem (Egypt) *see* Khepri.

Tem-Asar (Egypt) *see* Atum.

Tem-Sep (Egypt) *see* Assessors.

Temazcalteci (Mexico) *see* Ciuacoatl; Tonantzin.

Temt (Egypt)
Creator goddess. Little known ancient deity who is associated with or counterpart of the creator god, Tem.

Temtemtch (Egypt) *see* Aai.

Temu (Egypt)
Also known as: *Atem, Atmu, Atum, Tem, Tum.*
Sun deity. He either replaced Amen, or he is a form of Amen and Amen-Ra. *See also* Amen; Atem; Ra.

Tenages (Greek)
He is one of the Heliades and reputed to be the smartest. *See also* Heliades.

Tenazuchi-no-kami (Japan)
"Hand-Stroking-Elder." Asi-na-duti, an earthly deity, and Tenazuchi-no-kami are the parents of the rice goddess, Kushinada-hime, who is the youngest of eight daughters. *See also* Kushi-nada-hime.

Tenen (Egypt) *see* Tanunen.

Tengere Kaira Kan (Altaic, Tartars)
"Compassionate Heavenly Lord." *See also* Bai Ulgan.

Tengeri (Buryats) *see* Tangri.

Tengri (Kalmyks, Mongol People) *see* Tangri.

Tengu, The (Buddhist; Japan)
Spirits. Minor deities. Goblins. The Tengu are playful and sometimes evil spirits who live in the treetops, especially among the mountains. They hatch from eggs and live in colonies with a leader. The leader, Sojobo, is served by a messenger Tengu. Sojobo wears red robes and a small coronet and carries a fan made of feathers in his right hand. He has a large, aquiline nose and wears a fierce expression. His inferiors, known as Koppatengu, have mouths like beaks and bodies with small wings. The Tengu like to play tricks but do not like to be tricked. They are responsible for volcanoes and bad storms. The Tengu are thought to be reincarnated spirits of arrogant, malevolent people, particularly priests or warriors. These demons are depicted as small, bird-like men. They are sometimes shown wearing cloaks of feathers or leaves. The Tengu messenger is dressed in leaves. The aquiline nose is said to be a symbol of pride. Compare the Tenju to the Oni and Kappa. *See also* Gaki; Shiko-me.

Tenochtitlan (Mexico) *see* Huitzilopochtli.

Tenshodaijin (Japan)
A name for the goddess of light, Amaterasu (q.v.). *See also* Ama-Terasu-o-mi-kami.

Tenshoko-dagin (Japan) *see* Amaterasu.

Tenshoko-Daijin (Japan) *see* Amaterasu.

Tenshokokdaijin (Japan) *see* Amaterasu.

Tent-Baiu (Egypt)
The name of the Third Hour in Tuat. The gods of the country the souls pass through are called "Hidden Souls," and the Field (country?) is called Net-neb-ua-kheper-autu, mastered by the god Khatra. The boat of Ra is preceded by three other boats containing the nine forms of Osiris. *See also* Tuat.

Tentamides (Greek)
During a celebration in honor of his return (according to other sources the event was the funeral games of the father of Tentamides of Larissa), Perseus threw a discus (said to be his invention) and accidentally killed Acrisius. *See also* Perseus.

Tentit-uhesqet-khat-ab (Egypt)
The name of the Tenth Hour of Tuat. The region Osiris passes through is called Akert and the city is called Metchet-qat-utebu which has the pylon Aa-kheperu-mes-aru. The serpents mentioned are Thes-hrau and Ankh-ta. The gods who are identified in this hour are Tepthera, Shesera, Temau, Utu, Setu, Rau, Khesfu, Nekenu, Pesthi, Shemerthi, Thesu, and Kha-a. There is also mentioned the living beetle, P-ankhi, two additional serpents, Menenui, and the goddesses Netheth and Kenat, and Seftit. Eight more gods called Ermenui, Neb-aqet, Tua-khu, Her-she-taiu, Sem-Heru, Tua-Heru, Khenti-ast-f, and Khenti-ment are met on the journey of Osiris through this realm. *See also* Tuat.

Teoti-Husn (Mexico) *see* Teotihuancan.

Teotihuacan (Mexico) *see* Teotihuancan.

Teotihuancan *Teotihuacan* (Aztec People, Mexico)
Also known as: *Teoti-Husn.*
"City of the Gods." Sacred city. Although an actual city, mythically, it is the place where the gods met to create the fifth and final sun. The fifth sun is now, our present age. It is called Nahui Ollin, meaning four motion. Nahui Ollin is ruled by the sun god Tonatiuh or some say Xiuhtecuhth. The largest of the ancient cities, Teotihuancan is the site of the great pyramids of Mexico. Originally inhabited by the Nahua-speaking people around 400 B.C.E., the Toltecs invaded and ransacked the area in about C.E. 650. The Temple of Quetzalcoatl, the Pyramid of the Moon and the Pyramid of the Sun are located in Teotihuancan.

Teoyaoimquit *Teoyaomiqui* (Aztec People, Mexico)
Also known as: *Huahuantli* ("Striped One").
He is the god of warriors who die in battle. Teoyaoimquit is also the Lord of the Sixth Hour of the Day. *See also* Huahuantli; Lords of the Day Hours; Tepeyollotl.

Tep-tu-f (Egypt) *see* Anubis.

Tepen (Egypt)
A monster serpent in the Fifth Sector of Tuat. He carries offerings made by the living to the hawk-headed god, Seker. *See also* Seker; Tuat.

Tepeu (Maya People, Yucatan)
Creator. One of the seven regents, or gods that created everything. The council of seven solar gods decided to change the existing vegetation world and made several attempts. Tepeu is generally found with Gucumatz and Hurakan. *See also* Gucumatz; Huracan; Ixmucane; Ixpiyacoc.

Tepeyollotl *Tepeyolohtli* (Aztec, Zapotec People, Mexico)
Also known as: *Jaguar God, Teoyaoimquit, Tlaltecutli.*
His name means "Heart of the Mountains." He is the Lord of the eighth hour of the night. He is described as the spotted jaguar monster who leaps out to seize the declining sun. He is also called Tlaltecutli, the "Lord of the Earth," and the "Toad with Gaping Jaws." Tepeyollotl is probably the same as Mictlantecutli. *See also* Legend of the Four Suns; "L"; Lords of the Night Hours; Teoyaoimquit; Tlaltecutli.

Tepeyolohtli (Mexico) *see* Tepeyollotl.

Tepi (Egypt)
This monster serpent has four human heads, four breasts, and four pairs of human arms and legs. It is found in the Ninth Sector of Tuat. *See also* Ab-ta; Tepui.

Tepictoton (Aztec People, Mexico)
The Tepictoton are mountain dwarfs who are protectors of mountains. They might be related to the underground caverns called Tepeyollotl.

Tepoztecatl (Aztec People, Mexico)
Tepoztecatl is a local deity of Tepoztlan, who was born of a virgin.

Tepui (Egypt)
Afterworld deity. A two-headed god who appears in the eleventh sector of Tuat.

Ter (Egypt)
This two-headed monster serpent is found in the Fifth Sector of Taut.

Tera (Greek) *see* Rhea.

Tera, Mount (Persia) *see* Alburz (Mount).

Terah (Middle Eastern) *see* Elohim.

Teraphim *Teraph* (Hebrew)
The Teraphim are small household gods who provide protection for the family members. These gods are connected with ancestors.

Tere (Banda People, Africa)
Sky deity. Brother of Ngakola. His task is to take animals and seeds to earth. Once, he dropped the basket, releasing the contents of life-giving water. He chased the animals and the ones he caught became the domestic animals; the ones who got away are now the wild animals.

Tereus (Greek)
Deified mortal. According to different legends, Tereus either cut out his wife Procne's tongue and married her sister, Philomela, or he dishonored Philomela and cut out her tongue so that she might not reveal his misdeed. In any case, the sisters communicated with each other and Procne killed her son Itys and served up his flesh to Tereus out of revenge. When the sisters fled, pursued by Tereus, the gods changed all three into birds; Procne, a swallow; Philomela, a nightingale; and Tereus, a hawk. *See also* Aedon; Ares; Boreas.

Terminus (Roman)
Guardian. A lesser god of the Romans. Terminus is a boundary god who guards the edges of property. A stone dedicated to him was oiled and covered with plants, then placed in a hole which had been hallowed with the blood of a victim, usually a pig or lamb.

Terminalius (Greek)
"Protector of Boundaries." An epithet of Zeus. *See also* Terminus.

Terpimbrotos (Greek) *see* Helius.

Terpsichore (Greek)
One of the Muses. Terpsichore, goddess of dance, is usually seen wearing a crown of laurel and carrying a lyre. *See also* Muses; Sirens.

Terra (Roman)
Also known as: *Gaea* (Greek), *Tellus, Titaea.*
Goddess of the earth. *See also* Aello; Gaea; Harpies.

Tertiana (Roman) *see* Febris.

Teshub (Hittite)
God of rain and thunderstorms. King of gods. His brother is Tashmishu. His consort is Khepan, or Hepit. (Hepit's sister is Shoushka the Hurrian goddess of sexuality and marriage.) Teshub is the owner of the storm bulls Sheri and Khurri. Kumarbi slept with a rock and created a giant stone son, Ullikummi, to kill Teshup. Teshub and Tashmishu fought valiantly to overcome Ullikummi. Finally the great god Ea came to the rescue and with the giant who holds up the earth, Upelluri, they emerged the victors. A relief from the New Empire

shows Teshub in the form of a bull. This is the only case in the Hittite pantheon in which an animal stood for a god. In other representations he is standing on a bull or bulls pull his chariot. Teshub has also been depicted carrying a single ax. *See also* Adad; Ea; Hepit; Telipinu.

Tessub (Cassite) *see* Rimmon (Babylon).

Tet *Djed* (Egypt)
The symbol of Osiris. It is usually an amulet that represents stability or durability. It is similar in nature to Thet (Djet) which was the girdle, buckle or knot of Isis.

Tetenen (Egypt) *see* Tanunen.

Teteoinnan (Aztec People, Mexico)
"Mother of the Deities." An earth goddess. *See also* Ciuacoatl; Huitzilopochtli; Tlazolteutl; Tonantzin.

Tethus (Greek) *see* Tethys.

Tethys *Tethus* (Greek)
Rhea (the earth personified) took her daughter Hera (also earth) to Tethys to be cared for, since without water earth cannot exist. In the Pelasgian creation myth Tethys and Oceanus were the rulers of the planet Venus. Tethys is the Titaness daughter of Uranus and Gaea who married her brother, Oceanus. *See also* Achelous; Acheron; Alpheus; Amphitrite; Apsyrtus; Asopus; Calypso; Cephissus; Clytia; Cocytus; Cronus; Eurynome (A); Gaea; Hera; Inachus; Naiads; Oceanids; Oceanus; Styx; Themis.

Tetzcotzingo (Aztec People, Central Mexico)
Also known as: *Bald Rock.*
Sacred place. Worship takes place at Tetzcotzingo for rain, water, earth, and vegetation.

Teu (Teutonic) *see* Tyr.

Teucer (Greek)
He is the founder of the city of Salamis. His parents are Telamon and Hesione. Ajax is his half-brother. *See also* Ajax the Greater; Cinyras; Hesione.

Teuhie (Polynesia)
Creator. Teuhie is one of the foster parents of Eel (also known as Tuna) who was lover of Hina. The other parent was Kaloafu. *See also* Hina.

Teutamias (Greek) King of Larissa. *See also* Danae.

Teutates (Celtic)
Supreme deity. The human sacrifices to this god were killed by having the victim plunged headlong into a vat.

Tezcatlipoca *Tezcatepuca, Texcatlipoca, Tezcatlipo'ca* (Mexico, Aztec, Toltec)
Also known as: *Camaxte, Camaxtli, Chalchiuhtotolin, Huitzilopochtli, Ipalnemoani* (Lord of the Near and the Nigh), *Itzlacoliuhqui, Ixtlilton, Iztli, Iztli-Tezcatlipoca* (Stone Knife God of the Underworld), *Metztli* (moon god), *Moquequeloa, Moyocoyani* (Maker of Himself), *Omacatl, Telpochtli* (Lord of Festivities and Banquets), *Tepeyollotl* (Heart of the Mountain), *Tezcatlipoca, Titlacauan* (He who is closest to the shoulder),

Tloque Nauaque, Toueyo, Xipe Totec, Yaotl, Yoalli Ehecatl (Night Wind), *Yaotl* (The Enemy).
"Smoking Mirror." Supreme deity. Sun god. God of darkness. Foremost recipient of human sacrifice. Giver and taker of life. Bringer of fortune and misfortune. Patron of rulers. Protector of warriors. God of the north. God of fate and punitive justice. God of cold. God of darkness. Patron of sorcerers, magicians, and thieves. Patron of Trecena 1 Ocelotl in the Tonalamatl (Aztec calendar). Shape-changer. Representative of the sun in the four directions of the Universe. Tezcatlipoca, the foremost of the gods, is the son of Ometeotl and his spouse who is also himself, Omecihuatl. His brothers are Huitzilopochtli, Quetzalcoatl and Xipe Totec. With the advent of their births the cycle of birth and death, creation and destruction was put into motion. Before humans were created, Tezcatlipoca put out his gargantuan foot to tempt the Earth Monster also known as Cipactli, the great crocodile, to come up from the primordial waters. Earth Monster rose up and snapped off his foot. In retaliation, Tezcatlipoca ripped off her jaw. Earth Monster would never again sink into the waters. From that day she became the earth. It was on her back that all humans were created and to this day live. In place of his missing foot, Tezcatlipoca wears a dark obsidian mirror. His obsidian mirror reflects the future. It also allows him to see everything, including what is within the hearts of mortals. (Later, one of Tezcatlipoca's favorite disguises was that of a turkey wearing a mirror in place of his amputated foot.) Many myths relate the constant struggle between Tezcatlipoca and Quetzalcoatl. As Tezcatlipoca is an imperfect god, he is never able to approach the Pole Star, home of the omnipotent, omniscient great dual god, his father, Ometeotl. Instead he is relegated to hopping around on one foot leaving the tracks that make up the Great Bear constellation. He is depicted with his obsidian mirrors and broad bands of yellow and black across his face. He is one of gods of the "Four Eras or Four Suns." He was the god of the First Sun called Nahui Ocelotl, "four tiger." This sun lasted 676 years, then all men perished, devoured by tigers. In this role he is depicted dressed in a tiger skin. *See* Legend of the Four Suns for more information about this period. *See also* Camaxtli; Chimalmat; Citlallatonac; Coxcoxtli; Ehecatl; Huitzilopochtli; Ipalnemoani; Itzcoliuhqui; Quetzalcoatl.

Texcatzoncatl *Tezcatzontecatl* (Aztec; Mexico)
"Straw Mirror." God of drunkards. Pulque deity. Flower god. He is one of the group of brothers called Centzon Totochtin (q.v.). *See also* Cinteotl.

Teyron (Celtic) *see* Rhiannon.

Tez-Katli-Poka (Aztec) *see* Tezcatlipoca.

Tezcatepuca (Aztec) *see* Tezcatlipoca.

Tezcatlipo'ca (Aztec) *see* Tezcatlipoca.

Tezcatzontecatl (Mexico) *see* Texcatzoncatl.

Tgorem (Ugarit)
Also known as: *Num, Torum.*
God of the sky, of order and balance. *See also* Ec; Num.

Thakurani (India) *see* Gramadeveta.

Thalassa (Greek)
Also known as: *Dione.*

Thalassa is the goddess of the sea, personified. She is the mother of the Telchines and Halia. The father is possibly the sea god, Poseidon. *See also* Curetes; Telechines.

Thalath (Babylonia) *see* Belus (B).

Thalestris (Greek) *see* Amazons.

Thalia (A) (Greek)
"Rejoicing." Her parents are the illustrious Zeus and Themis the Titan, who is the personification of order and justice. Her siblings are Aglaea, Pasithea and Euphrosyne. By her father Zeus, she became the mother of the Sicilian twin volcanoes known as the Palici. (Others say that Hephaistos and Aetna are their parents.) Thalia is one of the Graces. *See also* Graces; Hephaistos; Palici.

Thalia (B) (Greek)
One of the nine Muses, Thalia is the muse of comedy. She is the daughter of Zeus and Mnemosyne, the personification of Memory. She carries the mask of comedy and a shepherd's staff. *See also* Corybantes; Muses.

Thalia (C) (Greek)
One of the fifty mermaids known as the Nereids (q.v.).

Thallo (Greek)
One of the Horae (goddesses of the seasons). Thallo is the personification of spring. She is the daughter of Zeus and Themis. Her sister, Carpo, the personification of autumn, is worshipped with her. *See also* Carpo; Horae.

Thaloc (Aztec) *see* Poseidon (Greek).

Thammuz (Babylonian) *see* Tammuz.

Thanantos (Greek) *see* Keres.

Thanatos *Thantos* (Greek)
Also known as: *Mors* (Roman); *Paean.*
God of death. Thanatos is the son of Nox and Erebus and brother of Hypnos. He sent those he struck with his sword to the realm of Hades. Thanatos is depicted as a winged or black-robed man carrying a sword. *See also* Aether; Erebus; Mors; Nemesis; Nox; Sarpedon (B).

Thantos (Greek) *see* Thanatos.

Thasus (Greek)
Thasus is the son of Agenor and Telephassa. *See also* Agenor (A).

Thauk (Teutonic) *see* Thok.

Thaukt (Teutonic) *see* Thok.

Thaumas (Greek)
Sea god. Thaumas is the son of Oceanus and Gaea or Pontus and Gaea. He married his half-sister Electra, the daughter of Oceanus and Tethys. *See also* Aello; Gaea; Harpies; Nereus; Oceanids; Oceanus; Phorcys.

Theano (Greek)
Theano is the daughter of the king of Thrace, Cisseus. It was Theano who gave the Palladium to Diomedes and Odysseus. She also founded Padua after the fall of Troy. She married

Antenor. Her children are Acamas, Agenor, Archelous, Coon, Crino, Demoleon, Iphidamas, Laodamas, Polybus, Glaucus, Helicaon, Laocoon, Lycaon and Polydamas. She also had two children by Metapontus, who killed her and two of her sons when he discovered that they were not his children. *See also* Agenor; Antenor; Diomedes; Metapontus; Odysseus; Polybus.

Theb-ka (Egypt) *see* Anhur.

Thebe (A) (Greek)
She is the daughter of Asopus, the river god, and Metope who was also the daughter of one of the river gods, either Ladon or Peneius. Thebe was abducted by Zeus. *See also* Antaeus; Asopus; Ladon; Zethus.

Thebe (B) (Greek)
She is the daughter of Zeus and the spouse of Ogyges.

Thegn (Teutonic) *see* Heimdall.

Theia (A) *Thia* (Greek)
She is the daughter of the Centaur Cheiron, who was raped by Aeolus. The sea god Poseidon changed her into Evippe, a mare. She became the mother of a foal named Melanippe, who changed into a girl. *See also* Aeolus; Cheiron; Poseidon.

Theia (B) (Greek) The daughter of Memnon.

Theia (C) (Greek)
She is the Titan daughter of Uranus and Gaea, sister spouse of her brother Hyperion, and the mother of Helius, Eos, and Selene. *See also* Cronus; Eos; Eurynome (A); Gaea; Helius; Hyperion; Oceanids; Oceanus.

Thein (Burma)
Rain nats (spirits) who live in the stars. When engaged in fights, they cause thunder and lightning. When rain is needed, the people hold a formal tug-of-war in an attempt to rouse the Thein. *See also* Nats.

Theiodamas (Greek) *see* Hydras.

Theispas (Urartian People, Armenia)
A weather or storm god. One of the triad of deities worshiped by the early Urartians. The other gods were Khaldi who was the supreme or moon deity, and Artinis the sun-god. All may have been forerunners of the Babylonian triad of Sin, Shamas and Ramman. *See also* Artinis.

Thelxiepeia (Greek) She is one of the Sirens (q.v.).

Thelxion (Greek)
Thelxion and Telchin wrenched the throne from Apis. *See also* Apis (B); Cassandra; Niobe (B).

Themehu (Egypt) *see* Aamu.

Themis *Themiste* (Greek)
Also known as: *Ananke.*
Goddess of law and justice. The Titan Themis is the daughter of Uranus and Gaea and the sister of the Titans and the Giants. When the Oceanid Metis, the first wife of Zeus (Hesiodic tradition), was swallowed by Zeus, Themis married the great god. She became the mother of the Moirae (Fates), the Horae (Seasons), Astraea (Justice) and possibly Prometheus

(Forethought) and Clymene. The original goddess of prophecy, she originated the Delphic Oracle and presented it to Zeus as a birthday present. A brilliant deity, advisor and inventor, she personified justice and order. Themis, Ocean, Tethys, Hyperion, Mnemosyne, Iapetus (because of his sons Atlas and Prometheus) were deities from the group known as the Elder Gods. These Titans were not ousted when Zeus toppled Cronus and the Olympians came into power. They were only reduced to a lower rung on the heavenly ladder. In the Pelasgian creation myth, Themis and Eurymedon are the deities who ruled the planet Jupiter. Themis is depicted carrying a cornucopia and scales. Compare Themis to Ananke. *See also* Atlas; Cronus; Dike; Eurynome (C); Evander (B); Fates; Gaea; Giants; Hesperides; Horae; Hyperion; Metis; Mnemosyne; Moirae; Ocean; Prometheus; Tethys; Titans; Uranus; Zeus.

Themiste (Greek)

Themiste is the daughter of Ilus and Eurydice and the sister of Laomedon. Her children are Anchises and Laocoon. *See also* Anchises; Laocoon; Laomedon.

Themisto (Greek)

The daughter of Hypseus, her siblings are Astyagyia, Cyrene, Stilbe and her husband is Athamas. (She was his third wife.) Her children are Erythrius, Leucon, Ptous and Schoeneus. When Themisto found that she had killed her own sons instead of the sons of Athamas and Ino, she committed suicide. *See also* Athamas; Ino.

Then-Aru (Egypt) *see* Aai.

Thenemi (Egypt) *see* Assessors.

Thenenet (Greek) *see* Isis.

Theno (Greek) *see* Acamas (B).

Thenti (Egypt) *see* Aai.

Theonoe (A) (Greek)

Also known as: *Eidothea*.

She is the daughter of Thestor and Megara. Her siblings are Alcmaon, Calchas and Leucippe. *See also* Alcmaon; Calchas.

Theonoe (B) (Greek)

Proteus and the Nereid Psamathe, the daughter of Nereus and Doris, are her parents. Her siblings are Cabeiro and Theoclymenus. *See also* Doris; Nereids; Proteus.

Theophane (Greek)

The beautiful Theophane was kidnapped by Poseidon and she became the mother of the ram who was born with the Golden Fleece. *See also* Golden Fleece; Poseidon.

Theoris *Thoeris* (Egypt, Greek)

Also known as: *Taurt*.

The goddess of women in childbirth and protector of babies, Theoris was called the "Great." She presided over toilet rites. She is sometimes identified with Hathor and is the female counterpart of Bes. She is shown as a female hippopotamus squatting on her haunches. Since the Archaic Period, she is depicted as standing upright with human arms and legs. She held either the attribute of the "sa" (a symbol of protection) or the ankh or a torch as attributes. Her image was often attached to beds and headrests. *See also* Bes; Hathor; Taueret.

Thermuthis (Egypt) *see* Renenet.

Thessalus (A) (Greek)

King of Thessaly. His parents are Heracles and Chalciope. His two sons took thirty ships to the Trojan War. *See also* Pheres (A).

Thessalus (B) (Greek)

His parents are Jason and Medea. For a list of his siblings, see Pheres (A). *See also* Jason; Medea.

Thestius (A) (Greek)

If his father was Ares, he is the possible father of Althea, Hypermnestra, Plexippus and several others. *See also* Althea; Ares.

Thestius (B) (Greek)

His son, Calydon, accidentally killed him.

Thestor (Greek)

Thestor is the son of Apollo or possibly Idmon. He married Megara and became the father of Alcmaon, Calchas, Leucippe and Thenoe. *See also* Calchas.

Theta-enen (Egypt) *see* Aai.

Thethu (Egypt)

A serpent demon mentioned in a magical formula of Unas. *See also* Akeneh.

Thetis (Greek)

Thetis "of the silver feet" is the daughter of Nereus and Doris. Hera raised her. Thetis' sisters are the Nereids. She had been wooed by Zeus and Poseidon until they heard an oracle announce that if Thetis had a son, he would be greater than his father. So, they dropped her in a hurry and forced her to marry Peleus. The goddess of strife, Eris, rolled the Golden Apple at her wedding. When her son Achilles was born, she dipped him in the Styx river to make him invulnerable. She was holding him by the heel and of course, that became his only vulnerable spot. *See also* Achilles; Doris; Eris; Peleus; Styx.

Thevadas (India) *see* Devis.

Thia (Greek) *see* Theia.

Thialfi *Thjalfi* (Norse; Teutonic)

Also known as: *Swift Runner*.

Lightning deity. Brother of Roskva and servant of Thor. Thialfi, encouraged by Loki, broke one of the magic bones of Thor's goat and because of this the peasant family gave their daughter and son to Thor as servants. Associated with Skrymir. Thialfi was beaten in a race with Hugi. *See also* Roskva.

Thiassi *Thjasse, Thjazi, Thiazi* (Norse; Teutonic)

Also known as: *Voland*.

Storm giant. Thiassi is the son of Ivalde and Greip and brother of Egil and possibly Idun. Idun is the guardian of the magic apples which Thiassi coveted to give him back his youth. Idun was finally restored to Valhalla by Loki. Thiassi was killed and burned by the Aesir. *See also* Idun.

Thiazi (Teutonic) *see* Thiassi.

Thing (Iceland. Norse; Teutonic)

Also known as: *Thingstead, Ting*.

The Thing is an assembly of the gods where matters of importance were discussed.

Thingstead (Teutonic) *see* Thing.

Thingsus (Teutonic) *see* Tyr; Ziv.

Thir (Teutonic) *see* Heimdall; Thor.

Thixo (Ponda, Xhosa People, Africa)
Also known as: *Dxui* (Bushmen), *Tsui'* (Hottentot).
Creator god. For details, *see* Tsui'goab.

Thjalfi (Teutonic) *see* Thialfi.

Thjasse (Teutonic) *see* Thiassi.

Thjazi (Teutonic) *see* Thiassi.

Tho-Ag *The Eternal Mother* (Tibet) *see* Aditi.

Tho-Og *The Eternal Mother* (Tibet) *see* Aditi.

Thoas (A) (Greek)
The son of Dionysus or Theseus and Ariadne. When the Lymnian women went insane and killed their spouses, he was the only survivor.

Thoas (B) (Greek)
Also known as: *Deiplus.*
He is the son of Jason and Hypsipyle. He was about to sacrifice Orestes and Pylades when Iphigeneia rescued them. *See also* Jason; Orestes; Pylades.

Thoas (C) (Greek)
King of Aetolia. Thoas was one of Helen's many suitors. He took forty ships to Troy. He was in the Wooden Horse.

Thoas (D) (Greek)
He was killed by Menelaus in the Trojan War.

Thoas (E) (Greek)
He is the giant son of Uranus and Gaea, killed by the Fates.

Thoas (F) (Greek) Aeneas' companion. *See also* Aeneas.

Thoas (G) (Greek)
He is the son of Ornytion, who is the son of Sisyphus and Merope. His brother is Phocus. *See also* Merope; Ornytion; Phocus; Sisyphus.

Thobadzistshini *Thobadestchin* (Navajo People)
He is either the son of Yolkai Estsan or Estanatlehi. *See also* Anaye; Atseatsine.

Thoeris (Greek) *see* Theoris.

Thok (Norse; Teutonic)
Also known as: *Loki* (possibly), *Thauk, Thaukt, Thokk.*
This female giant, representing darkness, is likely an aspect of the trickster fire god Loki. She was the only one who refused to weep for Balder after his death. This prevented him from returning to earth from Hel. *See also* Balder; Loki.

Thokk (Teutonic) *see* Thok.

Thomagata (Chibcha People, Columbia)
Also known as: *Fomagata.*
Thunder deity. Opponent of the sun god Bochicha. Thoma-

gata, an evil deity, with one eye, four ears and a long tail, turns men into animals.

Thomagostad (Niquiran People, Nicaragua)
Chief deity. He lives with his consort, Zipaltonal, in the east. Thomagostad and Zipaltonal created everything.

Thonenli (Navajo People, North America)
He is a water god who belongs to a group of household and nature deities, known as the Yei (q.v.). *See also* Ganaskid.

Thoon (Greek)
Thoon is the giant son of the earth, personified as Gaea. *See also* Giants; Hippolytus (B).

Thoosa (Greek)
Thoosa is the mother of the one-eyed Cyclops, Polyphemus, by the sea god, Poseidon. *See also* Phorcys; Polyphemus.

Thor *Thur, Tor, Tror* (Norse; Teutonic)
Also known as: *Akethor* (a corruption of Ukko-Thor), *Aku-Thor, Donar, Einridi, Finnish, Hloride, Hloridi, Hlorrida, Hlor-ridi, Lorridi, Lothurr* ("The Fighter"), *Thunaer, Thunar, Thunaraz, Thunor, Vingthor.*
God of thunder and lightning. Protector. God of fertility. God of the sky. God of the household. Thor follows Odin as a principal deity in the Norse pantheon. He is Odin's son by Jord or Fjorgyn, or Munon with one of Priamus' daughters, or his mother could be the giant Hlodyn. As a protector who watches over mortals he is always in battle with the wild forces of natures personified by the giant Jotuns. Thunder and lightning are his primary ways of gaining attention. Even his chariot produces its own thunder as it rolls through the skies pulled by the great god's goats Tanngnjost and Tanngrisni. When Thor is holding the reins he is known as Riding-Thor. These goats are amazing animals. Thor, who has to have a voracious appetite because of his size and the energy he expels, kills and eats the goats constantly. As long as he wraps their bones in their hides, they come back to life and are ready to cook and eat again. He is the spouse of the beautiful, blonde Sif. Their children are Modi and Throd (Thrud), or according to some Lorride and Thrud. He is also the father of Magni by the giant Jarnsaxa (Iarnsaxa) and according to other sources, Lorride, or Magni and Modi. Other male children said to be Thor's sons are Veggdegg, Beldegg (another name for Balder), Skjold, Saeming, and Yngve. Thor resides in Bilskirnir, a 540 room palace located in Thrudheim. He owns a few magnificent, magical objects: a hammer called Mjollnir that never misses its target and always returns to him; a pair of iron gauntlets called Iarngreiper to grasp his hammer; and a belt of strength called Megin-giord. Some say that he killed his foster-mother and father, Vingnir and Hlora, then took possession of the kingdom of Thracia. He assumed the names Vingthor and Hlorrida after his foster parents. Thor is the only god who cannot use the bridge Bifrost because of the heat he generates. It did not bother him as he found short cuts to reach the meeting place of the gods at Yggdrasil. As a god of the peasants and a household god his likeness was carved on the master of the household's chair. Thor is always more interested in deeds of strength than in craftsmanship. Thor is described as burly, red-headed, immensely strong, with blazing eyes and a beard. Like Odin, he wears a broad-brimmed hat. He is often

depicted holding his hammer Mjollnir in his hand. Thursday is named after this god (Thunar's Day). As Donar his symbol is the swastika. He resembles the Greek Zeus and Roman Jupiter. Compare Thor to the Celtic god Sucellos, the Yoruba deity, Shango, the Indian gods Indra and Pushan and the Celtic god Dagda. *See also* Aegir; Aesir; Alviss; Ares; Asgard; Balder; Bifrost; Brisingamen; Donar; Heimdall; Hrungnir; Jord; Jotuns; Loki; Magni; Midgard; Mjollnir; Modi; Ragnarok; Saeming; Sif (A); Thialfi; Thrall; Thrud; Thrudheim; Thunor.

Thora (A) (Norse; Teutonic)

Thora, the daughter of Hakon (or possibly Heroth), wife of Elf (or Ragnar Lodbrog), gave refuge to Gudrun and her daughter Svanhild in Denmark for seven and a half years. *See also* Elf.

Thora (B) (Africa) *see* Kaang.

Thot (Egypt) *see* Osiris.

Thoth *Thouth* (Egypt)

Also known as: *Aah, Aah-te-huti, Aah Tehuti, Djehuti, Tehuti, Thout, Thouti, Zehuti.*

God of wisdom, time, astromony, music, magic, medicine, drawing, writing, surveying. Messenger and secretary of the gods. Author of 42 books. He was the protector of Horus (he cured him from scorpion poison) who later followed him as ruler. Thoth attempted to revive Osiris when he had been pulled apart. His followers claim that he creates by sound. The sound of his voice caused the birth of the early deities of Nun by the sound of his voice. The baboon was incorporated into Thoth's cult and became an aspect of his being. When he was sent to retrieve Tefnut, Ra's estranged daughter, he and Shu were disguised as baboons. Thoth is represented as either an ibis or an ibis-headed man, or as a baboon, and sometimes with the head of a dog. His attributes are often a writing palette or a palm leaf. The Greeks identified Thoth with Hermes, and he was also known as Aah. When Thoth was god of the city of Hermopolis, he was either a baboon or an ibis; in Khnum, he was a he-goat, in Memphis, a bull. Thoth's female counterpart is Seshat. *See also* Aah; Aani; Amenhotep; Amit; Maat; Neith; Nut; Osiris; Sopdu.

Thott (Egypt) *see* Aani.

Thoueris (Greek) *see* Theoris.

Thout (Egypt) *see* Thoth.

Thouth (Egypt) *see* Thoth.

Thouti (Egypt) *see* Thoth.

Thraell (Teutonic) *see* Thrall.

Thraetana (Persian) *see* Thraetaona.

Thraetaona (Persian) *see* Ahura Mazda; Haoma; Thrita.

Thrall (Norse; Teutonic)

Also known as: *Thraell.*

Founder of the race of Serfs. He is the son of Heimdall and Edda. Heimdall spent three days in the hut with Rig and Edda and somehow Edda bore Thrall. There are some who say Thrall is the brother of Churl and Jarl. Thrall's wife is Thyr, the drudge. They had ten sons and ten daughters. Thrall has a dark complexion and is heavy set. *See also* Heimdall.

Thrasymedes (Greek)

He is the son of Nestor and Anaxibia or Eurydice. For the names of his siblings, *see* Stratius. *See also* Antilochus.

Thrbadestchin (Navajo People, North America)

A creator god. Son of Estanatlehi.

Three Emperors (China) *see* Fu-Hsi.

Three Goddesses of Munakata (Shinto; Japan)

Daughters of Amaterasu. The three goddesses of Munakata were born of the mist of the sun goddess Amaterasu's breath. Their names and affiliations follow. Takiri-bime-no-mikoto, also known as Okitsushima-hime-no-mikoto (Mist-Princess-Goddess), is thought to have married Opo-kuni-nusi. She is the mother of a daughter, Taka-pime-no-mikoto, and a son, Adi-siki-taka-pikone-no-kami. The second goddess of Munakata is Ichikishima-hime-no-mikoto (variant spellings, Ikiti-simapime-no-mikoto, Ikiti-sima-pime-no-mikoto), also known as Sayori-bime-no-mikoto (variant spelling, Sa-yori-bime-no-mikoto). The third goddess of Munakata is Takitsu-hime-no-mikoto (variant spelling, Takitu-pime-no-mikoto) (Seething-Water-Princess-Goddess). These goddesses are recorded in the *Kojiki* and the *Nihongi* and are included among the Hachi-o-jo or "Eight Rulers." The three goddesses of Munakata are described by Susanowo as graceful maidens. For the Shinto creation myth and additional details about the *Kojiki* and *Nihongi*, *see* Ama-no-minaka-nushi. *See also* Amaterasu; Susanowo.

Three Legged Ass (Persia)

The Three Legged Ass is a benevolent deity of disease and pests. He has three feet, six eyes, nine mouths, two ears and a horn. He is as big as a mountain and each foot covers as much ground as a thousand sheep. His task is to destroy the worst disease and pests.

Three Norns, The (Scandinavia) *see* Eumenides.

Thrita (Persian)

Also known as: *Faridun* (name in later times), *Thraetana, Thraetaona, Thrita Athwya, Trita Aptya.*

As Thrita he is the healer and preparer of haoma and the one who drives away serious illness and death from mortals. Thrita was the third man who prepared haoma for the corporeal world. (His name means third.) His prayers to Ahura Mazda brought all the healing plants that grow round the Gaokerena tree in Vourukasha, the cosmic ocean. As Thraetaona (Faridun in the later texts), he is a healer and a victorious warrior. He battled the three-headed, three-jawed, six-eyed mighty dragon, Azhi Dahaka. He is called upon to relieve itches, fevers, incontinency, and to keep evil people away. These discomforts are all attributed to the power of Azhi-Dahak. Thrita defeated the dragon with his club but could not slay him. When he finally took a sword and stabbed the evil dragon, a multitude of horrible creatures crept from his loathsome body. Fearful of the world being filled with such vile creatures as snakes, toads, scorpions, lizards, tortoises, and frogs, Thrita refrained from cutting the monster to pieces. Instead he bound and imprisoned him in Mount Demavand, where to this day he causes earthquakes. It is said that mortals will one day regret Thrita's action. It is Thraetaona who seized Yima's "khvarenanh" (his glory) when it left his body and then became the ruler of Yima's realm. He divided the kingdom between his sons Airya, Cairima, and Tura. In other legends, Thrita is represented as the father of Thraetaona. Thrita is killed by Azhi Dahaka (who represents frost). Thraetaona avenges his father's death by tying Azhi Dahaka to Mount Demavend. Traetasona sometimes reveals himself in the shape of a vulture. *See also* Ahura Mazda; Gaokerna Tree; Haoma; Kava; Trita (India); Vourukasha; Yima; Zahhak.

Thronia (Greek)

Thronia is the daughter of Belus, the king of the Egyptians, and Anchinoe, the daughter of the river god Nile. *See also* Agenor (A); Danaus.

Thrud (Teutonic)

Also known as: *Might.*

Thrud is the giant daughter of Thor and Sif and the sister of Lorride. Her lover was the dwarf, Alvis, who was petrified by sunlight because he failed to prove his mental powers to Thor. *See also* Magni; Thor.

Thrud-Heim (Teutonic) *see* Thrudheim.

Thrud-Vang (Teutonic) *see* Thrudheim.

Thrudgelmer (Teutonic) *see* Thrudgelmir.

Thrudgelmir *Thrudgelmer* (Norse; Teutonic)

Thrudgelmir, a six-headed frost giant, was born from the feet of Ymir. In turn, Thrudgelmir bore the giant Bergelmir, father of all frost giants. *See also* Bergelmir; Ymir.

Thrudheim *Thrud-Heim* (Norse; Teutonic)

Also known as: *Thrud-Vang, Thrudheimr, Thrudvangr, Thrudvarg.*

Home of gods. Thor's home in Asgard. Thor's mansion in Thrudheim is named Bilskirnir.

Thrudheimr (Teutonic) *see* Thrudheim.

Thrudvangr (Teutonic) *see* Thrudheim.

Thrudvarg (Teutonic) *see* Thrudheim.

Thrym (Teutonic)

Also known as: *Thrymr.*

Thrym is the frost giant who stole Thor's hammer. He was killed by Thor. Sometimes called the King of the Frost Giants. *See also* Loki.

Thrymr (Teutonic) *see* Thrym.

Thu (China) *see* She-chi.

Thunaer (Teutonic) *see* Thor.

Thunar (Teutonic) *see* Thor; Thunor.

Thunaraz (Teutonic) *see* Thor.

Thuner (Teutonic) *see* Thunor.

Thunor (Norse; Teutonic)

Also known as: *Thor, Thunar, Thuner.*

A Germanic sky god, Thunor is similar to Jupiter of the Romans. His symbols are the great oaks of central and western Europe. The name Thunor is one of Thor's alternate names. Thunor may have been the forerunner of Thor. Some say Thunor is Thor (q.v.). *See also* Jupiter.

Thunor (Teutonic) *see* Thor.

Thunupa (Inca People, Peru)

Also known as: *Virococha.*

High god. Thunupa's legends are similar to the legends of Virococha. Thunupa has one unique tale. He is said to have arrived from the north with five unnamed disciples. With the advent of Christianity, a cross was added to his back in his depictions. *See also* Virococha.

Thuremlin (Australia) *see* Baiame; Duramulun.

Thviti (Norse; Teutonic)

Thviti is the black boulder where Fenrir the wolf was chained by the fetter, Gleipnir (also called Gelgia). The gods pulled the end of Gleipnir through Gioll, the rock, and fastened it to Thviti. *See also* Fenrir; Gleipnir.

Thyestes (Greek)

He is the son of Pelops and the brother of Atreus. *See also* Aegisthus; Atreus; Pelops.

Thyia (A) (Greek)

Thyia is the daughter of the river god, Cephissus, or possibly Castalius. She had a child by Apollo. *See also* Cephissus.

Thyia (B) (Greek)

She is the daughter of Deucalion, the king of Perae, and his cousin Pyrrha, who is the daughter of Epimetheus and Pandora. Thyia and her father survived the Great Deluge.

Thyone (A) (Greek)

Thyone is the name given to Semele when she was deified. *See also* Semele.

Thyone (B) (Greek)

Thyone is one of the women who are said to be the mother of Dionysus.

Thyoneus (Greek) Another name for Dionysus.

Ti-Jean Petro (Haitian)

He is the serpent son of Dan Petro. His wife is the Haitian earth goddess, Marinette. Ti-Jean Petro likes to climb posts or trees. *See also* Marinette.

Ti-Kuan (Taoist; China)

Also known as: *San Kuan.*

God of forgiveness. Ti-Kuan, who has the power to forgive sins, is one of the Agents of Earth. He is one of the triad Shui-Kuan and T'ien-Kuan.

Ti-mu (China) *see* Ti-ya.

Ti-shih (China)

Ti-shih is the Chinese equivalent of the god Indra of India.

Ti-tsang-wang-pu-sa (Buddhist; China)

Also known as: *Jizo-Bosatsu* (Japan), *Kshitigarbha* (Central Asia), *Maudgalyayana* (India), Ti-tsang, Yu-ming Kio-shi.

Underworld deity. God of mercy. Ti-tsang was appointed by Buddha Sakyamuni with the job description of protecting the souls of those sent to the underworld, deciding who can be reincarnated and delivering souls to paradise (Si-fang ki-lo shi-kiai or Tsing-tsing t'u), the abode of Amitabha, and the task of emptying all the hells. He preaches to the damned and must remain in hell until the last soul is saved. He can assume any one of six forms or all of them at the same time. Ti-tsang is usually shown in the dress of the Chinese bonzes with a crown on his head. Sometimes he has two assistants, one of whom is Mu-lien, known as Maudgalyayana in India. He is sometimes worshiped along with Amitabha. In some instances, Ti-tsang-wang-pu-sa is shown as a smiling monk, robed, with a halo about his body and head; he carries the pearl of light and the staff with metal rings, which tinkle at his approach. For information about the underworld, see Ti-yu. See also Amitabha; Ch'eng-huang; Jizo-Bosatsu; Kshitigarbha; Kuan Yin; Tung-yo ta-ti; Yama Kings.

Ti-ya (China)
Also known as: *Ti-mu.*
Earth mother and goddess of children. Her title is Ancestress of the World.

Ti-yu (China)
Also known as: *Kings of Hell.*
Ti-yu is the home of the ten Yama Kings. They are judges of the dead. There are ten levels or hells in Ti-yu which are ruled by various kings. The first and chief of the rest is Yen-lo Wang or Yen-Wang, but he was replaced by Ts-in-kuang-wang. He receives the dead and decides where they go by placing them in front of the mirror Sie-king T'ai. After this they are taken to Wang-si ch'eng, who is in charge of those who die by accident. Various versions say they either can or cannot return. The second hell consists of sixteen sub-hells and is ruled by Ch'u-kiang wang (Ch'u Chiang). He decides the punishment of the go-betweens in the process of marriage rites. The third hell is ruled by Sung-ti, who punishes those mandarins who behaved badly to their superiors. The fourth hell, under Wu-kuan wang, is where those who are miserly are punished. The fifth hell is ruled by King Yama or Yen-lo Wang, who judges those who commit the worst sins: killing, destruction of sacred books, etc. King Pien'ch'eng is in charge of the sixth hell. He punishes those guilty of sacrilege or who curse other gods. The seventh hell is ruled by T'ai-shan kun wang (King of the Eastern Peak), who punishes those who desecrate graves, use or eat human flesh, or sell their wives to be slaves. The eighth hell has King of P'ing-teng in charge. He punishes those who fail to be pious. The ninth hell is ruled by King of Tu-shi, who punishes those who read or write obscene material, and the tenth hell is ruled by Chuan-lun-wang, who turns the Wheel of transmigration. He decides where the soul will be placed in the future life. In a sense he is a god of reincarnation. He also takes the soul to Meng'p'o niang-niang, who gives them the broth of oblivion. See also K'u-ch'u K'iao.

Tiamat *Tihamtu* (Assyro-Babylonian; Chaldea, Semite)
Also known as: *Baau* (beneficent form), *Bis-Bis, Hubar, Mummu-Tiamat, Omorca, Omoroka, Tamtu, Tauthe, Tehom, Thalass, Thalatth, Thamte, Thlavatth, Tiawath, Tisalat, Ummukhubar.*
The goddess of the primeval sea, visualized as a dragon and

representing the forces of chaos and evil, Tiamat is the salt water personified, the counterpart of Apsu, the sweet water. The gods and the world were born of Apsu and Tiamat. She is described as being 300 miles long, with a mouth 10 feet wide. Her circumference was 100 feet and she moved with undulations six miles high. In her own image she created multitudes of offspring. She is also credited with populating the earth with hornets, scorpions, spiders, apes, vultures, and hyenas. Her conflict with Marduk became aggressive when her mate, Apsu, was killed. Placing her son, Kingu, in command of the zoomorphic beings she had created, she went into battle against Marduk. She armed her group with horrific weapons and was assisted by the gods of the night sky and the star gods. Marduk slaughtered Tiamat, and made half her body the firmament, half the earth, and with her blood the sea was formed. Tiamat as Hubar is the personification of the underworld river, Hubar. She is depicted as a winged seven-headed dragon with a scaly body, and claws. Tiamat is similar to Apepi (Apep) of the Egyptians, and the Egyptian goddess Ta-Urt. She corresponds to the Greek Thalassa as a sea goddess and the Greek Hydra and Pistris as a dragon. Compare Tiamat to the dragon-slayer Indra (India). There may be a connection between Tiamat in her aspect as Bis-Bis, and Ishtar in her aspect as Bisi-Bisi. Tiamat and Yam parallel Zeus as rain providers. See also Apsu; Bau; Chaos; Damkina; Ea; Enlil; Ishtar; Kishar; Lahamu; Marduk; Nammu (Sumerian primeval sea personified as a mother goddess).

Tiamuni (Acoma People, North America)
The First Man. See also Katsinas; Mayoching; Tsichtinaka.

Tianquiztli (Aztec People, Mexico)
"Marketplace." The Pleiades were known as Tianquiztli to the Aztec People. See also Tlauixcalpantecuhtli.

Ticholtsodi (Navajo People, North America)
Water monster. See also Tonenili.

T'ie-kuai (China) see T'ie-Kuai Li.

T'ieh-Kuai Li *T'ie-kuai Li* (China)
Also known as: *Li, Li T'ieh-kuai.*
Deity of beggars. He is one of the Eight Immortals, who is sometimes called "Li with the Iron Crutch." T'ieh-Kuai Li lost his body after his servant cremated it too soon. His soul was placed in the body of a beggar who had died of hunger. He is shown as a beggar leaning on a crutch and carrying a large calabash on his back. T'ieh-Kuai Li is associated with Lao-tzu and Wang-kiu. See also Arhats; Eight Immortals; Pa-hsien.

Tieholtsodi (Navajo People, North America) Water Monster.

Tien *T'ien* (China)
Also known as: *Thien, Tian, Ti'in, Yu Huang.*
High god. Heaven. God of the Vault of Heaven. In some interpretations, Tien is the supreme god of the early Zhou people. Tien ("Heaven") is the supreme god, superior to ancestors and other gods. It was necessary for rulers to have and to hold Heaven's approval which could be lost if they were cruel or unfair. As heaven, Tien consists of Li (the active principle), Li (the mover), Ki (matter). Heaven is also known as the Chinese imperial heaven, Huang T'ien, where the ruler is Huang T'ien Shang Ti. Tien is often shown with a large round head. See also Yin and Yang.

T'ien-chu (China) *see* Kei-kung.

T'ien-Hou (China) *see* Sheng-mu.

Tien-Hou (China) *see* T'ien Hou.

T'ien Hou *Tien-Hou* (China)
Also known as: *Ch'uan Hou* (Goddess of Streams), *Ma-tsu-p'o, Nai-nai Niang-niang, Sheng-Mu, T'ien-Shang.*
Protector of merchants and ships. T'ien Hou is a sea goddess, although many say she was a deity of navigators. Once, as a mortal girl, she found that her four brothers were at sea, each on a different ship. She fell into a faint. After she was revived and three brothers came back safely, they told her it was the vision of their sister appearing to them that saved them from the dangers of a tempest each one had met. The brother who did not return had not seen his sister, because she had been brought out of her faint before she could reach him. In later mythology, she was given the title of "Empress of Heaven." Sometimes she is shown seated on a lotus, sometimes on a throne, sometimes on a cloud or on the waves. She holds either a tablet or scepter. T'ien Hou usually wears a long robe with a girdle and has a bonnet on her head. A variation of her name is Ch'uan Hou, goddess of streams. She is generally paired with An-kung, a god of sailors. *See also* An-kung; Hsi-Ho; Shengmu; Shiu-mu niang niang.

T'ien-Kuan (China) *see* San Kuan.

Tien-Kuan *T'ien-Kuan* (Taoist; China)
God of happiness. The Agent of Heaven, a god with the power to bestow happiness and well-being. One of a triad with Ti-Kuan and Shui-kuan. On special family occasions and before the performance in a theater, Tien-Kuan appears dressed in the robes of a mandarin and carrying a scroll filled with good wishes for those present. *See also* San Kuan.

Tien Mu *Tien-mu* (China)
Goddess of lightning. She works with Lei-Kung, the thunder god. She uses mirrors to produce flashes of lightning. Tien Mu is possibly the wife of Lei-Kung (also called Kei-Kung). She is associated with the Feng-Po, Jade Emperor, the Dragon King, Yu-Tzu and Yun-T'ung. Tien Mu is shown standing on a cloud holding two mirrors above her head. *See also* Kei-Kung.

T'ien Pao (China) *see* Cheng Wu; Yu Ch'ing.

T'ien-Shang (China) *see* T'ien Hou.

T'ien Tsu (China) The father of husbandry.

T'ien-Wang (China) *see* Men Shen; Ssu ta Chin-kang.

Tien-Wang (Buddhist; China)
Also known as: *Mo-Li.*
Deities of the doors. The door deities are four brothers who are guardians of the four directions. Their symbols are a sword, a guitar, an umbrella and a marten (animal) which they use to control the elements. They are the same as Vaisravana, Virudhaka, Virupasa and Dhrtarastra of India. *See also* Men Shen; Ssu Ta Chin-Kang; Ts'in Shu-Pao.

Tigranes (Iranian) *see* Nabu.

Tigris (Mesopotamia)
The sky god Anu poured the Tigris river from a great water pot. In another myth, Anu impregnated Kumbaris with the Tigris after being castrated by him. *See also* Anu (B).

Tii (Polynesia) *see* Atea; Tane; Tii-Maaraatai; Tiki.

Tii-Maaraatai (Polynesia)
Also known as: *Ta'aroa, Tane, Tii, Tiki.*
The mortal form of the creator god, Ta'aroa. He is the first man, considered evil. He was created by Ta'aroa from earth, and he was clothed in sand. A wife, named Hina, was created for Tii-Maaraatai. A white heron is associated with him. *See also* Atea; Hina; Ta'aroa; Tane; Tiki.

Tii-Tapu (Polynesia) *see* Atea; Tiki.

Tii-Tokerau (Polynesia)
Also known as: *Tahiti Tokerau.*
The goddess Tii-Tokerau was blinded and held prisoner by the god Puna. He also murdered her husband, Wahieroa. The great hero-god Rata rescued his mother, Tii-Tokerau. *See also* Rata.

Ti'in (China) *see* Tien.

Tiitii (Samoa) *see* Maui.

Tijuskeha (North America) *see* Ioskeha.

Tiki (Marquesas, Society Islands; Maori People, New Zealand)
Also known as: *Ki'i* (Hawaii), *Ti'i, Tii.*
Creator. The Maori replaced Tane with Tiki, and made him the husband of Hine. Once thought of as the first man, he is an artisan and messenger of Tane and represents virility. The Maori people called Tane's reproductive power and penis Tiki, while others used Tiki, Ti'i or Ki'i as the name for a separate deity. In Hawaiian mythology, Tiki is the husband/brother of Hina-famed-in-story, who was adept at using magic. When Tiki fell seriously ill, Hina-famed-in-story tried her magic and it did not work. Tiki succumbed and with him all mankind. *See also* Ihoiho; Tane; Tangaroa; Ti'i.

Tiki-Kapakapa (Polynesia, New Zealand) *see* Tikitohau.

Tikitohua (Polynesia, New Zealand)
First bird. In his last attempt to have a human child, Tane took Hine-ahu-one as his wife. First she gave birth to an egg that became Tikitohau, the ancestor of all birds. Then she gave birth to Tiki-kapakapa who was the first female human. *See also* Hine-ahu-one; Papa; Tane.

Tiksnamanjusri (India)
"Charming Splendor." A manifestation of Manjusri, the god of learning, speech, science and wisdom. *See also* Manjusri.

Til-bu-ma (Tibet)
Til-bu-ma is another name for Kinkini-Dhari, the serpent-headed door-keeper of the north.

Tilo (Baranga People, Africa; Mozambique)
Tilo, the storm god, is present in every rain storm. His voice is heard as the thunder. This god is connected with all that is mysterious in the universe.

Tilottama (India) A Nymph. *See also* Arjuna.

Timirau (Polynesia) *see* Tinirau.

Timi-iti (Polynesia)

In the beginning, Ta'aroa, the supreme deity, developed himself. He existed in Fa'a-ti, the place within the shell named Timi-iti. The outer portion of this shell, named Rumia, existed before creation, in a primeval void of darkness named Po. *See also* Ta'aroa.

Timo-Taata (Polynesia)

Creator god. Second to Ihoiho. *See also* Ihoiho.

Timondonar *Tamendonar, Tamanduare* (Tupi-Guarani People, Brazil) *see* Ariconte.

Tina *Tinia* (Etruscan)

He is the chief god of the people. With the goddess of wisdom, Minerva, and Cupra, the goddess of fertility, he is a member of the Great Triad. He is represented as a thunderbolt. As chief god, he has three thunderbolts and Minerva and Cupra have one each. Tina, Uni and Minerva became the Capitoline Triad, imposed on the Romans to replace Jupiter, Mars and Quirinus. Tina exhibits traits similar to the great Zeus. Some say he is identified with the Roman Summanus. An authority calls Summanus an epithet, "probably of Hades, referring to his power over the night sky." *See also* Cupra; Minerva.

Ting (Teutonic) *see* Thing.

Tinga (Greek) *see* Antaeus.

Tingir (Beltirs) *see* Tangri.

Tinia (Etruscan) *see* Tina.

Tinilau (Polynesia) *see* Tinirau.

Tinirau *Timirau, Tinilau* (Polynesia)

Also known as: *Kinilau, Sinilau.*

God of the Ocean. King of fish. Tinirau is generally thought of as the lover of Hina or Ina, as she is called in some cases. He lived on Motu-tapu or Vavau (the sacred islands). Motu-tapu was given to him by the great goddess, Vari-ma-te-takere. Tinirau has two forms and two faces. One form was human, the other was fish-like. *See also* Hina; Ina; Maui; Ru; Rupe; Vatea.

Tiphys (Greek)

Until his death, Tiphys, the son of Hagnias or Phorbas and Hyrmina, was the pilot of the Argos. The subsequent pilot was Ancaeus. *See also* Actor (B); Argonauts.

Tir (Iranian, Persian)

This demon of fatal accidents is the son of Iblis and the brother of Awar, Dasim, Sut, and Zalambur. *See also* Azazel; Tishtrya; Tiur.

Tir na-nog *Tir na n'og* (Celtic) *see* Tuatha De Danann.

Tirawa (Pawnee People, North America)

Also known as: *Atius Tirawa, Shakura, Tirawa Atius.*

A creator deity known as the Great Power or the Great Father, Tirawa lives in heaven with his wife Atira. He is in charge of the other gods. Knowledgeable about astrology, he placed Shakuru, the sun, in the heavens to give daylight, and Pah, the moon, for light in the evening. He set the Evening Star who was called Mother of All Things, the Morning Star (a soldier god) to guard the east, the Pole Star for the north and the Death Star for the south. Tirawa then placed four other stars as supports for the sky. He is also the god of good buffalo hunting. Some think of him as a god of thunder or a god of the sun. In the Creation Legend, Tirawa attempted to destroy the world by fire, but it was extinguished by a great deluge. *See also* Kitshi Manito; Pah; Wakonda.

Tirawa Atius (Pawnee Indian) *see* Tirawa.

Tiresias *Teiresias* (Greek)

Deified mortal. A Theban whom the gods blinded. In compensation for the loss of his sight, they gave him the power of prophecy. Tiresias is associated with Athena.

Tisandrus (Greek)

He is the son of Jason, the Argonaut, and Medea. *See also* Jason; Medea; Pheres (A).

Tishtrya *Tir* (Chaldean, Persian)

A yazata (celestial being), Tishtrya is in constant battle with the life destroying demon of drought, Apaosha. Tishtrya is Sirius, the dog-star, and a god of rain. In the *Bundahish* (q.v.), he is said to be the primeval producer of all water. In the "Yashts" (Zoroastrian hymns to divine spirits), he is shown as the continual source of water, the protector of Aryan lands, the lord of all stars, the giver of children and the victor over sorcerers. He produced the first rain at the creation. Each raindrop became as big as a bowl so the earth was covered to the height of a man. From the rains, the cosmic ocean Vourukasha was formed. When prayers reach him during droughts, he descends to Vourukasha as a white horse with golden ears to battle Apaosha, who appears as a dark horse. When he is able to overcome the demon, Vourukasha boils over. The vapors rise and are blown to earth. In one battle with Apaosha, he was losing ground. Ahura Mazda heard Tishtrya's cries of despair and offered prayers and sacrifices on his behalf. This gave him the strength of ten horses, ten camels, ten bulls, ten mountains and ten rivers and he overcame Apaosha, and the waters flowed freely. The fourth month of the year, June–July, is dedicated to him. During the first ten days of this period, he is said to take the form of a fifteen-year-old male, an age thought to be ideal in Persian thought. In the second ten days he takes the form of a bull and in the third, the form of a horse. It was in these forms that he created Vourukasha. In Chaldean astrology, Tishtrya as the dog-star is venerated with Hvare-Khshaeta, the sun; Mah, the moon; and Anahita, who was identified with the planet Venus. Tishtrya is depicted as a bull with golden horns or as a beautiful young man of about fifteen years of age. In this form, he is appealed to by believers for male children and wealth. Sometimes he is depicted in female form. *See also* Ahura Mazda; Aktar (The); Anahita; Apaosha; Bundahish; Hapto-iringa; Hvare-Khshaeta; Mah; Rapithwin; Sirius; Tir; Vourukasha (B); Yazatas.

Tisiphone (Greek)

Vengeance. One of the three Erinyes, Tisiphone wreaks vengeance on the evil. Her sisters are Alecto and Megaera. *See also* Erinyes; Eumenides.

Titae-Aretia (Greek) *see* Aretia.

Titaea (Greek)
An epithet of Gaea, goddess of the earth, and Rhea, mother of the gods (qq.v.).

Titaea Magna (Greek) *see* Aretia.

Titania (Anglo-Franco) *see* Alfheim.

Titans (Greek)
Giants. The Titans, who preceded the Olympian gods, are the giant, half-man, half-snake children of the god of the sky, Uranus, and the earth mother, Gaea (who are the offspring of Nox, meaning night). The Giants waged a ten year war with Zeus in which they were ultimately conquered and imprisoned in a cavern near the underworld, known as Tartarus. The Giants names are Agrius, Alcyoneus, Aloeus, Anax, Anteaus, Clytius, Cyclops, Enceladus, Epihialtes, Gration, Hecatonchires, Hippolytus, Mimas, Pallas, Polybotes, Porphyrion, Rhoetus, Thoas, Thoon and Tityus. The Cyclopes are the one-eyed monster giants: Arges, Brontes, and Steropes (some add Geraestus and Acmonides). The Hecatonchires, Briareus, Cottus and Gyges, are each equipped with 50 heads and 100 hands. *See also* Cyclopes; Gaea; Hecatonchires; Nox; Themis.

Tithonus (Greek)
Deified mortal. Son of Laomedon and brother of Priam, for whom his wife, Eos, secured immortality. Because she forgot to ask also for eternal youth, he continued to grow older until Eos changed him into a grasshopper. *See also* Eos; Priam.

Titlacauan (Mexico, Aztec) An aspect of Tezcatlipoca (q.v.).

Tityos (Greek) *see* Tityus.

Tityus *Tityos* (Greek)
A Euboeoan giant, Tityus is the son of Gaea (the earth) or Zeus and Elara (the daughter of Orchomenus). After Tityus attempted to rape Leto, who is the mother of Apollo and Artemis, he was killed either by Zeus or Apollo and Artemis. He was sent to Tartarus, the underworld, where his regenerating liver is ripped apart and eaten daily by vultures. *See also* Apollo; Artemis; Giants; Tartarus; Zeus.

Tiu (German) Name for Zeus.

Tiur (Armenia; Possibly Babylon, Persia, or Iran)
Also known as: *Tir* (Iranian).
The scribe of Aramazd who writes what Aramazd dictates about the events of each human life. He is probably a deity of writing and eloquence. Tiur is identified with the Greek Apollo, the prophet god of healing and music, and as a writer, Tiur is also identified with Nabu of the Babylonians and Hermes of the Greeks. *See also* Aramazd.

Tiw (Teutonic) *see* Tyr.

Tiwaz (Teutonic) *see* Tyr.

Tjausul and Othale (Teutonic) Deities of restlessness.

Tjikantja Brothers (Aborigine People, Australia)
Creators. Sky gods who created all things on earth.

Tjinimin the Bat (Australia) *see* Rainbow Snake.

Tlacauepan (Aztec, Mexico)
Magician. Tlacauepan is the younger brother of Tezcatlipoca (who is also Huitzilopochtli) and Titlacauan. Skilled magicians and adversaries of Quetzalcoatl, they tried to drive Quetzalcoatl from power.

Tlachgo (Celtic) *see* Eire.

Tlacht (Celtic) *see* Eire.

Tlahuitzin (Aztec) *see* Yappan.

Tlahuizcalpantecuhtli (Mexico) *see* Tlauixcalpantecuhtli.

Tlaloc (Aztec People, Mexico)
Also known as: *Atonatiuh, Chac* (Mayan) *Cocijo* (Zapotec), *Dzaui* (Mixtec), *Muye* (Otomi), *Nahualpilli, Tohil* (Quiche of Guatemala).
Tlaloc is the god of thunder, rain, moisture, and mountains. He is one of the four sons of Ometecuhtli and Omeciuatl. He was worshiped as a creator god in Mexico before the Aztecs conquered the region. He lived in the mountains with the goddesses of grain. His mate, who is sometimes called his sister, is Chalchihuitlicue, the "Emerald Lady." The rain gods known as the Tlalocs are his children. Huixtocihuatl, the goddess of salt, is his eldest sister. Infants and children were sacrificed to Tlaloc. He is the god of the south, and was the ruler of the sun of the third universe, which was consumed by fire. Tlaloc is also the lord of the eighth hour of the day and the ninth hour of the night. In some renditions of myths involving Tlaloc he is known as the husband of the flower-goddess Xochiquetzal. His home is in Tlalocan. Tlaloc is depicted with a mask of serpents similar to that of Quetzalcoatl, except Quetzalcoatl has only one serpent. His incense is the smell of burning rubber. Some of the legends attributed to Tlaloc are similar to those of Quetzalcoatl (q.v.). *See also* Atonatiuh; Chalchiuhtlicue; Choc Mol; Huitzilopochtli; Iztac Ciuatl; Lords of the Day Hours; Lords of the Night Hours; Ometecuhtli; Quetzalcoatl; Tezcatlipoca; Tlalocan; Tlaloques.

Tlalocan (Mexico, Aztec)
Also known as: *Mount Tlaloc, The Place of Tlaloc.*
Abode of the Rain God. In the Postclassic period, Tlaloc lived in magnificently decorated mountain caves. By the time of the Conquest, he had moved up to the fourth level of the upperworld, known as Tlalocan, where he lives with his consort, Chalchihuitlicue, and remains the ruler.
His tenants are all dead souls who died in the water, including flood water or a disease associated with water; the souls of dead Dwarfs; and souls of everyone who lived with a handicap. Tlalocan is a tranquil place, a place of abundance. The air is filled with the scent of flowers and the music of song is always heard in the background. All souls in Tlalocan stay for four years before they return to earth. *See also* Ciuateteo; Xolotl.

Tlalocs *Tlaloques* (Aztec)
Minor rain gods who are the children of Tlacoc (q.v.).

Tlaloques (Aztec) *see* Tlaloc.

Tlaltecuhtli *Tlaltecutli, Tlatecutli* (Aztec People, Mexico)
Also known as: *Coatlicue, Earth Lord or Earth Lady.*
The name of this giant monster, who looks like a crocodile,

indicates the male gender although most depictions indicate the female gender. Once, when the earth was covered in water from the Great Deluge that had destroyed the fourth age, Tlaltecuhtli was swimming around looking for flesh to eat. Quetzalcoatl and his companion, Tezcatlipoca, changed themselves into serpents and dove into the waters. They grabbed Tlaltecuhtli and ripped her in half. To please the gods they threw one half to the sky and it became the heavens and the stars. The other half became the surface of the earth. Other gods came to earth to comfort her. Tlaltecuhtli cried during the first night for the hearts of men to eat. Fruit would not console her unless it was sprinkled with the blood of men. She is one of the thirteen Companions of the Day who preside over the daylight hours. She is invoked by midwives when infant warriors threaten to kill the mother. Prayers to Tezcatlipoca often invoked Tlaltecuhtli as the sun. Tlaltecuhtli is usually represented with claws at the elbows and knees, a full-face death's head at the back, and skulls and crossbones at the sides. Often she is depicted as a crouching figure in the birth position, head upturned with a grinning mask, her mouth open showing flint blades. On her back there is the symbol of a skull. Sometimes she is represented as a toad swallowing a stone knife. Under the name Tlatecutli she is a form of Cihuacoatl or Tonantzin. She is associated with Tonatiuh and Tlaleutli. Tlaltecuhtli is a variant of Coatlicue. See also Chalchiuhtlicue; Mictlantecutli; Tepeyollotl.

Tlaltecutli (Aztec) see Tlaltecuhtli.

Tlanit Pene Baal (Carthage) see Tanit.

Tlanuwa (Cherokee Indian)

Deified bird. The Great Hawk, a magic bird. Tlanuwa is the same name the Natchez call their magical bird with metal feathers.

Tlaoque (Mexico) see Tlaloc.

Tlapallan (Aztec People, Mexico)

The Bright Land. Quetzalcoatl went to Tlapallan when he was driven out by the evil magicians. See also Quetzalcoatl.

Tlatecutli (Aztec) see Tlaltecuhtli.

Tlauixcalpantecuhtli *Tlahuizcalpantecuhtli* (Aztec People, Mexico)

Also known as: *Quetzalcoatl, Venus.*

"Lord of the House of Dawn." Lord of the twelfth hour of the day. When the sun (personified as Huitzilopochtli) was in a particular position in the sky in relation to the position of Venus, the planet (which is Tlauixcalpantecuhtli) and Tianquiztli (the Pleiades), special rituals took place. Tlauixcalpantecuhtli is an aspect of Quetzalcoatl. See also Acatl.

Tlazolteotl (Mexico) see Tlazolteutl.

Tlazolteutl *Tlazolteutl-Ixcuina, Tlazolteotl* (Aztec People, Mexico)

Also known as: *Ixcuiname, Teteoinan, Teteoinnan, Toci.*

"Sacred Filth Eater." "Lady of Witches."

Moon Goddess. Earth Goddess. Goddess of Excrement. Goddess of Purification, and Curing. Goddess of Love and Fertility. Goddess of Childbirth. Lifegiver. Forgiver of Sins. Goddess of Sexual Pleasure. Patron of Gambling. Great Spinner of Thread and Weaver of the Fabric of Life. One of the nine Lords of the Night Hours. Patron of the Day Ocelotl, and the Trecena 1 Ollin in the Tonalamatl (Aztec calendar). Once in a lifetime, confession could be given to a priest. This act was usually delayed until it was thought that age would nullify temptation. The "sinner" would appear before the priest and list all misdeeds. Wrong-doing would include disobeying the gods, deviating from the sexual mores of the community, cowardice during battle, and neglect of sacrifices. Offerings were made to the gods, and absolution was granted by Tlazolteutl's priest. If the confession was honest, Tlazolteutl would absorb the sins of the confessor, and purify the soul. Tlazolteutl could bring tranquility to the home and bestow fertility. Paradoxically, it is Tlazolteutl who tempted Quetzalcoatl. She is the power behind all magic in the Aztec world. Cinteotl, god of corn, is her son; another child is the eternally young Xochiquetzal. (Xochiquetzal was used by the gods to test the virtue of the aesthetic Yappan. Yappan succumbed to her beauty and was killed by the demon Yaotl.) As Tlazolteutl she appears nude, riding on a broom. She wears a horned headdress with a crescent moon and she holds a red snake. She also has a crescent moon decoration on her nose. Sometimes the area around her mouth is painted black. Tlazolteutl represents the planet Venus. She is often depicted wearing a flayed human skin (which represents her ties with the fertility and renewal of spring). As Ixcuiname, she is the spouse of Mictlantecuhtli, the lord of the underworld. Tlazolteutl is associated with her daughter Xochiquetzal, Toci the patron of midwives, and she is affiliated with Mayahuel, the goddess of maguey. See also Chalchiuhtlicue; Itztli; Ixcuiname; Ixmacane; Legend of the Four Suns; Lords of the Day Hours; Lords of the Night Hours; Mayahuel; Quetzalcoatl; Tlahuizcalpantecuhtli; Toci; Yappan; Xipe Totec; Xochiquetzal.

Tlazolteotl (Mexico) A variant spelling for Tlazolteutl.

Tlehanoai (Apache, Navajo, Papago People, North America)

"Carrier of the Night." A moon god.

Tlenamaw (Haida, Kwakiutl, Tlingit, Tsimshian People, North America)

Dragon. A monstrous dragon.

Tlepolemus (Greek) see Helen.

Tletonatiuh (Aztec)

Also known as: *Tonatiuh.*

The sun. Men were sacrificed so their blood would nourish Tletonatiuh. He is usually associated with Tlaltecutli, Huitzilopochtli and Tezcatlipoca in sacrifice. See also Huitzilopochtli; Legend of the Four Suns; Mictlan; Mictlantecutli; Tezcatlica; Tlaltecutli.

Tloquenahuaque *Tloque Nahuaque, Tloque Nauaque* (Aztec; Toltec People, Mexico)

Also known as: *Chicomexochit, Citalicue, Citlallatonac, Ipalnemoani* ("He Who Is Very Near"), *Ipalnemohuani, Omeciuatl, Ometecutli, Tonacaciutl, Tonacatecutli.*

"Lord of all Existence." High god or creator. Ancient Toltec god. The unknown god, creator of all things. Tloquenahuaque ruled the first of four or five worlds, known as the "water sun." After 1716 years it was destroyed by floods and lightning. He created the first man and the first woman. Other than a nine story building erected in his honor, there are no depictions or statues of Tloquenahuaque. *See also* Ipalnemoani.

To-Kabinana and To-Karvuvu (New Hebrides, Polynesia)

First humans. In legend a being (god) drew figures of men on the ground and sprinkled them with his blood. They came to life as To-Kabinana and To-Karvuvu. To-Kabinana climbed a coconut tree and threw down two yellow nuts which burst on impact and changed into two women. To-Karvuvu did the same but his changed into ugly women. In some various versions the two first men exchanged or stole coconuts from each other and caused the differences in dark and light races of people. In some tales one of the two is credited with creating death, and teaching the art of fire, building houses and other benefits of mankind. Some of the tales are similar to those of Qat (q.v.).

To-Kwatsu (Japan) *see* Jigoku.

To-Matauenga (Polynesia)

Supreme god. Son of Rangi and Papa. God of man. *See also* Rangi.

Toafa (Samoa) *see* Foge and Toafa.

Tobadzistsini (Apache, Navajo, Papago People, North America)

War god. Child of the Waterfall, a war spirit.

Tobardasum (Saora People, India) God of the banyan tree.

To'bilhaski'di (Navajo Indians)

The first world. At the east was a place called Tan, the south a place called Nahodoola and west, a place called Lokatsosakad. In the east at Essalai where was located Leyahogan whose chief was Tieholtsodi. The chief of the south was Thaltlahale and the chief of the west was Tsal. The chief of the north was Idni'd-slkai. In the west was a place called Tse'-Iitsibehogan where lived the twelve first people: Holatsi Dilyi'le who were dark ants; Holatsi Litsi, red ants; Tanilai, dragon flies; Tsaltsa, yellow beetles; Wointli'zi, hard beetles; Tse'yoali, stone-carrier beetles; Kinli'zin, black beetles; Maitsan, coyote-dung beetles; Tsapani, bats; Totso', white faced beetles; Wonistsidi, locusts; and Wonistsidikai, white locusts.

Tocay (Peru) *see* Manco Capac; Tahuantin Suyu Kapac.

Tochtli (Aztec)

God of the south. One of four year-bearers or year gods. Tochtli is in charge of the south region. He is god of those people who reside in that space and time. There is some disagreement as to which god was in charge of the North. Various writers place Tecpatl and Texcatlipoca in this function. *See also* Acatl; Calli; Tecpatl.

Toci (Aztec People, Mexico)

Mother goddess of the earth and curing. She was also identified with war. *See also* Tlazolteutl.

Todote (Samoyed of Siberia) God of evil and death.

Tohil (Mexico) *see* Quetzalcoatl; Tlaloc; Xumucane.

Tohil-Heumac (Mexico) *see* Quetzalcoatl.

Tokakami (Mexico)

God of death. Described as black and blood-smeared who come from the underworld to devour the Indians.

Tokay (Inca) *see* Ayar Uchi; Manco Capac; Viracocha.

Tokelau *Tokelo* (Polynesia)

Also known as: *Tui-Tokelo.*

Supreme deity. Similar to Ta'aroa (q.v.)

Tokelo (Polynesia) *see* Tokelau.

Tolocan (Aztec People, Mexico) Home of the gods.

Toma (Tibet)

Also known as: *Vajra-Yogini.*

Toma is a wrathful goddess associated with Yogic rites. Her followers are instructed to visualize her red in color, with three eyes, dancing nude, except for symbolic ornaments. She is an aspect of Vajra-Yogini (q.v.). *See also* Dorje-Naljorma.

Tominagatoo (Warrau People, South America)

Also known as: *Kononatoo.*

Possibly a creator. No function shown. Both names indicate a great father figure, but not necessarily a god.

Tomituka (Aborigine People, Australia)

Monsoon rain goddess. *See also* Pakadringa.

Tonacacihuatl (Aztec People, Mexico)

She is the wife of Tonacatecuhtli. *See also* Chicomecoatl; Omeciutal; Ometecutli; Tonacacuhtli.

Tonacaciuatl (Mexico) *see* Tonacacihuatl; Xochiquetzal.

Tonacaciutl (Mexico) *see* Omeciutal.

Tonacajoha (Mexico) *see* Cinteotl.

Tonacatecuhtli *Tonacatecutli* (Male), *Tonacacihuatl or Tonacaciutl* (Female); (Aztec People, Mexico)

Also known as: *Chicomexochit, Chicomexochitl, Omeciutal, Ometecutli.*

Creator and food giver. Tonacatecuhtli separated the waters from the heaven and was the first Lord of the World. He is usually considered a bisexual deity and is known under various names. In most cases he is paired with Tonacaciutl, who is the female principle. He is shown with a crown filled with grain. He is the same as Ometecuhtli (q.v.). *See also* Huitzilopochtli; Ipalnemoani; Ometecuhtli.

Tonacatecutli and Tonacaciutl (Aztec, Toltec People, Mexico)

Also known as: *Citlallatonac and Citalicue, Lord and Lady of Our Flesh, Lord and Lady of Our Sustenance.*

Male/female version of Tloque Nahuaque. Some say these two represent a single deity as a divine pair. In some versions they gave birth to red Tezcatlipoca (Xipe Totec or Camaxtli), black Tezcatlipoca, white Tezcatlipoca or Quetzalcoatl; blue Tezcatlipoca; Huitzilopochtli. *See also* Citalicue; Citlallatonac; Tloque Nahuaque; Tloquenahuaque.

Tonantzin (Aztec People, Mexico)

Also known as: *Cihuacoatl, Ciuacoatl, Coatlicue, Ilamatecutli, Itzpapalotl, Tamazcalteci, Teteoinnan, Tlatecutli.*

The Mother Goddess. Earth goddess. Her best known name was Ciuacoatl, but her titles, Old Goddess, Obsidian Butterfly, and Grandmother of the Sweat-Bath, and Mother of the Gods indicate she was worshiped in many ways, but primarily she was regarded as an earth deity. In her various roles she is represented as a toad swallowing a knife or a deer. *See also* Ciuacoatl; Coatlicue.

Tonapa (Peru) A name for Virocracha, the teacher of the world.

Tonatiuh *Tonatiuhichan* (Aztec People, Mexico)
Also known as: *Piltzintecutli.*
War or sun god. An ancient sun-god and god of warriors. His home, the House of the Sun, was the home of the warriors. Tonatiuh was fed and cooled by human sacrifice. Each day he was raised to the zenith by warriors, and in the evening, women who died in childbirth lowered him to the darkness of the underworld. Tonatiuh was also known as Piltzintecutli. Those who die in his service are rewarded with eternal life. He is also said to be the ruler of fate. In one version Tonatiuhichan is a type of heaven where warriors who died in battle became Quauteca (eagle's companion) and went to this eastern paradise. Others who die go either to Tlalocan (Tlaloc's home) or to Mictlan. Tonatiuh is depicted as the sun in the center of the Aztec calendar. Associated with Meztli (the dawn) and Tlahuizcalpantecuhtli. *See also* Tezcatlipoca.

To'nenile *Tonenili* (Apache, Navajo, Papago People, North America)
"Water Sprinkler." To'nenile ia a rain god and trickster. He is shown carrying a water pot. It is To'nenile who saved the people from Ticholtsodi, the water monster.

Tonenili (North America) *see* To'nenile.

Tonga-Iti (Polynesia) *see* Tangaroa.

Tongaiti (Polynesia) *see* Tangaroa.

Tootega (Eskimo)
Deity of boats. She is able to walk on water. She lives in a stone house on an island. Said to look like a little old woman.

Tooth Grinder (Norse) *see* Tanngnost; Thor.

Tope (A) (Norse) Deity of insanity.

Tope (B) (Buddhist) *see* Stupa.

Topielce (Slavic) Spirits who dwell in lake water.

Topiltzin *Toplitzin-Quetzalcoatl* (Toltec) (Mexico)
Also known as: *Ce Actl, Hueymac* (Aztec) *Papa, Xipe.*
Probably a deified mortal. Some versions claim this was the name of the priest who performed the actual slaying of the victim of sacrifice. He is shown with a red beard turning slightly white. *See also* Mixcoatl; Xipe Totec.

Toplitzin-Quetzalcoatl (Mexico) *see* Topiltzin

Tora-Galles (Lapp) *see* Hora-Galles.

Torch (Indo-European, Armenian)
Also known as: *Torx.*
Demons. Mythical demon of gigantic or dwarfish size. Usually benevolent, but sometimes a mischievous, spiteful genie. He falls into the same class as both the Telchines and Cyclopes.

This group of spirits were often referred to as blacksmiths. Similar to the Telchines and Cyclopes of Greece.

Tore (Pygmy of Africa)
God of thunderstorms. Some pygmies seized fire and ran off with it while Tore pursued them on his swing, up to the sky and down to the valley, in vain. He returned home to find his mother dead. As punishment he decreed that men should also die. Tore is interchangeable with mythical animals. Also known as lord of the dead.

Torgarsoak (Eskimo) *see* Tornarsuk.

Tornait (Eskimo) *see* Tornaq.

Tornaq (Eskimo)
Also known as: *Innua, Inua, Inuat, Tornait, Torngak.*
Spirit. A spirit being, the familiar of a shaman (Angakok). The Tornaq is called the owner or in-dweller of everything in nature. Normally invisible, but as Tornait they are helpers or guardians and sometimes appear as a light or fire prior to the death of someone. They are ruled by Tornarsuk, who is sometimes called the Great Tornak. *See also* Ingnersuit (Cliff Inua); Inua; Sedna; Umiarissat (Sea Inua).

Tornaq (Eskimo) *see* Inuat.

Tornarsuk (Inuit; Eskimo)
Also known as: *Tornatik or Tornarsuk* (Greenland), *Torngarsoak* (Labrador), *Torngasoak, Tungrangayak* (Alaska).
Ruling spirit. A higher spirit than the Tornaq. Generally thought of as the ruler of the Tornaq. Known in Alaska as Tungrangayak. Variously depicted as bear, a tall man with one arm, a tiny figure, and some say he is invisible. Some say his body is covered with eyes. Some say he is a sea monster or a large white bear. Same as Torngak, Tornaq and Tungrangayak.

Tortali (New Hebrides)
Sun deity. Tortali, the god of the sun and day, discovered his wife, Avin (a mortal), was having an affair with Ul, master of the moon and night. Tortali drove her from the garden and ever since, women had the menstrual cycle and had to work in the earth for food.

Tortoise Shell Goddess (West Africa) *see* Isong.

Toru (Polynesian)
He is the god of the deep ocean. His function is to paint fish and seashells.

Torum (Ugarit) *see* Ec; Num; Tgorem.

Torx (Indo-European, Armenian) *see* Torch.

Tos-khan (Altaic, Tartars) *see* Bai Ulgan.

Tosotsu-Ten *Tosotsa-Ten* (Japan)
Also known as: *Ryojusen, Tushita.*
Tosotsu-Ten is the Japanese Buddhist "Heaven of Contentment" situated somewhere high in the sky. *See also* Gokuraku; Jodo; Miroku-Bosatsu; Ryojusen; Tushita.

Totates (Celtic) *see* Teutates.

Totepeuh (Mexico) *see* Mixcoatl.

Tou Mu (China)

Also known as: *Chandi* (India), *Marichi* (India), *Mo-li-chi*.

Supreme goddess. The goddess of the North Star. Known as the "Bushel Mother," she is the mother of nine sons, who were the earliest of earthly rulers. Her palace is the center of the stellar system, and all other stars revolve around it. Tou Mu holds sway over life and death, but she is beneficent and sympathetic in the use of her power. She writes down the time of the life and death of mortals and in this she is a goddess of destiny. She is depicted with three eyes and eighteen arms, holding weapons, the solar and lunar disks, a dragon's head, and five chariots in her hands. *See also* Chandi; Marichi (A).

Tou-Shen (China)

Goddess of disease. One of the Tao-shi or Ministry of Epidemics and a goddess of smallpox. She is said to punish those guilty of infanticide. Associated with Sha-shen. *See also* Chenshen.

Tounela *Tuomela* (Finland) *see* Kipu-Tytto; Manala.

Touni (Finnish) *see* Kiyamat-Tora.

Toxeus (Greek)

Oeneus, the king of Calydon, and his niece, Althea, who later hanged herself, are the parents of Toxeus. He is the brother of Gorge, who, some think, was changed into a guinea fowl by the goddess of the hunt, Artemis. Toxeus is the half-brother of Deianeira, who commited suicide after accidentally killing Heracles (Deianeira was also turned into a guinea fowl after death by Artemis), and Meleager, the Argonaut and slayer of the Calydonian Boar. Meleager was also turned into a guinea fowl by Artemis. *See also* Althea; Artemis; Calydonian Boar Hunt; Deianeira; Meleager.

Toyo-kumu-no Mikoto (Japan)

"Rich Form Plain of Augustness." *See also* Ama-no-minaka-nushi.

Toyo-mike-nu (Japan) *see* Jimmu Tenno.

Toyo-Tama-Bime *Toyo-Tama-Bime-No-Mikoto, Toyo-Tama-Hime, Toyotama* (Shinto; Japan).

Sea goddess. Princess. Toya-Tama-Bime (Abundant Pearl Princess also called Lady Abundant Jewel) is the daughter of the ocean god O-Wata-Tsu-Mi. Her younger sister is Princess Tama-Yori-Bime (Jewel-Goodness-Princess or perhaps Spirit-Medium-Princess). They live in a castle on the bottom of the sea. She married Hikohohodemi (Prince Fire Subside), the son of Ninigi (Prosperity Man) and Kono-Hana-Sakuya-Hime (Blossoms-of-the-Trees-Blooming-Princess). She met her husband when he came to the ocean's depths in search of his brother Hosuseri's magic fishing hook. He was so happy with his new wife that he forgot his original intent. Three years later when he remembered, he was full of remorse. The magic hook was retrieved and O-Wata-Tsu-Mi gave him instructions to follow when he returned it to Hosuseri. He left for the upperworld (Japan) and was gone for a long time. Toyo-Tama-Bime, who was pregnant, decided to join her husband. She took her younger sister, Tama-Yori-Bime, on the journey. They settled in a small hut by the edge of the shore. When the time came to give birth, she warned her husband not to follow her into the

hut. His curiosity prevailed and he spied on her through a window. Horrified, he saw that she had assumed the shape of a mammoth sea crocodile. The princess was deeply offended by her husband's actions. After the birth of her son, Amatupiko-Pikonagisa (Ama-tu-Piko-nasgisa-take-U-gaya-puki-apezu-no-mikoto), she gave the child to her sister and returned to her father's home. In later years, Tami-Yori-Bime married her nephew Amatupiko-Pikonagisa. They became the parents of the first emperor of Japan, Waka-mi-ke-nu-no-mikoto, also known as Toyo-mike-nu and posthumously given the name of Jimmu Tenno. Toyo-Tama-Bime and her father, O-Wata-Tsu-Mi, are represented in a combination of human and dragon form. For a description of their undersea castle, *see* O-Wata-Tsu-Mi. *See* Hikohohodemi for the early relationship of Hikohohodemi and Toyo-Tama-Bime and for details about the magic hook and Hikohohodemi's relationship with Hosuseri. For the events that transpired when he returned the magic fishhook to his brother, *see also* Amaterasu; Haya-akitsu-hime-no-kami (goddess of the sea); Hosuseri; Jimmu Tenno; O-Wata-Tsu-Mi.

Toyo-Tama-Bime-No-Mikoto (Japan) *see* Toya-Tama-Bime.

Toyo-Tama-Hime (Japan) *see* Toyo-Tama-Bime.

Toyo-Uke-Bime (Japan) *see* Amaterasu; Ukemochi.

Toyo-Uke-Hime (Japan) *see* Amaterasu; Ukemochi.

Toyo-Uke-Hime-No-Himi (Japan) *see* Amaterasu. *See also* Ukemochi.

Toyo-Uke-No-Kami (Japan) *see* Amaterasu; Ukemochi.

Toyotama (Japan) *see* Toyo-Tama-Bime.

Tpereakl (Pelew Islands)

Tpereakl is the wife of the sky god, Latmikaik. Typereakl lived in the sea where she gave birth to two sons and all fish. The fish built a tower which became the earth, and mankind was the result of the mating of gods and fish.

Traetaona (Persia) *see* Yima.

Trailokaya (Tibet) *see* Trailokyavijaya.

Trailokya-Vijaya-Raja (Tibet) *see* Trailokyavijaya.

Trailokyavijaya *Trailokya-Vijaya-Raja* (Buddhistic Hinduism, Tibetan Tantrism)

Also known as: *Akshobhya, Gozanze-Myoo* (Japan), *hJig-rTen-gsum-rgyal* (Tibet), *Jig-ten-sum-gyal* (Tibet).

Trailokyavijaya, a Dhyanibodhisattva, is the lord of the three Buddhist worlds known as Trailokaya. Trailokayavijaya corresponds to the Japanese Gozanze-Myoo, one of the Godai-Myoo (Five Great Kings), who are the protectors of Buddhism. He is thought to be a terrible aspect of Akshobhya. A grotesque figure, Trailokyavijaya has bristling hair, four faces, a forehead eye, and eight arms. He holds a bell, sword, hook and arrow in right hands and a discus, bow and noose in the left hands. He is shown with his right foot on Parvati, the Hindu great virgin goddess, who is one of Shiva's consorts, and his left foot on Mahesvara, the spouse of the goddess Uma, who is an incarnation of Parvati. In some depictions, he is shown trampling on

Shiva's head. His emblem is the ghanta (bell). *See also* Dhyani-bodhisattvas; Godai-Myoo; Gozanze-Myoo; Parvati; Shiva; Uma.

Trambaka (India) *see* Shiva.

Tree of Many Seeds (Persia)
Two trees stand in Vourukasha, the cosmic ocean; the Tree of Many Seeds, from which all trees derive, and the Gaokerena tree, which will provide the elixir of immortality for all mortals at the renovation of the universe. In its branches lives the great Saena bird. When it beats its wings it breaks the branches, scattering the seeds which are then carried over the earth in the wind and the rain. *See also* Alburz (Mount); Haoma; Vourukasha.

Treta (India) *see* Tretayuga.

Tretayuga *Treta* (Hindu; India)
Part of the Kalpa cycle, Tretayuga lasts 1,296,000 years. In this cycle the god Dharma has only three legs and is red in color. Virtue is one-quarter less than perfect during this period. *See also* Dharma; Dwaparayuga; Kaliyuga; Kalpa.

Tri-Loka (India) *see* Triloka.

Triad, Capitoline (Roman) *see* Tinia.

Triad of Deities (Egypt) *see* Amum-Mut-Khons; Horus-Hathor-Harsomtus (Horus the Younger); Khnum-Anukis-Satis; Osiris-Isis-Horus (Harpocrates); Ptah-Sekhmet-Nefertem.

Triad of Elephantine (Egyptian) *see* Anukis.

Triambika (Hindu; India)
Wife of Rudra-Shiva. *See also* Devi; Rudra; Shiva.

Triloka (India) The Three Worlds. *See also* Bali (B); Loka.

Trimurti Trinity (Hindu; India)
The Hindu Trimurti consists of Brahma the creator, Vishnu the preserver and Shiva the destroyer. The symbol of this trinity is a,u,m, (pronounced om). Lakshmi, Sarasvati and Devi form a Trimurti of goddesses.

Trinavarta (India) Whirlwind, the Demon. *See also* Krishna.

Triopas (A) (Greek)
A Heliad. King of Rhodes. He is the son of the sun god, Helios and Rhode. *See also* Heliades; Helios.

Triopas (B) (Greek)
King of Thessaly. His parents are Poseidon and Canace. For the names of his siblings, *see* Canace. He married Hiscilla and became the father of Erysichthon, Iphimedeia and Phorbas. *See also* Erysichthon; Iphimedeia (A).

Triopas (C) (Greek)
He is the father of Pelasgus by Sois. *See also* Pelasgus (D).

Tripada (India) God of fever, usually malaria.

Triptolemus (Greek) *see* Abas (C); Demeter; Oceanus.

Trisala (India)
Also known as: *Priyakarini.*

The embryo of Mahavira ("Great Man") was transferred from the womb of Devananda to the womb of Trisala. She is the wife of the Kshatriya, Siddhartha. *See also* Mahavira.

Trishna *Trisna* (India)
She is the sister of the god of love, Kama, and daughter of Lakshmi. *See also* Kama; Lakshmi.

Trisiras (Hindu; India)
Possibly a three-headed water god. Trita, Aptya and Indra killed Trisiras and set his cows free. Some say Indra stole the cows. It was Trisiras' father, Tvashtri Tvastar, who forged Indra's bolt. Some say that Trisiras and Indra are half-brothers, and that Indra killed Tvastar. Trisiras is sometimes referred to as the twin of the goddess of the morning light Saranyu, and the son of Tvashtri. He is sometimes associated with the serpent Visvarupa, who is the son of Tvashtri. *See also* Saranyu; Tvashtri.

Trita Aptya *Thrita* (Hindu; India. Persian)
Trita is the slayer of the serpent Visvarupa. An air, water, lightning, moon, and storm god, he brought fire to earth in the form of lightning and prepared the elixir of the gods, soma. Not to be confused with Tretayuga of the Kalpa cycle. Comparable to the Iranian Thrita (q.v.). This myth is sometimes attributed to Agni or Indra. *See also* Agni; Indra; Soma; Trisiras; Varuna.

Tritogeneia (A) *Trigoneia, Tritonis* (Greek)
She is the daughter of Aeolus and some say the wife of Minyas, who was wealthy enough to build his own treasure house. *See also* Aeolus; Minyas.

Tritogeneia (B) (Greek)
Tritogeneia is a surname used for Athena.

Triton (Greek)
Also known as: *Tritons.*
Sea deity. A divinity of the sea, Triton is a son of Poseidon and Amphitrite or Kelaino. He makes the roaring of the ocean by blowing thorough his shell. Triton is human with fish tails for legs. He could be connected with the trident of Poseidon. He is also connected with the Muses. *See also* Amphitrite.

Tritonis (Greek)
She is the wife of Amphithemis. *See also* Acacallis.

Trivia (Roman) Trivia is the Latin equivalent of Artemis (q.v.). *See also* Diana.

Troezen (Greek)
Troezen is the son of Pelops and Hippodameia. *See also* Pelops.

Tronubeina (Teutonic) *see* Heimdall.

Tros (A) (Greek)
His parents are the wealthy king of Dardania, Erichthonius, and Astyoche. He is married to Callirrhoe. They are the parents of Assaracus, Cleopatra, Ganymede and Ilus. When Ganymede was kidnapped, he received two immortal horses from Zeus and a golden vine from Hephaistos. *See also* Callirrhoe; Cleopatra; Erichthonius; Ganymede; Hephaistos.

Tros (B) (Greek)
The son of Alastor, Tros was killed by Achilles in the Trojan War.

Tryambaka (India)

"Three-Mothered" or "Three-Eyed." *See also* Agni; Rudra; Shiva.

Tsagan-Sukuty (Mongol) *see* Ocirvani.

Ts'ai Lun (China)

God of stationers. Inventor of paper. Ts'ai is associated with Meng-T'ien, who made the first brush for writing, and Ts'ang Chieh, who invented writing.

Ts'ai Shen *Ts'shen Yeh* (China)

God of wealth. God of happiness. The widely venerated god of wealth. His birthday, which falls on the fifth day of the first month of the Chinese year, is celebrated with sacrifice and special acts of honor. The most common mortal identified with this deity was Chao Kung-ming although there were others. Ts'ai Shen owns a casket that holds an inexhaustible supply of gold. He is associated with Tseng-fu-ts'ai-shen, god of happiness, and Pi Kan, a deified mortal. *See also* Fu Shen; Shou Hsing.

Tsalu (Cherokee People, North America)

Tobacco. A name given to the tobacco plant by the Cherokees. It may or may not be a deity.

Ts'an Nu (China)

Also known as: *Ma't'ou Naing* (Lady with a Horse's Head). Goddess of silkworms. Ts'an Nu, the goddess of silkworms, is the second-rank wife of the Jade Emperor. She is shown wrapped in a horse's skin.

Ts'ana-Pa (Tibet) "White Brahma." *See also* Brahma.

Ts'ang Chien (China)

Ts'ang Chien is the inventor of writing. He is associated with Meng T'ien, who invented the first brush for writing, and Ts'ai Lun, who invented paper. *See also* Meng T'ien; Ts'ai Lun.

Ts'ang Kie (China) *see* Ts'ang Chien.

Tsao Chun (China)

God of fire or furnace or hearth. *See also* Chung-liu; Tsao Shen; Tsao-Wang.

Tsao-kuo-chia *Ts'ao Kuo-kiu* (China)

He is usually found with Ho-hsien-ku, the only female in the group known as the "Eight Immortals." In some legends, he is the brother of an empress in the Sung dynasty. Tsao-kuo-chia is shown dressed in imperial robes, wearing a bonnet and holding a tablet. *See also* Arhats; Eight Immortals; Ho-hsien-ku.

Ts'ao Kuo-Kiu (China) *see* Tsao-kuo-chia.

Tsao Shen (China)

Also known as: *Chung-Liu, Tsao Chun, Tsao Wang, Tse Shen.* Kitchen god. Prince of the Furnace. God of the Hearth. He was also known as Ch'an Tzu-fang, but in this form, dressed in yellow garments and having unkempt hair, he wasn't very popular. There is some confusion about Tsao Shen, Tsao Chun, Tsao-wang, and Ch'an Tzu-fang, since they were all gods of fire or furnace/hearth. The term Tsao can be used as furnace or stove. Associated with the Jade Emperor. Sometimes found with Oki-Tsu-Hiko and Oki-Tsu-Hime, both kitchen gods. *See also* Ho Shen.

Tsao-wang (China)

Also known as: *Tsao Chun, Tsao Shen.*

God of the Hearth. The hearth god, who resides in the home, near the hearth, keeps watch over the family. He makes his report before Tung Wang Kung, the Jade Emperor, when he appears once a year in heaven. He is assisted in his task by his wife, Tsao-wang nai-nai. When Tsao-wang has left the house on his mission to the Jade Emperor, the family offers sacrifice, and firecrackers are set off to guide his path. His way home is again indicated by firecrackers, and he is welcomed with sacrifice. He usually appears as an old man with a white beard sitting in an armchair with his wife beside him.

Tsaphon, Mount (Ugarit) *see* Zaphon.

Tse Shen (China) *see* Tsao Shen.

Tsects (North American Indian, Haida, Kwakiutl, Tlingit, Tsimshian)

Good spirit. Grandmother white mouse and a friendly spirit.

Ts'en-kuang (China) *see* Kshitigarbha.

Tseng Chang (China) *see* Mo-Li Ch'ing.

Tsentsa (Huron People, North America)

The good Creator-Twin. *See also* Heng.

Tseurima (India, Tibet) Cemetery goddess.

Tshindi (Navajo People, North America) *see* Anaye.

Ts'i-fu-shen (China)

Gods of happiness. Seven gods who give happiness.

Tsi-ku *Ts'iku* (China) *see* K'eng-san-ku.

Tsi-zhui (Osage People, North America)

Sky gods. The Tsi-zhui are known as the "Sky People."

Tsichtinaka (Acoma People, North America)

Guide. The guide of mankind during the emergence.

Ts'in-kuang-wang *Ts'en Kuang, Ts'kuang-wang* (China)

High god. Ts'in-kuang-wang replaced Yen-lo wang (also known as Yen-wang) as the chief of Ti-yu, the Chinese hell. He is the first god to see the dead. It is his function to receive the deceased and place them in front of the mirror known as Sieking t'ai, which shows their history. After this he decides on which level of hell the soul is to be placed. *See also* Ti-yu.

Ts'in Shu-pao (China)

God of the doorway. He is usually paired with Hu King-te. Once they were generals of the T'ang Emperor. These two deities replaced Shen-t'u and Yu-lu. Ts'in Shu-pao is shown as a leaf on one half of the outer door of the residence. Hu King-te is represented as a leaf on the other half. *See also* Hu King-te; Shen-t'u.

Ts'kuang-wang (China) *see* Ts'in-kuan-wang.

Tsmok (Russia) *see* Domovoj; Zmek (Slavic).

Tsoede (Sudan) God of canoe builders, smiths, and fertility.

Tsotsil (Navajo People, North America)
Deified mountain. Magical boundary mountain.

Tsui'goab *Tsui'*(Hottentot People, Africa)
Also known as: *Dxui* (Bushmen), *Thixo* (Pondo, Xhosa People), *Tsui-Goab, Tsui-Goam, Tsuni Goam.*
Supreme god. Sky god. God of rain, storms and thunder. He fought and killed the evil being Gaunab (chief of the dead) and received a wound in his knee which gave him his name. Tsui'-goab made the first man and woman or the rocks where they emerged. He is similar to or the same as Dxui of the Bushmen and Thixo of Xhosa and Ponda people of Africa. He may be the same as Haitsi-aibeb or Gurikhoisib. *See also* Gaunab; Heitsi-Eibib.

Tsui-Goam (Africa) *see* Tsui-Goab.

Tsuikiyomi (Japan) *see* Tsuikiyomi-no-mikoto.

Tsuki-Yomi (Shinto) Japan
Also known as: *Tsuikiyomi Mikoto, Tsuikiyomi-no-Mikoto.*
Tsuki-Yomi, god of the moon, and ruler of the night, was the son of Izanagi (Male who Invites) and Izanami (Female who Invites). He was born when Izanagi washed his right eye as he bathed in the sea following his return from Yumi, the world of the dead. Tsuki-Yomi, assigned the role of god of the moon and ruler of the night, played a minor role in Shinto mythology compared to two of his most famous siblings. His sister was the beautiful sun goddess Amaterasu and his brother Susanowo was the sea, thunder, rain and fertility god. Amaterasu was created from her father's left eye and Susanowo was born when his father washed his nose or sneezed. When smallpox was widespread, adherents appealed to Tsuki-Yomi for protection. For the Shinto creation myth, *see* Ama-no-minaka-nushi; Amaterasu; Hiurko; Izanagi and Izanami; Susanowo; Ukemochi.

Tsuikiyomi Mikoto (Japan) *see* Tsuki-Yomi.

Tsukiyomi-no-Mikoto (Japan) *see* Tsuki-Yomi.

Tsuni Goam (Africa) *see* Tsui'goab.

Ttlaya (Fox People, North America) A ghost.

Tu (Hawaii, New Zealand, Polynesia)
Also known as: *Ku* (Hawaiian), *Tu-matauenga, Tu-metua, Tu-of-the-angry-face.*
War god. Rangi is the sky father of Tu and Papa is the earth mother of Tu. When Rangi and Papa were cleaved together as sky and earth, they had already created Tane, Tangoroa, Tu, Rongo, Haumia and Tawhiri, who were within their warm embrace. There did not seem to be a way for the children to separate the parents. The children became restless in their cramped quarters. Tu suggested that they kill Rangi and Papa. Following their parents' separation, the brothers deserted Tu. His anger led him to catch the birds in Tane's forests, net the fish in Tangaroas' waters and pull from the ground the cultivated and uncultivated plants, which were the children of his brothers Tane and Haumia. In the Society Islands, legends replaced Tu with Oro, the son of and assistant to the creator, Ta'aroa. Known in Hawaii as Ku, he is the founder of the Ku family of war gods. He accepted human sacrifices. *See also* Ku and Hina; Papa; Rangi; Rongo; Ta'aroa; Tangoroa; Tawhiri; Tu-metua.

Tu-ka-nguha (Polynesia) *see* Tu-matauenga.

Tu-ka-taua (Polynesia) *see* Tu-matauenga.

Tu K'ang (China)
God of distillers. He is probably a mortal who discovered alcohol. Tu K'ang is generally associated with I-ti, the god of wine.

Tu-kariri (Polynesia) *see* Tu-matauenga.

Tu-mata-what-iti (Polynesia) *see* Tu-matauenga.

Tu-matauenga *Tu-ma-tauenga* (Polynesia)
Also known as: *Maru* (South Island of Maori), *Tu, Tu-ka-nguha, Tu-ka-taua, Tu-kariri, Tu-mata-what-iti, Tu-whake-ticke-tangata.*
God of War. An aspect of the god of war, Tu. Tu-matauenga is his name on the North Island; to the Maori of the South Island he is known as Maru. *See also* Maru; Maui; Papa; Po; Rangi.

Tu-Metua (Polynesia)
Also known as: *Tu, Tu-Papa, Tumateanaoa.*
Mother goddess. Papa is the goddess Tu-metua who is the daughter of Timatekore (Tima-te-kore) and his wife Tamaitingava-ringavari. Papa is the consort of Vatea. They had five children: Tangaroa, Rongo, Tonga-iti, Tangiia, and Tane. In another legend, Tu-Metua is the sixth and final child of the great mother goddess Vari-ma-te-takere who created her from a bit of her right side. The mother gave Tu-Metua the land called Te-enua-te-ki which is located at the very bottom of Avaiki. She is sometimes linked with her nephew, Tangaroa. *See also* Papa; Rangi; Tangaroa; Vatea.

Tu-nui-ka-re (Oceanic) see Faumea.

Tu-Papa (Polynesia) *see* Tu-Metua.

Tu-qu-aat (Egypt) *see* Aaru.

Tu-te-wanawana (Polynesia) *see* Tu-te-wehi.

Tu-te-wehi (Polynesia)
Also known as: *Tu-te-wanawana.*
Father of reptiles. *See also* Ika-tere; Po; Tangaroa.

T'u-Ti (China) *see* T'u-ti Lao-Yeh.

T'u-Ti Lao-Yeh (China)
Also known as: *T'u-Ti.*
Deified mortal. This name is usually given to a high official after death, placing him in the category of a local god. Anyone could be made a T'u-Ti Lao-Yeh after death, but the position was not stable. Failure to avert one disaster meant the individual lost his divine status and a replacement was brought in immediately.

T'u-Ti Shen (China)
Also known as: *Hou-T'u Shen.*
Patron god of the soil. God of the Place. God of Walls and Moats. *See also* Hou-Tu.

Tu-whake-ticke-tangata (Polynesia) *see* Tu-matauenga.

Tua-heru (Egypt) *see* Ap-taui.

Tuamutef (Egypt)
Also known as: *Duamutef.*

Tuamutef, a jackal-headed god, is one of the four divine sons of Horus and Isis. He is the guardian of the east, and the Canopic guardian of the stomach. His brothers are Amset, Hapi, and Qebhsneuf. *See also* Amset; Hapy (A); Horus; Isis; Qebhsneuf.

Tuart Rert (Egypt) *see* Taueret.

Tuat (Egypt)
Also known as: *Duat, Khert Neter, Neter-khertet, Ta-Djesant, Ta-tchesert, Twet.*
The underworld or otherworld. Divided into twelve sectors or nomes, each of which has its own demons or ordeals that the deceased must pass in order to be worthy of life with Osiris. Sometimes the place is called Ta-djesant, Ta-tchesert, Neter-khertet, or Khert Neter. A river flows through this underworld realm into twelve sections. The gates separating the twelve sections (fields) are guarded with serpents and demons. Ta, the sun god, must know the names of the these monsters to secure passage. Reference is made to seven arrets or circles within the divisions. These arrets are guarded by a doorkeeper, watcher, and herald. The first by Sekhet-hra-asht-aru, Semetu, and Hukheru; the second by Tun-pehti, Seqet-hra, and Sabes; the third by Am-haut-ent-peh-fi, Res-hra, and Uaau; the fourth by Khesef-hra-ash-kheru, Res-ab, and Neteqa-hr-khesef-atu; the fifth by Ankh-em-fentu, Ashebu, and Teb-her-kehaat; the sixth by Aken-tau-k-ha-kheru, An-her, and Metes-hra-ari-she; the seventh by Metes-sen, Aa-kheru, and Khesef-hra-khemiu. All the other entrances are guarded by a serpent god and a host of other gods. The first division, or first hour, is the entrance which is guarded by the serpent, Saa-Set. The second division is guarded by Mehen. The third division (Tent-Baiu) is guarded by the serpent and arch-fiend Apepi. The fourth division is guarded by Tchetbi (possibly Tekhi). The fifth division is guarded by Teka-hra. The sixth division is guarded by Maa-ab. The seventh division is guarded by Akhan-maati. The eighth division is guarded by Set-hra. The ninth division is guarded by Ab-ta. The tenth division (known as Tentit-uhesqet-khat-ab) is guarded by the serpent, Sethu. The eleventh division is guarded by Am-net-f, and the twelfth division is guarded by Sebi. There are twenty-one pylons in Tuat, but only ten have the names of the guards. These are Neri or Nerau, Mes-Peh or Mes-Ptah, Ertat-Sebanqa or Beq, Nekau or Hu-tepa, Henti-requ or Ertahen-er-reqau, Semamti or Samti, Akenti or Am-Nit, Khu-tchet-f or Netchses, Tchesef or Kau-tchet-f, Sekhen-ur whose name was not changed as the others were at a later date. Compare Tuat to Tartarus (Greek), Yomi and Jigoku (Japan). *See also* Aaru; Aati; Aau; Ab; Amentet Antiu; Arkharokh; Elysian Fields; Gehenna; Hentiu; Sekhet-Aarru (the domain of Osiris).

Tuatet-maket-neb-s (Egypt)
Afterworld. The name of the Ninth Hour of Tuat. Osiris passes through the city of Bes-aru which has the pylon Sa-Akeb. The deities mentioned are Akhem-sek-f, Akhem-urt-f, Akhem-hemi-f, Akhem-khemes-f, Khen-unnut-f, Hapti-ta-f, Hetep-uaa, Neter-neteru, Teha-Tuat, Tepi, Muti-khenti-Tuat, Nesti-khenti-Tuat, Nebt-au-khent-Tuat, Nehata, Teba, Ariti, Menkhet, Hebs, Nebti, Asti-neter, Asti-paut, Hetemet-khu, Neb-pat, Temtu, Men-a, Perit, Shemat-khu, Nebt-shat, Nebt-shef-shefet, Aat-aatet, Nebt-setau, Hent-nut-s, Nebt-mat, Tesert-ant,

Aat-khu, Sekhet-metu, Netert-en-khentet-Ra and Her-she-tauti. *See also* Tuat.

Tuatha De Danann *Tuatha de Danaan, Tuatha-Dedanan* (Celtic)
The Tuatha De Danann are a legendary race of gods, sometimes called "the Children of Don" (or Dan, Dana, Danann), who inhabited Ireland. They are the descendants of Nemed who came to the island from Greece. Skilled in the art of magic, they brought four talismans with them known as the "Hallows of Ireland." The Hallows are the Stone of Fal, the Sword of Nuada, the Lance of Lugh and the Cauldron of the Dagda. They defeated the evil giants, the Fomorians, who had defeated the original race, the Firbolgs. The Tuatha De Dananns were in turn defeated by the Milesians, who were ancestors of the Gaels. It is said that the agreement was made to divide the country into two sections. The upper section was for the Gaels and the Tuatha would retreat to the other section, or Otherworld, also known as Tir na n'og, or the Sidhe or Hollow Hills. The chief female deity of the Tuatha De Danann is the goddess Dana and one of the chief male deities is Dagda who is also known as the "Good God," because of his wisdom and skills. Their queen-goddess is Banbha. The symbols of the Tuatha De Danann are the stone, sword (or spear), lance and cauldron. It is said in some myths that the Tuatha De Danann and their treasures came from four cities: Gorias in the east, the origin of Lugh's lance; Falias in the north, which yielded the Stone of Destiny; Finias in the south, the origin of the sword or spear of Nuada; and Murias the city of the west (which later sank beneath the seas) is the origin of Undry, Dagda's magic cauldron. *See also* Amergin; Anu (A); Banbha; Beltine; Bress; Brigit; Cesair; Cian; Curoi Mac Daire; Dagda; Dana; Dia'necht; Domnu; Goibniu; Lugh; Manannan Mac Llyr; Nuada.

Tuatha-Dedanan (Celtic) *see* Tuatha De Danann.

Tuati (Egypt) *see* Aai.

Tubal-Cain (Sumer) Patron of the forge. *See also* Lumha.

Tucana People — Creation Legend (Amazon, South America) *see* Dyai.

Tuchita (India) *see* Tushita.

Tucupacha (Tarascan People, Mexico)
Tucupacha created heaven and earth, then created men and women from clay. After they melted in water, he created them again in cinders and metals. Apparently disappointed with his creations he caused a flood but saved a priest (Texpi) and his wife and some seeds and animals.

Tues (Greek) *see* Ares.

Tueris (Egypt) *see* Taueret.

Tuetates *Totates* (Gaul)
Also known as: *Alborix, Caturix, Loucetius, Rigisamos.*
God of war.

Tug'ny'gat (Eskimo People) *see* Tungat.

Tui-tokelo (Polynesia) *see* Tokelau.

Tuil (Kamchatka Peninsula, Siberia)
God of earthquakes. He rides his sleigh beneath the earth.

Tuil can be convinced to go elsewhere with his sleigh by poking holes in the ground with a very sharp stick of the proper length.

Tuirenn, Children of (Celtic) *see* Cian.

Tuku (Babylonia) *see* Marduk.

Tulasi (India)

The leaves of this sacred plant are used for the ceremonial worship of Shiva. Thought to remove all evils, it is sinful to break its branches. The juice of its leaves is said to have a curative effect. The goddess of plants who bears the same name is identified with Lakshmi (q.v.). *See also* Vilva.

Tule (Zande People, Siberia)

Water and trickster deity. He is the counterpart of Tere. *See also* Bele; Tere.

Tuleyone People — Creation Legend (North America) *see* Olle.

Tuli (Polynesia)

Messenger bird. Tangaloa sent Tuli to earth to establish land. After Tuli complained of lack of shade trees, Tangaloa gave Tuli a vine known as the "Peopling Vine," from which came humans. *See also* Tangaloa.

Tullius (Greek)

King of Rome. He is the son of Hephaistos and Ocrisia. *See also* Hephaistos.

Tulungusaq (Eskimo)

First creature. The first entity to appear was the Swallow. She showed Tulungusaq the clay soil at the bottom of a great abyss, which he uses to disguise himself as a Crow, and to create everything living.

Tum (Egypt)

Also known as: *Atum, Tem.*

Sun deity. He existed before creation. God of the setting sun, Tum presides over darkness. Some say he is the father of Ra who was born without a mother. His mate is possibly Akusaa, goddess of sunset. *See also* Atum; Tem.

Tumateanaoa (Polynesia) *see* Tu-metua.

Tumburu (India) *see* Gandharvas.

Tuminikar (Taruma People, Guiana)

Culture hero. He is a good deity whose twin brother, Duid, is a trickster god who causes worries for men.

Tumuteanaoa (Polynesia)

Also known as: *Echo.*

She is a child of the goddess Vari-ma-te-takere, who created her from a piece of her left side. This was Vari's fourth child, and the goddess gave her the land called Te-parai-tea. *See also* Vari.

Tun Huang T'ai (China) *see* Tung Huang T'ai I.

Tun Huang T'ai I (China) *see* Tung Huang T'ai I.

Tuna (Tongan People, Polynesia)

Also known as: *The Eel.*

God of trees. Tuna, the foster son of Kaloafu and Teuhie, was the spouse or lover of Hina. Hina grew tired of the relationship and left him. Finding a replacement lover was difficult as everyone was frightened of Tuna. Soon, the great hero-god Maui came along and was immensely attracted to Hina. Tuna and Maui engaged in a spectacular fight resulting in Tuna being chopped up in pieces. His head was planted and from it the first coconut tree sprouted. *See also* Hina; Maui.

Tung-Ak (Mongol)

God of managers and chiefs. Tung-Ak controls minor spirits.

Tung Chun (China)

Tung Chun, the god of the sun rising in the east, is also one of the nine heroes. Nine Songs.

Tung-Hua (China)

Tung-Hua is the official residence of male fairies. Tung Wang, also known as Tung Wang Kung, is in charge of Tung-Hua. *See also* Hsi-hua.

Tung Huang T'ai I (China)

Also known as: *T'ai Shan, T'ai-yueh-ta-ti, Tung-yueh-ta-te.*

Eastern Emperor. Great Emperor of the Eastern Peak. One of the nine heroes. Tung Huang T'ai I was placed in his position by the Jade Emperor. He is the protector of men and animals and he attends to the prosperity of both. His daughter, Pi-hsia-yuan-chung-mu, is a protector of children and goddess of birth. *See also* Nine Songs; Pi-hsia-yuan-chung-mu; T'ai shan.

Tung Wang Kung (China) *see* Yu Huang.

Tung-yo ta-ti (Buddhist)

After the judging, dead souls are sent to Tung-yo ta-ti, who is called the Emperor of the Eastern Peak. *See also* Sukhavati; Tung Huang T'ai I.

Tunkan Ingan (Dakota People, North America) Sex god.

Tuonela (Finnish)

Tuonela is the underworld ruled by Tuoni, the god of death. A beautiful black swan swimming on a black river protects the kingdom. *See also* Manala; Tuonetar.

Tuonetar (Finnish)

Queen of the underworld. She is the wife of Tuoni who is the king of the land of the dead, known as Tuonela. *See also* Kivutar; Loviatar; Manala; Tuoni; Vammatar.

Tuoni (Finnish)

God of the underworld. Lord of Tuonela, the underworld, he is the husband of Tuonetar and father of some vicious daughters and equally vicious sons. *See also* Kivutar; Kiyamat-Tora; Lemminkainen; Loviatar; Manala; Vainamoinen; Vammatar.

Tupan (Guarani, Tupinamba People, Brazil)

Also known as: *St. Thomas, Thunder, Toupan, Tumpa, Tupa, Tupi.*

God of thunder and lightning. Tupan is acknowledged as a god but is not worshiped. He is the son of the hero Nanderevusu and his wife, Nandecy. Whenever he visits his mother he causes storms; the creaking of his boat makes thunder. Tupan is a stocky young man with wavy hair. *See also* Milomaki.

Tupi (Brazil) *see* Tupan.

Tura (Persia) *see* Thrita.

Turachogue (Chibcha People, South America) *see* Bachue.

Turan (Etruscan)
Love goddess. She is associated with the moon goddess Zirna (q.v.).

Turi-a-faumea (Oceanic)
Turi-a-faumea is the son of the eel-woman, Faumea (q.v.).

Turms (Etruscan) *see* Hermes.

Turnus (Greek)
Turnus, the king of Rutuli, fought against the Trojans in the Trojan War. He fled Troy and went to Italy. In a battle with one of the three leaders of the Dardanians, Aeneas, Turnus was killed and sent to the underworld. Aeneas later married Lavina, the daughter of Turnus. *See also* Abas (A); Actor (C); Aeneas; Evander (B).

Turquoise Man-woman *see* Ahsonnutli.

Tushita *Tuchita, Tosotsa-Ten* (Buddhist; Japan).
The heaven for contented souls. Tushita is one of the twenty-four Buddhist heavens. It is the abode of Maitreya, the coming Buddha. Gautama Buddha resided in Tushita when he chose Maya as his mortal mother. Bodhisattvas are reborn in this realm before they become Buddhas. Each term of residence in Tushita is four hundred Tushita years. One Tushita day is four hundred years on earth. *See also* Buddha; Maitreya; Miroku-Bosatsu; Ryojusen; Sukhavati.

Tushna (Greek) *see* Apollo.

Tushnamatay (Persia) Goddess of meditation.

Tut (Babylon) *see* Marduk.

Tutates (Celtic) *see* Teutates.

Tute-Mute-Anaoa (Polynesia) *see* Vari (A).

Tuto-Tamu (Japan)
Tuto-Tamu is one of the gods who convinced the great goddess of light, Amaterasu, to leave her cave and restore light to the world. *See also* Amaterasu.

Tutruica (Choco People, Columbia, South America)
The rival of the creator, Caragabi (q.v.).

Tutsu-nushi No Kami (Japan)
Iha-tsutsu no wo and Ihatsutsu-nome are the parents of the god Tutsu-nushi No Kami. They are early generation deities in the creation legend. They are depicted hovering over the "Ocean of Chaos" just before the creation of the island of Onogoro. *See also* Izanami.

Tutu-F (Egypt) *see* Assessors.

Tvaksh-tri (India) *see* Tvashtri.

Tvashta (India) *see* Tvashtri.

Tvashtar (India) *see* Tvashtri.

Tvashtr (India) *see* Tvashtri.

Tvashtri (India)
Also known as: *Tvaksh-tri, Tvashta, Tvashtar, Tvashtr, Twashtar* (Sanskrit; Form Fashioner), *Twashtri, Visvakarma.* (Vedic; India)
Tvashtri, the divine artisan, architect and god of war, is the son of the sky god Dyaus. He is the father of the goddess of morning light, Saranyu, and the serpent Visvarupa. In some renditions he appears as the father of Indra, and in other legends, he is Indra's brother. Tvashtri is the creator of the magic thunderbolt known as the Vajra. He made thunderbolts as weapons for Indra and other deities. Another unique creation was the magic bowl that never emptied of soma, the ambrosia of the gods. Indra fortified himself with soma frequently, particularly before his battles with the serpent Vritra. Tvashtri taught his grandchildren, known as the Ribhus, their skills. In early times, his power was far-reaching and he was considered a creator god who gave life to all forms of creation, including heaven and earth. He created fire in the form of the god Agni. His far-reaching powers allowed him to form the men and women who were destined to marry, while they were still in the womb. During this period, Indra killed Tvashtri's son, Visvarupa, and Tvashtri and Indra became enemies. Some writers say Visvarupa was the same as Tvashtri. He could be the grandfather of Yama. He is said to be the father-in-law of Vayu, the god of wind. In later times, Tvashtri was known as Visvakarma. The vajra (vadjra), an important symbol to many Vedic, Hindu and Buddhist deities, is from the Sanskrit and means diamond and is usually translated as thunderbolt. It is a symbol of divine or mystic energy. It also symbolizes the male principle and the universal axis. It is usually represented in the form of a club or hammer, sometimes as weapon that looks like a discus with a hole in the middle. Compare Tvashtri to the Greek smith, Hephaistos, the Roman Vulcan, the Slavic Ilmarinen, and the Celtic Goibniu. *See also* Dyaus; Indra; Meru Mountain; Ribhus (The); Saranyu; Surya; Swarga; Vayu; Visvakarma; Yama; Yami.

Tviti (Teutonic) *see* Gleipnir.

Twashtar (India) *see* Tvashtri.

Twashtri (India) *see* Tvashtri.

Twet (Egypt) *see* Tuat.

Twilight of the Gods (Teutonic)
Another name for Ragnarok (q.v.).

Two Lady (Mexico) *see* Omeciutal; Ometecuhtli.

Two Lord (Mexico) *see* Omeciutatl; Ometecuhtli.

Twrch Trwyth (Celtic) *see* Cian.

Ty (Teutonic) *see* Odin; Tyr.

Tyche (Greek)
Also known as: *Tyche Agathe.*
The mate of Agathos Diamon, Tyche is a mother goddess and the goddess of fate. She is usually depicted winged, wearing a turreted crown and carrying a scepter. She is also shown standing on a ball or wheel or steering a wheel, wearing a blindfold. Compare Tyche to Fortuna, Allatu, and Astarte. *See also* Agathos Daimom; Allat; Fates.

Tydeus (Greek)

One of the Seven Against Thebes. He is the son of Oeneus and Gorge, or possibly Periboea. He married Deipyle and became the father of Diomedes, who became the king of Aetolia and who was deified after his death. Tydeus did not make out as well as his son. Near death, he killed his killer, Melanippus, and ate his brains. His actions did not sit well with the goddess Athena, who would not save his life, nor would she deify him. *See also* Calydonian Boar Hunt; Diomedes; Melanippus; Seven Against Thebes.

Tydus (Greek) *see* Adrestus.

Tyko (Greek) *see* Sisyphus.

Tyndareus (Greek)

Deified mortal. Husband of Leda and father of Clytemnestra and Castor; also king of Sparta. *See also* Agamemnon; Gorgophone; Helen; Leda.

Typheon (Greek) *see* Typhon (A).

Typhoeus (Greek) *see* Typhon (A).

Typhon (A) *Typhaon, Typheon* (Greek)

Also known as: *Typhoeus.*

Typhon, the demon of the whirlwind and a volcano deity, is the monster son of Typhoeus, who is a son of Tartarus and Gaea (Earth). As a son of Typhoeus, his aunt was the half-nymph, half-serpent Echidna. (Typhon and Typhoeus are often mistaken for the same person.) Typhon is the father by Echidna of a monstrous brood of offspring: the Crommyonian Sow, the Caucasian Eagle, Cerberus, the two-headed dog Orthus (Orthrus), Chimaera, the Nemean lion, the Vultures and the Sphinx. When the gods saw Typhon heading for Olympus, they fled to Egypt and transformed themselves into various animals. The great god Zeus remained behind. To allow the monster to take over Olympus was to allow him to become master of the world. A mighty battle ensued and at one point, Typhon felled his opponent, cut the muscles of his hands and feet, hid him in a cave and secreted his sinews under a bearskin, charging the dragon Delphyne to guard them. Hermes and Aegipan were able to regain them and restore them to Zeus' body. Zeus returned to Olympus for a new supply of thunderbolts and again engaged in battle with Typhon. The Fates entered the scene and tricked the monster into eating mortal food to weaken him. In the next bloody battle, Zeus the victor flung his enemy into the deepest region of the underworld, Tartarus. He is described as a giant monster having a hundred dragon heads, each shooting flames from mouth, eyes, and nostrils, and uttering blood curdling screams at the same time. Compare Typhon

to the Vedic deity Indra's victory over the serpent Vrita, and to the Egyptian Set and Osiris. *See also* Aegipan; Cerberus; Enceladus; Gaea; Hecatonchires; Hydra; Phorcys; Scylla; Set; Tartarus; Zeus.

Typhon (B) *Typheon, Tyhaon* (Greek)

Typhon is the son of Zeus and the mortal Niobe. His siblings are Argus, Osiris and Pelasgus. *See also* Aello; Agrus (A); Niobe (B); Pelasgus.

Tyr (Norse; Teutonic)

Also known as: *Reidi-tyr, Sig-tyr, Teu, Thingsus, Tiw, Tiwaz, Ty, Tyw, Zio, Ziu, Ziv, Ziw.*

Sky god. As Tiwaz (German) he is a god of battle who is associated with Mars by the Romans. He is the god of law and order and one who holds up the universe. He is also known as a god of the sky and of battle. He is either the son of Odin or Hymir. Some say Tyr was the son of Frigga by Odin and brother of Balder and Hermod. Tyr was the only brave one to fasten the fetter around the neck of Fenrir, the wolf, and lost his hand because Fenrir was mistrustful of the strength of the binding called Gleipnir. He is associated with the Valkyries. As Thingsus, Ziv is God of Assembly. *See also* Fenrir; Thing; Ziu.

Tyro (Greek)

The daughter of Salmoneus and Alcidice, she married her uncle (who was also her stepfather), Cretheus. Her children are Aeson, Amythaon, Pheres, and Promachus. A liason with the sea god Poseidon produced twin sons, Neleus, the king of Pyros, and Pelias, the king of Iolcus. *See also* Crethus; Neleus; Pelias; Salmoneus; Sisyphus.

Tyt (Egypt) *see* Ab.

Tyw (Teutonic) *see* Tyr.

Tzakol (Maya People, Yucatan) *see* Ixpiyacoc.

Tzakor (Maya People, Yucatan)

Creator. One of the four regents who attempted to create mankind. *See also* Ixpiyac (Xpiyacoc).

Tzinteotl (Aztec)

Also known as: Possibly *Xochiquetzal.*

Goddess of maize. Little known of her history, but she is probably related to Xilonen. *See also* Cinteotl; Xilonen.

Tzitzimime (Aztec People, Mexico)

Star demons. They are called "Monsters Descending from Above."

Tzontemoc (Mexico) *see* Mictlantecutli.

U

Uadjit (Egypt) *see* Buto (Greek); Uatchet.

Uaj (Slavic) God of the earth.

Uajet (Egypt) *see* Buto (A); Uatchet.

Uajyt (Egypt) *see* Uatchet.

Uamemti (Egypt) *see* Assessors.

Uasir (Egypt) *see* Osiris.

Uatch-Nes (Egypt) *see* Assessors.

Uatchet (Egypt)
Also known as: *Buto, Per Uadjit* (The Dwelling Place of Uadjit), *Uajyt, Uatchit, Uatchura, Uazet, Uto.*
Cobra goddess. Protector and guardian of royalty. Uatchet assisted Isis in hiding the infant Horus in the swamps. Uatchet is shown with wings and the red crown of Lower Egypt is on her head. She is mentioned in one of the old hymns along with Amen-Ra, Nekhebet and Mehen. *See also* Buto (A); Nekhbet; Wadjet.

Uatchit (Egypt) *see* Buto; Uatchet.

Uatchura (Egypt) *see* Buto (A); Uatchet.

Uazai (Egypt) *see* Buto (A); Uatchet.

Uazet (Egypt) *see* Uatchet.

Ubelluris (Hittite)
This mountain god carries the edge of the western sky on his shoulders.

Uben (Egypt) *see* Aai.

Uboze (Slavic) *see* Khoromozitel.

Uc-Zip (Maya)
Underworld deity. Uc-Zip announces the Vision Serpent when he emerges from Xibalba, the underworld.

Uchchaih-sravas (India) Sacred Horse. *See also* Kurma.

Uchtsiti (Acoma People, North America)
"Nothing Lacking." Uchtsiti is the "Father of the Gods."

Udar (Teutonic)
Udar, the son of Nott, is a water god. *See also* Nott.

Uddushunamir (Assyro-Babylonian) *see* Asushunamir.

Udumbara (India) "Man of the Ficus Tree." *See also* Yama.

Udzume (Japan) *see* Ama No Uzume.

Ueuecoyotl (Mexico, Aztec, Otomi)
Also known as: *Coyote* or *Old Coyote.*
God of fecundity. Trickster deity. He is the manifestation of unacceptable impulses. Some sources believe the name Xolotl was borrowed from Ueuecoyotl. He is also confused with Xolotl. Ueuecoyotl is generally considered the same as the North American Coyote (q.v.).

Ufa (Egypt)
Ufa is a serpent mentioned with Akeneh, the serpent demon, and other serpents in the text of *Unas*, a king in the fifth dynasty. This text describes magical methods to destroy serpents and barbarous beasts.

Ugar (Ugaric)
Ugar is one of Baal's messengers. *See also* Baal.

Uggerus (Teutonic) A name for Odin (q.v.).

Ugra (India) "Dread." *See also* Agni.

Ugra Tara (Buddhist; Tibet)
A dreadful manifestion of the goddess Khadga Jogina (q.v.).

Ugrasena, King (India)
The demon Drumalika assumed the body of King Ugrasena and raped his wife, Queen Pavanarekha. She became pregnant and gave birth to the demon Kansa. For additional details, *see* Kansa. *See also* Yadavas.

Uhiji-ni No Mikoto (Japan)
"Mud Earth." One of the third "generation" of deities to spring from Chaos. *See also* Ama-no-minaka-nushi.

Uhlanga (Africa)
Uhlanga is another name for the supreme god, Unkulunkulu (q.v.).

Uhumakaikai (Hawaii, Polynesia)
Local evil shark or fish gods of Kauai.

Uiracocha (Inca) *see* Virococha.

Uitzilopochtli (Aztec) *see* Huitzilopochtli.

Uitztlampa (Mexico, Aztec)
Also known as: *Place of Thorns.*
The mountain refuge of the brothers of Huitzilopochtli who escaped his wrath. *See also* Coatlicue; Huitzilopochtli.

Uixtochihuatl *Huixtocihuatl, Uixtociuatl* (Aztec People, Mexico)
She is the goddess of salt, and considered to be the eldest sister of Tlaloc. She is also known as the sister of the rain gods. Uixtochihuatl is sometimes identified as one of the wives of Tezcatlipoca. *See also* Atlantonan; Tlaloc; Xilonen; Xochiquetzal.

Uixtociuatl (Mexico) *see* Uixtochihuatl.

Uja-Jin (Japan)

Uja-Jin is an obsure deity who is associated with Benten, the sea goddess of good luck. *See also* Benten.

Ujikami (Japan)

The Ujikami are the ghosts of old rulers. *See also* Okuni-Nushino-Mikoto.

Uka-no-kami (Japan)

Uka-no-kami is another name for the androgynous deity of rice and good luck, Inari (q.v.).

Ukanipo (Hawaii) Great shark god of Hawaii. *See also* Moaalii.

Uke-mochi (Japan) *see* Ukemochi.

Uke-mochi-no-kami (Japan) *see* Ukemochi.

Ukemochi *Uke-mochi, Uki-mochi* (Japan)

Also known as: *Ogetsu-hime-no-kami* (Great-Food-Princess), *Toyo-uke-bime* (Princess-of-Rich-Food) *Toyo-uke-hime* (Plentiful-Food-August), *Toyo-uke-hime-no-hime, Toyo-uke-hime-no-himi, Toyo-uke-no-kami* (Abundance-Bounty-Goddess), *Uke-mochi-no-kami, Ukemochi-no-kami, Waka-uke-nomi* (Young-Woman-with-Food).

Goddess of food. Goddess of sustenance. Domestic deity. Ukemochi (Food-Possessing-Goddess) produced the food that the sun goddess Amaterasu used as seeds to grow in the fields she developed and irrigated. The ancient records of the *Nihongi* and the *Kojiki* vary in the interpretation of this myth. The *Nihongi* records that the sun goddess Amaterasu sent her brother Tsuki-yomi to visit Ukemochi. In the *Kojiki*, it is her brother Susanowo who is sent on the mission. The following myth, based on the *Nihongi*, is generally thought to be the most original rendition. Tsuki-yomi was sent to earth to see that Ukemochi was performing her duties. While being hospitable, she opened her mouth while facing the field, and boiled rice streamed from it. As she faced the sea, she regurgitated fish and edible seaweed. When she faced the wooded hills, game of various kinds came forth. Tsuki-yomi did not appreciate this banquet. He killed her. Death did not stop the food goddess from being productive. The ox and the horse emerged from her head, silkworms from her eyebrows, millet grew from her forehead, rice from her stomach, and wheat and beans from her genitals. Amaterasu, upset by her brother's actions, separated from him. The name Ogetsu-hime-no-kami may be another name for Ukemochi but it is not certain as the *Kojiki* is not clear about the name. It refers to Ogetsu-hime-no-kami as Ukemochi and also names a separate entity Ukemochi. The name is used as another name of the land of Apa. It also refers to Ogetsu-hime-no-kami as the wife of Pa-yama-to-no-kami, who is said to be the husband of Ukemochi. As wife and mother Ukemochi had eight children. Three of her daughters were Waka-sana-me-no-kami, Natu-taka-mi-no-kami (also known as Natu-no-me-no-kami) and Aki-bime-no-kami. Ukemochi may be the same as Waka-Uke-Nomi (Young-Woman-with-Food). She may be the same as Toyo-Uke-Bimi (Princess-of-Rich-Food) and Toyo-uke-no-kami (Abundance-Bounty-Goddess). Toyo-uke-no-kami was known as companion of the sun goddess Amaterasu.

Ukemochi is often confused with the god of rice Inari, who is often presented as a goddess. Ukemochi represents kindness, nourishment and the maternal cord. Rice is considered an emblem of happiness and nourishment. Seaweed signifies joyousness. Fish represent abundance, wisdom, generative power and woman. In some Asian cultures bones of the fish are thrown back into the sea so the fish can return to life for the next fishing season. The ox toils for others and is a symbol of agriculture. Wheat is also a symbol of agriculture. The horse symbolizes creativity and endurance. In Japan, beans, as well as being nourishing, were used to dispel evil spirits. (In ancient Greece and Rome, one could spit beans to expel ghosts.) Ise, the principal shrine dedicated to Amaterasu, has reserved the outer shrine for worship of Ukemochi. For information about the *Nihongi*, the *Kojiki* and the Shinto creation story, *see* Ama-no-minaka-nushi. Compare Ukemochi to Kami-mimusubi, who collected the seeds produced by Ogetsu-hime-no-kami. *See also* Amaterasu; Inari; Kaya-no-hime-no-kami (goddess of herbs).

Ukemochi-no-kami *see* Toyo-uke-hime-no-hime; Ukemochi.

Ukhukh (Egypt)

Local deity. He was worshiped near the site of modern Meir. His symbol is a staff decorated with two feathers and two serpents.

Uki-Mochi (Japan) *see* Ukemochi.

Ukibashi (Japan) *see* Izanami.

Ukko (Finnish)

Also known as: *Jumala.*

God of air. God of thunderstorms. Ukko replaced the sky and thunder god Jumala. He created fire when he struck his sword against his fingernail. Ukko is associated Vainamoinen and Ilmarinen. *See also* Ilmarinen; Jumala; Thor.

Ukko-Thor (Finnish) *see* Thor; Ukko.

Uksakka (Lapp)

Door goddess. Uksakka lives under the door. Her function is to protect the newborn and the owners of the house. She is similar to Dorr-Karing of the Swedish people.

Uktena (Cherokee People, North America)

The Great Water Serpent. *See also* Ukteni; Unktehi.

Ukteni (Natchez People, North America) Magical water snake.

Ul (New Hebrides) Spirit of moon and night. *See also* Tortali.

Ulgan (Siberia) Supreme god of heaven.

Uli (Hawaii, Polynesia)

Sorcery goddess. She is the most commonly invoked sorcery deity in Hawaii. Uli, Maka-ku-koae, the god who brings madness, and Alae-a-Hina, the goddess who had the secret of fire, are invoked to bring death to an enemy. *See also* Keoloewa; Ku-Kali-Moku; Kupua.

Ull (Norse; Teutonic)

Also known as: *Auler, Holler* (German), *Oller, Ollerus, Uller, Ullerus, Ullr, Wuldor* (Anglo-saxon).

God of winter. God of skiing. God of archery. Major god. Ull, Hod, Vali and Vidar are the four major gods in Norse mythology. In the mythology of the *Eddas*, Ull is one of twelve major deities. The others are Odin, Thor, Njord, Frey, Balder, Tyr, Heimda, Bragi, Forseti, Hod, Vidar and Vali. Ull is an excellent skier and archer. His mother is the beautiful, golden-haired protector of homes, Sif, and his stepfather is Thor. His natural father is unknown. Ull resides in Ydalir (Valley of Rain). *See also* Holler; Skadi.

Uller (Teutonic) *see* Ull.

Ullerus (Teutonic) *see* Ull.

Ulligarra (Sumer)
One of the two first ancestors of mankind. The other was Zalgarra. They were born from the blood of the gods known as Lamga. *See also* Cosmology of Assur.

Ullikummi (Hittite, Hurrian) *see* Ullikummis.

Ullikummis *Ullikummi* (Hittite, Hurrite)
His father, Kumbaris, had Ullikummis created specifically to oppose the gods. After being born he was first placed on the lap of Kumarbis by the goddesses Gul-shes and Makh, then placed on the right shoulder of Upelluris, the giant who sustained the world. Ullikummis' body, made of dioritic stone, grew to immense proportions. By the fifteenth day he stood in the sea, so tall, the sea only reached his belt. He grew to a height of 9,000 leagues with a girth of 9,000 leagues. As his height reached to the heavens, the other gods feared him. After he decided to destroy humanity and the storm god Kummiya, the other gods defeated him. They were helped by the great god Ea who weakened Ullikummis to the point where he could be overtaken. *See also* Alalus; Anus; Ea; Hepat; Kumarbis; Teshub; Upelluris.

Ullr (Teutonic) *see* Ull.

Ullur (Teutonic) *see* Aesir.

Ulmuka (India) Son of Bala-Rama (q.v.).

Ulu Tojon (Yakut People, Siberia)
Also known as: *Arsan-Duolai, Arson Duolai, Syga-Tojon.*
Creator. God of thunder and lightning. He is called the "stranger" or "white creator." Ulu Tojon is from the third heaven. He rules the underworld and the Abaasy. Mortals received fire from him. He is possibly the same as Arson Duolai (q.v.) *See also* Abassy.

Ulupi (India)
A Nagi serpent princess. *See also* Arjuna; Nagas and Nagis.

Ulysses (Roman) Ulysses is the Roman equivalent to Odysseus.

Uma (Hindu; India)
Also known as: *Devi, Parvati*
Uma is an aspect of the great goddess Devi and her name means "Light" as she personifies light and beauty. She is depicted with a golden skin and is attributed with inspiring the gods with love. Parvati was reborn as Uma. In one legend, Uma is the wife of the god Mahesvara. They had three thousand chil-

dren; the eldest son was Vinayaka. *See also* Daksha; Devi; Devis; Durga; Gozanze-Myoo; Kali; Parvati; Sati (A); Shashthi; Shiva; Trailokyavijaya.

Uma Haimavati (India) *see* Rudra.

Umai (Mongol, Turkey)
Also known as: *Mai, Ymai.*
Fire deity. Although a fire god or goddess to the Mongols, she is a Goddess of Fire in the sense of household use to the Turks. If her flame should be extinguished, so would that of the Turk family. Umai is possibly the same as Ummu of the Assyrians. *See also* Akha; Ot.

Umhlanga (Africa) *see* Unkulunkulu.

Umiarissat (Eskimo) *see* Inuat; Inue.

Umina (Ecuador)
God of medicine. He is represented by a large emerald.

Umlungu (Africa) *see* Mulungu.

Umm Kulthum (Islamic) *see* Mohammed.

Umunmutamku (Assyro-Babylonia)
The Great God, Ea, created Umunmutamku and Umunmutamnag as deities to present offerings to other gods. *See also* Ea.

Unas (Egypt)
Also known as: *Ashem, Sekhem, Unis.*
A god who eats other gods. The gods were snared by Amkehuu, and after an examination for fitness by Tcheser-tep-f, they were bound by Her-thertu and the god Khensu cut their throats and took out their intestines. Next, they were butchered and cooked by Shesemu. Unas ate their words, power and spirits. He ate the largest and finest at daybreak, the smaller ones at sunset, and the smallest for his evening meal. The old and worn out gods were rejected and used for fuel in his furnace. The result of his eating the gods was that he changed into Sekhem and Ashem. *See also* Shesemu.

Undines (Teutonic) Female water spirits. *See also* Nixie.

Undry (Celtic) *see* Dagda.

Unelanuhi (Cherokee People, North America)
Also known as: *Aghyu Gugu*
Unelanuhi is a sun goddess.

Ung (Egypt)
Ung is a god who is sometimes called "Son of the Solar Deity." He is a messenger of the gods. He is identified with Osiris and Shu.

Ungud (Aborigine People, Australia)
Also known as: *Rainbow Serpent, Wongar.*
Ungud is a bi-sexual snake god. He caused rain after Wallanganda threw water on the earth. He is possibly the same as Wuraka (q.v.). *See also* Rainbow Snake.

Unis (Egypt) *see* Unas.

Universal Egg (Greek) *see* Eurynome (A).

Universal Mother (India) *see* Maya (B).

Universal Shakti (India) *see* Maya (B).

Univirae (Etruscan, Roman) *see* Fortuna.

Unkulunkulu (Kaffir, Zulu People, Africa)

Also known as: *Nkulnkulu, Uhlanga, Umhlanga.*

Supreme deity. Son of Unvelingange, creator of civilization. Unkulunkulu's impatience is indirectly responsible for death because he couldn't wait for the message of creation to be spread among mortals. He chose the messenger. Another version from the Zulu people of Africa places Unkulunkulu as a creator god or a place of beginning. Other authorities state that Unkulunkulu was the first man. The name is associated with a reed or reed bed. He is similar to Mulungu and Ribimbi.

Unmatta (India) "Raging." *See also* Shiva.

Unnefer (Egypt)

Also known as: *Onnophris, Osiris, Unnofre, Wenen-nefer, Wenenefer.*

Unnefer is one of the titles applied to Osiris, meaning "he who is continually happy," in his role as god of resurrection. *See also* Onophris.

Unnet (Egypt) *see* Wenut.

Unnofre (Egypt) *see* Unnefer.

Unsas, The (Arabic)

A triad of powerful goddesses known as Al-Uza, Menat and Allat (also known as Lat, Uzza and Manat). *See also* Allat; Al-Uza.

Unt (Egypt) *see* Aaru.

Untunktahe (Dakota People, North America)

With Waukheon, the thunderbird, Untunktahe, the water god, is a primary deity.

Unummuzida (Sumer) *see* Ningishzida.

Unvelingange (Kaffir)

First god. The god who existed before anything else.

Upamanya (India)

His eyesight was restored by the twin deities of healing, the Asvins (q.v.).

Upananda (India)

Nanda and Upananda, two Naga kings, gave Buddha in his mortal form as Gautama his first bath. *See also* Naga Naga Knaya.

Upao (Polynesia)

Upao is a name for the creator god of the ocean and of fishers, Tangaroa.

Upasunda (India)

Upasunda and Sunda are two of the Asura brothers, who are constantly in conflict with the gods. *See also* Arjuna; Asuras.

Upelluri (Hittite) *see* Upelluris.

Upelluris *Upelluri* (Hittite, Hurrite)

The Isirra deities placed Ullikummis on the shoulders of this giant, so he could grow to immense proportions and oppose the gods. Like Atlas, Upelluris carried the world on his shoulders. *See also* Atlas; Ullikummis.

Upset (Egypt)

Upset is often identified with Isis and other goddesses worshipped at Philae.

Upshukina (Sumer)

Home of gods. In the great hall the gods meet to hold council. The Igigi held a banquet there and gave Marduk full powers as king and Ruler of the World. *See also* Igigi; Marduk.

Upuaut (Egypt) *see* Khenti Amenti.

Ur (Sumer)

He is an ancient Mesopotamian god, thought by some to be Nabu. *See also* Nabu.

Ur-Nammu (Sumer)

Originally the king of the city of Lagash, this tall, thin ruler was later deified.

Ur-Shanabi (Babylon) *see* Urshanabi.

Urshanabi (Babylon)

He is the sailor who takes dead souls across the Sea of Hades. *See also* Gilgamesh.

Ura (Assyro-Babylonia) A demon of pestilence.

Uraeus (Egypt)

Divine cobra. A flame-breathing asp who protects the sun god Ra by destroying his foes. Ra is sometimes depicted wearing on his head the disk of the sun surrounded by the uraeus, a symbol of royalty and power. Uraeus is the divine snake, a cobra, identified with the goddess Buto of Lower Egypt. It appears in the headdresses or crowns of many gods and goddesses of Egypt. It is said to spit fire at anyone who is an enemy of the gods or who invades the tombs of the dead.

Uragas (India) *see* Nagas and Nagis.

Urania (Greek)

Urania is the Muse of astronomy and astrology. She is the mother of Hymenaeus by Dionysus and the possible mother of the poet and musician, Linus. Urania is depicted with a globe and a pair of compasses. *See also* Hymen; Linus; Muses; Uranie.

Uranus (Greek)

Also known as: *Caelus, Coelus* (Roman), *Ouranos, Summano* (Etruscan).

Sky god. Most ancient of deities. His father is sometimes said to be Aether (Air). His mother and later his wife is Gaea (earth). He is the father of the Cyclopes, Hecatonchires and Titans. He sequestered his children by lock and key. Cronus, however, was able to castrate him and throw his genitals into the sea. From his genitals the goddess Aphrodite was created and rose from the sea. From his semen and blood the Erinyes, Giants and Meliae were born. The Telchines and Halia are possibly his children by Thalassa, personification of the sea. Compare Uranus to Varuna (India) and Indra (India). *See also* Aegaeon; Aether; Alcyoneus; Ceos; Chaos; Cronus; Cybele; Demeter; Enceladus;

Erinyes; Gaea; Giants; Hecatonchires; Meliae; Muses; Oceanus; Styx; Telechine; Theia (C); Themis; Thoas (E); Titans.

Urcaguary (Peru) *see* Urcaguay.

Urcaguay *Urcaguary* (Inca People, Peru)

He is a god of the underground and guardian of the underground treasures. Urcaguay is shown as a large snake with the head of a deer with little gold chains on the tail.

Urd *Urdh, Urdhr, Urdur* (Norse; Teutonic)

Also known as: *Urpr, Urth, Wurd, Wyrd* (Anglo-Saxon).

Goddess of destiny. One of the Norns. The better known of the numerous Norns are Urd, Verdandi and Skuld. There are both good and evil Norns. They oversee the destiny of all mortals and gods. At every birth, one of the Norns is present. They reside beneath the Tree of Life, Yggdrasil, next to Urd's Well. The gods assemble at this location. Some say Urd is the chief of the Norns and the daughter of Mimir. She is shown looking back. *See* Fates; Hel; Mimer; Mimer's Well; Norns; Odin; Yggdrasil.

Urdh (Teutonic) *see* Urd.

Urdhr (Teutonic) *see* Urd.

Urdur (Teutonic) *see* Urd.

Urien (Celtic)

Urien is one of the names for Bran's decapitated head. *See also* Bran.

Urin Cuzco (Inca)

Urin Cuzco is another name for Tahuantin Suyu Kapac, the four brothers who are the sons of the sun and the first people. *See also* Tahuantin Suyu Kapac.

Urion (Greek) *see* Orion.

Uris (Greek)

Uris is one of the attendants of Artemis, the moon goddess and goddess of hunting. Some say that Uris was possibly the lover of the hunter Orion (q.v.).

Urja (India)

Urja is one of Daksha's daughters. *See also* Daksha; Vasistha.

Urmila (India)

She is described as a beautiful sister of Sita, the goddess of fertility and agriculture. *See also* Sita.

Urpihuachac (Andean People, Peru)

Urpihuachac was the lucky recipient of the few fish in the world, a gift from the creator of all things, Coniraya (q.v.). *See also* Viracocha.

Urpr (Teutonic) *see* Urd.

Urshanabi *Ur-Shanabi* (Babylonia)

Urshanabi is the sailor who steered the ark built by Utnapishtim, during the great Deluge. *See also* Gilgamesh; Utnapishtim.

Urshiu (Egypt) *see* Aai.

Urt (A) (Egypt)

Also known as: *Osiris.*

Urt is one of the four earthly forms of Osiris in the sixth sector of Tuat.

Urt (B) (Finnish) *see* Ort.

Urth (Teutonic)

Urth is a name for the goddess of the underworld, Hel (q.v.).

Uruasi (India) *see* Urvasi.

Uruki (India) *see* Urvasi.

Urun Ai Toyon (Yakuts)

The god of the seventh heaven, who does only good, but can bring punishment.

Urutaetae (Polynesia, Tahiti)

God of the underworld (afterworld). Some say Urutaetae presides as the head of the underworld. *See also* Hiro.

Urutonga (Maori People, New Zealand)

"South West." In Maori mythology, she is the goddess wife of Hema and the mother Tawhaki and Kariki. *See also* Hema; Tawhaki.

Urvashi (India) *see* Urvasi.

Urvasi *Uruki, Uruasi, Urvashi* (Vedic, Hindu; India)

Goddess of success in love. An Apsaras. She is the daughter of the sage Naranarayana. The power that he acquired from his rigorous austerities alarmed the gods. They sent a beautiful nymph to distract him. When he saw her, he was not disturbed. He put a flower on his thigh and from it Urvasi, even more alluring than the nymph, blossomed. Her father sent her to the celestial realm where she created a major disturbance among the deities for they all wanted her for a mate. Varuna and Surya (sometimes Mitra) both loved her at the same time. She aroused them so that their sperm fell to the ground. It was collected in a jar of water and from it Agastya was born in the shape of a beautiful fish. She is also known as the mother of Vasishtha by Mithra or Varuna, or some say Agni. In other legends, she is the spouse of the mortal king Pururavas, the gleaming one, who is an aspect of the sun and the founder of the lunar dynasty. When a flash of lightning revealed her husband's brilliance, it was more than she could endure. Urvasi vanished into the water, and became a naiad with a fish tail. Distraught, Pururavas searched everywhere for her and finally found her on the last day of the year. In a slight variation of this tale, she lived with the king on the condition that she never wanted to see him naked. He forgot and when she came upon him without clothing, she was filled with disgust and fled. He promised her that if she returned he would give up his throne for her and become an erotic dancer. She is one of the few Apsarases with her own mythology. Her earthly counterpart is the swan or the lotus. Compare Urvasi to the Greek Psyche and Daphne. *See also* Agastya; Apsarases; Manaka; Marisha; Mitra; Varuna; Vasihtha.

Usanas (India) *see* Brihaspati.

Usekht-Nemmat (Egypt) *see* Assessors.

Usert (Egypt) *see* Isis.

Usha (India)

She is the demon daughter of Bana. *See also* Bana; Daityas; Krishna.

Ushas *Dyotana* (The Light-Bearer), *Marichi, Marishi, Usas* (Vedic, Hindu; India)

Ushas, goddess of the dawn, is the daughter of the earth goddess Prithiva and the sky god Dyaus. Her siblings are Agni the fire god, Ratri the night goddess (also known as Ratridevi), Varuna the king of the universe, Bhaga the god of prosperity and probably Indra the god of the heavens. Ushas may be the sister of the Adityas. She is the mother of the storm god Rudra and possibly the twin healing deities, the Asvins. If not their mother she is a close friend. Ratri and Ushas are reputed to be joint mothers of the sun god Surya. Others say she is the lover, bride or daughter of Surya. Chandra the moon god is also her husband. Their marriage can never be consummated, as the moon and the sun are constantly in pursuit of one another. Eternally youthful, she brings age to mortals. She is also a fertility goddess and a goddess of poetry. In some renditions, it is said that she was created by Indra. There is an ancient Vedic goddess named Asva who was called "The Dawn" and "The Mare." She closely corresponds to the goddess of dawn Ushas. Holding a bow and arrow, Ushas is depicted draped in the gentle colors of dawn, crossing the eastern sky in a vehicle drawn by red cows. As a fertility goddess, she is shown with three heads; one head is a pig's head, the symbol of fecundity. Seven pigs draw her vehicle. Ushas, the beautiful dawn goddess, is a source of delight to all living creatures. It is said that Marichi, who is a Buddhist goddess, is Ushas in her fierce form. In this aspect she is shown with an eye in her forehead, three faces, ten arms, her head crowned with skulls and wreathed in flame. Compare Ushas to the Greek goddess of dawn, Eos. *See also* Adityas; Agni; Asvins; Aurora; Bhaga; Chandra; Dyaus; Indra; Marichi (A); Marichi-ten; Prithiva; Ratri; Rudra; Saranyu; Surya; Varuna.

Ushemet Hatu Khefti Ra (Egypt)

Underworld time. The name of the first hour of Tuat. The dead (Af) make their journey along the river of Tuat in the Sektet boat. With them are Ap-uat, Sa, Heru-Hekenu, Nehes, Hu (the double of Shu, and the captain and lady of the boat). *See also* Tuat.

Ushnishavijaya (Buddhist; India)

This goddess abolishes fear and is also considered a goddess of charity. Her attributes are Buddha on the lotus, a bow and arrow, a noose and a water-pot. She is shown with three faces and eight arms.

Ushodevatas (India) *see* Devis.

Usma (Babylon)

He is one of the attendants of the great god, Ea. It is possible that he is a god of the sea. Usma is shown as two-faced.

Usukun (Maya People, Yucatan)

Evil deity. He is one of the brothers of Hapikern. Usukun hates mankind. His assistant is Kisin, the earthquake. Usukun is associated with Nohochacyum.

Usur-Apa (Egypt) *see* Serapis.

Usur-Api (Egypt) *see* Serapis.

Uta-Napishtim (Babylon) *see* Utnapishtim.

Uta-Napistim (Babylon) *see* Utnapishtim.

Utanapishtim (Babylon) *see* Utnapishtim.

Utnapishtim *Ut-Napishtim* (Babylon)

Also known as: *Uta-Napishtim, Ziusudra* (Sumerian).

A mortal who was deified. When the gods sent the Deluge, Utnapishtim built an ark and saved himself, his family and the beasts who inhabit the earth. The sailor who steered the craft was Urshanabi. Enlil the storm god made Utnapishtim immortal. It was Utnapishtim who Gilgamesh consulted in his search for immortality. Utnapishtim gave Gilgamesh a plant to eat for this purpose. *See also* Ea; Enlil; Gilgamesh; Siduri; Ziusudra.

Utathya (India) *see* Rishi; Sarasvati.

Utennu Apes (Egypt) *see* Aani.

Utet (Egypt) The heron god.

Utgard (Teutonic)

Also known as: *Jotunheim.*

Realm of the giants. Utgard is the home of Skrymir located in Jotunheim. Utgard-Loki may be the ruler. *See also* Fjalar; Utgard-Loki.

Utgard-Loki *Utgard-Loke* (Teutonic)

Also known as: *Loki, Skrymir.*

Giant. Utgard-Loki is the nemesis of Thor. As Loki he rules Utgard, the home of the giants in Jotunheim. For additional details of the shape-changer, *see* Loki. *See also* Fjalar; Skrymir.

Uther Ben (Celtic)

One of the names given to Bran's decapitated head. It means "Wonderful Head."

Uther Pendragon (Celtic)

One of the several names given to Bran's decapitated head. *See also* Arthur; Bran.

Uthra (Gnostic) *see* Abathur.

Uto (Egypt) *see* Uatchet.

Utsanati (Cherokee People, North America)

Rattlesnake, helper of man.

Utset and Bowutset (Sia People, India) The First Mothers.

Uttara (India)

Abhimanya and Uttara are the parents of Parikshit, the king of Hastinapura and patron of poetry. His grandfather is the warrior, Arjuna. *See also* Abhimanya; Parikshit.

Uttu (Sumer)

She is the goddess of clothing, earth, plants, and general vegetation. One of her responsibilities is weaving cloth and making clothing. Her mother, Ninkurra, is the daughter of Ninsar and Enki. Ninsar is the daughter of Ninhursag and Enki. Enki had an incestuous relationship with his daughter Ninsar and Ninkurra was born. He did the same with his granddaughter, Ninkurra, and Uttu was born. He tried to molest Uttu but her great grandmother Ninhursag intervened. *See also* Enki; Ninhursag; Ninkurra; Ninmu.

Utu (Sumer)

Also known as: *Babbar.*

He is the counterpart of the Babylonian god Shamash. The brother of Inanna, he wanted her to marry the farmer god Enkidu rather than the shepherd god Dumuzi. He is connected with legislation and justice. In some myths he is the moon god, son of Enlil and the goddess Ninlil. *See also* Babbar; Dumuzi; Enkidu; Enlil; Inanna; Ninlil; Shamash.

Utu-Rekhit (Egypt) *see* Assessors.

Utukki (Assyro-Babylonian)

The Utukki are the seven evil demons created from the union of Anu and Antu. Their siblings are the underworld gods, known as the Anunnaki. *See also* Anat; Antu; Anu.

Utukku (Sumer)

The Utukku are the genies who are spirits holding a position subordinate to that of the gods. Those called the Edimmu were forces of evil; the Shedu, forces of good. *See also* Edimmu; Shedu; Utukki.

Uuodan (German) *see* Odin.

Uyitzin (Maya People, Yucatan)

Benevolent deity. He is one of three brothers of Nohochacyu, the creator, who is the enemy of the evil Nohochacyum (q.v.).

Uyungsum (Saora People, India) *see* Adununkisum.

Uzzah (Arabic) *see* Al-Uza.

V

Vac (India) see Sarasvati.

Vach Vac, Vacha (Brahmanic, Hindu; India)

Also known as: *Bak, Madhyama, Para, Pashyanti, Sata-rupa, Savitri (A), Shatarupa* (She of the Thousand Forms), *Vaikhari.*

A charming, seductive and mysterious goddess, Vach, meaning "voice," was originally known as the goddess of thunder. Later, she became known as the goddess of knowledge and speech. All intelligent beings were created through Vach by Prajapati. In the Vedas, Vach is called the "melodious four-uddered cow." Her milk sustains all and her udders sustain the four quarters of the universe. She is variously known as the spouse of Indra, the bull As (meaning breath) and possibly Vata (the wind). In one legend, Vach, as one of Indra's wives and goddess of waters, gave the nectar of the gods Soma to the Gandharvas. As Sata-rupa she is an aspect of the female half of Brahma and the daughter of Kama (love). She is sometimes represented as a cow. She is similar in some aspects to the goddess Sarasvati and in some legends she is referred to as Sarasvati's mother. Vach corresponds to Diti and Aditi and closely parallels Kwan-Yin. *See also* Aditi; Brahma; Brihaspati; Indra; Kama; Karttikeya; Prajapati; Soma.

Vach-Sarasvati (India) *see* Sarasvati.

Vacha (India) *see* Vach.

Vacuna (Roman)

Vacuna is a Sabine goddess, often said to be the same as the Roman goddess of victory, Victoria. She is identified with Ceres, Diana, Minerva or Venus. *See also* Victoria.

Vadaba (India) *see* Vadava.

Vadava *Badava, Vadaba* (India)

This mare goddess is also a being of flame, with a horse's head, who licks up water, and causes clouds and rain. *See also* Asvins; Vivasvat.

Vadjra (India) *see* Vajra.

Vafthrudni (Teutonic) *see* Vafthrudnir.

Vafthrudnir (Teutonic)

Also known as: *Vafthrudni.*

Frost Giant. Possibly a god of riddles. A giant of great intelligence, Vafthrudnir matched wits with Odin who used the name Gangrad supplied by Frigga. The stakes were that the loser would also lose his head. Odin won, but it is not known if the giant lost his head.

Vafud (Teutonic) A name for Odin. *See also* Odin.

Vaghan (Tierra del Fuego)

Vaghan is another name for the supreme deity, Alakaluf.

Vagisvara *Vagiswara* (India) A name for Manjusri (q.v.).

Vagiswara (India) *see* Vagisvara.

Vague (Antilles Islands, Haiti)

Another name for the supreme being, Guamaonocon.

Vah (Persian) *see* Vahran; Verethraghna.

Vahagn (Armenia)

"Dragon Killer." God of fire. One of a triad with Aramazd and Anahit. This triad is similar to the Persian Auramazda, Anahita, and Mithra. Vahagn was once a rival of Ba'al Shamin and Mihr, both sun-gods. He had been accused of stealing straw and the wife of Ba'al Shamin. He used the straw to form the Milky Way. Vahagn might be the same as the Armenian storm god known as Dsovean. (Both gods were sea-born.) There is even a possibility of him being preceded by the pre–Vedic Vrtra-han. Vahagn's consort is sometimes said to be love goddess Arusyak ("Little Bride"). Vahagn bears some similarity to the fire god Agni. *See also* Anahit; Aramazd; Astaik; Ba'al Shamim; Dsovean.

Vahran (Persian)

Vahran is the name for Verethraghna, the genius of victory, in the Pahlavi dialect. *See also* Verethraghna.

Vahu (Polynesia)

A name for Tangaroa, the creator god. *See also* Tangaroa.

Vaidya-nath (India)

"Lord of the Knowing Ones," or "Lord of Physicians." *See also* Shiva.

Vaijayanta (India) Indra's palace. *See also* Indra; Swarga.

Vaikhari (India)

A name for Vach, the goddess of knowledge and speech. *See also* Vach.

Vaikuntha *Vaijayanta* (Hindu; India)

Vishnu's celestial abode is a city of gold and jeweled palaces. It is located on Mount Meru and has a circumference of 80,000 miles. The river Ganges, sometimes said to have its origin in Vishnu's foot, runs through his kingdom. Blue, red and white lotuses bloom in the five surrounding pools. Vishnu and his wife, the goddess of beauty Lakshmi, radiate like the sun as they sit amid the white lotuses. *See also* Amaravati; Lakshmi; Loka; Meru Mountain; Swarga; Vishnu.

Vainamoinen *Wainamoinen* (Finland)

Vainamoinen, the hero, god of music, magician and the enchanter, invented the zither. According to some legends Vainamoinen is the brother of Lemminkainen and Ilmarinen. When he plays his instrument he quiets the elements and all wild animals. Vainamoinen remained in his mother Luonno-tar's womb until he became bored, thirty years later. He married the daughter of the evil sorcerer Louhi, the Lady of Pohja (also spelled Pohjola). Vainamoinen had the smith god, Ilmari-nen, manufacture the talisman known as Sampo. Joukahainen promised Vainamoinen that he could marry his sister, Aino. Repulsed by the thought of marriage to the elderly man she ran away, fell into the sea and became a water spirit. Vainamoinen is the same as the Estonian god of music, Vanemuine. Forged from magic metals, Sampo is a mill that grinds out grain, salt and even gold upon demand. It represents a source of pros-perity. *See also* Aino; Hiisi; Ilmarinen; Ilmatar; Jumala; Lem-minkainen; Louhi; Luonnotar; Pohja; Sampo.

Vairagis *Vairajas* (India) *see* Loka.

Vairajas (India) *see* Vairagis.

Vairocana *Vairochana* (Buddhist; India, Nepal); (Ryobu-Shinto; Japan)

Also known as: *Dainichi Nyorai* (Japan), *Kun-Rig, Marichi* (possibly), *P'i-Lu-Cha-Na* (China), *rNam-parsnon-sras* (Tibet).

Vairocana is the fourth of the five contemplative Buddhas, known as the Dhyani Buddhas, except in Nepal, where he is placed as the first contemplative Buddha. The Buddha of com-passion, his consort (shakti) is Vajradhatvisvari, known as the Queen of Vajra Space. Other references name his consort as the Shakti Nam-kha-ing-kya-wang-chug-ma, the Divine Mother of Infinite Space, also known as Akasha Dhatu Ishvari. He is a pious Buddha who respects law and the scriptures. He is the master of the temple and its contents. Vairochana represents the cosmic element of form known as rupa and he presides over the autumn season. In the mandala of the five tathagatas (also known as five families), Vairocana is placed in the center of the first tathagata. In this position, he represents the basic poison of confusion and also its opposite, the reversal of ignorance. Akshobhya, the ruler of the Vajra family, is the second tathagata, who generally appears in the eastern side of the mandala, at the bottom. In some texts, he appears in the center with Vairochana. The poison of the Vajra family is hatred. The hatred is transmuted into wisdom. On the southern side of the mandala is Ratnasambhava (the jewel bearer), ruler of the ratna family. The ratna is the jewel which grants all desires. The poison of the ratna family is pride resulting from the possession of riches. The antidote is the wis-dom of equality and equanimity. In the five tathagatas mandala, Amitabha is placed above, in the west. His family, the padma (lotus), symbolizes desire and passion. The antidote is discrim-ination, which provides coolness and detachment. The passion is transformed into compassion. On the northern side (the right) is Amoghasiddhi who represents the karma family (meaning action). It is symbolized by the sword or the double Vajra (thun-derbolt). The poison of the karma family is the energy of envy and some say confrontation (sanskara). The antidote is wisdom which accomplishes all actions. Sanskara is also refinement, eru-dition and education. In China, Vairocana is known as P'i-Lu-Cha-Na and is considered a god of light. Vairocana's color is blue and sometimes white. (His attributes are sometimes alter-nated with the attributes of Aksobhya.) He is seated in a med-itative position (dhyana) with his two hands held against his chest, the tips of the fingers united. This mudra (pose) signifies preaching and turning the wheel of the law. It is also the mudra of Gautama and Maitreya. Vairocana's mount is the lion, some-times depicted as a dragon. His emblems are the wheel (chakra) and bell (ghanta). Without form (rupa) there cannot be indi-vidual existence. Autumn represents the disintegration of forms. Vairocana is often depicted in the meditative pose, white in color with four faces, holding an eight-spoked wheel. This pose indi-cates that he is both the center and everywhere. The wheel rep-resents transcending the concepts of direction and time. In the Ryobu-Shinto tradition, the Shinto sun goddess Amaterasu is Vairocana. *See also* Akshobhya; Amaterasu; Amrtakundali; Bud-dha; Dainichi-Nyorai; Dhyani Buddhas; Fudo-Myoo; Herukas; Marichi (A); Namasangiti; Ratnasambhava; Shakti; Tara (B); Vajrasatwa.

Vairochana (India) *see* Vairocana.

Vairochi (India)

Vairochi is another name for the demon with a thousand arms, Bana (q.v.)

Vaishnavi (India) Wife of Vishnu. *See also* Devi; Manasa.

Vaisravana (India)

Vaisravana is another name for the giant snake Vasuki, who is one of the three rulers of the Nagas in Patala, the underworld. *See also* Kuvera; Nagas; Patala; Takshaka; Vasuki.

Vaitarani (India) Hindu river of death. *See also* Yama.

Vaivasvata (India)

"Son of Vivasvat." Vaivasvata is the Manu for the seventh and present world cycle. Vaivasvata was the pilot of the ship that was tied to the horn of the great fish, Matsya, who is an avatar of Vishnu, during the great flood. Ida, an earth goddess and goddess of speech and vital air, is the daughter and possible wife of Vaivasvata. She is also called the instructor of Vaivasvata. *See also* Ida (B); Manu; Matsya; Vasuki; Vishnu; Yama.

Vaja (India)

Vaja and his brother Vibhan (also called Vibhu) are known as the Ribhus. They are the sons of Indra and the goddess of the morning light Saranyu, who is the daughter of Tvashtri. In some legends, they are the sons of Sudhanvan, the "good archer." The Ribhus, artisan elves, learned their skills from their grandfather, Tvashtri. For additional details, *see* Ribhus (The).

Vajra (India) Magic Thunderbolt. *See also* Tvashtri; Vairocana.

Vajra Dakinis (India) *see* Dakinis.

Vajra-Pani (India; Sanskrit) *see* Vajrapani.

Vajra-shringhala *Vajra-shringkhala* (Tibet)

Vajra-shringhala is found in the Bardo World on the Sixth Day. For a list of her companions, *see* Ankusha. *See also* Chadog-ma.

Vajra Tara (India)

Another name for Tara. *See also* Khadga Jogina; Tara.

Vajra-Varahi (Tibet) *see* Varahi.

Vajra-Yogini (Tibet)

Also known as: *Dorje-Naljorma; Toma.*

She is a Tantric goddess. For details, *see* Dorje-Naljorma; Toma.

Vajrabarahi (India)

Another name for Dorje Phogmo, the Thunderbolt Sow. *See also* Dorje Phogmo; Sambara (B); Varahi.

Vajradhara *Adibuddha* (Buddhist; Nepal)

Vajradhara, an aspect of Adibuddha, is presented in a single form and in yabyum (male, female). In single form he is decorated with jewels and sits in an attitude of meditation (vajra-paryanka), with the thunderbolt or wand that destroys ignorance (the vajra) in the right hand and the bell (ghanta) in his left hand. His two hands are crossed against his chest. In yabyum, his form is the same except that he embraces his female counterpart. Vajradhara and Vajrasawta are sometimes confused with one another. *See also* Adibuddha; Vajrasawta.

Vajradhatvisvari (Nepal)

"Queen of Vajra Space." Vajradhatvisvari is the consort of Vairocana, the fourth of the five contemplative Buddhas. *See also* Dhyani Buddhas; Vairocana.

Vajradhupa (Buddhist; India) Goddess of Incense.

Vajradipa (India)

Another name for the goddess of the lamp, Vajraloka.

Vajragandha (Buddhist; India) Goddess of Fragrance.

Vajragiti (Buddhist; India) Goddess of Song.

Vajrahara (India)

Vajrahara is another name for Manjusri, the god of learning, speech, science, and wisdom (q.v.).

Vajraheruka (Tibet) *see* Herukas.

Vajrajogini (India) *see* Kali; Khadga Jogini.

Vajraloka *Vajradipa* (Buddhist; India) Goddess of the Lamp.

Vajranga (Buddhist; India) Another name for Manjusri (q.v.).

Vajranrtya (Buddhist; India)

Goddess of the Exuberant Dance.

Vajrapani *Vajra-Pani* (Buddhist, Hindu; India)

Also known as: *Acala, Acaryavajrapani, Bodhisattva Chakdor* (Tibet), *Hayagriva* (Horse-Necked), *Heruka, Phyag-nardorje* (Bearing the Dorge in Hand; Tibet), *P'yag-na-rdo-rje* (Tibet), *Sakyamuni, Sotshirvani* (Siberia).

"Wielder of the Thunderbolt." Vajrapani is a Dhyanibodhisattva and the second of the five Buddhist creators of the universe. The other Dhyanibodhisattvas are Avalokitesvara, Ratnapani, Samantabhadra and Visvapani. Vajrapani is the spiritual son of Dhyani Buddha Akshobhya and his shaki (consort) Mamaki. Vajrapani means the vajra-holder. Vajra means thunderbolt. The thunderbolt is the symbol of extraordinary mystical power and divine energy. It also denotes the male principle, and the axis of the universe. Vajrapani's realm is "The Realm of Those of Long Hair." It is his paradise and not a Buddha Realm. He is known as the clearer of obstructions. In legend, he manifested himself as Hayagriva to subjugate the wrathful deity, Rudra, known as "The God of Storms" and "The Lord of Time and Death." Vajrapani as Hayagriva has a horse's head and is red in color. He entered Rudra's body through his anus. Rudra acknowledged the domination and offered himself as a throne to Vajrapani. Rudra's costume and attributes were transmuted into the Heruka Buddha costume. As a rain god, Vajrapani protects the nagas (serpents), who bring the rain from the garuda birds. Acala and Acaryavajrapani are manifestations of Vajrapani. In an early incarnation, Vajrapani was Sakyamuni, who is the third Buddha and the fourth Manushi-Buddha. Vajrapani as Vajrapani, and in his manifestations as the Supreme Heruka or Hayagriva, is an exorciser of evil spirits. He is a Dharmapala one of the hideous giants who are the Protectors of Religion in Buddhist tradition. Vajrapani, white in color, holds the vajra and the lotus. He is often depicted with a naked upper body. Vajrapani appears in the Gandharva (also called Gandhara) sculptures as a Zeus, Eros, Pan, Heracles or a Dionysus. The Gandharva school was of Greek influence and represented Buddha standing. In the mixed Hindu-Buddhist tradition, Vajrapani is the same as Indra (q.v.). *See also* Akshobhya; Amoghasiddhi; Avalokitesvara; Buddha; Dhyanibodhisattvas; Heng and Ha; Heruka; Indra; Lhamo; Mamaki; Manushi-Buddhas; Nagas; Otshirvani; Samantabhadra.

Vajraraga (Buddhist; India) God of love.

Vajrasattva (India) *see* Vajrasatwa.

Vajrasattvamika (Nepal)
She is the consort of Vajrasatwa and the mother of the Bodhisattva, Ghantapani (q.v.).

Vajrasatwa *Vajrasawta* (Buddhist; Nepal)
Also known as: *Dhyani Buddha, Dorje-sem-pa* (Tibet), *P'i-lu-cha-na* (China), *rDorje-sems-dpa* (Tibet), *Vajra-sattva, Vajrasattva, Vajrassattvamika* (Nepal).
"Courageous Thunderbolt Soul." Vajrasatwa is regarded by Nepali Buddhists as the priest of the five contemplative Buddhas, known as the Dhyani Buddhas. Independent shrines are dedicated to Vajrasatwa and his worship is always performed in secret for those initiated into the mysteries of Vajrayana. Vajrasatwa is worshiped as Adibuddha by the Red Cap sect in Tibet. Sometimes Vajrasatwa is included as a sixth Dhyani Buddha. His consort is Vajrasattvatmika and their son is the Bodhisattva Ghantapani. Vajrasatwa is represented in two forms, single and yab-yum. Yab means the "honorable father" and yum means the "honorable mother." The combined word means father in company of or the embrace of mother. Vajrasatwa, white in color, wears ornaments and a crown upon his head. Like the other Dhyani Buddhas, he sits cross-legged in a meditative pose. He carries the vajra and ghanta (bell) in his right hand with his palm upwards against his chest. His left hand rests upon his left thigh or in his lap. Vajrasatwa originates from the syllable HUM. *See also* Akshobhya; Amitabha; Amoghasiddhi; Amrtakundali; Dainichi-nyorai; Dhyani Buddhas; Mamaki; Ratnasambhava; Vairocana; Vajradhara.

Vajravarahi (Tibet) *see* Varahi.

Vajravina (India)
A name for the goddess of speech and learning, Sarasvati (q.v.).

Vajrayana (Nepal) *see* Chakra Sambara; Sambara.

Vaka (India)
Vaka is a demon killed by the ferocious Pandava, Bhima. *See also* Bhima (A).

Vakea (Polynesia) *see* Vatea.

Valaskjalf (Norse; Teutonic)
Also known as: *Shelf of the Slain.*
Home of the gods. Valaskjalf is one of the mansions of Odin, in Asgard. In Valaskjalf, he sits on his throne named Hlidskjalf and he rests his feet on a footstool of gold, as he surveys the world. Valaskjalf contains furniture and utensils of silver and gold manufactured by the gods. *See also* Asgard; Hlidskjalf; Valhalla; Vali (C).

Vale (Teutonic) *see* Boe; Odin; Vali.

Valetudo (Italy) Health and victory goddess.

Valfadir (Teutonic) *see* Odin.

Valfather (Teutonic)
Also known as: *Allfather.*
Valfather is an aspect or another name for Odin. *See also* Odin.

Valhal (Teutonic) *see* Valhalla.

Valhalla *Valhal, Walhalla* (Norse; Teutonic)
Also known as: *Hall of the Slain.*
Home of the gods. A great hall, the beautiful dwelling place of Odin and the other Scandinavian gods. Odin feasted in this temple of immortality daily on wine and boar's meat with all his chosen slain warriors who had fallen in battle. Some say he never ate, but subsisted on mead alone. Valhalla had five hundred and forty doors wide enough to allow eight hundred warriors to enter abreast. A boar's head and an eagle were above the principal gate. The walls of the building were fashioned of spears and the roof was made of golden shields. Compare to Amaravati. *See also* Valaskjalf.

Vali (Norse; Teutonic)
Also known as: *Ali (A), Beav, Bous, Vale, Voli.*
Possibly a god of vegetation and god of archery, Vali is the son of Odin by his third wife Rinda (also called Rind). Vali was born and reached full stature in one day and killed Hodur in revenge for the death of his half-brother Baldur (Balder). Vali will survive Ragnarok. Possibly the same Vali is the son of Loki and Sigyn and brother of Nari or Narvi. This Vali was turned into a wolf by the gods. He is usually shown as an archer. *See also* Odin.

Valkjosandi *Chooser of the Slain* (Teutonic) *see* Odin.

Valkyr (Teutonic) *see* Valkyrie.

Valkyrie *Valkyr, Valkyries* (Plural), *Valkyrja, Valkyrs, Walkure, Walkyrie* (Teutonic)
Also known as: *Alaisiagae.*
Goddesses of fate. Odin sent the beautiful Valkyries into battle to decide who would survive, and who would die. There are two classes of Valkyrie: the celestial, and the half-mortal, half-divine group. The latter group often lives among mortals for a time. Later, they return to Odin in Valhalla. When not on duty as goddesses of fate, they served as cup-bearers to Odin and the fallen heroes. Some of the goddesses serve in menial positions. They ride around on their horses in groups of three. The number of Valkyries, however, varies widely. A few of the better known Valkyries are Gundul, Hild, Lokk, Mist, Skogul, and Skuld. The Valkyries are closely related to the Norns (q.v.). They are similar to the Celtic Morrigan.

Valkyrja (Teutonic) *see* Valkyrie.

Valkyrs (Teutonic) *see* Valkyrie.

Valland (Teutonic) *see* Volund.

Vamana *Vamen, Vamena* (Hindu; India)
Also known as: *Bamun Owtar* (Vamana Avatar).

Vamana, a dwarf, is the fifth avatar of Vishnu. He returned to earth as the son of Kasyapa and Aditi. Another reference records that Vamana was the son of Kusht and Arwut and that he lived one thousand years. The gods had requested that he rid heaven and earth of the giant demon Bali, who was a Daitya. Bali was not evil but he had developed into a powerful ruler of the three worlds. Vamana approached King Bali under the pretense of being a poor man in need of land. He finally talked the king into giving him as much land as he could cover in three steps. Because of his diminutive size, the king agreed to his request. Vamana then grew into his omnipresent size and covered the entire earth with his first step, and the heavens with his second step. His third step could have encompassed the lower worlds but he decided to give a section of Patala to Bali. Bali is the grandson of Prahlada and the great-grandson of Hiranya-kasipu, who were involved with Vishnu during his avatar as the half-male, half-lion named Nara-Simha. Bali the demon represents darkness and the gods represent light. *See also* Daityas; Dikpalas; Hiranya-kasipu; Lakshmi; Lokapalas; Nara-Simha (Vishnu's avatar as half-man, half-lion); Parashur Rama; Patala; Prahlada; Vishnu.

Vamen (India) *see* Vamana.

Vamena (India) *see* Vamana.

Vammatar (Finnish)
Goddess of disease. Daughter of Tuoni and Tuonetar. Sister of Loviatar, Kipu-Tytto, and Kivutar. They live in Tuonela. *See also* Tuonetar.

Vamsa (Buddhist; India) Goddess of the Flute.

Vanadevatas (India) *see* Devis.

Vanadis (Teutonic)
Vanadis is another name for Freya given to her because she came from the Vanir race. As Vanadis she was worshiped in Disir at Uppsala. She is a member of a group of goddesses called Disir. The Disir were known for their concern for the good of the home and family. *See also* Aesir; Disir; Frejya; Vanir.

Vanagods (Teutonic)
The sea and wind gods, also referred to as Vanas (q.v.). *See also* Vanir.

Vanaheim (Norse; Teutonic)
Home of the gods. Home of the Vanir who were later integrated with the Aesir.

Vanant (Zoroastrian; Persia)
An unidentified star or constellation, and a Yazata (q.v.).

Vanas (Teutonic) see Vanir.

Vanavasas (India)
The Vanavasas are forest dwellers ruled over by Sugriva, the brother of Bali. *See also* Sugriva.

Vandya (India) A Yakshini. *See also* Yaksha and Yakshini.

Vanemuine (Estonian)
He is a god of music who is the same as the Finnish Vainamoinen (q.v.).

Vaner (Teutonic) *see* Vanas; Vanir.

Vanir (Norse; Teutonic)
Also known as: *Vanagods, Vaner, Vanir.*
Race of fertility gods. The Vanir, a peace-loving group who lived in Vanaheim, watched over the fruits of earth and all living things. The Aesir and the Vanir were constantly at odds with one another. Finally the two races were able to negotiate a peace treaty. As well as exchanging hostages, the Vanir were at last admitted to Asgard, the celestial home of the Aesir. *See also* Aesir; Asgard; Njord (re: terms of the hostage exchange); Frejya; Vanaheim.

Var (Teutonic) *see* Vor.

Vara (Teutonic) *see* Vor.

Varaha (Hindu; India) *Varaha-Avatara, Varahavatar.*
Also known as: *Vishnu.*
Varaha, the wild boar, is the third avatar of Vishnu. He assumed this form to drive the demon Hiranyaksha from power. After the Great Deluge, as he searched for the earth, he found that Hiranyaksha had hidden the earth under water. A battle lasting a thousand years ensued. Varaha emerged the victor and brought the planet to the surface again. In another rendition, Varaha overthrew the evil giant Hirnakess (or possibly Hiranyaksha) thought to be a Daitya, who attempted to keep him from his mission. He reached to the ocean's depths and rescued the earth goddess Bhumidevi. The tusks of Varaha supported her and enabled her to bear the weight of her creation. Lakshmi is his wife once again, in her avatar as Varahini. Sukapreyasi the sow goddess also appears as his wife during this period. In another rendition of this tale, the world is overpopulated. Varaha has to lift it with one tusk from time to time. The shift causes earthquakes, which keep the population in check. The wild boar is an earth symbol. *See also* Daityas; Hiranya-Kasipu (regarding Hiranyaksha); Kurma (the tortoise avatar of Vishnu); Lakshmi; Manu; Matsya (the fish avatar of Vishnu); Nara-Simha (Vishnu's avatar as half-man, half-lion); Vishnu.

Varaha-Avatara (India) *see* Varaha; Vishnu.

Varahavatar (India) *see* Varaha.

Varahi (Buddhist; Nepal)
The Varahi protect temples and buildings. Four Varahi protect the four corners of Kathmandu Valley in Nepal. They are Vajravarahi (also known as Dorje Phagmo), who is red and protects the livestock in the western quarter of the Kathmandu valley in Nepal; Nilavarahi, who is blue and protects the east; Swetavarahi, white, guards the south; and Dhumbarahi, grey, guards the north and is said to protect the valley from cholera. Vajravarahi is also known as the goddess of pleasure. As well as the embodiment of pleasure, she is the essence of five types of knowledge. Vajravarahi has two arms, one head with disheveled hair, three eyes, and is depicted nude. On her head she wears a garland of heads said to be wet from the blood she drinks. She is shown standing on the gods Bhiarav and Kalratri. In her right hand she holds the vajra, which is the thunderbolt or diamond that destroys ignorance. *See also* Dakinis; Dikpalas; Dorje Phagmo; Sambara.

Varahini (India)

An avatar of the beautiful goddess, Lakshmi (q.v.). *See also* Varaha.

Varanga (India)

A name for Manjusri, the god of speech and learning. *See also* Manjusri.

Varcin (Hindu; India)

A demon hostile to mortals who was overcome by Indra.

Vardhamana (India)

A name for the "Great Man," Mahavira (q.v.).

Varegan (Persian, Iranian) *see* Vareghna.

Vareghna *Varegan, Varengan* (Persian, Iranian)

The raven form of the god of war and victory, Verethraghna (q.v.).

Varengan (Iranian, Persian) *see* Vareghna.

Vari (A) (Indonesia, Polynesia)

Also known as: *Atea, Vari-Ma-Te-Takere, Wakea.*

In some accounts, Vari is the self existent being who lives at the bottom of the coconut shell called Avaiki, the land of the dead. (Avaiki, meaning "mud," was said to be the source of all life.) Below Vari is Take, the root of the universe. In another version of this myth, Vari-Ma-Te-Takere is the mother of Vatea, Tinirau, Tango, Tu-Mute-Anaoa, Raka, and Tu-metua. In still another version, she is the great mother goddess Vari-Ma-Te-Takere who plucked the gods and men from her left side. Parts of her body were distributed to Tinirau, Tango, Te-paraitea, and Raka. From her right side she plucked Tu-metua. In the Polynesian island of Mangaia's Creation Legend, Vari's daughter Vatea rules the underworld. Vari is the grandmother of the sky god Tangaroa, and the god of the underworld, Rongo. *See also* Atea; Avaiki; Raki; Tangaroa; Tango; Tinirau; Tu-Metua; Vari (A); Vatea.

Vari (B) (India) "Fair Faced." *See also* Devi.

Vari-Ma-Te-Takere (Polynesia) *see* Vari (A).

Varpulis (Slavic)

Wind god. Varpulis causes the noise of storms. He belongs to a group of wind gods who are associated with Perun. Varpulis is equated with Erisvorsh. He is possibly related to Stribog, the god of winter, and Dogoda, the west wind. *See also* Perun; Stribog.

Varshayanti (India) A Krittika sister. *See also* Rishi.

Varuna (Brahmanic, Buddhist, Hindu, Vedic; India; Persia)

Also known as: *Ahura Mazda* (Persia), *Amburaja, Jadapati, Jalpati* (Lord of the Waters), *Pasi, Prasetas* (Supremely Wise), *The Aditya* (Eternal Celestial Light), *Trita, Yadahpati* (Lord of the Living Beings in Water).

In early times, Varuna was the universal monarch and the guardian of cosmic law. He created the three worlds: the heavens, earth, and the air between them. He was all-seeing and a judge of the actions of mortals. His name means "the coverer," meaning the sky. He was the son of the sun goddess Aditi. His siblings were Mitra, Aryaman, Indra, Savitri, Bhaga, Ansa and Martanda (Vivasvat), and a sister, the goddess of dawn, Ushas. Later, he fell to the ranks of a secondary deity. He was a Dyad with the Vedic solar deity Mitra. As Mitra and Varuna (Mitra-Varuna), the sun and the moon, they are always present to guard and witness all actions and events. Endowed with magical powers, they understood the powers of certain devas (gods) and demons. Mitra-Varuna, the divine two-in-one, is coupled with the goddess Danu. He is part of a triad with Mitra and Aryaman. He is also one of the Vedic triad with Mitra and Agni (Divine Father, Divine Son and Holy Spirit). His early name was Asura (Lord), which is the same word as Ahura in the Parsi language. As ruler of the western direction, his domain included the Arabian sea. In Persia, he became Ahura Mazda, the Wise-Lord of the *Avesta*. In Vedic hymns he has a Hebraic quality, resembling the Yahweh of the Old Testament. His Sanskrit name means "sky" and in later times he was the head of the pantheon of Indo-European gods (the Adityas), who represent the military power of the gods. World order was maintained by their use of magical powers. In the *Mahabharata*, Varuna is the son of Kardama. He mated with the nymph Urvasi, and they had a son, the sage Vasistha, who was born from her soul. Varuna's kingdom is Sukha (happiness), located on Pushpa-giri (flower-mountain). In other versions, his wife is Gauri or Varunani, the goddess of wine, and his consorts are Ganges and Jumna. With Varunani a daughter, Varuni, was born, who is known as the Goddess of Spirituous Liquor. Varuna presides over the care of the sacrificial ambrosia, Soma, which is stored in the moon. There is a possibility that Varuna and the goddess Lakshmi were married. In some traditions, Varuna was usurped by Indra. When that happened, Varuna was relegated to the role of one of the Asuras (demons) and was removed from the celestial realm to the bottom of the ocean. He still retained his power, for in Indian mythology, gods and demons are of equal strength. Other scholars say that Indra reestablished the rule of Varuna. Indra and Varuna are often invoked together as a dual deity, as are Mitra and Varuna. Varuna is considered a Vedic rain god, as are Indra, the Maruts and Parjanya. He is often associated as lord of the dead with Yama, who was the first man to die. In later times he became known as the receiver of souls who died by drowning, and as guardian of the night. In the Buddhist tradition, Varuna emanated from the belly of the Dhyani Buddha, Avalokitesvara (The Lord Gifted with Complete Enlightenment). Varuna is depicted as white skinned, with a thousand eyes and four arms. Draped in a golden mantle, he sits on a throne. In later times he was shown riding a sea monster, half-crocodile, half-bird, known as Makara (q.v.). He holds a noose or lasso to snare non-believers. The lasso noose also indicates his function as a judge. The noose, often called "The Noose of Varuna" is called the Naga-pasa, or "snake noose," from which the wicked cannot escape. The god of death Yama (q.v.) also casts a noose over his candidates. Astovidad, the Persian demon of death, is another deity who uses a noose to perform his duties. Varuna also holds a container of gems which symbolize fertility. The horse is Varuna's sacred animal. Varuna also appears as Capricornus. In this form, he has the head and forelegs of an antelope and the body and tail of a fish. This is the same emblem as the Babylonian god Ea. Repentance for sins is granted at a festival known as Varunapragh. Compare Varuna to Uranus, Poseidon (Greek), Odin (Teutonic) and Lugh

(Celtic). Varuna is associated with the Japanese sea deity Suit-engu (q.v.). Varuna is sometimes confused with Indra and Agni. Trita is an aspect of Indra and Agni. Varuna is often identified with the god of ecstasy, Soma (q.v.) *See also* Aditi; Adityas; Asuras; Avalokitesvara; Brihaspati; Daityas; Dipkalas; Diti; Krishna; Lokapalas; Mitra; Parashur Rama (Vishnu's avatar as a dwarf); Ravana; Soma; Surya; Urvasi; Ushas; Vasistha; Vedas (The); Yama.

Varunani (India) *see* Varuni.

Varuni *Varunani* (India)
Also known as: *Shakti.*
(India) Goddess of Spirituous Liquor. *See also* Gauri; Kurma; Shakti; Soma; Varuna.

Vasa (Finnish) *see* Kul.

Vasanta (India)
The Deity of Blossoming Flowers. *See also* Kama.

Vasanta-Bandhu (Hindu; India)
"Friend of Spring," God of Love.

Vashita (Hindu; India) Goddess of Discipline.

Vashti (Semitic)
A little known Elamite goddess. Possibly associated with Varuna.

Vasishta (India) *see* Vasistha.

Vasistha *Vasishtha* (Brahmanic, Hindu, Vedic; India)
Also known as: *Adi.*
"Most Wealthy." Vasistha is the son of Varuna or some say Surya or Mitra. He was born from his mother Urvasi's soul. He is one of the seven Rishis who are divine sages, poets, and prophets, and one of the ten Prajapatis, the ten beings created by Brahma or by Manu who were assigned to carry out specific tasks in the creation of the world. A solar deity, and pupil of Agni, he composed the *Rig-Veda* hymns. He once owned the miraculous "Cow of Desires," Kamadhenu. The goddess Arund-hati, thought to be one of the seven Krittikas, is Vasistha's wife. There is a possibility that she was the mother of seven or one hundred sons. In one legend, Vasistha is said to have had a hundred sons who were all murdered by a Rakshasa who devoured them. Grief-stricken, he attempted suicide several times but was unsuccessful. He threw himself from a high mountain but the rocks below turned soft. He walked into a burning forest but the flames would not burn him. He jumped from a ship and was washed ashore. Finally, he tied his hands and threw himself into a river. The river Byas untied him and moved him safely to the shore. The Byas is still called "the Untier." Later, he wed Urja, a daughter of Daksha, and they had seven sons. Adi, an incarnation of Vasistha, is a demon who can take the shape of a bird or a snake. *See also* Agni; Brahma; Daksha; Kamadhenu; Kasyapa; Manu; Mitra; Nandi; Parashur Rama; Prajapati; Rakshasa; Rishi; Surya; Urvasi; Varuna; Vishnu.

Vasu (India) *see* Vasus.

Vasu Deva (India) *see* Vasudeva.

Vasud (Teutonic)
Icy Wind. He is the father of Vindsual who is the father of

Winter (god of winter). These winds were set in motion by the giant Hraesvelgr. *See also* Hraesvelgr; Winter.

Vasudeva *Vasu Deva* (India)
The Universal Spirit. *See also* Bala-Rama; Brahma; Devaki; Kunti.

Vasuki *Vairavana* (Hindu; India)
This gigantic snake is one of the three rulers of the Nagas in Patala. He served as a rope for the gods to churn the sea of milk and again for Vaivasvata to moor his ship to the horn of Mat-sya (the fish avatar of Vishnu) during the great flood. He is the ruler of the West and the snakes he rules are gods of the rains and of prosperity who can assume human shape. He is often identified with Vishnu's snake, Sesha. In some renditions, Sesha and Vasuki were both tied around Mount Mandara to serve as ropes for Kasyapa when he churned the ocean of milk. Vasuki sent Garuda a serpent a day to eat, to avoid having the Nagas annihilated. Vasuki is usually depicted in human form wearing the crest of a serpent. *See also* Devas (A); Garuda; Kurma (Vishnu's avatar as a tortoise); Lokapalas; Matsya; Nagas and Nagis; Patala; Sesha; Shiva; Vishnu; Yaksha and Yakshini.

Vasundhara (Buddhist, Hindu; India)
Vasundhara, an earth goddess and goddess of wealth, is the mother of the goddess of agriculture, Sita, and a son, Naraka. Vasundhara is the Buddhist counterpart of the Hindu Lakshmi. Vasundhara has four hands and holds a sheaf of paddy, a full vase, and jewels. She has three faces with different complex-ions. The right face is brown, the middle face is yellow and her left face is reddish. She is also shown as a six-armed crowned goddess in a dancing pose. Four of her hands hold symbols of abundance. Two of her hands are held in the varada (gift-giv-ing) mudra. This gesture shows the arms pendant, all fingers extended downward and the palms facing outward. Vasund-hara symbolizes the earth. She is honored to prevent poverty. *See also* Amoghapasa Lokeswara; Lakshmi; Sita.

Vasus, The (Vedic; India)
The Vasus are a group of seven, eight or nine demi-gods, children of Aditi, who are the attendants of Indra. Their names are Vasu (wealth), Apa (water), Anala (fire), Dhara (earth), Dhurva (the pole-star), Prabhasa (dawn), Pratyusha, (light), and Soma (moon). Anila (wind) is added in some descriptions. Chandra the moon god is sometimes included in the group of eight attendants to Indra. Nakshatras, meaning "stars," is some-times included as one of the attendants. Groups of Vedic gods, like the Adityas, Maruts, Ribhus and Vasus, often are repre-sented as rays of the sun, as stars or as constellations. The Vasus are symbols and personifications of natural phenomena. *See also* Aditi; Adityas; Chandra; Ganga; Indra; Maruts; Ribhus.

Vasusena (India)
A name for Karna, the great warrior, born of miraculous birth. *See also* Karna.

Vata (Iran) The god of the winds. *See also* Vayu.

Vatea *Vakea* (Polynesia)
Also known as: *Atea, Avatea.*
Vatea is known as the first man and the father of gods and mortals. In one version of this myth, Vatea was half-man and

half-fish. He came from the demon woman Vari-Ma-Te-Takere (Vari). She in turn came from Avaiki, the lowest part of the shell which is the universe. In another version, Vatea and Tangaroa argued about who was the first born of Papa. To settle the dispute Papa was cut in two and Vatea took the upper half and threw it into the sky where it become the sun. Tangaroa left the lower half of Papa on the ground until it was drained of blood and decomposing. Then he threw it into the sky where it became the pale moon. Vatea was given the land named Te'-papa-rairai or Te enua marama o Vatea by the great goddess, Vari-Ma-Te-Takere. In still another version, Vatea is the lover and wife of Papa. In the Mangaia Islands, Vatea is the husband of Papa, and the father of Rongo and Tangaroa. Papa influenced him to favor his son Rongo and disown Tangaroa. The other demons in Avaiki were Te-aka-ia-oe, Te-tangaengae or Te-vaerua, and Te-manava-roa. Some say one eye of Vatea was like a fish and the other like a human, others say one eye is the sun and the other eye the moon. Vatea's brothers are Tinirau, Tango, Raki, and Tumuteanaoa. (Some myths refer to Tumuteanaoa as a female.) There is another child of Vari, named Tu-metua (Tu), who was the principal god or goddess of the Polynesian people. Tu was also thought to be the aunt of Tangaroa. In some legends, Tumateanaoa or Tu-metua is the wife of Vatea and she was really named Papa. See also Atea; Avaiki; Papa (A); Raki; Rangi; Rongo; Tu-metua; Tumuteanaoa; Vari (A).

Vatsasura (India) A female cow demon. See also Krishna.

Vayu (Indo-Iranian, Persian, Vedic; India)

Also known as: *Marut, Maruta, Pavana* (Purifying), *Vata*.

Vayu, a nature deity, god of breath, life, air and wind, is said to have been created by the breath of Purusha. As he was created by breath, so does his breath give life to god and mortals. In early times, he was one of a triad with Agni and Surya. Later, Indra supplanted him in the triad. He is the father of the monkey-god Hanuman and of the Pandava, Bhima. His father-in-law is the artisan god Tvashtri. Vayu brings life in the rain clouds and death in the storm. He makes the dawn and lightning appear. Usually gentle, he does have a violent aspect. Angry with Indra, he broke off the peak of the sacred Mount Meru and it became Sri Lanka. He is considered by some to be one of the Maruts (storm gods) and by others to be one of the Vasus who were the attendants of Indra. In the Hindu tradition, with his elephant Pushpa-danta, he is also the guardian of the west. In Persia, Ahura Mazda (the creator), who rules in the light above, and Angra Mainyu (the devil), who rules in the darkness below, offer sacrifice to Vayu, who rules in the void between heaven and hell. Vayu is an assistant of Vohu Manah of the Ameshà Spentas. Vayu helps the souls of just mortals surmount any obstacles during the journey they must make after death. Prayers are offered to Vayu in times of danger for he is capable of moving as the wind, swiftly through both worlds. In the Zoroastrian tradition, Vayu is a Yazata (celestial being). He is described as a fearsome broad-breasted warrior wearing the raiment of warfare, and carrying a sharp spear and weapons made of gold. He is also shown in antelope form with a thousand eyes. This symbolizes his swiftness and his ability to be all-seeing. He may be seen driving a carriage pulled by red and purple steeds or in a chariot drawn by two red horses as the storm god Indra's charioteer. He is also shown in a gold char-iot, which touches the sky and is drawn by a thousand horses, or in a chariot drawn by three deer. His mount is the deer and his symbol the wheel. Vayu relates to Prana (the breath) and to the practice of Pranayama (breath control). Other nature gods are Tvashtri (the Thunderbolt), Parjanya (the Rain), Apa (the Waters), and Prithivi (the Earth). See also Agni; Ahura Mazda; Ameshas Spenta (Persian); Angra Mainyu; Dikpalas; Hanuman; Indra; Kunti; Lokapalas; Maruts; Mitra; Pandavas; Ravana; Soma; Vasus; Vedas (The); Vohu Manah (Persian); Yazatas (Persian).

Vazimba (Madagascar)

Spirit. Mother of Rasoalao and Ravola. Spirits of the dead. See also Rasoalao; Ravola.

Vazishta (Iranian)

Vazishta, who represents lightning, killed the demon Spenjaghrya, who represents darkness or winter.

Ve *We* (Norse; Teutonic)

He is the son of Bor and Bestla, and the brother of Odin and Vili. Ve helped create the first man and woman, Ask and Embla, from two trees. They were given senses, expression, and speech. Odin specifically gave them breath. Ve gave them color and body temperature. Vili gave them understanding. They also created the celestial bodies by employing the sparks that flew out of Muspells-heim. With his brothers, Ve killed the giant Ymir. Some identify Ve with Henir (q.v.). See also Ask; Audhumla; Bestla; Bor; Embla; Henir; Midgard; Muspells-heim; Odin; Vili; Ymir.

Vedams, The (India) see Vedas, The.

Vedas, The *Vedams, The* (Divine Knowledge); (Vedic, Hindu; India)

In the sacred Sanskrit scriptures known as the Vedas, there are four books called the Samhitas: the *Rig-Veda* or *Book of Hymns*, with 1,028 hymns (associated with speech); the *Soma-Veda* or *Book of Songs* (associated with song), a book of chants, mantras, and tunes; the *Yajur-Veda* or *Book of Liturgical Formulae* (associated with expression), sacrificial formulas, prayers, and explanatory material; the *Atharva-Veda* or *Book of Magic Formulae* (associated with emotion), charms and spells and the making of the shastra (law). The Rishis (divine sages, poets and teachers) preserved and handed down the knowledge imparted by the Vedas. The Vedic hymns created the first Hindu mythology. These hymns were addressed to the Vedic gods: Agni (fire), Indra (thunder), Surya (sun), Vayu (wind), Aditi (earth), Varuna (rain and sea), the Ashvins (healers) and Dyaus-piter (father of light). The feared deities are Yama (death), Vrita (drought), Rudra (storm), and the Maruts (whirlwinds). See also Agni; Ashvins; Indra; Maruts; Rishis; Rudra; Surya; Vrita; Yama.

Vedavyasa (India) see Vyasa.

Vedfolnir (Teutonic) The falcon of the Yggdrasil Tree (q.v.).

Vedic Creation Legend see Purusha.

Vediovis (Etruscan, Roman) An early name for Jove (q.v.). See also Jove; Jupiter.

Vedius (Roman) see Jupiter; Vejovis.

Vega (Persia) The constellation.

Veggdegg (Teutonic) *see* Thor

Vegtam (Teutonic) *see* Odin.

Vejamat (Latvia) Goddess of the wind.

Vejovis *Vedius* (Roman)
"Little Jupiter." An epithet of Jupiter when he appears without his thunder. The name Vedius is also used under these circumstances.

Vele (Prussia) Spirits of water and the woods.

Veles (Russia) The patron of flocks and harvests. *See also* Volos.

Velint (Teutonic) *see* Volund.

Vema (India) Goddess of sexual love.

Vemacitra (India)
"Splendid Robe." He is the sage of jealous gods. *See also* Amrtakundali.

Venus (A) (Roman)
Also known as: *Acidalia, Anahit* (Armenia), *Anahita* (Persia), *Aphrodite* (Greek), *Bennu-asar, Pi-neter-tauau* (Egypt), *Verticordia.*
Goddess of love and beauty. Mother of Amor by Mars. She is the Roman Aphrodite. Veneralia, her festival, takes place April 1 and August 19. August 19 is also the festival date for Jupiter. Some say Venus is the daughter of Jupiter and Dione, and that she is the mother of Aeneas and Pitho, the goddess of persuasion (by Mercury). *See also* Aphrodite (Greek); Astarte (Phoenician); Anahit (Armenia); Anahita (Persia); Ishtar (Babylon); Isis (Egypt).

Venus (B) The planet. *See also* Anahita (Chaldean); Brihaspati (India); Eurynome (A) (Greek); Ishtar (Babylonia); Tishtrya (Chaldean); Tlahuizcalpantecuhtli (Aztec); Xolotl (Aztec).

Verbeia (Celtic) River goddess. *See also* Sequana.

Verdandi (Teutonic)
Spirits. One of three Norns (goddesses of destiny) who decide the fates of men.

Verethraghna (Persia)
Also known as: *Bahram* (name in later times), *Bairam, Vah, Vahagn* (Armenian), *Vahran* (Pahlavi dialect), *Varegan, Vareghna, Varengan.*
Born in the ocean, he is the chief of the fravashis and the genius of victory. He overcame the dragon Azhi Dahaka, who symbolizes darkness and drought, and tied him to Mount Demavand. His name means "Victory Over Adverse Attack." Some writers describe him as a personification of aggressiveness and the irresistible force of victory and proclaim that he did not kill monsters or dragons. He is depicted as the victor over evilness in mortals and demons, and the administrator of punishment. He has ten incarnations: that of a strong wind which brings health and strength and carries the glory of Ahura Mazda; a golden-horned bull representing rays; a white horse with golden trappings; a youth of the ideal age of fifteen; a burden-bearing camel, shown sharp-toothed and stamping for-

ward, who represents a fertile cloud; a sharp-toothed boar who can kill at one stroke; a swift bird named Vareghna (possibly a raven); a wild ram; a fighting buck; and a man holding a sword with a golden blade (representing the hero). In his boar form, he accompanied Mithra. As a god of war, he is popular with soldiers. In later times, he was known as Bahram, the protector of travelers. Verethraghna is comparable in the Hindu god Indra who as Vritrahan constantly fought to overcome Vrita the drought demon. *See also* Azhi Dahaka; Azurha Mazda; Fravashi; Mithra; Vareghna.

Vergelmir Well (Teutonic)
An alternate spelling for Hvergelmir Well (q.v.).

Vergil *Virgil* (Greek) *see* Styx.

Vertimnus (Roman)
Also known as: *Vertumnus, Vortumnus.*
God of buying and selling. God of the changing seasons. God of gardens. He is the shape changer god who seduced Pomona, the goddess of fruit trees and orchards.

Vesna (Slavic) Goddess of spring.

Vesper (Greek)
Also known as: *Hesperus* (Greek).
Vesper is Venus as the Evening Star. *See also* Eos; Venus.

Vesperus (Greek) *see* Hesperides.

Vessavana (Buddhist, Cambodia)
Lord of benevolent demons. An amulet of this deity is often placed on a child's bed for protection.

Vesta (Roman, Greek)
Also known as: *Caca, Hestia, Prisca.*
The Roman Vesta, who is the Greek Hestia, is the virgin goddess of fire and the guardian of home and hearth. She was worshipped in every household. Her other function was to intervene to save the innocent. Her handmaidens, known as priestesses, are called Vestal Virgins or the King's Daughters and were treated as their names implied. It was the sacred obligation of the Vestal Virgins to keep the holy fires burning upon the royal hearth. Their term of service was thirty years and upon completion they had the option of returning to secular life. If their chastity was violated, they died a horrible death by being buried alive. Vesta's animal was the ass and her symbol the flame. A festival in honor of Vesta and known as the Vestalia was held on the ninth of June. Another Roman goddess, known as Fornax, the deity of ovens, is comparable to Vesta. A festival in honor of Fornax, known as Fornacalia, was celebrated in February. The oven is considered a mother symbol. For additional details, *see* Inari (Japan). The ancient Roman goddess Caca was replaced by Vesta. Vesta is etymologically connected with the Greek Hestia (q.v.). Compare Vesta to Agni (India), Fuji (Japan), Inari (Japan) and Pele (Hawaii). *See also* Silvanus.

Vetala (Hindu; India)
"Ghoul." An evil spirit who dwells in Smashana, Vetala is also known as the guardian of Deccan villages. In human form he is shown with his hands and feet turned backwards and hair that stands on end. He lives in a stone smeared with red paint

or in one of the stones in the prehistoric stone circles scattered around the hills. He haunts cemeteries and animates dead bodies. He is often portrayed as a mischievous demon who likes to play practical jokes. *See also* Durga; Shiva.

Vetanda (India)
"Like an Elephant." An epithet of Durga (q.v.).

Vialis (Roman) An epithet of Mercury (q.v.).

Viaroacocha (Inca) *see* Virococha.

Vibhishana (India)
A variant spelling of Vihishana, one of the eclectic members of the demon family of Visravas.

Vibhu (India) An alternate spelling for Ribhus (q.v.).

Vibhvan (India)
He is the artisan elf brother of Vaja and Ribhus, who collectively are known as the Ribhus (q.v.).

Vibishana (India) *see* Vihishana.

Vichitravirya (India)
He is the half-brother of the demigod poet, Vyasa (q.v.).

Victoria (Sabine, Roman)
Also known as: *Nike* (Greek), *Vacuna* (Sabine).
Originally Victoria was an early agricultural goddess who became the Sabine goddess of frivolity known as Vacuna. The Romans worshiped her as a goddess of war and victory and identified her with Bellona. *See also* Bellona; Nike.

Vid (Teutonic)
Vid is one of the eleven or twelve rivers springing from the well in Nifl-heim, known as Hvergelmir. The ice on the rivers created the clay giant Ymir. *See also* Elivagar.

Vidar *Vidor* (Norse; Teutonic)
Also known as: *Vidor, Vitharr*
"God of Few Words." God of peace. He is the son of Odin and the giant Grid. After Odin, he is the strongest of the gods. Vidar is the personification of the primeval forest. He lives in Landvidi, often shortened to Vidi. A tall, handsome man, he is depicted in his armor, carrying a broad-bladed sword and wearing a great iron or leather shoe. His shoe will be pushed against Fenrir the wolf's throat during the Twilight of the Gods, Ragnarok. *See also* Fenrir; Odin; Ragnarok; Vali.

Vidarbha (India) *see* Vidharba.

Vidforull (Teutonic) An epithet of Odin (q.v.).

Vidharba *Vidarbha* (India)
Vidharba is the father of Kesini, one of Sagara's wives. She is the mother of an emotionally disturbed son, Asamanjas, whom Sagara abandoned. *See also* Sagara.

Vidor (Scandinavian)
God of silence who walks on water and in the air. He is the same as the Norse Vidar (q.v.).

Vidura (India)
An incarnation of Dharma who as Vidura was the son of a maid and Vyasa. *See also* Dharma; Vyasa.

Vidyadevis (Jain; India) Goddesses of knowledge.

Vidyadhara *Bijadari, Wijadari* (Hindu; India)
The benevolent demigods Vidyadhara are shape changers who often appear as swan-maidens. They often take on human form and marry mortals. In the regions between earth and sky, they maintain their own kingdom. They supplanted the Yakshas and are analogues of the Melanesian swan maidens, the Vinmara. The Vidyadhara are not to be confused with the Vidyadhari, who are Hindu nymphs known to charm travelers. They live in ponds, on riverbanks and in woods. Swans are known as the preachers of gospels in the courts of kings. *See also* Kasyapa; Visvakarma; Yaksha.

Vidyadhari (India)
Wood and water nymphs. *See also* Vidyadhara.

Vigaya (India) "Victorious." *See also* Devi.

Vigona (San Cristobal)
Vigona is a variant spelling for the serpent-shaped creator spirits, Figonas.

Vigrid (Norse; Teutonic)
Also known as: *Battle Shaker.*
Vigrid is the plain in Asgard where the final battle known as Ragnarok, between the sons of Muspell and the forces of Surtr, will take place. *See also* Asgard; Muspells-heim; Ragnarok; Surtr.

Vihishana *Bibhishan, Vibishana, Vibhishana, Vihishana* (India)
He is the good-natured monster demon son of Visravas. His brothers are Kumbhakarna, Kuvera and Ravana. *See also* Kuvera; Nikasha; Rakshasas; Ravana; Vishravas.

Vii (Serbian) God of lightning.

Vijaya (India)
"The Victorious Guardian." He is the spouse of the goddess Ankusha (q.v.). *See also* Amrtakundali; Yaksha and Yakshini; Yamantaka.

Vijayasri (India) Goddess of victory.

Vikathikarala (India) "Fearful." An epithet of Durga (q.v.).

Vikrama (India) An epithet of Vishnu.

Vikramaditya (India) An epithet of Vishnu.

Vila (Slavic)
Also known as: *Russalka* (Russian).
Spirits of the forests, clouds and mountains. The eternally youthful Vila protects national heroes and are capable of calling forth whirlwinds, hailstorms and rain. They are long-haired and winged and are quite beautiful. *See also* Russalka.

Vile (Teutonic) *see* Vili.

Vili *Vile* (Norse; Teutonic)
First members of the race of Aesir. Vili is the brother of Odin and Ve. With his brothers, he helped create the first man and woman, Ask and Embla, from two trees. They were given senses, expression, and speech. Odin specifically gave them breath, Ve

gave them color and body temperature. Vili gave them understanding. From Ask and Embla all mortals were born. The brothers also created the celestial bodies from the sparks that flew out of Muspells-heim. Some say Vili later assimilated with Loki (q.v.). *See also* Ask; Audhumla; Bestla; Bor; Embla; Midgard; Muspells-heim; Odin; Ve; Ymir.

Vilin (Sumer)

The Vilin are malicious, attractive, female spirits who can change shape at will.

Vilva *Bel* (India)

The leaves of this sacred tree are used for the ceremonial worship of Shiva and Shakti. It is forbidden to break its branches. During the Durga-puga festival, Durga is invoked on a twig of this tree (q.v.). *See also* Durga; Tulasi.

Vinata (India)

"Mother of Eagles." She is the daughter of Daksha, the spouse of Kasyapa and the mother of Garuda. *See also* Daksha; Garuda; Kasyapa; Sumati.

Vinayaka (India)

"God of Difficulties." An epithet of Ganesha (q.v.). *See also* Uma.

Vindhyavali (Hindu; India)

She is the wife of Bali and the mother of Bana (also called Vairochi), the demon with a thousand arms, and a demon daughter, Putana, known for her poisonous breasts. *See also* Bali (B); Putana.

Vindhyavarini (India)

"Dwelling in the Vindhya Mountains." *See also* Devi.

Vindhyavasini (India) *see* Devi.

Vindsual (Teutonic)

Also known as: *Vindsval.*

Icy wind. He is the son of the icy wind, Vasud, and father of Winter, the enemy of Summer. *See also* Hraesvelgr; Winter.

Vindsval (Teutonic) *see* Vindsual.

Vingnir (Teutonic)

He is the foster father of Thor (q.v.). *See also* Vingthor.

Vingolf (Teutonic)

Vingolf is the sanctuary of Frigga and her goddesses. *See also* Gladsheim.

Vingthor (Teutonic)

Vingthor is the name Thor assumed from his foster father, Vingnir. *See also* Thor.

Vinmara (Melanesian) Swan-maidens. *See also* Vidyadhara.

Vipasyin (India) One of the seven Manushi-Buddhas (q.v.).

Virabhadra (India)

This monster of destruction, who is an emanation of Shiva, is a gigantic demon with a thousand eyes, arms and feet and enormous tusks. He killed Yajna while Daksha performed the first sacrifice. He also blinded Bhaga, knocked out Pushan's teeth, and beheaded Daksha. *See also* Bhaga; Daksha; Parvati; Shiva; Yajna.

Viracocha (Inca People; Peru) *see* Virococha.

Viraj (India)

Also known as: *Ambika, Purusha, Prajapati.*

According to some, Viraj is the child of Nari, the "Mother of the Earth," the primordial woman, who is the spouse of Nara. In other renditions, Purusha broke out of the golden cosmic egg after floating on the primeval waters for a thousand years. Fearful and lonely, the lord of the universe divided himself into a male and female half and created Ambika (also known as Viraj). *See also* Nari; Prajapati; Purusha; Sarasvati.

Virbius (Greek)

Also known as: *Auriga* ("The Charioteer" constellation), *Hippolytus.*

Hippolytus, the son of Theseus and Hippolyte, was named Virbius when he was deified after death. *See also* Hippolytus.

Virochana (India)

Virochana is the demon son of Prahalada, father of Bali and Kalanemi. *See also* Bali (B); Kalanemi; Prahalada.

Virococha *Uira-Cocha, Uiracocha, Viaracocha, Viracocha* (Inca People, Peru)

Also known as: *Arunaua, Choun, Con Ticci Viracocha, Con Ticci Viracocha Pachayachachic, Coniraya Viracocha, Illa Tici Viracocha* (Peru), *Manco Capac, Pachacamac, Taapac, Tarapaca, Thunupa, Ticci Viracocha, Tonapa, Tuapaca, Vicchaycamayoc, Virococharapacha Yachipachan.*

"Sea Foam." Supreme god. God of law. Teacher of the world. He sculpted in stone all the races of men and his work can still be seen today. He is the god of water and growing things, the creator and spirit of life. Like Pachacamac, Viracocha antedated the Incas in Peru and was taken by them as one of their gods. He lived in the depths of Lake Titicaca. He is the creator of the sun, moon, and stars and was lord of thunder, lightning and rain. His father is the Sun and his brothers are Pachacamac and Manco Capac. His sister and wife is Mama Cocha, also a deity of the water. Children and animals were sacrificed to him. His servants or assistants are named Tonapa and Tarapaca. Somehow, Virococha, who is without flesh and bones, has a beard, wears the sun as his crown and carries a thunderbolt. He also has a reputation of being a swift runner. Sometimes, Virococha wanders the earth as a beggar. Some say Virococha's opponent was named Taguacipa. *See also* Bochica; Coniraya; Manco Capac; Pachacamac; Rimac; Thunupa.

Virtus (Roman) God of male courage.

Virudaka (India) *see* Virudhaka.

Virudhaka *Virudaka* (Buddhist; India)

Also known as: *hPhags-skyes-po* (Tibet), *P'ags-Skyes-po, Zocho-ten* (Japan).

A Lokapalas and one of the Four Great Kings, Virudhaka is the King of the South, and lord of the giant demons and gnomes known as the Kumbhandas. He holds a sword and an elephant head skin. His color is blue. For a description of the abode of the Four Great Kings, *see* Dhartarastra, for the Buddhist Universe, *see* Chakravala. *See also* Kuvera; Lokapalas; Naga Naga Knaya; Virupaksha; Yakshas; Zocho-ten.

Virupaksha (Buddhist; India)

Also known as: *Komoku-ten* (Japan), *Mig-mi-bzan* (Tibet).

A Lokapala, he is the Lord of the Nagas in the west. His color is red. He holds a serpent, jewel and a receptacle. *See also* Dhartarastra; Komoku-ten; Lokapalas; Naga Naga Knaya; Sesha; Virudhaka.

Vis (Inca)
Also known as: *Earth.*
Harvest god. *See also* Ni; Si.

Vishapa (Armenian)
"Whose Saliva Is Poison." Vishap is an epithet of the evil dragon, Azi Dahaka, who is determined to wipe mortals from the earth. *See also* Azi Dahaka.

Vishnu *Primeval Being, Lord of the Universe, Lord Creator and Generator of All, Lord of Sacred Wisdom, Lord of Waters, World Maintainer.* (Brahmanic, Hindu, Jain, Vaishnava, Vedic; India)
Also known as: *Achyuta, Aditi, Ananta (Eternal), Ananta-Shayana (Sleeping on Ananta), Badari (Lord of Badari), Buddha (his ninth avatar), Hara, Hari (The Sun), Hayagriva, Jala-Shayin (Sleeping on the Water), Janardana, Jagannath, Kalki, Kalkin (his tenth and future avatar), Kesava, Krishna (his eighth avatar), Kurma (his second avatar as a tortoise), Manmatha, Madhava, Matsya (his first avatar as a fish), Mohini (feminine incarnation), Nara-Simbha, (his fourth avatar as a Man-Lion), Narasimba, Narasimbha, Narasinha, Narayana (Protector of Men), Parasu-Rama, Parashur Rama (his sixth avatar as Rama with an ax), Parasurama, Phra Narai (Siam), Phra Noreai-Narayana (Cambodia), Rama, Rama-candra, Rama-Chandra, (his seventh avatar as the gentle hero), Ramachandra, Surya-Narayana (Moving in the Waters), Vamana (Vishnu's fifth avatar as a dwarf), Varaha, Varaha-Avatara, Varahavatar, (his third avatar as a boar), Vikrama, Vikramaditya, Yajnesvara.*

Vishnu is variously known as the god of blue water, a sun god, a god of love, and later as a protector of worlds and conqueror of demons. In the Vedic period, Vishnu was a minor deity who was occasionally associated with Indra. In the *Rig-Veda*, a hymn to Vishnu celebrates his three strides. Two steps are visible to mortals and the third step is beyond sight and the bird's flight. With these steps, he brought into being the earth, the air and heaven. He is called the "All-pervader," the "Wide-stepper" and the preserver. This feat is also performed by Vamana who is the fifth avatar of Vishnu (in the form of a dwarf) in Brahmanic mythology. The Vedics believed in personal immortality. The good went to heaven or the world of Vishnu and others to the domain of Yama (although Yama was also thought of as the ruler of all departed spirits). During the Brahmanic period Vishnu rose in status and became the second member of the Hindu Trimurti (triad) along with Brahma the Creator and Shiva the Destroyer. In this representation, he is self-existent and embodies all good and mercy. His numerous avatars are enacted in order to overcome evil in the world and each avatar carries its own tale. He appears in human or supernatural form. Vishnu also appears in amsavataras or partial incarnations. This method permits him to invest a portion of himself to two or more men at once, with varying degrees of power. In his non-avatar form, he was childless and had a divided male-female essence. The male essence descended into Rama and Krishna and the female essence into Sita and Radha.

When Vishnu is in an avatar form, his wife, the beautiful goddess Lakshmi, often appears in another form with the same or another name. Vishnu is the husband or possible son of Aditi. His father is the sun god Vaivasvata. In the Bengali tradition, the Great Mother Devi as an avatar named Kali is his mother. He is also named as the husband of the earth goddess Bhu (also spelled Bhumi and Bhumidevi). Vishnu and Lakshmi reside in his heaven named Vaikuntha, an abode made of gold and precious stones, where he watches over the universe. In another rendition, Vishnu was married to Sarasvati. Their union was so unhappy that Vishnu suggested that she marry Brahma, which she attempted to do. The goddess of the Ganges, Ganga, was also his wife, Shiva's wife, and the spouse of several other deities. Manasa, also known as Manasa-devi was the wife of Vishnu and Shiva. Another wife was Sinivali, the goddess of fecundity, easy birth and goddess of the day of the new moon. Vishnu absorbed all the sun gods into himself as Surya-Narayana. In an attempt to obtain perfection, the other deities offered a sacrifice. Vishnu, who ended the ritual before the other gods, became the most powerful and the most perfect. This displeased the gods, so they decided to murder him. They approached but could not attack, for he was upright on his feet, his head resting on his bow. It was decided that an army of ants would be employed to carry out the plan. The ants gnawed on the string of his bow until it sprang back and decapitated Vishnu. The great god's power was seized by his murderers and divided into three parts, which became the three principal phases of sacrifice. Followers of Vishnu are known as Vaishnavas. Ten Avatars of Vishnu according to the *Bhagavad Gita*: 1. Matsya or Fish. 2. Kurma or Tortoise. 3. Varaha (Varahavatar) or Boar. 4. Nara-Simbha or Man-Lion. 5. Vamana or Dwarf. 6. Parashur Rama. 7. Rama, also called Ramachandra, the gentle Rama hero of the *Ramayana*. 8. Krishna. 9. Buddha. 10. Kalki, his future avatar with a white horse head. The first five avatars are mythological, the next three heroic, the ninth religious, the tenth to come. In the *Bhagavata Purana*, twenty-two avatars are mentioned and it is stated that the avatars of Vishnu are innumerable. Rama (also known as Ramachandra) and Krishna are Vishnu's two most popular aspects. He is often represented holding a mace, conch shell (his traditional emblem), wheel or sun disk (chakra), and a Padma (lotus) in each of his four hands, and with blue skin, and clothed in yellow. On his breast he wears the Kaustubha jewel, symbolizing the sun and the calf mark (vatsa). His disk was forged by Visvakarma from the shavings of the sun god Surya. In later times, he is shown riding the half-man, half-bird, Garuda. His other vehicle is an eight-wheeled chariot (symbolizing the eight directions). It is drawn by demons (representing blazing heat). He is also depicted reclining on a couch formed by the seven-headed serpent Sesha, whose length is endless. His seven raised heads provide shade. Once Vishnu appeared in his "real" form to Arjuna, one of the Pandava brothers whom Vishnu as Parashur Rama instructed in the art of military skills. This "real" form depicted hundreds of bodies, heads and arms and was said to be a terrifying sight. In the Vedic tradition, Vishnu is the manifestation of solar energy. His three steps are manifestations of light in the form of the sun, lightning and fire. They can also be interpreted as the three phases of the sun: sunrise, noon and sunset. His divine sword is named Nandaka and his bow Sarnga. Another of

Vishnu's symbols is the knot, which symbolizes life without beginning and without end. In the Vedic tradition there are three earths corresponding to three heavens. One earth, the fourth, is called Bhumi. She is described by some as the mother of Mars. Later, in the Tantric and Puranic periods of Hinduism (about C.E. 500–1500), Vishnu is identified with the lion. The pipal tree, a type of fig tree, is regarded as a representation of Vishnu. Throbbing pain in eyes and arms and also nightmares can be removed by sprinkling the sacred tree with water while reciting a prayer. In the Hindu tradition, in the Vaikuntha heaven, Vishnu is seated on white lotus flowers. His wife Lakshmi is seated to his right. Another common depiction is Vishnu reclining in a state of deep meditation on Shesha, who has one thousand cobra heads. A lotus rises up from his navel which is partly covered by the world-ocean. Brahma, also in deep meditation, is seated on the lotus. In the *Bhagavad Gita*, Yajna or sacrifice is said to be Vishnu. As Vishnu-Narayana, he is associated with the primordial waters and represents the creative principle from which universes emerge and into which they are reassimilated. The setting sun represents Vishnu dying. As Manmatha, Vishnu is the god of love who carries bows and arrows and is associated with Priti and Rati. As Hayagriva, Vishnu is depicted with a horse's head and is known as the god of learning. Lakshmi, who was originally worshiped through the sacred fire, symbolizes the abundance that comes through fire. Lakshmi and Bhumidevi are always represented with a blue or pink lotus in their hands. Vishnu is the central deity of worship in the Vaishnava tradition. Vishnu shares characteristics with Indra and Prajapati (q.v.). Vishnu is associated with Indra in relation to Vritra (q.v.). *See* Vivasvat, who is thought by some to be the forerunner of Vishnu. The sun god Savitri closely resembles Vishnu (q.v.). Compare to the Greek deities, Apollo and Zeus, the Egyptian Horus and the Norse Thor. *See* Pandora for a parallel myth. *See* Narayana who is said to be an aspect of Vishnu. The goddess Bhumi closely corresponds to Prithivi and some feel they are two forms of the same goddess. *See also* Aditi; Adityas; Agastya; Agni; Ahalya; Amrita; Andhaka; Arjuna; Asura; Badari; Bala-Rama; Bali (B); Bhumi; Brahma; Brighus; Buddha; Deva (A); Devaki; Devi; Dharti Mai (also known as Bhu Devi); Durga; Gandharvas; Ganesha; Ganga; Garuda; Gramadeveta; Hansa; Hara; Hiranya-Kasipu (regarding Hiranyaksha) Rama; Jagannath; Kali; Kaliyuga; Kalki; Kama (A); Kasyapa; Krishna; Kurma; Kuvera; Lakshmi; Manjusri (Buddhist); Manu; Mari; Matsya; Nagas and Nagis; Nara-Simha; Narayana (A); Narayana (B); Narayana (D); Parashur Rama; Patala; Prahlada; Prithivi; Priti; Rahu; Rati; Ravana; Sagara; Salagramas (stone representing Vishnu); Saranyu; Sarasvati; Sesha; Shiva; Siddhas; Sita (for details about Vaivasvata); Surya; Tulasi (sacred plant); Vaikuntha; Vamana; Varaha; Vasuki; Visvakarma; Yajna; Yama.

Vishvabhu (India) *see* Manushi-Buddhas.

Vishvakarman (India) *see* Visvakarma.

Vishvanatha (India) "Lord of All." *See also* Shiva.

Visnanatha (India)
   Visnanatha is Shiva's name as the presiding deity of the sacred city of Benares.

Visnu (India) *see* Vishnu.

Vispala (India)
   Vispala is one of the patients of the healing twin deities, known as the Asvins. The brothers fitted Vispala with an iron leg. *See also* Asvins.

Visravas (India)
   The son of Pulastya, father of Kuvera with Ilavida and with a Rakshasi, three sons, Ravana, Kumbhakarna and Vibishana. *See also* Kuvera; Ravana.

Visva-Karma (India) *see* Visvakarma.

Visva-Krit (India) *see* Visvakarma.

Visvakarma *Tvashtri, Vishvakarman, Visva-Karma, Visva-Krit, Viswakarman* (Buddhist, Hindu, Vedic; India)
   Originally, the name Visvakarma was an epithet used for gods of great power, such as Indra or Surya. In early times, Visvakarma was known as Tvashtri. Later, known as Visvakarma, he was the divine architect and divine smith for gods and demons. Beyond the understanding of mortals, he produced heavens and earths. In the post–Vedic period he was known as the divine architect. Visvakarma created the universe from an unknown tree and was responsible for the maintenance of his creation. He built the paradisiacal city of Amaravati in Swarga, and Vaijayanta, Indra's palace on Mount Meru. Krishna employed him to design his divine abode Dwarka in one night, and he built the dwelling place for the Rakshasas, Sri Lanka. He was also the architect for the assembly hall of Yudhisthira, and Chandrapura, city of the king of the Vidyadharas. Indraprastha, the palace of the Pandavas, was also his creation. He was a Rishi, one of the seven (some say fourteen) sages born from Brahma's brain. He designed the bridge to Lanka for Rama (one of the three avatars of Vishnu), and generated the ape Nala who acted as chief engineer and supervisor for the construction crew of monkeys who built the bridge. Indra's fabulous horses were produced by Visvakarma and he constructed the chariots of the gods. When his daughter Sanja was unable to stand the dazzling brightness of her mate, Surya the sun, he shaved off one eighth of his rays. With the shavings Visvakarma gave Nala material for his work on the bridge and forged metal to make weapons for the gods. He also forged Shiva's trident and Karttikeya's spear, and Vishnu's discus. Visvakarma is said to be all-seeing, with faces, eyes and arms on all sides. In the middle provinces of India, festivals were held four times yearly in Visvakarma's honor. During these periods, their book on architecture and their tools of the trade are revered. Visvakarma is also honored for introducing sacrifice and then giving the example by sacrificing himself. Visvakarma is sometimes identified with Indra, Tvashtri and Brahma and sometimes confused with Tvashtri. The confusion may stem from early times when Visvakarma was known as Tvashtri. Visvakarma is also confused with Vivasvat and is identified with Prajapati. *See also* Amaravati; Brahma; Chakravala the Buddhist Universe; Indra; Jagannath; Karttikeya; Krishna; Kuvera; Meru mountain; Pandavas; Rakshasas; Rama; Rishi; Sanja; Shiva; Surya; Swarga; Tvashtri; Vidyadhara; Vishnu; Vivasvat; Yadavas.

Visvamitra (India)
   He is a Rishi. The names and numbers of the Rishis varies.

Visvamitra is listed on the oldest list of seven rishis which includes Atri, Bharadvaja, Gautama, Jamadagni, Kasyapa and Vasistha. Together, the seven Rishis form the constellation of the Great Bear. *See also* Rishi.

Visvapani (Buddhist; India) A Dhyanibodhisattva (q.v.).

Visvapani is one of the five Buddhist creators of the universe. The other four are Avalokitesvara, Ratnapani, Samantabhadra, Vajrapani. *See also* Dhyani Buddhas; Samantabhadra; Vajrapani.

Visvarupa (India)

Visvarupa is the serpent son of Tvashtri. He is associated with Trisiras, the three-headed water god. *See also* Ahi; Trisiras; Tvashtri.

Visvavasu (India) *see* Vivasvat.

Viswakarman (India) *see* Visvakarma.

Vitharr (Teutonic) *see* Vidar.

Vivanghat (Persian) *see* Vivanghvant.

Vivanghvant *Vivanghat* (Persian)

"The Vivifier." *See also* Haoma; Hoshang; Jamshid.

Vivasvan (India) *see* Martanda; Vivasvat.

Vivasvant (India)

"The Bright One." *See also* Martanda; Vivasvat.

Vivasvat *Visvavasu, Vivasvan, Vivasvant* (Vedic; India)

Also known as: *Martanda, Marttanda, Savita, Surya.*

Vivasvat, also known as Martanda, emerged from an egg as an unformed lump. His mother, the "Mother of the Worlds," Aditi, took one look at him and hurled him into the heavens. The divine artificer Tvashtri molded the lump into Vivasvat the sun god. The excessive material fell to earth and became elephants. Vivasvat, an Aditya, was the eighth son born to Aditi. An extravagant wedding took place when Vivasvat married Saranyu, the goddess of morning light, who was the daughter of Tvashtri. The extensive guest list included the whole world and every deity. Eventually, the couple became the parents of twins, a son Yama and a daughter Yami who became the parents of all mortals. Saranyu found it difficult staying with Vivasvat because of his brightness. She assumed the shape of a mare and disappeared. Vadava (also spelled Vadaba) the mare goddess was formed in her likeness to take her place. She bore the twin healing deities, known as the Asvins. When Vivasvat realized that a clone of his wife was with him, he assumed the form of a horse and galloped off in search of his original bride. He found her and they reunited. In later times, Vivasvat and Saranyu became aspects of the chief sun god, Surya. Often the mythology of Vivasvat is attributed to Surya, as in time Surya absorbed Vivasvat and Savitri. Vivasvat crosses the sky daily, in a chariot drawn by seven red or white horses. Vivasvat's son Vaivasvata is the seventh and present Manu of the earth. *See* Manu; Matsya. For Vivasvat's siblings, *see* Aditi. *See also* Adityas; Asvins; Kasyapa; Martanda; Mitra; Saranyu; Surya; Tvashtri; Visvakarma; Yama; Yami.

Vivian (Arthurian) *see* Vivien.

Vivien *Vivian, Vivienne* (Arthurian)

Also known as: *Anatis, Dame du Lac, Ellen Douglas, Lady of the Lake, Nimue, Niniane, Rhiannon* (Possibly).

Lake goddess. Water nymph. Sorceress. Vivian, an enchantress, accorded the Excalibur sword to King Arthur. She was the mistress of Merlin the magician and prophet, and lived in a palace in the middle of a magic lake. In early times, as Niniane (in the writing of Malory), she imprisoned the same Merlin in a rock or a tree. In other traditions, Vivien is the same as Nimue, the daughter of Dinas, who seduced the older Merlin under the pretext of wanting to know how to build a tower out of air. He succumbed to her charms at a high price. He was imprisoned in her edifice, a walless tower, and died. Vivien as Ellen Douglas is from a poem by Scott and in Cabel's Jurgen she is called Anatis. It is thought that Vivien is an aspect of Rhiannon, the Cymric goddess. Vivien and the aspects of Vivien are the goddess personified. Her emblems are the sword and fish. *See also* Arthur; Rhiannon.

Vivienne (Arthurian) *see* Vivien.

Vizetot (Nicaragua)

God of famine. Vizetot is one of the creation deities who are ruled by Tamagostad and Zipaltonal. He is associated with Ecalchot, Ciaga, Quiateot, Misca, and Chiquinau.

Vjofn (Teutonic)

Goddess of love and peace. She is an attendant of Frigga. Her job is to maintain peace among mortals and to reconcile quarrels.

Vlkodlak *Vrkolak, Vukodlak* (Serbian, Slavic)

Also known as: *Volkum.*

Vlkodlak is a Slavic man who can turn into a werewolf. In Serbia, Vlkodlak is the spirit of the hungry wolf who causes eclipses of the sun and moon.

Voden (German) *see* Odin.

Vodu (Dahomey, Fon People, Africa)

Supreme beings. Masters of the divisions of nature. Sagbata, the earth god; Xevioso, the thunder god; Gun, the god of iron; Avlekete or Agbe, god of the sea. They are associated with Legba (q.v.) Some versions claim the vodu is the power, the force of a cult. *See also* Olodumare; Xevioso.

Vodyanoi *Vodyany* (Slavic, Russian)

Also known as: *Vodyany-Ye.*

"Grandfather." Water sprites. These immortal shape changers are very dangerous. They lure people to the water and drag them in to become their slaves. They keep their souls and allow the bodies to float to the top. Some of the Vodyanoi have a human face, paws in place of hands, long horns, eyes that glow and large toes. Others are men with red eyes, very long noses and black skin. A diverse group, other Vodyanoi are old men with green hair and beards. They can be depicted as a fish or a tree trunk with wings. The Vodyanoi can be propitiated by sacrificing a black pig. *See also* Kul.

Vodyanoy (Finnish) *see* Kul; Vodyanoi.

Vodyany-Ye (Slavic) *see* Vodyanoi.

Vohu Mana (Persia) *see* Vohu Manah.

Vohu Manah *Vohu Mana, Vohu Mano* (Zoroastrian; Persia)

Also known as: *Bahman* (Pahlavi dialect).

An Amesha Spentas, he is the advisor of Ahura Mazda and sits at his right hand. He keeps a daily record of men's thoughts, words and deeds. At death, he greets mortals and leads them to the highest heaven. Vohu Manah also protects domestic animals. He is particularly opposed to the demon Aka Manah (Vile Thoughts or Discord), and the demons Aeshma (Wrath), and Az (Wrong Mindedness). When he was thirty years old, Zarathustra Spitama, known as Zoroaster, the founder of Zoroastrianism, had a vision of Vohu Manah. He appeared to him as an angel nine times the size of a man, and proclaimed that Zoroaster would become the prophet of Ahura Mazda, the one true god. See also Ahura Mazda; Aka Manah; Ameshas Spenta; Asha Vahista; Az; Daevas; Haoma; Kshasthra Vairya; Vayu; Zoroaster.

Vohu Mano (Persia) see Vohu Manah.

Voice of the Void (Bambara People, Africa)
Creator spirits. They are primordial spirits who created everything. Pemba created women; Faro, the water. There was constant strife between Pemba, who was good, and his wife, Musso Koroni, who was evil. Faro gave mortals agriculture. See also Musso Koroni; Pemba.

Vol Vola, Volla (Norse; Teutonic) see Fulla.

Voland (Teutonic) see Valland; Volund.

Volcano Woman (North Pacific Coast People, North America)
Volcano Woman is another name for the mountain spirit Dzelarhons.

Voli (Teutonic) see Vali.

Volkun (Serbian, Slavic)
Another name for the werewolf, Vlkodlak.

Volla (Norse; Teutonic) see Vol.

Volos (Slavic)
Also known as: Veles, Vyelyes.
Volos is the god of cattle and commerce, the protector of the herds and flocks. The Christians later absorbed him into their religion as St. Blaise, or St. Vlas. Because he was worshiped by warriors he might have been considered a god of war at one time. The only physical description of him is that he had curly hair. He is identified with Pyerun (q.v.).

Volsung (Norse; Teutonic)
Volsung is the son of Rerir and one of the grandsons of Sigi, Odin's son. His mate is Liod. They had ten sons (Sigmund is the eldest) and a daughter, Signy. Signy's husband Siggeir murdered Volsung. The name Volsung is used for all members of Volsung's family. See also Odin; Sigmund.

Volsunga Saga, The (Teutonic; Norse)
The Volsunga Saga originated in 13th century Iceland. They are the stories of the gods, goddesses, heroes of the Volsungs. The main Volsung character is Sigurd, son of Sigmund and Hiordis. Others in the Volsunga Saga cast are Bryhild, Hiordis, Gudrun and Gunnar. See also Sigmund; Volsung.

Voltan (Maya) God of Earth.

Voltumna (Etruscan) Mother goddess.

Volturnus (Roman) God of the river Tiber.

Volund Foland, Phaland, Valland, Velint, Voland, (Norse; Teutonic)
Also known as: Wayland, Weland, Wieland, Woland.
Deity of smiths. The brothers Egil, Slagfinn and Volund lived with three Valkyries: Olrun, Alvit, and Svanhvit. After nine years the Valkyries left. Egil and Slagfinn followed and were lost. Voland stayed behind and, being a smith, copied the ring Alvit had given him. He made seven hundred duplicate rings, one of which King Nidud (who captured Volund) gave to his daughter Bodvild. In a clever ruse Volund escaped after killing all of Nidud's family. Volund went to Alfheim where he manufactured suits of impenetrable armor, the swords Balmung and Joyeuse, and was also said to have fashioned Miming for his son Heime.

Volundr (Teutonic) see Weland.

Voluptas (Roman)
Voluptas is the goddess of sexual delight. She is the daughter of Cupid and Psyche.

Volva, The (Teutonic)
The Volva is a name used for the evil goddess Gullveig.

Vor (Norse; Teutonic)
Also known as: Frigga (possibly), Var, Vara.
"Vow." Goddess of faith. Vor, an attendant of Frigga, is a goddess from whom nothing can be hidden. She is a goddess of marriage and contracts. She punishes those who do not keep their vows. See also Frigga.

Vortumnus (Roman) see Vertimnus.

Votan (A) (Teutonic) see Odin.

Votan (B) (Yucatan, Mayan)
Also known as: Heart of the People.
Culture hero, first man, or god. Votan descended from Imos (a genie or guardian of the days), and traveled on subterranean roads going beneath the Earth and ending at the roots of the sky. His successor was Canam-Lum (Serpent of the Earth). Votan appears to be the same as Quetzalcoatl, or similar. He is associated with Palenque, Zamna, Itzamna and Kukulcan.

Vourukasha (A) (Indo-Iranian and Hindu)
The sea godfather of Apam Napat ("Grandson of the Waters"), who was born on a cloud and who loved Anahita (q.v.).

Vourukasha (B) (Persian)
Vourukasha is the boundless ocean, so wide that it contains a thousand lakes, and the springs of the water goddess Anahita. Rain created by the god Tishtrya formed the waters of Vourukasha. From it the world is supplied with water. In the midst of Vourukasha stands Gaokerna the sacred plant and The Tree of Many Seeds. After the cosmic ocean was created, twenty-three seas followed; three great seas, and twenty smaller seas. Two rivers ran through the earth, one from north to west and the other from north to east. They ran over the edge of the world and their waters mingled with Vourukasha. The rains caused the earth to split into seven pieces. One half of the land mass is known as Khwanirath, and the surrounding six portions are the Keshvars. Passage from one portion to the other was impossible except by riding on the back of Srishok, or Hadhayos, the heavenly bull. Vourukasha is watched over by the fantastic half-

man, half-ox Gopatshah. *See also* Alburz (Mount); Anahita; Angra Mainyu; Gandarewa; Khara (A); Simburgh; Thrita; Tishtrya; Tree of Many Seeds.

Vretil (Hebrew) *see* Nabu.

Vrihaspati (India) *see* Tara.

Vrikdevatas (India) *see* Devis.

Vrikodara (India) "Wolf's Belly." *See also* Bhima (A).

Vrikshakas (India) *see* Apsarases.

Vrinda (India) *see* Asuras.

Vrishakapayi (India) Wife of Vrishakapi (q.v.).

Vrishakapi (India) The Ape. *See also* Hanuman; Indrani.

Vrita *Vrtra* (The Covering); (Hindu, Vedic; India)
Vrita the archdemon, serpent of darkness and draught, is an Asura. He is the offspring of the goddess Danu and is called a Danava. A Danava is a descendant of Danu or something having the character of Danu. Danavas became known as subordinates of Vrita. In later times, Danavas were called Rakshas and sometimes Vritas or Daitya or Adityas. The Adityas represent good and are hostile to the Danavas. In a variation of Vrita's origins, it is said that he was manifested by the father of a youth killed by Indra. The young man had three heads, one for studying, one for eating and one for watching. Indra was extremely jealous of the peaceful, studious youth. He tried unsuccessfully to distract him from his meditations and studies. Finally, Indra was so enraged that he hurled a thunderbolt at him and cut off his heads. Vita, a huge dragon or serpent, emerged and swallowed Indra's cows which were the rain clouds. He also blocked the seven great rivers of India with his ninety-nine coils or by lapping up the water. He terrified all the deities except Indra. With the advice and possible aid of Vishnu, or some say, Krishna, and enough soma to fortify him, he set out to slay the dragon. His method, either drowning him in a great mass of foam that emanated from his belly or attacking him with his magic thunderbolt, was successful. The hideous corpse frightened the courageous god and he leapt over the rivers that sprang free when Vrita's coils were removed. Upon Vrita's belly, his mother, who was slain in the battle, lay dead. His brave action caught the attention of the gods, and from that time, they were at Indra's side whenever he needed assistance. Vrita's name means the "Enemy" or the "Enveloper." There are variations of this myth, and Indra always emerges the victor. Vrita is depicted as strong and wily. Darkness symbolizes the pain and misery caused by drought. The seven great rivers are said by some to be the seven planets. Danu means "bondage" and Vrita, as a Danava and the offspring of Danu, therefore personifies restraint. Vrita is comparable to the celestial Egyptian snake, Ahi. Compare Vrita to Typhon (Greek). *See also* Adityas; Agastya; Asuras; Drukh; Indra; Maruts; Nagas and Nagis; Rakshasas; Sesha; Shiva; Soma; Tvashtri; Varuna; Vedas (The).

Vritra (India) *see* Vrita.

Vritrahan *Vritrahana, Vrtrahanna* (India)
Slayer of Vrita. *See also* Indra.

Vritrahana (India) *see* Vritrahan.

Vrkolak (Serbian, Slavic) *see* Vlkodlak.

Vrou-elde (Germanic) *see* Bertha.

Vrtra (India) *see* Vrita.

Vrtrahanna (India) *see* Vritrahan.

Vukodlak (Serbian, Slavic) *see* Vlkodlak.

Vukub-Ahpu (Maya) *see* Hunhun-Ahpu.

Vukub-Cakix (Maya People, Yucatan)
Sun and Moon deity. According to the "Popul Vuh," Vukub-Cakix was the first of the giants of one of the ages of the earth. He had two sons, Zipacna and Cabrakan. Vukub-Cakix owned a fruit tree which was for his food. The two brothers Hunahpu and Xbalanque hid in the branches and shot this giant with a poisoned arrow. The giant tore off one of Hunahpu's arms, which his wife, Chimalmat, proceeded to roast on a spit. Disguising themselves as physicians the two brothers managed to convince Vukub-Cakix that his teeth were causing him trouble and substituted maize for the emeralds that were his real teeth. The transplant robbed the giant of his power and soon killed him. After recovering, both brothers went on to their next adventures where they killed Zipacna and Cabrakan. *See also* Hunahpu; Xbalanque; Xibalba.

Vukubcame *Vukub-Came* (Quiche People, Guatemala)
One of the Lords of the Underworld. *See also* Hun-cane; Xibalba.

Vulcan *Vulcanus* (Roman)
Also known as: *Hephaistos* (Greek), *Mulciber the Smelter*.
God of Fire. God of metal working. Patron of iron workers. Vulcan might have been the husband of Maia (Maiestas). With Medusa, he had two children, Caca, the goddess of latrines, and Cacus, the fire-breathing giant. His festival, Vulcania, was held outside of the city on August 23. Small fish were thrown into fire to assuage him. He is similar to, and identified with, the Greek god Hephaistos. Compare to the Vedic deity Tvastri and the Celtic Goibniu. *See also* Caca; Hephaistos; Maia; Medusa.

Vulcania (Roman)
Festivals held in honor of Vulcan, celebrated August 23.

Vulcanus (Roman) *see* Vulcan.

Vultures (Greek)
They are the children of Typhon and Echidna. *See also* Typhon (A).

Vushkapariks (Armenia)
The Vushkapariks are spirits similar to the Pairikas (q.v.). *See also* Hambaris.

Vuub-Hunapu (Guatelmala) *see* Hun-cane.

Vyaghrini (Nepal) Female guardian demon.

Vyasa (Hindu; India)
Also known as: *Krishna Dwaipayana, Vedavyasa*.
Vyasa, the demigod son of the sage Parashara and the water nymph Satyavati, lived as a hermit in the forest. He became the poet of some of the books of the *Mahabharata*. His half-broth-

ers by King Shantanu of Hastinapura, Chitrangada and Vichi-travirya, died leaving their widows childless. Satyavati asked Vyasa to impregnate his sisters-in-law, Ambika and Ambalika. He agreed, but they were not overjoyed when they saw his appearance. They were expecting the handsome Bhishma, not a wild-looking man with long, matted hair. Ambika could not bear to open her eyes, so her son Dhritarashtra was born blind. Ambalika was so frightened that the color drained from her face. Her son was the pale Pandu. These births were not deemed

successful by Satyavati and she insisted that Ambika and Vyasa make another attempt. The thought horrified Ambika and although she consented, she substituted her maid as Vyasa's partner. The maid gave birth to Vidura who was an incarnation of Dharma. *See also* Bhishma; Brihaspati; Dhritarashtra; Ganesha; Pandavas; Parashara; Satyavati.

Vyelyes (Slavic) *see* Volos.

W

Wa (China)

Little is known about the divine woman, Wa, who, according to Chinese writings in the first century C.E., "produced ten thousand beings through metamorphosis."

Wa Cinaci (Arawak People, South America) *see* Ifilici Wacinaci.

Wa Murreta Kwonci (Arawak People, South America) *see* Ifilici Wacinaci.

Wabun (North America) *see* Manibozho.

Wadd (Arabic)

"The Loving." Wadd is a name used for the twin sons of El, Shahar, the god of dawn, and Shalim, the god of sunset. *See also* Shahar.

Wadjet (Egypt)

"Green One." Wadjet is the Goddess of Buto and the national goddess of Lower Egypt. She symbolizes the forces of growth. She is a fire-spitting serpent who is also known as the "Eye of Re." Wadjet is the most important serpent-deity. The uraeus, her sacred animal, is said to have wound herself around the king's diadem. Wadjet's counterpart is Nekhbet of Upper Egypt. She is sometimes seen with a leonine head topped by the solar disc and uraeus. *See also* Buto (Greek); Isis; Nekhbet; Uatchet.

Wagilag Sisters (Australia) *see* Wawalag Sisters.

Wahieroa (Oceanic)

Wahieroa is the mortal son of Tawhaki and a goddess. His grandparents are Hema and a goddess. His paternal uncle is Kariki. Wahieroa and his wife are the parents of Rata. Like his father and grandfather, Wahieroa was captured and killed (in his case, by a flying monster, named Matu'u-ta'u-ta'uo, although in some stories, it is a shark named Matuku tago-tago who bites off his head). As in generations past, Rata set out to avenge his father's death. His adventures comprise an exciting and enduring saga. Finally, Rata encounters Matuku, the shark. He rips open the shark's belly and finds his father's head. Other

body parts were found in the stomachs of Matuku's monster associates. Rata went on to rescue his mother, Puna, and to restore her eyesight. Mother, son and father's body parts went home together. *See also* Kariki; Rata; Tawhaki.

Wailing River (Greek)

Wailing River is a name used for the Cocytus river. As a river, the Cocytus is a tributary of the River of Sadness, the Acheron in Epirus. The souls of the dead not buried wander along the banks of the Cocytus where they will wail and groan for one hundred years after death. For the names of other rivers in the Underworld, *see* Cocytus. *See also* Charon.

Wainamoinen (Finland) *see* Vainomoinen.

Waka (Galla People, Ethiopia, Africa)

Waka will bring the needed rain, if the right devotee asks.

Waka-hiru-me *Wakahirume* (Japan)

The sun goddess, Amaterasu, thought highly of her weaving maiden, Waka-hiru-me. When Amaterasu's brother, the volatile Susanowo, threw a skinned colt through the roof of the "Heavenly Weaving Wall," Waka-hiru-me was so frightened that she fell onto her shuttle and punctured her vagina. Her death infuriated the sun goddess, who sealed herself into the cave known as Ame-no-Iwato (Sky-Rock-Cave) and withdrew the light of the world. *See also* Amaterasu; Amatsu-Mikaboshi.

Waka-mi-ke-nu-no-mikoto (Japan)

Jimmu Tenno, the first emperor and founder of the Imperial Line of Japan, was born Kama-Yamato-Iware-Biko but was also called Waka-mi-ke-nu-no-mikoto. He acquired the name Jimmu Tenno posthumously. *See also* Jimmu Tenno.

Waka-sana-me-no-kami (Japan)

A name for the goddess of food, Ukemochi (q.v.).

Waka-uke-nomi (Japan)

"Young woman with food." Another name for the goddess of food, Ukemochi (q.v.).

Wakahirume (Japan) *see* Waka-hiru-me.

Wakan (Oglala People, North America)
Another name for the supreme spirit, Kitshi Manito.

Wakan-Tanka (Dakota, Sioux People, North America)
Assembly of gods. The Wakan-Tanka is a collective unity of the gods which has tremendous power. It is similar to a gathering of world leaders, but far more effective. It is necessary to be of the right mind before calling on these gods. To quote a priest of the Dakotas, "It is not fitting that a man should suddenly go out and make a request of Wakan-Tanka." *See also* Kitshi Manito.

Wakanda (North American) *see* Wakonda.

Wakataka (Sioux People, North America)
Wakataka, the creator god, made the earth, the parents of the Sioux people, all fur animals that swim and all animals that hunt for food.

Wakcexi *Waktcexi* (Algonquin, Chippewa, Cree, Nascopie People, North America)
A water monster.

Wakea (Polynesia) *see* Vari (A).

Wakonda *Wakanda* (Osage, Omaha, Sioux and Dakota Indian, North America)
Wakonda is the power above; a supreme invisible being who created everything. Among the Nebraska Omaha People, Wakanda stands for the mysterious life power embodied in all natural forces and creatures, as well as in man. Compare to Tirawa of the Pawnee Indians. *See also* Kitshi Manito.

Wakonyingo (Pygmy or Wachaga People, Africa)
The Wakonyingo are dwarf spirits or elves who live at the peak of Kilimanjaro. They have their own ladders to climb to heaven. Though they are small of stature, their heads are so large that they carry a horn to call for help if they start to lose their balance.

Waktcexi (North American) *see* Wakcexi.

Wala (Fox People, North America) The Dawn.

Walangada (Aborigine People, Australia)
Walangada is one of the law-giving spirits who live in caves. *See also* Wondjina.

Walangala (Aborigine People, Australia)
He is a god of culture and social institutions. He is similar to Wallanganda, but Walangala did not create anything. If people do not follow the proper procedures, he will send floods. Walangala is associated with the maker of bull-roarers, Nyunyari. *See also* Ungud; Wallanganda.

Walhalla (Teutonic) *see* Valhalla.

Walkure (Teutonic) *see* Valkyrie.

Walkyrie (Teutonic) *see* Valkyrie.

Wallanganda (Aborigine People, Australia)
Wallanganda and Ungud created everything. They could be associated with the Wawalag sisters. *See also* Ungud.

Walumbe (Vedic; India)
Walumbe is mentioned in the *Rig-Veda* (approximately 1500 B.C.E.), as the god of death.

Wamara (Baziba People, Africa)
Father of gods. He has four sons: Kagoro; Mugasha, god of water; Kazoba, god of the sun and moon; and Ryangombe, god of cattle.

Wandjina (Aborigine People, Australia)
Ancestral spirits. When a Wandjina completes his task, he turns himself into a picture, which contains his spirit and power. According to Worora People, in eastern Australia, Wandjinas are giant human beings who came out of the sea. They created the world, spirit children and animals. In caves, they are painted as large figures with no mouths. The bodies are striped and dotted red, yellow, black and pale blue. The Worora repainted the Wandjinas as part of a ceremony to increase the number of animals. This ritual probably originated in Melanesia.

Wang (China)
The Jade Emperor Yu Huang's guardian of the palace door, Wang was also called upon to drive away evil spirits. *See also* Yu Huang.

Wang-chugmas *Wangchugmas* (Buddhist; Tibet)
There are twenty-eight of Wang-chugmas, who are bird and animal-headed goddesses. They appear in the Bardo World. *See also* Amrtakundali.

Wang-Mu-Niang-Niang (China)
Also known as: *Hsi-Wang-Mu, Lady Wang, Queen Mother Wang.*
Guardian. She is a beautiful young woman, who is the keeper of the peaches of immortality (known as P'an-T'ao or Shen-T'ao). Her husband is the Jade Emperor, or Yu-Huang-Shang-Ti. Wang-Mu-Niang-Niang is depicted in ceremonial dress, sometimes alone, sometimes with female attendants or with a peacock. *See also* Hsi Wang Mu.

Wantu Su (Africa; Sudan)
Creator. Wantu Su wanted to send gifts down to earth for humans, so he had his son, Wantu, slide down a rope and announce his arrival by drum-beating. A crow hit the drum which broke and scattered all the creatures of earth.

Warah (Arabic) *see* Shahar.

Waramurungundja *Waramurungundju* (Aborigine People, Australia)
Also known as: *Imberombera, Kunapipi.*
Mother goddess. She came out of the sea and from her body she produced children, animals and plants. She established the language for each group of people. *See also* Nuba; Wuraka.

Warana (Australia) *see* Wondjina; Yalungur.

Wasicong (Dakota People, North America)
Protective spirit.

Wata-tsu-mi (Japan) *see* O-wata-tsu-mi.

Watatsumi (Japan) *see* O-wata-tsu-mi.

Watchdog of Chulain (Celtic) *see* Cuchulain.

Water Mother (China) *see* Hsi-Ho.

Water Nymphs (Greek) *see* Naiads.

Wati and Kutjara (Aborigine People, Australia)
Also known as: *Two-Men.*
Spirits. Wati and Kutjara are ancestral spirits who gave men the ceremonial instruments that keep them in contact with the "Dreaming." They circumcised each other and the older brother gave his sister to his younger brother.

Waukheon (Dakota People, North America)
Waukheon is the thunder bird god. He and the water god, Untunktahe, are principal deities.

Wauwalak Sisters (Australia) *see* Wawalag Sisters.

Wawalag Sisters (Aborigine People, Australia)
Also known as: *Wagilag, Wauwalak, or Wawilak Sisters.*
Possibly fertility deities. They are generally associated with Yurlunggur and possibly Julunggul, Muit, Mumuna, Kunapipi. In legend one sister is pure and the other is not. Sometimes, they are identified with the Mungamunga girls who are said to be the daughters of Kunapipi. *See also* Djanggawuls; Rainbow Snake.

Wawalug (Australia) *see* Wawalag Sisters.

Wawilak Sisters (Australia) *see* Wawalag Sisters.

Waxcpini Xedera (Algonquian, Chippewa, Cree, Nascopie People, North America)
The Great Spirit.

Wayland the Smith (Teutonic)
Ruler of the dark elves. *See also* Alfar; Elves; Freyja.

We (A) (Kasena People, Africa)
Supreme god. This deity left earth because an old woman sliced bits from him for her stew pot.

We (B) (Teutonic) *see* Ve.

Weaver Damsel (China) *see* Chin Nu; Spinner Damsel.

Weendigo (North America) *see* Windigo.

Wehtiko (North America) *see* Windigo.

Wei-to *Wei-t'o* (China)
Also known as: *Bodhisattva, Celestial General Wei.*
Underworld deity. Overlord of all Hells. Guardian of the entrance. Chief of thirty-two generals who are subjects of the Four Kings. Wei-to is shown in armor including the helmet of a general. He is usually leaning with both hands on a club. Wei-to is the same as the Buddhist, Veda. He is identified with the Yaksha, Vajrapani. *See also* Ida-Ten.

Weiwobo (Japan)
Also known as: *Queen Mother of the West.*
One of the Sennins. Weiwobo, the Queen Mother, lives on a plateau, close to heaven, far to the west of China. *See also* Sennins.

Weland (Teutonic) see Wayland.

Weldegg (Teutonic) *see* Odin

Well of Urd (Teutonic) *see* Urd.

Wen Ch'ang (China)
Also known as: *Wen Ch'ang Ti Chun, Wen-ch'ang Ti-kun, Wen-chang-ta-ti, Wen-ti.*
God of literature. An ancient god, he is the emperor of literature, an honor bestowed on him by Tung Wang Kung (Yu-ti), the Jade Emperor, after he had lived a number of active, eventful lives. His original name as a mortal was Chang Ya, who was born during the T'ang dynasty. Another name given him was Chang Ya Tzu, and the dates of his life were either around C.E. 265–316 or some say C.E. 900–1280. In both cases he was killed during a fight. Wen Ch'ang is depicted in the blue dress of a mandarin and is usually seated, with a scepter in his hand. Sometimes only a tablet represents this god. Sometimes he is shown riding a white horse. His symbol is the crane. The god of examinations, K'uei-Hsing (Kuei-sing), was his helper. Another of his helpers is called "Red Jacket or Red Coat" (Chu I). In some versions his helpers are Hsuan T'ung-tzu and Ti-mu or T'ien-lung and Ti-ya. He is often confused with Tzu T'ung and K'uei-Hsing. *See also* Confucius.

Wen-chang-ta-ti (China) *see* Wen Ch'ang.

Wen Ch'ang Ti Chun (China) *see* Wen Ch'ang.

Wen-ch'ang Ti-kun (China) *see* Wen Ch'ang.

Wen-Ch'en (China) *see* Tara (B).

Wen-shu (China)
Wen-shu is the same as Manjusri, the god of learning. *See also* Manjusri; Dhyanibodhisattvas.

Wen-ti (China)
God of scholars. He is the same as Wen Ch'ang. *See also* Wen Ch'ang.

Wenen-Nefer (Egypt) *see* Unnefer.

Wenenefer (Egypt) *see* Unnefer.

Wenenut (Egypt)
Deified rabbit-headed goddess. Wenenut is the female counterpart of the hare-headed god, Wenenu. In some texts, Wenenu is identified as a form of Osiris. She is depicted with a knife in each hand, although she is also seen with the ankh and a scepter. *See also* Osiris.

Wenut (Egypt)
Also known as: *Unnet.*
Goddess of the hours. Shown as a woman with a star upon her head.

Wep-Rehewh (Egypt)
Also known as: *Thoth.*
"Judge of the Two Opponent Gods," Wep-Rehewh is an aspect of Thoth which refers to Thoth's role as judge in the strife between the gods Horus and Set for control of Egypt.

Weres Urs (Egypt) *see* Ab.

Weret Hekau (Egypt) The goddess of magic.

West, The (Egypt) *see* Ament; Amenti.

West Wind (Greek) The god Zephyrus is the West Wind.

Westre (Teutonic) *see* Westri.

Westri *Westre* (Norse; Teutonic)

Westri is one of the dwarfs who supports the heavens made from the skull of Ymir. His name is synonymous with South. His colleagues are Nordi, Sudri and Austri. *See also* Aarvak; Nordri.

Whaitiri *Whatitari, Whatitiri* (Maori People, Polynesia)

Cannibal chieftainess. Sky deity. Inventor of the latrine. She came down from the sky and married Kaitangata. They had two children, Hema and Punga. In several tales, Whaitiri, an evil woman, went blind and returned to the sky. In a Maori tale, Kaitangata complained constantly about the mess his children made and the smell of their excrement. Whaitiri invented the toilet, left the family behind and went to her home in the sky. *See also* Hema; Kaitangata; Tawhaki.

Whatitiri (Polynesia) *see* Whaitiri.

Whenua (Polynesia) Another name for Papa (q.v.).

Whisky Jack (North America) *see* Wisagatcak.

White Goddess, The (Greek)

The White Goddess is a name given to Leucothea, the sea goddess (known as Ino before deification) the by the Nereids. *See also* Ino; Nereids.

White Haoma (Persia) *see* Haoma.

White Hom (Persia) *see* Haoma.

Whitigo (North America) *see* Windigo.

Whitiko (North America) *see* Windigo.

Wieland (Teutonic) *see* Volund; Weland.

Wigan (Ifugao People, Philippines)

Also known as: *Muntalog*.

Wigan and her brother, Bugan, were survivors of the great deluge. Considered deities by some, there are many tales of how they created the human race. The god above them, Maknongan or Mumbonang, forgave their sin of incest in order to re-inhabit the earth. Their first son was Kabigat. *See also* Huginn.

Wijadari (India)

Benevolent demigods. *See also* Vidyadhara.

Wild Huntsman (Teutonic) A title for Odin.

Wild Men of the West (Tierra del Fuego) *see* Oulapatou.

Wilobo (Africa)

Wilobo, his brother Woko and Wilobo's son Ru-piny are the deities who fix things. *See also* Jok; Woko.

Wilolane (Zuni People, North America) The Lightning.

Wimpe (Algonquin People, North America)

This sorcerer, involved in a contest with Gluskap, grew taller than the pine forest. Gluskap, the power of good, grew even taller and defeated him. *See also* Gluskap.

Winabojo (North America) *see* Nanabozho.

Windigo (Algonquin, Chippewas, Ojibwa People, North America)

Also known as: *Weendigo, Wehtiko, Whitiko, Witigo*.

Evil giants. The Windigo are a race of giant cannibals who prey upon human beings in the winter when food is scarce.

These creatures have twisted mouths, emaciated bodies and hearts of ice. They emit a series of eerie whistles and also roar loudly. The only known way to destroy a Windigo is to hack it to pieces and burn it to melt its heart.

Wintua People — Creation Legend (North America) *see* Katochild.

Wisagatcak *Wisakedjak, Whiskey Jack* (Cree Indian People of Canada)

When Wisagatcak attempted to catch one of the large beavers who lived at the beginning of the world, he failed. The beavers used magic against him and caused water to cover the land. Wisagatcak made a raft. Many varieties of animals climbed aboard. After a time, a muskrat dove into the water looking for land. He drowned. A raven flew about in search of land, without luck. Wisagatcak with the help of a wolf magically made a ball of moss which turned into earth. It spread across the whole world and rested on water.

Wisakedjak (North America) *see* Wisagatcak.

Witana (Aborigine People, Australia)

A creator being. He made the gorges, cliffs, and water-holes. He also established the rites of initiation of male children into manhood. He made a cut in each arm. From one arm came blood which became red ocher, and from the other black blood came out which turned into reefs of black pigment. These colors are used in initiation ceremonies.

Witigo (North America) *see* Windigo.

Wlenenu (Egypt)

"Opener of the Ways." Wlenenu is a deified animal who is a door god. He is a battle god who appears on one of the four sacred standards of Pharaoh. His female counterpart is Wenenut. Wlenenu is sometimes identified as a form of Osiris. *See also* Wepwawet.

Wodan *Wode, Wodemus, Woden, Wodhen, Wodin, Wotan* (Germanic)

Wodan is a later form of Odin (q.v.).

Wode (Germanic) *see* Bertha; Wodan.

Wodemus (Germanic) *see* Wodan.

Woden (Germanic) *see* Wodan.

Wodhen (Germanic) *see* Wodan.

Wodin (Germanic) *see* Wodan.

Woko (Acholi People, Africa)

The deity Woko, his brother Wilobo, and Wilobo's son Ru-piny are called upon when things go wrong. They are "fixer-uppers." The family is related to the Joks. *See also* Jok.

Woland (Teutonic) *see* Volund.

Wollunka *Wollunqua* (Aborigine People, Australia)

Also known as: *Rainbow Snake*.

A snake god. He was a snake so large he could travel for miles and his tail would still be in the waterhole he left. His companion is a mortal named Mumumanugara who was supposed to have come from the great snake's body. *See also* Rainbow Snake.

Wollunqua (Australia) *see* Wollunka.

Wolverine (North America) *see* Nanabozho.

Wonaambi (Australia) *see* Rainbow Snake.

Wondjina (Aborigine People, Australia)
Also known as: *Djunggun, Walangada, Warana.*
Spirits. The Wondjina are the spirits of the sky and rain. The Rainbow Serpent (Galeru, Kaleru, Galaru, Ungur) is a Wondjina. They live in caves and are the law givers. Other Wondjinas are Warana the Eaglehawk, Wodoi the Rock Pigeon and Djunggun the Owl. Another Wondjina is an unidentified deity named Walangada. They are depicted on their sides with their heads haloed. The Wondjina do not have mouths and their eyes and noses are joined. *See also* Gidja; Rainbow Snake.

Wongar (Australia) *see* Ungud.

Wonungur (Australia) *see* Rainbow Snake.

Worombi (Australia) *see* Rainbow Snake.

Wotan (Germanic) *see* Wodan.

Woutan (Teutonic) *see* Odin.

Wowta (Warrau People, Guyana)
An evil frog-woman. *See also* Abore.

Woyengi (Ijo People, Nigeria, Africa).
Mother, Creator goddess.

Wu-Ch'ang (China)
Also known as: *Kou-hun-shih-che, Mr. Black, Mr. White.*
Messengers. The Wu-Ch'ang are the gods who conduct the souls to hell. It is the two Wu-Ch'ang rather than Ox-head (Niu-t'ou) and Horse-face (Ma-mien) who are in charge. One of the Wu-Ch'ang is black and the other is white. They are called Mr. White and Mr. Black. The Wu-Ch'ang are dressed in black or white robes. A rope hangs around their necks and they wear tall pointed hats. Both gods have their tongues hanging out. They are opposed by the Door Guards. *See also* Ma-mien; Niu-t'ou; Yama Kings.

Wu Kuan (Central Asia)
One of the Kings of Hell. He presides over punishments that are dispensed by the Yakshas. *See also* Kshitigarbha; Yakshas.

Wuhuu (Waranjui People, Africa)
Wuhuu is a name for Heaven or the "World Above." The ruler of Wuhuu is Ruwa, Mrule, Mrile, or Nrile. Some say Mrule is different from the others and that he is associated with the Masai people.

Wulbari (Krachi People, Africa)
Supreme deity. Wulbari once dwelled on top of mother earth, but it became too crowded so he left for heaven. He is associated with the spider Anansi. Wulbari's legends are similar to the god Nyankopon (q.v.).

Wuldor (Teutonic) *see* Ull.

Wulgis (Aborigine People, Australia)
Spirits of dead medicine men. The Wulgis take a possible candidate and conduct him to the sky many times. This is where he learns the secrets of magic and healing. The Wulgis are often consulted by medicine men to help in healing the sick.

Wuni (Dagamba People, Africa)
Supreme god. In old times, men did not die but were slaves forever. They wanted to be free so they sent Dog and Goat to ask Wuni to free them. Because Goat confused the message and said men wanted to die, Wuni made the arrangements. This legend is similar to Kalumba's legend.

Wuotan (German) *see* Odin.

Wuraka (Aborigine People, Australia)
Probably a god of procreation. He is the companion of the mother creator, Imberombera. His penis was so heavy he wore it around his neck. *See also* Waramurungundja.

Wurd (Anglo-Saxon) *see* Urd.

Wuriupranili (Aborigine People, Australia)
The Sun Woman. Wuriupranili is a sun goddess who travels across the sky carrying her flaming torch of bark. She paints the sunset colors in the sky. *See also* Ilara; Tuniruna; Yuwuku.

Wurusemu (Hittite) Sun goddess. *See also* Arinna; Hepat.

Wyrd (Anglo-Saxon) *see* Urd.

Wyrra-Warre (Australian aborigines)
The sky or sky god.

X

Xamaniqinqu (Maya People, Yucatan)
God of the north. His brother is the creator god, Nohoyum (q.v.). *See also* Hapikern; Uyitzin; Yantho.

Xanthippe (Greek)
She is the daughter of Dorus (who is the son of Apollo and Phthia). She married Pleuron and became the mother of Agenor and three other children. *See also* Agenor; Dorus; Pleuron.

Xanthos (Greek) *see* Xanthus.

Xanthus (A) (Greek) *Xanthos*

Achilles' immortal horses, Xanthus and Balius, have the power of speech. They are the offspring of the west wind Zephyrus, and the Harpy Podarge. *See also* Achilles; Harpies; Oceanus; Zephyrus.

Xanthus (B) (Greek)

"Yellow." Another name for Scamander (q.v.).

Xbalanque *Xbalemque* (Maya People, Yucatan) *see* Hunahpu; Vukub-Cakix.

Xecotcovach (Maya People, Yucatan)

Demon bird. After the gods created mankind from various materials they decided their work was not sufficient so destroyed what they created by a flood. Other demons helped in the destruction. Xecotcovach devoured their eyes. Camalotz cut off their heads. Cotzbalam ate their flesh, and Tucumbalam smashed their sinews and bones. Mankind was not destroyed, but those who were left were changed into monkeys. Most of the legends come from the "Popul Vuh." *See also* Alom; Bitol; Camalotz; Cotzbalam.

Xelhua (Aztec People, Mexico)

He is a giant who survived the Great Deluge. *See also* Atonatiuh; Legend of the Four Suns; Nata and Nena; Tlazolteotl.

Xenodice (Greek)

Xenodice is the daughter of the wealthy Minos and Pasiphae (the daughter of the sun god, Helius). *See also* Acacallis; Ariadne; Minos; Pasiphae.

Xevioso (Fon People, Africa)

Also known as: *Heviosso.*

God of thunder. Xevioso is the son of Mahu and Lisa and the twin of Gun. At one time he was offered human sacrifices. Associated with Legba. *See also* Legba; Vodu.

Xi Wang Mu *Xi Wang-Mu* (Taoist; China)

Also known as: *Hsi-Wang-Mu, Queen Mother of the West.*

Xi Wang Mu is a powerful goddess who reigns over a paradise in the west. Her believers are promised immortality. *See also* Hsi-Wang-Mu.

Xib Chac (Yucatan)

The name for the rain god who is commonly called Chac (q.v.).

Xibalba *Xibalha* (Maya People, Yucatan; Quiche People, Guatemala)

"Place of Fright." The underworld realm of the dead. The Celestial Monster dives into Xibalba with the mortal soul on its back. The soul must confront the Lord of Death, and other obnoxious creatures such as the God of Zero, and the Vision Serpent. The Hero Twins, Hunahpu and Xbalanque, once descended into the depths of Xibalba to take control of this land by means of defeating the creatures in a series of ball games. The lords of Xibalba are Hun-Came, meaning "One Death," and Vukub-Cakix, meaning Seven Deaths. In the mythology of the Quiche People, Xibalba is a region of phantoms. Xibalba is the equivalent of Hades (Greek). Compare to Hades. *See also* Hell; Hun-cane; Hunahpu.

Xilonen (Aztec People, Mexico)

Also known as: *Chalchiuhcihuatl, Chicomecoatl, Princess of the Unripe Maize.*

Goddess of maize. Fertility goddess. Protector of the home. When the early corn appeared and turned green, it took on divine form and was Xilonen, the counterpart of the god Cinteotl. Households kept a basket in front of the maize bin which held five ears of dried corn. It was formed into and dressed as a woman. This represented Xilonen. She is sometimes identified as a wife of Tezcatlipoca. Extremely pretty, Xilonen is depicted seated primly with bare breasts. In her hands she holds fresh maize cobs. Her festival is in July when the maize turns ripe. The feasts feature maize, gruel and tamales. *See also* Atlantonan; Chicomecoatl; Cinteotl; Tzinteotl; Uixtochihuatl; Xochiquetzal.

Xipe (Aztec) *see* Xipe Totec.

Xipe Itzpapalotl (Aztec People, Mexico)

Also known as: *Camaxtle.*

Agricultural or star goddess. Little known but she is designated Obsidian Knife Butterfly.

Xipe Totec *Xipe* (Aztec, Mixtec, Nahua, Zapotec People, Mexico)

Also known as: *Camaxtle, Camaxtli, God 7 Rain (Mixtec people), Nanautzin, Red Tezcatlipoca, Yopi.*

"Our Flayed Lord." Vegetation Deity (particularly of seeds). God of suffering. God of spring. God of renewal. Healer of eye ailments. God of flowers. Patron of goldsmiths and jewellers. God of the sunset. Patron of gladiatorial combat. Xipe is identified with suffering and sacrifice, particularly gladiator sacrifice. Xipe is one of the four sons of Ometeotl and Omecihuatl. His brothers are Tezcatlipoca, Quetzalcoatl and Huitzilopochtli. Quetzalcoatl and Huitzilopochtli were charged with creating the earth, other gods, and people. When Xipe and his brothers were born the universal cycle of creation and destruction was put in motion. As the Red Tezcatlipoca, Xipe is the brother of the Blue, Black and White Tezcatlipoca and Quetzalcoatl.

During the year, soldiers captured young gladiators and held them captive until Xipe's feast, known as Tlacaxipehualiztli (meaning, "Flaying of the Men"). At the time of the Conquest the festival took place March 6–March 25. Numerous references indicate that the festival went on many days longer than scheduled. The gladiators were flayed (skinned) alive and offered for sacrifice. Their skins were worn by impersonators, who were usually the captors of the victims. Some say the flayed skins were considered holy.

The four cardinal points are associated with the four sons of the supreme dual god: Quetzalcoatl, Xipe Totec, Camaxtli, and Huitzilopochtli. They are also connected with the Four Suns which preceded our world and ended in destruction. Xipe is similar to the Mayan god of sacrifice, and patron of the day Manik. As god of the sunset, Xipe is associated with the west and wears the eagle down of sacrifice on his robe. He is generally depicted as a human inside the flayed skin of another man. Vertical stripes run from his forehead to chin, running over or broken by the eyes. The puckered flayed skin usually displays an incision where the heart was removed; the penis is absent.

The flayed skin is elaborately tied on at the back. *See also* Camaxtli; Coatlicue; Tezcatlipoca; Topiltzin.

Xiuhcoatl (Aztec People, Mexico)

Xiuhcoatl is the serpent that Huitzilopochtli used as a weapon to kill his sister, Coyolxauhqui. *See also* Coyolxauhqui.

Xiuhtecuhtli (Aztec People, Mexico)

Also known as: *Huehueteotl, Xiuhtecutli.*

"Turquois Lord." God of fire. God of time. One of five gods who rule the suns: Tezcatlipoca, god of the north and first sun; Quetzalcoatl, god of the west, and the second sun; Tlaloc, god of the south and the third sun; Chalchihuitlicue, goddess of the east and fourth sun; and Xiuhtecuhtli, god of fire. Xiuhtecuhtli is the god of the present day sun. This is the fifth and last sun known as "nahui ollin" (four earthquake) which will end in earthquakes and fire. He lives in Chicunauhmictlan (abbreviated Mictlan), the underworld, with Mictlantecutli and Mictlanciuatl. *See also* Huehueteotl; Hueytonantzin; Huitzilopochtli; Legend of the Four Suns; Tezcatlipoca.

Xiuhtecutli (Mexico) *see* Xiuhtecuhtli.

Xmucane (Yucatan) *see* Ocomoco.

Xochipilli *Cinteotl* (Aztec People, Mexico)

Also known as: *Flower Lord, Flower Prince, Huehuecoyotl.*

God of flowers. God of sport. God of dance. God of games. God of beauty. God of love. God of youth. Husband (others say twin and husband) of the eternally young Xochiquetzal. His father is Cinteotl. Xochipilli is one of the brothers of the Centzon Totchtin (q.v.). He is associated with Patecatl. Some say his consort was the female form of Pilzintecutli. *See also* Centzon Totochtin; Huehuecoyotl; Macuilxochtli; Xochiquetzal.

Xochiquetal (Aztec People, Mexico) *see* Cinteotl.

Xochiquetzal *Xochiquetzalli* (Aztec, Toltec People, Mexico)

Also known as: *Itzcuinan, Nina, Tonacaciuatl, Xochipilli.*

"Flower Quetzal." "Flower of the Rich Plume." Flower deity. Patroness of unmarried women. Patroness of weavers. Guardian of childbirth. Guardian of the new mother. She is the goddess of flowers and love, daughter of Tlazolteutl, wife of Tlaloc or as some say, Coxcoxtli (Coxcox) They survived on Colhuacan mountain. Their children, who could not speak, were given the gift of speech by a dove (some say it was a pigeon) and spoke a multiplicity of tongues, each unintelligible to the others. Tezcatlipoca fell in love with Xochiquetzal, taking her from the rain-god. (Some say it was Nina and her husband, Nala, who escaped the flood in a hollowed out tree.) In some versions, Xochiquetzal, Xilonen, Atlantonan, and Uixtociuatl are wives of Tezcatlipoca. In other versions, Xochiquetzal is identical with Tonacaciuatl and is the consort of Tonacatecutli. She lives in Xochitlicacan, Itzeecayan, or Tamoanchan. Some say she is the patroness of unmarried women who went to the battleground with warriors. Another story indicates that one of the hairs of Xochiquetzal was made into the wife of the first man who was either Oxomoco or Piltzintecutli (qq.v.) One of her aspects is that of Itzcuinan who was a goddess of childbirth and sexual pleasure. The marigold is the favorite flower of Xochiquetzal. *See also* Tezcatlipoca; Tlaloc; Tonacaciuatl; Tzinteotl; Xilonen.

Xochiquetzalli (Mexico) *see* Xochiquetzal.

Xochitl (Mexico, Toltec, Aztec)

Probably a goddess of Pulque. According to some sources Xochitl appeared about the same time as Tezcatlipoca and Huitzilopochtli. Although not particularly recorded as creating Pulque, the intoxicating drink became popular during her time. There were many deities of the ancient Maya, Aztecs, and Toltecs who were said to have created Pulque. There is indication she was a mortal and the wife of one of the early kings. *See also* Colhuatzincatl; Mayauel; Patecatl; Texcatzoncatl.

Xocotl (Aztec) *see* Huitzilopochtli; Otontecutli.

Xolotl (Aztec People, Mexico)

God of monsters. God of magicians. Dispenser of bad luck. God of twins. God of double ears of maize. Twin brother of Quetzalcoatl. As the god of magicians, he has the power to assume different shapes. Xolotl represents the evening star, the planet Venus. His Quetzalcoatl is the morning star. Xolotl is the god of the game, play-ball. Xolotl, in the form of a dog, accompanies the souls and the sun during their journey into the realm of paradise and down to the underworld. In dog form, he is also the companion of Quetzalcoatl. According to some, Xolotl may have been a deified leader or chieftain of a group of people called the Chicimecs. This legend indicates he had a son named Nopaltzin who in turn had a son named Tlohtzin. Xolotl is described as being deformed with both feet pointing backward. Sometimes, he is depicted as a dog. He is identified with deformity and illness. He is similar to Coyote and Ueuecoyotl. *See also* Ciuateteo; Mayauel; Miclantecutli; Quetzalcoatl.

Xpiyacoc (Maya) *see* Hunhun-Ahpu; Ixpiyacoc; Vukub-Ahpu; Xmucane.

Xquiq (Maya People, Yucatan)

Creator mother. Xquiq became the mother of Hunahpu and Xbalanque from Hunhun-Ahpu's spittle when his head was on a fruit tree in the underworld. *See also* Hunahpu; Hunhun-Ahpu; Vukub Hunahpu; Xbalanque.

Xubchasgagua (Colombia)

Xubchasgagua is another name for the moon goddess, Chia (q.v.).

Xue (South America)

Xue is a name for the supreme creator and law-giver, Bochica (q.v.).

Xumucane (Maya People, Yucatan)

Creator. According to myth the gods created men from white and yellow maize while Xumacane made the broth that gave the humans life. The first people were named Balam-Quitze, who was the head of his clan and whose god was Tohil, Balam-Agab whose god was Avilix, Mahucutah whose god was Hacavitz, and Iqi-Balam whose god was Nicahtagah. Although they were like gods, the gods were not pleased, so they clouded the mortal's vision to make them just human beings. *See also* Cipactonal; Gucumatz; Hunhun-Ahpu; Ocomoco; Vukub-Ahpu; Xpiyacoc.

Xuthus (Greek)

Xuthus is the son of Hellen, the king of Phthia, and the nymph, Ortheis. His siblings are Aeolus, who married Enarete and Dorus. Creusa (who was raped by Apollo) became his wife.

Their children are Achaeus, Diomede, Ion and possibly Dorus. *See also* Achaeus; Aeolus (A).

Y

Ya-sima-zinumi-no-kami (Japan)

He is the husband of Konohana-chiru-hime (Blossoms-of-the-Trees-Falling-Princess). They are the parents of a son, Pupa-no-modi-kunusunu-no-kami. Konohana-chiru-hime is the descendant of Kushi-nada-hime, the rice goddess. *See also* Kushi-nada-hime.

Yacatecuhtli (Aztec People, Mexico)

Also known as: *Lord Nose.*

"He Who Goes Before." Yacatecuhtli is the god of commerce and traveling traders. He is shown as a bundle of staves. *See also* "M" (the Mayan god of travelers).

Yaccy-Ma (Tierra del Fuego)

Also known as: Possibly the same as *Taquatu* (q.v.).

Evil spirit. Yaccy-Ma is responsible for all evil deeds. His opposition is Yerri Yuppon, a giant black man, who is called upon in times of danger. *See also* Taquatu.

Yachihoko-no Kami (Japan)

"God of Eight Thousand Spears." Yachihoko-no Kami is a name for Okuni-Nushino-Mikoto, the god of medicine and sorcery.

Yachimata-Hiko (Japan)

God of the road. He and his female counterpart, Yachimato-hime, guard the cross-roads or as some say, all roads.

Yachimato-Himi (Japan) *see* Yachimata-Hiko.

Yadahpati (India)

"Lord of the Living Beings in Water." *See also* Varuna.

Yadavas (India)

The Yadavas are the Aryan descendants of King Yadu. Krishna is thought by some to have been born into this dynasty. When he became weary of battling demons, he assigned the divine architect Visvakarma the task of building a new kingdom. Upon completion, he led the Yadavas to their new home, the fortress city of Dvarka. Their first king was Ugrasena and the queen was his spouse Pavanarekha, the mother of the demon Kansa. Many Yadavas perished in the great flood but the survivors became the ancestors of kings. *See also* Jambavan; Kansa; Krishna; Syamantaka; Visvakarma.

Yagrush (Ugarit) A magic weapon. *See also* Khasis; Kothar.

Yahata (Buddhist, Shinto; Japan)

Yahata is another name for the god of war, Hachiman (q.v.).

Yahu (Semite) *see* Yahweh.

Yahveh (Hebrew) *see* Yahweh.

Yahweh *Yahveh* (Semite, Hebrew, Canaanite, Christian)

Also known as: *Elohim, Iaeuo, Iao, Jehova, Jehovah, Jhvh, Jhwh, Ya-w, Yaho, Yahu, Yahwe, Yahweh Elohim, Yau, Yaw, Yeuo, Yhvh, Yhwh.*

Supreme god. He is said to be an extremely jealous god who cannot tolerate the presence of other divinities. In the thirteenth century B.C.E. the Israelites overran the Canaanite cities. Their god Yahweh is obscure, but some think he may have been connected with the moon, since desert nomads travel by night and orient themselves by the moon. Yahweh may have been a weather god, which links him with Baal. His original name, Elohim, had first meant a collection of sacred or divine beings. Early Christian writers thought the diacritical marks placed under the consonants YHWH or JHVH by the ancient Hebrews indicated vowel sounds, but used the vowels for Adonai which ended up as the name Jehovah. Most scholars believe the correct pronunciation is Yahveh. There is a version where Yahweh is referred to as an Arabian volcanic god. In the first two chapters of Genesis in the Old Testament, two creation myths are presented. In the first chapter, the original state of the universe is watery chaos. The creator god Elohim divided creation into six separate periods, each belonging to one day. The order of creation is: Light; the firmament and heaven; the dry land (earth), separation of earth from the sea, vegetation; the celestial bodies; birds and fish; animals, and male and female together. In the second chapter of Genesis, in the beginning, the universe is waterless waste. Yahweh Elohim created man out of dust, the Garden of Eden, all trees, including the Tree of Life, and the Tree of the Knowledge of Good and Evil, animals and birds, and woman created from man. Recent discoveries indicate the goddess Ashura may have been the wife or consort of the Canaanite or Semitic god Yahweh. Remotely connected with Baal, Yam, Marduk and Tiamat. Possibly associated with Anat as her consort. *See also* Ashura; Varuna (India).

Yajna (Hindu; India)

When Daksha performed the first sacrifice, Yajna, a demigod

Xvarenah (Persia) *see* Khvarenanh.

with a deer's head, was killed by Virabhadra. *See also* Daksha; Virabhadra; Vishnu.

Yajnesvara (India) *see* Vishnu.

Yakami, Princess (Japan)
The princess was offered to Okuni-Nushino-Mikoto, a medicine man and a sorcerer (among numerous other attributes), as a gift from the skinned hare of Inaba for healing him. *See also* Okuni-Nushino-Mikoto.

Yakamouch (Tierra del Fuego)
Yakamouch is a shaman similar to the Eskimo Angakok. While the Angakok can speak to Sedna, the Yakamouch converses with a being called Aiapakal and they gain their power from a spirit named Hoakils. The Yakamouch can be either a man or woman (usually old) and can be recognized by their hair which is covered by a grey or white clay. The Yakamouch can cure or cause disease or death and are able to control the weather. Other than their hair style, they look like any other human. *See also* Angakok.

Yakho (India) *see* Yaksha and Yakshini.

Yakka (India) *see* Yaksha and Yakshini.

Yaksa (India) *see* Yaksha and Yakshini.

Yaksha and Yakshini (Hindu; India)
Also known as: *Agnimukha* (Fire-Face), *Ashvamukhi* (Horse-face, applies to female Yakshinis in half-woman, half-horse form), *Punyajana* (Friendly Folk), *Supporters of the Houses*, *Yakho, Yakka, Yaksa, Yakshas* (masculine plural), *Yakshinis* (feminine plural).
The Yakshas and Yakshinis are minor deities of the air, forest, and trees. Shape changers, they are attendants who accompany their king, Kuvera the god of wealth. When Kuvera wants to travel the Yakshas carry him through the sky. These deities are usually good and are considered harmless but they can be wicked. They are ferocious guardians of their master's gates and are known as protectors of good. As shape changers they can appear in any form. Yakshini is the female counterpart of Yaksha. She lives in the forest and appears in a seductive female form who smiles invitingly at unsuspecting travelers, who will then lose their way. Once, a Yakshini led Prince Vijaya and his men away from their trail in the forest. She immobilized them but could not devour them because they were protected by special charms. The prince followed her deep into the forest. When she turned around, she appeared as a beautiful woman named Kuvanna. She agreed to release his men only if he married her. He did and they had two children, Pulinda and Pulindi. Eventually, Vijaya, who had slain many demons, became king. The Yakshinis are also known to be ferocious and have been known to devour children. Some of the Yakshinis are Vandya, Sumitra, Sringatpadini (who produces horns and changes men into animals), Sulochana, and Saudamani. A type of Yakshas known as Agnimukha live in hell. They torture sinners with their blazing red faces, hands and feet. The Yakshas can appear as handsome men but sometimes appear as ugly, black dwarfs with distended stomachs. Yakshinis are often found carved on temple pillars as sensual women with accentuated hips. One depiction shows a Yakshini grasping the branch of a tree while giving the trunk a gentle kick. The kick is thought to make the tree burst into blossom. Other carvings show them clinging to mango trees like acrobats. The swelling curves of their bodies are said to suggest the fertility of tropical nature. Chakrisvari, a Yakshini with sixteen arms, is represented with the Yaksha Gaumuh in a Jaina temple at Palitana as the guardian of the main entrance. Sometimes the Yakshinis are depicted as half-woman, half-horse. In this form they are known as Ashvamukhi ("Horse-face"). The Yakshas were supplanted by the Vidyadhara (q.v.) The Yakshas and Yakshinis are comparable to the Greek fauns and satyrs. *See also* Bhima (A); Dikpala; Hariti; Kuvera; Panchika; Pretas; Rakshasas; Shiva; Takshaka; Vasuki; Vijaya; Virudaka; Wu Kuan.

Yakshi (India) *see* Kuvera.

Yakshinis (India)
Nature and Air Deities. *See also* Yaksha and Yakshini.

Yakushi-Nyorai *Yakushi-Rurikwo-Nyorai* (Japan)
Also known as: *Bhaishajyaguru* (Sanskrit).
He is a divine physician who governs the land of Joruri in the East. Humans are protected against disease by him. He has twelve generals called Yakushi juni shinsho. *See also* Dainichinyorai.

Yakushi-Rurikwo-Nyorai (Japan) *see* Yakushi-Noyorai.

Yalungur (Australia)
Also known as: *Eagle Hawk, Warana.*
Gidja, the moon god, made the first woman by castrating Yalungur, Eagle Hawk.
For a different rendition see Gidja.

Yam (Ugarit) *see* Yam-Nahar.

Yam-Nahar (Ugarit)
Also known as: *Yam, Yamm.*
The son of the Father of the Gods, El, and brother of the god of fertility, Baal, Yam-Nahar is the god of the seas and rivers. Yam-Nahar demanded that the gods turn Baal over to his messengers. Frightened of Yam-Nahar, the gods bowed their heads. El, who favored his son Yam-Nahar, promised to turn Baal over to his messengers. Baal shamed the gods for being frightened of Yam-Nahar and attacked his brother's messengers. He was restrained by Anat and Astoreth. The god Kothar-u-Khasis gave Baal two magic weapons, known as "Yagrush" (Chaser) and "Aymur" (Driver), to use against Yam-Nahar. Baal managed to subdue Yam-Nahar and was about to kill him when he was restrained by Astoreth. In celebration of his victory, Baal's sister Anat in her aspect as a goddess of war arranged a massive feast. Dressed in her festive finery, she closed the palace doors on Mount Zaphon, and murdered all of Baal's enemies. It is said that she waded in blood up to her knees and hung the heads and hands of the dead on her body. Yam-Nahar represents the waters in their hostile aspect. Baal represents the waters as rain that fertilizes the earth. Compare this myth to the Mesopotamian myth of Marduk and Tiamat (qq.v.). *See also* Anath; Baal; El; Kothar and Khasis.

Yama (Brahmanic, Hindu, Vedic; India; Buddhist; Tibet).
Also known as: *Antaka* (Antiquity or He Who Ends Life),

Asu-niti, Chos-Rgyal Phyi-Sgrub (Tibetan Buddhist), *Dandadhara* (Club-bearer), *Dharmaraha, Dharmaraja* (King of Virtue), *Kala* (Time), *King Yama* (Tibet), *Kritanta, Mitra, Mritya* (Death), *Pitripati* (Lord of the Fathers), *Preta-Raja* (King of Ghosts), *Samana* (The Leveller), *Samavurti* (The Impartial Judge), *Sraddeheva, Sraddhadeva* (God of Funeral Ceremonies), *Udumbara* (the Man of the Ficus Tree), *Vaivasvata* (Son of Vivasvat), *Yen-lo* (Central Asia).

In Vedic literature, Yama was the first man. He is considered an immortal who chose a mortal destiny. He is also described as a deified hero and the first man to die. In the Vedas Yama's kingdom is for good souls. In the Puranas, it is also a place for wicked souls. Yama, Soma and Varuna are the rulers of Pitriyana, the Vedic Path of the Fathers. Yama and his twin sister Yami are the children of Vivasvat, the rising sun, and Saranyu, the daughter of Tvashtri. In the Hindu tradition, Yama is the king of the dead. Later, as Dharmaraha, who was a form of Mitra and associated with Varuna, he became the judge of dead souls. Yama and Yami are the first man and woman and the founders of the human race. When Yama died, his soul traveled the path to the otherworld in the southern section of the upper sky and arrived in the Land of the Dead. He became the guardian of the south. His city is known as Yamapura and his palace is Yamasadana also known as Kalachi. The bloody river Vaitarani flows between this region and the land of the living. All souls must cross this water. Yama has two four-eyed, striped dogs with broad noses, Syama (also spelled Sarameya), the "courser," and Sabala (also called Svanau) the "hound." They are the offspring of Indra's heavenly dog Sarama ("Quick"). Some scholars believe that the dogs are Indra and Agni. Their duties are to guard the otherworld path and act as messengers as they visit dying souls. Sometimes an owl or a pigeon takes over their duties. Yama's ever vigilant messengers of death are known as the Yama-dutas. The emissaries lasso the spirit with a noose and deliver it to Yamapura. The trip from earth to the land of the dead takes four hours and forty minutes and cremation cannot take place until that time has passed. All humans will follow the same route after death, known as the "Path of the Fathers," or the "Path of the Manes" (Pitris, in Sanskrit). Yama and Varuna are the judges of the dead souls. (In later mythological times, Varuna became the lord of the ocean and had his own heaven.) In the Land of the Dead, Chitragupta the accountant produced a list of the mortal's deeds. This register is known as the Agrasandhani. A judgment, always fair, is handed down. The spirit is hurried back to the place of cremation where it feeds on oblations and receives a new body. The new body is led to Swarga (heaven) or to one of twenty-one hells, known as Naraka. If the destination is heaven, the faithful will be given the sacred beverage of the gods, Soma, to make them immortal. If the soul is headed to hell, the realm of darkness, known as Put, it must travel two hundred leagues a day through inconceivable tortures. Two of Yama's associates are the Vedic god Nirrita who is the guardian of the southwest, and Nirriti the goddess of decay. In the Buddhist tradition in China and Tibet, Yama became King Yama of the Ten Hells. In later times, Agni, representing the fire of the funeral pyre, presided over the "Path of the Fathers." Yama is depicted with a bull's head, a third eye and a crown of skulls. He stands to the right of a bull and under the bull is a woman. In another depiction, he appears similar but is naked except for a belt of heads and many jewels. As the judge of the dead he is shown riding a buffalo. He is green in color, often with a flower in his hair. He wears red clothing, and holds a noose and a club. He is also depicted as heavy set, with a greenish complexion, riding a black thunder horse. Around the first of November a festival known as Yama-dyitya is held in honor of Yama and Yami. The dog Syama, which means "black," is also a name given to Shiva. The first of the eight stages of yoga is called Yama. Yama corresponds to Varuna, who also uses a noose to capture the wicked. Compare to Manu, who is sometimes called Yama's twin; together they are known as the twin fathers of the human race. Yama corresponds to Yima (Persian). Compare to Osiris (Egypt), and Emma-O (Japan). *See also* Savitri (B) for a myth pertaining to Yama. Yama is sometimes identified with Kala, the god of time (q.v.). Compare Yama's dogs to Cerberus (Greek). *See also* Agni; Daksha; Dharma; Dikpalas; Indra; Lokapalas; Mara; Mrtyu; Parashur Rama; Parvati; Sanja; Saranyu; Shiva; Soma; Surya; Swarga; Tvashtri; Varuna; Vedas (The); Vishnu; Vivasvat; Yama Kings; Yamantaka; Yami.

Yama-Dutas (India) Messengers of death. *See also* Yama.

Yama-Dyitya (India)
    Festival for Yama and Yami. *See also* Yama.

Yama-Isvara (India) *see* Yami.

Yama Kings, The (Buddhist; China, Tibet)
    Also known as: *Shi-tien Yen-wang, Shi-wang.*
    The ten kings, known as the Yama Kings, sit as rulers and judges of the ten courts of Ti-yu (Hell). Each king has jurisdiction over the punishment of distinct and clearly outlined crimes committed during the offender's life. The kings live in the chief town of Ti-yu, Feng-tu. The principal Yama King or King Yama, who some say is Yeng-Wang-Yeh (others say he was dismissed by the Jade Emperor), reviews the deeds of the newly arrived souls and determines whether he or one of the other judges will carry out punishment, basing his decision on the type and severity of the crime, whether it be sacrilege, arson, dishonesty, murder, or lying. It is the province of the tenth judge to determine whether the soul is to be reborn in the form of a human or an animal. The virtuous souls and those without blame may return to life on earth almost at once or may achieve a place among the immortals. Several versions give different categories to the functions of these judges. The deities who are sent to retrieve the souls of the dead are Ox-Head (Niu-t'ou) and Horse-Face (also known as Ma Mien). They are opposed by the door guards. In Tibet Yama or Gsin-rje gsed is a god of the dead. Yamantaka conquered death. The Yama Kings are generally shown in imperial dress garments with a roll of paper in front of them. The Yama Kings correspond to the Indian Bodhisattva Kshitigarbha and the Chinese Ti-tsang (q.v.). The opposite of hell is the Kun-lun Mountain (q.v.). *See also* Fengtu; Kshitigarbha; Ma-Mien; Niu-t'ou; Ti-tsang-wang-pu-sa; Ti-yu; Yamataka; Yen-wang.

Yama-no-Kami (Japan)
    Also known as: *Yama-no-Shinbo.*
    Goddess of the hunt. Goddess of the forest. Goddess of agriculture. Goddess of vegetation.

Yama-Tsu-Mi (Japan) *see* O-Yama-Tsu-Mi.

Yama-Uba (Japan)
The Yama-Uba are evil female demons. They are possibly the same as Yuki-onna (the snow woman).

Yamai (Koli People, India)
She is a form of the Great Mother worshiped by people who fish. Newborns are shown her form which is represented as a stupa daubed with red clay. Goats are sacrificed to her yearly. *See also* Stupa.

Yamantaka *Yamantakha* (Buddhistic Hinduism; India, Tibet)
Also known as: *Dai Itoku-Myoo* (Japan), *Gsin-rje gsed* (Tibet), *Manjusri, Shin-je-she-chi-chyil-khor* (Tibet), *sSin-rje-gsed-kyi-dkyil-kor* (Tibet), *Yamari* (Foe of Yama).
Yamantaka, the Destroyer of Death, is the ferocious aspect of the deity Manjusri. He conquered the demon king Yama and exiled him to the infernal regions. Yamantaka is one of the four male guardians of the doors in Bardo. He guards the south gate. The other three male guardians are Armtakundali, the Coil of Nectar, Vijaya, the Victorious and Hayagriva, the Horse-necked, who is Vishnu as the god of learning, depicted with a horse's head. Yamantaka is the fierce form of Manjusri. His consort is Yamantakasakti, also a doorkeeper on the south gate. His consort is also referred to as Zhag-pa-ma, who is also known as Pashadhari, a sow-headed goddess. Yamantaka is depicted with the head of a bull, with a third eye and wearing a crown of skulls. His colors are black, blue or red. He has two arms and carries a karttrika (chopper) in his right hand and a kapala (human skull cup) in his left. He wears a belt of heads and is shown stepping to the right. He is usually accompanied by birds and demons. In paintings he is shown to have nine heads, sixteen feet, and thirty-four arms holding all the *Tantra* symbols. He is often green in color with flaming eyes. *See also* Armtakundali, for other deities, who appear with Yamantaka in Bardo on the sixth day. *See also* Ankusha; Dai Itoku-Myoo (Japan); Manjusri; Vishnu; Yama; Yima (Persian); Zhag-pa-ma.

Yamantakasakti (Tibet) *see* Yamantaka.

Yamantakha (Tibet) *see* Yamantaka.

Yamapura (India) City of the dead. *See also* Yama.

Yamari (India) *see* Dai Itoku-Myoo; Manjusri; Yamantaka.

Yamasadana (India) Yama's palace. *See also* Yama.

Yami (Hindu, Vedic; India)
Also known as: *Goddess of the River Yamuna, The Jumna, Kalinda-Kanya, Suryi, Yama-isvara, Yamuna.*
Yami is the twin sister and wife of the god of death Yama and the daughter of Vivasvat, the sun god, and Saranyu. They are described as the first couple and parents of the first human beings. She is identified with the sacred river Jumna, formerly called Yamuna. As the river Jumna, she protected the baby Karna and arranged for the goddess Radha to look after him. Bala-Rama is thought to have diverted her waters to irrigate the land. In one description, Yami has a swine's head. *See also* Bala-Rama; Ganga; Jumna; Karna; Kunti; Radha; Saranyu; Sarasvati; Vivasvat; Yama.

Yamma-Raja (Japan) *see* Emma-O.

Yamri (Afghanistan) *see* Imra.

Yamuna (India) *see* Yami.

Yan Tachu (Zuni People, North America)
Creator. Yan Tachu was created by Awonawilona and in turn he created mankind along with his wife, Tsita.

Yananamca Intanamca (Andean People, Peru)
Also known as: *Huacas.*
Spirits. The Yamanamca Intanamca are a group of spirits who walked upright and belonged to a group known as the Huacas. They were destroyed by a Huaca by the name of Huallallo Caruincho, who was evil. He was called Lord and instructed the women to have only two children. One of the children had to be sacrificed for him to eat. Huallallo Caruincho in turn was overthrown by a hero deity named Pariacaca (q.v.). *See also* Coniraya; Huacas; Viracocha.

Yanari (Japan) Goblin of earthquakes.

Yanauluha (Zuni People, North America)
The First Priest.

Yang (China) *see* Yin and Yang.

Yang-Chen (Buddhist, China)
Goddess of teaching and learning. Protector of sacred books. *See also* Sarasvati.

Yang Ch'eng (China)
Also known as: *Star of Happiness.*
God of happiness. He was once an official or mandarin who was quite small. Now he is worshiped as a deity. *See also* Shou-sing.

Yang Ching (China)
The goat god appealed to for protection against wild animals. He wears a goatskin and has a goat's head.

Yang Ki-Sheng (China) *see* Ch'eng Huang.

Yang-Ku (China) *see* Yang-Wu.

Yang-Wu *Yang-Ku* (China)
Yang-Wu is a valley in the east where the ten suns and their mother lived. Every day, each in turn, corresponding to one hour of the day, the suns crossed the sky, each one in his own chariot with the mother the charioteer, to a mountain in the west. Once, when all ten suns once appeared together, the Excellent Archer, Yi, took his magic bow and brought down all but one of the suns, saving the earth from the overpowering heat. *See also* Yi.

Yangombi (Bantu People, Africa) God of creation.

Yansan (Yoruban People, Africa) Wind deity.

Yantho (Maya) *see* Nohochacyum.

Yao (China)
God of writing. He authored works about regulating floods and binding rivers to their banks.

Yao-Shih Fu (China)
God of healing and sex change. He is the same as Buddhist god, Bhaishajyaguru.

Yaotl (Aztec, Toltec People, Mexico)

Also known as: *Texcatlipoca, Tezcatlipoca.*

"The Enemy." Yaotl spied on the ascetic, Yappan, until he caught him in a compromising position with the eternally young and beautiful goddess Xochiquetzal. Yaotl beheaded Yappan and the gods changed the fallen ascetic into a scorpion. *See also* Xochiquetzal; Yappan.

Yappan (Toltec People, Mexico)

Also known as: *Jappan.*

Deified mortal. Yappan was an ascetic mortal who wanted to win the favor of the gods. Leaving the world behind, he moved to the top of a huge rock and lived as a hermit. The gods, suspicious of Yappan, sent numerous women to seduce him. He did not bite the bait. So, Yaotl was sent to spy on him. In the meantime, the goddess Xochiquetzal decided to entice him. Yappan came down from his rock to help her climb up. He was lured into her net. After her conquest, she left him. Yaotl, who was privy to the episode, beheaded him. The gods turned Yappan into a scorpion, doomed to life under a rock instead of on top of a rock. Yappan's wife, Tlahuitzin, was also killed by Yaotl and changed into another variety of scorpion. *See also* Tlazolteutl; Yaotl.

Yaparamma (India)

She is one of the Mutalamma goddesses who are deities of the household. Yaparamma presides over business transactions. *See also* Mutalamma.

Yareah (Canaanite)

Moon god. He is worshiped with Shemesh, the deity of the sun. They are similar to Shahar and Shalem who are deities of dawn and sunset.

Yarikh (Mesopotamia; Syria, Ugarit)

Yarikh, the moon god, is the mate of the goddess of fruits of the earth, Nikkal. She is the daughter of Hiribi, the god of summer, and thought to be the youngest of the wise goddesses known as the Kathirat. When they married, the Kathirat provided all the necessities for the wedding. *See also* Baal; Kathirat.

Yarilo (Slavic)

God of love. He is generally thought to be connected with spring sown corn. Most legends associate him with carnal love. Yarilo is depicted as a young handsome man dressed in white. He carries flowers and sheaves of corn, is barefoot and rides a white horse. Sometimes he is shown with phallic attributes. Similar in some respects to Kupala (q.v.).

Yarovit (Slavic) God of victory.

Yasha (Nepal) *see* Dikpalas.

Yashts *Yasts* (Zoroastrian)

Hymns to the divine spirits, the Yashts form the Khorda-Avesta. *See also* Avesta; Bundahish; Tishtrya; Yazatas.

Yasoda (A) *Jesodha* (India)

Yasoda and Nanda, poor cowherds, were the parents of eight children. When their eighth child, a female, was born, Krishna and the gods replaced her with Krishna, as a newborn, to avoid the wrath of the evil Kansa. Yasoda and Nanda's daughter was assumed to be the child of Vasuveta and Devaki. For details, *see* Devaki; Devi; Kansa.

Yasoda (B) (India) Wife of Mahavira (q.v.).

Yasodhara (India) *see* Buddha; Shakti.

Yasts (Zoroastrian) *see* Yashts.

Yata *Yatis, Yatu, Yatus* (Zoroastrian; Persia)

Male counterparts of the Pairikas, the Yata are demon magicians and sorcerers who are the friends of the spirits of evil. Their chief is Akhtya. Compare to Daevas. *See also* Amesha Spentas; Angra Mainyu; Druj; Pairikas.

Yata-Kayami (Japan) *see* Amaterasu; Kagami.

Yatagarasu *Yata-Garasu* (Shinto, Japan)

Yatagarasu is the sacred crow of the sun-goddess Amaterasu. This tale corresponds to that of Yang-Wu in Chinese mythology. *See also* Amaterasu.

Yatis (Persia) *see* Yata.

Yatpan (Ugarit) *see* Khasis and Kothar.

Yatu (Persia, India)

A race of demons who take the shape of vultures or dogs. *See also* Yata.

Yatudhanis (India)

Female goblins and fiends who are associated with the sun. *See also* Devas (A).

Yatus (Persia)

Another spelling for Yata. *See also* Ameshas Spenta; Angra Mainyu; Yata.

Yau (Semite) *see* Yahweh.

Yauhahu (New Guinea) *see* Kenaima.

Yavishta (India) *see* Agni.

Yaw (Canaan)

The Hebrew people attached Babylonian myths to Yaw. *See also* Yahweh.

Yaya-Zakurai (Japan) Cherry tree goddess.

Yayu (India) God of air.

Yazatas (Zoroastrian; Persia)

Also known as: *Yajata* (Sanskrit), *Yazata* (singular), *Yazdan* (New Persian), *Zyed.*

"Adorable Ones." The Yazatas rank below Ahura Mazda and the Ameshas Spenta in the celestial realm. They are said to be innumerable; however, only about forty are mentioned in Zoroastrian texts. Of this number, the three most popular Yazatas are Sraosha, the guardian of humanity; his sister Ashi Vanguhi, the rewarder of good deeds; and Mithra. They are expressions of Ahura Mazda, and their duty is to transmit his will to mortals. They are divided into two classes: the spiritual, who personify truth and victory; and the material who are the guardian spirits of the elements, heaven, the planets, and stars. Other Yazatas are Anahita, Haoma, Atar, Verethraghna, Rapithwin, Apo, Hvarekhshaeta, Mah, Tishtrya, Hapto-iringa,

Satavaesa, Vanant, Dervaspa, Rashnu, Vayu, Tishtryas, and the twelve Akhtar or constellations. It is said that Ormazd was the first celestial Yazata while Zoroaster (the founder of the Zoroastrians) was the first terrestrial Yazata. The Yazata is also a part of the soul. It is created by Ormazd before a human's birth, and remains in the realm of the immaterial during life and survives death. The Yazatas are associated with the Fravashis (q.v.). *See also* Aeshma; Ahura Mazda; Akhtar (The); Ameshas Spenta; Asha Vahishta; Atar; Chinvat Bridge; Dervaspa; Haoma; Khshasthra Vairya; Mithra; Tishtrya; Vayu; Zoroaster.

Yazdan (Persia) *see* Ameshas Spenta; Yazatas.

Ydaler (Teutonic) *see* Ydalir.

Ydalir *Ydaler* (Teutonic) The abode of Ull (q.v.).

Y'den (Teutonic) *see* Idun.

Yeba Ka (Apache, Navajo, Papago People, North America)
   Male leader of the gods.

Yebaad (Apache, Navajo, Papago People, North America)
   Female leader of the gods. Female counterpart of Yeba Ka. *See also* Yeba Ka.

Yebitsai (North America) *see* Yebitshai.

Yebitshai (North America) *see* Yei.

Yebitshai *Yebitsai, Yepitsai* (North America) *see* Hasteseyalti; and Yei.

Yehl (Athapascan, Haida, Kwakiutl, Tlingit, Tsimshian People, North America)
   Also known as: *Yetl.*
   A name for the sacred bird, often called the Great Raven. Yehl is a demiurge and a trickster. In some myths, he is in the form of a crane. An Athapascan myth tells of Yehl the raven raising the earth from the waters after the great deluge. He became their ancestor and taught the people the uses of fire.

Yei (Navajo People, North America)
   Also known as: *Yeibechi, Yeibichai.*
   Household or nature spirits. A group of deities that can be classified as household or nature spirits. They are beneficial to mankind, and are opponents of the Anaye and Tshindi who are generally thought of as being evil. The Yei consist of Ganaskidi (harvest god), Thonenli (water god), Hastseyalti or Yebitshai (Yebitsai) (Maternal Grandfather of the gods and god of the east and dawn), and Hastshehogan (house god and god of the evening and the west). The highest of all is Estsanatlehi, a goddess of youth who grows old, then transforms herself into a girl again. Two brothers, Nayanezgani and Thobadzistshini, are worshiped as the destroyers of the Anaye. *See also* Anaye; Estsanatlehi; Ganaskidi; Hasteseyalti.

Yeibechi *Yeibichai* (North America) *see* Yei.

Yeibichai (North America) *see* Yei.

Yeitso (Navajo People, North America)
   The Sun's child, a giant.

Yelafaz *Yelafath* (Yap People, Marshall Islands, Micronesia)
   Also known as: *Luk.*

A creator deity. A huge tree hung from the sky, its roots touching the sea. A woman was born in this tree. Yelafaz gave her sand which she threw on the sea and thus created the earth. *See also* Lukelang.

Yellow Book of Lecan (Celtic) *see* Amergin.

Yemahya (Africa, Caribbean, Central America)
   God of the deep sea.

Yemanja (Brazil)
   Also known as: *Yemoja.*
   Goddess of the sea. On New Year's Eve, at midnight, those who love Yemanja go to a beach and light a candle in her name. Then, little boats constructed of flowers are set adrift on the waves. If they are taken out to the sea by Yemanja, a good year will come. If they are refused and thrown back onto the sand, it will be a bad year. *See also* Yemoja.

Yemaya (Yoruba People, Africa)
   Goddess of salt water. Goddess of the surface of the ocean. She is the wife of Olokun. *See also* Olodumare; Olokun.

Yembo (Africa) *see* Oduduwas.

Yemma (Japan) *see* Emma-O.

Yemoja *Yemaja, Yemanja, Yemaya* (Cuba), *Yemonja;* (Yoruba People, Africa)
   Mother of the gods. Yoruban goddess of the Ogun river and sometimes known as Ogun's wife. She is sometimes called the goddess of rivers and fish. In some legends, she is the wife of Aganju. Worship of Yemoja was carried to Cuba and Brazil (where she is known as Yemanja or Yemaya). *See also* Obatala; Ogun; Yemanja.

Yemonja (Africa) *see* Yemoja.

Yemowo (Africa) *see* Obatala.

Yen Kung (China)
   Weather god. He has the power to calm winds and waves.

Yen-lo Wang (China) *see* Yen-Wang.

Yen-Wang (China)
   Also known as: *Yen-lo Wang, Yen-Wang-Yeh.*
   Underworld deity. The god of the world of the dead, the chief of the Yama Kings. Yen-Wang controls the manner and time of death and decides the destiny of the souls of the dead, determining the shape, human or animal, those who return to earth will take, selecting those who will receive immortality and judging the punishments for the wicked. One version says Yen-Wang was dismissed by the Jade Emperor as chief of the underworld because he was too merciful. His replacement was Ts-in-kuang-wang. Yen-Wang corresponds to the Bodhisattva Kshitigarbha. (The chief of hell is Ti-tsang Wang-p'u-sa.) *See also* Kshitigarbha; Ts-in-kuang-wang; Yama Kings; Yen-lo Wang.

Yepitsai (North America) *see* Yebitshai.

Yero (Australia) *see* Rainbow Snake.

Yerri Yuppon (Tierra del Fuego) *see* Yaccy-Ma.

Yeshe-Khahdoma (Tibet) *see* Khadomas.

Yeshu (Hebrew) *see* Jesus.

Yetl (North American Indian) *see* Yehl.

Yeuo (Semite) *see* Yahweh.

Yew of Ross (Celtic) *see* Abellio.

Ygdrasil (Teutonic) *see* Yggdrasil.

Ygdrasili (Teutonic) *see* Yggdrasil.

Ygg (Teutonic) *see* Odin.

Yggdrasil *Iggdrasil, Ygdrasil, Yggr-drasill, Ygdrasili*; (Norse; Teutonic)

Also known as: *Ashyggr-drasil, Hoddmimir's Wood, Laerad, Ledrad.*

The ash tree Yggdrasil is the sacred tree of life, the universal tree. Yggdrasil's branches spread across the universe. It connects and shelters all the worlds. It has three roots: one is among the Aesir where Urd's Well, named after the wisest of the three goddess of Fate, is located. It is here that the gods and the Aesir have their principal meeting place. Another root is in the land of the giants, Jotun-heim, near Mimir's Well, the well of wisdom. The third root is deep in Nifl-heim, the underworld, where the Hvergelmir well is located. Here the dreaded serpent Nidhod constantly gnaws at Yggdrasil's roots. Yggdrasil was created by the All-Father after Odin and his colleagues established Midgard. An eagle perches on Lerad, the topmost bough of the sacred tree. Between his eyes Vedfolnir the falcon sits watching all. In some myths it is the golden cock, Gullinkambi, who watches. Always green, the tree provides food for Odin's goat Heidrun, who provides Odin's warriors with milk. The stags Dain, Dvalin, Duneyr, and Durathor nibble at the new buds and drip honeydew or water on the earth for all the rivers. The tree also has another occupant, a squirrel or rabbit named Ratatosk who constantly attempts to cause strife between the dragon and the eagle. The three goddesses of destiny known as the Norns are responsible for taking care of Yggdrasil. They sprinkle it with sacred waters from Urd's fountain. Heimdall's horn Gjall is hidden under one of Yggdrasil's roots. Compare Yggdrasil to the myth of the serpent Abyrga of Central Asia. *See also* Aesir; Alfheim; Ask; Dain; Davalin; Gjall; Gullinkambi; Haoma (Persian); Heidrun; Hvergelmir; Jotun-heim; Lif; Midgard; Mimir; Mimir's Well; Nidhod; Nifl-heim; Norns; Odin; Ratatosk; Urd; Verdandi; Ymir.

Yggr (Teutonic) *see* Odin.

Yggr-drasill (Teutonic) *see* Yggdrasil.

Y H V H (Hebrew) *see* Yahweh.

Y H W H (Hebrew) *see* Yahweh.

Yi (China)

Also known as: *Excellent Archer.*

Probably a sun god. Yi is the husband of Chang-o. There were once ten suns in the sky. When the excessive heat threatened the earth, Yi used his magic bow, given to him by emperor Ti-suin, to shoot down nine of the suns. This is why we have only one sun. In one version Si-wang-mu, who was the queen of the immortals, gave him the drink of immortality, but Yi's wife stole it. The drink allowed her to fly, but because Yi interfered she only drank part so was unable to fly to heaven. Stopping half-way she became a goddess of the moon, while Ye went all the way and became a sun deity. *See also* Yang-Wu.

Yi-dvag (Tibet) *see* Pretas.

Yidak (Buddhist; India)

Yidak is the spirit world of thirst and hunger. One is relegated to this world after death if during life it was necessary to always have the upper hand. These spirits have distended stomachs and suffer from colic. The water they drink turns to fire. The Yidak have long, thin necks and small mouths. *See also* Chakravala; Sukhavati.

Yim (Persian) *see* Yimi.

Yima (Indo-Iranian, Persian)

Also known as: *Jam, Jamshid* (later form of the name), *Jemshid, Yim, Yima Khshaeta, Yimi.*

Yima is the divine aspect of Jamshid, the first Iranian mortal. Known as the first king, he ruled the earth for a thousand years. During this golden period, the earth was plentiful and peaceful. As hunger, illness, cold, heat, and death did not exist, the population increased and Yima had to enlarge the world three different times. At the end of his reign, the world was twice as large as it was in the beginning. Yima is the creator of three fires: Burzhin Mitro, Frobak and Gushasp. When Yima was warned by the creator, Ahura Mazda, that Mahrkusha would send three wretched winters that would encompass the world, he built a Vara (cavern) to ensure the continuity of the earth's population. Here he placed the best of men, animals, and plants. Unfortunately, Yima had a dark side. He broke Zoroaster's law by bribing men with ox flesh in one rendition, and in another by lying and delighting in his lies. Three different times his lies caused his Khvarenanh (spirit or glory) to fly from him in the form of a bird. The first time, Mithra caught it; the second time, Traetaona; and the third, Keresaspa. In some renditions, at this point, he was seized by Azhi Dahaka. He either died by his brother Spityura's hand or was killed by the evil Azhi Dahaka in the form of a mortal named Zahhak, who took over his kingdom. In later times, Yima was known as a builder. As a cultural hero, he taught men to lay foundations and mold bricks. Yima initiated the Persian festival, Nauroz. In a variation of this myth, Yima is the first man, son of Vivanghvant or Yama. He lived in a Vara where he endured a horrible winter. Ahura Mazda sent a bird with the message that he was to leave the Vara and till the earth. The Vara, made of kneaded clay, was two miles long and two miles wide. It had only one window that was self-luminous, and one door which was sealed up. Within it he had all the seeds necessary to proceed with his mission. In addition, he was given a ring and a dagger by Ahura Mazda. During his 900 winters on earth, he filled it with people, birds and animals in a 600-year span. He then expanded the earth three times during the next three years by one-third its size each time. His reign was a golden period; people were happy living under the *Avesta* (law) of Ahura Mazda, and they lived for 150 years. Takhmoruw and Hoshang are also known as first kings in Persian mythology. According to some Yima's father was Takhmoruw who was the son of Husheng, who was son of Siyamek, who was son of Gayomort. In this case, Yima was not the first mortal. He was, however, the first immortal to chose mortality. Compare to Ymir (Teutonic). *See also* Ahura Mazda; Azhi Dahaka; Drujs; Haoma; Hoshang and Takhmoruw; Jamshid; Keresapa; Khvarenanh; Mahrkusha; Mithra; Thrita; Vivanghvant; Yama.

Yimak (Iranian) *see* Yimeh.

Yimaka (Iranian) *see* Yimeh.

Yimeh (Iranian)
Also known as: *Yimak, Yimaka.*
Creator. Wife of Yima, and, like him, she is a creator of the human race. *See also* Yima.

Yimi (Persian) *see* Yimi.

Yin and Yang (China)
Creators. Yin and Yang are the two ethers that came from the dividing of the original cell of primeval chaos, Ch'i. Yin is female, dark, negative and of the earth, and symbolized by a divided or broken line. Yang is male, bright, positive and of the heavens, and is symbolized by an unbroken line. Yin came to be identified with demons; Yang, to represent the gods. Yin and Yang are the foundation of the doctrine of dualism, in which alternating and opposing forces brought about the creation of the universe, Yin forming the earth and Yang the sky. Yin and Yang shaped the fundamental nature of all living things. In one version Yin and Yang became mixed and this resulted in the creation of man. This first man was named Huang-lao. Corresponds to In and Yo of the Japanese people. *See also* Chaos; Tien.

Yinewumana (Pueblo People, North America)
Goddess of Gems.

Yiyantsinni (Navaho, Pueblo, and Iroquois People, North America)
The Yiyantsinni are twelve men who hold up the sun or the heavens with their poles. *See also* Atseatsan and Atseatsine.

Ylg (Teutonic) *see* Elivagar.

Ymai (Turkey) *see* Umai.

Ymer (Teutonic) *see* Ymir.

Ymir *Ymer* (Norse; Teutonic)
Also known as: *Augelmir, Aurgelmir, Aurgenimir, Fornjotnr, Hrim-Thurs* (Ice Giant), *Hrimthursar, Orgelmir, Yme.*
The first of the supreme gods, Ymir is an evil frost giant. He was created in Ginnunga-gap, a vast place of emptiness, at the beginning of the universe. Created from the mist of ice rime of Nifl-heim when it encountered and was melted by the warmth from Muspells-heim, the land of fire, he was called a Hrim-Thurs (ice-giant). Ymir was nourished by the divine cow, Aud-humla, who was formed from the drips of ice before he came into existence. While Ymir rested, a man and a woman came from the sweat from under his left armpit, and a son from the union of one of his legs to the other. After the birth of the son and daughter, Ymir produced a six-headed giant named Thrudgelmir from his feet. Thrudgelmir in turn brought forth the giant Bergelmir who was the producer of all the evil frost giants. After being killed by Odin and his family, Ymir's flesh was turned into the garden Midgard which had a hedge surrounding it made from Ymir's eyebrows. Ymir's blood or sweat formed the ocean surrounding Midgard. His bones were the hills, his teeth the cliffs, his hair the trees and vegetation and his skull became heaven along with his brains which became the clouds. In another myth, it is Fornjotnr rather than Ymir who produced the first gods. Fornjotnr had three sons, Hler, Kari and Loki. It is also said that the tree Yggdrasil grew from his body. In one version, the first man was named Buri. With his sister/spouse, they had a son Bor who in turn had three sons, Odin, Vili, and Ve. From them came the Aesir (gods). There is a version that relates that when Ymir was killed the blood inundated the earth. Only a man and woman survived and from them a new race of giants descended. In the same version Ymir's flesh crawled with maggots which the gods gave wits and human appearance, and they turned into dwarfs. Compare Ymir to Yima (Indo-Iranian). *See also* Aesir; Ask; Audhumla; Bergelmir; Bestla; Buri; Dwarfs; Elivagar; Embla; Fornjotnr; Ginnunga-gap; Jotun-heim; Loki; Midgard; Mimir; Muspells-heim; Nifl-heim; Odin; Thrudgelmir; Ve; Vili; Westri; Yggdrasil.

Ynakhsyt (Yakut People, Siberia) Goddess of cattle.

Ynawc (Celtic)
Ynawc is one of the seven survivors of the battle between Bran and Matholwch. *See also* Bran.

Yngri (Teutonic) *see* Freyr.

Yngve (Teutonic) *see* Thor.

Yngvi (Teutonic) *see* Odin.

Yo and In (Japan)
The female and male principles, analogous to the Chinese Yin and Yang, of the egg of chaos that split to form the earth and heavens. *See also* Izanagi; Yin and Yang.

Yo-Elat (Ugarit) *see* Anath-Yahu

Yo Po (China) Fish god. *See also* Nine Songs; Shui Shen.

Yo-shi-wang Fo (China) *see* Yo-wang.

Yo-wang *Yo-shi-wang Fo* (Buddhist; China)
God of healing and medicines.

Yoalli (Mexico) *see* Texcatlipoca.

Yoalliehecatl (Mexico) *see* Teczatlipoca.

Yoamaxtli (Mexico) *see* Camaxtli.

Yocahu (Antilles Islands) *see* Guamaonocon.

Yocahuguama (Antilles) *see* Iocauna.

Yoga-Siddha (India)
The Monkey Queen. *See also* Visvakarma.

Yogini (Hindu; India)
One of the eight female demon servants of the goddess Durga (q.v.)

Yogisvari (India) "Adept in Yoga." *See also* Devi.

Yohual-Tecuhtin (Aztec People, Mexico)
Lords of the night. Ten deities who determine the fate of men.

Yohaulticetl (Anahauac People, Mexico)

Also known as: *Metztli, Tecciztecatl.*

"The Lady of the Night." Goddess of night. Guardian of babies. She is also the moon god, Tecciztecatl, who is also known as Meztli. *See also* Coyolxauhqui; Metzli; Tecciztecatl.

Yohualtonatiuh (Aztec) *see* Legend of the Four Suns.

Yolaikaiason (North America) *see* Atseatsan and Atseatsine.

Yolcuatl (Mexico) *see* Quetzalcoatl.

Yolkai Estsan (Navajo People, North America)

Also known as: *Yolaikaiason.*

Water goddess. Yolkai Estsan was created from a white shell. She is the sister of Estsanatlehi, the wife of the moon carrier, Klehanoai, and the mother of Thobadzistshini. *See also* Ataentsic; Klehanoai.

Yomanua-Borna (Antilles)

He is a rain god with two assistants, who has a shrine in a cavern.

Yomi (Shinto; Japan)

Also known as: *Meido, Ne-no-kuni* (Land of Roots), *Nenokatatsu-kuni, Soko-no-kuni* (Deep Land), *Sokotsu-kuni* (Bottom Land), *Yomi-no-kuni, Yomi-no-yo, Yomi-tsu-kuni* (Land of Darkness), *Yomotsukuni* (Land of Gloom).

Underworld. Yomi is the realm of the dead, a bottomless chasm and kingdom of darkness lying below the earth. It is reached from the edge of the sea or by a twisting, downhill road that leads to a subterranean level. The populace of Komi, rich, poor, good and bad, appear to lead lives similar to their mortal existence; they eat, have homes and move around. Punishment and rewards are not a part of this dark world. Once one eats the food cooked in Yomi then he or she is incorporated into the underworld realm. The grotesque female inhabitants of Yomi are known as Yomo-tsu-shiko-me (ugly-female-of-the-world-of-the-dead), also known as Shiko-Me. In some versions, Yomi is ruled by Tsuikiyomi-no-Mikoto, who is often called Tsuki-yomi. Tsuki-yomi is the ruler of the moon and the ruler of the night. It is also said that Yomo-tsu-kuni is the god of the realm of the dead. Yomi is referenced in the legend of Izanagi and Izanami and Okuni-nushi and Susanowo. Izanami (Female Who Invites) became the ruler of death and ills in Yomi after her death. The Peach Tree of Life grows on the border of Yomi. The peach is a symbol of the mother-goddess. Izanagi threw three peaches at his pursuers in Yomi. (The Chinese also have a gigantic sacred Peach Tree.) According to some, Yomi is possibly derived from Yama as other names associated with Yama or Yomi are deities of the underworld. The opposite of Yomi is Ama (heaven). Compare to Jigoku (Buddhist), Tuat (Egypt), Tartarus and Hades (Greek). *See also* Izanagi and Izanami; Kami; O-Wata-Tsu-Mi; Okuni-Nushino-Mikoto; Shiko-Me; Susanowo; Yomo-tsu-kami.

Yomi-no-kuni (Japan) *see* Yomi.

Yomi-no-yo (Japan) *see* Yomi.

Yomo-tsu-kami (Japan)

God of the dead. Possibly a male version of Yomo-tsu-shiko-me. *See also* Soko-no-kuni; Yomi.

Yomi-tsu-kuni *Yomotsukuni* (Japan)

"Land of Darkness." "Land of Gloom." *See also* Yomi.

Yomo-tsu-shiko-me (Japan)

"Ugly-female-of-the-world-of-the-dead." She is a resident of the underworld realm of the dead, Yomi. *See also* Shiko-Me; Yomi.

Yomotsukuni (Japan) *see* Yomi-tsu-kuni.

Yondung Halmoni (Korea)

Ancient wind goddess. She is given rice cakes during her celebrations in shamanic rituals.

Yorodzu-Hime (Japan) *see* Kami-Mimusubi.

Yoskeha and Taweskare *Yoskeha and Tawisara, Yoskeha and Tawiscara;* (Huron, Iroquois People, North America)

Also known as: *Hahgwehdiyu and Hahgwehdaetgah, Sapling and Flint, Yoskeha and Teharaonhiawagon.*

In an Iroquois version of this myth, Yoskeha and Taweskare are the twins of the mother goddess Ataentsic (also spelled Ataensic). The twins, bitter enemies, caused their mother's death. Ataentsic, who created the sun and moon from Taweskare (Flint), cast Yoskeha (Sapling) out for not telling the truth about who caused her death. Flint became a trickster and maker of malevolent beings and spirit of winter. In some versions, Ataentsic is their grandmother. In another version Yoskeha, known as Teharaonhia-wakon, still a sapling, changed himself into a youth each time he grew old. For a different version of this myth, *see* Taweskare. *See also* Ataentsic; Hadui.

Yoyolche (Aztec People, Mexico)

These evil demons live underground. When they walk at night they shake the house with their giant steps. *See also* Kisin; Yumchakob.

Yryn-ai-tojon (Siberia) *see* Yryn-aja-tojon.

Yryn-aja-tojon (Siberia)

Also known as: *Yryn-ai-tojon.*

Supreme deity. He is the white lord who created earth by challenging Satan to bring a piece of earth from the bottom of the sea. Yryn sat on this piece of earth and Satan stretched it to force him off. The more he stretched the larger the earth became. *See also* Ullu Tojon.

Ytzmatul (Maya) *see* Itzamna.

Yu-Ch'iang (China)

God of the sea wind. He is responsible for great storms. Depictions show him with a human face and the body of a bird. Sometimes two green serpents hang from his ears and two more cling to his feet. Yu-Ch'iang is also shown with the body of a fish. He rides on two dragons.

Yu-Ch'ih Ching-Te (China) *see* Men-shen.

Yu Ch'ing (Taoist; China)

Also known as: *Lo Ching Hsin, T'ien Pao, Yu Huang, Yuanshih T'ien-tsun.*

Supreme deity. God of the "Jade Heaven." In some versions this is one of three heavens called San Ch'ing. Yu Ch'ing is either the first heaven or the ruler of the first heaven. *See also* Ling-Pao T'ien-Tsun; Shang Ch'ing.

Yu-Huan-Shang-Ti (Taoist; China)

Also known as: *August Personage of Jade, August Supreme Emperor of Jade, Father Heaven, Huang T'ien Shang Ti, Jade Emperor, The Jade God, Lao-tien-heh, Lao-tien-yeh, Mu Kung, T'ai Ching, T'ien, Tien, Yu Ch'ing, Yu'ti.*

"The August Supreme Emperor of Jade." Emperor of the gods. God of purity. God of nature. Creator deity. Yu-Huang-Shang-Ti, the son of Pao Yu and Ching Te, lives on the highest level of heaven with his wife, the Queen Mother Wang (also known as Wang-mu-niang-niang and Hsi Wang Mu). All lesser gods in his court report to Yu-Huan-Shang-Ti about human activities. The emperor created mortals from clay. The clay figures were put out to dry but rain came and some of the figures were damaged. The damaged figures constitute the sick who live on earth; the healthy mortals are the clay figures that he saved. The door to his palace is guarded by Wang. According to Taoist tradition, as Yuan-shih T'ien-tsun, his agents are Tsao Chun and Lei Tsu. Yu-Huan-Shang-Ti is part of a triad of three deities from heaven (known as Ta-lo or San Ch'ing). The first member of the triad is Yuan-shi T'ien-tsun or Lo Ching Hsin or T'ien Pao. The second is Yu-Huang or Ling-pao T'ien-Tsun, and the third is Kin-k'ue Yu-chen T'ien-tsun or Lao Tzu. He is depicted seated on a throne, wearing the formal robes and headdress of a Chinese emperor. *See also* Si-wang-mu; Yu Ch'ing; Yuan-shih T'ien-tsun.

Yu-K'ien (China) *see* Ch'eng Huang.

Yu-Lu (China)

Door god. Guardian of the left side of the door. His brother, Shen-T'u, guards the right side. These two deities have been replaced by Ts'in Shu-pao and Hu King-te. Like most deities these were formerly mortals, in this case generals of the army of the T'ang Emperor. One has a red face, the other black. *See also* Celestial Kings; Men-shen; Shen-T'u.

Yu-ming Kio-shi (China) *see* Ti-tsang.

Yu Nu (China)

Also known as: *Jade Lady, T'ien Hsien Yu Nu Pi Hsia Yuan Chu (First Lord of the Blue Sky, Heavenly Fairy, Jade Lady).*

Goddess of rain. Yu Nu is the daughter of Tung Hai (Eastern Sea) and wife of Hsi Hai (Western Sea). She brings rain during periods of drought.

Yu Po (China)

Water deity. One of the Nine Songs. Similar to Shui Shen. *See also* Nine Songs.

Yu Shih (China)

Lord of the Winds. Yu Shih is a rain god, who has the gift of magic, and lives in K'un Lun Mountain. He walks through water without getting wet and fire without being burned. He is shown standing on a cloud pouring rain from a water can. He may be the same as Yu-Tzu (q.v.). *See also* Nine Songs; Yu Huang; Yu Nu.

Yu-ti (China) *see* Yu Huang.

Yu-tzu (China)

Also known as: *Master of Rain.*

God of rain. Yu-tzu carries rain in a ceramic pot and distributes it with his sword. He is generally found with Tien Mu

(lightning) and Lei-kung, the thunder god. Possibly same as Yu-Shih.

Yuan Shi (China) *see* Chen Wu.

Yuan-Shih T'ien-Tsun (Taoist, China)

Also known as: *The First Cause, Lo Ching Hsin, Yu Ch'ing.*

The Highest God. Invisible and immortal, he existed before creation. Some say he was part of a triad of high deities. Others say he is the highest of the high deities. He appears to have been replaced by Yu Huang. Yuan-Shih is associated with Tsao Chun (kitchen god) and Lei Tsu (thunder god) and Yu Ch'ing.

Yuan-shih T'ien-wang (China) *see* P'an Ku.

Yuddhisthira (India) *see* Yudhisthira.

Yudhishthira (India) *see* Yudhisthira.

Yudhisthira *Yuddhisthira, Yudhishthira* (India)

The son of Kunti and the god of justice, Dharma. *See also* Arjuna; Bhima (A); Brahma; Dharma; Duryodhana; Krishna; Kunti; Pandavas; Visvakarma.

Yuga (India) *see* Dwaparayuga.

Yuke (Norse; Teutonic) *see* Hiuke.

Yuki-onne (Japan) *see* Yukionna

Yukionna *Yuki-onne* (Japan)

Goddess of winter. Snow Woman. A ghastly, ghostly white spirit. Her custom is to appear in snowstorms and lull men to sleep and to death. She is young and has a beautiful body and a seemingly nice disposition, but she kills her husbands.

Yul-khor-bsrun (Tibet) *see* Dhartarastra.

Yum Caax *Yum Kaax* (Maya People, Yucatan)

Also known as: *Ghanan.*

The god of maize, coca and agriculture. Yum Caax is a handsome young deity. He is honored at planting and harvest time, particularly for coca and maize. The dried leaves of the coca, when masticated, create a state of euphoria. It was known as the "divine plant" by the Incas and was used by the ruling class. The coca plant has been revered by many groups. The leaves are used for purification or to ward off evil spirits. It has also been used to heal wounds, stomach problems and intestinal disorders. Maize is often a symbol of fertility and sustenance. *See also* Cinteotl.

Yum Chung Chun (China)

The god of the clouds. One of the nine heroes. *See also* Nine Songs.

Yum Cimil (Maya People, Yucatan)

Death god. Lord of the underworld. *See also* Hanhau.

Yum Kaax (Mexico) *see* Yum Caax.

Yumbalamob (Maya People, Yucatan)

Protectors. The ancient Yumbalamob are deities who protect Christians. They reside in the first heaven above the earth. The legend is similar to that of Tezcatlipoca in that they guard entrances and crossroads. *See also* Tezcatlipoca.

Yumchakob (Maya People, Mexico)

Also known as: *Nukuchyumchakob.*

Yumchakob is an ancient white-haired god who is fond of smoking. He produces rain and protects mortals. Yumchakob resides in the sixth of seven heavens which is ruled by the Christian god El Gran Dios, who might be Kukulcan. Kukulcan also has white hair and likes to smoke. Compare the Yumchakob to the Chacs. *See also* Kisin; Nohochacyum.

Yun Chung Chun (China)

God of clouds. One of the Nine Songs. *See also* Nine Songs.

Yun-T'ung (China)

Also known as: *Little Boy of the Clouds.*

God of clouds. Generally found with Lei-kung, Yu-tzu and Feng-po.

Yuncemil (Maya) *see* Acat; Becabs.

Yurlunggur or Julunggul (Australia) *see* Rainbow Snake.

Yurupari (Brazil, Tupiian people)

Demons. Some people say Yurupareu is a generic term for all evil demons or spirits. Others say Yurupari is god, spirit or ogre of the forest.

Yu'ti (China) *see* Yu Huang.

Yzamna (Maya) *see* Itzamna.

Z

Zababa (Kish) Supreme god of gods.

Zabba (Hurrite) God of war.

Zabel (Ugarit) The Lord of the Sea. *See also* Bod-Baal.

Zaden (Armenia)

Also known as: *Zatik.*

God or goddess of Fishermen. Little known deity during the reign of Queen Sathenik of Albania, about 190 B.C.E. May have been a representative of Ishtar. *See also* Zatik.

Zagreus (Greek)

Zagreus is the son of the great god, Zeus, and Persephone, goddess of the underworld. *See also* Dionysus; Sabizios.

Zaguaguaya *Zaquaguayu* (Guarayo People, South America) *see* Abaangui.

Zahgurim (Babylonia)

Zahgurim is a name for Marduk taken from the "Hymn of Fifty Names of Marduk." *See also* Marduk.

Zahhak *Zohak* (Middle Eastern) *see* Zohak.

Zahrim (Babylonia)

Zahrim is a name for Marduk taken from the "Hymn of Fifty Names of Marduk." *See also* Marduk.

Zainab (Islamic)

Zainab is one of the four daughters of Mohammed by his first wife, Khadija. Her sisters are Fatima, Ruqaiyah and Umm Kulthum. Mohammed and Khadija also had two (others say three) sons. *See also* Fatima; Mohammed.

Zairisha *Zari* (Persia)

The archdemons Zairisha and Taurvi degrade men, lead them to failure and cause old age. They are in opposition to the goddess of health, Haurvatat, and the goddess of immortality, Ameretat. *See also* Ameretat; Daevas; Haurvatat.

Zal (Persia)

Hero and deified king. The long legend of Zal depicts him as the father of the hero Rustam. He has adventures similar to those of Hercules. In one of the stories Zal is rescued by the vulture Simurgh, who also saves him in later times from his enemy, Isfandiyar. The bird also heals the wounds of Zal and his horse, Rakhsh.

Zalambur (Islamic)

The son of Iblis, and brother of Awar, Dasim, Sut, and Tir, Zalambur is the demon of dishonesty in business. *See also* Azazel.

Zalgarra (Sumer)

One of the two first ancestors of mankind. The other was Elligarra. *See also* Cosmology of Assur.

Zalmoxis *Salmoxis* (Greek)

Also known as: *Dionysus* (possibly), *Gebelzeizis.*

Zalmoxis is known as a Thracian god. At death's doorsteps, his followers asked him for immortality. Zalmoxis is possibly an epithet of Dionysus. *See also* Bacchus; Dionysus.

Zaltu (Assyro-Babylonia)

Zaltu is a goddess of strife who was created by Ea to complement Ishtar.

Zam-Armatay (Persia) She is an earth goddess.

Zam Zam *Zem Zem* (Islamic)

The prophet Ibrahim abandoned his son Ismail (also called Ishmael) and the child's mother Hajar (also called Hagar), who was his Egyptian slave, in Mecca. Hajar was left with a few dates and a small amount of water. In her search for more water, she traveled the hilly terrain between Safa and Marwah seven times until she came upon the sacred well Zam Zam. Pilgrims to Mecca still follow her route. *See also* Abram.

Zamama (Babylonian)

Corn, sun, and war deity. He subdued the eagle (storm) with his weapon, Sharur (cyclone). He was later identified with Marduk. *See also* Marduk.

Zamba (Cameroons, Africa)

Creator. He created the earth and made it his residence. He has four sons: N'Kokon, Otukut, Ngi, and Wo. He is probably the same as Zambi.

Zambi (Angola, Africa)

Supreme being. He lives in the sky and is connected with a flood legend. He is the supreme judge of the dead. Zambi may be the same or similar to Zamba (q.v.)

Zamin (Persian)

Some think that Zamin and the Greek Semele are Zemelo, an ancient earth goddess of the Phrygians. *See also* Semele.

Zamna (Yucatan) *see* Itzamna.

Zanaharibe (Madagascar) *see* Zanahary.

Zanahary (Madagascar)

Also known as: *Andriamanitra, Zanaharibe.*

Supreme god. Zanaharibe is supreme over the Zanahary hierarchy. There are many Zanahary deities, both good and bad, and they all were instrumental in creating earth and mankind.

Zanaru (Assyro-Babylonian)

An name for Ishtar, meaning "Lady of the Islands."

Zandagahih (Zoroastrian; Persia)

Zandagahih is another name for the "Bundahish," an important Zoroastrian work. For details *see* Bundahish.

Zaphon, Mount *Tsaphon* (Ugaritic)

Sacred Mountain. *See also* Baal; Yam-Nahar.

Zapotec Quetzalcoatl (Mexico) *see* Coqui-Xee.

Zaqar *Zakar* (Babylonia, Sumer)

Also known as: *Dzakar.*

Zaqar, the god Sin's messenger, brings messages from the god, to mortals through dreams.

Zaramama (Peru) Grain Mother. *See also* Mama Zara.

Zarathustra Spitama (Persia) A name for Zoroaster (q.v.).

Zari (Persia) *see* Daevas.

Zarik (Persia)

Zarik is one of the evil spirits created by Ahriman to be his assistant. *See also* Darvands.

Zarpandit (Assyro-Babylonian) *see* Zerpanitum.

Zarpanit (Assyro-Babylonian) *see* Zerpanitum.

Zarvan-akarana (Persian) *see* Zurvan.

Zarya (Slavic) *see* Zorya.

Zatik (Armenia)

Also known as: *Zaden.*

Little known god or goddess of vegetation. Probably a misspelling of the Iberian god of fishermen named "Zaden." Possibly associated in some way with Ishtar. Some say Zaden may have been a representative of Ishtar. In some versions Zatik appears related to the Palestinian god Sedeq or possibly the Babylonian sons of the god Shamash who were called Kettu and Misharu. These were later identified as Sydyk and Misor. *See also* Zaden.

Zcernoboch (Slavic) *see* Chernobog.

Zcernoch (Slavic) *see* Chernobog.

Zd (Slavic) *see* Shahpet.

Zduh *Zduhacz* (Slavic)

Zduh is the soul or spirit that leaves the body of a sleeping person or animal at night. During its travels, it engages in battles and could be killed. *See also* Domovoi; Kikimora.

Zduhacz (Slavic) *see* Zduh.

Zehuti (Egypt) *see* Djehuti Orzehuti; Thoth.

Zelos *Zelus* (Greek)

"Zeal." "Jealousy." Zelos is the son of the Titan Pallas and the Oceanid Styx. *See also* Styx.

Zelus (Greek) *see* Zelos.

Zem Zem (Islamic) *see* Zam Zam.

Zemelo (Phrygian)

Zemelo is an ancient earth goddess thought by some to be the fore-runner of the Greek Semele. *See also* Semele.

Zemes *Zems, Zemi, Zemis* (North America, South America)

Spirits. Believed to be intermediaries between the people and their god. This god can be considered both singular and plural. The people pray to the Zemes for rain or sun and in some versions the Zemes help lessen pain for women during the birth process. *See also* Guamaonocon; Iella; Iocauna.

Zemina *Sieroji Zemele, Zemyna, Zemynele* (Lithuania)

An earth goddess, she is the source of all life. Particular attention is given to her at the birth of each child. She is associated with plant life, particularly the spruce, oak, and linden trees.

Zempat (Prussian) God of earth and cattle.

Zemyna (Lithuania) *see* Zemina.

Zemynele (Lithuania) *see* Zemina.

Zend (Persia)

A translation and exposition of the *Avesta* in a form of Middle Persian used in Zoroastrian literature of the 3rd to 10th centuries, known as Pahlavi.

Zend-Aves'ta The *Avesta* together with the Zend.

Zeniari (Japan)

A name for Benten, goddess of the sea and goddess of good luck. *See also* Benten.

Zephyr (Greek) *see* Zephyrus.

Zephyros (Greek) *see* Zephyrus.

Zephyrus *Zephyr, Zephyros;* (Greek)

Also known as: *Caurus, Favonius* (Roman), *West Wind.*

God of the west wind. Zephyrus is the son of Astraeus (starry night) and Eos, goddess of dawn. He is the mild and gentle West Wind who resides in a cave in Thrace with his brother and close companion, Boreas, the North Wind. Their siblings are Notus, the south wind, and Eurus, the southeast wind. Zephyrus and his mate, the athlete Chloris, also known as Flora, have a son, Carpus (fruit). He is also the father of Achilles' immortal horses, Xanthus and Balius, by the Harpy Podarge. Zephyrus is held responsible by some writers for his jealousy and the subsequent death of the beautiful young man, Hyacinthos, who adored Apollo and was turned into a hyacinth or a lily. Zephyrus, who began life as a wild wind and deity, turned mellow over the years and is described as mild and gentle with flowers in his lap. He is comparable to the Roman Favonius. Compare to Fu-jin (Japan). *See also* Aeolus; Boreas; Chimaera; Chloris; Eos; Harpies; Hyacinthos.

Zeraili (Africa) *see* Azazel.

Zerbanit (Assyro-Babylonia) *see* Zerpanitum.

Zerbanitu (Assyro-Babylonia) *see* Zerpanitum.

Zerpanitum (Assyro-Babylonia)

Also known as: *Beltiya, Gamsu, Sarpanit, Zarpandit, Zarpanit, Zerbanitu, Zirbanit.*

Mother goddess. Creator and destroyer. In early times, Zerpanitum was depicted as pregnant and was worshipped as the moon rose. She may be the same as or an aspect of Ishtar and Beltis. Gamsu, a Chaldean sea goddess, eventually assimilated with Zerpanitum. *See also* Beltis; Gasmu; Ishtar.

Zervan (Persia) *see* Zurvan.

Zetes and Calais (Greek)

Also known as: *Boreadae, Boreades, Prodromes.*

Zetes and his twin Calais are the sons of Boreas (also known as Aquilo), the north wind, and the river nymph Oreithyia, who is the daughter of Erechtheus and Praxithea. Their siblings are Cleopatra, Haemus and Chione. The twins have wings that sprouted when they reached puberty although it is also said that their father presented the wings to them before they sailed on the Argo. Zetes and Calais are credited with saving the life of their brother-in-law, the old and starving king Phineus of Thrace, who had been beset by the wretched winged creatures, the Harpies. In some versions of this myth, the twins chased the monster birds through the sky and, unable to capture them, died of exhaustion. A more popular rendition is that they pursued their prey to the islands of Strophades and were told by either Hermes or Iris to desist with the promise that the Harpies would not trouble Phineus again. Some say it was their sister, Cleopatra, the wife of Phineus, whom they rescued. In one tale, Phineus imprisoned Cleopatra and her children because of the jealousy of another of Phineus' wives. They met their fate through Heracles who had heard that the twins were responsible for encouraging their shipmates to abandon him in Mysia. As the twins were en route home from the funeral games of

Pelias, Heracles killed them with his bow and arrows at Tenos. After death the twins became the Prodromes or winds from the northeast. When Boreas the north wind blew, one of the two pillars marking their graves would sway. Zetes and Calais have purple wings or purple hair. Compare to storm deities; Chimaera; Harpies. *See also* Argonauts; Boreas; Phineus.

Zethus (Greek)

Zethus is the son of Zeus and Antiope and the twin brother of Amphion. Abandoned at birth, he later married either Thebe or Aedon, the daughter of Pandareus, and became the father of Itylus. Zethus shared the kingship of Thebes with his brother, Amphion. Although they were opposites in many ways, the twins appeared to share their duties well. Zethus was known for his agricultural abilities and his brother for his musical abilities. Aedon accidentally killed their son, Itylus, and she turned into a nightingale. It is said that Zethus died of a broken heart. *See* Antiope for details of his mother's life and his birth. For additional information about his relationship with his brother, *see* Amphion; Thebe. *See* Aedon for details about the death of Itylus.

Zeus (Greek)

Also known as: *Amen* (Egyptian), *Ammon* (Egyptian), *Basileus* (the king), *Beelsamin* (Early Phoenician), *Deipatyros* (Illyrians), *Dyaus Pitar* (Aryan), *Gamelios* (God of Marriage), *Herkeios* (Protector of the Home), *Jove* (Roman), *Jupiter* (Roman), *Ktesios* (Guardian of Property), *Mechaneus* (manager and contriver), *Meilichios* (Zeus in Serpent Form), *Moiragete* (guide of the Moirae), *Panhellenius* (God of all Greeks), *Phyxios* (God of Escape), *Soter* (Father and Savior of Man), *Terminalius* (protector of boundaries), *Tiu* (German), *Zeus Chthonios* (God of Earth and Fertility).

Father of gods and men, god of the sky, and lord of Olympus, where he resides, Zeus is founder of the Olympian dynasty. Connected with the upper air, he is the god of all that is high, including mountain tops, eagles, oaks and thunderstorms. He was brought up in a cave on Mount Ida to be safe from his father, Cronus, the god of the world and time, who had swallowed his other children. Rhea, the mother of the gods and Zeus' mother, left him in the care of a nurse on Crete. The name of the nurse who hid the baby is given variously as Neda, Helice, Aega, Cynosura, Adrastea, Ida or Adamanthea. Zeus' siblings are Hades, the king of the underworld; Hera, the queen of heaven, whom Zeus seduced in the form of a cuckoo or a hummingbird; Hestia, the virginal goddess of the hearth; Poseidon, god of the sea; Demeter (also known as Ceres), the goddess of agriculture, who was also seduced by Zeus. Cronus had bound the one-eyed, monsters known as the Cyclopes. Zeus liberated them, and was rewarded by them with the gift of thunder and lightning. His thunderbolts were forged by the talented smith Hephaistos. The Cyclopes were invaluable assistants to Zeus as he traveled his path to become the leader of the gods. Using his thunder and lightning as weapons he conquered the race of giants known as the Titans (who are the siblings of the Cyclopes and the Hecatonchires). Zeus turned them upon the goddess of the earth Gaea, whom he deposed from her throne after a struggle with Typhoeus, the son of Gaea and Tartarus (who was born from Chaos). With the help of the Cyclopes (others say it was his mother Rhea and his first wife Metis, a daughter of Oceanus and Tethys, who helped him) he defeated Cronus and the other Titans and thus became master of the world. He gave the sea to his brother Poseidon to rule and the underworld to his other brother, Hades, reserving the heavens for himself. Zeus successfully fought two battles to keep his throne. One engagement was with the screaming monster whirlwind, Typhon, who has a hundred dragon heads that shoot flames from his nostrils and eyes. The other battle was with the most powerful of the giants, Enceladus. Both opponents had been sent by Gaea to punish Zeus. As Metis, the first wife of Zeus, was residing in his stomach, he married again. His second wife, the Titan Themis, the personification of order and justice, gave birth to daughters who are the seasons, personified as the Horae; the goddess of fate, personified as the Moirae; and the goddess of justice, Astraea. Another mate of Zeus was the Oceanid Eurynome, who gave birth to the Graces and personifies beauty and grace. By his sister, Demeter, Zeus fathered Persephone, goddess of the underworld. Persephone later succumbed to her father in the form of a snake and gave birth to Zagreus. The other child of Persephone and Zeus is Dionysus, who as an embroyo was swallowed by Zeus and placed in the body of Semele. Other wives and mistresses included Mnemosyne, the personification of memory and the mother of the Muses; Leto, a Titan, who became the mother of Apollo and Artemis; Hera, whom Zeus seduced in the form of a cuckoo or hummingbird and who gave birth to Ares, Hebe, Eileithyia, and possibly the god of fire, Hephaistos. It is generally agreed that his sister Hera is his important mate.

By Dione he was the father of the goddess of love Aphrodite (possibly). His affairs with mortal women produced more children. Disguised as Amphitryon, the spouse of Alcmene, she bore him Hercules. With Danae he fathered Perseus. Disguised as a white bull he kidnapped and had sex with Europa. She birthed Minos, Rhadamanthus, and Sarpedon. With Io he became the father of Epaphus. Disguised as a swan he seduced Leda. She hatched Castor and Pollux and Helen. He is also the father of Arcas by Callisto. Some of his other lovers were Aegina, Calliope, Carme, Electra, Eos, Eris, Laodamia, Leda, Niobe, Pandora, Selene, Semele, Styx, Tethys, Thalassa and Thymbris.

The ancient Persians called the sky Zeus. They climbed the highest peaks to offer sacrifices to Zeus. The Olympic Games were held every four years on Mt. Olympus in his honor. Zeus was possibly worshiped as early as 1500 B.C.E. Worshiped all over Greece, his principal shrines were at Dodona and Olympia. Zeus possesses the goatskin shield known as the aegis. His sacred bird is the eagle. Zeus is usually depicted seated on a throne, with thunderbolts in one hand and a scepter of cypress in the other, wearing a wreath of olive or myrtle. Most legends of Zeus parallel those of Jupiter (Roman). Compare Zeus to Dyaus (India); the Vedic god Vishnu; the Norse gods Odin, and Thor. See also Acrisius; Adrastia; Adrestus; Aegina; Aegipan; Aeolus (A); Aeolus (B); Agdistis; Aglaia; Amaltheia; Amen (A); Amen (B); Anchises; Antiope; Apis (A); Ares; Argus (A); Argus (C); Artemis; Asopus; Astrae; Atalanta; Bellerophon; Calypso; Chaos; Cian; Corybantes; Cronus; Cybele; Cyclops; Danae; Enceladus; Eris; Eurynome; Fates; Graces; Harmonia (A); Harpies; Hecatonchires; Hephaistos; Hermaphroditus; Hesperides; Hestia; Horae; Ino; Ixion; Lamia; Leto; Metis; Minos; Moirae; Muses; Naiads; Nephele; Niobe (B); Oceanus; Orion; Persephone; Perseus; Phineus; Poseidon; Rhadamantus; Rhea; Sarpedon (A); Sarpedon (B); Semele; Serapis; Sinope; Sisyphus; Styx; Tartarus; Tethys; Themis; Titans; Typhon.

Zhag-pa-ma (Tibet)
Also known as: *Pashadhari* (India).
This sow-headed goddess, associated with fondness, is a Shakti, and with her mate, Yamantaka, is the Door-Keeper of the South. Her other name, Pashadhari, indicates that she is a noose-bearer. See also Kinkini-Dhari; Shakti; Yamantaka.

Zhal-zas-ma (Tibet) see Amoghasiddhi.

Zi (Sumer)
Also known as: *Sige, Ziku.*
Spirits. As the ancient spirits, the Zi, became important, they were given new names. In general, they are controlling life spirits of everything in nature. Sometimes, Zi is singular and known as a goddess of life. Ziku is one of the names bestowed upon Marduk by Anu. See also Marduk; Sigi; Ti.

Ziapsu (Sumer) see Dumuzi.

Zib (Babylonia)
Zib is Ishtar as the evening star who generates desire. See also Ishtar.

Zigarun (Akkadia) see Apsu.

Ziku (Sumer, Babyloni) see Marduk; Zi.

Zima (Slavic) Mother Winter.

Zin (Nigeria, Africa)
Also known as: *Zin-Kibaru.*
Water spirits. The Zin, who are depicted as dragons, are associated with musical instruments. The Zin were possibly adapted from the Islamic Jinn. See also Zinkibaru.

Zin-Kibaru (Africa) see Zinkibaru.

Zinkibaru *Zin-Kibaru* (Songhoi, Africa)
Also known as: *Zin.*
A djinn, Zinkibaru is the blind Master of Fish.

Zio (Teutonic) see Tyr.

Zipacna (Guatemala, Central America)
Deity of the dawn. Every morning, Zipacna slays four hundred stars. Every evening, Hunahpu restores the stars to the sky. See also Gukup Cakix; Hunahpu; Ixbalanque.

Zipaltonal (Nicaragua)
Creator. Zipaltonal and her husband, Tamagostad, created earth and everything on it. Good souls go to them in their heaven. Bad souls go to Mictlantecuhtli (q.v.). See also Masaya.

Zirna (Etruscan)
She is a moon goddess who is depicted with a half moon hanging from her neck. Her companion is the love goddess Turan.

Zisa (German) see Cisa.

Zisi (Babylonia) see Marduk.

Ziu (Teutonic)

Also known as: *Mars, Othin* (possibly).

Ziu is thought to be the original father and sky god among the Teutonic People. He is identified with sun symbols, the circle, the wheel, the swastika. The Romans identified Ziu as Mars. *See also* Tyr; Zeus.

Ziukkinna (Babylonia) *see* Marduk.

Ziusudra (Sumer)

Also known as: *Utnapishtim* (Babylonia).

He is the pious king of Sippar, a mortal who was instructed by Enki to build a boat to save himself and others, along with some animals, from the great flood. In later times in Babylonian mythology, Ziusudra was known as Utnapishtim. *See also* Ea; Enki; Gilgamesh; Noah; Urshanabi; Utnapishtim.

Ziv (Teutonic)

Also known as: *Thingsus, Tyr.*

God of Assembly. *See also* Tyr.

Ziva (Slavic)

Also known as: *Siva, Zywie* (Polish).

Goddess of life.

Zivena *Vitzcatl* (Aztec People, Mexico) Highest heaven.

Ziw (Norse) *see* Tyr.

Ziz *Ziv* (Hebrew)

Ziz, an ancient giant bird, devours vegetation.

Zleja (Lithuania) Goddess of high day. *See also* Breksta.

Zluidni (Slavic) Malicious fairies.

Zmek (Slavic)

Also known as: *Cmok, Smok.*

Zmek, a guardian angel, has as his symbol the snake or serpent. *See also* Tsmok.

Zocho (Japan) *see* Zocho-Ten.

Zocho-ten (Buddhist; Japan)

Also known as: *Virudhaka, Zocho.*

Zocho-ten is one of the four heavenly kings known as Shi Tenno. As a guardian of the four directions, established to ward off evil spirits, he is responsible for the south in some versions and the west in others. He is known as the destroyer of evil, dispenser of good and a god of growth. Zocho-ten is shown dressed as a soldier, wearing a ferocious expression and holding a sword and a shield. Compare to the Nio guards (q.v.). *See also* Bishamon-Ten; Jikoku-Ten; Komoku-Ten; Shi Tenno; Virudhaka (India).

Zohak *Zahak, Zahhak* (India, Iran, Persia)

Deified mortal. Demon. Said to be the incarnation of the druj, Azhi Dahaka. Not originally evil, he came under the spell of Ahriman (Angra Mainyu) and later vanquished (or killed) Jemshid (another name for Yima). Zohak introduced meat to the people who were always vegetarians. The demon Zohak was later defeated and chained to a mountain by Feridun. In some interpretations, Zohak, the drought demon, was slain by Thraetaona. Zohak is not a pleasant sight. He has serpents growing from his shoulders. *See also* Azhi Dahaka; Yima.

Zonget (Siberia)

Zonget is the ancient goddess of hunting and ruler of all bird and animal life and ruler of all who hunt.

Zoroaster (Persia)

Also known as: *Ardusht, Mazdayasni-Zaroshtis, Zarathustra Spitama.*

He is said by some to have been born c. 590 B.C.E. Others place his birth at various points between 1000 and 600 B.C.E. Conceived by a ray of light that entered his mother's bosom, he was born of a virgin birth. It is said that he laughed at birth. His mother is Dughda (also known as Dughdhova), and his putative father is Pourushaspa. A light hero and prophet, Zoroaster had three wives, three sons, and three daughters. Yima's Khvarenanh (Glory) was transferred to him. The Ameshas Spenta appeared to him with revelations. Ahura Mazda revealed the path of truth to him on Mount Elburz and he founded Zoroastrianism. His rule of moral conduct is good thought, good word, and good action. During his life on earth, he performed many miracles, and endured temptation by the arch-demon Angra Mainyu. Eventually slain by demons, Zoroaster descended to the underworld and three days later ascended to heaven. He left his sperm in Lake Kasu where it is preserved. It is guarded by 99,999 Fravashis. Every millennium for three millenniums, a virgin bathing in the lake will receive his sperm and give birth to a savior. The first savior will be Aushedar who is known as the developer of righteousness. The second savior will be Aushedar-mah and the third savior, Soshyant. *See also* Ahura Mazda; Amesha Spentas; Angra Mainyu; Avesta; Fravashi; Haoma; Khvarenanh; Spenta Armaiti; Vohu Manah; Yazatas; Yima.

Zoroastrian — Creation Legend *see* Ahura Mazda.

Zorya, The (Slavic)

Also known as: *Aurora,* (Greek, Roman), *Zarya* (Slavic).

Guardians. Dawn goddesses. The Zorya are two or three goddesses who guard the universe. They are either Zvezda Dennitsa or Zorya Utrennyaya, the morning star, and Zvezda Vechernyaya, the evening star, and the midnight Zorya. They keep watch over the hound chained to the constellation of the Little Bear for if the chain should break it would be the end of the world. In some legends Dennitsa replaces the Sun as wife of Myesyats (moon). Dennitsa is almost equal to the greatest gods. The Zorya are the same as the Auroras. *See also* Perun.

Zorys, The Two (Serbian) *see* Auroras, The Two.

Zotzilaha Chimalman (Maya)

He is a bat god who is the same as Camazotz (q.v.).

Zu (Mesopotamia)

Also known as: *Anzu, Imgig.*

A minor deity, and perhaps an underworld god, Zu is the son of the bird goddess Siris. He lived with his wife and children, and worked as the valet of Ellil, the supreme god. Zu stole the Tablets of Fate from Ellil while he was washing. Ea, god of the earth and waters, persuaded the goddess of the womb, Belet-Ili, to conceive and deliver a divine hero who could overcome Zu. Ninurta was born, and fulfilled his destiny by recovering the Tablets of Fate. In another record of this myth, we are told that the gods were dismayed when the theft occurred but none volunteered to pursue Zu. Finally, Lugalbanda, the father of

Gilgamesh, undertook the task and killed Zu. In yet another record, *The Hymn of Ashurbanipal*, it is said that Marduk crushed Zu's skull. Zu and Siris are described as enormous birds who breathe fire and water. Zu is also depicted as a lion-headed eagle. *See also* Ea; Marduk.

Zulu People — Creation Legend (Africa) *see* Unkulunkulu.

Zulum (Babylonia) *see* Marduk.

Zumiang-nui (India) *see* Shuzanghu.

Zuni People — Creation Legend (North America) *see* Awonawilona; Shiwanni and Shiwanokia.

Zunto-zang-po (Tibet) *see* Samantabhadra.

Zurvan (Zurvanites; Persia)

Also known as: *Zarvan-akarana, Zervan* (this spelling is from a later sect of Zoroastrians), *Zrvan Akarana.*

Before the creation of heaven and earth, Zurvan, generally believed to mean "boundless time," existed alone. Androgynous, Zurvan desired a son. After offering sacrifices for a thousand years, Zurvan doubted that his desire would be fulfilled. In this moment of doubt, twins were conceived, Ohramazd and Ahriman. Ohramazd represented the fulfillment of his desire (all good), and Ahriman represented his doubt (evil). In Armenia, Zervan, Titan, and Japhet were worshiped, possibly the same as Shem, Ham, and Japhet of the Book of Genesis. Zurvanism is thought by some to be pre–Zoroastrian. The myths of the Zurvanites were incorporated into Zoroastrianism. *See also* Ahura Mazda; Angira Mainyu; Japhet.

Zvezda Dennitsa (Slavic)

Goddess of the Morning Star. According to some she and her sister represent the planet Venus. This goddess tends the horses of the sun. She may be linked with Zorya. *See also* Zvezda Vechernyaya.

Zvezda Vechernyaya (Slavic)

Goddess of the Evening Star. Sister of Zvezda Dennitsa. Possibly a moon deity.

Zvoruna (Lithuania) Goddess of the hunt and of animals.

Zyed (Persia) *see* Yazatas.

Zywie (Polish) *see* Ziva.

BIBLIOGRAPHY

Aldington, Richard and Delano Ames, trans. *Larousse Encyclopedia of Mythology*, 3rd impression. London: Paul Hamlyn, 1960.

Allen, Louis A. *Time Before Morning: Art and Myth of the Australian Aborigines*. New York: Crowell, 1975.

Altizer, Thomas J. J. *Truth, Myth, and Symbol*. Englewood Cliffs, NJ: Prentice-Hall, 1962.

Andersen, Johannes Carl. *Myths and Legends of the Polynesians*. New York: Farrar and Rinehart, 1931.

Andrews, Lynn V. *Windhorse Woman: A Marriage of Spirit*. New York: Warner Books, 1989.

Anton, Ferdinand. *Ancient Mexican Art*. London: Thames and Hudson, 1969.

Arnott, Kathleen. *African Myths and Legends, retold by Kathleen Arnott*. New York: Walck, 1963.

Asimov, Isaac. *Asimov's Guide to the Bible, The Old Testament*. New York: Equinox Books, Published by Avon Books, a division of the Hearst Corp., 1971.

Bachofen, J. J. *Myth, Religion, & Mother Right*. Bollingen Series LXXXIV, Princeton, NJ: Princeton University Press, 1973.

Balin, Peter. *The Flight of Feathered Serpent*. Venice, CA: Wisdom Garden Books, 1978.

Barbeau, Marius. *Huron and Wyandot Mythology; with an Appendix Containing Earlier Published Records, by C. M. Barbeau*. Ottawa: Goverment Printing Bureau, 1915.

Baumgartner, Anne S. *Ye Gods!* New Jersey: Lyle Stuart Inc., 1984.

Beck, Mary Giraudo. *Heroes and Heroines: Tlingit-Haida Legend*. Anchorage: Alaska Northwest Books, 1989.

Beckwith, Martha. *Hawaiian Mythology*. Honolulu: University of Hawaii Press, 1970.

Bell, Robert, E. *Women of Classical Mythology: A Biographical Dictionary*. Santa Barbara, CA: ABC-CLIO, 1991.

Bierhorst, John. *Mythology of South America*. New York: William Morrow and Company Inc., 1350 Avenue of the Americas, 1988.

_____. *The Mythology of Mexico and Central America*. New York: William Morrow and Company, 1990.

_____. *The Mythology of North America*. New York: William Morrow and Company, 1985.

Birch, Cyril. *Chinese Myths and Fantasies*. London: Oxford University Press, 1961.

Blackwell, Thomas. *Letters Concerning Mythology*. (The Printer or distributor may be J. Oswald, whose advertisement appears on the last page.) DNB attributes the printing to Andrew Millar, London, c. 1748.

Branston, Brian. *Lost Gods of England*. England: Oxford University Press, 1974.

Bratton, Fred Gladstone. *Myths and Legends of the Ancient Near East*. New York: Crowell, 1970.

Bray, Frank Chapin. *Bray's University Dictionary of Mythology*. New York: Thomas Y. Crowell Co., 1964.

Briggs, Katharine. *An Encyclopedia of Fairies*. New York: Pantheon Books, 1976.

Brinton, Daniel Garrison. *American Hero-Myths: A Study in the Native Religions of the Western Continent*. Philadelphia: H. C. Watts, 1882.

_____. *Religions for Primitive Peoples*. New York; London: G. P. Putnam's Sons, 1897.

Brock, Sebastian P. *The Syriac Vewsion of the Pseudo-Nonnos Mythological Scholia*. England: Cambridge University Press, 1971.

Bruce S., Roberto D. *Lacandon Dream Symbolism: Dream Symbolism and Interpretation Among the Lacandon Mayas of Chiapas, Mexico*. 2 vols. Mexico: Ediciónes Euroamericanas, 1975–79.

Brundage, Burr Cartwright. *The Fifth Sun: Aztec Gods, Aztec World*. Austin: University of Texas Press, 1979.

Bryant, Page. *The Aquarian Guide to Native American Mythol-*

ogy. London, England: The Aquarian Press, an Imprint of Harper Collins, 1991.

Budge, E. A. Wallis. *Amulets & Superstitions.* New York: Dover Publications, 1978.

_____. *The Gods of the Egyptians.* Volumes I and II. New York: Dover Publications, 1969.

Bulfinch, Thomas. *Bulfinch's Mythology, Illustrated Edition.* New York: Avenel Books, 1978.

Burland, C. A. *The Gods of Mexico.* New York: Putnam, 1967.

Burland, Cottie. *North American Indian Mythology.* New York: Tudor Publishing Company, 1965.

Campbell, Joseph. *Creative Mythology: The Masks of God.* New York: Penguin Books Ltd., 1968.

_____. *Occidental Mythology: The Masks of God.* New York: Penguin Books Ltd., 1976.

_____. *Oriental Mythology: The Masks of God.* New York: Penguin Books Ltd., 1976.

_____. *Primitive Mythology, The Masks of God.* New York: Penguin Books Ltd., 1976.

_____, with Bill Moyers. *The Power of Myth.* New York: Anchor Book, 1991.

Carrasco, David. *Quetzalcoatl and the Irony of Empire: Myths and Prophecies in the Aztec Tradition.* Chicago: University of Chicago Press, 1982.

Caso, Alfonso. *The Aztecs: People of the Sun.* Norman: University of Oklahoma, 1958.

Cassirer, Ernst. *Philosophie der Symbolischen Formen.* English, *The Philosophy of Symbolic Forms.* Translated by Ralph Manheim. 3 vols. New Haven: Yale University Press, 1953–57.

Cavendish, Richard, ed. *Man, Myth and Magic: The Illustrated Encyclopedia of Mythology, Religion and the Unknown.* Marshall Cavendish, 1983.

Ceram, C. W. *Gods, Graves, & Scholars: The Story of Archaeology.* Translated from the German by E. B. Garside and Sophie Wilkins. (Second, revised and substantially enlarged edition.) A Borzoi Book. Alfred A. New York: Knopf, 1968.

Chamberlain, Basil Hall. *The Language, Mythology, and Geographical Nomenclature of Japan Viewed in the Light of Aino Studies.* Toyko: Imperial University, 1887.

Chant, Joy. *The High Kings.* Toronto; New York: Bantam, 1983.

Christie, Anthony. *Chinese Mythology.* New York: Peter Bedrick Books, 1983.

Cirlot, J. E. *A Dictionary of Symbols.* (Translated from the Spanish) New York: Routledge & Kegan Paul (English translation). Published by Philosophical Library, 1962.

Clark, R. T. Rundle. *Myth and Symbol in Ancient Egypt.* London: Thames and Hudson Ltd, 1959.

Coffer, William E. *Spirits of the Sacred Mountains: Creation Stories of the American Indians.* New York: Van Nostrand Reinhold Co., 1978.

Conger, Jean. *The Velvet Paw: A History of Cats in Life, Mythology, and Art.* New York: I. Obolensky, 1963.

Conrad, Jack Randolph. *The Horn and the Sword: The History of the Bull as Symbol of Power and Fertility.* New York: Dutton, 1975.

Conway, Moncure Daniel. *Demonology and Devil-lore.* London: Chatto, 1879.

Coomaraswamy, Anadad K. & Sister Nivedita. *Myths of the Hindus & Buddhists.* New York: Dover Publications Inc., 1967.

Coyajee, Sir Jehanigir Cooverjee. *Cults & Legends of Ancient Iran & China.* Fort Bombay: J. B. Karani's Sons, 1936.

Craigie, Sir William A. *The Religion of Ancient Scandinavia.* Freeport, NY: Books for Libraries Press, 1969.

Cross, Frank Moore. *Canaanite Myth and Hebrew Epic: Essays in the History of the Religion of Israel.* Cambridge, MA: Harvard University Press, 1973.

Cushing, Frank Hamilton. *Outlines of Zuni Creation Myths.* New York: AMS Press, 1976.

Davidson, H. R. Ellis. *Gods and Myths of Northern Europe.* New York: Penguin Books Ltd., 1975.

Delphian Course, The. *The Delphian Society.* Indiana: W.B. Conkey Co., 1913.

Deren, Mary. *Divine Horsemen: The Living Gods of Haiti.* London; New York: Thames and Hudson, 1953.

Diner, Helen. *Mothers and Amazons.* New York: Doubleday Anchor, 1938.

Diop, Cheikh Anta. *The African Origin of Civilization, Myth or Reality.* Edited and translated by Mercer Cook. Chicago, IL: Lawrence Hill Books, 1974.

Dixon, Roland Burrage. *Oceanic Mythology.* Boston: Marshall Jones Company, 1916.

Dunne, John S., C.S.C. *The City of the Gods: A Study in Myth and Mortality.* New York: The Macmillan Company; London: Collier-Macmillan Limited, 1965.

Duran, Fray Diego (a translation). *Book of the Gods and Rites and the Ancient Calendar.* Norman: University of Oklahoma Press, 1971.

Durdin-Robertson, Lawrence. *God the Mother.* Wexford, Ireland: Cesara Publications, Redmond Print.

_____. *The Goddesses of Chaldea, Syria and Egypt.* Dublin, Ireland: Cesara Publications, 1975.

_____. *The Goddesses of India, Tibet, China, and Japan.* Dublin, Ireland: Cesara Publications, 1976.

Dwight, M. A. *Grecian and Roman Mythology.* New York: A.S. Barnes & Co., 1856.

Ecun, Oba. *Ita Mythology of the Yoruba Religion.* Miami, FL: Obaecun Books, 1989.

Edda (the younger). *Selections. The Prose Edda of Snorri Sturluson: Tales from Norse Mythology.* Introduced by Sigurdur Nordal; Selected and Translated by Jean I. Young. Berkeley: University of California Press, 1954.

Eisner, Robert. *The Road to Daulis: Psychoanalysis, Psychology, and Classical Mythology.* Syracuse, NY: Syracuse University Press, 1987.

Eliade, Mircea. *Australian Religions: An Introduction.* Ithaca and London: Cornell University Press, 1973.

_____. *Gods, Goddesses, and Myths of Creation.* New York: Harper & Row, Publishers, Inc., 1974.

Elmendorf, William Welcome. *Structure of Twana Culture.* New York: Garland Pub. Inc., 1974.

Evslin, Bernard. *Gods Demigods and Demons.* New York: Scholastic Book Services, 1975.

_____, and Hoopes. *Heros and Monsters of Greek Myth.* New York: Scholastic Book Services, Fourwinds Press, 1967.

Farnell, Lewis Richard. *Greece and Babylon: A Comparative Sketch of Mesopotamian, Anatolian and Hellenic Religions.* Edinburgh: T. & T. Clark, 1911.

Farugi, Isma'il Ragial, ed., David E. Sopher, map ed. *Historical Atlas of the Religions of the World.* New York: Macmillan Publishing Co., Inc., 1974.

Feibleman, James K. *Understanding Oriental Philosophy.* New York: A Mentor Book, New American Library, 1976.

Fell, Barry. *America B.C.* New York: Pocket Books, Simon & Schuster, Inc., 1989.

Fiske, John. *Myths and Myth-makers: Old Tales and Superstitions Interpreted by Comparative Mythology.* Boston: Houghton, 1900.

Flornoy, Bertram. *The World of the Inca.* (Translated from the original French, *L'Aventure Inca,* by Winifred Bradford.) New York: The Vanguard Press, 1956.

Fontein, Jan. *The Sculpture of Indonesia.* Washington, DC: National Gallery of Art, 1990.

Frawley, David. *Gods, Sages and Kings, Vedic Secrets of Ancient Civilization.* Salt Lake City, Utah: Passage Press (a division of Morson Publishing), 1991.

Frazer, Sir James George. *The Golden Bough: A Study in Magic and Religion.* New York: Abridged Edition, Collier Books, Macmillan Publishing Company, 1963.

_____. Edited and with notes and foreword by Dr. Theodor H. Gaster. *The New Golden Bough: A New Abridgment of the Classic Work.* New York: Criterion Books, 1959.

Furlong, J. G. R. *Encyclopedia of Religions.* 3 vols. New York: University Books Inc., 1964.

_____. *Faiths of Man.* 3 vols. New York: University Books Inc., 1964.

Gardner, Ernest Arthur. *Religion and Art in Ancient Greece.* London and New York: Harper & Brothers, 1910.

Gardner, Robert L. *The Rainbow Serpent: Bridge to Consciousness.* Toronto: Inner City Books, 1990.

Gaster, Theodor H. *The Oldest Stories in the World.* Boston, IL: Beacon Press, 1952.

_____. *Translations of Ancient Near Eastern Dramatic Texts.* New York: Schuman, 1950.

Gifford, Douglas. *Warriors, Gods & Sprits from Central & South American Mythology.* New York: Schocken Books; Vancouver (B. C.): Douglas & McIntyre, 1983.

Glueck, Nelson. *Deities and Dolphins; The Story of the Nabataeans.* New York: Farrar, Straus and Giroux, 1965.

Goldsmith, Elizabeth Edwards. *Life Symbols as Related to Sex Symbolism: A brief study into the origin and significance of certain symbols which have been found in all civilisations.* N.Y. and London: Pitnam's Sons, 1924.

Goodrich, Norma Lorre. *Ancient Myths.* New York: Meridian, 1994.

_____. *Priestesses.* New York: HarperPerennial, 1990.

Graves, Robert. *The Greek Myths.* 2 vols. New York: Penguin Books, 1985.

_____. *The White Goddess* New York: The Noonday Press, Farrar, Straus and Giroux, 1989.

Gray, John. *Near Eastern Mythology.* New York: Peter Bedrick Books, 1982.

Gray, Louis Herbert, ed. *The Mythology of All Races.* XIII vols. George Foot Moore, consulting editor. Boston: Marshall Jones Company, 1916–32.

Great Religions of Modern Man. 6 vols. New York: George Braziller Publisher, 1961.

Greenway, John. *The Primitive Reader.* Hatboro, PA: Folklore Associates, 1965.

Grey, Sir George. *Polynesian Mythology and Ancient Traditional History of the Maori as told by their Priests and Chiefs.* New York: Taplinger Pub. Co., 1970.

Grimm, Jacob. *Teutonic Mythology.* 3 vols. Translated from the 4th ed., by James Steven Stallybrass. London: G. Bell, 1883–1888.

Guerber, H.A. *The Norseman.* New York: Avenel Books, 1985.

Hamilton, Edith. *Mythology, Timeless Tales of Gods and Heroes.* New York: New American Library, 1969.

Hawkes, Jacquetta. *Man and the Sun.* New York: Random House, 1962.

Hays, H. R. *In the Beginnings.* New York: G. P. Putman's Sons, 1963.

Henderson, Joseph L. and Maud Oaks. *The Wisdom of the Serpent.* Canada: Ambassador Books, 1963.

Hewitt, James Francis Katherinus. *History and Chronology of the Myth-Making Age.* London: J. Parker, 1901.

Highwater, Jamake. *Myth and Sexuality.* New York: NAL Books, 1990.

Hinnells, John R. *Persian Mythology.* London; New York: Hamlyn, 1973.

Hodges, Margaret. *The Other World: Myths of the Celts.* New York: Farrar, Straus and Giroux, 1973.

Hooke, S. H. *Babylonian and Assyrian Religion.* Norman: University of Oklahoma Press, 1963.

Hopfe, Lewis M. *Religions of the World.* Canada: Collier Macmillan Canada, Ltd., 1979.

Horn, Siegfried H., Ph.D. *Seventh Day Adventist Bible Dictionary.* No. 1 of 8 vols. Washington, DC: Review and Herald Publishing Association, 1960.

Hospital, Clifford. *The Righteous Demon: A Study of Bali.* Vancouver: University of British Columbia Press, 1984.

Hultkrantz, Ake. *The Religions of the American Indians.* Translated by Monica Setterwall. Berkeley: University of California Press, 1980.

Hveberg, Harald. *Of Gods and Giants, Norse Mythology.* Translated by Pat Shaw Iversen. Norway: Johan Grundt Tanum Forlag, Office of Cultural Relations, Norwegian Ministry of Foreign Affairs, 4th edition, 1969.

Ions, Veronica. *Indian Mythology.* New York: Paul Hamlyn Publishers, 1968.

James, Edwin Oliver. *Myth and Ritual in the Ancient Near East: An Archeological and Documentary Study.* New York: Praeger, 1958.

James, William. *The Varieties of Religious Experience.* New York: Mentor Books, the New American Library, 1958.

Janson, H. W. *History of Art.* New York: Harry N. Abrams, Inc., 1977.

Jayne, Walter Addison. *The Healing Gods of Ancient Civilizations.* New Haven: Yale University Press, 1925.

Jaynes, Julian. *The Origins of Unconsciousness in the Breakdown of the Bicameral Mind.* Boston, MA: Houghton Mifflin Company, 1976.

Jenness, Diamond. *Indians of Canada.* Canada: Diamond Press, Ministry of Supply and Supplies, 1989.

Jobes, Gertrude. *Dictionary of Mythology, Folklore and Symbols.* 2 vols. New York: Scarecrow Press Inc., 1962.

Jorgensen, Joseph G. *The Sun Dance Religion: Power for the Powerless.* Chicago: University of Chicago Press, 1972.

Jung, Carl G. *Analytical Psychology, Its Theory and Practice (The Tavistock Lectures).* New York: Vintage Books, A Division of Random House, 1970.

_____. *Memories, Dreams, Reflections.* Recorded and Edited by Aniela Jaffe, Translated from the German by Richard and Clara Winston. New York: Vintage Books, a Division of Random House, 1965.

_____. *Symbols of Transformation: An Analysis of the Prelude to a Case of Schizophrenia.* Translated by R. F. C. Hull. Princeton, N.J.: Bollingen Series XX, Second Edition, Princeton University Press, 1976.

_____. *Two Essays on Analytical Psychology.* Translated by R. F. C. Hull. Cleveland Ohio: Meridian Book, The World Publishing Company, 1961.

_____, and M. L. von Franz, Joseph L. Henderson, Jolande Jacobi, Aniela Jaffé. *Man and His Symbols.* Garden City, NY: Doubleday & Company, 1964.

Kalakaua, His Majesty. *Legends and Myths of Hawaii: The Fables and Folk-Lore of a Strange People.* Rutland, VT: Charles Tuttle Co., 1979.

Karanitz, David. *Who's Who in Greek and Roman Mythology.* New York: Clarkson N. Potter, Inc., Publishers, 1975–76.

Keeler, Clyde E. *Secrets of the Cuna Earthmother: A Comparative Study of Ancient Religions.* New York: Exposition Press, Inc., 1960.

Keightley, Thomas. *Mythology of Ancient Greece and Italy.* New York: D. Appleton and Company, 1836.

Kellett, E. *The Story of Myths.* New York: Harcourt, 1927.

King, L. W. *Babylonian Religion and Mythology.* New York: AMS Press, 1976.

King, Noel Q. *Religions of Africa: A Pilgrimage Into Traditional Religions.* New York: Harper & Row, Publishers, 1970.

Kinsley, David R. *The Sword and the Flute, Kali and Krsna, Dark Visions of the Terrible and the Sublime in Hindu Mythology.* Berkeley and Los Angeles: University of California Press, 1975.

Knappert, Jan. *The Aquarian Guide to African Mythology.* Wellingborough, Northamptonshire, England: Aquarian Press, Thorsons Publishing Group, 1990.

_____. *An Encyclopedia of Myth and Legend, Indian Mythology.* Hammersmith, London, England: Aquarian Press, Thorsons Publishing Group, 1991.

_____. *An Encyclopedia of Myth and Legend, Pacific Mythology.* Hammersmith, London, England: Aquarian Press/Thorsons Publishing Group, 1992.

Korean Folklore. Edited by the Korean National Commission for Unesco, Pace International Research, U.S.A. Korea: The Si-Sa-Yong-O-Sa Publishers, Inc., 1983.

Kramer, Samuel Noah. *Mythologies of the Ancient World.* Edited and with an introduction by Samuel Noah Kramer. Garden City, NY: Anchor Books, Doubleday & Company, Inc., 1961.

La Barre, Weston. *The Ghost Dance, Origins of Religion.* Garden City, NY: Doubleday & Company, Inc., 1970.

Larousse World Mythology. New York: Prometheus Press, 1965.

Larson, Geral James, ed. *Myth in Indo-European Antiquity.* Co-edited by C. Scott Littleton and Jaan Puhvel. Berkeley: University of California Press, 1974.

Larue, Gerald A. *Ancient Myth and Modern Man.* Englewood Cliffs, NJ: Prentice Hall, 1975.

Leach, Edmund, ed. *The Structural Study of Myth and Totemism.* London: Tavistock Publications, 1967.

Leach, Maria, ed. *Funk & Wagnalls Standard Dictionary of Folklore Mythology & Legend.* New York: Funk & Wagnalls, 1949.

Leon-Portilla, Miguel, ed. *Native Mesoamerican Spirituality: Ancient Myths, Discourses, Stories, Doctrines, Hymns, Poems from the Aztec, Yucatec, Quiche-Maya and Other Sacred Traditions.* New York: Paulist Press, 1980.

Leonard, W. E. *Gilgamish.* New York: Viking Press, 1934.

Lessa, William A. *Tales from Ulithi Atoll, Oceanic Folklore.* Berkeley: University of California, 1961.

Lin, Hsu-tien. *The Nature and Characteristics of Chinese Myths and Legends*. Singapore: Dept. of Chinese Studies, National University of Singapore, 1983.

Long, Charles H. *Alpha: The Myths of Creation*. New York: George Braziller, 1963.

Lopez Lujan, Leonardo. *The Offerings of the Templo Mayor of Tenochtitlan*. Translated by Bernard R. Ortiz de Montellano and Thelma Ortiz de Montellano. Niwot: University of Colorado, 1994.

Lukker, Manfred. *The Gods and Symbols of Ancient Egypt*. London, England: Thames and Hudson, 1980.

MacCana, Proinsias. *Celtic Mythology*. Middlesex, England: The Hamlyn Publishing Group, 1975.

McConnel, Ursula. *Myths of the Munkan*. Carleton: Victoria: Melbourne University Press, 1957.

MacKenzie, Donald A. *China and Japan*. London, England: Studio Editions Ltd., Princess House, 1986.

Majupuria, Trilok Chandra. *Sacred and Symbolic Animals of Nepal: Animals in the Art, Culture, Myths and Legends of the Hindus and Buddhists*. Kathmandu: Sahayogi Prakashan, 1977.

Malinowski, Bronislaw. *Myth in Primitive Psychology*. New York: Norton, 1926.

_____. *Sex, Culture, and Myth*. New York, Harcourt, Brace & World, 1962.

Marriott, Alice Lee. *Plains Indian Mythology*. New York: Crowell, 1975.

Martin, Richard P., ed. *Bulfinch's Mythology. The Age of Fable, the Age of Chivalry, Legends of Charlemagne*. HarperCollins, 1991.

Masaharu, Anesaki. *History of Japanese Religion*. Rutland, VT: Charles E. Tuttle Company, 1975.

Mason, J. Alden. *The Ancient Civilizations of Peru*. Middlesex, England: Penguin Books Ltd., 1968.

Massey, Gerald. *Ancient Egypt, the Light of the World*. 2 vols. California: Mokelume Hill, Reprint 1988.

Matthew, John & Caitlin. *British & Irish Mythology*. London: Aquarian Press, Thorson Publishing Group, 1988.

Mercatante, Anthony S. *Who's Who in Egyptian Mythology*. New York: Clarkson N. Potter, Inc. Publishers, 1978.

Miller, Mary and Karl Taube. *The Gods and Symbols of Ancient Mexico and the Maya*. London: Thomas and Hudson Ltd., 1993.

Modder, Ralph P. *Chinese Temple Festivals, Origins and Religious Beliefs*. Hong Kong: South China Morning Post, 1983.

Mohanty, Sri Mangala Prasad. "Saora Tribals." *Hinduism Today*, March 1995. Pg. 1.

Monaghan, Patricia. *The Book of Goddesses & Heroines*. St. Paul, MN: Llewellyn Publications, 1990.

Morgan, Harry Titterton. *Chinese Symbols and Superstitions*. South Pasadena CA: P.D. and Ione Perkins, 1942.

Mortensen, Karl Andreas. *A Handbook of Norse Mythology*. Ann Arbor, MI: University Microfilms, 1971.

Mountford, Charles Pearcy. *Aboriginal Conception Beliefs*. Melbourne: Hyland House, 1981.

_____. *The Dawn of Time*. Australia: Rigby Press, 1974.

_____. *The Dreamtime*. Australia: Rigby Press, 1974.

_____. *The First Sunrise*. Australia: Rigby Press, 1974.

Munsterberg, Hugo. *The Arts of Japan: An Illustrated History*. Rutland, VT: Charles E. Tuttle Company, 1981.

Myerhoff, Barbara G. *Peyote Hunt: The Sacred Journey of the Huichol Indians*. Ithaca, NY: Cornell University Press, 1974.

Neumann, Erich. *The Great Mother; An Analysis of the Archetype*. Translated by Ralph Manheim. Princeton, NJ: Princeton University Press, 1963.

Noel, Ruth S. *The Mythology of Middle-earth*. Boston: Houghton Mifflin, 1977.

Okpewho, Isidore. *Myth in Africa: A Study of Its Aesthetic and Cultural Relevance*. New York: Cambridge University Press, 1983.

Olcott, William Tyler. *Sun Lore of All Ages: A Collection of Myths and Legends Concerning the Sun and Its Worship*. New York: Putnam, 1914.

Osborne, Harold. *South American Mythology*. New York: Peter Bedrick Books, 1983.

Otto, Walter Friedrich. *Dionysos, Mythos und Kultus*. English: *Dionysus, Myth and Cult*. Translated by Robert B. Palmer. Bloomington: Indiana University Press, 1965.

Overmyer, Daniel L. *Religions of China: The World as a Living System*. New York: Harper and Row Publishers, 1986.

Pagels, Elaine. *The Gnostic Gospels*. New York: Vintage Books, 1979.

Palmer, Robin. *Centaurs, Sirens, and Other Classical Creatures: A Dictionary, Tales and Verse from Greek & Roman*. New York: H. Z. Walck, 1969.

Parrinder, Geoffrey. *African Mythology*. Middlesex, England: The Hamlyn Publishing Group, 1967.

_____, ed. *World Religions: From Ancient History to the Present*. Facts on File, 1984.

The Pawnee: Mythology (Part 1). Collected under the Auspices of the Carnegie Institution of Washington, by George A. Dorsey. Washington: Carnegie Institution of Washington, 1906.

Payne, Robert. *The World of Art*. New York: Doubleday & Company, Inc., 1972.

Perry, John Weir. *Roots of Renewal in Myth and Madness*. San Francisco: Jossey-Bass, 1976.

Petrankos, Basil. *Ephor of Antiquities in Attica*. Athens, Greece: National Museum, Clio Editions, 1981.

Piggot, Juliet. *Japanese Mythology*. New York: The Hamlyn Publishing Group, 1975.

Platt, Rutherford H. (Jr.), ed. *The Forgotten Books of Eden*. New York: Bell Publishing Company, 1980.

Poetical Prose Quotations, Mythology. Watford, England: Reference Library. The Greycaine Book Manufacturing Company Limited, c. early 1800s.

Poignant, Roslyn. *Oceanic Mythology.* London, England: Paul Hamblyn Limited, 1967.

Polome, Edgar C. *Old Norse Literature and Mythology: A Symposium.* Austin: University of Texas Press, 1969.

Popol Vuh: The Great Mythological Book of the Ancient Maya. Translated by Ralph Nelson. Boston: Houghton Mifflin, 1976.

Popol Vuh: The Sacred Book of the Ancient Quiche Maya. English version by Delia Goetzand Sylvanus G. Morley from the Spanish translation by Adrian Recinos. Norman: University of Oklahoma Press, 1950.

Portillo, Jose Lopes, Demetrio Sodi, Fernando Diaz Infante. *Quetzalcoatl, in Myth, Archeology, and Art.* New York: Continuum, 1982.

Puhvel, Jaan. *Comparative Mythology.* Baltimore and London: The Johns Hopkins University Press. 1987.

Radhakrishnan, Sarvepalli, and Charles A. Moore, eds. *A Sourcebook in Indian Philosophy.* Princeton, NJ: Princeton University Press, 1967.

Reed, A. W. *Myths and Legends of Australia.* New York: Taplinger Publishing Co., 1973.

Rees, Alwyn D., and Brinley Ree. *Celtic Heritage: Ancient Tradition in Ireland and Wales.* New York: Grove Press, 1961.

Ringgren, Helmer. *Religions of the Ancient Near East.* Translated by John Sturdy. Philadelphia, PA: The Westminster Press, 1973.

Rinpoche, Guru, according to Karma Lingpa. *The Tibetan Book of the Dead. The Great Liberation through Hearing in Bardo.* Commentary by Francesca Fremantle and Chögyam Trungpa. Boulder, CO: Shambhala Publications, 1975.

Roberts, Ainslie. *The Dreamtime Book: Australian Aboriginal Myths in Paintings.* Adelaide, Australia: Rigby, 1973.

Robinson, Roland E. *The Feathered Serpent: The mythological genesis and recreative ritual of the aboriginal tribes of the Northern Territory of Australia.* Sydney: Edwards & Shaw, 1956.

Rose, H. J. *A Handbook of Greek Mythology.* New York: E. P. Dutton & Co., Inc., 1959.

Ross, Anne, Ph.D. *Druids, Gods, and Heroes from Celtic Mythology.* New York: Schocken, 1986.

Rowland, Beryl. *Animals with Human Faces, A Guide to Animal Symbolism.* Knoxville, Tennessee: The University of Tennessee Press, 1973.

Roys, Ralph L. *The Books of Chilam Balam of Chumayel.* Norman: University of Oklahoma Press, 1967.

Russell, Bertrand. *History of Western Philosophy and Its Connection with Political and Social Circumstances from the Earliest Time to the Present Day.* England: George Allen & Unwin Ltd., Ruskin House, 1965.

Rutherford, Ward. *Celtic Mythology.* Northamptonshire, England: Aquarian Press, Thorsons Publishing Group, 1987.

Rydberg, Viktor, Ph.D. *Teutonic Mythology, Gods and Goddesses of the Northland, Volume II.* London, England: Norrcena Society, 1906.

Sanders, Tao Tao Liu. *Dragons, Gods & Spirits from Chinese Mythology.* New York: Schocken Books, 1983.

Schafer, Edward H. *The Divine Woman; Dragon Ladies and Rain Maidens in T'ang Literature.* Berkeley: University of California Press, 1973.

Scherer, Margaret Roseman. *The Legends of Troy in Art and Literature.* New York: Phaidon Press for the Metropolitan Museum of Art, 1963.

Shapiro, Max S. & Rhoda A. Hendricks. *Mythologies of the World.* New York: Doubleday & Co., 1979.

Short Description of Gods, Goddesses and Ritual Objects of Buddhism and Hinduism in Nepal. Nepal: OM Printers, 1989.

Shryock, John Knight. *The Temples of Anking and Their Cults: A Study of Modern Chinese Religion.* New York: AMS Press, 1973.

Smith, Homer W. *Man and His Gods.* New York: Grossett's Universal Library, Grossett & Dunlap, 1957.

Spence, Lewis. *Mexico and Peru, Myths and Legends.* England: Thomas Y. Crowell Company, 1920.

_____. *Myths & Legends of Babylonia & Assyria.* Detroit: Gale Research Co., 1975.

_____. *The Outlines of Mythology.* London, England: Watts & Company, 1949.

_____. *The Popol Vuh: The Mythic and Heroic Sagas of the Kiches of Central America.* New York: AMS Press, 1972.

Sproul, Barbara C. *Primal Myths, Creating the World.* San Francisco: Harper & Row Publishers, 1979.

Squire, Charles. *Celtic Myth and Legend: Poetry & Romance.* Hollywood, CA: Newcastle Publishing Co., 1975.

Stace, W. T. *Mysticism & Philosophy.* Los Angeles, CA: Jeremy P. Tarcher, Inc., 1960.

Stapleton, Michael. *The Illustrated Dictionary of Greek and Roman Mythology.* New York: Peter Bedrick Books, 1986.

Thomas, Lawson E. *Religions of Africa.* San Francisco: Harper & Row, Publishers, 1984.

Townsend, Richard F. *The Aztecs.* London, England. Thames & Hudson Ltd., 1992.

Tripp, Edward. *The Meridian Handbook of Classical Mythology.* New York: A Meridian Book, New American Library, 1970.

Turnbull, Stephen R. *The Book of the Samurai: The Warrior Class of Japan.* New York: Gallery Books, An Imprint of W. H. Smith, Publishers, 1982.

Vaillant, C. R. *Aztecs of Mexico.* New York: Pelican Book–Penguin Books, 1966.

Velikovsky, Immanuel. *Oedipus and Akhnaton: Myth and History.* Garden City, NY: Doubleday, 1960.

Vermaseren, M. J. *The Legend of Attis in Greek and Roman Art.* Leiden, The Netherlands: E. J. Brill, 1966.

Visser, Marinus Willem de. *The Dragon in China and Japan.* Amsterdam: J. Muller, 1913.

Waddell, Laurence Austine. *The Buddhism of Tibet. Tibetan*

Buddhism, with its Mystic Cults, Symbolism and Mythology, and in its relation to Indian Buddhism. New York: Dover Publications, 1972.

Walker, Barbara G. *The Woman's Encyclopedia of Myths and Secrets.* San Francisco: Harper and Row, 1983.

Warren, Elizabeth. *Heroes, Monsters, and Other Worlds from Russian Mythology.* New York: Schocken Books, 1985.

Watterson, Barbara. *The Gods of Ancient Egypt.* New York: Facts on File Publications, 1984.

Watts, Alan W. *The Two Hands of God.* New York: George Braziller, 1963.

Weigle, Marta. *Spiders and Spinsters: Women and Mythology.* Albuquerque: University of New Mexico Press, 1982.

Werner, E. T. C. *Myths and Legends of China.* London: G. G. Harrop, 1922; reprinted Singapore: G. Brash, 1984.

Williamson, Robert Wood. *Religion and Social Organization in Central Polynesia.* New York: AMS Press, 1977.

Wolf, Eric *Sons of the Shaking Earth.* Illinois: University of Chicago Press, 1959.

Wolkstein, Diane and Samuel Kramer. *Inanna.* London, England: Rider and Co., 1983.

Woodcock, P. G. *Dictionary of Mythology.* New York: Philosophical Library, 1953.

Yumoto, John M. *The Samurai Sword, a Handbook.* Rutland, VT: Charles E. Tuttle Company, 1985.

Zimmer, Heirick Robert. *The Art of Indian Asia: Its Mythology and Transformations.* 2 vols. New York: Pantheon Books, 1955.

INDEX

CPSIA information can be obtained
at www.ICGtesting.com
Printed in the USA
BVHW010818020322
630414BV00009B/122